MUSIC MASTER

MUSIC MASTER

SPOKEN WORD CATALOGUE

W Waterlow

Published by Waterlow Information Services Limited, London.

First edition, June, 1992.

Published by Music Master, Music House, 1 De Cham Avenue, Hastings, East Sussex. TN37 6HE.

Advertising enquiries: Telephone: 071-490-0049. Fax: 071-608-1163.

Editorial enquiries: Telephone: (0424) 715181. Fax: (0424) 422805.

Book trade enquiries: Music Sales, 8/9 Frith Street, London, W1V 5TZ. Telephone: 071-434-0066. Fax: 071-439-2848.

Private orders and record trade enquiries: Music Master Customer Services, Unit 4, Durham Road, Borehamwood, Hertfordshire, WD6 1LW. Telephone: 081-953-5433. Fax: 081-207-5814.

ISBN 0 904520 69 2

THE MUSIC MASTER TEAM: Production Manager: George Rankin. **Production:** Dave Kent, Jason Philpott, Fiona Allman, Marianne Hyne. **Editorial Manager:** Liz O' Connor. **Product Development Manager:** Chris Spalding. **Editorial:** Pete Smith, Sylvia Davis, Karen Blackman, Jimmy Kent, Jenny Bellerose. **Research:** Anita Ferrario, Clive Brown. **Administration:** Pam Brown.

© **Copyright warning:** It is a condition of sale of this publication that it may not be used to compile other directories or mailing lists without the express written permission of the Publisher. Persons or companies wishing to offer a list broking service are invited to contact the Publisher. Any persons or companies found to be offering a mailing list service derived in whole or part from this publication will be prosecuted. Any persons or companies found to be assisting others in producing mailing lists, or machine-readable versions derived from this publication will be prosecuted for copyright infringement.

All rights reserved. No part of this publication may be reproduced, stored in a retrieval system or transmitted in any form, or by any means, electronic, mechanical, photocopying, recording or otherwise, without the prior written permission of the copyright owner.

Printed and bound in Great Britain by Richard Clays Limited, Bungay, Suffolk.

Cover design by Jonathan Clegg, Design Communication.

MUSIC MASTER
SPOKEN WORD CATALOGUE

CONTENTS

Introduction 5
About This Book 7
Biographies Index 11
Bird Songs Index 16
Children Index 17
Educational Index 35
Environmental Index 48
Health & Fitness Index 49
History Index 51
Humour Index 52
Languages Index 57
Plays Index 63
Poetry Index 66
Radio Index 70
Religious Index 71
Self Improvement Index 73
Sound Effects Index 77
Sport Index 78
Transport Index 79
Fiction Section 83
Non-Fiction Section 269
Titles (alphabetical listing) 347

THE LIBRARY ON TAPE

THOUSANDS OF BOOKS IN STOCK

If the idea of having your own library on tape appeals then Travellers' Tales will be of particular interest.

As the UK's first postal audio library, we offer thousands of unabridged books on tape for you to enjoy when driving in the car, working with your hands or simply relaxing.

Join Travellers' Tales and you can 'read' a whole host of titles when you don't have time to pick up a book.

Choose from classics, fiction, non-fiction, thrillers, plays, poetry, biographies and childrens' books read by professional actors.

RUTH RENDELL
TROLLOPE
ALISTAIR McLEAN
VICTORIA HOLT
CHARLES DICKENS
GRAHAM GREENE
DAPHNE DU MAURIER

If you are interested in joining Travellers' Tales please write or telephone for further details: Great Weddington, Ash, Canterbury, Kent CT3 2AR.

☎ **0304 812531**

INTRODUCTION

The written word will never be completely replaced and man's quest for knowledge will always demand an almost unlimited array of books from which to glean this information. However, as the above quotation illustrates vividly, the proper use of the spoken word can be every bit as effective as the written word.

There is a growing demand for spoken word cassettes, whether it be for educational purposes, for example languages or GCSE studies, hobbies or interests such as keep-fit or a whole range of literature now available on cassette.

This book lists all the information available to us at time of going to press. The range of topics covered is summarised in our list of indices published at the beginning of the book, whether it be biographies, bird songs or a general work of fiction. The book is divided into two sections - fiction and non-fiction. The purpose of the indices at the beginning of the book is to allow an entry in either of the main sections of the book to be found quickly. A full alphabetical list of recordings by title is published at the end of the book.

For instance, if you wish to find a particular biography, the Biographies index should be consulted. This index will give a list, in alphabetical order, of all such recordings listed in this book and will indicate the section of the book under which it can be found (i.e. fiction or non-fiction) and the name of the heading or "black strip" under which it is listed. Therefore, the biography *Backcloth* will be listed in the non-fiction section under the heading *Bogarde, Dirk*.

Wherever possible, details of narrators have also been published, although this information is not always supplied when we receive details of recordings. The general principle we have worked to is that, where appropriate, recordings will be listed under a "black strip" heading of the author's name - *David Copperfield* will therefore be listed under the heading *Dickens, Charles* within the fiction section.

Where authors do not apply, the "black strip" heading will be an eponymous title or or one of a more general nature.

We hope you will find this book, a new title from Music Master, interesting, useful and informative. Thank you for purchasing our first Spoken Word Catalogue.

BBC RADIO COLLECTION

THE №1 NAME IN SPOKEN WORD

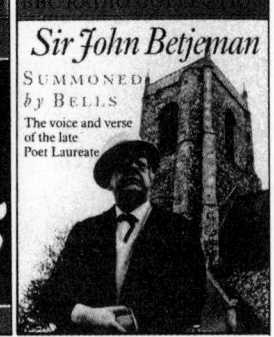

TOUJOURS *provence*
Written and read by PETER MAYLE
By the bestselling author of A YEAR IN PROVENCE

ROUND THE HORNE

Sir John Betjeman
SUMMONED by BELLS
The voice and verse of the late Poet Laureate

As heard on National BBC Radio

BBC Radio Collection, Room A2117, BBC Enterprises, 80 Wood Lane, London W12 0TT

Distributed to record shops in the U.K. by Pinnacle Records Tel:0689 870622
and to bookshops by DMS/Excel Logistics Tel: 0622 882000

GET THE FULL STORY WITH

isis AUDIO BOOKS

Complete & Unabridged

- Bestselling titles
- Popular authors

Isis Audio Books
55 St Thomas' Street,
Oxford OX1 1JG.
Tel: (0865) 250333

LIBRARIANS: MAKE SURE YOU'RE ON THE RIGHT TRACK.

For the most comprehensive spoken word stockholding and library supply service available contact:–

MORLEY ▷▷AUDIO SERVICES
THE NAME IN AUDIO SUPPLY

Morley Audio Services
Elmfield Road
Morley Leeds LS27 0NN
Tel 0532 538811
Fax 0532 527925

Morley Audio Services
116–120 Golden Lane
London EC1Y 0UD
Tel 071 251 2551
Fax 071 490 2338

ABOUT THIS BOOK

The spoken word cassette market is one of the fastest growing areas of sound recordings, with an increasing number of publishers and record companies involved.

Many book shops now carry ranges of fiction and non-fiction titles and some record shops also include ranges. You are unlikely to see the wide range of titles featured in this book in any one shop, but by providing the shop with the details given here, you will help them to accurately order the titles they do not have in stock.

Alternatively, you can order from mail order suppliers, again providing them with the details given in this book.

Restricted Availability
Certain publishers' catalogues, notably Ulverscroft and Chivers (except for Cavalcade and Word For Word series) are not available in shops, but entries from them are included in this book because they are important current titles. Prospective purchasers should enquire directly to the publishers.

Rental Entries
Entries marked Rental refer to commercial rental to members of the Travellers' Tales rental club only. No permission is given or implied by their inclusion in this book as to their availability for commercial rental by Travellers' Tales or any other trader.

Spoken word cassettes are available for loan from many public libraries. A small administration fee may be levied.

Retailers
Spoken word cassettes are generally available from the usual trade source for the publisher of the cassette, or from a wholesaler, unless they are non-trade ranges (see above).

Book Shops
If you are a book shop, your normal book distributors will handle those publishers with whom you already deal. Publishers you are unfamiliar with may well be from record company sources and you may need to consider opening new accounts or using a wholesaler.

Record Shops
If you are a record retailer, many of the labels may be unfamiliar, normally being associated with the book trade. Apart from your normal record company accounts, you may therefore need to open new accounts in the book trade, or else use a wholesaler.

"A word fitly spoken is like apples of gold in pictures of silver."
(Proverbs, 11)

BIOGRAPHIES

TITLE	HEADING	SECTION
Adolf Hitler	Hitler, Adolf	Non-Fiction
Adolph Hitler: My Part In His Downfall	Milligan, Spike	Non-Fiction
Albert Einstein	Einstein, Albert	Non-Fiction
Alexander Fleming	Fleming, Alexander	Non-Fiction
Allan Border: An Autobiography	Border, Allan	Non-Fiction
Amateur Emigrant, The	Stevenson, Robert Louis	Non-Fiction
Amazing Grace	Dessau, Joanna	Non-Fiction
Amy Johnson	Johnson, Amy	Non-Fiction
Anne: The Princess Royal	Hoey, Brian	Non-Fiction
Around The World In Wanderer III	Hiscock, E	Non-Fiction
As I Walked Out One Midsummer Morning	Lee, Laurie	Non-Fiction
Autobiography, An	Cushing, Peter	Non-Fiction
Back To The Forest	Foley, Winifred	Non-Fiction
Backcloth	Bogarde, Dirk	Non-Fiction
BBC-Readings By:	BBC...	Non-Fiction
Be My Baby	Spector, Ronnie	Non-Fiction
Below Stairs	Powell, Margaret	Non-Fiction
Berry, Me And Motown	Gordy Singleton, Raynoma	Non-Fiction
Billy The Kid	Utley, Robert M.	Non-Fiction
Born Free	Adamson, Joy	Non-Fiction
Boy Growing Up, A	Thomas, Dylan	Non-Fiction
Bring On The Empty Horses	Niven, David	Non-Fiction
Butler's Revenge, The	Powell, Margaret	Non-Fiction
By The Waters Of Liverpool	Forrester, Helen	Non-Fiction
Cary Grant, The Light Touch	Godfrey, L	Non-Fiction
Catherine De Medici	De Medici, Catherine	Non-Fiction
Charles Darwin	Darwin, Charles	Non-Fiction
Charles Dickens	Orwell, George	Non-Fiction
Child Alone, A	Bardot, Brigitte	Non-Fiction
Child Alone, A - Memoirs	Watkins-Pitchford	Non-Fiction
Child In The Forest, A	Foley, Winifred	Non-Fiction
Christopher Columbus	Columbus, Christopher	Non-Fiction
Cider With Rosie	Lee, Laurie	Non-Fiction
Climbing The Stairs	Powell, Margaret	Non-Fiction
Coming Attractions	Stamp, Terence	Non-Fiction
Common Years, The	Cooper, Jilly	Non-Fiction
Constable Around The Village	Rhea, Nicholas	Non-Fiction
Constable On The Hill	Rhea, Nicholas	Non-Fiction
Constable On The Prowl	Rhea, Nicholas	Non-Fiction
Cotswold Characters	Cotswolds	Non-Fiction
Cotswold Craftsmen	Cotswolds	Non-Fiction
Cotswold Voices	Cotswolds	Non-Fiction
Country Diary Of An Edwardian Lady	Holden, Edith	Non-Fiction
Crowdie And Cream	MacDonald, Finlay J	Non-Fiction
Dalesman's Diary, A	Mitchell, W.R.	Non-Fiction
Dame Margot Fonteyn	Fonteyn, Dame Margot	Non-Fiction
Daughter Of The Dales	Hauxwell, Hannah	Non-Fiction
Diaries 1915-1918, The	Sassoon, Siegfried	Non-Fiction
Diary Of Anne Frank, The	Frank, Anne	Non-Fiction
Diary Of Samuel Pepys	Pepys, Samuel	Non-Fiction

BIOGRAPHIES

Double Feature	Stamp, Terence	Non-Fiction
Down And Out In Paris And London	Orwell, George	Non-Fiction
Down To Earth	Elliot, Emily	Non-Fiction
Drunk Man Looks At The Thistle, A	MacDiarmid, Hugh	Non-Fiction
Dust In The Lion's Paw	Stark, Freya	Non-Fiction
Early Stages	Gielgud, Sir John	Non-Fiction
Ebdon's England	Ebdon, John	Non-Fiction
Ebdon's Odyssey	Ebdon, John	Non-Fiction
Eight Feet In The Andes	Murphy, Devia	Non-Fiction
Elizabeth I	Elizabeth I	Non-Fiction
Elizabeth Taylor	Kelly, Kitty	Non-Fiction
Emma And Co.	Hocken, Sheila	Non-Fiction
Emma Hamilton	Hamilton, Emma	Non-Fiction
Escape From Germany	Crawley, Aidan	Non-Fiction
Evening Gull, The	Tangye, Derek	Non-Fiction
Falling Towards England	James, Clive	Non-Fiction
Farce About Face	Rix, Sir Brian	Non-Fiction
Florence Nightingale	Nightingale, Florence	Non-Fiction
Florence Nightingale	Strachey, Lytton	Non-Fiction
Foolish Virgin, The	Penn, Margaret	Non-Fiction
Fortunate Grandchild, A	Read, Miss	Non-Fiction
Four Linmill Stories	McLellan, Robert	Non-Fiction
Francis Drake	Drake, Sir Francis	Non-Fiction
Franz Joseph Haydn 1732 -1809	Haydn (composer)	Non-Fiction
Freedom Come All Ye	Henderson, Hamish	Non-Fiction
Full Tilt - Ireland To India With A Bicycle	Murphy, Devia	Non-Fiction
Further Tales From A Country Practice	Jackson, Arthur	Non-Fiction
Gandhi	Gandhi	Non-Fiction
George And Elizabeth	Duff, David	Non-Fiction
George Frederic Handel	Handel (composer)	Non-Fiction
George Gershwin Remembered	Gershwin (composer)	Non-Fiction
George Washington	Washington, George	Non-Fiction
Giuseppe Verdi	Verdi (composer)	Non-Fiction
Giuseppe Verdi 1813-1901	Verdi (composer)	Non-Fiction
Gracie	Burns, George	Non-Fiction
Grass Is Greener, The	Brown, Fred	Non-Fiction
Grey Is The Colour Of Hope	Ratushinskaya, Irina	Non-Fiction
Growing Up In The Gorbals	Glasser, Ralph	Non-Fiction
Guglielmo Marconi	Marconi, Guglielmo	Non-Fiction
Gull On The Roof	Tangye, Derek	Non-Fiction
Happy	Brown, Fred	Non-Fiction
He Being Dead Yet Speaketh	Kilvert, Rev. Francis	Non-Fiction
Henry Ford	Ford, Henry	Non-Fiction
Her Life And Art	Teyte, Dame Maggie	Non-Fiction
High, Wide And Lonesome	Borland, Hal	Non-Fiction
Homage To Catalonia	Orwell, George	Non-Fiction
Horatio Nelson	Nelson	Non-Fiction
How To Grow Old Gracefully	Gingold, Hermione	Non-Fiction
How Was It For You?	Lipman, Maureen	Non-Fiction
Hugh MacDiarmid	MacDiarmid, Hugh	Non-Fiction
I Can't Stay Long	Lee, Laurie	Non-Fiction
I Know Why The Caged Bird Sings	Angelou, Maya	Non-Fiction
I Leap Over The Wall	Baldwin, Monica	Non-Fiction
I Light A Candle	Turgel, Gena	Non-Fiction
In Trouble Again	O'Hanlon, Redmond	Non-Fiction
Innocent Abroad, An	Hauxwell, Hannah	Non-Fiction
Invisible Friendship	Grenfell & Moore	Non-Fiction
Isaac Newton	Newton, Isaac	Non-Fiction
Isabella Of Castile & Leon	Isabella	Non-Fiction

BIOGRAPHIES

It's A Vet's Life	Duncan, Alex	Non-Fiction
J Kingston Platt	Kingston Platt, J	Non-Fiction
Jason Voyage, The	Severin, Tim	Non-Fiction
Jeannie	Tangye, Derek	Non-Fiction
Joan Of Arc	Joan Of Arc	Non-Fiction
Johann Sebastian Bach	Bach, J.S. (composer)	Non-Fiction
Johann Sebastian Bach 1685 - 1750	Bach, J.S. (composer)	Non-Fiction
Johann Strauss 1825-1899	Strauss, J. (composer)	Non-Fiction
Johann Strauss The Younger	Strauss, J. (composer)	Non-Fiction
John Barrymore: From Matinee Idol To Buffoon	Barrymore, John	Non-Fiction
John Wayne Story, The	Carpozi, George Jnr.	Non-Fiction
Journey Through Britain	Hillaby, John	Non-Fiction
Journey To The Jade Sea	Hillaby, John	Non-Fiction
Julius Caesar	Caesar, Julius	Non-Fiction
Just Williams	Williams, Kenneth	Non-Fiction
Kon-Tiki Expedition	Heyerdahl, Thor	Non-Fiction
Lama	Tangye, Derek	Non-Fiction
Lang Syne In The East Neuk O Fife	Kermack, Mary	Non-Fiction
Last Days Of General Gordon	Strachey, Lytton	Non-Fiction
Last Grain Race, The	Newby, Eric	Non-Fiction
Ledge Between The Streams, The	Metha, Ved	Non-Fiction
Lenin	Lenin	Non-Fiction
Letters From A Bomber Pilot	Hodgson, David	Non-Fiction
Life And Times Of Lord Mountbatten,the	Lord Mountbatten	Non-Fiction
Life In The Country, A	Fletcher, Cyril	Non-Fiction
Life Of Charlotte Bronte, The	Cleghorn Gaskell	Non-Fiction
Life On The Mississippi	Twain, Mark	Non-Fiction
Life's Rich Pageant	Marshall, Arthur	Non-Fiction
Lillee: Over And Out	Cricket	Non-Fiction
Lime Street At Two	Forrester, Helen	Non-Fiction
Longest Walk, The	Meegan, George	Non-Fiction
Love And War In The Apennines	Newby, Eric	Non-Fiction
Ludwig Van Beethoven 1770-1827	Beethoven (composer)	Non-Fiction
Maids And Mistresses	Powell, Margaret	Non-Fiction
Man From Odessa, The	Wynne, Greville	Non-Fiction
Manchester Fourteen Miles	Penn, Margaret	Non-Fiction
Mao Tse-Tung	Mao Tse-Tung	Non-Fiction
Martin Luther King	King, Martin Luther	Non-Fiction
Mary Baker Eddy	Baker Eddy, Mary	Non-Fiction
Me	Hepburn, Katherine	Non-Fiction
Memoirs Of The Hammer Years	Cushing, Peter	Non-Fiction
Memories Of Highland Lady	Grant, Elizabeth	Non-Fiction
Memories Of Osborne	Blake, Dorothy	Non-Fiction
Minerva's Stepchild	Forrester, Helen	Non-Fiction
Moment Of War, A	Lee, Laurie	Non-Fiction
Monarch: Life And Times Of Elizabeth II	Fisher, Graham	Non-Fiction
Monocled Mutineer, The	Allison & Fairley	Non-Fiction
Moon's A Balloon, The	Niven, David	Non-Fiction
More Tales From A Country Practice	Jackson, Arthur	Non-Fiction
Mortar Fire - Normandy To Germany 1944-45	Francia, Paul	Non-Fiction
Mussolini: His Part In My Downfall	Milligan, Spike	Non-Fiction
My Family And Other Animals	Durrell, Gerald	Non-Fiction
My Small Country Living	Mcmullen, Jeanine	Non-Fiction
My Turn To Make The Tea	Dickens, Monica	Non-Fiction
Nancy Reagan	Kelly, Kitty	Non-Fiction
Napoleon Bonaparte	Napoleon	Non-Fiction
Nice One, Cyril	Fletcher, Cyril	Non-Fiction
Nikita Khrushchev	Krushchev, Nikita	Non-Fiction
Nothing Quite Like It	Wallace, Ian	Non-Fiction

BIOGRAPHIES

O, The Northern Muse	Heaney, Seamus	Non-Fiction
Odd Man Out	Mason, James	Non-Fiction
One Man And His Dog	Richardson, Anthony	Non-Fiction
One Pair Of Feet	Dickens, Monica	Non-Fiction
One Pair Of Hands	Dickens, Monica	Non-Fiction
Orderly Man, An	Bogarde, Dirk	Non-Fiction
Oscar Wilde	Wilde, Oscar	Non-Fiction
Our Gracie	Fields, Gracie	Non-Fiction
Our Kate	Cookson, Catherine	Non-Fiction
Our Story	Kray, Reg & Ron	Non-Fiction
Out Of Africa	Blixen, Karen	Non-Fiction
Particular Friendship, A	Bogarde, Dirk	Non-Fiction
Past Forgetting	Cushing, Peter	Non-Fiction
Path Of Morning, The	De Valois, Dame Ninette	Non-Fiction
Peter Ilyich Tchaikovsky	Tchaikovsky (composer)	Non-Fiction
Peter Ilyich Tchaikovsky 1840 - 1893	Tchaikovsky (composer)	Non-Fiction
Queen's Travels, The	Fisher, Graham	Non-Fiction
Question Of Balance, A	Duke Of Edinburgh	Non-Fiction
Rasputin	Fulop-Miller, Rene	Non-Fiction
Recollections No. 1: A Railway Guard	Trains...	Non-Fiction
Recollections No. 2: Life On The Canal	Canals	Non-Fiction
Recollections No. 3: Silent Days Of The Cinema	Cinema	Non-Fiction
Recollections No. 4: Foot Plate Days	Trains...	Non-Fiction
Recollections No. 5: British Motorcycle Industry	Motorcycling	Non-Fiction
Robert Owen & New Lanark	Owen, Robert Dale	Non-Fiction
Rodgers & Hammerstein	Rodgers & Hammerstein	Non-Fiction
Rommel? Gunner Who?	Milligan, Spike	Non-Fiction
Ronald Reagan: An American Life	Reagan, Ronald	Non-Fiction
Sailing Alone Around The World	Slocum, Joshua	Non-Fiction
Samuel Beckett	Beckett, Samuel	Non-Fiction
Scottish Sketches	Cunningham Graham, R.B.	Non-Fiction
Seasons Of My Life	Hauxwell, Hannah	Non-Fiction
Shoes Were For Sunday	Weir, Molly	Non-Fiction
Short Walk In The Hindu Kush, A	Newby, Eric	Non-Fiction
Sigmund Freud	Freud, Sigmund	Non-Fiction
Slow Boats Home	Young, Gavin	Non-Fiction
Something To Fall Back On	Lipman, Maureen	Non-Fiction
South	Shackleton, Sir Ernest	Non-Fiction
Stalker	Stalker, John	Non-Fiction
Stamp Album	Stamp, Terence	Non-Fiction
Stare Back And Smile	Lumley, Joanna	Non-Fiction
Still On My Way To Hollywood	Wise, Ernie	Non-Fiction
Story Of Charles Dickens, The	Dickens, Charles	Non-Fiction
Story Of Robert Burns	Burns, Robert	Non-Fiction
Story Of William Shakespeare, The	Shakespeare, William	Non-Fiction
Surviving The Killing Fields	Ngor, Haing	Non-Fiction
Tales From A Country Practice	Jackson, Arthur	Non-Fiction
Tenement Tales	Weir, Molly	Non-Fiction
Testament Of Friendship	Brittain, Vera	Non-Fiction
Thanks For The Memory	Carrick, Peter	Non-Fiction
Thanks For The Memory	Hope, Bob	Non-Fiction
There's Lovely	Morris, Johnny	Non-Fiction
Thomas Alva Edison	Edison, Thomas Alva	Non-Fiction
To Be A Country Doctor	Duncan, Alex	Non-Fiction
To The Navel Of The World	Somerville-Large	Non-Fiction
Tomorrow Is Too Late	Moore, Ray	Non-Fiction
Travels Of Sir John Mandeville	Mandeville, John	Non-Fiction
Travels On My Elephant	Shand, Mark	Non-Fiction
Tribute To Fred Astaire, A	Carrick, Peter	Non-Fiction

BIOGRAPHIES

True Britt	Ekland, Britt	Non-Fiction
Tunnelling Into Colditz	Rogers, Jim	Non-Fiction
Two Worlds Of Joseph Race	Race, Steve	Non-Fiction
Twopence To Cross The Mersey	Forrester, Helen	Non-Fiction
Two-Way Story	Michelmore, Cliff	Non-Fiction
Uncooking Old Sherry	Thompson, John Cargill	Non-Fiction
Under The Eye Of The Clock	Nolan, Christopher	Non-Fiction
Unreliable Memoirs	James, Clive	Non-Fiction
Walking Tall	Weston, Simon	Non-Fiction
Wallis And Edward	Bloch, Michael	Non-Fiction
War: A Memoir	Duras, Marguerite	Non-Fiction
Welcome To The Peach Tree Cottage	Kane, Charlotte	Non-Fiction
We'll Meet Again	Lynn, Vera	Non-Fiction
Where Have All The Bullets Gone?	Milligan, Spike	Non-Fiction
While I Work I Whistle	Cotswolds	Non-Fiction
Whimpering In The Rhododendrons	Marshall, Arthur	Non-Fiction
Wilbur And Orville Wright	Wright Brothers	Non-Fiction
Winston Churchill	Churchill, Sir Winston	Non-Fiction
Wise Man From The West, The	Cronin, Vincent	Non-Fiction
Wolfgang Amadeus Mozart	Mozart (composer)	Non-Fiction
Wolfgang Amadeus Mozart 1756-1791	Mozart (composer)	Non-Fiction
Words Of Gandhi, The	Gandhi	Non-Fiction
World Of, The	Ashcroft, Peggy	Non-Fiction
Wright Brothers	Wright Brothers	Non-Fiction
Young Mrs. Burton, The	Penn, Margaret	Non-Fiction

BIRD SONGS

TITLE	HEADING	SECTION
All The Bird Songs Of Britain & Europe	Bird Songs	Non-Fiction
All The Bird Songs Of Europe Vol.1	Bird Songs	Non-Fiction
All The Bird Songs Of Europe Vol.3	Bird Songs	Non-Fiction
All The Bird Songs Of Europe Vol.2	Bird Songs	Non-Fiction
All The Bird Songs Of Europe Vol.4	Bird Songs	Non-Fiction
Bird Songs Volume 1	Bird Songs	Non-Fiction
Bird Songs Volume 2	Bird Songs	Non-Fiction
Bird Songs Volume 3	Bird Songs	Non-Fiction
Bird Songs Volume 4	Bird Songs	Non-Fiction
Bird Songs Volume 5	Bird Songs	Non-Fiction
Bird Songs Volume 6	Bird Songs	Non-Fiction
Bird Songs Volume 7	Bird Songs	Non-Fiction
Bird Songs Volume 8	Bird Songs	Non-Fiction
Bird Songs Volume 9	Bird Songs	Non-Fiction
Bird Songs Volume 10	Bird Songs	Non-Fiction
Bird Songs Volume 11	Bird Songs	Non-Fiction
Bird Songs Volume 12	Bird Songs	Non-Fiction
Bird Songs Volume 13	Bird Songs	Non-Fiction
Bird Songs Volume 14	Bird Songs	Non-Fiction
Bird Songs Volume 15	Bird Songs	Non-Fiction
Bird Spot	Bird Songs	Non-Fiction
Birds Awakening	Bird Songs	Non-Fiction
British Bird Songs And Calls	Bird Songs	Non-Fiction
British Wild Birds In Stereo	Bird Songs	Non-Fiction
Larger Thrushes	Bird Songs	Non-Fiction
Larks Ascending	Bird Songs	Non-Fiction
Nocturnal And Diurnal Birds Of Prey	Bird Songs	Non-Fiction
Nocturne Of Nightingales	Bird Songs	Non-Fiction
Our Favourite Garden Birds	Bird Songs	Non-Fiction
Sound Guide To British Waders	Bird Songs	Non-Fiction
Warblers	Bird Songs	Non-Fiction
Woodland And Garden Birds	Bird Songs	Non-Fiction
World's Best Bird Songs	Bird Songs	Non-Fiction
Your Favourite Bird Songs	Bird Songs	Non-Fiction

CHILDREN

TITLE	HEADING	SECTION
3 Hours Of Favourite Children's Stories	Children's Stories..	Fiction
6 Children's Classics	Andersen, Hans Christian	Fiction
15 Minute Tales	Blyton, Enid	Fiction
101 Dalmatians	Films	Fiction
ABC (Alphabet)	Early Learning	Non-Fiction
ABC Rhymes	Early Learning	Non-Fiction
Ace	King-Smith, Dick	Fiction
Action Force	Television	Fiction
Add On ... Take Away	Early Learning	Non-Fiction
Adventures Of Black Beauty, The	Sewell, Anna	Fiction
Adventures Of Creamcake And Company	Zabel, Jennifer	Fiction
Adventures Of Doctor Snuggles	O'Kelly, Jeffrey	Fiction
Adventures Of Dusty And The Dinosaurs	Croft, Mike	Fiction
Adventures Of Fireman Sam, The	Wilmer, Diane	Fiction
Adventures Of Heggarty Haggerty	Lindsay, Eliza	Fiction
Adventures Of Huckleberry Finn	Twain, Mark	Fiction
Adventures Of Mary Mouse	Blyton, Enid	Fiction
Adventures Of Mask	Jackson, Steve	Fiction
Adventures Of Milly-Molly-Mandy	Lankester Brisley	Fiction
Adventures Of Mr. Chatterbox	Hargreaves, Roger	Fiction
Adventures Of Mr. Greedy	Hargreaves, Roger	Fiction
Adventures Of Mr. Messy	Hargreaves, Roger	Fiction
Adventures Of Mr. Noisy	Hargreaves, Roger	Fiction
Adventures Of Mr. Pinkwhistle	Blyton, Enid	Fiction
Adventures Of Mr. SIlly	Hargreaves, Roger	Fiction
Adventures Of Mr. Small	Hargreaves, Roger	Fiction
Adventures Of Mr. Sneeze	Hargreaves, Roger	Fiction
Adventures Of Mr. Tickle	Hargreaves, Roger	Fiction
Adventures Of Naughty Amelia Jane	Blyton, Enid	Fiction
Adventures Of Orlando	Hale, Kathleen	Fiction
Adventures Of Portland Bill	Armitage, David	Fiction
Adventures Of Postman Pat, The	Cunliffe, John	Fiction
Adventures Of Robin Hood, The	Traditional	Fiction
Adventures Of Roger And The Rotten Trolls, The	Children's Stories..	Fiction
Adventures Of Rupert Bear	Bestall, Alfred	Fiction
Adventures Of Sinbad The Sailor	Traditional	Fiction
Adventures Of Snuffy Steam Train	Adamson, Jean	Fiction
Adventures Of The Gumby Gang, The	Oldfield, Pamela	Fiction
Adventures Of The Secret Seven	Blyton, Enid	Fiction
Adventures Of The Space Dog, The	Standiford, Natalie	Fiction
Adventures Of Tom Sawyer, The	Twain, Mark	Fiction
Adventures Of Topsy And Tim	Adamson, Jean	Fiction
Adventures Of Victoria Plum	Hyks, Veronika	Fiction
Adventures Of Worzel Gummidge, The	Waterhouse, Keith	Fiction
Adventures, The	Aiken Hodge, Jane	Fiction
Adventurous Four, The	Blyton, Enid	Fiction
Aesop Fables	Aesop	Fiction
Aesop In Fableland	Aesop	Fiction
Aesop's Fables	Aesop	Fiction
Aesop's Fables Book 1	Aesop	Fiction
Aesop's Fables Book 2	Aesop	Fiction
Aimer Gates	Garner, Alan	Fiction
Aince For Pleisure And Twice For Joy	Annand, JK	Fiction
Aladdin	Traditional	Fiction

CHILDREN

Aladdin And Ali Baba	Traditional	Fiction
Aladdin And His Lamp	Traditional	Fiction
Aladdin And His Magic Lamp	Traditional	Fiction
Aladdin And The Wonderful Lamp	Traditional	Fiction
Alexander And The Terrible, Horrible, No Good...	Viorst, Judith	Fiction
Alexander The Great	Traditional	Fiction
Alfie Gives A Hand	Hughes, Shirley	Fiction
Alfie's Feet	Hughes, Shirley	Fiction
Ali Baba	Traditional	Fiction
Ali Baba And The Forty Thieves	Traditional	Fiction
Alice In Wonderland	Carroll, Lewis	Fiction
Alice Through The Looking Glass	Carroll, Lewis	Fiction
Alice's Adventures In Wonderland	Carroll, Lewis	Fiction
All About My Naughty Little Sister	Edwards, Dorothy	Fiction
All Join In And Other Nonsense	Blake, Quentin	Fiction
Alphabet, The	Early Learning	Non-Fiction
Amazing Monsters	Fisher, Robert	Fiction
Andy Pandy And Teddy At The Zoo	Bird, Maria	Fiction
Andy Pandy And The Badger	Bird, Maria	Fiction
Andy Pandy And The Dovecot	Bird, Maria	Fiction
Andy Pandy And The Ducklings	Bird, Maria	Fiction
Andy Pandy And The Red Motor Car	Bird, Maria	Fiction
Andy Pandy And The Spotted Cow	Bird, Maria	Fiction
Andy Pandy And The Willow Tree	Bird, Maria	Fiction
Animal Alphabet, The	Craig, Bobbie	Fiction
Animal Fairyland	Children's Stories..	Fiction
Animal Magic	Early Learning	Non-Fiction
Animals Of Farthing Wood	Dann, Colin	Fiction
Animals Went In Two By Two, The	Children's Stories..	Fiction
Antelope Company Ashore, The	Hall, Willis	Fiction
Antelope Company At Large, The	Hall, Willis	Fiction
Arabian Nights: Aladdin	Traditional	Fiction
Arabian Tales, Legends And Romances	Traditional	Fiction
Are You There God? It Is Me, Margaret	Blume, Judy	Fiction
Aristocats	Disney	Fiction
Arthur And The Belly Button Diamond	Coren, Alan	Fiction
Asterix And The Gladiator	Goscinny & Uderzo	Fiction
Asterix And The Magic Carpet	Goscinny & Uderzo	Fiction
Asterix In Britain	Goscinny & Uderzo	Fiction
Asterix The Gaul	Goscinny & Uderzo	Fiction
Baa Baa Black Sheep	Children's Stories..	Fiction
Babar And Father Christmas	De Brunhoff, Jean	Fiction
Babar At Home	De Brunhoff, Jean	Fiction
Babar The Elephant	De Brunhoff, Jean	Fiction
Babar The King	De Brunhoff, Jean	Fiction
Babar's Choice	De Brunhoff, Jean	Fiction
Babar's First Step	De Brunhoff, Jean	Fiction
Babar's Mystery	De Brunhoff, Jean	Fiction
Bag Of Moonshine, A	Garner, Alan	Fiction
Ballet Shoes	Streatfield, Noel	Fiction
Bambi	Salten, Felix	Fiction
Bangers And Mash	Television	Fiction
Barbie	Mandeville, A	Fiction
Batman	Shaw Gardner, Craig	Fiction
Batman In Rhymes, Riddles And Riots	Shaw Gardner, Craig	Fiction
Battle Of The Bubble And Squeak	Pearce, Philippa	Fiction
Bear Called Paddington, A	Bond, Michael	Fiction
Bears' Christmas	Berenstain, Stan & Jan	Fiction
Bears' Picnic, The	Berenstain, Stan & Jan	Fiction
Beauty And The Beast	Grimm	Fiction
Beaver Towers	Hinton, Nigel	Fiction
Bedtime Fairy Stories	Children's Stories..	Fiction
Bedtime For Frances	Hoban, Russell	Fiction
Bedtime Stories	Children's Stories..	Fiction

CHILDREN

Title	Author	Type
Beezus And Ramona	Cleary, Beverly	Fiction
Bertha	Television	Fiction
Best Of Milly Molly Mandy	Lankester Brisley	Fiction
Best Of Teddy Robinson	Robinson, Joan	Fiction
B.F.G, The	Dahl, Roald	Fiction
Big Alfie And Annie	Hughes, Shirley	Fiction
Big Alfie Out Of Doors Storybook, The	Hughes, Shirley	Fiction
Big Pancake, The	Children's Stories..	Fiction
Biggles	Johns, Capt. W.E	Fiction
Biggles Defies The Swastika	Johns, Capt. W.E	Fiction
Biggles Flies East	Johns, Capt. W.E	Fiction
Bill The Minder	Forder, Timothy	Fiction
Bill's New Frock	Fine, Anne	Fiction
Billy And Blaze	Anderson, C.W.	Fiction
Billy Bunter Gets The Boot	Richards, Frank	Fiction
Birthday Burglar, The	Mahy, Margaret	Fiction
Birthday Treat, A	Bond, Michael	Fiction
Black Beauty	Children's Stories..	Fiction
Black Beauty	Sewell, Anna	Fiction
Black Fairy Tales	Traditional	Fiction
Blackground	Aiken, Joan	Fiction
Blood-And-Thunder Adventure On Hurricane Peak	Mahy, Margaret	Fiction
Blossoms And The Green Phantom	Byars, Betsy	Fiction
Blossoms Meet The Vulture Lady	Byars, Betsy	Fiction
Bobby Brewster's Scarecrow	Todd, H.E.	Fiction
Bonkers Clocks	Fisk, Nicholas	Fiction
Book Of Dragons, The	Nesbitt, E	Fiction
Borrowers Afield, The	Norton, Mary	Fiction
Borrowers, The	Norton, Mary	Fiction
Box Of Nothing, A	Dickinson, Peter	Fiction
Brambly Hedge	Barklem, Jill	Fiction
Brave Little Tailor	Children's Stories..	Fiction
Bravestarr	Television	Fiction
Brer Rabbit	Uncle Remus	Fiction
Brontonappers, The	Television	Fiction
Bunnicula	Howe, Deborah & James	Fiction
Burglar Bill	Ahlberg, Janet	Fiction
Calendar, The	Early Learning	Non-Fiction
Canterville Ghost, The	Wilde, Oscar	Fiction
Captain Beaky	Lloyd, Jeremy	Fiction
Captain Pugwash	Ryan, John	Fiction
Car Wars	Jackson, Steve	Fiction
Carrie's War	Bawden, Nina	Fiction
Castle Of Adventure, The	Blyton, Enid	Fiction
Castle Of The Golden Sun, The	Reeves, James	Fiction
Castle Of Yew, The	Boston, Lucy M.	Fiction
Cat Ate My Gymsuit, The	Danziger, Paula	Fiction
Challenge In The Dark	Leeson, Robert	Fiction
Chant Village Stories	Children's Stories..	Fiction
Charlie And The Chocolate Factory	Dahl, Roald	Fiction
Charlie And The Great Glass Elevator	Dahl, Roald	Fiction
Charlie Brown's All Stars	Schultz, Charles	Fiction
Charlie Lewis Plays For Time	Kemp, Gene	Fiction
Charlie Moon And The Big Bonanza Bust-up	Hughes, Shirley	Fiction
Chatterbox Classics 1	Chatterbox	Non-Fiction
Chatterbox Humour 1	Chatterbox	Non-Fiction
Chatterbox Mixed Bag 1	Chatterbox	Non-Fiction
Chatterbox Pops 1	Chatterbox	Non-Fiction
Chestnut Soldier, The	Nimmo, Jenny	Fiction
Chewing Gum Rescue, The	Mahy, Margaret	Fiction
Chicken Licken	Children's Stories..	Fiction
Children Of Green Knowe, The	Boston, Lucy M.	Fiction
Children's Bible In 365 Stories, The	Bible	Non-Fiction
Children's Hour	Radio	Fiction

CHILDREN

Children's Hour	Television	Fiction
Childrens Number Songs And Stories	Early Learning	Non-Fiction
Children's Stories	Children's Stories..	Fiction
Children's Tales From Around The World	Children's Stories..	Fiction
Child's Garden Of Verses, A	Stevenson, Robert Louis	Fiction
Chip 'n' Dale	Television	Fiction
Chitty Chitty Bang Bang	Fleming, Ian	Fiction
Chocolate War, The	Cormier, Robert	Fiction
Christmas Activity Box	Christmas	Fiction
Christmas Carol, A	Dickens, Charles	Fiction
Christmas Stories	Lurtsema, Robert J.	Fiction
Chronicles Of Narnia Soundbook	Lewis, C.S	Fiction
Chronicles Of Narnia, The	Lewis, C.S	Fiction
Church Mouse And Church Cat	Oakley, Graham	Fiction
Cinderella	Traditional	Fiction
Circles Of Deceit	Bawden, Nina	Fiction
Clever Polly And The Stupid Wolf	Storr, Catherine	Fiction
Clock, The	Early Learning	Non-Fiction
Clock Tower Ghost, The	Kemp, Gene	Fiction
Collected Stories From Europe	Children's Stories..	Fiction
Colours	Early Learning	Non-Fiction
Colours (The Rainbow Ship)	Early Learning	Non-Fiction
Complete Alice In Wonderland, The	Carroll, Lewis	Fiction
Cops And Robbers	Ahlberg, Janet & Allan	Fiction
Coral Island	Ballantyne, R.M.	Fiction
Count Duckula	Television	Fiction
Count To Ten With Mr. Men	Hargreaves, Roger	Fiction
Countdown	Early Learning	Non-Fiction
Counting Is Fun	Early Learning	Non-Fiction
Counting Songs	Early Learning	Non-Fiction
Couples	Updike, John	Fiction
Cracker Jackson	Byars, Betsy	Fiction
Crow	Hughes, Ted	Fiction
Crow And Wodwo	Hughes, Ted	Fiction
Cuckoo Sister, The	Alcock, Vivien	Fiction
Cyril Bonhamy	Gathorne-Hardy, Jonathan	Fiction
Dan Dare	Radio	Fiction
Dancing Granny, The	Bryan, Ashley	Fiction
Dangermouse And Public Enemy No.1	Television	Fiction
Danny, The Champion Of The World	Dahl, Roald	Fiction
Day At The Zoo, A	Early Learning	Non-Fiction
Daylight Dig, The	Miscellaneous	Fiction
Deenie	Blume, Judy	Fiction
Demon Bike Rider, The	Leeson, Robert	Fiction
Demon Headmaster, The	Cross, Gillian	Fiction
Dick Tracy	Gould, Chester	Fiction
Dick Whittington	Children's Stories..	Fiction
Dick Whittington	Traditional	Fiction
Dick Whittington And His Cat	Traditional	Fiction
Diddakoi, The	Godden, Rumer	Fiction
Dinosaurs	Early Learning	Non-Fiction
Dirty Beasts	Dahl, Roald	Fiction
Disaster With The Fiend	Lavelle, Sheila	Fiction
Doctor De Soto	Steig, William	Fiction
Dod And Davie	Busch, Wilhelm	Fiction
Dodos Are Forever	King-Smith, Dick	Fiction
Dog Crusoe, The	Ballantyne, R.M.	Fiction
Donald's Pooch Parlour	Disney	Fiction
Donkey Cabbages, The	Children's Stories..	Fiction
Don't Know Boy, The	Traditional	Fiction
Double Trouble	Superman	Fiction
Dracula	Stoker, Bram	Fiction
Dragon Den, The	Murray, William	Fiction
Dragon Slayer	Sutcliff, Rosemary	Fiction

CHILDREN

Dream-Time, Splintered Sword	Treece, Henry	Fiction
Dream-Time, The	Treece, Henry	Fiction
Ducktails	Disney	Fiction
Dumbo	Disney	Fiction
Edward Gets The Hiccups	Cole, Michael	Fiction
Edward, Gordon And Henry	Awdry, Rev. W.	Fiction
Edward Joins The Band	Cole, Michael	Fiction
Edward Lear's Nonsense Rhymes	Lear, Edward	Fiction
Eighteenth Emergency, The	Byars, Betsy	Fiction
Elephant's Child, The	Kipling, Rudyard	Fiction
Ellie And The Hagwitch	Cresswell, Helen	Fiction
Elves And The Shoemaker, The	Children's Stories..	Fiction
Elves And The Shoemaker, The	Grimm	Fiction
Emil In The Soup Tureen	Lindgren, Astrid	Fiction
Emlyn's Moon	Nimmo, Jenny	Fiction
Emma Dilemma, The	Sefton, Catherine	Fiction
Emma's Ghost	Sefton, Catherine	Fiction
Emperor And The Nightingale, The	Traditional	Fiction
Emperor's New Clothes, The	Andersen, Hans Christian	Fiction
Emu's Pink Windmill Adventures	Hull, Rod & Emu	Fiction
Enchanted Orchestra, The	Niven, David	Fiction
Enchanted Wood, The	Blyton, Enid	Fiction
End Of The Tale, The	Corbett, W.J.	Fiction
Enormous Crocodile, The	Dahl, Roald	Fiction
E.T. The Extra Terrestrial	Films	Fiction
Evening At Alfie's, An	Hughes, Shirley	Fiction
Everyday Stories	Children's Stories..	Fiction
Everything Comes Up Blank	Gould, Chester	Fiction
Fables Of Aesop, The	Aesop	Fiction
Fables Of India	Traditional	Fiction
Faerie Queen	Spenser, Edmund	Fiction
Fairy Rebel, The	Reid Banks, Lynne	Fiction
Fairy Tales	Traditional	Fiction
Fairy Tales For You	Traditional	Fiction
Fanny And The Monsters	Lively, Penelope	Fiction
Fantastic Mr. Fox	Dahl, Roald	Fiction
Favourite European Tales	Traditional	Fiction
Favourite Fairy Stories	Traditional	Fiction
Favourite Fairy Tales	Traditional	Fiction
Favourite Rupert Bear Stories	Bestall, Alfred	Fiction
Favourite Rupert Stories	Bestall, Alfred	Fiction
Fiend Next Door, The	Lavelle, Sheila	Fiction
Fiery Dragon, The	Nesbitt, E	Fiction
Final Test, The	Owen, Gareth	Fiction
Firebird, The	Children's Stories..	Fiction
Fireman Sam	Wilmer, Diane	Fiction
First Anansi Story, The	Traditional	Fiction
First Queen Elizabeth	Elizabeth 1	Non-Fiction
First Story In The World, The	Bible	Non-Fiction
First Term At Malory Towers	Blyton, Enid	Fiction
First Words	Early Learning	Non-Fiction
Fisherman And His Wife, The	Children's Stories..	Fiction
Five Children And It	Nesbitt, E	Fiction
Five Get Into A Fix	Blyton, Enid	Fiction
Five Get Into Trouble	Blyton, Enid	Fiction
Five Go Adventuring Again	Blyton, Enid	Fiction
Five Go Off In A Caravan	Blyton, Enid	Fiction
Five Go Off To Camp	Blyton, Enid	Fiction
Five Go To Billycock Hill	Blyton, Enid	Fiction
Five Go To Demon's Rock	Blyton, Enid	Fiction
Five Go To Mystery Moor	Blyton, Enid	Fiction
Five Have A Mystery To Solve	Blyton, Enid	Fiction
Five Have A Wonderful Time	Blyton, Enid	Fiction
Five Have Plenty Of Fun	Blyton, Enid	Fiction

CHILDREN

Five Hundred Mile Walkies	Wallington, Mark	Fiction
Five On A Hike Together	Blyton, Enid	Fiction
Five On A Secret Trail	Blyton, Enid	Fiction
Five On A Treasure Island	Blyton, Enid	Fiction
Five On Finniston Farm	Blyton, Enid	Fiction
Five On Kirrin Island Again	Blyton, Enid	Fiction
Five Tales Of The Brothers Grimm	Grimm	Fiction
Flash Gordon	Raymond, Alex	Fiction
Flat Stanley	Brown, Jeff	Fiction
Flossie Teacake - Again	Davies, Hunter	Fiction
Flossie Teacake Strikes Back	Davies, Hunter	Fiction
Flossie Teacake's Fur Coat	Davies, Hunter	Fiction
Folk Of The Faraway Tree, The	Blyton, Enid	Fiction
Folk Tales From Around The World	Traditional	Fiction
Folk Tales Of The Tribes Of Africa	Traditional	Fiction
Follow Me To The Seaside	Trower, Terry	Fiction
Forgotten Heritage, A	Aitken, Hannah	Fiction
Four Classic Stories	Children's Stories..	Fiction
Four Dragon Stories	Nesbitt, E	Fiction
Four Of Your Favourite Stories From Grimm	Grimm	Fiction
Four Stories	Grimm	Fiction
Four Traditional Fairy Tales	Traditional	Fiction
Fox Busters, The	King-Smith, Dick	Fiction
Foxwood Tales	Paterson, Cynthia	Fiction
Frankie's Hat	Mark, Jan	Fiction
Fred The Fisherman	Television	Fiction
Fun And Games With Postman Pat	Cunliffe, John	Fiction
Fun For The Secret Seven	Blyton, Enid	Fiction
Funny Bones	Ahlberg, Janet & Allan	Fiction
Further Adventures Of Spot, The	Hill, Eric	Fiction
Further Railway Stories	Awdry, Rev. W.	Fiction
Gaffer Sampson's Luck	Paton Walsh, Jill	Fiction
Gawain And The Green Knight	Traditional	Fiction
Gawain And The Green Knight And The Pearl	Traditional	Fiction
George's Marvellous Medicine	Dahl, Roald	Fiction
Gerald Mcboing Boing	Children's Stories..	Fiction
Gertrude Gooseberry And Belinda Blackcurrant	Garden Gang	Fiction
Ghost And Bertie Boggin, The	Sefton, Catherine	Fiction
Ghost Boast	Miscellaneous	Fiction
Ghost Downstairs, The	Garfield, Leon	Fiction
Ghost Of Blacklake, The	Miscellaneous	Fiction
Ghost Of Thomas Kempe, The	Lively, Penelope	Fiction
Ghostbuster Of The Year	Spurgeon, Maureen	Fiction
Ghostly Companions	Alcock, Vivien	Fiction
Ghosts Of Hungry House Land, The	McBratney, Sam	Fiction
Giants, Gods, Gold And Greece	Greek Mythology	Fiction
Gingerbread Boy, The	Children's Stories..	Fiction
Gingerbread Man, The	Traditional	Fiction
Gingerbread Rabbit, The	Jarrell, Randall	Fiction
Giraffe, The Pelley And Me, The	Dahl, Roald	Fiction
Girl From The Candle-Lit Bath	Smith, Dodie	Fiction
Girl Of The Great Mountain, The	Traditional	Fiction
Glenda Jackson Reads From Her Storybook	Jackson, Glenda	Fiction
Glo Bug	Miscellaneous	Fiction
Glo Butterfly	Miscellaneous	Fiction
Glo Cricket	Miscellaneous	Fiction
Glo Worm	Miscellaneous	Fiction
Goblins At The Bath House	Manning-Sanders, Ruth	Fiction
Going Home	Peyton, K.M.	Fiction
Going To The Zoo	Children's Stories..	Fiction
Golden Fox	Valentine, Anthony	Fiction
Golden Goose, The	Grimm	Fiction
Goldilocks	Traditional	Fiction
Goldilocks And The Three Bears	Children's Stories..	Fiction

CHILDREN

Title	Author	Category
Goldilocks And The Three Bears	Traditional	Fiction
Good Work Secret Seven	Blyton, Enid	Fiction
Goodnight Stories	Children's Stories..	Fiction
Goose Girl, The	Children's Stories..	Fiction
Gowie Corby Plays Chicken	Kemp, Gene	Fiction
Grandma And The Ghowlies	Moray Williams, Ursula	Fiction
Granny Reardun	Garner, Alan	Fiction
Granny Was A Buffer Girl	Doherty, Berlie	Fiction
Great Fairy Tales Of The World	Traditional	Fiction
Great Piratical Rumbustification, The	Mahy, Margaret	Fiction
Great Switcheroo, The	Dahl, Roald	Fiction
Green Smoke	Manning, Rosemary	Fiction
Grimm Brothers Fairy Tales	Grimm	Fiction
Grimm's Fairy Tales	Grimm	Fiction
Grinny	Fisk, Nicholas	Fiction
Growing Pains Of Adrian Mole, The	Townsend, Sue	Fiction
Gulliver's Travels	Swift, Jonathan	Fiction
Gumby Gang Again, The	Oldfield, Pamela	Fiction
Gumby Gang On Holiday, The	Oldfield, Pamela	Fiction
Gumby Gang Strikes Again, The	Oldfield, Pamela	Fiction
Gumdrop	Biro, Val	Fiction
Hairs In The Palm Of The Hand	Mark, Jan	Fiction
Hand Rhymes	Brown, Marc	Fiction
Hans Andersen	Andersen, Hans Christian	Fiction
Hans Andersen Stories	Andersen, Hans Christian	Fiction
Hans Christian Andersen Fairy Tales	Andersen, Hans Christian	Fiction
Hansel And Gretel	Children's Stories..	Fiction
Hansel And Gretel	Grimm	Fiction
Happy Adventure Tales	Children's Stories..	Fiction
Happy Families	Ahlberg, Allan	Fiction
Happy Families Stories	Children's Stories..	Fiction
Happy Prince, The	Wilde, Oscar	Fiction
Harry's Mad	King-Smith, Dick	Fiction
Haunting, The	Mahy, Margaret	Fiction
Heidi	Spyri, Johanna	Fiction
Heidi Grows Up	Tritten, Charles	Fiction
Helen Oxenbury's Nursery Stories	Oxenbury, Helen	Fiction
Henry's Cat	Television	Fiction
Henry's Cat Becomes Prime Minister	Television	Fiction
Herbert The Hedgehog	Kelham, John	Fiction
Here Comes Charlie Moon	Hughes, Shirley	Fiction
Hermit And The Bear, The	Yeoman, John	Fiction
He's Your Dog, Charlie Brown	Schultz, Charles	Fiction
Higglety Pigglety Pop	Sendak, Maurice	Fiction
Hobbit, The	Tolkien, J.R.R.	Fiction
Holiday With The Fiend	Lavelle, Sheila	Fiction
Home Sweet Home	Grahame, Kenneth	Fiction
Hornbook For Witches, A	Sendak, Maurice	Fiction
Horse And His Boy, The	Lewis, C.S	Fiction
Hour Of Fairy Stories, An	Traditional	Fiction
House At Pooh Corner	Milne, A.A.	Fiction
House Inside Out, A	Lively, Penelope	Fiction
How Robin Became An Outlaw	Traditional	Fiction
How The Leopard Got His Spots	Kipling, Rudyard	Fiction
How The Rhinoceros Got His Skin	Kipling, Rudyard	Fiction
How Tiger Got His Stripes	Traditional	Fiction
Huckleberry Finn	Twain, Mark	Fiction
Hunting Of The Snark, The	Carroll, Lewis	Fiction
Huxley Pig At The Circus	Peppe, Rodney	Fiction
I Can Count	Early Learning	Non-Fiction
I Capture The Castle	Smith, Dodie	Fiction
Ice House, The	Bawden, Nina	Fiction
Iggie's House	Blume, Judy	Fiction
Indian In The Cupboard, The	Reid Banks, Lynne	Fiction

CHILDREN

Title	Author	Category
Iron Man, The	Hughes, Ted	Fiction
Island Of Adventure	Blyton, Enid	Fiction
It's A Children's World	Children's Stories..	Fiction
It's The Great Pumpkin, Charlie Brown	Schultz, Charles	Fiction
It's Too Frightening For Me!	Hughes, Shirley	Fiction
Ivor The Engine	Television	Fiction
Jack And The Beanstalk	Children's Stories..	Fiction
Jack And The Beanstalk	Traditional	Fiction
James And The Giant Peach	Dahl, Roald	Fiction
Jason Bodger And The Priory Ghost	Kemp, Gene	Fiction
Jeffy, The Burglar's Cat	Moray Williams, Ursula	Fiction
Jelly Pie	Mcgough, Roger	Fiction
Jennings Goes To School	Buckeridge, Anthony	Fiction
Jenny And James Learn To Count	Early Learning	Non-Fiction
Jenny And James Start School	Miscellaneous	Fiction
Jenny And The Cat Club	Averill, Esther	Fiction
Jeremiah In The Dark Woods	Ahlberg, Janet & Allan	Fiction
Jim At The Corner	Farjeon, Eleanor	Fiction
Jimbo Flies To France	Maddocks, Pete	Fiction
Jimbo Flies To Spain	Maddocks, Pete	Fiction
Jimmy's Golden Mile	Cammell, Jim	Fiction
Jive Bunny Finds Fame	Miscellaneous	Fiction
Jive Bunny Saves The Day	Miscellaneous	Fiction
Johnny Tomorrow	Bear, Carolyn	Fiction
Jolly Postman, The	Ahlberg, Janet & Allan	Fiction
Jolly Tall	Hissey, Jane	Fiction
Josh's Panther	Sampson, Fay	Fiction
Journey To The Centre Of The Earth	Verne, Jules	Fiction
Julie Of The Wolves	Craighead, Jean-George	Fiction
Jungle Book Stories	Kipling, Rudyard	Fiction
Jungle Book, The	Kipling, Rudyard	Fiction
Juniper: A Mystery	Kemp, Gene	Fiction
Just So Stories	Kipling, Rudyard	Fiction
Just William	Crompton, Richmal	Fiction
Just William Stories	Crompton, Richmal	Fiction
Kelpie	Mayne, William	Fiction
Kenny's Window	Sendak, Maurice	Fiction
Kept In The Dark	Bawden, Nina	Fiction
Kidnapped	Stevenson, Robert Louis	Fiction
Kim	Kipling, Rudyard	Fiction
King Arthur	Traditional	Fiction
King Arthur And Excalibur	Children's Stories..	Fiction
King Arthur And His Knights	Traditional	Fiction
King Arthur And Merlyn's Animal Council	Traditional	Fiction
King Arthur - Excalibur	Traditional	Fiction
King Richard The Lionheart	Children's Stories..	Fiction
Kingdom Under The Sea, The	Aiken, Joan	Fiction
Kitchen Warriors, The	Aiken, Joan	Fiction
Knox The Fox	Harvey, Richard	Fiction
Labours Of Heracles, The	Greek Mythology	Fiction
Lady And The Tramp	Disney	Fiction
Land Of Make Believe	Children's Stories..	Fiction
Land Of Oz, The	Baum, L. Frank	Fiction
Lark's Castle	York, Susannah	Fiction
Last Battle, The	Lewis, C.S	Fiction
Last Of The Mohicans, The	Cooper, James Fenimore	Fiction
Last Slice Of The Rainbow, The	Aiken, Joan	Fiction
Last Vampire, The	Hall, Willis	Fiction
Learn The Alphabet	Early Learning	Non-Fiction
Learn To Count	Early Learning	Non-Fiction
Learning Colours	Early Learning	Non-Fiction
Learning The Alphabet	Early Learning	Non-Fiction
Learning The Alphabet And Learning To Count	Early Learning	Non-Fiction
Learning To Spell	Early Learning	Non-Fiction

CHILDREN

Title	Author	Type
Learning Your Tables	Early Learning	Non-Fiction
Legends Of The Clans	Traditional	Fiction
Let's Listen	Aesop	Fiction
Let's Play	Children's Stories..	Fiction
Light Princess, The	Macdonald, Geoff	Fiction
Lion At School	Pearce, Philippa	Fiction
Lion Children's Bible, The	Bible	Non-Fiction
Lion, The Witch And The Wardrobe, The	Lewis, C.S	Fiction
Lionel's Car	Cole, Michael	Fiction
Lionel's Party	Cole, Michael	Fiction
Listen To This	Cecil, Laura	Fiction
Listen With Mother	Radio	Fiction
Little Bear Lost	Hissey, Jane	Fiction
Little Blue Brontosaurus	Priess & Stout	Fiction
Little Bo Peep	Children's Stories..	Fiction
Little Broomstick, The	Stewart, Mary	Fiction
Little Drummer Girl, The	Le Carre, John	Fiction
Little Gingerbread Man, The	Children's Stories..	Fiction
Little Grey Rabbit Collection, The	Uttley, Alison	Fiction
Little Grey Rabbit Stories	Uttley, Alison	Fiction
Little Grey Rabbit, The	Uttley, Alison	Fiction
Little Match Girl, The	Andersen, Hans Christian	Fiction
Little Mermaid, The	Andersen, Hans Christian	Fiction
Little Miss Stories	Hargreaves, Roger	Fiction
Little Old Mrs. Pepperpot	Proysen, Alf	Fiction
Little Oz Stories	Baum, L. Frank	Fiction
Little Prince, The	De Saint-Exupery	Fiction
Little Princess, A	Hodgson Burnett	Fiction
Little Red Fox Book	Uttley, Alison	Fiction
Little Red Hen, The	Southgate, Vera	Fiction
Little Red Riding Hood	Children's Stories..	Fiction
Little Red Riding Hood	Perrault, Charles	Fiction
Little Tin Soldier, The	Children's Stories..	Fiction
Little Toot Stories	Gramatsky, Hardie	Fiction
Little Women	Alcott, Louisa May	Fiction
Lizzie Dripping	Cresswell, Helen	Fiction
London Snow	Theroux, Paul	Fiction
Lord Of The Rings	Tolkien, J.R.R.	Fiction
Lucy And The Big Bad Wolf	Jungman, Ann	Fiction
Lucy And The Wolf In Sheep's Clothing	Jungman, Ann	Fiction
Ludo And The Star Horse	Stewart, Mary	Fiction
Machine Gunners, The	Westhall, Robert	Fiction
Magic Faraway Tree, The	Blyton, Enid	Fiction
Magic Finger, The	Dahl, Roald	Fiction
Magic Quern, The	Traditional	Fiction
Magic Sword, The	Traditional	Fiction
Magician's Nephew, The	Lewis, C.S	Fiction
Magnus Powermouse	King-Smith, Dick	Fiction
Man Who Would Be King, The	Kipling, Rudyard	Fiction
Maple Town	Miscellaneous	Fiction
Marmaduke The Lorry Goes To Italy	Chapman, Elizabeth	Fiction
Marriage Of Gawain, The	Traditional	Fiction
Martin's Mice	King-Smith, Dick	Fiction
Mary Poppins	Travers, P.L.	Fiction
Mary Poppins And The Banks Family	Travers, P.L.	Fiction
Mary Poppins Comes Back	Travers, P.L.	Fiction
Mary Poppins Opens The Door	Travers, P.L.	Fiction
Mask	Jackson, Steve	Fiction
Mask-a-Raid	Jackson, Steve	Fiction
Master Of Ballantrae	Stevenson, Robert Louis	Fiction
Masters Of The Universe	Television	Fiction
Mathilde Mouse	Gallico, Paul	Fiction
Matilda	Dahl, Roald	Fiction
Meet Posy Bates	Cresswell, Helen	Fiction

CHILDREN

Title	Author	Category
Meg And Mog	Nicoll, Helen	Fiction
Merlin And Perceval	Traditional	Fiction
Mervyn Mouse	Poetry	Fiction
Miffy	Bruna, Dick	Fiction
Miffy Stories	Bruna, Dick	Fiction
Milly Molly Mandy Stories	Lankester Brisley, Joyce	Fiction
Minpins, The	Dahl, Roald	Fiction
Missing Ambassador, The	Miscellaneous	Fiction
Moby Dick	Melville, Herman	Fiction
Mogg's Christmas	Kerr, Judith	Fiction
Mom, The Wolfman And Me	Klein, Norma	Fiction
Monster Maker	Fisk, Nicholas	Fiction
Moon Princess, The	Traditional	Fiction
Mop And Smiff	Television	Fiction
Mop And Smiff Go To School	Television	Fiction
Mop And Smiff In Search Of A Pedigree	Television	Fiction
Mop And Smiff On Bunny Hill	Television	Fiction
Mop And Smiff's Day Sunnyseas	Television	Fiction
More About Paddington Bear	Bond, Michael	Fiction
More About The Gumby Gang	Oldfield, Pamela	Fiction
More Adventures Of My Little Pony	Zabel, Jennifer	Fiction
More From Ten In A Bed	Ahlberg, Allan	Fiction
More Grimm's Fairy Tales	Grimm	Fiction
More Jungle Book Stories	Kipling, Rudyard	Fiction
More Little Grey Rabbit Stories	Uttley, Alison	Fiction
More Naughty Little Sister Stories	Edwards, Dorothy	Fiction
More Postman Pat Stories	Cunliffe, John	Fiction
More Railway Stories (1)	Awdry, Rev. W.	Fiction
More Railway Stories (2)	Awdry, Rev. W.	Fiction
More Tales From Ten In A Bed	Ahlberg, Allan	Fiction
More William Stories	Crompton, Richmal	Fiction
More Will O' The Wisp Stories	Television	Fiction
Mortimer Says Nothing	Aiken, Joan	Fiction
Mortimer's Cross	Aiken, Joan	Fiction
Mother Goose	Traditional	Fiction
Mountain Of Adventure	Blyton, Enid	Fiction
Mouse Butcher, The	King-Smith, Dick	Fiction
Mouse Tales	Potter, Beatrix	Fiction
Mr Grumpy's Outing	Burningham, John	Fiction
Mr. Majeika	Carpenter, Humphrey	Fiction
Mr. Men	Hargreaves, Roger	Fiction
Mr. Men And Little Miss	Hargreaves, Roger	Fiction
Mr. Men Ride Again, The	Hargreaves, Roger	Fiction
Mr. Men Stories	Hargreaves, Roger	Fiction
Mr. Plod And Little Noddy	Blyton, Enid	Fiction
Mrs Frisby And The Rats Of Nimh	O'Brien, Robert C	Fiction
Mrs. Pepperpot Stories	Proysen, Alf	Fiction
Mrs. Tiggy-Winkle And Friends	Potter, Beatrix	Fiction
Multiplication	Early Learning	Non-Fiction
Mummy, The	Sibley, Raymond	Fiction
Munch Bunch	Read, Giles	Fiction
Munch Bunch Stories	Read, Giles	Fiction
Munch Bunch Stories And Songs	Read, Giles	Fiction
Musical Sounds	Early Learning	Non-Fiction
Musical Sums	Early Learning	Non-Fiction
Musical Times Tables	Early Learning	Non-Fiction
Musicians Of Bremen, The	Grimm	Fiction
My Book Of Pets	Early Learning	Non-Fiction
My Book Of Words	Early Learning	Non-Fiction
My Favourite Fairy Stories	Traditional	Fiction
My Friend Walter	Morpurgo, Michael	Fiction
My Little Pony	Zabel, Jennifer	Fiction
Mystery Of Tally-Ho Cottage, The	Blyton, Enid	Fiction
Mystery Of The Burnt Cottage, The	Blyton, Enid	Fiction

CHILDREN

Title	Author	Type
Mystery Of The Secret Room, The	Blyton, Enid	Fiction
Nana	Zola, Emile	Fiction
Napoleon	Napoleon	Non-Fiction
Nature Of The Beast	Howker, Janni	Fiction
Necklace Of Raindrops, A	Aiken, Joan	Fiction
Nellie The Elephant	Children's Stories..	Fiction
Nelson	Nelson	Non-Fiction
Never Smile At A Crocodile	Children's Stories..	Fiction
Nickums, The	Bell, J.J.	Fiction
Night Before Christmas, The	Children's Stories..	Fiction
Nightingale, The	Children's Stories..	Fiction
Night-Watchmen, The	Cresswell, Helen	Fiction
No Place Like	Kemp, Gene	Fiction
Noddy And The Magic Boots	Blyton, Enid	Fiction
Noddy And The Tootles	Blyton, Enid	Fiction
Noddy Goes To Sea	Blyton, Enid	Fiction
Noddy Has An Adventure	Blyton, Enid	Fiction
Noddy Makes Everyone Cross	Blyton, Enid	Fiction
Noddy Stories	Blyton, Enid	Fiction
Noddy's Big Balloon	Blyton, Enid	Fiction
Noddy's Unlucky Day	Blyton, Enid	Fiction
Nonsense Poems	Lear, Edward	Fiction
Nonsense Poetry	Poetry	Fiction
Nonstop Nonsense	Mahy, Margaret	Fiction
Nothing To Be Afraid Of	Mark, Jan	Fiction
Not-Just-Anybody Family, The	Byars, Betsy	Fiction
Now We Are Six	Milne, A.A.	Fiction
Numbers	Early Learning	Non-Fiction
Odd Flamingo, The	Bawden, Nina	Fiction
Odysseus - The Greatest Hero Of Them All	Robinson, Tony	Fiction
Oi, Get Off Our Train	Burningham, John	Fiction
Old Bear	Hissey, Jane	Fiction
Old Macdonald	Children's Stories..	Fiction
Old Macdonald Had A Farm	Children's Stories..	Fiction
Old Man Of Lochnagar	H.R.H. Prince Of Wales	Fiction
Oliver And Company	Disney	Fiction
Oliver Cromwell	Cromwell, Oliver	Non-Fiction
Oliver Twist	Dickens, Charles	Fiction
Once Upon A Time	Biro, Val	Fiction
Once Upon A Time	Children's Stories..	Fiction
Once Upon A Time	Oldfield, Pamela	Fiction
Once Upon A Time	Traditional	Fiction
Once Upon A World	Bible	Non-Fiction
One Hundred And One Dalmatians	Smith, Dodie	Fiction
Open Road, The	Grahame, Kenneth	Fiction
Opposites	Early Learning	Non-Fiction
Ordinary Princess, The	Kaye, M.M.	Fiction
Orville And Cuddles	Harris, Keith	Fiction
Outlaw Band Of Sherwood Forest, The	Traditional	Fiction
Outsiders, The	Hinton, S.E.	Fiction
Owl Who Was Afraid Of The Dark, The	Tomlinson, Jill	Fiction
Paddington	Bond, Michael	Fiction
Paddington Abroad	Bond, Michael	Fiction
Paddington And Pantomine Time	Bond, Michael	Fiction
Paddington And The Disappearing Trick	Bond, Michael	Fiction
Paddington At Large	Bond, Michael	Fiction
Paddington At The Station	Bond, Michael	Fiction
Paddington Bear	Bond, Michael	Fiction
Paddington Does It Himself	Bond, Michael	Fiction
Paddington Goes To The Sales	Bond, Michael	Fiction
Paddington Goes To Town	Bond, Michael	Fiction
Paddington Helps Out	Bond, Michael	Fiction
Paddington Hits Out	Bond, Michael	Fiction
Paddington Marches On	Bond, Michael	Fiction

CHILDREN

Title	Author	Category
Paddington On The River	Bond, Michael	Fiction
Paddington Takes A Bath	Bond, Michael	Fiction
Paddington's Birthday Party	Bond, Michael	Fiction
Paddington's Golden Record	Bond, Michael	Fiction
Paddington's New Room	Bond, Michael	Fiction
Pam Parsnip And Lawrence Lemon	Garden Gang	Fiction
Past Eight O'Clock	Aiken, Joan	Fiction
Patrick Pear And Colin Cucumber	Garden Gang	Fiction
Paul Bunyan	Children's Stories..	Fiction
Pearl Of Babar Shah, The	Traditional	Fiction
Pecos Bill	Children's Stories..	Fiction
Pedro Pepper And The Cherry Twins	Garden Gang	Fiction
Pegasus The Winged Horse	Greek Mythology	Fiction
Peppermint Pig, The	Bawden, Nina	Fiction
Percival Pea And Polly Pomegranate	Garden Gang	Fiction
Percy And Harold	Awdry, Rev. W.	Fiction
Percy Runs Away	Awdry, Rev. W.	Fiction
Percy's Predicament	Awdry, Rev. W.	Fiction
Peter And The Wolf	Children's Stories..	Fiction
Peter And The Wolf	Prokofiev (composer)	Fiction
Peter And The Wolf And Tubby The Tuba	Children's Stories..	Fiction
Peter Pan	Barrie, J.M.	Fiction
Peter Potato And Alice Apple	Garden Gang	Fiction
Phantom Of The Lake	Miscellaneous	Fiction
Phantom Ship And Mr Midshipman Easy, The	Captain Marryat	Fiction
Phoenix And The Carpet, The	Nesbitt, E	Fiction
Pied Piper Of Hamelin	Browning, Robert	Fiction
Piemakers, The	Cresswell, Helen	Fiction
Piggo	Ayres, Pam	Fiction
Pigwig Papers	Harvey, Richard	Fiction
Pinocchio	Collodi, Carlo	Fiction
Pirate Uncle, The	Mahy, Margaret	Fiction
Pirates' Mixed-Up Voyage, The	Mahy, Margaret	Fiction
Pistachio Prescription, The	Danziger, Paula	Fiction
Planet Of The Elves, The	Miscellaneous	Fiction
Play Listen And Learn With Ronald Mcdonald	Early Learning	Non-Fiction
Poems, Riddles And Songs	Soutar, William	Fiction
Poetry Of Browning, The	Browning, Robert	Fiction
Polly Put The Kettle On	Children's Stories..	Fiction
Pop Goes The Diesel	Awdry, Rev. W.	Fiction
Portland Bill	Armitage, David	Fiction
Portland Bill And The Storm	Armitage, David	Fiction
Portland Bill's Busy Day	Armitage, David	Fiction
Portland Bill's Important Message	Armitage, David	Fiction
Postman Pat	Cunliffe, John	Fiction
Postman Pat And The Breezy Day	Cunliffe, John	Fiction
Postman Pat And The Christmas Pudding	Cunliffe, John	Fiction
Postman Pat And The Dinosaur Bones	Cunliffe, John	Fiction
Postman Pat And The Greendale Ghost	Cunliffe, John	Fiction
Postman Pat And The Letter Puzzle	Cunliffe, John	Fiction
Postman Pat Goes On Safari	Cunliffe, John	Fiction
Postman Pat Makes A Splash	Cunliffe, John	Fiction
Postman Pat - More Stories	Cunliffe, John	Fiction
Postman Pat Plays For Greendale	Cunliffe, John	Fiction
Postman Pat Stories, The	Cunliffe, John	Fiction
Postman Pat Takes A Message	Cunliffe, John	Fiction
Postman Pat's 123 Story	Cunliffe, John	Fiction
Postman Pat's ABC Story	Cunliffe, John	Fiction
Postman Pat's Bedtime Stories	Cunliffe, John	Fiction
Postman Pat's Breezy Day	Cunliffe, John	Fiction
Postman Pat's Day In Bed	Cunliffe, John	Fiction
Postman Pat's Messy Day	Cunliffe, John	Fiction
Postman Pat's Parcel Of Fun	Cunliffe, John	Fiction

CHILDREN

Title	Author	Category
Postman Pat's Secret	Cunliffe, John	Fiction
Postman Pat's Treasure Hunt	Cunliffe, John	Fiction
Postman Pat's Wet Day	Cunliffe, John	Fiction
Primary French	Early Learning	Non-Fiction
Primary German	Early Learning	Non-Fiction
Primary Science	Early Learning	Non-Fiction
Prince And The Pauper The	Twain, Mark	Fiction
Prince At Black Pony Inn	Pullein-Thompson, Christine	Fiction
Prince Caspian	Lewis, C.S	Fiction
Prince Ivan And The Frog Princess	Traditional	Fiction
Princess And The Frog	Traditional	Fiction
Princess And The Goblin	MacDonald, George	Fiction
Princess And The Pea	Andersen, Hans Christian	Fiction
Princess Ferozshah And The Horse Prince	Traditional	Fiction
Puddle Lane	McCullagh, Sheila	Fiction
Puff The Magic Dragon	Children's Stories..	Fiction
Puffalumps And The Caves	Riley, Phil	Fiction
Puffalumps And The Wizard, The	Riley, Phil	Fiction
Puss In Boots	Traditional	Fiction
Queen's Nose, The	King-Smith, Dick	Fiction
Raging Robots And Unruly Uncles	Mahy, Margaret	Fiction
Railway Cat, The	Arkle, Phyllis	Fiction
Railway Children, The	Nesbitt, E	Fiction
Railway Stories	Awdry, Rev. W.	Fiction
Rainbow - The Square	Television	Fiction
Ramona And Her Mother	Cleary, Beverly	Fiction
Ramona Forever	Cleary, Beverly	Fiction
Ramona Quimby, Age 8	Cleary, Beverly	Fiction
Ramona The Pest	Cleary, Beverly	Fiction
Rapunzel	Grimm	Fiction
Real Fairies	Van Gelder, Dora	Fiction
Rebecca Of Sunnybrook Farm	Wiggin, Kate Douglas	Fiction
Red Dog	Kipling, Rudyard	Fiction
Red Riding Hood	Perrault, Charles	Fiction
Red Riding Hood	Traditional	Fiction
Reluctant Dragon, The	Grahame, Kenneth	Fiction
Rescuers, The	Disney	Fiction
Return Of The Antelope, The	Hall, Willis	Fiction
Return Of The Gumby Gang	Oldfield, Pamela	Fiction
Return Of The Indian	Reid Banks, Lynne	Fiction
Return Of The Jedi	Science Fiction	Fiction
Return Of The Mr. Men, The	Hargreaves, Roger	Fiction
Revolting Rhymes	Dahl, Roald	Fiction
Rhyme Stew	Dahl, Roald	Fiction
Rhyming Words	Early Learning	Non-Fiction
Rikki-Tikki-Tavi	Kipling, Rudyard	Fiction
Roald Dahl Collection, The	Dahl, Roald	Fiction
Roald Dahl Slipcase	Dahl, Roald	Fiction
Robert Raspberry And Grace Grape	Garden Gang	Fiction
Robert The Bruce	Robert The Bruce	Non-Fiction
Robin And His Merry Men	Traditional	Fiction
Robin Hood	Traditional	Fiction
Robin's Adventures With Little John	Traditional	Fiction
Robinson Crusoe	Traditional	Fiction
Rock A Bye Baby	Romer, Jane	Fiction
Rocking Horse Secret, The	Godden, Rumer	Fiction
Roland And Oliver	Traditional	Fiction
Roland, The Minstrel Pig	Steig, William	Fiction
Romany Tales	Traditional	Fiction
Rose Storytape	Hughes, Shirley	Fiction
Rumpelstiltskin	Children's Stories..	Fiction
Runaway Train, The	Children's Stories..	Fiction
Runaways, The	Thomas, Ruth	Fiction
Rupert And The Frog Song	Bestall, Alfred	Fiction

CHILDREN

Title	Author	Category
Rupert And The Magic Seeds	Bestall, Alfred	Fiction
Rupert And The Nutwood Stage	Bestall, Alfred	Fiction
Rupert And The Old Hat	Bestall, Alfred	Fiction
Rupert And The Wobbly Witch	Bestall, Alfred	Fiction
Rupert Bear	Bestall, Alfred	Fiction
Rupert Bear And The Chocolate Buttons Gang	Bestall, Alfred	Fiction
Rupert Bear And The Hidden Lake	Bestall, Alfred	Fiction
Rupert Bear And The Lonely Bird	Bestall, Alfred	Fiction
Rupert Bear And The Muddled Magic	Bestall, Alfred	Fiction
Rupert Bear And The Yellow Elephant	Bestall, Alfred	Fiction
Rupert Bear And The Young Dragon	Bestall, Alfred	Fiction
Rupert Bear - Stories From The 1982 Annual	Bestall, Alfred	Fiction
Rupert Bear's New Adventures	Bestall, Alfred	Fiction
Saddlebottom	King-Smith, Dick	Fiction
Sam Smells A Rat	Wilmer, Diane	Fiction
Sam To The Rescue	Wilmer, Diane	Fiction
Sameep And The Parrots	Abrahams, Elaine	Fiction
Sam's Bumper Jumper	Wilmer, Diane	Fiction
Sam's Night Watch	Wilmer, Diane	Fiction
Sam's Rabbit Rescue	Wilmer, Diane	Fiction
Scenes From Watership Down	Adams, Richard	Fiction
Seal Boy, The	Traditional	Fiction
Secret Diary Of Adrian Mole	Townsend, Sue	Fiction
Secret Diary Of Adrian Mole Aged 13 & 3/4	Townsend, Sue	Fiction
Secret Garden, The	Hodgson Burnett	Fiction
Secret Island, The	Blyton, Enid	Fiction
Secret Of Kelly's Mill, The	Carus, Zena	Fiction
Secret Of The Indian, The	Reid Banks, Lynne	Fiction
Secret Seven Fireworks	Blyton, Enid	Fiction
Secret Seven Mystery	Blyton, Enid	Fiction
Secret Seven, The	Blyton, Enid	Fiction
Secret Seven Win Through	Blyton, Enid	Fiction
Secret Staircase, The	Barklem, Jill	Fiction
Selected Bosh	Lear, Edward	Fiction
Selections From Crow And Wodwo	Hughes, Ted	Fiction
Seven Dwarfs And Their Diamond Mine	Disney	Fiction
Shadow The Sheepdog	Blyton, Enid	Fiction
Sheep-Pig, The	King-Smith, Dick	Fiction
Sheila Shallot And Benny	Garden Gang	Fiction
She-Ra	Television	Fiction
Ship Of Adventure, The	Blyton, Enid	Fiction
Shock For The Secret Seven	Blyton, Enid	Fiction
Shoe People, The	Driscoll, Jim	Fiction
Shrinking Of Treehorn, The	Heide, Florence Parry	Fiction
Shuffle The Shoemaker	Children's Stories..	Fiction
Siege Of Troy, The	Greek Mythology	Fiction
Signalman, The	Dickens, Charles	Fiction
Silver Chair, The	Lewis, C.S	Fiction
Silver Jackanory	Television	Fiction
Silver Skates, The	Dodge, Mary M.	Fiction
Silverhawks	Television	Fiction
Simon Swede And Avril Apricot	Garden Gang	Fiction
Simple Adding Sums	Early Learning	Non-Fiction
Simple Spelling	Early Learning	Non-Fiction
Simple Take-Away Songs	Early Learning	Non-Fiction
Sinbad The Sailor	Traditional	Fiction
Singing Stones, The	Traditional	Fiction
Sings A Golden Hour Of Nursery Rhymes	Bestall, Alfred	Fiction
Sir Francis Drake	Drake, Sir Francis	Non-Fiction
Sir Gibbie	Macdonald, George	Fiction
Six Little Ducks	Children's Stories..	Fiction
Sleeping Beauty	Children's Stories..	Fiction
Sleeping Beauty	Perrault, Charles	Fiction
Sly Fox And The Little Red Hen	Southgate, Vera	Fiction

CHILDREN

Title	Author	Category
Sniff Stories, The	Whybrow, Ian	Fiction
Snitchnose Switch	Miscellaneous	Fiction
Snow Queen, The	Andersen, Hans Christian	Fiction
Snow Spider, The	Nimmo, Jenny	Fiction
Snow White	Grimm	Fiction
Snow White And Rose Red	Grimm	Fiction
Snow White And The Seven Dwarfs	Grimm	Fiction
Snowbird And The Sunbird	Traditional	Fiction
Snowman Postman	Cunliffe, John	Fiction
Snowman, The	Briggs, Raymond	Fiction
Soldier Tale, The	Traditional	Fiction
Sonal Splash	Abrahams, Elaine	Fiction
Sorcerer's Apprentice, The	Hosier, John	Fiction
Soria Moria Castle	Traditional	Fiction
Sounds Of Music	Early Learning	Non-Fiction
Space Boat, The	Miscellaneous	Fiction
Special Present, The	Miscellaneous	Fiction
Spell Me A Witch	Willard, Barbara	Fiction
Spid	Moray Williams, Ursula	Fiction
Spot The Dog	Hill, Eric	Fiction
Spot's First Picnic	Hill, Eric	Fiction
Spot's Hospital Visit	Hill, Eric	Fiction
Squib	Bawden, Nina	Fiction
Squirrel Of Wirral	Harvey, Richard	Fiction
Stanley Bagshaw	Wilson, Bob	Fiction
Starlight Barking, The	Smith, Dodie	Fiction
Starting School	Early Learning	Non-Fiction
Steadfast Tin Soldier, The	Andersen, Hans Christian	Fiction
Stig Of The Dump	King, Clive	Fiction
Stone Book	Garner, Alan	Fiction
Stonewalkers, The	Alcock, Vivien	Fiction
Stories For Children	Andersen, Hans Christian	Fiction
Stories For Children	Wilde, Oscar	Fiction
Stories From Pippi Longstocking	Lindgren, Astrid	Fiction
Stories Grandad Tells Me	Reid, George	Fiction
Stories Of Rupert Bear	Bestall, Alfred	Fiction
Story Of Babar	De Brunhoff, Jean	Fiction
Story Of Hatim Tai, The	Traditional	Fiction
Story Of Peter Pan	Barrie, J.M.	Fiction
Story Of Sir Galahad, The	Traditional	Fiction
Story Of Sir Lancelot, The	Traditional	Fiction
Story Of Star Wars	Science Fiction	Fiction
Story Of Swan Lake	Traditional	Fiction
Story Of The Empire Strikes Back	Science Fiction	Fiction
Story Of The Little Black Sambo	Bannerman, Helen	Fiction
Story Of The Return Of The Jedi	Science Fiction	Fiction
Story Of The Taj Mahal, The	Traditional	Fiction
Story Of The Three Kings	Bible	Non-Fiction
Story, The	Superman	Fiction
Storybook	Children's Stories..	Fiction
Storytime	Lavitz, T	Fiction
Storytime For 2 Year Olds	Stimson, Joan	Fiction
Storytime For 3 Year Olds	Stimson, Joan	Fiction
Storytime For 4 Year Olds	Stimson, Joan	Fiction
Storytime For 5 Year Olds	Stimson, Joan	Fiction
Storytime For 6 Year Olds	Stimson, Joan	Fiction
Storytime Top Ten	Berg, Leila	Fiction
Storytime Top Ten	Biro, Val	Fiction
Storytime Top Ten	Chapman, Elizabeth	Fiction
Storytime Top Ten	Children's Stories..	Fiction
Storytime Top Ten	Oldfield, Pamela	Fiction
Storytime Top Ten	Todd, H.E.	Fiction
Strange Case Of Dr. Jekyll And Mr. Hyde	Stevenson, Robert Louis	Fiction
Strange Riders At Black Pony Inn	Pullein-Thompson, Christine	Fiction

CHILDREN

Title	Author	Category
Streetwise	Early Learning	Non-Fiction
Strega Nona's Magic Lessons	De Paola, Tomie	Fiction
Stuff And Nonsense	Cecil, Laura	Fiction
Super Gran	Wilson, Forrest	Fiction
Superman And Nightmare	Children's Stories..	Fiction
Superted And Bubbles The Clown	Television	Fiction
Superted And The Lumberjacks	Television	Fiction
Superted And The Space Beavers	Television	Fiction
Superted In Superted's Dream	Television	Fiction
Swallows And Amazons	Ransome, Arthur	Fiction
Sweet Sally Lunn	Oldfield, Pamela	Fiction
Swiss Family Robinson	Wyss, Johann	Fiction
Sword In The Anvil, The	Traditional	Fiction
Tailor Of Gloucester, The	Potter, Beatrix	Fiction
Tale Of A Donkey's Tail	Children's Stories..	Fiction
Tale Of A One-Way Street	Aiken, Joan	Fiction
Tale Of Benjamin Bunny	Potter, Beatrix	Fiction
Tale Of Jemima Puddle-Duck	Potter, Beatrix	Fiction
Tale Of Mrs Tiggy-Winkle, The	Potter, Beatrix	Fiction
Tale Of Peter Rabbit, The	Potter, Beatrix	Fiction
Tale Of Scheherezade	Traditional	Fiction
Tale Of Squirrel Nutkin, The	Potter, Beatrix	Fiction
Tale Of The Cuddly Toys, The	Blyton, Enid	Fiction
Tale Of The Shining Princess, The	Gish, Lillian	Fiction
Tale Of Tom Kitten	Potter, Beatrix	Fiction
Tale Of Tuppeny	Potter, Beatrix	Fiction
Tale Of Two Bad Mice, The	Potter, Beatrix	Fiction
Tales From Lavender Shoes	Uttley, Alison	Fiction
Tales From Moomin Valley	Jansson, Tove	Fiction
Tales From Ten In A Bed	Ahlberg, Allan	Fiction
Tales From The Arabian Nights	Traditional	Fiction
Tales From The Jungle Book	Kipling, Rudyard	Fiction
Tales Of Ancient Greece	Greek Mythology	Fiction
Tales Of Hans Christian Andersen	Andersen, Hans Christian	Fiction
Tales Of King Arthur	Traditional	Fiction
Tales Of Rupert Bear	Bestall, Alfred	Fiction
Tales Of The Desert	Traditional	Fiction
Tales Of Toad	Grahame, Kenneth	Fiction
Tales Of Witches, Ghosts And Goblins	Ghost Stories	Fiction
Talking Bird, The	Traditional	Fiction
Tanya Moves House	Abrahams, Elaine	Fiction
Tarka The Otter	Williamson, Henry	Fiction
Tatty Apple	Nimmo, Jenny	Fiction
Teddy Bear's Picnic, The	Children's Stories..	Fiction
Teddy Ruxpin	Miscellaneous	Fiction
Teenage Mutant Hero Turtles	Television	Fiction
Telling The Time	Early Learning	Non-Fiction
Terribly Plain Princess, The	Oldfield, Pamela	Fiction
Then Again, Maybe I Won't	Blume, Judy	Fiction
There's A Wolf In My Pudding	Wilson, David Henry	Fiction
Third Class Genie, The	Leeson, Robert	Fiction
Thomas And Bertie	Awdry, Rev. W.	Fiction
Thomas And Terence	Awdry, Rev. W.	Fiction
Thomas And The Missing Christmas Tree	Awdry, Rev. W.	Fiction
Thomas And Trevor	Awdry, Rev. W.	Fiction
Thomas Comes To Breakfast	Awdry, Rev. W.	Fiction
Thomas Goes Fishing	Awdry, Rev. W.	Fiction
Thomas, Percy And The Coal	Awdry, Rev. W.	Fiction
Thomas's Christmas Party	Awdry, Rev. W.	Fiction
Three Bears, The	Traditional	Fiction
Three Billy Goats Gruff	Traditional	Fiction
Three Cheers Secret Seven	Blyton, Enid	Fiction
Three Little Pigs	Traditional	Fiction
Three Musketeers, The	Dumas, Alexandre	Fiction

CHILDREN

Title	Author	Genre
Through The Looking Glass	Carroll, Lewis	Fiction
Thumbelina	Andersen, Hans Christian	Fiction
Thumper's Race	Disney	Fiction
Thunder And Lightnings	Mark, Jan	Fiction
Thundercats	Television	Fiction
Tiger Who Came To Tea, The	Kerr, Judith	Fiction
Time For Tea	Miscellaneous	Fiction
Tinder Box, The	Andersen, Hans Christian	Fiction
Tintin And The Picaros	Herge	Fiction
Tintin And The Seven Crystal Balls	Herge	Fiction
Tintin: The Broken Ear	Herge	Fiction
Tiny Lifeboat, The	Traditional	Fiction
Toby And The Stout Gentleman	Awdry, Rev. W.	Fiction
Toby Man, The	King-smith, Dick	Fiction
Tom And Jerry	Television	Fiction
Tom Brown's Schooldays	Hughes, Thomas	Fiction
Tom Fobbles Day	Garner, Alan	Fiction
Tom Sawyer	Twain, Mark	Fiction
Tom Thumb	Traditional	Fiction
Tom's Midnight Garden	Pearce, Philippa	Fiction
Tony Ross' Fairy Tales	Ross, Tony	Fiction
Top Brain Anansi	Traditional	Fiction
Topiwalo The Hat Maker	Abrahams, Elaine	Fiction
Topsy And Tim Go Swimming	Adamson, Jean	Fiction
Topsy And Tim On Holiday	Adamson, Jean	Fiction
Tottie	Godden, Rumer	Fiction
Tough Ted	Bond, Simon	Fiction
Town Mouse And The Country Mouse, The	Mckie, Anne	Fiction
Traditional Stories Collection	Traditional	Fiction
Transformers	Television	Fiction
Treasure Island	Stevenson, Robert Louis	Fiction
Treasury Of Fairy Tales	Traditional	Fiction
Trillions	Fisk, Nicholas	Fiction
Trouble At The Airport	Bond, Michael	Fiction
Trouble With Product X, The	Aiken, Joan	Fiction
Trouble With The Fiend	Lavelle, Sheila	Fiction
Tshindao	Aardema, Verna	Fiction
Tumbleweed	King-Smith, Dick	Fiction
Turbulent Term Of Tyke Tiler, The	Kemp, Gene	Fiction
Twain Soundbook	Twain, Mark	Fiction
Twelve Dancing Princesses, The	Grimm	Fiction
Twinkle Twinkle Little Star	Children's Stories..	Fiction
Twits, The	Dahl, Roald	Fiction
Two Brothers, The	Traditional	Fiction
Two Stories From Button Moon	Parkinson, Robin	Fiction
Two Thousand Pound Goldfish, The	Byars, Betsy	Fiction
Ugly Duckling, The	Andersen, Hans Christian	Fiction
Ugly Duckling, The	Children's Stories..	Fiction
Uninvited Ghosts	Lively, Penelope	Fiction
Vampire's Holiday, The	Hall, Willis	Fiction
Vanishment Of Thomas Tull, The	Ahlberg, Janet	Fiction
Vassili Lackluck	Traditional	Fiction
Velveteen Rabbit, The	Williams, Margery	Fiction
Victoria Plum	Hyks, Veronika	Fiction
Victoria Plum Gives Ben A Surprise	Hyks, Veronika	Fiction
Victoria Plum Has A Treasure Hunt	Hyks, Veronika	Fiction
Victoria Plum Helps The Badgers	Hyks, Veronika	Fiction
Victoria Plum Stories	Hyks, Veronika	Fiction
Visionaries	Television	Fiction
Visit To The Dentist, A	Bond, Michael	Fiction
Voyage Of The Dawn Treader, The	Lewis, C.	Fiction
Voyages Of Sinbad	Traditional	Fiction
Walt Disney Stories For Children	Disney	Fiction
Water Babies, The	Kingsley, Charles	Fiction

CHILDREN

Title	Author	Category
Watership Down	Adams, Richard	Fiction
We Can Say No	Pithers & Greene	Non-Fiction
Wee Willie Water Melon And Betty Beetroot	Garden Gang	Fiction
Well Done Secret Seven	Blyton, Enid	Fiction
What Katy Did	Coolidge, Susan M.	Fiction
What The Neighbours Did	Pearce, Philippa	Fiction
What's The Time ?	Early Learning	Non-Fiction
Wheel Of Danger, The	Leeson, Robert	Fiction
Wheels On The Bus, The	Children's Stories..	Fiction
When Jenny Lost Her Scarf	Averill, Esther	Fiction
When We Were Very Young	Milne, A.A.	Fiction
Where The Wild Things Are	Sendak, Maurice	Fiction
Whipping Boy, The	Fleischman, Sid	Fiction
White Witch, The	Goudge, Elizabeth	Fiction
Who Framed Roger Rabbit?	Wold, Gary K	Fiction
Whoever Heard Of A Fird?	Bach, Othello	Fiction
Why Mosquitos Buzz In Peoples' Ears...	Aardema, Verna	Fiction
Why The Whales Came	Morpurgo, Michael	Fiction
Willerby's And The Bank Robbers, The	Oldfield, Pamela	Fiction
Will O' The Wisp	Television	Fiction
Wind In The Willows	Grahame, Kenneth	Fiction
Winnie The Pooh	Milne, A.A.	Fiction
Winnie The Pooh	Radio	Fiction
Winnie The Pooh And Christopher Robin	Milne, A.A.	Fiction
Winnie The Pooh And Eeyore	Milne, A.A.	Fiction
Winnie The Pooh And Kanga And Roo	Milne, A.A.	Fiction
Winnie The Pooh And The Blustery Day	Milne, A.A.	Fiction
Winnie The Pooh And The Honey Tree	Milne, A.A.	Fiction
Winnie The Pooh And Tigger	Milne, A.A.	Fiction
Winnie The Pooh And Tigger Too	Milne, A.A.	Fiction
Witches Revenge, The	Miscellaneous	Fiction
Witches, The	Dahl, Roald	Fiction
Wizard Of Oz, The	Baum, L. Frank	Fiction
Wolf And The Seven Little Kids	Grimm	Fiction
Wolves Of Willoughby Chase, The	Aiken, Joan	Fiction
Womble Stories	Beresford, Elizabeth	Fiction
Wonderful Story Of Henry Sugar, The	Dahl, Roald	Fiction
Wonderful World Of Children's Christmas	Christmas	Fiction
Wooden Horse	Williams, Eric	Fiction
Woolly Rhino, The	Miscellaneous	Fiction
World Of Colours, The	Early Learning	Non-Fiction
World Of Stories	Children's Stories..	Fiction
Worst Witch, The	Murphy, Jill	Fiction
Worzel Gives A Lecture	Waterhouse, Keith	Fiction
Worzel Gummidge	Waterhouse, Keith	Fiction
Wu And The Dragon	Traditional	Fiction
Your Favourite Fairy Stories	Traditional	Fiction
Your First Animal Book And Safety First At Home	Early Learning	Non-Fiction
You're In Love, Charlie Brown	Schultz, Charles	Fiction
Yours Affectionately Peter Rabbit	Potter, Beatrix	Fiction
Zadig, Man Of Destiny	Traditional	Fiction
Zulu	Aardema, Verna	Fiction

EDUCATIONAL

TITLE	HEADING	SECTION
16th Century Scotland	History	Non-Fiction
17th Century France; Continuity And Change	France	Non-Fiction
19th And 20th Century British Trade Unionism	Social Sciences	Non-Fiction
19th Century Russia	Russia	Non-Fiction
110% Solution, The	McCormack, Mark	Non-Fiction
325,000 Francs	Vailland, R	Non-Fiction
A Travers Sis Chansons	Brel, Jacques	Non-Fiction
ABC (The Alphabet Hunt)	Early Learning	Non-Fiction
Across The Limpopo	Nicholson, Michael	Non-Fiction
Age Of Appeasement In Europe 1918-1929, The	History	Non-Fiction
Age Of Unreason	Handy, C	Non-Fiction
Agnes Bernauer	Hebbel, F	Non-Fiction
Agriculture In England	History	Non-Fiction
Alfred Lord Tennyson	Tennyson, Alfred Lord	Non-Fiction
Among The Russians	Thubron, Colin	Non-Fiction
Andalusins, The	Spain...	Non-Fiction
Andorra	Frisch, Max	Non-Fiction
Andromaque	Racine, Jean	Non-Fiction
Anna Karenina	Tolstoy, Leo	Non-Fiction
Ansichten Eines Clowns	Boll, Heinrich	Non-Fiction
Anthony And Cleopatra	A-Level	Non-Fiction
Anthony And Cleopatra	Shakespeare, William	Non-Fiction
Antigone	Anouilh, J	Non-Fiction
Approach To Poetry Criticism	English Literature	Non-Fiction
Approach To The Nineteenth Century Novel	English Literature	Non-Fiction
Arab Culture And The West	Middle East	Non-Fiction
Arab - Israeli Conflict, The	Middle East	Non-Fiction
Archpriest Avvakum And The Russian Church Schism	Russia	Non-Fiction
Art And Design	G.C.S.E.	Non-Fiction
Art Of The General Prologue, The	A-Level	Non-Fiction
Artists Struggle For Integrity, The	Baldwin, James	Non-Fiction
As You Like It	A-Level	Non-Fiction
As You Like It	Shakespeare, William	Non-Fiction
Asquith	Social Sciences	Non-Fiction
Asya / Pervaya Lyubov	Turgenev, Ivan	Non-Fiction
Attitudes To War In England Before 1914	Military History	Non-Fiction
Aus Dem Leben Eines Taugenichts	Eichendorff	Non-Fiction
Background	Yesenin, S	Non-Fiction
Background To Gide	Gide, Andre	Non-Fiction
Background To Hamlet	English Literature	Non-Fiction
Background To Jean Paul Sartre	Sartre, Jean Paul	Non-Fiction
Barboche	Bosco, H	Non-Fiction
Basques, The	Spain...	Non-Fiction
Becket	Anouilh, J	Non-Fiction
Behind The Wall	Thubron, Colin	Non-Fiction
Beleet Parus Odinokii	Kataev, V	Non-Fiction
Beowulf	English Literature	Non-Fiction
Biedermann Und Die Brandstifter	Frisch, Max	Non-Fiction
Big Deal, The	Business	Non-Fiction
Biology (course)	G.C.S.E.	Non-Fiction

EDUCATIONAL

Bismarck And The German Problem	Germany	Non-Fiction
Bismarck And Germany	Germany	Non-Fiction
Black Africa: Yesterday And Today	Africa	Non-Fiction
Blue Nile, The	Moorehead, Alan	Non-Fiction
Bodas De Sangre	Lorca, F. Garcia	Non-Fiction
Bonjour Tristesse	Sagan, Francoise	Non-Fiction
Bonnie Prince Charlie	Bonnie Prince Charlie	Non-Fiction
Boulevard Durand	Salacrou, A	Non-Fiction
Bourges And Berry	France	Non-Fiction
Brecht And The Actor	Brecht, Bertolt	Non-Fiction
Britain Between The Wars	Social Sciences	Non-Fiction
Britannicus	Racine, Jean	Non-Fiction
British Appeasement	Social Sciences	Non-Fiction
British Political Economy 1919-1939, The	Social Sciences	Non-Fiction
Bruce Memorial Window	Scotland	Non-Fiction
Burden Of Population	Social Sciences	Non-Fiction
Business Studies (course)	G.C.S.E.	Non-Fiction
Business Trading Ethics	Business	Non-Fiction
Byron's Rhetoric	English Literature	Non-Fiction
Caligula	Camus, A	Non-Fiction
Candide	Voltaire	Non-Fiction
Canti	Leopardi, Giacomo	Non-Fiction
Catalans, The	Spain...	Non-Fiction
Centre And The Provinces, The	History	Non-Fiction
Cezanne	Cezanne	Non-Fiction
Chamberlain	Social Sciences	Non-Fiction
Charles Dickens	Dickens, Charles	Non-Fiction
Charles I And Puritanism	History	Non-Fiction
Charles II	History	Non-Fiction
Charles V	France	Non-Fiction
Chartism	History	Non-Fiction
Chartism And The 1870 Education Act	Social Sciences	Non-Fiction
Chemistry (course)	G.C.S.E.	Non-Fiction
China - Revolution And Foreign Policy	History	Non-Fiction
Chinese - English Dictionaries And How To Use Them	Chinese	Non-Fiction
Christopher Columbus	Columbus, Christopher	Non-Fiction
Church Of England	History	Non-Fiction
Church Of England And The English Reformation	Religious	Non-Fiction
Cinema E Letteratura In Italia 1945-1965	Italy	Non-Fiction
Classical Revolution In Italian Theatre 1500-152	Italy	Non-Fiction
Cold War In Europe 1945-1950, The	History	Non-Fiction
Colloquial Russian	Russian	Non-Fiction
Colomba	Merimee, Prosper	Non-Fiction
Compleat Angler, The	Walton, Izaak	Non-Fiction
Computer Studies	G.C.S.E.	Non-Fiction
Conflict In Europe	Social Sciences	Non-Fiction
Conrad	Conrad, Joseph	Non-Fiction
Conservative Party From Peel To Gladstone	Social Sciences	Non-Fiction
Continuity Of Conflict In French Society	France	Non-Fiction
Cooper's Creek	Moorehead, Alan	Non-Fiction
Coriolanus	Shakespeare, William	Non-Fiction
Court And Kingdom	History	Non-Fiction
Craft, Design And Technology	G.C.S.E.	Non-Fiction
Cromwell, Science And Society	History	Non-Fiction
Cymbeline	Shakespeare, William	Non-Fiction
D H Lawrence	Lawrence, D.H.	Non-Fiction
D H Lawrence: Sons And Lovers	A-Level	Non-Fiction
D H Lawrence: The Rainbow	A-Level	Non-Fiction
Dama's Sobachkoi	Chekhov, Anton	Non-Fiction

Daniel Defoe	Defoe, Daniel	Non-Fiction
Dantons Tod	Buchner, G	Non-Fiction
Darwin And Utilitarianism	History	Non-Fiction
Das Brot Der Fruhen Jahre	Boll, Heinrich	Non-Fiction
Das Geteilte Deutschland: Geschichte Und Gegenwa	Germany	Non-Fiction
Das Wrack And Other Stories	Lenz, S	Non-Fiction
De Gaulle And The French Political Scene	De Gaulle, Charles	Non-Fiction
Decembrists, The	Russia	Non-Fiction
Decline Of The Habsburg Monarchy, The	Germany	Non-Fiction
Decolonization	France	Non-Fiction
Defence In The Fifth Republic	France	Non-Fiction
Democracy In America	De Tocqueville, Alexis	Non-Fiction
Demon	Lermontov, M	Non-Fiction
Der Besuch Der Alten Dame	Durrenmatt, F	Non-Fiction
Der Gute Mensch Von Sezuan	Brecht, Bertolt	Non-Fiction
Der Prozess	Kafka, Franz	Non-Fiction
Der Richter Und Sein Henker Und Die Tradition...	Durrenmatt, F	Non-Fiction
Der Schimmelreiter	Storm, Theodor	Non-Fiction
Der Tod In Venedig	Mann, Thomas	Non-Fiction
Des Teufels General	Zuckmayer, Carl	Non-Fiction
Detstvo	Tolstoy, Leo	Non-Fiction
Development Of British Society - 1914-1945, The	Social Sciences	Non-Fiction
Development Of India, The	History	Non-Fiction
Development Of Jane Austen's Comic Art, The	A-Level	Non-Fiction
Dickens	Dickens, Charles	Non-Fiction
Die Judenbuche	Von Droste-Hulshoff, Annette	Non-Fiction
Die Leiden Des Jungen Werthers	Von Goethe, J.W.	Non-Fiction
Die Verlorene Ehre Der Katharina Blum	Boll, Heinrich	Non-Fiction
Die Verwandlung	Kafka, Franz	Non-Fiction
Disraeli	History	Non-Fiction
Disraeli	Social Sciences	Non-Fiction
Dni Turbinykh	Bulgakov, M	Non-Fiction
Don Carlos	Von Schiller, F	Non-Fiction
Don Juan: The Sorcerer	Casteaneda, Carlos	Non-Fiction
Draussen Vor Der Tur	Borchert, W	Non-Fiction
Drei Novellen	Storm, Theodor	Non-Fiction
Dreyfus Affair, The	Social Sciences	Non-Fiction
Dutch Republic In The 17th Century, The	Netherlands	Non-Fiction
E M Forster	Forster, E.M.	Non-Fiction
Early Soviet Cinema	Russia	Non-Fiction
Economics	G.C.S.E.	Non-Fiction
Education In The Federal Republic Of Germany	Germany	Non-Fiction
Effi Briest	Fontaine, T.H.	Non-Fiction
Egmont	Von Goethe, J.W.	Non-Fiction
El Caballero De Olmedo	De Vega Carpio, Lope	Non-Fiction
Elise Ou La Vraie Vie	Etcherelli, Claire	Non-Fiction
Elizabeth I	History	Non-Fiction
Elizabethan England	History	Non-Fiction
Emilia Galotti	Lessing G.E.	Non-Fiction
Emily Bronte	Bronte, Emily	Non-Fiction
Emperor Charles V, The	France	Non-Fiction
Empire To Commonwealth	Social Sciences	Non-Fiction
End Of Romanov Russia, The	Russia	Non-Fiction
English And Dutch Trade	History	Non-Fiction
English (course)	G.C.S.E.	Non-Fiction
English Language	G.C.E. O Level...	Non-Fiction
English Literature	G.C.E. O Level...	Non-Fiction
English Literature (course)	G.C.S.E.	Non-Fiction
English Monarchs	History	Non-Fiction

English Novel Today: From Dickens To Snow, The	English Literature	Non-Fiction
English Parliaments In Perspective	Social Sciences	Non-Fiction
Enlightenment, The	Social Sciences	Non-Fiction
Enrico IV - Two Tragic Humorists	Pirandello, Luigi	Non-Fiction
Ethnic Prince	Machiavelli	Non-Fiction
European Socialism In The 19th Century	Social Sciences	Non-Fiction
Evangelical Religion And Society From 1789-1859	Religious	Non-Fiction
Evelyn Waugh	Waugh, Evelyn	Non-Fiction
Existentialist Writing	Mailer, Norman	Non-Fiction
Expressionism	Picasso & Rouault	Non-Fiction
F Scott Fitzgerald	A-Level	Non-Fiction
Fables	De La Fontaine, J	Non-Fiction
Far From The Madding Crowd	A-Level	Non-Fiction
Fascism	Social Sciences	Non-Fiction
Fascism In Italy 1919-1945	Italy	Non-Fiction
First Industrial Revolution, The	Social Sciences	Non-Fiction
First Twenty Years, The	Calvino	Non-Fiction
First World War Poets	English Literature	Non-Fiction
First World War Poets: Wilfred Owen And Isaac Rosenburg	A-Level	Non-Fiction
Five Examples Of Sense And Sensibility In Modern	Ginzburg, Natalia	Non-Fiction
Fonvizin - His Life And Literary Career	Fonvizin, D	Non-Fiction
Food For Millions	Social Sciences	Non-Fiction
Formation Of The Russian State, The	Russia	Non-Fiction
Forrestal Lecture At The U.S. Naval Academy	Heinlein, Robert	Non-Fiction
Four Modern Poets	English Literature	Non-Fiction
Framework For New Knowledge	Social Sciences	Non-Fiction
Franco: The Man And The Ruler	Spain...	Non-Fiction
Frau Jenny Treibel	Fontaine, T.H.	Non-Fiction
French Alexandrine And The Sonnet, The	French Literature	Non-Fiction
French (course)	G.C.S.E.	Non-Fiction
French Local Government	France	Non-Fiction
French Political Parties - Part 1	France	Non-Fiction
French Political Parties - Part 2	France	Non-Fiction
French Press, The	France	Non-Fiction
French Revolution And The Peasants, The	France	Non-Fiction
French Revolution, The	France	Non-Fiction
French Youth And Its Problems	France	Non-Fiction
Frenchness Of French Literature, The	French Literature	Non-Fiction
From Revolution To Industrialisation	Russia	Non-Fiction
Fruhlings Erwachen	Wedekind, Franz	Non-Fiction
Gedichte	Morike, E	Non-Fiction
General Strike, The	Social Sciences	Non-Fiction
Geography (course)	G.C.S.E.	Non-Fiction
George Elliot	Elliot, George	Non-Fiction
George III	History	Non-Fiction
George Orwell	Orwell, George	Non-Fiction
Gerard Manley Hopkins	Hopkins, Gerard Manley	Non-Fiction
Gerard Manley Hopkins: Modern Or Victorian Poet?	A-Level	Non-Fiction
Gerard Manley Hopkins: The Wreck Of The Deutschland	A-Level	Non-Fiction
German Foreign Policy 1918-1970	History	Non-Fiction
German Poetry Since 1945	German Literature	Non-Fiction
Germany 1914-1945	Germany	Non-Fiction
Germinal	Zola, Emile	Non-Fiction
Geroi Nashego Vremeni	Russia	Non-Fiction
Giving A Talk	Webb & Lee	Non-Fiction
Gladstone	Social Sciences	Non-Fiction
Gladstone And The Liberal Party	History	Non-Fiction

EDUCATIONAL

Glencoe	Prebble, John	Non-Fiction
Gore Ot Uma	Griboedov, A	Non-Fiction
Government And Science In Britain, USA & USSR	Social Sciences	Non-Fiction
Grammatika Lyubvi	Bunin, I	Non-Fiction
Great Depression Of 1990, The	Social Sciences	Non-Fiction
Great Railway Bazaar By Train Through Asia	Theroux, Paul	Non-Fiction
Great Slump, The	Social Sciences	Non-Fiction
Guide To Good Gardening	Thrower, Percy	Non-Fiction
Hamlet	Shakespeare, William	Non-Fiction
Hamlet As Play Of Revenge	A-Level	Non-Fiction
Hamlet: Book Or Play?	A-Level	Non-Fiction
Hapsburg And Ottoman Empires, The	Germany	Non-Fiction
Hard Times	Terkel, Studs	Non-Fiction
Hardy And Manchild	Hardy, Thomas	Non-Fiction
Hardy's Tragic Fiction	A-Level	Non-Fiction
Hardy's Wessex Novels	A-Level	Non-Fiction
Harold Pinter: The Caretaker	A-Level	Non-Fiction
Hear All About It - What Makes News?	Webb & Lee	Non-Fiction
Henry Fielding	Fielding, Henry	Non-Fiction
Henry IV	Shakespeare, William	Non-Fiction
Heroic Villains, The	English Literature	Non-Fiction
Historian On History, A	History	Non-Fiction
Historical Demography	Social Sciences	Non-Fiction
History And Hardware Of Computers	Computing	Non-Fiction
History Reflected, Elizabeth 1, The Armada 1588	History	Non-Fiction
Hitler's World Policy	Germany	Non-Fiction
Home Economics (course)	G.C.S.E.	Non-Fiction
How French Poetry Works	French Literature	Non-Fiction
How People Change	Mean, Margaret	Non-Fiction
How Spanish Poetry Works	Spanish Literature	Non-Fiction
How To Solve The Rubik Cube	Rubik's Cube	Non-Fiction
Human Biology	G.C.S.E.	Non-Fiction
Human Geography	Social Sciences	Non-Fiction
I Promessi Sposi	Manzoni, Alessandro	Non-Fiction
I Suoni Dell Italiano E Le Varainti Regionali	Italy	Non-Fiction
Ibn Khaldun - His Life. His Works And His Source	Middle East	Non-Fiction
Idea Of The Frontier, The	American...	Non-Fiction
Il Cinema Italiano Durante Il Fascismo	Italy	Non-Fiction
Il Contesto	Sciascia	Non-Fiction
Il Futurismo In Italia	Italy	Non-Fiction
Il Giardino Dei Finzi-Contini	Bassini, G	Non-Fiction
Improve Your Driving	Driving...	Non-Fiction
Improve Your Typing	Business	Non-Fiction
In Search Of Excellence	Peters, Thomas. J.	Non-Fiction
In Search Of The Trojan War	Wood, Michael	Non-Fiction
Industrial And Agrarian Change In The 18th Century England	Social Sciences	Non-Fiction
Industrial Espionage	Business	Non-Fiction
Industrial Relations In France	France	Non-Fiction
Industrial Revolution, The	Social Sciences	Non-Fiction
International Relations Between The Wars	Social Sciences	Non-Fiction
Interview With Lillian Hellman, An	Hellman, Lillian	Non-Fiction
Interviews And Interviewing	Webb & Lee	Non-Fiction
Introducing The Arab World	Middle East	Non-Fiction
Introduction To Brittany, An	France	Non-Fiction
Introduction To Computing, An	Computing	Non-Fiction
Introduction To No Drama, An	Japan	Non-Fiction
Introduction To Petrarch's Selected Poems	Petrarch	Non-Fiction
Introduction To The German Democratic Republic	Germany	Non-Fiction

EDUCATIONAL

Iphigenie Auf Tauris	Von Goethe, J.W.	Non-Fiction
Iranian Revolution, The	Middle East	Non-Fiction
Irish Question 1800-1922, The	Social Sciences	Non-Fiction
Isaac Newton	Newton, Isaac	Non-Fiction
Talian Politics Since World War Ii	Italy	Non-Fiction
Italian Risorgimento, The	Italy	Non-Fiction
J R R Tolkien	Guerolt, Denis	Non-Fiction
James I	History	Non-Fiction
James Joyce	Joyce, James	Non-Fiction
James Joyce Stephen Hero	Joyce, James	Non-Fiction
Jane Austen	Austen, Jane	Non-Fiction
Jane Eyre By Charlotte Bronte	Bronte, Charlotte	Non-Fiction
Jean Calvin	France	Non-Fiction
Jean Stafford Reads One Of Her Short Stories	Stafford, Jean	Non-Fiction
Joan Of Arc	Joan Of Arc	Non-Fiction
Job Satisfaction	Social Sciences	Non-Fiction
John Dos Passos Reads His Poetry	Dos Passos, John	Non-Fiction
Jonathan Swift	Swift, Jonathan	Non-Fiction
Joyce James	Joyce, James	Non-Fiction
Jude The Obscure	A-Level	Non-Fiction
Judith	Hebbel, F	Non-Fiction
Julius Caesar	Caesar, Julius	Non-Fiction
Julius Caesar	Shakespeare, William	Non-Fiction
Kabale Und Liebe	Von Schiller, F	Non-Fiction
Kaiser's Germany, The	Germany	Non-Fiction
Kalendergeschichten	Brecht, Bertolt	Non-Fiction
Katz Und Maus	Grass, Gunther	Non-Fiction
Keats	Keats	Non-Fiction
King Lear	A-Level	Non-Fiction
King Lear	Shakespeare, William	Non-Fiction
Kingdom By The Sea, The	Theroux, Paul	Non-Fiction
Kings And Queens Of England	History	Non-Fiction
Kira Georgievna	Nekrasov, V	Non-Fiction
Knock	Romains, J	Non-Fiction
Koln - Ein Horbild	Germany	Non-Fiction
Konig Ottokars Gluck Und Ende	Grillparzer, F	Non-Fiction
Kruschev And Eastern Europe	Russia	Non-Fiction
La Chute	Camus, A	Non-Fiction
La Condition Humaine	Malraux, Andre	Non-Fiction
La Dentelliere	Laine, Pascal	Non-Fiction
La Divina Commedia	Dante	Non-Fiction
La France Sous Mitterrand, 1981-1988	France	Non-Fiction
La Gloire De Mon Pere	Pagnol, M	Non-Fiction
La Guerre De Troie	Giraudoux, Jean	Non-Fiction
La Luna E I Falo	Pavese, C	Non-Fiction
La Machine Infernale	Cocteau, Jean	Non-Fiction
La Modification	Butor, M	Non-Fiction
La Neige En Devil	Troyat, H	Non-Fiction
La Politique Francaise Du Temps Libre	France	Non-Fiction
La Porte Etroite	Gide, Andre	Non-Fiction
La Provence - Part 1	France	Non-Fiction
La Provence - Part 2	France	Non-Fiction
La Reine Morte	De Montherlant, H	Non-Fiction
Labour Government, The	Social Sciences	Non-Fiction
Ladri De Biciclette	De Sica, Vittorio	Non-Fiction
L'Affaire Dreyfus	France, Anatole	Non-Fiction
L'Amante Anglaise	Duras, Marguerite	Non-Fiction
Language Course - Welsh	Welsh	Non-Fiction
Language Of Poetry, The	English Literature	Non-Fiction

EDUCATIONAL

Lawrence And Joyce	Lawrence, D.H.	Non-Fiction
Le Barbier De Seville	Beaumarchais	Non-Fiction
Le Bete Humaine	Zola, Emile	Non-Fiction
Le Ble En Herbe	Colette	Non-Fiction
Le Bourgeois Gentil Homme	Moliere	Non-Fiction
Le Chateau De Ma Mere	Pagnol, M	Non-Fiction
Le Cid	Corneille, P	Non-Fiction
Le Cinema Francais Depuis 1945	France	Non-Fiction
Le Clos Du Roi	Scipion, M	Non-Fiction
Le Colonel Chabert: Gobseck	De Balzac, Honore	Non-Fiction
Le Cure De Tours	De Balzac, Honore	Non-Fiction
Le Grand Meaulnes	Fournier, Alain	Non-Fiction
Le Jeu De L' Amour Et Du Hasard	Marivaux	Non-Fiction
Le Legende Des Siecles	Hugo, Victor	Non-Fiction
Le Maitre De Santiago	De Montherlant, H	Non-Fiction
Le Malade Imaginaire	Moliere	Non-Fiction
Le Mariage De Figaro	Beaumarchais	Non-Fiction
Le Massif Central	France	Non-Fiction
Le Monde Des Annees 80	France	Non-Fiction
Le Notaire Du Havre	Duhamel, G	Non-Fiction
Le Pere Goriot	De Balzac, Honore	Non-Fiction
Le Rouge Et Le Noir	Stendhal	Non-Fiction
Le Silence De La Mer	Vercours	Non-Fiction
League Of Nations, The	History	Non-Fiction
Learning To Touch Type	Business	Non-Fiction
Learning To Write Fiction	Welty, Eudora	Non-Fiction
Lenin	Russia	Non-Fiction
Lenin And Leninism	Russia	Non-Fiction
Leo Ferre	Ferre, Leo	Non-Fiction
Les Allumettes Suedoises	Sabatier, R	Non-Fiction
Les Fausses Confidences	Marivaux	Non-Fiction
Les Fleurs Du Mal	Baudelaire	Non-Fiction
Les Gommes	Robbe-Grillet, Alain	Non-Fiction
Les Jeux Sont Faits	Sartre, Jean Paul	Non-Fiction
Les Liaisons Dangereuses	Laclos, P	Non-Fiction
Les Mains Sales	Sartre, Jean Paul	Non-Fiction
Les Petits Enfants Du Siecle	Rochefort, C	Non-Fiction
Les Relations Entre La France Et L'Algerie	France	Non-Fiction
Les Sequestres D'Altona	Sartre, Jean Paul	Non-Fiction
L'Espace Francais: Rural France	France	Non-Fiction
L'Eesprit Francais	France	Non-Fiction
L'Etranger	Camus, A	Non-Fiction
L'Exil Et Le Royaume	Camus, A	Non-Fiction
Liberals In The 20th Century, The	Social Sciences	Non-Fiction
Life In Chaucer's England	A-Level	Non-Fiction
L'Ile Des Pingouins	France, Anatole	Non-Fiction
L'Immigration En France	France	Non-Fiction
Listening And Understanding	Webb, Edwin	Non-Fiction
Literature And Society In The '30's For Universities	English Literature	Non-Fiction
Lloyd George	Social Sciences	Non-Fiction
Lloyd George To Beveridge	Social Sciences	Non-Fiction
Lord Of The Flies	A-Level	Non-Fiction
Los Pazos De Ulloa	Pardo Bazan, E	Non-Fiction
Lost World Of The Kalahari, The	Van Der Post, Laurens	Non-Fiction
Louis XIV	France	Non-Fiction
Lyrics	Pushkin & Lermontov	Non-Fiction
Lyudi	Zoshchenko, M	Non-Fiction
MacBeth	Shakespeare, William	Non-Fiction
MacBeth As A Tragedy	A-Level	Non-Fiction

EDUCATIONAL

Machiavelli And The Medici	Machiavelli	Non-Fiction
Madame Bovary	Flaubert, Gustave	Non-Fiction
Making It Happen	Harvey-Jones, John	Non-Fiction
Manon Lescaut	Prevost, Abbe	Non-Fiction
Mansfield Park: The Symbol Of The House	A-Level	Non-Fiction
Marriage Group, The	A-Level	Non-Fiction
Marx And Marxism	Russia	Non-Fiction
Marx And The Material Concept Of History	Germany	Non-Fiction
Mary Tudor	History	Non-Fiction
Mathematics (course)	G.C.S.E.	Non-Fiction
Matryonin Dvor	Solzhentizyn, Alexander	Non-Fiction
Measure For Measure	A-Level	Non-Fiction
Measure For Measure	Shakespeare, William	Non-Fiction
Mednyi Vsadnik	Pushkin, Alexander S.	Non-Fiction
Meeting, The	Webb, Edwin	Non-Fiction
Mercantilism	Social Sciences	Non-Fiction
Merchant Of Venice, The	Shakespeare, William	Non-Fiction
Mesyats V Derevne	Turgenev, Ivan	Non-Fiction
Metternich And The Napoleonic Wars 1809-1815	Military History	Non-Fiction
Moderato Cantabile	Duras, Marguerite	Non-Fiction
Modern Italian Cinema	Italy	Non-Fiction
Modern Poetry	English Literature	Non-Fiction
Modern Soviet Cinema	Russia	Non-Fiction
Morality Of Strikes	Social Sciences	Non-Fiction
Mozart I Salieri	Pushkin, Alexander S.	Non-Fiction
Much Ado About Nothing	A-Level	Non-Fiction
Mussolini	Italy	Non-Fiction
Mutter Courage Und Ihre Kinder	Brecht, Bertolt	Non-Fiction
My	Zamyatin, Evgeny	Non-Fiction
Napoleon Bonaparte	France	Non-Fiction
Napoleon II	France	Non-Fiction
Napoleon III	France	Non-Fiction
Naturalism And The American Novel	Caldwell, Erskine	Non-Fiction
Nature And Structure Of Shakespearean Comedy	A-Level	Non-Fiction
Nature Of Keats' Great Odes, The	A-Level	Non-Fiction
Necessary Treason, A	English Literature	Non-Fiction
Neeps And Tatties	Scotland	Non-Fiction
Nep And Soviet Industrialisation, The	Russia	Non-Fiction
New Alignments, The	Social Sciences	Non-Fiction
New Imperialism 1870 - 1914, The	Germany	Non-Fiction
Night Sky, The	Astronomy	Non-Fiction
Nineteen Eighty-Four, George Orwell	Orwell, George	Non-Fiction
Nineteenth Century Imperialism	Social Sciences	Non-Fiction
Nineteenth Century Russia	Russia	Non-Fiction
No More Cocoons	Biafra, Jello	Non-Fiction
Novels Of Graham Greene, The	Greene, Graham	Non-Fiction
Nun's Priest's Tale, The	A-Level	Non-Fiction
Oblomov	Goncharov, I.A	Non-Fiction
Obscure Beauty: Difficulty In Poetry, The	English Literature	Non-Fiction
Oil A World Crisis	Social Sciences	Non-Fiction
Old Patagonian Express, The	Theroux, Paul	Non-Fiction
On Ne Badine Pas Avec L'Amour	De Musset, A	Non-Fiction
On The Side Of Laughter	Muggeridge, Malcolm	Non-Fiction
One Man's War	Social Sciences	Non-Fiction
Oregon Trail, The	Parkman, Francis	Non-Fiction
Origins And Development Of The French Revolution	France	Non-Fiction
Origins Of The First World War, The	Military History	Non-Fiction
Orlando Furioso	Ariosto, L	Non-Fiction
Othello	A-Level	Non-Fiction

EDUCATIONAL

Othello	Shakespeare, William	Non-Fiction
Ottsy I Deti	Turgenev, Ivan	Non-Fiction
Outline Of Russian Music, An	Russia	Non-Fiction
Outline Of Soviet Music, An	Russia	Non-Fiction
Overview Of Transport In France	France	Non-Fiction
Paradise Lost	A-Level	Non-Fiction
Parliamentary Monarchy In France 1815-1848	France	Non-Fiction
Paroles	Prevert, Jacques	Non-Fiction
Party Politics Between The Wars	Social Sciences	Non-Fiction
Party Politics, The	Germany	Non-Fiction
Path To World War II, The	Military History	Non-Fiction
Peaceful Revolution	Social Sciences	Non-Fiction
Peel	Social Sciences	Non-Fiction
Pennine Journey, A	Wainwright, A	Non-Fiction
People And Communications In Business	Webb, Edwin	Non-Fiction
Peoples Of The U.S.S.R., The	Russia	Non-Fiction
Perfect Interview, The	Social Sciences	Non-Fiction
Perfect Sales Presentation, The	Business	Non-Fiction
Peter The Great And Catherine The Great	Russia	Non-Fiction
Petrol And Pollution	Social Sciences	Non-Fiction
Phedre	Racine, Jean	Non-Fiction
Philip Larkin And Ted Hughes	A-Level	Non-Fiction
Phonetic Transcription	French Literature	Non-Fiction
Physics (course)	G.C.S.E.	Non-Fiction
Pierre Et Jean	De Maupassant, Guy	Non-Fiction
Pikovaya Dama	Pushkin, Alexander S.	Non-Fiction
Pirandello's Theatre	Pirandello, Luigo	Non-Fiction
Planning For Peace 1914-1918	History	Non-Fiction
Poemes	Verlaine, Paul	Non-Fiction
Poesies	Gautier, T.H.	Non-Fiction
Poet Among Scientists, A	Graves, Robert	Non-Fiction
Poet As A Translator, The	English Literature	Non-Fiction
Poetic Vision And Modern Literature	English Literature	Non-Fiction
Poetry And Audience	French Literature	Non-Fiction
Poetry Of Anne Sexton, The	Sexton, Anne	Non-Fiction
Poetry Of Boris Pasternak, The	Pasternak, Boris	Non-Fiction
Poetry Of Dylan Thomas, The	Thomas, Dylan	Non-Fiction
Poetry Of George Herbert And Andrew Marvell, The	A-Level	Non-Fiction
Poetry Of John Ciardi, The	Ciardi, John	Non-Fiction
Poetry Of Robert Lowell, The	Lowell, Robert	Non-Fiction
Poetry Of Stephen Spender, The	Spender, Stephen	Non-Fiction
Poetry Of Theodore Roathke, The	Roathke, Theodore	Non-Fiction
Political Parties And Walpole	Social Sciences	Non-Fiction
Politics In Post-War Italy: An Assessment	Italy	Non-Fiction
Pollution And Industry	Social Sciences	Non-Fiction
Pope And Augustan Poetry	English Literature	Non-Fiction
Population	Social Sciences	Non-Fiction
Position Of Women In 20th Century Britain, The	Social Sciences	Non-Fiction
Post-War Division In Europe, The	History	Non-Fiction
Povest'O Tom Kak Possorilsya Ivan Ivanovich S IV	Gogol, Nikolai Vasilievich	Non-Fiction
Practical Criticism: Poetry	A-Level	Non-Fiction
Practical Criticism: Prose	A-Level	Non-Fiction
Pre-Eminence And Competition	Social Sciences	Non-Fiction
Prehistoric Scandinavia	Galica, Divina	Non-Fiction
Premiership Of Stanley Baldwin, The	Social Sciences	Non-Fiction
Press In The German - Speaking Countries, The	Germany	Non-Fiction
Pride And Prejudice	A-Level	Non-Fiction
Primary French	Early Learning	Non-Fiction
Prinz Friedrich Von Homburg	Von Kleist, H	Non-Fiction

EDUCATIONAL

Title	Author/Subject	Category
Prose And Poetry	English Literature	Non-Fiction
Prose And Poetry Of John Updike, The	Updike, John	Non-Fiction
Prose Appreciation	English Literature	Non-Fiction
Prose Readings	Burgess, Anthony	Non-Fiction
Purgatorio	Dante	Non-Fiction
Questions And Answers	Social Sciences	Non-Fiction
Rape Of The Lock, The	A-Level	Non-Fiction
Rasskazy	Babel, Isaak	Non-Fiction
Reading Difficult Poetry	English Literature	Non-Fiction
Reappraisal Of What Went Wrong In Palestine, A	Middle East	Non-Fiction
Reb Moishe Babba	Singer, Isaac Bashevis.	Non-Fiction
Recent Poetry	Walker, Ted	Non-Fiction
Reformation In England, The	History	Non-Fiction
Reformation, The	Social Sciences	Non-Fiction
Regain	Giono, J	Non-Fiction
Regionalism In France	France	Non-Fiction
Reign Of Catherine The Great, 1762-1796, The	Russia	Non-Fiction
Reign Of Edward VI, The	History	Non-Fiction
Religion In The Soviet Union	Russia	Non-Fiction
Religious Studies	G.C.S.E.	Non-Fiction
Renaissance, The	Social Sciences	Non-Fiction
Restoration, The	History	Non-Fiction
Revolution Of 1848, The	Social Sciences	Non-Fiction
Revolutionary China	China	Non-Fiction
Revolutions Of 1848 In France And Central Europe	France	Non-Fiction
Rhinoceros	Ionesco, E	Non-Fiction
Richard II	A-Level	Non-Fiction
Richard II	Shakespeare, William	Non-Fiction
Richard III	Shakespeare, William	Non-Fiction
Rise And Fall Of Sweden, The	Sweden	Non-Fiction
Rise And Fall Of The Dutch Republic, The	Holland	Non-Fiction
Rise Of The Labour Party 1885-1906, The	Social Sciences	Non-Fiction
Rise Of The Nazi Party, The	History	Non-Fiction
Rise Of The Spanish Empire, The	Spain...	Non-Fiction
Road To Munich, The	Germany	Non-Fiction
Robert Browning	Browning, Robert	Non-Fiction
Robert Cecil, Lord Salisbury	History	Non-Fiction
Robert Frost Reads His Poems	Frost, Robert	Non-Fiction
Role Of Personality In Science, The	English Literature	Non-Fiction
Role Of The Church In Modern Italian History, The	Italy	Non-Fiction
Romans Et Contes	Voltaire	Non-Fiction
Romantic Hero, The	French Literature	Non-Fiction
Romantics, The	English Literature	Non-Fiction
Romeo And Juliet	Shakespeare, William	Non-Fiction
Roots Of Inflation	Social Sciences	Non-Fiction
Roots Of Marxism-Leninism, The	Russia	Non-Fiction
Russia 1917: Year Of Revolution	Russia	Non-Fiction
Russian Classicism	Russia	Non-Fiction
Russian Folk Theatre, The	Russia	Non-Fiction
Russian Icons	Russia	Non-Fiction
Russian Revolution, The	Russia	Non-Fiction
Russian Revolutionary Novel, The	Russian Literature	Non-Fiction
Samuel Pepys	History	Non-Fiction
Scenes De La Vie De Province	De Maupassant, Guy	Non-Fiction
Science	G.C.S.E.	Non-Fiction
Science Fiction	Science Fiction	Non-Fiction
Scientists And Responsibility	Social Sciences	Non-Fiction
Secrets Of Success	Business	Non-Fiction
Selected Stories	Kazakov, Yu	Non-Fiction

EDUCATIONAL

Sergeant Lamb's America	Graves, Robert	Non-Fiction
Seventeenth Century Literature	English Literature	Non-Fiction
Shakespeare's Women	A-Level	Non-Fiction
Shinel	Gogol, Nikolai Vasilievich	Non-Fiction
Sicilian World	Verga, Giovanni	Non-Fiction
Silas Marner	A-Level	Non-Fiction
Silicon Chips - Their Impact	Business	Non-Fiction
Silicon Chips - Their Uses	Business	Non-Fiction
Sinbad Voyage, The	Severin, Tim	Non-Fiction
Sir Robert Peel	History	Non-Fiction
Six Analyses	Rilke	Non-Fiction
Sixteenth Century France	France	Non-Fiction
Smert' Ivana Il'icha	Tolstoy, Leo	Non-Fiction
Social And Economic History	G.C.S.E.	Non-Fiction
Social Change	Social Sciences	Non-Fiction
Social Change In The Sixteenth Century	Social Sciences	Non-Fiction
Social Impact Of The Industrial Revolution	Social Sciences	Non-Fiction
Society And Literature In The 1930's For Schools	English Literature	Non-Fiction
Some Problems In Reading Canterbury Tales	English Literature	Non-Fiction
Something About Poetry	Auden, W.H.	Non-Fiction
Sonata De Otono	Valle-Inclan, R	Non-Fiction
Songs Of Georges Brassens, The	Brassens, Georges	Non-Fiction
Sounds Of Classical Latin, The	Latin (language)	Non-Fiction
Sounds Of Germany, The - Parts 1 And 2	Germany	Non-Fiction
Sounds Of Poetry, The	English Literature	Non-Fiction
Sources Of Energy	Social Sciences	Non-Fiction
Soviet Economic Development 1917-1953	Russia	Non-Fiction
Soviet Economy: The Brezhnev Era	Russia	Non-Fiction
Soviet Economy Under Khrushchev, The	Russia	Non-Fiction
Soviet Jews	Russia	Non-Fiction
Soviet Political System, The	History	Non-Fiction
Soviet Union's Geographical Problems, The	Russia	Non-Fiction
Spain	Spain...	Non-Fiction
Spain Travel Kit	Spanish	Non-Fiction
Sport And Politics	Social Sciences	Non-Fiction
Sport In Soviet Society	Russia	Non-Fiction
Stalin	Russia	Non-Fiction
Stalin And Soviet Economic Development	Russia	Non-Fiction
Stalin And Stalinism	Russia	Non-Fiction
Sud'ba Cheloveka	Sholokhov, M	Non-Fiction
Surviving The Great Depression Of 1990	Social Sciences	Non-Fiction
Switzerland In Question	Switzerland...	Non-Fiction
T S Elliot: Prufrock, Portrait Of A Lady & The Wasteland	A-Level	Non-Fiction
Tartuffe	Moliere	Non-Fiction
Teenagers In The Family	Social Sciences	Non-Fiction
Tempest, The	Shakespeare, William	Non-Fiction
Tempest: Unity	A-Level	Non-Fiction
Ten Kittle Quirks In Scottish History	History	Non-Fiction
Terre Des Hommes	De Saint-Exupery	Non-Fiction
Therese Desqueyroux	Mauriac, F	Non-Fiction
Third Reich - A Social Revolution?	Germany	Non-Fiction
Thirty Years War, The	Military History	Non-Fiction
Thomas Hardy	Hardy, Thomas	Non-Fiction
Thomas Jefferson	American	Non-Fiction
Thomas Wolsey	History	Non-Fiction
Three Novels	Silone	Non-Fiction
Thriving On Chaos	Peters, Tom	Non-Fiction
To Be A Slave	Social Sciences	Non-Fiction
Tonio Kroger	Mann, Thomas	Non-Fiction

EDUCATIONAL

Trade Union Movement And The General Strike	Social Sciences	Non-Fiction
Trade Unions In France	France	Non-Fiction
Traffic Control	Social Sciences	Non-Fiction
Transport Revolution, The	Social Sciences	Non-Fiction
Troilus And Cressida	A-Level	Non-Fiction
Troilus And Cressida	Shakespeare William	Non-Fiction
Trois Contes	Flaubert, Gustave	Non-Fiction
Trotsky And Trotskyism	Russia	Non-Fiction
Tudor Foreign Policy	Social Sciences	Non-Fiction
Tudor Regime Reconsidered, The	Social Sciences	Non-Fiction
Tueur Sans Gages	Ionesco, E	Non-Fiction
Twelfth Night	Shakespeare, William	Non-Fiction
Two Views Of Italian Rural Society	Silone & Levi	Non-Fiction
Typewriting	G.C.S.E.	Non-Fiction
Ubu Roi	Jarry, A	Non-Fiction
Un Recteur De L'ile De Sein	Queffelec, H	Non-Fiction
Unconscious Factors In Creativity	Koestler, Arthur	Non-Fiction
Unexpected Masterpiece, The	De Tormes, Lazarillo	Non-Fiction
Unification Of Italy, The	Italy	Non-Fiction
Unwilling To School	Social Sciences	Non-Fiction
Urban Geography	Social Sciences	Non-Fiction
USSR And Comecon, The	Russia	Non-Fiction
Veil: The Secret Wars Of The CIA	Social Sciences	Non-Fiction
Victorian England	History	Non-Fiction
Vietnam - The History Of American Involvement	History	Non-Fiction
Virginia Woolf	Woolf, Virginia	Non-Fiction
Vishnyovyi Sad	Chekhov, Anton	Non-Fiction
Voina I Mir	Tolstoy, Leo	Non-Fiction
Vremya Vperyod	Kataev, V	Non-Fiction
W B Yeats	Yeats, W.B.	Non-Fiction
W B Yeats And The Romantic Tradition	A-Level	Non-Fiction
W B Yeats: Poet Of Love, Politics And The Other	A-Level	Non-Fiction
W B Yeats: The Natural And The Supernatural	A-Level	Non-Fiction
Waiting For Godot	Beckett, Samuel	Non-Fiction
Walpole, Pitt And Foreign Policy	Social Sciences	Non-Fiction
War And Society From 1914	Social Sciences	Non-Fiction
War Of 1812, The	American...	Non-Fiction
Webster: The White Devil	A-L:evel	Non-Fiction
Weimar Republic, The	Germany	Non-Fiction
Westward Expansion	American...	Non-Fiction
White Nile, The	Moorehead, Alan	Non-Fiction
Why Overtime?	Social Sciences	Non-Fiction
Why Save Wild Animals	Mountford, G	Non-Fiction
Wilhelm Tell	Von Schiller, F	Non-Fiction
William Blake	Blake, William	Non-Fiction
William Cecil, Lord Burghley	History	Non-Fiction
William Golding	Golding, William	Non-Fiction
William Styron Reads His Work	Styron, William	Non-Fiction
Winter's Tale, The	Shakespeare, William	Non-Fiction
Woman Writers In Italy 1943-1956	Italy	Non-Fiction
Wordsworth	Wordsworth, William	Non-Fiction
Wordsworth: The Lyrical Ballads	A-Level	Non-Fiction
Wordsworth's 'The Prelude'	A-Level	Non-Fiction
World Development And Europe's Long-Term Rise	Social Sciences	Non-Fiction
World History	G.C.S.E.	Non-Fiction
World Of King Lear, The	Shakespeare, William	Non-Fiction
World War II	Military History	Non-Fiction
World Wars 1914/1939	Military History	Non-Fiction
Woyzeck	Buchner, G	Non-Fiction

EDUCATIONAL

Writer In Wales Today, The	Wales...	Non-Fiction
Zapiski Iz Podpol'ya	Dostoevsky, Fyodor	Non-Fiction
Zavist	Olesha, Yu	Non-Fiction
Zen: The Eternal Now	Social Sciences	Non-Fiction

ENVIRONMENTAL

TITLE	HEADING	SECTION
African Forests And Savannahs	Environmental Sounds	Non-Fiction
American Forests And Lakes	Environmental Sounds	Non-Fiction
Babbling Brook	Environmental Sounds	Non-Fiction
Babbling Brook / Summer Rain	Environmental Sounds	Non-Fiction
Dawn At Josiah's Bay	Environmental Sounds	Non-Fiction
Early Cape Morning	Environmental Sounds	Non-Fiction
Early Cape Morning / Sunset Surf	Environmental Sounds	Non-Fiction
Environmental Atmospheres: Australia	Environmental Sounds	Non-Fiction
Forests And Mountains Of Asia	Environmental Sounds	Non-Fiction
Forests Of The Amazon	Environmental Sounds	Non-Fiction
Frogs And Toads	Environmental Sounds	Non-Fiction
Gloucestershire Wildlife Tapestry	Wildlife (Natural)	Non-Fiction
Marsh Melodies	Environmental Sounds	Non-Fiction
Mid-Day On Jost Vandyke	Environmental Sounds	Non-Fiction
Mountain Medley	Environmental Sounds	Non-Fiction
Songs From The Deep	Whales	Non-Fiction
Songs Of The Humpback Whale	Whales	Non-Fiction
South Atlantic Islands	Wildlife (Natural)	Non-Fiction
Summer Rain	Environmental Sounds	Non-Fiction
Sunset Surf	Environmental Sounds	Non-Fiction
Wild Animals (Europe)	Environmental Sounds	Non-Fiction

HEALTH & FITNESS

TITLE	HEADING	SECTION
Aerobic Exercise Music	Health & Fitness	Non-Fiction
Aerobicise	Health & Fitness	Non-Fiction
Aids - The Facts	Health & Fitness	Non-Fiction
American Cancer Society's "Freshstart"	Self Improvement	Non-Fiction
Anger Workout	Self Improvement	Non-Fiction
Arnold Schwarzenegger's Total Body Workout	Health & Fitness	Non-Fiction
As Young As You Feel With Eileen Fowler	Health & Fitness	Non-Fiction
Banish Pain - Mind Power And Pain Relief	Self Improvement	Non-Fiction
Bio- Feedback	Self Improvement	Non-Fiction
Breathe, Relax And Imagine	Self Improvement	Non-Fiction
Callanetics For Your Back	Health & Fitness	Non-Fiction
Calm And Peaceful Mind, A	Self Improvement	Non-Fiction
Complete Fitness Course, The	Health & Fitness	Non-Fiction
Complete Yoga	Health & Fitness	Non-Fiction
Control Your Weight	Self Improvement	Non-Fiction
Curing Depression	Self Improvement	Non-Fiction
Dance Keep Fit & Slim To Music	Health & Fitness	Non-Fiction
Discover Inner Energy And Overcome Stress	Self Improvement	Non-Fiction
Emotions And Cancer	Self Improvement	Non-Fiction
Enjoy Your Slimming With Eileen Fowler	Health & Fitness	Non-Fiction
Everyday Yoga	Health & Fitness	Non-Fiction
Ex 'n' Dans	Health & Fitness	Non-Fiction
Expectant Father	Health & Fitness	Non-Fiction
Expectant Mother	Health & Fitness	Non-Fiction
Family Keep Fit With Eileen Fowler	Health & Fitness	Non-Fiction
Fit To Ski	Health & Fitness	Non-Fiction
Get Fit With The Green Goddess	Health & Fitness	Non-Fiction
Get Into Shape After Childbirth	Health & Fitness	Non-Fiction
Healing Force - Using Your Mind To Help Heal	Self Improvement	Non-Fiction
Hip And Thigh Workout	Health & Fitness	Non-Fiction
Inch Loss Plan	Health & Fitness	Non-Fiction
Inflight Relaxation	Self Improvement	Non-Fiction
Jane Fonda Workout	Health & Fitness	Non-Fiction
Jane Fonda's Workout Record	Health & Fitness	Non-Fiction
Jane Fonda's Workout Record For Pregnancy, Birth	Health & Fitness	Non-Fiction
Keep In Shape System	Health & Fitness	Non-Fiction
Keep In Shape, Vol.2	Health & Fitness	Non-Fiction
Learning To Control Pain	Self Improvement	Non-Fiction
Lotte Berk Exercise Record - Get Physical	Health & Fitness	Non-Fiction
Medicine The Human Aspect	Self Improvement	Non-Fiction
Meditation	Self Improvement	Non-Fiction
Meditations For Personal Harmony	Self Improvement	Non-Fiction
Mental Stress And Physical Fitness	Self Improvement	Non-Fiction
Mind Over Illness	Self Improvement	Non-Fiction
Mind-Body Tempo	Health & Fitness	Non-Fiction
Music 'n' Motion	Health & Fitness	Non-Fiction
Myths Of Mental Illness	Szasz, Thomas S.	Non-Fiction
Natural Way To Alleviate Stress	Health & Fitness	Non-Fiction
Natural Way To Control Agoraphobia	Health & Fitness	Non-Fiction
Natural Way To Control Nail Biting	Health & Fitness	Non-Fiction

HEALTH & FITNESS

Natural Way To Learn Self Hypnosis And Relax....	Health & Fitness	Non-Fiction
Natural Way To Overcome Fear Of Flying	Health & Fitness	Non-Fiction
Natural Way To Overcome Insomnia	Health & Fitness	Non-Fiction
Natural Way To Slim, The	Health & Fitness	Non-Fiction
Natural Way To Stop Smoking	Health & Fitness	Non-Fiction
Pathway To Healing, A	Self Improvement	Non-Fiction
Peace Of Mind	Self Improvement	Non-Fiction
Perfect Health	Self Improvement	Non-Fiction
Perfect Weight - Perfect Body	Self Improvement	Non-Fiction
Picture Yourself Relaxed	Self Improvement	Non-Fiction
Prime Time Workout With Jane Fonda	Health & Fitness	Non-Fiction
Radiant Health And A Strong Immune System	Self Improvement	Non-Fiction
Rational Emotive Therapy	Self Improvement	Non-Fiction
Relieve Stress And Anxiety	Self Improvement	Non-Fiction
Schizophrenia - A Viewpoint	Medical	Non-Fiction
Shape Up And Dance	Health & Fitness	Non-Fiction
Shape Up For Motherhood	Health & Fitness	Non-Fiction
Sleep Like A Baby	Self Improvement	Non-Fiction
Sleep Peacefully	Self Improvement	Non-Fiction
Sleeping Easy	Self Improvement	Non-Fiction
Slim To Rhythm With Eileen Fowler	Health & Fitness	Non-Fiction
Spend Your Life In Slender	Self Improvement	Non-Fiction
Strategies For Stress Free Living	Self Improvement	Non-Fiction
Stress Proof Child	Self Improvement	Non-Fiction
Surviving Loss	Self Improvement	Non-Fiction
Techniques For Greater Beauty & Greater Vitality	Health & Fitness	Non-Fiction
Techniques For Greater Energy And Vitality	Health & Fitness	Non-Fiction
Techniques For PMS Relief And Greater Vitality	Health & Fitness	Non-Fiction
Techniques For Weight Loss And Greater Vitality	Health & Fitness	Non-Fiction
Teenagers And Sexuality	Self Improvement	Non-Fiction
Teenagers Under Stress	Self Improvement	Non-Fiction
Ultimate Relaxation	Self Improvement	Non-Fiction
Understanding And Coping With Anxiety	Self Improvement	Non-Fiction
Weight Lost	Self Improvement	Non-Fiction
Work That Body	Health & Fitness	Non-Fiction
Work That Body Into Ski Shape	Health & Fitness	Non-Fiction
Workout Record New And Improved	Health & Fitness	Non-Fiction
Yoga For All	Health & Fitness	Non-Fiction
Your Last Cigarette - No Exceptions!	Self Improvement	Non-Fiction

HISTORY

TITLE	HEADING	SECTION
Alexander The Great	Alexander The Great	Non-Fiction
Antarctica	Johnson, Stanley	Non-Fiction
Aviators, The	Aviation	Non-Fiction
Battle Of Britain	Military History	Non-Fiction
Battle Of Jutland, The	Military History	Non-Fiction
Battle Of Midway, The	Military History	Non-Fiction
Battle Of Waterloo	Military History	Non-Fiction
Brides In The Bath Case & The Penge Mystery, The	Lustgarten, Edgar	Non-Fiction
Brief History In Time, A	Hawking, Stephen	Non-Fiction
Brighton Trunk Case & The Blazing Car Case, The	Lustgarten, Edgar	Non-Fiction
Classic Motorcycles	Motorcycling	Non-Fiction
Culloden - The Last Jacobite Rising	Prebble, John	Non-Fiction
Dambusters, The Great Escape	Brickhill, Paul	Non-Fiction
D-Day Despatches	Military History	Non-Fiction
Flagship Hood	Briggs, Ted	Non-Fiction
Fourteen Minutes: The Sinking Of The Empress Of Ireland	Croall, James	Non-Fiction
Great British Aircraft	Aviation	Non-Fiction
Great Escape, The	Brickhill, Paul	Non-Fiction
Grey Widow Maker, The	Edwards, Bernard	Non-Fiction
Hindenburg Disaster, The	Military History	Non-Fiction
In Search Of The Trojan War	Wood, Michael	Non-Fiction
Last Gunboat Blockade, The	Military History	Non-Fiction
Lizzie Borden Took An Axe	Lustgarten, Edgar	Non-Fiction
MG Just For The Record	MG Cars	Non-Fiction
Monkeyville Case, The	Lustgarten, Edgar	Non-Fiction
Mrs Maybrick & Mrs Merryfield	Lustgarten, Edgar	Non-Fiction
Murder At The Follies	Lustgarten, Edgar	Non-Fiction
Newcastle Train Murder & Death On The Crumbles	Lustgarten, Edgar	Non-Fiction
Second World War	Military History	Non-Fiction
Sinking Of The Lusitania	Military History	Non-Fiction
Spanish Armada, The	Military History	Non-Fiction
State Funeral Of Sir Winston Churchill,K.G.,OM,C	Churchill, Sir Winston	Non-Fiction
Trial Of Mrs Maybrick (1889) & Mrs Merrifield.	Lustgarten, Edgar	Non-Fiction
Under The Crab Apple Tree	Lustgarten, Edgar	Non-Fiction
Victory In Europe	Military History	Non-Fiction
Wings Of History	Aviation	Non-Fiction

HUMOROUS

TITLE	HEADING	SECTION
1001 Gelignites	Bates, Blaster	Fiction
Ad Nauseam	Derek & Clive	Fiction
After Henry	Brett, Simon	Fiction
Alas Smith And Jones	Smith & Jones	Fiction
All Good Stuff, Mary	Miller, Max	Fiction
'Allo 'Allo	Television	Fiction
Alternative Government	Stuart, Francis	Fiction
Another Monty Python Record	Monty Python	Fiction
At His Best Entertaining The Troops	Hope, Bob	Fiction
At The Oxford Union	Hoffnung, Gerard	Fiction
Atlantic Bridge	Connolly, Billy	Fiction
Bean Bag	Bean, Billy	Fiction
Belgravia	Bingham, Charlotte	Fiction
Berkeley Concert	Bruce, Lenny	Fiction
Best Of Bob Newhart	Newhart, Bob	Fiction
Best Of Bob Newhart (2)	Newhart, Bob	Fiction
Best Of Hysteria 3	Comedy...	Fiction
Best Of Irish Humour	Roach, Hal	Fiction
Best Of Jimmy Jones	Jones, Jimmy	Fiction
Best Of Lee Sutton: Uncensored	Sutton, Lee	Fiction
Best Of Mike Harding, The	Harding, Mike	Fiction
Best Of Roy Chubby Brown	Brown, Roy 'Chubby'	Fiction
Best Of Sellers	Sellers, Peter	Fiction
Best Of The Goon Shows	Goons	Fiction
Beyond The Fringe	Comedy...	Fiction
Big Yin Double Helping, A	Connolly, Billy	Fiction
Bills Best Friend	Cosby, Bill	Fiction
Billy And Albert	Connolly, Billy	Fiction
Birds, Beasts And Relatives	Durrell, Gerald	Fiction
Bitter And Twisted	Smith & Jones	Fiction
Blastermind	Bates, Blaster	Fiction
Blood Donor	Hancock, Tony	Fiction
Blowing His Mind And Yours Too	Lord Buckley	Fiction
Bob Newhart	Newhart, Bob	Fiction
Brand New	Mason, Jackie	Fiction
British Comedy Classics	Comedy...	Fiction
Can You Hear Me, Mother?	Powell, Sandy	Non-Fiction
Captain Kremmen	Everett, Kenny	Fiction
Captain Paralytic And The Brown Ale Cowboy	Harding, Mike	Fiction
Carrott's Condensed Classics	Carrott, Jasper	Fiction
Carry On Jeeves	Wodehouse, P.G.	Fiction
Change Is As Good As A Rest, A	Connolly, Billy	Fiction
Clean Tapes	Cook, Peter	Fiction
Code Of The Woosters, The	Wodehouse, P.G.	Fiction
Colin Campbell's Local Radio	Campbell, Colin	Fiction
Collection: Joyce Grenfell	Grenfell, Joyce	Fiction
Collection Of Spikes, A	Milligan, Spike	Fiction
Come Again	Derek & Clive	Fiction
Comedian	Murphy, Eddie	Fiction
Comedy Countdown	Kelly, Frank	Fiction

HUMOROUS

Title	Author/Source	Category
Comedy Spectacular	Comedy...	Fiction
Comic Strip	Comedy...	Fiction
Comical Cuts	Comedy...	Fiction
Commercial Road	Digance, Richard	Fiction
Contractual Obligation	Monty Python	Fiction
Cop Yer Whack Of This	Connolly, Billy	Fiction
Cosmic Carrot	Carrott, Jasper	Fiction
Country Comedy Time - Lonzo And Oscar	Comedy...	Fiction
Crack, The	Connolly, Billy	Fiction
Dad's Army	Television	Fiction
Dangerous In Love	Thomas, Leslie	Fiction
Dark Side Of The Goons	Goons	Fiction
Darling Buds Of May, The	Bates, H.E.	Fiction
Derek And Clive Come Again	Derek & Clive	Fiction
Dice	Dice Clay, Andrew	Fiction
Doctor At Large	Gordon, Richard	Fiction
Doctor On The Boil	Gordon, Richard	Fiction
Don't Crush That Dwarf, Hand Me The Pliers	Firesign Theatre	Fiction
Eve Of St. Venus	Burgess, Anthony	Fiction
Evening Wasted With Tom Lehrer, An	Lehrer, Tom	Fiction
Evening With Spike Milligan	Milligan, Spike	Fiction
Evening With Wally Londo, An	Carlin, George	Fiction
Farewell To The North Enclosure	Boyce, Max	Fiction
Fawlty Towers	Television	Fiction
Fillets Of Plaice	Durrell, Gerald	Fiction
Final Rip Off, The	Monty Python	Fiction
Flotsam And Jetsam	Flotsam & Jetsam (2)	Fiction
Foo Foo Shufflewick And Her Exotic Banana	Harding, Mike	Fiction
Fool Britannia	Comedy...	Fiction
For Adults Only	Cosby, Bill	Fiction
Four Faces Of Chubby Brown, The	Brown, Roy 'Chubby'	Fiction
From Inside The Helmet	Brown, Roy 'Chubby'	Fiction
Fun At One	Radio	Fiction
Fundamental Frolics	Comedy...	Fiction
Funny Commercials And Other Radio Fluffs	Radio	Fiction
Gala Week	Clarke, Roy	Fiction
Garden Of The Gods, The	Durrell, Gerald	Fiction
Gellybabe	Bates, Blaster	Fiction
Get Right Intae Him	Connolly, Billy	Fiction
Gobshite	Sadowitz, Jerry	Fiction
God's Own Drunk	Harding, Mike	Fiction
Golden Hour Of Comedy, A	Comedy...	Fiction
Golden Hour Of Mike Reid	Reid, Mike (1)	Fiction
Golden Hour Of Tony Hancock	Hancock, Tony	Fiction
Goon Show Classics	Goons	Fiction
Grand Prix Of Gibraltar	Ustinov, Peter	Fiction
Hancock	Hancock, Tony	Fiction
Hancock's Half Hour	Hancock, Tony	Fiction
Hedgehog Sandwich	Not The Nine O'Clock News	Fiction
Here Comes The Judge	Cook, Peter	Fiction
Hinge And Bracket In Concert	Hinge & Bracket	Fiction
Hitch-Hiker's 1	Adams, Douglas	Fiction
Hitch-Hiker's Guide To The Galaxy	Adams, Douglas	Fiction
Hobo Sexual, The	Nicol, Hector	Fiction
Hoffnung - A Last Encore	Hoffnung, Gerard	Fiction
Homework	Digance, Richard	Fiction
Housewife Superstar	Humphries, Barry	Fiction
How To Win An Election	Goons	Fiction
Hunting And Shooting Stories	Bates, Blaster	Fiction

HUMOROUS

Hurricane Jack Of The Vital Spark	Munro, Neil	Fiction
I Know Cos I Was There	Boyce, Max	Fiction
I'm The Greatest Comedian In The World	Mason, Jackie	Fiction
In Highland Harbours	Munro, Neil	Fiction
Incredible Plan, The	Boyce, Max	Fiction
Inimitable Jeeves, The	Wodehouse, P.G.	Fiction
Innocent Anthropologist, The	Barley, Nigel	Fiction
Inside Shelley Berman	Berman, Shelley	Fiction
Instant Record Collection	Monty Python	Fiction
Is It Something I Said	Pryor, Richard	Fiction
Isle Of Illusion	Munro, Neil	Fiction
It Ain't Half Hot Mum	Television	Fiction
I.T.M.A.	Radio	Fiction
Jeeves	Wodehouse, P.G.	Fiction
Jeeves In The Offing	Wodehouse, P.G.	Fiction
Joy In The Morning	Wodehouse, P.G.	Fiction
Joyce Grenfell Requests The Pleasure	Grenfell, Joyce	Fiction
Keepsake	Grenfell, Joyce	Fiction
Komic Kutz	Harding, Mike	Fiction
Kremmen The Movie	Everett, Kenny	Fiction
Lady And The Champ, The	Nicol, Hector	Fiction
Last Goon Show Of All	Goons	Fiction
Last Night Of The Poms	Everage, Dame Edna	Fiction
Laughing Stock Of The BBC	Comedy...	Fiction
Laughter With A Bang	Bates, Blaster	Fiction
Laurel And Hardy	Laurel & Hardy	Fiction
Laurel And Hardy On The Air	Laurel & Hardy	Fiction
Lenin Of The Rovers	Radio	Fiction
Liar, The	Fry, Stephen	Fiction
Life Of Brian	Monty Python	Fiction
Life, The Universe And Everything	Adams, Douglas	Fiction
Lift Off	Bates, Blaster	Fiction
Lift, The	Hancock, Tony	Fiction
Live And Unleashed	Henry, Lenny	Fiction
Live At Drury Lane	Monty Python	Fiction
Live At Jongleurs	Comedy...	Fiction
Live At The Embassy Club	Manning, Bernard	Fiction
Live At The Morgue	Bednarczyk, Stefan	Fiction
Live At The Talk Of East Anglia	Jones, Jimmy (comedy)	Fiction
Live At Treorchy	Boyce, Max	Fiction
Live In America	Carrott, Jasper	Fiction
Live In Belfast	Atkinson, Rowan	Fiction
Live In Concert - Wanted	Pryor, Richard	Fiction
Look At Life, A	O'Connor, Tom	Fiction
Man Upstairs, The	Wodehouse, P.G.	Fiction
Matching Tie And Handkerchief	Monty Python	Fiction
Me And Billy Williams	Boyce, Max	Fiction
Memories Of Great Wireless Comedy Shows	Comedy...	Fiction
Memory Kinda Lingers, The / Not In Front Of The Audience	Not The Nine O'Clock News	Fiction
Milligan Preserved	Milligan, Spike	Fiction
Monarch Of The Glen, The	Mackenzie, Compton	Fiction
Monty Python And The Holy Grail	Monty Python	Fiction
Monty Python's Flying Circus	Monty Python	Fiction
Monty Python's Meaning Of Life	Monty Python	Fiction
Moonbather, The	Clarke, Roy	Fiction
More Fun At One	Radio	Fiction
More Junk	Corbett, Harry H.	Fiction
More Monologues And Songs	Holloway, Stanley	Fiction

HUMOROUS

More Of The Best Of Round The Horne	Radio	Fiction
Most Immaculately Hip Aristocrat	Lord Buckley	Fiction
Motormouth	Elton, Ben	Fiction
Motorvation	Elton, Ben	Fiction
Mrs.'Ardin's Kid	Harding, Mike	Fiction
Much Binding In The Marsh	Radio	Fiction
Much Obliged, Jeeves	Wodehouse, P.G.	Fiction
Navy Lark, The	Radio	Fiction
News Quiz, The	Radio	Fiction
Nightclub Years (1964-1968)	Allen, Woody	Fiction
Noel Coward And Gertrude Lawrence	Coward, Noel	Fiction
Noel's Funny Phone Calls	Edmonds, Noel	Fiction
Not Just A Pretty Face	Atkinson, Rowan	Fiction
Not Just A Pretty Face	Cool, Phil	Fiction
Not That I'm Biased	Boyce, Max	Fiction
Not The Double Album	Not The Nine O'Clock News	Fiction
Not The Nine O'Clock News	Not The Nine O'Clock News	Fiction
Oh Baby	Cosby, Bill	Fiction
On Tour With The Big Yin	Connolly, Billy	Fiction
Once More With Cook	Cook, Peter	Fiction
One Hundred Comedy Inserts	Comedy...	Fiction
Only A World Cup Excuse	Watson, Jonathan	Fiction
Only An Excuse	Watson, Jonathan	Fiction
Only Another Excuse	Watson, Jonathan	Fiction
Ordinary Copper, An	Warner, Jack	Fiction
Peter Sellers Collection	Sellers, Peter	Fiction
Phantom Of The Soap Opera	Simple, Lee J.	Fiction
Pick Of Billy Connolly, The	Connolly, Billy	Fiction
Picnic And Suchlike Pandemonium, The	Durrell, Gerald	Fiction
Pieces Of Hancock	Hancock, Tony	Fiction
Pink Medicine Album	Beetles, Chris	Fiction
Porridge	Television	Fiction
Porterhouse Blue	Sharpe, Tom	Fiction
Portrait, The	Connolly, Billy	Fiction
Previous Album	Monty Python	Fiction
Private Eye Golden Satiricals	Comedy...	Fiction
Puckoon	Milligan, Spike	Fiction
Rabbits On And On And On...	Carrott, Jasper	Fiction
Raw Meat For The Balcony	Connolly, Billy	Fiction
Ray's A Laugh	Ray, Ted	Fiction
Record Size Willy	Humour	Fiction
Re-Joyce	Grenfell, Joyce	Fiction
Restaurant At The End Of The Universe	Adams, Douglas	Fiction
Right Ho, Jeeves	Wodehouse, P.G.	Fiction
Road And The Miles, The	Boyce, Max	Fiction
Rochdale Cowboy Rides Again, The	Harding, Mike	Non-Fiction
Roll Over Cecil Sharpe	Harding, Mike	Fiction
Rooted	Harding, Mike	Fiction
Round The Horne	Radio	Fiction
Scoop	Waugh, Evelyn	Fiction
Scotch And Full Of It	Nicol, Hector	Fiction
Scratch 'n' Sniff	Smith & Jones	Fiction
Secret Policeman's Ball	Comedy...	Fiction
Secret Policeman's Other Ball	Comedy	Fiction
Secret Policeman's Third Ball	Comedy	Fiction
Sellers Market	Sellers, Peter	Fiction
Short Stories	Wodehouse, P.G.	Fiction
Sir Henry At Rawlinson End	Stanshall, Vivian	Fiction
Snow Goose, The	Milligan, Spike	Fiction

HUMOROUS

So Long, And Thanks For All The Fish	Adams, Douglas	Fiction
Something Fresh	Wodehouse, P.G.	Fiction
Songs And Dialogue	Laurel & Hardy	Fiction
Songs And Monologues Of Joyce Grenfell, The	Grenfell, Joyce	Fiction
Sound Of Edna,the	Humphries, Barry	Fiction
Spit In Your Ear	Spitting Image	Fiction
Stand Up...Get Down	Henry, Lenny	Fiction
Standing Room Only	Duffus, George	Fiction
Steptoe & Son	Steptoe & Son	Fiction
Steptoe & Son	Radio	Fiction
Suspense	Buchan, John	Fiction
Sweet Dreams	Frayn, Michael	Fiction
Take Your Fingers Off It	Harding, Mike	Fiction
Taking Over	Lowe & Ince	Fiction
Thank You, Jeeves	Wodehouse, P.G.	Fiction
There Was This Bloke	Humour	Fiction
They All Laughed	Humour	Fiction
This Is Hancock	Hancock, Tony	Fiction
Those Of You With Or Without Children	Cosby, Bill	Fiction
Three Men In A Boat	Jerome, Jerome K.	Fiction
Three Men On The Bummel	Jerome, Jerome K.	Fiction
Three Of A Kind	Television	Fiction
Throwback, The	Sharpe, Tom	Fiction
Titmuss Regained	Mortimer, John	Fiction
TNT For Two	Bates, Blaster	Fiction
Toledo Window Box	Carlin, George	Fiction
Tribute To The Kings Of Scottish Comedy	Beattie, Johnny	Fiction
True Blue Comedy Vol 1	Lucky Grills	Fiction
True Blue Comedy Vol 2	Lucky Grills	Fiction
True Blue Comedy Vol 3	Lucky Grills	Fiction
Two Ronnies	Two Ronnies	Fiction
Unspun Socks From A Chickens Laundry	Milligan, Spike	Fiction
Utterly Utterly Live	Comedy...	Fiction
Very Best Of Me And The Very Best Of Him, The	Two Ronnies	Fiction
Very Best Of Rowan Atkinson, The (live)	Atkinson, Rowan	Fiction
Vice Versa	Anstey, F	Fiction
Victoria Wood	Wood, Victoria	Fiction
Vintage Stuff	Sharpe, Tom	Fiction
Vital Spark, The	Munro, Neil	Fiction
Voices On The Stairheid	Humour	Fiction
Watch Out For The Bits	Bates, Blaster	Fiction
We All Had Doctors Papers	Boyce, Max	Fiction
Weekend Sounds	Morecambe & Wise	Fiction
What Goes Up Might Come Down	Gunson, David	Fiction
Wild And Crazy Guy	Martin, Steve	Fiction
Wit And Wisdom Of Ronald Reagan	Reagan, Ronald	Fiction
Wolves, Witches And Giants	Milligan, Spike	Fiction
Words And Music	Connolly, Billy	Fiction
World Of Paddy Roberts	Roberts, Paddy	Fiction
World Of Pete And Dud	Cook, Peter	Fiction
World Of Tony Hancock, The	Hancock, Tony	Fiction
Yes Minister	Radio	Fiction

LANGUAGES

TITLE	HEADING	SECTION
A Vous La France	French	Non-Fiction
A Vous La France (2)	French	Non-Fiction
Afrikaans	African	Non-Fiction
Arabic Cassette Course	Arabic	Non-Fiction
Arabic Travel Pack	Arabic	Non-Fiction
Articulos	Spanish	Non-Fiction
Aspects Of Russian Grammar	Russian	Non-Fiction
Basic Cantonese	Chinese	Non-Fiction
Basic French (Part A)	French	Non-Fiction
Basic French (Part B)	French	Non-Fiction
Basic German	German	Non-Fiction
Basic German Advanced Level	German	Non-Fiction
Basic German Intermediate	German	Non-Fiction
Basic Hungarian	Hungarian	Non-Fiction
Basic Saudi Arabic	Arabic	Non-Fiction
Basic Spanish (Advanced Level)	Spanish	Non-Fiction
Basic Spanish (Beginners)	Spanish	Non-Fiction
Basic Spanish (Intermediate)	Spanish	Non-Fiction
Basic Turkish	Turkish	Non-Fiction
Beginning Japanese	Japanese	Non-Fiction
Bol Chaal	Hindi	Non-Fiction
Branche Entre Nous	French	Non-Fiction
Buongiorno Italia	Italian	Non-Fiction
Business Spanish	Spanish	Non-Fiction
Canseo	Gaelic	Non-Fiction
Carmen	French	Non-Fiction
Celtic Language, The	Celtic	Non-Fiction
Chinese Cassette Course	Chinese	Non-Fiction
Chinese - English Dictionaries And How To Use Them	Chinese	Non-Fiction
Chinese Travel Pack	Chinese	Non-Fiction
Church Slavonicisms In Russian	Russian	Non-Fiction
Contemporary Czech	Czech	Non-Fiction
Contes De La Becasse	French	Non-Fiction
Conversational Polish: A Beginners Course	Polish	Non-Fiction
Czech Phonology	Czech	Non-Fiction
Czech Travel Pack	Czech	Non-Fiction
Danish Cassette Course	Danish	Non-Fiction
Danish Travel Pack	Danish	Non-Fiction
Das Fraulein Von Scuderi	German	Non-Fiction
Declension Of Adjectives, The	German	Non-Fiction
Declension Of Nouns, The	German	Non-Fiction
Decollage	French	Non-Fiction
Deutsch Direkt	German	Non-Fiction
Deutsch Express	German	Non-Fiction
Development Of The German Language, The	German	Non-Fiction
Development Of The Russian Language, The	Russian	Non-Fiction
Die Marquise Von O And Das	German	Non-Fiction
Digame	Spanish	Non-Fiction
Discovering Portuguese	Portuguese	Non-Fiction
Discussion Of Modern Greek Poetry	Greek	Non-Fiction

LANGUAGES

Doing Business In Japan	Japanese	Non-Fiction
Dutch Cassette Course	Dutch	Non-Fiction
Dutch For Travel	Dutch	Non-Fiction
Dutch Language Basics	Dutch	Non-Fiction
Dutch Travel Pack	Dutch	Non-Fiction
Eastern Arabic	Arabic	Non-Fiction
El Ingles Simplificado	English	Non-Fiction
El Ingles Simplificado Cassette Course	English	Non-Fiction
English Cassette Course	English	Non-Fiction
English Child In France, An	French	Non-Fiction
English Simplified	English	Non-Fiction
English With A Dialect	English	Non-Fiction
English With An Accent	English	Non-Fiction
Entre Nous	French	Non-Fiction
Espana Viva	Spanish	Non-Fiction
Executive Japanese	Japanese	Non-Fiction
Fables	French	Non-Fiction
Finnish For Foreigners	Finnish	Non-Fiction
Franc Parler	French	Non-Fiction
French At The Wheel	French	Non-Fiction
French Business Cassette Course	French	Non-Fiction
French Cassette Course	French	Non-Fiction
French Extra	French	Non-Fiction
French For Business	French	Non-Fiction
French For Travel	French	Non-Fiction
French Language Basics	French	Non-Fiction
French Legal And Commercial Professions	French	Non-Fiction
French Outside France: French Speaking Switzerland	French	Non-Fiction
French Outside France: Le Francais Du Quebec	French	Non-Fiction
French Phonology	French	Non-Fiction
French Travel Kit	French	Non-Fiction
French Travel Packs	French	Non-Fiction
FSI Basic Amharic	African	Non-Fiction
FSI Swedish Basic Course	Swedish	Non-Fiction
Fula Basic Course	African	Non-Fiction
Ganz Spontan	German	Non-Fiction
Gender In Russian	Russian	Non-Fiction
Gender Of Nouns, The	German	Non-Fiction
German At The Wheel	German	Non-Fiction
German Business Cassette Course	German	Non-Fiction
German Cassette Course	German	Non-Fiction
German For Business	German	Non-Fiction
German For Travel	German	Non-Fiction
German Language Basics	German	Non-Fiction
German Travel Kit	German	Non-Fiction
German Travel Packs	German	Non-Fiction
German-English Dictionaries And How To Use Them	German	Non-Fiction
Get By Arabic	Arabic	Non-Fiction
Get By In Chinese	Chinese	Non-Fiction
Get By In French	French	Non-Fiction
Get By In German	German	Non-Fiction
Get By In Greek	Greek	Non-Fiction
Get By In Hindi	Hindi	Non-Fiction
Get By In Italian	Italian	Non-Fiction
Get By In Japanese	Japanese	Non-Fiction
Get By In Portuguese	Portuguese	Non-Fiction
Get By In Russian	Russian	Non-Fiction
Get By In Spanish	Spanish	Non-Fiction
Get By In Turkish	Turkish	Non-Fiction

LANGUAGES

Get By Travel Packs	Arabic	Non-Fiction
Get By Travel Packs	Chinese	Non-Fiction
Get By Travel Packs	French	Non-Fiction
Get By Travel Packs	German	Non-Fiction
Get By Travel Packs	Greek	Non-Fiction
Get By Travel Packs	Italian	Non-Fiction
Get By Travel Packs	Japanese	Non-Fiction
Get By Travel Packs	Portuguese	Non-Fiction
Get By Travel Packs	Russian	Non-Fiction
Get By Travel Packs	Spanish	Non-Fiction
Get By Travel Packs	Turkish	Non-Fiction
Gleg	Scottish	Non-Fiction
Greek Cassette Course	Greek	Non-Fiction
Greek For Travel	Greek	Non-Fiction
Greek Language And People	Greek	Non-Fiction
Greek Language Basics	Greek	Non-Fiction
Greek Travel Pack	Greek	Non-Fiction
Hausa Basic Course	African	Non-Fiction
Hebrew Travel Pack	Hebrew	Non-Fiction
How To End A Japanese Sentence	Japanese	Non-Fiction
Hungarian Travel Pack	Hungarian	Non-Fiction
Il Problema Dell' Unificazione Linguistica Itali	Italian	Non-Fiction
Immensee	German	Non-Fiction
Improve Your English	English	Non-Fiction
Improve Your French	French	Non-Fiction
Improve Your Word Power	English	Non-Fiction
Interviews In French	French	Non-Fiction
Interviews In French	French	Non-Fiction
Introducing Ancient Greek	Greek	Non-Fiction
Introducing The Arabic Language	Arabic	Non-Fiction
Introducing The Byelorussian Language	Slavonic	Non-Fiction
Introducing The Dutch Language	Dutch	Non-Fiction
Introducing The Japanese Language	Japanese	Non-Fiction
Introducing The Romanian Language	Romanian	Non-Fiction
Introducing The Turkish Language	Turkish	Non-Fiction
Irish-English Dictionaries And How To Use Them	Irish	Non-Fiction
Italia, Anni '80: Corso Di Lingua E Cultura	Italian	Non-Fiction
Italian At The Wheel	Italian	Non-Fiction
Italian Between Past And Present	Italian	Non-Fiction
Italian Cassette Course	Italian	Non-Fiction
Italian For Travel	Italian	Non-Fiction
Italian Language Basics	Italian	Non-Fiction
Italian Travel Kit	Italian	Non-Fiction
Italian Travel Pack	Italian	Non-Fiction
Japanese Cassette Course	Japanese	Non-Fiction
Japanese Language And People	Japanese	Non-Fiction
Japanese Travel Pack	Japanese	Non-Fiction
Kein Problem	German	Non-Fiction
Korva Tarkkana	Finnish	Non-Fiction
La Questione Della Lingua Nel Rinasciments	Italian	Non-Fiction
Lallans	Scotland	Non-Fiction
L'Anglais Simplifie	English	Non-Fiction
L'Anglais Simplifie Cassette Course	English	Non-Fiction
Language Course - Arabic (Modern Standard)	Arabic	Non-Fiction
Language Course - Chinese (Mandarin)	Chinese	Non-Fiction
Language Course - Danish	Danish	Non-Fiction
Language Course - Dutch	Dutch	Non-Fiction
Language Course - English	English	Non-Fiction
Language Course - Ensemble	French	Non-Fiction

LANGUAGES

Language Course - Finnish	Finnish	Non-Fiction
Language Course - French	French	Non-Fiction
Language Course - French At Home	French	Non-Fiction
Language Course - German	German	Non-Fiction
Language Course - Greek (Modern)	Greek	Non-Fiction
Language Course - Hebrew (Modern)	Hebrew	Non-Fiction
Language Course - Hindi	Hindi	Non-Fiction
Language Course - Icelandic	Icelandic	Non-Fiction
Language Course - Irish	Irish...	Non-Fiction
Language Course - Italian	Italian	Non-Fiction
Language Course - Japanese	Japanese	Non-Fiction
Language Course - Make Sentences In French 1	French	Non-Fiction
Language Course - Malay (Bahasa Malaysia)	Malay	Non-Fiction
Language Course - Norwegian	Norwegian	Non-Fiction
Language Course - Polish	Polish	Non-Fiction
Language Course - Portuguese	Portuguese	Non-Fiction
Language Course - Russian	Russian	Non-Fiction
Language Course - Spanish	Spanish	Non-Fiction
Language Course - Spanish (Castilian)	Spanish	Non-Fiction
Language Course - Spanish (Latin-American)	Spanish	Non-Fiction
Language Course - Swedish	Swedish	Non-Fiction
Language Course - Welsh	Welsh	Non-Fiction
Languages Of India - Part 1 Indo-european	Indian	Non-Fiction
Languages Of India - Part 2 Non-Indo European	Indian	Non-Fiction
Lawyers And Industry In Germany	German	Non-Fiction
Learn To Speak Danish	Danish	Non-Fiction
Levantine Arabic Pronounciation	Arabic	Non-Fiction
Lexis Of Russian, The	Russian	Non-Fiction
Leyendas	Spanish	Non-Fiction
Linguaphone French Travellers	French	Non-Fiction
Linguaphone German Travellers	German	Non-Fiction
Linguaphone Greek Travellers	Greek	Non-Fiction
Linguaphone Italian Travellers	Italian	Non-Fiction
Linguaphone Portuguese Travellers	Portuguese	Non-Fiction
Linguaphone Spanish Travellers	Spanish	Non-Fiction
L'Italia Dal Vivo	Italian	Non-Fiction
Make Sentences In French 2	French	Non-Fiction
Making Sense Of The Verb	German	Non-Fiction
Mexico Vivo	Spanish	Non-Fiction
Modal Auxiliary Verbs, The	German	Non-Fiction
Modern Greek Basic Course	Greek	Non-Fiction
Modern Russian	Russian	Non-Fiction
Modern Spoken Italian	Italian	Non-Fiction
Modern Written Arabic	Arabic	Non-Fiction
Moroccan Arabic	Arabic	Non-Fiction
Norsk Fonetikk For Utlendinger	Norwegian	Non-Fiction
Norsk For Utlendinger	Norwegian	Non-Fiction
Norwegian Cassette Course	Norwegian	Non-Fiction
Norwegian Travel Pack	Norwegian	Non-Fiction
Outstanding Greek Modern Poetry	Greek	Non-Fiction
Paso Doble	Spanish	Non-Fiction
Penguin Basic Russian	Russian	Non-Fiction
Polish Travel Pack	Polish	Non-Fiction
Por Aqui	Spanish	Non-Fiction
Portuguese Cassette Course	Portuguese	Non-Fiction
Portuguese For Travel	Portuguese	Non-Fiction
Portuguese Language Basics	Portuguese	Non-Fiction
Portuguese Travel Pack	Portuguese	Non-Fiction
Prepositions And The Cases Which They Govern	German	Non-Fiction

LANGUAGES

Programmatic Portuguese	Portuguese	Non-Fiction
Pronunciation And Reading Of Ancient Greek, The	Ancient Greek	Non-Fiction
Pronunciation And Reading Of Classical Latin	Latin	Non-Fiction
Protestant Church In Germany, The	Golka, F.W.	Non-Fiction
Reading Japanese	Japanese	Non-Fiction
Recital Of Ancient Greek Poetry, A	Ancient Greek	Non-Fiction
Romance Languages, The	Romance Languages	Non-Fiction
Russian And The Languages Of The U.S.S.R.	Russian	Non-Fiction
Russian Approach To Literature, The	Russian	Non-Fiction
Russian Cassette Course	Russian	Non-Fiction
Russian Dialects	Russian	Non-Fiction
Russian Language And People	Russian	Non-Fiction
Russian Listening Comprehension	Russian	Non-Fiction
Russian Stress	Russian	Non-Fiction
Russian Travel Pack	Russian	Non-Fiction
Selection From Catullus And Horace	Latin	Non-Fiction
Selections From The Greek Orators	Latin	Non-Fiction
Selections From Virgil	Latin	Non-Fiction
Senilita	Italian	Non-Fiction
Separable And Inseparable Verbs, The	German	Non-Fiction
Serbo Croat	Serbo Croat	Non-Fiction
Shona Basic Course	African	Non-Fiction
Slavonic Language, The	Slavonic	Non-Fiction
Sounds And Alphabet Of Czech, The	Czech	Non-Fiction
Sounds And Alphabet Of Polish, The	Polish	Non-Fiction
Sounds And Alphabet Of Romanian	Romanian	Non-Fiction
Sounds And Alphabet Of Russian, The	Russian	Non-Fiction
Sounds And Alphabet Of Serbo Croatian, The	Serbo Croat	Non-Fiction
Sounds And Alphabet Of Spanish, The	Spanish	Non-Fiction
Sounds And Alphabet Of Welsh, The	Welsh	Non-Fiction
Sounds Of Arabic, The - Part 1	Arabic	Non-Fiction
Sounds Of Arabic, The - Part 2	Arabic	Non-Fiction
Sounds Of Classical Latin, The	Latin	Non-Fiction
Sounds Of Spanish, The	Spanish	Non-Fiction
Spanish At The Wheel	Spanish	Non-Fiction
Spanish Cassette Course	Spanish	Non-Fiction
Spanish For Travel	Spanish	Non-Fiction
Spanish Language Basics	Spanish	Non-Fiction
Spanish Language In America, The	Spanish	Non-Fiction
Spanish Travel Kit	Spanish	Non-Fiction
Spanish Travel Pack	Spanish	Non-Fiction
Speak Dutch Today	Dutch	Non-Fiction
Speak English Today	English	Non-Fiction
Speak French Today	French	Non-Fiction
Speak German Today	German	Non-Fiction
Speak Greek Today	Greek	Non-Fiction
Speak Italian Today	Italian	Non-Fiction
Speak Portuguese Today	Portuguese	Non-Fiction
Speak Spanish Today	Spanish	Non-Fiction
Speaking Chinise In China	Chinese	Non-Fiction
Spoken Egyptian Arabic	Arabic	Non-Fiction
Spoken Romanian	Romanian	Non-Fiction
Sure Le Vif	French	Non-Fiction
Swahili, Active Introduction	African	Non-Fiction
Swahili Basic Course	African	Non-Fiction
Swedish Cassette Course	Swedish	Non-Fiction
Swedish Travel Pack	Swedish	Non-Fiction
Syrian Arabic	Arabic	Non-Fiction
Thai Travel Pack	Thai	Non-Fiction

Turkish Cassette Course	Turkish	Non-Fiction
Turkish For Travel	Turkish	Non-Fiction
Turkish Language Basics	Turkish	Non-Fiction
Turkish Travel Pack	Turkish	Non-Fiction
Twa Leids And Da Chanan	Scottish	Non-Fiction
TWI Basic Course	African	Non-Fiction
Use Of Cases In Russian, The	Russian	Non-Fiction
Verbs Of Motion	Russian	Non-Fiction
When In France	French	Non-Fiction
When In Germany	German	Non-Fiction
When In Italy	Italian	Non-Fiction
When In Spain	Spanish	Non-Fiction
Yoruba Basic Course	African	Non-Fiction
Yugoslav Travel Pack	Slavonic	Non-Fiction
Zulu	African	Non-Fiction

PLAYS

TITLE	HEADING	SECTION
Adolphe	Constant, B	Fiction
After Henry	Brett, Simon	Fiction
All's Well That Ends Well	Shakespeare, William	Fiction
Anthony And Cleopatra	Shakespeare, William	Fiction
Antigone	Sophocles	Fiction
Arsenic And Old Lace	Christie, Agatha	Fiction
As You Like It	Shakespeare, William	Fiction
Athalie	Racine, Jean	Fiction
Background	Voltaire	Non-Fiction
Bajazet	Racine, Jean	Fiction
Berenice	Racine, Jean	Fiction
Bhowani Junction	Masters, John	Fiction
Breakfast At Tiffany's	Capote, Truman	Fiction
Browning Version, The	Rattigan, Terence	Fiction
Butley	Gray, Simon	Fiction
Caesar And Cleopatra	Shaw, George Bernard	Fiction
Charley's Aunt	Plays	Fiction
Cinna	Corneille, P	Fiction
Comedy Of Errors, The	Shakespeare, William	Fiction
Contes A Ninon	Zola, Emile	Fiction
Coriolanus	Shakespeare, William	Fiction
Crucible, The	Miller, Arthur	Fiction
Cymbeline	Shakespeare, William	Fiction
Cyrano De Bergerac	Rostand, Edmund	Fiction
Death Of A Salesman	Miller, Arthur	Fiction
Don Juan	Moliere	Fiction
Double Bill	Coward, Noel	Fiction
Double Bill	Rattigan, Terence	Fiction
Duchess Of Malfi, The	Webster, John	Fiction
Edward II	Marlowe, Christopher	Fiction
Emperor Jones, The	O'Neill, Eugene	Fiction
Enquiry	Francis, Dick	Fiction
Essential Shakespeare, The	Shakespeare, William	Fiction
Family Reunion	Eliot, T.S.	Fiction
Fatal Eggs, The	Samuels, Arthur	Fiction
Five One-Act Plays	Yeats, W.B.	Fiction
Forty Years On	Bennett, Alan	Fiction
Front Page, The	Hecht, Ben	Fiction
Glass Menagerie, The	Williams, Tennessee	Fiction
Great Shakespeareans	Shakespeare, William	Fiction
Hamlet	Shakespeare, William	Fiction
Heartbreak House	Shaw, George Bernard	Fiction
Henry IV	Shakespeare, William	Fiction
Henry V	Shakespeare, William	Fiction
Henry VI	Shakespeare, William	Fiction
Homecoming, The	Pinter, Harold	Fiction
Horace	Corneille, P	Fiction
Ice Man Cometh, The	O'Neill, Eugene	Fiction
Importance Of Being Earnest, The	Wilde, Oscar	Fiction
Jeeves And The Feudal Spirit	Wodehouse, P.G.	Fiction

PLAYS

John Bull's Other Island	Shaw, George Bernard	Fiction
Julius Caesar	Shakespeare, William	Fiction
Juno And The Paycock	O'Casey, Sean	Fiction
King Henry VIII	Shakespeare, William	Fiction
King John	Shakespeare, William	Fiction
King Lear	Shakespeare, William	Fiction
L'Avare	Moliere	Fiction
Le Misanthrope	Moliere	Fiction
L'Ecole Des Femmes	Moliere	Fiction
Les Femmes Savantes	Moliere	Fiction
Long Day's Journey Into Night	O'Neill, Eugene	Fiction
Love's Labour's Lost	Shakespeare, William	Fiction
Luther	Osborne, John	Fiction
MacBeth	Shakespeare, William	Fiction
MacGowran Speaking Beckett	Beckett, Samuel	Fiction
Major Barbara	Shaw, George Bernard	Fiction
Master Builder, The	Ibsen, Henrik	Fiction
Measure For Measure	Shakespeare, William	Fiction
Medea	Euripides	Fiction
Merchant Of Venice, The	Shakespeare, William	Fiction
Merry Wives Of Windsor, The	Shakespeare, William	Fiction
Midsummer Night's Dream, A	Shakespeare, William	Fiction
Misalliance	Shaw, George Bernard	Fiction
Mithridate	Racine, Jean	Fiction
Monk's Hood	Peters, Ellis	Fiction
Much Ado About Nothing	Shakespeare, William	Fiction
Murder In The Cathedral	Eliot, T.S.	Fiction
Murder Must Advertise	Sayers, Dorothy L.	Fiction
No Exit	Sartre, Jean-paul	Fiction
Oedipus Rex	Sophocles	Fiction
Old Possum's Book Of Practical Cats	Eliot, T.S.	Fiction
Othello	Shakespeare, William	Fiction
Our Man In Havana	Greene, Graham	Fiction
Pericles	Shakespeare, William	Fiction
Playboy Of The Western World, The	Synge, John	Fiction
Poirot	Christie, Agatha	Fiction
Polyeucte	Corneille, P.	Fiction
Present Laughter	Coward, Noel	Fiction
Price Of Fear, The	Ghost Stories	Fiction
Private Lives	Coward, Noel	Fiction
Pygmalion	Shaw, George Bernard	Fiction
Richard II	Shakespeare, William	Fiction
Richard III	Shakespeare, William	Fiction
Rodogune	Corneille, P	Fiction
Romeo And Juliet	Shakespeare, William	Fiction
Rose Tattoo, The	Williams, Tennessee	Fiction
Rosencrantz And Guildenstern Are Dead	Stoppard, Tom	Fiction
Rumpole 2	Mortimer, John	Fiction
Saint Joan	Shaw, George Bernard	Fiction
Shakespeare Sonnets-2	Shakespeare, William	Fiction
She Stoops To Conquer	Goldsmith, Oliver	Fiction
Six Plays	Plays	Fiction
Smiley's People	Le Carre, John	Fiction
Sonnets	Shakespeare, William	Fiction
Sound Of Classical Drama, The	Plays	Fiction
Sound Of Modern Drama, The	Plays	Fiction
Streetcar Named Desire, A	Williams, Tennessee	Fiction
Tale Of Two Cities, A	Dickens, Charles	Fiction
Talking Heads	Bennett, Alan	Fiction

PLAYS

Taming Of The Shrew	Shakespeare, William	Fiction
Tempest, The	Shakespeare, William	Fiction
Timon Of Athens	Shakespeare, William	Fiction
Tinker Tailor Soldier Spy	Le Carre, John	Fiction
Titus Andronicus	Shakespeare, William	Fiction
Titus Groan And Gormenghast	Peake, Mervyn	Fiction
Tragedy Of Richard III, The	Shakespeare, William	Fiction
Troilus And Cressida	Shakespeare, William	Fiction
Twelfth Night	Shakespeare, William	Fiction
Two Gentlemen Of Verona	Shakespeare, William	Fiction
Uncle Mort's North Country	Tinniswood, Peter	Fiction
Uncle Mort's South Country	Tinniswood, Peter	Fiction
Under Milk Wood	Thomas, Dylan	Fiction
Unsuitable Job For A Woman, A	James, P.D.	Fiction
Venus And Adonis	Shakespeare, William	Fiction
Winesburg, Ohio	Anderson, Sherwood	Fiction
Winter's Tale, The	Shakespeare, William	Fiction
World Of Shakespeare, The	Shakespeare, William	Fiction

POETRY

TITLE	HEADING	SECTION
10 Medieval Makars	Poetry	Fiction
18 Poems From The Bird Path	White, Kenneth	Fiction
20th Century Poetry	Poetry	Fiction
41 Poems From Handbook For The Diamond Country	White, Kenneth	Fiction
Alexander Montgomerie	Montgomerie, Alexander	Fiction
Alexander Scott	Scott, Alexander	Fiction
Allan Ramsay	Ramsay, Allan	Fiction
Alligator Pie	Poetry	Fiction
And Death Shall Have No Domination	Thomas, Dylan	Fiction
Another Round Of Poems And Pints	Poetry	Fiction
Anthology - Poetry Readings	Poetry	Fiction
Argo Treasury Of Comic And Curious Verse	Poetry	Fiction
Argo Treasury Of English Poetry (Volume 1)	Poetry	Fiction
Argo Treasury Of English Poetry (Volume 2)	Poetry	Fiction
Argo Treasury Of English Poetry (Volume 3)	Poetry	Fiction
Argo Treasury Of Love Poems	Poetry	Fiction
Argo Treasury Of Readings From Longer Poems	Poetry	Fiction
Argo Treasury Of Religious Verse	Poetry	Fiction
Argo Treasury Of Romantic Verse	Poetry	Fiction
Argo Treasury Of Victorian Poetry	Poetry	Fiction
Assessment And Choice	MacDiarmid, Hugh	Fiction
Assessment And Selection	Burns, Robert	Fiction
Bad Ballads And Cautionary Verses, The	Gilbert, W.S.	Fiction
Bailtean (Villages)	Campbell, Myles	Fiction
Banana Blush	Betjeman, Sir John	Fiction
Bennygoak	Garry, Flora	Fiction
Beowulf, The Battle Of Malden	Poetry	Fiction
Best Loved Verse	Poetry	Fiction
Betjeman Reads Betjeman	Betjeman, Sir John	Fiction
Betjeman's Britain	Betjeman, Sir John	Fiction
Blackmore By The Stour	Barnes, William	Fiction
Bonnie Fechter, A	Scott, Alexander	Fiction
Brian Patten Reading His Poems	Patten, Brian	Fiction
Burns Cottage Selection	Burns, Robert	Fiction
C. Day Lewis Reads C. Day Lewis	Day Lewis, C	Fiction
Cantico Del Sole, Canto 99...	Poetry	Fiction
Cautionary Verses	Poetry	Fiction
Choice And Commentary	Garioch, Robert	Fiction
Collected Poems	Poetry	Fiction
Come Love With Me	Poetry	Fiction
Comic Rhymes	Poetry	Fiction
Commentary And Choice	Barbour, John	Fiction
Commentary And Choice	Douglas, Gavin	Fiction
Commentary And Selection	Poetry	Fiction
Companions In A Death Boat	Childish, Wild Billy	Fiction
Conversations With Doctor X	Childish, Wild Billy	Fiction
Crossing Brooklyn Ferry	Whitman, Walt	Fiction
Currie Flavour	Poetry	Fiction
David Rorie	Rorie, David	Fiction
Day Of Rhymes, A	Pooley, Sarah	Fiction

POETRY

Derek Mahon Reads His Own Poetry	Mahon, Derek	Fiction
Discovering Rhythm & Rhyme In Poetry	Untermeyer, Louis	Fiction
Dogmatic	Barker, Les	Fiction
Dylan Thomas And Edith Sitwell Read Her Poems	Sitwell, Dame Edith	Fiction
Dylan Thomas Reading His Poetry	Thomas, Dylan	Fiction
Dylan Thomas Reads A Personal Anthology	Thomas, Dylan	Fiction
Edinburgh Calendar, The	Fergusson, Robert	Fiction
Edith Sitwell Reading Her Poems	Sitwell, Dame Edith	Fiction
E.E. Cummings Reading	Cummings, E.E.	Fiction
E.E. Cummings Reads His Poetry	Cummings, E.E.	Fiction
Epic Poems	Poetry	Fiction
Essential McGough, The	McGough, Roger	Fiction
Extracts From Paradise Lost	Milton, John	Fiction
Farmer's Ingle And Other Poems, The	Fergusson, Robert	Fiction
Favourite Poems	Poetry	Fiction
Fifty Pawky Poems	Poetry	Fiction
Four Twentieth Century Poets	Poetry	Fiction
Granny's Button Box	Everill, Joyce	Fiction
Gunga Din	Kipling, Rudyard	Fiction
Hairst Gaitherins	Maitland, William	Fiction
Hamewith	Murray, Charles	Fiction
I Hear America Singing	Whitman, Walt	Fiction
I Remember, I Remember	Duce, Joan	Fiction
In Country Heaven	Thomas, Dylan	Fiction
In Mind O A Makar	Garioch, Robert	Fiction
John Betjeman Reads John Betjeman	Betjeman, Sir John	Fiction
Langholm Memorial Sculpture	MacDiarmid, Hugh	Fiction
Late Flowering Love	Betjeman, Sir John	Fiction
Lewis, Cecil Day	see under Day Lewis, C	Fiction
Living Ghosts	Kennelly, Brendan	Fiction
Love Poems Of John Donne, The	Donne, John	Fiction
Love Song Of J. Alfred Prufrock, The	Eliot, T.S.	Fiction
Lydlinch Bells	Barnes, William	Fiction
Man Be My Metaphor	Thomas, Dylan	Fiction
Matter Of Choice	Poetry	Fiction
Merry Matanzie	Soutar, William	Fiction
Metamorphoses	Ovid	Fiction
Millay Reading Her Poetry	Millay, Edna	Fiction
More Favourite Poems	Poetry	Fiction
My Last Duchess	Browning, Robert	Fiction
My Little Pony	Zabel, Jennifer	Fiction
My Old Chap	Goodland, Norman	Fiction
Nightmares	Poetry	Fiction
Noel Coward Reading	Coward, Noel	Fiction
Nonsense Verse	Carroll, Lewis	Fiction
Over Sir John's Hill	Thomas, Dylan	Fiction
People And Places	Fergusson, Robert	Fiction
Pied Piper Of Hamelin	Poetry	Fiction
Poems	Poetry	Fiction
Poems And A Selection From Summoned By Bells	Betjeman, Sir John	Fiction
Poems And Letters	Dickinson, Emily	Fiction
Poems And Songs Of Middle Earth	Tolkien, J.R.R.	Fiction
Poems Chiefly In The Scottish Dialect	Burns, Robert	Fiction
Poems From Black Africa	Jones, James Earl	Fiction
Poems From The Barrier Block	Childish, Wild Billy	Fiction
Poems In Scots	Poetry	Fiction
Poems In Scots And Gaelic	Poetry	Fiction
Poems In The Thrie Leids O Alba	Neill, William	Fiction
Poems Of Laughter And Violence	Childish, Wild Billy	Fiction

67

POETRY

Poems Of Thomas Hardy, The	Hardy, Thomas	Fiction
Poems Without Rhyme	Childish, Wild Billy	Fiction
Poems You Love	Poetry	Fiction
Poet Speaks, The	Poetry	Fiction
Poetry And Voice Of Margaret Atwood	Atwood, Margaret	Fiction
Poetry From World War I And Ii	Poetry	Fiction
Poetry In Motion	Poetry	Fiction
Poetry Of Catullus	Poetry	Fiction
Poetry Of Coleridge, The	Coleridge, Samuel Taylor	Fiction
Poetry Of Gerald Manley Hopkins	Hopkins, Gerard Manley	Fiction
Poetry Of Keats	Keats	Fiction
Poetry Of Robert Burns, The	Burns, Robert	Fiction
Poetry Of W.H. Auden, The	Auden, W.H.	Non-Fiction
Poetry Of William Blake	Blake, William	Fiction
Poetry Of William Butler Yeats, The	Yeats, W.B.	Fiction
Poetry Of Wordsworth, The	Wordsworth, William	Fiction
Poetry Olympics	Poetry	Fiction
Poetry Please	Poetry	Fiction
Poetry Prose And Piano	Poetry	Fiction
Poetry Selection	Day Lewis, C	Fiction
Poet's Gold	Poetry	Fiction
Poets Of The West Indies	Poetry	Fiction
Portrait Of Four Poets In Prose And Poetry, A	Poetry	Fiction
Profile	Andi, Su	Fiction
Quite Early One Morning	Thomas, Dylan	Fiction
Randall Jarrell Reads Poems Against War	Jarrell, Randall	Fiction
Ravenswood Poems	Poetry	Fiction
Reading His Poetry	Betjeman, Sir John	Fiction
Reading His Poetry	Spender, Stephen	Fiction
Reading His Poetry	Wilbur, Richard	Fiction
Requiem For The Living	Day Lewis, C	Fiction
Reverend James Currie And Friends	Currie, James	Fiction
Richard Eberhart Reading	Eberhart, Richard	Fiction
Rime Of The Ancient Mariner, The	Poetry	Fiction
Road Not Taken, The	Frost, Robert	Fiction
Robert Graves Reads	Graves, Robert	Fiction
Robert Henryson Selections	Henryson, Robert	Fiction
Robert Lowell: A Reading	Lowell, Robert	Fiction
Robert Penn Warren Reads	Warren, Robert Penn	Fiction
Sangshaw	Macdiarmid, Hugh	Fiction
Scots Poems	Soutar, William	Fiction
Selected Poems	Warren, Robert Penn	Fiction
Selection Of Favourite Poetry, A	Poetry	Fiction
Selections	Dunbar, William	Fiction
Self Portrait, A	Dickinson, Emily	Fiction
Siamese Boyfriends	Langley, Gerard	Fiction
Sir Smasham Uppe	Rieu, E.V.	Fiction
Soliloquy	Andi, Su	Fiction
Some More Of Me Poems And Songs	Ayres, Pam	Fiction
Some Of Me Poems And Songs	Ayres, Pam	Fiction
Song Of The Open Road	Whitman, Walt	Fiction
Sonnets From The Portuguese	Poetry	Fiction
Take My Youth	Poetry	Fiction
Tempo Favourite Poems	Poetry	Fiction
Ten Poets Of The 20th Century	Poetry	Fiction
Theodore Roethke Reads	Roethke, Theodore	Fiction
Tickets, Please	Lawrence, D.H.	Fiction
To The Quick	Childish, Wild Billy	Fiction
Tony The Turtle	Poetry	Fiction

Twa Chiels And A Lass	Poetry	Fiction
Twa Three Sangs And Stories	Graham, William	Fiction
Twelve Poets Of The 20th Century	Poetry	Fiction
Under The Eildon Tree	Goodsir Smith, Sydney	Fiction
Virgil, Dante Et Al	Poetry	Fiction
Visit To America, A	Thomas, Dylan	Fiction
Wallace Stevens Reading	Stevens, Wallace	Fiction
Waste Land	Eliot, T.S.	Fiction
W.H. Auden Reading	Poetry	Fiction
With A Little Help	Richardson, John	Fiction
Your Favourite Poems	Poetry	Fiction
Zip Style Method	Cooper Clarke, John	Fiction

RADIO

TITLE	HEADING	SECTION
50 Years Of Royal Broadcasts	Radio	Non-Fiction
Adventures Of Sherlock Holmes	Conan Doyle, Arthur	Fiction
Al Read Show	Radio	Fiction
Archers - The Wedding, The	Radio	Fiction
Beachcomber - By The Way	Radio	Fiction
Bradshaws Vol. 1	Bradshaws	Fiction
Bradshaws Vol. 2	Bradshaws	Fiction
Bradshaws Vol. 3	Bradshaws	Fiction
Clitheroe Kid, The	Radio	Fiction
Crown House	Ling & Ace	Fiction
Dad's Army	Television	Fiction
Deceiver, The	Forsyth, Frederick	Fiction
Diana's Story	Longden, Deric	Fiction
Diary Of A Somebody	Matthew, Christopher	Fiction
Dick Barton	Radio	Fiction
Doctor Who	Radio	Fiction
Emma	Radio	Fiction
Fashion In Shrouds, The	Allingham, Margery	Fiction
Father Brown	Chesterton, G.K.	Fiction
Flywheel, Shyster And Flywheel	Radio	Fiction
Goon Show Classics	Goons	Fiction
Hitch-Hiker's Guide To The Galaxy	Adams, Douglas	Fiction
I'm Sorry I'll Read That Again	Radio	Fiction
Journey Into Space	Chilton, Charles	Fiction
Lake Wobegon Days	Keillor, Garrison	Fiction
Leaving Home	Keillor, Garrison	Fiction
Maigret	Simenon, Georges	Fiction
Memoirs Of A Sword Swallower	Mannix, Dan	Fiction
My Uncle Silas	Bates, H.E.	Fiction
News From Lake Wobegon	Keillor, Garrison	Fiction
Not A Penny More, Not A Penny Less	Archer, Jeffrey	Fiction
Official Guide To CB Radio	CB Radio	Non-Fiction
On Radio	Marx, Groucho	Fiction
Parent's Survival Guide	Grahame, Laurie	Non-Fiction
Plain Tales From The Raj	Radio	Non-Fiction
Poirot	Christie, Agatha	Fiction
Radio Active	Radio Active	Fiction
Round The Horne	Radio	Fiction
Rumpole	Mortimer, John	Fiction
Sherlock Holmes	Conan Doyle, Arthur	Fiction
Silent Partner	Kellerman, Jonathan	Fiction
Star Is Born, A	Radio	Fiction
Steptoe And Son	Radio	Fiction
Symphony Of The Body	Radio	Fiction
Vintage Archers	Radio	Fiction
Voice Of Richard Dimbleby	Dimbleby, Richard	Non-Fiction
We Are Still Married	Keillor, Garrison	Fiction
Well Schooled In Murder	George, Elizabeth	Fiction
Yes Minister	Radio	Fiction

RELIGIOUS

TITLE	HEADING	SECTION
Acts (part 1)	Bible	Non-Fiction
Acts (part 2)	Bible	Non-Fiction
Bible Stories	Bible	Non-Fiction
Boys From Beersheba, The	Bible	Non-Fiction
Bring Us Together	Bible	Non-Fiction
Centuries	Religious	Non-Fiction
Changes The World	Bible	Non-Fiction
Corinthians	Bible	Non-Fiction
Cross, The	Bible	Non-Fiction
Following Jesus	Bible	Non-Fiction
Galatians To Thessalonians	Bible	Non-Fiction
Gives Us The Future	Bible	Non-Fiction
His Holiness Pope John Paul II	Pope John-Paul II	Non-Fiction
Holy Spirit	Bible	Non-Fiction
In Praise Of Buddha	Religious	Non-Fiction
James To Jude	Bible	Non-Fiction
Jehovah's Witnesses	Religious	Non-Fiction
Jesus	Bible	Non-Fiction
John	Bible	Non-Fiction
John (part 1)	Bible	Non-Fiction
John (part 2)	Bible	Non-Fiction
John Paul II	Pope John-Paul II	Non-Fiction
Luke	Bible	Non-Fiction
Luke (part 1)	Bible	Non-Fiction
Luke (part 2)	Bible	Non-Fiction
Makes All The Difference	Bible	Non-Fiction
Makes Us Useful	Bible	Non-Fiction
Mark	Bible	Non-Fiction
Matter Of Life And Death, A	Bible	Non-Fiction
Matthew	Bible	Non-Fiction
Mission England Vol.2	Religious	Non-Fiction
Moonies, The	Religious	Non-Fiction
Mormons	Religious	Non-Fiction
New Testament	Bible	Non-Fiction
New Testament In Scots	Bible	Non-Fiction
New Testament - Vol.12	Bible	Non-Fiction
New Testament - Vol.13	Bible	Non-Fiction
New Testament - Vol.14	Bible	Non-Fiction
New Testament - Vol.15	Bible	Non-Fiction
Night On't Town, A	Bible	Non-Fiction
Normal Procedure	Bible	Non-Fiction
Old Testament	Bible	Non-Fiction
Old Testament - The Authorised Version	Bible	Non-Fiction
Old Testament - Vol.1	Bible	Non-Fiction
Old Testament - Vol.2	Bible	Non-Fiction
Old Testament - Vol.3	Bible	Non-Fiction
Old Testament - Vol.4	Bible	Non-Fiction
Old Testament - Vol.5	Bible	Non-Fiction
Old Testament - Vol.6	Bible	Non-Fiction
Old Testament - Vol.7	Bible	Non-Fiction

RELIGIOUS

Old Testament - Vol.10	Bible	Non-Fiction
Old Testament - Vol.11	Bible	Non-Fiction
Out Of The Blue	Religious	Non-Fiction
Pilgrim Pope, The	Pope John-Paul II	Non-Fiction
Revelation	Bible	Non-Fiction
Romans	Bible	Non-Fiction
Rubaiyat Of Omar Khayyam, The	Khayyam, Omar	Non-Fiction
Sometimes Hurts	Bible	Non-Fiction
Start The Day With Colossians	Bible	Non-Fiction
Start The Day With Ephesians	Bible	Non-Fiction
Start The Day With Exodus	Bible	Non-Fiction
Start The Day With Galatians	Bible	Non-Fiction
Start The Day With Hebrews	Bible	Non-Fiction
Start The Day With Isaiah	Bible	Non-Fiction
Start The Day With James	Bible	Non-Fiction
Start The Day With Job	Bible	Non-Fiction
Start The Day With John	Bible	Non-Fiction
Start The Day With Luke	Bible	Non-Fiction
Start The Day With Mark	Bible	Non-Fiction
Start The Day With Matthew	Bible	Non-Fiction
Start The Day With Philippians	Bible	Non-Fiction
Start The Day With Psalms	Bible	Non-Fiction
Start The Day With Romans	Bible	Non-Fiction
Start The Day With Timothy	Bible	Non-Fiction
Story Box	Bible	Non-Fiction
Story Box 2	Bible	Non-Fiction
Story Box 3	Bible	Non-Fiction
Story Box 4	Bible	Non-Fiction
Teach Us To Pray	Religious	Non-Fiction
Timothy To Hebrews	Bible	Non-Fiction
Who Needs God?	Religious	Non-Fiction

SELF IMPROVEMENT

TITLE	HEADING	SECTION
5-00pm Refresher, The	Self Improvement	Non-Fiction
Accelerated (High-Speed) Learning	Self Improvement	Non-Fiction
Achievement	Heyerdahl, Thor	Non-Fiction
Alternatives To Marriage	Self Improvement	Non-Fiction
American Cancer Society's "Freshstart"	Self Improvement	Non-Fiction
Ancient Ways To New Freedom	Lessing, Doris	Non-Fiction
Anger Workout	Self Improvement	Non-Fiction
Aquarian Conspiracy: Tools For Change	Self Improvement	Non-Fiction
Attracting Perfect Love	Self Improvement	Non-Fiction
Awakened Life	Self Improvement	Non-Fiction
Banish Pain - Mind Power And Pain Relief	Self Improvement	Non-Fiction
Be A Confident Winner	Self Improvement	Non-Fiction
Be Happy Attitudes	Self Improvement	Non-Fiction
Be Positive	Self Improvement	Non-Fiction
Become A New Person	Self Improvement	Non-Fiction
Being The Best	Self Improvement	Non-Fiction
Believe And Be Happy	Self Improvement	Non-Fiction
Between The Words	Self Improvement	Non-Fiction
Bio- Feedback	Self Improvement	Non-Fiction
Breathe, Relax And Imagine	Self Improvement	Non-Fiction
Calm And Peaceful Mind, A	Self Improvement	Non-Fiction
Case Against It	Self Improvement	Non-Fiction
Charisma - Drawing People To You	Self Improvement	Non-Fiction
Choices	Self Improvement	Non-Fiction
Choosing Your Own Greatness	Self Improvement	Non-Fiction
Co-Dependents Guide To The Twelve Steps	Self Improvement	Non-Fiction
Concentration - Power Plus	Self Improvement	Non-Fiction
Constructive Anger	Self Improvement	Non-Fiction
Control Freaks	Self Improvement	Non-Fiction
Control Your Weight	Self Improvement	Non-Fiction
Create Wealth - Power Programming	Self Improvement	Non-Fiction
Creating Positive Relationships	Self Improvement	Non-Fiction
Curing Depression	Self Improvement	Non-Fiction
Different Drum, The	Self Improvement	Non-Fiction
Discover Inner Energy And Overcome Stress	Self Improvement	Non-Fiction
Discover What You're Best At	Self Improvement	Non-Fiction
Do More In Less Time	Self Improvement	Non-Fiction
Dream Solutions-Find Your Answers In Your Dreams	Self Improvement	Non-Fiction
Dreams And Dreaming	Self Improvement	Non-Fiction
Emotions And Cancer	Self Improvement	Non-Fiction
Everyday Heroics Of Living And Dying	Self Improvement	Non-Fiction
Experience High Self-Esteem	Self Improvement	Non-Fiction
Families And How To Survive	Skynner, Dr Robin	Non-Fiction
Feel Secure Now	Self Improvement	Non-Fiction
Feel The Fear And Do It Anyway	Self Improvement	Non-Fiction
Find Your Inner Happiness	Self Improvement	Non-Fiction
Five Days To An Organized Life	Self Improvement	Non-Fiction
Further Along The Road Less Travelled	Self Improvement	Non-Fiction
Garden Of Peace	Self Improvement	Non-Fiction
Gently And Deeply	Self Improvement	Non-Fiction

SELF IMPROVEMENT

Get It Done Now	Self Improvement	Non-Fiction
Getting Unstuck: Breaking Through The Barriers Of Change	Self Improvement	Non-Fiction
Goal Setting	Self Improvement	Non-Fiction
Goals	Self Improvement	Non-Fiction
Good Life, The - Health, Wealth And Happiness	Self Improvement	Non-Fiction
Great Memory, A	Self Improvement	Non-Fiction
Greatest Of These Is Love	Self Improvement	Non-Fiction
Healing Force - Using Your Mind To Help Heal	Self Improvement	Non-Fiction
How To Be A No-Limit Person	Self Improvement	Non-Fiction
How To Change Ideas	Self Improvement	Non-Fiction
How To Decide Exactly What You Want	Self Improvement	Non-Fiction
How To Develop Your ESP Power	Self Improvement	Non-Fiction
How To Get Whatever You Want Out Of Life	Self Improvement	Non-Fiction
How To Improve Your Memory	Self Improvement	Non-Fiction
How To Make Love To A Man	Self Improvement	Non-Fiction
How To Turn A Friendship Into A Love Affair	Self Improvement	Non-Fiction
Husbands And Wives	Self Improvement	Non-Fiction
I Never Know What To Say	Self Improvement	Non-Fiction
Imagineering	Self Improvement	Non-Fiction
Incredible Self-Confidence	Self Improvement	Non-Fiction
Inflight Relaxation	Self Improvement	Non-Fiction
Intensify Creative Ability	Self Improvement	Non-Fiction
Kreskin On Mind Power	Self Improvement	Non-Fiction
Learning And Memory	Self Improvement	Non-Fiction
Learning To Control Pain	Self Improvement	Non-Fiction
Lifespring	Self Improvement	Non-Fiction
Living Without Limits	Self Improvement	Non-Fiction
Love Myself - Self-Esteem Programming	Self Improvement	Non-Fiction
Magic Of Believing	Self Improvement	Non-Fiction
Magic Of Thinking	Self Improvement	Non-Fiction
Magic Of Thinking Big, The	Self Improvement	Non-Fiction
Making Relationships Last	Self Improvement	Non-Fiction
Meditation	Self Improvement	Non-Fiction
Meditations For Personal Harmony	Self Improvement	Non-Fiction
Melody Of Life	Baldursson	Non-Fiction
Mental Stress And Physical Fitness	Self Improvement	Non-Fiction
Mind Over Illness	Self Improvement	Non-Fiction
Natural Way To Alleviate Stress	Health & Fitness	Non-Fiction
Natural Way To Control Agoraphobia	Health & Fitness	Non-Fiction
Natural Way To Control Nail Biting	Health & Fitness	Non-Fiction
Natural Way To Increase Confidence	Health & Fitness	Non-Fiction
Natural Way To Learn Self Hypnosis And Relax...	Health & Fitness	Non-Fiction
Natural Way To Overcome Fear Of Flying	Health & Fitness	Non-Fiction
Natural Way To Overcome Insomnia	Health & Fitness	Non-Fiction
Natural Way To Reduce Driving Test Nerves	Health & Fitness	Non-Fiction
Natural Way To Reduce Exam Nerves	Health & Fitness	Non-Fiction
Natural Way To Slim, The	Health & Fitness	Non-Fiction
Natural Way To Stop Smoking	Health & Fitness	Non-Fiction
Never Be Nervous Again	Self Improvement	Non-Fiction
Overcoming Fearful Flying	Self Improvement	Non-Fiction
Overcoming Shyness	Self Improvement	Non-Fiction
Pathway To Healing, A	Self Improvement	Non-Fiction
Peace Of Mind	Self Improvement	Non-Fiction
Perfect Health	Self Improvement	Non-Fiction
Perfect Weight - Perfect Body	Self Improvement	Non-Fiction
Picture Yourself Relaxed	Self Improvement	Non-Fiction
Power And Success - Get It, Keep It, Use It	Self Improvement	Non-Fiction
Power Of Persistence, The	Self Improvement	Non-Fiction

SELF IMPROVEMENT

Title	Category	Type
Power Of Positive Thinking, The	Self Improvement	Non-Fiction
Power Of Self Talk	Self Improvement	Non-Fiction
Power Of Your Own Voice	Self Improvement	Non-Fiction
Power Words	Self Improvement	Non-Fiction
Powerful Person - Programming	Self Improvement	Non-Fiction
Psychology Of Achievement	Self Improvement	Non-Fiction
Psychology Of Winning	Self Improvement	Non-Fiction
Radiant Health And A Strong Immune System	Self Improvement	Non-Fiction
Relieve Stress And Anxiety	Self Improvement	Non-Fiction
Right-Brain Solutions	Self Improvement	Non-Fiction
Road Less Travelled, The	Self Improvement	Non-Fiction
Satisfaction And Happiness	Self Improvement	Non-Fiction
Schizophrenia - A Viewpoint	Medical	Non-Fiction
Scientific View Of Meditation, A	Self Improvement	Non-Fiction
Self Defeating Behaviours	Self Improvement	Non-Fiction
Seth: The Voice And The Message	Self Improvement	Non-Fiction
Seven Habits Of Highly Effective People	Self Improvement	Non-Fiction
Silva Mind Control Method Of Mental Dynamics	Self Improvement	Non-Fiction
Six Thinking Hats	Self Improvement	Non-Fiction
Sleep Like A Baby	Self Improvement	Non-Fiction
Sleep Peacefully	Self Improvement	Non-Fiction
Sleeping Easy	Self Improvement	Non-Fiction
Speak Up - Say What You Want To Say	Self Improvement	Non-Fiction
Speed Reading	Self Improvement	Non-Fiction
Spend Your Life In Slender	Self Improvement	Non-Fiction
Staying On Top When Your World Turns Upside Down	Self Improvement	Non-Fiction
Strategies For Stress Free Living	Self Improvement	Non-Fiction
Strengthen Your Ego	Self Improvement	Non-Fiction
Stress Proof Child	Self Improvement	Non-Fiction
Success And Excellence	Self Improvement	Non-Fiction
Successful Independent Lifestyle	Self Improvement	Non-Fiction
Super Learning	Self Improvement	Non-Fiction
Surviving Loss	Self Improvement	Non-Fiction
Take Control Of Your Life	Self Improvement	Non-Fiction
Teenagers And Sexuality	Self Improvement	Non-Fiction
Teenagers Under Stress	Self Improvement	Non-Fiction
Tennis: Concentration,Timing, Strokes & Strategy	Self Improvement	Non-Fiction
Thriving Self	Self Improvement	Non-Fiction
Tough Times Never Last But Tough People Do	Self Improvement	Non-Fiction
Transformation: The Next Step For The No-Limit Person	Self Improvement	Non-Fiction
Traveller's Refresher, The	Self Improvement	Non-Fiction
Turning Your Stress Into High Energy Performance	Self Improvement	Non-Fiction
Ultimate Relaxation	Self Improvement	Non-Fiction
Ultimate Secret To Getting Absolutely Everything You Want	Self Improvement	Non-Fiction
Understanding And Coping With Anxiety	Self Improvement	Non-Fiction
Understanding And Managing Jealousy	Self Improvement	Non-Fiction
Understanding And Overcoming Loneliness	Self Improvement	Non-Fiction
Unlimited Power	Self Improvement	Non-Fiction
Upper Hand, The	Self Improvement	Non-Fiction
Valuable As You Are	Self Improvement	Non-Fiction
Wake-Up Refresher, The	Self Improvement	Non-Fiction
Waters Of The World	Self Improvement	Non-Fiction
Weight Lost	Self Improvement	Non-Fiction
When All You've Ever Wanted Isn't Enough	Self Improvement	Non-Fiction
When I Say No, I Feel Guilty	Self Improvement	Non-Fiction
Woulda, Shoulda, Coulda	Self Improvement	Non-Fiction
You Are The Power	Self Improvement	Non-Fiction

SELF IMPROVEMENT

You Can Become The Person You Want To Be	Self Improvement	Non-Fiction
You Can Do It	Self Improvement	Non-Fiction
You Can If You Think You Can	Self Improvement	Non-Fiction
Your Last Cigarette - No Exceptions!	Self Improvement	Non-Fiction

SOUND EFFECTS

TITLE	HEADING	SECTION
All In A Diesel Day	Trains...	Non-Fiction
Changing Trains	Trains...	Non-Fiction
Courage The Guard Dog	Sound Effects	Non-Fiction
Diesels On Dainton	Trains...	Non-Fiction
Diesels On The Lickey Incline	Trains...	Non-Fiction
Dynamic Diesels	Trains...	Non-Fiction
Essential Combat And Disaster Sound Effects	Sound Effects	Non-Fiction
Essential Death And Horror 1	Sound Effects	Non-Fiction
Essential Death And Horror 2	Sound Effects	Non-Fiction
Essential Hi-Tech	Sound Effects	Non-Fiction
Essential Home Video Sound Effects	Sound Effects	Non-Fiction
Essential Science Fiction	Sound Effects	Non-Fiction
Essential Sound Effects	Sound Effects	Non-Fiction
Essential Sound Effects (2)	Sound Effects	Non-Fiction
Farewell To The Deltics	Trains...	Non-Fiction
Farewell To The Forties	Trains...	Non-Fiction
Great British Aircraft	Aviation	Non-Fiction
Great Train Record, The	Trains...	Non-Fiction
HST 125 & DMU	Trains...	Non-Fiction
London Live	Sound Effects	Non-Fiction
Mid-Day On Jost Van Dyke	Environmental Sounds	Non-Fiction
Motive Power Vol.1	Trains...	Non-Fiction
Motive Power Vol.2	Trains...	Non-Fiction
Motive Power Vol.3	Trains...	Non-Fiction
Motive Power Vol.4	Trains...	Non-Fiction
Music And Sound Library Vols.1 & 2	Sound Effects	Non-Fiction
Sci-Fi And Futuristic	Sound Effects	Non-Fiction
Sound Effects And Lindrum Fills	Sound Effects	Non-Fiction
Sound Effects Nos.1 To 29	Sound Effects	Non-Fiction
Sounds For Wargames	Sound Effects	Non-Fiction
Spectacular Sound Effects Vol. I	Sound Effects	Non-Fiction
Spectacular Sound Effects Vol. II	Sound Effects	Non-Fiction
Star Trek - Sound Effects: The TV Series	Sound Effects	Non-Fiction
This Is York	Trains...	Non-Fiction
Vermont Hearth	Sound Effects	Non-Fiction
Vermont Stream	Sound Effects	Non-Fiction
West Somerset Railway	Trains...	Non-Fiction
Western Ways	Trains...	Non-Fiction
Wings Of History Vol. 1	Aviation	Non-Fiction
Wings Of History Vol. 2	Aviation	Non-Fiction
Wings Of History Vol. 3	Aviation	Non-Fiction
Wings Of History Vol. 4	Aviation	Non-Fiction
World Of Railways	Trains...	Non-Fiction

SPORT

TITLE	HEADING	SECTION
Allan Border: An Autobiography	Border, Allan	Non-Fiction
Another Bloody Tour	Frances, Edmond	Non-Fiction
Ashes 1948-1981, The	Cricket	Non-Fiction
Australia's Greatest Cricket Characters	Cricket	Non-Fiction
Bradman - The Don Declares	Cricket	Non-Fiction
Roarin' Game, The	Curling	Non-Fiction
England V The West Indies	Cricket	Non-Fiction
European Cup Final - 1968	Football	Non-Fiction
European Cup Final - 1977	Football	Non-Fiction
European Cup Final - 1978	Football	Non-Fiction
European Cup Final - 1981	Football	Non-Fiction
European Cup Final - 1982	Football	Non-Fiction
European Cup Finals - 1979 And 1980	Football	Non-Fiction
F.A. Cup Final - 1972	Football	Non-Fiction
Five Grand Nationals 1973-1977	Horse Racing	Non-Fiction
Golden Age, The	Cricket	Non-Fiction
Golf Courses At Turnberry, The	Golf	Non-Fiction
Great Cricket Matches	Cricket	Non-Fiction
History And The Humour, The	Rugby Union	Non-Fiction
Isle Of Man TT Races, 1967	Motorcycling	Non-Fiction
League Cup Final - 1981	Football	Non-Fiction
League Cup Final - 1982	Football	Non-Fiction
Lord's: The Home Of Cricket	Cricket	Non-Fiction
Peter O'Sullevan Talks Turf	O'Sullevan, Peter	Non-Fiction
Roarin' Game, The	Curling	Non-Fiction
Scottish Cup - 1976	Football	Non-Fiction
So You Think You Know About Football	Football	Non-Fiction
Straight Down The Middle	Golf	Non-Fiction
TT Highlights	Motorcycling	Non-Fiction
UEFA Cup-1976	Football	Non-Fiction
View From The Boundary	Cricket	Non-Fiction
Voice Of Cricket, The	Cricket	Non-Fiction

TRANSPORT

TITLE	HEADING	SECTION
Against The Grade	Trains...	Non-Fiction
Age Of Steam, The	Trains...	Non-Fiction
Aviators, The	Aviation	Non-Fiction
Big Four, The	Trains...	Non-Fiction
Black Fives	Trains...	Non-Fiction
British Railways Standard Locomotives	Trains...	Non-Fiction
Built Swindon	Trains...	Non-Fiction
Castles And Kings	Trains...	Non-Fiction
Classic Motorcycles	Motorcycling	Non-Fiction
Copper Capped Engines	Trains...	Non-Fiction
Deltic Duties	Trains...	Non-Fiction
Double Head Of Steam	Trains...	Non-Fiction
Early 60's Steam	Trains...	Non-Fiction
Echoes Of Engines	Trains...	Non-Fiction
Engines From Derby And Crewe	Trains...	Non-Fiction
Engines With Accents	Trains...	Non-Fiction
Farewell To Steam	Trains...	Non-Fiction
Flying Scotsman And Other Locomotives	Trains...	Non-Fiction
From The Footplate	Trains...	Non-Fiction
Gone With Regret	Trains...	Non-Fiction
Great Little Trains Of England	Trains...	Non-Fiction
Great Northern For The North	Trains...	Non-Fiction
Great Western In Gloucestershire	Trains...	Non-Fiction
Great Western, The	Trains...	Non-Fiction
Gresley Beat, The	Trains...	Non-Fiction
G.W.R.	Trains...	Non-Fiction
Iron-Ore Steamers	Trains...	Non-Fiction
Last Grain Race, The	Newby, Eric	Non-Fiction
Last Train To Ryde	Trains...	Non-Fiction
Little Trains Of Wales, The	Trains...	Non-Fiction
L.M.S.	Trains...	Non-Fiction
L.N.E.R.	Trains...	Non-Fiction
Locomotives From Leeds	Trains...	Non-Fiction
Magnificent Severn, The	Trains...	Non-Fiction
Main Line Steam Specials	Trains...	Non-Fiction
MG Just For The Record	MG Cars	Non-Fiction
Midland And North Western	Trains...	Non-Fiction
Nocturnal Steam	Trains...	Non-Fiction
North Of Kings Cross	Trains...	Non-Fiction
Pacific Power	Trains...	Non-Fiction
Passengers No More	Trains...	Non-Fiction
Power Of Steam, The	Trains...	Non-Fiction
Railway Rhythms	Trains...	Non-Fiction
Railway To Riccarton	Trains...	Non-Fiction
Railways Recalled	Trains...	Non-Fiction
Railways Round The Clock	Trains...	Non-Fiction
Rainhill Remembered	Trains...	Non-Fiction
Real Days Of Steam	Trains...	Non-Fiction
Recollections No. 1: A Railway Guard	Trains...	Non-Fiction
Recollections No. 2: Life On The Canal	Canals	Non-Fiction

TRANSPORT

Recollections No. 5: British Motorcycle Industry	Motorcycling	Non-Fiction
Regional Round No. 1 Eastern	Trains...	Non-Fiction
Regional Round No. 2 Southern	Trains...	Non-Fiction
Severn Valley Steam	Trains...	Non-Fiction
Shap	Trains...	Non-Fiction
Shunting The Yard	Trains...	Non-Fiction
Somerset And Dorset, The	Trains...	Non-Fiction
Somerset & Dorset	Trains...	Non-Fiction
Sounds Of Severn Valley Railway	Trains...	Non-Fiction
Southern Steam	Trains...	Non-Fiction
Specials In Steam	Trains...	Non-Fiction
Steam And Harness	Trains...	Non-Fiction
Steam From A To V	Trains...	Non-Fiction
Steam Hauled By A Stanier Black 5	Trains...	Non-Fiction
Steam In All Directions	Trains...	Non-Fiction
Steam In Scotland	Trains...	Non-Fiction
Steam In The Fifties	Trains...	Non-Fiction
Steam In The Seventies	Trains...	Non-Fiction
Steam In Twilight	Trains...	Non-Fiction
Steam Locomotives On The Gradient	Trains...	Non-Fiction
Steam On The Lickey Incline	Trains...	Non-Fiction
Steam Over The Pennines	Trains...	Non-Fiction
Steam Railway Miscellany, A	Trains...	Non-Fiction
Steam Specials Of The 70s	Trains...	Non-Fiction
Steam Through All Seasons	Trains...	Non-Fiction
Steam Weekend, A	Trains...	Non-Fiction
Steam's Final Hours	Trains...	Non-Fiction
Storefield In The Rain	Trains...	Non-Fiction
Storefield Story	Trains...	Non-Fiction
Sunset Of Steam	Trains...	Non-Fiction
Trains In The Hills	Trains...	Non-Fiction
Trains In The Night	Trains...	Non-Fiction
Trains In Trouble	Trains...	Non-Fiction
Trains To Remember	Trains...	Non-Fiction
Triumph Of An A4 Pacific, The	Trains...	Non-Fiction
West Of Exeter	Trains...	Non-Fiction
Western Steam In The Midlands	Trains...	Non-Fiction
Working On The Footplate	Trains...	Non-Fiction
World Of Steam Vol 1	Trains...	Non-Fiction
World Of Steam Vol 2	Trains...	Non-Fiction
York Collection, The	Trains...	Non-Fiction

FICTION SECTION

Aardema, Verna

TSHINDAO (Ossie Davis & Ruby Dee).
LP. Cat no: **1499**. Released on Caedmon (USA), '88 by Caedmon Records (USA), Bond Street Music.

WHY MOSQUITOS BUZZ IN PEOPLES' EARS... (Ossie Davis & Ruby Dee).
MC. Cat no: **1592**. Released on Caedmon (USA), '88 by Caedmon Records (USA), Bond Street Music.
MC. Cat no: **0001051555**. Released on Collins-Caedmon, '91 by Collins Audio, Taylors, Bond Street Music.

ZULU (And Other African Folktales) (Ossie Davis & Ruby Dee).
MC. Cat no: **1474**. Released on Caedmon (USA), '88 by Caedmon Records (USA), Bond Street Music.
MC. Cat no: **0001051571**. Released on Collins-Caedmon, '91 by Collins Audio, Taylors, Bond Street Music.

Abraham, Cyril

BLAZING OCEAN, THE (Unknown narrator(s)).
MCSET. Cat no: **0008**. Released on Bramhope, '91 by Ulverscroft Soundings.
MCSET. Cat no: **1259F**. Released on Travellers Tales, '91 by Travellers Tales.

ONEDIN LINE: IRON SHIPS (Ray Dunbobbin).
MCSET. Cat no: **1002F**. Released on Travellers Tales, '91 by Travellers Tales. Note: 4 Cassettes.
MCSET. Cat no: **1854960024**. Released on Bramhope, '91 by Ulverscroft Soundings.

ONEDIN LINE: THE HIGH SEAS (Ray Dunbobbin).
MCSET. Cat no: **1003F**. Released on Travellers Tales, '91 by Travellers Tales.
MCSET. Cat no: **1854960016**. Released on Bramhope, '91 by Ulverscroft Soundings.

ONEDIN LINE: THE SHIPMASTER (Ray Dunbobbin).
MCSET. Cat no: **1001F**. Released on Travellers Tales, '91 by Travellers Tales. Note: 4 Cassettes.
MCSET. Cat no: **1854960032**. Released on Bramhope, '91 by Ulverscroft Soundings. Note: 4 Cassettes.

ONEDIN LINE: THE WHITE SHIPS (Ray Dunbobbin).
MCSET. Cat no: **1249F**. Released on Travellers Tales, '91 by Travellers Tales. Note: 4 Cassettes.
MCSET. Cat no: **185490059**. Released on Bramhope, '91 by Ulverscroft Soundings. Note: 4 Cassettes.

ONEDIN LINE: TRADE WINDS (Ray Dunbobbin).
MCSET. Cat no: **1004F**. Released on Travellers Tales, '91 by Travellers Tales. Note: 4 Cassettes.
MCSET. Cat no: **1854960040**. Released on Bramhope, '91 by Ulverscroft Soundings.

Abrahams, Elaine

SAMEEP AND THE PARROTS (English and Bengali) (Cliff Norgate & Afroza Hassan).
MCSET. Cat no: **0948998075**. Released on Harmony Books, '91 by Harmony Books. Note: 2 Cassettes.

SAMEEP AND THE PARROTS (English and Gujarati) (Cliff Norgate & Kanchan Jogia).
MCSET. Cat no: **0948998040**. Released on Harmony Books, '91 by Harmony Books. Note: 2 Cassettes.

SAMEEP AND THE PARROTS (English and Punjabi) (Cliff Norgate & K Singh).
MCSET. Cat no: **0948998067**. Released on Harmony Books, '91 by Harmony Books. Note: 2 Cassettes.

SAMEEP AND THE PARROTS (English and Urdu) (Cliff Norgate & Zareena Hashmi).
MCSET. Cat no: **0948998059**. Released on Harmony Books, '91 by Harmony Books. Note: 2 Cassettes.

SONAL SPLASH (English Version) (Clifford Norgate).
MCSET. Cat no: **0948998121**. Released on Harmony Books, '91 by Harmony Books. Note: 2 Cassettes.

SONAL SPLASH (English and Bengali) (Cliff Norgate & Afroza Hassan).
MCSET. Cat no: **0948998113**. Released on Harmony Books, '91 by Harmony Books. Note: 2 Cassettes.

SONAL SPLASH (English and Gujarati) (Cliff Norgate & Kanchan Jogia).
MCSET. Cat no: **0948998083**. Released on Harmony Books, '91 by Harmony Books. Note: 2 Cassettes.

SONAL SPLASH (English and Punjabi) (Cliff Norgate & K Singh).
MCSET. Cat no: **0948998105**. Released on Harmony Books, '91 by Harmony Books. Note: 2 Cassettes.

SONAL SPLASH (English and Urdu) (Cliff Norgate & Zareena Hashmi).
MCSET. Cat no: **0948998091**. Released on Harmony Books, '91 by Harmony Books. Note: 2 Cassettes.

TANYA MOVES HOUSE (English and Arabic) (Cliff Norgate & S. Fattoum).
MCSET. Cat no: **0948998245**. Released on Harmony Books, '91 by Harmony Books. Note: 2 Cassettes.

TANYA MOVES HOUSE (English and Bengali) (Cliff Norgate & K Singh).
MCSET. Cat no: **0948998210**. Released on Harmony Books, '91 by Harmony Books. Note: 2 Cassettes.

TANYA MOVES HOUSE (English and French) (Cliff Norgate & Janine Harris).
MCSET. Cat no: **0948998229**. Released on Harmony Books, '91 by Harmony Books. Note: 2 Cassettes.

TANYA MOVES HOUSE (English and German) (Cliff Norgate & Bridget Newman).
MCSET. Cat no: **0948998237**. Released on Harmony Books, '91 by Harmony Books. Note: 2 Cassettes.

TANYA MOVES HOUSE (English and Gujarat) (Cliff Norgate & Hansa Patei).
MCSET. Cat no: **0948998180**. Released on Harmony Books, '91 by Harmony Books. Note: 2 Cassettes.

TANYA MOVES HOUSE (English and Punjabi) (Cliff Norgate & H. Singh).
MCSET. Cat no: **0948998202**. Released on Harmony Books, '91 by Harmony Books. Note: 2 Cassettes.

TANYA MOVES HOUSE (English and Urdu) (Cliff Norgate & Zareena Hashmi).
MCSET. Cat no: **0948998199**. Released on Harmony Books, '91 by Harmony Books. Note: 2 Cassettes.

TOPIWALO THE HAT MAKER (English and Gujarati) (Cliff Norgate & Zareena Hashmi).
MCSET. Cat no: **0948998008**. Released on Harmony Books, '91 by Harmony Books. Note: 2 Cassettes.

TOPIWALO THE HAT MAKER (English and Punjabi) (Cliff Norgate & K Singh).
MCSET. Cat no: **0948998024**. Released on Harmony Books, '91 by Harmony Books. Note: 2 Cassettes.

TOPIWALO THE HAT MAKER (English and Urdu) (Cliff Norgate & Zareena Hashmi).
CDSIN. Cat no: **0948998016**. Released on Harmony Books, '91 by Harmony Books.

Ackroyd, Peter

GREAT FIRE OF LONDON, THE (Anthony Homyer).
MCSET. Cat no: **1592F**. Released on Travellers Tales, '91 by Travellers Tales.
MCSET. Cat no: **TCL 22**. Released on Complete Listener, '91 by Complete Listener. Note: 5 Cassettes (BB) Playing time: 420 minutes.

Adams, Douglas

HITCH-HIKER'S 1 (Various narrator(s).
LP. Cat no: **HNBL 2301**. Released on Hannibal, May '89 by Rykodisc, Roots Records, Topic Records, Charly Records, W.R.P.M., Sterns Records, Jazz Music, Cadillac Music.
MC. Cat no: **HNBC 2301**. Released on Hannibal, May '89 by Rykodisc, Roots Records, Topic Records, Charly Records, W.R.P.M., Sterns Records, Jazz Music, Cadillac Music.

HITCH-HIKER'S GUIDE TO THE GALAXY (Stephen Moore).
MCSET. Cat no: **LFP 7088**. Released on Listen For Pleasure, Nov '83 by EMI Records **Deleted** Apr '90.

MCSET. Cat no: **1001S.** Released on Travellers Tales, '91 by Travellers Tales. Note: 2 Cassettes.

HITCH-HIKER'S GUIDE TO THE GALAXY (Radio Adaptation) (Various artists).
MCSET. Cat no: **1028S.** Released on Travellers Tales, '91 by Travellers Tales. Note: 2 Cassettes.

HITCH-HIKER'S GUIDE TO THE GALAXY (Various artists).
Note: The original radio production in presentation box.
MCSET. Cat no: **ZBBC 1035.** Released on BBC Radio Collection, Sep '88 by BBC Records. Note: 6 Cassettes. ISBN No: 0563 225602
CDSET. Cat no: **BBCCD 6001.** Released on BBC Radio Collection, Sep '88 by BBC Records. Note: ISBN No: 0563 226153

LIFE, THE UNIVERSE AND EVERYTHING (Stephen Moore).
MCSET. Cat no: **LFP 7174.** Released on Listen For Pleasure, Oct '84 by EMI Records **Deleted** Apr '90.

MCSET. Cat no: **1002S.** Released on Travellers Tales, '91 by Travellers Tales.

RESTAURANT AT THE END OF THE UNIVERSE (Stephen Moore).
MCSET. Cat no: **LFP 7115.** Released on Listen For Pleasure, Apr '83 by EMI Records **Deleted** Apr '90.

MCSET. Cat no: **1003S.** Released on Travellers Tales, '91 by Travellers Tales. Note: 2 Cassettes.

SO LONG, AND THANKS FOR ALL THE FISH (Stephen Moore).
MCSET. Cat no: **LFP 7208.** Released on Listen For Pleasure, Sep '85 by EMI Records **Deleted** Apr '90.

MCSET. Cat no: **1013S.** Released on Travellers Tales, '91 by Travellers Tales. Note: 2 Cassettes.

Adams, Richard
SCENES FROM WATERSHIP DOWN (Roy Dotrice).
Note: Abridged.
MC. Cat no: **MCFR 117.** Released on Conifer, '86 by Conifer Records, Jazz Music.
MC. Cat no: **0600560589.** Released on Hamlyn Books On Tape, '88, Bond Street Music.

WATERSHIP DOWN (Roy Dotrice).
MCSET. Cat no: **MCFR 110/2.** Released on Conifer, '86 by Conifer Records, Jazz Music. Note: 3 Cassettes.
MCSET. Cat no: **9001F.** Released on Travellers Tales, '91 by Travellers Tales. Note: 3 Cassettes.

WATERSHIP DOWN (Various narrator(s)).
LPS. Cat no: **ZSW 574/7.** Released on Argo, Nov '76 by Decca International.
MCSET. Cat no: **K 30K 44.** Released on Argo, Nov '76 by Decca International.

Adamson, Jean
ADVENTURES OF SNUFFY STEAM TRAIN (Unknown narrator(s)).
MCSET. Cat no: **0411370073.** Released on Tempo, '91 by Warwick Records, Celtic Music, Henry Hadaway Organisation. Note: 2 Cassettes

ADVENTURES OF TOPSY AND TIM (Julie Peasgood).
MCSET. Cat no: **0411370286.** Released on Tempo, '91 by Warwick Records, Celtic Music, Henry Hadaway Organisation. Note: 2 Cassettes

TOPSY AND TIM GO SWIMMING (Elizabeth Lindsay).
MCSET. Cat no: **0411395912.** Released on Tempo, '91 by Warwick Records, Celtic Music, Henry Hadaway Organisation. Note: 2 Cassettes

TOPSY AND TIM ON HOLIDAY (Elizabeth Lindsay).
MCSET. Cat no: **0411395920.** Released on Tempo, '91 by Warwick Records, Celtic Music, Henry Hadaway Organisation. Note: 2 Cassettes

Aesop
AESOP FABLES (Clifford Simak).
MC. Cat no: **CP 1649.** Released on Caedmon (USA), Jan '81 by Caedmon Records (USA), Bond Street Music.

AESOP IN FABLELAND (Arthur Lowe with the London Symphony Orchestra).
LP. Cat no: **MFP 50538.** Released on MFP, Nov '81 by EMI Records, Solomon & Peres **Deleted** '88.
MC. Cat no: **TCMFP 50538.** Released on MFP, Nov '81 by EMI Records, Solomon & Peres **Deleted** '88.
LP. Cat no: **FOUR 2.** Released on Arista, Nov '79 by BMG Records (UK) Ltd., Outlet Records **Deleted** '84.

AESOP'S FABLES (Boris Karloff).
Tracks / Ant And The Grasshopper, The / Oak And The Reed, The / Mice In Council, The / Lion In Love, The.
MC. Cat no: **1221.** Released on Caedmon (USA), '88 by Caedmon Records (USA), Bond Street Music.

AESOP'S FABLES BOOK 1 (For Ages 7-12) (Various narrators).
MC. Cat no: **PLB 114.** Released on Tell-A-Tale, '88 by Pickwick Records, Taylors, Clyde Factors.

AESOP'S FABLES BOOK 2 (For Ages 7-12) (Various narrators).
MC. Cat no: **PLB 128.** Released on Tell-A-Tale, Oct '84 by Pickwick Records, Taylors, Clyde Factors.

FABLES OF AESOP, THE (Helen Lloyd).
Note: Includes The Hare And The Tortoise, The Wolf In Sheep's Clothing and The Lion And The Mouse.
MC. Cat no: **AC 111.** Released on Audicord, May '83 by Audicord Cassettes.

LET'S LISTEN (Unknown narrator(s)).

Note: Includes 6 Aesop's Fables.
MC. Cat no: **1182.** Released on Caedmon (USA), Jul '88 by Caedmon Records (USA), Bond Street Music.

Agee, James
LET US NOW PRAISE FAMOUS MEN (Various narrators).
MC. Cat no: **1324.** Released on Caedmon (USA), by Caedmon Records (USA), Bond Street Music.

Ahlberg, Allan
HAPPY FAMILIES (Martin Jarvis).
MC. Cat no: **881670.** Released on Puffin Cover To Cover, '88, Green Dragon Audio Visual.

HAPPY FAMILIES (Unknown narrator(s)).
LP. Cat no: **LAP 1001.** Released on Shangri-La, Nov '84 **Deleted** '85.
MC. Cat no: **CLAP 1001.** Released on Shangri-La, Nov '84 **Deleted** '85.

MORE FROM TEN IN A BED (Carole Boyd).
MC. Cat no: **TS 340.** Released on Tellastory, '88 by Random Century Audiobooks.

MORE TALES FROM TEN IN A BED (Carole Boyd).
MC. Cat no: **TS 340.** Released on Bartlett Bliss, '91 by Bartlett Bliss Productions Ltd..

TALES FROM TEN IN A BED (Carole Boyd).
MCSET. Cat no: **TS 401.** Released on Tellastory, Feb '92 by Random Century Audiobooks. Note: 2 Cassettes. ISBN no. 1856560353

Ahlberg, Janet
BURGLAR BILL (Bernard Cribbins).
MC. Cat no: **0 00 102199 0.** Released on Tempo, '88 by Warwick Records, Celtic Music, Henry Hadaway Organisation.
MC. Cat no: **000101003-6.** Released on Harper Collins, '91 by Harper Collins.

VANISHMENT OF THOMAS TULL, THE (Nigel Carrington).
MC. Cat no: **TS 356.** Released on Tellastory, '88 by Random Century Audiobooks.

Ahlberg, Janet & Allan
COPS AND ROBBERS (Bernard Cribbins).
MC. Cat no: **0 00 102198 2.** Released on Tempo Storytime, '88 by Warwick Records, Celtic Music.
MC. Cat no: **0001010034.** Released on Harper Collins, '91 by Harper Collins.

FUNNY BONES (Bernard Cribbins).
MC. Cat no: **0 00 102197 4.** Released on Tempo Storytime, '88 by Warwick Records, Celtic Music.
MC. Cat no: **0001010042.** Released on Harper Collins, '91 by Harper Collins.

JEREMIAH IN THE DARK WOODS (Johnny Morris).
MC. Cat no: **881 549**. Released on Puffin Cover To Cover, Apr '88, Green Dragon Audio Visual.
MC. Cat no: **TS 335**. Released on Tellastory, Jun '83 by Random Century Audiobooks.

JOLLY POSTMAN, THE (Janet & Allan Ahlberg).
MC. Cat no: **0 00 109029 1**. Released on Tempo Storytime, '88 by Warwick Records, Celtic Music.

JOLLY POSTMAN, THE (Susan Sheridan & Charles Collingwood). Note: Also available on hanging format, Cat. No: 0411380869.
MC. Cat no: **041140041X**. Released on Harper Collins, '91 by Harper Collins. Note: ISBN no. 1856560566

Aiken Hodge, Jane

ADVENTURES, THE (Judeth Franklyn).
MCSET. Cat no: **1001R**. Released on Travellers Tales, '91 by Travellers Tales. Note: 6 Cassettes

Aiken, Joan

BLACKGROUND (Rosemary Davis).
MCSET. Cat no: **1638F**. Released on Travellers Tales, '91 by Travellers Tales. Note: 8 Cassettes.
CDSET. Cat no: **OAS 91023**. Released on Oasis Audio Books, '91 by Isis Audio Books. Note: 4 Cassettes.

KINGDOM UNDER THE SEA, THE (And Other Stories) (Deirdre Edwards).
MCSET. Cat no: **2CCA 3007**. Released on Chivers Audio Books, '91 by Chivers Audio Books, Green Dragon Audio Visual. Note: 2 Cassettes.
MCSET. Cat no: **9002F**. Released on Travellers Tales, '91 by Travellers Tales. Note: 2 Cassettes.
MCSET. Cat no: **0862220407**. Released on Chivers Calvacade, Apr '88 by Chivers Audio Books, Green Dragon Audio Visual.

KITCHEN WARRIORS, THE (Susan Skipper).
MCSET. Cat no: **2CCA 3032**. Released on Chivers Audio Books, '91 by Chivers Audio Books, Green Dragon Audio Visual. Note: 2 Cassettes.
MCSET. Cat no: **9098F**. Released on Travellers Tales, '91 by Travellers Tales. Note: 2 Cassettes.

LAST SLICE OF THE RAINBOW, THE (Carole Boyd).
MC. Cat no: **TS 376**. Released on Tellastory, '91 by Random Century Audiobooks. Note: ISBN no. 1856561003

MORTIMER SAYS NOTHING (Judy Bennett).
MCSET. Cat no: **2CCA 3151**. Released on Chivers Audio Books, '91 by Chivers Audio Books, Green Dragon Audio Visual. Note: 2 Cassettes.

MORTIMER'S CROSS (Judy Bennett).
MCSET. Cat no: **2CCA 3047**. Released on Chivers Audio Thrillers, '88 by Chivers Audio Books, Green Dragon Audio Visual. Note: 2 Cassettes.
MCSET. Cat no: **9130F**. Released on Travellers Tales, '91 by Travellers Tales. Note: 2 Cassettes.

NECKLACE OF RAINDROPS, A (Unknown narrator(s)).
MC. Cat no: **1690**. Released on Caedmon (USA), '88 by Caedmon Records (USA), Bond Street Music.

PAST EIGHT O'CLOCK (Jane Asher).
MCSET. Cat no: **2CCA 3081**. Released on Chivers Audio Books, '91 by Chivers Audio Books, Green Dragon Audio Visual. Note: 2 Cassettes.
MCSET. Cat no: **9161F**. Released on Travellers Tales, '91 by Travellers Tales. Note: 2 Cassettes.

RIBS OF DEATH, THE (Neil Appelt).
MCSET. Cat no: **1854965832**. Released on Bramhope, Apr '92 by Ulverscroft Soundings. Note: Playing time: 60 minutes.

TALE OF A ONE-WAY STREET (And Other Stories) (Jane Asher).
MCSET. Cat no: **2CCA 3099**. Released on Chivers Audio Books, '91 by Chivers Audio Books, Green Dragon Audio Visual. Note: 2 Cassettes.
MCSET. Cat no: **9169F**. Released on Travellers Tales, '91 by Travellers Tales. Note: 2 Cassettes.

TROUBLE WITH PRODUCT X, THE (Unknown narrator(s)).
MCSET. Cat no: **1854964895**. Released on Bramhope, '91 by Ulverscroft Soundings. Note: 5 Cassettes.

WOLVES OF WILLOUGHBY CHASE (Sir Michael Hordern).
MC. Cat no: **ZCTER 8311**. Released on T. E. R., Dec '89 by That's Entertainment Records, Silva Screen.
CD. Cat no: **CDTER 8311**. Released on T. E. R., Dec '89 by That's Entertainment Records, Silva Screen.

WOLVES OF WILLOUGHBY CHASE, THE (Unknown narrator(s)).
MC. Cat no: **1540**. Released on Caedmon (USA), '88 by Caedmon Records (USA), Bond Street Music.

Aird, Catherine

COMPLETE STEEL, THE (Robin Bailey).
MCSET. Cat no: **CAB 425**. Released on Chivers Audio Books, '91 by Chivers Audio Books, Green Dragon Audio Visual. Note: 4 Cassettes.
MCSET. Cat no: **1451T**. Released on Travellers Tales, '91 by Travellers Tales. Note: 4 Cassettes.

DEAD LIBERTY, A (Robin Bailey).
MCSET. Cat no: **CAB 234**. Released on Chivers Audio Books, '91 by Chivers Audio Books, Green Dragon Audio Visual. Note: 6 Cassettes.
MCSET. Cat no: **1184T**. Released on Travellers Tales, '91 by Travellers Tales. Note: 6 Cassettes.

HENRIETTA WHO? (Robin Bailey).
MCSET. Cat no: **CAB 517**. Released on Chivers Audio Books, '91 by Chivers Audio Books, Green Dragon Audio Visual. Note: 4 Cassettes
MCSET. Cat no: **1597T**. Released on Travellers Tales, '91 by Travellers Tales. Note: 4 Cassettes.

LATE PHOENIX, A (Robin Bailey).
MC. Cat no: **CAT 4031**. Released on Chivers Audio Thrillers, Jul '88 by Chivers Audio Books, Green Dragon Audio Visual. Note: 4 Cassettes.
MCSET. Cat no: **1254T**. Released on Travellers Tales, '91 by Travellers Tales. Note: 4 Cassettes.

RELIGIOUS BODY, THE (Robin Bailey).
MCSET. Cat no: **1001T**. Released on Travellers Tales, '91 by Travellers Tales. Note: 4 Cassettes.

Aitken, Hannah

FORGOTTEN HERITAGE, A (Various narrator(s)).
MC. Cat no: **SSC 022**. Released on Scotsoun, '91 by Scotsoun Recordings, Morley Audio Services.

Albee, Edward

DELICATE BALANCE, A (Various narrator(s)).
MCSET. Cat no: **0360**. Released on Caedmon (USA), by Caedmon Records (USA), Bond Street Music. Note: 3 cassettes

Alcock, Vivien

CUCKOO SISTER, THE (Carole Hayman).
MC. Cat no: **3CCA 3057**. Released on Chivers Audio Thrillers, Oct '88 by Chivers Audio Books, Green Dragon Audio Visual. Note: 3 Cassettes.
MCSET. Cat no: **9134F**. Released on Travellers Tales, '91 by Travellers Tales. Note: 3 Cassettes.

GHOSTLY COMPANIONS (Kenneth Shanley).
MCSET. Cat no: **3CCA 3042**. Released on Chivers Audio Books, '91 by Chivers Audio Books, Green Dragon Audio Visual. Note: 3 Cassettes.
MCSET. Cat no: **9164F**. Released on Travellers Tales, '91 by Travellers Tales. Note: 3 Cassettes.

STONEWALKERS, THE (Carole Hayman).
MCSET. Cat no: **3CCA 3015**. Released on Chivers Audio Books, '91 by Chivers Audio Books, Green Dragon Audio Visual. Note: 3 Cassettes.
MCSET. Cat no: **9004F**. Released on Travellers Tales, '91 by Travellers Tales. Note: 3 Cassettes.

Alcott, Louisa May
LITTLE WOMEN (Glenda Jackson). Note: Abridged.
MCSET. Cat no: **SAY 99**. Released on Argo (Polygram), Apr '84 by PolyGram Classics **Deleted** Jan '89. Note: Playing time: 3 hours
MCSET. Cat no: **ARGO 1175**. Released on Argo (EMI), Oct '89 by EMI Records. Note: 2 Cassettes.
MCSET. Cat no: **9003F**. Released on Travellers Tales, '91 by Travellers Tales. Note: 2 Cassettes.

LITTLE WOMEN (Julie Harris).
MC. Cat no: **1470**. Released on Caedmon (USA), '88 by Caedmon Records (USA), Bond Street Music.

LITTLE WOMEN (Elaine Stritch).
MC. Cat no: **P 90041**. Released on Pinnacle, '79 by Pinnacle Records, Outlet Records, Music Sales Records.

Aldiss, Brian W.
BEST SCIENCE FICTION OF BRIAN ALDISS, THE (Volume 1) (Brian Aldiss).
MC. Cat no: **MCLIS 500**. Released on Listen, '91, Cartel. Note: 60 mins.

BEST SCIENCE FICTION OF BRIAN ALDISS, THE (Volume 2) (Brian Aldiss).
MC. Cat no: **MCLIS 501**. Released on Listen, '91, Cartel. Note: 60 mins.

BEST SCIENCE FICTION OF BRIAN W. ALDISS (Unknown narrator(s)).
MCSET. Cat no: **LISF 0003/0004**. Released on Listen Productions, Nov '84.

Alexander, L.G.
OPERATION JANUS (And Other Stories) (Unknown narrator(s)).
MC. Cat no: **058256977 X**. Released on Longman/Pickwick, '91 by Pickwick Records.

Allan, Margaret
DOCTOR DAVID (Unknown narrator(s)).
MCSET. Cat no: **1854963953**. Released on Trio, '91 by EMI Records. Note: 3 Cassettes.

Allan, Stella
KISS YESTERDAY GOODBYE (Jill Shilling).
MCSET. Cat no: **MRC 1087**. Released on Chivers Audio Books, '91 by Chivers Audio Books, Green Dragon Audio Visual. Note: 2 Cassettes.

Allbeury, Ted
ALL OUR TOMORROWS (Nigel Davenport).
MC. Cat no: **LFP 41 7188 5**. Released on Listen For Pleasure, May '85 by EMI Records.

ALPHA LIST, THE (Gordon Griffin).
MCSET. Cat no: **1568T**. Released on Travellers Tales, '91 by Travellers Tales. Note: 5 Cassettes.

MCSET. Cat no: **1854963279**. Released on Bramhope, '91 by Ulverscroft Soundings. Note: 5 Cassettes.

CHILDREN OF TENDER YEARS (Denis Quilley).
MCSET. Cat no: **1003T**. Released on Travellers Tales, '91 by Travellers Tales. Note: 6 Cassettes

CHOICE OF ENEMIES, A (Denis Quilley).
MCSET. Cat no: **1452T**. Released on Travellers Tales, '91 by Travellers Tales. Note: 6 Cassettes.
MCSET. Cat no: **185496254X**. Released on Bramhope, '91 by Ulverscroft Soundings.

CHOICE, THE (Gordon Griffin).
MCSET. Cat no: **1595/1596F**. Released on Travellers Tales, '91 by Travellers Tales. Note: 9 cassettes.
MCSET. Cat no: **1854963775**. Released on Bramhope, '91 by Ulverscroft Soundings.

CODEWORD CROMWELL (Gordon Griffin).
MCSET. Cat no: **1571T**. Released on Travellers Tales, '91 by Travellers Tales. Note: 5 Cassettes.
MCSET. Cat no: **1854963112**. Released on Bramhope, '91 by Ulverscroft Soundings.

CROSSING, THE (Steven Pacey).
MCSET. Cat no: **CAB 571**. Released on Chivers Audio Books, '91 by Chivers Audio Books, Green Dragon Audio Visual. Note: 6 Cassettes.
MCSET. Cat no: **1719T**. Released on Travellers Tales, '91 by Travellers Tales. Note: 6 Cassettes.

DEEP PURPLE (Christian Rodska).
MCSET. Cat no: **CAB 449**. Released on Chivers Audio Books, '92 by Chivers Audio Books, Green Dragon Audio Visual. Note: 6 Cassettes.
MCSET. Cat no: **1507T**. Released on Travellers Tales, '91 by Travellers Tales. Note: 6 Cassettes.

GIRL FROM ADDIS, THE (Denis Quilley).
MCSET. Cat no: **CAB 235**. Released on Chivers Audio Books, '91 by Chivers Audio Books, Green Dragon Audio Visual. Note: 6 Cassettes.
MCSET. Cat no: **1185T**. Released on Travellers Tales, '91 by Travellers Tales. Note: 6 Cassettes.

ITALIAN ASSETS (Christian Rodska).
MCSET. Cat no: **CAB 526**. Released on Chivers Audio Books, '91 by Chivers Audio Books, Green Dragon Audio Visual. Note: 6 Cassettes
MCSET. Cat no: **1646T**. Released on Travellers Tales, '91 by Travellers Tales. Note: 6 Cassettes.

JUDAS FACTOR, THE (Denis Quilley).
MCSET. Cat no: **1004T**. Released on Travellers Tales, '91 by Travellers Tales. Note: 6 Cassettes.

LANTERN NETWORK, THE (Gordon Griffin).

MCSET. Cat no: **1443T**. Released on Travellers Tales, '91 by Travellers Tales. Note: 5 Cassettes.
MCSET. Cat no: **1854962361**. Released on Bramhope, '91 by Ulverscroft Soundings.

LONELY MARGINS, THE (Christopher Kay).
MCSET. Cat no: **1854964577**. Released on Soundings, '91 by Soundings Records, Bond Street Music.

MOSCOW QUADRILLE (Peter Wheeler).
MCSET. Cat no: **1246T**. Released on Travellers Tales, '91 by Travellers Tales. Note: 5 Cassettes.
MCSET. Cat no: **1854960067**. Released on Bramhope, '91 by Ulverscroft Soundings.

NO PLACE TO HIDE (Denis Quilley).
MCSET. Cat no: **CAB 271**. Released on Chivers Audio Books, '91 by Chivers Audio Books, Green Dragon Audio Visual. Note: 6 Cassettes.
MCSET. Cat no: **1214TT**. Released on Chivers Audio Books, '91 by Chivers Audio Books, Green Dragon Audio Visual.

NO PLACE TO HIDE (John Nettles).
MC. Cat no: **060056049X**. Released on Hamlyn Books On Tape, '88, Bond Street Music.

ONLY GOOD GERMAN, THE (Gordon Griffin).
MCSET. Cat no: **1652T**. Released on Travellers Tales, '91 by Travellers Tales.
MCSET. Cat no: **1854963597**. Released on Bramhope, '91 by Ulverscroft Soundings.

OTHER KINDS OF TREASON (Unknown narrator(s)).
MCSET. Cat no: **1854965239**. Released on Soundings, '91 by Soundings Records, Bond Street Music. Note: 8 Cassettes.

OTHER SIDE OF SILENCE (Gordon Griffin).
MCSET. Cat no: **1739T**. Released on Travellers Tales, '91 by Travellers Tales. Note: 7 Cassettes.
MCSET. Cat no: **1854964178**. Released on Soundings, '91 by Soundings Records, Bond Street Music.

PALOMINO BLONDE (Gordon Griffin).
MCSET. Cat no: **1440T**. Released on Travellers Tales, '91 by Travellers Tales. Note: 4 Cassettes.
MCSET. Cat no: **1854962302**. Released on Bramhope, '91 by Ulverscroft Soundings.

PAY ANY PRICE (Jerry Harte).
MC. Cat no: **CAB 307**. Released on Chivers Audio Books, Jul '88 by Chivers Audio Books, Green Dragon Audio Visual.
MCSET. Cat no: **1357T**. Released on Travellers Tales, '91 by Travellers Tales. Note: 6 Cassettes.

SECRET WHISPERS, THE (Bernard Hepton).
MCSET. Cat no: **CAB 074**. Released on Chivers Audio Books, '91 by Chivers Audio Books, Green Dragon Audio Visual. Note: 6 Cassettes.
MCSET. Cat no: **1005T**. Released on Travellers Tales, '91 by Travellers Tales. Note: 6 Cassettes.

SEEDS OF TREASON, THE (Denis Quilley).
MCSET. Cat no: **CAB 408**. Released on Chivers Audio Books, '91 by Chivers Audio Books, Green Dragon Audio Visual. Note: 8 Cassettes
MCSET. Cat no: **1453T**. Released on Travellers Tales, '91 by Travellers Tales. Note: 8 Cassettes.

SHADOW OF SHADOWS (Christian Rodska).
MCSET. Cat no: **CAB 619**. Released on Chivers Audio Books, '91 by Chivers Audio Books, Green Dragon Audio Visual. Note: 8 Cassettes

SNOWBALL (Gordon Griffin).
MCSET. Cat no: **1578T**. Released on Travellers Tales, '91 by Travellers Tales. Note: 5 Cassettes.
MCSET. Cat no: **185496335X**. Released on Bramhope, '91 by Ulverscroft Soundings. Note: 5 Cassettes.

SPECIAL COLLECTION, THE (Peter Wheeler).
MCSET. Cat no: **1242T**. Released on Travellers Tales, '91 by Travellers Tales. Note: 5 Cassettes.
MCSET. Cat no: **1854960075**. Released on Bramhope, '91 by Ulverscroft Soundings.

TIME WITHOUT SHADOWS, A (Gordon Griffin).
MCSET. Cat no: **1581T**. Released on Travellers Tales, '91 by Travellers Tales. Note: 7 Cassettes.
MCSET. Cat no: **1854963481**. Released on Soundings, '91 by Soundings Records, Bond Street Music.

TWENTIETH DAY OF JANUARY, THE (David Rintoul).
MCSET. Cat no: **CAB 658**. Released on Chivers Audio Books, Jan '92 by Chivers Audio Books, Green Dragon Audio Visual. Note: 6 Cassettes.

WHERE ALL THE GIRLS ARE SWEETER (Christian Rodska).
MCSET. Cat no: **CAB 481**. Released on Chivers Audio Books, '91 by Chivers Audio Books, Green Dragon Audio Visual. Note: 4 Cassettes.
MCSET. Cat no: **1561T**. Released on Travellers Tales, '91 by Travellers Tales. Note: 4 Cassettes.

WILDERNESS OF MIRRORS, A (Michael Culver).
MCSET. Cat no: **CAB 364**. Released on Chivers Audio Books, '92 by Chivers Audio Books, Green Dragon Audio Visual. Note: 8 Cassettes.
MCSET. Cat no: **1397T**. Released on Travellers Tales, '91 by Travellers Tales. Note: 8 Cassettes.

Allen, Maudie
TRAVELLER'S JOY (Kate Lock).
MCSET. Cat no: **MRC 1045**. Released on Chivers Moonlight Romances, Apr '88 by Chivers Audio Books, Green Dragon Audio Visual. Note: 2 Cassettes.

Allen, Woody
NIGHTCLUB YEARS (1964-1968) (EMI Comedy Classics) (Woody Allen).
Note: Contains The Nightclub Years Parts 1 - 4.
MCSET. Cat no: **ECC 3**. Released on EMI, Mar '90 by EMI Records. Note: UK cat. no.'s ECC 31/32. International cat. no.'s 7939694/704.

Allingham, Margery
CAMPION (Flowers for the Judge) (Peter Davison).
MCSET. Cat no: **LFP 7484**. Released on Listen For Pleasure, Oct '90 by EMI Records.

CORONER'S PIDGIN (Francis Matthews).
MCSET. Cat no: **1006T**. Released on Travellers Tales, '91 by Travellers Tales. Note: 6 Cassettes.
MCSET. Cat no: **CAB 182**. Released on Chivers Audio Books, '91 by Chivers Audio Books, Green Dragon Audio Visual.

CRIME AT BLACK DUDLEY, THE (Francis Matthews).
MCSET. Cat no: **CAB 580**. Released on Chivers Audio Books, '91 by Chivers Audio Books, Green Dragon Audio Visual. Note: 8 Cassettes.
MCSET. Cat no: **1723T**. Released on Travellers Tales, '91 by Travellers Tales. Note: 8 Cassettes.

DEATH OF A GHOST (Francis Matthews).
MCSET. Cat no: **CAB 228**. Released on Chivers Audio Books, '91 by Chivers Audio Books, Green Dragon Audio Visual. Note: 8 Cassettes.
MCSET. Cat no: **1181T**. Released on Travellers Tales, '91 by Travellers Tales. Note: 8 Cassettes.

FASHION IN SHROUDS, THE (Jeremy Nicholas).
MCSET. Cat no: **ZBBC 1166**. Released on BBC Radio Collection, Feb '91 by BBC Records. Note: ISBN No: 0563 411155

HIDE MY EYES (Bernard Archard).
MC. Cat no: **CAB 025**. Released on Chivers Audio Books, Aug '81 by Chivers Audio Books, Green Dragon Audio Visual.
MCSET. Cat no: **1007T**. Released on Travellers Tales, '91 by Travellers Tales. Note: 6 Cassettes.

LOOK TO THE LADY (Francis Matthews).
MCSET. Cat no: **CAB 365**. Released on Chivers Audio Books, '91 by Chivers Audio Books, Green Dragon Audio Visual. Note: 6 Cassettes.

MCSET. Cat no: **1420T**. Released on Travellers Tales, '91 by Travellers Tales. Note: 6 Cassettes.

MORE WORK FOR THE UNDERTAKER (Francis Matthews).
MC. Cat no: **CAB 334**. Released on Chivers Audio Books, Oct '88 by Chivers Audio Books, Green Dragon Audio Visual. Note: 6 Cassettes.
MCSET. Cat no: **1363T**. Released on Travellers Tales, '91 by Travellers Tales. Note: 6 Cassettes.

MYSTERY MILE (Francis Matthews).
MCSET. Cat no: **CAB 651**. Released on Chivers Audio Books, Dec '91 by Chivers Audio Books, Green Dragon Audio Visual. Note: 8 cassettes.

POLICE AT THE FUNERAL (Francis Matthews).
MCSET. Cat no: **CAB 434**. Released on Chivers Audio Books, '91 by Chivers Audio Books, Green Dragon Audio Visual. Note: 6 Cassettes.
MCSET. Cat no: **1454T**. Released on Travellers Tales, '91 by Travellers Tales. Note: 6 Cassettes.

STORIES FROM THE ALLINGHAM CASEBOOK (Bernard Archard).
MCSET. Cat no: **1188T**. Released on Travellers Tales, '91 by Travellers Tales. Note: 4 Cassettes.

SWEET DANGER (Francis Matthews).
MCSET. Cat no: **1010T**. Released on Travellers Tales, '91 by Travellers Tales. Note: 6 Cassettes.
MCSET. Cat no: **CAB 093**. Released on Chivers Audio Books, '91 by Chivers Audio Books, Green Dragon Audio Visual.

TIGER IN THE SMOKE (Francis Matthews).
MCSET. Cat no: **CAB 482**. Released on Chivers Audio Books, '91 by Chivers Audio Books, Green Dragon Audio Visual. Note: 8 Cassettes.
MCSET. Cat no: **1563T**. Released on Travellers Tales, '91 by Travellers Tales. Note: 8 Cassettes.

TRAITOR'S PURSE (Francis Matthews).
MCSET. Cat no: **CAB 259**. Released on Chivers Audio Books, '91 by Chivers Audio Books, Green Dragon Audio Visual. Note: 6 Cassettes.
MCSET. Cat no: **1215T**. Released on Travellers Tales, '91 by Travellers Tales. Note: 6 Cassettes.

Allsop, Kenneth
LETTERS FROM MY FATHER (John Moffat & Abigail McKern).
MCSET. Cat no: **ZBBC 1161**. Released on BBC, Jul '90 by BBC Records, Taylors. Note: ISBN No: 0563 410868

Alverson, Charles
GOODEY'S LAST STAND (Frank Muller).

MCSET. Cat no: **RB 81050.** Released on Recorded Books, Jul '92 by Isis Audio Books. Note: 4 Cassettes. Playing time: 6 hours.

Ambler, Eric

EPITAPH FOR A SPY (Alexander Spencer).
MCSET. Cat no: **IAB 91123.** Released on Isis Audio Books, Dec '91. Note: 6 Cassettes. Playing time 7 hours.

JOURNEY INTO FEAR (Edward Fox).
MCSET. Cat no: **1011T.** Released on Travellers Tales, '91 by Travellers Tales. Note: 6 Cassettes.

Amis, Kingsley

LUCKY JIM (Tom Courtenay).
MC. Cat no: **0600560562.** Released on Hamlyn Books On Tape, Jul '88, Bond Street Music.

RUSSIAN HIDE-AND-SEEK (Edward Woodward).
MCSET. Cat no: **1004S.** Released on Travellers Tales, '91 by Travellers Tales. Note: 6 Cassettes.

TAKE A GIRL LIKE YOU (Steve Hodson).
MCSET. Cat no: **1149/1150r.** Released on Travellers Tales, '91 by Travellers Tales. Note: 12 Cassettes.

MCSET. Cat no: **OAS 89112.** Released on Oasis Audio Books, '91 by Isis Audio Books.

Andersen, Hans Christian

6 CHILDREN'S CLASSICS (Peter Whitbread & Gillian Blake).
Note: For children aged 3 - 9 years. Includes The Kings New Clothes, The Nightingale, The Ugly Duckling, The Princess and the Pea, The Little Tin Soldier and The Snow Queen.
MC. Cat no: **STC 103.** Released on VFM Cassettes, '85 by VFM Cassettes, Midland Records, Crusader Marketing Co., Taylors, Morley Audio Services.

EMPEROR'S NEW CLOTHES, THE (Sir John Gielgud & Mark Isham).
CD. Cat no: **WD 0719.** Released on Windham Hill, Jun '91 by Windham Hill Records (USA), New Note.

MC. Cat no: **WT 0719.** Released on Windham Hill, Jun '91 by Windham Hill Records (USA), New Note.

EMPEROR'S NEW CLOTHES, THE (And Other Stories) (Unknown narrator(s)).
Tracks / Emperor's New Clothes, The / Salt, Pepper and Mustard / Kastchey the Deathless / John and Jane / Shortshanks and Sturdy-oh.
MC. Cat no: **ANV 651.** Released on Anvil Cassettes, Feb '83 by Anvil Cassettes, Chivers Audio Books. Note: Cassette plus book.

EMPEROR'S NEW CLOTHES, THE (Well Loved Tales Up to Age 9) (Unknown narrator(s)).
MC. Cat no: **PLB 50.** Released on Tell-A-Tale, Jul '82 by Pickwick Records, Taylors, Clyde Factors.
Note: Book and Cassette

EMPEROR'S NEW CLOTHES, THE (Jane Asher).
MC. Cat no: **LPMC 210.** Released on Listen, '88, Cartel.

EMPEROR'S NEW CLOTHES, THE (And Other Stories) (Sir Michael Redgrave).
Note: Also available on hanging format, Cat. No: 0001845691.
MC. Cat no: **000184590X.** Released on Harper Collins, '91 by Harper Collins.

HANS ANDERSEN (Various narrators).
MC. Cat no: **STC 003.** Released on VFM Cassettes, Jun '88 by VFM Cassettes, Midland Records, Crusader Marketing Co., Taylors, Morley Audio Services.

HANS ANDERSEN STORIES (Unknown narrator(s)).
Tracks / Emperor's New Clothes, The / Tinder box / Nightingale, The / Princess and the Pea.
LP. Cat no: **KPM 7008.** Released on Unicorn-Kanchana, Oct '80 by Unicorn - Kanchana Records, Outlet Records **Deleted** Oct '85.

HANS C. ANDERSEN FAIRY TALES. (Unknown narrators)
MC. Cat no: **BBMLB 6.** Released on Bibi (Budget Cassettes), Feb '82.

HANS CHRISTIAN ANDERSEN (Volume 1) (Various narrators).
Note: The Nightingale read by Michelle Dotrice. The Princess And The Pea read by Fiona Fullerton. The Flying Trunk read by Ian Ogilvy. The Tinder Box read by Jane Asher.
MC. Cat no: **MCLIS 180.** Released on Listen, '91, Cartel. Note: 60 mins.

HANS CHRISTIAN ANDERSEN (Volume 2) (Jane Asher).
Note: Contains the following stories:- Emperors New Clothes, Thumbelina, Ugly Ducking and Little Match Girl.
MC. Cat no: **MCLIS 101.** Released on Listen, '91, Cartel. Note: 70 mins.

HANS CHRISTIAN ANDERSEN (Volume 1).(Unknown narrators)
MC. Cat no: **VCA 104.** Released on VFM Cassettes, Jan '85 by VFM Cassettes, Midland Records, Crusader Marketing Co., Taylors, Morley Audio Services.

HANS CHRISTIAN ANDERSEN FAIRY TALES (Wendy Craig).
Note: Includes The Ugly Duckling, The Nightingale, The Emperor's New Clothes, The Princess and The Pea and The Little Mermaid.
MC. Cat no: **TC LFP 7105.** Released on Listen For Pleasure, Oct '82 by EMI Records. Note: Approx. 2 hours.

LITTLE MATCH GIRL, THE (And Other Tales) (Boris Karloff).
Tracks / Swinehered, The / Top and the Ball, The / Red shoes, The / Thumbelina / Little Match Girl, The.
MC. Cat no: **1117.** Released on Caedmon (USA), '88 by Caedmon Records (USA), Bond Street Music.

LITTLE MERMAID, THE (Barbara Bliss).
MC. Cat no: **TS 319.** Released on Tellastory, Jun '92 by Random Century Audiobooks. Note: ISBN no. 1856560090

LITTLE MERMAID, THE (Well Loved Tales Age Up to 9) (Unknown narrator(s)).
Note: Book and cassette.
MC. Cat no: **PLB 73.** Released on Tell-A-Tale, '83 by Pickwick Records, Taylors, Clyde Factors.

LITTLE MERMAID, THE (Unknown narrator(s)).
MC. Cat no: **DIS 020.** Released on Disney (Read-a-long), Sep '90 by Disneyland Records.

LITTLE MERMAID, THE (Cathleen Nesbitt).
Note: Also available on hanging format, Cat. No: 0001389769.
MC. Cat no: **1230.** Released on Caedmon (USA), '88 by Caedmon Records (USA), Bond Street Music.
MC. Cat no: **0001389777.** Released on Harper Collins, '91 by Harper Collins.

PRINCESS AND THE PEA (And The Three Musicians) (Fiona Fullerton).
MC. Cat no: **LP 202.** Released on Listen Productions, Nov '84.

PRINCESS AND THE PEA (Well Loved Tales Age Up To 9) (Unknown narrator(s)).
Note: Book and cassette.
MC. Cat no: **PLB 62.** Released on Tell-A-Tale, '83 by Pickwick Records, Taylors, Clyde Factors.

SNOW QUEEN, THE (Cathleen Nesbitt).
MC. Cat no: **1229.** Released on Caedmon (USA), '88 by Caedmon Records (USA), Bond Street Music.

SNOW QUEEN, THE (Well Loved Tales Up to Age 9) (Unknown narrator(s)).
Note: Book and cassette.
MC. Cat no: **PLB 111.** Released on Tell-A-Tale, '88 by Pickwick Records, Taylors, Clyde Factors.

SNOW QUEEN, THE (Various narrators).
MC. Cat no: **TS 313.** Released on Tellastory, Oct '79 by Random Century Audiobooks.

SNOW QUEEN, THE (Pamela Matthew).
LP. Cat no: **TMP 9004.** Released on Tempo, Nov '79 by Warwick Records, Celtic Music, Henry Hadaway Organisation.
MC. Cat no: **TMP4 9004.** Released on Tempo, Nov '79 by Warwick Records, Celtic Music, Henry Hadaway Organisation.

SNOW QUEEN, THE (A Fairy Tale) (Natalia Makarova).
MC. Cat no: **13491 6004 4.** Released on Delos, Dec '90.

STEADFAST TIN SOLDIER, THE (Jeremy Irons).
CD. Cat no: **WD 0702.** Released on Windham Hill, Jan '92 by Windham Hill Records (USA), New Note.
MC. Cat no: **WT 0702.** Released on Windham Hill, Jan '92 by Windham Hill Records (USA), New Note.

STORIES FOR CHILDREN (Volume 2).(Unknown narrators)
Note: For children aged 3 - 9 years. Includes The Flying Trunk and Elfin Mount.
MC. Cat no: **VCA 105.** Released on VFM Cassettes, Jan '85 by VFM Cassettes, Midland Records, Crusader Marketing Co., Taylors, Morley Audio Services.

TALES OF HANS CHRISTIAN ANDERSEN (Sir Michael Redgrave).
Tracks : Tinder Box, The / Steadfast Tin Soldier, The.
MC. Cat no: **1073.** Released on Caedmon (USA), '88 by Caedmon Records (USA), Bond Street Music.

THUMBELINA (Well Loved Tales Age Up to 9) (Unknown narrator(s)).
Note: Book and cassette.
MC. Cat no: **PLB 65.** Released on Tell-A-Tale, '83 by Pickwick Records, Taylors, Clyde Factors.

THUMBELINA (Jane Asher).
MC. Cat no: **LPMC 211.** Released on Listen, '88, Cartel.

THUMBELINA (Unknown narrator(s)).
MC. Cat no: **STK 014.** Released on Stick-A-Tale, Jan '89 by Pickwick Records.

THUMBELINA (And The Little Match Girl) (Unknown narrator(s)).
MC. Cat no: **LP 211.** Released on Listen Productions, Nov '84.

THUMBELINA (Music by Mark Isham) (Kelly McGillis).
CD. Cat no: **WD 0712.** Released on Windham Hill, Jan '92 by Windham Hill Records (USA), New Note.
MC. Cat no: **WT 0712.** Released on Windham Hill, Jan '92 by Windham Hill Records (USA), New Note.

TINDER BOX, THE (Well Loved Tales Up to Age 9) (Unknown narrator(s)).
Note: Book and cassette.
MC. Cat no: **PLB 205.** Released on Tell-A-Tale, '88 by Pickwick Records, Taylors, Clyde Factors.

TINDER BOX, THE (Jane Asher).
MC. Cat no: **LPMC 209.** Released on Listen, '88, Cartel.

UGLY DUCKLING, THE (Peter Bartlett).
MC. Cat no: **TS 309.** Released on Tellastory, '91 by Random Century Audiobooks. Note: ISBN no. 1856560031

UGLY DUCKLING, THE (Music by Patrick Ball) (Cher).
CD. Cat no: **WD 0705.** Released on Windham Hill, Jan '92 by Windham Hill Records (USA), New Note.
MC. Cat no: **WT 0705.** Released on Windham Hill, Jan '92 by Windham Hill Records (USA), New Note.

UGLY DUCKLING, THE (Unknown narrator(s)).
MC. Cat no: **1856560031.** Released on Random Century, '91 by Random Century Audiobooks, Conifer Records. Note: Playing time: 60 Minutes.
MC. Cat no: **STK 005.** Released on Stick-A-Tale, Jan '89 by Pickwick Records.

UGLY DUCKLING, THE (Well Loved Tales Up to Age 9) (Unknown narrator(s)).
Note: Book and cassette.
MC. Cat no: **PLB 52.** Released on Tell-A-Tale, Feb '83 by Pickwick Records, Taylors, Clyde Factors.

UGLY DUCKLING, THE (Susan Hampshire).
MC. Cat no: **3603.** Released on Storytime Cassettes, Aug '83 by VFM Cassettes, Iona Records, Rio Communications.

Anderson, C.W.

BILLY AND BLAZE (David Cassidy).
MC. Cat no: **1737.** Released on Caedmon (USA), Sep '84 by Caedmon Records (USA), Bond Street Music.

Anderson, Sherwood

WINESBURG, OHIO (The Conscience of Winesburg) (Various narrators).
MC. Cat no: **SBRC 504.** Released on Caedmon (USA), '84 by Caedmon Records (USA), Bond Street Music.

Andi, Su

PROFILE (Su Andi).
MC. Cat no: **BIP 602.** Released on Bop, Jun '89 by Bop Records, Bop Records.

SOLILOQUY (Su Andi).
MC. Cat no: **BIP 601.** Released on Bop, Jul '89 by Bop Records, Bop Records.

Andrews, Lucilla

CRYSTAL GULL, THE (Unknown narrator(s)).
MCSET. Cat no: **185496285X.** Released on Bramhope, '91 by Ulverscroft Soundings. Note: 4 Cassettes.

EDINBURGH EXCURSION (Unknown narrator(s)).
MCSET. Cat no: **1854960083.** Released on Bramhope, '91 by Ulverscroft Soundings. Note: 4 Cassettes.

FLOWERS FROM THE DOCTOR (Marie Clarke).
MCSET. Cat no: **SOUND 16.** Released on Soundings, Mar '85 by Soundings Records, Bond Street Music.

HIGHLAND INTERLUDE (Unknown narrator(s)).
MCSET. Cat no: **1854960105.** Released on Bramhope, '91 by Ulverscroft Soundings. Note: 5 Cassettes.

HOSPITAL CIRCLES (Unknown narrator(s)).
MCSET. Cat no: **1854960113.** Released on Bramhope, '91 by Ulverscroft Soundings. Note: 4 Cassettes.

HOSPITAL SUMMER (Unknown narrator(s)).
MCSET. Cat no: **1854960121.** Released on Bramhope, '91 by Ulverscroft Soundings. Note: 4 Cassettes.

HOUSE FOR SISTER MARY (Unknown narrator(s)).
MCSET. Cat no: **185496013X.** Released on Bramhope, '91 by Ulverscroft Soundings. Note: 4 Cassettes.

IN STORM AND IN CALM (Unknown narrator(s)).
MCSET. Cat no: **1854960148.** Released on Bramhope, '91 by Ulverscroft Soundings. Note: 4 Cassettes.

LIGHT IN THE WARD, THE (Unknown narrator(s)).
MCSET. Cat no: **1854960156.** Released on Bramhope, '91 by Ulverscroft Soundings. Note: 5 Cassettes.

MY FRIEND THE PROFESSOR (Jean Wallace).
MCSET. Cat no: **SOUND 13.** Released on Soundings, Mar '85 by Soundings Records, Bond Street Music.

NEW SISTER THEATRE, THE (Jane Jermyn).
MCSET. Cat no: **SOUND 14.** Released on Soundings, Mar '85 by Soundings Records, Bond Street Music.

NURSE ERRANT (Unknown narrator(s)).
MCSET. Cat no: **1854960180.** Released on Soundings, '91 by Soundings Records, Bond Street Music. Note: 2 Cassettes.

ONE NIGHT IN LONDON (Unknown narrator(s)).
MCSET. Cat no: **1854964291.** Released on Bramhope, '91 by Ulverscroft Soundings. Note: 5 Cassettes.

PHOENIX SYNDROME, THE (Unknown narrator(s)).
MCSET. Cat no: **1854964399.** Released on Bramhope, '91 by Ulverscroft Soundings. Note: 5 Cassettes.

PRINT PETTICOAT, THE (Unknown narrator(s)).
MCSET. Cat no: **1854960199.** Released on Soundings, '91 by Soundings Records, Bond Street Music. Note: 2 Cassettes.

QUIET WARDS, THE (Unknown narrator(s)).
MCSET. Cat no: **1854960202.** Released on Bramhope, '91 by Ulverscroft Soundings. Note: 4 Cassettes.

SECRET ARMOUR, THE (Unknown narrator(s)).

MCSET. Cat no: **1854963287.** Released on Bramhope, '91 by Ulverscroft Soundings. Note: 4 Cassettes.
YOUNG DOCTOR DOWNSTAIRS, THE (Unknown narrator(s)).
MCSET. Cat no: **1854960210.** Released on Bramhope, '91 by Ulverscroft Soundings. Note: 4 Cassettes.

Andrews, Virginia
FLOWERS IN THE ATTIC (Dorothy Lyman).
MCSET. Cat no: **067162850X.** Released on Simon & Schuster, '91 by Simon & Schuster Ltd.
PETALS ON THE WIND (Leslie Charleson).
MCSET. Cat no: **0671683535.** Released on Simon & Schuster, '91 by Simon & Schuster Ltd. Note: 4 Cassettes.
WEB OF DREAMS (Unknown narrator(s)).
MCSET. Cat no: **0671-70003-0.** Released on Simon & Schuster, '91 by Simon & Schuster Ltd.

Annand, J.K.
AINCE FOR PLEASURE AND TWICE FOR JOY (J.K. Annand & Lavinia Derwent).
MC. Cat no: **SSC 009.** Released on Scotsoun, '91 by Scotsoun Recordings, Morley Audio Services.

Anstey, F
VICE VERSA (Michael Elder).
Note: Abridged version.
MCSET. Cat no: **1044H.** Released on Travellers Tales, '91 by Travellers Tales. Note: 4 Cassettes.
MCSET. Cat no: **SPF 020-1.** Released on Schiltron Audio Books, '91 by Schiltron Publishing. Note: 4 Cassettes. Playing time: 5 hours 47 minutes.

Antek, Chris
LIGHTHOUSE CIRCLE 1, THE (Suicide on Stage) (Chris Antek & Cast).
MC. Cat no: **75730.** Released on Cantext, '91.
MADE IN GERMANY 1 (1954, A Ship is Coming) (Chris Antek & Cast).
MC. Cat no: **75749.** Released on Cantext, '91.

Anthony, Evelyn
ALBATROSS (Carol Drinkwater).
MCSET. Cat no: **CAB 129.** Released on Chivers Audio Books, '91 by Chivers Audio Books, Green Dragon Audio Visual. Note: 6 Cassettes.
MCSET. Cat no: **1012T.** Released on Travellers Tales, '91 by Travellers Tales. Note: 6 Cassettes.
ASSASSIN, THE (Carolyn Pickles).
MCSET. Cat no: **CAB 296.** Released on Chivers Audio Books, Apr '88 by Chivers Audio Books, Green Dragon Audio Visual. Note: 6 Cassettes.

MCSET. Cat no: **1255T.** Released on Travellers Tales, '91 by Travellers Tales. Note: 6 Cassettes.
COMPANY OF SAINTS, THE (Carolyn Pickles).
MCSET. Cat no: **CAB 351.** Released on Chivers Audio Books, '91 by Chivers Audio Books, Green Dragon Audio Visual. Note: 8 Cassettes
MCSET. Cat no: **1381T.** Released on Travellers Tales, '91 by Travellers Tales. Note: 8 Cassettes.
GRAVE OF TRUTH, THE (Terrence Hardiman).
MCSET. Cat no: **CAB 610.** Released on Chivers Audio Books, '91 by Chivers Audio Books, Green Dragon Audio Visual. Note: 8 Cassettes.
HOUSE OF VANDEKAR, THE (Carolyn Pickles).
MCSET. Cat no: **CAB 393.** Released on Chivers Audio Books, '91 by Chivers Audio Books, Green Dragon Audio Visual. Note: 8 Cassettes.
MCSET. Cat no: **1455T.** Released on Travellers Tales, '91 by Travellers Tales. Note: 8 Cassettes.
MALASPIGA EXIT, THE (Carolyn Pickles).
MCSET. Cat no: **CAB 441.** Released on Chivers Audio Books, '91 by Chivers Audio Books, Green Dragon Audio Visual. Note: 8 Cassettes.
MCSET. Cat no: **1509T.** Released on Travellers Tales, '91 by Travellers Tales. Note: 8 Cassettes.
NO ENEMY BUT TIME (Carolyn Pickles).
MCSET. Cat no: **CAB 251.** Released on Chivers Audio Books, '91 by Chivers Audio Books, Green Dragon Audio Visual. Note: 8 Cassettes.
MCSET. Cat no: **1193T.** Released on Travellers Tales, '91 by Travellers Tales. Note: 8 Cassettes.
SCARLET THREAD, THE (Rula Lenska).
MCSET. Cat no: **CAB 544.** Released on Chivers Audio Books, '91 by Chivers Audio Books, Green Dragon Audio Visual. Note: 10 cassettes.
MCSET. Cat no: **1611/1612F.** Released on Soundings, '91 by Soundings Records, Bond Street Music. Note: 10 cassettes.
SILVER FALCON, THE (Carolyn Pickles).
MCSET. Cat no: **CAB 472.** Released on Chivers Audio Books, '91 by Chivers Audio Books, Green Dragon Audio Visual. Note: 8 Cassettes.
MCSET. Cat no: **1508T.** Released on Travellers Tales, '91 by Travellers Tales. Note: 8 Cassettes.
TAMARIND SEED, THE (Carolyn Pickles).
MCSET. Cat no: **CAB 216.** Released on Chivers Audio Books, '91 by Chivers Audio Books, Green Dragon Audio Visual. Note: 8 Cassettes.
MCSET. Cat no: **1158T.** Released on

Travellers Tales, '91 by Travellers Tales. Note: 8 Cassettes.
VOICES ON THE WIND (Carolyn Pickles).
MCSET. Cat no: **CAB 183.** Released on Chivers Audio Books, '91 by Chivers Audio Books, Green Dragon Audio Visual.
MCSET. Cat no: **1013T.** Released on Travellers Tales, '91 by Travellers Tales. Note: 8 Cassettes.

Archer, Jeffrey
AS THE CROW FLIES (Alec McCowen).
MCSET. Cat no: **0001046535.** Released on Harper Collins, Mar '92 by Harper Collins.
FIRST AMONG EQUALS (Tony Britton).
MCSET. Cat no: **CAB 327.** Released on Chivers Audio Books, '91. Note: 10 Cassettes.
MCSET. Cat no: **1404/1405T.** Released on Travellers Tales, '91 by Travellers Tales. Note: 10 Cassettes.
LOOPHOLE, THE (And Other Stories from 'A Twist In The Tale') (Nigel Havers).
MCSET. Cat no: **LFP 7400.** Released on Listen For Pleasure, Jul '89 by EMI Records. Note: Playing time: 2 hours 45 minutes.
MATTER OF HONOUR, A (Martin Jarvis).
MCSET. Cat no: **LFP 7280.** Released on Listen For Pleasure, Feb '87 by EMI Records. Note: Playing time: 3 hours.
MCSET. Cat no: **1208T.** Released on Travellers Tales, '91 by Travellers Tales. Note: 2 Cassettes.
MATTER OF HONOUR, A (David Rintoul).
MCSET. Cat no: **CAB 450.** Released on Chivers Audio Books, '91 by Chivers Audio Books, Green Dragon Audio Visual.
MCSET. Cat no: **1510T.** Released on Travellers Tales, '91 by Travellers Tales. Note: 8 Cassettes.
NOT A PENNY MORE, NOT A PENNY LESS (Paul Daneman).
MCSET. Cat no: **LFP 7274.** Released on Listen For Pleasure, Sep '86 by EMI Records. Note: 2 Cassettes.
MCSET. Cat no: **1144T.** Released on Travellers Tales, '91 by Travellers Tales.
NOT A PENNY MORE, NOT A PENNY LESS (Various narrators).
MCSET. Cat no: **ZBBC 1040.** Released on BBC Radio Collection, Sep '88 by BBC Records. Note: ISBN No: 0563 225645
PERFECT MURDER, A (And Other Stories From 'A Twist in the Tale') (Martin Jarvis & Rosalind Ayres).
MCSET. Cat no: **LFP 7382.** Released on Listen For Pleasure, Mar '89 by EMI Records. Note: Playing time: 3 hours.
QUIVER FULL OF ARROWS, A (Volume 1) (Martin Jarvis).

Note: 6 short stories.
MCSET. Cat no: **TTDMC 408.** Released on CSA Tell Tapes, Jun '91 by CSA Tell-Tapes. Note: 2 Cassettes. ISBN No: 1873859082.

QUIVER FULL OF ARROWS, A (Volume 2) (Martin Jarvis).
MCSET. Cat no: **TTDMC 410.** Released on CSA Tell Tapes, Sep '91 by CSA Tell-Tapes. Note: 2 Cassettes. ISBN No: 1873859104.

QUIVER FULL OF ARROWS, A (Paul Scofield).
MCSET. Cat no: **LISF 0005/0006.** Released on Listen Productions, Nov '84.

SHALL WE TELL THE PRESIDENT (E.C. Kelly).
MCSET. Cat no: **CAB 319.** Released on Chivers Audio Books, '91 by Chivers Audio Books, Green Dragon Audio Visual. Note: 6 Cassettes.

MCSET. Cat no: **1456T.** Released on Travellers Tales, '91 by Travellers Tales. Note: 6 Cassettes.

Arkle, Phyllis
RAILWAY CAT, THE (Andrew Branch).
MC. Cat no: **881980.** Released on Puffin Cover To Cover, Oct '88, Green Dragon Audio Visual.

Armitage, David
ADVENTURES OF PORTLAND BILL (Norman Rossington).
LP. Cat no: **STMP 9032.** Released on Super Tempo, Aug '84 by Warwick Records, Taylors, Solomon & Peres, Sony Music Operations.
MC. Cat no: **STMP 49032.** Released on Super Tempo, Aug '84 by Warwick Records, Taylors, Solomon & Peres, Sony Music Operations.

PORTLAND BILL (Norman Rossington).
MC. Cat no: **TTS 9816.** Released on Tempo, Aug '84 by Warwick Records, Celtic Music, Henry Hadaway Organisation.

PORTLAND BILL AND THE STORM (Norman Rossington).
MC. Cat no: **TTS 9818.** Released on Tempo, Aug '84 by Warwick Records, Celtic Music, Henry Hadaway Organisation.

PORTLAND BILL'S BUSY DAY (Norman Rossington).
MC. Cat no: **TTS 9802.** Released on Tempo, Aug '84 by Warwick Records, Celtic Music, Henry Hadaway Organisation.

PORTLAND BILL'S IMPORTANT MESSAGE (Norman Rossington).
MC. Cat no: **TTS 9817.** Released on Tempo, Aug '84 by Warwick Records, Celtic Music, Henry Hadaway Organisation.

Ashwell, Julia
FUGITIVE FROM LOVE (Elizabeth Proud).
MC. Cat no: **85 1001.** Released on Cover to Cover, Nov '86 by Cover to Cover Cassettes.

Asimov & Ballard
STORIES FROM THE SCIENCE FICTION MAGAZINE (And the Crystal World) (Clifford Norgate).
Note: Written by Isaac Asimov and J G Ballard.
MCSET. Cat no: **1023S.** Released on Travellers Tales, '91 by Travellers Tales. Note: 9 Cassettes.

Asimov, Isaac
FOUNDATION AND EMPIRE (The Mule) (Isaac Asimov).
MC. Cat no: **0001071408.** Released on Collins-Caedmon, '91 by Collins Audio, Taylors, Bond Street Music.

FOUNDATION: THE PSYCHOHISTORIANS (William Shatner).
MCSET. Cat no: **0001071424.** Released on Collins-Caedmon, '91 by Collins Audio, Taylors, Bond Street Music. Note: 2 Cassettes.

FOUNDATION TRILOGY, THE (Various artists).
MCSET. Cat no: **ZBBC 8001.** Released on BBC Radio Collection, 5 Mar '90 by BBC Records. Note: 8 Cassettes. ISBN No: 0563 410221

FOUNDATIONS EDGE (Isaac Asimov).
MC. Cat no: **1710.** Released on Caedmon (USA), Apr '83 by Caedmon Records (USA), Bond Street Music.
MC. Cat no: **0001071416.** Released on Collins-Caedmon, '91 by Collins Audio, Taylors, Bond Street Music.

MULE, THE (Unknown narrator(s)).
MC. Cat no: **CP 1661.** Released on Caedmon (USA), Oct '81 by Caedmon Records (USA), Bond Street Music.

NEMESIS (Peter MacNicol).
MCSET. Cat no: **ZBBC 1229.** Released on BBC, '91 by BBC Records, Taylors. Note: ISBN No: 0563 409991

ROBOTS OF DAWN, THE (Isaac Asimov).
MC. Cat no: **CDL 51732.** Released on Caedmon (USA), '84 by Caedmon Records (USA), Bond Street Music.

SCIENCE FICTION FAVOURITES (Isaac Asimov).
MCSET. Cat no: **1024S.** Released on Travellers Tales, '91 by Travellers Tales. Note: 6 Cassettes.

MCSET. Cat no: **CSL 013.** Released on Chivers Audio Books, '91 by Chivers Audio Books, Green Dragon Audio Visual.

Atkinson, Rowan
LIVE IN BELFAST (Rowan Atkinson).
Tracks / Man in seat 23c / Sir Marcus Browning MP / Mary Jane / I hate the French / Interval announcement / Do bears sha la la / Senator Brea / Devil, The / Impatient man in queue behind student / Joke / Wedding / Station announcement.
LP. Cat no: **SPART 1150.** Released on Arista, Aug '83 by BMG Records (UK) Ltd., Outlet Records.
MC. Cat no: **TCART 1150.** Released on Arista, Aug '83 by BMG Records (UK) Ltd., Outlet Records.

NOT JUST A PRETTY FACE (Rowan Atkinson).
Tracks / Gobble D. Gook / Tom, Dick and Harry / Vicar's point / Perkins intro / Fatal beatings / 37-0 / I believe / Indian waiter / Madonna / Awards / Zak / Fish / CND / Peace camp / Perkins outro / Cana / Nasty end, A.
Note: Originally released in November 1987.
LP. Cat no: **POLD 5217.** Released on Polydor, Jul '90 by Polydor Ltd, Solomon & Peres **Deleted** Aug '91.
MC. Cat no: **POLDC 5217.** Released on Polydor, Jul '90 by Polydor Ltd, Solomon & Peres.

VERY BEST OF ROWAN ATKINSON, THE (LIVE) (Rowan Atkinson).
MC. Cat no: **LAFFC 1.** Released on Laughing Stock, Sep '91.

Atwood, Margaret
CAT'S EYE (Unknown narrator(s)).
MCSET. Cat no: **RC 66.** Released on Random Century, '92 by Random Century Audiobooks, Conifer Records.

HANDMAID'S TALE, THE (Joanna David).
MCSET. Cat no: **CAB 518.** Released on Chivers Audio Books, '91 by Chivers Audio Books, Green Dragon Audio Visual. Note: 8 Cassettes.
MCSET. Cat no: **1598T.** Released on Travellers Tales, '91 by Travellers Tales. Note: 8 Cassettes.

HANDMAID'S TALE, THE (Julie Christie).
Note: From the 'Virago' collection.
MCSET. Cat no: **RC 21.** Released on Random Century, '91 by Random Century Audiobooks, Conifer Records. Note: 2 Cassettes. ISBN no.1856860493. Playing time 3hrs approx.

POETRY AND VOICE OF MARGARET ATWOOD (Margaret Atwood).
MC. Cat no: **CDL 51537.** Released on Caedmon (USA), Aug '79 by Caedmon Records (USA), Bond Street Music.

Aubrey, John
BRIEF LIVES (Roy Dotrice).
MCSET. Cat no: **SAY 49.** Released on Argo (Polygram), Jul '83 by PolyGram Classics **Deleted** Jan '89.
2LP. Cat no: **ZSW 522/3.** Released on Argo, Nov '74 by Decca International.
MCSET. Cat no: **1002P.** Released on Travellers Tales, '91 by Travellers Tales. Note: 2 Cassettes.

Auel, Jean
PLAINS OF PASSAGE, THE (Part 1) (Barbara Rosenblat).

MCSET. Cat no: **RB 91212**. Released on Recorded Books, Aug '92 by Isis Audio Books. Note: 15 Cassettes. Playing time: 21 1/2 hours.
PLAINS OF PASSAGE, THE (Part 2) (Barbara Rosenblat).
MCSET. Cat no: **RB 91213**. Released on Recorded Books, Aug '92 by Isis Audio Books. Note: 11 Cassettes. Playing time: 15 hours, 30 mins.

Austen, Jane

EMMA (Jane Laportaire).
MCSET. Cat no: **CTC 014**. Released on Cover to Cover, Jun '85 by Cover to Cover Cassettes.
MCSET. Cat no: **1001/1002C**. Released on Travellers Tales, '91 by Travellers Tales. Note: 12 Cassettes.
EMMA (Prunella Scales).
Note: Abridged version.
MCSET. Cat no: **1055C**. Released on Travellers Tales, '91 by Travellers Tales. Note: 2 Cassettes.
EMMA (Prunella Scales).
MCSET. Cat no: **CTC 056**. Released on Cover to Cover, '91 by Cover to Cover Cassettes. Note: 11 Cassettes. 14 hrs 30 mins.
MCSET. Cat no: **ARGO 1109**. Released on Argo (EMI), '91 by EMI Records.
LOVE AND FRIENDSHIP (Norma West).
MCSET. Cat no: **OAS 20292**. Released on Oasis Audio Books, Feb '92 by Isis Audio Books. Note: 4 Cassettes. Playing time: 4 hrs
MANSFIELD PARK (Maureen O'Brien).
MCSET. Cat no: **CTC 036**. Released on Cover to Cover, '87 by Cover to Cover Cassettes. Note: 12 Cassettes. Playing time:16hrs 25 mins.
MCSET. Cat no: **1053/1054C**. Released on Travellers Tales, '91 by Travellers Tales. Note: 12 Cassettes.
NORTHANGER ABBEY (Anna Massey).
MCSET. Cat no: **CTC 055**. Released on Cover to Cover, '91 by Cover to Cover Cassettes. Note: 6 Cassettes. Playing time:8 hrs.
PERSUASION (Anna Massey).
MCSET. Cat no: **CTC 022**. Released on Cover to Cover, '87 by Cover to Cover Cassettes. Note: 6 Cassettes. Playing time:8 hrs.
MCSET. Cat no: **1003C**. Released on Travellers Tales, '91 by Travellers Tales. Note: 6 Cassettes.
PERSUASION (Prunella Scales).
MCSET. Cat no: **ARGO 1178**. Released on Argo (EMI), Oct '89 by EMI Records. Note: 2 Cassettes. Playing time: 2 hours 30 minutes.
PRIDE AND PREJUDICE (Irene Sutcliffe).
MCSET. Cat no: **CTC 001**. Released on Cover to Cover, '87 by Cover to Cover Cassettes. Note: 10 Cassettes. Playing time:11 hrs 30 mins.
MCSET. Cat no: **1004/1005C**. Released on Travellers Tales, '91 by Travellers Tales. Note: 10 Cassettes
PRIDE AND PREJUDICE (Celia Johnson).
MCSET. Cat no: **LFP 7224**. Released on Listen For Pleasure, Oct '85 by EMI Records.
PRIDE AND PREJUDICE (Claire Bloom).
MC. Cat no: **1595**. Released on Caedmon (USA), by Caedmon Records (USA), Bond Street Music.
PRIDE AND PREJUDICE (Anna Massey).
MCSET. Cat no: **1870521300**. Released on Eloquent Reels, '91, Bond Street Music, Morley Audio Services.
PRIDE AND PREJUDICE (Celia Johnson).
Note: Abridged version.
MCSET. Cat no: **1056C**. Released on Travellers Tales, '91 by Travellers Tales. Note: 2 Cassettes.
SENSE AND SENSIBILITY (Claire Bloom).
MC. Cat no: **1627**. Released on Caedmon (USA), '88 by Caedmon Records (USA), Bond Street Music.
SENSE AND SENSIBILITY (Sarah Badel).
MCSET. Cat no: **CTC 033**. Released on Cover to Cover, '87 by Cover to Cover Cassettes. Note: 9 Cassettes. Playing time:10 hrs 30 mins.
MCSET. Cat no: **1006/1007C**. Released on Travellers Tales, '91 by Travellers Tales. Note: 9 Cassettes.
WOMAN'S HOUR, THE (Various narrators).
Note: Read by Juliet Stevenson, Janet Suzman, Penelope Keith, Patricia Hodge, Maria Aitken and Annette Crosbie.
MCSET. Cat no: **ZBBC 1207**. Released on BBC Radio Collection, Sep '91 by BBC Records. Note: 9 Double Cassettes. ISBN No: 0563 409827

Averill, Esther

JENNY AND THE CAT CLUB (And Jenny's First Party) (Tammy Grimes).
MC. Cat no: **1577**. Released on Caedmon (USA), '88 by Caedmon Records (USA), Bond Street Music.
WHEN JENNY LOST HER SCARF (And Jenny's Adopted Brother) (Tammy Grimes).
MC. Cat no: **CDL 51608**. Released on Caedmon (USA), by Caedmon Records (USA), Bond Street Music.

Awdry, Rev. W.

EDWARD, GORDON AND HENRY (Up to Age 8) (Unknown narrator(s)).
Note: Book and cassette.
MC. Cat no: **PLBE 159**. Released on Tell-A-Tale, '88 by Pickwick Records, Taylors, Clyde Factors.
FURTHER RAILWAY STORIES (Willie Rushton).
Note: Stories include: Main Line Engines, Small Railway Engines, Enterprising Engines, Oliver the Western Engine, Duke the Lost Engine and Tramway Engines.
MCSET. Cat no: **SAY 100**. Released on Argo (Polygram), Jun '84 by PolyGram Classics **Deleted** Jan '89.
MORE RAILWAY STORIES (1) (Willie Rushton).
Note: Stories include: The Twin Engine, Branch Line Engines, Gallant Old Engine, Stepney, Mountain Engines and Very Old Engines.
MCSET. Cat no: **SAY 75**. Released on Argo (Polygram), Nov '83 by PolyGram Classics **Deleted** Jan '89.
MCSET. Cat no: **ARGO 1151**. Released on Argo (EMI), Oct '89 by EMI Records. Note: 2 Cassettes. Playing time: 2 hours.
MORE RAILWAY STORIES (2) (Johnny Morris).
Note: Includes stories: Troublesome Engines, Henry the Green Engine, Toby the Tram Engine and Gordon the Big Engine.
MCSET. Cat no: **SAY 90**. Released on Argo (Polygram), Nov '83 by PolyGram Classics **Deleted** Jan '89.
PERCY AND HAROLD (Up to Age 8) (Unknown narrator(s)).
Note: Book and cassette.
MC. Cat no: **PLBE 223**. Released on Tell-A-Tale, '88 by Pickwick Records, Taylors, Clyde Factors.
PERCY RUNS AWAY (Up to Age 8) (Unknown narrator(s)).
Note: Book and cassette.
MC. Cat no: **PLBE 156**. Released on Tell-A-Tale, '88 by Pickwick Records, Taylors, Clyde Factors.
PERCY'S PREDICAMENT (Up to Age 8) (Unknown narrator(s)).
Note: Book and cassette.
MC. Cat no: **PLBE 230**. Released on Tell-A-Tale, '88 by Pickwick Records, Taylors, Clyde Factors.
POP GOES THE DIESEL (Up to Age 8) (Unknown narrator(s)).
Note: Book and cassette.
MC. Cat no: **PLBE 228**. Released on Tell-A-Tale, '88 by Pickwick Records, Taylors, Clyde Factors.
RAILWAY STORIES (Featuring Thomas the Tank Engine) (Johnny Morris).
MC. Cat no: **0600560872**. Released on Hamlyn Books On Tape, '88, Bond Street Music.
RAILWAY STORIES (Willie Rushton).
Note: Stories include: Duck the Diesel Engine and Little Old Engine.
LP. Cat no: **SPA 559**. Released on Decca, Sep '79 by PolyGram Classics, Thames Distributors Ltd. **Deleted** '84.
RAILWAY STORIES (Willie Rushton).
Note: Stories include: Edward the Blue

Engine and Four Little Engine.
LP. Cat no: **SPA 560**. Released on Decca, Sep '79 by PolyGram Classics, Thames Distributors Ltd. **Deleted** '84.

RAILWAY STORIES (Willie Rushton).
Note: Stories include: Percy the Small Engine and Eight Famous Engines.
LP. Cat no: **SPA 561**. Released on Decca, Sep '79 by PolyGram Classics, Thames Distributors Ltd. **Deleted** '84.

RAILWAY STORIES (Volume 3) (Johnny Morris).
MCSET. Cat no: **ARGO 1235**. Released on Argo (EMI), Oct '90 by EMI Records. Note: 2 Cassettes.

RAILWAY STORIES (1) (Willie Rushton).
MCSET. Cat no: **SAY 29**. Released on Argo (Polygram), Jul '82 by PolyGram Classics **Deleted** Jan '89.
MCSET. Cat no: **ARGO 1058**. Released on Argo (EMI), May '89 by EMI Records. Note: 2 Cassettes.

RAILWAY STORIES (2) (Johnny Morris).
MCSET. Cat no: **SAY 87**. Released on Argo (Polygram), Jun '88 by PolyGram Classics **Deleted** Jan '89.

THOMAS AND BERTIE (Up to Age 8) (Unknown narrator(s)).
Note: Book and cassette.
MC. Cat no: **PLBE 155**. Released on Tell-A-Tale, '88 by Pickwick Records, Taylors, Clyde Factors.

THOMAS AND TERENCE (Up to Age 8) (Unknown narrator(s)).
Note: Book and cassette.
MC. Cat no: **PLBE 158**. Released on Tell-A-Tale, '88 by Pickwick Records, Taylors, Clyde Factors.

THOMAS AND THE MISSING CHRISTMAS TREE (Up to Age 8) (Unknown narrator(s)).
Note: Book and cassette.
MC. Cat no: **PLBE 234**. Released on Tell-A-Tale, '88 by Pickwick Records, Taylors, Clyde Factors.

THOMAS AND TREVOR (Up to Age 8) (Unknown narrator(s)).
Note: Book and cassette.
MC. Cat no: **PLBE 190**. Released on Tell-A-Tale, '88 by Pickwick Records, Taylors, Clyde Factors.

THOMAS COMES TO BREAKFAST (Up to Age 8) (Unknown narrator(s)).
Note: Book and cassette.
MC. Cat no: **PLBE 229**. Released on Tell-A-Tale, '88 by Pickwick Records, Taylors, Clyde Factors.

THOMAS GOES FISHING (Up to Age 8) (Unknown narrator(s)).
Note: Book and cassette.
MC. Cat no: **PLBE 157**. Released on Tell-A-Tale, '88 by Pickwick Records, Taylors, Clyde Factors.

THOMAS, PERCY AND THE COAL (Up to Age 8) (Unknown narrator(s)).
Note: Book and cassette.

MC. Cat no: **PLBE 189**. Released on Tell-A-Tale, '88 by Pickwick Records, Taylors, Clyde Factors.

THOMAS'S CHRISTMAS PARTY (Up to Age 8) (Unknown narrator(s)).
Note: Book and cassette.
MC. Cat no: **PLBE 198**. Released on Tell-A-Tale, '88 by Pickwick Records, Taylors, Clyde Factors.

TOBY AND THE STOUT GENTLEMAN (Up to Age 8) (Unknown narrator(s)).
Note: Book and cassette.
MC. Cat no: **PLBE 160**. Released on Tell-A-Tale, '88 by Pickwick Records, Taylors, Clyde Factors.

Ayckbourn, Alan

DOUBLE BILL (Michael Aldridge & Nicky Henson).
Note: Includes Relatively Speaking and Season's Greetings.
MCSET. Cat no: **ZBBC 1043**. Released on BBC Radio Collection, Sep '88 by BBC Records. Note: ISBN No: 0563 225688

Ayres, Pam

PIGGO.
MCSET. Cat no: **ZBBC 1203**. Released on BBC Audio Collection, '91 by BBC Records. Note: ISBN No: 0563 409096

SOME MORE OF ME POEMS AND SONGS.
LP. Cat no: **GAL 6010**. Released on Galaxy (1), Oct '76 by President Records.
MC. Cat no: **GALC 6010**. Released on Galaxy (1), Oct '76 by President Records.

SOME OF ME POEMS AND SONGS.
Tracks / Battery hen / Oh I wish I looked after my teeth / Minnie Dyer / In fear of the butcher / Like you would / Hegg / Time / Embarrassing experience with the parrot / Don't sell our Edgar no more violins / Not you Basil / In defence of hedgehogs / Stuffed horse / Bike / I'm a starling, me darling / Fling another chair leg on the fire mother / Father dear father / Goodwill to men, give us your money / Oh no, I got a cold.
LP. Cat no: **MFP 50461**. Released on MFP, Jan '80 by EMI Records, Solomon & Peres **Deleted** '85.
MC. Cat no: **TCMFP 50461**. Released on MFP, Jan '80 by EMI Records, Solomon & Peres **Deleted** '85.
LP. Cat no: **GAL 6003**. Released on Galaxy (1), Mar '76 by President Records **Deleted** '80.

Ayres, Ruby M.

MAN IN HER LIFE, THE (Jane Ballard).
MCSET. Cat no: **SOUND 37**. Released on Soundings, Feb '85 by Soundings Records, Bond Street Music.

RETURN JOURNEY (Rosemary Davis).
MCSET. Cat no: **OAS 21091**. Released on Oasis Audio Books, Oct '91 by Isis Audio Books. Note: 8 cassettes. Playing time 8hrs 15mins.

Babson, Marian

DEATH IN FASHION (Rosemary Leach).
MCSET. Cat no: **1014T**. Released on Travellers Tales, '91 by Travellers Tales. Note: 4 Cassettes.

REEL MURDER (Rosemary Leach).
MCSET. Cat no: **CAT 4025**. Released on Chivers Audio Thrillers, Apr '88 by Chivers Audio Books, Green Dragon Audio Visual. Note: 4 Cassettes.
MCSET. Cat no: **1247T**. Released on Travellers Tales, '91 by Travellers Tales. Note: 4 Cassettes.

UNFAIR EXCHANGE (Carole Boyd).
MCSET. Cat no: **CAT 4055**. Released on Chivers Audio Books, '91 by Chivers Audio Books, Green Dragon Audio Visual. Note: 4 Cassettes.
MCSET. Cat no: **1599T**. Released on Travellers Tales, '91 by Travellers Tales. Note: 4 Cassettes.

Bach, Othello

WHOEVER HEARD OF A FIRD? (Joel Gray).
MC. Cat no: **1735**. Released on Caedmon (USA), '84 by Caedmon Records (USA), Bond Street Music.

Bach, Richard

ILLUSIONS (Adventures of a Reluctant Messiah) (Richard Bach).
MC. Cat no: **1585**. Released on Caedmon (USA), '88 by Caedmon Records (USA), Bond Street Music.

JONATHAN LIVINGSTONE SEAGULL (Unknown narrator(s)).
MC. Cat no: **CDL 51639**. Released on Caedmon (USA), May '82 by Caedmon Records (USA), Bond Street Music **Deleted** '87.

Bagley, Desmond

BAHAMA CRISIS (Brian Greene).
MCSET. Cat no: **CAB 362**. Released on Chivers Audio Books, '91 by Chivers Audio Books, Green Dragon Audio Visual. Note: 8 Cassettes.
MCSET. Cat no: **1392T**. Released on Travellers Tales, '91 by Travellers Tales. Note: 8 Cassettes.

ENEMY, THE (Nigel Davenport).
MCSET. Cat no: **CAB 592**. Released on Chivers Audio Books, '91 by Chivers Audio Books, Green Dragon Audio Visual. Note: 8 Cassettes.
MCSET. Cat no: **1752T**. Released on Travellers Tales, '91 by Travellers Tales. Note: 8 Cassettes.

FLYAWAY (Keith Barron).
MCSET. Cat no: **ZC SWD 361**. Released on ASV (Academy Sound & Vi-

sion), Oct '89 by Academy Sound & Vision Records. Note: 2 Cassettes. Playing time: 2 hours 45 minutes.

FLYAWAY (Unknown narrator(s)).
MCSET. Cat no: **1854964879**. Released on Soundings, '91 by Soundings Records, Bond Street Music. Note: 7 Cassettes.

FREEDOM TRAP, THE (Nigel Davenport).
MCSET. Cat no: **CAB 652**. Released on Chivers Audio Books, Jan '92 by Chivers Audio Books, Green Dragon Audio Visual. Note: 8 Cassettes.

GOLDEN KEEL, THE (Nigel Davenport).
MCSET. Cat no: **CAB 272**. Released on Chivers Audio Books, '91 by Chivers Audio Books, Green Dragon Audio Visual. Note: 8 Cassettes.

MCSET. Cat no: **1216T**. Released on Travellers Tales, '91 by Travellers Tales. Note: 8 Cassettes.

HIGH CITADEL (Nigel Davenport).
MCSET. Cat no: **CAB 394**. Released on Chivers Audio Books, '91 by Chivers Audio Books, Green Dragon Audio Visual. Note: 8 Cassettes.

MCSET. Cat no: **1501T**. Released on Travellers Tales, '91 by Travellers Tales. Note: 8 Cassettes.

JUGGERNAUT (Peter Marinker).
MC. Cat no: **0600560503**. Released on Hamlyn Books On Tape, '88, Bond Street Music.

JUGGERNAUT (Unknown narrator(s)).
MCSET. Cat no: **1854960237**. Released on Soundings, '91 by Soundings Records, Bond Street Music. Note: 8 Cassettes.

JUGGERNAUT (Peter Wheeler).
MCSET. Cat no: **1380T**. Released on Travellers Tales, '91 by Travellers Tales. Note: 6 Cassettes.

LANDSLIDE (Nigel Davenport).
MCSET. Cat no: **CAB 473**. Released on Chivers Audio Books, '91 by Chivers Audio Books, Green Dragon Audio Visual. Note: 8 Cassettes.

MCSET. Cat no: **1511T**. Released on Travellers Tales, '91 by Travellers Tales. Note: 8 Cassettes.

NIGHT OF ERROR (Nigel Davenport).
MCSET. Cat no: **CAB 451**. Released on Chivers Audio Books, '91 by Chivers Audio Books, Green Dragon Audio Visual. Note: 8 Cassettes.

MCSET. Cat no: **1512T**. Released on Travellers Tales, '91 by Travellers Tales. Note: 8 Cassettes.

RUNNING BLIND (Martin Jarvis).
MCSET. Cat no: **1187T**. Released on Travellers Tales, '91 by Travellers Tales. Note: 2 Cassettes.

MCSET. Cat no: **LFP 7292**. Released on Listen For Pleasure, '91 by EMI Records.

RUNNING BLIND (Peter Joyce).
MCSET. Cat no: **1649T**. Released on Travellers Tales, '91 by Travellers Tales. Note: 6 Cassettes.

MCSET. Cat no: **1854963562**. Released on Soundings, '91 by Soundings Records, Bond Street Music. Note: 6 Cassettes.

SNOW TIGER, THE (Nigel Davenport).
MCSET. Cat no: **CAB 302**. Released on Chivers Audio Books, Apr '88 by Chivers Audio Books, Green Dragon Audio Visual. Note: 8 Cassettes

MCSET. Cat no: **1256T**. Released on Travellers Tales, '91 by Travellers Tales. Note: 8 Cassettes.

TIGHTROPE MEN, THE (Tim Pigott-Smith).
MCSET. Cat no: **1015T**. Released on Travellers Tales, '91 by Travellers Tales. Note: 8 Cassettes.

VIVERO LETTER, THE (Nigel Davenport).
MCSET. Cat no: **CAB 222**. Released on Chivers Audio Books, '91 by Chivers Audio Books, Green Dragon Audio Visual. Note: 8 Cassettes.

MCSET. Cat no: **1159T**. Released on Travellers Tales, '91 by Travellers Tales. Note: 8 Cassettes.

WYATT'S HURRICANE (Nigel Davenport).
MCSET. Cat no: **CAB 509**. Released on Chivers Audio Books, '91 by Chivers Audio Books, Green Dragon Audio Visual. Note: 8 Cassettes.

MCSET. Cat no: **1600T**. Released on Travellers Tales, '91 by Travellers Tales. Note: 8 Cassettes.

Bailey, Don

NO ADMITTANCE, NO EXIT (And The Willoughby Obession) (Various narrators).
Note: Authors are Don Bailey and Milo Ringham.
MC. Cat no: **NF 8**. Released on Nightfall Tapes, '89 by BMG Records (UK) Ltd..

Bainbridge, Beryl

WATSON'S APOLOGY (Terrence Hardiman).
MCSET. Cat no: **CAB 175**. Released on Chivers Audio Books, '91 by Chivers Audio Books, Green Dragon Audio Visual. Note: 8 Cassettes.

MCSET. Cat no: **1016T**. Released on Travellers Tales, '91 by Travellers Tales. Note: 8 Cassettes.

Ballantyne, R.M.

CORAL ISLAND (Martin Heller).
MCSET. Cat no: **COL 3001**. Released on Colophone, Sep '81 by AVLS (Audio-Visual Library Services).

DOG CRUSOE, THE (Arthur Boland & Martin Heller).
Note: Abridged.
MCSET. Cat no: **COL 3007**. Released on Colophone, Nov '81 by AVLS

(Audio-Visual Library Services).
MCSET. Cat no: **9010F**. Released on Travellers Tales, '91 by Travellers Tales. Note: 2 Cassettes.

Ballard, J.G.

CRYSTAL WORLD, THE (Clifford Norgate).
MCSET. Cat no: **CAB 260**. Released on Chivers Audio Books, '91 by Chivers Audio Books, Green Dragon Audio Visual.

DROWNED WORLD, THE (Clifford Norgate).
MCSET. Cat no: **1190F**. Released on Travellers Tales, '91 by Travellers Tales. Note: 6 Cassettes.

MCSET. Cat no: **CAB 194**. Released on Chivers Audio Books, '91 by Chivers Audio Books, Green Dragon Audio Visual.

EMPIRE OF THE SUN (Peter Egan).
MCSET. Cat no: **CAB 152**. Released on Chivers Audio Books, '91 by Chivers Audio Books, Green Dragon Audio Visual. Note: 8 Cassettes.

MCSET. Cat no: **1006F**. Released on Travellers Tales, '91 by Travellers Tales. Note: 8 Cassettes.

EMPIRE OF THE SUN (Unknown narrator(s)).
MCSET. Cat no: **0671652389**. Released on Simon & Schuster, '91 by Simon & Schuster Ltd.

EMPIRE OF THE SUN (Jeremy Irons).
MCSET. Cat no: **0600558703**. Released on Hamlyn Books On Tape, Apr '88, Bond Street Music. Note: 2 Cassettes

KINDNESS OF WOMEN, THE (Joss Ackland).
MCSET. Cat no: **HCA 84**. Released on Harper Collins, Oct '91 by Harper Collins.

Bannerman, Helen

STORY OF THE LITTLE BLACK SAMBO (And Others) (Unknown narrator(s)).
Tracks / Story of little black Quibba, The / Story of little black Quasha, The / Story of Sambo and the twins, The / Story of little black Bobtail, The / Story of little black Mingo, The.
MC. Cat no: **TS 322**. Released on Tellastory, Dec '86 by Random Century Audiobooks.

Barber, Noel

DAUGHTERS OF THE PRINCE (David Rintoul).
MCSET. Cat no: **CAB 491**. Released on Chivers Audio Books, '91 by Chivers Audio Books, Green Dragon Audio Visual. Note: 12 Cassettes.

MCSET. Cat no: **1508/1509F**. Released on Travellers Tales, '91 by Travellers Tales. Note: 12 Cassettes.

WEEPING AND THE LAUGHTER, THE (David Rintoul).

MCSET. Cat no: **CAB 426**. Released on Chivers Audio Books, '91 by Chivers Audio Books, Green Dragon Audio Visual. Note: 12 cassettes.
MCSET. Cat no: **1442/1443F**. Released on Travellers Tales, '91 by Travellers Tales. Note: 12 cassettes.

Barbour, John
COMMENTARY AND CHOICE (Thomas Crawford & Derrick McClure).
MC. Cat no: **SSC 041**. Released on Scotsoun, '91 by Scotsoun Recordings, Morley Audio Services.

Barker, Clive
BODY POLITIC, THE (Bob Peck).
MCSET. Cat no: **0600558568**. Released on Hamlyn Books On Tape, Apr '88, Bond Street Music. Note: 2 Cassettes.

IMAJICA (Peter MacNicol).
MCSET. Cat no: **HCA 83**. Released on Harper Collins, Dec '91 by Harper Collins.

Barker, Les
DOGMATIC (Les Barker).
LP. Cat no: **AVA 111**. Released on Avada, Nov '80, Celtic Music **Deleted** Nov '85.

Barklem, Jill
BRAMBLY HEDGE (John Baddeley & Susan Sheridan).
Note: Also available on hanging format, Cat No: 0411380877
MC. Cat no: **0411400428**. Released on Harper Collins, '91 by Harper Collins.

SECRET STAIRCASE, THE (And The High Hills) (Unknown narrator(s)).
MC. Cat no: **00 104 1282**. Released on Tempo, Apr '88 by Warwick Records, Celtic Music, Henry Hadaway Organisation.

Barley, Nigel
INNOCENT ANTHROPOLOGIST, THE (Notes from a Mud Hut) (Nigel Barley).
MCSET. Cat no: **CAB 659**. Released on Chivers Audio Books, Jan '92 by Chivers Audio Books, Green Dragon Audio Visual. Note: 6 Cassettes.

Barnard, Robert
AT DEATH'S DOOR (Richard Mitchley).
MCSET. Cat no: **CAT 4067**. Released on Chivers Audio Books, '91 by Chivers Audio Books, Green Dragon Audio Visual. Note: 6 Cassettes.

BODIES (Richard Mitchley).
MCSET. Cat no: **CAT 4026**. Released on Chivers Audio Thrillers, Apr '88 by Chivers Audio Books, Green Dragon Audio Visual. Note: 6 Cassettes.

MCSET. Cat no: **1248T**. Released on Travellers Tales, '91 by Travellers Tales. Note: 4 Cassettes.

CITY OF STRANGERS, A (Keith Barron).
MCSET. Cat no: **CAB 670**. Released on Chivers Audio Books, Jan '92 by Chivers Audio Books, Green Dragon Audio Visual. Note: 6 Cassettes.

POLITICAL SUICIDE (Richard Mitchley).
MCSET. Cat no: **1160T**. Released on Travellers Tales, '91 by Travellers Tales. Note: 4 Cassettes.

Barnes, Julian
FLAUBERT'S PARROT (Crawford Logan).
MCSET. Cat no: **OAS 89066**. Released on Oasis Audio Books, '91 by Isis Audio Books. Note: 6 cassettes.
MCSET. Cat no: **1384F**. Released on Travellers Tales, '91 by Travellers Tales. Note: 6 Cassettes.

FLAUBERT'S PARROT (Julian Barnes).
MCSET. Cat no: **RC 63**. Released on Random Century, Jul '92 by Random Century Audiobooks, Conifer Records. Note: ISBN no. 1856860396

HISTORY OF THE WORLD IN TEN AND A HALF CHAPTERS, A (Unknown narrator(s)).
MCSET. Cat no: **RC 62**. Released on Random Century, Jul '92 by Random Century Audiobooks, Conifer Records. Note: ISBN no. 1856860388

HISTORY OF THE WORLD IN TEN AND HALF CHAPTERS (Tony Robinson).
MCSET. Cat no: **1448F**. Released on Travellers Tales, '91 by Travellers Tales. Note: 8 Cassettes.
MCSET. Cat no: **IAB 90052**. Released on Isis Audio Books, '91. Note: 8 Cassettes.

TALKING IT OVER (Various narrators).
Note: Narrators are Jonathan Coy, William Gaminara and Suzanna Hamilton.
MCSET. Cat no: **RC 9**. Released on Random Century, '91 by Random Century Audiobooks, Conifer Records. Note: 2 cassettes. ISBN 1856860094. 3 hrs approx.

Barnes, William
BLACKMORE BY THE STOUR (Poems of William Barnes) (Various narrators).
MC. Cat no: **FTC 6020**. Released on Forest Tracks, '88.

LYDLINCH BELLS (Poems of William Barnes) (Various narrators).
MC. Cat no: **FTC 6021**. Released on Forest Tracks, '88.

Baroness Orczy
SCARLET PIMPERNEL, THE (Robert Powell).
MC. Cat no: **LFP 7469**. Released on Listen For Pleasure, Oct '90 by EMI Records.

Barras, Leonard
TAPIOCA BY MOONLIGHT (Leonard Barras).
MC. Cat no: **7197**. Released on Bridge Studios, '91 by Bridge Studios.

Barrie, J.M.
PETER PAN (Roy Dotrice & Family).
MCSET. Cat no: **MCFR 108/9**. Released on Conifer, Dec '85 by Conifer Records, Jazz Music. Note: 2 cassettes.

PETER PAN (Lyn Redgrave).
MC. Cat no: **1856560996**. Released on Random Century, '91 by Random Century Audiobooks, Conifer Records. Note: Playing time: 60 Minutes.

PETER PAN (Children's Classics) (Unknown narrator(s)).
Note: Book and cassette.
MC. Cat no: **PLBC 138**. Released on Tell-A-Tale, Oct '84 by Pickwick Records, Taylors, Clyde Factors.

PETER PAN (Unknown narrator(s)).
MC. Cat no: **0 00 109030 5**. Released on Tempo, '88 by Warwick Records, Celtic Music, Henry Hadaway Organisation.

PETER PAN (Wendy Craig).
MCSET. Cat no: **LFP 7086**. Released on Listen For Pleasure, Jan '84 by EMI Records.
MCSET. Cat no: **9011F**. Released on Travellers Tales, '91 by Travellers Tales. Note: 2 Cassettes.

PETER PAN (Carnival Classics) (George Layton).
MC. Cat no: **0001010816**. Released on Harper Collins, Dec '91 by Harper Collins.

STORY OF PETER PAN (Glynis Johns).
MC. Cat no: **1395**. Released on Caedmon (USA), '88 by Caedmon Records (USA), Bond Street Music.

WINDOW IN THRUMS, A (Sheila Donald & Michael Elder).
MCSET. Cat no: **SPF 055-1**. Released on Schiltron Audio Books, '91 by Schiltron Publishing. Note: 4 Cassettes. Playing time 3 hours 30 minutes.
MCSET. Cat no: **1370F**. Released on Travellers Tales, '91 by Travellers Tales. Note: 4 Cassettes.

Barstow, Stan
B MOVIE (Christine Rodska).
MCSET. Cat no: **1151F**. Released on Travellers Tales, '91 by Travellers Tales. Note: 4 cassettes.
MCSET. Cat no: **CAB 246**. Released on Chivers Audio Books, '91 by Chivers Audio Books, Green Dragon Audio Visual.

JUST YOU WAIT AND SEE (Unknown narrator(s)).
MCSET. Cat no: **1854960245**. Released on Bramhope, '91 by Ulverscroft Soundings. Note: 4 Cassettes.

KIND OF LOVING, A (Stephen Thorne).
MCSET. Cat no: **OAS 11291**. Released on Oasis Audio Books, '91 by

Isis Audio Books. Note: 8 Cassettes. Playing time 9 hours 30 minutes.

Basker, Joe
COMANCHE GOLD (Unknown narrator(s)).
MCSET. Cat no: **1854964259**. Released on Trio, '91 by EMI Records. Note: 3 Cassettes.

Bates, Blaster
1001 GELIGNITES (Volume 2) (Blaster Bates).
LP. Cat no: **BB 00 03**. Released on Big Ben, Nov '80 by Tangent Records, Roots Records, Swift, Celtic Music, Spartan, Topic Records, Duncans, Projection.
MC. Cat no: **BBMC 00 03**. Released on Big Ben, Nov '80 by Tangent Records, Roots Records, Swift, Celtic Music, Spartan, Topic Records, Duncans, Projection.

BLASTERMIND (Volume 7) (Blaster Bates).
LP. Cat no: **BB 00 13**. Released on Big Ben, Nov '80 by Tangent Records, Roots Records, Swift, Celtic Music, Spartan, Topic Records, Duncans, Projection.
MC. Cat no: **BBMC 00 13**. Released on Big Ben, Nov '80 by Tangent Records, Roots Records, Swift, Celtic Music, Spartan, Topic Records, Duncans, Projection.

GELLYBABE (Volume 6) (Blaster Bates).
LP. Cat no: **BB 00 11**. Released on Big Ben, Nov '80 by Tangent Records, Roots Records, Swift, Celtic Music, Spartan, Topic Records, Duncans, Projection.
MC. Cat no: **BBMC 00 11**. Released on Big Ben, Nov '80 by Tangent Records, Roots Records, Swift, Celtic Music, Spartan, Topic Records, Duncans, Projection.

HUNTING AND SHOOTING STORIES (Volume 8) (Blaster Bates).
LP. Cat no: **BB 00 15**. Released on Big Ben, Nov '84 by Tangent Records, Roots Records, Swift, Celtic Music, Spartan, Topic Records, Duncans, Projection.
MC. Cat no: **BBMC 00 15**. Released on Big Ben, Nov '84 by Tangent Records, Roots Records, Swift, Celtic Music, Spartan, Topic Records, Duncans, Projection.

LAUGHTER WITH A BANG (Volume 1) (Blaster Bates).
LP. Cat no: **BB 00 01**. Released on Big Ben, Nov '80 by Tangent Records, Roots Records, Swift, Celtic Music, Spartan, Topic Records, Duncans, Projection.
MC. Cat no: **BBMC 00 01**. Released on Big Ben, Nov '80 by Tangent Records, Roots Records, Swift, Celtic Music, Spartan, Topic Records, Duncans, Projection.
CD. Cat no: **BBCD 00 01**. Released on Big Ben, '91 by Tangent Records, Roots Records, Swift, Celtic Music, Spartan, Topic Records, Duncans, Projection.

LIFT OFF (Volume 5) (Blaster Bates).
LP. Cat no: **BB 00 09**. Released on Big Ben, Nov '80 by Tangent Records, Roots Records, Swift, Celtic Music, Spartan, Topic Records, Duncans, Projection.
MC. Cat no: **BBMC 00 09**. Released on Big Ben, Nov '80 by Tangent Records, Roots Records, Swift, Celtic Music, Spartan, Topic Records, Duncans, Projection.

TNT FOR TWO (Volume 3) (Blaster Bates).
LP. Cat no: **BB 00 05**. Released on Big Ben, Oct '80 by Tangent Records, Roots Records, Swift, Celtic Music, Spartan, Topic Records, Duncans, Projection.
MC. Cat no: **BBMC 00 05**. Released on Big Ben, Oct '80 by Tangent Records, Roots Records, Swift, Celtic Music, Spartan, Topic Records, Duncans, Projection.

WATCH OUT FOR THE BITS (Volume 4) (Blaster Bates).
LP. Cat no: **BB 00 07**. Released on Big Ben, Nov '80 by Tangent Records, Roots Records, Swift, Celtic Music, Spartan, Topic Records, Duncans, Projection.
MC. Cat no: **BBMC 00 07**. Released on Big Ben, Nov '80 by Tangent Records, Roots Records, Swift, Celtic Music, Spartan, Topic Records, Duncans, Projection.

Bates, H.E.
DARLING BUDS OF MAY, THE (Bruce Montague).
MCSET. Cat no: **1027H**. Released on Travellers Tales, '91 by Travellers Tales. Note: 4 Cassettes.
MCSET. Cat no: **CAB 178**. Released on Chivers Audio Books, Dec '91 by Chivers Audio Books, Green Dragon Audio Visual. Note: 4 Cassettes.

FAIR STOOD THE WIND FOR FRANCE (Nigel Havers).
MCSET. Cat no: **CAB 211**. Released on Chivers Audio Books, '91 by Chivers Audio Books, Green Dragon Audio Visual. Note: 8 Cassettes.
MCSET. Cat no: **1188F**. Released on Travellers Tales, '91 by Travellers Tales.

HOUSE OF WOMEN, A (Unknown narrator(s)).
MCSET. Cat no: **1854964992**. Released on Soundings, '91 by Soundings Records, Bond Street Music. Note: 7 Cassettes.

LIGHTHOUSE, THE (And The Kimono) (Martin Jarvis).
MC. Cat no: **PTB 614**. Released on Pickwick Talking Books, '83 by Pickwick Records, Clyde Factors.

LOVE FOR LYDIA (Christopher Kay).
MCSET. Cat no: **1157/1158R**. Released on Travellers Tales, '91 by Travellers Tales. Note: 9 Cassettes.
MCSET. Cat no: **1854963570**. Released on Soundings, '91 by Soundings Records, Bond Street Music. Note: 9 Cassettes.

MOMENT IN TIME, A (Cheryl Campbell).
MCSET. Cat no: **CAB 562**. Released on Chivers Audio Books, '91 by Chivers Audio Books, Green Dragon Audio Visual. Note: 6 Cassettes.
MCSET. Cat no: **1653F**. Released on Travellers Tales, '91 by Travellers Tales. Note: 6 Cassettes.

MY UNCLE SILAS (David Neal). Note: 12 Short Stories.
MCSET. Cat no: **ZBBC 1243**. Released on BBC Radio Collection, Aug '91 by BBC Records. Note: ISBN No: 0563 365161

PURPLE PLAIN, THE (Brian Deacon).
MCSET. Cat no: **CAB 631**. Released on Chivers Audio Books, Oct '91 by Chivers Audio Books, Green Dragon Audio Visual.

SPELLA-HO. (Unknown narrators)
MCSET. Cat no: **1683/1684F**. Released on Travellers Tales, '91 by Travellers Tales. Note: 9 Cassettes.
MCSET. Cat no: **1854964186**. Released on Soundings, '91 by Soundings Records, Bond Street Music. Note: 9 Cassettes.

Baum, L. Frank
LAND OF OZ, THE (A Sequel to the Wizard of Oz) (Sheila Donald).
MCSET. Cat no: **SPJ 060-1**. Released on Schiltron Audio Books, '91 by Schiltron Publishing. Note: 4 Cassettes. Playing time 5 hours.
MCSET. Cat no: **9167F**. Released on Travellers Tales, '91 by Travellers Tales. Note: 4 Cassettes.

LAND OF OZ, THE (Unknown narrator(s)).
MC. Cat no: **1618**. Released on Caedmon (USA), '88 by Caedmon Records (USA), Bond Street Music.

LITTLE OZ STORIES (Ray Bolger).
MC. Cat no: **1716**. Released on Caedmon (USA), Aug '83 by Caedmon Records (USA), Bond Street Music.

WIZARD OF OZ, THE (Unknown narrator(s)).
MC. Cat no: **STK 027**. Released on Stick-A-Tale, Jul '90 by Pickwick Records.

WIZARD OF OZ, THE (Various narrators).
LP. Cat no: **D 347**. Released on Disneyland, Dec '82 by Disneyland-Vista Records (USA).
MC. Cat no: **D 13DC**. Released on Disneyland, Dec '82 by Disneyland-Vista Records (USA).

WIZARD OF OZ, THE (Unknown narrator(s)).

Note: Abridged.
MC. Cat no: **1512.** Released on Caedmon (USA), '89 by Caedmon Records (USA), Bond Street Music.

WIZARD OF OZ, THE (Well Loved Tales up to Age 9) (Unknown narrator(s)).
Note: Book and cassette.
MC. Cat no: **PLB 179.** Released on Tell-A-Tale, '88 by Pickwick Records, Taylors, Clyde Factors.

WIZARD OF OZ, THE (Stephen Moore).
MCSET. Cat no: **TC LFP 417142 5.** Released on Listen For Pleasure, Mar '84 by EMI Records.
MCSET. Cat no: **LFP 7448.** Released on Listen For Pleasure, Apr '90 by EMI Records.

WIZARD OF OZ, THE (Carnival Classics) (George Layton).
MC. Cat no: **0001010794.** Released on Harper Collins, Dec '91 by Harper Collins.

Bawden, Nina

CARRIE'S WAR (Zela Clark).
MC. Cat no: **881999.** Released on Puffin Cover To Cover, '88, Green Dragon Audio Visual.
MCSET. Cat no: **9112F.** Released on Travellers Tales, '91 by Travellers Tales. Note: 3 Cassettes.

CIRCLES OF DECEIT (Richard Owens).
MCSET. Cat no: **1478F.** Released on Travellers Tales, '91 by Travellers Tales. Note: 12 Cassettes.
MCSET. Cat no: **OAS 90083.** Released on Oasis Audio Books, '91 by Isis Audio Books. Note: 12 Cassettes.

ICE HOUSE, THE (Susannah York).
MCSET. Cat no: **1008F.** Released on Travellers Tales, '91 by Travellers Tales.

KEPT IN THE DARK (Carole Boyd).
MCSET. Cat no: **3CCA 3044.** Released on Chivers Audio Books, '91 by Chivers Audio Books, Green Dragon Audio Visual. Note: 3 Cassettes.

ODD FLAMINGO, THE (Richard Mitchley).
MCSET. Cat no: **CAT 4049.** Released on Chivers Audio Books, '92 by Chivers Audio Books, Green Dragon Audio Visual. Note: 6 Cassettes.
MCSET. Cat no: **1513T.** Released on Travellers Tales, '91 by Travellers Tales. Note: 6 Cassettes.

PEPPERMINT PIG, THE (Carole Boyd).
MCSET. Cat no: **9170F.** Released on Travellers Tales, '91 by Travellers Tales. Note: 3 Cassettes.
MCSET. Cat no: **3CCA 3067.** Released on Chivers Audio Books, '91 by Chivers Audio Books, Green Dragon Audio Visual. Note: 3 Cassettes.

SQUIB (Eve Karpf).
MCSET. Cat no: **3CCA 3019.** Released on Chivers Audio Books, '91 by Chivers Audio Books, Green Dragon Audio Visual. Note: 3 Cassettes.
MCSET. Cat no: **9012F.** Released on Travellers Tales, '91 by Travellers Tales. Note: 3 Cassettes.

Baxter, Olive

FORGIVING HEART (Sheila Donald).
MCSET. Cat no: **CLT 1003.** Released on Candlelight, Jun '81 by AVLS (Audio-Visual Library Services).

Bean, Billy

BEAN BAG (An Album of Adult Humour) (Billy Bean).
LP. Cat no: **CLIB 1.** Released on Climber, May '85 by Climber Records **Deleted** '86.
MC. Cat no: **CLIC 1.** Released on Climber, May '85 by Climber Records **Deleted** '86.

Bear, Carolyn

JOHNNY TOMORROW (Jon Pertwee).
Note: Includes Johnny Escapes to Earth and Johnny and Tim Return to Utopia.
MC. Cat no: **VCA 097.** Released on VFM Cassettes, Jan '85 by VFM Cassettes, Midland Records, Crusader Marketing Co., Taylors, Morley Audio Services.

Beattie, Johnny

TRIBUTE TO THE KINGS OF SCOTTISH COMEDY.
LP. Cat no: **KLP 67.** Released on Igus, Nov '88 by Klub Records.
MC. Cat no: **ZCKLP 67.** Released on Igus, Dec '88 by Klub Records.

Beckett, Samuel

MACGOWRAN SPEAKING BECKETT (Jack MacGowran).
LP. Cat no: **CCT 3.** Released on Claddagh (Ireland), Aug '88 by Claddagh Records (Ireland), Projection, Impetus Records, Jazz Music, Roots Records, C.M. Distribution, Outlet Records, Taylors.

MOLLOY/ MALONE DIES (The Unnameable) (Cyril Cusack).
MC. Cat no: **0001071202.** Released on Collins-Caedmon, '91 by Collins Audio, Taylors, Bond Street Music.

Bednarczyk, Stefan

LIVE AT THE MORGUE (Stefan Bednarczyk).
Tracks : Pusillaninimity / 'Sunny View Rest Home' commercial / Taboo / N.W.3 / Gold day of youth / Seance humoresque / Visual aids / Dinosaur can-can / Champagne aria, The / With a charm that is all your own / Valentine's song / Twelve days of warning / Young executives square dance / Children's action workshop (When Santa kissed the fairy on the Christmas tree).
LP. Cat no: **ALA 3005.** Released on ASV (Academy Sound & Vision), Oct '83 by Academy Sound & Vision Records **Deleted** Feb '89.
MC. Cat no: **ZC ALA 3005.** Released on ASV (Academy Sound & Vision), Oct '83 by Academy Sound & Vision Records **Deleted** Feb '89.

Beetles, Chris

PINK MEDICINE ALBUM (Chris Beetles & Rob Buckman).
LP. Cat no: **SCX 6616.** Released on Columbia (EMI), Oct '79 by EMI Records **Deleted** '84.

Bell, J.J.

NICKUMS, THE (Sheila Donald).
MCSET. Cat no: **SPF 066-1.** Released on Schiltron Audio Books, '91 by Schiltron Publishing. Note: 2 Cassettes. Playing time 3 hours.

Bell, John. S.

WEE MACGREEGOR (James Copeland).
MCSET. Cat no: **COL 2013.** Released on Colophone, Jun '81 by AVLS (Audio-Visual Library Services).

Bell, Josephine

DEATH OF A CON MAN (Kenneth Shanley).
MCSET. Cat no: **CAT 4056.** Released on Chivers Audio Books, '91 by Chivers Audio Books, Green Dragon Audio Visual. Note: 6 Cassettes.
MCSET. Cat no: **1601T.** Released on Travellers Tales, '91 by Travellers Tales. Note: 6 Cassettes.

WELL-KNOWN FACE, A (Trevor Nichols).
MCSET. Cat no: **CAT 4043.** Released on Chivers Audio Books, '91 by Chivers Audio Books, Green Dragon Audio Visual. Note: 4 Cassettes.
MCSET. Cat no: **1457T.** Released on Travellers Tales, '91 by Travellers Tales. Note: 4 Cassettes.

Bellow, Saul

HERZOG (Unknown narrator(s)).
MC. Cat no: **1584.** Released on Caedmon (USA), '88 by Caedmon Records (USA), Bond Street Music.

Benchley, Peter

BEAST, THE (David Rasche).
MCSET. Cat no: **RC 41.** Released on Random Century, '91 by Random Century Audiobooks, Conifer Records. Note: 2 Cassettes. ISBN 1856860582. 3 hrs approx.

GIRL OF THE SEA OF CORTEZ, THE (Jenny Agutter).
MCSET. Cat no: **1010F.** Released on Travellers Tales, '91 by Travellers Tales. Note: 6 Cassettes.

Q - CLEARANCE (Jerry Farden).
MCSET. Cat no: **1675/1676T.** Released on Travellers Tales, '91 by Travellers Tales. Note: 10 Cassettes.
MCSET. Cat no: **IAB 90111.** Released on Isis Audio Books, '91. Note: 10 Cassettes.

Benét, Stephen Vincent
DEVIL AND DANIEL WEBSTER, THE (Pat Hingle).
MC. Cat no: **1591**. Released on Caedmon (USA), Apr '83 by Caedmon Records (USA), Bond Street Music.

Bennett, Alan
FORTY YEARS ON (And A Woman Of No Importance) (Sir John Gielgud & Patricia Routledge).
MCSET. Cat no: **ZBBC 1029**. Released on BBC Radio Collection, '91 by BBC Records. Note: ISBN No: 0563 225580

FORTY YEARS ON (Unknown narrator(s)).
MC. Cat no: **ZCF 504**. Released on BBC, May '84 by BBC Records, Taylors **Deleted** Apr '89.

TALKING HEADS (Various narrators).
Note: Voices include Thora Hird and Julie Walters.
MCSET. Cat no: **ZBBC 1097**. Released on BBC Radio Collection, Nov '90 by BBC Records. Note: ISBN No: 0563 227214

Bennett, Arnold
ANNA OF THE FIVE TOWNS (Peter Jeffrey).
MCSET. Cat no: **418 150-4**. Released on Argo (Polygram), Jun '88 by PolyGram Classics **Deleted** Jan '89. Note: 2 Cassettes

ANNA OF THE FIVE TOWNS (Unknown narrator(s)).
MCSET. Cat no: **IAB 92043**. Released on Isis Audio Books, Apr '92. Note: 6 Cassettes. Playing time 7hrs 42mins.

OLD WIVE'S TALE, THE (Phyllis Calvert).
Note: Abridged version.
MCSET. Cat no: **1360F**. Released on Travellers Tales, '91 by Travellers Tales. Note: 2 Cassettes.

OLD WIVE'S TALE, THE (Phyllis Calvert).
MCSET. Cat no: **418 198-4**. Released on Argo (Polygram), Apr '88 by PolyGram Classics **Deleted** Jan '89.

PRETTY LADY, THE (Alistair Maydon).
MCSET. Cat no: **OAS 89075**. Released on Oasis Audio Books, '91 by Isis Audio Books.
MCSET. Cat no: **1428F**. Released on Travellers Tales, '91 by Travellers Tales.

Benson, E.F
LUCIA IN LONDON (Geraldine McEwan).
MCSET. Cat no: **IAB 92033**. Released on Isis Audio Books, Mar '92. Note: 8 Cassettes. Playing time 9hrs 20mins.

LUCIA'S PROGRESS (Prunella Scales).
MCSET. Cat no: **IAB 92072**. Released on Isis Audio Books, Jul '92. Note: 8 Cassettes. Playing time: 9 hours, 10 mins.

MAPP AND LUCIA (Prunella Scales).
MC. Cat no: **0600560481**. Released on Hamlyn Books On Tape, '88, Bond Street Music.

MCSET. Cat no: **1511/1512F**. Released on Travellers Tales, '91 by Travellers Tales. Note: 10 Cassettes.

MCSET. Cat no: **HCA 85**. Released on Harper Collins, Jan '92 by Harper Collins.

MCSET. Cat no: **IAB 90084**. Released on Isis Audio Books, '91. Note: 10 Cassettes.

MISS MAPP (Prunella Scales).
MCSET. Cat no: **IAB 90113**. Released on Isis Audio Books, '91. Note: 8 Cassettes.

MCSET. Cat no: **1510F**. Released on Travellers Tales, '91 by Travellers Tales. Note: 8 Cassettes.

QUEEN LUCIA (Unknown narrator(s)).
MCSET. Cat no: **ZBBC 1120**. Released on BBC Radio Collection, Jun '90 by BBC Records. Note: ISBN No: 0563 410361

QUEEN LUCIA (Geraldine McEwan).
MCSET. Cat no: **1609F**. Released on Travellers Tales, '91 by Travellers Tales. Note: 8 Cassettes.

Berenstain, Stan & Jan
BEARS' CHRISTMAS (And Other Stories) (Stan & Jan Berenstain).
Note: Includes five bear books: The Bears' Christmas, He Bear, She Bear, The Bear Detectives, The Bear Almanac and The Bike Lesson.
MC. Cat no: **1573**. Released on Caedmon (USA), '88 by Caedmon Records (USA), Bond Street Music.

BEARS' PICNIC, THE (And Other Stories) (Stan & Jan Berenstain).
MCSET. Cat no: **1549**. Released on Caedmon (USA), '90 by Caedmon Records (USA), Bond Street Music.

Beresford, Elizabeth
WOMBLE STORIES (Bernard Cribbins).
LP. Cat no: **REC 253**. Released on BBC, Oct '76 by BBC Records, Taylors **Deleted** '87.

Berg, Leila
STORYTIME TOP TEN (Volume 4) (Ronnie Stevens).
Note: For children aged 4 - 8 years. Music by De Wolfe. Includes Mr. Fox, Anansi and the Pudding Tree, Rabbit and Elephant and Mr. Wolf and his Tail.
MC. Cat no: **VCA 058**. Released on VFM Cassettes, Jan '85 by VFM Cassettes, Midland Records, Crusader Marketing Co., Taylors, Morley Audio Services.

STORYTIME TOP TEN (Volume 5) (Ronnie Stevens).
Note: For children aged 4 - 8 years. Music by De Wolfe. Includes Uncle Bouki and the Horse and The Man who Rode the Tiger.
MC. Cat no: **VCA 059**. Released on VFM Cassettes, Jan '85 by VFM Cassettes, Midland Records, Crusader Marketing Co., Taylors, Morley Audio Services.

Berman, Shelley
INSIDE SHELLEY BERMAN.
LP. Cat no: **CLP 1300**. Released on Capitol, Nov '60 by EMI Records **Deleted** '65.

Bestall, Alfred
ADVENTURES OF RUPERT BEAR (Unknown narrator(s)).
MCSET. Cat no: **DTO 10540**. Released on Ditto, '88 by Pickwick Records, Midland Records.

FAVOURITE RUPERT BEAR STORIES (Unknown narrator(s)).
MC. Cat no: **0411400452**. Released on Harper Collins, '91 by Harper Collins.

FAVOURITE RUPERT STORIES (Judy Bennett).
MC. Cat no: **00 1034588**. Released on Tempo, '88 by Warwick Records, Celtic Music, Henry Hadaway Organisation.

RUPERT AND THE FROG SONG (For Ages 5-10) (Unknown narrator(s)).
MC. Cat no: **PLBR 212**. Released on Tell-A-Tale, '88 by Pickwick Records, Taylors, Clyde Factors.

RUPERT AND THE MAGIC SEEDS (Unknown narrator(s)).
MC. Cat no: **PLBR 280**. Released on Tell-A-Tale, '89 by Pickwick Records, Taylors, Clyde Factors.

RUPERT AND THE NUTWOOD STAGE (Unknown narrator(s)).
MC. Cat no: **00 00 102128 1**. Released on Tempo, '88 by Warwick Records, Celtic Music, Henry Hadaway Organisation.

RUPERT AND THE OLD HAT (Unknown narrator(s)).
MC. Cat no: **PLBR 281**. Released on Tell-A-Tale, '89 by Pickwick Records, Taylors, Clyde Factors.

RUPERT AND THE WOBBLY WITCH (Unknown narrator(s)).
MC. Cat no: **00 00 102127 3**. Released on Tempo, '88 by Warwick Records, Celtic Music, Henry Hadaway Organisation.

RUPERT BEAR (Nutwood Chums) (Unknown narrators).
LP. Cat no: **CMAE 1**. Released on Animated Expressions, Nov '86.
MC. Cat no: **CMAEC 1**. Released on Animated Expressions, Nov '86.

RUPERT BEAR AND THE CHOCOLATE BUTTONS GANG (Various narrators).
MC. Cat no: **0001010220**. Released on Harper Collins, '91 by Harper Collins.
MC. Cat no: **0001021257**. Released on Tempo, '88 by Warwick Records,

Celtic Music, Henry Hadaway Organisation.

RUPERT BEAR AND THE HIDDEN LAKE (Judy Bennett).
MC. Cat no: **TTS 9811**. Released on Tempo, Aug '84 by Warwick Records, Celtic Music, Henry Hadaway Organisation.

RUPERT BEAR AND THE LONELY BIRD (Judy Bennett).
MC. Cat no: **TTS 9810**. Released on Tempo, Aug '84 by Warwick Records, Celtic Music, Henry Hadaway Organisation.

RUPERT BEAR AND THE MUDDLED MAGIC (Judy Bennett).
MC. Cat no: **TTS 9812**. Released on Tempo, Aug '84 by Warwick Records, Celtic Music, Henry Hadaway Organisation.

RUPERT BEAR AND THE YELLOW ELEPHANT (Various narrators).
MC. Cat no: **0001010204**. Released on Harper Collins, '91 by Harper Collins.
MC. Cat no: **0001021265**. Released on Tempo, '88 by Warwick Records, Celtic Music, Henry Hadaway Organisation.

RUPERT BEAR AND THE YOUNG DRAGON (Judy Bennett).
MC. Cat no: **TTS 9801**. Released on Tempo, Aug '84 by Warwick Records, Celtic Music, Henry Hadaway Organisation.

RUPERT BEAR - STORIES FROM THE 1982 ANNUAL (Unknown narrator(s)).
MC. Cat no: **PTB 636**. Released on Pickwick Talking Books, Mar '84 by Pickwick Records, Clyde Factors.

RUPERT BEAR'S NEW ADVENTURES (Unknown narrator(s)).
Note: Four books & 1 long play cassette in presentation pack.
MC. Cat no: **00 104 132 0**. Released on Tempo, Apr '88 by Warwick Records, Celtic Music, Henry Hadaway Organisation.

SINGS A GOLDEN HOUR OF NURSERY RHYMES (Unknown narrator(s)).
LP. Cat no: **SPR 8524**. Released on Spot, Feb '83 by Pickwick Records.
MC. Cat no: **SPC 8524**. Released on Spot, Feb '83 by Pickwick Records.

STORIES OF RUPERT BEAR (Volume 1) (Unknown narrator(s)).
MCSET. Cat no: **DTO 10519**. Released on Ditto, '88 by Pickwick Records, Midland Records.

STORIES OF RUPERT BEAR (Volume 2) (Unknown narrator(s)).
MCSET. Cat no: **DTO 10525**. Released on Ditto, '88 by Pickwick Records, Midland Records.

TALES OF RUPERT BEAR (Joanna Lumley).
MC. Cat no: **PTB 616**. Released on Pickwick Talking Books, '83 by Pickwick Records, Clyde Factors.

Bester, Alfred

DEMOLISHED MAN, THE (Joe Dunlop).
MCSET. Cat no: **1458T**. Released on Travellers Tales, '91 by Travellers Tales. Note: 7 Cassettes.
MCSET. Cat no: **OAS 89114**. Released on Oasis Audio Books, '91 by Isis Audio Books. Note: 7 Cassettes.

Betjeman, Sir John

BANANA BLUSH (Unknown narrator(s)).
Tracks / Indoor games near Newbury / Business girls / Agricultural caress / Youth and age on Beaulieu River Hants / Arrest of Oscar Wilde at the Cadogan Hotel / Lenten thoughts / Cockney amorist, The / Longfellow's visit to Venice / Flight from Bootle, The / Shropshire lad, A / On a portrait of a deaf man / Child ill, A.
LP. Cat no: **CHC 26**. Released on Charisma, Aug '88 by Virgin Records **Deleted** Mar '91.

BETJEMAN READS BETJEMAN (Sir John Betjeman).
Tracks / Middlesex / Harrow-on-the-hill / Upper Lambourne / Wantage bells / Trebetherick / Heart of Thomas Hardy, The / Arrest of Oscar Wilde at the Cadogan Hotel / I.M.Walter Ramsden / Devonshire Street W.1. / In a Bath tea shop / Attempt, The / Irish unionist's farewell, The / Lincolnshire church, The / Potpourri from a Surrey garden / Henley-on-Thames / Diary of a church mouse / In the public gardens / Eunice / Last of her order, The / Matlock bath.
Note: John Betjeman, the Poet Laureate, here reads a selection of his best-loved poems, and excerpts from his autobiographical work ,"Summoned by Bells".
MCSET. Cat no: **SAY 59**. Released on Argo (Polygram), '83 by PolyGram Classics **Deleted** Jan '89.
MCSET. Cat no: **ARGO 1037**. Released on Argo (EMI), May '89 by EMI Records. Note: 2 Cassettes.

BETJEMAN'S BRITAIN (Sir John Betjeman).
Tracks / Hunter trials / Autumn 1964 / Subaltern's love song, A / Seaside golf / Upper Lambourne / Death of King George V / Middlesex / South London 1844 / South London 1944 / Harrow-on-the-Hill / City / Parliament hill fields.
LP. Cat no: **CHC 28**. Released on Charisma, '88 by Virgin Records **Deleted** Jun '91.

JOHN BETJEMAN READS JOHN BETJEMAN (Sir John Betjeman).
MCSET. Cat no: **TTC 1011**. Released on Talking Tape Company, Apr '91, Conifer Records. Note: Playing time: 36 minutes. ISBN No: 872520898

LATE FLOWERING LOVE (Sir John Betjeman).
Tracks / Narcissus / Olympic girl, The / Invasion exercise on a poultry farm / Licorice fields at Pontefract, The / Russell flint, A / Station syren / Myfanwy and Myfanwy at Oxford / In the public gardens / Eunice / Senex / Late flowering lust / Sun and fun.
LP. Cat no: **CHC 27**. Released on Charisma, '88 by Virgin Records **Deleted** Jun '91.

POEMS AND A SELECTION FROM SUMMONED BY BELLS (Sir John Betjeman).
MCSET. Cat no: **ZBBC 1249**. Released on BBC Radio Collection, Aug '91 by BBC Records. Note: ISBN No: 0563 365188
MCSET. Cat no: **1003Y**. Released on Travellers Tales, '91 by Travellers Tales. Note: 2 Cassettes.

READING HIS POETRY (Sir John Betjeman).
MC. Cat no: **1557**. Released on Caedmon (USA), '90 by Caedmon Records (USA), Bond Street Music.
LP. Cat no: **TC 1557**. Released on Caedmon (USA), '78 by Caedmon Records (USA), Bond Street Music.

Bierce, Ambrose

OCCURRENCE AT OWL CREEK BRIDGE, AN (Mark Hammer).
Note: Includes stories: An Occurrence at Owl Creek Bridge, The Damned Thing, A Watcher by the Dead, An Inhabitant of Carosa, The Famous Gilson Bequest, The Eyes of the Panther, The Secret of Macarger's Gulch and The Night-Doings at Deadman's.
MCSET. Cat no: **RB 82041**. Released on Recorded Books, Dec '91 by Isis Audio Books. Note: 2 Cassettes. Playing time 3hrs.

Binchy, Maeve

CIRCLE OF FRIENDS (Kate Binchy).
MCSET. Cat no: **CAB 563**. Released on Chivers Audio Books, '91 by Chivers Audio Books, Green Dragon Audio Visual. Note: 12 Cassettes.
MCSET. Cat no: **RC 84**. Released on Random Century, Mar '93 by Random Century Audiobooks, Conifer Records. Note: ISBN no. 1856861066
MCSET. Cat no: **1649/1650F**. Released on Travellers Tales, '91 by Travellers Tales.

DUBLIN 4 (Kate Binchy).
MCSET. Cat no: **CAB 308**. Released on Chivers Audio Books, Jul '88 by Chivers Audio Books, Green Dragon Audio Visual. Note: 4 cassettes.
MCSET. Cat no: **1315F**. Released on Travellers Tales, '91 by Travellers Tales. Note: 4 Cassettes.
MCSET. Cat no: **0745128033**. Released on Word For Word, May '92 by Chivers Audio Books.

LIGHT A PENNY CANDLE (Kate Binchy).
MCSET. Cat no: **RC 1**. Released on Random Century, '91 by Random Century Audiobooks, Conifer Records. Note: 2 Cassettes. ISBN 1856860000. 3 hrs approx.

LILAC BUS, THE (Kate Binchy).
MCSET. Cat no: **CAB 198.** Released on Chivers Audio Books, '91 by Chivers Audio Books, Green Dragon Audio Visual. Note: 6 Cassettes.

MCSET. Cat no: **1089R.** Released on Travellers Tales, '91 by Travellers Tales. Note: 6 Cassettes.

LONDON TRANSPORTS (Kate Binchy).
MCSET. Cat no: **CAB 247.** Released on Chivers Audio Books, '91 by Chivers Audio Books, Green Dragon Audio Visual. Note: 6 Cassettes.

MCSET. Cat no: **1028H.** Released on Travellers Tales, '91 by Travellers Tales. Note: 6 Cassettes.

SILVER WEDDING, THE (Kate Binchy).
MCSET. Cat no: **CAB 384.** Released on Chivers Audio Books, '91 by Chivers Audio Books, Green Dragon Audio Visual. Note: 8 Cassettes.

MCSET. Cat no: **1373F.** Released on Travellers Tales, '91 by Travellers Tales. Note: 8 Cassettes.

Bingham, Charlotte
BELGRAVIA (Liza Goddard).
MCSET. Cat no: **1001H.** Released on Travellers Tales, '91 by Travellers Tales. Note: 6 Cassettes.

Bird, Maria
ANDY PANDY AND TEDDY AT THE ZOO (Ysanne Churchman).
MC. Cat no: **LL 41 8022 4.** Released on Look & Listen, Nov '84.

ANDY PANDY AND THE BADGER (Ysanne Churchman).
MC. Cat no: **LL 41 8021 4.** Released on Look & Listen, Nov '84.

ANDY PANDY AND THE DOVECOT (Various narrators).
MC. Cat no: **LL 41 8007 4.** Released on Listen For Pleasure, Jun '84 by EMI Records.

ANDY PANDY AND THE DUCKLINGS (Various narrators).
MC. Cat no: **LL 41 8012 4.** Released on Listen For Pleasure, Jun '84 by EMI Records.

ANDY PANDY AND THE RED MOTOR CAR (Various narrators).
MC. Cat no: **LL 41 8008 4.** Released on Listen For Pleasure, Jun '84 by EMI Records.

ANDY PANDY AND THE SPOTTED COW (Various narrators).
MC. Cat no: **LL 41 8010 4.** Released on Listen For Pleasure, Jun '84 by EMI Records.

ANDY PANDY AND THE WILLOW TREE (Various narrators).
MC. Cat no: **LL 41 8011 4.** Released on Listen For Pleasure, Jun '84 by EMI Records.

Biro, Val
GUMDROP (Richard Briers).
Note: For 4 to 8 year olds.
MC. Cat no: **CS 009.** Released on Times Cassettes, '82.
MC. Cat no: **A 001.** Released on Green Dragon, '91 by Green Dragon Audio Visual.

ONCE UPON A TIME (Richard Briers).
Note: For children aged 3 - 9 years. Includes The Adventures of a Vintage Car, Gumdrop on the Move, Gumdrop and the Farmer's Friend, Gumdrop goes to London and Gumdrop on the Brighton Run.
MC. Cat no: **OTC 004.** Released on VFM Cassettes, '85 by VFM Cassettes, Midland Records, Crusader Marketing Co., Taylors, Morley Audio Services.

STORYTIME TOP TEN (Volume 3) (Richard Briers).
Note: Music by Major Records. Includes Gumdrop on the Move, Gumdrop and the Farmer's Friend, Gumdrop Goes to London and Gumdrop on the Brighton Run. For children aged 4 - 8 years.
MC. Cat no: **VCA 057.** Released on VFM Cassettes, Jan '85 by VFM Cassettes, Midland Records, Crusader Marketing Co., Taylors, Morley Audio Services.

Blackmore, R.D.
LORNA DOONE (Anthony Homyer).
MCSET. Cat no: **1097C.** Released on Travellers Tales, '91 by Travellers Tales. Note: 8 cassettes.

MCSET. Cat no: **TCL 21.** Released on Complete Listener, '91 by Complete Listener. Note: 8 Cassettes. Playing time: 12 hours.

LORNA DOONE (Peter Gilmore).
MCSET. Cat no: **LFP 7244.** Released on Listen For Pleasure, May '86 by EMI Records.

LORNA DOONE (Peter Gilmore).
Note: Abridged version.
MCSET. Cat no: **1008C.** Released on Travellers Tales, '91 by Travellers Tales. Note: 2 Cassettes.

LORNA DOONE (Unknown narrator(s)).
Note: Book and cassette.
MC. Cat no: **PLBC 207.** Released on Tell-A-Tale, '88 by Pickwick Records, Taylors, Clyde Factors.

Blair, Emma
JESSIE GRAY (Eve Karpf).
MCSET. Cat no: **CAB 677.** Released on Chivers Audio Books, Mar '92 by Chivers Audio Books, Green Dragon Audio Visual. Note: 8 Cassettes.

MAGGIE JORDAN (Eve Karpf).
MCSET. Cat no: **CAB 629.** Released on Chivers Audio Books, '91 by Chivers Audio Books, Green Dragon Audio Visual. Note: 12 cassettes.

THIS SIDE OF HEAVEN (Eve Karpf).
MCSET. Cat no: **CAB 527.** Released on Chivers Audio Books, '91 by Chivers Audio Books, Green Dragon Audio Visual. Note: 8 Cassettes.
MCSET. Cat no: **1537F.** Released on Travellers Tales, '91 by Travellers Tales. Note: 8 Cassettes.

Blake, Michael
DANCES WITH WOLVES (Michael Blake).
MCSET. Cat no: **CAB 630.** Released on Chivers Audio Books, '91 by Chivers Audio Books, Green Dragon Audio Visual. Note: 6 Cassettes.

Blake, Quentin
ALL JOIN IN AND OTHER NONSENSE (Richard Briers).
MC. Cat no: **TS 400.** Released on Tellastory, Feb '92 by Random Century Audiobooks. Note: ISBN no. 1856561313

Blake, Veronica
TICKET TO TENERIFE (Susan Skipper).
MCSET. Cat no: **MRC 1033.** Released on Chivers Audio Books, '91 by Chivers Audio Books, Green Dragon Audio Visual.

Blake, William
POETRY OF WILLIAM BLAKE (Sir Ralph Richardson).
MC. Cat no: **1101.** Released on Caedmon (USA), '88 by Caedmon Records (USA), Bond Street Music.

Blanchard, Kenneth
TALKING WITH THE ONE MINUTE MANAGER (Kenneth Blanchard & Spencer Johnson).
MC. Cat no: **0600560651.** Released on Hamlyn Books On Tape, '88, Bond Street Music.

Bleasdale, Alan
BOYS FROM THE BLACKSTUFF (Bernard Hill).
MCSET. Cat no: **LFP 7487.** Released on Listen For Pleasure, Oct '90 by EMI Records.

Bloch, Robert
PSYCHO (Kevin McCarthy).
MCSET. Cat no: **LFP 7343.** Released on Listen For Pleasure, Jun '88 by EMI Records **Deleted** Apr '90. Note: Playing time: 3 hours

Blume, Judy
ARE YOU THERE GOD? IT'S ME, MARGARET (Susannah Fellows).
MCSET. Cat no: **3CCA 3045.** Released on Chivers Audio Books, '91 by Chivers Audio Books, Green Dragon Audio Visual. Note: 3 Cassettes.

MCSET. Cat no: **9142F.** Released on Travellers Tales, '91 by Travellers Tales. Note: 3 cassettes

DEENIE (Kim Braden).
MCSET. Cat no: **LFP 7278.** Released on Listen For Pleasure, Feb '87 by EMI Records.

IGGIE'S HOUSE (Susannah Fellows).
MCSET. Cat no: **2CCA 3003.** Re-

leased on Chivers Audio Books, '91 by Chivers Audio Books, Green Dragon Audio Visual. Note: 2 Cassettes.
MCSET. Cat no: **9013F.** Released on Travellers Tales, '91 by Travellers Tales. Note: 2 Cassettes.
MCSET. Cat no: **086 222 0415.** Released on Chivers Calvacade, '91 by Chivers Audio Books, Green Dragon Audio Visual.

THEN AGAIN, MAYBE I WON'T (Blain Fairman).
MCSET. Cat no: **3CCA 3068.** Released on Chivers Audio Books, '91 by Chivers Audio Books, Green Dragon Audio Visual. Note: 3 Cassettes.
MCSET. Cat no: **9158F.** Released on Travellers Tales, '91 by Travellers Tales. Note: 3 Cassettes.

Blyton, Enid

15 MINUTE TALES (Unknown narrator(s)).
MC. Cat no: **PTB 635.** Released on Pickwick Talking Books, '84 by Pickwick Records, Clyde Factors.

ADVENTURES OF MARY MOUSE (Cindy Kent).
LP. Cat no: **STMP 9023.** Released on Super Tempo, May '84 by Warwick Records, Taylors, Solomon & Peres, Sony Music Operations.
MC. Cat no: **STMP 49023.** Released on Super Tempo, May '84 by Warwick Records, Taylors, Solomon & Peres, Sony Music Operations.

ADVENTURES OF MR. PINK-WHISTLE (Clive Bennett).
LP. Cat no: **STMP 9022.** Released on Super Tempo, May '84 by Warwick Records, Taylors, Solomon & Peres, Sony Music Operations.
MC. Cat no: **STMP4 9022.** Released on Super Tempo, May '84 by Warwick Records, Taylors, Solomon & Peres, Sony Music Operations.

ADVENTURES OF NAUGHTY AMELIA JANE (Su Pollard).
LP. Cat no: **STMP 9021.** Released on Super Tempo, May '84 by Warwick Records, Taylors, Solomon & Peres, Sony Music Operations.
MC. Cat no: **STMP4 9021.** Released on Super Tempo, May '84 by Warwick Records, Taylors, Solomon & Peres, Sony Music Operations.

ADVENTURES OF THE SECRET SEVEN (Roy Castle).
MC. Cat no: **PTB 606.** Released on Pickwick Talking Books, Oct '81 by Pickwick Records, Clyde Factors.

ADVENTUROUS FOUR, THE (Philip Schofield).
MCSET. Cat no: **LFP 7328.** Released on Listen For Pleasure, Apr '88 by EMI Records.

CASTLE OF ADVENTURE, THE (Bernard Cribbins).
MCSET. Cat no: **LFP 7478.** Released on Listen For Pleasure, Jun '90 by EMI Records. Note: Playing time: 2 3/4 hours.

ENCHANTED WOOD, THE (Jill Shilling).
MC. Cat no: **TS 392.** Released on Tellastory, '91 by Random Century Audiobooks. Note: ISBN no, 1856561348. 2 Cassettes.

FIRST TERM AT MALORY TOWERS (Unknown narrator(s)).
MCSET. Cat no: **DTO 10502.** Released on Ditto, '88 by Pickwick Records, Midland Records.

FIVE GET INTO A FIX (Nanette Newman).
MCSET. Cat no: **418 201-4.** Released on Argo (Polygram), Apr '88 by Poly-Gram Classics **Deleted** Jan '89. Note: 2 Cassettes.

FIVE GET INTO TROUBLE (Judy Bennett & Charles Collingwood).
MC. Cat no: **0 00 102259 8.** Released on Tempo, '88 by Warwick Records, Celtic Music, Henry Hadaway Organisation.

FIVE GO ADVENTURING AGAIN (Unknown narrator(s)).
LP. Cat no: **STMP 9028.** Released on Super Tempo, May '84 by Warwick Records, Taylors, Solomon & Peres, Sony Music Operations.
MC. Cat no: **STMP 49028.** Released on Super Tempo, May '84 by Warwick Records, Taylors, Solomon & Peres, Sony Music Operations.

FIVE GO OFF IN A CARAVAN (Judy Bennett & Charles Collingwood).
MC. Cat no: **0 00 102256 3.** Released on Tempo, '88 by Warwick Records, Celtic Music, Henry Hadaway Organisation.

FIVE GO OFF TO CAMP (Judy Bennett & Charles Collingwood).
MC. Cat no: **0 00 102254 7.** Released on Tempo Storytime, '88 by Warwick Records, Celtic Music.

FIVE GO TO BILLYCOCK HILL (Nanette Newman).
MCSET. Cat no: **418 213-4.** Released on Argo (Polygram), Apr '88 by Poly-Gram Classics **Deleted** Jan '89.

FIVE GO TO DEMON'S ROCK (Nanette Newman).
MCSET. Cat no: **418 210-4.** Released on Argo (Polygram), Apr '88 by Poly-Gram Classics **Deleted** Jan '89. Note: 2 Cassettes

FIVE GO TO MYSTERY MOOR (Sarah Greene).
MCSET. Cat no: **LFP 7248.** Released on Listen For Pleasure, Jun '86 by EMI Records.
MCSET. Cat no: **9015F.** Released on Travellers Tales, '91 by Travellers Tales. Note: 2 Cassettes.

FIVE HAVE A MYSTERY TO SOLVE (Ann Beach).
MCSET. Cat no: **3CCA 3108.** Released on Chivers Audio Books, '91 by Chivers Audio Books, Green Dragon Audio Visual. Note: 3 Cassettes.

FIVE HAVE A WONDERFUL TIME (Nanette Newman).
MCSET. Cat no: **418 207-4.** Released on Argo (Polygram), Apr '88 by Poly-Gram Classics **Deleted** Jan '89. Note: 2 Cassettes.

FIVE HAVE PLENTY OF FUN (Judy Bennett & Charles Collingwood).
MC. Cat no: **0 00 102258 X.** Released on Tempo, '88 by Warwick Records, Celtic Music, Henry Hadaway Organisation.

FIVE ON A HIKE TOGETHER (Judy Bennett & Charles Collingwood).
MC. Cat no: **0 00 102255 5.** Released on Tempo, '88 by Warwick Records, Celtic Music, Henry Hadaway Organisation.

FIVE ON A SECRET TRAIL (Nanette Newman).
MCSET. Cat no: **418 204-4.** Released on Argo (Polygram), Apr '88 by Poly-Gram Classics **Deleted** Jan '89. Note: 2 Cassettes.

FIVE ON A TREASURE ISLAND (Jan Francis).
MCSET. Cat no: **LFP 7418.** Released on Listen For Pleasure, Sep '89 by EMI Records. Note: Playing time: 2 3/4 hours.

FIVE ON FINNISTON FARM (Sarah Greene).
MCSET. Cat no: **LFP 7300.** Released on Listen For Pleasure, Sep '87 by EMI Records. Note: Playing time: 2 1/2 hours

FIVE ON KIRRIN ISLAND AGAIN (Judy Bennett & Charles Collingwood).
MC. Cat no: **0 00 102257 1.** Released on Tempo, '88 by Warwick Records, Celtic Music, Henry Hadaway Organisation.

FOLK OF THE FARAWAY TREE, THE (Jill Shilling).
MCSET. Cat no: **TS 409.** Released on Tellastory, Jun '92 by Random Century Audiobooks. Note: 2 Cassettes. ISBN no. 1856561437

FUN FOR THE SECRET SEVEN (Sue Sheridan & Nigel Anthony).
MC. Cat no: **0 00 102266 0.** Released on Tempo, '88 by Warwick Records, Celtic Music, Henry Hadaway Organisation.

GOOD WORK SECRET SEVEN (Sue Sheridan & Nigel Anthony).
MC. Cat no: **0 00 102260 1.** Released on Tempo, '88 by Warwick Records, Celtic Music, Henry Hadaway Organisation.

ISLAND OF ADVENTURE (Peter Davison).
MCSET. Cat no: **LFP 7216.** Released on Listen For Pleasure, '88 by EMI Records.
MCSET. Cat no: **9016F.** Released on Travellers Tales, '91 by Travellers Tales. Note: 2 Cassettes.

MAGIC FARAWAY TREE, THE (Jill Shilling).
MCSET. Cat no: **TS 392.** Released on Tellastory, '91 by Random Century

Audiobooks. Note: 2 Cassettes.

MOUNTAIN OF ADVENTURE (Roger Blake & Elizabeth Lindsay).
MC. Cat no: **0 00 102263 6**. Released on Tempo, '88 by Warwick Records, Celtic Music, Henry Hadaway Organisation.

MR. PLOD AND LITTLE NODDY (Ernest Burden).
LP. Cat no: **CMCR 802**. Released on Golden Wand, Nov '83, Taylors.
MC. Cat no: **CMC 802**. Released on Golden Wand, Nov '83, Taylors.

MYSTERY OF TALLY-HO COTTAGE, THE (Liz Morgan & John Baddeley).
MC. Cat no: **0 00 102267 9**. Released on Tempo, '88 by Warwick Records, Celtic Music, Henry Hadaway Organisation.

MYSTERY OF THE BURNT COTTAGE, THE (Liz Morgan & John Baddeley).
MC. Cat no: **0 00 102268 7**. Released on Tempo, '88 by Warwick Records, Celtic Music, Henry Hadaway Organisation.

MYSTERY OF THE SECRET ROOM, THE (Liz Morgan & John Baddeley).
MC. Cat no: **0 00 102265 2**. Released on Tempo, '88 by Warwick Records, Celtic Music, Henry Hadaway Organisation.

MYSTERY OF THE SECRET ROOM, THE (Ann Beach).
MCSET. Cat no: **3CCA 3139**. Released on Chivers Audio Books, '91 by Chivers Audio Books, Green Dragon Audio Visual. Note: 3 Cassettes.

NODDY AND THE MAGIC BOOTS (Denise Bryer).
MC. Cat no: **TTS 9803**. Released on Tempo, Aug '84 by Warwick Records, Celtic Music, Henry Hadaway Organisation.

NODDY AND THE TOOTLES (Ernest Burden).
MC. Cat no: **CMC 804**. Released on Children's Wand, Jan '84.

NODDY GOES TO SEA (Ernest Burden).
LP. Cat no: **CMCR 801**. Released on Golden Wand, Nov '83, Taylors.
MC. Cat no: **CMC 801**. Released on Golden Wand, Nov '83, Taylors.

NODDY HAS AN ADVENTURE (Ernest Burden).
LP. Cat no: **CMCR 800**. Released on Golden Wand, Nov '82, Taylors.
MC. Cat no: **CMC 800**. Released on Golden Wand, Nov '82, Taylors.

NODDY MAKES EVERYONE CROSS (Denise Bryer).
MC. Cat no: **TTS 9815**. Released on Tempo, Aug '84 by Warwick Records, Celtic Music, Henry Hadaway Organisation.

NODDY STORIES (Volume 1) (Unknown narrator(s)).

MCSET. Cat no: **DTO 10500**. Released on Ditto, '88 by Pickwick Records, Midland Records.

NODDY STORIES (Volume 2) (Unknown narrator(s)).
MCSET. Cat no: **DTO 10507**. Released on Ditto, '88 by Pickwick Records, Midland Records.

NODDY STORIES (Volume 3) (Unknown narrator(s)).
MCSET. Cat no: **DTO 10542**. Released on Ditto, '88 by Pickwick Records, Midland Records.

NODDY STORIES (Richard Briers).
MC. Cat no: **PTB 605**. Released on Pickwick Talking Books, '83 by Pickwick Records, Clyde Factors.

NODDY STORIES (Unknown narrator(s)).
MCSET. Cat no: **DTO 10536**. Released on Ditto, '88 by Pickwick Records, Midland Records.
MCSET. Cat no: **DTO 10550**. Released on Ditto, '88 by Pickwick Records, Midland Records.
MCSET. Cat no: **DTO 10545**. Released on Ditto, '88 by Pickwick Records, Midland Records.

NODDY'S BIG BALLOON (Denise Bryer).
MC. Cat no: **TTS 9813**. Released on Tempo, Aug '84 by Warwick Records, Celtic Music, Henry Hadaway Organisation.

NODDY'S UNLUCKY DAY (Denise Bryer).
MC. Cat no: **TTS 9814**. Released on Tempo, Aug '84 by Warwick Records, Celtic Music, Henry Hadaway Organisation.

SECRET ISLAND, THE (Jan Francis).
MCSET. Cat no: **LFP 7514**. Released on Listen For Pleasure, Apr '91 by EMI Records.

SECRET SEVEN FIREWORKS (Unknown narrator(s)).
MCSET. Cat no: **DTO 10511**. Released on Ditto, '88 by Pickwick Records, Midland Records.

SECRET SEVEN MYSTERY (Geoffrey Matthews).
MCSET. Cat no: **2CCA 3103**. Released on Chivers Audio Books, '91 by Chivers Audio Books, Green Dragon Audio Visual. Note: 2 Cassettes.
MCSET. Cat no: **9171F**. Released on Travellers Tales, '91 by Travellers Tales. Note: 2 Cassettes.

SECRET SEVEN, THE (Volume 1) (Unknown narrator(s)).
MCSET. Cat no: **DTO 10501**. Released on Ditto, '88 by Pickwick Records, Midland Records.

SECRET SEVEN, THE (Volume 2) (Unknown narrator(s)).
MCSET. Cat no: **DTO 10527**. Released on Ditto, '88 by Pickwick Records, Midland Records.

SECRET SEVEN WIN THROUGH

(Sue Sheridan & Nigel Anthony).
MC. Cat no: **0 00 102261 X**. Released on Tempo, '88 by Warwick Records, Celtic Music, Henry Hadaway Organisation.

SHADOW THE SHEEPDOG (Christopher Timothy).
MCSET. Cat no: **LFP 7409**. Released on Listen For Pleasure, Jul '89 by EMI Records.

SHIP OF ADVENTURE, THE (Roger Blake & Elizabeth Lindsay).
MC. Cat no: **0 00 102264 4**. Released on Tempo, '88 by Warwick Records, Celtic Music, Henry Hadaway Organisation.

SHOCK FOR THE SECRET SEVEN (Unknown narrator(s)).
MCSET. Cat no: **DTO 10532**. Released on Ditto, '88 by Pickwick Records, Midland Records.

TALE OF THE CUDDLY TOYS, THE (Ernest Burden).
LP. Cat no: **CMCR 803**. Released on Golden Wand, Nov '83, Taylors.
MC. Cat no: **CMC 803**. Released on Golden Wand, Nov '83, Taylors.

THREE CHEERS SECRET SEVEN (Sue Sheridan & Nigel Anthony).
MC. Cat no: **0 00 102262 8**. Released on Tempo, '88 by Warwick Records, Celtic Music, Henry Hadaway Organisation.

WELL DONE SECRET SEVEN (Unknown narrator(s)).
LP. Cat no: **STMP 9029**. Released on Super Tempo, May '84 by Warwick Records, Taylors, Solomon & Peres, Sony Music Operations.
MC. Cat no: **STMP4 9029**. Released on Super Tempo, May '84 by Warwick Records, Taylors, Solomon & Peres, Sony Music Operations.

Boccaccio, Giovanni

DECAMERON (David McCallum).
MC. Cat no: **CDL 51650**. Released on Caedmon (USA), Oct '81 by Caedmon Records (USA), Bond Street Music.

Boland, John

CATCH, THE (Stephen Thorne).
MCSET. Cat no: **CAT 4057**. Released on Chivers Audio Books, '91 by Chivers Audio Books, Green Dragon Audio Visual. Note: 6 Cassettes.
MCSET. Cat no: **1602T**. Released on Travellers Tales, '91 by Travellers Tales. Note: 6 Cassettes.

Bomphray, Clint

LATE SPECIAL (And Wildcats) (Various narrators).
Note: Dramatised by Otto Lowry.
MC. Cat no: **NF 7**. Released on Nightfall Tapes, '89 by BMG Records (UK) Ltd..

Bond, Michael

BEAR CALLED PADDINGTON, A (Sir Michael Hordern).
Note: Also available on hanging format, Cat. No: **0001031910**.

MC. Cat no: **1580**. Released on Caedmon (USA), '88 by Caedmon Records (USA), Bond Street Music.
MC. Cat no: **0001072706**. Released on Harper Collins, '91 by Harper Collins.
BIRTHDAY TREAT, A (And Other Stories) (Unknown narrator(s)).
MC. Cat no: **1767**. Released on Caedmon (USA), '88 by Caedmon Records (USA), Bond Street Music.
MONSIEUR PAMPLEMOUSSE (George Guidall).
MCSET. Cat no: **IAB 92014**. Released on Isis Audio Books, Jan '92. Note: 5 cassettes. Playing time 5hrs 45mins.
MONSIEUR PAMPLEMOUSSE INVESTIGATES (George Guidall).
MCSET. Cat no: **IAB 92058**. Released on Isis Audio Books, May '92. Note: 5 Cassettes. Playing time: 6 1/2 hours.
MORE ABOUT PADDINGTON BEAR (Bernard Cribbins).
MC. Cat no: **P 90025**. Released on Pinnacle, '79 by Pinnacle Records, Outlet Records, Music Sales Records.
PADDINGTON (Sir Michael Hordern).
MC. Cat no: **39557**. Released on Tempo, Oct '89 by Warwick Records, Celtic Music, Henry Hadaway Organisation.
PADDINGTON ABROAD (Bernard Cribbins).
MC. Cat no: **P 90029**. Released on Pinnacle, '79 by Pinnacle Records, Outlet Records, Music Sales Records.
PADDINGTON AND PANTOMINE TIME (Sir Michael Hordern).
Note: Also available on hanging format, Cat. No: 0001035576.
MC. Cat no: **0001035576**. Released on Harper Collins, '91 by Harper Collins.
PADDINGTON AND THE DISAPPEARING TRICK (Bernard Cribbins).
MC. Cat no: **1599**. Released on Caedmon (USA), '88 by Caedmon Records (USA), Bond Street Music.
PADDINGTON AT LARGE (Bernard Cribbins).
MC. Cat no: **P 90030**. Released on Pinnacle, '79 by Pinnacle Records, Outlet Records, Music Sales Records.
PADDINGTON AT THE STATION (Sir Michael Hordern).
MC. Cat no: **0 00 109081 X**. Released on Tempo, '88 by Warwick Records, Celtic Music, Henry Hadaway Organisation.
PADDINGTON BEAR (Volume 1) (Bernard Cribbins).
LP. Cat no: **LP 8304**. Released on Pinnacle, Oct '75 by Pinnacle Records, Outlet Records, Music Sales Records.
PADDINGTON BEAR (Volume 2) (Bernard Cribbins).
MC. Cat no: **P 90024**. Released on Pinnacle, '79 by Pinnacle Records, Outlet Records, Music Sales Records.

PADDINGTON DOES IT HIMSELF (Sir Michael Hordern).
MC. Cat no: **00 103529**. Released on Tempo, '88 by Warwick Records, Celtic Music, Henry Hadaway Organisation. Note: Book and tape set
PADDINGTON GOES TO THE SALES (Sir Michael Hordern).
MC. Cat no: **0 00 102189 3**. Released on Tempo, '88 by Warwick Records, Celtic Music, Henry Hadaway Organisation.
PADDINGTON GOES TO TOWN (Bernard Cribbins).
MC. Cat no: **P 90037**. Released on Pinnacle, '79 by Pinnacle Records, Outlet Records, Music Sales Records.
PADDINGTON HELPS OUT (Bernard Cribbins).
MC. Cat no: **P 90026**. Released on Pinnacle, '79 by Pinnacle Records, Outlet Records, Music Sales Records.
PADDINGTON HITS OUT (Sir Michael Hordern).
MC. Cat no: **00 1034510**. Released on Tempo, '88 by Warwick Records, Celtic Music, Henry Hadaway Organisation. Note: Book and tape set
PADDINGTON MARCHES ON (Bernard Cribbins).
MC. Cat no: **P 90035**. Released on Pinnacle, '79 by Pinnacle Records, Outlet Records, Music Sales Records.
PADDINGTON ON THE RIVER (Sir Michael Hordern).
MC. Cat no: **0001010255**. Released on Harper Collins, '91 by Harper Collins. Note: 25 mins.
PADDINGTON TAKES A BATH (Sir Michael Hordern).
MC. Cat no: **0 00 109084 4**. Released on Tempo, '88 by Warwick Records, Celtic Music, Henry Hadaway Organisation.
PADDINGTON'S BIRTHDAY PARTY (Sir Michael Hordern).
MC. Cat no: **0001010018**. Released on Harper Collins, '91 by Harper Collins.
PADDINGTON'S GOLDEN RECORD (Unknown narrator(s)).
LP. Cat no: **ATXLP 7**. Released on Audiotrax, Nov '84 **Deleted** '86.
MC. Cat no: **ZCATX 7**. Released on Audiotrax, Nov '84 **Deleted** '86.
PADDINGTON'S NEW ROOM (Sir Michael Hordern).
MC. Cat no: **0 00 102190 7**. Released on Tempo, '88 by Warwick Records, Celtic Music, Henry Hadaway Organisation.
TROUBLE AT THE AIRPORT (And Other Stories) (Unknown narrator(s)).
MC. Cat no: **1780**. Released on Caedmon (USA), '88 by Caedmon Records (USA), Bond Street Music.
VISIT TO THE DENTIST, A (Unknown narrator(s)).
MC. Cat no: **1773**. Released on Caedmon (USA), '88 by Caedmon Records

(USA), Bond Street Music.

Bond, Simon
TOUGH TED (Roger Blake).
MC. Cat no: **00 1034596**. Released on Tempo, '88 by Warwick Records, Celtic Music, Henry Hadaway Organisation.

Booth, Pat
MALIBU (Morgan Fairchild).
MCSET. Cat no: **RC 10**. Released on Random Century, '91 by Random Century Audiobooks, Conifer Records. Note: 2 Cassettes. ISBN 1856860108. 3 hrs approx.

Boston, Lucy M.
CASTLE OF YEW, THE (David Goodland).
Note: Abridged.
MC. Cat no: **88162X**. Released on Puffin Cover To Cover, '88, Green Dragon Audio Visual.
CHILDREN OF GREEN KNOWE, THE (William Franklyn).
MCSET. Cat no: **3CCA 3132**. Released on Chivers Audio Books, '91 by Chivers Audio Books, Green Dragon Audio Visual. Note: 3 Cassettes.

Bosworth, Frank
OXYOKE, THE (Unknown narrator(s)).
MCSET. Cat no: **1854960253**. Released on Trio, '91 by EMI Records. Note: 3 Cassettes.

Boulle, Pierre
BRIDGE ON THE RIVER KWAI (Robert Hardy).
MC. Cat no: **LFP 41 7152 5**. Released on Listen For Pleasure, May '84 by EMI Records.
BRIDGE ON THE RIVER KWAI (Sir John Mills).
MCSET. Cat no: **CAB 021**. Released on Chivers Audio Books, '91 by Chivers Audio Books, Green Dragon Audio Visual. Note: 4 Cassettes.
MCSET. Cat no: **1021W**. Released on Travellers Tales, '91 by Travellers Tales. Note: 4 Cassettes.

Bowen, John
PLAIN TALES OF THE AFGHAN BORDER (Garard Green).
MCSET. Cat no: **OAS 89122**. Released on Oasis Audio Books, '91 by Isis Audio Books. Note: 3 cassettes.
MCSET. Cat no: **1081N**. Released on Travellers Tales, '91 by Travellers Tales. Note: 3 Cassettes.

Boyce, Max
FAREWELL TO THE NORTH ENCLOSURE.
Tracks / Sospan fach / I am an entertainer / I wandered lonely / I gave my love a debenture / Slow, men at work / Pontypool front row, The / Sospan fach / Divine intervention, The / Ode to Barry Island / Incredible plan, The / I was there interpolating brief extract from

103

'Delilah' / Day that Gareth was dropped, The / Childhood memories / What does she know about music? / Y deryn pur (gentle bird) / 100,000,000,000 green bottles / French trip interpolating 'The Stripper' / Day we lost to England, The / Paul Ringer's song interpolating 'Captain Beaky' / Tarquin's letter / Oggie song, The / Farewell to the north enclosure / Play off - brief extract only from 'Hymns and Arias'.
MCSET. Cat no: **ECC 8.** Released on EMI, Oct '90 by EMI Records.

I KNOW COS I WAS THERE.
LP. Cat no: **MAX 1001.** Released on EMI, May '78 by EMI Records **Deleted** '83.

INCREDIBLE PLAN, THE.
Tracks / It's over / Sospan Fach / Hymns and arias / Pontypool front row, The / Asso asso yogishi / Divine intervention, The / Ode to Barry Island / Incredible plan, The (Interpolating Convoy march, Cardiff Arms.) / Gypsy, The / What does she know about music / Morning star / Bugail Aberdyfi / One hundred thousand million green bottles / French trip, The (Interpolating The Stripper.).
LP. Cat no: **MFP 5580.** Released on MFP, Nov '82 by EMI Records, Solomon & Peres **Deleted** '86.
MC. Cat no: **TCMFP 5580.** Released on MFP, Nov '82 by EMI Records, Solomon & Peres **Deleted** '86.
LP. Cat no: **MB 102.** Released on EMI, Nov '76 by EMI Records **Deleted** '81.

LIVE AT TREORCHY.
Tracks / 9-3 / Scottish trip, The / Ballad of Morgan the moon / Outside-half factory, The / Asso asso yogishi / Duw it's hard / Ten thousand instant Christians / Did you understand? / Hymns and arias.
LP. Cat no: **OU 2033.** Released on One-Up, May '74 by EMI Records.
MC. Cat no: **TC OU 2033.** Released on One-Up, Jul '81 by EMI Records **Deleted** '83.
LP. Cat no: **MFP 41 5699 1.** Released on MFP, Jun '85 by EMI Records, Solomon & Peres **Deleted** '88.
LP. Cat no: **OU 54053.** Released on One-Up, Mar '78 by EMI Records **Deleted** '83.

ME AND BILLY WILLIAMS.
Tracks / Day we lost to England / Paul Ringer's song / Tarquin's letter / Two soldiers / Y deryn pur / Me and Billy Williams / Dowlais top / Morgan and Rhys / Oggie song / Eli Jenkin's prayer.
LP. Cat no: **MAX 1003.** Released on EMI, Nov '80 by EMI Records **Deleted** '85.

NOT THAT I'M BIASED.
Tracks / I think it's a spring onion / 27-3 / One night in Oldham / When we walked to Merthyr Tydfil / Young Davy / Mae nghariad in Fenws / Seagulls of Llandudno / El terible / There but for

Johnny Walters / I don't like cabbage / Coats on the bed / How fast was Gerald Davies, Dad? / Collier lad / Ben Thomas and Mr Pocock / There were many babies born.
LP. Cat no: **MAX 1002.** Released on EMI, Oct '79 by EMI Records **Deleted** '84.

ROAD AND THE MILES, THE.
LP. Cat no: **MB 103.** Released on EMI, Jan '78 by EMI Records **Deleted** '83.

WE ALL HAD DOCTORS PAPERS.
LP. Cat no: **MB 101.** Released on EMI, Nov '75 by EMI Records **Deleted** '80.

Boyd, Neil
BLESS ME FATHER (Peter Wheeler).
MCSET. Cat no: **SOUND 30.** Released on Soundings, Mar '85 by Soundings Records, Bond Street Music. Note: 4 Cassettes.
MCSET. Cat no: **1001N.** Released on Travellers Tales, '91 by Travellers Tales. Note: 4 Cassettes

Boyd, William
MY GIRL IN SKIN TIGHT JEANS (And Other Stories) (Martin Jarvis).
MCSET. Cat no: **TTDMC 409.** Released on CSA Tell Tapes, Jun '91 by CSA Tell-Tapes. Note: 2 Cassettes. ISBN No: 1873859090.

Bradbury, Ray
FANTASTIC TALES (Ray Bradbury).
MCSET. Cat no: **1020S.** Released on Travellers Tales, '91 by Travellers Tales. Note: 6 Cassettes.
MCSET. Cat no: **CSL 001.** Released on Chivers Audio Books, '91 by Chivers Audio Books, Green Dragon Audio Visual. Note: 6 Cassettes.
ILLUSTRATED MAN, THE (Leonard Nimoy).
MC. Cat no: **1479.** Released on Caedmon (USA), Jul '88 by Caedmon Records (USA), Bond Street Music.
MARTIAN CHRONICLES, THE (Ray Bradbury).
MCSET. Cat no: **1025S.** Released on Travellers Tales, '91 by Travellers Tales. Note: 6 Cassettes.
MCSET. Cat no: **CSL 014.** Released on Chivers Audio Books, '91 by Chivers Audio Books, Green Dragon Audio Visual.
MARTIAN CHRONICLES, THE (Leonard Nimoy).
Note: Includes There Will Come Soft Rains and Usher II.
MC. Cat no: **1466.** Released on Caedmon (USA), '88 by Caedmon Records (USA), Bond Street Music.
SMALL ASSASSIN, THE (Ray Bradbury).
MC. Cat no: **CDL 51677.** Released on Caedmon (USA), '82 by Caedmon Records (USA), Bond Street Music.

Bradford, B. Taylor
REMEMBER (Diana Quick).
MCSET. Cat no: **0001046454.** Released on Harper Collins, Mar '92 by Harper Collins.
WOMAN OF SUBSTANCE (Volume 1) (Unknown narrator(s)).
MCSET. Cat no: **1854962426.** Released on Soundings, '91 by Soundings Records, Bond Street Music. Note: 10 Cassettes.
WOMAN OF SUBSTANCE (Volume 2) (Unknown narrator(s)).
MCSET. Cat no: **1854962434.** Released on Soundings, '91 by Soundings Records, Bond Street Music. Note: 12 Cassettes.
WOMAN OF SUBSTANCE, A (Diana Quick).
MCSET. Cat no: **HCA 82.** Released on Harper Collins, Nov '91 by Harper Collins.
WOMAN OF SUBSTANCE, A (Judeth Franklyn).
MCSET. Cat no: **1410/1/2/3F.** Released on Travellers Tales, '91 by Travellers Tales. Note: 27 Cassettes.Bradshaws

BRADSHAWS VOL. 1 (In Their Own Words).(Unknown narrators).
Tracks / What was it like in olden days / Monkey with the funny coloured bum, The / God's spy 'ole / Mam's fys / 2 wheeler, influence and wee, The / Ragbone & dad's brown mac / Marbses / Fixin the window / Bonfire night / Fog an' dad's bike lamp, The / Can I 'ave a budgie / Dad's coat and the scruffy dog.
MC. Cat no: **ZW 26.** Released on Piccadilly Radio, Feb '88.
BRADSHAWS VOL. 2 (In Their Own Voices).(Unknown narrators).
Tracks / Tooth fairy, The / Split the kipper / Taking plaster off / Hiccups / Are you in a good mood or a bad mood / Runaway / Wot's your belly button for / Old tin bath, The / Chapped legs / Will you fix me roller skate / Dad's black eye / Snowball, The.
MC. Cat no: **ZV 27.** Released on Piccadilly Radio, Feb '88.
BRADSHAWS VOL. 3 (In Their Own Backyard).(Unknown narrators).
Tracks / Empty bottles / Bent cigs and corn dog / Politics and beans / Clubman cometh, The / Tea-time / Whit walks / Love letters / Pickles / Man's 'eadache and rickers / Heaster heggs / Fun at the fair / Two balls.
MC. Cat no: **ZB 28.** Released on Piccadilly Radio, Feb '88.

Bragg, Melvin
HIRED MAN, THE (Gordon Griffin).
CDSIN. Cat no: **1854965506.** Released on Soundings, '92 by Soundings Records, Bond Street Music. Note: 6 Cassettes.
JOSH LAWTON (Geoffrey Banks).
MCSET. Cat no: **1327F.** Released on

Travellers Tales, '91 by Travellers Tales. Note: 5 Cassettes.
MCSET. Cat no: **185496027X**. Released on Bramhope, '91 by Ulverscroft Soundings. Note: 5 Cassettes.

Brahmabhatti, Prahlad
ADHOCRA ARMAN (GUJARATI) (Unknown narrator(s)).
MCSET. Cat no: **94888**. Released on Sonex, '91. Note: 3 Cassettes.

Brahms & Simon
BULLET IN THE BALLET (Gretel Davis).
Note: Authors are Caryl Brahms and S.J. Simon.
MCSET. Cat no: **OAS 20791**. Released on Oasis Audio Books, '91 by Isis Audio Books. Note: 6 Cassettes.

Braine, John
ONE AND LAST LOVE (Richard Earthy).
MCSET. Cat no: **1143R**. Released on Travellers Tales, '91 by Travellers Tales. Note: 7 Cassettes.
MCSET. Cat no: **OAS 89105**. Released on Oasis Audio Books, '91 by Isis Audio Books. Note: 7 Cassettes.

Brambell, Wilfred
See under Steptoe & Son

Brand, Christianna
DEATH IN HIGH HEELS (Carole Boyd).
MCSET. Cat no: **CAT 4037**. Released on Chivers Audio Books, '91 by Chivers Audio Books, Green Dragon Audio Visual. Note: 6 Cassettes.
MCSET. Cat no: **1428T**. Released on Travellers Tales, '91 by Travellers Tales. Note: 6 Cassettes.

DEATH OF JEZEBEL (William Franklyn).
MCSET. Cat no: **CAT 4050**. Released on Chivers Audio Books, '91 by Chivers Audio Books, Green Dragon Audio Visual. Note: 6 Cassettes.
MCSET. Cat no: **1514T**. Released on Travellers Tales, '91 by Travellers Tales. Note: 6 Cassettes.

Brand, Max
BLACKJACK (Leonard Zola).
MCSET. Cat no: **CAB 253**. Released on Chivers Audio Books, '91 by Chivers Audio Books, Green Dragon Audio Visual. Note: 6 Cassettes

BLACKSIGNAL (Martin R. Anderson).
MCSET. Cat no: **CAB 188**. Released on Chivers Audio Books, '91 by Chivers Audio Books, Green Dragon Audio Visual. Note: 4 Cassettes.
MCSET. Cat no: **1014W**. Released on Travellers Tales, '91 by Travellers Tales. Note: 4 Cassettes.

MAX BRAND'S BEST WESTERN STORIES (Edited by William F. Nolan) (Jack Clancy).
MCSET. Cat no: **CAB 254**. Released on Chivers Audio Books, Apr '88 by Chivers Audio Books, Green Dragon Audio Visual. Note: 6 Cassettes.

THREE ON THE TRAIL (Steven Aveson).
MCSET. Cat no: **CAB 190**. Released on Chivers Audio Books, '91 by Chivers Audio Books, Green Dragon Audio Visual. Note: 6 Cassettes.
MCSET. Cat no: **1015W**. Released on Travellers Tales, '91 by Travellers Tales. Note: 6 Cassettes.

TRAIL TO SAN TRISTE, THE (Nat Warren-White).
MCSET. Cat no: **CAB 192**. Released on Chivers Audio Books, '91 by Chivers Audio Books, Green Dragon Audio Visual. Note: 6 Cassettes.
MCSET. Cat no: **1018W**. Released on Travellers Tales, '91 by Travellers Tales. Note: 6 Cassettes.

WILD FREEDOM (Kerry Shale).
MCSET. Cat no: **CAB 095**. Released on Chivers Audio Books, '91 by Chivers Audio Books, Green Dragon Audio Visual. Note: 6 Cassettes.
MCSET. Cat no: **1002W**. Released on Travellers Tales, '91 by Travellers Tales. Note: 6 Cassettes.

Brayshaw, Margaret
RIVIERA MASQUERADE (Deirdre Edwards).
MCSET. Cat no: **MRC 1061**. Released on Chivers Audio Books, '91 by Chivers Audio Books, Green Dragon Audio Visual. Note: 2 Cassettes

Brennan, Will
CHEYENNE DAWN (Unknown narrator(s)).
MCSET. Cat no: **1854960288**. Released on Trio, '91 by EMI Records. Note: 3 Cassettes.

HOUR-GLASS, THE (Unknown narrator(s)).
MCSET. Cat no: **1854960296**. Released on Trio, '91 by EMI Records. Note: 3 Cassettes.

Brent, Madeleine
CAPRICORN STONE, THE (Christine Dawe).
MCSET. Cat no: **1270T**. Released on Travellers Tales, '91 by Travellers Tales. Note: 8 Cassettes.
MCSET. Cat no: **185496030X**. Released on Soundings, '91 by Soundings Records, Bond Street Music. Note: 8 Cassettes.

HERITAGE OF SHADOWS, A (Unknown narrator(s)).
MCSET. Cat no: **1854962558**. Released on Soundings, '91 by Soundings Records, Bond Street Music. Note: 9 Cassettes.

KIRBY'S CHANGELING (Melissa Jane Sinden).
MCSET. Cat no: **1495/1496F**. Released on Travellers Tales, '91 by Travellers Tales. Note: 9 cassettes.
MCSET. Cat no: **1854963163**. Released on Soundings, '91 by Soundings Records, Bond Street Music. Note: 9 Cassettes.

LONG MASQUERADE, THE (Christine Dawe).
MCSET. Cat no: **1336/1337F**. Released on Travellers Tales, '91 by Travellers Tales. Note: 12 cassettes.
MCSET. Cat no: **1854960318**. Released on Soundings, '91 by Soundings Records, Bond Street Music. Note: 12 Cassettes.

MERLIN'S KEEP (Judeth Franklyn).
MCSET. Cat no: **1854962604**. Released on Soundings, '91 by Soundings Records, Bond Street Music. Note: 10 Cassettes.
MCSET. Cat no: **1439/1440F**. Released on Travellers Tales, '91 by Travellers Tales. Note: 10 Cassettes.

MOONRAKER'S BRIDE (Judeth Franklyn).
MCSET. Cat no: **1134R**. Released on Travellers Tales, '91 by Travellers Tales. Note: 8 Cassettes.
MCSET. Cat no: **1854960326**. Released on Soundings, '91 by Soundings Records, Bond Street Music. Note: 8 Cassettes.

STORMSWIFT (Unknown narrator(s)).
MCSET. Cat no: **1854962825**. Released on Soundings, '91 by Soundings Records, Bond Street Music. Note: 8 Cassettes.

TREGARON'S DAUGHTER (Unknown narrator(s)).
MCSET. Cat no: **1854962906**. Released on Soundings, '91 by Soundings Records, Bond Street Music. Note: 9 Cassettes.

Brett, Simon
AFTER HENRY (Various narrators).
Note: Starring Prunella Scales.
MCSET. Cat no: **ZBBC 1030**. Released on BBC Radio Collection, Sep '88 by BBC Records. Note: ISBN No: 0563 225548

AFTER HENRY (Various narrators).
MCSET. Cat no: **CAB 290**. Released on Chivers Audio Books, '91 by Chivers Audio Books, Green Dragon Audio Visual. Note: 6 Cassettes.
MCSET. Cat no: **1031H**. Released on Travellers Tales, '91 by Travellers Tales. Note: 6 Cassettes

CAST, IN ORDER OF DISAPPEARANCE (Simon Brett).
MCSET. Cat no: **1017T**. Released on Travellers Tales, '91 by Travellers Tales. Note: 4 Cassettes.

COMEDIAN DIES, A (Simon Brett).
MCSET. Cat no: **1161T**. Released on Travellers Tales, '91 by Travellers Tales. Note: 4 Cassettes.

MRS. PARGETER'S PACKAGE (Simon Brett).
MCSET. Cat no: **1699T**. Released on Travellers Tales, '91 by Travellers

Tales. Note: 6 Cassettes
MCSET. Cat no: **IAB 91061.** Released on Isis Audio Books, '91. Note: 6 Cassettes.

MRS. PRESUMED DEAD (Simon Brett).
MCSET. Cat no: **1391T.** Released on Travellers Tales, '91 by Travellers Tales. Note: 6 Cassettes.
MCSET. Cat no: **IAB 89042.** Released on Isis Audio Books, '91. Note: 6 Cassettes.

MURDER UNPROMPTED (Simon Brett).
MCSET. Cat no: **CAB 686.** Released on Chivers Audio Books, Apr '92 by Chivers Audio Books, Green Dragon Audio Visual. Note: 4 Cassettes.

NICE CLASS OF CORPSE, A (Simon Brett).
MCSET. Cat no: **1213T.** Released on Travellers Tales, '91 by Travellers Tales. Note: 6 Cassettes.
MCSET. Cat no: **IAB 87122.** Released on Isis Audio Books, '91. Note: 6 Cassettes.

SERIES OF MURDERS, A (Simon Brett).
MCSET. Cat no: **CAB 427.** Released on Chivers Audio Books, '91 by Chivers Audio Books, Green Dragon Audio Visual. Note: 4 Cassettes.
MCSET. Cat no: **1459T.** Released on Travellers Tales, '91 by Travellers Tales. Note: 4 Cassettes.

SHOCK TO THE SYSTEM, A (Simon Brett).
MCSET. Cat no: **1515T.** Released on Travellers Tales, '91 by Travellers Tales. Note: 7 Cassettes.
MCSET. Cat no: **IAB 90062.** Released on Isis Audio Books, '91. Note: 7 Cassettes.

WHAT BLOODY MAN IS THAT? (Simon Brett).
MCSET. Cat no: **CAB 632.** Released on Chivers Audio Books, Oct '91 by Chivers Audio Books, Green Dragon Audio Visual. Note: 6 Cassettes.

Bridge, Ann

EPISODE AT TOLEDO, THE (Jacqueline King).
MCSET. Cat no: **IAB 92073.** Released on Isis Audio Books, Jul '92. Note: 7 Cassettes. Playing time: 8 hours, 44 mins.

Briggs, Raymond

SNOWMAN, THE (Film Soundtrack & Story) (Bernard Cribbins).
LP. Cat no: **CBS 71116.** Released on CBS, Dec '83 by Sony Music, Solomon & Peres, Outlet Records.
MC. Cat no: **40 71116.** Released on CBS, Dec '83 by Sony Music, Solomon & Peres, Outlet Records.
CD. Cat no: **CD 71116.** Released on CBS (Masterworks), Nov '87 by Sony Music.
MC. Cat no: **711164.** Released on Columbia, Nov '91 by Sony Music.
CD. Cat no: **711162.** Released on Columbia, Nov '91 by Sony Music.

Bromige, Iris

ALEX AND THE RAYNHAMS (Gwen Cherrell).
MCSET. Cat no: **OAS 20392.** Released on Oasis Audio Books, Apr '92 by Isis Audio Books. Note: 6 Cassettes. Playing time: 7hrs 11mins.

FAIR PRISONER (Carol Marsh).
MCSET. Cat no: **IAB 92074.** Released on Isis Audio Books, Jul '92. Note: 7 Cassettes. Playing time: 8 hours, 35 mins.

NEW LIFE FOR JOANNA, A (Helen Bourne).
MCSET. Cat no: **IAB 92064.** Released on Isis Audio Books, Jun '92. Note: 7 Cassettes. Playing time: 8 hours, 16 mins.

NIGHT OF THE PARTY, THE (Helen Bourne).
MCSET. Cat no: **1472F.** Released on Travellers Tales, '91 by Travellers Tales. Note: 6 Cassettes.
MCSET. Cat no: **OAS 90035.** Released on Oasis Audio Books, '91 by Isis Audio Books.

SHELTERING TREE, A (Carol Marsh).
MCSET. Cat no: **1646F.** Released on Travellers Tales, '91 by Travellers Tales. Note: 6 Cassettes.
MCSET. Cat no: **OAS 30591.** Released on Oasis Audio Books, '91 by Isis Audio Books. Note: 6 Cassettes.

Bronte, Anne

AGNES GREY (Rosemary Davis).
MCSET. Cat no: **OAS 89064.** Released on Oasis Audio Books, '91 by Isis Audio Books. Note: 6 Cassettes. Playing time 7hrs 45mins.
MCSET. Cat no: **1082C.** Released on Travellers Tales, '91 by Travellers Tales.

AGNES GREY (Anthony Homyer).
MCSET. Cat no: **TCL 5.** Released on Complete Listener, '91 by Complete Listener. Note: 5 Cassettes (BB) Playing Time: 450 Minutes.

TENANT OF WILDFELL HALL, THE (Anthony Homyer).
MCSET. Cat no: **1095/1096C.** Released on Travellers Tales, '91 by Travellers Tales. Note: 10 Cassettes.
MCSET. Cat no: **TCL 6.** Released on Complete Listener, '91 by Complete Listener. Note: 10 Cassettes. Playing time: 9 hours 10 minutes.

Bronte, Charlotte

JANE EYRE (Maureen O'Brien).
MCSET. Cat no: **1011/1012C.** Released on Travellers Tales, '91 by Travellers Tales. Note: 15 Cassettes.
MCSET. Cat no: **CTC 008.** Released on Cover to Cover, '87 by Cover to Cover Cassettes. Note: 15 Cassettes. Playing time 21 hours 40 minutes.

JANE EYRE (Dame Wendy Hiller). Note: Abridged version.
MCSET. Cat no: **1057C.** Released on Travellers Tales, '91 by Travellers Tales. Note: 2 Cassettes.

JANE EYRE (Claire Bloom & Anthony Quayle).
Note: Also available on hanging format, catalogue number:- 0001389637.
MCSET. Cat no: **HCA 14.** Released on Harper Collins, Jan '92 by Harper Collins.

JANE EYRE (Hilary Chadwick).
MCSET. Cat no: **1870524152.** Released on Eloquent Reels, '91, Bond Street Music, Morley Audio Services. Note: 4 Cassettes.

JANE EYRE (Anthony Homyer).
MCSET. Cat no: **TCL 1.** Released on Complete Listener, '91 by Complete Listener. Note: 14 Cassettes. (BB) Playing Time: 1,260 Minutes.

JANE EYRE (Claire Bloom).
MCSET. Cat no: **3003.** Released on Caedmon (USA), '88 by Caedmon Records (USA), Bond Street Music.

JANE EYRE (Dame Wendy Hiller).
MCSET. Cat no: **LFP 7160.** Released on Listen For Pleasure, Jul '84 by EMI Records.

PROFESSOR, THE (Anthony Homyer).
MCSET. Cat no: **TCL 4.** Released on Complete Listener, '91 by Complete Listener. Note: 6 Cassettes. (BB) Playing Time: 540 Minutes.

SHIRLEY (Anthony Homyer).
MCSET. Cat no: **TCL 3.** Released on Complete Listener, '91 by Complete Listener. Note: 14 Tapes. (BB). Playing Time: 1,290 Minutes.
MCSET. Cat no: **1092/1093C.** Released on Travellers Tales, '91 by Travellers Tales. Note: 14 Cassettes.

VILLETTE (Anthony Homyer).
MCSET. Cat no: **TCL 2.** Released on Complete Listener, '91 by Complete Listener. Note: 14 Cassettes. (BB) Playing Time: 1,260 Minutes.
MCSET. Cat no: **1090/1091C.** Released on Travellers Tales, '91 by Travellers Tales.

Bronte, Emily

WUTHERING HEIGHTS (Patricia Routledge).
MCSET. Cat no: **CTC 002.** Released on Cover to Cover, '87 by Cover to Cover Cassettes. Note: 10 Cassettes. Playing time:14 hrs 15 mins.

WUTHERING HEIGHTS (Anthony Homyer).
MCSET. Cat no: **TCL 7.** Released on Complete Listener, '91 by Complete Listener. Note: 9 Cassettes. (BB) Playing Time: 810 Minutes.

WUTHERING HEIGHTS (Daniel Massey).
Note: Abridged.
MCSET. Cat no: **LFP 7168.** Released on Listen For Pleasure, Sep '84 by EMI Records.

MCSET. Cat no: **1058C**. Released on Travellers Tales, '91 by Travellers Tales.

WUTHERING HEIGHTS (Various narrators).
MC. Cat no: **SAG/CAS/2**. Released on Sagittarius, Mar '88 by Sagittarius Records.
LP. Cat no: **SAG/LPR/2**. Released on Sagittarius, Mar '88 by Sagittarius Records.

WUTHERING HEIGHTS (Peter McEnery).
MC. Cat no: **0600560465**. Released on Hamlyn Books On Tape, '88, Bond Street Music.

WUTHERING HEIGHTS (Claire Bloom).
MCSET. Cat no: **2086**. Released on Caedmon (USA), '89 by Caedmon Records (USA), Bond Street Music.

WUTHERING HEIGHTS (Andrew Sachs).
MCSET. Cat no: **1870524209**. Released on Eloquent Reels, '91, Bond Street Music, Morley Audio Services. Note: 4 Cassettes.

Brookner, Anita

BRIEF LIVES (Anna Massey).
MCSET. Cat no: **1654F**. Released on Travellers Tales, '91 by Travellers Tales. Note: 8 Cassettes.

HOTEL DU LAC (Anna Massey).
MCSET. Cat no: **CAB 217**. Released on Chivers Audio Books, '91 by Chivers Audio Books, Green Dragon Audio Visual. Note: 4 cassettes.

MCSET. Cat no: **1194F**. Released on Travellers Tales, '91 by Travellers Tales. Note: 4 Cassettes.

LATECOMERS (Andrew Sachs).
MCSET. Cat no: **CAB 405**. Released on Chivers Audio Books, '91 by Chivers Audio Books, Green Dragon Audio Visual. Note: 6 Cassettes.

MCSET. Cat no: **1386F**. Released on Travellers Tales, '91 by Travellers Tales. Note: 6 Cassettes.

LEWIS PERCY (Judith Whale).
MCSET. Cat no: **IAB 92034**. Released on Isis Audio Books, Mar '92. Note: 8 Cassettes. Playing time 12hrs.

LOOK AT ME (Judith Whale).
MCSET. Cat no: **IAB 92084**. Released on Isis Audio Books, Aug '92. Note: 6 Cassettes. Playing time: 7 hours.

MISALLIANCE, THE (Margaret Hilton).
MCSET. Cat no: **1670F**. Released on Travellers Tales, '91 by Travellers Tales. Note: 6 Cassettes.

MCSET. Cat no: **RB 88510**. Released on Recorded Books, '91 by Isis Audio Books.

PROVIDENCE (Judith Whale).
MCSET. Cat no: **IAB 92055**. Released on Isis Audio Books, May '92. Note: 6 Cassettes. Playing time: 6 1/2 hours.

Brooks, Walter R.

FREDDY THE DETECTIVE (Pat Carroll).
MC. Cat no: **CP 1698**. Released on Caedmon (USA), Sep '82 by Caedmon Records (USA), Bond Street Music.

Brown, Jeff

FLAT STANLEY (David Healy).
MCSET. Cat no: **CTC 011**. Released on Cover to Cover, Sep '86 by Cover to Cover Cassettes.

Brown, Marc

HAND RHYMES (Joanna Lumley).
MC. Cat no: **0001010425**. Released on Harper Collins, '91 by Harper Collins.

Brown, Roy 'Chubby'

BEST OF ROY CHUBBY BROWN.
MC. Cat no: **RDC 1202**. Released on Rio Digital, Dec '90 by Rio Digital Records.

FOUR FACES OF CHUBBY BROWN, THE.
LP. Cat no: **RDLP 1205**. Released on Rio Digital, Dec '89 by Rio Digital Records.

MC. Cat no: **RDC 1205**. Released on Rio Digital, Dec '89 by Rio Digital Records.

FROM INSIDE THE HELMET.
MC. Cat no: **849 094 4**. Released on Polydor, Apr '91 by Polydor Ltd, Solomon & Peres.
CD. Cat no: **849 094 2**. Released on Polydor, Apr '91 by Polydor Ltd, Solomon & Peres.
LP. Cat no: **849 094 1**. Released on Polydor, Apr '91 by Polydor Ltd, Solomon & Peres.

Browning, Robert

MY LAST DUCHESS (And Other Poems) (James Mason).
MC. Cat no: **1201**. Released on Caedmon (USA), '88 by Caedmon Records (USA), Bond Street Music.

PIED PIPER OF HAMELIN (Well Loved Tales Age Up To 9) (Unknown narrator(s)).
Note: Book and cassette.
MC. Cat no: **PLB 180**. Released on Tell-A-Tale, '88 by Pickwick Records, Taylors, Clyde Factors.

PIED PIPER OF HAMELIN (Various narrators).
Note: Also includes The Ugly Duckling by Hans Christian Anderson.
EP. Cat no: **MP 9042**. Released on Mr.Pickwick, Aug '83 **Deleted** '85.

PIED PIPER OF HAMELIN (Various artists).
MC. Cat no: **TS 304**. Released on Tellastory, Oct '79 by Random Century Audiobooks.

PIED PIPER OF HAMELIN (And Other Famous Poems) (Various artists).
MC. Cat no: **TS 328**. Released on Tellastory, Jul '82 by Random Century Audiobooks.

POETRY OF BROWNING, THE (James Mason).
MC. Cat no: **1048**. Released on Caedmon (USA), '88 by Caedmon Records (USA), Bond Street Music.

Bruce, Lenny

BERKELEY CONCERT (Lenny Bruce).
Tracks / Intro: Crap house / Law, The / Prejudice / Faggots / Midgets / Religion / Postman, The / Chicks / Ralph Gleason / Alaska.
CD. Cat no: **VERB CD 7**. Released on Demon Verbals, Oct '89 by Demon Records.

Bruckner, Anita

FRIEND FROM ENGLAND, A (Cherie Lunghi).
MCSET. Cat no: **CAB 335**. Released on Chivers Audio Books, '91 by Chivers Audio Books, Green Dragon Audio Visual. Note: 6 Cassettes.
MCSET. Cat no: **1321F**. Released on Travellers Tales, '91 by Travellers Tales. Note: 6 Cassettes.

Bruna, Dick

MIFFY (And Other Stories) (Dick Bruna).
MC. Cat no: **3S 321**. Released on Tellastory, Dec '86 by Random Century Audiobooks.

MIFFY STORIES (Barbara Bliss).
MC. Cat no: **TS 321**. Released on Tellastory, Aug '92 by Random Century Audiobooks. Note: ISBN no. 1856560112

Bryan, Ashley

DANCING GRANNY, THE (And Other African Stories) (Unknown narrator(s)).
MC. Cat no: **1765**. Released on Caedmon (USA), Sep '85 by Caedmon Records (USA), Bond Street Music.

Buchan, John

GREENMANTLE (Christian Rodska).
MCSET. Cat no: **1182T**. Released on Travellers Tales, '91 by Travellers Tales. Note: 8 Cassettes.

MCSET. Cat no: **CAB 229**. Released on Chivers Audio Books, '91 by Chivers Audio Books, Green Dragon Audio Visual.

HUNTINGTOWER (Michael Elder).
MCSET. Cat no: **SPF 090-1**. Released on Schiltron Audio Books, Jun '91 by Schiltron Publishing. Note: 6 Cassettes. Playing time 7 hours.

SELECTED STORIES OF JOHN BUCHAN (Iain Cuthbertson).
MCSET. Cat no: **TTDMC 405**. Released on CSA Tell Tapes, Jul '90 by CSA Tell-Tapes. Note: 2 Cassettes. ISBN No: 18743859058.

SUSPENSE (James Cagney & Herbert Marshall).
Note: Includes: No Escape and Thirty-Nine Steps.
LP. Cat no: **LP 103**. Released on Radio Archives (USA), Feb '88 by Kiner Ents.(USA).

THIRTY-NINE STEPS, THE (Robert Powell).
MCSET. Cat no: **CAB 024**. Released on Chivers Audio Books, '91 by Chivers Audio Books, Green Dragon Audio Visual. Note: 4 Cassettes.
MCSET. Cat no: **1018T**. Released on Travellers Tales, '91 by Travellers Tales. Note: 4 Cassettes.
MCSET. Cat no: **LFP 7379**. Released on Listen For Pleasure, '91 by EMI Records.

THIRTY-NINE STEPS, THE (Sam Waterston).
MCSET. Cat no: **2098**. Released on Caedmon (USA), '89 by Caedmon Records (USA), Bond Street Music.

Buckeridge, Anthony
JENNINGS GOES TO SCHOOL.(Unknown narrators)
MC. Cat no: **P 90004**. Released on Pinnacle, '79 by Pinnacle Records, Outlet Records, Music Sales Records.

JENNINGS GOES TO SCHOOL (And Jennings Again) (Stephen Fry).
MCSET. Cat no: **ZBBC 1226**. Released on BBC Radio Collection, Jul '91 by BBC Records. Note: ISBN No: 0563 409983

Buckingham, Nancy
CLOUD OVER MALVERTON (Hazel Temperley).
MCSET. Cat no: **1854964690**. Released on Bramhope, '91 by Ulverscroft Soundings. Note: 5 Cassettes.

DARK SUMMER, THE (Anne Cater).
MCSET. Cat no: **1854964496**. Released on Soundings, '91 by Soundings Records, Bond Street Music. Note: 5 Cassettes.

QUEST FOR ALEXIS (Judith Porter).
MCSET. Cat no: **1854965689**. Released on Bramhope, Mar '92 by Ulverscroft Soundings. Note: Playing time: 60 minutes.

ROMANTIC JOURNEY (Margaret Holt).
MCSET. Cat no: **1854965387**. Released on Bramhope, Jan '92 by Ulverscroft Soundings.

STORM IN THE MOUNTAINS (Unknown narrator(s)).
MCSET. Cat no: **1854965131**. Released on Bramhope, '91 by Ulverscroft Soundings. Note: 4 Cassettes.

VALLEY OF THE RAVENS (Anne Dover).
MCSET. Cat no: **1854965840**. Released on Bramhope, Apr '92 by Ulverscroft Soundings. Note: Playing time: 60 minutes.

VICTIM OF LOVE (Unknown narrator(s)).
MCSET. Cat no: **1854965255**. Released on Bramhope, '91 by Ulverscroft Soundings. Note: 4 Cassettes.

Bunyan, John
PILGRIM'S PROGRESS, THE (Sir John Gielgud).
MCSET. Cat no: **SAY 111**. Released on Argo (Polygram), Jun '84 by PolyGram Classics **Deleted** Jan '89.
MCSET. Cat no: **ARGO 1100**. Released on Argo (EMI), Jun '89 by EMI Records.
MCSET. Cat no: **1013F**. Released on Travellers Tales, '91 by Travellers Tales. Note: 2 Cassettes.

PILGRIM'S PROGRESS, THE (James Mason).
MC. Cat no: **CP 1666**. Released on Caedmon (USA), Oct '81 by Caedmon Records (USA), Bond Street Music.

Burgess, Alan
SMALL WOMAN, THE (Ingrid Bergman).
Note: Abridged.
MCSET. Cat no: **1014F**. Released on Travellers Tales, '91 by Travellers Tales. Note: 2 Cassettes.
MCSET. Cat no: **SAY 17**. Released on Argo (Polygram), Jul '82 by PolyGram Classics **Deleted** Jan '89.

Burgess, Anthony
CLOCKWORK ORANGE, A (Anthony Burgess).
MC. Cat no: **1417**. Released on Caedmon (USA), '91 by Caedmon Records (USA), Bond Street Music.

EVE OF ST. VENUS (And Nothing Like The Sun) (Anthony Burgess).
MC. Cat no: **1442**. Released on Caedmon (USA), '88 by Caedmon Records (USA), Bond Street Music.

PIANO PLAYERS, THE (Carole Boyd).
MCSET. Cat no: **1441F**. Released on Travellers Tales, '91 by Travellers Tales. Note: 6 Cassettes.
MCSET. Cat no: **IAB 89113**. Released on Isis Audio Books, '91. Note: 6 Cassettes.

Burley, W.J.
DEATH IN WILLOW PATTERN (Gordon Griffin).
MCSET. Cat no: **1854964704**. Released on Bramhope, '91 by Ulverscroft Soundings. Note: 5 Cassettes.

HOUSE OF CARE, THE (Peter Joyce).
MCSET. Cat no: **1674T**. Released on Travellers Tales, '91 by Travellers Tales. Note: 4 Cassettes.
MCSET. Cat no: **1854964003**. Released on Bramhope, '91 by Ulverscroft Soundings. Note: 4 Cassettes.

SCHOOL MASTER, THE (Unknown narrator(s)).
MCSET. Cat no: **1854964909**. Released on Bramhope, '91 by Ulverscroft Soundings. Note: 4 Cassettes

WYCLIFFE AND DEATH IN A SALUBRIOUS PLACE (Gordon Griffin).
MCSET. Cat no: **185496450 X**. Released on Bramhope, '91 by Ulverscroft Soundings. Note: 5 Cassettes.

WYCLIFFE AND DEATH IN STANLEY STREET (Unknown narrator(s)).
MCSET. Cat no: **1854965018**. Released on Bramhope, '91 by Ulverscroft Soundings. Note: 5 Cassettes

WYCLIFFE AND THE BEALES (Unknown narrator(s)).
MCSET. Cat no: **1854962698**. Released on Bramhope, '91 by Ulverscroft Soundings. Note: 5 Cassettes.

WYCLIFFE AND THE CYCLE OF DEATH (Unknown narrator(s)).
MCSET. Cat no: **1854965263**. Released on Bramhope, '91 by Ulverscroft Soundings. Note: 5 Cassettes.

WYCLIFFE AND THE DEAD FLAUTIST (Gordon Griffin).
MCSET. Cat no: **18549655301**. Released on Bramhope, Feb '92 by Ulverscroft Soundings.

WYCLIFFE AND THE FOUR JACKS (Gordon Griffin).
MCSET. Cat no: **1503T**. Released on Travellers Tales, '91 by Travellers Tales. Note: 5 Cassettes.
MCSET. Cat no: **185496612**. Released on Bramhope, '91 by Ulverscroft Soundings. Note: 5 cassettes.

WYCLIFFE AND THE GUILT EDGED ALIBI (Gordon Griffin).
MCSET. Cat no: **1670T**. Released on Travellers Tales, '91 by Travellers Tales. Note: 4 Cassettes.
MCSET. Cat no: **1854963902**. Released on Bramhope, '91 by Ulverscroft Soundings. Note: 4 Cassettes.

WYCLIFFE AND THE PEA-GREEN BOAT (Gordon Griffin).
MCSET. Cat no: **1664T**. Released on Travellers Tales, '91 by Travellers Tales. Note: 5 Cassettes.
MCSET. Cat no: **1854963708**. Released on Bramhope, '91 by Ulverscroft Soundings. Note: 5 Cassettes.

WYCLIFFE AND THE QUIET VIRGIN (Gordon Griffin).
MCSET. Cat no: **1576T**. Released on Travellers Tales, '91 by Travellers Tales. Note: 5 Cassettes.
MCSET. Cat no: **1854963198**. Released on Bramhope, '91 by Ulverscroft Soundings. Note: 5 Cassettes.

WYCLIFFE AND THE SCAPEGOAT (Unknown narrator(s)).
MCSET. Cat no: **1854962930**. Released on Bramhope, '91 by Ulverscroft Soundings. Note: 5 Cassettes.

WYCLIFFE AND THE SCHOOLGIRLS (Unknown narrator(s)).
MCSET. Cat no: **1854962566**. Released on Bramhope, '91 by Ulverscroft Soundings. Note: 4 Cassettes.

WYCLIFFE AND THE TANGLED WEB (Gordon Griffin).
MCSET. Cat no: **1738T**. Released on Travellers Tales, '91 by Travellers Tales. Note: 4 Cassettes.

MCSET. Cat no: **1854964097**. Released on Bramhope, '91 by Ulverscroft Soundings. Note: 4 Cassettes.

WYCLIFFE AND THE THREE TOED MYSTERY (Gordon Griffin).
MCSET. Cat no: **1854965859**. Released on Bramhope, Apr '92 by Ulverscroft Soundings. Note: 5 Cassettes.

WYCLIFFE AND THE WINDSOR BLUE (Unknown narrator(s)).
MCSET. Cat no: **1854962485**. Released on Bramhope, '91 by Ulverscroft Soundings. Note: 5 Cassettes.

WYCLIFFE IN PAUL'S COURT (Gordon Griffin).
MCSET. Cat no: **1743T**. Released on Travellers Tales, '91 by Travellers Tales. Note: 4 Cassettes.

MCSET. Cat no: **1854964321**. Released on Bramhope, '91 by Ulverscroft Soundings. Note: 4 Cassettes.

WYCLIFFE'S WILD GOOSE CHASE (Gordon Griffin).
MCSET. Cat no: **1582T**. Released on Travellers Tales, '91 by Travellers Tales. Note: 4 Cassettes.

MCSET. Cat no: **1854963430**. Released on Bramhope, '91 by Ulverscroft Soundings. Note: 4 Cassettes.

Burningham, John

MR GRUMPY'S OUTING (Stephen Thorne).
MC. Cat no: **TS 329**. Released on Tellastory, '91 by Random Century Audiobooks. Note: ISBN no. 185656018X

OI, GET OFF OUR TRAIN (Stephen Thorne).
MC. Cat no: **TS 391**. Released on Tellastory, Oct '91 by Random Century Audiobooks. Note: ISBN no. 1856561070

Burns, Robert

ASSESSMENT AND SELECTION (Volume 1) (Various narrators).
MC. Cat no: **SSC 035**. Released on Scotsoun, '91 by Scotsoun Recordings, Morley Audio Services.

ASSESSMENT AND SELECTION (Volume 2) (Various narrators).
MC. Cat no: **SSC 036**. Released on Scotsoun, '91 by Scotsoun Recordings, Morley Audio Services.

ASSESSMENT AND SELECTION (Volume 3) (Various narrators).
MC. Cat no: **SSC 037**. Released on Scotsoun, '91 by Scotsoun Recordings, Morley Audio Services.

BURNS COTTAGE SELECTION (Various narrators).
MC. Cat no: **SSC 067**. Released on Scotsoun, '91 by Scotsoun Recordings, Morley Audio Services.

POEMS CHIEFLY IN THE SCOTTISH DIALECT (Irvine Burns).

MC. Cat no: **SSC 008**. Released on Scotsoun, '91 by Scotsoun Recordings, Morley Audio Services.

POETRY OF ROBERT BURNS, THE (And Border Ballads) (Various narrators).
MC. Cat no: **1103**. Released on Caedmon (USA), '88 by Caedmon Records (USA), Bond Street Music.

Burroughs, William S.

BREAKTHROUGH IN GREY ROOM (William S Burroughs).
Tracks / Canine was in combat with the alien / Origin and theory of the tape cutup / Recalling all active agents / Silver smoke of dreams / Junkie relations / Joujouka (x 4) / Curse go back / Present time excersises / Working with the popular forces / Interview with Mr Martin / Soundpiece / Burroughs called the law.
LP. Cat no: **SUB 33005-8**. Released on Sub Rosa, Feb '87 by Sub Rosa Records.

DEAD CITY RADIO.(Unknown narrators).
CD. Cat no: **ANCD 8760**. Released on Antilles (Import), Apr '92. Note: Originally released 4/91

MC. Cat no: **ANC 8760**. Released on Antilles (Import), Apr '92. Note: Originally released 4/91

DOCTOR IS ON THE MARKET, THE (William S Burroughs).
Tracks / Twilight's last gleaming / Doctor is on the market, The/ Green nun, The / From here to eternity / Meeting of international conference of technical... / Ah pook is here / Junkie / Towers open fire.
LP. Cat no: **IM 003**. Released on Interior Music, Jan '88 by Interior Music Records.
LP. Cat no: **LTMV.XX**. Released on Les Moumtures Terrestes, Oct '86 by Red Rhino Records.

Burton, Betty

CONSEQUENCES OF WAR, THE (Judith Porter).
MCSET. Cat no: **1687F**. Released on Travellers Tales, '91 by Travellers Tales. Note: 8 Cassettes.

MCSET. Cat no: **1854964372**. Released on Soundings, '91 by Soundings Records, Bond Street Music.

Busch, Wilhelm

DOD AND DAVIE (J.K. Annard).
MC. Cat no: **SSC 075**. Released on Scotsoun, '91 by Scotsoun Recordings, Morley Audio Services.

Butler, Gwendoline

COFFIN FROM THE PAST, A (Philip Talbot).
MCSET. Cat no: **1162T**. Released on Travellers Tales, '91 by Travellers Tales. Note: 4 Cassettes.

COFFIN IN MALTA (Philip Talbot).
MCSET. Cat no: **CAT 4038**. Released on Chivers Audio Books, '91 by Chivers Audio Books, Green Dragon Audio Visual. Note: 4 Cassettes.

MCSET. Cat no: **1429T**. Released on Travellers Tales, '91 by Travellers Tales. Note: 4 Cassettes.

COFFIN IN THE BLACK MUSEUM (Philip Talbot).
MCSET. Cat no: **CAT 4068**. Released on Chivers Audio Books, '91 by Chivers Audio Books, Green Dragon Audio Visual. Note: 6 Cassettes.

Butterworth, Michael

MAN WHO BROKE THE BANK AT MONTE CARLO (Richard Mitchley).
MCSET. Cat no: **1163T**. Released on Travellers Tales, '91 by Travellers Tales. Note: 4 Cassettes.

MCSET. Cat no: **CAT 4020**. Released on Chivers Audio Books, '91 by Chivers Audio Books, Green Dragon Audio Visual.

Byars, Betsy

BLOSSOMS AND THE GREEN PHANTOM (Blain Fairman).
MCSET. Cat no: **3CCA 3070**. Released on Chivers Audio Books, '91 by Chivers Audio Books, Green Dragon Audio Visual. Note: 3 Cassettes.

MCSET. Cat no: **9182F**. Released on Travellers Tales, '91 by Travellers Tales. Note: 3 Cassettes.

BLOSSOMS MEET THE VULTURE LADY (Blain Fairman).
MCSET. Cat no: **2CCA 3071**. Released on Chivers Audio Books, '91 by Chivers Audio Books, Green Dragon Audio Visual. Note: 2 Cassettes.

MCSET. Cat no: **9172F**. Released on Travellers Tales, '91 by Travellers Tales. Note: 2 Cassettes

CRACKER JACKSON (Kerry Shale).
MCSET. Cat no: **3CCA 3028**. Released on Chivers Audio Books, '91 by Chivers Audio Books, Green Dragon Audio Visual. Note: 3 Cassettes.

MCSET. Cat no: **9100F**. Released on Travellers Tales, '91 by Travellers Tales. Note: 3 Cassettes.

EIGHTEENTH EMERGENCY, THE (James Aubery).
MC. Cat no: **881387**. Released on Puffin Cover To Cover, '88, Green Dragon Audio Visual.

NOT-JUST-ANYBODY FAMILY, THE (Blain Fairman).
MC. Cat no: **3CCA 3043**. Released on Chivers Audio Books, '88 by Chivers Audio Books, Green Dragon Audio Visual. Note: 3 Cassettes.

MCSET. Cat no: **9127F**. Released on Travellers Tales, '91 by Travellers Tales. Note: 3 Cassettes.

TWO THOUSAND POUND GOLDFISH, THE (Blain Fairman).
MCSET. Cat no: **2CCA 3090**. Released on Chivers Audio Books, '91 by Chivers Audio Books, Green Dragon Audio Visual. Note: 2 Cassettes.

MCSET. Cat no: **9151F**. Released on Travellers Tales, '91 by Travellers Tales. Note: 2 Cassettes.

Byatt, A.S.
POSSESSION (Alan Howard).
MCSET. Cat no: **RC 2**. Released on Random Century, '91 by Random Century Audiobooks, Conifer Records. Note: 2 Cassettes. ISBN 1856860019. 3 hrs approx.

Cadell, Elizabeth
EMPTY NEST, THE (Ciaran Madden).
MCSET. Cat no: **CAB 223**. Released on Chivers Audio Books, '91 by Chivers Audio Books, Green Dragon Audio Visual. Note: 6 Cassettes.
MCSET. Cat no: **1164F**. Released on Travellers Tales, '91 by Travellers Tales.
FAMILY GATHERING (Judith Porter).
MCSET. Cat no: **1854965549**. Released on Bramhope, Feb '92 by Ulverscroft Soundings. Note: Playing time: 60 minutes.
GREEN EMPRESS, THE (Jane Jermyn).
MCSET. Cat no: **1014R**. Released on Travellers Tales, '91 by Travellers Tales. Note: 4 Cassettes.
MCSET. Cat no: **1854960342**. Released on Bramhope, '91 by Ulverscroft Soundings. Note: 4 Cassettes.
LANGUAGE OF THE HEART (Jane Jermyn).
MCSET. Cat no: **1015R**. Released on Travellers Tales, '91 by Travellers Tales. Note: 4 Cassettes.
MCSET. Cat no: **1854960350**. Released on Bramhope, '91 by Ulverscroft Soundings. Note: 4 Cassettes.
OUT OF THE RAIN (Ciaran Madden).
MCSET. Cat no: **CAB 309**. Released on Chivers Audio Books, Jul '88 by Chivers Audio Books, Green Dragon Audio Visual. Note: 6 Cassettes.
MCSET. Cat no: **1316F**. Released on Travellers Tales, '91 by Travellers Tales. Note: 6 Cassettes.
WAITING GAME (Ciaran Madden).
MCSET. Cat no: **1254F**. Released on Travellers Tales, '91 by Travellers Tales. Note: 6 Cassettes.

Cain, James M
DOUBLE INDEMNITY (Barry Bostiwick).
Note: Also available on hanging format, catalogue number: 0001031597
MCSET. Cat no: **HCA 7**. Released on Harper Collins, Jan '92 by Harper Collins.

Caldwell & Stearn
I, JUDAS (Grover Gardner).
Note: Authors are Taylor Caldwell and Jess Stearn.
MCSET. Cat no: **RB 82040**. Released on Recorded Books, May '92 by Isis Audio Books. Note: 9 Cassettes. Playing time: 13 hours.

Cameron, James
INDIAN SUMMER, AN (Paul Shelley).
MCSET. Cat no: **ZBBC 1247**. Released on BBC Radio Collection, Aug '91 by BBC Records. Note: ISBN No: 0563 365153

Cammell, Jim
JIMMY'S GOLDEN MILE (Volume 1) (Krankies).
Note: For children aged 3 to 9 years. Includes The Case of the Kidnapped Clown and The Case of the Missing Sea Turtle.
MC. Cat no: **VCA 627**. Released on VFM Cassettes, '85 by VFM Cassettes, Midland Records, Crusader Marketing Co., Taylors, Morley Audio Services.
JIMMY'S GOLDEN MILE (Volume 2) (Krankies).
Note: For children aged 3 - 9 years. Includes The Case of the Vanishing Zebra and The Case of the Missing Models.
MC. Cat no: **VCA 628**. Released on VFM Cassettes, '85 by VFM Cassettes, Midland Records, Crusader Marketing Co., Taylors, Morley Audio Services.
JIMMY'S GOLDEN MILE (Volume 3) (Krankies).
Note: For children aged 3 - 9 years. Includes The Case of the Missing Jack-in-the-Box and The Case of the Bearded Lady.
MC. Cat no: **VCA 629**. Released on VFM Cassettes, '85 by VFM Cassettes, Midland Records, Crusader Marketing Co., Taylors, Morley Audio Services.

Campbell, Colin
COLIN CAMPBELL'S LOCAL RADIO (Volume 1).
MC. Cat no: **CJR 004**. Released on Ross (1), Dec '85 by Ross Records, Taylors, Celtic Music, Duncans, Record Merchandisers, Terry Blood Dist.
COLIN CAMPBELL'S LOCAL RADIO (Volume 2).
MC. Cat no: **CJR 007**. Released on Ross (1), Dec '86 by Ross Records, Taylors, Celtic Music, Duncans, Record Merchandisers, Terry Blood Dist.
COLIN CAMPBELL'S LOCAL RADIO (Volume 3).
Tracks / Radio Caithness / North of the Ord / Radio Bettyhill / Blach Isle radio / Eilean Dubh / Radio Morningside / Perthshire autumn, A / Radio back / Loch Duich once more / Radio Auchnagatt / Radio Papa Westray / Peedie boy.
MC. Cat no: **CWGRTV 4**. Released on Ross (1), Dec '87 by Ross Records, Taylors, Celtic Music, Duncans, Record Merchandisers, Terry Blood Dist.
COLIN CAMPBELL'S LOCAL RADIO (Volume 4).
Tracks / Radio Caithness intro / Radio Bettyhill / Radio Auchnagatt / Kilbaddie's bonnie quine / Radio Caithness / Caithness and you / Radio Caithness quiz / Deserted Highland discs / Song of the Spey / Radio back / Radio Morningside / Let me show you the Highlands / Radio Auchnagatt - Campbells of Slacktacktit / Lass of Suie Hill / Radio back - News / Radio Caithness - book at bedtime / Time is but a sigh.
MC. Cat no: **CWGRTV 10**. Released on Ross (1), Nov '88 by Ross Records, Taylors, Celtic Music, Duncans, Record Merchandisers, Terry Blood Dist..
COLIN CAMPBELL'S LOCAL RADIO (Volume 5) (Colin Campbell).
Tracks / Radio Caithness - intro / Radio Bettyhill - news / Radio Back - weather forecast and letter spot / Celtic Queen / Radio Caithness - Nirex phone in / Radio Papa Westray - news / Radio Bettyhill - mastermind / Banffshire braes / Radio Caithness - It's your line phone in / Black Isle radio - news / Radio Auchnagatt - Campbells of Slacktackit / Radio Ballinluig - news / Menzies tree / Radio Back - Evening service / Radio Caithness - Nuclear fishin'? / Radio Scallowag - news / Slipway at Sandsayre / Findhorn challenge, The.
MC. Cat no: **CWGR TV 14**. Released on Ross (1), Nov '90 by Ross Records, Taylors, Celtic Music, Duncans, Record Merchandisers, Terry Blood Dist.

Campbell, Myles
BAILTEAN VILLAGES (Accompanying Music by Donald Shaw) (Various artists).
Note: Donald Shaw (Capercaillie) provides a musical underlay to Myles Campbell's poems narrated, in Gaelic, by himself and, in English, by others.
MC. Cat no: **MR 1018**. Released on Mull Recordings, '90 by Mull Recordings.

Campbell, Patrick
WAVING ALL EXCUSES (James Villiers).
MCSET. Cat no: **LISF 0007/0008**. Released on Listen Productions, Nov '84.

Canitz, William J.
SUSPECTS (Edward Asner).
MCSET. Cat no: **0600558584**. Released on Hamlyn Books On Tape, Apr '88, Bond Street Music.

Canning, Victor
HOUSE OF THE SEVEN FLIES (Valentine Dyall).
MC. Cat no: **CAB 027**. Released on Chivers Audio Books, Aug '81 by

Chivers Audio Books, Green Dragon Audio Visual.
MCSET. Cat no: **1019T**. Released on Travellers Tales, '91 by Travellers Tales. Note: 6 Cassettes.

WHIP HAND, THE (Valentine Dyall).
MCSET. Cat no: **1020T**. Released on Travellers Tales, '91 by Travellers Tales. Note: 6 Cassettes.

Capote, Truman
BREAKFAST AT TIFFANY'S (Various narrators).
MCSET. Cat no: **0502**. Released on Caedmon (USA), '89 by Caedmon Records (USA), Bond Street Music. Note: 2 Cassettes

Captain Marryat
PHANTOM SHIP AND MR MIDSHIPMAN EASY, THE (Joss Ackland).
Note: For 8 to 16 year olds.
MC. Cat no: **C 004**. Released on Green Dragon, '91 by Green Dragon Audio Visual.

Carey, Peter
OSCAR AND LUCINDA (Nigel Graham).
MCSET. Cat no: **1350/1351F**. Released on Travellers Tales, '91 by Travellers Tales. Note: 12 Cassettes.
MCSET. Cat no: **IAB 89052**. Released on Isis Audio Books, '91. Note: 12 Cassettes.

Carlin, George
EVENING WITH WALLY LONDO, AN.
Tracks / New news / Teenage masturbation / Mental hot foots / High on the plane / Bodily functions / Wurds / For name's sake / Baseball - football / Good sports / Flesh colored band parts / Religious life / Radio dial / Y'ever unrelated things.
LP. Cat no: **K 59655**. Released on Little David (USA), '88.

TOLEDO WINDOW BOX.
Tracks / Goofy shit / Toledo window box / Nursery rhymes / Some werds / Water sex / Metric system, The / God gay lib / Snot the original rubber cement / Urinals are 50% universal / Few more farts, A.
LP. Cat no: **K 59652**. Released on Little David (USA), '88.

Carpenter, Humphrey
MR. MAJEIKA (Humphrey Carpenter).
MCSET. Cat no: **2CCA 3130**. Released on Chivers Audio Books, '91 by Chivers Audio Books, Green Dragon Audio Visual. Note: 2 Cassettes.

Carr, Margaret
BLINDMAN'S BLUFF (Unknown narrator(s)).
MCSET. Cat no: **1854965271**. Released on Bramhope, '91 by Ulverscroft Soundings. Note: 4 Cassettes.

DAGGERS DRAWN (Unknown narrator(s)).
MCSET. Cat no: **1854964917**. Released on Bramhope, '91 by Ulverscroft Soundings. Note: 4 Cassettes.

SHARANDEL (Melissa Jane Sinden).
MCSET. Cat no: **1854964798**. Released on Bramhope, '91 by Ulverscroft Soundings. Note: 5 Cassettes.

Carroll, Lewis
ALICE IN WONDERLAND (Margaretta Scott & Jane Asher).
MCSET. Cat no: **SAY 7**. Released on Argo (Polygram), '82 by PolyGram Classics **Deleted** Jan '89.

ALICE IN WONDERLAND (Unknown narrator(s)).
LP. Cat no: **REC 563**. Released on BBC, May '85 by BBC Records, Taylors **Deleted** 31 Aug '88.
MC. Cat no: **ZCM 563**. Released on BBC, May '85 by BBC Records, Taylors **Deleted** 31 Aug '88.
MC. Cat no: **SBC 127**. Released on Caedmon (USA), Sep '85 by Caedmon Records (USA), Bond Street Music.
MC. Cat no: **STC 014**. Released on VFM Cassettes, Jun '88 by VFM Cassettes, Midland Records, Crusader Marketing Co., Taylors, Morley Audio Services.
MC. Cat no: **DIS 006**. Released on Disney (Read-a-long), Jul '90 by Disneyland Records.
MC. Cat no: **STK 026**. Released on Stick-A-Tale, Jul '90 by Pickwick Records.
MLP. Cat no: **D 306**. Released on Disneyland, '82 by Disneyland-Vista Records (USA).
MC. Cat no: **D 23DC**. Released on Disneyland, '82 by Disneyland-Vista Records (USA).

ALICE IN WONDERLAND (Joan Greenwood & Stanley Holloway).
MC. Cat no: **1097**. Released on Caedmon (USA), '88 by Caedmon Records (USA), Bond Street Music.

ALICE IN WONDERLAND (Willie Rushton).
MCSET. Cat no: **9020F**. Released on Travellers Tales, '91 by Travellers Tales. Note: 2 Cassettes.

ALICE IN WONDERLAND (Children's Classics) (Unknown narrator(s)).
Note: Book and cassette.
MC. Cat no: **PLBC 194**. Released on Tell-A-Tale, '88 by Pickwick Records, Taylors, Clyde Factors.

ALICE IN WONDERLAND (Various narrators).
Tracks / All on a golden afternoon: Various artists / Readin, riting and rithmetic: Dotrice, Karen / Decisions: Connor, Kenneth / Speak roughly to your little boy: Reid, Beryl/Dorothy Squires / Lobster quadrille, The: Howerd, Frankie / Beautiful soup: Howerd, Frankie/Harry H. Corbett/Karen Dotrice / Mad hatters tea party, The: Forsyth, Bruce/Karen Dotrice/Fenella Fielding/Tommy Cooper / Ceremonial march: Dotrice, Karen/Peggy Mount/Arthur Haynes / Love makes the world go round: Reid, Beryl (nar) / I'll have you executed on the spot: Haynes, Arthur/Peggy Mount / I remember the incident: Connor, Kenneth / All on a golden afternoon (reprise): Various artists.
2LP. Cat no: **MFP 1013**. Released on MFP, Sep '81 by EMI Records, Solomon & Peres **Deleted** Sep '86.
MCSET. Cat no: **TCMFP 1013**. Released on MFP, Sep '81 by EMI Records, Solomon & Peres **Deleted** Sep '86.

ALICE IN WONDERLAND (Stanley Holloway).
Note: Also available on hanging format, Cat. No: 0001387781.
MC. Cat no: **0001034308**. Released on Harper Collins, '91 by Harper Collins.

ALICE IN WONDERLAND (And Alice Through the Looking Glass) (Alan Bennett).
MCSET. Cat no: **ZBBC 1013**. Released on BBC, Sep '88 by BBC Records, Taylors. Note: ISBN No: 0563 225505.

ALICE IN WONDERLAND (Willie Rushton).
MCSET. Cat no: **LFP 7391**. Released on Listen For Pleasure, Jun '89 by EMI Records. Note: Reissue. Formerly LFP 4170635 released 10/85.

ALICE THROUGH THE LOOKING GLASS (Unknown narrator(s)).
MCSET. Cat no: **DTO 10575**. Released on Ditto, '88 by Pickwick Records, Midland Records.

ALICE THROUGH THE LOOKING GLASS (Margaretta Scott & Jane Asher).
MCSET. Cat no: **SAY 43**. Released on Argo (Polygram), Jun '88 by PolyGram Classics **Deleted** Jan '89.

ALICE'S ADVENTURES IN WONDERLAND (Unknown narrator(s)).
MCSET. Cat no: **DTO 10573**. Released on Ditto, '88 by Pickwick Records, Midland Records.

ALICE'S ADVENTURES IN WONDERLAND (Patricia Routledge).
MCSET. Cat no: **9019F**. Released on Travellers Tales, '91 by Travellers Tales. Note: 3 Cassettes.
MCSET. Cat no: **CTC 020**. Released on Cover to Cover, '90 by Cover to Cover Cassettes. Note: 3 Cassettes. Playing time: 3 hours 10 minutes.

ALICE'S ADVENTURES IN WONDERLAND (Nigel Hawthorne).
MC. Cat no: **0600560600**. Released on Hamlyn Books On Tape, '88, Bond Street Music.

COMPLETE ALICE IN WONDERLAND, THE (Christopher Plummer).
MC. Cat no: **0001042696**. Released

on Collins-Caedmon, '88 by Collins Audio, Taylors, Bond Street Music.

HUNTING OF THE SNARK, THE (Various narrators).
Tracks / Hunting of the snark / Two old bachelors, The / Jumblies, The / Mr. & Mrs. Discobbolos / Jackdaw of Rheims:
MC. Cat no: **ANV 627.** Released on Anvil Cassettes, Jan '81 by Anvil Cassettes, Chivers Audio Books.

NONSENSE VERSE (Stanley Holloway).
MC. Cat no: **1078.** Released on Caedmon (USA), '88 by Caedmon Records (USA), Bond Street Music.

THROUGH THE LOOKING GLASS (Joan Greenwood & Stanley Holloway).
MC. Cat no: **1098.** Released on Caedmon (USA), '88 by Caedmon Records (USA), Bond Street Music.

THROUGH THE LOOKING GLASS (And What Alice Saw There) (Christopher Plummer).
Note: Contains *The Wasp in a Wig*, a previously missing chapter.
MCSET. Cat no: **129.** Released on Caedmon (USA), '88 by Caedmon Records (USA), Bond Street Music.

THROUGH THE LOOKING GLASS (Willie Rushton).
MCSET. Cat no: **TCLFP 417 116-5.** Released on Listen For Pleasure, '83 by EMI Records.
MCSET. Cat no: **9021F.** Released on Travellers Tales, '91 by Travellers Tales. Note: 2 Cassettes.

Carrott, Jasper
CARROTTS CONDENSED CLASSICS.
Tracks / Mole, The / Magic roundabout / Car insurance / America / Truck drivers / Zits / Football / Driving lesson, The / Scunthorpe baths / Tribute to Eric my idol / Explosive gases.
CD. Cat no: **CCD 30.** Released on Dover, Nov '91 by Chrysalis Records, EMI Distribution (M & D) Services.
LP. Cat no: **ADD 30.** Released on Dover, Nov '91 by Chrysalis Records, EMI Distribution (M & D) Services.
MC. Cat no: **ZDD 30.** Released on Dover, Nov '91 by Chrysalis Records, EMI Distribution (M & D) Services.

COSMIC CARROTT
Tracks / 60's, The / Cowards / Alternatives / Plumbers / Mechanics / Boy scouts / Store detectives / Cruise missiles / More cars / Fear / Animals / Xmas time / Cosmic carrott.
LP. Cat no: **LAUGH 1.** Released on Portrait, Dec '86 by Sony Music Operations **Deleted** Aug '88.
MC. Cat no: **LAUGH 401.** Released on Portrait, Dec '86 by Sony Music Operations **Deleted** Aug '88.

LIVE IN AMERICA.
LP. Cat no: **RNLP 817.** Released on Rhino (USA), Jan '86 by Rhino Records (USA).

RABBITS ON AND ON AND ON...
Tracks / Introduction / Spaghetti junction / Boggery, The / In concert / Local radio / BBC medical / Magic roundabout / Waggy's testimonial / Learner driver / Tribute to Eric Idle my idol.
LP. Cat no: **DJF 20462.** Released on DJM, Nov '76.
MC. Cat no: **DJH 40462.** Released on DJM, Nov '76.

Carter, Angela
WISE CHILDREN (Dora Bryan).
MCSET. Cat no: **RC 83.** Released on Random Century, Apr '92 by Random Century Audiobooks, Conifer Records.

Cartland, Barbara
CRUEL COUNT, THE (Jeremy Sinden).
MCSET. Cat no: **IAB 88113.** Released on Isis Audio Books, '91. Note: 4 Cassettes.
MCSET. Cat no: **1139R.** Released on Travellers Tales, '91 by Travellers Tales. Note: 4 Cassettes.

FLOWERS FOR THE GOD OF LOVE (Jeremy Sinden).
MCSET. Cat no: **1133R.** Released on Travellers Tales, '91 by Travellers Tales. Note: 4 Cassettes.
MCSET. Cat no: **IAB 88053.** Released on Isis Audio Books, '91. Note: 4 Cassettes.

GIFT OF THE GODS (Leslie Clack).
MCSET. Cat no: **1125R.** Released on Travellers Tales, '91 by Travellers Tales. Note: 4 Cassettes.
MCSET. Cat no: **IAB 88023.** Released on Isis Audio Books, '91. Note: 4 Cassettes.

KING IN LOVE, A (Christian Rodska).
MCSET. Cat no: **IAB 88103.** Released on Isis Audio Books, '91. Note: 4 cassette set.
MCSET. Cat no: **1138R.** Released on Travellers Tales, '91 by Travellers Tales. Note: 4 cassette

LITTLE WHITE DOVES OF LOVE (Jeremy Sinden).
MCSET. Cat no: **IAB 88073.** Released on Isis Audio Books, '91. Note: 4 Cassettes.
MCSET. Cat no: **1132R.** Released on Travellers Tales, '91 by Travellers Tales.

LOVE LOCKED IN (John Green).
MCSET. Cat no: **1129R.** Released on Travellers Tales, '91 by Travellers Tales. Note: 4 Cassettes.
MCSET. Cat no: **IAB 880033.** Released on Isis Audio Books, '91.

LOVE, LORDS AND LADYBIRDS (John Green).
MCSET. Cat no: **1123R.** Released on Travellers Tales, '91 by Travellers Tales. Note: 4 Cassettes.
MCSET. Cat no: **IAB 87116.** Released on Isis Audio Books, '91. Note: 4 Cassettes.

LOVERS IN PARADISE (Christian Rodska).
MCSET. Cat no: **1130R.** Released on Travellers Tales, '91 by Travellers Tales. Note: 4 Cassettes.
MCSET. Cat no: **IAB 88063.** Released on Isis Audio Books, '91. Note: 4 Cassettes.

PASSION AND THE FLOWER, THE (Leslie Clack).
MCSET. Cat no: **1131R.** Released on Travellers Tales, '91 by Travellers Tales. Note: 4 Cassettes.
MCSET. Cat no: **IAB 88043.** Released on Isis Audio Books, '91. Note: 4 Cassettes.

PRINCE AND THE PEKINESE, THE (Christian Rodska).
MCSET. Cat no: **IAB 88083.** Released on Isis Audio Books, '91. Note: 4 Cassettes.
MCSET. Cat no: **1136R.** Released on Travellers Tales, '91 by Travellers Tales.

SIGN OF LOVE, THE (Leslie Clack).
MCSET. Cat no: **1124R.** Released on Travellers Tales, '91 by Travellers Tales. Note: 4 Cassettes.
MCSET. Cat no: **IAB 87123.** Released on Isis Audio Books, '91. Note: 4 Cassettes.

WALTZ OF HEARTS, THE (Jeremy Sinden).
MCSET. Cat no: **1137R.** Released on Travellers Tales, '91 by Travellers Tales. Note: 4 Cassettes.
MCSET. Cat no: **IAB 88093.** Released on Isis Audio Books, '91. Note: 4 Cassettes.

WOMEN HAVE HEARTS (John Green).
MCSET. Cat no: **1126R.** Released on Travellers Tales, '91 by Travellers Tales. Note: 4 Cassettes.
MCSET. Cat no: **IAB 88013.** Released on Isis Audio Books, '91. Note: 4 Cassettes.

Carus, Zena
SECRET OF KELLY'S MILL, THE (Nigel Greaves).
MCSET. Cat no: **086 222 042-3.** Released on Chivers Calvacade, Apr '88 by Chivers Audio Books, Green Dragon Audio Visual. Note: 2 Cassettes
MCSET. Cat no: **9022F.** Released on Travellers Tales, '91 by Travellers Tales. Note: 2 Cassettes

Castle, Arthur
FLIGHT INTO DANGER See under Hailey, John

Cather, Willa
O PIONEERS (Barbara McCulloch).
MCSET. Cat no: **RB 89460.** Released on Recorded Books, Mar '92 by Isis Audio Books. Note: 5 Cassettes.

Cecil, Laura
LISTEN TO THIS (Stories For Young Children) (Prunella Scales).

MC. Cat no: **TS 404.** Released on Tellastory, Mar '92 by Random Century Audiobooks.
STUFF AND NONSENSE (Prunella Scales).
Note: Advanced release.
MC. Cat no: **TS 415.** Released on Tellastory, Aug '92 by Random Century Audiobooks. Note: ISBN no. 1856561844

Challis, Simon
DEATH ON A QUIET BEACH (Tom Hunsinger).
MCSET. Cat no: **1434T.** Released on Travellers Tales, '91 by Travellers Tales. Note: 4 Cassettes.
MCSET. Cat no: **1854962183.** Released on Bramhope, '91 by Ulverscroft Soundings. Note: 4 Cassettes.

Chambers, Peter
DON'T BOTHER TO KNOCK (John Keyworth).
MCSET. Cat no: **1376T.** Released on Travellers Tales, '91 by Travellers Tales. Note: 4 Cassettes.
MCSET. Cat no: **1854960377.** Released on Bramhope, '91 by Ulverscroft Soundings. Note: 4 Cassettes.
FEMALE HANDLE WITH CARE (Brian Rapkin).
MCSET. Cat no: **1585T.** Released on Travellers Tales, '91 by Travellers Tales. Note: 4 Cassettes.
MCSET. Cat no: **1854962981.** Released on Bramhope, '91 by Ulverscroft Soundings. Note: 4 Cassettes.
HOT MONEY CAPER, THE (John Chancer).
MCSET. Cat no: **1854964852.** Released on Trio, '91 by EMI Records. Note: 3 Cassettes.
LONG TIME DEAD, A (Garrick Hagon).
MCSET. Cat no: **1650T.** Released on Travellers Tales, '91 by Travellers Tales. Note: 4 Cassettes.
MCSET. Cat no: **1854963511.** Released on Bramhope, '91 by Ulverscroft Soundings. Note: 4 Cassettes.
MINIATURE MURDER MYSTERY (A Gentle Little Murder) (John Keyworth & Christopher Kay).
Note: Authors are Peter Chambers and Philip Daniels.
MCSET. Cat no: **1198T.** Released on Travellers Tales, '91 by Travellers Tales. Note: 6 Cassettes.
MCSET. Cat no: **1854960385.** Released on Bramhope, '91 by Ulverscroft Soundings. Note: 3 Cassettes.
MURDER IS FOR KEEPS (Unknown narrator(s)).
MCSET. Cat no: **185496514X.** Released on Bramhope, '91 by Ulverscroft Soundings. Note: 5 Cassettes.
NO GOLD WHEN YOU GO (John Keyworth).
MCSET. Cat no: **1203T.** Released on Travellers Tales, '91 by Travellers Tales. Note: 4 Cassettes.

MCSET. Cat no: **1854960393.** Released on Bramhope, '91 by Ulverscroft Soundings. Note: 4 Cassettes.
SPEAK ILL OF THE DEAD (John Keyworth).
MCSET. Cat no: **1504T.** Released on Travellers Tales, '91 by Travellers Tales. Note: 4 Cassettes.
MCSET. Cat no: **1854962620.** Released on Bramhope, '91 by Ulverscroft Soundings. Note: 4 Cassettes.

Chand, Prem
PRATIGVA (HINDI) (Pramod Kaul).
MCSET. Cat no: **86706.** Released on Sonex, '91. Note: 4 Cassettes.

Chander, Krishan
SHIKAST (URDU) (Iqbal Warsi).
MCSET. Cat no: **86680.** Released on Sonex, '91.

Chandler, Raymond
BIG SLEEP, THE (Daniel Massey).
MCSET. Cat no: **LFP 7113.** Released on Listen For Pleasure, Apr '83 by EMI Records Deleted '89.
HIGH WINDOW, THE (Elliot Gould).
Note: Also available on hanging format, catalogue number:- 0001031554
MCSET. Cat no: **0001072420.** Released on Harper Collins, '91 by Harper Collins. Note: 2 Cassettes.
LADY IN THE LAKE, THE (Elliot Gould).
Note: Also available on hanging format, catalogue number:- 0001031562.
MCSET. Cat no: **0001072439.** Released on Harper Collins, '91 by Harper Collins. Note: 2 Cassettes.
LITTLE SISTER, THE (Ed Bishop).
MCSET. Cat no: **CAB 057.** Released on Chivers Audio Books, '91 by Chivers Audio Books, Green Dragon Audio Visual. Note: 6 Cassettes.
MCSET. Cat no: **1021T.** Released on Travellers Tales, '91 by Travellers Tales. Note: 6 Cassettes.
LITTLE SISTER, THE (Elliot Gould).
Note: Also available on hanging format, catalogue number:- 0001031546.
MCSET. Cat no: **0001072927.** Released on Harper Collins, '91 by Harper Collins. Note: 2 Cassettes.
LONG GOODBYE, THE (Elliot Gould).
Note: Also available on hanging format, catalogue number:- 0001031538.
MCSET. Cat no: **0001072919.** Released on Harper Collins, '91 by Harper Collins. Note: 2 Cassettes.
RED WIND (Elliot Gould).
Note: Also available on hanging format
MC. Cat no: **0001388258.** Released on Harper Collins, '91 by Harper Collins.
TROUBLE IS MY BUSINESS (Elliot Gould).
Note: Also available on hanging format, catalogue number:- 0001387804.
MCSET. Cat no: **0001387790.** Re-

leased on Harper Collins, '91 by Harper Collins. Note: 2 Cassettes.

Chandos, Fay
SWEET ROSEMARY (June Andrews).
MCSET. Cat no: **CLT 1008.** Released on Candlelight, '88 by AVLS (Audio-Visual Library Services). Note: 2 Cassettes.

Chaplin, Sid
DAY OF THE SARDINE (Christopher Kay).
MCSET. Cat no: **1016F.** Released on Travellers Tales, '91 by Travellers Tales. Note: 4 Cassettes.
MCSET. Cat no: **1854960407.** Released on Bramhope, '91 by Ulverscroft Soundings. Note: 4 Cassettes.

Chapman, Elizabeth
MARMADUKE THE LORRY GOES TO ITALY (Kenneth Williams).
Note: For 4 to 6 year olds.
MC. Cat no: **A 005.** Released on Green Dragon, '91 by Green Dragon Audio Visual.
STORYTIME TOP TEN (Volume 9) (Kenneth Williams).
Note: Music by Major Records. Includes Marmaduke is Stolen, Marmaduke Goes to Venice, Marmaduke in a Film and A Rainy Day. For children aged 4 - 8 years.
MC. Cat no: **VCA 063.** Released on VFM Cassettes, Jan '85 by VFM Cassettes, Midland Records, Crusader Marketing Co., Taylors, Morley Audio Services.

Chard, Judy
BETRAYED (Elizabeth Henry).
MCSET. Cat no: **1854965484.** Released on Trio, '92 by EMI Records.
ENCHANTMENT (Unknown narrator(s)).
MCSET. Cat no: **1854963961.** Released on Trio, '91 by EMI Records. Note: 3 Cassettes.
TIME TO LOVE, A (Unknown narrator(s)).
MCSET. Cat no: **1854962574.** Released on Trio, '91 by EMI Records. Note: 3 Cassettes.
WILD JUSTICE (Unknown narrator(s)).
MCSET. Cat no: **1854965212.** Released on Bramhope, '91 by Ulverscroft Soundings. Note: 3 Cassettes.
WINGS OF THE MORNING (Unknown narrator(s)).
MCSET. Cat no: **1854964054.** Released on Bramhope, '91 by Ulverscroft Soundings. Note: 3 Cassettes.

Charles, Caroline
SMILE OF THE TIGER (Jill Kidstone).
MCSET. Cat no: **MRC 1088.** Released on Chivers Audio Books, '91 by Chivers

Audio Books, Green Dragon Audio Visual. Note: 2 Cassettes.

Charles, Cathy
SECRET OF THE GLEN (Karen Craig).
MCSET. Cat no: **MRC 1041.** Released on Chivers Moonlight Romances, Apr '88 by Chivers Audio Books, Green Dragon Audio Visual. Note: 2 Cassettes.

Charlton, Ann
IRRESISTIBLE FORCE, AN (Ann Charlton).
MCSET. Cat no: **PMB 019.** Released on Mills & Boon, '91. Note: 2 Cassettes

Charteris, Leslie
SAINT ERRANT (Charles Collingwood).
MCSET. Cat no: **1165T.** Released on Travellers Tales, '91 by Travellers Tales. Note: 2 Cassettes.
MCSET. Cat no: **CAT 11015.** Released on Chivers Audio Books, '91 by Chivers Audio Books, Green Dragon Audio Visual. Note: 4 Cassettes

THANKS TO THE SAINT (Charles Collingwood).
MCSET. Cat no: **1022T.** Released on Travellers Tales, '91 by Travellers Tales. Note: 4 Cassettes.
MCSET. Cat no: **CAT 4008.** Released on Chivers Audio Books, '91 by Chivers Audio Books, Green Dragon Audio Visual.

Chase, James Hadley
HIT THEM WHERE IT HURTS (Blain Fairman).
MCSET. Cat no: **1023T.** Released on Travellers Tales, '91 by Travellers Tales. Note: 4 Cassettes.

MORE DEADLY THAN THE MALE (Barry Lankester).
MCSET. Cat no: **SOUND 28.** Released on Soundings, Mar '85 by Soundings Records, Bond Street Music. Note: 4 Cassettes
MCSET. Cat no: **1024T.** Released on Travellers Tales, '91 by Travellers Tales. Note: 4 Cassettes.

TRY THIS ONE FOR SIZE (Blain Fairman).
MCSET. Cat no: **1166T.** Released on Travellers Tales, '91 by Travellers Tales. Note: 4 Cassettes.

Chaucer, Geoffrey
CANTERBURY TALES, THE (The Wife of Bath - Prologue and Tale) (Trevor Eaton).
MC. Cat no: **THE 612.** Released on Pearl, '91 by Pavilion Records, Harmonia Mundi (UK).

CANTERBURY TALES, THE (The Wife of Bath's Tale) (Prunella Scales & Richard Bebb).
Note: Read in Middle English.
MCSET. Cat no: **ARGO 1091.** Released on Argo (EMI), Jun '89 by EMI Records. Note: 2 Cassettes.
MCSET. Cat no: **1007Y.** Released on Travellers Tales, '91 by Travellers Tales. Note: 2 Cassettes.
MCSET. Cat no: **SAY 23.** Released on Argo (Polygram), Jul '82 by PolyGram Classics **Deleted** Jan '89.

CANTERBURY TALES, THE (The Canan Yeomans Prologue and Tale) (Douglas Mensforth).
Note: Original Middle English Reading.
MC. Cat no: **TWC 7.** Released on Tellways, '91.

CANTERBURY TALES, THE (Various narrators).
Note: Includes: Nun's Priests Tale and Knight's Tale. Read in middle English by: Nevil Cogill, Normal Davis, Lena Davis, John Burrow, Roy Spencer, Richard Bebb, Frank Duncan, Peter Orr, Denis McCarthy and Prunella Scales.
MCSET. Cat no: **SAY 91.** Released on Argo (Polygram), '83 by PolyGram Classics **Deleted** Jan '89.

CANTERBURY TALES, THE (Parson's Tale) (J.B. Bessinger).
Note: Read in the original Middle English.
MC. Cat no: **1151.** Released on Caedmon (USA), '88 by Caedmon Records (USA), Bond Street Music.

CANTERBURY TALES, THE (The Miller's Tale) (Trevor Eaton).
MC. Cat no: **THE 595.** Released on Pearl, '91 by Pavilion Records, Harmonia Mundi (UK).

CANTERBURY TALES, THE (Wife of Bath) (Dame Peggy Ashcroft).
MC. Cat no: **1102.** Released on Caedmon (USA), '88 by Caedmon Records (USA), Bond Street Music.

CANTERBURY TALES, THE (The Merchant's Prologue and Tale) (Trevor Eaton).
MC. Cat no: **THE 618.** Released on Pearl, '91 by Pavilion Records, Harmonia Mundi (UK).

CANTERBURY TALES, THE (Unknown narrator(s)).
MCSET. Cat no: **SAY 24.** Released on Argo (Polygram), '82 by PolyGram Classics **Deleted** Jan '89.

CANTERBURY TALES, THE (The Merchant's Prologue and Tale) (Douglas Mensforth).
Note: Original Middle English Recordings.
MC. Cat no: **TWC 6.** Released on Tellways, '91.

CANTERBURY TALES, THE (Prunella Scales & Martin Starkie).
MCSET. Cat no: **LFP 7320.** Released on Listen For Pleasure, Feb '88 by EMI Records.

CANTERBURY TALES, THE (The Knight's Tale) (Professor John Burrow).
Note: Original Middle English reading.
MCSET. Cat no: **TWC 1/2.** Released on Tellways, '91.

CANTERBURY TALES, THE (The Miller's Tale) (Professor Norman Davis).
Note: Original Middle English Reading.
MC. Cat no: **TWC 3.** Released on Tellways, '91.

CANTERBURY TALES, THE (Franklin's Tale, The) (Carl Schmidt).
Note: Original Middle English reading. Carl Schmidt is a fellow and tutor of Balliol College, Oxford.
MC. Cat no: **TWC 4.** Released on Tellways, '91.

CANTERBURY TALES, THE (The Wife of Bath's - Prologue and Tale) (Cecily Longrigg).
Note: Original Middle English Reading.
MC. Cat no: **TWC 5.** Released on Tellways, '91.

CANTERBURY TALES, THE (The Nun's Priest's Tale and Shipman's Tale) (Trevor Eaton).
Note: And also the Prioress's Prologue and Tale.
MC. Cat no: **THE 619.** Released on Pearl, '91 by Pavilion Records, Harmonia Mundi (UK).

CANTERBURY TALES, THE (The Reeve's Tale) (Trevor Eaton).
MC. Cat no: **THE 606.** Released on Pearl, '91 by Pavilion Records, Harmonia Mundi (UK).

CANTERBURY TALES, THE (The Friar's Prologue and Tale) (Trevor Eaton).
MC. Cat no: **THE 620.** Released on Pearl, Mar '91 by Pavilion Records, Harmonia Mundi (UK).

CANTERBURY TALES, THE (The Nun's Priest's Tale) (George Sayer).
Note: Original Middle English Recording.
MC. Cat no: **TWC 9.** Released on Tellways, '91.

CANTERBURY'S TALE, THE (The Pardoner's Tale) (General Prologue) (Trevor Eaton).
MC. Cat no: **THE 607.** Released on Pearl, '91 by Pavilion Records, Harmonia Mundi (UK).

GENERAL PROLOGUE FROM THE CANTERBURY TALES, THE (George Sayer).
Note: Original Middle English Reading.
MC. Cat no: **TWC 8.** Released on Tellways, '91.

GLORY OF THE GARDEN, THE (Various narrators).
Note: Performed by Margaret Howard, Bernard Palmer and Three's Company Plus.
MC. Cat no: **GEMM 7352.** Released on Pearl, '91 by Pavilion Records, Harmonia Mundi (UK).

KNIGHT'S TALE, THE (Trevor Eaton).
Note: Read in Middle English.

MCSET. Cat no: **THES 625**. Released on Pearl, Feb '92 by Pavilion Records, Harmonia Mundi (UK).
TROILUS AND CRISEYDE (Various narrators).
Note: Read in Middle English by Gary Watson, Prunella Scales and others. Abridged.
MCSET. Cat no: **SAY 74**. Released on Argo (Polygram), Jun '88 by PolyGram Classics **Deleted** Jan '89.
MCSET. Cat no: **1008Y**. Released on Travellers Tales, '91 by Travellers Tales. Note: 2 Cassettes.

Chawla, Harcharan

CHIRAGH KE ZAKHAM (Harcharan Chawla).
MCSET. Cat no: **86671**. Released on Sonex, '91. Note: 4 Cassettes

Cheever, John

SWIMMER, THE (And Death of Justina) (Unknown narrator(s)).
MC. Cat no: **CDL 51668**. Released on Caedmon (USA), Oct '81 by Caedmon Records (USA), Bond Street Music.

Chekhov, Anton

THREE SISTERS (Various narrators).
MCSET. Cat no: **0325**. Released on Caedmon (USA), '88 by Caedmon Records (USA), Bond Street Music. Note: 3 cassettes

Chesterton, G.K.

FATHER BROWN (Various artists).
Note: Four stories starring Andrew Sachs and Olivier Pierre.
MCSET. Cat no: **ZBBC 1175**. Released on BBC Radio Collection, Feb '91 by BBC Records. Note: ISBN No: 0563 411198
INNOCENCE OF FATHER BROWN, THE (Father Brown Stories) (John Horton).
Note: Contains the following stories:- The Blue Cross, The Secret Garden, The Queer Feet, The Flying Stars, The Invisible Man, The Honour Of Isreal Gow, The Wrong Shape, The Sins Of Prince Saradine, The Hammer Of God, The Eye Of Apollo, The Sign Of The Broken Sword, The Three Tools Of Death.
MCSET. Cat no: **IAB 91091**. Released on Isis Audio Books, Sep '91. Note: 8 Cassettes. Playing time 9hrs.
INNOCENCE OF FATHER BROWN, THE (Nigel Hawthorne).
MCSET. Cat no: **1217T**. Released on Travellers Tales, '91 by Travellers Tales. Note: 4 Cassettes.
MCSET. Cat no: **418 054-4**. Released on Argo (Polygram), Jun '88 by PolyGram Classics **Deleted** Jan '89.
INNOCENCE OF FATHER BROWN, THE (Volume 2) (Nigel Hawthorne).
MCSET. Cat no: **418 057-4**. Released on Argo (Polygram), Jun '88 by Poly-Gram Classics **Deleted** Jan '89.
MORE FATHER BROWN STORIES (Nigel Hawthorne).
MCSET. Cat no: **ARGO 1268**. Released on Argo (EMI), May '91 by EMI Records.
NAPOLEON OF NOTTINGHILL, THE (Paul Scofield).
Note: Abridged.
MCSET. Cat no: **SAY 93**. Released on Argo (Polygram), Oct '83 by PolyGram Classics **Deleted** Jan '89.
MCSET. Cat no: **1017F**. Released on Travellers Tales, '91 by Travellers Tales. Note: 2 Cassettes.
SCANDAL OF FATHER BROWN, THE (John Graham).
MCSET. Cat no: **CAT 4027**. Released on Chivers Audio Thrillers, Apr '88 by Chivers Audio Books, Green Dragon Audio Visual. Note: 4 Cassettes.
MCSET. Cat no: **1249T**. Released on Travellers Tales, '91 by Travellers Tales. Note: 4 Cassettes.
SECRET OF FATHER BROWN, THE (Geoffrey Matthews).
MCSET. Cat no: **CAB 428**. Released on Chivers Audio Books, '91 by Chivers Audio Books, Green Dragon Audio Visual. Note: 6 Cassettes.
MCSET. Cat no: **1497T**. Released on Travellers Tales, '91 by Travellers Tales. Note: 6 Cassettes
THREE FATHER BROWN STORIES (Nigel Hawthorne).
MCSET. Cat no: **ARGO 1007**. Released on Argo (EMI), May '89 by EMI Records. Note: Playing time: 2 1/4 hours. 2 Cassettes.
WISDOM OF FATHER BROWN, THE (John Graham).
MCSET. Cat no: **1025T**. Released on Travellers Tales, '91 by Travellers Tales. Note: 4 Cassettes.
MCSET. Cat no: **CAT 4003**. Released on Chivers Audio Books, '91 by Chivers Audio Books, Green Dragon Audio Visual.

Cheyney, Peter

CALLING MR CALLAGHAN (Unknown narrator(s)).
MCSET. Cat no: **1854960423**. Released on Trio, '91 by EMI Records. Note: 3 Cassettes.
DANGEROUS CURVES (Unknown narrator(s)).
MCSET. Cat no: **185496237X**. Released on Bramhope, '91 by Ulverscroft Soundings. Note: 5 Cassettes.
IT COULDN'T MATTER LESS (David Wade).
MCSET. Cat no: **1651T**. Released on Travellers Tales, '91 by Travellers Tales. Note: 4 Cassettes.
MCSET. Cat no: **185496237X**. Released on Bramhope, '91 by Ulverscroft Soundings.
UNEASY TERMS (David Wade).
MCSET. Cat no: **1579T**. Released on Travellers Tales, '91 by Travellers Tales. Note: 4 Cassettes.
MCSET. Cat no: **1854963368**. Released on Bramhope, '91 by Ulverscroft Soundings. Note: 4 Cassettes.
URGENT HANGMAN, THE (Nigel Stanger).
MCSET. Cat no: **1441T**. Released on Travellers Tales, '91 by Travellers Tales. Note: 5 Cassettes.
MCSET. Cat no: **1854962310**. Released on Bramhope, '91 by Ulverscroft Soundings. Note: 5 Cassettes.

Childers, Erskine

RIDDLE OF THE SANDS, THE (Martin Jarvis).
MCSET. Cat no: **ZC SWD 358**. Released on ASV (Academy Sound & Vision), Oct '89 by Academy Sound & Vision Records. Note: 2 Cassettes. Playing time 3 hours.
RIDDLE OF THE SANDS, THE (Leon Sinden).
MCSET. Cat no: **COL 2024**. Released on Colophone, '88 by AVLS (Audio-Visual Library Services).
MCSET. Cat no: **1026T**. Released on Travellers Tales, '91 by Travellers Tales. Note: 2 Cassettes.
RIDDLE OF THE SANDS, THE (Patrick Tull).
MCSET. Cat no: **1413T**. Released on Travellers Tales, '91 by Travellers Tales. Note: 8 Cassettes.
MCSET. Cat no: **IAB 89033**. Released on Isis Audio Books, '91. Note: 8 Cassettes.

Childish, Wild Billy

COMPANIONS IN A DEATH BOAT (Wild Billy Childish & The Black Hands).
LP. Cat no: **WORDUP 001**. Released on Hangman, Jun '88 by Hangman Records, Cartel.
CONVERSATIONS WITH DOCTOR X (Wild Billy Childish & The Black Hands).
LP. Cat no: **WORDUP 006**. Released on Hangman, Jun '88 by Hangman Records, Cartel.
POEMS FROM THE BARRIER BLOCK (Unknown narrator(s)).
LP. Cat no: **WORDUP 003**. Released on Hangman, Jun '88 by Hangman Records, Cartel.
POEMS OF LAUGHTER AND VIOLENCE (Unknown narrator(s)).
Tracks / People don't need poetry / Warts grown like flys / Talking lites, The / Me 'n' my father / Hawk and spitfire / Heaven she said / In here we believe / Terrible buti, The / Catastrophy / Mercy.
LP. Cat no: **HANG 16 UP**. Released on Hangman, Jun '88 by Hangman Records, Cartel.
POEMS WITHOUT RHYME (Unknown narrator(s)).
LP. Cat no: **WORDUP 004**. Released on Hangman, Jun '88 by Hangman Records, Cartel.
TO THE QUICK (Unknown narrator(s)).

LP. Cat no: **WORDUP 007.** Released on Hangman, Jun '88 by Hangman Records, Cartel.

Children's Stories

3 HOURS OF FAVOURITE CHILDREN'S STORIES (Various narrators).
MCSET. Cat no: **TR 1542.** Released on Trio, Oct '84 by EMI Records **Deleted** Aug '89.

ADVENTURES OF ROGER AND THE ROTTEN TROLLS, THE (Colin Baker).
CD. Cat no: **CDMFP 5952.** Released on MFP, Dec '91 by EMI Records, Solomon & Peres.
MC. Cat no: **TCMFP 5952.** Released on EMI, Dec '91 by EMI Records.

ANIMAL FAIRYLAND (14 Favourite Songs and Stories) (Various artists).
Note: For children aged 2 - 9 years. Includes Pussy Cat, Pussy Cat, Five Little Ducks, My Little Kitten, Gee Up Neddy, My Little Pony, Knox the Fox, The Kangaroo of Waterloo, 1 2 3 4 5, The Squirrel of Wirral, Where Oh Where Has My Little Dog Gone, To Market To Market, Three Little Kittens, Hey De Ho and Panda Monium.
MC. Cat no: **STC 110.** Released on VFM Cassettes, Jun '88 by VFM Cassettes, Midland Records, Crusader Marketing Co., Taylors, Morley Audio Services.

ANIMALS WENT IN TWO BY TWO, THE (And Other Favourite Songs and Stories) (Various artists).
Note: For children aged 2 - 9 years. Includes The Animals Went in Two by Two, Pookie Doodle Puppy, Old Mother Hubbard, There Was a Crooked Man, Touch Your Toes, Pop Goes the Weasel, Hop, Skip and Jump, Good Dog Spot, Dick Whittington and The Little Tin Soldier.
MC. Cat no: **SFC 403.** Released on VFM Cassettes, '85 by VFM Cassettes, Midland Records, Crusader Marketing Co., Taylors, Morley Audio Services.

BAA BAA BLACK SHEEP (And Other Favourite Nursery Rhymes & Stories) (Gillian Blake).
Note: Includes Baa Baa Black Sheep, Little Miss. Muffet, Ride a Cock Horse, Girls and Boys Come Out to Play, The Selfish Giants, Jack and Jill, Pat a Cake Pat a Cake, Simple Simon and The Dancing Princesses. For ages 3 - 9
MC. Cat no: **STC 118.** Released on VFM Cassettes, Jun '86 by VFM Cassettes, Midland Records, Crusader Marketing Co., Taylors, Morley Audio Services.
MC. Cat no: **STC 309B.** Released on VFM Cassettes, Jun '86 by VFM Cassettes, Midland Records, Crusader Marketing Co., Taylors, Morley Audio Services.

BEDTIME FAIRY STORIES (Unknown narrator(s)).

MCSET. Cat no: **DTO 10534.** Released on Ditto, '88 by Pickwick Records, Midland Records.

BEDTIME STORIES (Hayley Mills).
MC. Cat no: **0600560902.** Released on Hamlyn Books On Tape, '88, Bond Street Music.

BIG PANCAKE, THE (Unknown narrator(s)).
Note: Book and cassette. Well loved tales up to age 9.
MC. Cat no: **PLB 95.** Released on Tell-A-Tale, '88 by Pickwick Records, Taylors, Clyde Factors.

BLACK BEAUTY (And Other Favourite Stories) (Peter Whitbread & Gillian Blake).
Note: For ages 3 - 7. Includes Black Beauty, The Magic Bean, Brer Rabbit's Travels and The Magic Clogs.
MC. Cat no: **VCA 602.** Released on VFM Cassettes, Jul '85 by VFM Cassettes, Midland Records, Crusader Marketing Co., Taylors, Morley Audio Services.

BRAVE LITTLE TAILOR (Unknown narrator(s)).
Note: Well loved tales up to age 9. Book and cassette.
MC. Cat no: **PLB 206.** Released on Tell-A-Tale, '88 by Pickwick Records, Taylors, Clyde Factors.

BRAVE LITTLE TAILOR (Donald Pleasance).
MC. Cat no: **BKK 401.** Released on Kiddy Kassettes, Aug '77.

CHANT VILLAGE STORIES (Isla St.Clair).
Note: Book and cassette.
MC. Cat no: **TBC 9503.** Released on Tempo Storytime, May '84 by Warwick Records, Celtic Music.

CHICKEN LICKEN (Well Loved Tales up to Age 9) (Unknown narrator(s)).
Note: Book and cassette.
MC. Cat no: **PLB 94.** Released on Tell-A-Tale, '88 by Pickwick Records, Taylors, Clyde Factors.

CHILDREN'S STORIES (Felicity Kendal).
MC. Cat no: **OTC 002.** Released on VFM Cassettes, '85 by VFM Cassettes, Midland Records, Crusader Marketing Co., Taylors, Morley Audio Services.

CHILDREN'S STORIES (Paul Eddington).
MC. Cat no: **OTC 003.** Released on VFM Cassettes, '85 by VFM Cassettes, Midland Records, Crusader Marketing Co., Taylors, Morley Audio Services.

CHILDREN'S TALES FROM AROUND THE WORLD (James, Sally).
LP. Cat no: **STMP 9011.** Released on Super Tempo, May '84 by Warwick Records, Taylors, Solomon & Peres, Sony Music Operations.
MC. Cat no: **STMP4 9011.** Released on Super Tempo, May '84 by Warwick Records, Taylors, Solomon & Peres,

Sony Music Operations.

COLLECTED STORIES FROM EUROPE (Volume 1) (Michele Dotrice).
Note: The Glass Axe, The Wicked Prince and The Wonderful Musician.
MC. Cat no: **MCLIS 205.** Released on Listen, '91, Cartel. Note: 40 mins.

DAYLIGHT DIG, THE (Various narrators).
Note: Read by Miriam Margoyles and featuring the Keypers characters.
MC. Cat no: **00 102151 6.** Released on Tempo, '88 by Warwick Records, Celtic Music, Henry Hadaway Organisation.

DICK WHITTINGTON (And Other Favourite Children's Stories) (Peter Whitbread & Gillian Blake).
Note: Includes Dick Whittington, King Rolphus the Wise and The Magic Ring. For children aged 5 - 9 years.
MC. Cat no: **VCA 608.** Released on Storyteller Cassettes, '85.

DICK WHITTINGTON (And Other Favourite Children's Stories) (Peter Whitbread & Gillian Blake).
Note: Includes Dick Whittington, The Little Match Girl, Robin Hood and The Tinker and the Donkey. For ages 3 - 7.
MC. Cat no: **STC 303C.** Released on VFM Cassettes, '88 by VFM Cassettes, Midland Records, Crusader Marketing Co., Taylors, Morley Audio Services.

DONKEY CABBAGES, THE (Various artists).
Tracks / Donkey cabbages, The Drummer, The / Simeli mountain / Hop o' my thumb / Professor know-all.
MC. Cat no: **ANV 618.** Released on Anvil Cassettes, Jan '81 by Anvil Cassettes, Chivers Audio Books.

ELVES AND THE SHOEMAKER, THE (And Other Favourite Children's Stories) (Peter Whitbread & Gillian Blake).
Note: Includes The Elves and the Shoemaker, The Magic Clock and Prince Parian's Secret. For ages 3 - 9.
MC. Cat no: **STC 307A.** Released on VFM Cassettes, '88 by VFM Cassettes, Midland Records, Crusader Marketing Co., Taylors, Morley Audio Services.

EVERYDAY STORIES (Volume 1) (Unknown narrator(s)).
Note: Four stories suitable for the under-sevens with a picture for colouring.
MC. Cat no: **AC 107.** Released on Audicord, '91 by Audicord Cassettes.

EVERYDAY STORIES (Volume 2) (Unknown narrator(s)).
Note: Four more stories for the under-sevens with a picture for colouring.
MC. Cat no: **AC 108.** Released on Audicord, '91 by Audicord Cassettes.

FIREBIRD, THE (Unknown narrator(s)).
Note: Well loved tales for up to 9 years old.
MC. Cat no: **PLB 213.** Released on Tell-A-Tale, '88 by Pickwick Records, Taylors, Clyde Factors.

FISHERMAN AND HIS WIFE, THE (Music by Van Dyke Parks) (Jodie Foster).
CD. Cat no: **WD 0714.** Released on Windham Hill, Jan '92 by Windham Hill Records (USA), New Note.
MC. Cat no: **WT 0714.** Released on Windham Hill, Jan '92 by Windham Hill Records (USA), New Note.

FOUR CLASSIC STORIES (And Twenty Popular Nursery Rhymes) (Sheila Southern).
Tracks / Boys and girls come out to play / Cock-a-doodle-doo / Pata cake pata cake / Tom Thumb (story) / Hey diddle dumplin' / Little Jack Horner / One two buckle my shoe / Three blind mice / Goldilocks & the three bears / What are little boys made of / Peter Piper / Owl & the pussy cat / Old woman in a shoe / Frog he would a wooin' go, A / Dance to your daddy / Little Red Riding Hood (story) / Doctor Foster / Tom Thumb the pipers son / Twinkle twinkle little star / Little Bo Peep / Dick Whittington (story) / Ride a cock horse / Pussy cat where have you been / Horsey horsey / Hush a baby baby / Boys and girls come out to play.
LP. Cat no: **HN 3100.** Released on Horatio Nelson, Nov '86 by Horatio Nelson Records & Tapes Ltd..
MC. Cat no: **CHN 3100.** Released on Horatio Nelson, Nov '86 by Horatio Nelson Records & Tapes Ltd..

GERALD MCBOING BOING (And Other Stories) (Various narrators).
MC. Cat no: **13491 6001 4.** Released on Delos, Dec '90.

GINGERBREAD BOY, THE (Well Loved Tales Up To Age 9) (Unknown narrator(s)).
Note: Book and cassette.
MC. Cat no: **PLB 90.** Released on Tell-A-Tale, '88 by Pickwick Records, Taylors, Clyde Factors.

GLO BUG (Unknown narrator(s)).
Note: Book and cassette. Up to the age of 6.
MC. Cat no: **PLBG 202.** Released on Tell-A-Tale, '88 by Pickwick Records, Taylors, Clyde Factors.

GLO BUTTERFLY (Unknown narrator(s)).
Note: Book and cassette. Up to the age of 6.
MC. Cat no: **PLBG 184.** Released on Tell-A-Tale, '88 by Pickwick Records, Taylors, Clyde Factors.

GLO CRICKET (Unknown narrator(s)).
Note: Book and cassette. Up to the age of 6.
MC. Cat no: **PLBG 183.** Released on Tell-A-Tale, '88 by Pickwick Records, Taylors, Clyde Factors.

GLO WORM (Unknown narrator(s)).
Note: Book and cassette. Up to the age of 6.
MC. Cat no: **PLBG 203.** Released on Tell-A-Tale, '88 by Pickwick Records, Taylors, Clyde Factors.

GOING TO THE ZOO (And Other Favourite Songs and Stories) (Peter Whitbread & Gillian Blake).
Note: For children aged 2 - 9 years. Includes Going To the Zoo, The Penguin and his Dinner Suit, Don't Shake Hands With an Octopus, Never Play Cards With a Cheetah, Don't Upset the Camel, The Puffin Song, My Little Kitten, The Yellow Elephant, The Laughing Hyena, The Three Little Pigs and The Town Mouse and the Country Mouse.
MC. Cat no: **SFC 410.** Released on VFM Cassettes, '85 by VFM Cassettes, Midland Records, Crusader Marketing Co., Taylors, Morley Audio Services.

GOLDILOCKS AND THE THREE BEARS (6 Favourite Children's Stories) (Peter Whitbread & Gillian Blake).
Note: For children aged 3 - 9 years. Includes Goldilocks and the Three Bears, The Little Match Girl, Robin Hood and Maid Marian, Ali Baba and the Forty Thieves, Harlequin the Rag Doll and Aladdin and his Magic Lamp.
MC. Cat no: **STC 108.** Released on VFM Cassettes, '85 by VFM Cassettes, Midland Records, Crusader Marketing Co., Taylors, Morley Audio Services.

GOLDILOCKS AND THE THREE BEARS (And Other Favourite Stories) (Peter Whitbread & Gillian Blake).
Note: For ages 3 - 7. Includes Goldilocks and the Three Bears, Old Mother Started It All, The Three Children of Fortune and The Mad Hatter.
MC. Cat no: **VCA 601.** Released on VFM Cassettes, Jul '85 by VFM Cassettes, Midland Records, Crusader Marketing Co., Taylors, Morley Audio Services.

GOODNIGHT STORIES (Unknown narrator(s)).
MCSET. Cat no: **DTO 10505.** Released on Ditto, '88 by Pickwick Records, Midland Records.

GOOSE GIRL, THE (Well Loved Tales Age Up To 9) (Unknown narrator(s)).
Note: Book and cassette.
MC. Cat no: **PLB 130.** Released on Tell-A-Tale, Oct '84 by Pickwick Records, Taylors, Clyde Factors.

HANSEL AND GRETEL (And Other Favourite Children's Stories) (Peter Whitbread & Gillian Blake).
Note: Includes Hansel and Gretel, Josh and the Golden Sword and The Golden Sword to the Rescue. For ages 3 - 9.
MC. Cat no: **STC 306A.** Released on VFM Cassettes, '88 by VFM Cassettes, Midland Records, Crusader Marketing Co., Taylors, Morley Audio Services.

HAPPY ADVENTURE TALES (Unknown narrator(s)).
MCSET. Cat no: **DTO 10547.** Released on Ditto, '88 by Pickwick Records, Midland Records.

HAPPY FAMILIES STORIES (And Mrs Wobble and the Waitress) (Unknown narrator(s)).
MC. Cat no: **TS 333.** Released on Tellastory, Mar '83 by Random Century Audiobooks.

IT'S A CHILDREN'S WORLD (Unknown narrator(s)).
LP. Cat no: **PRCC 100.** Released on Peerless (USA), Jan '75 by Discos Latin International (USA) **Deleted** May '78.

JACK AND THE BEANSTALK (And Other Favourite Children's Stories) (Peter Whitbread & Gillian Blake).
Note: Includes Jack and the Beanstalk, The Tortoise and the Hare, The Goose That Laid the Golden Egg and The Brown Bear and the Fox. For ages 3 - 7.
MC. Cat no: **STC 303A.** Released on VFM Cassettes, '88 by VFM Cassettes, Midland Records, Crusader Marketing Co., Taylors, Morley Audio Services.

JENNY AND JAMES START SCHOOL (Unknown narrator(s)).
MC. Cat no: **STK 035.** Released on Stick-A-Tale, Sep '90 by Pickwick Records.

KING ARTHUR AND EXCALIBUR (Plus Other Favourite Children's Stories) (Peter Whitbread).
Note: Includes King Arthur and Exalibur, Gulliver's Travels, Daniel and the Lion's Den and Sinbad. For ages 5 - 9.
MC. Cat no: **STC 301A.** Released on VFM Cassettes, '88 by VFM Cassettes, Midland Records, Crusader Marketing Co., Taylors, Morley Audio Services.
MC. Cat no: **SBC 118.** Released on Caedmon (USA), '81 by Caedmon Records (USA), Bond Street Music. Note: ISBN no. 185656021X

KING RICHARD THE LIONHEART (And Other Favourite Children's Stories) (Peter Whitbread).
Note: Includes Richard the Lionheart, King Alfred the Great, Robinson Crusoe, Christopher Columbus. For ages 5 - 9.
MC. Cat no: **STC 301C.** Released on VFM Cassettes, '88 by VFM Cassettes, Midland Records, Crusader Marketing Co., Taylors, Morley Audio Services.

LAND OF MAKE BELIEVE (20 More Favourite Songs and Stories) (Various artists).
Note: For children aged 2 - 9 years. Includes The Yellow Elephant, I'm a Fluffy Cloud, Old Mother Started It All, Oh Dear, What Can the Matter Be, Little Boy Blue, Hey Diddle Diddle, Hickory Dickory Dock, Old Mother Hubbard, There Was a Crooked Man, Little Tommy Tucker, Where Oh Where's My Teddy Bear, Finn McCoull, I Had a Little Nut Tree, Touch Your Toes, Dancing 'Round the Maypole, 'Round and 'Round the Garden, Hop, Skip and Jump, The Man in the Moon, This Old Man (Nick Nack Paddywak) and Pop

Goes the Weasel.
MC. Cat no: **STC 111**. Released on VFM Cassettes, '85 by VFM Cassettes, Midland Records, Crusader Marketing Co., Taylors, Morley Audio Services.

LET'S PLAY (Unknown narrator(s)).
MC. Cat no: **RWM 002**. Released on Tell-A-Tale, Sep '90 by Pickwick Records, Taylors, Clyde Factors.

LITTLE BO PEEP (Various narrators).
MC. Cat no: **STC 308A**. Released on VFM Cassettes, '88 by VFM Cassettes, Midland Records, Crusader Marketing Co., Taylors, Morley Audio Services.

LITTLE GINGERBREAD MAN, THE (And Other Favourite Children's Stories) (Peter Whitbread & Gillian Blake).
Note: Includes The Little Gingerbread Man, The Duckling Who Couldn't Quack and The Hut at the End of the Lane. For Ages 3 - 9.
MC. Cat no: **STC 305 C**. Released on VFM Cassettes, '88 by VFM Cassettes, Midland Records, Crusader Marketing Co., Taylors, Morley Audio Services.

LITTLE RED RIDING HOOD (6 Favourite Children's Stories) (Peter Whitbread & Gillian Blake).
Note: For children aged 3 - 9 years. Includes Little Red Riding Hood, Dick Whittington, Robinson Crusoe, the Three Billy Goats Gruff, King Midas (the King Who Loved Gold) and The Town Mouse and the Country Mouse.
MC. Cat no: **STC 106**. Released on VFM Cassettes, '85 by VFM Cassettes, Midland Records, Crusader Marketing Co., Taylors, Morley Audio Services.

LITTLE RED RIDING HOOD (And Other Favourite Children's Stories) (Peter Whitbread & Gillian Blake).
Note: Includes Little Red Riding Hood, The King's New Clothes, Sleeping Beauty and Harlequin, the Rag Doll. For ages 3 - 7.
MC. Cat no: **VCA 606**. Released on VFM Cassettes, Jul '85 by VFM Cassettes, Midland Records, Crusader Marketing Co., Taylors, Morley Audio Services.

LITTLE TIN SOLDIER, THE (And Other Favourite Children's Stories) (Peter Whitbread & Gillian Blake).
Note: Includes The Little Tin Soldier, Sam and his Musket, Little Bear's First Feather and Finn McCoull. For ages 3 - 9.
MC. Cat no: **STC 308C**. Released on VFM Cassettes, '88 by VFM Cassettes, Midland Records, Crusader Marketing Co., Taylors, Morley Audio Services.

MISSING AMBASSADOR, THE (Unknown narrator(s)).
Note: (Book & cassette)o
MC. Cat no: **PLB 136**. Released on Tell-A-Tale, Aug '84 by Pickwick Records, Taylors, Clyde Factors.

NELLIE THE ELEPHANT (And Other Favourite Songs and Stories) (Various artists).

Note: For children aged 2 - 9 years. Includes Nellie the Elephant, Panda Monium, My Pretend Friend, Oranges and Lemons, In a Land of Princes and Dragons, Comb and Paper Band, Hansel and Gretel and The Gingerbread Man.
MC. Cat no: **SFC 402**. Released on VFM Cassettes, '85 by VFM Cassettes, Midland Records, Crusader Marketing Co., Taylors, Morley Audio Services.

NEVER SMILE AT A CROCODILE (And Other Favourite Songs and Stories) (Various artists).
Note: For children aged 2 - 9 years. Includes Never Smile at a Crocodile, Froggy Went a Courting, Wee Willie Winkie, Diddle Diddle Dumpling, Frere Jacques, Hush Little Baby, Lucy Locket, My Little Pony, A Tisket a Tasket, If You're Happy Clap Your Hands, The Grand Old Duke of York, Tom Thumb and The King's New Clothes.
MC. Cat no: **SFC 408**. Released on VFM Cassettes, '85 by VFM Cassettes, Midland Records, Crusader Marketing Co., Taylors, Morley Audio Services.

NIGHT BEFORE CHRISTMAS, THE (And Other Favourite Children's Stories) (Various narrators).
Note: For children aged 3 - 9 years. Includes I Want a Teddy for Christmas, The Fairy on the Christmas Tree, It's Teddy's First Christmas, Galloping Through the Snow, The Lonely Christmas Tree, Pookie Doodles Christmas Party, It's Christmas Day Today, The Runaway Snowman, Snowy The Snowflake and The Night Before Christmas.
MC. Cat no: **STC 310C**. Released on VFM Cassettes, '88 by VFM Cassettes, Midland Records, Crusader Marketing Co., Taylors, Morley Audio Services.

NIGHTINGALE, THE (And Other Favourite Children's Stories) (Peter Whitbread & Gillian Blake).
Note: Includes The Nightingale, A Tale of Three Wishes, Snow White and the Seven Dwarfs and The Fisherman and the Mermaid. For ages 3 - 9.
MC. Cat no: **STC 307 C**. Released on Storytime Cassettes, '85 by VFM Cassettes, Iona Records, Rio Communications.

OLD MACDONALD (Various narrators).
MC. Cat no: **STC 309C**. Released on VFM Cassettes, Jun '88 by VFM Cassettes, Midland Records, Crusader Marketing Co., Taylors, Morley Audio Services.

OLD MACDONALD HAD A FARM (And Other Favourite Songs, Nursery Rhymes and Stories) (Various artists).
Note: For children aged 2 - 9 years. Includes Old MacDonald Had a Farm, Old Mother Hubbard (story), The Yellow Elephant, Willie the Whale, Sing a Song of Sixpence, Polly Put the Kettle On, Emerald the Engine, The Emu and the Kangaroo and Nick Nack Paddywack.
MC. Cat no: **STC 116**. Released on VFM Cassettes, '85 by VFM Cassettes, Midland Records, Crusader Marketing Co., Taylors, Morley Audio Services.

ONCE UPON A TIME (Richard Briers & Felicity Kendall).
Note: For 4 to 8 year olds.
MCSET. Cat no: **B 001A/B**. Released on Green Dragon, '91 by Green Dragon Audio Visual. Note: 2 Cassettes.

PAUL BUNYAN (Music by Leo Kottke) (Jonathan Winters).
CD. Cat no: **WD 0717**. Released on Windham Hill, Jan '92 by Windham Hill Records (USA), New Note.
MC. Cat no: **WT 0717**. Released on Windham Hill, Jan '92 by Windham Hill Records (USA), New Note.

PECOS BILL (Music by Ry Cooder) (Robin Williams).
CD. Cat no: **WD 0709**. Released on Windham Hill, Jan '92 by Windham Hill Records (USA), New Note.
MC. Cat no: **WT 0709**. Released on Windham Hill, Jan '92 by Windham Hill Records (USA), New Note.

PETER AND THE WOLF (Unknown narrator(s)).
LP. Cat no: **PLB 271**. Released on Tell-A-Tale, '89 by Pickwick Records, Taylors, Clyde Factors.

PETER AND THE WOLF AND TUBBY THE TUBA (Carol Channing).
LP. Cat no: **TC 1623**. Released on Caedmon (USA), Jan '81 by Caedmon Records (USA), Bond Street Music **Deleted** '86.

PLANET OF THE ELVES, THE (Unknown artist(s)).
Note: Book and cassette.
MC. Cat no: **PLB 145**. Released on Tell-A-Tale, '84 by Pickwick Records, Taylors, Clyde Factors.

POLLY PUT THE KETTLE ON (And Other Favourite Nursery Rhymes and Stories) (Various artists).
Note: For children aged 2 - 6 years. Includes Polly Put the Kettle On, Little Miss. Muffet, I Love Little Pussy, Round and Round the Garden, Pat a Cake, Pat a Cake, The Man in the Moon, Higgledy Piggledy, Dancing Round the Maypole, The Muffin Man, Diddle Diddle Dumpling, Cock a Doodle Doo, The Little Nut Tree, Hickory Dickory Dock, Bye Baby Bunting, Gee Up Neddy, Little Boy Blue, Little Jack Horner, Hot Cross Buns, Jack and Jill, Little Bo Peep, The Princess and the Pea and The Little Red Hen.
MC. Cat no: **SFC 404**. Released on VFM Cassettes, '85 by VFM Cassettes, Midland Records, Crusader Marketing Co., Taylors, Morley Audio Services.

PUFF THE MAGIC DRAGON (15 Favourite Songs and Stories) (Peter Whitbread & Gillian Blake).
Note: For children aged 2 - 9 years.

Includes Puff the Magic Dragon, This Old Man (Nick Nack Paddywack), Little Bo Peep, Sing a Song of Sixpence, Little Miss. Muffet, Polly Put the Kettle On, Three Blind Mice, Simple Simon Met a Pieman, Jack and Jill, The Muffin Man, Here We Go Round the Mulberry Bush, Girls and Boys Come OUt to Play, The Three Little Pigs, Black Beauty and Jack and the Beanstalk.
MC. Cat no: **STC 115**. Released on VFM Cassettes, '85 by VFM Cassettes, Midland Records, Crusader Marketing Co., Taylors, Morley Audio Services.

PUFF THE MAGIC DRAGON (And Other Favourite Children's Songs & Stories) (Gillian Blake).
Note: Includes Puff the Magic Dragon, Here We Go Round the Mulberry Bush, Lavender Blue, The Muffin Man, Goosey Goosey Gander, Golden Slumbers and Little Beau Peep. For ages 3 - 9.
MC. Cat no: **STC 308b**. Released on VFM Cassettes, by VFM Cassettes, Midland Records, Crusader Marketing Co., Taylors, Morley Audio Services.

RUMPELSTILTSKIN (And Other Favourite Children's Stories) (Gillian Blake).
Note: Includes Rumpelstiltskin, The Queen's Hat Pin and Hobnob the Garden Gnome. For ages 3 - 9.
MC. Cat no: **STC 306B**. Released on VFM Cassettes, '88 by VFM Cassettes, Midland Records, Crusader Marketing Co., Taylors, Morley Audio Services.

RUNAWAY TRAIN, THE (And Other Favourite Songs and Stories) (Various artists).
Note: For children aged 2 - 9 years. Includes The Runaway Train, The Big Ship Sails On the Alley Alley O, I'm the King of the Castle, Pandora's Puppies, My Bicycle Has a Bell, One Finger, One Thumb, Nick Nack Paddywack, Riding Along in my Sleigh, A B C D E F G, Goldilocks and the Three Bears and The Pied Piper of Hamelin.
MC. Cat no: **SFC 401**. Released on VFM Cassettes, '85 by VFM Cassettes, Midland Records, Crusader Marketing Co., Taylors, Morley Audio Services.

SHUFFLE THE SHOEMAKER (Unknown narrator(s)).
MCSET. Cat no: **DTO 10552**. Released on Ditto, '88 by Pickwick Records, Midland Records.

SIX LITTLE DUCKS (And Other Favourite Songs and Stories) (Various artists).
Note: For children aged 2 - 9 years. Includes Six Little Ducks, Why Did the Butterfly Flutterby, Rat a Tat Tat, There Was an Old Lady, I'm a Silly Old Bear Called Bizzley, Good Morning Mrs. Hen, Bought Me a Cat, The Quick Brown Fox, My Little Kitten, Pop Goes the Weasel, The Brown Bear and the Fox, Rapunzel and The Sleeping Beauty.
MC. Cat no: **SFC 407**. Released on VFM Cassettes, '85 by VFM Cassettes, Midland Records, Crusader Marketing Co., Taylors, Morley Audio Services.

SLEEPING BEAUTY (And Other Favourite Children's Stories) (Peter Whitbread & Gillian Blake).
Note: Includes The Sleeping Beauty, Tom Thumb, King Midas (the King Who Loved Gold) and Aladdin and his Magic Lamp. For ages 3 - 7.
MC. Cat no: **STC 302B**. Released on VFM Cassettes, '88 by VFM Cassettes, Midland Records, Crusader Marketing Co., Taylors, Morley Audio Services.

STORYBOOK (Glenda Jackson).
MCSET. Cat no: **ARGO 1274**. Released on Argo (EMI), Jul '91 by EMI Records.

STORYTIME TOP TEN (Volume 2) (Penelope Keith).
MC. Cat no: **VCA 056**. Released on VFM Cassettes, Jan '85 by VFM Cassettes, Midland Records, Crusader Marketing Co., Taylors, Morley Audio Services.

STORYTIME TOP TEN (Volume 7) (Ian Gelder & Hazel Clyne).
Note: Music by Major Records. Includes St. George and the Dragon, Medusa the Gorgon, The Sphinx, The Phoenix, The Unicorn, Choiron the Centaur, The Werewolf and The Salamander. For children aged 4 - 7 years.
MC. Cat no: **VCA 061**. Released on VFM Cassettes, Jan '85 by VFM Cassettes, Midland Records, Crusader Marketing Co., Taylors, Morley Audio Services.

STORYTIME TOP TEN (Volume 10) (Penelope Keith & Richard Briers).
Note: For children aged 4 - 8 years. With music by Major Records. Includes Adventures of a Vintage Car, The Soldier Doll, Gumdrop and the Farmer's Friend and The Terribly Plain Princess.
MC. Cat no: **VCA 064**. Released on VFM Cassettes, '91 by VFM Cassettes, Midland Records, Crusader Marketing Co., Taylors, Morley Audio Services.

SUPERMAN AND NIGHTMARE (Unknown narrator(s)).
MC. Cat no: **TCMFP 5712**. Released on MFP, Oct '85 by EMI Records, Solomon & Peres **Deleted** '88.

TALE OF A DONKEY'S TAIL (And Other Playschool Stories) (Various narrators).
LP. Cat no: **REC 232**. Released on BBC, Jun '76 by BBC Records, Taylors **Deleted** '87.
MC. Cat no: **MRMC 045**. Released on BBC, Jun '76 by BBC Records, Taylors **Deleted** '87.

TEDDY BEAR'S PICNIC, THE (And Other Favourite Children's Songs & Stories) (Gillian Blake).
Note: Includes the Teddy Bear's Picnic, My Grandfathers Clock, Hey Diddle Diddle, Hickory Dickory Dock, There Was a Crooked Man, Little Tommy Tucker, Touch Your Toes, Hop Skip and Jump, The Cuckoo Clock, The King Who Nearly Drowned, and The Wicked Witch. For ages 3 - 9.
MC. Cat no: **STC 017**. Released on VFM Cassettes, Jun '88 by VFM Cassettes, Midland Records, Crusader Marketing Co., Taylors, Morley Audio Services.
MC. Cat no: **STC 309A**. Released on VFM Cassettes, by VFM Cassettes, Midland Records, Crusader Marketing Co., Taylors, Morley Audio Services.

TEDDY RUXPIN (To The Rescue) (Unknown narrator(s)).
MC. Cat no: **STK 008**. Released on Stick-A-Tale, Jan '89 by Pickwick Records.

TEDDY RUXPIN (Fun At The Fair) (Unknown narrator(s)).
MC. Cat no: **PLBX 279**. Released on Tell-A-Tale, '89 by Pickwick Records, Taylors, Clyde Factors.

TEDDY RUXPIN (A Surprise Visitor) (Unknown narrator(s)).
MC. Cat no: **PLBX 278**. Released on Tell-A-Tale, '89 by Pickwick Records, Taylors, Clyde Factors.

TEDDY RUXPIN (Teddy's Dream) (Unknown narrator(s)).
MC. Cat no: **STK 007**. Released on Stick-A-Tale, Jan '89 by Pickwick Records.

THREE BILLY GOATS GRUFF (And Other Favourite Children's Stories) (Peter Whitbread & Gillian Blake).
Note: Includes The Three Billy Goats Gruff, The Snow Queen, The Emperor's New Clothes and The Mad Hatter's Tea Party. For ages 3 - 7.
MC. Cat no: **STC 303 B**. Released on VFM Cassettes, '88 by VFM Cassettes, Midland Records, Crusader Marketing Co., Taylors, Morley Audio Services.

THREE LITTLE PIGS (And Other Favourite Stories) (Peter Whitbread & Gillian Blake).
Note: For children aged 3-7 years. Includes The Three Little Pigs, The Little Red Hen, Cats and Dogs and The Brown Bear and the Fox.
MC. Cat no: **VCA 605**. Released on VFM Cassettes, Jul '85 by VFM Cassettes, Midland Records, Crusader Marketing Co., Taylors, Morley Audio Services.

TWINKLE TWINKLE LITTLE STAR (And Other Favourite Songs and Stories) (Various artists).
Note: For children aged 2 - 9 years. Includes Twinkle Twinkle Little Star, London Bridge is Falling Down, Pussy Cat Pussy Cat, Hushabye Baby, Here We Go Looby Loo, Mary Mary Quite Contrary, Ring a Ring o Roses, Ten Green Bottles, Aladdin and his Magic Lamp, Achmed and the Sultan's Daughters.
MC. Cat no: **STC 405**. Released on VFM Cassettes, '85 by VFM Cassettes, Midland Records, Crusader Marketing Co., Taylors, Morley Audio Services.

UGLY DUCKLING, THE (And Other

Favourite Children's Stories) (Peter Whitbread & Gillian Blake).
Note: For children aged 3 - 9 years. Includes The Ugly Duckling, King Rolphus the Wise, Snow White and the Seven Dwarfs, The Boy Who Cried Wolf, The Little Red Hen and The Nightingale.
MC. Cat no: **STC 119**. Released on VFM Cassettes, '85 by VFM Cassettes, Midland Records, Crusader Marketing Co., Taylors, Morley Audio Services.

UGLY DUCKLING, THE (And Other Favourite Songs and Stories) (Various artists).
Note: For children aged 2 - 9 years. Includes There Once Was an Ugly Duckling, My Grandfather's Clock, Put Your Finger in the Air, Flying in my Balloon, Sur Le Pont D'Avignon, Ding Dong Bell, 1 2 3 4 5, Old King Cole, She'll Be Coming Round the Mountain, The Ugly Duckling and Puss in Boots.
MC. Cat no: **SFC 409**. Released on VFM Cassettes, '85 by VFM Cassettes, Midland Records, Crusader Marketing Co., Taylors, Morley Audio Services.

WHEELS ON THE BUS, THE (And Other Favourite Songs and Stories) (Various artists).
Note: For children aged 2 - 9 years. Includes The Wheels on the Bus, Rolling on Your Roller Skates, And More for the Skylark, Incey Wincey Spider, Riding in a Rickshaw, The Paddles on the Steamer, Eight Rowers in a Boat, Little Red Riding Hood, Ali Baba and the Forty Thieves.
MC. Cat no: **SFC 406**. Released on VFM Cassettes, '85 by VFM Cassettes, Midland Records, Crusader Marketing Co., Taylors, Morley Audio Services.

WORLD OF STORIES (Katherine Hepburn).
MCSET. Cat no: **LFP 7180**. Released on Listen For Pleasure, '88 by EMI Records.

Chilton, Charles

JOURNEY INTO SPACE (Operation Luna) (Various narrators).
MCSET. Cat no: **ZBBC 4002**. Released on BBC Radio Collection, May '89 by BBC Records. Note: 4 Cassettes. ISBN No: 0563 226323
MCSET. Cat no: **1029S**. Released on Travellers Tales, '91 by Travellers Tales. Note: 4 Cassettes.

JOURNEY INTO SPACE (The Red Planet) (Various narrators).
Note: Includes a special introduction by Charles Chilton.
MCSET. Cat no: **ZBBC 1223**. Released on BBC Radio Collection, Nov '91 by BBC Records. Note: 8 Cassettes. ISBN No: 0563 409924

Christie, Agatha

4.50 FROM PADDINGTON (Rosemary Leach).
MCSET. Cat no: **CAB 312**. Released on Chivers Audio Books, '91 by Chivers Audio Books, Green Dragon Audio Visual. Note: 6 Cassettes.
MCSET. Cat no: **1398T**. Released on Travellers Tales, '91 by Travellers Tales. Note: 6 Cassettes.

ABC MURDERS, THE (Geoffrey Matthews).
MCSET. Cat no: **IAB 92052**. Released on Isis Audio Books, May '92. Note: 6 Cassettes. Playing time: 7 hours, 20 mins.

AND THEN THERE WERE NONE (Norman Barrs).
MCSET. Cat no: **CAB 317**. Released on Chivers Audio Books, '91 by Chivers Audio Books, Green Dragon Audio Visual. Note: 6 Cassettes.
MCSET. Cat no: **1588T**. Released on Travellers Tales, '91 by Travellers Tales. Note: 6 Cassettes.

ARSENIC AND OLD LACE (And Kind Hearts And Coronets) (Various narrators).
Note: Starring Dame Sybil Thorndike and Robert Powell.
MCSET. Cat no: **ZBBC 1125**. Released on BBC Radio Collection, Aug '90 by BBC Records. Note: ISBN No: 0563 410612

AT BERTRAM'S HOTEL (Rosemary Leach).
MCSET. Cat no: **CAB 313**. Released on Chivers Audio Books, '91 by Chivers Audio Books, Green Dragon Audio Visual. Note: 6 Cassettes.
MCSET. Cat no: **1461T**. Released on Travellers Tales, '91 by Travellers Tales. Note: 6 Cassettes.

BLUE GERANIUM (And More Stories) (Joan Hickson).
MCSET. Cat no: **LFP 7340**. Released on Listen For Pleasure, Jun '88 by EMI Records.

BODY IN THE LIBRARY, THE (Gwen Watford).
MCSET. Cat no: **1681T**. Released on Travellers Tales, '91 by Travellers Tales. Note: 5 Cassettes.
MCSET. Cat no: **TE 856**. Released on Isis Audio Books, '91. Note: 5 Cassettes.
MCSET. Cat no: **IAB 91012**. Released on Isis Audio Books, '91. Note: 5 Cassettes.

CARIBBEAN MYSTERY, A (Rosemary Leach).
MCSET. Cat no: **CAB 581**. Released on Chivers Audio Books, '91 by Chivers Audio Books, Green Dragon Audio Visual. Note: 6 Cassettes.
MCSET. Cat no: **1724T**. Released on Travellers Tales, '91 by Travellers Tales. Note: 6 Cassettes.

CLOCKS, THE (Robin Bailey).
MCSET. Cat no: **CAB 640**. Released on Chivers Audio Books, Oct '91 by Chivers Audio Books, Green Dragon Audio Visual. Note: 8 Cassettes.

DEAD MAN'S FOLLY (David Suchet).
MCSET. Cat no: **CAB 314**. Released on Chivers Audio Books, '91 by Chivers Audio Books, Green Dragon Audio Visual. Note: 6 Cassettes.
MCSET. Cat no: **1462T**. Released on Travellers Tales, '91 by Travellers Tales. Note: 6 Cassettes.

DEATH ON THE NILE (David Suchet).
MCSET. Cat no: **CAB 601**. Released on Chivers Audio Books, Mar '92 by Chivers Audio Books, Green Dragon Audio Visual. Note: 8 cassettes

HERB OF DEATH (Joan Hickson).
MCSET. Cat no: **LFP 7394**. Released on Listen For Pleasure, Jun '89 by EMI Records.

LABOURS OF HERCULES, THE (John Woodvine).
MCSET. Cat no: **CAB 134**. Released on Chivers Audio Books, '91 by Chivers Audio Books, Green Dragon Audio Visual. Note: 6 Cassettes.
MCSET. Cat no: **1027T**. Released on Travellers Tales, '91 by Travellers Tales. Note: 6 Cassettes.

MURDER AT THE VICARAGE, THE (Gwen Watford).
MCSET. Cat no: **1700T**. Released on Travellers Tales, '91 by Travellers Tales. Note: 6 Cassettes.

MURDER AT THE VICARAGE, THE (James Saxon).
MCSET. Cat no: **CAB 611**. Released on Chivers Audio Books, '91 by Chivers Audio Books, Green Dragon Audio Visual. Note: 8 Cassettes.

MURDER IN MESOPOTAMIA (Anne Rosenfield).
MCSET. Cat no: **IAB 91071**. Released on Isis Audio Books, '91. Note: 6 Cassettes.

MURDER IN THE MEWS (Nigel Hawthorne).
MCSET. Cat no: **LFP 7134**. Released on Listen For Pleasure, Mar '84 by EMI Records.
MCSET. Cat no: **1028T**. Released on Travellers Tales, '91 by Travellers Tales. Note: 2 Cassettes.

MURDER IS ANNOUNCED, A (Rosemary Leach).
MCSET. Cat no: **CAB 297**. Released on Chivers Audio Books, Apr '88 by Chivers Audio Books, Green Dragon Audio Visual. Note: 8 Cassettes.
MCSET. Cat no: **1257T**. Released on Travellers Tales, '91 by Travellers Tales. Note: 8 Cassettes.

MURDER OF ROGER ACKROYD (Robin Bailey).
MCSET. Cat no: **CAB 199**. Released on Chivers Audio Books, '91 by Chivers Audio Books, Green Dragon Audio Visual. Note: 6 Cassettes.
MCSET. Cat no: **1146T**. Released on Travellers Tales, '91 by Travellers Tales. Note: 6 Cassettes.

MURDER ON THE ORIENT EXPRESS (David Suchet).
MCSET. Cat no: **CAB 315**. Released on Chivers Audio Books, '91 by Chivers

Audio Books, Green Dragon Audio Visual. Note: 6 Cassettes.
MCSET. Cat no: **1447T**. Released on Travellers Tales, '91 by Travellers Tales. Note: 6 Cassettes.
MCSET. Cat no: **0745128017**. Released on Word For Word, Apr '92 by Chivers Audio Books.

MYSTERIOUS MR QUIN, THE (Geoffrey Matthews).
Note: Contains these stories:- The Coming Of Mr Quin, The Shadow On The Glass, At The Bells and Motley, The Sign in the Sky, The Soul of the Croupier, The Man From the Sea, The Voice in the Dark, The Face of Helen, The Dead Harlequin, The Bird With the Broken Wing, The World's End and Harlequin Lane.
MCSET. Cat no: **IAB 91114**. Released on Isis Audio Books, Nov '91. Note: 7 Cassettes. Playing time 8 hours and 30 minutes.

N OR M ? (James Warwick).
MCSET. Cat no: **CAB 653**. Released on Chivers Audio Books, Dec '91 by Chivers Audio Books, Green Dragon Audio Visual. Note: 6 Cassettes.

NEMESIS (Gwen Watford).
MCSET. Cat no: **1678T**. Released on Travellers Tales, '91 by Travellers Tales. Note: 6 Cassettes.

ONE, TWO, BUCKLE MY SHOE (Geoffrey Matthews).
MCSET. Cat no: **IAB 91121**. Released on Isis Audio Books, '91. Note: 6 Cassettes. Playing time 7 hours 15 minutes.

ORDEAL BY INNOCENCE (Robin Bailey).
MCSET. Cat no: **CAB 593**. Released on Chivers Audio Books, '91 by Chivers Audio Books, Green Dragon Audio Visual. Note: 8 Cassettes.
MCSET. Cat no: **1753T**. Released on Travellers Tales, '91 by Travellers Tales. Note: 8 Cassettes.

POCKET FULL OF RYE, A (Rosemary Leach).
MCSET. Cat no: **CAB 099**. Released on Chivers Audio Books, '91 by Chivers Audio Books, Green Dragon Audio Visual. Note: 6 Cassettes.
MCSET. Cat no: **1029T**. Released on Travellers Tales, '91 by Travellers Tales. Note: 6 Cassettes.

POIROT (Various narrators)
Note: Includes: The Murder of Roger Ackroyd and Murder on the Links.
MCSET. Cat no: **ZBBC 1057**. Released on BBC Radio Collection, Sep '89 by BBC Records. Note: ISBN No: 0563 226099

POIROT (Lord Edgeware Dies) (Various narrators).
MCSET. Cat no: **ZBBC 1309**. Released on BBC Radio Collection, '91 by BBC Records.

POIROT INVESTIGATES (Volume 1) (David Suchet).
MCSET. Cat no: **LFP 7421**. Released on Listen For Pleasure, Sep '89 by EMI Records. Note: Playing time: 3 hours

POIROT INVESTIGATES (Volume 2) (David Suchet).
MCSET. Cat no: **LFP 7460**. Released on Listen For Pleasure, Mar '90 by EMI Records. Note: Playing time: 2 hours 45 minutes.

SITTAFORD MYSTERY, THE (Original cast).
MCSET. Cat no: **ZBBC 1126**. Released on BBC, Apr '90 by BBC Records, Taylors. Note: ISBN No: 0563 410620

SLEEPING MURDER (Rosemary Leach).
MCSET. Cat no: **CAB 620**. Released on Chivers Audio Books, '91 by Chivers Audio Books, Green Dragon Audio Visual. Note: 6 Cassettes.

SPARKLING CYANIDE (Robin Bailey).
MCSET. Cat no: **CAB 316**. Released on Chivers Audio Books, '91 by Chivers Audio Books, Green Dragon Audio Visual. Note: 6 Cassettes.
MCSET. Cat no: **1418T**. Released on Travellers Tales, '91 by Travellers Tales. Note: 6 Cassettes.

THEY DO IT WITH MIRRORS (Rosemary Leach).
MCSET. Cat no: **CAB 086**. Released on Chivers Audio Books, '91 by Chivers Audio Books, Green Dragon Audio Visual. Note: 6 Cassettes.
MCSET. Cat no: **1031T**. Released on Travellers Tales, '91 by Travellers Tales. Note: 6 Cassettes.

THIRD GIRL (John Woodvine).
MCSET. Cat no: **CAB 105**. Released on Chivers Audio Books, '91 by Chivers Audio Books, Green Dragon Audio Visual. Note: 6 Cassettes.
MCSET. Cat no: **1030T**. Released on Travellers Tales, '91 by Travellers Tales. Note: 6 Cassettes.

THIRTEEN PROBLEMS, THE (Joan Hickson).
MCSET. Cat no: **LFP 7312**. Released on Listen For Pleasure, Oct '87 by EMI Records.

UNEXPECTED GUEST (Unknown narrator(s)).
MC. Cat no: **ZCF 533**. Released on BBC, Sep '84 by BBC Records, Taylors **Deleted** Apr '89.

Christmas

CHRISTMAS ACTIVITY BOX (Unknown narrator(s)).
MC. Cat no: **TATAB 2**. Released on Pickwick International, '88 by Pickwick International Inc.(USA), Taylors, Clyde Factors.

WONDERFUL WORLD OF CHILDREN'S CHRISTMAS (Various narrators).
LP. Cat no: **HDY 1932**. Released on Audio Fidelity(USA), Oct '84 by Audio Fidelity (USA).
MC. Cat no: **ZCHDY 1932**. Released on Audio Fidelity(USA), Oct '84 by Audio Fidelity (USA).

Clancy, Tom

HUNT FOR RED OCTOBER, THE (Richard Crenna).
Note: Also available on hanging format, catalogue number:- 000138855X
MCSET. Cat no: **HCA 12**. Released on Harper Collins, Jan '92 by Harper Collins.

HUNT FOR RED OCTOBER, THE (Frank Muller).
MCSET. Cat no: **1603/1604T**. Released on Travellers Tales, '91 by Travellers Tales. Note: 10 Cassettes.
MCSET. Cat no: **IAB 90103**. Released on Isis Audio Books, '91. Note: 10 Cassettes.

Clarke, Arthur C

2001: A SPACE ODYSSEY (Arthur C Clarke).
MC. Cat no: **001042475**. Released on Collins-Caedmon, '88 by Collins Audio, Taylors, Bond Street Music.

2001: A SPACE ODYSSEY (Unknown narrator(s)).
Note: Additional music by Richard Strauss.
MC. Cat no: **CDL 51504**. Released on Caedmon (USA), Jul '88 by Caedmon Records (USA), Bond Street Music.

2010: ODYSSEY TWO (Unknown narrator(s)).
MC. Cat no: **1709**. Released on Caedmon (USA), Apr '83 by Caedmon Records (USA), Bond Street Music.

FOUNTAINS OF PARADISE (Unknown narrator(s)).
MC. Cat no: **1606**. Released on Caedmon (USA), '88 by Caedmon Records (USA), Bond Street Music.

TRANSIT OF EARTH (And Other Stories) (Unknown narrator(s)).
MC. Cat no: **1566**. Released on Caedmon (USA), '88 by Caedmon Records (USA), Bond Street Music.

Clarke, Austin

BEYOND THE PALE (Unknown narrator(s)).
LP. Cat no: **CCT 2**. Released on Claddagh (Ireland), Aug '88 by Claddagh Records (Ireland), Projection, Impetus Records, Jazz Music, Roots Records, C.M. Distribution, Outlet Records, Taylors.

Clarke, Roy

GALA WEEK (Summer Wine Chronicles) (Peter Sallis).
MCSET. Cat no: **CAB 298**. Released on Chivers Audio Books, Apr '88 by Chivers Audio Books, Green Dragon Audio Visual. Note: 6 Cassettes.
MCSET. Cat no: **1035H**. Released on Travellers Tales, '91 by Travellers Tales. Note: 6 Cassettes

MOONBATHER, THE (Peter Sallis).
MCSET. Cat no: **CAB 371**. Released on Chivers Audio Books, '91 by Chivers Audio Books, Green Dragon Audio Visual. Note: 6 Cassettes.

Cleary, Beverly

BEEZUS AND RAMONA (Stockard Channing).
MCSET. Cat no: **2CCA 3142**. Released on Chivers Audio Books, '91 by Chivers Audio Books, Green Dragon Audio Visual. Note: 2 Cassettes.

RAMONA AND HER MOTHER (Stockard Channing).
MCSET. Cat no: **2CCA 3072**. Released on Chivers Audio Books, '91 by Chivers Audio Books, Green Dragon Audio Visual. Note: 2 Cassettes.
MCSET. Cat no: **9192F**. Released on Travellers Tales, '91 by Travellers Tales. Note: 2 Cassettes.

RAMONA FOREVER (Stockard Channing).
MCSET. Cat no: **9193F**. Released on Travellers Tales, '91 by Travellers Tales. Note: 2 Cassettes.

RAMONA QUIMBY, AGE 8 (Stockard Channing).
MCSET. Cat no: **2CCA 3074**. Released on Chivers Audio Books, '91 by Chivers Audio Books, Green Dragon Audio Visual. Note: 2 Cassettes.
MCSET. Cat no: **9183F**. Released on Travellers Tales, '91 by Travellers Tales. Note: 2 Cassettes.

RAMONA THE PEST (Stockard Channing).
MCSET. Cat no: **2CCA 3152**. Released on Chivers Audio Books, Sep '91 by Chivers Audio Books, Green Dragon Audio Visual. Note: 2 Cassettes.

Cleary, Jon

FALL OF AN EAGLE, THE (Carole Boyd).
MCSET. Cat no: **1240F**. Released on Travellers Tales, '91 by Travellers Tales. Note: 8 Cassettes.

GREEN HELMET, THE (Unknown narrator(s)).
MCSET. Cat no: **1854960431**. Released on Bramhope, '91 by Ulverscroft Soundings. Note: 4 Cassettes.

HIGH COMMISSIONER, THE (Peter Wheeler).
MCSET. Cat no: **SOUND 33**. Released on Soundings, Feb '85 by Soundings Records, Bond Street Music. Note: 4 Cassettes.

JUSTIN BAYARD (Unknown narrator(s)).
MCSET. Cat no: **1854960458**. Released on Bramhope, '91 by Ulverscroft Soundings. Note: 4 Cassettes.

LONG PURSUIT (Unknown narrator(s)).
MCSET. Cat no: **1854960466**. Released on Bramhope, '91 by Ulverscroft Soundings.

MASK OF THE ANDES (Unknown narrator(s)).
MCSET. Cat no: **1854960474**. Released on Soundings, '91 by Soundings Records, Bond Street Music. Note: 6 Cassettes.

PETER'S PENCE (Unknown narrator(s)).
MCSET. Cat no: **1854760482**. Released on Soundings, '91 by Soundings Records, Bond Street Music. Note: 6 Cassettes.

SUNDOWNERS, THE (Christopher Kay).
MCSET. Cat no: **1195F**. Released on Travellers Tales, '91 by Travellers Tales. Note: 5 Cassettes.
MCSET. Cat no: **1854960490**. Released on Bramhope, '91 by Ulverscroft Soundings. Note: 5 Cassettes.

VERY PRIVATE WAR, A (Christopher Kay).
MCSET. Cat no: **1024W**. Released on Travellers Tales, '91 by Travellers Tales. Note: 6 Cassettes.

VORTEX (Unknown narrator(s)).
MCSET. Cat no: **1854960512**. Released on Bramhope, '91 by Ulverscroft Soundings. Note: 5 Cassettes.

Cleland, John

FANNY HILL (Memoirs of a Woman of Pleasure) (Barbara McCulloch).
MCSET. Cat no: **RB 86860**. Released on Recorded Books, '91 by Isis Audio Books. Note: 6 Cassettes.

Clinton-Baddeley, U.C.

NO CASE FOR THE POLICE (Unknown artist(s)).
MCSET. Cat no: **1854963600**. Released on Bramhope, '91 by Ulverscroft Soundings. Note: 5 Cassettes.

ONLY A MATTER OF TIME (Unknown narrator(s)).
MCSET. Cat no: **1854963376**. Released on Bramhope, '91 by Ulverscroft Soundings. Note: 4 Cassettes.

Cocteau, Jean

HUMAN VOICE, THE (Ingrid Bergman).
MC. Cat no: **1118**. Released on Caedmon (USA), '88 by Caedmon Records (USA), Bond Street Music.

Coetzee, J.M.

IN THE HEART OF THE COUNTRY (Norma West).
MCSET. Cat no: **OAS 89086**. Released on Oasis Audio Books, '91 by Isis Audio Books. Note: 6 Cassette.
MCSET. Cat no: **1391F**. Released on Travellers Tales, '91 by Travellers Tales. Note: 6 Cassettes.

Coffman, Virginia

LOOKING GLASS, THE (Pat Starr).
MCSET. Cat no: **1018F**. Released on Travellers Tales, '91 by Travellers Tales. Note: 6 Cassettes.

ORCHID TREE, THE (Pat Starr).
MCSET. Cat no: **1271F**. Released on Travellers Tales, '91 by Travellers Tales. Note: 8 Cassettes.
MCSET. Cat no: **CAB 265**. Released on Chivers Audio Books, '91 by Chivers Audio Books, Green Dragon Audio Visual.

Cole, Michael

EDWARD GETS THE HICCUPS (Unknown narrator(s)).
Note: Book and cassette.
MC. Cat no: **PLBL 232**. Released on Tell-A-Tale, '88 by Pickwick Records, Taylors, Clyde Factors.

EDWARD JOINS THE BAND (And Clive's Kite) (Unknown narrator(s)).
MC. Cat no: **PLBL 250**. Released on Tell-A-Tale, Jan '89 by Pickwick Records, Taylors, Clyde Factors.

LIONEL'S CAR (And Edward To The Rescue) (Unknown narrator(s)).
MC. Cat no: **PLBL 249**. Released on Tell-A-Tale, Jan '89 by Pickwick Records, Taylors, Clyde Factors.

LIONEL'S PARTY (Unknown narrator(s)).
Note: Book and cassette.
MC. Cat no: **PLBL 231**. Released on Tell-A-Tale, '88 by Pickwick Records, Taylors, Clyde Factors.

Colegate, Isabel

GLIMPSE OF SION'S GLORY, A (Judith Whale).
MCSET. Cat no: **1513F**. Released on Travellers Tales, '91 by Travellers Tales. Note: 4 Cassettes.
MCSET. Cat no: **OAS 90092**. Released on Oasis Audio Books, '91 by Isis Audio Books. Note: 4 Cassettes.

Coleridge, Samuel

POETRY OF COLERIDGE, THE (Sir Ralph Richardson).
Note: Includes: The Rime of the Ancient Mariner.
MC. Cat no: **1092**. Released on Caedmon (USA), '88 by Caedmon Records (USA), Bond Street Music.

Collins, Jackie

CHANCES (Unknown narrator(s)).
MCSET. Cat no: **0671738070**. Released on Simon & Schuster, '91 by Simon & Schuster Ltd.

LADY BOSS (Unknown narrator(s)).
MCSET. Cat no: **0671726331**. Released on Simon & Schuster, '91 by Simon & Schuster Ltd. Note: 2 Cassettes.

LUCKY (Unknown narrator(s)).
MCSET. Cat no: **0671738089**. Released on Simon & Schuster, '91 by Simon & Schuster Ltd.

Collins, Joan

LOVE AND DESIRE AND HATE (Joan Collins).
MCSET. Cat no: **RC 23**. Released on Random Century, '91 by Random Century Audiobooks, Conifer Records. Note: 2 Cassettes. ISBN 1856860590. 3 hrs approx.

Collins, Wilkie

MOONSTONE, THE (Peter Jeffrey).
MCSET. Cat no: **CTC 052**. Released on Cover to Cover, '90 by Cover to

Cover Cassettes. Note: 14 Cassettes. Playing time: 18 hrs 30 mins.
MCSET. Cat no: **1339/1340F.** Released on Travellers Tales, '91 by Travellers Tales. Note: 14 Cassettes.

WOMAN IN WHITE, THE (Ian Holm).
MCSET. Cat no: **CTC 018.** Released on Cover to Cover, Jun '85 by Cover to Cover Cassettes. Note: 18 Cassettes. Playing time: 24 hrs 45 mins.
MCSET. Cat no: **1215/6/7F.** Released on Travellers Tales, '91 by Travellers Tales. Note: 18 cassettes.

Collodi, Carlo

PINOCCHIO (Unknown narrator(s)).
MCSET. Cat no: **41 7030 5.** Released on Listen For Pleasure, Oct '85 by EMI Records.

PINOCCHIO (Bernard Cribbins).
MCSET. Cat no: **SAY 9.** Released on Argo (Polygram), Jul '82 by PolyGram Classics **Deleted** Jan '89.

PINOCCHIO (Unknown narrator(s)).
Note: Book and cassette.
LP. Cat no: **D 311.** Released on Disneyland, Dec '82 by Disneyland-Vista Records (USA).
MC. Cat no: **D 2DC.** Released on Disneyland, Dec '82 by Disneyland-Vista Records (USA).
LP. Cat no: **D 3905.** Released on Disneyland, Dec '82 by Disneyland-Vista Records (USA).
LPPD. Cat no: **D 3102.** Released on Disneyland, Dec '82 by Disneyland-Vista Records (USA).
MC. Cat no: **PLB 69.** Released on Tell-A-Tale, '83 by Pickwick Records, Taylors, Clyde Factors.

PINOCCHIO (Cyril Ritchard).
MC. Cat no: **1262.** Released on Caedmon (USA), '88 by Caedmon Records (USA), Bond Street Music.

PINOCCHIO (Unknown narrator(s)).
MC. Cat no: **DIS 003.** Released on Disney (Read-a-long), Jul '90 by Disneyland Records.
MC. Cat no: **STK 013.** Released on Stick-A-Tale, Jan '89 by Pickwick Records.

PINOCCHIO (Alan Haines).
MC. Cat no: **TS 332.** Released on Tellastory, '91 by Random Century Audiobooks. Note: ISBN no. 1856561151

Colum, Padraic

TWELVE LABOURS OF HERACLES, THE (Anthony Quayle).
MC. Cat no: **1256.** Released on Caedmon (USA), '88 by Caedmon Records (USA), Bond Street Music.

Comedy...

BEST OF HYSTERIA 3 (Various artists).
Tracks / Introduction to Hysteria 3: *Fry, Stephen* / Sexuality: *Bragg, Billy* / Contraception: *Elton, Ben* / Being happy: *Lederer, Helen* / Together again: *Holland, Jools & Sam Brown* / I, an actor: *Craig, Nicholas* / Awards acceptance speech: *Wax, Ruby & Tony Slattery* / Wilderness years, The: *Izzard, Eddie* / Take me in your arms: *Henry, Lenny & Steve Nieve* / Celebrity sticky moments: *Clary, Julian* / Why fish wear socks: *Wright, Steven* / Interviews Elton John: *Atkinson, Rowan & Elton John* / I wish I knew how it would feel to be free: *Starr, Edwin*.
CD. Cat no: **CDEMC 3606.** Released on EMI, Oct '91 by EMI Records.
MC. Cat no: **TCEMC 3606.** Released on EMI, Oct '91 by EMI Records.

BEYOND THE FRINGE (At the Fortune Theatre/On Broadway) (Various artists).
Tracks / Royal box, The: *Cook, Peter & Dudley Moore* / Heat, The-Death of the universe: *Miller, Jonathan* / Bollard: *Moore, Dudley* (Dudley Moore at the piano.) / T.V.P.M.: *Cook, Peter* / Aftermyth of war: *Company* / Real class: *Company* / Little Miss Britten: *Moore, Dudley* / Black equals white: *Cook, Peter & Jonathan Miller* / Take a pew: *Bennett, Alan* / End of the world: *Company* / Sadder and the wiser beaver, The: *Cook, Peter & Alan Bennett* / Sitting on the bench: *Cook, Peter* / And the same to you/Colonel Bogey: *Moore, Dudley* (Dudley Moore at the piano.) / Portrait from memory: *Miller, Jonathan* / So that's the way you like it: *Company* / English way of death, The: *Bennett, Alan* / Song: *Whitehead, Paxton/Dudley Moore* / Home thoughts from abroad: *Various artists* / One leg too few: *Cook, Peter & Dudley Moore* / Two English songs: *Whitehead, Paxton/Dudley Moore* / Lord Cobbold/The Duke: *Cook, Peter/Paxton Whitehead/Dudley Moore* / Piece of my mind, A: *Whitehead, Paxton* / Great train robbery: *Cook, Peter & Alan Bennett*.
MCSET. Cat no: **ECC 1.** Released on EMI, Mar '90 by EMI Records. Note: UK cat. no.'s ECC 11/12. International cat. no.'s 7939634/44.
MC. Cat no: **92055.4.** Released on Silva Screen, '90 by Silva Screen, Conifer Records.
CD. Cat no: **92055.2.** Released on Silva Screen, '90 by Silva Screen, Conifer Records.

BRITISH COMEDY CLASSICS (Various artists).
Tracks / Song of the Australian outlaw: *Williams, Kenneth* / Society wedding stakes, The: *Hudd, Roy* / Football results: *Bentine, Michael* / Stop press: *Cope, Kenneth/David Frost* / You need feet: *Bresslaw, Bernard* / Ton up boy: *Morecambe & Wise* / Gossip calypso: *Cribbins, Bernard* / Letter from Bill, A: *Various artists* (The Rag Trade) / Lovely lunch: *Bird, John/John Fortune* / Goodness gracious me: *Sellers, Peter/Sophia Loren* / Impressions: *Morecambe & Wise* / Holiday commercial: *Bentine, Michael* / Right said Fred: *Cribbins, Bernard* / Drats: *Bentine, Michael* / My boomerang won't come back: *Drake, Charlie* / Green grow my nadgers oh: *Williams, Kenneth* / Phoney folk-lore: *Ustinov, Peter* / Ad nauseum (That was the week that was): *Various artists* / Gnu song, The: *Flanders & Swann* / Mad passionate love: *Bresslaw, Bernard* / Royal box, The: *Cook, Peter & Dudley Moore* / Get it right corporal: *Morecambe & Wise* / Lolly commercial: *Bentine, Michael* / Boom oo yatta ta ta: *Morecambe & Wise* / Notice to quit: *Hudd, Roy* / Old girls school reunion: *Grenfell, Joyce* / Funny game politics: *Various artists* / Moscow radio commercial: *Bentine, Michael* / Ballad of the woggler's moulie: *Williams, Kenneth* / Take a pew: *Bennett, Alan* / You gotto go oww: *Milligan, Spike* / Indians: *Morecambe & Wise* / Ice cream commercial: *Bentine, Michael* / Q5 piano tune, The: *Milligan, Spike* / Fly buttons: *Martin, Millicent/Roy Kinnear/* / Hole in the ground: *Cribbins, Bernard* / Hippopotamus song, The: *Flanders & Swann* / Sitting on the bench: *Cook, Peter* / Narcissus: *Grenfell, Joyce & Norman Wisdom* / Horse show, The: *Bentine, Michael* / Madeira m'dear: *Flanders & Swann* / Drop of the hard stuff, A: *Sellers, Peter* / And the same to you/Colonel Bogey: *Moore, Dudley*.
MCSET. Cat no: **ECC 7.** Released on EMI, Jul '90 by EMI Records.

BRITISH COMEDY CLASSICS (Volume 2) (Various artists).
Tracks / Judge not: *Cleese, John, Tim Brooke Taylor, Bill Oddie* / Mock Mozart: *Ustinov, Peter* / Grieg's piano concerto: *Morecambe & Wise* / French for beginners: *Bentine, Michael* / Bus driver: *Hudd, Roy* / Transport of delight, A: *Flanders & Swann* / Car commercial: *Bentine, Michael* / Couple: *Bron, Eleanor & John Fortune* / Shame and scandal in the family: *Percival, Lance* / Wormwood Scrubs tango: *Various artists* / My dear Prime Minister: *Percival, Lance & William Rushton* / Runcorn splod cobbler's song: *Williams, Kenneth* / Charlie Brown: *Bresslaw, Bernard* / Real class: *Various artists* (Beyond the Fringe Company) / Singing the blues: *Morecambe & Wise* / Finale: *Milligan, Spike* / Astronauts, The: *Bentine, Michael* / Nursery school: *Grenfell, Joyce* / Balham - Gateway to the South: *Sellers, Peter* / How green was my button hole: *Various artists* / Gas man cometh, The: *Flanders & Swann* / Terrible tale of the Somerset nog, The: *Williams, Kenneth* / Underneath it all: *Milligan, Spike* / Train commercial: *Bentine, Michael* / Stroll down Memory Lane, A: *Hudd, Roy* (Interpolating 'Together' - Munro/Smith/Perci-

val.) / BBC B.C.: *Hatch, David & John Cleese* / My September love: *Milligan, Spike* / Scotland Yard: *Bentine, Michael* / Ambassador of Khasiland: *Morecambe & Wise* / Song of the bogle clencher: *Williams, Kenneth* / Fuller's earth: *Sellers, Peter/Graham Stark* / End of the world: *Various artists* (The Company).

MCSET. Cat no: **ECC 17**. Released on EMI, May '91 by EMI Records.

COMEDY SPECTACULAR (Various artists).
LP. Cat no: **REB 249**. Released on BBC, Oct '76 by BBC Records, Taylors **Deleted** '87.

COMIC STRIP (Various artists).
LP. Cat no: **HAHA 6001**. Released on Springtime, Nov '81 by Springtime Records.
MC. Cat no: **CHACHA 6001**. Released on Springtime, Nov '81 by Springtime Records.

COMICAL CUTS (Volume 3) (Various artists).
Tracks / Interviewed: *Oliver, Vic* (With Jeradyne Jarvis) / Vic Oliver calling: *Oliver, Vic* / Knock knock, who's there?: *Oliver, Vic* (With Sarah Churchill) / Vic Oliver ambles on: *Oliver, Vic* / Vic Oliver versus Gloria Day - butting in: *Oliver, Vic* / Vic Oliver goes naughty: *Oliver, Vic* / Vic Oliver's twists: *Oliver, Vic* / Tickling your fancy/Tickling the ivories: *Oliver, Vic* / O dear dear: *Frankau, Ronald* / Good morning Mr. Barlow: *Frankau, Ronald* / They have a much better time when they're naughty: *Frankau, Ronald* / I'd like to have a honeymoon with her: *Frankau, Ronald* / Uncle Bill has much improved: *Frankau, Ronald* / I'd rather be a woman than a man: *Frankau, Ronald* / Through a momentary loss of self-control: *Frankau, Ronald* / Upper class love: *Frankau, Ronald* / Chinese nights: *Frankau, Ronald* / He's a twirp: *Frankau, Ronald* / Headmistress, The: *Marshall, Arthur* / School girls story, A: *Marshall, Arthur* / Showing the school: *Marshall, Arthur* / Games mistress: *Marshall, Arthur* / Hostess, The: *Marshall, Arthur* / Nature walk, A: *Marshall, Arthur* / Botany class, The: *Marshall, Arthur* / Reading with children: *Marshall, Arthur* / Out with the guides: *Marshall, Arthur* / Miss Pritchard's tricycle: *Marshall, Arthur* / Cabaret boys, The: *Byng, Douglas* (With Lance Lister) / Sunday school has done a lot for me: *Byng, Douglas* / Oriental Emma of the 'arem: *Byng, Douglas* / Sex appeal Sarah: *Byng, Douglas* / Mexican Minnie: *Byng, Douglas* / I'm one of the Queens of England: *Byng, Douglas* / I'm the pest of Budapest: *Byng, Douglas* / I must have everything Hungarian: *Byng, Douglas* / I'm a bird: *Byng, Douglas* / Mayoress of Mould On The Puddle, The: *Byng, Douglas*.

MCSET. Cat no: **ECC 19**. Released on EMI, May '91 by EMI Records.

COMICAL CUTS (Volume 2) (Various artists).
Tracks / Goodnight, everybody goodnight: *Wilton, Robb* (Comedian with orchestra.) / I should say so: *Wilton, Robb* (Comedian with orchestra.) / Fire station, The (part 1): *Wilton, Robb* (Comedy sketch.) / Fire station, The (part 2): *Wilton, Robb* (Comedy sketch by Robb Wilton with Florence Palmer.) / Police station, The: *Wilton, Robb* (Comedy sketch by Robb Wilton with Florence Palmer.) / Home guard, The: *Wilton, Robb* (Comedy sketch by Robb Wilton.) / Munitions worker, The: *Wilton, Robb* (Comedy sketch by Robb Wilton.) / Fourth form at St Michael's (part 1): *Hay, Will* / Fourth form at St Michael's (part 2): *Hay, Will* / Fourth form at St Michael's (part 3): *Hay, Will* / Fourth form at St Michael's (part 4): *Hay, Will* / Fourth form at St Michael's (part 5): *Hay, Will* / Fourth form at St Michael's (part 6): *Hay, Will* / Convict 99 (part 1): *Hay, Will* (With Moore Marriott & Graham Moffatt) / Convict 99 (part 2): *Hay, Will* (With Moore Marriott & Graham Moffatt) / Nell: *Bennett, Billy* / Green tie on the little yellow dog, The: *Bennett, Billy* / No power on earth: *Bennett, Billy* / Charge of the tight brigade: *Bennett, Billy* / Ogul mogul (A kanakanese love lyric): *Bennett, Billy* / Tightest man I know, The: *Bennett, Billy* / Mandalay: *Bennett, Billy & Orchestra* / Coffee stall keeper, The: *Bennett, Billy & Orchestra* / Foreign legion, The: *Bennett, Billy* (With piano.) / Bookmaker's daughter, The: *Bennett, Billy* (With piano.) / Funny face - a few drinks: *Howard, Sydney/Leslie Henson* / Our village concert (part 1): *Howard, Sydney* (With Vera Pearce, Leonard Henry & Co. with orchestra .) / Our village concert (part 2): *Howard, Sydney* (With Vera Pearce, Leonard Henry & Co. with orchestra .) / Swanker's 'You don't say so', The: *Howard, Sydney* (With Vera Pearce and the Four Bright Sparks.) / Happiest couple in Lancashire, The: *Howard, Sydney & Orchestra* / Sex, sobs and slaughter (part 1): *Howard, Sydney* (With Company.) / Sex, sobs and slaughter (part 2): *Howard, Sydney* (With Company.).

MCSET. Cat no: **ECC 14**. Released on EMI, Mar '91 by EMI Records.

COMICAL CUTS (The 1930's and 40's) (Various artists).
Tracks / Laurel & Hardy: *Laurel & Hardy* / Dance of the cuckoos: *Laurel & Hardy* / Mr Potter wanders on: *Potter, Gillie* / Laughing gas: *Courtneidge, Cicely & Company* / Trip to Brighton, A: *Constandurous, Mabel/Michael Hogan & Company* (Recorded on the Southern Railway.) / Digging holes parts 1 & 2: *Flanagan & Allen* (Whatever happened to the breakdown man.) / Old school tie, The: *Western Brothers* / Joe Ramsbottam sells pills: *Evans, Norman* / Spot of fishing, A: *Clapham & Dwyer* / Cycling: *Tilley, John* / Kids and the char (part 2) out shopping, The: *Hemsley, Harry/Suzette Tarri* / Kids and the char (part 2) doin' a bit of busking, The: *Hemsley, Harry/Suzette Tarri* / It wouldn't have done for the Duke; sir: *Long, Norman* / Cyril Fletcher tells a couple: *Fletcher, Cyril* / Little Red Hooding Ride: *Bacon, Max* / Common sense: *King, Nosmo* (Introductory dialogue with Hubert.) / Dizzy: *Burns, George & Gracie Allen* / With her head tucked underneath her arm: *Holloway, Stanley* / Beefeater, The: *Holloway, Stanley* / Crazy Gang at sea, The: *Crazy Gang* / On behalf of the working classes: *Russell, Billy* (Recorded live in the Theatre.) / Tommy introduces McChumley & sings 'You lucky people': *Trinder, Tommy* / Tommy lets you into a few pilgrim family secrets: *Trinder, Tommy* / Tommy picks one out from 'The Classics' and recites: *Trinder, Tommy* / Tommy sings S'artnoon: *Trinder, Tommy* / Gardening: what to do with your aspidistra: *Wakefield, Oliver* (The voice of inexperience.) / Rags, bottles and bones: *Walker, Syd* / Old mother Riley's budget: *Lucan & McShane* / Old mother Riley takes her medicine: *Lucan & McShane* / Sid Field plays golf: *Field, Sid.*

MCSET. Cat no: **ECC 12**. Released on EMI, Oct '90 by EMI Records.

COUNTRY COMEDY TIME - LONZO AND OSCAR (Various artists).
LP. Cat no: **HAT 3123**. Released on Stetson, '89 by Hasmick Promotions, Taylors, Swift, Wellard Dist., Jazz Music, Hot Shot, Crusader Marketing Co..

FOOL BRITANNIA (Various artists).
LP. Cat no: **CEL 902**. Released on Ember, Sep '63 by Bulldog Records (UK) **Deleted** Sep '69.

FUNDAMENTAL FROLICS (Various artists).
LP. Cat no: **REB 435**. Released on BBC, Jan '82 by BBC Records, Taylors **Deleted** Jan '87.

GOLDEN HOUR OF COMEDY, A (Various artists).
MC. Cat no: **KGHMC 157**. Released on Masterpiece, Jul '91 by Knight Records Ltd., BMG Distribution Operations.
CD. Cat no: **KGHCD 157**. Released on Masterpiece, Jul '91 by Knight Records Ltd., BMG Distribution Operations.

LAUGHING STOCK OF THE BBC (Various artists).
LP. Cat no: **LAF 1**. Released on BBC, Apr '82 by BBC Records, Taylors **Deleted** '87.
MC. Cat no: **ZCLAF 1**. Released on BBC, Apr '82 by BBC Records, Taylors **Deleted** '88.

LIVE AT JONGLEURS (Various artists).
LP. Cat no: **JONG 1**. Released on Spartan, Feb '88, Outlet Records, Music Sales Records.
MC. Cat no: **JONGC 1**. Released on

Spartan, Feb '88, Outlet Records, Music Sales Records.

MEMORIES OF GREAT WIRELESS COMEDY SHOWS (1939-41) (Various artists).
LP. Cat no: **SH 388**. Released on Retrospect, Nov '80 by EMI Records **Deleted** Nov '85.

ONE HUNDRED COMEDY INSERTS (Volume 3) (Various artists).
LP. Cat no: **EAP 1007 SLP**. Released on East Anglian Productions, '81 by East Anglian Productions.
MC. Cat no: **EAP 1007 CAS**. Released on East Anglian Productions, '81 by East Anglian Productions.

ONE HUNDRED COMEDY INSERTS (Volume 2) (Various artists).
LP. Cat no: **EAP 1006 SLP**. Released on East Anglian Productions, '81 by East Anglian Productions.
MC. Cat no: **EAP 1006 CAS**. Released on East Anglian Productions, '81 by East Anglian Productions.

PRIVATE EYE GOLDEN SATIRICALS (Various artists).
LP. Cat no: **HAHA 6002**. Released on Springtime, Nov '81 by Springtime Records.
MC. Cat no: **CHACHA 6002**. Released on Springtime, Nov '81 by Springtime Records.

SECRET POLICEMAN'S BALL (Original Soundtrack) (Various artists).
Tracks / Interesting facts: *Various artists* / Country and western supersong: *Various artists* / How do you do it?: *Various artists* / School master: *Various artists* / Pregnancy test: *Various artists* / Name's the game: *Various artists* / Stake your claim: *Various artists* / Entirely a matter for you: *Various artists* / Cheese shop: *Various artists* / Please: *Various artists* / Four Yorkshiremen: *Various artists* / Two little boys in blue: *Various artists* / End of the world: *Various artists*.
LP. Cat no: **ILPS 9601**. Released on Island, Dec '79 by Island Records, Outlet Records, Solomon & Peres, Projection, Jetstar **Deleted** Jun '88.
MC. Cat no: **ICT 9601**. Released on Island, Dec '79 by Island Records, Outlet Records, Solomon & Peres, Projection, Jetstar **Deleted** Jun '88.
MC. Cat no: **LAFFC 3**. Released on Laughing Stock, Sep '91.

SECRET POLICEMAN'S OTHER BALL (Various artists).
Tracks / Word of thanks, A: *Cleese, John* / Road safety: *Atkinson, Rowan* / Australian motor insurance claims: *Carrott, Jasper* / Clothes off: *Cleese, John, Pamela Stephenson & Graham Chapman* / Had it up to here: *Wood, Victoria* / Men's talk: *Fortune, John & Alan Bennett* / What's on in Stoke Newington: *Sayle, Alexei* / Royal Australian prostate foundation, The: *Everage, Dame Edna* / Denis on the menace: *Wells, John* / Beekeeping: *Atkinson,* *Rowan & John Cleese* / Song in a french accent: *Innes, Neil* / Divorce service: *Atkinson, Rowan, Griff Rhyss Jones, Pamela Stephenson & John* / Reading the riot act: *Langham, Chris* / Top of the form: *Cleese, John & Company* / Drinking: *Connolly, Billy*.
LP. Cat no: **HAHA 6003**. Released on Springtime, '81 by Springtime Records **Deleted** '84.
MC. Cat no: **CHACHA 6003**. Released on Springtime, '81 by Springtime Records **Deleted** '84.

SECRET POLICEMAN'S THIRD BALL (The Comedy) (Various artists).
Note: Intro: Mike Hurley as Bill Bore & Chris Langham/Phil Cool/Emo Phillips/Spitting Image/Hale & Pace as The Two Rons/Mel Smith & Griff Rhys-Jones (inc. Walk on the wild Side)/Lenny Henry/French & Saunders/Andrew Sachs as Manuel/Warren Mitchell as Alf Garnett/Rory Bremner/Ben Elton/Outro: Mike Hurley as Bill Bore
LP. Cat no: **V 2459**. Released on Virgin, Sep '87 by Virgin Records, Music Sales Records **Deleted** Feb '89.
MC. Cat no: **TCV 2459**. Released on Virgin, Sep '87 by Virgin Records, Music Sales Records **Deleted** Feb '89.
CD. Cat no: **CDV 2459**. Released on Virgin, '87 by Virgin Records, Music Sales Records **Deleted** Feb '89.

UTTERLY UTTERLY LIVE (Comic Relief) (Unknown narrator(s)).
LP. Cat no: **WX 51**. Released on WEA, May '86 by Warner Music International (WEA), Solomon & Peres, Outlet Records, Music Sales Records.
MC. Cat no: **WX 51C**. Released on WEA, May '86 by Warner Music International (WEA), Solomon & Peres, Outlet Records, Music Sales Records.

Compton-Burnett, Ivy

PRESENT AND THE PAST, THE (Elizabeth Proud).
MCSET. Cat no: **OAS 21291**. Released on Oasis Audio Books, Dec '91 by Isis Audio Books. Note: 7 Cassettes. Playing time 7 hours.

Conan Doyle, Arthur

ADVENTURES OF SHERLOCK HOLMES (Volume 1) (Various artists).
Note: Starring Clive Merrison and Michael Williams. Includes, A Scandal in Bohemia, The Red-Headed League, A Case of Identity and The Boscombe Valley Mystery.
MCSET. Cat no: **ZBBC 1200**. Released on BBC Radio Collection, Feb '91 by BBC Records. Note: ISBN No: 0563 409061

ADVENTURES OF SHERLOCK HOLMES (Volume 2) (Various artists).
Note: Includes: The Five Orange Pips, The Man With The Twisted Lip, The Adventure of The Blue Carbuncle and The Adventure of The Speckled Band.
MCSET. Cat no: **ZBBC 1201**. Released on BBC Radio Collection, Feb '91 by BBC Records. Note: ISBN No: 0563 40907X.

ADVENTURES OF SHERLOCK HOLMES (Volume 3) (Various artists).
Note: Includes: The Adventure of The Engineer's Thumb, The Adventure of The Noble Bachelor, The Adventure of The Beryl Coronet, The Adventure of The Copper Beeches.
MCSET. Cat no: **ZBBC 1202**. Released on BBC Radio Collection, Feb '91 by BBC Records. Note: ISBN No: 0563 409088

ADVENTURES OF SHERLOCK HOLMES, THE (Patrick Tull).
MCSET. Cat no: **IAB 90064**. Released on Isis Audio Books, '91. Note: 10 cassette set.

ADVENTURES OF SHERLOCK HOLMES, THE (Donald Pickering).
MC. Cat no: **PTB 601**. Released on Pickwick Talking Books, Jan '83 by Pickwick Records, Clyde Factors.

ADVENTURES OF SHERLOCK HOLMES, THE (Robert Hardy).
MCSET. Cat no: **418 141-4**. Released on Argo (Polygram), Jun '88 by PolyGram Classics **Deleted** Jan '89.

CASE BOOK OF SHERLOCK HOLMES, THE (Robert Hardy).
Note: Stories include: Adventure of The Three Garridebs, Adventures of The Lions Mane and The Adventure of The Retired Colourman.
MCSET. Cat no: **414 748-4**. Released on Argo (Polygram), Oct '85 by PolyGram Classics **Deleted** Jan '89.

EXPLOITS OF BRIGADIER GERARD (Martin Heller).
MCSET. Cat no: **SPF 170-1**. Released on Schiltron Audio Books, '91 by Schiltron Publishing. Note: 4 Cassettes. Playing time 5 hours 30 minutes.
MCSET. Cat no: **1363F**. Released on Travellers Tales, '91 by Travellers Tales. Note: 4 cassettes.

FAMOUS CASES OF SHERLOCK HOLMES (John Brewster).
MCSET. Cat no: **1272F**. Released on Travellers Tales, '91 by Travellers Tales. Note: 6 cassettes.

FOUR SHERLOCK HOLMES STORIES (Robert Hardy).
Note: Stories include: The Adventure of The Three Students, The Greek Interpreter, The Adventure of The Sussex Vampire and The Adventure of Charles Augustus Milverton.
MCSET. Cat no: **SAY 2**. Released on Argo (Polygram), Jul '82 by PolyGram Classics **Deleted** Jan '89.
MCSET. Cat no: **ARGO 1004**. Released on Argo (EMI), May '89 by EMI Records.

HOLMES COLLECTION, THE (Volume 1) (Unknown narrator(s)).
Note: Roy Marsden plays Sherlock Hol-

mes and John Moffatt plays Dr. Watson. Includes:- The Priory School, The Second Stain, Charles Augustus Milverton and the Boscombe Valley mystery.
MCSET. Cat no: TTC 2001. Released on Talking Tape Company, Apr '91, Conifer Records. Note: 2 cassettes. ISBN no.1872520944. Playing time 1hr. 50 mins.

HOLMES COLLECTION, THE (Volume 2) (Unknown narrator(s)).
Note: Stories include: The Six Napoleons, The Abbey Grange, The Norwood Builder and The Naval Treaty.
MCSET. Cat no: TTC 2002. Released on Talking Tape Company, Apr '91, Conifer Records. Note: 2 cassettes. Playing time 1hr 53mins. ISBN no. 1872520952

HOLMES COLLECTION, THE (Volume 3) (Unknown narrator(s)).
Note: Includes the Red Headed League, The Solitary Cyclist, A Scandal In Bohemia and The Blue Carbuncle.
MCSET. Cat no: TTC 2003. Released on Talking Tape Company, '91, Conifer Records. Note: 2 cassettes. Playing time 1hr 45mins. ISBN no. 1872520952

HOLMES COLLECTION, THE (Volume 4) (Unknown narrator(s)).
Note: Includes: The Speckled Band, Black Peter and The Golden Prince Nez And The Man With The Twisted Lip.
MCSET. Cat no: TTC 2004. Released on Talking Tape Company, Apr '91, Conifer Records. Note: 2 cassettes. ISBN no. 187520979. Playing time 1 hr 55 mins.

HOLMES COLLECTION, THE (Volume 5) (Unknown narrator(s)).
Note: Includes: The Copper Beeches, The Engineers Thumb, The Sussex Vampire And Shoscombe Old Place.
MCSET. Cat no: TTC 2005. Released on Talking Tape Company, Apr '91, Conifer Records. Note: 2 cassettes. Playing time 1hr 47mins . ISBN no.1872520987

HOLMES COLLECTION, THE (Volume 6) (Unknown narrator(s)).
Note: Include: The Devils Foot, The Bruce Partington Plans, The Cardboard Box and Thor Bridge.
MCSET. Cat no: TTC 2006. Released on Talking Tape Company, Apr '91, Conifer Records. Note: 2 cassettes. Playing time 1hr 5mins. ISBN no. 1872520995

HOUND OF THE BASKERVILLES, THE (Unknown narrator(s)).
Note: Book and cassette.
MC. Cat no: PLBC 82. Released on Tell-A-Tale, '88 by Pickwick Records, Taylors, Clyde Factors.

HOUND OF THE BASKERVILLES, THE (Patrick Tull).
MCSET. Cat no: IAB 92045. Released on Isis Audio Books, Apr '92. Note: 4 cassettes. Playing time 5hrs.

HOUND OF THE BASKERVILLES, THE (Hugh Burden).
MCSET. Cat no: LFP 7212. Released on Listen For Pleasure, Sep '85 by EMI Records.
MCSET. Cat no: 001042424. Released on Collins-Caedmon, '88 by Collins Audio, Taylors, Bond Street Music.

HOUND OF THE BASKERVILLES, THE (Nicol Williamson).
MCSET. Cat no: 505. Released on Caedmon (USA), Jul '88 by Caedmon Records (USA), Bond Street Music.

HOUND OF THE BASKERVILLES, THE (Peter Emmens).
MCSET. Cat no: 1267 F. Released on Travellers Tales, '91 by Travellers Tales. Note: 4 cassettes.

LOST WORLD, THE (Anthony Homyer).
MCSET. Cat no: TCL 17. Released on Complete Listener, '91 by Complete Listener. Note: 6 Cassettes. (BB) Playing Time: 540 Minutes.
MCSET. Cat no: 1568F. Released on Travellers Tales, '91 by Travellers Tales. Note: 6 Cassettes.

LOST WORLD, THE (Unknown narrator(s)).
Note: Book and cassette.
MC. Cat no: PLBC 81. Released on Tell-A-Tale, '88 by Pickwick Records, Taylors, Clyde Factors.

LOST WORLD, THE (Daniel Massey).
MCSET. Cat no: ARGO 1226. Released on Argo (EMI), Nov '90 by EMI Records. Note: 2 Cassettes.

LOST WORLD, THE (James Mason).
MC. Cat no: TC LFP 7070. Released on Listen For Pleasure, Dec '80 by EMI Records.

MEMOIRS OF SHERLOCK HOLMES (Robert Hardy).
Tracks / Yellow face, The / Stockbroker's clerk, The / "Gloria Scott", The / Final problem, The.
MCSET. Cat no: SAY 108. Released on Argo (Polygram), '86 by PolyGram Classics **Deleted** Jan '89.

MEMOIRS OF SHERLOCK HOLMES (Alex Spencer).
Note: A collection of short stories.
MCSET. Cat no: RB 86960. Released on Recorded Books, '91 by Isis Audio Books. Note: 7 cassettes.
MCSET. Cat no: 1573F. Released on Travellers Tales, '91 by Travellers Tales. Note: 7 Cassettes.

MORE SHERLOCK HOLMES STORIES (Robert Hardy).
Note: Stories include: The Adventure of the Dying Detective, The Adventure of Shoscombe Old Place, The Musgrave Ritual and The Crooked Man.
MCSET. Cat no: SAY 98. Released on Argo (Polygram), Mar '84 by PolyGram Classics **Deleted** Jan '89.
MCSET. Cat no: ARGO 1202. Released on Argo (EMI), May '90 by EMI Records. Note: 2 Cassettes.

NORWOOD BUILDER, THE (Various artists).
Note: Robert Hardy as Sherlock Holmes and Nigel Stock as Dr. Watson with full supporting cast. Includes: Lady Frances Carfax.
MC. Cat no: ANV 643. Released on Anvil Cassettes, Jan '81 by Anvil Cassettes, Chivers Audio Books.

RETURN OF SHERLOCK HOLMES, THE (Robert Hardy).
Note: Stories include: The Adventure of the Empty House, The Adventure of the Solitary Cyclist, The Adventure of the Red Cycle and The Adventure of the Mazarin Stone.
MCSET. Cat no: SAY 109. Released on Argo (Polygram), Jun '84 by PolyGram Classics **Deleted** Jan '89.

SHERLOCK HOLMES (Volume 2) (Various artists).
Note: Includes: The Blue Carbuncle, The Silver Blaze, The Final Problem and The Empty House.
MCSET. Cat no: ZBBC 1091. Released on BBC Radio Collection, Sep '89 by BBC Records. Note: ISBN No: 0563 227036

SHERLOCK HOLMES (Various artists).
Note: Stories are Charles Augustus Milverton and Black Peter. Starring Robert Hardy as Sherlock Holmes and Nigel Stock as Doctor Watson with full supporting cast.
MC. Cat no: ANV 642. Released on Anvil Cassettes, Jan '81 by Anvil Cassettes, Chivers Audio Books.

SHERLOCK HOLMES (Volume 3) (Various artists).
Note: Includes: The Musgrave Ritual, Black Peter, The Bruce Partington Plans and The Dancing Men.
MCSET. Cat no: ZBBC 1123. Released on BBC Radio Collection, Apr '90 by BBC Records. Note: ISBN No: 0563 410590

SHERLOCK HOLMES (Various artists).
Note: The classic radio production with Carleton Hobbs and Norman Shelley. Includes: A Scandal in Bohemia, The Red-Headed League, Charles Augustus Milverton and The Speckled Band.
MCSET. Cat no: ZBBC 1031. Released on BBC Radio Collection, Sep '88 by BBC Records. Note: ISBN No: 0563 225718

SHERLOCK HOLMES ADVENTURES (John Wood).
MCSET. Cat no: IAB 90093. Released on Isis Audio Books, '91. Note: 11 cassettes.

SHERLOCK HOLMES AND THE DANCING MEN (And The Storm) (Various narrators).
MC. Cat no: 0582526507. Released on Longman/Pickwick, '91 by Pickwick

Records. Note: 8 Cassettes.

SHERLOCK HOLMES SOUNDBOOK (Various artists).
MC. Cat no: **SBC 107**. Released on Caedmon (USA), Oct '81 by Caedmon Records (USA), Bond Street Music.

SHERLOCK HOLMES STORIES (Volume 4) (Basil Rathbone).
MC. Cat no: **CDL 51240**. Released on Caedmon (USA), Oct '81 by Caedmon Records (USA), Bond Street Music.

SHERLOCK HOLMES STORIES (Volume 1) (Basil Rathbone).
MC. Cat no: **CDL 51172**. Released on Caedmon (USA), Oct '81 by Caedmon Records (USA), Bond Street Music.

SHERLOCK HOLMES STORIES (Volume 2) (Basil Rathbone).
MC. Cat no: **CDL 51208**. Released on Caedmon (USA), Oct '81 by Caedmon Records (USA), Bond Street Music.

SHERLOCK HOLMES STORIES (Part 1) (Robert Hardy).
MCSET. Cat no: **1238F**. Released on Travellers Tales, '91 by Travellers Tales. Note: 6 cassettes.

SHERLOCK HOLMES STORIES (Part 2) (Robert Hardy).
MCSET. Cat no: **1239F**. Released on Travellers Tales, '91 by Travellers Tales. Note: 6 cassettes.

SHERLOCK HOLMES STORIES (Volume 3) (Basil Rathbone).
MC. Cat no: **CDL 51220**. Released on Caedmon (USA), Oct '81 by Caedmon Records (USA), Bond Street Music.

SHOSCOMBE OLD PLACE (Various artists).
Note: Robert Hardy as Sherlock Holmes and Nigel Stock as Dr. Watson with full supporting cast. Includes: The Illustrious Client.
MC. Cat no: **ANV 644**. Released on Anvil Cassettes, Jan '81 by Anvil Cassettes, Chivers Audio Books.

SIGN OF FOUR, THE (Patrick Tull).
MCSET. Cat no: **1514F**. Released on Travellers Tales, '91 by Travellers Tales. Note: 4 cassettes.

SPECKLED BAND, THE (Various artists).
Note: Robert Hardy as Sherlock Holmes and Nigel Stock as Dr. Watson with full supporting cast. Includes: The Blue Carbuncle.
MC. Cat no: **ANV 641**. Released on Anvil Cassettes, Jan '81 by Anvil Cassettes, Chivers Audio Books.

STUDY IN SCARLET, A (Robert Powell).
MC. Cat no: **ZCF 501**. Released on BBC, May '84 by BBC Records, Taylors.

STUDY IN SCARLET, A (Tony Britton).
MC. Cat no: **TCLFP 417130**. Released on Listen For Pleasure, '83 by EMI Records.

STUDY IN SCARLET, A (Peter Mesney).
MCSET. Cat no: **IAB 91044**. Released on Isis Audio Books, '91. Note: 4 cassette set.

TALES OF TERROR (Clive Champney & Robert Trotter).
MCSET. Cat no: **SPF 170-2**. Released on Schiltron Audio Books, '91 by Schiltron Publishing. Note: 2 Cassettes. Playing time 2 hours 21 minutes.

VALLEY OF FEAR, THE (Patrick Tull).
MCSET. Cat no: **IAB 91083**. Released on Isis Audio Books, '91. Note: 5 cassette set

Congreve, William

WAY OF THE WORLD, THE (Various artists).
MCSET. Cat no: **339**. Released on Caedmon (USA), May '88 by Caedmon Records (USA), Bond Street Music. Note: 2 cassettes

Connell, Evan S.

MR. BRIDGE (George Guidall).
MCSET. Cat no: **RB 91214**. Released on Recorded Books, Sep '91 by Isis Audio Books. Note: 9 cassettes. Playing time 12hrs 15mins.

MRS. BRIDGE (Sally Darling).
MCSET. Cat no: **RB 91201**. Released on Recorded Books, Nov '91 by Isis Audio Books. Note: 7 cassettes. Playing time 9hrs 15mins

Connolly, Billy

ATLANTIC BRIDGE (Billy Connolly).
LP. Cat no: **2383 419**. Released on Polydor, Dec '76 by Polydor Ltd, Solomon & Peres **Deleted** Dec '81.

BIG YIN DOUBLE HELPING, A (Billy Connolly).
Tracks / Donkey / Crucifixion / Travel away / Telling lies / Nobody's child / Joe Dempsey / Near you / 9 and a half guitars / Oh dear / Good love / Jobbie weecha / Leo McGuire's song / Little blue lady.
2LP. Cat no: **CR 133**. Released on Cambra, Apr '84 by Cambra Records **Deleted** '88.
MCSET. Cat no: **CRT 133**. Released on Cambra, Apr '84 by Cambra Records **Deleted** '88.

BILLY AND ALBERT (Billy Connolly).
Tracks / President of America / Pope, The / Australian talent show / Edinburgh festival / Learning the banjo / Dachshund / Nuclear / Jet lag / Box of chocolates / Hotel room in Perth / Condoms / Variety theatre / Childhood songs / Visiting Scotland / Wee brown dogs / Neck lumps / Casual vomit, The / Driving the porcelain truck / Something has to give.
LP. Cat no: **DIX 65**. Released on Ten, 21 Nov '87 by 10 Records.
MC. Cat no: **CDIX 65**. Released on Ten, 21 Nov '87 by 10 Records.
CD. Cat no: **DIXCD 65**. Released on Ten, '87 by 10 Records.

CHANGE IS AS GOOD AS A REST, A (Billy Connolly).
Tracks / Jesus Christ I'm nearly 40 / Bram Stoker sucks / Hey Dolores / Jack's rap / You take my photograph (I break your face) / Day in the country, A / Oz moz / Goodbye Wranglers, hello Calvin Klein / Half bottle, The / I wish I was in Glasgow.
LP. Cat no: **POLD 5077**. Released on Polydor, Jul '83 by Polydor Ltd, Solomon & Peres.
MC. Cat no: **POLDC 5077**. Released on Polydor, Jul '83 by Polydor Ltd, Solomon & Peres.
MC. Cat no: **SPELP 89**. Released on Polydor, Feb '85 by Polydor Ltd, Solomon & Peres **Deleted** '87.
MC. Cat no: **SPEMC 89**. Released on Polydor, Feb '85 by Polydor Ltd, Solomon & Peres.

COP YER WHACK OF THIS (Billy Connolly).
LP. Cat no: **2383 310**. Released on Polydor, Jan '75 by Polydor Ltd, Solomon & Peres **Deleted** Jan '80.

CRACK, THE.
MC. Cat no: **LAFFC 10**. Released on Laughing Stock, Apr '92.

GET RIGHT INTAE HIM (Billy Connolly).
LP. Cat no: **2383 368**. Released on Polydor, Dec '75 by Polydor Ltd, Solomon & Peres **Deleted** Dec '80.

ON TOUR WITH THE BIG YIN (Billy Connolly).
Tracks / Glasgow accents / Nine and a half guitars / Marie's wedding / Jobbie wheecha, The / Short haired police cadet, The / Harry Campbell and the heavies / Life in the day of, A / Stainless steel wellies / Crucifixion, The.
2LP. Cat no: **CCSLP 218**. Released on Castle Collector Series, 21 Aug '89 by Castle Communications PLC, Pinnacle, Castle Sales & Marketing.
MC. Cat no: **CCSMC 218**. Released on Castle Collector Series, 21 Aug '89 by Castle Communications PLC, Pinnacle, Castle Sales & Marketing. Note: Double play cassette.
CD. Cat no: **CCSCD 218**. Released on Castle Collector Series, 21 Aug '89 by Castle Communications PLC, Pinnacle, Castle Sales & Marketing.

PICK OF BILLY CONNOLLY, THE (Billy Connolly).
Tracks / D.I.V.O.R.C.E. / Tell Laura I love her / Football violence / Welly boot song / When in Rome / Scottish highland national dress / Sexy Sadie and lovely Raquel / C & W super song, The / Marvo and the lovely Doreen / In appreciation.
LP. Cat no: **SPELP 57**. Released on Polydor, Nov '83 by Polydor Ltd, Solomon & Peres **Deleted** Apr '91.
MC. Cat no: **SPEMC 57**. Released on Polydor, Nov '83 by Polydor Ltd, Solomon & Peres.

LP. Cat no: **POLTV 15.** Released on Polydor, Dec '81 by Polydor Ltd, Solomon & Peres **Deleted** Dec '86.

PORTRAIT, THE (Billy Connolly). Tracks / Glasgow accents / Nine and a half guitars / Maries wedding / Harry Campbell and the Heavies / Nobody's child / Life in the day of, A / Short haired police cadet / Jobbie wheecha, The / Leo McGuires song / Crucifixion.
LP. Cat no: **ITV 451.** Released on Scotdisc, Feb '89 by Scotdisc Records, Ross Records, Taylors.
MC. Cat no: **KITV 451.** Released on Scotdisc, Feb '89 by Scotdisc Records, Ross Records, Taylors.
CD. Cat no: **CDITV 451.** Released on Scotdisc, Feb '89 by Scotdisc Records, Ross Records, Taylors.

RAW MEAT FOR THE BALCONY (Billy Connolly).
LP. Cat no: **2383 463.** Released on Polydor, Jan '78 by Polydor Ltd, Solomon & Peres **Deleted** Jan '83.

WORDS AND MUSIC (Billy Connolly).
LP. Cat no: **TRA SAM 32.** Released on Transatlantic, Sep '75 by Logo Records, Celtic Music **Deleted** Sep '80.

Conrad, Joseph

END OF THE TETHER, THE (And Heart of Darkness) (Harry Andrews & Paul Scofield).
MCSET. Cat no: **1026f.** Released on Travellers Tales, '91 by Travellers Tales. Note: 4 Cassettes.

END OF THE TETHER, THE (Harry Andrews).
MCSET. Cat no: **418 003-4.** Released on Argo (Polygram), Jun '88 by PolyGram Classics **Deleted** Jan '89.

HEART OF DARKNESS (Anthony Quayle).
MCSET. Cat no: **2043.** Released on Caedmon (USA), '88 by Caedmon Records (USA), Bond Street Music.

HEART OF DARKNESS (Paul Scofield).
MCSET. Cat no: **414 700-4.** Released on Argo (Polygram), Apr '85 by PolyGram Classics **Deleted** Jan '89.

HEART OF DARKNESS (Alistair Maydon).
MCSET. Cat no: **OAS 89084.** Released on Oasis Audio Books, '91 by Isis Audio Books. Note: 8 cassettes. Playing time 11hrs.
MCSET. Cat no: **1390 F.** Released on Travellers Tales, '91 by Travellers Tales. Note: 8 Cassettes.

LORD JIM (Michael Elder). Note: Abridged Version.
MCSET. Cat no: **SPF 130-1.** Released on Schiltron Audio Books, '91 by Schiltron Publishing. Note: 4 Cassettes. Playing time 4 hours 15 minutes.
MCSET. Cat no: **1366 F.** Released on Travellers Tales, '91 by Travellers Tales. Note: 4 Cassettes.

NOSTROMA (Frank Muller).
MCSET. Cat no: **1671/1672 F.** Released on Travellers Tales, '91 by Travellers Tales. Note: 11 cassettes.
MCSET. Cat no: **RB 87930.** Released on Recorded Books, '91 by Isis Audio Books. Note: 11 Cassettes.

SECRET AGENT, THE (Garard Green).
MCSET. Cat no: **IAB 89053.** Released on Isis Audio Books, '91. Note: 8 cassette set. Playing time 9hrs.
MCSET. Cat no: **1412T.** Released on Travellers Tales, '91 by Travellers Tales. Note: 8 Cassettes.

SECRET AGENT, THE (Tim Pigott-Smith).
MCSET. Cat no: **418 192-4.** Released on Argo (Polygram), Apr '88 by PolyGram Classics **Deleted** Jan '89. Note: 2 Cassettes.

Constanduros, Denis

MY GRANDFATHER (And Father Dear Father) (Benjamin Whitrow).
MCSET. Cat no: **ZBBC 1095.** Released on BBC Radio Collection, Oct '89 by BBC Records. Note: ISBN No: 0563 227079

Constant, B

ADOLPHE (Edited By Peter Wagstaff) (Unknown narrator(s)).
MC. Cat no: **F 7817.** Released on Exeter Tapes, '91 by Drakes Educational Associates.

Cook, Bob

DISORDERLY ELEMENTS (Unknown narrator(s)).
MCSET. Cat no: **1854962450.** Released on Bramhope, '91 by Ulverscroft Soundings. Note: 4 Cassettes.

Cook, Peter

AD NAUSEAM (See under Derek & Clive).

CLEAN TAPES (Peter Cook & Dudley Moore). Tracks / Newsreel overture, The / Music teacher, The / Tramponuns / Lovely lady of the roses / Dud and Pete on sex / Isn't she a sweetie / Real stuff, The / Aversion therapy / Father and son / Lengths / Goodbye-ee.
LP. Cat no: **HIFLY 26.** Released on Cube, '81.
MC. Cat no: **ZCFLY 26.** Released on Cube, '81.
MC. Cat no: **RDC 1206.** Released on Rio Digital, Feb '91 by Rio Digital Records.

DEREK AND CLIVE COME AGAIN (Peter Cook & Dudley Moore).
LP. Cat no: **V 2094.** Released on Virgin, '77 by Virgin Records, Music Sales Records **Deleted** '88.
MC. Cat no: **TCV 2094.** Released on Virgin, '77 by Virgin Records, Music Sales Records **Deleted** '88.

HERE COMES THE JUDGE (Live in Concert) (Peter Cook).

LP. Cat no: **VR 4.** Released on Virgin, '79 by Virgin Records, Music Sales Records **Deleted** '88.

ONCE MORE WITH COOK (Peter Cook & Dudley Moore).
LP. Cat no: **LK 4785.** Released on Decca, May '66 by PolyGram Classics, Thames Distributors Ltd. **Deleted** May '71.

WORLD OF PETE AND DUD (Peter Cook & Dudley Moore). Tracks / Art gallery / Bit of a chat including all things bright and beautiful / Lengths / Psychiatrist, The / Dud dreams / Ravens, The / Father and son / Six of the best.
LP. Cat no: **SPA 311.** Released on Decca, '74 by PolyGram Classics, Thames Distributors Ltd..
MC. Cat no: **LAFFC 5.** Released on Laughing Stock, Oct '91.

Cooke, Alistair

LETTERS FROM AMERICA (Unknown narrator(s)).
MC. Cat no: **TC LFP 7055.** Released on Listen For Pleasure, '79 by EMI Records.
MCSET. Cat no: **ZBBC 1039.** Released on BBC, Sep '88 by BBC Records, Taylors **Deleted** '89.

Cookson, Catherine

BILL BAILEY (Susan Jameson).
MCSET. Cat no: **CAB 241.** Released on Chivers Audio Books, '91 by Chivers Audio Books, Green Dragon Audio Visual. Note: 6 Cassettes.
MCSET. Cat no: **1241 F.** Released on Travellers Tales, '91 by Travellers Tales. Note: 6 Cassettes.

BILL BAILEY'S DAUGHTER (Susan Jameson).
MCSET. Cat no: **CAB 377.** Released on Chivers Audio Books, '91 by Chivers Audio Books, Green Dragon Audio Visual. Note: 6 Cassettes.
MCSET. Cat no: **1374 F.** Released on Travellers Tales, '91 by Travellers Tales. Note: 6 Cassettes.

BILL BAILEY'S LOT (Susan Jameson).
MCSET. Cat no: **CAB 273.** Released on Chivers Audio Books, '91 by Chivers Audio Books, Green Dragon Audio Visual. Note: 8 Cassettes
MCSET. Cat no: **1274 F.** Released on Travellers Tales, '91 by Travellers Tales. Note: 8 Cassettes.

BLACK CANDLE, THE (Susan Jameson).
MCSET. Cat no: **CAB 519.** Released on Chivers Audio Books, '91 by Chivers Audio Books, Green Dragon Audio Visual. Note: 12 Cassettes.
MCSET. Cat no: **1515/1516F.** Released on Travellers Tales, '91 by Travellers Tales. Note: 12 cassettes.

BLACK VELVET GOWN, THE (Elizabeth Henry).
MCSET. Cat no: **1490/1491F.** Re-

leased on Travellers Tales, '91 by Travellers Tales. Note: 12 cassettes
MCSET. Cat no: **1854963325.** Released on Soundings, '91 by Soundings Records, Bond Street Music. Note: 12 Cassettes.

CINDER PATH, THE (Susan Jameson).
MCSET. Cat no: **CAB 058.** Released on Chivers Audio Books, '91 by Chivers Audio Books, Green Dragon Audio Visual. Note: 6 Cassettes.
MCSET. Cat no: **1225 F.** Released on Travellers Tales, '91 by Travellers Tales. Note: 6 Cassettes.

CULTURED HANDMAIDEN, THE (Susan Jameson).
MCSET. Cat no: **CAB 336.** Released on Chivers Audio Books, '88 by Chivers Audio Books, Green Dragon Audio Visual. Note: 8 Cassettes.
MCSET. Cat no: **1322 F.** Released on Travellers Tales, '91 by Travellers Tales. Note: 8 Cassettes.

DEVIL AND MARY ANN (Susan Jameson).
MCSET. Cat no: **CAB 013.** Released on Chivers Audio Books, '81 by Chivers Audio Books, Green Dragon Audio Visual.
MCSET. Cat no: **CAB 080.** Released on Chivers Audio Books, '91 by Chivers Audio Books, Green Dragon Audio Visual. Note: 6 Cassettes
MCSET. Cat no: **1226F.** Released on Travellers Tales, '91 by Travellers Tales. Note: 6 cassettes.

FANNY MCBRIDE (Susan Jameson).
MCSET. Cat no: **CAB 212.** Released on Chivers Audio Books, '91 by Chivers Audio Books, Green Dragon Audio Visual. Note: 6 Cassettes
MCSET. Cat no: **1227 F.** Released on Travellers Tales, '91 by Travellers Tales. Note: 6 cassettes.

FENWICK HOUSES (Elizabeth Henry).
MCSET. Cat no: **1250F.** Released on Travellers Tales, '91 by Travellers Tales. Note: 8 cassettes.
MCSET. Cat no: **1854960520.** Released on Soundings, '91 by Soundings Records, Bond Street Music. Note: 8 Cassettes.

FIFTEEN STREETS, THE (Susan Jameson).
MCSET. Cat no: **1228F.** Released on Travellers Tales, '91 by Travellers Tales. Note: 6 cassettes.
MCSET. Cat no: **CAB 135.** Released on Chivers Audio Books, Jan '92 by Chivers Audio Books, Green Dragon Audio Visual. Note: 6 cassettes.

GAMBLING MAN, THE (Gordon Griffin).
MCSET. Cat no: **1685/1686F.** Released on Travellers Tales, '91 by Travellers Tales. Note: 9 cassettes.
MCSET. Cat no: **1854964275.** Released on Soundings, '91 by Soundings Records, Bond Street Music. Note: 9 Cassettes.

GARMENT, THE (Elizabeth Henry).
MCSET. Cat no: **1260F.** Released on Travellers Tales, '91 by Travellers Tales. Note: 8 cassettes.
MCSET. Cat no: **1854960539.** Released on Soundings, '91 by Soundings Records, Bond Street Music. Note: 8 Cassettes.

GILLYVORS, THE (Susan Jameson).
MCSET. Cat no: **CAB 564.** Released on Chivers Audio Books, '91 by Chivers Audio Books, Green Dragon Audio Visual. Note: 8 Cassettes.
MCSET. Cat no: **1647F.** Released on Travellers Tales, '91 by Travellers Tales. Note: 8 cassettes.

GLASS VIRGIN, THE (Elizabeth Henry).
MCSET. Cat no: **1854965808.** Released on Soundings, Apr '92 by Soundings Records, Bond Street Music. Note: 9 cassettes

GOODBYE HAMILTON (Elizabeth Henry).
MCSET. Cat no: **1378F.** Released on Travellers Tales, '91 by Travellers Tales. Note: 8 cassettes.
MCSET. Cat no: **1854962329.** Released on Soundings, '91 by Soundings Records, Bond Street Music. Note: 8 Cassettes.

GRAND MAN, A (Susan Jameson).
MCSET. Cat no: **CAB 006.** Released on Chivers Audio Books, '81 by Chivers Audio Books, Green Dragon Audio Visual. Note: 4 Cassettes.
MCSET. Cat no: **1028F.** Released on Travellers Tales, '91 by Travellers Tales. Note: 4 cassettes.
MCSET. Cat no: **0745128009.** Released on Word For Word, May '92 by Chivers Audio Books.

HAMILTON (Elizabeth Henry).
MCSET. Cat no: **1376F.** Released on Travellers Tales, '91 by Travellers Tales. Note: 8 cassettes.
MCSET. Cat no: **1854962191.** Released on Soundings, '91 by Soundings Records, Bond Street Music. Note: 8 Cassettes.

HANNAH MASSEY (Elizabeth Henry).
MCSET. Cat no: **1333F.** Released on Travellers Tales, '91 by Travellers Tales. Note: 6 cassettes.
MCSET. Cat no: **1854960547.** Released on Soundings, '91 by Soundings Records, Bond Street Music. Note: 6 Cassettes.

HAROLD (Elizabeth Henry).
MCSET. Cat no: **1429F.** Released on Travellers Tales, '91 by Travellers Tales. Note: 8 cassettes.
MCSET. Cat no: **1854962582.** Released on Soundings, '91 by Soundings Records, Bond Street Music. Note: 8 Cassettes.

HARROGATE SECRET, THE (Susan Jameson).
MCSET. Cat no: **CAB 415.** Released on Chivers Audio Books, '91 by Chivers Audio Books, Green Dragon Audio Visual. Note: 10 Cassettes
MCSET. Cat no: **1444/1445F.** Released on Travellers Tales, '91 by Travellers Tales. Note: 10 cassettes.

INVISIBLE CHORD, THE (Elizabeth Henry).
MCSET. Cat no: **1676/1677F.** Released on Travellers Tales, '91 by Travellers Tales. Note: 9 cassettes.
MCSET. Cat no: **1854964070.** Released on Soundings, '91 by Soundings Records, Bond Street Music. Note: 9 Cassettes.

INVITATION, THE (Susan Jameson).
MCSET. Cat no: **CAB 474.** Released on Chivers Audio Books, '91 by Chivers Audio Books, Green Dragon Audio Visual. Note: 8 Cassettes.
MCSET. Cat no: **1449F.** Released on Travellers Tales, '91 by Travellers Tales. Note: 8 cassettes.

KATE HANNIGAN (Juliet Stevenson).
MCSET. Cat no: **CAB 063.** Released on Chivers Audio Books, '91 by Chivers Audio Books, Green Dragon Audio Visual. Note: 6 Cassettes
MCSET. Cat no: **1229F.** Released on Travellers Tales, '91 by Travellers Tales. Note: 6 cassettes.

LIFE AND MARY ANN (Susan Jameson).
MCSET. Cat no: **CAB 022.** Released on Chivers Audio Books, Apr '81 by Chivers Audio Books, Green Dragon Audio Visual.
MCSET. Cat no: **CAB 081.** Released on Chivers Audio Books, Apr '81 by Chivers Audio Books, Green Dragon Audio Visual. Note: 6 Cassettes
MCSET. Cat no: **1230F.** Released on Travellers Tales, '91 by Travellers Tales. Note: 6 cassettes.

LONG CORRIDOR, THE (Unknown narrator(s)).
MCSET. Cat no: **1854960555.** Released on Bramhope, '91 by Ulverscroft Soundings. Note: 5 cassettes.
MCSET. Cat no: **1288F.** Released on Travellers Tales, '91 by Travellers Tales. Note: 5 cassettes.

LORD AND MARY ANN, THE (Susan Jameson).
MCSET. Cat no: **CAB 011.** Released on Chivers Audio Books, '91 by Chivers Audio Books, Green Dragon Audio Visual. Note: 4 Cassettes.
MCSET. Cat no: **1231F.** Released on Travellers Tales, '91 by Travellers Tales. Note: 4 cassettes .

LOVE AND MARY ANN (Susan Jameson).
MCSET. Cat no: **CAB 017.** Released on Chivers Audio Books, May '81 by Chivers Audio Books, Green Dragon

Audio Visual. Note: 4 Cassettes
MCSET. Cat no: **1232F.** Released on Travellers Tales, '91 by Travellers Tales. Note: 4 cassettes.

MAGGIE ROWAN (Unknown narrator(s)).
MCSET. Cat no: **1854965115.** Released on Soundings, '91 by Soundings Records, Bond Street Music. Note: 9 Cassettes.

MALLEN GIRL, THE (Unknown narrator(s)).
MCSET. Cat no: **1854962744.** Released on Soundings, '91 by Soundings Records, Bond Street Music. Note: 8 Cassettes.

MALLEN LITTER (Unknown narrator(s)).
MCSET. Cat no: **1854962833.** Released on Soundings, '91 by Soundings Records, Bond Street Music. Note: 9 Cassettes.

MALLEN STREAK, THE (Unknown narrator(s)).
MCSET. Cat no: **1854962671.** Released on Soundings, '91 by Soundings Records, Bond Street Music. Note: 8 cassettes.

MAN WHO CRIED, THE (Gordon Griffin).
MCSET. Cat no: **1600F.** Released on Travellers Tales, '91 by Travellers Tales. Note: 8 cassettes.
MCSET. Cat no: **185496397X.** Released on Soundings, '91 by Soundings Records, Bond Street Music.

MARRIAGE AND MARY ANN (Susan Jameson).
MCSET. Cat no: **CAB 026.** Released on Chivers Audio Books, '91 by Chivers Audio Books, Green Dragon Audio Visual. Note: 4 Cassettes.
MCSET. Cat no: **1233F.** Released on Travellers Tales, '91 by Travellers Tales. Note: 4 cassettes.

MARY ANN AND BILL (Susan Jameson).
MCSET. Cat no: **CAB 030.** Released on Chivers Audio Books, '91 by Chivers Audio Books, Green Dragon Audio Visual. Note: 4 Cassettes.
MCSET. Cat no: **1234F.** Released on Travellers Tales, '91 by Travellers Tales. Note: 4 cassettes.

MARY ANN'S ANGELS (Susan Jameson).
MCSET. Cat no: **CAB 029.** Released on Chivers Audio Books, '91 by Chivers Audio Books, Green Dragon Audio Visual. Note: 4 Cassettes.
MCSET. Cat no: **1235F.** Released on Travellers Tales, '91 by Travellers Tales. Note: 4 cassettes.

MENAGERIE, THE (Susan Jameson).
MCSET. Cat no: **CAB 172.** Released on Chivers Audio Books, '91 by Chivers Audio Books, Green Dragon Audio Visual. Note: 6 Cassettes.
MCSET. Cat no: **1236F.** Released on Travellers Tales, '91 by Travellers Tales. Note: 6 cassettes.

MOTH, THE (Elizabeth Henry).
MCSET. Cat no: **1598/1599F.** Released on Travellers Tales, '91 by Travellers Tales. Note: 10 cassettes
MCSET. Cat no: **1854963872.** Released on Soundings, '91 by Soundings Records, Bond Street Music. Note: 10 Cassettes.

MY BELOVED SON (Unknown narrator(s)).
MCSET. Cat no: **1854964585.** Released on Soundings, '91 by Soundings Records, Bond Street Music. Note: 10 Cassettes.

NICE BLOKE, THE (Elizabeth Henry).
MCSET. Cat no: **1294F.** Released on Travellers Tales, '91 by Travellers Tales. Note: 6 cassettes.
MCSET. Cat no: **1854960563.** Released on Soundings, '91 by Soundings Records, Bond Street Music. Note: 6 Cassettes.

PARSON'S DAUGHTER, THE (Betty Henry).
MCSET. Cat no: **1330/1331F.** Released on Travellers Tales, '91 by Travellers Tales. Note: 12 cassettes.
MCSET. Cat no: **1854960571.** Released on Soundings, '91 by Soundings Records, Bond Street Music. Note: 12 Cassettes.

ROONEY (John Woodvine).
MCSET. Cat no: **1237F.** Released on Travellers Tales, '91 by Travellers Tales. Note: 6 Cassettes.
MCSET. Cat no: **CAB 163.** Released on Chivers Audio Books, '91 by Chivers Audio Books, Green Dragon Audio Visual.

ROUND TOWER, THE (Unknown narrator(s)).
MCSET. Cat no: **1854963031.** Released on Soundings, '91 by Soundings Records, Bond Street Music. Note: 4 cassettes.

ROUND TOWER, THE (Gordon Griffin).
MCSET. Cat no: **1483/1484F.** Released on Travellers Tales, '91 by Travellers Tales. Note: 9 cassettes.

SLINKY JANE (Judeth Franklyn).
MCSET. Cat no: **1257F.** Released on Travellers Tales, '91 by Travellers Tales. Note: 6 cassettes.
MCSET. Cat no: **185496058X.** Released on Soundings, '91 by Soundings Records, Bond Street Music. Note: 6 Cassettes.

TILLY TROTTER (Part 1) (Elizabeth Henry).
MCSET. Cat no: **1196F.** Released on Travellers Tales, '91 by Travellers Tales. Note: 6 cassettes.
MCSET. Cat no: **1854960598.** Released on Soundings, '91 by Soundings Records, Bond Street Music. Note: 6 Cassettes.

TILLY TROTTER (Part 2) (Elizabeth Henry).

MCSET. Cat no: **1197F.** Released on Travellers Tales, '91 by Travellers Tales. Note: 6 cassettes.
CDSET. Cat no: **1854960601.** Released on Soundings, '91 by Soundings Records, Bond Street Music. Note: 6 Cassettes.

TILLY TROTTER WED (Elizabeth Henry).
MCSET. Cat no: **1246F.** Released on Travellers Tales, '91 by Travellers Tales. Note: 8 cassettes.
MCSET. Cat no: **185496061X.** Released on Soundings, '91 by Soundings Records, Bond Street Music. Note: 8 Cassettes.

TILLY TROTTER WIDOWED (Elizabeth Henry).
MCSET. Cat no: **1261F.** Released on Travellers Tales, '91 by Travellers Tales. Note: 8 cassettes.
MCSET. Cat no: **1854960628.** Released on Soundings, '91 by Soundings Records, Bond Street Music. Note: 8 Cassettes.

UNBAITED TRAP, THE (Elizabeth Henry).
MCSET. Cat no: **1296F.** Released on Travellers Tales, '91 by Travellers Tales. Note: 6 cassettes.
MCSET. Cat no: **1854960636.** Released on Soundings, '91 by Soundings Records, Bond Street Music. Note: 6 Cassettes.

WINGLESS BIRD, THE (Unknown narrator(s)).
MCSET. Cat no: **185496447X.** Released on Soundings, '91 by Soundings Records, Bond Street Music. Note: 10 Cassettes.

Cool, Phil
NOT JUST A PRETTY FACE (Phil Cool).
Tracks / Trouble with being an impressionist, The / Practising in the bathroom / Academy awards, The / Whicker's world / Hellraisers / Caviar to pigs / Billy Connolly / Mike Harding / Depression / Adverts / Wogan - the space creature / Day after / Reagan / Australians / Pope, The / Rolf Harris.
LP. Cat no: **OVED 228.** Released on Virgin, Nov '86 by Virgin Records, Music Sales Records **Deleted** Mar '91.
MC. Cat no: **OVEDC 228.** Released on Virgin, Nov '86 by Virgin Records, Music Sales Records **Deleted** Mar '91. Note: (MM)

Coolidge, Susan M.
WHAT KATY DID (Gwen Watford).
MCSET. Cat no: **LFP 7322.** Released on Listen For Pleasure, Feb '88 by EMI Records.

Coonts, Stephen
FLIGHT OF THE INTRUDER, THE (Frank Muller).
MCSET. Cat no: **1625F.** Released on Travellers Tales, '91 by Travellers

Tales. Note: 8 cassettes.
MCSET. Cat no: **RB 86980.** Released on Recorded Books, '91 by Isis Audio Books. Note: 8 Cassettes.

Cooper Clarke, John
ZIP STYLE METHOD. (Unknown narrators)
Tracks / Midnight shift / New assasin / Face behind the scream / I travel in biscuits / Day the world stood still, The / Heart disease called love / Ghost of Al Capone / Ninety degrees in my shades / Day my pad went mad, The / I wanna be yours / Drive she said / Night people.
LP. Cat no: **EPC 85667.** Released on Epic, Jun '82 by Sony Music **Deleted** Jun '87.

Cooper, Duff
OPERATION HEARTBREAK (Simon Calburn).
MCSET. Cat no: **1304F.** Released on Travellers Tales, '91 by Travellers Tales. Note: 4 cassettes.

Cooper, James Fenimore
LAST OF THE MOHICANS, THE (James Mason).
MC. Cat no: **1239.** Released on Caedmon (USA), '88 by Caedmon Records (USA), Bond Street Music.
MC. Cat no: **0001051830.** Released on Collins-Caedmon, '91 by Collins Audio, Taylors, Bond Street Music.

LAST OF THE MOHICANS, THE (Children's Classics) (Unknown narrator(s)).
MC. Cat no: **PLBC 125.** Released on Tell-A-Tale, Sep '84 by Pickwick Records, Taylors, Clyde Factors.

LAST OF THE MOHICANS, THE (Larry McKeever).
MCSET. Cat no: **RB 89630.** Released on Recorded Books, Nov '91 by Isis Audio Books. Note: 11 cassettes. Playing time 15hrs 30mins.

Cooper, Jilly
CLASS (Penelope Keith).
MCSET. Cat no: **LFP 7406.** Released on Listen For Pleasure, Jul '89 by EMI Records. Note: Playing time: 2 hours.

EMILY (Jan Francis).
MCSET. Cat no: **CAB 200.** Released on Chivers Audio Books, '91 by Chivers Audio Books, Green Dragon Audio Visual. Note: 4 Cassettes.
MCSET. Cat no: **1189F.** Released on Travellers Tales, '91 by Travellers Tales. Note: 4 cassettes

HARRIET (Jan Francis).
MCSET. Cat no: **1002H.** Released on Travellers Tales, '91 by Travellers Tales. Note: 6 cassettes.

IMOGEN (Tammy Ustinov).
MCSET. Cat no: **CAB 536.** Released on Chivers Audio Books, '91 by Chivers Audio Books, Green Dragon Audio Visual. Note: 6 cassettes.

MCSET. Cat no: **1614F.** Released on Travellers Tales, '91 by Travellers Tales. Note: 6 cassettes.

OCTAVIA (Judy Bennett).
MCSET. Cat no: **CAB 641.** Released on Chivers Audio Books, Nov '91 by Chivers Audio Books, Green Dragon Audio Visual. Note: 6 Cassettes.

Copper, Basil
PRESSURE POINT (Unknown narrator(s)).
MCSET. Cat no: **1854964518.** Released on Bramhope, '91 by Ulverscroft Soundings. Note: 4 Cassettes.

Corbett, Harry H.
See under Steptoe & Son

Corbett, W.J.
END OF THE TALE, THE (And Other Stories) (Christian Rodska).
MCSET. Cat no: **2CCA 3038.** Released on Chivers Audio Books, '91 by Chivers Audio Books, Green Dragon Audio Visual. Note: 2 Cassettes.
MCSET. Cat no: **9115F.** Released on Travellers Tales, '91 by Travellers Tales. Note: 2 Cassettes.

Cordell, Alexander
RAPE OF THE FAIR COUNTRY (Philip Madoc).
MCSET. Cat no: **1696F.** Released on Travellers Tales, '91 by Travellers Tales. Note: 8 cassettes.
MCSET. Cat no: **CAB 594.** Released on Chivers Audio Books, '91 by Chivers Audio Books, Green Dragon Audio Visual. Note: 8 Cassettes.

Coren, Alan
ARTHUR AND THE BELLY BUTTON DIAMOND (Tom Baker).
MC. Cat no: **TTC 1035.** Released on Talking Tape Company, Apr '91, Conifer Records. Note: Playing time 1 hr-8mins. ISBN no. 187252074X
MC. Cat no: **TTCK 05.** Released on Talking Tape Company, '88, Conifer Records.

Cormier, Robert
CHOCOLATE WAR, THE (Frank Muller).
MCSET. Cat no: **4CCA 3127.** Released on Chivers Audio Books, '91 by Chivers Audio Books, Green Dragon Audio Visual. Note: 4 Cassettes.

Corneille, P
CINNA (Edited By Christopher J. Gossip) (Unknown narrator(s)).
MC. Cat no: **F 7999.** Released on Exeter Tapes, '91 by Drakes Educational Associates.

HORACE (Edited By Christopher J. Gossip) (Unknown narrator(s)).
MC. Cat no: **F 7612.** Released on Exeter Tapes, '91 by Drakes Educational Associates.

POLYEUCTE (Edited By Jean D. Biard) (Unknown narrator(s)).
Note: A discussion of the main characters of the play and their development with an analysis of the tragedy. In French.

MC. Cat no: **F 7749.** Released on Exeter Tapes, '91 by Drakes Educational Associates.

RODOGUNE (Edited By Peggy Chaplin) (Unknown narrator(s)).
Note: Includes a discussion of Corneille's theories of heroic drama and a commentary on Act II Scene I, Cleopatre's great monologue of self revelation.
MC. Cat no: **F 7765.** Released on Exeter Tapes, '91 by Drakes Educational Associates.

Cornwell, Bernard
COURTESANS AND FALLEN WOMEN (An Anthology) (Morag Hood & Diana Olsson).
MCSET. Cat no: **SPF 9801.** Released on Schiltron Audio Books, '91 by Schiltron Publishing.

CRACKDOWN (Terrence Hardiman).
MCSET. Cat no: **CAB 565.** Released on Chivers Audio Books, '91 by Chivers Audio Books, Green Dragon Audio Visual. Note: 8 Cassettes.
MCSET. Cat no: **1718T.** Released on Travellers Tales, '91 by Travellers Tales. Note: 8 Cassettes.

SEA LORD (Peter Joyce).
MCSET. Cat no: **1570T.** Released on Travellers Tales, '91 by Travellers Tales.
MCSET. Cat no: **1854963171.** Released on Soundings, '91 by Soundings Records, Bond Street Music. Note: 8 Cassettes.

SHARPE'S REVENGE (William Gaminara).
MCSET. Cat no: **CAB 642.** Released on Chivers Audio Books, Nov '91 by Chivers Audio Books, Green Dragon Audio Visual. Note: 10 Cassettes.

SHARPE'S WATERLOO (William Gaminara).
MCSET. Cat no: **CAB 671.** Released on Chivers Audio Books, Jan '92 by Chivers Audio Books, Green Dragon Audio Visual. Note: 10 cassettes.

SHARPE'S EAGLE (William Gaminara).
MCSET. Cat no: **CAB 429.** Released on Chivers Audio Books, '91 by Chivers Audio Books, Green Dragon Audio Visual. Note: 8 Cassettes
MCSET. Cat no: **1496T.** Released on Travellers Tales, '91 by Travellers Tales. Note: 8 Cassettes.

SHARPE'S GOLD (William Gaminara).
MCSET. Cat no: **CAB 510.** Released on Chivers Audio Books, '91 by Chivers Audio Books, Green Dragon Audio Visual. Note: 8 Cassettes
MCSET. Cat no: **1605T.** Released on Travellers Tales, '91 by Travellers Tales. Note: 8 Cassettes.

SHARPE'S RIFLES (William Gaminara).
MCSET. Cat no: **CAB 352.** Released on Chivers Audio Books, '91 by Chivers

Audio Books, Green Dragon Audio Visual. Note: 8 Cassettes.
MCSET. Cat no: **1423T**. Released on Travellers Tales, '91 by Travellers Tales. Note: 8 Cassettes.

SHARPE'S SIEGE (William Gaminara).
MCSET. Cat no: **CAB 573**. Released on Chivers Audio Books, '91 by Chivers Audio Books, Green Dragon Audio Visual. Note: 10 Cassettes
MCSET. Cat no: **1720/1721T**. Released on Travellers Tales, '91 by Travellers Tales. Note: 10 Cassettes.

WILDTRACK (Christopher Kay).
MCSET. Cat no: **1505/1506T**. Released on Travellers Tales, '91 by Travellers Tales. Note: 9 Cassettes.
MCSET. Cat no: **1854962639**. Released on Soundings, '91 by Soundings Records, Bond Street Music. Note: 9 Cassettes.

Cosby, Bill

BILLS BEST FRIEND (Bill Cosby).
Tracks / English language, The / Henry Kissinger / UFO / My father confused me / Glazed donut monster, The / Mothers enunciate / FCC and mothers, The / Mothers will hit you for nothing / Fathers are the funniest people / Marriage and duties / New husbands kill things / Lizard and the mouse, The / Dudes on dope.
MCSET. Cat no: **ECC 21**. Released on EMI, Aug '91 by EMI Records.

FOR ADULTS ONLY (Bill Cosby).
MC. Cat no: **LAFFC 2**. Released on Laughing Stock, Sep '91.

OH BABY.
LP. Cat no: **GEF 24428**. Released on Geffen, Nov '91 by MCA Records, New Note, Pinnacle.
MC. Cat no: **GEFC 24428**. Released on Geffen, Nov '91 by MCA Records, New Note, Pinnacle.
CD. Cat no: **GEFD 24428**. Released on Geffen, Nov '91 by MCA Records, New Note, Pinnacle.

THOSE OF YOU WITH OR WITHOUT CHILDREN (Bill Cosby).
Note: Full title of album: Those of you with or without children, you'll understand
LP. Cat no: **9241041**. Released on Geffen, Jul '86 by MCA Records, New Note, Pinnacle.

Courtney, Caroline

FORTUNES OF LOVE, THE (Barbara Murray).
MCSET. Cat no: **1030F**. Released on Travellers Tales, '91 by Travellers Tales. Note: 6 cassettes.

LIBERTINE IN LOVE (Barbara Murray).
MCSET. Cat no: **1031F**. Released on Travellers Tales, '91 by Travellers Tales. Note: 6 cassettes.

LOVE UNMASKED (Barbara Murray).
MCSET. Cat no: **1032F**. Released on Travellers Tales, '91 by Travellers Tales. Note: 4 cassettes.

Coward, Noel

DOUBLE BILL (Paul Scofield & Dame Peggy Ashcroft).
Note: Includes: Private Lives and Hayfever.
MCSET. Cat no: **ZBBC 1042**. Released on BBC, Sep '88 by BBC Records, Taylors. Note: ISBN No: 0563 225661

NOEL COWARD AND GERTRUDE LAWRENCE (Noel Coward & Gertrude Lawrence).
Tracks / Parisian Pierrot (from 'London Calling') / Mad dogs and Englishmen / Do-do-do (from 'Oh Kay!') / Love scene, Act 1 (from 'Private lives') / Honeymoon scene, Act II (from 'Private lives') / Lover of my dreams (from 'Cavalcade') / Someone to watch over me (from 'Oh Kay!') / Mary- make me believe (from 'This year of Grace') / Here's a toast / Room with a view, A (from 'This year of Grace') / Mad about the boy / Any little fish / Has anybody seen our ship? / Man about town / World weary / We were dancing (from 'Tonight at 8:30') / Then play, orchestra, play (from 'Shadow play') / You were there (from 'Shadow play') / Let's say goodbye.
CD. Cat no: **PAST CD 9715**. Released on Flapper, '90 by Pavilion Records, Taylors, Pinnacle.

NOEL COWARD READING (Noel Coward).
Note: A selection of Coward's verses, also containing Shaw's Interlude from *The Apple Cart*.
MC. Cat no: **1094**. Released on Caedmon (USA), '88 by Caedmon Records (USA), Bond Street Music.

PRESENT LAUGHTER (And Private Lives) (Various artists).
Note: With Paul Scofield, Fenella Fielding and Miriam Margolyes.
MC. Cat no: **TCC/NCW2**. Released on Talking Tape Company, '84, Conifer Records.
MCSET. Cat no: **1048P**. Released on Travellers Tales, '91 by Travellers Tales. Note: 2 Cassettes.

PRIVATE LIVES (Various artists).
Note: Narrators are: Paul Scofield, Fennella Fielding, Miriam Margolyes and Patricia Routledge.
MC. Cat no: **TTC/NCW1**. Released on Talking Tape Company, '84, Conifer Records.

Coyle, Harold

TEAM YANKEE (Charles Durning).
MCSET. Cat no: **067166252X**. Released on Simon & Schuster, '91 by Simon & Schuster Ltd. Note: 2 cassettes.

Craig, Bobbie

ANIMAL ALPHABET, THE (Well Loved Tales Up to Age 9) (Unknown narrator(s)).
Note: Book and cassette.
MC. Cat no: **PLB 204**. Released on Tell-A-Tale, '88 by Pickwick Records, Taylors, Clyde Factors.

Craighead, Jean-George

JULIE OF THE WOLVES (Worth, Irene).
MC. Cat no: **1534**. Released on Caedmon (USA), '88 by Caedmon Records (USA), Bond Street Music.

Crane, Stephen

MAGGIE - A GIRL OF THE STREETS (Diana Olsson).
MCSET. Cat no: **SPF 980-18**. Released on Schiltron Audio Books, '91 by Schiltron Publishing. Note: 2 cassettes.

RED BADGE OF COURAGE, THE (Edmund O'Brien).
MC. Cat no: **1040**. Released on Caedmon (USA), '88 by Caedmon Records (USA), Bond Street Music.
MCSET. Cat no: **0001060317**. Released on Collins-Caedmon, '91 by Collins Audio, Taylors, Bond Street Music.

RED BADGE OF COURAGE, THE (Frank Muller).
MCSET. Cat no: **RB 81240**. Released on Recorded Books, '91 by Isis Audio Books. Note: 3 cassettes.

RED BADGE OF COURAGE, THE (Jack Dahlby).
MCSET. Cat no: **1301F**. Released on Travellers Tales, '91 by Travellers Tales. Note: 6 cassettes
MCSET. Cat no: **CSL 015**. Released on Chivers Audio Books, '91 by Chivers Audio Books, Green Dragon Audio Visual. Note: 6 cassettes.

Crane, Teresa

FRAGILE PEACE, A (Unknown narrator(s)).
MCSET. Cat no: **1854962914**. Released on Soundings, '91 by Soundings Records, Bond Street Music. Note: 12 Cassettes.

TOMORROW, JERUSALEM (Volume 1) (Unknown narrator(s)).
MCSET. Cat no: **1854963333**. Released on Soundings, '91 by Soundings Records, Bond Street Music. Note: 8 Cassettes.

TOMORROW, JERUSALEM (Volume 2) (Unknown narrator(s)).
MCSET. Cat no: **1854963341**. Released on Soundings, '91 by Soundings Records, Bond Street Music. Note: 9 Cassettes.

TOMORROW, JERUSALEM (Judith Porter).
MCSET. Cat no: **1492/3/4F**. Released on Travellers Tales, '91 by Travellers Tales. Note: 17 cassettes.

Craven, Margaret

I HEARD THE OWL CALL MY NAME (Frank Muller).
MCSET. Cat no: **RB 87400**. Released

on Recorded Books, '91 by Isis Audio Books. Note: 3 cassettes.

Craven, Sara
FLAME OF DIABLO (Lesley Seaward).
MCSET. Cat no: **PMB 011.** Released on Mills & Boon, '88. Note: 2 Cassettes.

Creasey, John
BUNDLE FOR THE TOFF, A (Clifford Norgate).
MCSET. Cat no: **CAT 4061.** Released on Chivers Audio Books, '91 by Chivers Audio Books, Green Dragon Audio Visual. Note: 4 Cassettes.

MCSET. Cat no: **1727T.** Released on Travellers Tales, '91 by Travellers Tales. Note: 4 Cassettes.

INSPECTOR WEST CRIES WOLF (Clifford Norgate).
MCSET. Cat no: **CAT 4058.** Released on Chivers Audio Books, '91 by Chivers Audio Books, Green Dragon Audio Visual. Note: 6 Cassettes.

MCSET. Cat no: **1606T.** Released on Travellers Tales, '91 by Travellers Tales. Note: 6 Cassettes.

THREE DAY'S TERROR (Clifford Norgate).
MCSET. Cat no: **1258T.** Released on Travellers Tales, '91 by Travellers Tales. Note: 4 Cassettes.

MCSET. Cat no: **CAT 4032.** Released on Chivers Audio Thrillers, '91 by Chivers Audio Books, Green Dragon Audio Visual.

Cresswell, Helen
ELLIE AND THE HAGWITCH (Marise Hepworth).
MCSET. Cat no: **2CCA 3017.** Released on Chivers Audio Books, '91 by Chivers Audio Books, Green Dragon Audio Visual. Note: 2 Cassettes.

MCSET. Cat no: **9025F.** Released on Travellers Tales, '91 by Travellers Tales. Note: 2 Cassettes.

MCSET. Cat no: **086222043-1.** Released on Tempo, Apr '88 by Warwick Records, Celtic Music, Henry Hadaway Organisation. Note: 2 Cassettes.

LIZZIE DRIPPING (Tina Heath).
MCSET. Cat no: **CC/044.** Released on Cover to Cover, '88 by Cover to Cover Cassettes.

MEET POSY BATES (Judy Bennett).
MCSET. Cat no: **2CCA 3162.** Released on Chivers Audio Books, Sep '91 by Chivers Audio Books, Green Dragon Audio Visual. Note: 2 Cassettes.

NIGHT-WATCHMEN, THE (Stephen Thorne).
MCSET. Cat no: **3CCA 3114.** Released on Chivers Audio Books, '91 by Chivers Audio Books, Green Dragon Audio Visual. Note: 3 Cassettes.

MCSET. Cat no: **9194F.** Released on Travellers Tales, '91 by Travellers Tales. Note: 3 Cassettes.

PIEMAKERS, THE (Patricia Routledge).
MCSET. Cat no: **2CCA 3076.** Released on Chivers Audio Books, '91 by Chivers Audio Books, Green Dragon Audio Visual. Note: 2 Cassettes.

MCSET. Cat no: **9143F.** Released on Travellers Tales, '91 by Travellers Tales. Note: 2 Cassettes.

Crichton, M
JURASSIC PARK (John Heard).
MCSET. Cat no: **RC 3.** Released on Random Century, '91 by Random Century Audiobooks, Conifer Records. Note: 2 cassettes. ISBN 1856860027. 3 hrs approx.

Crisp, N.J.
ODD JOB MAN, THE (Bruce Montague).
MCSET. Cat no: **1569T.** Released on Travellers Tales, '91 by Travellers Tales. Note: 5 Cassettes.

MCSET. Cat no: **1854963295.** Released on Bramhope, '91 by Ulverscroft Soundings. Note: 5 Cassettes.

Crockett, S.R.
STICKIT MINISTER, THE (And Other Stories) (Robert Trotter, Shelia Donald & Paul Young).
MCSET. Cat no: **SPF 135-1.** Released on Schiltron Audio Books, '91 by Schiltron Publishing. Note: 2 Cassettes. Playing time 2 hours 20 minutes.

Croft, Mike
ADVENTURES OF DUSTY AND THE DINOSAURS (Nanette Newman).
MC. Cat no: **TBC 9508.** Released on Tempo Storytime, May '84 by Warwick Records, Celtic Music.

Crompton, Richmal
JUST WILLIAM (Volume 2) (Martin Jarvis).
Note: Stories include: The Sweet Little Girl in White, A Birthday Treat, The Outlaws and Triplets, A Bit of Blackmail, William Makes a Noise About It, William and The Lost Tourist, The Leopard Hunter, The New Neighbour, William the Philanthropist,and William and The Prize Cat.

MCSET. Cat no: **ZBBC 1180.** Released on BBC Radio Collection, Nov '90 by BBC Records. Note: ISBN no: 0563 411244

JUST WILLIAM (Martin Jarvis).
MCSET. Cat no: **ZBBC 1165.** Released on BBC Radio Collection, Jul '90 by BBC Records. Note: ISBN No: 0563 410825

JUST WILLIAM STORIES (Kenneth Williams).
MCSET. Cat no: **0600560880.** Released on Hamlyn Books On Tape, '88, Bond Street Music.

MCSET. Cat no: **SAY 4.** Released on Argo (Polygram), Jul '82 by PolyGram Classics **Deleted** Jan '89.

MCSET. Cat no: **ARGO 1010.** Released on Argo (EMI), May '89 by EMI Records. Note: 2 Cassettes.

MORE WILLIAM STORIES (Kenneth Williams).
MCSET. Cat no: **SAY 84.** Released on Argo (Polygram), Jun '88 by PolyGram Classics **Deleted** Jan '89.

MCSET. Cat no: **ARGO 1259.** Released on Argo (EMI), Apr '91 by EMI Records.

Cronin, A.J.
JUDAS TREE, THE (Peter Wheeler).
MCSET. Cat no: **1328F.** Released on Travellers Tales, '91 by Travellers Tales. Note: 8 cassettes.

MCSET. Cat no: **1854960652.** Released on Soundings, '91 by Soundings Records, Bond Street Music. Note: 8 Cassettes.

KEYS OF THE KINGDOM (Christopher Kay).
MCSET. Cat no: **1033F.** Released on Travellers Tales, '91 by Travellers Tales. Note: 6 cassettes.

MCSET. Cat no: **1854960660.** Released on Soundings, '91 by Soundings Records, Bond Street Music. Note: 6 Cassettes.

LADY WITH CARNATIONS (Judy Geeson).
MC. Cat no: **CAB 007.** Released on Chivers Audio Books, '81 by Chivers Audio Books, Green Dragon Audio Visual.

MCSET. Cat no: **1034F.** Released on Travellers Tales, '91 by Travellers Tales. Note: 4 cassettes.

MINSTREL BOY, THE (Peter Wheeler).
MCSET. Cat no: **1332F.** Released on Travellers Tales, '91 by Travellers Tales. Note: 8 cassettes.

MCSET. Cat no: **1854960679.** Released on Soundings, '91 by Soundings Records, Bond Street Music. Note: 8 Cassettes.

SHANNON'S WAY (Ray Dunbobbin).
MCSET. Cat no: **1198F.** Released on Travellers Tales, '91 by Travellers Tales. Note: 6 cassettes.

MCSET. Cat no: **1854960687.** Released on Soundings, '91 by Soundings Records, Bond Street Music. Note: 6 Cassettes.

SPANISH GARDENER, THE (Christopher Kay).
MCSET. Cat no: **1035F.** Released on Travellers Tales, '91 by Travellers Tales. Note: 4 cassettes.

MCSET. Cat no: **1854960695.** Released on Bramhope, '91 by Ulverscroft Soundings. Note: 4 Cassettes.

Cross, Gillian
DEMON HEADMASTER, THE (Judy Bennett).
MCSET. Cat no: **3CCA 3115.** Released on Chivers Audio Books, '91 by Chivers Audio Books, Green Dragon

Audio Visual. Note: 3 Cassettes.

Cruz Smith, Martin
GORKY PARK (Henry Strozier).
MCSET. Cat no: **1688/1689T**. Released on Travellers Tales, '91 by Travellers Tales. Note: 10 Cassettes.
MCSET. Cat no: **IAB 91014**. Released on Isis Audio Books, '91. Note: 10 Cassettes.

POLAR STAR (Robert O'Keefe).
MCSET. Cat no: **RC 11**. Released on Random Century, '91 by Random Century Audiobooks, Conifer Records. Note: 2 cassettes. ISBN 1856860116. 3 hrs approx.

POLAR STAR (Frank Muller).
MCSET. Cat no: **1640T**. Released on Travellers Tales, '91 by Travellers Tales. Note: 8 Cassettes.
MCSET. Cat no: **IAB 90091**. Released on Isis Audio Books, '91. Note: 8 Cassettes.

Cullingford, Guy
POST MORTEM (John Rye).
MCSET. Cat no: **IAB 92054**. Released on Isis Audio Books, May '92. Note: 7 Cassettes. Playing time: 7 hours, 50 mins.

Cummings, E.E.
E.E. CUMMINGS READING (E.E. Cummings).
Note: *The Acrobat Passage* (from *Him*), *Lenin's Tomb (Eimi)* and others.
MC. Cat no: **1017**. Released on Caedmon (USA), '88 by Caedmon Records (USA), Bond Street Music.

E.E. CUMMINGS READS HIS POETRY (1920-1940) (E.E. Cummings).
Note: Includes *Next to of Course God America*, *Anyone Lived in a Pretty how Yown*, *My Father Moved Through Dooms of Love*.
MCSET. Cat no: **2080**. Released on Caedmon (USA), '88 by Caedmon Records (USA), Bond Street Music. Note: 2 cassettes

E.E. CUMMINGS READS HIS POETRY (1943-1958) (E.E. Cummings).
Note: Includes *YgUDuh*, *Pity This Busy Monster*, *Manunkind*, *(Once Like a Spark)*, *Stand With Your Lover on the Unending Earth*.
MCSET. Cat no: **2081**. Released on Caedmon (USA), '88 by Caedmon Records (USA), Bond Street Music. Note: 2 cassettes

Cunliffe, John
ADVENTURES OF POSTMAN PAT, THE (Ken Barrie).
MC. Cat no: **UNKNOWN**. Released on Tempo, '88 by Warwick Records, Celtic Music, Henry Hadaway Organisation.

FUN AND GAMES WITH POSTMAN PAT (Ken Barrie).
MC. Cat no: **00 103 44 99**. Released on Tempo, '88 by Warwick Records, Celtic Music, Henry Hadaway Organisation.

MORE POSTMAN PAT STORIES (Ken Barrie).
MC. Cat no: **TS 341**. Released on Tellastory, '88 by Random Century Audiobooks.
CD. Cat no: **U 4076**. Released on Tellastory, '88 by Random Century Audiobooks.

POSTMAN PAT (Ken Barrie).
Tracks / Postman Pat / Jesse the cat / Walking in Greendale / Mobile shop / Reverend Timms / Travelling music / Handyman song / Valley waltz / Miss Rebecca Hubbard / Farmer's song / Dawn and countryside waltz / Greendale jig / Busy day.
LP. Cat no: **PPLP101**. Released on Post Music, Jan '84 **Deleted** Jan '89.
MC. Cat no: **ZCPLP 101**. Released on Post Music, Jan '84 **Deleted** Jan '89.

POSTMAN PAT (Ken Barrie).
MCSET. Cat no: **00 104 125 8**. Released on Tempo, Apr '88 by Warwick Records, Celtic Music, Henry Hadaway Organisation. Note: Cassette & book set

POSTMAN PAT AND THE CHRISTMAS PUDDING (Ken Barrie).
MC. Cat no: **0 00 109026 7**. Released on Tempo, '88 by Warwick Records, Celtic Music, Henry Hadaway Organisation.

POSTMAN PAT AND THE DINOSAUR BONES (Ken Barrie).
MC. Cat no: **0 00 109025 9**. Released on Tempo, '88 by Warwick Records, Celtic Music, Henry Hadaway Organisation.

POSTMAN PAT AND THE GREENDALE GHOST (Ken Barrie).
MC. Cat no: **0 00 109024 0**. Released on Tempo, '88 by Warwick Records, Celtic Music, Henry Hadaway Organisation.

POSTMAN PAT AND THE LETTER PUZZLE (Ken Barrie).
MC. Cat no: **TS 372**. Released on Tellastory, '91 by Random Century Audiobooks. Note: ISBN no. 1856560945

POSTMAN PAT GOES ON SAFARI (Ken Barrie).
MC. Cat no: **0 00 102175 3**. Released on Tempo, '88 by Warwick Records, Celtic Music, Henry Hadaway Organisation.

POSTMAN PAT MAKES A SPLASH (Ken Barrie).
MC. Cat no: **0 00 109022 4**. Released on Tempo, '88 by Warwick Records, Celtic Music, Henry Hadaway Organisation.

POSTMAN PAT - MORE STORIES (Ken Barrie).
Note: Also available on hanging format, Cat. No: 0411380974.
MC. Cat no: **0411400487**. Released on Harper Collins, '91 by Harper Collins.

POSTMAN PAT PLAYS FOR GREENDALE (Ken Barrie).
MC. Cat no: **0 00 102177 X**. Released on Tempo, '88 by Warwick Records, Celtic Music, Henry Hadaway Organisation.

POSTMAN PAT STORIES, THE (Ken Barrie).
MC. Cat no: **TS 336**. Released on Tellastory, Dec '86 by Random Century Audiobooks.

POSTMAN PAT TAKES A MESSAGE (Ken Barrie).
MC. Cat no: **TS 373**. Released on Tellastory, '91 by Random Century Audiobooks. Note: ISBN no. 185656097X

POSTMAN PAT TAKES A MESSAGE (And Postman Pat's Treasure Hunt) (Ken Barrie).
MCSET. Cat no: **TS 386**. Released on Tellastory, '91 by Random Century Audiobooks. Note: 2 cassettes. ISBN no. 1856561321

POSTMAN PAT'S 123 STORY (Ken Barrie).
Note: Book and cassette.
MCSET. Cat no: **00 103 208 9**. Released on Tempo, Apr '88 by Warwick Records, Celtic Music, Henry Hadaway Organisation.

POSTMAN PAT'S ABC STORY (Ken Barrie).
Note: Book and cassette.
MCSET. Cat no: **00 103 207 0**. Released on Tempo, Apr '88 by Warwick Records, Celtic Music, Henry Hadaway Organisation.

POSTMAN PAT'S BEDTIME STORIES (Ken Barrie).
Note: Also available on hanging format, Cat. No: 0411386575.
MC. Cat no: **0411400312**. Released on Harper Collins, '91 by Harper Collins.

POSTMAN PAT'S BREEZY DAY (Ken Barrie).
MC. Cat no: **TS 371**. Released on Tellastory, '91 by Random Century Audiobooks. Note: ISBN no. 1856560953

POSTMAN PAT'S DAY IN BED (Ken Barrie).
Note: Postman Pat's Easy Reader series.
MC. Cat no: **0 00 109023 2**. Released on Tempo, '88 by Warwick Records, Celtic Music, Henry Hadaway Organisation.

POSTMAN PAT'S MESSY DAY (Ken Barrie).
MC. Cat no: **0 00 102176 1**. Released on Tempo, '88 by Warwick Records, Celtic Music, Henry Hadaway Organisation.

POSTMAN PAT'S PARCEL OF FUN (Ken Barrie).
MC. Cat no: **00 1034502**. Released on Tempo, '88 by Warwick Records, Celtic Music, Henry Hadaway Organisation.

POSTMAN PAT'S SECRET (Ken Barrie).

MC. Cat no: **1856560961**. Released on Random Century, '91 by Random Century Audiobooks, Conifer Records. Note: Playing time: 45 Minutes.

POSTMAN PAT'S TREASURE HUNT (Ken Barrie).
MC. Cat no: **TS 370**. Released on Tellastory, '91 by Random Century Audiobooks. Note: ISBN no. 1856560961

POSTMAN PAT'S WET DAY (Ken Barrie).
MC. Cat no: **0 00 102178 8**. Released on Tempo, '88 by Warwick Records, Celtic Music, Henry Hadaway Organisation.

SNOWMAN POSTMAN (Ken Barrie).
MC. Cat no: **TS 394**. Released on Tellastory, '91 by Random Century Audiobooks. Note: ISBN no. 1856561690

Currie, James

REVEREND JAMES CURRIE AND FRIENDS (Various artists).
MC. Cat no: **SSC 078**. Released on Scotsoun, '91 by Scotsoun Recordings, Morley Audio Services.

Curtiss, Ursula

SECOND SICKLE, THE (Jan Carey).
MCSET. Cat no: **CAT 4044**. Released on Chivers Audio Books, '91 by Chivers Audio Books, Green Dragon Audio Visual. Note: 6 Cassettes.

MCSET. Cat no: **1463T**. Released on Travellers Tales, '91 by Travellers Tales. Note: 6 Cassettes.

Custer, Clint

MATANZAS (Unknown narrator(s)).
MCSET. Cat no: **1854960709**. Released on Trio, '91 by EMI Records. Note: 3 Cassettes.

Dahl, Roald

AH, SWEET MYSTERY OF LIFE (Nigel Lambert).
MCSET. Cat no: **1691F**. Released on Travellers Tales, '91 by Travellers Tales. Note: 4 cassettes.

MCSET. Cat no: **IAB 91052**. Released on Isis Audio Books, '91. Note: 4 Cassettes.

B.F.G, THE (Book 2) (Jeremy Bullock).
Note: Also available on hanging format cat. no. 0411387014.
MC. Cat no: **0411870130**. Released on Harper Collins, '91 by Harper Collins. Note: Playing time 2hrs 56mins.

B.F.G, THE (Unknown narrator(s)).
Note: Also available on hanging format cat. no. 0411380613. Adapted as a play with sound effects.
MC. Cat no: **0411400231**. Released on Harper Collins, '91 by Harper Collins.

CHARLIE AND THE CHOCOLATE FACTORY (Unknown narrator(s)).

MCSET. Cat no: **000101076X**. Released on Harper Collins, Sep '91 by Harper Collins. Note: 3 Cassettes.

CHARLIE AND THE CHOCOLATE FACTORY (Roald Dahl).
MCSET. Cat no: **LFP 7104**. Released on Listen For Pleasure, Nov '85 by EMI Records.
MC. Cat no: **1476**. Released on Caedmon (USA), '88 by Caedmon Records (USA), Bond Street Music.
MCSET. Cat no: **9027F**. Released on Travellers Tales, '91 by Travellers Tales. Note: 3 Cassettes.

CHARLIE AND THE CHOCOLATE FACTORY (Kerry Shale).
Note: Also available on hanging format cat. no. 0411387030.
MC. Cat no: **041187033X**. Released on Harper Collins, '91 by Harper Collins. Note: Playing time 3hrs 6mins.

CHARLIE AND THE CHOCOLATE FACTORY (Unknown narrator(s)).
Note: Also available on hanging format cat. no. 0411380656. Adapted as a play with sound effects.
MC. Cat no: **0411400258**. Released on Harper Collins, '91 by Harper Collins. Note: 3 Cassettes.

CHARLIE AND THE CHOCOLATE FACTORY (Roald Dahl).
Note: Also available on hanging format cat. no. 0001031880.
MC. Cat no: **0001034189**. Released on Harper Collins, '91 by Harper Collins.

CHARLIE AND THE GREAT GLASS ELEVATOR (Kerry Shale).
Note: Also available on hanging format. Cat. No: 0411387049.
MC. Cat no: **0411870432**. Released on Harper Collins, '91 by Harper Collins.

CHARLIE AND THE GREAT GLASS ELEVATOR (Jonathan Cecil).
MCSET. Cat no: **3CCA 3146**. Released on Chivers Audio Books, '91 by Chivers Audio Books, Green Dragon Audio Visual. Note: 3 Cassettes.

CHARLIE AND THE GREAT GLASS ELEVATOR (Various artists).
Note: Also available on hanging format cat.no. 0411380648. Adapted as a play with sound effects.
MC. Cat no: **0411400266**. Released on Harper Collins, '91 by Harper Collins.

DANNY, THE CHAMPION OF THE WORLD (Unknown narrator(s)).
Note: Also available on hanging format cat. no. 0411380680. Adapted as a play with sound effects.
MC. Cat no: **0411400304**. Released on Harper Collins, '91 by Harper Collins.

DANNY, THE CHAMPION OF THE WORLD (Jimmy Hibert).
Note: Also available on hanging format, Cat. No: 0411387065.

MC. Cat no: **0411876637**. Released on Harper Collins, '91 by Harper Collins. Note: Playing time: 2 hours, 49 mins.

DIRTY BEASTS (Prunella Scales).
Note: Also available on hanging format cat. no:- 0411380796
MC. Cat no: **0411400347**. Released on Harper Collins, '91 by Harper Collins.

ENORMOUS CROCODILE, THE (And The Magic Finger) (Roald Dahl).
Note: Also available on hanging format catalogue number: 0001031899.
LP. Cat no: **TC 1633**. Released on Caedmon (USA), Sep '80 by Caedmon Records (USA), Bond Street Music.
MC. Cat no: **1633**. Released on Caedmon (USA), '88 by Caedmon Records (USA), Bond Street Music.
MC. Cat no: **0001034170**. Released on Harper Collins, '91 by Harper Collins.

ENORMOUS CROCODILE, THE (Roger Blake).
Note: Also available on hanging format cat. no. 0411380842.
MC. Cat no: **00 1022113**. Released on Tempo, '88 by Warwick Records, Celtic Music, Henry Hadaway Organisation.
MC. Cat no: **0411400398**. Released on Harper Collins, '91 by Harper Collins.

FANTASTIC MR. FOX (Unknown narrator(s)).
MC. Cat no: **1576**. Released on Caedmon (USA), '88 by Caedmon Records (USA), Bond Street Music.

FANTASTIC MR. FOX (John Baddley).
MCSET. Cat no: **0001010751**. Released on Harper Collins, Sep '91 by Harper Collins.
MC. Cat no: **0411400401**. Released on Harper Collins, '91 by Harper Collins.
MC. Cat no: **0001034197**. Released on Harper Collins, '91 by Harper Collins.

FANTASTIC MR. FOX (Unknown narrator(s)).
Note: Also available on hanging format cat. no. 0411380656. Adapted as a play with sound effects.
MC. Cat no: **0411400274**. Released on Harper Collins, '91 by Harper Collins.

FANTASTIC MR. FOX (Lionel Jeffries).
Note: Suitable for 5-7 year olds.
MCSET. Cat no: **CC/016**. Released on Cover to Cover, Nov '86 by Cover to Cover Cassettes.

GEORGE'S MARVELLOUS MEDICINE (Derek Griffiths).
Note: Also available on hanging format cat. no. 0411380834
MC. Cat no: **041140038**. Released on Harper Collins, '91 by Harper Collins.

135

GEORGE'S MARVELLOUS MEDICINE (Unknown narrator(s)).
Note: Also available on hanging format cat. no. 0411380621. Adapted as a play with sound effects.
MC. Cat no: **041140024X**. Released on Harper Collins, '91 by Harper Collins.

GIRAFFE, THE PELLEY AND ME, THE (Roald Dahl).
Note: Also available on hanging format cat. no. 041138080X
MC. Cat no: **0411400355**. Released on Harper Collins, '91 by Harper Collins.
MC. Cat no: **001022105**. Released on Tempo, '88 by Warwick Records, Celtic Music, Henry Hadaway Organisation.

GREAT SWITCHEROO, THE (Patricia Neal).
Note: Also available on hanging format, cataglogue number:- 000138967X
MC. Cat no: **1545**. Released on Caedmon (USA), '88 by Caedmon Records (USA), Bond Street Music.
MC. Cat no: **0001389661**. Released on Harper Collins, '91 by Harper Collins.

JAMES AND THE GIANT PEACH (Unknown narrator(s)).
Note: Also available on hanging format. cat. no. 0411380605. Adapted as a play with sound effects.
MC. Cat no: **0411400223**. Released on Harper Collins, '91 by Harper Collins.

JAMES AND THE GIANT PEACH (Brian Trueman).
Note: Also available on hanging format, Cat. No: 0411387057.
MC. Cat no: **041187053 X**. Released on Harper Collins, '91 by Harper Collins. Note: Playing time: 2 hours, 47 mins.

JAMES AND THE GIANT PEACH (Roald Dahl).
Note: Also available on hanging format cat. no. 0001031872
MC. Cat no: **0001031872**. Released on Harper Collins, '91 by Harper Collins.

JAMES AND THE GIANT PEACH (Unknown narrator(s)).
MC. Cat no: **1543**. Released on Caedmon (USA), '88 by Caedmon Records (USA), Bond Street Music.

MAGIC FINGER, THE (Anne Clements).
MC. Cat no: **0411400371**. Released on Harper Collins, '91 by Harper Collins.

MATILDA (Unknown narrator(s)).
Note: Also available on hanging format cat. no. 0411 380664. Adapted as a play with sound effects
MC. Cat no: **0411400282**. Released on Harper Collins, '91 by Harper Collins.

MATILDA (Sarah Greene).
MCSET. Cat no: **3CCA 3100**. Released on Chivers Audio Books, '91 by Chivers Audio Books, Green Dragon Audio Visual. Note: 3 Cassettes.
MCSET. Cat no: **9150F**. Released on Travellers Tales, '91 by Travellers Tales. Note: 3 Cassettes.

MATILDA (Jenny Hanley).
Note: Also available on hanging format, Cat. No: 0411387022.
MC. Cat no: **0411870238**. Released on Harper Collins, '91 by Harper Collins. Note: Playing time: 3 hours, 3 mins.

MINPINS, THE (Richard Pasco).
MC. Cat no: **TS 396**. Released on Tellastory, '91 by Random Century Audiobooks. Note: ISBN no. 1856561186

REVOLTING RHYMES (Prunella Scales & Timothy West).
Note: Also available on hanging format cat. no.:- 04114003391.
MC. Cat no: **0411400339**. Released on Harper Collins, '91 by Harper Collins.
CD. Cat no: **U 4073**. Released on Spectrum (1), '88 by PolyGram UK Ltd, Terry Blood Dist..

RHYME STEW (Derek Griffiths & Julie Dawn Cole).
Note: Also available on hanging format cat. no. 0411380753
MC. Cat no: **0411400622**. Released on Harper Collins, '91 by Harper Collins.

ROALD DAHL COLLECTION (Volume 2) (Various artists).
Note: Include stories: The Magic Finger, The Twits and George's Marvellous Medicine. Narrators are Roger Blake, Richard Griffiths and Ann Clement.
MCSET. Cat no: **00 104 130-4**. Released on Tempo, Apr '88 by Warwick Records, Celtic Music, Henry Hadaway Organisation. Note: 3 cassette set

ROALD DAHL COLLECTION, THE (Roald Dahl).
MC. Cat no: **0001042718**. Released on Collins-Caedmon, '88 by Collins Audio, Taylors, Bond Street Music.

ROALD DAHL SLIPCASE (OLDER) (Roald Dahl).
MC. Cat no: **0001016520**. Released on Harper Collins, '91 by Harper Collins.

ROALD DAHL SLIPCASE (YOUNGER) (Roald Dahl).
MC. Cat no: **000101651**. Released on Harper Collins, '91 by Harper Collins.

TWITS, THE (Roger Blake).
Note: Also available on hanging format cat. no. 0411380818
MC. Cat no: **0411400363**. Released on Harper Collins, '91 by Harper Collins. Note: NNYunused

WITCHES, THE (Unknown narrator(s)).
Note: Also available on hanging format cat. no. 0411380672. Adapted as a play with sound effects.
MC. Cat no: **0411400290**. Released on Harper Collins, '91 by Harper Collins.

WITCHES, THE (Richard Briers).
MCSET. Cat no: **3CCA 3085**. Released on Chivers Audio Books, '91 by Chivers Audio Books, Green Dragon Audio Visual. Note: 3 Cassettes.
MCSET. Cat no: **9159F**. Released on Travellers Tales, '91 by Travellers Tales. Note: 3 Cassettes.

WITCHES, THE (Judy Bennett).
Note: Also available on hanging format, Cat. No: 0411387073.
MC. Cat no: **0411870734**. Released on Harper Collins, '91 by Harper Collins. Note: Playing time: 3 hours, 3 mins.

WONDERFUL STORY OF HENRY SUGAR, THE (Martin Jarvis).
MCSET. Cat no: **2CCA 3109**. Released on Chivers Audio Books, '91 by Chivers Audio Books, Green Dragon Audio Visual. Note: 2 Cassettes.
MCSET. Cat no: **9196F**. Released on Travellers Tales, '91 by Travellers Tales. Note: 2 Cassettes.

Dailey, Janet

MASQUERADE (Kate Harper).
MCSET. Cat no: **CAB 552**. Released on Chivers Audio Books, '91 by Chivers Audio Books, Green Dragon Audio Visual. Note: 8 cassettes.
MCSET. Cat no: **1707T**. Released on Travellers Tales, '91 by Travellers Tales. Note: 8 Cassettes.

RIVALS (Kate Harper).
MCSET. Cat no: **CAB 612**. Released on Chivers Audio Books, '91 by Chivers Audio Books, Green Dragon Audio Visual. Note: 12 Cassettes.

Daniels, Philip

ALIBI OF GUILT (Philip Daniels).
MCSET. Cat no: **SOUND 9**. Released on Soundings, Apr '85 by Soundings Records, Bond Street Music.
MCSET. Cat no: **1039T**. Released on Travellers Tales, '91 by Travellers Tales.

CINDERELLA SPY (Judith Porter).
MCSET. Cat no: **1654T**. Released on Travellers Tales, '91 by Travellers Tales. Note: 5 Cassettes.
MCSET. Cat no: **1854963619**. Released on Bramhope, '91 by Ulverscroft Soundings. Note: 5 Cassettes.

DRACULA MURDERS, THE (Peter Joyce).
MCSET. Cat no: **1744T**. Released on Travellers Tales, '91 by Travellers Tales. Note: 4 Cassettes.
MCSET. Cat no: **185496433X**. Released on Bramhope, '91 by Ulverscroft Soundings. Note: 4 Cassettes.

GENTEEL LITTLE MURDER, A (Unknown narrator(s)).
MCSET. Cat no: **1854960725**. Released on Trio, '91 by EMI Records. Note: 3 cassettes.

GOLDMINE LONDON W1 (Peter Chambers).
MCSET. Cat no: **SOUND 3**. Released on Soundings, Apr '85 by Soundings Records, Bond Street Music.

MCSET. Cat no: **1040T**. Released on Travellers Tales, '91 by Travellers Tales. Note: 4 Cassettes.

INCONVENIENT CORPSE, THE (Unknown narrator(s)).
MCSET. Cat no: **1854962868**. Released on Bramhope, '91 by Ulverscroft Soundings. Note: 4 Cassettes.

MINIATURE MURDER MYSTERY (See under Chambers, Peter).

NICE KNIGHT FOR MURDER (Unknown narrator(s)).
MCSET. Cat no: **1854964453**. Released on Trio, '91 by EMI Records. Note: 3 Cassettes.

Dann, Colin

ANIMALS OF FARTHING WOOD (Hannah Gordon).
MCSET. Cat no: **LFP 7505**. Released on Listen For Pleasure, 16 Oct '90 by EMI Records.

Dante

DIVINE COMEDY, THE (Inferno Cantos 1-6) (Ian Richardson).
MC. Cat no: **CDL 51632**. Released on Caedmon (USA), Sep '80 by Caedmon Records (USA), Bond Street Music.

Danziger, Paula

CAT ATE MY GYMSUIT, THE (Paula Danziger).
MC. Cat no: **1745**. Released on Caedmon (USA), '88 by Caedmon Records (USA), Bond Street Music.

PISTACHIO PRESCRIPTION, THE (Pat Starr).
MCSET. Cat no: **3CCA 3046**. Released on Chivers Audio Books, '91 by Chivers Audio Books, Green Dragon Audio Visual. Note: 3 Cassettes.
MCSET. Cat no: **9165F**. Released on Travellers Tales, '9 by Travellers Tales. Note: 3 Cassettes.

Darke, Susan

VITAL SPARK, THE (Unknown narrator(s)).
MCSET. Cat no: **1854964755**. Released on Trio, '91 by EMI Records. Note: 3 Cassettes.

Davidson, Jean

MANHATTAN MAGIC (Unknown narrator(s)).
MCSET. Cat no: **1854964925**. Released on Bramhope, '91 by Ulverscroft Soundings. Note: 5 Cassettes.

Davidson, Lionel

NIGHT OF WENCESLAS (Timothy Bentinck).
MCSET. Cat no: **CAT 4045**. Released on Chivers Audio Books, '91 by Chivers Audio Books, Green Dragon Audio Visual. Note: 6 Cassettes.

MCSET. Cat no: **1464T**. Released on Travellers Tales, '91 by Travellers Tales. Note: 6 Cassettes.

Davidson, Peter

GREY AREAS (Peter Davidson).
MC. Cat no: **MC 7070**. Released on Magic Carpet, '91 by Morley Audio Services.

SIGNS OF THE TIMES (Peter Davidson).
MC. Cat no: **MC 5050**. Released on Magic Carpet, '91 by Morley Audio Services.

SPIRELLI NAMES NAMES (Peter Davidson).
MC. Cat no: **MC 4040**. Released on Magic Carpet, '91 by Morley Audio Services.

TELLING TALES (Peter Davidson).
MC. Cat no: **MC 3030**. Released on Magic Carpet, '91 by Morley Audio Services.

Davies, Hunter

FLOSSIE TEACAKE - AGAIN (Eve Karpf).
MCSET. Cat no: **2CCA 3086**. Released on Chivers Audio Books, '91 by Chivers Audio Books, Green Dragon Audio Visual. Note: 2 Cassettes.
MCSET. Cat no: **9156F**. Released on Travellers Tales, '91 by Travellers Tales. Note: 2 Cassettes.

FLOSSIE TEACAKE STRIKES BACK (Eve Karpf).
MCSET. Cat no: **2CCA 3104**. Released on Chivers Audio Books, '91 by Chivers Audio Books, Green Dragon Audio Visual. Note: 2 Cassettes.
MCSET. Cat no: **9173F**. Released on Travellers Tales, '91 by Travellers Tales. Note: 2 Cassettes.

FLOSSIE TEACAKE'S FUR COAT (Eve Karpf).
MCSET. Cat no: **2CCA 3033**. Released on Chivers Audio Books, '91 by Chivers Audio Books, Green Dragon Audio Visual. Note: 2 Cassettes.
MCSET. Cat no: **9104F**. Released on Travellers Tales, '91 by Travellers Tales. Note: 2 Cassettes.

Day Lewis, C

C. DAY LEWIS READS C. DAY LEWIS (C. Day Lewis).
MC. Cat no: **TTC 1010**. Released on Talking Tape Company, Apr '91, Conifer Records. Note: Playing time 48 mins. ISBN no. 1872520901

POETRY SELECTION (C. Day Lewis).
MC. Cat no: **TTC/PS 02**. Released on Talking Tape Company, '84, Conifer Records.

REQUIEM FOR THE LIVING (C Day Lewis & Donald Swann).
LP. Cat no: **PLR 061**. Released on Plant Life, Jul '84 by Plant Life Records, Roots Records, Jazz Music, Celtic Music, Duncans, Topic Records, W.R.P.M..

De Brunhoff, Jean

BABAR AND FATHER CHRISTMAS (And Babar's Friend Zephir) (John Nettleton).
MC. Cat no: **TS 390**. Released on Tellastory, '91 by Random Century Audiobooks. Note: ISBN no. 1856561658

BABAR AND FATHER CHRISTMAS (And Babar And His Children) (Louis Jordan).
MC. Cat no: **1488**. Released on Caedmon (USA), '88 by Caedmon Records (USA), Bond Street Music.

BABAR AT HOME (And Other Stories) (John Nettleton).
MC. Cat no: **TS 343**. Released on Tellastory, '88 by Random Century Audiobooks.

BABAR THE ELEPHANT (Angela Rippon).
LP. Cat no: **K 53598**. Released on Manticore, Nov '79.

BABAR THE KING (And Babar At Home) (John Nettleton).
MC. Cat no: **TS 389**. Released on Tellastory, '91 by Random Century Audiobooks. Note: ISBN no. 185656049X

BABAR THE KING (And Babar And Zephir) (Louis Jordan).
MC. Cat no: **1487**. Released on Caedmon (USA), '88 by Caedmon Records (USA), Bond Street Music.

BABAR'S CHOICE (Various narrators).
MC. Cat no: **0001010050**. Released on Harper Collins, '91 by Harper Collins.

BABAR'S FIRST STEP (Various narrators).
MC. Cat no: **0001010069**. Released on Harper Collins, '91 by Harper Collins.

BABAR'S MYSTERY (And Babar and the Wully-Wully) (Laurent De Brunhoff).
MC. Cat no: **1583**. Released on Caedmon (USA), '88 by Caedmon Records (USA), Bond Street Music.

STORY OF BABAR (Unknown narrator(s)).
MC. Cat no: **TS 342**. Released on Tellastory, Dec '86 by Random Century Audiobooks.

STORY OF BABAR (And Travels of Babar) (Louis Jordan).
Note: Also available on hanging format, Cat. No: 0001848577.
MC. Cat no: **1486**. Released on Caedmon (USA), '88 by Caedmon Records (USA), Bond Street Music.
MC. Cat no: **0001848623**. Released on Harper Collins, '91 by Harper Collins.

STORY OF BABAR (And Babar's Travels) (John Nettleton).
MC. Cat no: **TS 388**. Released on Tellastory, '91 by Random Century Audiobooks. Note: ISBN no. 1856560481

De Cervantes, Miguel

DON QUIXOTE (Various artists).

MC. Cat no: **ANV 630**. Released on Anvil Cassettes, Jan '81 by Anvil Cassettes, Chivers Audio Books.
EXPLOITS OF DON QUIXOTE (Anthony Quayle).
MC. Cat no: **1289**. Released on Caedmon (USA), '88 by Caedmon Records (USA), Bond Street Music.

De La Roche, Mazo
BUILDING OF JALNA, THE (Dorothy Tutin).
MCSET. Cat no: **CAB 436**. Released on Chivers Audio Books, '91 by Chivers Audio Books, Green Dragon Audio Visual. Note: 8 cassettes.

DELIGHT (Kara Wilson).
MCSET. Cat no: **CAB 366**. Released on Chivers Audio Books, '91 by Chivers Audio Books, Green Dragon Audio Visual. Note: 6 Cassettes

MCSET. Cat no: **1346F**. Released on Travellers Tales, '91 by Travellers Tales. Note: 6 cassettes.

MARY WAKEFIELD (Vivien Heilbron).
MCSET. Cat no: **CAB 626**. Released on Chivers Audio Books, Sep '91 by Chivers Audio Books, Green Dragon Audio Visual. Note: 8 Cassettes

MORNING AT JALNA (Vivien Heilbron).
MCSET. Cat no: **CAB 561**. Released on Chivers Audio Books, '91 by Chivers Audio Books, Green Dragon Audio Visual. Note: 8 Cassettes.

MCSET. Cat no: **1622F**. Released on Travellers Tales, '91 by Travellers Tales. Note: 8 cassettes.

WHITEOAKS OF JALNA, THE (Part 1) (Dorothy Tutin).
MCSET. Cat no: **1517F**. Released on Travellers Tales, '91 by Travellers Tales. Note: 8 Cassettes.

De La Torre, Lilian
DR SAM: JOHNSON, DETECTOR (Alexander Spencer).
Note: Contains the stories: The Wax-Work Cadaver, The Second Sight of Dr Sam: Johnson,The Flying Highwayman, The Monboddo Ape Boy, The Manifestations in Mincing Lane,Prince Charlie's Ruby, The Stolen Christmas Box, The Conveyance of Emelina Grange and The Great Seal of England.
MCSET. Cat no: **RB 89691**. Released on Recorded Books, Dec '91 by Isis Audio Books. Note: 5 cassettes. Playing time 7hrs 30mins.

De Lampedusa, Giuseppe
LEOPARD, THE (John Houseman).
MC. Cat no: **1720**. Released on Caedmon (USA), by Caedmon Records (USA), Bond Street Music.

De Maupassant, Guy
BOULE DE SUIF / THE WOMAN WITH THE BLUE EYES (Morag Hood).
Note: Authors are Guy De Maupassant and Maxim Gorky.
MCSET. Cat no: **SPF 980-1A**. Released on Schiltron Audio Books, '91 by Schiltron Publishing. Note: 2 Cassettes. Playing time 2 hours 6 minutes

STORIES OF GUY DE MAUPASSANT (Claire Bloom).
MC. Cat no: **1268**. Released on Caedmon (USA), '88 by Caedmon Records (USA), Bond Street Music.

De Paola, Tomie
STREGA NONA'S MAGIC LESSONS (And Other Stories) (Tammy Grimes).
MC. Cat no: **1714**. Released on Caedmon (USA), '88 by Caedmon Records (USA), Bond Street Music.

De Saint-Exupery, Antoine
LITTLE PRINCE, THE (Peter Ustinov).
MCSET. Cat no: **9029F**. Released on Travellers Tales, '91 by Travellers Tales.

LITTLE PRINCE, THE (Louis Jordan).
Note: Also available on hanging format, Cat. No: 0001031856.
MC. Cat no: **1695**. Released on Caedmon (USA), '88 by Caedmon Records (USA), Bond Street Music.
MC. Cat no: **MCFR 113/4**. Released on Conifer, '88 by Conifer Records, Jazz Music.
MC. Cat no: **0001072749**. Released on Harper Collins, '91 by Harper Collins.

Defoe, Daniel
MOLL FLANDERS (Siobhan McKenna).
MC. Cat no: **1090**. Released on Caedmon (USA), '88 by Caedmon Records (USA), Bond Street Music.
MC. Cat no: **000105189X**. Released on Collins-Caedmon, '91 by Collins Audio, Taylors, Bond Street Music.
Note: NNYunused

MOLL FLANDERS (Anthony Homyer).
MCSET. Cat no: **TCL 12**. Released on Complete Listener, '91 by Complete Listener. Note: 9 Cassettes. (BB) Playing Time: 810 Mintues.
MCSET. Cat no: **1557/8F**. Released on Travellers Tales, '91 by Travellers Tales. Note: 9 Cassettes.

MOLL FLANDERS (Barbara Leigh-Hunt).
MCSET. Cat no: **ARGO 1244**. Released on Argo (EMI), Oct '90 by EMI Records **Deleted** '91. Note: 2 Cassettes.

ROBINSON CRUSOE (Frank Duncan).
MC. Cat no: **P 90010**. Released on Pinnacle, '79 by Pinnacle Records, Outlet Records, Music Sales Records.

ROBINSON CRUSOE (Anthony Homyer).
MCSET. Cat no: **TCL 13**. Released on Complete Listener, '91 by Complete Listener. Note: 8 Cassettes. (BB) Playing Time: 720 Minutes.
MCSET. Cat no: **1559F**. Released on Travellers Tales, '91 by Travellers Tales. Note: 8 Cassettes.

ROBINSON CRUSOE (Ian Richardson).
LP. Cat no: **TC 1461**. Released on Caedmon (USA), Jul '78 by Caedmon Records (USA), Bond Street Music.
MC. Cat no: **1461**. Released on Caedmon (USA), by Caedmon Records (USA), Bond Street Music.

ROBINSON CRUSOE (Unknown narrator(s)).
MCSET. Cat no: **DTO 10579**. Released on Ditto, '88 by Pickwick Records, Midland Records.

ROBINSON CRUSOE (Harry Andrews).
MCSET. Cat no: **414 766-4**. Released on Argo (Polygram), Oct '85 by PolyGram Classics **Deleted** Jan '89.
MCSET. Cat no: **ARGO 1073**. Released on Argo (EMI), May '89 by EMI Records. Note: 2 Cassettes.
MCSET. Cat no: **9030F**. Released on Travellers Tales, '91 by Travellers Tales. Note: 2 Cassettes.

ROBINSON CRUSOE (Clifford Norgate).
MC. Cat no: **SQRL 32**. Released on Squirrel, Nov '81.

Deighton, Len
BERLIN GAME (Paul Daneman).
MCSET. Cat no: **CAB 553**. Released on Chivers Audio Books, '91 by Chivers Audio Books, Green Dragon Audio Visual. Note: 8 Cassettes.
MCSET. Cat no: **1693T**. Released on Travellers Tales, '91 by Travellers Tales. Note: 8 Cassettes.

FUNERAL IN BERLIN (Paul Daneman).
MCSET. Cat no: **CAB 435**. Released on Chivers Audio Books, '91 by Chivers Audio Books, Green Dragon Audio Visual. Note: 8 Cassettes.
MCSET. Cat no: **1586T**. Released on Travellers Tales, '91 by Travellers Tales. Note: 6 Cassettes.

IPCRESS FILE, THE (Paul Daneman).
MCSET. Cat no: **CAB 423**. Released on Chivers Audio Books, '91 by Chivers Audio Books, Green Dragon Audio Visual. Note: 6 Cassettes.
MCSET. Cat no: **1465T**. Released on Travellers Tales, '91 by Travellers Tales. Note: 6 Cassettes.

MEXICO SET (Paul Daneman).
MCSET. Cat no: **CAB 621**. Released on Chivers Audio Books, '91 by Chivers Audio Books, Green Dragon Audio Visual. Note: 10 Cassettes.

SPY HOOK (Paul Daneman).
MCSET. Cat no: **CAB 395**. Released on Chivers Audio Books, '91 by Chivers

Audio Books, Green Dragon Audio Visual. Note: 8 Cassettes.
MCSET. Cat no: **1518T.** Released on Travellers Tales, '91 by Travellers Tales. Note: 8 Cassettes.

SPY STORY (Paul Daneman).
MCSET. Cat no: **CAB 520.** Released on Chivers Audio Books, '91 by Chivers Audio Books, Green Dragon Audio Visual. Note: 6 Cassettes
MCSET. Cat no: **1607T.** Released on Travellers Tales, '91 by Travellers Tales. Note: 6 Cassettes.

TWINKLE TWINKLE LITTLE SPY (Paul Daneman).
MCSET. Cat no: **CAB 492.** Released on Chivers Audio Books, '91 by Chivers Audio Books, Green Dragon Audio Visual. Note: 6 Cassettes
MCSET. Cat no: **1608T.** Released on Travellers Tales, '91 by Travellers Tales. Note: 6 Cassettes.

Delafield, E.M.
DIARY OF A PROVINCIAL LADY, THE (Judy Franklin).
MCSET. Cat no: **IAB 91095.** Released on Isis Audio Books, Sep '91. Note: 5 cassettes. Playing time 4hrs 39mins.

Delderfield, R.F.
ALL OVER THE TOWN (Ray Dunbobbin).
MCSET. Cat no: **1037F.** Released on Travellers Tales, '91 by Travellers Tales. Note: 5 cassettes.
MCSET. Cat no: **1854960741.** Released on Soundings, '91 by Soundings Records, Bond Street Music. Note: 5 Cassettes.

COME HOME CHARLIE AND FACE THEM (John Duttine).
MCSET. Cat no: **1242F.** Released on Travellers Tales, '91 by Travellers Tales. Note: 8 cassettes.

SPRING MADNESS OF MR SERMON (Peter Wheeler).
MCSET. Cat no: **1244F.** Released on Travellers Tales, '91 by Travellers Tales. Note: 8 cassettes.
MCSET. Cat no: **185496075X.** Released on Soundings, '91 by Soundings Records, Bond Street Music. Note: 8 Cassettes.

TOO FEW FOR DRUMS (Christopher Kay).
MCSET. Cat no: **1854965867.** Released on Bramhope, Apr '92 by Ulverscroft Soundings. Note: Playing time: 60 minutes.

Derek & Clive
AD NAUSEAM.
Tracks / Endangered species / Racing / T.V. / Bruce / Records / Soul time / Russia / Sir / Celebrity suicide / Politics / Labels / Street music / Horn / Mona / Critics.
LP. Cat no: **OVED 162.** Released on Virgin, Apr '86 by Virgin Records, Music Sales Records. Note: (MM)
MC. Cat no: **OVEDC 162.** Released on Virgin, Apr '86 by Virgin Records, Music Sales Records. Note: (MM)
LP. Cat no: **V 2112.** Released on Virgin, '78 by Virgin Records, Music Sales Records **Deleted** '88.
CD. Cat no: **CDOVD 162.** Released on Virgin, Dec '89 by Virgin Records, Music Sales Records. Note: (MM)

COME AGAIN.
Tracks / Coughing contest / Cancer / Non-stop dancer/My mum song / Joan Crawford / Norman the carpet / How's your mother / Back of the cab / Alfie Noakes / In the cubicles / Nurse / Ross Mc Pharter / Hello Colin / Having a wank / I saw this bloke / Parking offence / Members only.
LP. Cat no: **OVED 110.** Released on Virgin, Aug '88 by Virgin Records, Music Sales Records. Note: (MM)
MC. Cat no: **OVEDC 110.** Released on Virgin, '87 by Virgin Records, Music Sales Records. Note: (MM)
CD. Cat no: **CDOVD 110.** Released on Virgin, Dec '89 by Virgin Records, Music Sales Records. Note: (MM)

Desai, Anita
IN CUSTODY (Garard Green).
MCSET. Cat no: **1425F.** Released on Travellers Tales, '91 by Travellers Tales. Note: 6 cassettes.
MCSET. Cat no: **OAS 90024.** Released on Oasis Audio Books, '91 by Isis Audio Books.

Dessau, Joanna
BELOVED EMMA (Unknown narrator(s)).
MCSET. Cat no: **1854962779.** Released on Bramhope, '91 by Ulverscroft Soundings. Note: 5 Cassettes.

GREY GOOSE, THE (Anne Cater).
MCSET. Cat no: **1854964712.** Released on Bramhope, Jul '91 by Ulverscroft Soundings. Note: 4 Cassettes.

Dever, Joe
LONE WOLF (Edward De Souza).
MCSET. Cat no: **RC 48.** Released on Random Century, May '92 by Random Century Audiobooks, Conifer Records. Note: ISBN no. 1856860965

Deveraux, Jude
DUCHESS, THE (Unknown narrator(s)).
MCSET. Cat no: **0671747517.** Released on Simon & Schuster, '91 by Simon & Schuster Ltd.

KNIGHT IN SHINING ARMOUR (Stephanie Zimbalist).
MCSET. Cat no: **0671707426.** Released on Simon & Schuster, '91 by Simon & Schuster Ltd. Note: 2 cassettes.

MOUNTAIN LAUREL (Judith Light).
MCSET. Cat no: **0671708724.** Released on Simon & Schuster, '91 by Simon & Schuster Ltd. Note: 2 cassettes.

Dexter, Colin
DEAD OF JERICHO, THE (Colin Dexter).
MCSET. Cat no: **CAB 442.** Released on Chivers Audio Books, '91 by Chivers Audio Books, Green Dragon Audio Visual. Note: 6 Cassettes
MCSET. Cat no: **1519T.** Released on Travellers Tales, '91 by Travellers Tales. Note: 6 Cassettes.

RIDDLE OF THE THIRD MILE, THE (Michael Pennington).
MCSET. Cat no: **CAB 672.** Released on Chivers Audio Books, Feb '92 by Chivers Audio Books, Green Dragon Audio Visual. Note: 6 cassettes.

WENCH IS DEAD, THE (Colin Dexter).
MCSET. Cat no: **CAB 582.** Released on Chivers Audio Books, '91 by Chivers Audio Books, Green Dragon Audio Visual. Note: 6 Cassettes.
MCSET. Cat no: **1725T.** Released on Travellers Tales, '91 by Travellers Tales. Note: 6 Cassettes.

Dibdin, Michael
RATKING (William Gaminara).
MCSET. Cat no: **1495T.** Released on Travellers Tales, '91 by Travellers Tales. Note: 8 Cassettes.
MCSET. Cat no: **IAB 89122.** Released on Isis Audio Books, '91. Note: 8 Cassettes.

Dice Clay, Andrew
DICE (Andrew Dice Clay).
LP. Cat no: **8281621.** Released on Fontana, Sep '89 by Phonogram Ltd **Deleted** May '91.
MC. Cat no: **8281624.** Released on Fontana, Sep '89 by Phonogram Ltd.
CD. Cat no: **8281622.** Released on Fontana, Sep '89 by Phonogram Ltd.

Dickens, Charles
BLEAK HOUSE (Hugh Dickson).
MCSET. Cat no: **CTC 038.** Released on Cover to Cover, '90 by Cover to Cover Cassettes. Note: 30 cassette set. Playing time 38 hrs.
MCSET. Cat no: **1071/2/3/4C.** Released on Travellers Tales, '91 by Travellers Tales. Note: 30 Cassettes.

BLEAK HOUSE (Sir John Gielgud). Note: Abridged.
MCSET. Cat no: **414 751-4.** Released on Argo (Polygram), Jun '88 by PolyGram Classics **Deleted** Jan '89.
MCSET. Cat no: **ARGO 1070.** Released on Argo (EMI), May '89 by EMI Records. Note: 2 Cassettes.

BLEAK HOUSE (Sir John Gielgud).
MCSET. Cat no: **1016C.** Released on Travellers Tales, '91 by Travellers Tales. Note: 2 cassettes.

CHRISTMAS BOOKS, THE (Anthony Homyer).
Note: Includes:- A Christmas Carol, The Chimes, The Battle of Life, The

Cricket on the Hearth and The Haunted Man.
MCSET. Cat no: **TCL 27**. Released on Complete Listener, '91 by Complete Listener. Note: 14 Cassettes. (BB) Playing Time: 1,260 Minutes.

CHRISTMAS CAROL, A (Daniel Massey).
MCSET. Cat no: **414 775-4**. Released on Argo (Polygram), Jun '88 by Poly-Gram Classics **Deleted** Jan '89.
MCSET. Cat no: **ARGO 1142**. Released on Argo (EMI), Sep '89 by EMI Records. Note: 2 Cassettes.
MCSET. Cat no: **1017C**. Released on Travellers Tales, '91 by Travellers Tales.

CHRISTMAS CAROL, A (And the Snow Queen) (Peter Bartlett & Barbara Bliss).
MCSET. Cat no: **1856560082**. Released on Random Century, '91 by Random Century Audiobooks, Conifer Records. Note: Playing time: 42 minutes.
MCSET. Cat no: **TS 395**. Released on Tellastory, '91 by Random Century Audiobooks. Note: 2 Cassettes. ISBN No: 1856560082

CHRISTMAS CAROL, A (Unknown narrator(s)).
MC. Cat no: **LFP 41 7176 5**. Released on Listen For Pleasure, Oct '84 by EMI Records.
MC. Cat no: **TS 318**. Released on Tellastory, Dec '86 by Random Century Audiobooks.
MCSET. Cat no: **DTO 10583**. Released on Ditto, Jan '89 by Pickwick Records, Midland Records.
MCSET. Cat no: **1854960776**. Released on Trio, '91 by EMI Records. Note: 3 Cassettes.

CHRISTMAS CAROL, A (Martin Jarvis & Denise Briars).
Tracks / Christmas Eve / Marley's ghost / Christmas past / Christmas past, Christmas present / Cratchits' Christmas, The / Final visions, The / Scrooge perplexed / God bless us, every one.
MCSET. Cat no: **ZBBC 1033**. Released on BBC, Sep '88 by BBC Records, Taylors. Note: ISBN No: 0563 225734.

CHRISTMAS CAROL, A (Children's Classics) (Unknown narrator(s)).
Note: Book and cassette.
MC. Cat no: **PLBC 137**. Released on Tell-A-Tale, '88 by Pickwick Records, Taylors, Clyde Factors.

DAVID COPPERFIELD (Anthony Homyer).
MCSET. Cat no: **TCL 24**. Released on Complete Listener, '91 by Complete Listener. Note: 26 Cassettes. (BB) Playing Time: 2.310 Minutes.
MCSET. Cat no: **1101/2/3C**. Released on Travellers Tales, '91 by Travellers Tales. Note: 26 Cassettes.

DAVID COPPERFIELD (Peter Emmens).
MCSET. Cat no: **1870524403**. Re-leased on Eloquent Reels, '91, Bond Street Music, Morley Audio Services. Note: 4 cassettes.

DAVID COPPERFIELD (Roger Rees).
MC. Cat no: **1706**. Released on Caedmon (USA), Apr '83 by Caedmon Records (USA), Bond Street Music.

DAVID COPPERFIELD (Roy Dotrice).
Note: Abridged.
MCSET. Cat no: **1019C**. Released on Travellers Tales, '91 by Travellers Tales. Note: 2 cassettes.

DAVID COPPERFIELD (Paul Scofield).
Note: Also available on hanging format, catalogue number:- 000138855.
MCSET. Cat no: **0001388150**. Released on Harper Collins, '91 by Harper Collins. Note: 2 Cassettes.

DAVID COPPERFIELD (Anton Rodgers).
MCSET. Cat no: **LFP 7346**. Released on Listen For Pleasure, Sep '88 by EMI Records.

EXCERPTS FROM CHRISTMAS STORIES (Emlyn Williams).
MCSET. Cat no: **SAY 71**. Released on Argo (Polygram), Jun '88 by PolyGram Classics **Deleted** Jan '89.
MCSET. Cat no: **1020C**. Released on Travellers Tales, '91 by Travellers Tales. Note: 2 Cassettes.

GREAT EXPECTATIONS (Richard Pasco).
MC. Cat no: **0600560457**. Released on Hamlyn Books On Tape, '88, Bond Street Music.

GREAT EXPECTATIONS (Peter Jeffrey).
Note: Abridged.
MCSET. Cat no: **ARGO 1172**. Released on Argo (EMI), Oct '89 by EMI Records. Note: 2 Cassettes. Playing time 2 hours 15 minutes.
MCSET. Cat no: **414 709-4**. Released on Argo (Polygram), Sep '88 by PolyGram Classics **Deleted** Jan '89.
MCSET. Cat no: **1059C**. Released on Travellers Tales, '91 by Travellers Tales. Note: 2 Cassettes.

GREAT EXPECTATIONS (Martin Jarvis).
MCSET. Cat no: **CTC 010**. Released on Cover to Cover, '87 by Cover to Cover Cassettes. Note: 13 cassettes. Playing time: 17 hrs 30 mins.
MCSET. Cat no: **1021/1022C**. Released on Travellers Tales, '91 by Travellers Tales. Note: 2 Cassettes.

HARD TIMES (Peter Jeffrey).
MCSET. Cat no: **418 042-4**. Released on Argo (Polygram), Jun '88 by PolyGram Classics **Deleted** Jan '89.
MCSET. Cat no: **ARGO 1217**. Released on Argo (EMI), Jul '90 by EMI Records. Note: 2 Cassettes.
MCSET. Cat no: **1079C**. Released on Travellers Tales, '91 by Travellers Tales.

HARD TIMES (Various artists).
MC. Cat no: **TTT 832**. Released on Tale To Tell, '91 by Morley Audio Services.

HARD TIMES (Stephen Thorne).
MCSET. Cat no: **CC/019**. Released on Cover to Cover, '87 by Cover to Cover Cassettes.
MCSET. Cat no: **1023/1024C**. Released on Travellers Tales, '91 by Travellers Tales. Note: 9 cassettes.

NICHOLAS NICKELBY (Anthony Homyer).
MCSET. Cat no: **TCL 26**. Released on Complete Listener, '91 by Complete Listener. Note: 7 Cassettes. (BB) Playing Time: 2,430 Minutes.

NICHOLAS NICKLEBY (Roger Rees).
MC. Cat no: **CP 1702**. Released on Caedmon (USA), Sep '82 by Caedmon Records (USA), Bond Street Music.
MCSET. Cat no: **SAY 77**. Released on Argo (Polygram), Nov '82 by PolyGram Classics **Deleted** Jan '89.
MCSET. Cat no: **ARGO 1049**. Released on Argo (EMI), May '89 by EMI Records. Note: 2 Cassettes.
MCSET. Cat no: **1025C**. Released on Travellers Tales, '91 by Travellers Tales.

NICHOLAS NICKLEBY (Paul Scofield).
MCSET. Cat no: **0001072994**. Released on Harper Collins, '91 by Harper Collins. Note: 2 Cassettes.

OLIVER TWIST (Children's Classics) (Unknown narrator(s)).
Note: Book and cassette.
MC. Cat no: **PLBC 195**. Released on Tell-A-Tale, '88 by Pickwick Records, Taylors, Clyde Factors.

OLIVER TWIST (Four Chapters) (Anthony Quayle).
MC. Cat no: **1484**. Released on Caedmon (USA), '88 by Caedmon Records (USA), Bond Street Music.
MCSET. Cat no: **TCL 23**. Released on Complete Listener, '91 by Complete Listener.
MCSET. Cat no: **1098/1099C**. Released on Travellers Tales, '91 by Travellers Tales.

OLIVER TWIST (Paul Scofield).
Note: Also available on hanging format, catalogue number:- 0001388371.
MCSET. Cat no: **0001388177**. Released on Harper Collins, '91 by Harper Collins. Note: 2 Cassettes.

OLIVER TWIST (Ron Moody).
MCSET. Cat no: **LFP 7580**. Released on Listen For Pleasure, Feb '92 by EMI Records.

PICKWICK PAPERS (Julian Orchard).
MC. Cat no: **P 90011**. Released on Pinnacle, '79 by Pinnacle Records, Outlet Records, Music Sales Records.

PICKWICK PAPERS (Paul Scofield).

MCSET. Cat no: **0001388134**. Released on Harper Collins, '91 by Harper Collins. Note: 2 Cassettes.

PICKWICK PAPERS (Anthony Homyer).
MCSET. Cat no: **1104/5/6C**. Released on Travellers Tales, '91 by Travellers Tales.

MCSET. Cat no: **TCL 25**. Released on Complete Listener, '91 by Complete Listener. Note: 6 Cassettes. (BB)

SIGNALMAN, THE (And To Be Read At Dusk) (Various artists).
MC. Cat no: **TS 355**. Released on Tellastory, Apr '88 by Random Century Audiobooks.

TALE OF TWO CITIES, A (Volume 1) (Charles Dance).
MCSET. Cat no: **ZBBC 1074**. Released on BBC Radio Collection, Jun '89 by BBC Records. Note: ISBN No: 0563 226447

TALE OF TWO CITIES, A (Volume 2) (Charles Dance).
MCSET. Cat no: **ZBBC 1075**. Released on BBC Radio Collection, Jul '89 by BBC Records. Note: ISBN No: 0563 410302

TALE OF TWO CITIES, A (Richard Pasco).
MCSET. Cat no: **CTC 037**. Released on Cover to Cover, '87 by Cover to Cover Cassettes. Note: 11 cassettes. Playing time: 14 hrs 35 mins.

MCSET. Cat no: **1061/1062C**. Released on Travellers Tales, '91 by Travellers Tales. Note: 11 cassettes.

TALE OF TWO CITIES, A (James Mason).
MCSET. Cat no: **2079**. Released on Caedmon (USA), '88 by Caedmon Records (USA), Bond Street Music.

TALE OF TWO CITIES, A (John Carson).
MCSET. Cat no: **TCLFP 7059**. Released on Listen For Pleasure, '80 by EMI Records **Deleted** '85.

MCSET. Cat no: **LFP 7412**. Released on Listen For Pleasure, Jul '89 by EMI Records.

TALE OF TWO CITIES, A (Sir John Gielgud).
Note: Abridged version.
MCSET. Cat no: **1028C**. Released on Travellers Tales, '91 by Travellers Tales. Note: 2 cassettes.

MCSET. Cat no: **4147214**. Released on Argo (Polygram), '91 by PolyGram Classics.

TALE OF TWO CITIES, A (Unknown narrator(s)).
MCSET. Cat no: **1854960784**. Released on Soundings, '91 by Soundings Records, Bond Street Music. Note: 12 Cassettes.

Dickens, Monica

CLOSED AT DUSK (Eleanor Bron).
MCSET. Cat no: **CAB 521**. Released on Chivers Audio Books, '91 by Chivers Audio Books, Green Dragon Audio Visual. Note: 6 Cassettes

MCSET. Cat no: **1609T**. Released on Travellers Tales, '91 by Travellers Tales. Note: 6 Cassettes.

ENCHANTMENT (Jane Asher).
MCSET. Cat no: **1518F**. Released on Travellers Tales, '91 by Travellers Tales. Note: 5 cassettes.

MCSET. Cat no: **IAB 90082**. Released on Isis Audio Books, '91. Note: 5 Cassettes.

HAPPY PRISONER, THE (Sheila Mitchell).
MCSET. Cat no: **IAB 92081**. Released on Isis Audio Books, Aug '92. Note: 10 Cassettes. Playing time: 13 hours, 12 mins.

LAST YEAR WHEN I WAS YOUNG (Hywel Bennett).
MC. Cat no: **CAB 015**. Released on Chivers Audio Books, May '81 by Chivers Audio Books, Green Dragon Audio Visual.

MCSET. Cat no: **1038F**. Released on Travellers Tales, '91 by Travellers Tales. Note: 6 cassettes

MARIANA (Unknown narrator(s)).
MCSET. Cat no: **IAB 92023**. Released on Isis Audio Books, Feb '92. Note: 10 cassettes. Playing time 12hrs 45mins.

Dickinson, Emily

POEMS AND LETTERS (Julie Harris).
MC. Cat no: **1119**. Released on Caedmon (USA), '88 by Caedmon Records (USA), Bond Street Music.

SELF PORTRAIT, A (Julie Harris).
MCSET. Cat no: **2026**. Released on Caedmon (USA), '88 by Caedmon Records (USA), Bond Street Music. Note: 2 cassettes

Dickinson, Peter

BOX OF NOTHING, A (Gordon Fairclough).
MCSET. Cat no: **3CCA 3048**. Released on Chivers Audio Books, '91 by Chivers Audio Books, Green Dragon Audio Visual. Note: 3 Cassettes.

MCSET. Cat no: **9118F**. Released on Travellers Tales, '91 by Travellers Tales. Note: 3 Cassettes.

HINDSIGHT (Joe Dunlop).
MCSET. Cat no: **1466T**. Released on Travellers Tales, '91 by Travellers Tales. Note: 6 Cassettes.

MCSET. Cat no: **OAS 89073**. Released on Oasis Audio Books, '91 by Isis Audio Books. Note: 6 Cassettes.

PERFECT GALLOWS (Stephen Thorne).
MCSET. Cat no: **1373T**. Released on Travellers Tales, '91 by Travellers Tales. Note: 8 Cassettes.

MCSET. Cat no: **IAB 88102**. Released on Isis Audio Books, '91.

Dickson, Carter

AND SO TO MURDER (Nigel Lambert).

MCSET. Cat no: **CAT 4039**. Released on Chivers Audio Books, '91 by Chivers Audio Books, Green Dragon Audio Visual. Note: 6 Cassettes.

MCSET. Cat no: **1430T**. Released on Travellers Tales, '91 by Travellers Tales. Note: 6 Cassettes.

Digance, Richard

COMMERCIAL ROAD (Richard Digance).
Tracks / Suicide Sam / Jungle cup final / East End ding dong / Think of me / Jumping Jack frog / Nightingale sang in Berkeley Square, A / Beauty queen / Goodbye my friend / Goodbye heavyweight Albert / Backstreet international / Jimmy Greaves.
LP. Cat no: **CHR 1262**. Released on Chrysalis, Nov '79 by EMI Records, Solomon & Peres.

MC. Cat no: **ZCHR 1262**. Released on Chrysalis, '83 by EMI Records, Solomon & Peres.

HOMEWORK (Richard Digance).
LP. Cat no: **COASTAL 5**. Released on Coast, Jul '84 by Coast Records, Roots Records **Deleted** '88.

Disney

101 DALMATIANS (Unknown narrator(s)).
MC. Cat no: **DIS 018**. Released on Disney (Read-a-long), '92 by Disneyland Records.

ARISTOCATS, THE (Unknown narrator(s)).
MC. Cat no: **DIS 012**. Released on Disney (Read-a-long), Apr '91 by Disneyland Records.

DONALD'S POOCH PARLOUR (Various artists).
MC. Cat no: **DIS 026**. Released on Disney, May '91.

DUCKTAILS (Dinosaur Ducks) (Unknown narrator(s)).
MC. Cat no: **DIS 025**. Released on Pickwick, Jun '91 by Pickwick Records, Clyde Factors, Taylors, Arabesque, Solomon & Peres, I & B Records, Prism Leisure, Outlet Records.

DUMBO (Unknown narrator(s)).
MC. Cat no: **DIS 019**. Released on Disney (Read-a-long), Sep '90 by Disneyland Records.

LADY AND THE TRAMP (Unknown narrator(s)).
MC. Cat no: **DIS 011**. Released on Disney (Read-a-long), Apr '91 by Disneyland Records.

LADY AND THE TRAMP (Prunella Scales).
MCSET. Cat no: **UNKNOWN**. Released on Whinfrey Strachan, Jan '85 **Deleted** '86.

LADY AND THE TRAMP (Various artists).
MLP. Cat no: **D 307**. Released on Disneyland, Dec '82 by Disneyland-Vista Records (USA).

MC. Cat no: **D 22DC**. Released on Disneyland, Dec '82 by Disneyland-

141

Vista Records (USA).
LP. Cat no: **D 3917**. Released on Disneyland, '83 by Disneyland-Vista Records (USA) **Deleted** '88.

LPPD. Cat no: **D 3103**. Released on Disneyland, '83 by Disneyland-Vista Records (USA) **Deleted** '88.

OLIVER AND COMPANY (Unknown narrator(s)).
MC. Cat no: **DIS 010**. Released on Disney (Read-a-long), Jul '90 by Disneyland Records.

RESCUERS, THE (Unknown narrator(s)).
MC. Cat no: **DIS 017**. Released on Disney (Read-a-long), '92 by Disneyland Records.

SEVEN DWARFS AND THEIR DIAMOND MINE (Various artists).
EP. Cat no: **D 314**. Released on Disneyland, Apr '81 by Disneyland-Vista Records (USA). Note: Includes book

THUMPER'S RACE (Various artists).
EP. Cat no: **D 343**. Released on Disneyland, Apr '81 by Disneyland-Vista Records (USA).

WALT DISNEY STORIES FOR CHILDREN (Various artists).
Tracks / Peter and the wolf: *Various artists* / Mickey and the beanstalk: *Various artists* / Fee fi fo fum: *Various artists* / My favourite dream: *Various artists* / My what a happy day: *Various artists* / Three little pigs: *Various artists* / Who's afraid of the big bad wolf: *Various artists* / Little engine that could, The: *Various artists.*
LP. Cat no: **GH 858**. Released on Golden Hour, Jan '77, Outlet Records **Deleted** '80.

Dobbs, Michael
HOUSE OF CARDS (Peter Joyce).
MCSET. Cat no: **1547/1548F**. Released on Travellers Tales, '91 by Travellers Tales. Note: 10 cassettes.

MCSET. Cat no: **1854963643**. Released on Soundings, '91 by Soundings Records, Bond Street Music. Note: 10 Cassettes.

TO PLAY THE KING (Paul Eddington).
MCSET. Cat no: **0001046489**. Released on Harper Collins, Mar '92 by Harper Collins.

WALL GAMES (Gordon Griffin).
MCSET. Cat no: **1745/1746T**. Released on Travellers Tales, '91 by Travellers Tales. Note: 9 Cassettes.

MCSET. Cat no: **1854964380**. Released on Soundings, '91 by Soundings Records, Bond Street Music. Note: 9 Cassettes.

Doddington, Paula
SEPARATION (Eve Karpf).
MCSET. Cat no: **MRC 1042**. Released on Chivers Moonlight Romances, Apr '88 by Chivers Audio Books, Green Dragon Audio Visual. Note: 2 cassette set

Dodge, Mary M.
SILVER SKATES, THE (Claire Bloom).
MC. Cat no: **1493**. Released on Caedmon (USA), '88 by Caedmon Records (USA), Bond Street Music.

Doherty, Berlie
GRANNY WAS A BUFFER GIRL (Berlie Doherty).
MCSET. Cat no: **3CCA 3053**. Released on Chivers Audio Books, '91 by Chivers Audio Books, Green Dragon Audio Visual. Note: 3 Cassettes.

Donne, John
LOVE POEMS OF JOHN DONNE, THE (Richard Burton).
MC. Cat no: **41**. Released on Caedmon (USA), '88 by Caedmon Records (USA), Bond Street Music.

Dostoevsky, Fyodor
CRIME AND PUNISHMENT (Excerpts From) (James Mason).
MC. Cat no: **1691**. Released on Caedmon (USA), '88 by Caedmon Records (USA), Bond Street Music.

Douglas, Gavin
COMMENTARY AND CHOICE (Various artists).
Note: Readers are Jack Aitken (editor of DOST), David Munson (editor of SND) and Thomas Crawford.
MC. Cat no: **SSC 042**. Released on Scotsoun, '91 by Scotsoun Recordings, Morley Audio Services.

Douglas, George
HOUSE WITH THE GREEN SHUTTERS (Tom Watson).
MCSET. Cat no: **COL 4001**. Released on Colophone, Feb '81 by AVLS (Audio-Visual Library Services).

HOUSE WITH THE GREEN SHUTTERS (Tom Watson).
Note: Abridged version.
MCSET. Cat no: **1039F**. Released on Travellers Tales, '91 by Travellers Tales. Note: 4 cassettes.

Douglas Wiggin, Kate
REBECCA OF SUNNYBROOK FARM (Julie Harris).
MC. Cat no: **CDL 51637**. Released on Caedmon (USA), Feb '81 by Caedmon Records (USA), Bond Street Music.
LP. Cat no: **TC 1637**. Released on Caedmon (USA), Sep '80 by Caedmon Records (USA), Bond Street Music.

Drabble, Margaret
GARRICK YEAR, THE (Mel Martin).
MCSET. Cat no: **1243F**. Released on Travellers Tales, '91 by Travellers Tales. Note: 6 cassettes.

SUMMER BIRDCAGE, A (Paula Wilcox).
MCSET. Cat no: **1040F**. Released on Travellers Tales, '91 by Travellers Tales. Note: 6 cassettes.

Dracup, Angela
BAVARIAN OVERTURE (Eve Karpf).
MCSET. Cat no: **MRC 1057**. Released on Chivers Audio Books, '91 by Chivers Audio Books, Green Dragon Audio Visual. Note: 2 cassettes.

Driscoll, Jim
SHOE PEOPLE, THE (PC Boot Takes Charge) (Philip Whitchurch).
MC. Cat no: **00 1021869**. Released on Tempo, '88 by Warwick Records, Celtic Music, Henry Hadaway Organisation.

SHOE PEOPLE, THE (Trampy's Rainbow Surprise) (Philip Whitchurch).
MC. Cat no: **00 1021850**. Released on Tempo, '88 by Warwick Records, Celtic Music, Henry Hadaway Organisation.

Driver, Grace
ENGLISH GIRL, THE (Unknown narrator(s)).
MCSET. Cat no: **1854964402**. Released on Bramhope, '91 by Ulverscroft Soundings. Note: 4 cassettes.

LADY OF THE QUINTA (Judeth Franklyn).
MCSET. Cat no: **1854964607**. Released on Bramhope, Jun '91 by Ulverscroft Soundings. Note: 4 Cassettes.

SHOWER OF GOLD (Jean Waggoner).
MCSET. Cat no: **MRC 1062**. Released on Chivers Audio Books, '91 by Chivers Audio Books, Green Dragon Audio Visual. Note: 2 cassettes

Du Maurier, Daphne
DON'T LOOK NOW / THE BIRDS / OTHER ECHOES FROM THE MACABRE (Valentine Dyall).
MCSET. Cat no: **1189T**. Released on Travellers Tales, '91 by Travellers Tales. Note: 4 Cassettes.

FRENCHMAN'S CREEK (John Castle).
MCSET. Cat no: **CTC 021**. Released on Cover to Cover, '87 by Cover to Cover Cassettes. Note: 6 cassettes. Playing time: 8 hrs 50 mins.

MCSET. Cat no: **1043T**. Released on Travellers Tales, '91 by Travellers Tales. Note: 6 Cassettes.

FRENCHMAN'S CREEK (Daniel Massey).
MCSET. Cat no: **RC 27**. Released on Random Century, Apr '92 by Random Century Audiobooks, Conifer Records. Note: ISBN no. 185686099X

FRENCHMAN'S CREEK (Lorna Heilbron & Struan Rodger).
2LP. Cat no: **ZBBC 1106**. Released on BBC Radio Collection, May '90 by BBC Records. Note: ISBN No: 0563 410035

MCSET. Cat no: **0563410035**. Released on BBC Radio Collection, '91 by BBC Records. Note: 2 cassettes

JAMAICA INN (Unknown narrator(s)).
MCSET. Cat no: **RC 60**. Released on

Random Century, Jun '92 by Random Century Audiobooks, Conifer Records. Note: ISBN no. 1856860876

JAMAICA INN (Trevor Eve).
Note: Abridged.
MCSET. Cat no: **LFP 7114**. Released on Listen For Pleasure, Apr '83 by EMI Records.
MCSET. Cat no: **1044T**. Released on Travellers Tales, '91 by Travellers Tales. Note: 2 Cassettes.

MY COUSIN RACHEL (Mel Gibson).
Note: Also available on hanging format, catalogue number:- 0001035398.
MCSET. Cat no: **HCA 23**. Released on Harper Collins, '92 by Harper Collins.
MCSET. Cat no: **2095**. Released on Harper Collins, '92 by Harper Collins.

MY COUSIN RACHEL (Jonathan Price).
MCSET. Cat no: **CAB 378**. Released on Chivers Audio Books, '91 by Chivers Audio Books, Green Dragon Audio Visual. Note: 8 Cassettes
MCSET. Cat no: **1424T**. Released on Travellers Tales, '91 by Travellers Tales.

MY COUSIN RACHEL (Unknown narrator(s)).
MC. Cat no: **RC 22**. Released on Random Century, '91 by Random Century Audiobooks, Conifer Records.

REBECCA (Juliet Stevenson).
MCSET. Cat no: **RC 47**. Released on Random Century, Apr '92 by Random Century Audiobooks, Conifer Records. Note: ISBN no. 1856860973

REBECCA (Claire Bloom).
MCSET. Cat no: **TC FP 417118-5**. Released on Listen For Pleasure, '83 by EMI Records.

RENDEZVOUZ, THE (And Other Short Stories) (Edward De Souza).
MCSET. Cat no: **1368T**. Released on Travellers Tales, '91 by Travellers Tales. Note: 8 Cassettes.
MCSET. Cat no: **CAB 341**. Released on Chivers Audio Books, '88 by Chivers Audio Books, Green Dragon Audio Visual.

Duce, Joan
I REMEMBER, I REMEMBER (118 Favourite Poems) (Various artists).
MCSET. Cat no: **IAB 87115**. Released on Isis Audio Books, '91. Note: 4 cassette set.

Duffus, George
STANDING ROOM ONLY (George Duffus).
Tracks / It's George / Sex equality / Holidays / Ballad of Glencoe / Red cross / Capricorn / David and Goliath / Winning the pools / Earnin' a shillin' / Rubber legs / Scotland's oil / CB mad man.
LP. Cat no: **LILP 5121**. Released on Lismor, Nov '82 by Lismor Records, Duncans, Roots Records, Lismor Records, Outlet Records, Conifer Records, C.M. Distribution, Record Services.
MC. Cat no: **LICS 5121**. Released on Lismor, Nov '82 by Lismor Records, Duncans, Roots Records, Lismor Records, Outlet Records, Conifer Records, C.M. Distribution, Record Services.

Duke, Madelaine
DEATH AT THE WEDDING (Unknown narrator(s)).
MCSET. Cat no: **1854962787**. Released on Bramhope, '91 by Ulverscroft Soundings. Note: 4 cassettes.

DEATH OF A DANDIE DINMONT (Unknown narrator(s)).
MCSET. Cat no: **1854962493**. Released on Trio, '91 by EMI Records. Note: 3 cassettes.

DEATH OF A HOLY MURDERER (Sarah Newton).
MCSET. Cat no: **1379F**. Released on Travellers Tales, '91 by Travellers Tales. Note: 3 cassettes.
MCSET. Cat no: **1854962388**. Released on Trio, '91 by EMI Records. Note: 3 Cassettes.

ONCE IN AUSTRIA (Unknown narrator(s)).
MCSET. Cat no: **1854960792**. Released on Trio, '91 by EMI Records. Note: 3 cassettes.

Dumas, Alexandre
BLACK TULIP, THE (Morag Hood).
Note: Abridged version.
MCSET. Cat no: **1450F**. Released on Travellers Tales, '91 by Travellers Tales. Note: 4 cassettes.
MCSET. Cat no: **SPF 190-2**. Released on Schiltron Audio Books, '91 by Schiltron Publishing. Note: (MM)

COUNT OF MONTE CRISTO (Paul Daneman).
MC. Cat no: **BKK 403**. Released on Kiddy Kassettes, Aug '77.

COUNT OF MONTE CRISTO (Louis Jordan).
LP. Cat no: **TC 1554**. Released on Caedmon (USA), Jan '78 by Caedmon Records (USA), Bond Street Music.
MC. Cat no: **CDL 51554**. Released on Caedmon (USA), Jan '78 by Caedmon Records (USA), Bond Street Music.

COUNT OF MONTE CRISTO, THE (John Sheddon).
Note: Abridged version.
MCSET. Cat no: **1361F**. Released on Travellers Tales, '91 by Travellers Tales. Note: 4 cassettes
MCSET. Cat no: **SPF 190-1**. Released on Schiltron Audio Books, '91 by Schiltron Publishing. Note: 4 cassettes. Playing time 6 hours.

THREE MUSKETEERS, THE (Chapters 1-5) (Michael York).
MC. Cat no: **1692**. Released on Caedmon (USA), '88 by Caedmon Records (USA), Bond Street Music.

THREE MUSKETEERS, THE (Children's Classics) (Unknown narrator(s)).
MC. Cat no: **PLBC 78**. Released on Tell-A-Tale, '88 by Pickwick Records, Taylors, Clyde Factors.
Note: Book and cassette.

Dunbar, William
SELECTIONS (Various artists).
Note: Selected and introduced by Edwin Morgan. Other readers are Carol-Ann Crawford, Barbara Douglas, Eleanor Aitken, Dr Jack Aitken, Robert Garioch and Alexander Scott.
MC. Cat no: **SSC 020**. Released on Scotsoun, '91 by Scotsoun Recordings, Morley Audio Services.

Duncan, Alex
DIARY OF A COUNTRY DOCTOR (Brian Rapkin).
MCSET. Cat no: **1393F**. Released on Travellers Tales, '91 by Travellers Tales. Note: 5 cassettes.
MCSET. Cat no: **1854962507**. Released on Bramhope, '91 by Ulverscroft Soundings. Note: 5 Cassettes.

DOCTOR'S AFFAIRS ALL TOLD, THE (Christopher Kay).
MCSET. Cat no: **1597F**. Released on Travellers Tales, '91 by Travellers Tales. Note: 4 cassettes.
MCSET. Cat no: **1854963805**. Released on Bramhope, '91 by Ulverscroft Soundings. Note: 4 Cassettes.

GOD AND THE DOCTOR (Christopher Kay).
MCSET. Cat no: **1603F**. Released on Travellers Tales, '91 by Travellers Tales. Note: 4 cassettes.
MCSET. Cat no: **1854964011**. Released on Bramhope, '91 by Ulverscroft Soundings. Note: 4 Cassettes.

VET AMONG THE PIGEONS (Unknown narrator(s)).
MCSET. Cat no: **1854964267**. Released on Trio, '91 by EMI Records. Note: 3 cassette.

VET HAS NINE LIVES, THE (Various artists).
MCSET. Cat no: **SOUND 40**. Released on Soundings, Feb '85 by Soundings Records, Bond Street Music.
MCSET. Cat no: **1006N**. Released on Travellers Tales, '91 by Travellers Tales. Note: 4 Cassettes.

VET IN THE MANGER (Unknown narrator(s)).
MCSET. Cat no: **1854964151**. Released on Trio, '91 by EMI Records. Note: 3 cassettes.

VET'S CHOICE (Hazel Temperley).
MCSET. Cat no: **1594F**. Released on Travellers Tales, '91 by Travellers Tales. Note: 3 cassettes.
MCSET. Cat no: **1854963759**. Released on Trio, '91 by EMI Records. Note: 3 cassettes.

VET'S IN CONGRESS (Unknown narrator(s)).
MCSET. Cat no: **185496268X**. Re-

leased on Trio, '91 by EMI Records. Note: 3 cassettes.

VETS IN THE BELFRY (Brian Rapkin).
MCSET. Cat no: **1438F**. Released on Travellers Tales, '91 by Travellers Tales. Note: 4 cassettes.
MCSET. Cat no: **1045H**. Released on Travellers Tales, '91 by Travellers Tales. Note: 4 cassettes
MCSET. Cat no: **1854962590**. Released on Bramhope, '91 by Ulverscroft Soundings. Note: 4 Cassettes.

Dunkling, Leslie
BATTLE OF NEWTON ROAD (And Kate And The Clock) (Unknown narrator(s)).
MC. Cat no: **058252671X**. Released on Longman/Pickwick, '91 by Pickwick Records. Note: 2 cassette set.

Dunne, Dominick
TWO MRS. GRENVILLES, THE (F. Murray Abraham).
MCSET. Cat no: **0671640097**. Released on Simon & Schuster, '91 by Simon & Schuster Ltd. Note: 2 Cassettes

Duras, Marguerite
LOVER, THE (Leslie Caron).
MCSET. Cat no: **0671641050**. Released on Simon & Schuster, '91 by Simon & Schuster Ltd. Note: 2 Cassettes

Durbridge, Francis
PAUL TEMPLE AND THE CONRAD CASE (Various artists).
MCSET. Cat no: **ZBBC 1032**. Released on BBC Radio Collection, Apr '89 by BBC Records. Note: ISBN No: 0563 209852

Durham, John
APACHE MOON (David Horne).
MCSET. Cat no: **SOUND 5**. Released on Soundings, Mar '85 by Soundings Records, Bond Street Music. Note: 4 Cassettes.
MCSET. Cat no: **1006W**. Released on Travellers Tales, '91 by Travellers Tales. Note: 4 Cassettes.

Durrell, Gerald
BAFUT BEAGLES, THE (Nigel Davenport).
MCSET. Cat no: **CAB 484**. Released on Chivers Audio Books, '91 by Chivers Audio Books, Green Dragon Audio Visual. Note: 6 Cassettes.
MCSET. Cat no: **1052H**. Released on Travellers Tales, '91 by Travellers Tales. Note: 6 cassettes.
BEASTS IN MY BELFRY (Nigel Davenport).
MCSET. Cat no: **CAB 270**. Released on Chivers Audio Books, '91 by Chivers Audio Books, Green Dragon Audio Visual. Note: 6 Cassettes.
MCSET. Cat no: **1030H**. Released on Travellers Tales, '91 by Travellers Tales. Note: 6 cassettes.

BIRDS, BEASTS AND RELATIVES (Nigel Davenport).
MCSET. Cat no: **CAB 166**. Released on Chivers Audio Books, '91 by Chivers Audio Books, Green Dragon Audio Visual. Note: 6 Cassettes.
MCSET. Cat no: **1026H**. Released on Travellers Tales, '91 by Travellers Tales. Note: 6 cassettes.
FILLETS OF PLAICE (Nigel Davenport).
MCSET. Cat no: **CAB 379**. Released on Chivers Audio Books, '91 by Chivers Audio Books, Green Dragon Audio Visual. Note: 6 Cassettes.
MCSET. Cat no: **1043H**. Released on Travellers Tales, '91 by Travellers Tales. Note: 6 cassettes.
GARDEN OF THE GODS, THE (Christopher Timothy).
MCSET. Cat no: **1003H**. Released on Travellers Tales, '91 by Travellers Tales. Note: 6 cassettes
PICNIC AND SUCHLIKE PANDEMONIUM, THE (Nigel Davenport).
MCSET. Cat no: **1024H**. Released on Travellers Tales, '91 by Travellers Tales. Note: 4 cassettes.

Dwyer-Joyce, Alice
MOONLIT WAY, THE (Unknown narrator(s)).
MCSET. Cat no: **1854962876**. Released on Bramhope, '91 by Ulverscroft Soundings. Note: 4 cassettes.

Dyall, Valentine
ECHOES FROM THE MACABRE (Valentine Dyall).
MC. Cat no: **CAB 008**. Released on Chivers Audio Books, May '81 by Chivers Audio Books, Green Dragon Audio Visual.

Eberhart, Mignon G
FIVE PASSENGERS FROM LISBON (Pat Starr).
MCSET. Cat no: **CAT 4059**. Released on Chivers Audio Books, '91 by Chivers Audio Books, Green Dragon Audio Visual. Note: 6 Cassettes.
MCSET. Cat no: **1610T**. Released on Travellers Tales, '91 by Travellers Tales. Note: 6 cassettes.
TWO LITTLE RICH GIRLS (Kate Harper).
MCSET. Cat no: **CAT 4062**. Released on Chivers Audio Books, '91 by Chivers Audio Books, Green Dragon Audio Visual. Note: 6 Cassettes.
MCSET. Cat no: **1729T**. Released on Travellers Tales, '91 by Travellers Tales. Note: 6 cassettes.

Eberhart, Richard
RICHARD EBERHART READING (Richard Eberhart).
MC. Cat no: **1243**. Released on Caedmon (USA), '88 by Caedmon Records (USA), Bond Street Music.

Eccles, Marjorie
DEATH OF A GOOD WOMAN (Unknown narrator(s)).

MCSET. Cat no: **185496528X**. Released on Bramhope, '91 by Ulverscroft Soundings. Note: 5 cassettes.

Eden, Dorothy
AFTERNOON FOR LIZARDS (Angela Down).
MCSET. Cat no: **1854965395**. Released on Bramhope, Jan '92 by Ulverscroft Soundings.
AMERICAN HEIRESS, THE (Liza Ross).
MCSET. Cat no: **1854965514**. Released on Soundings, Feb '92 by Soundings Records, Bond Street Music. Note: 7 cassettes.
BELLA (Jane Jermyn).
MCSET. Cat no: **1028R**. Released on Travellers Tales, '91 by Travellers Tales. Note: 6 Cassettes.
MCSET. Cat no: **1854960849**. Released on Soundings, '91 by Soundings Records, Bond Street Music. Note: 6 Cassettes.
DEADLY TRAVELLERS, THE (Rowena Cooper).
MCSET. Cat no: **CAB 555**. Released on Chivers Audio Books, '91 by Chivers Audio Books, Green Dragon Audio Visual. Note: 6 cassettes.
MCSET. Cat no: **1618F**. Released on Travellers Tales, '91 by Travellers Tales. Note: 6 cassettes.
DEATH IS A RED ROSE (Delia Corrie).
MCSET. Cat no: **1029R**. Released on Travellers Tales, '91 by Travellers Tales. Note: 4 Cassettes.
MCSET. Cat no: **1854960857**. Released on Bramhope, '91 by Ulverscroft Soundings. Note: 4 Cassettes.
LAMB TO THE SLAUGHTER (Rowena Cooper).
MCSET. Cat no: **CAB 622**. Released on Chivers Audio Books, Sep '91 by Chivers Audio Books, Green Dragon Audio Visual. Note: 6 Cassettes.
MARRIAGE CHEST, THE (Rowena Cooper).
MCSET. Cat no: **CAB 490**. Released on Chivers Audio Books, '91 by Chivers Audio Books, Green Dragon Audio Visual. Note: 6 Cassettes.
MCSET. Cat no: **1564T**. Released on Travellers Tales, '91 by Travellers Tales.
MILLIONAIRE'S DAUGHTER (Pat Starr).
MCSET. Cat no: **CAB 153**. Released on Chivers Audio Books, '91 by Chivers Audio Books, Green Dragon Audio Visual. Note: 8 Cassettes.
MCSET. Cat no: **1043F**. Released on Travellers Tales, '91 by Travellers Tales. Note: 8 cassettes.
SAMANTHA (Rowena Cooper).
MCSET. Cat no: **CAB 396**. Released on Chivers Audio Books, '91 by Chivers Audio Books, Green Dragon Audio Visual. Note: 6 Cassettes
MCSET. Cat no: **1394F**. Released on

Travellers Tales, '91 by Travellers Tales. Note: 6 cassettes.

SPEAK TO ME OF LOVE (Rowena Cooper).
MCSET. Cat no: **CAB 452**. Released on Chivers Audio Books, '91 by Chivers Audio Books, Green Dragon Audio Visual. Note: 8 cassettes.
MCSET. Cat no: **1451F**. Released on Travellers Tales, '91 by Travellers Tales. Note: 8 cassettes.

STORRINGTON PAPERS, THE (Delia Corrie).
MCSET. Cat no: **CAB 230**. Released on Chivers Audio Books, '91 by Chivers Audio Books, Green Dragon Audio Visual. Note: 6 cassettes.
MCSET. Cat no: **1211F**. Released on Travellers Tales, '91 by Travellers Tales. Note: 6 cassettes.

VOICE OF THE DOLLS, THE (Rowena Cooper).
MC. Cat no: **CAB 322**. Released on Chivers Audio Books, '88 by Chivers Audio Books, Green Dragon Audio Visual. Note: 6 cassettes.
MCSET. Cat no: **1360T**. Released on Travellers Tales, '91 by Travellers Tales. Note: 6 Cassettes.

WAITING FOR WILLA (Claire Bloom).
MC. Cat no: **CAB 023**. Released on Chivers Audio Books, Apr '81 by Chivers Audio Books, Green Dragon Audio Visual. Note: 4 Cassettes.
MCSET. Cat no: **1044F**. Released on Travellers Tales, '91 by Travellers Tales. Note: 4 cassettes.

WHISTLE FOR THE CROWS (Rowena Cooper).
MCSET. Cat no: **CAB 353**. Released on Chivers Audio Books, '91 by Chivers Audio Books, Green Dragon Audio Visual. Note: 6 cassettes.
MCSET. Cat no: **1342F**. Released on Travellers Tales, '91 by Travellers Tales. Note: 6 cassettes.

Edmonds, Noel

NOEL'S FUNNY PHONE CALLS (Various artists).
Tracks / Telephone engineer, The: *Various artists* / Mickey mouse phone: *Various artists* / American parking ticket: *Various artists* / Playing cricket in prison: *Various artists* / Booking a band to play in the nude: *Various artists* / Telephone consumer service: *Various artists* / Spanish holiday: *Various artists* / Pony trekking in Wales: *Various artists* / New driving test with extras, The: *Various artists* / Emergency stop, The: *Various artists* / Wrong highway code, The: *Various artists* / Going into hospital: *Various artists* / Launderette: *Various artists* / Unusual gift, The: *Various artists* / Robin Cousins fit it: *Various artists* / Haggis shooting: *Various artists*.
LP. Cat no: **REC 433**. Released on BBC, Nov '81 by BBC Records, Taylors **Deleted** '88.

MC. Cat no: **ZCM 433**. Released on BBC, Nov '81 by BBC Records, Taylors **Deleted** '88.

Edmonstoune Aytoun, W.

GLENMUTCHKIN RAILWAY, THE (Paul Young).
MCSET. Cat no: **SPF 950-1A**. Released on Schiltron Audio Books, '91 by Schiltron Publishing. Note: Playing time 65 minutes.

Edmunds, Karen

WILD ISLAND AFFAIR (Anna Barry).
MCSET. Cat no: **MRC 1022**. Released on Chivers Audio Books, '91 by Chivers Audio Books, Green Dragon Audio Visual. Note: 2 cassettes.

Edwards, Dorothy

ALL ABOUT MY NAUGHTY LITTLE SISTER (Felicity Kendal).
MCSET. Cat no: **TC LFP 7013**. Released on Listen For Pleasure, Nov '77 by EMI Records **Deleted** '85.
MCSET. Cat no: **LFP 7334**. Released on Listen For Pleasure, Jun '88 by EMI Records.

EQUALITY OF LOVE (Marcia Steele).
MCSET. Cat no: **MRC 1031**. Released on Moonlight Romance, Jun '88.

MORE NAUGHTY LITTLE SISTER STORIES (Maggie McCarthy).
MC. Cat no: **881727**. Released on Puffin Cover To Cover, '88, Green Dragon Audio Visual.

Edwards, Olwen

DEVIL'S OWN, THE (Unknown narrator(s)).
MCSET. Cat no: **1854960865**. Released on Trio, '91 by EMI Records. Note: 3 Cassettes.

Edwards, Rowan

ISLAND MAGIC (Unknown narrator(s)).
MCSET. Cat no: **1854965034**. Released on Bramhope, '91 by Ulverscroft Soundings. Note: 4 cassettes.

MATURING SUN, THE (Unknown narrator(s)).
MCSET. Cat no: **1854964933**. Released on Bramhope, '91 by Ulverscroft Soundings. Note: 4 cassettes.

SWEET VENGEANCE (Unknown narrator(s)).
MCSET. Cat no: **1854963120**. Released on Bramhope, '91 by Ulverscroft Soundings. Note: 4 cassettes.

Egleton, Clive

CONFLICT OF INTERESTS, A (Patrick Tull).
MCSET. Cat no: **1611T**. Released on Travellers Tales, '91 by Travellers Tales. Note: 6 Cassettes.
MCSET. Cat no: **IAB 90101**. Released on Isis Audio Books, '91. Note: 6 Cassettes.

DIFFERENT DRUMMER, A (Simon Prebble).
MCSET. Cat no: **IAB 92088**. Released on Isis Audio Books, Aug '92. Note: 7 Cassettes. Playing time: 8 1/2 hours.

Elder, Michael

ALIEN EARTH, THE (Michael Elder).
MCSET. Cat no: **COL 2019**. Released on Colophone, '88 by AVLS (Audio-Visual Library Services).

NOWHERE ON EARTH (Michael Elder).
MCSET. Cat no: **COL 2023**. Released on Colophone, '88 by AVLS (Audio-Visual Library Services).

Eliot, George

MILL ON THE FLOSS, THE (Eileen Atkins).
MCSET. Cat no: **CTC 009**. Released on Cover to Cover, Jun '85 by Cover to Cover Cassettes. Note: Playing time: 19 hours 20 minutes.
MCSET. Cat no: **1029/1030C**. Released on Travellers Tales, '91 by Travellers Tales. Note: 14 cassettes.

MILL ON THE FLOSS, THE (Claire Bloom).
MC. Cat no: **1568**. Released on Caedmon (USA), '88 by Caedmon Records (USA), Bond Street Music.

SILAS MARNER (Judi Dench).
MCSET. Cat no: **SAY 5**. Released on Argo (Polygram), Jul '82 by PolyGram Classics **Deleted** Jan '89.
MCSET. Cat no: **ARGO 1136**. Released on Argo (EMI), Sep '89 by EMI Records. Note: 2 Cassettes.

SILAS MARNER (Basil Rathbone).
MCSET. Cat no: **2024**. Released on Caedmon (USA), '88 by Caedmon Records (USA), Bond Street Music.

SILAS MARNER (Margaret Hilton).
MCSET. Cat no: **RB 88270**. Released on Recorded Books, '91 by Isis Audio Books. Note: 5 cassettes. Playing time 7hrs 24mins.
MCSET. Cat no: **1089C**. Released on Travellers Tales, '91 by Travellers Tales. Note: 5 cassettes.

SILAS MARNER (Morag Hood). Note: Abridged version.
MCSET. Cat no: **1085C**. Released on Travellers Tales, '91 by Travellers Tales. Note: 4 cassettes
MCSET. Cat no: **SPF 210-1**. Released on Schiltron Audio Books, '91 by Schiltron Publishing. Note: 4 Cassettes. Playing time: 4 hours 20 minutes.

Eliot, T.S.

FAMILY REUNION (Unknown narrator(s)).
MCSET. Cat no: **0308**. Released on Caedmon (USA), '88 by Caedmon Records (USA), Bond Street Music. Note: 3 cassettes

LOVE SONG OF J. ALFRED PRUFROCK, THE (Unknown narrator(s)).
MC. Cat no: **1045**. Released on Caedmon (USA), '88 by Caedmon Records

(USA), Bond Street Music.
MURDER IN THE CATHEDRAL (Unknown narrator(s)).
MCSET. Cat no: **330**. Released on Caedmon (USA), '88 by Caedmon Records (USA), Bond Street Music. Note: 2 cassettes

MURDER IN THE CATHEDRAL (Richard Pasco & The Royal Shakespeare Company).
MCSET. Cat no: **SAY 26**. Released on Argo (Polygram), Jul '82 by PolyGram Classics **Deleted** Jan '89.
MCSET. Cat no: **1005P**. Released on Travellers Tales, '91 by Travellers Tales. Note: 2 Cassettes.

OLD POSSUM'S BOOK OF PRACTICAL CATS (Sir John Gielgud).
MC. Cat no: **1713**. Released on Caedmon (USA), '88 by Caedmon Records (USA), Bond Street Music.

WASTE LAND (And Other Poems) (Unknown narrator(s)).
MC. Cat no: **1326**. Released on Caedmon (USA), '88 by Caedmon Records (USA), Bond Street Music.

WASTE LAND (Alec Guinness).
MCSET. Cat no: **SAY 25**. Released on Argo (Polygram), Jul '82 by PolyGram Classics **Deleted** Jan '89.

WASTE LAND (Four Quartets And Other Poems) (Sir Alec Guinness).
MCSET. Cat no: **1009Y**. Released on Travellers Tales, '91 by Travellers Tales. Note: 2 Cassettes.

Ellerbeck, R
HAMMERSLEIGH (Unknown narrator(s)).
MCSET. Cat no: **1854962205**. Released on Bramhope, '91 by Ulverscroft Soundings. Note: 5 Cassettes.

Elton, Ben
MOTORMOUTH (Ben Elton).
LP. Cat no: **BENLP 1**. Released on Mercury, 21 Nov '87 by Phonogram Ltd **Deleted** Mar '91.
MC. Cat no: **BENMC 1**. Released on Mercury, 21 Nov '87 by Phonogram Ltd **Deleted** Mar '91.

MOTORVATION (Ben Elton).
LP. Cat no: **836 652-1**. Released on Mercury, '88 by Phonogram Ltd **Deleted** Mar '91.
MC. Cat no: **836 652-4**. Released on Mercury, '88 by Phonogram Ltd **Deleted** Mar '91.
CD. Cat no: **836 652-2**. Released on Mercury, '88 by Phonogram Ltd **Deleted** Jun '90.

Erdman, Paul
PANIC OF '89, THE (Nicol Williamson).
MCSET. Cat no: **0671651250**. Released on Simon & Schuster, '91 by Simon & Schuster Ltd. Note: 2 cassettes.

Euripides
MEDEA (Dame Judith Anderson).

MCSET. Cat no: **0302**. Released on Caedmon (USA), '88 by Caedmon Records (USA), Bond Street Music. Note: 2 cassettes

Evans, Alan
THUNDER AT DAWN (Kenneth Knowles).
MCSET. Cat no: **1046T**. Released on Travellers Tales, '91 by Travellers Tales. Note: 4 Cassettes.
MCSET. Cat no: **1854960873**. Released on Bramhope, '91 by Ulverscroft Soundings. Note: 4 Cassettes.

Everage, Dame Edna
LAST NIGHT OF THE POMS (Dame Edna Everage & Carl Davis).
LP. Cat no: **EDNA 81**. Released on EMI, Nov '81 by EMI Records **Deleted** Nov '86.

MY GORGEOUS LIFE (Barry Humphries).
Note: Also available on hanging format, catalogue number:- 0001035266.
MCSET. Cat no: **HCA 24**. Released on Harper Collins, '92 by Harper Collins.

HOUSEWIFE SUPERSTAR (See under Humphries, Barry).

SOUND OF EDNA, THE (See under Humphries, Barry).

Everett, Kenny
CAPTAIN KREMMEN (Greatest Adventure Yet).
LP. Cat no: **CBS 84761**. Released on CBS, '80 by Sony Music, Solomon & Peres, Outlet Records **Deleted** '86.

KREMMEN THE MOVIE (Various artists).
Tracks / Call for Kremmen: Various artists / Q's theme: Various artists / Pretty Pauline: Various artists / Announcer: Various artists / Kremmen and Q: Various artists.
LP. Cat no: **EMC 3342**. Released on EMI, Aug '80 by EMI Records **Deleted** '85.
MC. Cat no: **TCEMC 3342**. Released on EMI, Aug '80 by EMI Records **Deleted** '85.

Everill, Joyce
GRANNY'S BUTTON BOX (Joyce Everill).
Tracks / Memories / Granny's button box / Schoolday ruminations / Fishy story, A / Torry skipper, A / Fishwife in the green, A / Castlegate yestreen / Cocky Hunter's store / Seterday's penny / Divi day / Washin' day / Summers remembered / Doon the sanny dee / Mind yer mainners / Somebidy chappin' at the door / By Royal appointment / Standin' in the lobby / I kent best / Ca' canny noo / Laddie, far hae ye been / Baby-sitter, The / Progress? / Exile's return, The / Torry then / Children on the shore / His will - nae mine / Woman of the year.
MC. Cat no: **ACLMC 2**. Released on

City Arts, '89 by Aberdeen City Arts Department.

Ezrin, Arlene
DEADLY DEVELOPMENTS (And the Book of Hell) (Arlene Ezrin).
MC. Cat no: **NF 6**. Released on Nightfall Tapes, '89 by BMG Records (UK) Ltd..

Farjeon, Eleanor
JIM AT THE CORNER (Sir Michael Hordern).
MCSET. Cat no: **2CCA 3054**. Released on Chivers Audio Books, '91 by Chivers Audio Books, Green Dragon Audio Visual. Note: 2 Cassettes.
MCSET. Cat no: **9017F**. Released on Travellers Tales, '91 by Travellers Tales. Note: 2 Cassettes.

Farr, Diana
CHOOSING (Norma West).
MCSET. Cat no: **1436F**. Released on Travellers Tales, '91 by Travellers Tales. Note: 7 cassettes.
MCSET. Cat no: **OAS 90026**. Released on Oasis Audio Books, '91 by Isis Audio Books. Note: 7 Cassettes.

Farrant, Elizabeth
TRUANT HEART, THE (Judy Bennett).
MCSET. Cat no: **MRC 1049**. Released on Chivers Audio Books, '91 by Chivers Audio Books, Green Dragon Audio Visual. Note: 2 cassettes.

Fast, Howard
APRIL MORNING (Jamie Hanes).
MCSET. Cat no: **RB 88320**. Released on Recorded Books, Oct '91 by Isis Audio Books. Note: 4 cassettes. Playing time 4hrs 45mins.

FREEDOM ROAD (Norman Dietz).
MCSET. Cat no: **RB 88350**. Released on Recorded Books, '91 by Isis Audio Books. Note: 7 cassettes.

Ferber, Edna
SHOWBOAT AND THE GAY OLD DOG (Edna Ferber).
MC. Cat no: **1719**. Released on Caedmon (USA), Aug '83 by Caedmon Records (USA), Bond Street Music.

Ferguson, Max
WHERE DO WE GO FROM HERE? (Last Visit) (Unknown narrator(s)).
MC. Cat no: **NF 2**. Released on Nightfall Tapes, Sep '87 by BMG Records (UK) Ltd. **Deleted** Feb '92.

Fergusson, Robert
EDINBURGH CALENDAR, THE (Volume 1) (Various artists).
Note: Readers are Alec MacMillan, Jean Faulds, Robert Garioch, Alexander Scott, George Philp, Lord Birsay, Peter MacLaren and Jean Taylor Smith.

MC. Cat no: **SSC 001**. Released on Scotsoun, '91 by Scotsoun Recordings, Morley Audio Services.

FARMER'S INGLE AND OTHER POEMS, THE (Volume 3) (Various artists).
MC. Cat no: **SSC 007**. Released on Scotsoun, '91 by Scotsoun Recordings, Morley Audio Services.

PEOPLE AND PLACES (Volume 2) (Various artists).
MC. Cat no: **SSC 006**. Released on Scotsoun, '91 by Scotsoun Recordings, Morley Audio Services.

Fermor, Patrick Leigh

BETWEEN THE WOODS AND THE WATERFRONT (Raymond Adamson).
MCSET. Cat no: **IAB 88101**. Released on Isis Audio Books, '91. Note: 8 Cassettes.

MCSET. Cat no: **1040N**. Released on Travellers Tales, '91 by Travellers Tales. Note: 8 Cassettes.

Ferrars, Elizabeth

ALWAYS SAY DIE (Gwen Watford).
MCSET. Cat no: **CAT 4051**. Released on Chivers Audio Books, '91 by Chivers Audio Books, Green Dragon Audio Visual. Note: 6 Cassettes.

MCSET. Cat no: **1520T**. Released on Travellers Tales, '91 by Travellers Tales. Note: 6 Cassettes.

MARCH HARE MURDERS, THE (Eleanor Bron).
MC. Cat no: **CAT 4033**. Released on Chivers Audio Books, Jul '88 by Chivers Audio Books, Green Dragon Audio Visual. Note: 4 Cassettes.

MCSET. Cat no: **1259T**. Released on Travellers Tales, '91 by Travellers Tales. Note: 4 Cassettes.

MURDER TOO MANY, A (Nigel Graham).
MCSET. Cat no: **1613T**. Released on Travellers Tales, '91 by Travellers Tales. Note: 6 Cassettes.

MCSET. Cat no: **OAS 90103**. Released on Oasis Audio Books, '91 by Isis Audio Books. Note: 6 Cassettes.

REMOVE THE BODIES (Jeremy Sinden).
MCSET. Cat no: **CAT 4046**. Released on Chivers Audio Books, '91 by Chivers Audio Books, Green Dragon Audio Visual. Note: 6 Cassettes.

MCSET. Cat no: **1471T**. Released on Travellers Tales, '91 by Travellers Tales. Note: 6 Cassettes.

SMOKE WITHOUT FIRE (George Hagan).
MCSET. Cat no: **IAB 92085**. Released on Isis Audio Books, Aug '92. Note: 6 Cassettes. Playing time: 7 hours, 1 min

SOMETHING WICKED (James Saxon).
MCSET. Cat no: **CAT 4069**. Released on Chivers Audio Books, '91 by Chivers Audio Books, Green Dragon Audio Visual. Note: 4 Cassettes.

THINNER THAN WATER (Jane Asher).
MCSET. Cat no: **CAT 4063**. Released on Chivers Audio Books, '91 by Chivers Audio Books, Green Dragon Audio Visual. Note: 4 Cassettes.

MCSET. Cat no: **1731T**. Released on Travellers Tales, '91 by Travellers Tales. Note: 4 Cassettes.

TRIAL BY FURY (Gwen Cherrell).
MCSET. Cat no: **1612T**. Released on Travellers Tales, '91 by Travellers Tales. Note: 6 Cassettes

MCSET. Cat no: **OAS 90081**. Released on Oasis Audio Books, '91 by Isis Audio Books.

WOMAN SLAUGHTER (Frances Jeater).
MCSET. Cat no: **OAS 20891**. Released on Oasis Audio Books, '91 by Isis Audio Books. Note: 5 Cassettes.

Fielding, Henry

AMELIA (Anthony Homyer).
MCSET. Cat no: **TCL 10**. Released on Complete Listener, '91 by Complete Listener. Note: 12 Cassettes. (BB) Playing Time: 1,080 Minutes.

MCSET. Cat no: **1552/1553F**. Released on Travellers Tales, '91 by Travellers Tales. Note: 12 Cassettes.

JONATHAN WILD (Anthony Homyer).
MCSET. Cat no: **TCL 9**. Released on Complete Listener, '91 by Complete Listener. Note: 5 Cassettes (BB) Playing Time: 450 Minutes.

JOSEPH ANDREWS (Daniel Massey).
MCSET. Cat no: **418 162-4**. Released on Argo (Polygram), Jun '88 by PolyGram Classics **Deleted** Jan '89. Note: 2 cassette set

JOSEPH ANDREWS (Anthony Homyer).
MCSET. Cat no: **1550 F**. Released on Travellers Tales, '91 by Travellers Tales. Note: 8 cassettes.

MCS. Cat no: **TCL 8**. Released on Complete Listener, '91 by Complete Listener. Note: 8 Cassettes. (BB)

TOM JONES (Anthony Homyer).
MCS. Cat no: **TCL 11**. Released on Complete Listener, '91 by Complete Listener. Note: 22 Cassettes. (BB) Playing Time: 1,980 Minutes.

MCSET. Cat no: **1554/5/6F**. Released on Travellers Tales, '91 by Travellers Tales. Note: 22 Cassettes.

Fielding, Lucy

FROM GREECE WITH LOVE (Unknown narrator(s)).

MCSET. Cat no: **1854960881**. Released on Soundings, '91 by Soundings Records, Bond Street Music. Note: 2 cassettes.

Films

101 DALMATIANS (Film Soundtrack) (Various artists).
LP. Cat no: **ST 3934**. Released on Disneyland, Dec '78 by Disneyland-Vista Records (USA).

LP. Cat no: **REC 544**. Released on Walt Disney, Oct '84 by Walt Disney Productions **Deleted** '88.

MC. Cat no: **ZCM 544**. Released on Walt Disney, Oct '84 by Walt Disney Productions **Deleted** '88.

ANGEL AND THE SOLDIER BOY, THE (Film Soundtrack) (Clannad & Tom Conti).
Tracks / Dream in the night, A / Pirates, The / Soldier boy, The / Angel, The / Flies, The / Spider, The / Cat, The / Jolly Rodger, The / Into the picture / Pirates merrymaking / Finding the key / Pirates on the island / Sea and storm / Love theme, The / Chase, The / Toys, The / Rescue, The / Back to the book / Dream in the night (instrumental).
LP. Cat no: **PL 74328**. Released on RCA, Dec '89 by BMG Records (UK) Ltd., Solomon & Peres, Outlet Records.

MC. Cat no: **PK 74328**. Released on RCA, Dec '89 by BMG Records (UK) Ltd., Solomon & Peres, Outlet Records.

CD. Cat no: **PD 74328**. Released on RCA, Dec '89 by BMG Records (UK) Ltd., Solomon & Peres, Outlet Records.

E.T. THE EXTRA TERRESTRIAL (Michael Jackson).
LP. Cat no: **MCA 70000**. Released on MCA, Feb '83 by MCA Records **Deleted** Feb '88.

MC. Cat no: **MCAC 70000**. Released on MCA, Feb '83 by MCA Records **Deleted** Feb '88.

NIGHTMARE ON ELM STREET 5 (The Dream Child) (Robert Englund).
MC. Cat no: **0671687188**. Released on Simon & Schuster, '91 by Simon & Schuster Ltd.

Fine, Anne

BILL'S NEW FROCK (And the Country Pancake) (Tony Robinson).
MCSET. Cat no: **2CCA 3133**. Released on Chivers Audio Books, '91 by Chivers Audio Books, Green Dragon Audio Visual. Note: 2 Cassettes.

Firesign Theatre

DON'T CRUSH THAT DWARF, HAND ME THE PLIERS. (Unknown narrators).
CD. Cat no: **MFCD 880**. Released on Mobile Fidelity Sound Lab(USA), by

Mobile Fidelity Records (USA).

Fisher, Graham
WINDSOR SECRET, THE (Heather Fisher).
MCSET. Cat no: **1854962884**. Released on Bramhope, '91 by Ulverscroft Soundings. Note: 4 Cassettes.

Fisher, Robert
AMAZING MONSTERS (Martin Jarvis).
MC. Cat no: **CDSC 1**. Released on Delyse, Oct '80.

Fisk, Nicholas
BONKERS CLOCKS (Kenneth Shanley).
MCSET. Cat no: **2CCA 3031**. Released on Chivers Audio Books, '91 by Chivers Audio Books, Green Dragon Audio Visual. Note: 2 Cassettes.

MCSET. Cat no: **9099F**. Released on Travellers Tales, '91 by Travellers Tales. Note: 2 cassettes.

GRINNY (Andy Crane).
MCSET. Cat no: **2CCA 3116**. Released on Chivers Audio Books, '91 by Chivers Audio Books, Green Dragon Audio Visual. Note: 2 Cassettes.

MCSET. Cat no: **9197F**. Released on Travellers Tales, '91 by Travellers Tales. Note: 2 Cassettes.

MONSTER MAKER (Kenneth Shanley).
MCSET. Cat no: **3CCA 3001**. Released on Chivers Audio Books, '91 by Chivers Audio Books, Green Dragon Audio Visual. Note: 3 Cassettes.

MCSET. Cat no: **9032F**. Released on Travellers Tales, '91 by Travellers Tales. Note: 3 Cassettes.

TRILLIONS (Steve Hodson).
MCSET. Cat no: **CTC 039**. Released on Cover to Cover, '87 by Cover to Cover Cassettes. Note: 4 cassettes. Playing time: 5 hrs 10 mins.

MC. Cat no: **882146**. Released on Puffin Cover To Cover, '88, Green Dragon Audio Visual.

MCSET. Cat no: **9110F**. Released on Travellers Tales, '91 by Travellers Tales. Note: 4 Cassettes.

Fitzgerald, F. Scott
DIAMOND AS BIG AS THE RITZ, THE (And Other Stories) (Vincent Marzello).
MCSET. Cat no: **1045F**. Released on Travellers Tales, '91 by Travellers Tales. Note: 6 cassettes.

GREAT GATSBY, THE (And Other Stories) (Alexander Scourby).
MCSET. Cat no: **1302F**. Released on Travellers Tales, '91 by Travellers Tales. Note: 6 cassettes.

GREAT GATSBY, THE (Anthony Homyer).
MCSET. Cat no: **NO CAT. NO.**. Released on Complete Listener, '91 by Complete Listener. Note: 5 Cassettes. (BB) Playing time: 390 Minutes.

Flagg, Fannie
FRIED GREEN TOMATOES AT THE WHISTLE STOP CAFE (Fannie Flagg).
MCSET. Cat no: **RC 77**. Released on Random Century, Apr '92 by Random Century Audiobooks, Conifer Records. Note: ISBN no. 1856861112

Flaherty, Liam
ECSTASY OF ANGUS, THE (Unknown narrator(s)).
2LP. Cat no: **CCT 15/16**. Released on Claddagh (Ireland), Aug '88 by Claddagh Records (Ireland), Projection, Impetus Records, Jazz Music, Roots Records, C.M. Distribution, Outlet Records, Taylors.

Flanagan, Mary
TRUST (Gretel Davis).
MCSET. Cat no: **1395/1396F**. Released on Travellers Tales, '91 by Travellers Tales. Note: 12 cassettes.

MCSET. Cat no: **OAS 89074**. Released on Oasis Audio Books, '91 by Isis Audio Books. Note: 12 Cassettes.

Flaubert, Gustave
MADAME BOVARY (Irene Worth).
MC. Cat no: **CDL 51664**. Released on Caedmon (USA), Oct '81 by Caedmon Records (USA), Bond Street Music.

MCSET. Cat no: **000106051X**. Released on Collins-Caedmon, '91 by Collins Audio, Taylors, Bond Street Music.

MADAME BOVARY (Davina Porter).
MCSET. Cat no: **1083/1084C**. Released on Travellers Tales, '91 by Travellers Tales. Note: 12 cassettes.

MCSET. Cat no: **IAB 89093**. Released on Isis Audio Books, '91. Note: 12 Cassettes.

Fleischman, Sid
WHIPPING BOY, THE (Kerry Shale).
MCSET. Cat no: **2CCA 3089**. Released on Chivers Audio Books, '91 by Chivers Audio Books, Green Dragon Audio Visual. Note: 2 Cassettes.

MCSET. Cat no: **9155F**. Released on Travellers Tales, '91 by Travellers Tales. Note: 2 Cassettes.

Fleming, Ian
CASINO ROYALE (David Rintoul).
MCSET. Cat no: **CAB 345**. Released on Chivers Audio Books, '91 by Chivers Audio Books, Green Dragon Audio Visual. Note: 6 Cassettes

MCSET. Cat no: **1385T**. Released on Travellers Tales, '91 by Travellers Tales. Note: 6 Cassettes.

CHITTY CHITTY BANG BANG (Lionel Jeffries).
MCSET. Cat no: **LFP 7577**. Released on Listen For Pleasure, Feb '92 by EMI Records.

CHITTY CHITTY BANG BANG (Hermione Gingold).
MC. Cat no: **1390**. Released on Caedmon (USA), '88 by Caedmon Records (USA), Bond Street Music.

DIAMONDS ARE FOREVER (David Rintoul).
MCSET. Cat no: **CAB 511**. Released on Chivers Audio Books, '91 by Chivers Audio Books, Green Dragon Audio Visual. Note: 6 Cassettes

MCSET. Cat no: **1614T**. Released on Travellers Tales, '91 by Travellers Tales. Note: 6 Cassettes.

DIAMONDS ARE FOREVER (Ian Ogilvy).
MCSET. Cat no: **LFP 7172**. Released on Listen For Pleasure, Sep '84 by EMI Records.

DR. NO (David Rintoul).
MCSET. Cat no: **1390**. Released on Chivers Audio Books, '91 by Chivers Audio Books, Green Dragon Audio Visual.

MCSET. Cat no: **1048T**. Released on Travellers Tales, '91 by Travellers Tales. Note: 6 Cassettes.

LIVE AND LET DIE (Unknown narrator(s)).
MC. Cat no: **LFP 41 7166 5**. Released on Listen For Pleasure, Sep '84 by EMI Records.

LIVE AND LET DIE (David Rintoul).
MCSET. Cat no: **CAB 475**. Released on Chivers Audio Books, '91 by Chivers Audio Books, Green Dragon Audio Visual. Note: 6 Cassettes.

MCSET. Cat no: **1521T**. Released on Travellers Tales, '91 by Travellers Tales. Note: 6 Cassettes.

MAN WITH THE GOLDEN GUN, THE (David Rintoul).
MCSET. Cat no: **1225T**. Released on Travellers Tales, '91 by Travellers Tales. Note: 4 Cassettes.

MCSET. Cat no: **CAB 266**. Released on Chivers Audio Books, '91 by Chivers Audio Books, Green Dragon Audio Visual. Note: 4 Cassettes.

MOONRAKER (David Rintoul).
MCSET. Cat no: **CAB 147**. Released on Chivers Audio Books, '91 by Chivers Audio Books, Green Dragon Audio Visual. Note: 6 Cassettes.

MCSET. Cat no: **1052T**. Released on Travellers Tales, '91 by Travellers Tales. Note: 6 Cassettes.

ON HER MAJESTY'S SECRET SERVICE (David Rintoul).
MCSET. Cat no: **CAB 291**. Released on Chivers Audio Books, Apr '88 by Chivers Audio Books, Green Dragon Audio Visual. Note: 6 cassette set

MCSET. Cat no: **1238T**. Released on Travellers Tales, '91 by Travellers Tales. Note: 6 Cassettes.

SPY WHO LOVED ME, THE (Rula Lenska).
MCSET. Cat no: **CAB 406**. Released on Chivers Audio Books, '91 by Chivers Audio Books, Green Dragon Audio Visual. Note: 4 Cassettes.

MCSET. Cat no: **1472T.** Released on Travellers Tales, '91 by Travellers Tales. Note: 4 Cassettes.
YOU ONLY LIVE TWICE (David Rintoul).
MCSET. Cat no: **CAB 184.** Released on Chivers Audio Books, '91 by Chivers Audio Books, Green Dragon Audio Visual. Note: 6 Cassettes.
MCSET. Cat no: **1053T.** Released on Travellers Tales, '91 by Travellers Tales. Note: 6 Cassettes.

Floren, Lee
BLACK GUNSMOKE (Brian Rapkin).
MCSET. Cat no: **1025W.** Released on Travellers Tales, '91 by Travellers Tales. Note: 4 Cassettes.
MCSET. Cat no: **1854963201.** Released on Bramhope, '91 by Ulverscroft Soundings. Note: 4 Cassettes.
DEADLY DRAW (Unknown narrator(s)).
MCSET. Cat no: **1854963538.** Released on Bramhope, '91 by Ulverscroft Soundings. Note: 4 Cassettes.
LOBO VALLEY (Unknown narrator(s)).
MCSET. Cat no: **1854962949.** Released on Bramhope, '91 by Ulverscroft Soundings. Note: 4 Cassettes.
SADDLE WOLVES, THE (Unknown narrator(s)).
MCSET. Cat no: **1854962795.** Released on Bramhope, '91 by Ulverscroft Soundings. Note: 4 Cassettes.

Flotsam & Jetsam
FLOTSAM AND JETSAM.
Tracks / Introduction / King Canute / Mrs Peer Gynt / P.C. Lamb / Maude-Marie / Optimist and pessimist / Polonaise in the Mall / Melodrama of the mice / Only a few of us left / Business man's love song, The / Simon the bootlegger / Song of the air / Move into my house / Little Betty Bouncer / Weather reports / We never know what to expect / Schubert's toy shop / Village blacksmith, The / Alsation and the pekinese, The / Modern diver, The / Little Joan / What was the matter with Rachmaninov? / British pantomime, The / Ghost of old king's jester / High-brow sailor, The / When I grow old, dad / Postscript, The.
CD. Cat no: **PAST CD 9723.** Released on Flapper, '90 by Pavilion Records, Taylors, Pinnacle.

Follett, Ken
EYE OF THE NEEDLE (Graeme Malcom).
MCSET. Cat no: **1522T.** Released on Travellers Tales, '91 by Travellers Tales. Note: 8 Cassettes.
MCSET. Cat no: **IAB 90053.** Released on Isis Audio Books, '91. Note: 8 Cassettes.
KEY TO REBECCA, THE (Anthony Quayle).
MCSET. Cat no: **LFP 7198.** Released on Listen For Pleasure, '88 by EMI Records.

KEY TO REBECCA, THE (Anthony Quayle).
Note: Abridged.
MCSET. Cat no: **1055T.** Released on Travellers Tales, '91 by Travellers Tales. Note: 2 Cassettes.
KEY TO REBECCA, THE (Peter Fernandez).
MCSET. Cat no: **1615/1616T.** Released on Travellers Tales, '91 by Travellers Tales. Note: 10 Cassettes.
MCSET. Cat no: **IAB 90083.** Released on Isis Audio Books, '91. Note: 10 Cassettes.
MAN FROM ST. PETERSBURG, THE (Terrence Hardiman).
MCSET. Cat no: **CAB 387.** Released on Chivers Audio Books, '91 by Chivers Audio Books, Green Dragon Audio Visual. Note: 10 Cassettes
MCSET. Cat no: **1473/1474T.** Released on Travellers Tales, '91 by Travellers Tales. Note: 10 Cassettes.
MODIGLIANI SCANDAL, THE (Michael York).
Note: Also available on hanging format, catalogue number:- 0001348401.
MCSET. Cat no: **0001388207.** Released on Harper Collins, '91 by Harper Collins. Note: 2 Cassettes.
PAPER MONEY (John Standing).
Note: Also available on hanging format, catalogue number:- 0001388398
MCSET. Cat no: **0001388193.** Released on Harper Collins, '91 by Harper Collins. Note: 2 Cassettes.
PAPER MONEY (Patrick Tull).
MCSET. Cat no: **1701T.** Released on Travellers Tales, '91 by Travellers Tales. Note: 5 Cassettes.
MCSET. Cat no: **IAB 91034.** Released on Isis Audio Books, '91. Note: 5 Cassettes.
PILLARS OF THE EARTH, THE (Tim Pigott-Smith).
MCSET. Cat no: **0671690841.** Released on Simon & Schuster, '91 by Simon & Schuster Ltd. Note: 4 Cassettes.
TRIPLE (Terrence Hardiman).
MCSET. Cat no: **CAB 493.** Released on Chivers Audio Books, '91 by Chivers Audio Books, Green Dragon Audio Visual. Note: 10 Cassettes.
MCSET. Cat no: **1617/1618T.** Released on Travellers Tales, '91 by Travellers Tales. Note: 10 Cassettes.

Forbes, Bryan
ENDLESS GAME, THE (Bryan Forbes).
MCSET. Cat no: **TTDMC 407.** Released on CSA Tell Tapes, Jun '91 by CSA Tell-Tapes. Note: 2 Cassettes. ISBN No: 1873859309.

Forbes, Colin
AVALANCHE EXPRESS (Clifford Norgate).
MCSET. Cat no: **IAB 88092.** Released on Isis Audio Books, '91.

Note: 8 cassettes.
MCSET. Cat no: **1372T.** Released on Travellers Tales, '91 by Travellers Tales.
COVER STORY (David Rintoul).
MCSET. Cat no: **1703/1704T.** Released on Travellers Tales, '91 by Travellers Tales. Note: 10 Cassettes.
MCSET. Cat no: **IAB 91051.** Released on Isis Audio Books, '91. Note: 10 Cassettes.
DOUBLE JEOPARDY (Stephen Thorne).
MCSET. Cat no: **1683T.** Released on Travellers Tales, '91 by Travellers Tales. Note: 7 Cassettes.
MCSET. Cat no: **IAB 91021.** Released on Isis Audio Books, '91. Note: 7 Cassettes.
HEIGHTS OF ZERVOS, THE (Sean Barrett).
MCSET. Cat no: **1685T.** Released on Travellers Tales, '91 by Travellers Tales. Note: 8 Cassettes.
MCSET. Cat no: **IAB 91011.** Released on Isis Audio Books, '91. Note: 8 Cassettes.
JANUS MAN (Steven Pacey).
MCSET. Cat no: **1619/1620T.** Released on Travellers Tales, '91 by Travellers Tales. Note: 12 Cassettes.
MCSET. Cat no: **IAB 90092.** Released on Isis Audio Books, '91. Note: 12 Cassettes.
PALERMO AMBUSH, THE (Sean Barrett).
MCSET. Cat no: **1698T.** Released on Travellers Tales, '91 by Travellers Tales. Note: 6 Cassettes.
MCSET. Cat no: **IAB 91062.** Released on Isis Audio Books, '91. Note: 6 Cassettes.
STOCKHOLM SYNDICATE, THE (Sean Barrett).
MCSET. Cat no: **IAB 91104.** Released on Isis Audio Books, Oct '91. Note: 8 Cassettes, Playing time 11 hours.
STONE LEOPARD, THE (Peter McGowan).
MCSET. Cat no: **1437T.** Released on Travellers Tales, '91 by Travellers Tales. Note: 5 Cassettes.
MCSET. Cat no: **1854962248.** Released on Soundings, '91 by Soundings Records, Bond Street Music. Note: 5 Cassettes.
TARGET 5 (David Rintoul).
MCSET. Cat no: **IAB 91081.** Released on Isis Audio Books, '91. Note: 7 cassette set.
TERMINAL (Sean Barrett).
MCSET. Cat no: **1684T.** Released on Travellers Tales, '91 by Travellers Tales. Note: 8 Cassettes.
MCSET. Cat no: **IAB 91031.** Released on Isis Audio Books, '91. Note: 8 Cassettes.
TRAMP IN ARMOUR (Sean Barrett).
MCSET. Cat no: **IAB 91092.** Released

Forder, Timothy

BILL THE MINDER (Timothy Forder).
Tracks / Old Crispin / King, The / Navigator, The / Aunt Galladia / Respectable gentleman, The / Chloe / Doctor, The / Sicilian cleaning lady, The / Button crane of Bararoo, The / Waiter, The / Bosworth.
MC. Cat no: **TS 349**. Released on Tellastory, Apr '87 by Random Century Audiobooks.

Forester, C.S.

AFRICAN QUEEN, THE (Edward Woodward).
MC. Cat no: **TC LFP 7072**. Released on Listen For Pleasure, Dec '80 by EMI Records.
MCSET. Cat no: **LFP 7583**. Released on Listen For Pleasure, Feb '92 by EMI Records.
MR. MIDSHIPMAN HORNBLOWER (Christian Rodska).
MCSET. Cat no: **CAB 654**. Released on Chivers Audio Books, Dec '91 by Chivers Audio Books, Green Dragon Audio Visual. Note: 8 cassettes.

Forrester, Helen

LATCHKEY KID, THE (Carole Boyd).
MCSET. Cat no: **CAB 136**. Released on Chivers Audio Books, '91 by Chivers Audio Books, Green Dragon Audio Visual. Note: 6 Cassettes.
MCSET. Cat no: **1046F**. Released on Travellers Tales, '91 by Travellers Tales. Note: 6 cassettes.
LEMON TREE, THE (Anne Dover).
MCSET. Cat no: **1499/1500F**. Released on Travellers Tales, '91 by Travellers Tales. Note: 9 cassettes.
MCSET. Cat no: **1854963244**. Released on Soundings, '91 by Soundings Records, Bond Street Music. Note: 9 Cassettes.
LIVERPOOL DAISY (Christine Dawe).
MCSET. Cat no: **1295F**. Released on Travellers Tales, '91 by Travellers Tales. Note: 6 cassettes.
MCSET. Cat no: **1854960938**. Released on Soundings, '91 by Soundings Records, Bond Street Music. Note: 6 Cassettes.
MONEYLENDER OF SHAHPUR, THE (Christopher Kay).
MCSET. Cat no: **1096R**. Released on Travellers Tales, '91 by Travellers Tales. Note: 4 Cassettes.
MCSET. Cat no: **1854960954**. Released on Travellers Tales, '91 by Travellers Tales.
THREE WOMEN OF LIVERPOOL (Christine Dawe).
MCSET. Cat no: **SOUND 34**. Released on Soundings, Feb '85 by Soundings Records, Bond Street Music.

on Isis Audio Books, Sep '91. Note: 8 cassette set. Playing time 9hrs 15mins.
MCSET. Cat no: **1047F**. Released on Travellers Tales, '91 by Travellers Tales. Note: 4 Cassettes.
THURSDAY'S CHILD (Carolyn Pickles).
MCSET. Cat no: **CAB 171**. Released on Chivers Audio Books, '91 by Chivers Audio Books, Green Dragon Audio Visual. Note: 6 Cassettes
MCSET. Cat no: **1252F**. Released on Travellers Tales, '91 by Travellers Tales. Note: 6 cassettes.
YES MAMA (Christine Dawe).
MCSET. Cat no: **1329F**. Released on Travellers Tales, '91 by Travellers Tales. Note: 8 cassettes.
MCSET. Cat no: **1854960989**. Released on Soundings, '91 by Soundings Records, Bond Street Music. Note: 8 Cassettes.

Forster, E.M.

NEW COLLECTED SHORT STORIES, THE (Charles Kay).
MCSET. Cat no: **IAB 88052**. Released on Isis Audio Books, '91. Note: 8 cassettes. Playing time 9hrs 45mins.
MCSET. Cat no: **1300F**. Released on Travellers Tales, '91 by Travellers Tales. Note: 8 cassettes.
PASSAGE TO INDIA (Ben Kingsley).
MCSET. Cat no: **SAY 115**. Released on Argo (Polygram), Sep '84 by PolyGram Classics **Deleted** Jan '89.
MCSET. Cat no: **ARGO 1064**. Released on Argo (EMI), May '89 by EMI Records. Note: 2 Cassettes.
MCSET. Cat no: **1048F**. Released on Travellers Tales, '91 by Travellers Tales.
ROOM WITH A VIEW, A (Judi Dench).
MCSET. Cat no: **418 153-4**. Released on Argo (Polygram), Jun '88 by PolyGram Classics **Deleted** Jan '89.
MCSET. Cat no: **ARGO 1082**. Released on Argo (EMI), May '89 by EMI Records. Note: 2 Cassettes.
MCSET. Cat no: **1275F**. Released on Travellers Tales, '91 by Travellers Tales. Note: 2 Cassettes.
ROOM WITH A VIEW, A (Joanna David).
MCSET. Cat no: **CAB 545**. Released on Chivers Audio Books, '91 by Chivers Audio Books, Green Dragon Audio Visual. Note: 6 Cassettes
MCSET. Cat no: **1615F**. Released on Travellers Tales, '91 by Travellers Tales. Note: 6 cassettes.

Forsyth, Frederick

DAY OF THE JACKAL, THE (David Rintoul).
MCSET. Cat no: **CAB 328**. Released on Chivers Audio Books, '91 by Chivers Audio Books, Green Dragon Audio Visual.
MCSET. Cat no: **1406/1407T**. Released on Travellers Tales, '91 by Trav-

ellers Tales. Note: 10 Cassettes.
DECEIVER, THE (Charles Keating).
MCSET. Cat no: **ZBBC 1254**. Released on BBC, Aug '91 by BBC Records, Taylors. Note: ISBN No: 0563 365250
DEVIL'S ALTERNATIVE, THE (Peter Egan).
MCSET. Cat no: **LFP 7361**. Released on Listen For Pleasure, Nov '88 by EMI Records. Note: Playing time: 2 hours.
FOURTH PROTOCOL, THE (Charles Dance).
MCSET. Cat no: **LFP 7190**. Released on Listen For Pleasure, May '85 by EMI Records.
MCSET. Cat no: **1056T**. Released on Travellers Tales, '91 by Travellers Tales. Note: 2 Cassettes.
FOURTH PROTOCOL, THE (David Rintoul).
MCSET. Cat no: **CAB 458**. Released on Chivers Audio Books, '91 by Chivers Audio Books, Green Dragon Audio Visual. Note: 10 Cassettes.
MCSET. Cat no: **1523/1524T**. Released on Travellers Tales, '91 by Travellers Tales. Note: 10 Cassettes.
NEGOTIATOR, THE (Anthony Zerbe).
Note: Also available on hanging format, catalogue number:- 0001388533.
MCSET. Cat no: **HCA 26**. Released on Harper Collins, '92 by Harper Collins.
NO COMEBACKS (Frank Muller).
Note: Contains these stories:- No Comebacks, There Are No Snakes in Ireland, The Emperor, There Are Some Days..., Money With Menances, Used in Evidence, Privilege, Duty, A Careful Man and Sharp Practice.
MCSET. Cat no: **IAB 91113**. Released on Isis Audio Books, Nov '91. Note: 8 Cassettes. Playing time 9 hours.
NO COMEBACKS (Nigel Davenport).
MCSET. Cat no: **CAB 069**. Released on Chivers Audio Books, '91 by Chivers Audio Books, Green Dragon Audio Visual. Note: 6 Cassettes.
MCSET. Cat no: **1057T**. Released on Travellers Tales, '91 by Travellers Tales. Note: 6 Cassettes.
ODESSA FILE, THE (David Rintoul).
MC. Cat no: **CAB 333**. Released on Chivers Audio Books, '88 by Chivers Audio Books, Green Dragon Audio Visual.
MCSET. Cat no: **1361T**. Released on Travellers Tales, '91 by Travellers Tales. Note: 8 Cassettes.
ODESSA FILE, THE (Patrick Allen).
MC. Cat no: **TC-LFP 7030**. Released on Listen For Pleasure, Jul '78 by EMI Records.
SHEPHERD, THE (Robert Powell).
MC. Cat no: **PTB 600**. Released on Pickwick Talking Books, '83 by Pickwick Records, Clyde Factors.

Fowles, John
FRENCH LIEUTENANT'S WOMAN, THE (Jeremy Irons).
Note: Also available on hanging format, catalogue number:- 0001388541
MCSET. Cat no: **HCA 9.** Released on Harper Collins, '91 by Harper Collins.

Francis, Dick
BLOODSPORT (Tony Britton).
MCSET. Cat no: **CAB 087.** Released on Chivers Audio Books, '91 by Chivers Audio Books, Green Dragon Audio Visual. Note: 6 Cassettes.

MCSET. Cat no: **1059T.** Released on Travellers Tales, '91 by Travellers Tales. Note: 6 Cassettes.

BOLT (Nigel Havers).
MCSET. Cat no: **LFP 7306.** Released on Listen For Pleasure, Sep '87 by EMI Records. Note: Playing time: 2 1/2 hours.

BOLT. (See under Francis & Herbert) (Unknown narrator(s))

BONE CRACK (Tony Britton).
MCSET. Cat no: **CAB 167.** Released on Chivers Audio Books, '91 by Chivers Audio Books, Green Dragon Audio Visual. Note: 6 Cassettes.

MCSET. Cat no: **1060T.** Released on Travellers Tales, '91 by Travellers Tales. Note: 6 Cassettes.

BREAK IN (Nigel Havers).
MCSET. Cat no: **LFP 7260.** Released on Listen For Pleasure, Aug '86 by EMI Records.

MCSET. Cat no: **1145T.** Released on Travellers Tales, '91 by Travellers Tales. Note: 2 Cassettes.

COME BACK (Unknown narrator(s)).
MCSET. Cat no: **RC 43.** Released on Random Century, '91 by Random Century Audiobooks, Conifer Records. Note: 2 cassettes. ISBN 1856860663. 3 hrs approx.

DANGER, THE (Tim Pigott-Smith).
MCSET. Cat no: **LFP 7182.** Released on Listen For Pleasure, Mar '85 by EMI Records.

MCSET. Cat no: **1061T.** Released on Travellers Tales, '91 by Travellers Tales. Note: 2 Cassettes.

DANGER, THE (Tony Britton).
MCSET. Cat no: **CAB 303.** Released on Chivers Audio Books, '91 by Chivers Audio Books, Green Dragon Audio Visual. Note: 8 Cassettes.

MCSET. Cat no: **1260T.** Released on Travellers Tales, '91 by Travellers Tales. Note: 8 Cassettes.

DEAD CERT (Tony Britton).
MCSET. Cat no: **CAB 437.** Released on Chivers Audio Books, '91 by Chivers Audio Books, Green Dragon Audio Visual. Note: 6 Cassettes.

MCSET. Cat no: **1587T.** Released on Travellers Tales, '91 by Travellers Tales. Note: 6 Cassettes.

DEAD CERT (James Fox).

MCSET. Cat no: **RC 16.** Released on Random Century, '91 by Random Century Audiobooks, Conifer Records. Note: 2 cassettes. ISBN 185686037X. 3 hrs approx.

EDGE, THE (Peter Marinker).
MCSET. Cat no: **LFP 7424.** Released on Listen For Pleasure, Sep '89 by EMI Records.

ENQUIRY (Tony Britton).
MCSET. Cat no: **CAB 051.** Released on Chivers Audio Books, '91 by Chivers Audio Books, Green Dragon Audio Visual. Note: 6 Cassettes.

MCSET. Cat no: **1062T.** Released on Travellers Tales, '91 by Travellers Tales. Note: 6 Cassettes.

ENQUIRY (And Bonecrack) (Various artists).
MCSET. Cat no: **ZBBC 1055.** Released on BBC Radio Collection, May '90 by BBC Records. Note: ISBN No: 0563 226072

FLYING FINISH (Simon McCorkindale).
MCSET. Cat no: **RC 68.** Released on Random Century, Jun '92 by Random Century Audiobooks, Conifer Records. Note: ISBN no. 1856860604

FLYING FINISH (Tony Britton).
MCSET. Cat no: **CAB 453.** Released on Chivers Audio Books, '91 by Chivers Audio Books, Green Dragon Audio Visual. Note: 6 Cassettes.

MCSET. Cat no: **1525T.** Released on Travellers Tales, '91 by Travellers Tales. Note: 6 Cassettes.

FOR KICKS (Tony Britton).
MCSET. Cat no: **CAB 185.** Released on Chivers Audio Books, '91 by Chivers Audio Books, Green Dragon Audio Visual. Note: 6 Cassettes.

MCSET. Cat no: **1063T.** Released on Travellers Tales, '91 by Travellers Tales. Note: 6 Cassettes.

FORFEIT (Tony Britton).
MCSET. Cat no: **CAB 044.** Released on Chivers Audio Books, '91 by Chivers Audio Books, Green Dragon Audio Visual. Note: 6 Cassettes.

MCSET. Cat no: **1064T.** Released on Travellers Tales, '91 by Travellers Tales. Note: 6 Cassettes.

HIGH STAKES (James Bolam).
Note: Abridged.
MCSET. Cat no: **1449T.** Released on Travellers Tales, '91 by Travellers Tales. Note: 2 Cassettes.

HIGH STAKES (James Bolam).
MCSET. Cat no: **LFP 7358.** Released on Listen For Pleasure, Sep '88 by EMI Records. Note: Playing time: 2 hours 30 minutes.

HOT MONEY (Christopher Casenove).
MCSET. Cat no: **LFP 7326.** Released on Listen For Pleasure, Feb '88 by EMI Records.

HOT MONEY (Christopher Casenove).
Note: Abridged.

MCSET. Cat no: **1272T.** Released on Travellers Tales, '91 by Travellers Tales. Note: 2 Cassettes.

IN THE FRAME (Tony Britton).
MCSET. Cat no: **CAB 137.** Released on Chivers Audio Books, '91 by Chivers Audio Books, Green Dragon Audio Visual. Note: 6 Cassettes.

MCSET. Cat no: **1065T.** Released on Travellers Tales, '91 by Travellers Tales. Note: 6 Cassettes.

KNOCK DOWN (Tony Britton).
MCSET. Cat no: **CAB 613.** Released on Chivers Audio Books, '91 by Chivers Audio Books, Green Dragon Audio Visual. Note: 6 Cassettes.

KNOCK DOWN (Tim Pigott-Smith).
MCSET. Cat no: **RC 34.** Released on Random Century, '91 by Random Century Audiobooks, Conifer Records. Note: 2 cassettes. ISBN 1856860698. 3 hrs approx.

NERVE (Tony Britton).
MCSET. Cat no: **CAB 213.** Released on Chivers Audio Books, '91 by Chivers Audio Books, Green Dragon Audio Visual. Note: 6 Cassettes

MCSET. Cat no: **1153T.** Released on Travellers Tales, '91 by Travellers Tales. Note: 6 Cassettes.

ODDS AGAINST (Ian McShane).
MCSET. Cat no: **RC 30.** Released on Random Century, '91 by Random Century Audiobooks, Conifer Records. Note: 2 cassettes. ISBN 1856860620. 3 hrs approx.

ODDS AGAINST (Robert Powell).
MCSET. Cat no: **CTC 029.** Released on Cover to Cover, Sep '86 by Cover to Cover Cassettes. Note: 6 cassettes. Playing time: 7 hrs 40 mins.

MCSET. Cat no: **1066T.** Released on Travellers Tales, '91 by Travellers Tales. Note: 6 Cassettes.

PROOF (Charles Dance).
MCSET. Cat no: **LFP 7214.** Released on Listen For Pleasure, Sep '85 by EMI Records.

PROOF (Charles Dance).
Note: Abridged.
MCSET. Cat no: **1067T.** Released on Travellers Tales, '91 by Travellers Tales. Note: 2 Cassettes.

RAT RACE (Ian Ogilvy).
MCSET. Cat no: **CAB 020.** Released on Chivers Audio Books, '91 by Chivers Audio Books, Green Dragon Audio Visual. Note: 4 Cassettes.

MCSET. Cat no: **1068T.** Released on Travellers Tales, '91 by Travellers Tales. Note: 4 Cassettes.

MCSET. Cat no: **0745128025.** Released on Word For Word, May '92 by Chivers Audio Books.

RAT RACE (Simon Jones).
MCSET. Cat no: **RC 67.** Released on Random Century, May '92 by Random Century Audiobooks, Conifer Records. Note: ISBN no. 1856860612

REFLEX (Tony Britton).

MCSET. Cat no: **CAB 546**. Released on Chivers Audio Books, '91 by Chivers Audio Books, Green Dragon Audio Visual. Note: 8 cassettes.

MCSET. Cat no: **1690T**. Released on Travellers Tales, '91 by Travellers Tales. Note: 8 Cassettes.

RISK (Tony Britton).
MCSET. Cat no: **CAB 660**. Released on Chivers Audio Books, Feb '92 by Chivers Audio Books, Green Dragon Audio Visual. Note: 6 Cassettes.

RISK/ BOLT / THE FOG (Various narrators).
Note: Authors are Dick Francis and James Herbert. All stories are abridged.
MCSET. Cat no: **1221T**. Released on Travellers Tales, '91 by Travellers Tales. Note: 6 Cassettes.

SLAY-RIDE (Tony Britton).
MCSET. Cat no: **CAB 248**. Released on Chivers Audio Books, '91 by Chivers Audio Books, Green Dragon Audio Visual. Note: 6 Cassettes.

MCSET. Cat no: **1222T**. Released on Travellers Tales, '91 by Travellers Tales. Note: 6 Cassettes.

SMOKESCREEN (Edward Woodward).
MCSET. Cat no: **RC 28**. Released on Random Century, '91 by Random Century Audiobooks, Conifer Records. Note: 2 cassettes. ISBN 185686054X.

SMOKESCREEN (Tony Britton).
MCSET. Cat no: **CAB 486**. Released on Chivers Audio Books, '91 by Chivers Audio Books, Green Dragon Audio Visual. Note: 6 Cassettes.

MCSET. Cat no: **1562T**. Released on Travellers Tales, '91 by Travellers Tales. Note: 6 Cassettes.

STRAIGHT (Simon McCorkindale).
MCSET. Cat no: **LFP 7457**. Released on Listen For Pleasure, Apr '90 by EMI Records.

TRIAL RUN (Tony Britton).
MCSET. Cat no: **CAB 070**. Released on Chivers Audio Books, '91 by Chivers Audio Books, Green Dragon Audio Visual. Note: 6 Cassettes.

MCSET. Cat no: **1069T**. Released on Travellers Tales, '91 by Travellers Tales. Note: 6 Cassettes.

TWICE SHY (Tony Britton).
MCSET. Cat no: **CAB 407**. Released on Chivers Audio Books, '91 by Chivers Audio Books, Green Dragon Audio Visual. Note: 8 Cassettes.

MCSET. Cat no: **1467T**. Released on Travellers Tales, '91 by Travellers Tales. Note: 6 Cassettes.

WHIP HAND, THE (Tony Britton).
MCSET. Cat no: **1448T**. Released on Travellers Tales, '91 by Travellers Tales. Note: 8 Cassettes.

MCSET. Cat no: **CAB 358**. Released on Chivers Audio Books, '91 by Chivers Audio Books, Green Dragon Audio Visual. Note: 8 cassettes.

Francis, Helen

LIGHT WITHIN, A (Unknown narrator(s)).
MCSET. Cat no: **1854965042**. Released on Bramhope, '91 by Ulverscroft Soundings. Note: 4 cassettes.

Francome, John

EAVESDROPPER (Keith Barron).
MCSET. Cat no: **1167T**. Released on Travellers Tales, '91 by Travellers Tales. Note: 6 Cassettes.

MCSET. Cat no: **CAB 224**. Released on Chivers Audio Books, '91 by Chivers Audio Books, Green Dragon Audio Visual. Note: 6 cassettes.

RIDING HIGH (Keith Barron).
Note: Authors are: John Francome and James MacGregor.
MCSET. Cat no: **1223T**. Released on Travellers Tales, '91 by Travellers Tales. Note: 6 Cassettes.

MCSET. Cat no: **CAB 274**. Released on Chivers Audio Books, '91 by Chivers Audio Books, Green Dragon Audio Visual. Note: 6 cassettes.

Fraser, Alison

COMING HOME (Lesley Seaward).
MCSET. Cat no: **PMB 015**. Released on Mills & Boon, '88. Note: 2 Cassettes
MC. Cat no: **0263115051**. Released on Mills &Boon, 30 Jun '87.

Fraser, Anthea

DEATH SPEAKS SOFTLY (Unknown narrator(s)).
MCSET. Cat no: **1854965298**. Released on Bramhope, '91 by Ulverscroft Soundings. Note: 5 Cassettes.

NIGHT BRIGHT SHINERS, THE (Unknown narrator(s)).
MCSET. Cat no: **1854965158**. Released on Bramhope, '91 by Ulverscroft Soundings. Note: 5 cassettes.

SIX PROUD WALKERS (Peter Joyce).
MCSET. Cat no: **1854965697**. Released on Bramhope, Mar '92 by Ulverscroft Soundings. Note: Playing time: 60 minutes.

Fraser, Antonia

CAVALIER CASE, THE (Nichola McAuliffe).
MCSET. Cat no: **CAB 673**. Released on Chivers Audio Books, Feb '92 by Chivers Audio Books, Green Dragon Audio Visual. Note: 8 cassettes.

COOL REPENTANCE (Joanna Lumley).
MCSET. Cat no: **1070T**. Released on Travellers Tales, '91 by Travellers Tales. Note: 6 Cassettes.

JEMIMA SHORE'S FIRST CASE (And Other Stories) (Patricia Hodge).
Note: Unabridged.
MC. Cat no: **CAB 340**. Released on Chivers Audio Books, '88 by Chivers Audio Books, Green Dragon Audio Visual. Note: 6 Cassettes.

MCSET. Cat no: **1366T**. Released on Travellers Tales, '91 by Travellers Tales. Note: 6 Cassettes.

OXFORD BLOOD (Patricia Hodge).
MCSET. Cat no: **CAB 204**. Released on Chivers Audio Books, '91 by Chivers Audio Books, Green Dragon Audio Visual. Note: 6 Cassettes.

MCSET. Cat no: **1147T**. Released on Travellers Tales, '91 by Travellers Tales. Note: 6 Cassettes.

QUIET AS A NUN (Patricia Hodge).
MCSET. Cat no: **CAB 397**. Released on Chivers Audio Books, '91 by Chivers Audio Books, Green Dragon Audio Visual. Note: 6 Cassettes.

SPLASH OF RED, A (Patricia Hodge).
MCSET. Cat no: **CAB 101**. Released on Chivers Audio Books, '91 by Chivers Audio Books, Green Dragon Audio Visual. Note: 6 Cassettes.

WILD ISLAND, THE (Patricia Hodge).
MCSET. Cat no: **CAB 522**. Released on Chivers Audio Books, '91 by Chivers Audio Books, Green Dragon Audio Visual. Note: 6 Cassettes

MCSET. Cat no: **1621T**. Released on Travellers Tales, '91 by Travellers Tales. Note: 6 Cassettes.

YOUR ROYAL HOSTAGE (Patricia Hodge).
MCSET. Cat no: **CAB 261**. Released on Chivers Audio Books, '91 by Chivers Audio Books, Green Dragon Audio Visual. Note: 6 Cassettes.

Frayn, Michael

SWEET DREAMS (Martin Jarvis).
MCSET. Cat no: **1029H**. Released on Travellers Tales, '91 by Travellers Tales. Note: 6 cassettes.

MCSET. Cat no: **CAB 177**. Released on Chivers Audio Books, '91 by Chivers Audio Books, Green Dragon Audio Visual.

Freeborn, Peter

STARK TRUTH, THE (David Ogden Steirs).
MCSET. Cat no: **0071689304**. Released on Simon & Schuster, '91 by Simon & Schuster Ltd. Note: 2 cassettes.

Freeling, Nicolas

NOT AS FAR AS VELMA (Peter Wickham).
MCSET. Cat no: **1698F**. Released on Travellers Tales, '91 by Travellers Tales. Note: 6 cassettes.

MCSET. Cat no: **OAS 40691**. Released on Oasis Audio Books, '91 by Isis Audio Books. Note: 8 Cassettes.

Fresson, I.M.

THIS SAD FREEDOM (Karen Craig).
MCSET. Cat no: **MRC 1039**. Released on Chivers Audio Books, '91 by Chivers Audio Books, Green Dragon Audio Visual. Note: 2 Cassettes.

Frost, Robert

ROAD NOT TAKEN, THE (Robert Frost).
MC. Cat no: **1060**. Released on Caedmon (USA), '88 by Caedmon Records (USA), Bond Street Music.

Fry, Stephen

LIAR, THE (Stephen Fry).
MCSET. Cat no: **0001046438**. Released on Harper Collins, Mar '92 by Harper Collins.

Fugard, Athol

BLOOD KNOT (Various artists).
MCSET. Cat no: **0362**. Released on Caedmon (USA), '88 by Caedmon Records (USA), Bond Street Music. Note: 2 cassettes

Fullerton, Alexander

APHRODITE CARGO, THE (Alan Dunbavin).
MCSET. Cat no: **1168T**. Released on Travellers Tales, '91 by Travellers Tales. Note: 6 Cassettes.

MCSET. Cat no: **1854960997**. Released on Bramhope, '91 by Ulverscroft Soundings. Note: 5 Cassettes.

Fyfield, Frances

QUESTION OF GUILT, A (Rula Lenska).
MCSET. Cat no: **CAB 602**. Released on Chivers Audio Books, '91 by Chivers Audio Books, Green Dragon Audio Visual. Note: 8 cassettes

Gallagher, Jock

TO THE VICTOR, THE SPOILS (Nina Holloway).
MCSET. Cat no: **1426F**. Released on Travellers Tales, '91 by Travellers Tales. Note: 5 cassettes.

MCSET. Cat no: **OAS 90015**. Released on Oasis Audio Books, '91 by Isis Audio Books. Note: 5 Cassettes.

Galsworthy, John

FORSYTE SAGA, THE (The Man of Property) (Sir Michael Hordern).
MCSET. Cat no: **LFP 7234**. Released on Listen For Pleasure, Feb '86 by EMI Records.

FORSYTE SAGE, THE (PART 2) (In Chancery) (Sir Michael Hordern).
MCSET. Cat no: **LFP 7250**. Released on Listen For Pleasure, Jun '86 by EMI Records.

FORSYTE SAGA, THE (The Man of Property) (Neil Hunt).
MCSET. Cat no: **IAB 89123**. Released on Isis Audio Books, '91. Note: 12 cassette set. Playing time 15hrs.

FORSYTE SAGA, THE (Various artists).
MCSET. Cat no: **ZBBC 1252**. Released on BBC Radio Collection, Sep '91 by BBC Records. Note: 6 Cassettes. ISBN No: 0563 365218

FORSYTE SAGA, THE (Excerpts from) (Various narrators).
Note: Excerpts from Man Of Property, In Chancery and White Monkey.
MCSET. Cat no: **1224F**. Released on Travellers Tales, '91 by Travellers Tales. Note: 8 cassettes.

FORSYTE SAGA, THE (Part 1) (Neil Hunt).
MCSET. Cat no: **1430/31F**. Released on Travellers Tales, '91 by Travellers Tales. Note: 12 cassettes.

FORSYTE SAGA, THE (PART 2) (In Chancery) (Neil Hunt).
MCSET. Cat no: **1432F**. Released on Travellers Tales, '91 by Travellers Tales. Note: 8 cassettes.

MCSET. Cat no: **IAB 90013**. Released on Isis Audio Books, '91. Note: 8 Cassettes. Playing time: 11 hours.

FORSYTE SAGA, THE (PART 3) (To Let) (Neil Hunt).
MCSET. Cat no: **1433F**. Released on Travellers Tales, '91 by Travellers Tales. Note: 8 cassettes.

MCSET. Cat no: **IAB 90023**. Released on Isis Audio Books, '91. Note: 8 Cassettes. Playing time: 9 hours 30 minutes.

MCSET. Cat no: **LFP 7292**. Released on Listen For Pleasure, '87 by EMI Records.

FORSYTE SAGA, THE (PART 4) (The White Monkey) (Martin Jarvis).
MCSET. Cat no: **LFP 7367**. Released on Listen For Pleasure, Nov '88 by EMI Records. Note: Playing Time: 2 hours 30 minutes.

FORSYTE SAGA, THE (PART 5) (The Silverspoon) (Martin Jarvis).
Note: Abridged version.
MCSET. Cat no: **1447F**. Released on Travellers Tales, '91 by Travellers Tales. Note: 2 cassettes.

MCSET. Cat no: **LFP 7397**. Released on Listen For Pleasure, '89 by EMI Records. Note: Playing time: 2 hours 30 minutes.

FORSYTE SAGA, THE (PART 6) (The Swan Song) (Martin Jarvis).
Note: Abridged version.
MCSET. Cat no: **1699F**. Released on Travellers Tales, '91 by Travellers Tales. Note: 2 cassettes.

MCSET. Cat no: **LFP 7427**. Released on Listen For Pleasure, '91 by EMI Records. Note: Playing time: 3 hours.

Galt, John

ANNALS OF THE PARISH (John Sheddon).
MCSET. Cat no: **COL 4505**. Released on Colophone, '88 by AVLS (Audio-Visual Library Services).

ANNALS OF THE PARISH (John Sheddon).

Note: Abridged version.
MCSET. Cat no: **1052F**. Released on Travellers Tales, '91 by Travellers Tales. Note: 4 cassettes.

Gann, Ernest K.

IN THE COMPANY OF EAGLES (George Guidall).
MCSET. Cat no: **RB 91218**. Released on Recorded Books, Feb '92 by Isis Audio Books. Note: 7 cassettes. Playing time 10hrs 30mins.

Garden Gang

GERTRUDE GOOSEBERRY AND BELINDA BLACKCURRANT (Unknown artist(s)).
Note: Book and cassette.
MC. Cat no: **PLB 135**. Released on Tell-A-Tale, Oct '84 by Pickwick Records, Taylors, Clyde Factors.

PAM PARSNIP AND LAWRENCE LEMON (Unknown artist(s)).
Note: Book and cassette.
MC. Cat no: **PLB 144**. Released on Tell-A-Tale, '84 by Pickwick Records, Taylors, Clyde Factors.

PATRICK PEAR AND COLIN CUCUMBER (Unknown artist(s)).
Note: Book and cassette.
MC. Cat no: **PLB 133**. Released on Tell-A-Tale, Oct '84 by Pickwick Records, Taylors, Clyde Factors.

PEDRO PEPPER AND THE CHERRY TWINS (Unknown artist(s)).
Note: Book and cassette.
MC. Cat no: **PLB 132**. Released on Tell-A-Tale, Oct '84 by Pickwick Records, Taylors, Clyde Factors.

PERCIVAL PEA AND POLLY POMEGRANATE (Unknown artist(s)).
Note: Book and cassette.
MC. Cat no: **PLB 141**. Released on Tell-A-Tale, '84 by Pickwick Records, Taylors, Clyde Factors.

PETER POTATO AND ALICE APPLE (Unknown artist(s)).
Note: Book and cassette.
MC. Cat no: **PLB 134**. Released on Tell-A-Tale, Oct '84 by Pickwick Records, Taylors, Clyde Factors.

ROBERT RASPBERRY AND GRACE GRAPE (Unknown artist(s)).
Note: Book and cassette.
MC. Cat no: **PLB 131**. Released on Tell-A-Tale, Oct '84 by Pickwick Records, Taylors, Clyde Factors.

SHEILA SHALLOT AND BENNY (Unknown artist(s)).
Note: Book and cassette.
MC. Cat no: **PLB 142**. Released on Tell-A-Tale, '84 by Pickwick Records, Taylors, Clyde Factors.

SIMON SWEDE AND AVRIL APRICOT (Unknown artist(s)).
Note: Book and cassette.
MC. Cat no: **PLB 143**. Released on Tell-A-Tale, '84 by Pickwick Records, Taylors, Clyde Factors.

WEE WILLIE WATER MELON AND BETTY BEETROOT (Unknown artist(s)).
Note: Book and cassette.
MC. Cat no: **PLB 140**. Released on Tell-A-Tale, Aug '84 by Pickwick Records, Taylors, Clyde Factors.

Gardner, John

FOR SPECIAL SERVICES (Jonathan Oliver).
MCSET. Cat no: **1622T**. Released on Travellers Tales, '91 by Travellers Tales. Note: 8 Cassettes.
MCSET. Cat no: **OAS 90091**. Released on Oasis Audio Books, '91 by Isis Audio Books. Note: 8 Cassettes.
LICENCE TO KILL (David Rintoul).
MCSET. Cat no: **CAB 669**. Released on Chivers Audio Books, Dec '91 by Chivers Audio Books, Green Dragon Audio Visual. Note: 6 cassettes.
SCORPIUS (Tony Chambers).
MCSET. Cat no: **1499T**. Released on Travellers Tales, '91 by Travellers Tales. Note: 7 Cassettes.
MCSET. Cat no: **OAS 89126**. Released on Oasis Audio Books, '91 by Isis Audio Books. Note: 7 Cassettes.

Garfield, Leon

GHOST DOWNSTAIRS, THE (Clifford Norgate).
Note: Abridged.
MCSET. Cat no: **2CCA 3025**. Released on Chivers Audio Books, '91 by Chivers Audio Books, Green Dragon Audio Visual. Note: 2 Cassettes.
MCSET. Cat no: **9033F**. Released on Travellers Tales, '91 by Travellers Tales. Note: 2 Cassettes.
GHOST DOWNSTAIRS, THE (Clifford Norgate).
MCSET. Cat no: **086 222 044X**. Released on Chivers Calvacade, Apr '88 by Chivers Audio Books, Green Dragon Audio Visual. Note: 7 Cassettes.

Garioch, Robert

CHOICE AND COMMENTARY (1909-1981) (Norman MacCaig & Robert Garioch).
MC. Cat no: **SSC 045**. Released on Scotsoun, '91 by Scotsoun Recordings, Morley Audio Services.
IN MIND O A MAKAR (1909-1981) (Various artists).
Note: A Scotsoun tribute to Robert Garioch (1909-1981). Comments, recollections from Alexander Scott, James L Caird, David Murison, Norman MacCaig, Jack Sitken, Sorley MacLean, JK Annand, Albert MacKie, Edwin Morgan. Garioch reads from his own work and from Dubar, Fergusson and Ramsay.
MC. Cat no: **SSC 061**. Released on Scotsoun, '91 by Scotsoun Recordings, Morley Audio Services.

Garner, Alan

AIMER GATES (Unknown narrator(s)).
LP. Cat no: **ZDSW 726**. Released on Argo, Sep '79 by Decca International **Deleted** '84.
BAG OF MOONSHINE, A (Alan Garner).
MCSET. Cat no: **2CCA 3122**. Released on Chivers Audio Books, '91 by Chivers Audio Books, Green Dragon Audio Visual. Note: 2 Cassettes.
GRANNY REARDUN (Unknown narrator(s)).
LP. Cat no: **ZDSW 725**. Released on Argo, Sep '79 by Decca International **Deleted** '84.
STONE BOOK (Alan Garner).
LP. Cat no: **ZDSW 724**. Released on Argo, Sep '79 by Decca International **Deleted** '84.
TOM FOBBLES DAY (Unknown narrator(s)).
LP. Cat no: **ZDSW 727**. Released on Argo, Sep '79 by Decca International **Deleted** '84.

Garry, Flora

BENNYGOAK (Poems in the Buchan Dialect) (Various artists).
MC. Cat no: **SSC 016**. Released on Scotsoun, '91 by Scotsoun Recordings, Morley Audio Services.

Garve, Andrew

VERY QUIET PLACE, A (Michael Kitchen).
MCSET. Cat no: **CAT 4028**. Released on Chivers Audio Thrillers, Apr '88 by Chivers Audio Books, Green Dragon Audio Visual. Note: 4 Cassettes.
MCSET. Cat no: **1250T**. Released on Travellers Tales, '91 by Travellers Tales. Note: 4 Cassettes.

Gaskell, Elizabeth

COUSIN PHYLLIS (Kenneth Branagh).
MCSET. Cat no: **CTC 027**. Released on Cover to Cover, Sep '86 by Cover to Cover Cassettes. Note: 3 cassettes. Playing time: 3 hrs 55 mins.
MCSET. Cat no: **1053F**. Released on Travellers Tales, '91 by Travellers Tales. Note: 3 cassettes.
CRANFORD (Prunella Scales).
MCSET. Cat no: **418 018-4**. Released on Argo (Polygram), Jun '88 by PolyGram Classics **Deleted** Jan '89.
CRANFORD (Prunella Scales).
Note: Abridged version.
MCSET. Cat no: **1054F**. Released on Travellers Tales, '91 by Travellers Tales. Note: 2 cassettes.
FOUR SHORT STORIES (Judith Whale).
MCSET. Cat no: **OAS 89085**. Released on Oasis Audio Books, '91 by Isis Audio Books. Note: 4 Cassettes. Playing time 5hrs.
MCSET. Cat no: **1397F**. Released on Travellers Tales, '91 by Travellers Tales. Note: 4 cassettes.

Gaskin, Catherine

BLAKE'S REACH (Rowena Cooper).
MCSET. Cat no: **CAB 512**. Released on Chivers Audio Books, '91 by Chivers Audio Books, Green Dragon Audio Visual. Note: 10 Cassettes.
MCSET. Cat no: **1154/1155R**. Released on Travellers Tales, '91 by Travellers Tales. Note: 10 Cassettes.
DAUGHTER OF THE HOUSE (Jan Francis).
MCSET. Cat no: **CAB 278**. Released on Chivers Audio Books, '91 by Chivers Audio Books, Green Dragon Audio Visual. Note: 6 Cassettes.
MCSET. Cat no: **1277F**. Released on Travellers Tales, '91 by Travellers Tales. Note: 6 cassettes.
EDGE OF GLASS (Rosalind Ayres).
MCSET. Cat no: **CAB 359**. Released on Chivers Audio Books, '91 by Chivers Audio Books, Green Dragon Audio Visual. Note: 8 Cassettes.
MCSET. Cat no: **1394T**. Released on Travellers Tales, '91 by Travellers Tales. Note: 8 Cassettes.
FALCON FOR A QUEEN, A (Eve Karpf).
MCSET. Cat no: **CAB 463**. Released on Chivers Audio Books, '91 by Chivers Audio Books, Green Dragon Audio Visual. Note: 10 Cassettes.
MCSET. Cat no: **1452/3F**. Released on Travellers Tales, '91 by Travellers Tales. Note: 10 cassettes.
FILE ON DEVLIN, THE (Sinead Cusack).
MCSET. Cat no: **CAB 409**. Released on Chivers Audio Books, '91 by Chivers Audio Books, Green Dragon Audio Visual. Note: 8 Cassettes.
MCSET. Cat no: **1468T**. Released on Travellers Tales, '91 by Travellers Tales. Note: 8 Cassettes.
FIONA (Eve Karpf).
MCSET. Cat no: **CAB 574**. Released on Chivers Audio Books, '91 by Chivers Audio Books, Green Dragon Audio Visual. Note: 10 Cassettes.
MCSET. Cat no: **1655/6F**. Released on Travellers Tales, '91 by Travellers Tales. Note: 10 cassettes.

Gaston, Bill

WINTER AND THE WHITE WITCH (Unknown narrator(s)).
MCSET. Cat no: **SOUND 27**. Released on Soundings, Mar '85 by Soundings Records, Bond Street Music.
MCSET. Cat no: **1854961004**. Released on Soundings, '91 by Soundings Records, Bond Street Music. Note: 2 Cassettes.

Gater, Dilys

DARK STAR, THE (Unknown narrator(s)).
MCSET. Cat no: **1854963546**. Released on Bramhope, '91 by Ulverscroft Soundings. Note: 4 cassettes.

EMILY (Unknown narrator(s)).
MCSET. Cat no: **1854962957**. Released on Bramhope, '91 by Ulverscroft Soundings. Note: 4 Cassettes.

PREJUDICED WITNESS (Elizabeth Henry).
MCSET. Cat no: **1854965756**. Released on Trio, Mar '92 by EMI Records. Note: Playing time: 60 Minutes.

PROPHECY FOR A QUEEN (Unknown narrator(s)).
MCSET. Cat no: **1854962647**. Released on Trio, '91 by EMI Records. Note: 3 cassettes.

WITCH GIRL, THE (Unknown narrator(s)).
MCSET. Cat no: **185496321X**. Released on Bramhope, '91 by Ulverscroft Soundings. Note: 5 Cassettes.

Gathorne-Hardy, J.
CYRIL BONHAMY (And The Great Drain Robbery) (Hugh Laurie).
MC. Cat no: **2CCA 3058**. Released on Chivers Audio Books, '88 by Chivers Audio Books, Green Dragon Audio Visual. Note: 2 Cassettes

Gault, William
BLOODSTAINED BOKHARA, THE (Peter Whitman).
MCSET. Cat no: **CAT 4052**. Released on Chivers Audio Books, '91 by Chivers Audio Books, Green Dragon Audio Visual. Note: 4 Cassettes.

MCSET. Cat no: **1527T**. Released on Travellers Tales, '91 by Travellers Tales. Note: 4 Cassettes.

Gavin, Catherine
SNOW MOUNTAIN (Morag Hood).
MCSET. Cat no: **COL 4501**. Released on Colophone, Feb '81 by AVLS (Audio-Visual Library Services).

MCSET. Cat no: **1001G**. Released on Travellers Tales, '91 by Travellers Tales. Note: 4 Cassettes.

Genet, Jean
BALCONY, THE (Unknown narrator(s)).
MCSET. Cat no: **0316**. Released on Caedmon (USA), '88 by Caedmon Records (USA), Bond Street Music. Note: 3 cassettes

George, Catherine
RELUCTANT PARAGON (Carole Boyd).
MCSET. Cat no: **PMB 004**. Released on Mills & Boon, '91.

George, Elizabeth
GREAT DELIVERANCE, A (Michael Tudor Barnes).
MCSET. Cat no: **1715T**. Released on Travellers Tales, '91 by Travellers Tales. Note: 8 Cassettes.

MCSET. Cat no: **OAS 91013**. Released on Oasis Audio Books, '91 by Isis Audio Books. Note: 8 Cassettes.

PAYMENT IN BLOOD (Michael McStay).

MCSET. Cat no: **1680T**. Released on Travellers Tales, '91 by Travellers Tales. Note: 8 Cassettes.

MCSET. Cat no: **OAS 30691**. Released on Oasis Audio Books, '91 by Isis Audio Books. Note: 8 Cassettes.

WELL SCHOOLED IN MURDER (Derek Jacobi).
MCSET. Cat no: **ZBBC 1260**. Released on BBC, Aug '91 by BBC Records, Taylors. Note: ISBN No: 0563 365595

WELL SCHOOLED IN MURDER (Michael McStay).
MCSET. Cat no: **IAB 92065**. Released on Isis Audio Books, Jun '92. Note: 10 Cassettes. Playing time: 14 hours, 42 mins.

Gerson, Jack
ASSASSINATION RUN (Alan Dunbavin).
MCSET. Cat no: **1073T**. Released on Travellers Tales, '91 by Travellers Tales. Note: 4 Cassettes.

MCSET. Cat no: **1854961012**. Released on Bramhope, '91 by Ulverscroft Soundings. Note: 4 Cassettes.

BACK OF THE TIGER, THE (Gordon Griffin).
MCSET. Cat no: **1243T**. Released on Travellers Tales, '91 by Travellers Tales. Note: 5 Cassettes.

MCSET. Cat no: **1854961020**. Released on Bramhope, '91 by Ulverscroft Soundings. Note: 5 Cassettes.

WHITEHALL SANCTION (Christopher Kay).
MCSET. Cat no: **1074T**. Released on Travellers Tales, '91 by Travellers Tales. Note: 6 Cassettes.

MCSET. Cat no: **1854961039**. Released on Soundings, '91 by Soundings Records, Bond Street Music. Note: 6 Cassettes.

Ghost Stories
CLASSIC GHOST STORIES (Richard Pasco).
Note: Contains works by Stoker, Le Fanu, Saki and Poe.

MCSET. Cat no: **TTDMC 403**. Released on CSA Tell Tapes, Oct '89 by CSA Tell-Tapes. Note: 2 Cassettes. ISBN No: 1873859031.

CLASSIC TALES OF MYSTERY AND THE SUPERNATURAL (Robin Bailey).
Note: Contains works by Dickens, Wallace, Saki, M.R. James and Poe.

MCSET. Cat no: **TTDMC 404**. Released on CSA Tell Tapes, Oct '89 by CSA Tell-Tapes. Note: 2 Cassettes. ISBN No: 187385904X.

EXORCISM OF BROTHER SIMEON (Various artists).
MCSET. Cat no: **BS 18/21**. Released on Chiron Cassettes, '79.

GHOST BOAST (Various artists).
MC. Cat no: **PLBM 272**. Released on Tell-A-Tale, '89 by Pickwick Records, Taylors, Clyde Factors.

GHOST OF BLACKLAKE, THE (Unknown narrator(s)).
MC. Cat no: **PLBG 287**. Released on Tell-A-Tale, Jul '90 by Pickwick Records, Taylors, Clyde Factors.

GRIM TALES FROM THE SCOTS (John Sheddon).
Note: Stories by Robert Louis Stevenson, Sir Walter Scott and James Hogg.
MCSET. Cat no: **COL 4004**. Released on Colophone, '88 by AVLS (Audio-Visual Library Services).

MCSET. Cat no: **1018S**. Released on Travellers Tales, '91 by Travellers Tales. Note: 6 Cassettes.

MASK, THE (And Other Stories) (Various narrators).
Note: Narrators are:- Clive Champney, Richard Greenwood, Robert Trotter and Paul Young. Stories include The Mask, The Legend Of The Blue Rock, The Man In The Bell, The Middle Toe Of The Left Foot and The Boarded Window.
MCSET. Cat no: **SPF 970 3**. Released on Schiltron Audio Books, Feb '92 by Schiltron Publishing. Note: 2 cassettes. Playing time 2hrs 10mins.

MONSTERS OF THE EARTH (Various artists).
MC. Cat no: **BS 19**. Released on Chiron Cassettes, '79.

MOON'S GIBBET (And Other Stories) (Clive Champney & Robert Trotter).
Note: Includes:- Moon's Gibbet by Egerton Castle, The Lighthouse on Shivering Sand by J.S. Fletcher and Smeath by Barry Pain.
MCSET. Cat no: **SPF 970-2**. Released on Schiltron Audio Books, '91 by Schiltron Publishing. Note: 2 Cassettes. Playing time 2 hours 5 minutes.

PRICE OF FEAR, THE (Vincent Price).
Note: Four dramatisations.
MCSET. Cat no: **ZBBC 1118**. Released on BBC Radio Collection, Jun '90 by BBC Records. Note: ISBN No: 0563 410345

SCREAMING SKULL, THE (And Other Stories) (Richard Greenwood).
Note: Includes: The Screaming Skull by F. Marion Crawford, The Ghost Ship by Richard Middleton, My Favourite Murder by Ambrose Bierce and Oh, Whistle, and I'll Come To You by Mr James.
MCSET. Cat no: **SPF 970-1**. Released on Schiltron Audio Books, '91 by Schiltron Publishing. Note: 2 Cassettes. Playing time 2 hours 17 minutes.

TALES OF TERROR (Dyall, Valentine).
MC. Cat no: **P 90009**. Released on Storyteller Cassettes, '79.

TALES OF WITCHES, GHOSTS AND GOBLINS (Vincent Price).
MC. Cat no: **1393**. Released on Caedmon (USA), '89 by Caedmon Records (USA), Bond Street Music.

VIRAGO BOOK OF GHOST STORIES (Unknown narrator(s)).
MCSET. Cat no: **RC 37**. Released on Random Century, '91 by Random Century Audiobooks, Conifer Records. Note: 2 cassettes. ISBN no.1856860558. Playing time 3hrs approx

VIRAGO VICTORIAN GHOST STORIES (Patricia Hodge).
MCSET. Cat no: **RC 81**. Released on Random Century, Aug '92 by Random Century Audiobooks, Conifer Records. Note: ISBN no. 1856861090

Gibbon, Lewis Grassic

CLOUD HOWE (Eileen McCallum).
MCSET. Cat no: **SPF 320-3**. Released on Schiltron Audio Books, '91 by Schiltron Publishing. Note: 8 Cassettes. Playing time 9 hours 16 minutes.
MCSET. Cat no: **1454F**. Released on Travellers Tales, '91 by Travellers Tales. Note: 8 cassettes.

FORSAKEN (And the Wow O'Rivven) (Eileen McCallum).
Note: Authors are:- Lewis Grassic Gibbon and George MacDonald.
MC. Cat no: **SPF 320-5**. Released on Schiltron Audio Books, '91 by Schiltron Publishing. Note: Playing time 66 minutes.

GREY GRANITE (Eileen McCallum).
MCSET. Cat no: **SPF 320-4**. Released on Schiltron Audio Books, '91 by Schiltron Publishing. Note: 8 Cassettes. Playing time 9 hours.
MCSET. Cat no: **1549F**. Released on Travellers Tales, '91 by Travellers Tales. Note: 8 cassettes.

SMEDDUM, CLAY, GREENDEN AND SIM (Eileen McCallum).
MCSET. Cat no: **SPF 320-1**. Released on Schiltron Audio Books, '91 by Schiltron Publishing. Note: 2 Cassettes. Playing time 2 hours

SUNSET SONG (Eileen McCallum).
MCSET. Cat no: **SPF 320-2**. Released on Schiltron Audio Books, '91 by Schiltron Publishing. Note: 8 Cassettes. Playing time 10 hours 50 minutes.
MCSET. Cat no: **1398F**. Released on Travellers Tales, '91 by Travellers Tales. Note: 8 cassettes.

WOMAN OF LEADENHALL STREET, THE (And Other Stories) (Robert Trotter).
MCSET. Cat no: **SPF 320-6**. Released on Schiltron Audio Books, '91 by Schiltron Publishing. Note: 2 Cassettes. Playing time 1 hour 45 minutes.

Gibbons, Stella

COLD COMFORT FARM (Miriam Margoyles).
MCSET. Cat no: **ZBBC 1076**. Released on BBC Radio Collection, Jun '89 by BBC Records. Note: ISBN No: 0563 226617

COLD COMFORT FARM (Prunella Scales).
MCSET. Cat no: **SAY 15**. Released on Argo (Polygram), Jul '82 by PolyGram Classics **Deleted** Jan '89.
MCSET. Cat no: **ARGO 1148**. Released on Argo (EMI), Sep '89 by EMI Records. Note: 2 Cassettes.
MCSET. Cat no: **1055F**. Released on Travellers Tales, '91 by Travellers Tales.

Gielgud, Sir John

HIS GREATEST ROLES (Sir John Gielgud).
Note: Includes: Hamlet Speech, Richard II, King Lear, The Tempest, Forty Years On, No Mans Land, Ode To The West Wind.
LP. Cat no: **REGL 351**. Released on BBC, '80 by BBC Records, Taylors **Deleted** Apr '89.
MC. Cat no: **ZCF 351**. Released on BBC, '80 by BBC Records, Taylors **Deleted** Apr '89.

Gilbert, Anthony

BLACK STAGE, THE (Gordon Fairclough).
MCSET. Cat no: **CAT 4047**. Released on Chivers Audio Books, '91 by Chivers Audio Books, Green Dragon Audio Visual. Note: 6 Cassettes.
MCSET. Cat no: **1469T**. Released on Travellers Tales, '91 by Travellers Tales. Note: 6 Cassettes.

Gilbert, Jacqueline

CHEQUERED SILENCE, A (Carole Boyd).
MCSET. Cat no: **PMB 021**. Released on Mills & Boon, '88. Note: 2 Cassettes

Gilbert, Michael

BLOOD AND JUDGEMENT (Bruce Montague).
MCSET. Cat no: **IAB 91116**. Released on Isis Audio Books, Nov '91. Note: 8 Cassettes. Playing time 7 hours 12 minutes.

Gilbert, W.S.

BAD BALLADS AND CAUTIONARY VERSES, THE (Stanley Holloway & Joyce Grenfell).
MC. Cat no: **1104**. Released on Caedmon (USA), '88 by Caedmon Records (USA), Bond Street Music.

GOLDEN SLUMBERS (Unknown narrator(s)).
MC. Cat no: **1399**. Released on Caedmon (USA), Jul '88 by Caedmon Records (USA), Bond Street Music.

Gill, B.M.

DYING TO MEET YOU (Richard Morant).
MCSET. Cat no: **CAB 299**. Released on Chivers Audio Books, Apr '88 by Chivers Audio Books, Green Dragon Audio Visual. Note: 4 Cassettes.
MCSET. Cat no: **1261T**. Released on Travellers Tales, '91 by Travellers Tales. Note: 4 Cassettes.

DYING TO MEET YOU (Robert Hardy).
MCSET. Cat no: **CAB 161**. Released on Chivers Audio Books, '91 by Chivers Audio Books, Green Dragon Audio Visual. Note: 6 cassettes.

SEMINAR FOR MURDER (Robert Hardy).
MCSET. Cat no: **1075T**. Released on Travellers Tales, '91 by Travellers Tales. Note: 6 Cassettes.

TWELFTH JUROR, THE (John Atterbury).
MCSET. Cat no: **1403T**. Released on Travellers Tales, '91 by Travellers Tales. Note: 6 Cassettes.
MCSET. Cat no: **IAB 88122**. Released on Isis Audio Books, '91. Note: 6 Cassettes.

Gilliat, Penelope

WOMAN OF SINGULAR OCCUPATION, A (Stephen Thorne).
MCSET. Cat no: **1479F**. Released on Travellers Tales, '91 by Travellers Tales. Note: 5 Cassettes.
MCSET. Cat no: **OAS 90094**. Released on Oasis Audio Books, '91 by Isis Audio Books. Note: 5 Cassettes.

Gallico, Paul

MATHILDE MOUSE (And the Story of Silent Night) (Unknown narrator(s)).
MC. Cat no: **CDL 51681**. Released on Caedmon (USA), '82 by Caedmon Records (USA), Bond Street Music.
MC. Cat no: **TC 1681**. Released on Caedmon (USA), '86 by Caedmon Records (USA), Bond Street Music.

Gilman, Dorothy

AMAZING MRS. POLLIFAX, THE (Barbara Rosenblat).
MCSET. Cat no: **RB 89740**. Released on Recorded Books, Sep '91 by Isis Audio Books. Note: 5 cassettes. Playing time 6hrs 45mins.

ELUSIVE MRS. POLLIFAX, THE (Barbara Rosenblat).
MCSET. Cat no: **RB 90005**. Released on Recorded Books, Jan '92 by Isis Audio Books. Note: 5 cassettes. Playing time 6hrs 30mins.

MRS POLLIFAX ON THE CHINA STATION (Barbara Rosenblat).
MCSET. Cat no: **RB 90101**. Released on Recorded Books, Jun '92 by Isis Audio Books. Note: 5 Cassettes. Playing time: 7 hours, 15 mins.

UNEXPECTED MRS. POLLIFAX, THE (Unknown narrator(s)).
MCSET. Cat no: **RB 89730**. Released on Recorded Books, '91 by Isis Audio Books. Note: 6 cassettes.

Gish, Lillian

TALE OF THE SHINING PRINCESS, THE (Unknown narrator(s)).
MC. Cat no: **1707**. Released on Caedmon (USA), Apr '83 by Caedmon Records (USA), Bond Street Music.

Goddard, Robert
IN PALE BATTALIONS (Tony Britton).
MCSET. Cat no: **CAB 614.** Released on Chivers Audio Books, Mar '92 by Chivers Audio Books, Green Dragon Audio Visual. Note: 10 Cassettes.

Godden, Rumer
BATTLE OF VILLA FIORITA, THE (Sheri Blair).
MCSET. Cat no: **1574F.** Released on Travellers Tales, '91 by Travellers Tales. Note: 6 cassettes.

MCSET. Cat no: **RB 82038.** Released on Recorded Books, '91 by Isis Audio Books. Note: 6 Cassettes.

BLACK NARCISSUS (Sheri Blair).
MCSET. Cat no: **1580F.** Released on Travellers Tales, '91 by Travellers Tales. Note: 6 cassettes

MCSET. Cat no: **RB 82015.** Released on Recorded Books, '91 by Isis Audio Books.

DIDDAKOI, THE (Lynda Bellingham).
MCSET. Cat no: **3CCA 3091.** Released on Chivers Audio Books, '91 by Chivers Audio Books, Green Dragon Audio Visual. Note: 3 Cassettes.

MCSET. Cat no: **9152F.** Released on Travellers Tales, '91 by Travellers Tales. Note: 3 Cassettes.

GREENGAGE SUMMER, THE (Nicola Pagett).
MCSET. Cat no: **1056F.** Released on Travellers Tales, '91 by Travellers Tales. Note: 6 cassettes.

GREENGAGE SUMMER, THE (Susannah York).
MCSET. Cat no: **ZC SWD 363.** Released on ASV (Academy Sound & Vision), Oct '89 by Academy Sound & Vision Records. Note: 2 cassettes. Playing time: 3 hours.

KINGFISHER'S CATCH FIRE (Sheri Blair).
MCSET. Cat no: **1632F.** Released on Travellers Tales, '91 by Travellers Tales. Note: 6 cassettes.

MCSET. Cat no: **RB 81090.** Released on Recorded Books, '91 by Isis Audio Books. Note: 6 Cassettes.

ROCKING HORSE SECRET, THE (Unknown narrator(s)).
MCSET. Cat no: **DTO 10559.** Released on Ditto, '88 by Pickwick Records, Midland Records.

TOTTIE (Unknown narrator(s)).
MCSET. Cat no: **DTO 10564.** Released on Ditto, '88 by Pickwick Records, Midland Records.

Golding, William
CLOSE QUARTERS (To the Ends of the Earth) (William Golding).
MCSET. Cat no: **IAB 90061.** Released on Isis Audio Books, '91. Note: 8 cassette set. Playing time 9hrs 40mins.

MCSET. Cat no: **1456F.** Released on Travellers Tales, '91 by Travellers Tales. Note: 8 cassettes

FIRE DOWN BELOW (To the Ends of the Earth) (William Golding).
MCSET. Cat no: **IAB 90081.** Released on Isis Audio Books, '91. Note: 8 cassette set. Playing time 7hrs.

MCSET. Cat no: **1519F.** Released on Travellers Tales, '91 by Travellers Tales. Note: 8 cassettes.

LORD OF THE FLIES (William Golding).
MCSET. Cat no: **1278F.** Released on Travellers Tales, '91 by Travellers Tales. Note: 6 cassettes.

PINCHER MARTIN (Richard Earthy).
MCSET. Cat no: **OAS 30491.** Released on Oasis Audio Books, '91 by Isis Audio Books. Note: 6 cassettes. Playing time 6hrs 29mins.

MCSET. Cat no: **1689F.** Released on Travellers Tales, '91 by Travellers Tales. Note: 6 cassettes.

RITES OF PASSAGE (To the Ends of the Earth) (William Golding).
MCSET. Cat no: **IAB 90033.** Released on Isis Audio Books, '91. Note: 8 cassette set. Playing time 9hrs 50mins.

MCSET. Cat no: **1455F.** Released on Travellers Tales, '91 by Travellers Tales. Note: 8 cassettes.

Goldman, William
PRINCESS BRIDE, THE (Rob Reiner).
MCSET. Cat no: **0001386484.** Released on Collins-Caedmon, '91 by Collins Audio, Taylors, Bond Street Music. Note: 2 Cassettes.

Goldsmith, Oliver
SHE STOOPS TO CONQUER (Various artists).
MCSET. Cat no: **309.** Released on Caedmon (USA), '89 by Caedmon Records (USA), Bond Street Music.

VICAR OF WAKEFIELD, THE (Derek Jacobi).
MCSET. Cat no: **418 174-4.** Released on Argo (Polygram), Jun '88 by Poly-Gram Classics **Deleted** Jan '89. Note: 2 cassette set

Goodland, Norman
MY OLD CHAP (Norman Goodland).
Tracks / Cuckoo be come / I thank ee, Lard / I do luv ee / Poacher, The / When zun de dip.
Note: The atmosphere and country ways of old Wessex.
LP. Cat no: **SDL 320.** Released on Saydisc, by Amon Ra Records, Taylors, C.M. Distribution, Gamut Distribution **Deleted** '89.

MC. Cat no: **CSDL 320.** Released on Saydisc, by Amon Ra Records, Taylors, C.M. Distribution, Gamut Distribution **Deleted** '89.

Goodsir Smith, Sydney
UNDER THE EILDON TREE (Alexander Scott & Donald Campbell).
MC. Cat no: **SSC 024.** Released on Scotsoun, '91 by Scotsoun Recordings, Morley Audio Services.

Goodwin, Grace
ITALIAN SUMMER (Unknown narrator(s)).
MCSET. Cat no: **1854965336.** Released on Trio, '91 by EMI Records. Note: 3 Cassettes.

LOVE IS THE KEY (Unknown narrator(s)).
MCSET. Cat no: **1854964100.** Released on Bramhope, '91 by Ulverscroft Soundings. Note: 4 Cassettes.

NURSE AT RADLEIGH (Valerie Georgeson).
MCSET. Cat no: **MRC 1034.** Released on Chivers Audio Books, '91 by Chivers Audio Books, Green Dragon Audio Visual. Note: 2 Cassettes.

NURSE IN THE VALLEY (Unknown narrator(s)).
MCSET. Cat no: **185496299X.** Released on Bramhope, '91 by Ulverscroft Soundings. Note: 4 Cassettes.

PROMISE OF THE MORNING (Unknown narrator(s)).
MCSET. Cat no: **1854964194.** Released on Bramhope, '91 by Ulverscroft Soundings. Note: 4 Cassettes.

WAY TO HIS HEART, THE (Hazel Temperley).
MCSET. Cat no: **1854964801.** Released on Bramhope, Aug '91 by Ulverscroft Soundings. Note: 4 Cassettes.

Goons
BEST OF THE GOON SHOWS (Volume 1).
Tracks / Missing No 10 Downing Street, The / Red fort, The.
LP. Cat no: **EMC 3062.** Released on EMI, Dec '74 by EMI Records **Deleted** Nov '88.

MC. Cat no: **TCEMC 3062.** Released on EMI, Dec '74 by EMI Records **Deleted** May '91.

LP. Cat no: **PMC 1108.** Released on Parlophone, Nov '59 by EMI Records, Solomon & Peres **Deleted** '64.

BEST OF THE GOON SHOWS (Volume 2).
LP. Cat no: **PMC 1129.** Released on Parlophone, Dec '60 by EMI Records, Solomon & Peres **Deleted** '65.

DARK SIDE OF THE GOONS.

Tracks / Boiled bananas and carrots / Any old iron / You gotta go oow / Will I find my lover today? / Heart of a clown / Fuller's earth / Faith can move mountains / Wormwood Scrubs tango / One love, one lifetime / My September love / Wish I knew / My old dutch / Putting on the smile / I'll make you mine / Postman's knock / Drop of the hard stuff / I'm so ashamed / Here is my heart.
LP. Cat no: **OU 2232**. Released on One-Up, Nov '80 by EMI Records.
MC. Cat no: **TC OU 2232**. Released on One-Up, Nov '80 by EMI Records.

GOON SHOW CLASSICS (Volume 1).
Note: Featuring Peter Sellers, Harry Secombe, Spike Milligan, Ray Ellington, Max Geldray, Wallace Greenslade. Orchestra conducted by Angela Morley. Script by Spike Milligan. Includes: Dreaded Batter Pudding Hurler of Bexhill-on-Sea and The History of Pliny the Elder.
LP. Cat no: **REB 177**. Released on BBC, Sep '81 by BBC Records, Taylors **Deleted** Aug '88.
MC. Cat no: **RMC 4010**. Released on BBC, Sep '81 by BBC Records, Taylors **Deleted** Aug '88.

GOON SHOW CLASSICS (Volume 2).
Note: Featuring Peter Sellers, Spike Milligan, Harry Secombe, Ray Ellington, Max Geldray, Walter Greenslade, with guest A.E. Matthews. Includes: The Jet-Propelled Guided NAAFI and The Evils of Bushey Spon.
LP. Cat no: **REB 213**. Released on BBC, Sep '81 by BBC Records, Taylors **Deleted** Aug '88.
MC. Cat no: **RMC 4026**. Released on BBC, Sep '81 by BBC Records, Taylors **Deleted** Aug '88.

GOON SHOW CLASSICS (Volume 3).
Note: Featuring Peter Sellers, Spike Milligan, Harry Secombe, Ray Ellington, Max Geldray, Wallace Greenslade; orchestra conducted by Angela Morley; script by Spike Milligan. Includes: Lurgi Strikes Britain and The International Christmas Pudding.
LP. Cat no: **REB 246**. Released on BBC, Sep '81 by BBC Records, Taylors **Deleted** Aug '88.
MC. Cat no: **RMC 4046**. Released on BBC, Sep '81 by BBC Records, Taylors **Deleted** Aug '88.

GOON SHOW CLASSICS (Volume 4).
Note: Featuring Peter Sellers, Spike Milligan, Harry Secombe, Ray Ellington, Max Geldray, Wallace Greenslade. Includes: Napoleon's Piano and The Flea.
LP. Cat no: **REB 291**. Released on BBC, Sep '81 by BBC Records, Taylors **Deleted** Aug '88.
MC. Cat no: **ZCF 291**. Released on BBC, Sep '81 by BBC Records, Taylors **Deleted** Aug '88.

GOON SHOW CLASSICS (Volume 5).
Note: Featuring Peter Sellers, Spike Milligan, Harry Secombe. Includes: The Treasure in the Lake and The Greenslade Story.
LP. Cat no: **REB 339**. Released on BBC, Sep '81 by BBC Records, Taylors **Deleted** Apr '89.
MC. Cat no: **ZCF 339**. Released on BBC, Sep '81 by BBC Records, Taylors **Deleted** Apr '89.

GOON SHOW CLASSICS (Volume 6).
Note: Featuring Peter Sellers, Spike Milligan, Harry Secombe. Includes: Wings Over Dagenham and The Rent Collectors.
LP. Cat no: **REB 366**. Released on BBC, '79 by BBC Records, Taylors **Deleted** Apr '89.
MC. Cat no: **ZCF 366**. Released on BBC, '79 by BBC Records, Taylors **Deleted** Apr '89.

GOON SHOW CLASSICS (Volume 7).
Note: Featuring Peter Sellers, Spike Milligan, Harry Secombe. Includes: The Man Who Never Was and The Case of the Missing CD Plates.
LP. Cat no: **REB 392**. Released on BBC, Sep '80 by BBC Records, Taylors **Deleted** Apr '89.
MC. Cat no: **ZCF 392**. Released on BBC, Sep '80 by BBC Records, Taylors **Deleted** Apr '89.

GOON SHOW CLASSICS (Volume 8).
Note: Featuring Peter Sellers, Spike Milligan, Harry Secombe. Includes: World War 1 and Nasty Affair at the Burami Oasis.
LP. Cat no: **REB 422**. Released on BBC, Sep '81 by BBC Records, Taylors **Deleted** Apr '89.
MC. Cat no: **ZCF 422**. Released on BBC, Sep '81 by BBC Records, Taylors **Deleted** Apr '89.

GOON SHOW CLASSICS (Volume 9).
Note: Featuring Peter Sellers, Spike Milligan, Harry Secombe. Includes: Call of the West and The Last Smoking Seagoon.
MC. Cat no: **ZCF 444**. Released on BBC, Sep '82 by BBC Records, Taylors **Deleted** '88.
LP. Cat no: **REB 444**. Released on BBC, Sep '82 by BBC Records, Taylors **Deleted** '88.

GOON SHOW CLASSICS (Volume 10).
Note: Featuring Peter Sellers, Spike Milligan, Harry Secombe. Includes: The Whistling Spy Enigma and I Was Monty's Treble.
LP. Cat no: **REB 481**. Released on BBC, Oct '83 by BBC Records, Taylors **Deleted** '88.
MC. Cat no: **ZCF 481**. Released on BBC, Oct '83 by BBC Records, Taylors **Deleted** '88.

GOON SHOW CLASSICS (Volume 11).
Note: Featuring Peter Sellers, Spike Milligan, Harry Secombe. Includes: Shifting Sands and 1985.
LP. Cat no: **REB 565**. Released on BBC, Oct '85 by BBC Records, Taylors **Deleted** '88.
MC. Cat no: **ZCF 565**. Released on BBC, Oct '85 by BBC Records, Taylors **Deleted** '88.

GOON SHOW CLASSICS.
Note: Includes: 'The Dreaded Batter Pudding Hurler of Bexhill-on-Sea', 'The Histories of Pliny the Elder', 'The Jet-Propelled Naafi' and 'The Evils of Bushey Spon'.
MCSET. Cat no: **ZBBC 1007**. Released on BBC, '88 by BBC Records, Taylors. Note 2 casettes. ISBN No: 0563 225432

GOON SHOW CLASSICS (Volume 2).
Note: Includes: 'Lurgi strikes Britain', 'The International Christmas Pudding', 'Napoleon's Piano' and 'The Flea'.
MCSET. Cat no: **ZBBC 1016**. Released on BBC, Sep '88 by BBC Records, Taylors. Note: 2 Cassettes. ISBN No: 0563 225440

GOON SHOW CLASSICS (Volume 3).
Note: Includes: 'The Treasure of Loch Lomond, 'The Greenslade Story', 'Wings over Dagenham and 'The Rent Collectors'.
MCSET. Cat no: **ZBBC 1047**. Released on BBC, '89 by BBC Records, Taylors. Note: 2 Cassettes. ISBN No: 0563 226048.

GOON SHOW CLASSICS (Volume 4).
Note: Includes: 'The Man Who Never Was', 'The Case of the Missing CD Plates', 'World War' and 'The Nasty Affair at the Burami Oasis'.
MCSET. Cat no: **ZBBC 1048**. Released on BBC, '89 by BBC Records, Taylors. Note: 2 Cassettes. ISBN No: 0563 226056

GOON SHOW CLASSICS (Volume 5).
Note: Includes: "The Call of the West', 'The Last Smoking Seagoon', '1985', 'Shifting Sands'.
MCSET. Cat no: **ZBBC 1133**. Released on BBC, '90 by BBC Records, Taylors. Note: 2 Cassettes. ISBN No: 0563 410671

GOON SHOW CLASSICS (Volume 6).
Note: Includes: 'Rommel's Treasure', 'Ill Met by Goonlight', "I was Monty's Treble', 'The Seagoon Memoirs',.
MCSET. Cat no: **ZBBC 1149**. Released on BBC Radio Collection, '91 by BBC Records. Note: 2 Cassettes. ISBN No: 0563 409606

GOON SHOW CLASSICS (Volume 7).
Note: Includes, 'The Whistling Spy Enigma ', 'The Affair of the Lone Banana', The Great Tuscan Salami Scandal', 'Scradje'.
MCSET. Cat no: **ZBBC 1239**. Released on BBC Radio Collection, '91 by BBC Records. Note: 2 Cassettes. ISBN No: 0563 408456. Taylors. Note: 2 Cassettes. ISBN No: 0563 226048.,
GOON SHOW GREATS.
Note: Includes: Tales of Old Dartmoor, Dishonoured (Parts 1 and 2) and Six Charlies in in Search of an Author.
MC. Cat no: **TCPMC 7179**. Released on Parlophone, Sep '79 by EMI Records, Solomon & Peres **Deleted** May '91.
LP. Cat no: **PMC 7179**. Released on Parlophone, '79 by EMI Records, Solomon & Peres **Deleted** Nov '88.
GOON SHOW, THE.
Note: Featuring two episodes - "White Man Burden" and "The China Story", staring Peter Sellers, Harry Secombe and Spike Miligan.
LP. Cat no: **MFP 415650-1**. Released on MFP, Jan '84 by EMI Records, Solomon & Peres **Deleted** Jan '87.
MC. Cat no: **TCMFP 415650-4**. Released on MFP, Jan '84 by EMI Records, Solomon & Peres **Deleted** Jan '87.
GOON SHOWS (Volume 1).
Note: Cast: Spike Milligan, Peter Sellers, Harry Secombe. BBC recordings. Includes: Dartmoor, Tale of Men's Shirts, Dishonoured and The Scarlet Capsule.
MCSET. Cat no: **ECC 4**. Released on EMI, Mar '90 by EMI Records. Note: Individual cat. no.'s ECC 41/42.
GOON SHOWS (Volume 2).
Note: Includes: China Story, Macreekie Rising of '74, Six Charlies in Search of an Author and Insurance - The White Man's Burden.
MCSET. Cat no: **ECC 6**. Released on EMI, Aug '90 by EMI Records.
GOON SHOWS (Volume 3).
Note: Includes: The Missing No.10 Downing Street, The Red Fort, Foiled by President Fred and Robin Hood and his Merry Men.
MCSET. Cat no: **ECC 9**. Released on EMI, Oct '90 by EMI Records.
HOW TO WIN AN ELECTION.
LP. Cat no: **AL 3464**. Released on Philips, Dec '81 by Phonogram Ltd **Deleted** Dec '86.
LAST GOON SHOW OF ALL.
Note: The last Goon show of all from the Radio 4 broadcast with Peter Sellers, Harry Secombe, Spike Milligan, Ray Ellington, Max Geldray and Andrew Timothy - Orchestra conducted by Peter Knight. Script by Spike Milligan.
LP. Cat no: **REB 142**. Released on BBC, Oct '77 by BBC Records, Taylors.
MC. Cat no: **REMC 142**. Released on BBC, Oct '77 by BBC Records, Taylors.

Gordon, Richard
DOCTOR AT LARGE (Robin Nedwell).
MC. Cat no: **CAB 004**. Released on Chivers Audio Books, Oct '81 by Chivers Audio Books, Green Dragon Audio Visual.
MCSET. Cat no: **1006H**. Released on Travellers Tales, '91 by Travellers Tales. Note: 4 cassettes.
DOCTOR ON THE BOIL (Nigel Hawthorne).
MCSET. Cat no: **1005H**. Released on Travellers Tales, '91 by Travellers Tales. Note: 4 cassettes.

Goring, Anne
PENGARA SUMMER (Margaret Holt).
MCSET. Cat no: **1854964623**. Released on Bramhope, Jun '91 by Ulverscroft Soundings. Note: 4 Cassettes.

Goscinny & Uderzo
ASTERIX AND THE GLADIATOR (Willie Rushton).
Note: Adapted by Anthea Bell.
MCSET. Cat no: **LFP 7238**. Released on Listen For Pleasure, Feb '86 by EMI Records.
ASTERIX AND THE GLADIATOR (William Rushton).
Note: Abridged.
MCSET. Cat no: **9034F**. Released on Travellers Tales, '91 by Travellers Tales. Note: 2 Cassettes.
ASTERIX AND THE MAGIC CARPET (Willie Rushton).
MCSET. Cat no: **LFP 7370**. Released on Listen For Pleasure, Nov '88 by EMI Records.
ASTERIX IN BRITAIN (Willie Rushton).
Note: This recording of Astrix in Britain is adapted from its well-known comic strip format by Anthea Bell, who together with Derek Hockridge translated the stories.
MCSET. Cat no: **LFP 7294**. Released on Listen For Pleasure, Jun '87 by EMI Records.
ASTERIX THE GAUL (Willie Rushton).
MCSET. Cat no: **LFP 7493**. Released on Listen For Pleasure, Oct '90 by EMI Records.

Gosling, Paula
BACKLASH (John Chancer).
MCSET. Cat no: **1854965352**. Released on Soundings, Jan '92 by Soundings Records, Bond Street Music. Note: 6 cassettes.
MONKEY PUZZLE (Blain Fairman).
MCSET. Cat no: **1374T**. Released on Travellers Tales, '91 by Travellers Tales. Note: 7 Cassettes.
MCSET. Cat no: **IAB 88082**. Released on Isis Audio Books, '91. Note: 7 Cassettes.
WYCHFORD MURDERS, THE (Peter Wickham).
MCSET. Cat no: **1623T**. Released on Travellers Tales, '91 by Travellers Tales. Note: 8 Cassettes.
MCSET. Cat no: **OAS 90082**. Released on Oasis Audio Books, '91 by Isis Audio Books. Note: 8 Cassettes.

Goudge, Elizabeth
WHITE WITCH, THE (Gwyneth Guthrie).
MCSET. Cat no: **COL 2022**. Released on Colophone, Nov '81 by AVLS (Audio-Visual Library Services).
WHITE WITCH, THE (Gwyneth Guthrie).
Note: Abridged version.
MCSET. Cat no: **1002G**. Released on Travellers Tales, '91 by Travellers Tales. Note: 2 cassettes.

Gould, Chester
DICK TRACY (Big Boy Turns Up The Heat) (Unknown narrator(s)).
MC. Cat no: **DIS 023W**. Released on Disney (Read-a-long), Apr '91 by Disneyland Records.
EVERYTHING COMES UP BLANK (Unknown narrator(s)).
MC. Cat no: **DIS 024W**. Released on Disney (Read-a-long), Apr '91 by Disneyland Records.

Graham, Margaret
FRAGMENT OF TIME, A (Anne Dover).
MCSET. Cat no: **1160/1161R**. Released on Travellers Tales, '91 by Travellers Tales. Note: 10 Cassettes.
MCSET. Cat no: **1854963880**. Released on Soundings, '91 by Soundings Records, Bond Street Music. Note: 10 Cassettes.
FUTURE IS OURS, THE (Judith Porter).
MCSET. Cat no: **1854965360**. Released on Soundings, Jan '92 by Soundings Records, Bond Street Music. Note: 9 cassettes.
MEASURE OF PEACE, A (Anne Dover).
MCSET. Cat no: **1854964674**. Released on Soundings, Jul '91 by Soundings Records, Bond Street Music. Note: 12 Cassettes
ONLY THE WIND IS FREE (Unknown narrator(s)).
MCSET. Cat no: **185496500X**. Released on Soundings, '91 by Soundings Records, Bond Street Music. Note: 12 Cassettes.

Graham, Vanessa
SUCH MEN ARE DANGEROUS (Nicolette McKenzie).
MCSET. Cat no: **MRC 1043**. Released on Chivers Moonlight Romances, Apr '88 by Chivers Audio Books, Green Dragon Audio Visual. Note: 2 Cassettes.

Graham, William
TWA THREE SANGS AND STORIES (Various artists).
MC. Cat no: **SSC 040**. Released on Scotsoun, '91 by Scotsoun Recordings, Morley Audio Services.

Graham, Winston
CAMEO (David Rintoul).
MCSET. Cat no: **CAB 372**. Released on Chivers Audio Books, '91 by Chivers Audio Books, Green Dragon Audio Visual. Note: 6 Cassettes

FORGOTTEN STORY, THE (Patricia Hughes).
MCSET. Cat no: **OAS 30891**. Released on Oasis Audio Books, '91 by Isis Audio Books. Note: 8 cassettes.

FORTUNE IS A WOMAN (John Nettles).
MCSET. Cat no: **1076T**. Released on Travellers Tales, '91 by Travellers Tales. Note: 6 Cassettes.

GREEK FIRE (Gordon Griffin).
MCSET. Cat no: **1854965816**. Released on Soundings, Apr '92 by Soundings Records, Bond Street Music. Note: 7 cassettes.

NIGHT JOURNEY (Peter Joyce).
MCSET. Cat no: **1854965557**. Released on Bramhope, Feb '92 by Ulverscroft Soundings. Note: Playing time: 60 minutes.

TAKE MY LIFE (Maggie Ollerenshaw).
MCSET. Cat no: **1854965409**. Released on Bramhope, Jan '92 by Ulverscroft Soundings.

Grahame, Kenneth
HOME SWEET HOME (John Braddeley).
Note: Book and cassette.
MCSET. Cat no: **00 103 209 7**. Released on Tempo, Apr '88 by Warwick Records, Celtic Music, Henry Hadaway Organisation.

OPEN ROAD, THE (John Braddeley).
Note: Book and tape set.
MCSET. Cat no: **00 103 210 0**. Released on Tempo, Apr '88 by Warwick Records, Celtic Music, Henry Hadaway Organisation.

RELUCTANT DRAGON, THE (Boris Karloff).
MC. Cat no: **1074**. Released on Caedmon (USA), '88 by Caedmon Records (USA), Bond Street Music.

RELUCTANT DRAGON, THE (And Tarka the Otter) (Sir Michael Horden).
MCSET. Cat no: **SAY 70**. Released on Argo (Polygram), May '83 by PolyGram Classics **Deleted** Jan '89.
MCSET. Cat no: **9035F**. Released on Travellers Tales, '91 by Travellers Tales.

TALES OF TOAD (Unknown narrator(s)).
MCSET. Cat no: **DTO 10551**. Released on Ditto, '88 by Pickwick Records, Midland Records.

WIND IN THE WILLOWS (Unknown narrator(s)).
MC. Cat no: **STK 028**. Released on Stick-A-Tale, Jul '90 by Pickwick Records.

WIND IN THE WILLOWS (The Wild Wood) (John Braddeley).
MC. Cat no: **TTS 9835**. Released on Tempo, Aug '84 by Warwick Records, Celtic Music, Henry Hadaway Organisation.
MC. Cat no: **00 102117 6**. Released on Tempo, '88 by Warwick Records, Celtic Music, Henry Hadaway Organisation.

WIND IN THE WILLOWS (Carnival Classics) (George Layton).
MC. Cat no: **0001010859**. Released on Harper Collins, Dec '91 by Harper Collins.

WIND IN THE WILLOWS (The River Bank) (John Braddeley).
MC. Cat no: **00 102118 4**. Released on Tempo, '88 by Warwick Records, Celtic Music, Henry Hadaway Organisation.

WIND IN THE WILLOWS (Unknown narrator(s)).
Note: Book and cassette.
MC. Cat no: **PLBC 85**. Released on Tell-A-Tale, '88 by Pickwick Records, Taylors, Clyde Factors.

WIND IN THE WILLOWS (Unknown narrator(s)).
MCSET. Cat no: **SAY 8**. Released on Argo (Polygram), Jul '82 by PolyGram Classics **Deleted** Jan '89.
MCSET. Cat no: **ARGO 1124**. Released on Argo (EMI), Sep '89 by EMI Records. Note: 2 Cassettes.
MCSET. Cat no: **DTO 10566**. Released on Ditto, '88 by Pickwick Records, Midland Records. Note: 2 Cassettes.

WIND IN THE WILLOWS (Adapted By Anne McKie) (Lisa Abbott).
Note: Stories are The Further Adventures Of Mr. Toad, and The Battle For Toad Hall.
MC. Cat no: **ST 409**. Released on Cassettes For Young People, Aug '91 by Cassettes For Young People Lmd, DMS Dist..

WIND IN THE WILLOWS (Alan Bennett).
MCSET. Cat no: **ZBBC 1072**. Released on BBC, Jun '89 by BBC Records, Taylors. Note: ISBN No: 0563 226463.

WIND IN THE WILLOWS (John Braddeley).
MC. Cat no: **TTS 9833**. Released on Tempo, Aug '84 by Warwick Records, Celtic Music, Henry Hadaway Organisation.

WIND IN THE WILLOWS (The Open Door) (John Braddeley).
MC. Cat no: **TTS 9834**. Released on Tempo, Aug '84 by Warwick Records, Celtic Music, Henry Hadaway Organisation.

WIND IN THE WILLOWS (Unknown narrator(s)).
Tracks / Wind in the willows (Theme.) / On the river / Ducks ditty / Open road, The / Mr. Toad - the motorist / Wild wood, The / Mr. Badger / Dulce domum / Further adventures of toad, The / Hero's song, A / When the toad came home / Battle, The / Wind in the willows.
LP. Cat no: **RBDLP 1150**. Released on Red Bus, Mar '84 by Red Bus Records.
MC. Cat no: **ZCRBD 1150**. Released on Red Bus, Mar '84 by Red Bus Records.

WIND IN THE WILLOWS (Adapted By Anne McKie) (Lisa Abbott).
Note: Stories are The River Bank, and The Wild Wood.
MC. Cat no: **ST 407**. Released on Cassettes For Young People, Aug '91 by Cassettes For Young People Lmd, DMS Dist..

WIND IN THE WILLOWS (Adapted By Anne McKie) (Lisa Abbott).
Note: Stories are The Open Road, and The Adventures Of Mr. Toad.
MC. Cat no: **ST 408**. Released on Cassettes For Young People, Aug '91 by Cassettes For Young People Lmd, DMS Dist..

WIND IN THE WILLOWS (Kenneth Williams).
MCSET. Cat no: **LFP 7041**. Released on Listen For Pleasure, Jan '84 by EMI Records. Note: 2 Cassettes.
MCSET. Cat no: **9036F**. Released on Travellers Tales, '91 by Travellers Tales.

WIND IN THE WILLOWS (Frank Duncan).
MC. Cat no: **P 90022**. Released on Pinnacle, '79 by Pinnacle Records, Outlet Records, Music Sales Records.

Gramatsky, Hardie
LITTLE TOOT STORIES (Hans Conreid).
MC. Cat no: **1528**. Released on Caedmon (USA), '88 by Caedmon Records (USA), Bond Street Music.

Grant-Adamson, Lesley
FACE OF DEATH, THE (Delia Corrie).
MCSET. Cat no: **1200T**. Released on Travellers Tales, '91 by Travellers Tales. Note: 6 Cassettes.
MCSET. Cat no: **1854961063**. Released on Soundings, '91 by Soundings Records, Bond Street Music. Note: 6 Cassettes.

PATTERNS IN THE DUST (Jane Jermyn).
MCSET. Cat no: **1034R**. Released on Travellers Tales, '91 by Travellers Tales. Note: 4 Cassettes.
MCSET. Cat no: **1854961071**. Released on Bramhope, '91 by Ulverscroft Soundings. Note: 4 Cassettes.

Graves, Robert
CLAUDIUS THE GOD (Derek Jacobi).

MCSET. Cat no: **SAY 45**. Released on Argo (Polygram), Mar '83 by PolyGram Classics **Deleted** Jan '89.
MC. Cat no: **K 180K 22**. Released on Argo, Jan '80 by Decca International.
MCSET. Cat no: **ARGO 1163**. Released on Argo (EMI), Oct '89 by EMI Records. Note: 2 Cassettes.

GOODBYE TO ALL THAT (Sean Barrett).
MCSET. Cat no: **IAB 90051**. Released on Isis Audio Books, '91. Note: 10 cassette set. Playing time 12hrs.
MCSET. Cat no: **1056/1057A**. Released on Travellers Tales, '91 by Travellers Tales.

GREAT EUROPEAN SHORT STORIES (William Shust).
MCSET. Cat no: **CSL 004**. Released on Chivers Audio Books, '91 by Chivers Audio Books, Green Dragon Audio Visual. Note: 6 cassettes.

GREAT WOMEN WRITERS READ THEIR WORK (Various artists).
MCSET. Cat no: **CSL 007**. Released on Chivers Audio Books, '91 by Chivers Audio Books, Green Dragon Audio Visual. Note: 6 cassettes.

GREEN-SAILED VESSEL, THE (Unknown narrator(s)).
LP. Cat no: **CCT 14**. Released on Claddagh (Ireland), Aug '88 by Claddagh Records (Ireland), Projection, Impetus Records, Jazz Music, Roots Records, C.M. Distribution, Outlet Records, Taylors.

I CLAUDIUS (Derek Jacobi).
MCSET. Cat no: **SAY 16**. Released on Argo (Polygram), Jul '82 by PolyGram Classics **Deleted** Jan '89.
MCSET. Cat no: **ARGO 1022**. Released on Argo (EMI), May '89 by EMI Records. Note: 2 Cassettes.

I CLAUDIUS (Derek Jacobi).
Note: Abridged version.
MCSET. Cat no: **1057F**. Released on Travellers Tales, '91 by Travellers Tales. Note: 2 cassettes.

ROBERT GRAVES READS (Robert Graves).
MC. Cat no: **1066**. Released on Caedmon (USA), '88 by Caedmon Records (USA), Bond Street Music.

Gray, Caroline
FIRST CLASS (Margaret Holt).
MCSET. Cat no: **1199F**. Released on Travellers Tales, '91 by Travellers Tales. Note: 6 cassettes.
MCSET. Cat no: **185496108X**. Released on Soundings, '91 by Soundings Records, Bond Street Music. Note: 6 Cassettes.

Gray, Simon
BUTLEY.
MCSET. Cat no: **0362**. Released on Caedmon (USA), by Caedmon Records (USA), Bond Street Music. Note: 3 cassettes

Grayson, Richard
CRIME WITHOUT PASSION (Unknown narrator(s)).
MCSET. Cat no: **1854965166**. Released on Bramhope, '91 by Ulverscroft Soundings. Note: 5 Cassettes.

DEATH OF ABBE DIDIER, THE (Gordon Griffin).
MCSET. Cat no: **1854955700**. Released on Bramhope, Mar '92 by Ulverscroft Soundings. Note: Playing time: 60 minutes.

MONTMARTE MURDERS, THE (Gordon Griffin).
MCSET. Cat no: **1854964615**. Released on Bramhope, '91 by Ulverscroft Soundings. Note: 5 Cassettes.

Greek Mythology
GIANTS, GODS, GOLD AND GREECE (Edward De Souza).
Note: For 8 to 16 year olds.
MC. Cat no: **C 005**. Released on Green Dragon, '91 by Green Dragon Audio Visual.

JASON AND THE GOLDEN FLEECE (The Tanglewood Tales) (Cathleen Nesbitt).
Note: Adpated by Nathaniel Hawthorne.
MC. Cat no: **1367**. Released on Caedmon (USA), '88 by Caedmon Records (USA), Bond Street Music.

LABOURS OF HERACLES, THE (Various artists).
Tracks / Labours of Heracles, The: *Various artists* / Ion: *Various artists* / Phaethon: *Various artists* / Jason and the Argonauts: *Various artists* / Opheus and Eurydice: *Various artists*.
MC. Cat no: **ANV 647**. Released on Anvil Cassettes, Jul '82 by Anvil Cassettes, Chivers Audio Books.

PEGASUS THE WINGED HORSE (Various artists).
MC. Cat no: **TS 317**. Released on Tellastory, Oct '79 by Random Century Audiobooks.

SIEGE OF TROY, THE (Various artists).
Note: Includes: Perseus and the Gorgon and Theseus.
MC. Cat no: **ANV 646**. Released on Anvil Cassettes, Jul '82 by Anvil Cassettes, Chivers Audio Books.

TALES OF ANCIENT GREECE (The Travels of Ulysses) (Anthony Hyde).
Note: Adapted by Andrew Lang.
MC. Cat no: **TS 367**. Released on Tellastory, Feb '92 by Random Century Audiobooks. Note: ISBN no. 1856560473

TALES OF ANCIENT GREECE (Jason and the Golden Fleece) (Anthony Hyde).
Note: Adapted by Andrew Lang.
MC. Cat no: **TS 402**. Released on Tellastory, Feb '92 by Random Century Audiobooks. Note: ISBN no. 1856561887

TALES OF ANCIENT GREECE (The Siege of Troy) (Anthony Hyde).
Note: Adapted by Andrew Lang.
MC. Cat no: **TS 366**. Released on Tellastory, '91 by Random Century Audiobooks. Note: ISBN no. 1856560465

Greene, Graham
CAPTAIN AND THE ENEMY, THE (Kenneth Branagh).
MCSET. Cat no: **CAB 398**. Released on Chivers Audio Books, '91 by Chivers Audio Books, Green Dragon Audio Visual. Note: 4 Cassettes.
MCSET. Cat no: **1528T**. Released on Travellers Tales, '91 by Travellers Tales. Note: 4 Cassettes.

CONFIDENTIAL AGENT, THE (Patrick Tull).
MCSET. Cat no: **IAB 89072**. Released on Isis Audio Books, '91. Note: 5 cassette set. Playing time 7hrs 30mins.
MCSET. Cat no: **1470T**. Released on Travellers Tales, '91 by Travellers Tales. Note: 5 Cassettes.

DREAM OF A STRANGE LAND (Hugh Burden).
MC. Cat no: **TTC/GG 03**. Released on Talking Tape Company, '84, Conifer Records.

END OF THE AFFAIR, THE (Julia Glover & Kika Markham).
MCSET. Cat no: **ZBBC 1068**. Released on BBC Radio Collection, '91 by BBC Records. Note: ISBN No: 0563 226404. 2 cassettes.

GETTING TO KNOW THE GENERAL (Jonathan Oliver).
MCSET. Cat no: **OAS 90021**. Released on Oasis Audio Books, '91 by Isis Audio Books. Note: 6 cassette set. Playing time 7hrs 20mins.
MCSET. Cat no: **1073N**. Released on Travellers Tales, '91 by Travellers Tales. Note: 6 cassettes.

GUN FOR SALE, A (Patrick Tull).
MCSET. Cat no: **IAB 89043**. Released on Isis Audio Books, '91. Note: 6 cassette set. Playing time 7hrs 20mins.
MCSET. Cat no: **1414T**. Released on Travellers Tales, '91 by Travellers Tales. Note: 6 Cassettes.

HUMAN FACTOR, THE (Peter Jeffrey).
MCSET. Cat no: **ZBBC 1150**. Released on BBC Radio Collection, Jul '91 by BBC Records. Note: ISBN No: 0563 365145

MONSIGNOR QUIXOTE (Derek Jacobi).
MCSET. Cat no: **0671621416**. Released on Simon & Schuster, '91 by Simon & Schuster Ltd. Note: 2 Cassettes.

MONSIGNOR QUIXOTE (Cyril Cusack).
MCSET. Cat no: **1060F**. Released on Travellers Tales, '91 by Travellers Tales. Note: 6 cassettes.

OUR MAN IN HAVANA (Various artists).

MCSET. Cat no: **ZBBC 1067.** Released on BBC Radio Collection, May '90 by BBC Records. Note: ISBN No: 0563 226390

OUR MAN IN HAVANA (Alistair Maydon).
MCSET. Cat no: **OAS 90112.** Released on Oasis Audio Books, '91 by Isis Audio Books. Note: 6 cassette set. Playing time 7hrs.

MCSET. Cat no: **1053H.** Released on Travellers Tales, '91 by Travellers Tales. Note: 6 cassettes.

QUIET AMERICAN, THE (Simon Cadell).
MCSET. Cat no: **1061F.** Released on Travellers Tales, '91 by Travellers Tales. Note: 4 cassettes.

SENSE OF REALITY (And Other Stories) (Derek Jacobi).
MCSET. Cat no: **IAB 90063.** Released on Isis Audio Books, '91. Note: 6 cassette set. Playing time 7hrs 30mins.

MCSET. Cat no: **1506F.** Released on Travellers Tales, '91 by Travellers Tales. Note: 6 cassettes.

SHORT STORIES (Hugh Burden).
MCSET. Cat no: **1221F.** Released on Travellers Tales, '91 by Travellers Tales. Note: 4 cassettes.

STAMBOUL TRAIN (Roddy McDowall).
Note: Also available on hanging format, catalogue number:- 0001031589.

MCSET. Cat no: **2099.** Released on Caedmon (USA), '88 by Caedmon Records (USA), Bond Street Music.

MCSET. Cat no: **HCA 42.** Released on Harper Collins, '92 by Harper Collins.

THIRD MAN, THE (James Mason).
MC. Cat no: **TC LFP 7103.** Released on Listen For Pleasure, Sep '82 by EMI Records.

TRAVELS WITH MY AUNT (Geoffrey Palmer).
MCSET. Cat no: **IAB 88032.** Released on Isis Audio Books, '91. Note: 6 cassette set. Playing time 9hrs 25mins.

MCSET. Cat no: **1298F.** Released on Travellers Tales, '91 by Travellers Tales. Note: 8 cassettes.

TWENTY ONE STORIES (Derek Jacobi).
MCSET. Cat no: **IAB 90042.** Released on Isis Audio Books, '91. Note: 6 cassette set. Playing time 7hrs 10mins.

MCSET. Cat no: **1459F.** Released on Travellers Tales, '91 by Travellers Tales. Note: 6 cassettes.

VISIT TO MORIN, A (Hugh Burden).
MC. Cat no: **TTC/GG 02.** Released on Talking Tape Company, '84, Conifer Records.

Grenfell, Joyce

COLLECTION: JOYCE GRENFELL (Joyce Grenfell).
Tracks / I'm going to see you today / Encores / Picture postcard / Dear Francois / Old girls' school reunion / Re-union / Joyful noise / Nursery school - flowers / Rime / Three brothers / Shirley's girlfriend / Fanfare / Oh, Mr. Du Maurier / Boat train / I wouldn't go back / Old Joe Clarke (Songs my mother taught me) / Step light lady / All the pretty little horses / Nursery school - Free activity period / Olde tyme dancing.

LP. Cat no: **OU 1249.** Released on One-Up, Oct '76 by EMI Records.

MC. Cat no: **TCOU 1249.** Released on One-Up, 19 Sep '88 by EMI Records.

JOYCE GRENFELL REQUESTS THE PLEASURE (Joyce Grenfell).
Tracks / How was it for you / Life's rich pageant / Christmas carol / Joyce Grenfell requests the pleasure / Vintage Archers / Diary of a nobody, A / Clinging to the wrecking / Tales from a long room / Just Williams / Plain tales from Raj / Epic poems / Perfect spy, A.

MCSET. Cat no: **ZBBC 1049.** Released on BBC Radio Collection, Mar '89 by BBC Records. Note: ISBN NO: 0563 226064

KEEPSAKE (Joyce Grenfell).
Tracks / Mad about the boy / Sigh no more / Ziguener / I'd follow my secret heart / Parisian Pierrot / Some day I'll find you / Matelot / I'll see you again / Useful and acceptable gifts / Keepsake / Maud / Yellow rose of Texas / All the pretty little horses / I don't 'arf love you / Narcissus / If love were all / Some day I'll find you / Matelot / Party's over, The / I'm going to see you today / Drifting / There's nothing new to tell you / Village mother, The / American mother.

LP. Cat no: **SH 507.** Released on Retrospect, Jul '86 by EMI Records **Deleted** Nov '88.

MC. Cat no: **TCSH 507.** Released on Retrospect, Jul '86 by EMI Records **Deleted** Feb '91.

RE-JOYCE (Joyce Grenfell).
Tracks / Opera interval / American mother / Old girls' school reunion / I'm going to see you today / Committee / Useful and acceptable gifts / Hymn / Security song / Shirley's girlfriend / I like life / First flight / Maud / Life and literature / Nursery school / Three brothers / Terrible worrier, A / Narcissus / Time.

LP. Cat no: **EMS 1305.** Released on EMI, Sep '88 by EMI Records **Deleted** Nov '91.

MC. Cat no: **TCEMS 1305.** Released on EMI, Sep '88 by EMI Records.

CD. Cat no: **CDP 790 991 2.** Released on EMI, Sep '88 by EMI Records **Deleted** May '90. Note: UK cat. no. CZ 139.

CD. Cat no: **CZ 139.** Released on EMI, Sep '88 by EMI Records **Deleted** May '90.

SONGS AND MONOLOGUES OF JOYCE GRENFELL, THE (Joyce Grenfell).
Tracks / Opening numbers / Nursery school / Joyful noise / picture postcard / What shall I wear / Visitor / Dear Francois / Nursery school (flowers) / I'm going to see you today / Shirley's girlfriend "picnic" / Oh Mr. Du Maurier / Writer of children's books / Olde tyme dancing / Telephone call / Bring back the silence / Old girls' school re-union / Three brothers / Nicodemus / Hostess, The / Lally Tullet / Hymn / Wrong songs for wrong singers (or songs to make you sick) / Wedding is on Saturday, The / Fan / I wouldn't go back / Thursdays / Duet / Nursery school (going home) / Slow down.

MCSET. Cat no: **ECC 18.** Released on EMI, Jun '91 by EMI Records.

Grey, Zane

CALL OF THE CANYON (Leonard Corman).
MCSET. Cat no: **CAB 189.** Released on Chivers Audio Books, '91 by Chivers Audio Books, Green Dragon Audio Visual. Note: 6 Cassettes.

MCSET. Cat no: **1016W.** Released on Travellers Tales, '91 by Travellers Tales. Note: 6 Cassettes.

LONE STAR RANGER, THE (John Sheddon).
MCSET. Cat no: **SPF 335-1.** Released on Schiltron Audio Books, '91 by Schiltron Publishing. Note: 6 Cassettes. Playing time 8 hours 22 minutes.

RIDERS OF THE PURPLE SAGE (Donald Buka).
MCSET. Cat no: **IAB 91053.** Released on Isis Audio Books, '91. Note: 10 cassettes.

STAIRS OF SAND (Ken Cheeseman).
MCSET. Cat no: **CAB 191.** Released on Chivers Audio Books, '91 by Chivers Audio Books, Green Dragon Audio Visual. Note: 6 Cassettes.

MCSET. Cat no: **1017W.** Released on Travellers Tales, '91 by Travellers Tales. Note: 6 Cassettes

STRANGER FROM THE TONTO (Richard Provost).
MCSET. Cat no: **CAB 255.** Released on Chivers Audio Books, '91 by Chivers Audio Books, Green Dragon Audio Visual. Note: 6 Cassettes.

THUNDER MOUNTAIN (Leonard Zola).
MCSET. Cat no: **CAB 256.** Released on Chivers Audio Books, Apr '88 by Chivers Audio Books, Green Dragon Audio Visual. Note: 6 Cassettes.

MCSET. Cat no: **1023W.** Released on Travellers Tales, '91 by Travellers Tales. Note: 6 Cassettes.

TRAIL DRIVER, THE (Peter Guttmacher).
MCSET. Cat no: **CAB 193.** Released on Chivers Audio Books, '91 by Chivers Audio Books, Green Dragon Audio Visual. Note: 6 Cassettes.

MCSET. Cat no: **1019W.** Released on Travellers Tales, '91 by Travellers Tales. Note: 6 Cassettes.

Grimes, Martha
ANODYNE NECKLACE, THE (Peter Whitman).
MCSET. Cat no: **CAB 528**. Released on Chivers Audio Books, '91 by Chivers Audio Books, Green Dragon Audio Visual. Note: 8 Cassettes.
MCSET. Cat no: **1647T**. Released on Travellers Tales, '91 by Travellers Tales. Note: 8 Cassettes.

Grimm
BEAUTY AND THE BEAST (And Other Stories) (Douglas Fairbanks Jnr).
MC. Cat no: **1394**. Released on Caedmon (USA), Jul '88 by Caedmon Records (USA), Bond Street Music.

BEAUTY AND THE BEAST (Unknown narrator(s)).
MC. Cat no: **HA 2**. Released on Happy Learning, Aug '91 by Happy Learning Co.Ltd., Castle Sales & Marketing.

BEAUTY AND THE BEAST (Unknown narrator(s)).
Note: Well loved tales up to age 9. Book and cassette.
MC. Cat no: **PLB 58**. Released on Tell-A-Tale, Feb '83 by Pickwick Records, Taylors, Clyde Factors.
MC. Cat no: **TS 323**. Released on Tellastory, Apr '81 by Random Century Audiobooks.

ELVES AND THE SHOEMAKER, THE (Well Loved Tales Up to Age 9) (Unknown narrator(s)).
Note: Book and cassette.
MC. Cat no: **PLB 63**. Released on Tell-A-Tale, '83 by Pickwick Records, Taylors, Clyde Factors.

FIVE TALES OF THE BROTHERS GRIMM (Dr. David Luke).
MC. Cat no: **SSC 068**. Released on Scotsoun, '91 by Scotsoun Recordings, Morley Audio Services.

FOUR OF YOUR FAVOURITE STORIES FROM GRIMM (Unknown narrator(s)).
LP. Cat no: **TMP 9009**. Released on Tempo, Nov '79 by Warwick Records, Celtic Music, Henry Hadaway Organisation.
MC. Cat no: **TMP4 9009**. Released on Tempo, Nov '79 by Warwick Records, Celtic Music, Henry Hadaway Organisation.

FOUR STORIES (Ian Ogilvy & Fiona Fullerton).
Note: Rumplestiltskin, Rapunzel and The Frog Prince read by Ian Ogilvy. The Three Musicians read by Fiona Fullerton.
MC. Cat no: **MCLIS 200**. Released on Listen, '91, Cartel. Note: 40 mins.

GOLDEN GOOSE, THE (Well Loved Cassettes Age Up to 9) (Unknown narrator(s)).
Note: Book & cassette
MC. Cat no: **PLB 57**. Released on Tell-A-Tale, Feb '83 by Pickwick Records, Taylors, Clyde Factors.

GRIMM BROTHERS FAIRY TALES (Volume 1) (Hannah Gordon).
LP. Cat no: **P 0051**. Released on Pinnacle, '79 by Pinnacle Records, Outlet Records, Music Sales Records.

GRIMM BROTHERS FAIRY TALES (Volume 2) (Hannah Gordon).
LP. Cat no: **P 0052**. Released on Pinnacle, '79 by Pinnacle Records, Outlet Records, Music Sales Records.

GRIMM'S FAIRY TALES (Volume 1) (Unknown narrator(s)).
Note: For children aged 3 - 9 years. Includes Hansel and Gretel and The Little Brother and Sister.
MC. Cat no: **VCA 107**. Released on VFM Cassettes, Jan '85 by VFM Cassettes, Midland Records, Crusader Marketing Co., Taylors, Morley Audio Services.

GRIMMS FAIRY TALES (Various artists).
Tracks / Rumpelstiltskin: *Various artists* / Little Red-Cap: *Various artists* / Nose, The: *Various artists* / Tom Thumb: *Various artists* / Elves and the shoemaker, The: *Various artists* / Peter and the goatherd: *Various artists* / Golden goose, The: *Various artists* / Travelling musicians, The: *Various artists* / Rose-Bud: *Various artists* / Wolf and the seven little goats: *Various artists* / Valiant tailor, The: *Various artists* / Grateful beasts, The: *Various artists* / Three children of fortune, The: *Various artists* / Hans in luck: *Various artists*.
Note: 14 Stories read by Michael Hordern, Peter Jeffrey, Ben Kingsley, Peter Orr and Margaret Rawlings.
MCSET. Cat no: **ARGO 1196**. Released on Argo (EMI), Apr '90 by EMI Records. Note: 2 Cassettes.

GRIMMS FAIRY TALES (Sheila Hancock).
MCSET. Cat no: **TCLFP 4171245**. Released on Listen For Pleasure, '83 by EMI Records.
MCSET. Cat no: **9037F**. Released on Travellers Tales, '91 by Travellers Tales. Note: 2 Cassettes.

GRIMMS FAIRY TALES (Eve Watkinson & Christopher Casson).
MCSET. Cat no: **9106F**. Released on Travellers Tales, '91 by Travellers Tales. Note: 3 Cassettes.

GRIMMS FAIRY TALES (6 Children's Classics) (Peter Whitbread & Gillian Blake).
Note: For children aged 3 - 9. Includes Cinderella, Tom Thumb, The Goose Girl, Sleeping Beauty, Snow White and the Seven Dwarfs and Rapunzel.
MC. Cat no: **STC 113**. Released on VFM Cassettes, '85 by VFM Cassettes, Midland Records, Crusader Marketing Co., Taylors, Morley Audio Services.

HANSEL AND GRETEL (Well Loved Tales Age Up to 9) (Unknown narrator(s)).
Note: Book and cassette.

MC. Cat no: **PLB 70**. Released on Tell-A-Tale, '83 by Pickwick Records, Taylors, Clyde Factors.

HANSEL AND GRETEL (And Other Fairy Stories) (Claire Bloom).
MC. Cat no: **1274**. Released on Caedmon (USA), Jul '88 by Caedmon Records (USA), Bond Street Music.

HANSEL AND GRETEL (Unknown narrator(s)).
MC. Cat no: **HA 4**. Released on Happy Learning, Aug '91 by Happy Learning Co.Ltd., Castle Sales & Marketing.

MC. Cat no: **STK 019**. Released on Stick-A-Tale, '89 by Pickwick Records.

MORE GRIMM'S FAIRY TALES.
Tracks / Cinderella / Four accomplished brothers, The / Old Mother Frost / Little farmer, The / Goose girl, The / Wonderful musician, The / King Grisly - beard / Hansel and Gretel / Queen bee / Twelve dancing princesses, The / Tom Tit and the bear, The / Little brother and sister, The.
Note: Read by: Geraldine Newman, Joy Parker, Paul Schofield, Timothy West.
MCSET. Cat no: **414 715-4**. Released on Argo (Polygram), Apr '85 by Poly-Gram Classics **Deleted** Jan '89.

MUSICIANS OF BREMEN, THE (Well Loved Tales Age Up to 9) (Unknown narrator(s)).
Note: Book and cassette.
MC. Cat no: **PLB 68**. Released on Tell-A-Tale, '83 by Pickwick Records, Taylors, Clyde Factors.

RAPUNZEL (Michaela Strachan).
MC. Cat no: **STOR 3**. Released on Storytime Cassettes, Apr '92 by VFM Cassettes, Iona Records, Rio Communications.

RAPUNZEL (Well Loved Tales up to Age 9) (Unknown narrator(s)).
Note: Book and cassette.
MC. Cat no: **PLB 112**. Released on Tell-A-Tale, '88 by Pickwick Records, Taylors, Clyde Factors.

RUMPELSTILTSKIN (Ian Ogilvy).
MC. Cat no: **LP 208**. Released on Listen Productions, Nov '84.

RUMPELSTILTSKIN (Well Loved Tales Up to Age 9) (Unknown narrator(s)).
Note: Book and cassette.
MC. Cat no: **PLB 96**. Released on Tell-A-Tale, '88 by Pickwick Records, Taylors, Clyde Factors.

RUMPELSTILTSKIN (And the Flying Trunk) (Ian Ogilvy).
MC. Cat no: **LPMC 208**. Released on Listen, '88, Cartel.

SNOW WHITE (Unknown narrator(s)).
MC. Cat no: **1856560074**. Released on Random Century, '91 by Random Century Audiobooks, Conifer Records.
Note: Playing time: 60 Minutes.

SNOW WHITE (Various artists).
MC. Cat no: **ANV 619**. Released on Anvil Cassettes, Jan '81 by Anvil Cas-

settes, Chivers Audio Books.
SNOW WHITE (And Other Fairy Tales) (Claire Bloom).
MC. Cat no: **1266.** Released on Caedmon (USA), '89 by Caedmon Records (USA), Bond Street Music.

SNOW WHITE (Susan Hampshire).
MC. Cat no: **3604.** Released on Storytime Cassettes, Aug '83 by VFM Cassettes, Iona Records, Rio Communications.

SNOW WHITE AND ROSE RED (And Other Stories) (Unknown narrator(s)).
Tracks / Snow White and Rose Red / Little grey goose, The / Soldier boy.
LP. Cat no: **TMP 9006.** Released on Tempo, Nov '79 by Warwick Records, Celtic Music, Henry Hadaway Organisation.

SNOW WHITE AND ROSE RED (Well Loved Tales Up to Age 9) (Unknown narrator(s)).
Note: Book and cassette.
MC. Cat no: **PLB 71.** Released on Tell-A-Tale, '83 by Pickwick Records, Taylors, Clyde Factors.

SNOW WHITE AND THE SEVEN DWARFS (Miriam Margoyles).
MC. Cat no: **PTB 630.** Released on Pickwick Talking Books, '83 by Pickwick Records, Clyde Factors.

SNOW WHITE AND THE SEVEN DWARFS (Unknown narrator(s)).
MC. Cat no: **DIS 001.** Released on Disney (Read-a-long), Jul '90 by Disneyland Records **Deleted** Mar '92.
MC. Cat no: **STK 001.** Released on Stick-A-Tale, Jul '90 by Pickwick Records.

SNOW WHITE AND THE SEVEN DWARFS (Unknown narrator(s)).
Note: Book and cassette.
MC. Cat no: **DIS 030.** Released on Disney (Read-a-long), Mar '92 by Disneyland Records.

SNOW WHITE AND THE SEVEN DWARFS (And Other Stories) (Carole Boyd).
MC. Cat no: **TS 316.** Released on Tellastory, '91 by Random Century Audiobooks. Note: ISBN no. 1856560074

SNOW WHITE AND THE SEVEN DWARFS (Unknown narrator(s)).
Tracks / Snow White and the seven dwarfs / Water of life, The / Little people / Goose girl, The / King wren.
Note: Book and cassette.
MC. Cat no: **PLB 72.** Released on Tell-A-Tale, '83 by Pickwick Records, Taylors, Clyde Factors.
LP. Cat no: **D 3906.** Released on Disneyland, Dec '82 by Disneyland-Vista Records (USA).
LPPD. Cat no: **D 3101.** Released on Disneyland, Dec '82 by Disneyland-Vista Records (USA).
MLP. Cat no: **D 310.** Released on Disneyland, Dec '82 by Disneyland-Vista Records (USA).

MC. Cat no: **D 1DC.** Released on Disneyland, Dec '82 by Disneyland-Vista Records (USA).
TWELVE DANCING PRINCESSES, THE (Unknown narrator(s)).
Note: Book and cassette.
MC. Cat no: **PLB 239.** Released on Tell-A-Tale, '88 by Pickwick Records, Taylors, Clyde Factors. Note: Book and tape set

WOLF AND THE SEVEN LITTLE KIDS (Well Loved Tales Up to Age 9) (Unknown narrator(s)).
Note: Book and cassette.
MC. Cat no: **PLB 67.** Released on Tell-A-Tale, '88 by Pickwick Records, Taylors, Clyde Factors.

Grossmith, G. & W.
DIARY OF A NOBODY, THE (Arthur Lowe).
MCSET. Cat no: **ZBBC 1023.** Released on BBC Radio Collection, Sep '88 by BBC Records. Note: ISBN No: 0563 225742

DIARY OF A NOBODY, THE (Unknown narrator(s)).
MCSET. Cat no: **SAY 76.** Released on Argo (Polygram), Jun '88 by PolyGram Classics **Deleted** Jan '89.

DIARY OF A NOBODY, THE (Terence Hardiman).
MCSET. Cat no: **1020H.** Released on Travellers Tales, '91 by Travellers Tales. Note: 6 cassettes.

DIARY OF A NOBODY, THE
MCSET. Cat no: **CAB 231.** Released on Chivers Audio Books, '91 by Chivers Audio Books, Green Dragon Audio Visual. Note: 6 cassettes.

DIARY OF A NOBODY, THE (Richard Briers & Cast).
Note: Abridged version.
MCSET. Cat no: **1025H.** Released on Travellers Tales, '91 by Travellers Tales. Note: 2 cassettes

Grove, Fred
SANACO (Unknown narrator(s)).
MCSET. Cat no: **SOUND 26.** Released on Soundings, Mar '85 by Soundings Records, Bond Street Music.
MCSET. Cat no: **1008W.** Released on Travellers Tales, '91 by Travellers Tales. Note: 4 Cassettes.

Guest, Judith
ORDINARY PEOPLE (Aviva Skell).
MCSET. Cat no: **RB 84110.** Released on Recorded Books, '91 by Isis Audio Books. Note: 5 cassettes.

SECOND HEAVEN (Sheri Blair).
MCSET. Cat no: **RB 83049.** Released on Recorded Books, Dec '91 by Isis Audio Books. Note: 7 cassettes. Playing time 9hrs 30mins.

Gunson, David
WHAT GOES UP MIGHT COME DOWN (David Gunson).
MC. Cat no: **BBMC 00 12.** Released on Big Ben, '82 by Tangent Records, Roots Records, Swift, Celtic Music, Spartan, Topic Records, Duncans, Projection.
LP. Cat no: **BB 00 12.** Released on Big Ben, Dec '82 by Tangent Records, Roots Records, Swift, Celtic Music, Spartan, Topic Records, Duncans, Projection **Deleted** '87.
CD. Cat no: **BBCD 0012.** Released on Big Ben, '91 by Tangent Records, Roots Records, Swift, Celtic Music, Spartan, Topic Records, Duncans, Projection.

Hagar, Judith
DON'T RUN FROM LOVE (Judy Bennett).
MCSET. Cat no: **MRC 1058.** Released on Chivers Audio Books, '91 by Chivers Audio Books, Green Dragon Audio Visual. Note: 2 cassettes.

PLACE OF HAPPINESS, THE (Valerie Georgeson).
MCSET. Cat no: **MRC 1025.** Released on Chivers Audio Books, '91 by Chivers Audio Books, Green Dragon Audio Visual. Note: 2 cassettes.

Hailey, Arthur
EVENING NEWS, THE (Fritz Weaver).
MCSET. Cat no: **ZBBC 1228.** Released on BBC, '91 by BBC Records, Taylors. Note: ISBN No: 0563 408006

Hailey, John
FLIGHT INTO DANGER (Edward Albert).
Note: Authors are John Hailey and Arthur Castle.
MCSET. Cat no: **LFP 7290.** Released on Listen For Pleasure, Apr '87 by EMI Records **Deleted** Aug '89.
MCSET. Cat no: **1169T.** Released on Travellers Tales, '91 by Travellers Tales.

Hale, Kathleen
ADVENTURES OF ORLANDO (The Marmalade Cat) (Various artists).
Note: Includes: Orlando Buys A Farm and Orlando And The Water Cats.
MC. Cat no: **TS 311.** Released on Tellastory, Dec '86 by Random Century Audiobooks.
MC. Cat no: **TS 315.** Released on Tellastory, Oct '79 by Random Century Audiobooks.

Hall, Willis
ANTELOPE COMPANY ASHORE, THE (Nigel Lambert).
MCSET. Cat no: **3CCA 3077.** Released on Chivers Audio Books, '91 by Chivers Audio Books, Green Dragon Audio Visual. Note: 3 Cassettes.
MCSET. Cat no: **9141F.** Released on Travellers Tales, '91 by Travellers Tales. Note: 3 Cassettes.

ANTELOPE COMPANY AT LARGE, THE (Nigel Lambert).

MCSET. Cat no: **3CCA 3094.** Released on Chivers Audio Books, '91 by Chivers Audio Books, Green Dragon Audio Visual. Note: 3 Cassettes.

MCSET. Cat no: **9174F.** Released on Travellers Tales, '91 by Travellers Tales. Note: 3 Cassettes.

LAST VAMPIRE, THE (Geoffrey Matthews).
MCSET. Cat no: **3CCA 3034.** Released on Chivers Audio Books, '91 by Chivers Audio Books, Green Dragon Audio Visual. Note: 3 Cassettes.

MCSET. Cat no: **9107F.** Released on Travellers Tales, '91 by Travellers Tales. Note: 3 Cassettes.

RETURN OF THE ANTELOPE, THE (Nigel Lambert).
MCSET. Cat no: **3CCA 3049.** Released on Chivers Audio Books, '91 by Chivers Audio Books, Green Dragon Audio Visual. Note: 3 Cassettes.

MCSET. Cat no: **9124F.** Released on Travellers Tales, '91 by Travellers Tales. Note: 3 Cassettes.

VAMPIRE'S HOLIDAY, THE (And Dr Jekyll and Mr Hollins) (Victoria Wood).
MCSET. Cat no: **ZBBC 1205.** Released on BBC, Aug '91 by BBC Records, Taylors. Note: ISBN No: 0563 409118.

Hammett, Dashiell

THIN MAN, THE (Daniel J. Travanti & Lynne Lipton).
MCSET. Cat no: **2106.** Released on Caedmon (USA), Jul '88 by Caedmon Records (USA), Bond Street Music.
MCSET. Cat no: **0001042440.** Released on Collins-Caedmon, '91 by Collins Audio, Taylors, Bond Street Music. Note: 2 cassettes.

Hammond, Rosemary

TWO DOZEN RED ROSES (Georgina Melville).
MCSET. Cat no: **PMB 013.** Released on Mills & Boon, '88. Note: 2 Cassettes

Hancock, Tony

BLOOD DONOR (And Radio Ham) (Tony Hancock).
LP. Cat no: **PYL 22.** Released on PRT, Jul '89 by Castle Communications PLC.

CD. Cat no: **PYC 22.** Released on PRT, Jul '89 by Castle Communications PLC.

MC. Cat no: **PYM 22.** Released on PRT, Jul '89 by Castle Communications PLC.

GOLDEN HOUR OF TONY HANCOCK.
MC. Cat no: **KGHMC 115.** Released on Knight, Jun '90 by Knight Records Ltd., BMG Distribution Operations.

CD. Cat no: **KGHCD 115.** Released on Knight, Jun '90 by Knight Records Ltd., BMG Distribution Operations. Note: BB

HANCOCK (Tony Hancock).
MC. Cat no: **ZCMA 872.** Released on Marble Arch, Nov '71.

LP. Cat no: **NPL 18068.** Released on Pye, Mar '62 **Deleted** '67.

HANCOCK'S HALF HOUR (Volume 5) (Tony Hancock).
Note: Includes: 'The Diary', 'The Old School Reunion', 'Hancock in the Police', 'The East Cheam Drama Festival', 'Sleepless Night' and 'Fred's Pie Stall'.
LP. Cat no: **REB 485.** Released on BBC, Oct '83 by BBC Records, Taylors **Deleted** 31 Aug '88.

MC. Cat no: **ZCF 485.** Released on BBC, Oct '83 by BBC Records, Taylors **Deleted** 31 Aug '88.

HANCOCK'S HALF HOUR (Volume 1) (Tony Hancock).
Note: Inlcudes: Poetry Society and Sid's Mystery Tours.
LP. Cat no: **REB 394.** Released on BBC, Nov '80 by BBC Records, Taylors **Deleted** 31 Aug '88.

MC. Cat no: **ZCF 394.** Released on BBC, Nov '80 by BBC Records, Taylors **Deleted** 31 Aug '88.

HANCOCK'S HALF HOUR (Volume 2) (Various artists).
Note: Includes: 'The Scandal Magazine', 'Last of McHancocks', 'The Sleepless Night' and 'Fred's pie stall', 'The American's Hit Town', 'The Unexploded Bomb'.
LP. Cat no: **REB 423.** Released on BBC, Oct '81 by BBC Records, Taylors **Deleted** 31 Aug '88.

MC. Cat no: **ZCF 423.** Released on BBC, Oct '81 by BBC Records, Taylors **Deleted** 31 Aug '88.

MCSET. Cat no: **ZBBC 1018.** Released on BBC Radio Collection, '91 by BBC Records. Note: 2 Cassettes. ISBN No: 0563 225467.

HANCOCK'S HALF HOUR (Volume 3) (Tony Hancock).
Note: Includes: The Scandal Magazine and The Last of the McHancocks.
LP. Cat no: **REB 451.** Released on BBC, Oct '82 by BBC Records, Taylors **Deleted** 31 Aug '88.

MC. Cat no: **ZCF 451.** Released on BBC, Oct '82 by BBC Records, Taylors **Deleted** 31 Aug '88.

HANCOCK'S HALF HOUR (Various artists).
Note: Includes: 'The American's Hit Town', 'The Unexploded Bomb', 'The Poetry Society'and 'Sids Mystery Tour'.
MCSET. Cat no: **ZBBC 1008.** Released on BBC, Sep '88 by BBC Records, Taylors. Note: 2 Cassettes. ISBN No: 0563 225459.

HANCOCK'S HALF HOUR (Volume 4) (Various artists).
Note: Includes: The Diary, The Old School Reunion, Hancock In The Police, The East Cheam Dream Festival.
MCSET. Cat no: **ZBBC 1122.** Released on BBC, Jun '90 by BBC Records, Taylors. Note: 2 Cassettes. ISBN No: 0563 410388.

HANCOCK'S HALF HOUR (Volume 5) (Tony Hancock).
Note: Includes: Hancock's War and The Christmas Club.
LP. Cat no: **REB 526.** Released on BBC, Oct '84 by BBC Records, Taylors.

MC. Cat no: **ZCF 526.** Released on BBC, Oct '84 by BBC Records, Taylors.

LIFT, THE (And Twelve Angry Men).
LP. Cat no: **REB 260.** Released on BBC, Nov '76 by BBC Records, Taylors.

MC. Cat no: **RMC 4055.** Released on BBC, Nov '76 by BBC Records, Taylors.

PIECES OF HANCOCK (Tony Hancock).
LP. Cat no: **NPL 18054.** Released on Pye, Nov '60 **Deleted** '65.

THIS IS HANCOCK (Tony Hancock).
LP. Cat no: **NPL 18045.** Released on Pye, Apr '60 **Deleted** '65.

LP. Cat no: **GGL 0206.** Released on Golden Guinea, Sep '63 **Deleted** '68.

WORLD OF TONY HANCOCK, THE (Tony Hancock).
Note: Includes: The Missing Page and The Reunion Party.
LP. Cat no: **SPA 417.** Released on Decca, Oct '75 by PolyGram Classics, Thames Distributors Ltd..

MC. Cat no: **KCPA 417.** Released on Decca, Jan '79 by PolyGram Classics, Thames Distributors Ltd. **Deleted** Apr '91.

CD. Cat no: **8208952.** Released on Eclipse (3), Jun '91 by London Records Ltd.

MC. Cat no: **8208954.** Released on Eclipse (3), Jun '91 by London Records Ltd.

Harcourt, Palma

AT HIGH RISK (Christopher Kay).
MCSET. Cat no: **1671t.** Released on Travellers Tales, '91 by Travellers Tales. Note: 4 Cassettes.

MCSET. Cat no: **1854963929.** Released on Bramhope, '91 by Ulverscroft Soundings. Note: 4 Cassettes.

CLASH OF LOYALTIES (Unknown narrator(s)).
MCSET. Cat no: **1854962469.** Released on Soundings, '91 by Soundings Records, Bond Street Music. Note: 6 Cassettes.

CLIMATE FOR CONSPIRACY (David Learner).
MCSET. Cat no: **1854965875.** Released on Bramhope, Apr '92 by Ulverscroft Soundings. Note: Playing time: 60 minutes.

COVER FOR A TRAITOR (Claran Madden).
MCSET. Cat no: **CAB 537.** Released on Chivers Audio Books, '91 by Chivers Audio Books, Green Dragon Audio Visual. Note: 8 Cassettes.

MCSET. Cat no: **1708T**. Released on Travellers Tales, '91 by Travellers Tales. Note: 8 Cassettes.

DANCE FOR DIPLOMATS (Unknown narrator(s)).
MCSET. Cat no: **1854965301**. Released on Bramhope, '91 by Ulverscroft Soundings. Note: 5 Cassettes.

DISTANT STRANGERS, THE (Gordon Griffin).
MCSET. Cat no: **1375T**. Released on Travellers Tales, '91 by Travellers Tales. Note: 5 Cassettes.
MCSET. Cat no: **1854961101**. Released on Bramhope, '91 by Ulverscroft Soundings. Note: 5 Cassettes.

DOUBLE DECEIT (Christopher Kay).
MCSET. Cat no: **1673T**. Released on Travellers Tales, '91 by Travellers Tales. Note: 7 Cassettes.
MCSET. Cat no: **1854963988**. Released on Soundings, '91 by Soundings Records, Bond Street Music. Note: 7 Cassettes.

LIMITED OPTIONS (Unknown narrator(s)).
MCSET. Cat no: **1854962922**. Released on Soundings, '91 by Soundings Records, Bond Street Music. Note: 6 Cassettes.

MATTER OF CONSCIENCE, A (Christopher Kay).
MCSET. Cat no: **1854964488**. Released on Soundings, May '91 by Soundings Records, Bond Street Music. Note: 6 Cassettes.

SLEEP OF SPIES, A (David Learner).
MCSET. Cat no: **1834965565**. Released on Bramhope, Feb '92 by Ulverscroft Soundings. Note: Playing time: 60 minutes.

TOMORROWS TREASON (David Learner).
MCSET. Cat no: **1854965417**. Released on Bramhope, Jan '92 by Ulverscroft Soundings.

TURN OF TRAITORS, A (Unknown narrator(s)).
MCSET. Cat no: **1854965050**. Released on Bramhope, '91 by Ulverscroft Soundings. Note: 5 Cassettes.

TWISTED TREE, THE (Gordon Griffin).
MCSET. Cat no: **185496481X**. Released on Bramhope, Aug '91 by Ulverscroft Soundings. Note: 6 Cassettes.

Harding, Mike

BEST OF MIKE HARDING, THE (Volume 2) (Mike Harding).
LP. Cat no: **RUB 047**. Released on Rubber, May '86 by Mawson & Wareham Music, Roots Records, Projection, Celtic Music, Jazz Music, Pinnacle.
MC. Cat no: **RUBC 047**. Released on Rubber, May '86 by Mawson & Wareham Music, Roots Records, Projection, Celtic Music, Jazz Music, Pinnacle.

CAPTAIN PARALYTIC AND THE BROWN ALE COWBOY (Mike Harding).
Tracks / Brown ale cowboys play a bit / Enter Captain Paralytic / Brum and a giant tortoise / These are my uncles / God was a golliwog / Man'nited song / Rosy cheeked girls, The / Upper echelon, The / Bloody, bloody, bloody, bloody / Old green iron lamp, The / Egremont - Gateway to oblivia / Mr. Fat Cigar / Horizontal Lil / Akroyds funeral / Captain Paralytics polka - the pishtenstein wa / Sonny's pain / Manuel / PBI.NKD.NP.BAGA / Lochdale ploughboy / BACS play a bit more.
2LP. Cat no: **6641 798**. Released on Philips, Jun '78 by Phonogram Ltd **Deleted** '83.

FOO FOO SHUFFLEWICK AND HER EXOTIC BANANA (Mike Harding).
Tracks / Foo Foo Shufflewick and her exotic banana / I am dancing alone in the night / Dracula and the trendies / Hotel Transylvania, The / Ronald Reagan, my hero / God meets Ronnie / Son et lumiere / Sao Bras Albufeira.
Note: Mike's latest comedy album recorded live at the Leeds Grand Theatre on Mike's 'One For The Road' tour 1985.
LP. Cat no: **MOO 8**. Released on Moonraker, Nov '86 by Moonraker Records, Pinnacle, Projection.
MC. Cat no: **MOOC 8**. Released on Moonraker, Nov '86 by Moonraker Records, Pinnacle, Projection.

GOD'S OWN DRUNK (Mike Harding).
LP. Cat no: **MOO 10**. Released on Moonraker, 12 Apr '89 by Moonraker Records, Pinnacle, Projection.
MC. Cat no: **MOOC 10**. Released on Moonraker, 12 Apr '89 by Moonraker Records, Pinnacle, Projection.

KOMIC KUTZ (Mike Harding).
Tracks / Is that the sun / Cameo club, The / Unluckiest man in the world, The / Can't help looking on the bright side / Jiggery pokery / Posh parties / Roggers and I / Uming face, A / Scouting for balmpots / Ladies man, The / Professional hospital visitor, The / 'Ardins theory of umour / Hole in the elephant's bottom, The.
2LP. Cat no: **6625 041**. Released on Philips, Oct '79 by Phonogram Ltd.
MC. Cat no: **7649 131**. Released on Philips, Oct '79 by Phonogram Ltd.

MRS.'ARDIN'S KID (Mike Harding).
Tracks / Joseph Anthony Capstick / Suitcase, The / Away with rum / Ballad of Cowheel Lou / Sailor courted a farmer's daughter, A / What's what / Drunken tackler, The / Strangeways Hotel, The / Man from the Pru, The / Uncle Joe's mint balls.
LP. Cat no: **RUB 011**. Released on Rubber, Jun '82 by Mawson & Wareham Music, Roots Records, Projection, Celtic Music, Jazz Music, Pinnacle.
MC. Cat no: **RUBC 011**. Released on Rubber, Jun '82 by Mawson & Wareham Music, Roots Records, Projection, Celtic Music, Jazz Music, Pinnacle.

ROLL OVER CECIL SHARPE (Mike Harding).
Tracks / Buggeri, buggeri, buggeri / Just can't beat this family life / Yorkshireman in the court of King Ronnie,The / 3 legged pig,The / Roll over Cecil Sharpe / K-Tel folk song PLC. Inc..
LP. Cat no: **MOO 7**. Released on Moonraker, Apr '86 by Moonraker Records, Pinnacle, Projection.
MC. Cat no: **MOOC 7**. Released on Moonraker, Apr '86 by Moonraker Records, Pinnacle, Projection.

ROOTED (Mike Harding).
Tracks / Buckets of blue steam and square bubbles / Leroy and the foreman / When the Martians land in Huddersfield / Rooted / She'll be right mate / West Yorkshire Dobro-playin' hippy cowboy,The / Wath on dearne blues.
LP. Cat no: **MOO 2**. Released on Moonraker, Apr '86 by Moonraker Records, Pinnacle, Projection.
MC. Cat no: **MOOC 2**. Released on Moonraker, Apr '86 by Moonraker Records, Pinnacle, Projection.

TAKE YOUR FINGERS OFF IT (Mike Harding).
Tracks / Australia / Hail glorious St. Margaret / Take your fingers off it / Captain Legless meets Superdrunk / Ghost of the cafe Gungha Din, The / Crumpsall kid, The / Quasimodo meets the Virgin Mary / Viking helmet, The.
LP. Cat no: **MOO 1**. Released on Moonraker, Apr '86 by Moonraker Records, Pinnacle, Projection.
MC. Cat no: **MOOC 1**. Released on Moonraker, Apr '86 by Moonraker Records, Pinnacle, Projection.

Hardwick, Mollie

DUCHESS OF DUKE STREET (Unknown narrator(s)).
MC. Cat no: **CAB 002**. Released on Chivers Audio Books, '81 by Chivers Audio Books, Green Dragon Audio Visual.

DUCHESS OF DUKE STREET (Volume 1) (Carole Boyd).
MCSET. Cat no: **1854965379**. Released on Soundings, Jan '92 by Soundings Records, Bond Street Music. Note: 6 cassettes.

DUCHESS OF DUKE STREET, THE (Volume 2) (Carole Boyd).
MCSET. Cat no: **1834965573**. Released on Bramhope, Feb '92 by Ulverscroft Soundings.

GIRL WITH THE CRYSTAL DOVE (Jenny Seagrove).
MCSET. Cat no: **1066F**. Released on Travellers Tales, '91 by Travellers Tales. Note: 3 cassettes.
MCSET. Cat no: **CAB 186**. Released on Chivers Audio Books, '91 by Chivers Audio Books, Green Dragon Audio Vis-

ual. Note: 3 cassettes.
MALICE DOMESTIC (Jan Francis).
MCSET. Cat no: **1191T.** Released on Travellers Tales, '91 by Travellers Tales. Note: 6 Cassettes.

PARSON'S PLEASURE (Jan Francis).
MCSET. Cat no: **CAB 304.** Released on Chivers Audio Books, Apr '88 by Chivers Audio Books, Green Dragon Audio Visual. Note: 6 cassette set
MCSET. Cat no: **1262T.** Released on Travellers Tales, '91 by Travellers Tales. Note: 6 Cassettes.

Hardy, Thomas

BARBARA OF THE HOUSE OF GREBE (And the Fiddler of the Reels) (Richard Morant).
MC. Cat no: **TTC 2007.** Released on Talking Tape Company, Apr '91, Conifer Records. Note: 2 cassettes. Playing time 2hrs 2mins. ISBN no. 1872520928

FAR FROM THE MADDING CROWD (Stephen Thorne).
MCSET. Cat no: **CTC 003.** Released on Cover to Cover, Jun '85 by Cover to Cover Cassettes. Note: 11 cassettes. Playing time:14 hrs 15 mins.

MCSET. Cat no: **1033/1034C.** Released on Travellers Tales, '91 by Travellers Tales. Note: 11 cassettes.

FIDDLER OF THE REELS (Richard Morant).
MC. Cat no: **TTC/TH 03.** Released on Talking Tape Company, '84, Conifer Records.

IMAGINATIVE WOMAN, AN (Unknown narrator(s)).
MC. Cat no: **TTC/TH 04.** Released on Talking Tape Company, Sep '84, Conifer Records.

JUDE THE OBSCURE (Peter Jeffrey).
MCSET. Cat no: **418 171-4.** Released on Argo (Polygram), Jun '88 by PolyGram Classics **Deleted** Jan '89.

MAYOR OF CASTERBRIDGE (John Rowe).
MCSET. Cat no: **CTC 028.** Released on Cover to Cover, Sep '86 by Cover to Cover Cassettes. Note: 9 cassettes. Playing time: 12 hrs 30 mins.

MCSET. Cat no: **1036/1037C.** Released on Travellers Tales, '91 by Travellers Tales. Note: 9 cassettes.

MAYOR OF CASTERBRIDGE (Alan Bates).
MCSET. Cat no: **LFP 7237.** Released on Listen For Pleasure, Jun '88 by EMI Records.

MELANCHOLY HUSSAR, THE (And Other Stories) (Morag Hood).
Note: Also includes:- An Imaginative Woman, To Please His Wife and On the Western Circuit.
MCSET. Cat no: **SPF 352-1.** Released on Schiltron Audio Books, '91 by Schiltron Publishing. Note: 2 Cassettes. Playing time 3 hours

POEMS OF THOMAS HARDY, THE (Richard Burton).
MCSET. Cat no: **HCA 49.** Released on Harper Collins, '92 by Harper Collins.
MC. Cat no: **1140.** Released on Caedmon (USA), '88 by Caedmon Records (USA), Bond Street Music.

RETURN OF THE NATIVE, THE (Peter Jeffrey).
Note: Abridged version.
MCSET. Cat no: **1038C.** Released on Travellers Tales, '91 by Travellers Tales. Note: 2 cassettes.

RETURN OF THE NATIVE, THE (Peter Jeffrey).
MCSET. Cat no: **414 754-4.** Released on Argo (Polygram), Jun '88 by PolyGram Classics **Deleted** Jan '89.

RETURN OF THE NATIVE, THE (Alan Rickman).
MCSET. Cat no: **CTC 017.** Released on Cover to Cover, '87 by Cover to Cover Cassettes. Note: 12 cassettes. Playing time:15hrs 45 mins.

MCSET. Cat no: **1039/1040C.** Released on Travellers Tales, '91 by Travellers Tales. Note: 12 cassettes.

RETURN OF THE NATIVE, THE (Lee Richardson).
MC. Cat no: **CDL 51733.** Released on Caedmon (USA), '84 by Caedmon Records (USA), Bond Street Music.

MCSET. Cat no: **0001060333.** Released on Collins-Caedmon, '91 by Collins Audio, Taylors, Bond Street Music.

SHORT STORIES (Richard Morant).
MCSET. Cat no: **1066C.** Released on Travellers Tales, '91 by Travellers Tales. Note: 5 cassettes.

TESS OF THE D'URBERVILLES (Moira Shearer).
MCSET. Cat no: **SAY 56.** Released on Argo (Polygram), Nov '82 by PolyGram Classics **Deleted** Jan '89.

MCSET. Cat no: **ARGO 1187.** Released on Argo (EMI), Mar '90 by EMI Records.

MCSET. Cat no: **1067C.** Released on Travellers Tales, '91 by Travellers Tales. Note: 2 cassettes.

TESS OF THE D'URBERVILLES (Stephen Thorne).
MCSET. Cat no: **CTC 054.** Released on Cover to Cover, Oct '88 by Cover to Cover Cassettes. Note: 12 cassettes. 15 hrs 30 mins.

MCSET. Cat no: **1080/1081C.** Released on Travellers Tales, '91 by Travellers Tales. Note: 12 cassettes.

THOMAS HARDY AND LOVE (Various artists).
CD. Cat no: **SHECD 9622.** Released on Pearl, Aug '91 by Pavilion Records, Harmonia Mundi (UK).
MC. Cat no: **THE 7622.** Released on Pearl, Aug '91 by Pavilion Records, Harmonia Mundi (UK).

THOMAS HARDY AND MUSIC (Unknown narrator(s)).

MC. Cat no: **THE 587.** Released on Pearl, '90 by Pavilion Records, Harmonia Mundi (UK).

THREE STRANGERS (And the Withered Arm) (Richard Morant).
MCSET. Cat no: **TTC 2008.** Released on Talking Tape Company, Apr '91, Conifer Records. Note: 2 cassetttes. Playing time - 2hr. 14mins. ISBN no. 1872520936

THREE STRANGERS, THE (Richard Morant).
MC. Cat no: **TTCTH 01.** Released on Talking Tape Company, '84, Conifer Records.

TRUMPET MAJOR, THE (Unknown narrator(s)).
MCSET. Cat no: **IAB 92032.** Released on Isis Audio Books, Mar '92. Note: 10 cassettes. Playing time 13hrs. 24mins.

UNDER THE GREENWOOD TREE (Robert Hardy).
MCSET. Cat no: **1042C.** Released on Travellers Tales, '91 by Travellers Tales. Note: 4 cassettes.

WITHERED ARM, THE (Various narrators).
MC. Cat no: **E 30.** Released on Tutor Tape, '91 by Morley Audio Services.

WITHERED ARM, THE (Corin Redgrave).
MCSET. Cat no: **COL 2017.** Released on Colophone, Nov '81 by AVLS (Audio-Visual Library Services).

WITHERED ARM, THE (Richard Morant).
MCSET. Cat no: **TTCH/TH 02.** Released on Talking Tape Company, '84, Conifer Records.

Hargreaves, Roger

ADVENTURES OF MR. CHATTERBOX (Lance Percival).
MC. Cat no: **TTS 9806.** Released on Tempo, Aug '84 by Warwick Records, Celtic Music, Henry Hadaway Organisation.

ADVENTURES OF MR. GREEDY (Lance Percival).
MC. Cat no: **TTS 9819.** Released on Tempo, Aug '84 by Warwick Records, Celtic Music, Henry Hadaway Organisation.

ADVENTURES OF MR. MESSY (Lance Percival).
MC. Cat no: **TTS 9823.** Released on Tempo, Aug '84 by Warwick Records, Celtic Music, Henry Hadaway Organisation.

ADVENTURES OF MR. NOISY (Lance Percival).
MC. Cat no: **TTS 9805.** Released on Tempo, Aug '84 by Warwick Records, Celtic Music, Henry Hadaway Organisation.

ADVENTURES OF MR. SILLY (Lance Percival).
MC. Cat no: **TT5 9824.** Released on Tempo, Aug '84 by Warwick Records, Celtic Music, Henry Hadaway Organisation. Note: Playing time - 40 mins. ISBN no. 187252088X

ADVENTURES OF MR. SILLY (Lance Percival).
MC. Cat no: **TTS 9824.** Released on Tempo, Aug '84 by Warwick Records, Celtic Music, Henry Hadaway Organisation.

ADVENTURES OF MR. SMALL (Lance Percival).
MC. Cat no: **TT5 9820.** Released on Tempo, Aug '84 by Warwick Records, Celtic Music, Henry Hadaway Organisation. Note: Playing time: 36 minutes. ISBN No: 872520898

ADVENTURES OF MR. SMALL (Lance Percival).
Note: Cassette with 32 page book.
MC. Cat no: **TTS 9820.** Released on Tempo, Aug '84 by Warwick Records, Celtic Music, Henry Hadaway Organisation.

ADVENTURES OF MR. SNEEZE (Lance Percival).
MC. Cat no: **TTS 9822.** Released on Tempo, Aug '84 by Warwick Records, Celtic Music, Henry Hadaway Organisation. Note: Playing time: 36 minutes. ISBN No: 872520898

ADVENTURES OF MR. TICKLE (Lance Percival).
MC. Cat no: **TTS 9821.** Released on Tempo, Aug '84 by Warwick Records, Celtic Music, Henry Hadaway Organisation.

COUNT TO TEN WITH MR. MEN (Arthur Lowe & Roy Castle).
MC. Cat no: **TBC 9513.** Released on Tempo Storytime, May '84 by Warwick Records, Celtic Music.

LITTLE MISS STORIES (John Alderton & Pauline Collins).
LP. Cat no: **INGL 003.** Released on Ingot, Dec '83 by Ingot Records.
MC. Cat no: **INGC 003.** Released on Ingot, Dec '83 by Ingot Records.

MR. MEN (Arthur Lowe).
LP. Cat no: **REC 337.** Released on BBC, '78 by BBC Records, Taylors **Deleted** 31 Aug '88.
MC. Cat no: **ZCM 337.** Released on BBC, '78 by BBC Records, Taylors **Deleted** 31 Aug '88.

MR. MEN AND LITTLE MISS (Volume 2) (Various artists).
Note: Narrators are: Arthur Lowe, John Alderton and Pauline Collins. Includes: Mr Busy, Mr Clever, Mr Wrong, Mr Mischief, Mr Quiet, Mr Nonsense, Little Miss Neat, Little Miss Helpful, Little Miss Plump, Little Miss Bossy, Little Miss Trouble andLittle Miss Scatterbrain.

MCSET. Cat no: **KIDM 9004.** Released on PRT, Nov '87 by Castle Communications PLC.

MR. MEN AND LITTLE MISS (Volume 1) (Various artists).
Note: Narrators are: Arthur Lowe, John Alderton and Pauline Collins. Includes: Mr Grumpy, Mr Tall, Mr Clumsy, Mr Skinny, Mr Worry, Mr Slow, Little Miss Splendid, Little Miss Shy, Little Miss Sunshine, Little Miss Magic, Little Miss Tiny and Little Miss Naughty.
MCSET. Cat no: **KIDM 9003.** Released on PRT, Nov '87 by Castle Communications PLC.

MR. MEN RIDE AGAIN, THE (Various artists).
Note: Includes: Mr Tall, Mr Grumpy, Mr Skinny, Mr Slow, Mr Worry and Mr Clumsy.
LP. Cat no: **INGL 001.** Released on Ingot, Dec '82 by Ingot Records.
MC. Cat no: **INGC 001.** Released on Ingot, Dec '82 by Ingot Records.

MR. MEN STORIES (Volume 2) (Arthur Lowe).
LP. Cat no: **REC 386.** Released on BBC, Oct '80 by BBC Records, Taylors **Deleted** 31 Aug '88.
MC. Cat no: **ZCM 386.** Released on BBC, Oct '80 by BBC Records, Taylors **Deleted** 31 Aug '88.

MR. MEN STORIES (Volume 3) (Arthur Lowe).
LP. Cat no: **REC 457.** Released on BBC, Oct '82 by BBC Records, Taylors **Deleted** 31 Aug '88.
MC. Cat no: **ZCM 457.** Released on BBC, Oct '82 by BBC Records, Taylors **Deleted** 31 Aug '88.

RETURN OF THE MR. MEN, THE (Arthur Lowe).
Note: Includes: Mr Wrong, Mr Nonsense, Mr Quiet, Mr Busy, Mr Mischief and Mr Clever.
LP. Cat no: **INGL 002.** Released on Ingot, Dec '82 by Ingot Records.
MC. Cat no: **INGC 002.** Released on Ingot, Dec '82 by Ingot Records.

Harley Lewis, Roy
DEATH IN VERONA (Unknown narrator(s)).
MCSET. Cat no: **1854962817.** Released on Bramhope, '91 by Ulverscroft Soundings. Note: 5 cassettes.

WHERE AGENTS FEAR TO TREAD (Clive Champney).
MCSET. Cat no: **1577T.** Released on Travellers Tales, '91 by Travellers Tales. Note: 5 Cassettes.
MCSET. Cat no: **1854963228.** Released on Bramhope, '91 by Ulverscroft Soundings. Note: 6 Cassettes.

Harris, Keith
ORVILLE AND CUDDLES (Keith Harris).
MC. Cat no: **0 00 102214 8.** Released on Tempo, '88 by Warwick Records, Celtic Music, Henry Hadaway Organisation.

Harris, Thomas
SILENCE OF THE LAMBS (Unknown narrator(s)).
MCSET. Cat no: **0671673513.** Released on Simon & Schuster, '91 by Simon & Schuster Ltd.

SILENCE OF THE LAMBS (Thomas Harris).
MCSET. Cat no: **ZDS 32.** Released on Dover, Apr '92 by Chrysalis Records, EMI Distribution (M & D) Services.

Harrison, Elizabeth
SURGEON'S AFFAIR (Carole Boyd).
MCSET. Cat no: **PMB 009.** Released on Mills & Boon, '88. Note: 2 Cassettes.

Hart, Josephine
DAMAGE (Edward Petherbridge).
MCSET. Cat no: **RC 55.** Released on Random Century, Mar '92 by Random Century Audiobooks, Conifer Records. Note: ISBN no. 1856860922

Hart-Davis, Duff
HEIGHTS OF RIMRING, THE (Gordon Griffin).
MCSET. Cat no: **1170T.** Released on Travellers Tales, '91 by Travellers Tales. Note: 8 Cassettes.
MCSET. Cat no: **185496111X.** Released on Soundings, '91 by Soundings Records, Bond Street Music. Note: 8 Cassettes.

LEVEL FIVE (Christopher Kay).
MCSET. Cat no: **1077T.** Released on Travellers Tales, '91 by Travellers Tales. Note: 6 Cassettes.
MCSET. Cat no: **1854961128.** Released on Soundings, '91 by Soundings Records, Bond Street Music. Note: 6 Cassettes.

Hartland, Michael
SEVEN STEPS TO TREASON (Nicholas Lumley).
MCSET. Cat no: **1669T.** Released on Travellers Tales, '91 by Travellers Tales. Note: 6 Cassettes.
MCSET. Cat no: **1854963899.** Released on Soundings, '91 by Soundings Records, Bond Street Music.

Hartley, L.P.
GO-BETWEEN, THE (Edward Petherbridge).
MCSET. Cat no: **CAB 566.** Released on Chivers Audio Books, '91 by Chivers Audio Books, Green Dragon Audio Visual. Note: 8 Cassettes.
MCSET. Cat no: **1648F.** Released on Travellers Tales, '91 by Travellers Tales. Note: 8 cassettes.

Harvey, John
LONELY HEARTS (B. Montague).
MCSET. Cat no: **1666T.** Released on Travellers Tales, '91 by Travellers Tales. Note: 7 Cassettes.
MCSET. Cat no: **1854963783.** Released on Soundings, '91 by Soundings Records, Bond Street Music. Note: 7 Cassettes.

Harvey, Richard
KNOX THE FOX (And Other Favourite Story Rhymes) (Arthur Lowe).
Note: Includes Knox the Fox, The Kangaroo of Waterloo, The Pig in a Wig and

The Sparrow of Harrow. For ages 3 - 7.
MC. Cat no: **STC 304B**. Released on VFM Cassettes, '88 by VFM Cassettes, Midland Records, Crusader Marketing Co., Taylors, Morley Audio Services.

PIGWIG PAPERS (Arthur Lowe).
Note: Includes the stories, The Squirrel of Wirral, The Frog and his Dog, The Lion and Curiosity, Knox the Fox, The Kangaroo of Waterloo, The Pig in the Wig, Dolphin Dee and the Chimpanzee, The Tiger and the Monkey, The Dinosaur of Ilkley Moor and The Sparrow of Harrow.
MC. Cat no: **VCA 098**. Released on VFM Cassettes, Jan '85 by VFM Cassettes, Midland Records, Crusader Marketing Co., Taylors, Morley Audio Services.

SQUIRREL OF WIRRAL (And Other Favourite Storyrhymes) (Arthur Lowe).
Note: Includes The Squirrel of Wirral, Dolphin Dee and the Chimpanzee, The Frog and his Dog, The Lion and Curiosity, The Tiger and the Monkey, and The Dinosaur of Ilkley Moor. For ages 3 - 9.
MC. Cat no: **STC 305 A**. Released on VFM Cassettes, '88 by VFM Cassettes, Midland Records, Crusader Marketing Co., Taylors, Morley Audio Services.

Harvey, Roger
PERCY THE PIGEON (Unknown narrator(s)).
MCSET. Cat no: **1854961136**. Released on Soundings, '91 by Soundings Records, Bond Street Music. Note: 2 cassettes.

SILVER SPITFIRE, THE (Unknown narrator(s)).
MCSET. Cat no: **1854961144**. Released on Trio, '91 by EMI Records. Note: 3 cassettes.

Hatton, Cliff
SANTA FE TRAIL (Tom Hunsinger).
MCSET. Cat no: **1009W**. Released on Travellers Tales, '91 by Travellers Tales. Note: 2 Cassettes.
MCSET. Cat no: **1854961152**. Released on Soundings, '91 by Soundings Records, Bond Street Music. Note: 2 Cassettes.

Hawthorne, Nathaniel
GREAT STONE FACE, THE (Nelson Runger).
MCSET. Cat no: **RB 86120**. Released on Recorded Books, Mar '92 by Isis Audio Books. Note: 2 cassettes. Playing time 2hrs

Haycox, Ernest
STARLIGHT RIDER (Richard Provost).
MCSET. Cat no: **CAB 257**. Released on Chivers Audio Books, Apr '88 by Chivers Audio Books, Green Dragon Audio Visual. Note: 6 Cassettes.

Hayes, Lesley
OXFORD MARMALADE (Susannah Dawson).
MCSET. Cat no: **MRC 1046**. Released on Chivers Moonlight Romances, Apr '88 by Chivers Audio Books, Green Dragon Audio Visual. Note: 2 Cassettes.

Haymon, S.T.
DEATH AND THE PREGNANT VIRGIN (Patrick Romer).
MCSET. Cat no: **OAS 40791**. Released on Oasis Audio Books, '91 by Isis Audio Books. Note: 7 cassettes.

Heaton, Dorothy
TEMPT HER WITH DIAMONDS (Alison Skilbeck).
MCSET. Cat no: **MRC 1053**. Released on Chivers Audio Books, '91 by Chivers Audio Books, Green Dragon Audio Visual. Note: 2 cassettes.

WHERE HE GOES, THERE GO I (Eunice Roberts).
MCSET. Cat no: **MRC 1009**. Released on Chivers Audio Books, '91 by Chivers Audio Books, Green Dragon Audio Visual. Note: 2 cassettes.

Heaven, Constance
CASTLE OF EAGLES (Jenny Hanley).
MCSET. Cat no: **1067F**. Released on Travellers Tales, '91 by Travellers Tales. Note: 6 cassettes.

WILDCLIFFE BIRD, THE (Julie Covington).
MCSET. Cat no: **CAB 583**. Released on Chivers Audio Books, '91 by Chivers Audio Books, Green Dragon Audio Visual. Note: 8 Cassettes.
MCSET. Cat no: **1661F**. Released on Travellers Tales, '91 by Travellers Tales. Note: 8 Cassettes.

Hecht, Ben
FRONT PAGE, THE (Various artists).
MCSET. Cat no: **0351**. Released on Caedmon (USA), '88 by Caedmon Records (USA), Bond Street Music. Note: 3 cassettes

Heide, Florence Parry
SHRINKING OF TREEHORN, THE (And The Treehorn's Treasure) (Kerry Shale).
MC. Cat no: **881581**. Released on Puffin Cover To Cover, '88, Green Dragon Audio Visual.

Heinlein, Robert
CAT WHO WALKS THROUGH WALLS, THE (Robert Vaughan).
MCSET. Cat no: **0671621432**. Released on Simon & Schuster, '91 by Simon & Schuster Ltd. Note: 2 Cassettes.

GREEN HILLS OF EARTH (And Gentlemen Be Seated) (Leonard Nimoy).
MC. Cat no: **1526**. Released on Caedmon (USA), '88 by Caedmon Records (USA), Bond Street Music.
MCSET. Cat no: **0001071475**. Released on Collins-Caedmon, '91 by Collins Audio, Taylors, Bond Street Music. Note: 2 cassettes.

JOB: A COMEDY OF JUSTICE (John Rubinstein).
MCSET. Cat no: **0671625225**. Released on Simon & Schuster, '91 by Simon & Schuster Ltd. Note: 2 Cassettes.

Heller, Joseph
CATCH 22 (Alan Arkin).
Note: Abridged version.
MCSET. Cat no: **1068F**. Released on Travellers Tales, '91 by Travellers Tales. Note: 2 cassettes.

CATCH 22 (Unknown narrator(s)).
MC. Cat no: **1418**. Released on Caedmon (USA), '88 by Caedmon Records (USA), Bond Street Music.

Hemingway, Ernest
OLD MAN AND THE SEA, THE (Charlton Heston).
MCSET. Cat no: **2084**. Released on Caedmon (USA), '88 by Caedmon Records (USA), Bond Street Music.
MCSET. Cat no: **00107153X**. Released on Collins-Caedmon, '91 by Collins Audio, Taylors, Bond Street Music. Note: 2 cassettes.

STORIES OF ERNEST HEMINGWAY, THE (Alexander Scourby).
MCSET. Cat no: **1303F**. Released on Travellers Tales, '91 by Travellers Tales. Note: 6 cassettes.
MCSET. Cat no: **CSL 017**. Released on Chivers Audio Books, '91 by Chivers Audio Books, Green Dragon Audio Visual. Note: 6 cassettes.

Henry, Lenny
LIVE AND UNLEASHED (Lenny Henry).
Tracks / Line up, ragamuffin style / Bad jokes / Harrassing the paying public / In clubland / International negro / Delbert Wilkins kickin' it live / I come from Dudley / Tales from Disco City / Pay attention / Everybody knows... / Men and women / Cat flaps! / Animal heaven / Blues ya'll, The / Music scene, The / Mandela day / Deakus / Theophilus P Wildebeest / I don't wanna leave.
CD. Cat no: **CID 9937**. Released on Island, Aug '89 by Island Records, Outlet Records, Solomon & Peres, Projection, Jetstar.
MC. Cat no: **ICT 9937**. Released on Island, Aug '89 by Island Records, Outlet Records, Solomon & Peres, Projection, Jetstar.

LP. Cat no: **ILPS 9937.** Released on Island, Aug '89 by Island Records, Outlet Records, Solomon & Peres, Projection, Jetstar **Deleted** Nov '90.

MC. Cat no: **ICM 9937.** Released on Island, Apr '91 by Island Records, Outlet Records, Solomon & Peres, Projection, Jetstar.

STAND UP...GET DOWN (Lenny Henry).
Tracks / Hello everybody / Olympics / Kids' TV / School / Katanga / Blackpool / J.A. Deakus / Scratch joke / Sex and kids and growing up / Big love (it's a love thing, girl!) / Delbert / Delbert.
LP. Cat no: **CHR 1484.** Released on Chrysalis, Nov '84 by EMI Records, Solomon & Peres.

MC. Cat no: **ZCHR 1484.** Released on Chrysalis, Nov '84 by EMI Records, Solomon & Peres.

Henry, O

GIFT OF THE MAGI, THE (And Other Stories) (Julie Harris).
MC. Cat no: **1273.** Released on Caedmon (USA), '88 by Caedmon Records (USA), Bond Street Music.

HOUR WITH O HENRY, AN (Ed Bishop).
MC. Cat no: **4175.** Released on Drake, '91 by Morley Audio Services.

INDIAN SUMMER OF DRY VALLEY JOHNSON (And Other Stories by O Henry & Ring Lardner) (John Sheddon).
MC. Cat no: **SPF 990-1B.** Released on Schiltron Audio Books, '91 by Schiltron Publishing. Note: Playing time 85 minutes.

NEW YORK STORIES, THE (Ed Bishop).
MC. Cat no: **LD 8.** Released on Green Dragon, '91 by Green Dragon Audio Visual.

O HENRY FAVOURITES (R. Donley & J Whittaker).
MCSET. Cat no: **1279F.** Released on Travellers Tales, '91 by Travellers Tales. Note: 6 cassettes.

MCSET. Cat no: **CSL 005.** Released on Chivers Audio Books, '91 by Chivers Audio Books, Green Dragon Audio Visual. Note: 6 cassettes.

WORLD OF O HENRY (Frank Muller).
MCSET. Cat no: **1633F.** Released on Travellers Tales, '91 by Travellers Tales. Note: 4 cassettes.

MCSET. Cat no: **RB 84015.** Released on Recorded Books, '91 by Isis Audio Books. Note: 4 Cassettes.

Henryson, Robert

ROBERT HENRYSON SELECTIONS (Volume 1) (Matthew McDiarmid).
MC. Cat no: **SSC 018.** Released on Scotsoun, '91 by Scotsoun Recordings, Morley Audio Services.

ROBERT HENRYSON SELECTIONS (Volume 2) (Matthew McDiarmid).
MC. Cat no: **SSC 019.** Released on Scotsoun, '91 by Scotsoun Recordings, Morley Audio Services.

Herbert, Frank

BATTLE OF DUNE (Unknown narrator(s)).
MC. Cat no: **CDL 51601.** Released on Caedmon (USA), Oct '70 by Caedmon Records (USA), Bond Street Music.

DUNE TRILOGY SOUNDBOOK (Unknown narrator(s)).
MCSET. Cat no: **116.** Released on Caedmon (USA), '88 by Caedmon Records (USA), Bond Street Music. Note: 4 cassettes

HERETICS OF DUNE (Unknown narrator(s)).
MC. Cat no: **1742.** Released on Caedmon (USA), '88 by Caedmon Records (USA), Bond Street Music.

WHITE PLAGUE, THE (Dillman Bradford).
MCSET. Cat no: **LFP 7308.** Released on Listen For Pleasure, Sep '87 by EMI Records **Deleted** Aug '89.

Herbert, James

MOON (Rula Lenska).
MCSET. Cat no: **1007S.** Released on Travellers Tales, '91 by Travellers Tales. Note: 8 Cassettes.

THE FOG See under Risk, by Dick Francis.

Herge

TINTIN AND THE PICAROS (Various artists).
MC. Cat no: **LPMC 501.** Released on Listen, '88, Cartel.

TINTIN AND THE SEVEN CRYSTAL BALLS (Various artists).
MC. Cat no: **LPMC 504.** Released on Listen, '88, Cartel.

TINTIN: THE BROKEN EAR (Various artists).
MC. Cat no: **LPMC 500.** Released on Listen Productions, '88.

Herriot, James

ALL CREATURES GREAT AND SMALL (Christopher Timothy).
MCSET. Cat no: **LFP 7202.** Released on Listen For Pleasure, Jul '85 by EMI Records.

ALL THINGS WISE AND WONDERFUL (Christopher Timothy).
MCSET. Cat no: **LFP 7256.** Released on Listen For Pleasure, Jun '86 by EMI Records.

IF ONLY THEY COULD TALK (And It Shouldn't Happen) (Unknown narrator(s)).
MCSET. Cat no: **LFP 7024.** Released on Listen For Pleasure, Jan '84 by EMI Records.

MCSET. Cat no: **LFP 4170245.** Released on Listen For Pleasure, Oct '85 by EMI Records.

LORD GOD MADE THEM ALL, THE (Christopher Timothy).
MCSET. Cat no: **LFP 4171025.** Released on Listen For Pleasure, Oct '85 by EMI Records.

Hesse, Hermann

STEPPENWOLF (Curt Jurgens).
MC. Cat no: **1589.** Released on Caedmon (USA), '88 by Caedmon Records (USA), Bond Street Music.

MC. Cat no: **0001071289.** Released on Collins-Caedmon, '91 by Collins Audio, Taylors, Bond Street Music.

Heyer, Georgette

BEHOLD, HERE'S POISON (Hugh Dickson).
MCSET. Cat no: **CAB 687.** Released on Chivers Audio Books, Apr '92 by Chivers Audio Books, Green Dragon Audio Visual. Note: 6 Cassettes.

BLACK MOTH, THE (Maggie Jones).
MCSET. Cat no: **1153R.** Released on Travellers Tales, '91 by Travellers Tales. Note: 8 Cassettes.

MCSET. Cat no: **OAS 90113.** Released on Oasis Audio Books, '91 by Isis Audio Books. Note: 8 Cassettes.

BLUNT INSTRUMENT, A (Hugh Dickson).
MCSET. Cat no: **CAB 370.** Released on Chivers Audio Books, '91 by Chivers Audio Books, Green Dragon Audio Visual. Note: 6 Cassettes.

MCSET. Cat no: **1399T.** Released on Travellers Tales, '91 by Travellers Tales. Note: 6 Cassettes.

CORINTHIAN, THE (Eve Matheson).
MCSET. Cat no: **CAB 595.** Released on Chivers Audio Books, '91 by Chivers Audio Books, Green Dragon Audio Visual. Note: 8 Cassettes.

MCSET. Cat no: **1697F.** Released on Travellers Tales, '91 by Travellers Tales. Note: 8 cassettes

COUSIN KATE (Sian Phillips).
MCSET. Cat no: **CAB 501.** Released on Chivers Audio Books, '91 by Chivers Audio Books, Green Dragon Audio Visual. Note: 10 Cassettes.

MCSET. Cat no: **1520/1F.** Released on Travellers Tales, '91 by Travellers Tales. Note: 10 cassettes.

DUPLICATE DEATH (Clifford Norgate).
MCSET. Cat no: **CAB 643.** Released on Chivers Audio Books, Nov '91 by Chivers Audio Books, Green Dragon Audio Visual. Note: 8 Cassettes.

FOOTSTEPS IN THE DARK (Maureen O'Brien).
MCSET. Cat no: **CAB 464.** Released on Chivers Audio Books, '91 by Chivers Audio Books, Green Dragon Audio Visual. Note: 8 Cassettes.

MCSET. Cat no: **1529T.** Released on Travellers Tales, '91 by Travellers Tales. Note: 8 Cassettes.

GRAND SOPHY, THE (John Westbrook).
MCSET. Cat no: **1457/8F.** Released

on Travellers Tales, '91 by Travellers Tales. Note: 10 cassettes.
MCSET. Cat no: **OAS 90045.** Released on Oasis Audio Books, '91 by Isis Audio Books. Note: 10 Cassettes.

MASQUERADERS, THE (Rosemary Leach).
MCSET. Cat no: **CAB 410.** Released on Chivers Audio Books, '91 by Chivers Audio Books, Green Dragon Audio Visual. Note: 8 Cassettes.

MCSET. Cat no: **1144R.** Released on Travellers Tales, '91 by Travellers Tales. Note: 8 Cassettes.

PISTOL FOR TWO (And Hazzard) (Christopher Casenove).
MC. Cat no: **PTB 608.** Released on Pickwick, '83 by Pickwick Records, Clyde Factors, Taylors, Arabesque, Solomon & Peres, I & B Records, Prism Leisure, Outlet Records.

SPANISH BRIDE, THE (Alison Skilbeck).
MCSET. Cat no: **CAB 661.** Released on Chivers Audio Books, Jan '92 by Chivers Audio Books, Green Dragon Audio Visual. Note: 12 cassettes.

SYLVESTER, OR THE WICKED UNCLE (Judy Franklin).
MCSET. Cat no: **1688F.** Released on Travellers Tales, '91 by Travellers Tales. Note: 8 cassettes.

MCSET. Cat no: **OAS 20491.** Released on Oasis Audio Books, '91 by Isis Audio Books. Note: 8 Cassettes.

UNFINISHED CLUE, THE (Clifford Norgate).
MCSET. Cat no: **CAB 575.** Released on Chivers Audio Books, '91 by Chivers Audio Books, Green Dragon Audio Visual. Note: 6 Cassettes.

MCSET. Cat no: **1722T.** Released on Travellers Tales, '91 by Travellers Tales. Note: 6 Cassettes.

Higgins Clark, Mary

ANASTASIA SYNDROME, THE (Lynn Redgrave).
MCSET. Cat no: **067168812X.** Released on Simon & Schuster, '91 by Simon & Schuster Ltd. Note: 2 Cassettes.

DOUBLE VISION (Unknown narrator(s)).
MCSET. Cat no: **0671736140.** Released on Simon & Schuster, '91 by Simon & Schuster Ltd.

LOST ANGEL (Unknown narrator(s)).
MCSET. Cat no: **0671736132.** Released on Simon & Schuster, '91 by Simon & Schuster Ltd.

LOVES MUSIC, LOVES TO DANCE (Unknown narrator(s)).
MCSET. Cat no: **0671726234.** Released on Simon & Schuster, '91 by Simon & Schuster Ltd.

STRANGER IS WATCHING, A (Unknown narrator(s)).
MCSET. Cat no: **0671745492.** Released on Simon & Schuster, '91 by Simon & Schuster Ltd.

TERROR STALKS THE CLASS REUNION (Sally Kirkland).
MCSET. Cat no: **0671708929.** Released on Simon & Schuster, '91 by Simon & Schuster Ltd. Note: 2 Cassettes.

WEEP NO MORE MY LADY (Elizabeth Ashley).
MCSET. Cat no: **0671657348.** Released on Simon & Schuster, '91 by Simon & Schuster Ltd. Note: 2 Cassettes.

WHILE MY PRETTY ONE SLEEPS (Jessica Walter).
MCSET. Cat no: **0671675907.** Released on Simon & Schuster, '91 by Simon & Schuster Ltd. Note: 2 Cassettes

Higgins, George

MANDEVILLE TALENT, THE (Ed Bishop).
MCSET. Cat no: **IAB 92012.** Released on Isis Audio Books, Jan '92. Note: 7 cassettes. Playing time 9hrs 16mins.

Higgins, Jack

COLD HARBOUR (David McCallum).
MCSET. Cat no: **0671701940.** Released on Simon & Schuster, '91 by Simon & Schuster Ltd. Note: 2 cassettes.

EAGLE HAS FLOWN (Unknown narrator(s)).
MCSET. Cat no: **0671724657.** Released on Simon & Schuster, '91 by Simon & Schuster Ltd.

EAGLE HAS LANDED, THE (Edward Fox).
MCSET. Cat no: **LFP 7403.** Released on Listen For Pleasure, Jul '89 by EMI Records. Note: Playing time; 2 hours 30 minutes.

EAST OF DESOLATION (Stephen Rea).
MCSET. Cat no: **CAB 267.** Released on Chivers Audio Books, '91 by Chivers Audio Books, Green Dragon Audio Visual. Note: 6 Cassettes.

MCSET. Cat no: **1226T.** Released on Travellers Tales, '91 by Travellers Tales. Note: 6 Cassettes.

EXOCET (Martin Shaw).
MCSET. Cat no: **CAB 065.** Released on Chivers Audio Books, '91 by Chivers Audio Books, Green Dragon Audio Visual. Note: 6 Cassettes.

MCSET. Cat no: **1078T.** Released on Travellers Tales, '91 by Travellers Tales. Note: 6 Cassettes.

FINE NIGHT FOR DYING, A (Barry Foster).
MCSET. Cat no: **ZC SWD 359.** Released on ASV (Academy Sound & Vision), Oct '89 by Academy Sound & Vision Records. Note: 2 cassettes. Playing time: 2 hours 45 minutes.

FOUR ABRIDGED STORIES (Various artists).
MCSET. Cat no: **1190T.** Released on Travellers Tales, '91 by Travellers Tales. Note: 8 Cassettes.

HELL IS ALWAYS TODAY (Michael McKenzie).
MCSET. Cat no: **COL 2016.** Released on Colophone, Jun '81 by AVLS (Audio-Visual Library Services).

IN THE HOUR BEFORE MIDNIGHT (Stephen Rea).
MC. Cat no: **CAB 337.** Released on Chivers Audio Books, '88 by Chivers Audio Books, Green Dragon Audio Visual.

MCSET. Cat no: **1364T.** Released on Travellers Tales, '91 by Travellers Tales. Note: 4 Cassettes.

IRON TIGER, THE (Barry Foster).
MCSET. Cat no: **CAB 173.** Released on Chivers Audio Books, '91 by Chivers Audio Books, Green Dragon Audio Visual. Note: 4 Cassettes.

MCSET. Cat no: **1080T.** Released on Travellers Tales, '91 by Travellers Tales. Note: 6 Cassettes

LUCIANO'S LUCK (Barry Foster).
MCSET. Cat no: **CAB 107.** Released on Chivers Audio Books, '91 by Chivers Audio Books, Green Dragon Audio Visual. Note: 6 Cassettes.

MCSET. Cat no: **1081T.** Released on Travellers Tales, '91 by Travellers Tales. Note: 6 Cassettes.

NIGHT JUDGEMENT AT SINOS (Philip Talbot).
MCSET. Cat no: **COL 2027.** Released on Colophone, '88 by AVLS (Audio-Visual Library Services).

NIGHT OF THE FOX (Unknown narrator(s)).
MCSET. Cat no: **0671646354.** Released on Simon & Schuster, '91 by Simon & Schuster Ltd. Note: 2 Cassettes

PASSAGE BY NIGHT (Barry Foster).
MCSET. Cat no: **CAB 148.** Released on Chivers Audio Books, '91 by Chivers Audio Books, Green Dragon Audio Visual. Note: 4 Cassettes.

MCSET. Cat no: **1083T.** Released on Travellers Tales, '91 by Travellers Tales. Note: 4 Cassettes.

MCSET. Cat no: **0745128041.** Released on Word For Word, May '92 by Chivers Audio Books.

PRAYER FOR THE DYING (Unknown narrator(s)).
MCSET. Cat no: **0671646362.** Released on Simon & Schuster, '91 by Simon & Schuster Ltd.

SAVAGE DAY, THE (Stephen Rea).
MCSET. Cat no: **CAB 275.** Released on Chivers Audio Books, '91 by Chivers Audio Books, Green Dragon Audio Visual. Note: 4 Cassettes.

MCSET. Cat no: **1227T.** Released on Travellers Tales, '91 by Travellers Tales. Note: 6 Cassettes.

SEASON IN HELL, A (David McCallum).
MCSET. Cat no: **0671673505.** Re-

leased on Simon & Schuster, '91 by Simon & Schuster Ltd. Note: 2 cassettes.

STORM WARNING (Marius Goring).
MCSET. Cat no: **COL 2020.** Released on Colophone, '88 by AVLS (Audio-Visual Library Services).

TESTAMENT OF CASPAR SCHULTZ, THE (Clifford Rose).
MCSET. Cat no: **CAB 036.** Released on Chivers Audio Books, '91 by Chivers Audio Books, Green Dragon Audio Visual.

MCSET. Cat no: **1085T.** Released on Travellers Tales, '91 by Travellers Tales. Note: 4 Cassettes.

TOUCH THE DEVIL (Ian Holm).
MCSET. Cat no: **LFP 7186.** Released on Listen For Pleasure, Mar '85 by EMI Records **Deleted** Aug '89.

VIOLENT ENEMY, THE (Barry Foster).
MCSET. Cat no: **CAB 210.** Released on Chivers Audio Books, '91 by Chivers Audio Books, Green Dragon Audio Visual. Note: 4 cassettes.

MCSET. Cat no: **1148T.** Released on Travellers Tales, '91 by Travellers Tales. Note: 4 Cassettes.

Highsmith, Patricia

BLUNDERER, THE (Don Fellows).
MCSET. Cat no: **1087T.** Released on Travellers Tales, '91 by Travellers Tales. Note: 8 Cassettes.

RIPLEY UNDER GROUND (Nigel Lambert).
MCSET. Cat no: **IAB 91094.** Released on Isis Audio Books, Sep '91. Note: 8 cassette set. Playing time 9hrs 5mins.

RIPLEY UNDER WATER (Geoffrey Matthews).
MCSET. Cat no: **IAB 92061.** Released on Isis Audio Books, Jun '92. Note: 8 Cassettes. Playing time: 11 hours, 20 mins.

TALENTED MR. RIPLEY, THE (Nigel Lambert).
MCSET. Cat no: **1475T.** Released on Travellers Tales, '91 by Travellers Tales. Note: 8 Cassettes.

MCSET. Cat no: **IAB 89102.** Released on Isis Audio Books, '91. Note: 8 Cassettes.

Hill, David

GIFT OF FIRE, THE (And Other Stories) (Robert Trotter & Sheila Donald).
Note: Includes:- The Gift of Fire, The Black Spaniel, Rent and Seed, The Warlocks Tune and The Face.
MCSET. Cat no: **SPF 356-1.** Released on Schiltron Audio Books, '91 by Schiltron Publishing. Note: 2 Cassettes. Playing time 1 hour 45 minutes.

Hill, Eric

FURTHER ADVENTURES OF SPOT, THE (Peter Hawkins).
Note: Also available on hanging format,

Cat. No: 0411380583.
MC. Cat no: **0411400320.** Released on Harper Collins, '91 by Harper Collins. Note: Playing time: 38 mins.

SPOT THE DOG (Paul Nicholas).
CD. Cat no: **U 4074.** Released on Spectrum (1), '88 by PolyGram UK Ltd, Terry Blood Dist..

SPOT'S FIRST PICNIC (Unknown narrator(s)).
MC. Cat no: **0 00 109027 5.** Released on Tempo Storytime, '88 by Warwick Records, Celtic Music.

MC. Cat no: **0411395297.** Released on Harper Collins, '91 by Harper Collins.

SPOT'S HOSPITAL VISIT (Unknown narrator(s)).
MC. Cat no: **0411395300.** Released on Harper Collins, '91 by Harper Collins.

Hill, Pamela

DIGBY (Unknown narrator(s)).
MCSET. Cat no: **1854962701.** Released on Bramhope, '91 by Ulverscroft Soundings. Note: 5 Cassettes.

JEANNIE URQUHART (Unknown narrator(s)).
MCSET. Cat no: **1854962809.** Released on Bramhope, '91 by Ulverscroft Soundings. Note: 5 Cassettes.

WHITTON'S FOLLY (Gordon Green).
MCSET. Cat no: **1069F.** Released on Travellers Tales, '91 by Travellers Tales. Note: 6 cassettes.

MCSET. Cat no: **1854961160.** Released on Soundings, '91 by Soundings Records, Bond Street Music. Note: 6 Cassettes.

Hill, Susan

WOMAN IN BLACK, THE (Christopher Kay).
MCSET. Cat no: **1088T.** Released on Travellers Tales, '91 by Travellers Tales. Note: 4 Cassettes.

MCSET. Cat no: **1854961187.** Released on Bramhope, '91 by Ulverscroft Soundings. Note: 4 Cassettes.

Hillerman, Tony

BLESSING WAY, THE (George Guidall).
MCSET. Cat no: **IAB 92066.** Released on Isis Audio Books, Jun '92. Note: 6 Cassettes. Playing time: 8 hours, 15 mins.

LISTENING WOMAN (George Guidall).
MCSET. Cat no: **IAB 92044.** Released on Isis Audio Books, Apr '92. Note: 5 cassettes. Playing time 6hrs 30mins.

Hilton, James

GOODBYE MR. CHIPS (John Sheddon).
MCSET. Cat no: **COL 2007.** Released on Colophone, Feb '81 by AVLS (Audio-Visual Library Services).

GOODBYE MR. CHIPS (And Lost Horizon) (John Sheddon & Michael Elder).
Note: Abridged version.
MCSET. Cat no: **1253F.** Released on Travellers Tales, '91 by Travellers Tales. Note: 6 cassettes.

LOST HORIZON (Michael Elder).
MCSET. Cat no: **COL 4002.** Released on Colophone, Jun '81 by AVLS (Audio-Visual Library Services).

LOST HORIZON (Unknown narrator(s)).
MCSET. Cat no: **1854961195.** Released on Bramhope, '91 by Ulverscroft Soundings. Note: 5 Cassettes.

Hilton, John Buxton

DEATH OF AN ALDERMAN (Timothy West).
MC. Cat no: **CAT 4034.** Released on Chivers Audio Books, Jul '88 by Chivers Audio Books, Green Dragon Audio Visual.

MCSET. Cat no: **1263T.** Released on Travellers Tales, '91 by Travellers Tales. Note: 4 Cassettes.

Hines, Barry

GAMEKEEPER, THE (Keith Barron).
MCSET. Cat no: **1213F.** Released on Travellers Tales, '91 by Travellers Tales. Note: 6 cassettes.

MCSET. Cat no: **CAB 236.** Released on Chivers Audio Books, '91 by Chivers Audio Books, Green Dragon Audio Visual. Note: 6 cassettes.

KES (Collin Wellard).
MC. Cat no: **LFP 7060.** Released on Listen For Pleasure, May '80 by EMI Records.

Hinge & Bracket

HINGE AND BRACKET IN CONCERT.
Tracks / HMS Pinafore / Patience / Iolanthe / Pirates of Penzance / Yeoman of the Guard / Perchance to dream / Gondoliers / Il Trovatore.
LP. Cat no: **OU 2227.** Released on One-Up, Apr '79 by EMI Records **Deleted** Apr '84.

Hinton, Nigel

BEAVER TOWERS (Unknown narrator(s)).
MCSET. Cat no: **DTO 10562.** Released on Ditto, '88 by Pickwick Records, Midland Records.

Hinton, S.E.

OUTSIDERS, THE (Jim Fyfe).
MCSET. Cat no: **4CCA 3134.** Released on Chivers Audio Books, '91 by Chivers Audio Books, Green Dragon Audio Visual. Note: 4 Cassettes.

Hissey, Jane

JOLLY TALL (And Other Stories) (Anton Rodgers).
MC. Cat no: **TS 385.** Released on Tellastory, '91 by Random Century Audiobooks. Note: ISBN no. 1856560566

LITTLE BEAR LOST (And Other Stories) (Anton Rodgers).
MC. Cat no: **TS 368.** Released on Tellastory, '91 by Random Century Audiobooks. Note: ISBN no. 1856560937

OLD BEAR (And Little Bear Lost) (Unknown narrator(s)).
MCSET. Cat no: **TS 387.** Released on Random Century, Oct '91 by Random Century Audiobooks, Conifer Records. Note: 2 cassettes. ISBN no. 185656133X

OLD BEAR (And Other Stories) (Anton Rodgers).
MC. Cat no: **TS 369.** Released on Tellastory, '91 by Random Century Audiobooks. Note: ISBN no. 1856560929

Hoban, Russell

BARGAIN FOR FRANCES, A (Glynis Johns).
MC. Cat no: **1547.** Released on Caedmon (USA), '88 by Caedmon Records (USA), Bond Street Music.

BEDTIME FOR FRANCES (Jill Shilling).
Tracks / Best friends for Frances / Baby sister for Frances, A / Birthday for Frances, A / Bedtime for Frances.
MC. Cat no: **TS 348.** Released on Tellastory, Apr '87 by Random Century Audiobooks.

FRANCES (Glynis Johns).
MC. Cat no: **1546.** Released on Caedmon (USA), '88 by Caedmon Records (USA), Bond Street Music.

MOUSE AND HIS CHILD (Peter Ustinov).
LP. Cat no: **TC 1550.** Released on Caedmon (USA), Jan '78 by Caedmon Records (USA), Bond Street Music.
MC. Cat no: **CDL 51550.** Released on Caedmon (USA), Jan '78 by Caedmon Records (USA), Bond Street Music.
MC. Cat no: **1550.** Released on Caedmon (USA), '88 by Caedmon Records (USA), Bond Street Music.

Hocking, Mary

GOOD DAUGHTERS (Hugh Ross).
MCSET. Cat no: **OAS 90043.** Released on Oasis Audio Books, '91 by Isis Audio Books. Note: 8 cassettes.

MCSET. Cat no: **1460F.** Released on Travellers Tales, '91 by Travellers Tales. Note: 8 cassettes.

LETTERS FROM CONSTANCE (Jane Asher).
MCSET. Cat no: **IAB 92071.** Released on Isis Audio Books, Jul '92. Note: 7 Cassettes. Playing time: 8 hours, 5 mins

Hodge, Jane Aiken

ADVENTURERS, THE (Unknown narrator(s)).
MCSET. Cat no: **1854961217.** Released on Soundings, '91 by Soundings Records, Bond Street Music. Note: 6 cassettes.

HERE COMES A CANDLE (Unknown narrator(s)).
MCSET. Cat no: **1854961225.** Released on Soundings, '91 by Soundings Records, Bond Street Music. Note: 8 cassettes.

Hodgson Burnett, F.

LITTLE PRINCESS, A (Maureen Lipman).
MCSET. Cat no: **418 180-4.** Released on Argo (Polygram), Jun '88 by PolyGram Classics **Deleted** Jan '89. Note: 2 cassette set
MCSET. Cat no: **ARGO 1112.** Released on Argo (EMI), Jun '89 by EMI Records. Note: 2 Cassettes.

LITTLE PRINCESS, A (Children's Classics) (Unknown narrator(s)). Note: Book and cassette.
MC. Cat no: **PLBC 210.** Released on Tell-A-Tale, '88 by Pickwick Records, Taylors, Clyde Factors.

SECRET GARDEN, THE (Gwen Watford).
MCSET. Cat no: **LFP 7314.** Released on Listen For Pleasure, Oct '87 by EMI Records.

SECRET GARDEN, THE (Hannah Gordon).
MC. Cat no: **P 90027.** Released on Pinnacle, '79 by Pinnacle Records, Outlet Records, Music Sales Records.

SECRET GARDEN, THE (Glenda Jackson).
MCSET. Cat no: **SAY 51.** Released on Argo (Polygram), Nov '82 by PolyGram Classics **Deleted** Jan '89.

SECRET GARDEN, THE (Claire Bloom).
MC. Cat no: **1463.** Released on Caedmon (USA), '88 by Caedmon Records (USA), Bond Street Music.

SECRET GARDEN, THE (Miranda Richardson).
MC. Cat no: **0600560597.** Released on Hamlyn Books On Tape, '88, Bond Street Music.

SECRET GARDEN, THE (Unknown narrator(s)). Note: Book and cassette.
MC. Cat no: **PLBC 76.** Released on Tell-A-Tale, '88 by Pickwick Records, Taylors, Clyde Factors.

SECRET GARDEN, THE (Unknown narrator(s)).
MCSET. Cat no: **DTO 10574.** Released on Ditto, '88 by Pickwick Records, Midland Records.

SECRET GARDEN, THE (Glenda Jackson). Note: Abridged.
MCSET. Cat no: **9018F.** Released on Travellers Tales, '91 by Travellers Tales. Note: 2 Cassettes.

Hoffnung, Gerard

AT THE OXFORD UNION (Gerard Hoffnung).
LP. Cat no: **LF 1330.** Released on Decca, Sep '60 by PolyGram Classics, Thames Distributors Ltd. **Deleted** '65.

HOFFNUNG - A LAST ENCORE (Various artists).
Tracks / Speech day: *Various artists* / My life: *Various artists* / Talking about music: *Various artists* / Charles Richardson interviews, The: *Various artists* / Bricklayer, The: *Various artists* / Film fan, The: *Various artists* / Oxford union: *Various artists* / Hoffnung Gerard interviews, The: *Various artists*.
MCSET. Cat no: **ZBBC 1062.** Released on BBC, Jan '89 by BBC Records, Taylors. Note: 2 Cassettes. ISBN No: 0563 226161.

Hogg, James

BROWNIE OF THE BLACK HAGGS (And Other Stories) (Eileen McCallum, Robert Trotter & Paul Young).
Note: Also includes:- The Barber of Duncow, The Cameronian Preachers Tsle, George Dobson's Expedition To Hell and The Watchmaker.
MCSET. Cat no: **SPF 375-2.** Released on Schiltron Audio Books, '91 by Schiltron Publishing. Note: 2 Cassettes. Playing time 2 hours 40 minutes.

PRIVATE MEMORIES AND CONFESSIONS OF A JUSTIFIED SINNER (John Sheddon).
MCSET. Cat no: **SPF 375-1.** Released on Schiltron Audio Books, '91 by Schiltron Publishing. Note: 4 Cassettes. Playing time 5 hours

Holland, Lys

MAN OF HONOUR, A (Betty Henry).
MCSET. Cat no: **SOUND 8.** Released on Soundings, Mar '85 by Soundings Records, Bond Street Music.
MCSET. Cat no: **1039R.** Released on Travellers Tales, '91 by Travellers Tales. Note: 4 Cassettes.

SING NO SAD SONGS (Unknown narrator(s)).
MCSET. Cat no: **1854963449.** Released on Bramhope, '91 by Ulverscroft Soundings. Note: 4 Cassettes.

Holloway, Stanley

MORE MONOLOGUES AND SONGS (Stanley Holloway).
Tracks / Sam's Xmas / Old Sam's party / Sam goes to it / Recumbent posture / Three ha'pence a foot / Many happy returns / Jonah & the Grampus / Yorkshire pudding / Gunner Joe / Parson of puddle / With her head tucked underneath her arm / Careless talk / My missus / Sometimes I'm happy / Keep smiling / London pride / Comedy tonight / Burlington Bertie from Bow.
LP. Cat no: **ONCM 533.** Released on Encore, Oct '80 by EMI Records, Sterns Records **Deleted** Oct '85.

Holt, Victoria

CAPTIVE, THE (Vivien Heilbron).
MCSET. Cat no: **CAB 655.** Released on Chivers Audio Books, Dec '91 by Chivers Audio Books, Green Dragon

Audio Visual. Note: 10 cassettes.

DEVIL ON HORSEBACK, THE (Maureen O'Brien).
MCSET. Cat no: **CAB 411**. Released on Chivers Audio Books, '91 by Chivers Audio Books, Green Dragon Audio Visual. Note: 10 Cassettes.
MCSET. Cat no: **1145/1146R**. Released on Travellers Tales, '91 by Travellers Tales. Note: 10 Cassettes.

GOOD FRIDAY (Unknown narrator(s)).
MCSET. Cat no: **0671667793**. Released on Simon & Schuster, '91 by Simon & Schuster Ltd.

INDIA FAN, THE (Maureen O'Brien).
MCSET. Cat no: **CAB 688**. Released on Chivers Audio Books, Apr '92 by Chivers Audio Books, Green Dragon Audio Visual. Note: 12 Cassettes

KING OF THE CASTLE, THE (Susan Jameson).
MC. Cat no: **CAB 310**. Released on Chivers Audio Books, '88 by Chivers Audio Books, Green Dragon Audio Visual. Note: 8 Cassettes.
MCSET. Cat no: **1318F**. Released on Travellers Tales, '91 by Travellers Tales. Note: 8 cassettes

KIRKLAND REVELS (Kara Wilson).
MCSET. Cat no: **CAB 444**. Released on Chivers Audio Books, '91 by Chivers Audio Books, Green Dragon Audio Visual. Note: 8 Cassettes.
MCSET. Cat no: **1461F**. Released on Travellers Tales, '91 by Travellers Tales. Note: 8 cassettes.

LEGEND OF THE SEVENTH VIRGIN (Maureen O'Brien).
MCSET. Cat no: **CAB 494**. Released on Chivers Audio Books, '91 by Chivers Audio Books, Green Dragon Audio Visual. Note: 8 Cassettes.
MCSET. Cat no: **1156R**. Released on Travellers Tales, '91 by Travellers Tales. Note: 8 Cassettes.

MENFREYA (Susan Jameson).
MCSET. Cat no: **CAB 142**. Released on Chivers Audio Books, '91 by Chivers Audio Books, Green Dragon Audio Visual. Note: 8 cassettes.
MCSET. Cat no: **1072F**. Released on Travellers Tales, '91 by Travellers Tales. Note: 8 cassettes.

MISTRESS OF MELLYN (Felicity Kendal).
CDSET. Cat no: **CAB 014**. Released on Chivers Audio Books, Jan '81 by Chivers Audio Books, Green Dragon Audio Visual.
MCSET. Cat no: **1073F**. Released on Travellers Tales, '91 by Travellers Tales. Note: 6 Cassettes.
MCSET. Cat no: **CAB 082**. Released on Chivers Audio Books, '91 by Chivers Audio Books, Green Dragon Audio Visual.

PRIDE OF THE PEACOCK, THE (Eva Haddon).

MCSET. Cat no: **CAB 538**. Released on Chivers Audio Books, '91 by Chivers Audio Books, Green Dragon Audio Visual. Note: 10 Cassettes
MCSET. Cat no: **1642/1643F**. Released on Travellers Tales, '91 by Travellers Tales. Note: 10 cassettes.

ROAD TO PARADISE ISLAND, THE (Susan Jameson).
MCSET. Cat no: **CAB 329**. Released on Chivers Audio Books, '91 by Chivers Audio Books, Green Dragon Audio Visual. Note: 10 Cassettes.
MCSET. Cat no: **1352/1353F**. Released on Travellers Tales, '91 by Travellers Tales. Note: 12 cassettes

SPRING OF THE TIGER, THE (Eva Haddon).
MCSET. Cat no: **CAB 596**. Released on Chivers Audio Books, '91 by Chivers Audio Books, Green Dragon Audio Visual. Note: 10 Cassettes.
MCSET. Cat no: **1694/1695F**. Released on Travellers Tales, '91 by Travellers Tales. Note: 10 cassettes.

Holtby, Winifred
LAND OF GREEN GINGER (Elizabeth Proud).
MCSET. Cat no: **IAB 92076**. Released on Isis Audio Books, Jul '92. Note: 8 Cassettes. Playing time: 10 hours, 30 mins.

POOR CAROLINE (Frances Jeater).
MCSET. Cat no: **OAS 90111**. Released on Oasis Audio Books, '91 by Isis Audio Books. Note: 8 cassettes.
MCSET. Cat no: **1522F**. Released on Travellers Tales, '92 by Travellers Tales. Note: 8 Cassettes.

Homer
ILIAD, THE (Richard Lattimore).
MC. Cat no: **1196**. Released on Caedmon (USA), '88 by Caedmon Records (USA), Bond Street Music.

ODYSSEY, THE (Anthony Quayle).
MC. Cat no: **3001**. Released on Caedmon (USA), '88 by Caedmon Records (USA), Bond Street Music.

Hope, Bob
AT HIS BEST ENTERTAINING THE TROOPS (Bob Hope).
MC. Cat no: **CMR 1060**. Released on Derann Trax, Nov '91 by Pinnacle Records.
CD. Cat no: **CDCMR 1060**. Released on Derann Trax, Nov '91 by Pinnacle Records.

Hope, Sir Anthony
PRISONER OF ZENDA, THE (Derek Jacobi).
MCSET. Cat no: **414 763-4**. Released on Argo (Polygram), Jun '88 by PolyGram Classics **Deleted** Jan '89.
MCSET. Cat no: **ARGO 1214**. Released on Argo (EMI), Apr '90 by EMI Records.

PRISONER OF ZENDA, THE (Derek Jacobi).

Note: Abridged version.
MCSET. Cat no: **1074F**. Released on Travellers Tales, '91 by Travellers Tales. Note: 4 Cassettes.

Hopkins, Gerald Manley
POETRY OF GERALD MANLEY HOPKINS (Cyril Cusack).
MC. Cat no: **1111**. Released on Caedmon (USA), '88 by Caedmon Records (USA), Bond Street Music.

Hornung, E.W.
RAFFLES (Volume 1) (Michael Elder).
MCSET. Cat no: **COL 2002**. Released on Colophone, '88 by AVLS (Audio-Visual Library Services).

RAFFLES (Volume 2) (Michael Elder).
MCSET. Cat no: **COL 2012**. Released on Colophone, Feb '81 by AVLS (Audio-Visual Library Services).

RAFFLES: A THIEF IN THE NIGHT (Robin Browne).
MCSET. Cat no: **1502T**. Released on Travellers Tales, '91 by Travellers Tales. Note: 6 Cassettes.
MCSET. Cat no: **OAS 89096**. Released on Oasis Audio Books, '91 by Isis Audio Books.

RAFFLES - AMATEUR CRACKSMAN (Michael Elder).
MCSET. Cat no: **1207T**. Released on Travellers Tales, '91 by Travellers Tales. Note: 4 Cassettes.

RAFFLES - BLACK MASK (Volume 2) (Michael Elder).
MCSET. Cat no: **COL 2026**. Released on Colophone, '88 by AVLS (Audio-Visual Library Services).

RAFFLES - BLACK MASK (Volume 1) (Michael Elder).
MCSET. Cat no: **COL 2025**. Released on Colophone, '88 by AVLS (Audio-Visual Library Services).

Hosier, John
SORCERER'S APPRENTICE, THE (Well Loved Tales Up to Age 9) (Unknown narrator(s)).
Note: Book and cassette.
MC. Cat no: **PLB 97**. Released on Tell-A-Tale, '88 by Pickwick Records, Taylors, Clyde Factors.

Household, Geoffrey
SUMMON THE BRIGHT WATER (Clifford Norgate).
MCSET. Cat no: **CAB 169**. Released on Chivers Audio Books, '91 by Chivers Audio Books, Green Dragon Audio Visual. Note: 6 Cassettes.
MCSET. Cat no: **1157T**. Released on Travellers Tales, '91 by Travellers Tales. Note: 6 Cassettes.

Houston, Will
SAM'S VALLEY (Unknown narrator(s)).
MCSET. Cat no: **1854961241**. Released on Trio, '91 by EMI Records. Note: 3 cassettes.

Howard, Audrey
SKYLARK'S SONG, THE (Unknown narrator(s)).
MCSET. Cat no: **1854964887**. Released on Soundings, '91 by Soundings Records, Bond Street Music. Note: 7 Cassettes..

Howard, Hartley
LAST VANITY, THE (Blain Fairman).
MCSET. Cat no: **CAT 4040**. Released on Chivers Audio Books, '91 by Chivers Audio Books, Green Dragon Audio Visual. Note: 6 Cassettes.

MCSET. Cat no: **1431T**. Released on Travellers Tales, '91 by Travellers Tales. Note: 6 Cassettes.

Howard, Troy
EAGLE TRAIL (Unknown narrator(s)).
MCSET. Cat no: **185496125X**. Released on Trio, '91 by EMI Records. Note: 3 Cassettes.

Howatch, Susan
APRIL'S GRAVE (Rowena Cooper).
MCSET. Cat no: **CAB 416**. Released on Chivers Audio Books, '91 by Chivers Audio Books, Green Dragon Audio Visual. Note: 4 Cassettes.

MCSET. Cat no: **1476T**. Released on Travellers Tales, '91 by Travellers Tales. Note: 4 Cassettes.

CALL IN THE NIGHT (Pat Starr).
MCSET. Cat no: **CAB 305**. Released on Chivers Audio Books, Apr '88 by Chivers Audio Books, Green Dragon Audio Visual. Note: 4 Cassettes.

MCSET. Cat no: **1264T**. Released on Travellers Tales, '91 by Travellers Tales. Note: 4 Cassettes.

DARK SHORE, THE (Rowena Cooper).
MCSET. Cat no: **CAB 360**. Released on Chivers Audio Books, '91 by Chivers Audio Books, Green Dragon Audio Visual. Note: 6 Cassettes.

MCSET. Cat no: **1395T**. Released on Travellers Tales, '91 by Travellers Tales. Note: 6 Cassettes.

DEVIL ON LAMAS NIGHT, THE (Rowena Cooper).
MCSET. Cat no: **CAB 459**. Released on Chivers Audio Books, '91 by Chivers Audio Books, Green Dragon Audio Visual. Note: 6 Cassettes.

MCSET. Cat no: **1530T**. Released on Travellers Tales, '91 by Travellers Tales. Note: 6 Cassettes.

GLAMOROUS POWERS (Dermot Crowley).
MCSET. Cat no: **CAB 644**. Released on Chivers Audio Books, Nov '91 by Chivers Audio Books, Green Dragon Audio Visual. Note: 16 Cassettes.

GLITTERING IMAGES (Stephen Thorne).
MCSET. Cat no: **CAB 523**. Released on Chivers Audio Books, '91 by Chivers Audio Books, Green Dragon Audio Visual. Note: 12 Cassettes.

SHROUDED WALLS, THE (Rowena Cooper).
MCSET. Cat no: **CAB 218**. Released on Chivers Audio Books, '91 by Chivers Audio Books, Green Dragon Audio Visual. Note: 6 Cassettes.

MCSET. Cat no: **1171T**. Released on Travellers Tales, '91 by Travellers Tales. Note: 6 Cassettes.

WAITING SANDS, THE (Rowena Cooper).
MCSET. Cat no: **CAB 179**. Released on Chivers Audio Books, '91 by Chivers Audio Books, Green Dragon Audio Visual. Note: 6 Cassettes.

MCSET. Cat no: **1093T**. Released on Travellers Tales, '91 by Travellers Tales. Note: 6 Cassettes.

Howe, Deborah & James
BUNNICULA (A Rabbit-Tale of Mystery) (Lou Jacobi).
MC. Cat no: **CP 1700**. Released on Caedmon (USA), Sep '82 by Caedmon Records (USA), Bond Street Music.

Howker, Janni
NATURE OF THE BEAST (Christian Rodska).
MCSET. Cat no: **3CCA 3029**. Released on Chivers Audio Books, '91 by Chivers Audio Books, Green Dragon Audio Visual. Note: 3 Cassettes.

MCSET. Cat no: **9101F**. Released on Travellers Tales, '91 by Travellers Tales. Note: 3 Cassettes.

H.R.H. Prince of Wales
OLD MAN OF LOCHNAGAR (Peter Ustinov).
LP. Cat no: **MMT LP 109**. Released on Multi-Media, Apr '82.

MC. Cat no: **MMT TC 109**. Released on Multi-Media, Apr '82.

Hudson, Harriet
WHEN NIGHTINGALES SANG (Jane Asher).
MCSET. Cat no: **CAB 584**. Released on Chivers Audio Books, '91 by Chivers Audio Books, Green Dragon Audio Visual. Note: 10 Cassettes.

MCSET. Cat no: **1663/4F**. Released on Travellers Tales, '91 by Travellers Tales. Note: 10 cassettes.

Hudson, William H.
GREEN MANSIONS (Anthony Quayle).
MC. Cat no: **1241**. Released on Caedmon (USA), '88 by Caedmon Records (USA), Bond Street Music.

Hughes, Richard
HIGH WIND IN JAMAICA (Anthony Quayle).
LP. Cat no: **TC 1563**. Released on Caedmon (USA), '78 by Caedmon Records (USA), Bond Street Music.

MC. Cat no: **CDL 51563**. Released on Caedmon (USA), Jan '78 by Caedmon

Records (USA), Bond Street Music.
MC. Cat no: **0001071483**. Released on Collins-Caedmon, '91 by Collins Audio, Taylors, Bond Street Music.

Hughes, Shirley
ALFIE GIVES A HAND (Thora Hird).
MC. Cat no: **0001010123**. Released on Harper Collins, '91 by Harper Collins.

ALFIE'S FEET (Thora Hird).
MC. Cat no: **0001010492**. Released on Harper Collins, '91 by Harper Collins.

BIG ALFIE AND ANNIE (Thora Hird).
MC. Cat no: **0411380761**. Released on Harper Collins, '91 by Harper Collins.

BIG ALFIE OUT OF DOORS STORYBOOK, THE (Thora Hird).
MC. Cat no: **TS 403**. Released on Tellastory, Mar '92 by Random Century Audiobooks. Note: ISBN no. 1856561488

CHARLIE MOON AND THE BIG BONANZA BUST-UP (Gordon Fairclough).
MCSET. Cat no: **2CCA 3092**. Released on Chivers Audio Books, '91 by Chivers Audio Books, Green Dragon Audio Visual. Note: 2 Cassettes.

MCSET. Cat no: **9153F**. Released on Travellers Tales, '91 by Travellers Tales. Note: 2 Cassettes.

EVENING AT ALFIE'S, AN (Thora Hird).
MC. Cat no: **0001010131**. Released on Harper Collins, '91 by Harper Collins.

HERE COMES CHARLIE MOON (Gordon Fairclough).
MC. Cat no: **2CCA 3059**. Released on Chivers Audio Books, '88 by Chivers Audio Books, Green Dragon Audio Visual. Note: 2 Cassettes.

IT'S TOO FRIGHTENING FOR ME! (John Bennett).
MC. Cat no: **881573**. Released on Puffin Cover To Cover, '88, Green Dragon Audio Visual.

ROSE STORYTAPE (Thora Hird).
MC. Cat no: **0411400541**. Released on Harper Collins, '91 by Harper Collins.

Hughes, Ted
CROW (Unknown narrator(s)).
2LP. Cat no: **CCT 9/10**. Released on Claddagh (Ireland), '89 by Claddagh Records (Ireland), Projection, Impetus Records, Jazz Music, Roots Records, C.M. Distribution, Outlet Records, Taylors.

CROW AND WODWO (Unknown narrator(s)).
MC. Cat no: **CDL 51628**. Released on Caedmon (USA), May '80 by Caedmon Records (USA), Bond Street Music.

IRON MAN, THE (Bernard Cribbins).

MCSET. Cat no: **SAY 32.** Released on Argo (Polygram), Jul '82 by PolyGram Classics **Deleted** Jan '89.
SELECTIONS FROM CROW AND WODWO (Unknown narrator(s)).
MC. Cat no: **1628.** Released on Caedmon (USA), '88 by Caedmon Records (USA), Bond Street Music.

Hughes, Thomas

TOM BROWN'S SCHOOLDAYS (Brown Derby).
MCSET. Cat no: **COL 3006.** Released on Colophone, Sep '81 by AVLS (Audio-Visual Library Services).
TOM BROWN'S SCHOOLDAYS (Rowan Atkinson).
MCSET. Cat no: **LFP 7376.** Released on Listen For Pleasure, Mar '89 by EMI Records. Note: Playing time: 2 hours.
TOM BROWN'S SCHOOLDAYS (Brown Derby).
Note: Abridged
MCSET. Cat no: **9039F.** Released on Travellers Tales, '91 by Travellers Tales. Note: 2 Cassettes.

Hugo, Victor

LES MISERABLES (Martin Jarvis).
MCSET. Cat no: **LFP 7463.** Released on Listen For Pleasure, Mar '90 by EMI Records. Note: Playing time: 3 hours

Hull, Rod & Emu

EMU'S PINK WINDMILL ADVENTURES (Volume 1) (Rod Hull & Emu).
Note: For children aged 3 - 9 years. Includes The Little Lost Dog and Grotbags Makes it Hot.
MC. Cat no: **VCA 613.** Released on VFM Cassettes, Aug '85 by VFM Cassettes, Midland Records, Crusader Marketing Co., Taylors, Morley Audio Services.
EMU'S PINK WINDMILL ADVENTURES (Volume 2) (Rod Hull & Emu).
Note: For children aged 3 - 9 years. Includes A Windy Day and Two Pink Windmills.
MC. Cat no: **VCA 614.** Released on VFM Cassettes, Aug '85 by VFM Cassettes, Midland Records, Crusader Marketing Co., Taylors, Morley Audio Services.
EMU'S PINK WINDMILL ADVENTURES (Volume 3) (Rod Hull & Emu).
Note: For children aged 3 - 9 years. Includes Grotbags Moving Day, Grotbags Nearly Does It, The Thoughts of a Boy Looking Out of his Bedroom Window, Dad and Gardening and Miss Rix.
MC. Cat no: **VCA 615.** Released on VFM Cassettes, Aug '80 by VFM Cassettes, Midland Records, Crusader Marketing Co., Taylors, Morley Audio Services.
EMU'S PINK WINDMILL ADVENTURE (Volume 4) (Rod Hull & Emu).
Note: For children aged 3 - 9 years.

Includes Super Emu, Grotbags Eastern Magic, The Fish and The Bully.
MC. Cat no: **VCA 616.** Released on VFM Cassettes, Aug '85 by VFM Cassettes, Midland Records, Crusader Marketing Co., Taylors, Morley Audio Services.
EMU'S PINK WINDMILL ADVENTURES (Volume 5) (Rod Hull & Emu).
Note: For children aged 3 - 9 years. Includes Changed Places, A Proverb for Emu, A March Day, The Gnu, My First Day at School and Opposites
MC. Cat no: **VCA 617.** Released on VFM Cassettes, Aug '85 by VFM Cassettes, Midland Records, Crusader Marketing Co., Taylors, Morley Audio Services.
EMU'S PINK WINDMILL ADVENTURES (Volume 6) (Rod Hull & Emu).
Note: For children aged 3 - 9 years. Includes A Big Blow for Rod, Four Little Gnomes, The Garden Centre, The Lamb in Spring, Pig Food, The Pink Windmill and Miss Bleep.
MC. Cat no: **VCA 618.** Released on VFM Cassettes, Aug '85 by VFM Cassettes, Midland Records, Crusader Marketing Co., Taylors, Morley Audio Services.

Humour

RECORD SIZE WILLY (Unknown narrator(s)).
LP. Cat no: **WILLY 1.** Released on Lifestyle, Nov '87 by Jive Records **Deleted** Nov '89.
MC. Cat no: **WILLY C1.** Released on Lifestyle, Nov '87 by Jive Records **Deleted** Nov '89.
THERE WAS THIS BLOKE (Various artists).
Tracks / John Blunt: *Various artists* / Only friend I own, The: *Various artists* / Crazy words: *Various artists* / Polly had a poodle: *Various artists* / Four letters: *Various artists* / Camp in the country: *Various artists* / Sir Quincy De Bas: *Various artists* / She loved a Portuguese: *Various artists* / Irwell Delta blues: *Various artists* / My brudda Sylveste: *Various artists*.
Featuring Mike Harding, Tony Capstick, Derek Brimstone, Bill Barclay.
LP. Cat no: **RUB 010.** Released on Rubber, Jun '82 by Mawson & Wareham Music, Roots Records, Projection, Celtic Music, Jazz Music, Pinnacle.
THEY ALL LAUGHED (Various artists).
Tracks / Best of Spike Milligan, The: *Various artists* / Me and my tune: *Various artists* / Girls like, The: *Various artists* / Airport routine: *Various artists* / Willy: *Various artists* / End of my old cigar: *Various artists* / Goldyloppers: *Various artists* / Happy go lucky: *Various artists* / Sheik of Araby, The: *Various artists*.
Note: Featuring songs and sketches by Hylda Baker & Arthur Mullard, Dick Em-

ery, Spike Milligan, Benny Hill, Max Wall, Roy Hudd, Max Miller, Frankie Howerd and June Whitfield, Bobby Knutt, Eric Morecambe and Ernie Wise, George Formby, Mike Reid, Tommy Cooper, Roger De Courcey & Nookie Bear, Wounded John Scott Cree, Danny La Rue, Larry Grayson, Stanley Unwin.
2LP. Cat no: **PYL 7006.** Released on PRT, Jan '88 by Castle Communications PLC.
MC. Cat no: **PYM 7006.** Released on PRT, Jan '88 by Castle Communications PLC. Note: Extended-play cassette.
VOICES ON THE STAIRHEID (Scottish Monologues and Sketches) (Sheila Donald & Robert Trotter).
Note: Includes works by J J Bell, Willie MacCulloch, Neil Munro, M C Smith and Mike Wood.
MC. Cat no: **SPF 959-1.** Released on Schiltron Audio Books, '91 by Schiltron Publishing.

Humphries, Barry

HOUSEWIFE SUPERSTAR (Barry Humphries).
LP. Cat no: **CHC 18.** Released on Charisma, Mar '83 by Virgin Records **Deleted** May '90.
MC. Cat no: **CHCMC 18.** Released on Charisma, Mar '83 by Virgin Records **Deleted** Jun '90.
MC. Cat no: **HSC 3255.** Released on Pickwick, Jan '89 by Pickwick Records, Clyde Factors, Taylors, Arabesque, Solomon & Peres, I & B Records, Prism Leisure, Outlet Records.
SOUND OF EDNA, THE (Barry Humphries).
LP. Cat no: **CHC 60.** Released on Charisma, Oct '86 by Virgin Records **Deleted** '88.
LAST NIGHT OF THE POMS (See under Everage, Dame Edna).
MY GORGEOUS LIFE (See under Everage, Dame Edna).

Huxley, Elspeth

MURDER AT GOVERNMENT HOUSE (Jill Tanner).
MCSET. Cat no: **1626T.** Released on Travellers Tales, '91 by Travellers Tales. Note: 8 Cassettes.
MCSET. Cat no: **IAB 90073.** Released on Isis Audio Books, '91.
MURDER ON SAFARI (Janet Porter).
MCSET. Cat no: **IAB 90032.** Released on Isis Audio Books, '91. Note: 7 cassettes.
MURDER ON SAFARI (Jill Tanner).
MCSET. Cat no: **1531T.** Released on Travellers Tales, '91 by Travellers Tales. Note: 7 Cassettes

Hyde, Anthony

RED FOX, THE (Donald Sutherland).

MCSET. Cat no: **0671640089**. Released on Simon & Schuster, '91 by Simon & Schuster Ltd. Note: 2 Cassettes.

Hyks, Veronika

ADVENTURES OF VICTORIA PLUM (Angela Rippon).
LP. Cat no: **STMP 9024**. Released on Super Tempo, May '84 by Warwick Records, Taylors, Solomon & Peres, Sony Music Operations.

MC. Cat no: **STMP4 9024**. Released on Super Tempo, May '84 by Warwick Records, Taylors, Solomon & Peres, Sony Music Operations.

VICTORIA PLUM (Angela Rippon). Note: Book and cassette.

MCSET. Cat no: **TBC 9512**. Released on Tempo Storytime, May '84 by Warwick Records, Celtic Music.

MCSET. Cat no: **TTS 9827**. Released on Tempo, Aug '84 by Warwick Records, Celtic Music, Henry Hadaway Organisation.

VICTORIA PLUM GIVES BEN A SURPRISE (Angela Rippon).
MCSET. Cat no: **TTS 9826**. Released on Tempo, Aug '84 by Warwick Records, Celtic Music, Henry Hadaway Organisation.

VICTORIA PLUM HAS A TREASURE HUNT (Angela Rippon). Note: Book and cassette.

MCSET. Cat no: **TTS 9828**. Released on Tempo, Aug '84 by Warwick Records, Celtic Music, Henry Hadaway Organisation.

VICTORIA PLUM HELPS THE BADGERS (Angela Rippon).
MCSET. Cat no: **TTS 9825**. Released on Tempo, Aug '84 by Warwick Records, Celtic Music, Henry Hadaway Organisation.

VICTORIA PLUM STORIES (Angela Rippon).
LP. Cat no: **6381 043**. Released on Philips, May '81 by Phonogram Ltd **Deleted** '86.

Ibsen, Henrik

DOLL'S HOUSE, A (Claire Bloom).
LP. Cat no: **TRS 343**. Released on Caedmon (USA), '74 by Caedmon Records (USA), Bond Street Music.

MC. Cat no: **CDL 5343**. Released on Caedmon (USA), '74 by Caedmon Records (USA), Bond Street Music.

MASTER BUILDER, THE (Various artists).
LP. Cat no: **TRS 307**. Released on Caedmon (USA), '74 by Caedmon Records (USA), Bond Street Music.

MC. Cat no: **307**. Released on Caedmon (USA), May '88 by Caedmon Records (USA), Bond Street Music.

Inge, William

BUS STOP (And Come Back Little Sheba) (Unknown narrator(s)).
MC. Cat no: **1771**. Released on Caedmon (USA), Sep '85 by Caedmon Records (USA), Bond Street Music.

Innes, Hammond

ANGRY MOUNTAIN, THE (Stephen Thorne).
MCSET. Cat no: **CAB 430**. Released on Chivers Audio Books, '91 by Chivers Audio Books, Green Dragon Audio Visual. Note: 8 Cassettes.

MCSET. Cat no: **1498T**. Released on Travellers Tales, '91 by Travellers Tales. Note: 8 Cassettes.

ATLANTIC FURY (Ian Stuart).
MCSET. Cat no: **1532T**. Released on Travellers Tales, '91 by Travellers Tales. Note: 8 Cassettes.

MCSET. Cat no: **IAB 90043**. Released on Isis Audio Books, '91. Note: 8 Cassettes.

BLUE ICE, THE (Stephen Thorne).
MC. Cat no: **CAB 342**. Released on Chivers Audio Books, '88 by Chivers Audio Books, Green Dragon Audio Visual.

MCSET. Cat no: **1367T**. Released on Travellers Tales, '91 by Travellers Tales. Note: 6 Cassettes.

CAMPBELL'S KINGDOM (Ian Stuart).
MCSET. Cat no: **1450T**. Released on Travellers Tales, '91 by Travellers Tales. Note: 6 Cassettes.

MCSET. Cat no: **IAB 89062**. Released on Isis Audio Books, '91. Note: 6 Cassettes.

DEAD AND ALIVE (Bob Peck).
MCSET. Cat no: **CAB 195**. Released on Chivers Audio Books, '91 by Chivers Audio Books, Green Dragon Audio Visual. Note: 6 Cassettes.

MCSET. Cat no: **1094T**. Released on Travellers Tales, '91 by Travellers Tales. Note: 6 Cassettes.

DOOMED OASIS, THE (Stephen Thorne).
MCSET. Cat no: **CAB 539**. Released on Chivers Audio Books, '91 by Chivers Audio Books, Green Dragon Audio Visual. Note: 6 Cassettes.

MCSET. Cat no: **1709/1710T**. Released on Travellers Tales, '91 by Travellers Tales. Note: 6 Cassettes.

HIGH STAND (Barry Foster).
MCSET. Cat no: **CAB 154**. Released on Chivers Audio Books, '91 by Chivers Audio Books, Green Dragon Audio Visual. Note: 8 Cassettes

MCSET. Cat no: **1096T**. Released on Travellers Tales, '91 by Travellers Tales. Note: 8 Cassettes.

KILLER MINE, THE (Stephen Thorne).
MCSET. Cat no: **CAB 662**. Released on Chivers Audio Books, Jan '92 by Chivers Audio Books, Green Dragon Audio Visual. Note: 6 cassettes.

LAND GOD GAVE TO CAIN, THE (Michael Sinclair).
MCSET. Cat no: **1673F**. Released on Travellers Tales, '91 by Travellers Tales. Note: 7 cassettes

MCSET. Cat no: **RB 89500**. Released on Recorded Books, '91 by Isis Audio Books. Note: 7 Cassettes.

LAST VOYAGE, THE (Nelson Runger).
MCSET. Cat no: **RB 88995**. Released on Recorded Books, May '92 by Isis Audio Books. Note: 5 Cassettes. Playing time: 7 hours.

LEVKAS MAN (Stephen Thorne).
MCSET. Cat no: **CAB 292**. Released on Chivers Audio Books, Apr '88 by Chivers Audio Books, Green Dragon Audio Visual. Note: 8 cassette set

MCSET. Cat no: **1239T**. Released on Travellers Tales, '91 by Travellers Tales. Note: 8 Cassettes.

LONELY SKIER, THE (Patrick Allen).
MCSET. Cat no: **1097T**. Released on Travellers Tales, '91 by Travellers Tales. Note: 6 Cassettes.

MEDUSA (Stephen Thorne).
MCSET. Cat no: **CAB 373**. Released on Chivers Audio Books, '91 by Chivers Audio Books, Green Dragon Audio Visual. Note: 8 Cassettes

MCSET. Cat no: **1415T**. Released on Travellers Tales, '91 by Travellers Tales. Note: 8 Cassettes.

STRODE VENTURER, THE (Stephen Thorne).
MCSET. Cat no: **CAB 603**. Released on Chivers Audio Books, '91 by Chivers Audio Books, Green Dragon Audio Visual. Note: 10 Cassettes.

TROJAN HORSE, THE (Stephen Thorne).
MCSET. Cat no: **CAB 476**. Released on Chivers Audio Books, '91 by Chivers Audio Books, Green Dragon Audio Visual. Note: 6 Cassettes.

MCSET. Cat no: **1533T**. Released on Travellers Tales, '91 by Travellers Tales. Note: 6 Cassettes.

WRECK OF THE MARY DEARE, THE (Ian Stuart).
MCSET. Cat no: **IAB 90074**. Released on Isis Audio Books, '91. Note: 7 cassettes.

MCSET. Cat no: **1659T**. Released on Travellers Tales, '91 by Travellers Tales. Note: 7 Cassettes.

Innes, Michael

APPLEBY FILE, THE (Christopher Kay).
MCSET. Cat no: **1854965719**. Released on Bramhope, Mar '92 by Ulverscroft Soundings. Note: Playing time: 60 minutes.

HARE SITTING UP (Jeremy Sinden).
MCSET. Cat no: **1095T**. Released on Travellers Tales, '91 by Travellers Tales. Note: 4 Cassettes.

LORD MULLION'S SECRET (Hugh Laurie).
MCSET. Cat no: **CAT 4029**. Released on Chivers Audio Thrillers, Apr '88 by Chivers Audio Books, Green Dragon Audio Visual. Note: 4 cassette set

MCSET. Cat no: **1251T**. Released on Travellers Tales, '91 by Travellers Tales. Note: 4 Cassettes.

Iremonger, Valentin
BY SANDYMOUNT STRAND (Unknown narrator(s)).
LP. Cat no: **CCT 12**. Released on Claddagh (Ireland), Aug '88 by Claddagh Records (Ireland), Projection, Impetus Records, Jazz Music, Roots Records, C.M. Distribution, Outlet Records, Taylors.

Irving, Washington
LEGEND OF SLEEPY HOLLOW (And Ichabod Crane) (Ed Begley).
MC. Cat no: **1242**. Released on Caedmon (USA), '88 by Caedmon Records (USA), Bond Street Music.

LEGEND OF SLEEPY HOLLOW (Glenn Close).
CD. Cat no: **WD 0711**. Released on Windham Hill, Jan '92 by Windham Hill Records (USA), New Note.
MC. Cat no: **WT 0711**. Released on Windham Hill, Jan '92 by Windham Hill Records (USA), New Note.

Isherwood, Christopher
GOODBYE TO BERLIN (And Other Stories) (Christopher Isherwood).
MC. Cat no: **1752**. Released on Caedmon (USA), Apr '85 by Caedmon Records (USA), Bond Street Music.
MC. Cat no: **0001071459**. Released on Collins-Caedmon, '91 by Collins Audio, Taylors, Bond Street Music.

Jackson Braun, Lilian
CAT WHO ATE DANISH MODERN, THE (George Guidall).
MCSET. Cat no: **RB 90081**. Released on Recorded Books, Apr '92 by Isis Audio Books. Note: 4 cassettes. Playing time 5hrs.

CAT WHO COULD READ BACKWARDS, THE (Lilian Jackson Braun).
MCSET. Cat no: **RB 90082**. Released on Recorded Books, '91 by Isis Audio Books. Note: 4 cassettes.

CAT WHO KNEW SHAKESPEARE, THE (George Guidall).
MCSET. Cat no: **RB 91115**. Released on Recorded Books, Aug '92 by Isis Audio Books. Note: 4 Cassettes. Playing time: 6 hours.

CAT WHO SAW RED, THE (George Guidall).
MCSET. Cat no: **RB 90083**. Released on Recorded Books, Dec '91 by Isis Audio Books. Note: 4 cassettes. Playing time 5hrs 45mins.

Jackson, Glenda
GLENDA JACKSON READS FROM HER STORYBOOK (Glenda Jackson).
MCSET. Cat no: **9062F**. Released on Travellers Tales, '91 by Travellers Tales. Note: 2 Cassettes.

Jackson, Steve
ADVENTURES OF MASK (Various artists).
MC. Cat no: **00 1041983**. Released on Tempo, '88 by Warwick Records, Celtic Music, Henry Hadaway Organisation. Note: 4 books and 1 cassette

CAR WARS (Various artists).
Note: Read by Mask characters.
MC. Cat no: **00 1021338**. Released on Tempo, '88 by Warwick Records, Celtic Music, Henry Hadaway Organisation.

MASK (Various artists).
Note: Read by the Mask characters.
MC. Cat no: **0 00 102212 1**. Released on Tempo, '88 by Warwick Records, Celtic Music, Henry Hadaway Organisation.

MASK-A-RAID (Various artists).
Note: Read by Mask characters.
MC. Cat no: **00 102140 0**. Released on Tempo, '88 by Warwick Records, Celtic Music, Henry Hadaway Organisation.

Jacob, Naomi
LONG SHADOWS (Jenny Hanley).
MCSET. Cat no: **1075F**. Released on Travellers Tales, '91 by Travellers Tales. Note: 6 cassettes.

Jacobson, Howard
COMING FROM BEHIND (Raymond Sawyer).
MCSET. Cat no: **OAS 89083**. Released on Oasis Audio Books, '91 by Isis Audio Books. Note: 8 cassettes.
MCSET. Cat no: **1049H**. Released on Travellers Tales, '91 by Travellers Tales. Note: 8 Cassettes.

REDBACK (Raymond Sawyer).
MCSET. Cat no: **1047/8H**. Released on Travellers Tales, '91 by Travellers Tales. Note: 12 cassettes.
MCSET. Cat no: **OAS 89101**. Released on Oasis Audio Books, '91 by Isis Audio Books. Note: 12 Cassettes.

James, Henry
ASPERN PAPERS, THE (Adrian Cronauer).
MCSET. Cat no: **RB 86340**. Released on Recorded Books, '91 by Isis Audio Books. Note: 3 cassettes.

ASPERN PAPERS, THE (Anthony Homyer).
MCSET. Cat no: **TCL 28**. Released on Complete Listener, '91 by Complete Listener. Note: 5 Cassettes. (BB) Playing Time: 450 Minutes.

TURN OF THE SCREW, THE (Various artists).
MCSET. Cat no: **SAY 112**. Released on Argo (Polygram), Sep '84 by PolyGram Classics **Deleted** Jan '89.
MC. Cat no: **TC LFP 7076**. Released on Listen For Pleasure, Feb '81 by EMI Records.
MCSET. Cat no: **ARGO 1061**. Released on Argo (EMI), May '89 by EMI Records. Note: 2 Cassettes.

TURN OF THE SCREW, THE (Rosemary Davis).
MCSET. Cat no: **OAS 11091**. Released on Oasis Audio Books, Oct '91 by Isis Audio Books. Note: 6 Cassettes. Playing time: 5 hrs 50 mins.

TURN OF THE SCREW, THE (Anthony Homyer).
MCSET. Cat no: **TCL 29**. Released on Complete Listener, '91 by Complete Listener. Note: 6 Cassettes. (BB) Playing Time: 540 Minutes.

TURN OF THE SCREW, THE (Virginia McKenna).
Note: Abridged version.
MCSET. Cat no: **1077F**. Released on Travellers Tales, '91 by Travellers Tales. Note: 2 cassettes.

WASHINGTON SQUARE (Connie Booth).
MCSET. Cat no: **1202F**. Released on Travellers Tales, '91 by Travellers Tales. Note: 6 cassettes.
MCSET. Cat no: **CAB 226**. Released on Chivers Audio Books, '91 by Chivers Audio Books, Green Dragon Audio Visual. Note: 6 cassettes.

James, Kenneth
INSPECTOR THACKERY ARRIVES (Various narrators).
MC. Cat no: **0582541409**. Released on Longman/Pickwick, '91 by Pickwick Records. Note: 2 cassette set.

James, M.R.
GHOST STORIES (Sir Michael Hordern).
MCSET. Cat no: **SAY 62**. Released on Argo (Polygram), Nov '82 by PolyGram Classics **Deleted** Jan '89.
MCSET. Cat no: **ARGO 1145**. Released on Argo (EMI), Sep '89 by EMI Records. Note: 2 Cassettes.
MCSET. Cat no: **1268F**. Released on Travellers Tales, '91 by Travellers Tales. Note: 2 cassettes.

MORE GHOST STORIES (Sir Michael Hordern).
Note: Includes: There Was A Man Dwelt By A Churchyard, Lost Hearts, Oh, Whistle And I'll Come To You, My Lad and The Mezzotint.
MCSET. Cat no: **SAY 113**. Released on Argo (Polygram), Jun '84 by PolyGram Classics **Deleted** Jan '89.

NUMBER 13 (And Other Ghost Stories) (Sir Michael Hordern).
MCSET. Cat no: **ARGO 1247**. Released on Argo (EMI), Oct '90 by EMI Records. Note: 2 Cassettes.

OTHER GHOST STORIES (Sir Michael Hordern).
Note: Includes: Stories I Have Tried To Write, The Uncommon Prayer-Book, A Warning To The Curious, A Neighbours Landmark and The Rose Garden.
MCSET. Cat no: **418 045-4**. Released on Argo (Polygram), Jun '88 by PolyGram Classics **Deleted** Jan '89.

WARNING TO THE CURIOUS, A (Nigel Lambert).
MCSET. Cat no: **1022S**. Released on

Travellers Tales, '91 by Travellers Tales. Note: 4 Cassettes.
MCSET. Cat no: **IAB 87112.** Released on Isis Audio Books, '91. Note: 4 Cassettes.

WARNING TO THE CURIOUS, A (And Casting The Runes) (Geoff McGivern).
MCSET. Cat no: **RSJ 5005/1/2.** Released on Landfall, '91.

James, P.D.
BLACK TOWER, THE (Michael Jayston).
MCSET. Cat no: **CAB 445.** Released on Chivers Audio Books, '91 by Chivers Audio Books, Green Dragon Audio Visual. Note: 8 Cassettes

MCSET. Cat no: **1534T.** Released on Travellers Tales, '91 by Travellers Tales. Note: 8 Cassettes.

COVER HER FACE (Roy Marsden).
MCSET. Cat no: **CAB 138.** Released on Chivers Audio Books, '91 by Chivers Audio Books, Green Dragon Audio Visual. Note: 6 Cassettes.

MCSET. Cat no: **1098T.** Released on Travellers Tales, '91 by Travellers Tales. Note: 6 Cassettes.

DEATH OF AN EXPERT WITNESS (Michael Jayston).
MC. Cat no: **CAB 311.** Released on Chivers Audio Books, Jul '88 by Chivers Audio Books, Green Dragon Audio Visual. Note: 8 Cassettes.

MCSET. Cat no: **1358T.** Released on Travellers Tales, '91 by Travellers Tales. Note: 8 Cassettes.

DEVICES AND DESIRES (Michael Jayston).
MCSET. Cat no: **CAB 663.** Released on Chivers Audio Books, Jan '92 by Chivers Audio Books, Green Dragon Audio Visual. Note: 12 cassettes.

INNOCENT BLOOD (Michael Jayston).
MCSET. Cat no: **CAB 487.** Released on Chivers Audio Books, '91 by Chivers Audio Books, Green Dragon Audio Visual. Note: 10 Cassettes.

MCSET. Cat no: **1565/1566T.** Released on Travellers Tales, '91 by Travellers Tales. Note: 10 Cassettes.

MIND TO MURDER, A (Roy Marsden).
MCSET. Cat no: **CAB 131.** Released on Chivers Audio Books, '91 by Chivers Audio Books, Green Dragon Audio Visual. Note: 6 Cassettes.

MCSET. Cat no: **1099T.** Released on Travellers Tales, '91 by Travellers Tales. Note: 6 Cassettes.

SHROUD FOR A NIGHTINGALE, A (Michael Jayston).
MCSET. Cat no: **CAB 388.** Released on Chivers Audio Books, '91 by Chivers Audio Books, Green Dragon Audio Visual. Note: 8 Cassettes.

MCSET. Cat no: **1477T.** Released on Travellers Tales, '91 by Travellers Tales. Note: 8 Cassettes.

SKULL BENEATH THE SKIN, THE (Greta Scacchi & Cast).
MCSET. Cat no: **ZBBC 1083.** Released on BBC Radio Collection, Jul '89 by BBC Records. Note: ISBN No: 0563 226641

SKULL BENEATH THE SKIN, THE (Jane Asher).
MCSET. Cat no: **CAB 330.** Released on Chivers Audio Books, '91 by Chivers Audio Books, Green Dragon Audio Visual. Note: 10 Cassettes.

MCSET. Cat no: **1408/1409T.** Released on Travellers Tales, '91 by Travellers Tales. Note: 10 Cassettes.

TASTE FOR DEATH, A (Michael Jayston).
MCSET. Cat no: **CAB 547.** Released on Chivers Audio Books, '91 by Chivers Audio Books, Green Dragon Audio Visual. Note: 12 Cassettes.

MCSET. Cat no: **1686/1687T.** Released on Travellers Tales, '91 by Travellers Tales. Note: 12 Cassettes.

UNNATURAL CAUSES (Michael Jayston).
MCSET. Cat no: **CAB 072.** Released on Chivers Audio Books, '91 by Chivers Audio Books, Green Dragon Audio Visual. Note: 6 Cassettes.

MCSET. Cat no: **1100T.** Released on Travellers Tales, '91 by Travellers Tales. Note: 6 Cassettes.

MCSET. Cat no: **0745128068.** Released on Word For Word, May '92 by Chivers Audio Books. Note: 6 cassettes.

UNSUITABLE JOB FOR A WOMAN (Tammy Ustinov).
MCSET. Cat no: **CAB 180.** Released on Chivers Audio Books, '91 by Chivers Audio Books, Green Dragon Audio Visual. Note: 6 Cassettes.

MCSET. Cat no: **1101T.** Released on Travellers Tales, '91 by Travellers Tales. Note: 6 Cassettes.

UNSUITABLE JOB FOR A WOMAN, AN (Various artists).
Note: Starring Judi Bowker, Anna Massey and Michael Turner.
MCSET. Cat no: **ZBBC 1141.** Released on BBC Radio Collection, '91 by BBC Records. Note: ISBN No: 0563 409959

Jameson, Claudia
MELTING HEART, THE (Georgina Melville).
MCSET. Cat no: **PMB 010.** Released on Mills & Boon, '88. Note: 2 Cassettes

Jansson, Tove
TALES FROM MOOMIN VALLEY (Unknown narrator(s)).
Note: Includes: The Last Dragon On The World, The Invisible Child and Cedric.
MC. Cat no: **TS 344.** Released on Tellastory, Dec '86 by Random Century Audiobooks. Note: Playing time: 1 hour

Jarrell, Randall
GINGERBREAD RABBIT, THE (Unknown narrator(s)).
MC. Cat no: **1381.** Released on Caedmon (USA), '88 by Caedmon Records (USA), Bond Street Music.

RANDALL JARRELL READS POEMS AGAINST WAR.
MC. Cat no: **1363.** Released on Caedmon (USA), by Caedmon Records (USA), Bond Street Music.

Jefferson Parker, T
LAGUNA HEAT (Peter Fernandez).
MCSET. Cat no: **RB 89800.** Released on Recorded Books, Jun '92 by Isis Audio Books. Note: 7 Cassettes. Playing time: 10 hours, 15 mins.

Jenkins, Geoffrey
SCEND OF THE SEA (Patrick Malahide).
MCSET. Cat no: **CAB 634.** Released on Chivers Audio Books, Oct '91 by Chivers Audio Books, Green Dragon Audio Visual. Note: 8 cassettes

Jerome, Jerome K.
THREE MEN IN A BOAT (Martin Heller).
MCSET. Cat no: **COL 2001.** Released on Colophone, '88 by AVLS (Audio-Visual Library Services).

THREE MEN IN A BOAT (George Rose).
MC. Cat no: **1711.** Released on Caedmon (USA), '88 by Caedmon Records (USA), Bond Street Music.

THREE MEN IN A BOAT (Jeremy Nicholas).
MCSET. Cat no: **SAY 86.** Released on Argo (Polygram), Jun '88 by PolyGram Classics **Deleted** Jan '89.

MCSET. Cat no: **ARGO 1052.** Released on Argo (EMI), May '89 by EMI Records. Note: 2 Cassettes.

THREE MEN IN A BOAT (Ian Carmichael).
MCSET. Cat no: **1007H.** Released on Travellers Tales, '91 by Travellers Tales. Note: 4 cassettes.

THREE MEN ON THE BUMMEL (Martin Heller).
MCSET. Cat no: **SPF 430-1.** Released on Schiltron Audio Books, '91 by Schiltron Publishing. Note: 4 Cassettes. Playing time 4 hours 45 minutes.

MCSET. Cat no: **1042H.** Released on Travellers Tales, '91 by Travellers Tales. Note: 4 cassettes.

John, Phillipa
CARIBBEAN ENCOUNTER (Fiona Matheson).
MC. Cat no: **85 1002.** Released on Cover to Cover, Nov '86 by Cover to Cover Cassettes.

Johns, Capt. W.E
BIGGLES (Michael York).
MC. Cat no: **TCLFP 417136 5.** Released on Listen For Pleasure, '83 by EMI Records.

BIGGLES DEFIES THE SWAS-TIKA (Tim Pigott-Smith).
MCSET. Cat no: **TS 414.** Released on Tellastory, Jul '92 by Random Century Audiobooks. Note: 2 cassettes. ISBN no. 1856561372

BIGGLES FLIES EAST (Tim Pigott-Smith).
MCSET. Cat no: **TS 413.** Released on Tellastory, Jul '92 by Random Century Audiobooks. Note: 2 cassettes. ISBN no. 1856561364

Jones, James Earl
POEMS FROM BLACK AFRICA (James Earl Jones).
MC. Cat no: **1315.** Released on Caedmon (USA), '88 by Caedmon Records (USA), Bond Street Music.

Jones, Jimmy
BEST OF JIMMY JONES (Jimmy Jones).
LP. Cat no: **KIN 3.** Released on A.1, Nov '86 by A.1 Records, Telstar Records (UK), Total Distribution.
MC. Cat no: **KINC 3.** Released on A.1, Nov '86 by A.1 Records, Telstar Records (UK), Total Distribution.

LIVE AT THE TALK OF EAST ANGLIA (Jimmy Jones).
LP. Cat no: **KIN 1.** Released on Kin'ell, Nov '81.

Jordan, Penny
TIGER MAN (Georgina Melville).
MCSET. Cat no: **PMB 002.** Released on Mills & Boon, '88. Note: 2 cassettes.

Joseph, Marie
BETTER WORLD THAN THIS, A (Carole Boyd).
MCSET. Cat no: **CAB 399.** Released on Chivers Audio Books, '91 by Chivers Audio Books, Green Dragon Audio Visual. Note: 6 Cassettes.

MCSET. Cat no: **1147R.** Released on Travellers Tales, '91 by Travellers Tales. Note: 8 Cassettes.

CLOGGER'S CHILD, THE (Carole Boyd).
MCSET. Cat no: **CAB 585.** Released on Chivers Audio Books, '91 by Chivers Audio Books, Green Dragon Audio Visual. Note: 8 Cassettes.

MCSET. Cat no: **1662F.** Released on Travellers Tales, '91 by Travellers Tales. Note: 8 cassettes.

EMMA SPARROW (Carole Boyd).
MCSET. Cat no: **CAB 361.** Released on Chivers Audio Books, '91 by Chivers Audio Books, Green Dragon Audio Visual. Note: 8 Cassettes

MCSET. Cat no: **1344F.** Released on Travellers Tales, '91 by Travellers Tales. Note: 8 cassettes.

LISA LOGAN (Carole Boyd).
MCSET. Cat no: **CAB 176.** Released on Chivers Audio Books, '91 by Chivers Audio Books, Green Dragon Audio Visual. Note: 8 cassettes.

MCSET. Cat no: **1080F.** Released on Travellers Tales, '91 by Travellers Tales. Note: 8 cassettes.

LISTENING SILENCE, THE (Carole Boyd).
MCSET. Cat no: **CAB 262.** Released on Chivers Audio Books, '91 by Chivers Audio Books, Green Dragon Audio Visual. Note: 6 Cassettes

MCSET. Cat no: **1127R.** Released on Travellers Tales, '91 by Travellers Tales. Note: 6 Cassettes.

MAGGIE CRAIG (Carole Boyd).
MCSET. Cat no: **CAB 284.** Released on Chivers Audio Books, '91 by Chivers Audio Books, Green Dragon Audio Visual. Note: 8 Cassettes

MCSET. Cat no: **1289F.** Released on Travellers Tales, '91 by Travellers Tales. Note: 8 cassettes.

POLLYPILGRIM (Carole Boyd).
MCSET. Cat no: **CAB 219.** Released on Chivers Audio Books, '91 by Chivers Audio Books, Green Dragon Audio Visual. Note: 6 Cassettes

MCSET. Cat no: **1098R.** Released on Travellers Tales, '91 by Travellers Tales. Note: 6 Cassettes.

RING-A-ROSES (Carole Boyd).
MCSET. Cat no: **CAB 656.** Released on Chivers Audio Books, Dec '91 by Chivers Audio Books, Green Dragon Audio Visual. Note: 4 cassettes.

TRAVELLING MAN, THE (Carole Boyd).
MCSET. Cat no: **CAB 508.** Released on Chivers Audio Books, '91 by Chivers Audio Books, Green Dragon Audio Visual. Note: 8 Cassettes.

MCSET. Cat no: **1523F.** Released on Travellers Tales, '91 by Travellers Tales. Note: 8 cassettes

WORLD APART, A (Carole Boyd).
MCSET. Cat no: **1462F.** Released on Travellers Tales, '91 by Travellers Tales. Note: 8 cassettes

MCSET. Cat no: **CAB 460.** Released on Chivers Audio Books, '91 by Chivers Audio Books, Green Dragon Audio Visual.

Joseph, Mark
TO KILL THE POTEMKIN (Garrick Hagon).
MCSET. Cat no: **1442T.** Released on Travellers Tales, '91 by Travellers Tales. Note: 5 Cassettes.

MCSET. Cat no: **1854962337.** Released on Bramhope, '91 by Ulverscroft Soundings.

Joyce, James
DEAD, THE (And Other Stories From The Dubliners) (T.P. McKenna).
MCSET. Cat no: **TTDMC 415.** Released on CSA Tell Tapes, '91 by CSA Tell-Tapes. Note: 2 Cassettes. ISBN No: 1873859155

ULYSSES (Unknown narrator(s)).
MCSET. Cat no: **0328.** Released on Caedmon (USA), '88 by Caedmon Records (USA), Bond Street Music. Note: 2 cassettes

MCSET. Cat no: **0001063758.** Released on Collins-Caedmon, '91 by Collins Audio, Taylors, Bond Street Music. Note: 2 cassettes

Jungman, Ann
LUCY AND THE BIG BAD WOLF (Jane Asher).
MCSET. Cat no: **2CCA 3118.** Released on Chivers Audio Books, '91 by Chivers Audio Books, Green Dragon Audio Visual. Note: 2 Cassettes.

LUCY AND THE WOLF IN SHEEP'S CLOTHING (Jane Asher).
MCSET. Cat no: **2CCA 3147.** Released on Chivers Audio Books, '91 by Chivers Audio Books, Green Dragon Audio Visual. Note: 2 Cassettes.

Kafka, Franz
METAMORPHOSIS, THE (James Mason).
MC. Cat no: **1594.** Released on Caedmon (USA), '88 by Caedmon Records (USA), Bond Street Music.

STORIES OF FRANZ KAFKA (Lotte Lenya).
MC. Cat no: **1114.** Released on Caedmon (USA), '88 by Caedmon Records (USA), Bond Street Music.

Karlin, M.
TAILORS OF PENZANCE (Unknown narrator(s)).
LP. Cat no: **EMPL 1005.** Released on Amberlee, '71 by Amberlee Records.

Kaula, Edna Mason
AFRICAN VILLAGE FOLKTALES (Volume 1) (Brock Peters & Diana Sands).
MC. Cat no: **1309.** Released on Caedmon (USA), '88 by Caedmon Records (USA), Bond Street Music.

AFRICAN VILLAGE FOLKTALES (Volume 2) (Brock Peters & Diana Sands).
MC. Cat no: **1312.** Released on Caedmon (USA), '88 by Caedmon Records (USA), Bond Street Music.

AFRICAN VILLAGE FOLKTALES (Volume 3) (Brock Peters & Diana Sands).
MC. Cat no: **1310.** Released on Caedmon (USA), '88 by Caedmon Records (USA), Bond Street Music.

Kavanagh, Patrick
ALMOST EVERYTHING (Unknown narrator(s)).
LP. Cat no: **CCT 1.** Released on Claddagh (Ireland), Aug '88 by Claddagh Records (Ireland), Projection, Impetus Records, Jazz Music, Roots Records, C.M. Distribution, Outlet Records, Taylors.

Kaye, M.M.
DEATH IN BERLIN (Virginia McKenna).
MCSET. Cat no: **CAB 237.** Released

on Chivers Audio Books, '91 by Chivers Audio Books, Green Dragon Audio Visual. Note: 6 Cassettes.
MCSET. Cat no: **1186T**. Released on Travellers Tales, '91 by Travellers Tales. Note: 6 Cassettes.
DEATH IN CYPRUS (Virginia McKenna).
MCSET. Cat no: **CAB 201**. Released on Chivers Audio Books, '91 by Chivers Audio Books, Green Dragon Audio Visual. Note: 8 Cassettes.
MCSET. Cat no: **1149T**. Released on Travellers Tales, '91 by Travellers Tales. Note: 8 Cassettes.
DEATH IN KASHMIR (Virginia McKenna).
MCSET. Cat no: **CAB 367**. Released on Chivers Audio Books, '91 by Chivers Audio Books, Green Dragon Audio Visual. Note: 8 Cassettes.
MCSET. Cat no: **1400T**. Released on Travellers Tales, '91 by Travellers Tales. Note: 8 Cassettes.
DEATH IN KENYA (Virginia McKenna).
MCSET. Cat no: **CAB 088**. Released on Chivers Audio Books, '91 by Chivers Audio Books, Green Dragon Audio Visual. Note: 6 cassettes.
MCSET. Cat no: **1102T**. Released on Travellers Tales, '91 by Travellers Tales. Note: 6 Cassettes.
DEATH IN THE ANDAMANS (Virginia McKenna).
MCSET. Cat no: **CAB 293**. Released on Chivers Audio Books, Apr '88 by Chivers Audio Books, Green Dragon Audio Visual. Note: 8 Cassettes.
MCSET. Cat no: **1240T**. Released on Travellers Tales, '91 by Travellers Tales. Note: 8 Cassettes
DEATH IN ZANZIBAR (Virginia McKenna).
MCSET. Cat no: **CAB 143**. Released on Chivers Audio Books, '91 by Chivers Audio Books, Green Dragon Audio Visual. Note: 8 Cassettes.
MCSET. Cat no: **1103T**. Released on Travellers Tales, '91 by Travellers Tales. Note: 8 Cassettes.
ORDINARY PRINCESS, THE (Jan Francis).
MCSET. Cat no: **2CCA 3148**. Released on Chivers Audio Books, '91 by Chivers Audio Books, Green Dragon Audio Visual. Note: 2 Cassettes.

Keane, Molly
GOOD BEHAVIOUR (Kate Binchy).
MCSET. Cat no: **1082F**. Released on Travellers Tales, '91 by Travellers Tales. Note: 6 cassettes.
LOVING AND GIVING (Anne Dover).
MCSET. Cat no: **1854964771**. Released on Soundings, Aug '91 by Soundings Records, Bond Street Music. Note: 6 Cassettes.
TIME AFTER TIME (Sheila Mitchell).

MCSET. Cat no: **1083F**. Released on Travellers Tales, '91 by Travellers Tales. Note: 6 cassettes

Keating, H.R.F.
BODY IN THE BILLIARD ROOM, THE (Sam Dastor).
MCSET. Cat no: **1212T**. Released on Travellers Tales, '91 by Travellers Tales. Note: 6 Cassettes.
MCSET. Cat no: **IAB 87113**. Released on Isis Audio Books, '91. Note: 6 Cassettes.
GO WEST, INSPECTOR GHOTE (Garard Green).
MCSET. Cat no: **OAS 91024**. Released on Oasis Audio Books, '91 by Isis Audio Books. Note: 8 Cassettes.
MCSET. Cat no: **1705T**. Released on Travellers Tales, '91 by Travellers Tales.
INSPECTOR GHOTE DRAWS A LINE (Garard Green).
MCSET. Cat no: **1736T**. Released on Travellers Tales, '91 by Travellers Tales. Note: 6 Cassettes.
MCSET. Cat no: **OAS 30391**. Released on Oasis Audio Books, '91 by Isis Audio Books.
MRS. CRAGGS (Joe Dunlop).
MCSET. Cat no: **1560T**. Released on Travellers Tales, '91 by Travellers Tales. Note: 6 Cassettes.
MCSET. Cat no: **OAS 90061**. Released on Oasis Audio Books, '91 by Isis Audio Books. Note: 6 Cassettes.
MURDER OF THE MAHARAJAH, THE (Garrad Green).
MCSET. Cat no: **IAB 91105**. Released on Isis Audio Books, Oct '91. Note: 8 Cassettes. Playing time 11 hours.
PERFECT MURDER, THE (Garard Green).
MCSET. Cat no: **OAS 30791**. Released on Oasis Audio Books, '91 by Isis Audio Books. Note: 7 Cassettes.
SHERIFF OF BOMBAY (Garard Green).
MCSET. Cat no: **IAB 92022**. Released on Isis Audio Books, Feb '92. Note: 6 cassettes. Playing time 6hrs 45mins.
UNDER A MONSOON CLOUD (Sam Dastor).
MCSET. Cat no: **1434F**. Released on Travellers Tales, '91 by Travellers Tales. Note: 8 Cassettes.
MCSET. Cat no: **IAB 89073**. Released on Isis Audio Books, '91. Note: 8 Cassettes.

Keats
POETRY OF KEATS (Sir Ralph Richardson).
MC. Cat no: **1087**. Released on Caedmon (USA), '88 by Caedmon Records (USA), Bond Street Music.

Keillor, Garrison
LAKE WOBEGON DAYS (Garrison Keillor).
MCSET. Cat no: **ZBBC 1065**. Released on BBC Radio Collection, May '89 by BBC Records. Note: ISBN No: 0563 226139. 2 cassettes.

LAKE WOBEGON DAYS (Garrison Keillor).
MCSET. Cat no: **1389F**. Released on Travellers Tales, '91 by Travellers Tales. Note: 4 Cassettes.
LEAVING HOME (More Tales from Lake Wobegone) (Garrison Keillor).
MCSET. Cat no: **ZBBC 1066**. Released on BBC Radio Collection, May '89 by BBC Records. Note: ISBN No: 0563 226021
NEWS FROM LAKE WOBEGON (Fall/Winter) (Garrison Keillor).
MCSET. Cat no: **zbbc 1199**. Released on BBC Radio Collection, '91 by BBC Records. Note: ISBN No: 0563 409053
NEWS FROM LAKE WOBEGON (Spring/Summer) (Garrison Keillor).
MCSET. Cat no: **ZBBC 1198**. Released on BBC Radio Collection, '91 by BBC Records. Note: ISBN No: 0563 409045
WE ARE STILL MARRIED (Garrison Keillor).
MCSET. Cat no: **ZBBC 1156**. Released on BBC Radio Collection, Jul '90 by BBC Records. Note: ISBN No: 0563 410779

Kelham, John
HERBERT THE HEDGEHOG (Volumes 1 - 4) (Unknown narrator(s)).
MCSET. Cat no: **H1/H2/H3/H4**. Released on Herbert The Hedgehog, Nov '82.

Kellerman, Jonathan
SILENT PARTNER (John Rubinstein).
MCSET. Cat no: **ZBBC 1231**. Released on BBC, Aug '91 by BBC Records, Taylors. Note: ISBN No: 0563 408049

Kelly, Frank
COMEDY COUNTDOWN (Frank Kelly).
LP. Cat no: **SPL 402**. Released on Ritz, '88 by Ritz Records, Spartan, Celtic Music, Solomon & Peres, Prism Leisure, I & B Records, Terry Blood Dist., Taylors.

Kemp, Gene
CHARLIE LEWIS PLAYS FOR TIME (John Green).
MCSET. Cat no: **3CCA 3035**. Released on Chivers Audio Books, '91 by Chivers Audio Books, Green Dragon Audio Visual. Note: 3 Cassettes.
CLOCK TOWER GHOST, THE (Eve Karpf).
MCSET. Cat no: **2CCA 3004**. Released on Chivers Audio Books, '91 by Chivers Audio Books, Green Dragon Audio Visual. Note: 2 Cassettes.
MCSET. Cat no: **9040F**. Released on Travellers Tales, '91 by Travellers Tales. Note: 2 Cassettes.
MCSET. Cat no: **086 222 0458**. Released on Chivers Calvacade, '91 by Chivers Audio Books, Green Dragon Audio Visual.

GOWIE CORBY PLAYS CHICKEN (John Green).
MCSET. Cat no: **3CCA 3016.** Released on Chivers Audio Books, '91 by Chivers Audio Books, Green Dragon Audio Visual. Note: 3 Cassettes.
MCSET. Cat no: **9125F.** Released on Travellers Tales, '91 by Travellers Tales. Note: 3 Cassettes.

JASON BODGER AND THE PRIORY GHOST (John Green).
MCSET. Cat no: **3CCA 3082.** Released on Chivers Audio Books, '91 by Chivers Audio Books, Green Dragon Audio Visual. Note: 3 Cassettes.
MCSET. Cat no: **9166F.** Released on Travellers Tales, '91 by Travellers Tales. Note: 3 Cassettes.

JUNIPER: A MYSTERY (Sarah Greene).
MCSET. Cat no: **2CCA 3055.** Released on Chivers Audio Books, '91 by Chivers Audio Books, Green Dragon Audio Visual. Note: 2 Cassettes.
MCSET. Cat no: **9113F.** Released on Travellers Tales, '91 by Travellers Tales. Note: 2 Cassettes.

NO PLACE LIKE (John Green).
MCSET. Cat no: **3CCA 3105.** Released on Chivers Audio Books, '91 by Chivers Audio Books, Green Dragon Audio Visual. Note: 3 Cassettes.
MCSET. Cat no: **9175F.** Released on Travellers Tales, '91 by Travellers Tales. Note: 3 Cassettes.

TURBULENT TERM OF TYKE TILER, THE (Michael Cochrane).
MCSET. Cat no: **CC/031.** Released on Cover to Cover, '87 by Cover to Cover Cassettes.
MCSET. Cat no: **9041F.** Released on Travellers Tales, '91 by Travellers Tales.

Keneally, Thomas

FAMILY MADNESS, A (Steve Hodson).
MCSET. Cat no: **1749/1750T.** Released on Travellers Tales, '91 by Travellers Tales. Note: 10 Cassettes.

FLYING HERO CLASS (Patrick Tull).
MCSET. Cat no: **IAB 92024.** Released on Isis Audio Books, Feb '92. Note: 8 cassettes. Playing time 11hrs 30mins.

Kennedy, Adam

DOMINO PRINCIPLE, THE (Frank Muller).
MCSET. Cat no: **RB 82030.** Released on Recorded Books, '91 by Isis Audio Books. Note: 3 cassettes.

DOMINO VENDETTA, THE (Frank Muller).
MCSET. Cat no: **RB 85130.** Released on Recorded Books, Aug '92 by Isis Audio Books. Note: 4 Cassettes. Playing time: 5 hours.

Kennedy, Lena

DANDELION SEED, THE (Carole Boyd).
MCSET. Cat no: **CAB 323.** Released on Chivers Audio Books, by Chivers Audio Books, Green Dragon Audio Visual. Note: 6 Cassettes.
MCSET. Cat no: **1319F.** Released on Travellers Tales, '91 by Travellers Tales. Note: 6 cassettes.

DOWN OUR STREET (Carole Boyd).
MCSET. Cat no: **CAB 374.** Released on Chivers Audio Books, '91 by Chivers Audio Books, Green Dragon Audio Visual. Note: 6 Cassettes.
MCSET. Cat no: **1358F.** Released on Travellers Tales, '91 by Travellers Tales. Note: 6 cassettes.

EVE'S APPLES (Carole Boyd).
MCSET. Cat no: **CAB 513.** Released on Chivers Audio Books, '91 by Chivers Audio Books, Green Dragon Audio Visual. Note: 10 Cassettes.
MCSET. Cat no: **1524/5F.** Released on Travellers Tales, '91 by Travellers Tales. Note: 10 cassettes

INN ON THE MARSH, THE (Carole Boyd).
MCSET. Cat no: **CAB 454.** Released on Chivers Audio Books, '91 by Chivers Audio Books, Green Dragon Audio Visual. Note: 8 Cassettes
MCSET. Cat no: **1535T.** Released on Travellers Tales, '91 by Travellers Tales. Note: 8 Cassettes.

LADY PENELOPE (Carole Boyd).
MCSET. Cat no: **CAB 689.** Released on Chivers Audio Books, Apr '92 by Chivers Audio Books, Green Dragon Audio Visual. Note: 6 Cassettes

LIZZIE (Carole Boyd).
MCSET. Cat no: **CAB 279.** Released on Chivers Audio Books, '91 by Chivers Audio Books, Green Dragon Audio Visual. Note: 8 Cassettes.
MCSET. Cat no: **1128R.** Released on Travellers Tales, '91 by Travellers Tales. Note: 8 Cassettes.

MAGGIE (Carole Boyd).
MCSET. Cat no: **CAB 417.** Released on Chivers Audio Books, '91 by Chivers Audio Books, Green Dragon Audio Visual. Note: 10 Cassettes.
MCSET. Cat no: **1399/1400F.** Released on Travellers Tales, '91 by Travellers Tales. Note: 10 cassettes

NELLY KELLY (Carole Boyd).
MCSET. Cat no: **CAB 238.** Released on Chivers Audio Books, '91 by Chivers Audio Books, Green Dragon Audio Visual. Note: 8 Cassettes
MCSET. Cat no: **1105R.** Released on Travellers Tales, '91 by Travellers Tales. Note: 8 Cassettes.

SUSAN (Carole Boyd).
MCSET. Cat no: **CAB 205.** Released on Chivers Audio Books, '91 by Chivers Audio Books, Green Dragon Audio Visual. Note: 6 Cassettes
MCSET. Cat no: **1090R.** Released on Travellers Tales, '91 by Travellers Tales. Note: 6 Cassettes.

Kennedy Toole, John

CONFEDERACY OF DUNCES (Arte Johnson).
MC. Cat no: **SSC 027.** Released on Scotsoun, '91 by Scotsoun Recordings, Morley Audio Services.

Kennelly, Brendan

LIVING GHOSTS (Brendan Kennelly).
MC. Cat no: **LRCS 6.** Released on Livia, Jun '88, Record Services.

Kent, Alexander

HONOUR THIS DAY (Michael Jayston).
MCSET. Cat no: **CAB 529.** Released on Chivers Audio Books, '91 by Chivers Audio Books, Green Dragon Audio Visual. Note: 8 Cassettes
MCSET. Cat no: **1538F.** Released on Travellers Tales, '91 by Travellers Tales. Note: 8 cassettes.

INSHORE SQUADRON, THE (Christopher Kay).
MCSET. Cat no: **1104T.** Released on Travellers Tales, '91 by Travellers Tales. Note: 6 Cassettes.
MCSET. Cat no: **1854961268.** Released on Soundings, '91 by Soundings Records, Bond Street Music. Note: 6 Cassettes.

ONLY VICTOR, THE (Michael Jayston).
MCSET. Cat no: **CAB 586.** Released on Chivers Audio Books, '91 by Chivers Audio Books, Green Dragon Audio Visual. Note: 10 Cassettes.
MCSET. Cat no: **1665F.** Released on Travellers Tales, '91 by Travellers Tales. Note: 10 cassettes.

RICHARD BOLITHO - MIDSHIPMAN (Anthony Valentine).
MCSET. Cat no: **LFP 7252.** Released on Listen For Pleasure, Aug '86 by EMI Records.

Kerr, Carole

SHADOW OF THE HUNTER (Angela Down).
MCSET. Cat no: **1854964631.** Released on Bramhope, Jun '91 by Ulverscroft Soundings. Note: 5 Cassettes.

Kerr, Judith

MOGG'S CHRISTMAS (Geraldine McEwan).
MC. Cat no: **0001010565.** Released on Harper Collins, '91 by Harper Collins.

TIGER WHO CAME TO TEA, THE (Geraldine McEwan).
MC. Cat no: **0001010271.** Released on Harper Collins, '91 by Harper Collins.

Kerr, Madeleine

VIRTUOUS LADY (Carole Boyd).
MCSET. Cat no: **PMB 007.** Released on Mills & Boon, '91.

Kesey, Ken

ONE FLEW OVER THE CUCKOO'S NEST (Michael Moriaty).

MCSET. Cat no: **LFP 7264**. Released on Listen For Pleasure, Sep '86 by EMI Records.

Kilgore, John
DEADWOOD STAGE, THE (John Chancer).
MCSET. Cat no: **1854965638**. Released on Trio, Feb '92 by EMI Records. Note: Playing time: 60 minutes.

Kincaid, J.D.
SHOWDOWN AT MEDICINE CREEK (Unknown narrator(s)).
MCSET. Cat no: **1854965220**. Released on Trio, '91 by EMI Records. Note: 3 Cassettes.

King, Clive
STIG OF THE DUMP (Martin Jarvis).
MC. Cat no: **882162**. Released on Puffin Cover To Cover, '85, Green Dragon Audio Visual.
MCSET. Cat no: **CTC 006**. Released on Cover to Cover, '88 by Cover to Cover Cassettes.
MCSET. Cat no: **9042F**. Released on Travellers Tales, '91 by Travellers Tales. Note: 3 Cassettes.

King, Stephen
DARK TOWER, THE (Stephen King).
MCSET. Cat no: **1027S**. Released on Travellers Tales, '91 by Travellers Tales. Note: 4 Cassettes.

DARK TOWER, THE (Volume 2 - The Drawing Of The Three) (Stephen King).
MCSET. Cat no: **0453006434**. Released on N.A.L., '91 by Morley Audio Services. Note: 8 cassettes

DARK TOWER, THE (Volume 1 - The Gunslinger) (Stephen King).
MCSET. Cat no: **0453006361**. Released on N.A.L., '91 by Morley Audio Services. Note: 11 cassettes.

I AM THE DOORWAY (Ed Bishop). Note: Includes: 'One for the Road'.
MC. Cat no: **PTB 615**. Released on Pickwick Talking Books, '83 by Pickwick Records, Clyde Factors.

THINNER (Paul Sorvino).
MCSET. Cat no: **LFP 7254**. Released on Listen For Pleasure, Jun '86 by EMI Records **Deleted** Apr '90.

Kingsley, Charles
WATER BABIES, THE (Sarah Greene).
MCSET. Cat no: **LFP 7415**. Released on Listen For Pleasure, Sep '89 by EMI Records. Note: Playing time: 2 hours 30 minutes.

WATER BABIES, THE (Unknown narrator(s)).
MC. Cat no: **CDL 51728**. Released on Caedmon (USA), Jan '84 by Caedmon Records (USA), Bond Street Music.

King-Smith, Dick
ACE (Nigel Lambert).

MCSET. Cat no: **2CCA 3149**. Released on Chivers Audio Books, '91 by Chivers Audio Books, Green Dragon Audio Visual. Note: 2 Cassettes.

DODOS ARE FOREVER (Nigel Lambert).
MCSET. Cat no: **2CCA 3128**. Released on Chivers Audio Books, '91 by Chivers Audio Books, Green Dragon Audio Visual. Note: 2 Cassettes.

FOX BUSTERS, THE (Nigel Lambert).
MCSET. Cat no: **2CCA 3022**. Released on Chivers Audio Books, '91 by Chivers Audio Books, Green Dragon Audio Visual. Note: 2 Cassettes.
MCSET. Cat no: **9043F**. Released on Travellers Tales, '91 by Travellers Tales. Note: 2 Cassettes.

HARRY'S MAD (Nigel Lambert).
MCSET. Cat no: **2CCA 3036**. Released on Chivers Audio Books, '91 by Chivers Audio Books, Green Dragon Audio Visual. Note: 2 Cassettes.
MCSET. Cat no: **9108F**. Released on Travellers Tales, '91 by Travellers Tales. Note: 2 Cassettes.

MAGNUS POWERMOUSE (Nigel Anthony).
MCSET. Cat no: **881 557**. Released on Puffin Cover To Cover, Apr '88, Green Dragon Audio Visual. Note: 2 cassettes

MARTIN'S MICE (Nigel Lambert).
MCSET. Cat no: **2CCA 3101**. Released on Chivers Audio Books, '91 by Chivers Audio Books, Green Dragon Audio Visual. Note: 2 Cassettes.
MCSET. Cat no: **9176F**. Released on Travellers Tales, '91 by Travellers Tales. Note: 2 Cassettes.

MOUSE BUTCHER, THE (Stephen Thorne).
MC. Cat no: **881638**. Released on Puffin Cover To Cover, '88, Green Dragon Audio Visual.

QUEEN'S NOSE, THE (Eve Karpf).
MCSET. Cat no: **2CCA 3080**. Released on Chivers Audio Books, '91 by Chivers Audio Books, Green Dragon Audio Visual. Note: 2 Cassettes.
MCSET. Cat no: **9145F**. Released on Travellers Tales, '91 by Travellers Tales. Note: 2 Cassettes.

SADDLEBOTTOM (Nigel Lambert).
MCSET. Cat no: **2CCA 3013**. Released on Chivers Audio Books, '91 by Chivers Audio Books, Green Dragon Audio Visual. Note: 2 Cassettes.
MCSET. Cat no: **9044F**. Released on Travellers Tales, '91 by Travellers Tales. Note: 2 Cassettes.
MCSET. Cat no: **086 222 0512**. Released on Chivers Calvacade, Apr '88 by Chivers Audio Books, Green Dragon Audio Visual.

SHEEP-PIG, THE (Stephen Thorne).
MCSET. Cat no: **CC/030**. Released on Cover to Cover, '87 by Cover to Cover Cassettes.
MCSET. Cat no: **9045F**. Released on

Travellers Tales, '91 by Travellers Tales. Note: 2 Cassettes.

TOBY MAN, THE (Nigel Lambert).
MCSET. Cat no: **2CCA 3117**. Released on Chivers Audio Books, '91 by Chivers Audio Books, Green Dragon Audio Visual. Note: 2 Cassettes.
MCSET. Cat no: **9198F**. Released on Travellers Tales, '91 by Travellers Tales. Note: 2 Cassettes.

TUMBLEWEED (Nigel Lambert).
MCSET. Cat no: **2CCA 3056**. Released on Chivers Audio Books, '91 by Chivers Audio Books, Green Dragon Audio Visual. Note: 2 Cassettes.
MCSET. Cat no: **9114F**. Released on Travellers Tales, '91 by Travellers Tales.

Kingston, Beryl
KISSES AND HA'PENNIES (Judith Porter).
MCSET. Cat no: **1678/9F**. Released on Travellers Tales, '91 by Travellers Tales. Note: 12 cassettes.
MCSET. Cat no: **1854964089**. Released on Soundings, '91 by Soundings Records, Bond Street Music. Note: 12 Cassettes.

Kingston, Edna
LIFE TO SHARE, A (Delia Corrie).
MCSET. Cat no: **MRC 1035**. Released on Chivers Audio Books, '91 by Chivers Audio Books, Green Dragon Audio Visual. Note: 2 cassettes

Kinsella, Thomas
FAIR ELEANOR, CHRIST THEE SAVE (Unknown narrator(s)).
LP. Cat no: **CCT 6**. Released on Claddagh (Ireland), Aug '88 by Claddagh Records (Ireland), Projection, Impetus Records, Jazz Music, Roots Records, C.M. Distribution, Outlet Records, Taylors.

Kipling, Rudyard
ELEPHANT'S CHILD, THE (Jack Nicholson).
CD. Cat no: **WD 0701**. Released on Windham Hill, Jan '92 by Windham Hill Records (USA), New Note.
MC. Cat no: **WT 0701**. Released on Windham Hill, Jan '92 by Windham Hill Records (USA), New Note.

ELEPHANT'S CHILD, THE (Jack Nicholson).
MC. Cat no: **1856560988**. Released on Random Century, '91 by Random Century Audiobooks, Conifer Records. Note: Playing time: 30 Minutes.

GUNGA DIN (And Other Poems) (Boris Karloff).
MC. Cat no: **1193**. Released on Caedmon (USA), '88 by Caedmon Records (USA), Bond Street Music.

HOW THE LEOPARD GOT HIS SPOTS (Danny Glover).
CD. Cat no: **WD 0715**. Released on Windham Hill, Jan '92 by Windham Hill Records (USA), New Note.

MC. Cat no: **WT 0715.** Released on Windham Hill, Jan '92 by Windham Hill Records (USA), New Note.

HOW THE RHINOCEROS GOT HIS SKIN (And How the Camel got his Hump) (Jack Nicholson).
CD. Cat no: **WD 0704.** Released on Windham Hill, Jan '92 by Windham Hill Records (USA), New Note.
MC. Cat no: **WT 0704.** Released on Windham Hill, Jan '92 by Windham Hill Records (USA), New Note.

JUNGLE BOOK STORIES (Ian Richardson).
Note: Includes: Mowgli's Brothers, The King's Ankus, Kaa's Hunting.
MCSET. Cat no: **SAY 50.** Released on Argo (Polygram), Jun '88 by PolyGram Classics **Deleted** May '89. Note: Playing time: 2 hours 30 minutes.
MCSET. Cat no: **ARGO 1154.** Released on Argo (EMI), Oct '89 by EMI Records. Note: 2 Cassettes.

JUNGLE BOOK STORIES VOL.1, THE (Mowgli's Brothers) (Michael Palin).
MC. Cat no: **MCLIS 201.** Released on Listen, '91, Cartel. Note: 40 mins.

JUNGLE BOOK STORIES VOL.2, THE (How Fear Came) (Michael Palin).
MC. Cat no: **MCLIS 202.** Released on Listen, '91, Cartel. Note: 35 mins.
MC. Cat no: **LP 206.** Released on Listen Productions, Nov '84.
MC. Cat no: **LPMC 206.** Released on Listen, '88, Cartel.

JUNGLE BOOK STORIES VOL.3, THE (Letting In The Jungle) (Sir Anthony Quayle).
MC. Cat no: **MCLIS 203.** Released on Listen, '91, Cartel. Note: 60 mins.

JUNGLE BOOK STORIES VOL.4, THE (Kaa's Hunting) (Anthony Quayle).
MC. Cat no: **MCLIS 204.** Released on Listen, '91, Cartel.

JUNGLE BOOK, THE (Freddie James & Una Stubbs).
MC. Cat no: **Unknown**. Released on Whinfrey Strachan, Jan '85 **Deleted** '86.

JUNGLE BOOK, THE (Various artists).
LP. Cat no: **D 319.** Released on Disneyland, Dec '82 by Disneyland-Vista Records (USA).
MC. Cat no: **D 4DC.** Released on Disneyland, Dec '82 by Disneyland-Vista Records (USA). Note: Storyteller
LP. Cat no: **D 3948.** Released on Disneyland, Dec '82 by Disneyland-Vista Records (USA).
LPPD. Cat no: **D 3105.** Released on Disneyland, Dec '82 by Disneyland-Vista Records (USA). Note: 12" Picture disc

JUNGLE BOOK, THE (Unknown narrator(s)).
MC. Cat no: **DIS 002.** Released on Disney (Read-a-long), Jul '90 by Disneyland Records.
MC. Cat no: **STK 025.** Released on Stick-A-Tale, Jul '90 by Pickwick Records.

JUNGLE BOOK, THE (Windsor Davies).
MCSET. Cat no: **LFP 7120.** Released on Listen For Pleasure, Sep '83 by EMI Records.
MCSET. Cat no: **9046F.** Released on Travellers Tales, '91 by Travellers Tales.

JUST SO STORIES (Volume 2) (Various artists).
Note: Narrators are: Michael Horden, Barbara Jefford and Richard Johnson.
MCSET. Cat no: **SAY 44.** Released on Argo (Polygram), May '83 by PolyGram Classics **Deleted** Jan '89.

JUST SO STORIES (Volume 6) (Ian Ogilvy).
Note: The Crab That Played With The Sea and How The Rhinoceros Got His Skin
MC. Cat no: **KLP 006.** Released on Listen, '91, Cartel. Note: 30 mins.

JUST SO STORIES (Johnny Morris).
MCSET. Cat no: **CTC 005.** Released on Cover to Cover, '90 by Cover to Cover Cassettes. Note: 3 cassette set. Playing time 3hrs 25mins.
MCSET. Cat no: **9047F.** Released on Travellers Tales, '91 by Travellers Tales. Note: 3 Cassettes.

JUST SO STORIES (Volume 1) (Various artists).
MCSET. Cat no: **SAY 30.** Released on Argo (Polygram), Jul '82 by PolyGram Classics **Deleted** Jan '89.
MCSET. Cat no: **ARGO 1031.** Released on Argo (EMI), May '89 by EMI Records. Note: 2 Cassettes.

JUST SO STORIES (Volume 1) (Ian Ogilvy).
Note: How The Whale Got His Throat and The Beginning Of The Armadilloes.
MC. Cat no: **KLP 001.** Released on Listen, '91, Cartel. Note: 25 mins.

JUST SO STORIES (Volume 4) (Ian Ogilvy/ Jane Asher).
Note: How The Leopard Got His Spots and The Cat That Walked By Himself.
MC. Cat no: **KLP 004.** Released on Listen, '91, Cartel. Note: 40 mins

JUST SO STORIES (David Davis).
MC. Cat no: **P 90021.** Released on Pinnacle, '79 by Pinnacle Records, Outlet Records, Music Sales Records.

JUST SO STORIES (Selected Stories) (Roy Dotrice & Dorothy Tutin).
MC. Cat no: **0600560910.** Released on Hamlyn Books On Tape, '88, Bond Street Music.

JUST SO STORIES (Ian Ogilvy).
MC. Cat no: **LPMC 207.** Released on Listen Productions, '88.

JUST SO STORIES (David Davis).
Note: Includes: How Did The Leopard Get His Spots and How Did The Lazy Camel Find His Hump.
MCSET. Cat no: **ZBBC 1163.** Released on BBC, Jun '90 by BBC Records, Taylors. Note: ISBN No: 0563 410884.

JUST SO STORIES (Volume 5) (Jane Asher).
Note: The Butterfly That Stamped and How The First Letter Was Written.
MC. Cat no: **KLP 005.** Released on Listen, '91, Cartel. Note: 40 mins.

JUST SO STORIES (Volume 2) (Jane Asher).
Note: Sing Song Of Old Man Kangaroo and How The Alphabet Was Made.
MC. Cat no: **KLP 002.** Released on Listen, '91, Cartel. Note: 30 mins.

JUST SO STORIES (Volume 3) (Ian Ogilvy).
Note: The Elephant's Child and How The Camel Got His Hump.
MC. Cat no: **KLP 003.** Released on Listen, '91, Cartel. Note: 25 mins.

JUST SO STORIES (Carnival Classics) (George Layton).
MC. Cat no: **0001010824.** Released on Harper Collins, Dec '91 by Harper Collins. Note: 25 mins.

KIM (Ben Cross).
MCSET. Cat no: **LFP 7222.** Released on Listen For Pleasure, May '86 by EMI Records **Deleted** Aug '89.
MCSET. Cat no: **1086F.** Released on Travellers Tales, '92 by Travellers Tales.

KIM (Margaret Hilton).
MCSET. Cat no: **1381/2F.** Released on Travellers Tales, '91 by Travellers Tales. Note: 12 cassettes.
MCSET. Cat no: **IAB 89063.** Released on Isis Audio Books, '91. Note: 12 cassettes.

KIM (Tim Pigott-Smith).
MCSET. Cat no: **418 144-4.** Released on Argo (Polygram), Jun '88 by PolyGram Classics **Deleted** Jan '89.
MCSET. Cat no: **ARGO 1220.** Released on Argo (EMI), Oct '90 by EMI Records. Note: 2 Cassettes.

KIM (And Captain Courageous) (Various narrators).
MCSET. Cat no: **CSL 009.** Released on Chivers Audio Books, '91 by Chivers Audio Books, Green Dragon Audio Visual. Note: 2 cassettes.

MAN WHO WOULD BE KING, THE (Michael Elder).
MCSET. Cat no: **SPF 470-1.** Released on Schiltron Audio Books, '91 by Schiltron Publishing. Note: 4 Cassettes. Playing time 4 hours 10 minutes.

MAN WHO WOULD BE KING, THE (Anthony Quayle).
MC. Cat no: **1258.** Released on Caedmon (USA), '88 by Caedmon Records (USA), Bond Street Music.
MC. Cat no: **0001051857.** Released on Collins-Caedmon, '91 by Collins Audio, Taylors, Bond Street Music.

MAN WHO WOULD BE KING, THE

(And Other Stories) (George Taylor).
MCSET. Cat no: **1674F.** Released on Travellers Tales, '91 by Travellers Tales. Note: 3 cassettes.

MCSET. Cat no: **IAB 91063.** Released on Isis Audio Books, '91. Note: 3 Cassettes.

MORE JUNGLE BOOK STORIES (Ian Richardson).
Note: Includes: Tiger, Tiger, Rikki-Tikki-Tavi and Red Dog.
MCSET. Cat no: **SAY 68.** Released on Argo (Polygram), Jul '83 by PolyGram Classics **Deleted** Jan '89.

PLAIN TALES FROM THE HILLS (Martin Jarvis).
MCSET. Cat no: **TTDMC 401.** Released on CSA Tell Tapes, May '89 by CSA Tell-Tapes. Note: 2 Cassettes. ISBN No. 1873859015.

RED DOG (Anthony Quayle).
MC. Cat no: **1482.** Released on Caedmon (USA), '88 by Caedmon Records (USA), Bond Street Music.

RIKKI-TIKKI-TAVI (And Wee Willie Winkle) (Anthony Quayle).
MC. Cat no: **1257.** Released on Caedmon (USA), '88 by Caedmon Records (USA), Bond Street Music.

SHORT STORIES (Michael Elder).
MCSET. Cat no: **1367F.** Released on Travellers Tales, '91 by Travellers Tales. Note: 5 cassettes.

TALES FROM THE JUNGLE BOOK (Unknown narrator(s)).
Note: Book and cassette.
MC. Cat no: **PLBC 237.** Released on Tell-A-Tale, '88 by Pickwick Records, Taylors, Clyde Factors.

THEY AND MARY POSTGATE (Michael Elder).
MCSET. Cat no: **SPF 470-2.** Released on Schiltron Audio Books, '91 by Schiltron Publishing.

WHITE SEAL, THE (Anthony Quayle).
MC. Cat no: **0001060236.** Released on Collins-Caedmon, '91 by Collins Audio, Taylors, Bond Street Music. Note: 2 Cassettes.

Kirst, H.H.
NIGHT OF THE GENERALS (Jon Croft).
MCSET. Cat no: **COL 2014.** Released on Colophone, '88 by AVLS (Audio-Visual Library Services).

Klein, Norma
MOM, THE WOLFMAN AND ME (Alexandra Elizabeth Sheedy).
MC. Cat no: **1517.** Released on Caedmon (USA), '88 by Caedmon Records (USA), Bond Street Music.

Koestler, Arthur
DARKNESS AT NOON (John Le Carre).
Note: Advanced release.
MCSET. Cat no: **RC 72.** Released on Random Century, Aug '92 by Random Century Audiobooks, Conifer Records.

Note: ISBN no. 856860906

Koontz, Dean R.
LIGHTNING (Peter Marinker).
MCSET. Cat no: **0671652370.** Released on Simon & Schuster, '91 by Simon & Schuster Ltd. Note: 2 cassettes.

Kossoff, David
RABBI STORIES, THE (David Kossoff).
MCSET. Cat no: **LD 9/10/11.** Released on Green Dragon, '91 by Green Dragon Audio Visual.

Lamb, Charlotte
OBSESSION (Carole Boyd).
MCSET. Cat no: **PMB 014.** Released on Mills & Boon, '88. Note: 2 Cassettes.

SILKEN TRAP, THE (Lesley Seaward).
MCSET. Cat no: **PMB 020.** Released on Mills & Boon, '88. Note: 2 Cassettes

Lamb, Mary
TALES FROM SHAKESPEARE (Julie Harris).
MC. Cat no: **1469.** Released on Caedmon (USA), May '88 by Caedmon Records (USA), Bond Street Music.

Langland, William
EVERYMAN-VISIONS FROM PIERS PLOWMAN (Various artists).
MCSET. Cat no: **SAY 107.** Released on Argo (Polygram), Mar '84 by PolyGram Classics **Deleted** Jan '89.

Langley, Gerard
SIAMESE BOYFRIENDS (Langley, Gerard & Ian Kearey).
Note: Includes: Nicknames, Snow-Walking, Joe Taylor's, Good Weather, Dear Though The Night Is Gone, The Famous Aren't.
LP. Cat no: **FIRELP 4.** Released on Fire, Feb '87 by Fire Records **Deleted** Oct '91.

LP. Cat no: **FIRE 11004.** Released on Fire, Oct '91 by Fire Records.

Lankester Brisley, J.
ADVENTURES OF MILLY-MOLLY-MANDY (Janie Rayne).
LP. Cat no: **STMP 9026.** Released on Super Tempo, May '84 by Warwick Records, Taylors, Solomon & Peres, Sony Music Operations.

MC. Cat no: **STMP4 9026.** Released on Super Tempo, May '84 by Warwick Records, Taylors, Solomon & Peres, Sony Music Operations.

BEST OF MILLY MOLLY MANDY (Unknown narrator(s)).
Note: Includes: Milly Molly Mandy and Dum Dum, Milly Molly Mandy Finds A Train, Milly Molly Mandy And The Gang and Milly Molly Mandy Goes Sledging.
MC. Cat no: **TS 307.** Released on Tellastory, Dec '86 by Random Century Audiobooks.

MILLY MOLLY MANDY (Unknown narrator(s)).
MCSET. Cat no: **DTO 10539.** Released on Ditto, '88 by Pickwick Records, Midland Records.

MILLY MOLLY MANDY STORIES (Various narrators).
Note: Advanced release.
MCSET. Cat no: **TS 412.** Released on Tellastory, Aug '92 by Random Century Audiobooks. Note: 2 cassettes. ISBN no. 1856561852

MILLY MOLLY MANDY STORIES (Liza Goddard).
MC. Cat no: **TC LFP 7100.** Released on Listen For Pleasure, Sep '82 by EMI Records.

Lathen, Emma
ACCOUNTING FOR MURDER (Ed Bishop).
MCSET. Cat no: **CAB 245.** Released on Chivers Audio Books, '91 by Chivers Audio Books, Green Dragon Audio Visual. Note: 6 Cassettes.

MCSET. Cat no: **1192T.** Released on Travellers Tales, '91 by Travellers Tales. Note: 6 Cassettes.

BY HOOK OR BY CROOK (Ed Bishop).
MCSET. Cat no: **1229T.** Released on Travellers Tales, '91 by Travellers Tales. Note: 6 Cassettes.

DOUBLE DOUBLE OIL AND TROUBLE (Ed Bishop).
MCSET. Cat no: **CAB 503.** Released on Chivers Audio Books, '91 by Chivers Audio Books, Green Dragon Audio Visual. Note: 8 Cassettes.

MCSET. Cat no: **1627T.** Released on Travellers Tales, '91 by Travellers Tales. Note: 8 Cassettes.

MURDER WITHOUT ICING (Blain Fairman).
MCSET. Cat no: **1154T.** Released on Travellers Tales, '91 by Travellers Tales. Note: 6 Cassettes.

SOMETHING IN THE AIR (Ed Bishop).
MCSET. Cat no: **CAB 389.** Released on Chivers Audio Books, '91 by Chivers Audio Books, Green Dragon Audio Visual. Note: 6 Cassettes.

MCSET. Cat no: **1478T.** Released on Travellers Tales, '91 by Travellers Tales. Note: 6 Cassettes.

Laurel & Hardy
LAUREL AND HARDY.
Tracks / Introduction including the cuckoo song / Fresh fish / Victims of the depression / Furniture payment / Let me call you sweetheart / What flavours have you / Higher endeavours / Mistaken identity / Trail of the lonesome pine (Featuring Chill Wills) / Long distance / Oh Gaston / Stagecoach manners / At the ball (Featuring the Avalon Boys.) / New recruits, The including the cuckoo song / There's a dollar / Hard

boiled eggs including in the good old summertime / Where were you born / United we stand / Annual convention / We're going now / Way down south including I want to be in Dixie / Introduction including the cuckoo song / Turn on the radio / Ever as you are and I / Clean sweep, A / Future Mrs. Hardy, The / Every cloud has a silver lining / Lazy moon / When the cat's away / Danger by clockwork / Food for thought / Court again / Dual deceit including Honolulu baby & Sons of the desert / Goodbye.
MCSET. Cat no: **ECC 13.** Released on EMI, Mar '91 by EMI Records.

LAUREL AND HARDY ON THE AIR (Rare Recordings 1932-59).
CD. Cat no: **CDMR 1104.** Released on Radiola, Aug '91 by Derann Trax Distribution.
MC. Cat no: **CMR 1104.** Released on Radiola, Aug '91 by Derann Trax Distribution.
LP. Cat no: **MR 1104.** Released on Radiola, Jan '89 by Derann Trax Distribution.

SONGS AND DIALOGUE (Volume 1).
Tracks / Cuckoo song / At the ball / Trail of the Lonesome Pine / There's gonna be a fight / Eloping / We want to get married / All aboard / Ice cream shop / School room / Where's my clothes / Lazy moon / Higher endeavours / Four rounds tonight / Hat eating / Way down South / Dixie.
CD. Cat no: **MESSCD 1.** Released on Another Fine Mess, '89 by Wax Records, RTM Distribution, Pinnacle.
LP. Cat no: **MESSLP 1.** Released on Another Fine Mess, '89 by Wax Records, RTM Distribution, Pinnacle.

SONGS AND DIALOGUE (Volume 2) (Another Fine Mess).
Tracks / In the good old summertime / Oh Gaston / You are the ideal of my dreams / At the hotel / Phone call / Looking for Mr. Smith / We don't sell ice cream / Annual convention / Honolulu baby / Let me call you sweetheart / Box 204J / On the quayside / Get out of town / Hard boiled eggs and nuts.
LP. Cat no: **MESSLP 2.** Released on Another Fine Mess, Feb '90 by Wax Records, RTM Distribution, Pinnacle.
CD. Cat no: **MESSCD 2.** Released on Another Fine Mess, Feb '90 by Wax Records, RTM Distribution, Pinnacle.
LPPD. Cat no: **MESSLP 2P.** Released on Another Fine Mess, Feb '90 by Wax Records, RTM Distribution, Pinnacle.

SONGS AND DIALOGUE (Volume 3).
LP. Cat no: **MESSLPP 3.** Released on Another Fine Mess, Jun '90 by Wax Records, RTM Distribution, Pinnacle.
LPPD. Cat no: **MESSLPP 3.** Released on Another Fine Mess, Jun '90 by Wax Records, RTM Distribution, Pinnacle.
CD. Cat no: **MESSCD 3.** Released on Another Fine Mess, Jun '90 by Wax

Records, RTM Distribution, Pinnacle.

Lavelle, Sheila
DISASTER WITH THE FIEND (Judy Bennett).
MCSET. Cat no: **2CCA 3112.** Released on Chivers Audio Books, '91 by Chivers Audio Books, Green Dragon Audio Visual. Note: 2 Cassettes.
MCSET. Cat no: **9199F.** Released on Travellers Tales, '91 by Travellers Tales. Note: 2 Cassettes

FIEND NEXT DOOR, THE (Judy Bennett).
MCSET. Cat no: **2CCA 3026.** Released on Chivers Audio Books, '91 by Chivers Audio Books, Green Dragon Audio Visual. Note: 2 Cassettes.
MCSET. Cat no: **9048F.** Released on Travellers Tales, '91 by Travellers Tales. Note: 2 Cassettes.
MCSET. Cat no: **086 222 0466.** Released on Chivers Calvacade, Apr '88 by Chivers Audio Books, Green Dragon Audio Visual.

HOLIDAY WITH THE FIEND (Judy Bennett).
MC. Cat no: **2CCA 3060.** Released on Chivers Audio Books, '88 by Chivers Audio Books, Green Dragon Audio Visual. Note: 2 Cassettes.
MCSET. Cat no: **9136F.** Released on Travellers Tales, '91 by Travellers Tales. Note: 2 Cassettes.

TROUBLE WITH THE FIEND (Judy Bennett).
MCSET. Cat no: **2CCA 3087.** Released on Chivers Audio Books, '91 by Chivers Audio Books, Green Dragon Audio Visual. Note: 2 Cassettes.
MCSET. Cat no: **9157F.** Released on Travellers Tales, '91 by Travellers Tales. Note: 2 Cassettes.

Lavitz, T
STORYTIME (Unknown narrator(s)).
CD. Cat no: **PJCD 88012.** Released on Passport Jazz (USA), '87 by Jem Records Inc.(USA), Pacific Records Distribution.
LP. Cat no: **PJ 88012.** Released on Passport Jazz (USA), '87 by Jem Records Inc.(USA), Pacific Records Distribution.
MC. Cat no: **PJC 88012.** Released on Passport Jazz (USA), '87 by Jem Records Inc.(USA), Pacific Records Distribution.

Lawrence, D.H.
FOX, THE (Anna Massey).
Note: Abridged version.
MCSET. Cat no: **1359F.** Released on Travellers Tales, '91 by Travellers Tales. Note: 2 cassettes.
MCSET. Cat no: **418 183-4.** Released on Argo (Polygram), Jun '88 by Polygram Classics **Deleted** Jan '89.

FOX, THE (And Other Stories) (Diana Olsson).
Note: Also includes:- England, my Eng-

land, Tickets Please, Monkey Nuts.
MCSET. Cat no: **SPF 505-2.** Released on Schiltron Audio Books, '91 by Schiltron Publishing. Note: 4 Cassettes. Playing time 4 hours 40 minutes.

LADY CHATTERLEY'S LOVER (Pamela Brown).
MC. Cat no: **1116.** Released on Caedmon (USA), '88 by Caedmon Records (USA), Bond Street Music.
MC. Cat no: **0001063960.** Released on Collins-Caedmon, '91 by Collins Audio, Taylors, Bond Street Music.

LADY CHATTERLEY'S LOVER (Janet Suzman).
MCSET. Cat no: **LFP 7388.** Released on Listen For Pleasure, Jun '89 by EMI Records. Note: Playing time: 2 hours 30 minutes.

LADY CHATTERLEY'S LOVER (Margaret Hilton).
MCSET. Cat no: **1354/5F.** Released on Travellers Tales, '91 by Travellers Tales. Note: 12 cassettes.
MCSET. Cat no: **IAB 89023.** Released on Isis Audio Books, '91. Note: 12 Cassettes.

LOVE AMONG THE HAYSTACKS (And Other Stories) (Various narrators).
Note: Narrators are: Margaret Hilton, Victoria Seabrook and Davina Porter.
MCSET. Cat no: **1463F.** Released on Travellers Tales, '91 by Travellers Tales. Note: 6 cassettes.
MCSET. Cat no: **IAB 90031.** Released on Isis Audio Books, '91. Note: 6 Cassettes.

MOTHER AND DAUGHTER (And The Blind Man) (Diana Olsson & Morag Hood).
MC. Cat no: **SPF 505-3.** Released on Schiltron Audio Books, '91 by Schiltron Publishing. Note: Playing time 88 minutes.

PRINCESS, THE (And Other Stories) (Morag Hood).
Note: Includes:- The Princess, The Blue Mocassins, You Touched Me, Samson and Delilah and The Mortal Coil.
MCSET. Cat no: **SPF 505-1.** Released on Schiltron Audio Books, '91 by Schiltron Publishing. Note: 4 Cassettes. Playing time 4 hours 43 minutes.

PRUSSIAN OFFICER, THE (Jill Tanner).
MCSET. Cat no: **RB 89440.** Released on Recorded Books, Feb '92 by Isis Audio Books. Note: 6 cassettes. Playing time 9hrs 15mins.

SHORT STORIES (Diana Olsson & Morag Hood).
Note: Includes The Fox
MCSET. Cat no: **1364F.** Released on Travellers Tales, '91 by Travellers Tales. Note: 8 cassettes.

SONS AND LOVERS (Ian McKellen).
MCSET. Cat no: **SAY 78.** Released on Argo (Polygram), Mar '83 by PolyGram

Classics **Deleted** Jan '89.
MCSET. Cat no: **ARGO 1097.** Released on Argo (EMI), Jun '89 by EMI Records. Note: 2 Cassettes.
MCSET. Cat no: **1088F.** Released on Travellers Tales, '91 by Travellers Tales.

ST. MAWR (Davina Porter).
MCSET. Cat no: **RB 88190.** Released on Recorded Books, May '92 by Isis Audio Books. Note: 5 Cassettes. Playing time: 6 1/2 hours.

TICKETS, PLEASE (And Other Stories And Poems) (Various artists). Note: Includes: Goose Fair, Her Turn, Shadow in the Rose Garden and Tickets, Please.
MCSET. Cat no: **418 177-4.** Released on Argo (Polygram), Jun '88 by PolyGram Classics **Deleted** Jan '89. Note: 2 cassette set

VIRGIN AND THE GYPSY, THE (Margaret Hilton).
MCSET. Cat no: **IAB 91103.** Released on Isis Audio Books, Oct '91. Note: 3 Cassettes. Playing time 3 hours, 45 minutes.

VIRGIN AND THE GYPSY, THE (Robert Lindsay).
MC. Cat no: **0600560473.** Released on Hamlyn Books On Tape, '88, Bond Street Music.

VIRGIN AND THE GYPSY, THE (Elizabeth Bell).
MC. Cat no: **PTB 622.** Released on Pickwick, '83 by Pickwick Records, Clyde Factors, Taylors, Arabesque, Solomon & Peres, I & B Records, Prism Leisure, Outlet Records.

Le Carre, John

CALL FOR THE DEAD (Michael Jayston).
MCSET. Cat no: **CAB 668.** Released on Chivers Audio Books, Dec '91 by Chivers Audio Books, Green Dragon Audio Visual. Note: 4 cassettes.

CALL FOR THE DEAD (Part 2) (Unknown narrator(s)).
MCSET. Cat no: **1856860795.** Released on Random Century, '91 by Random Century Audiobooks, Conifer Records.

FLEDGLING SPY, THE (Book One of the Secret Pilgrim) (John Le Carre).
MCSET. Cat no: **LFP 7517.** Released on Listen For Pleasure, Apr '91 by EMI Records.

LITTLE DRUMMER GIRL, THE (John Le Carre).
MC. Cat no: **TCLFP 417126-5.** Released on Listen For Pleasure, '83 by EMI Records.

LOOKING GLASS WAR, THE (John Le Carre).
MCSET. Cat no: **RC 26.** Released on Random Century, Apr '92 by Random Century Audiobooks, Conifer Records. Note: 2 cassettes. ISBN 1856860426. 3 hrs approx.

MURDER OF QUALITY, A (John Le Carre).
MCSET. Cat no: **RC 17.** Released on Random Century, '91 by Random Century Audiobooks, Conifer Records. Note: 2 cassettes. ISBN 1856860361. 3 hrs approx.

PERFECT SPY, A (John Le Carre).
MCSET. Cat no: **ZBBC 1041.** Released on BBC Radio Collection, Sep '88 by BBC Records. Note: ISBN No: 0563 225785

RUSSIA HOUSE, THE (John Le Carre).
MCSET. Cat no: **LFP 7430.** Released on Listen For Pleasure, Oct '89 by EMI Records. Note: Playing time: 3 hours

SMILEY'S PEOPLE (Various artists).
Note: Starring Bernard Hepton.
MCSET. Cat no: **ZBBC 1131.** Released on BBC, Jun '90 by BBC Records, Taylors. Note: ISBN No: 0563 410736. 2 cassettes.

SMILEY'S PEOPLE (Unknown narrator(s)).
MCSET. Cat no: **TC LFP 7106.** Released on Listen For Pleasure, Oct '82 by EMI Records.

SPY WHO CAME IN FROM THE COLD, THE (Michael Jayston).
MCSET. Cat no: **CAB 500.** Released on Chivers Audio Books, '91 by Chivers Audio Books, Green Dragon Audio Visual. Note: 6 Cassettes.
MCSET. Cat no: **1628T.** Released on Travellers Tales, '91 by Travellers Tales. Note: 6 Cassettes.

SPY WHO CAME IN FROM THE COLD, THE (John Le Carre).
MCSET. Cat no: **LFP 7192.** Released on Listen For Pleasure, May '85 by EMI Records **Deleted** Apr '90.
MCSET. Cat no: **1106T.** Released on Travellers Tales, '91 by Travellers Tales. Note: 2 Cassettes.

SPY WHO CAME OF AGE (Book Two of The Secret Pilgrim) (John Le Carre).
MCSET. Cat no: **LFP 7523.** Released on Listen For Pleasure, Apr '91 by EMI Records. Note: Playing time: 2 3/4 hours.

TINKER TAILOR SOLDIER SPY (Various artists).
MCSET. Cat no: **ZBBC 1071.** Released on BBC, Jul '89 by BBC Records, Taylors. Note: ISBN No: 0563 226420

Le Guin, Ursula

FARTHEST SHORE (Morag Hood).
MCSET. Cat no: **COL 4504.** Released on Colophone, Nov '81 by AVLS (Audio-Visual Library Services) **Deleted** '88.

GWILAM'S HARP AND INTRACOM (Unknown narrator(s)).
MC. Cat no: **1556.** Released on Caedmon (USA), '88 by Caedmon Records (USA), Bond Street Music.

TOMBS OF ATUAN (Morag Hood).
MCSET. Cat no: **COL 4503.** Released on Colophone, Nov '81 by AVLS (Audio-Visual Library Services) **Deleted** '88.

WIZARD OF EARTHSEA (Morag Hood).
MCSET. Cat no: **COL 4502.** Released on Colophone, Nov '81 by AVLS (Audio-Visual Library Services) **Deleted** '88.

Lea, Constance

SCENT OF OLEANDER, A (Alison Skilbeck).
MCSET. Cat no: **MRC 1047.** Released on Chivers Moonlight Romances, Apr '88 by Chivers Audio Books, Green Dragon Audio Visual. Note: 2 cassette set

Lear, Edward

EDWARD LEAR'S NONSENSE RHYMES (Edward Lear).
MCSET. Cat no: **DTO 10581.** Released on Ditto, '88 by Pickwick Records, Midland Records.

NONSENSE POEMS (Sir John Gielgud & Others).
MCSET. Cat no: **1027Y.** Released on Travellers Tales, '91 by Travellers Tales. Note: 2 cassettes.

SELECTED BOSH (Alan Bennett).
MCSET. Cat no: **CC/043.** Released on Cover to Cover, '88 by Cover to Cover Cassettes.

Lee, Harper

TO KILL A MOCKINGBIRD (Sally Darling).
MCSET. Cat no: **1575/6F.** Released on Travellers Tales, '91 by Travellers Tales. Note: 9 cassettes.
MCSET. Cat no: **RB 86640.** Released on Recorded Books, '91 by Isis Audio Books. Note: 9 cassettes.

Lee, Jesse

LAST STAGE TO SUNSET CREEK (Tom Hunsinger).
MCSET. Cat no: **1011W.** Released on Travellers Tales, '91 by Travellers Tales. Note: 2 Cassettes.
MCSET. Cat no: **1854961306.** Released on Soundings, '91 by Soundings Records, Bond Street Music. Note: 2 Cassettes.

Leeming, John F.

GIRL LIKE WIGAN, A (Ray Dunbobbin).
MCSET. Cat no: **1091F.** Released on Travellers Tales, '91 by Travellers Tales. Note: 6 cassettes.
MCSET. Cat no: **1854961314.** Released on Soundings, '91 by Soundings Records, Bond Street Music. Note: 6 Cassettes.

IT ALWAYS RAINS IN ROME (Ray Dunbobbin).
MCSET. Cat no: **1092F.** Released on Travellers Tales, '91 by Travellers Tales. Note: 4 cassettes.
MCSET. Cat no: **1854961322.** Re-

Leeson, Robert

CHALLENGE IN THE DARK (Kenneth Shanley).
MCSET. Cat no: **2CCA 3095**. Released on Chivers Audio Books, '91 by Chivers Audio Books, Green Dragon Audio Visual. Note: 2 Cassettes.

MCSET. Cat no: **9177F**. Released on Travellers Tales, '91 by Travellers Tales. Note: 2 Cassettes.

DEMON BIKE RIDER, THE (Kenneth Shanley).
MCSET. Cat no: **2CCA 3078**. Released on Chivers Audio Books, '91 by Chivers Audio Books, Green Dragon Audio Visual. Note: 2 Cassettes.

MCSET. Cat no: **9144F**. Released on Travellers Tales, '91 by Travellers Tales. Note: 2 Cassettes.

THIRD CLASS GENIE, THE (Kenneth Shanley).
MCSET. Cat no: **3CCA 3011**. Released on Chivers Audio Books, '91 by Chivers Audio Books, Green Dragon Audio Visual. Note: 3 Cassettes.

MCSET. Cat no: **9053F**. Released on Travellers Tales, '91 by Travellers Tales. Note: 3 Cassettes.

WHEEL OF DANGER, THE (Kenneth Shanley).
MCSET. Cat no: **086 222 0474**. Released on Chivers Calvacade, Apr '88 by Chivers Audio Books, Green Dragon Audio Visual.

MCSET. Cat no: **9054F**. Released on Travellers Tales, '91 by Travellers Tales. Note: 2 Cassettes.

Legat, Michael

CAST IRON MAN, THE (Gordon Griffin).
MCSET. Cat no: **1293F**. Released on Travellers Tales, '91 by Travellers Tales. Note: 8 cassettes.

MCSET. Cat no: **1854961330**. Released on Soundings, '91 by Soundings Records, Bond Street Music. Note: 8 Cassettes.

SHAPIRO DIAMOND, THE (Gordon Griffin).
MCSET. Cat no: **1203F**. Released on Travellers Tales, '91 by Travellers Tales. Note: 5 cassettes.

MCSET. Cat no: **1854961349**. Released on Bramhope, '91 by Ulverscroft Soundings. Note: 5 Cassettes.

SILK MAKER, THE (Gordon Griffin).
MCSET. Cat no: **1258F**. Released on Travellers Tales, '91 by Travellers Tales. Note: 8 Cassettes.

MCSET. Cat no: **1854961357**. Released on Soundings, '91 by Soundings Records, Bond Street Music. Note: 8 cassettes.

SILVER FOUNTAIN, THE (Anne Dover).
MCSET. Cat no: **1545/6F**. Released on Travellers Tales, '91 by Travellers Tales. Note: 10 cassettes.

MCSET. Cat no: **1854963589**. Released on Soundings, '91 by Soundings Records, Bond Street Music. Note: 10 Cassettes.

Lehmann, Rosamund

INVITATION TO THE WALTZ (Joanna Lumley).
MCSET. Cat no: **1093F**. Released on Travellers Tales, '91 by Travellers Tales. Note: 6 cassettes

Lehrer, Tom

EVENING WASTED WITH TOM LEHRER, AN (Tom Lehrer).
LP. Cat no: **SKL 4097**. Released on Decca, Jun '80 by PolyGram Classics, Thames Distributors Ltd. **Deleted** Apr '91.

LP. Cat no: **RS 6199**. Released on Reprise, by Warner Music International (WEA).

LP. Cat no: **LK 4332**. Released on Decca, Jun '60 by PolyGram Classics, Thames Distributors Ltd. **Deleted** Jun '65.

Lemarchand, Elizabeth

AFFACOMBE AFFAIR, THE (James Saxon).
MCSET. Cat no: **CAT 4053**. Released on Chivers Audio Books, '91 by Chivers Audio Books, Green Dragon Audio Visual. Note: 6 Cassettes.

MCSET. Cat no: **1536T**. Released on Travellers Tales, '91 by Travellers Tales.

WHEEL TURNS, THE (Gretel Davis).
MCSET. Cat no: **OAS 90044**. Released on Oasis Audio Books, '91 by Isis Audio Books. Note: 6 cassettes.

MCSET. Cat no: **1537T**. Released on Travellers Tales, '91 by Travellers Tales. Note: 6 Cassettes.

Leonard, Elmore

52 PICK-UP (Unknown narrator(s)).
MCSET. Cat no: **067163528X**. Released on Simon & Schuster, '91 by Simon & Schuster Ltd.

CITY PRIMEVAL (Steve Dunn).
MCSET. Cat no: **CAB 402**. Released on Chivers Audio Books, '91 by Chivers Audio Books, Green Dragon Audio Visual. Note: 6 Cassettes.

MCSET. Cat no: **1589T**. Released on Travellers Tales, '91 by Travellers Tales. Note: 6 Cassettes.

KILLSHOT (Bruce Boxleitner).
Note: Also available on hanging format, catalogue number:- 0001388282.

MCSET. Cat no: **0001388088**. Released on Harper Collins, '91 by Harper Collins. Note: 2 Cassettes.

SWITCH, THE (Blain Fairman).
MCSET. Cat no: **CAB 477**. Released on Chivers Audio Books, '91 by Chivers Audio Books, Green Dragon Audio Visual. Note: 6 Cassettes.

MCSET. Cat no: **1464F**. Released on Travellers Tales, '91 by Travellers Tales. Note: 6 cassettes.

TOUCH (Ian Craig).
MCSET. Cat no: **OAS 90071**. Released on Oasis Audio Books, '91 by Isis Audio Books. Note: 7 Cassettes.

MCSET. Cat no: **1629T**. Released on Travellers Tales, '91 by Travellers Tales. Note: 5 Cassettes.

Leroux, Gaston

FLOATING PRISON, THE (John Sheddon).
Note: Abridged version.

MCSET. Cat no: **1507F**. Released on Travellers Tales, '91 by Travellers Tales. Note: 2 cassettes.

MCSET. Cat no: **SPF 515-2**. Released on Schiltron Audio Books, '9 by Schiltron Publishing. Note: 2 Cassettes. Playing time: 3 hours.

PHANTOM OF THE OPERA (John Sheddon).
MCSET. Cat no: **SPF 515-1**. Released on Schiltron Audio Books, '91 by Schiltron Publishing. Note: 2 Cassettes. Playing time 3 hours.

PHANTOM OF THE OPERA (Henry Butler).
MCSET. Cat no: **IAB 91022**. Released on Isis Audio Books, '91. Note: 8 cassettes.

MCSET. Cat no: **1032S**. Released on Travellers Tales, '91 by Travellers Tales. Note: 8 Cassettes.

PHANTOM OF THE OPERA (Anton Rodgers).
MCSET. Cat no: **LFP 7284**. Released on Listen For Pleasure, Feb '87 by EMI Records.

MC. Cat no: **001063618**. Released on Collins-Caedmon, Jul '88 by Collins Audio, Taylors, Bond Street Music.

MCSET. Cat no: **1014S**. Released on Travellers Tales, '91 by Travellers Tales. Note: 94 minutes

Lessing, Doris

FIFTH CHILD, THE (Susan Fleetwood).
MC. Cat no: **IAB 88112**. Released on Isis Audio Books, '88. Note: 4 Cassettes.

MCSET. Cat no: **1326F**. Released on Travellers Tales, '91 by Travellers Tales. Note: 4 cassettes.

Lester, Jane

DOCTOR BRENT'S BROKEN JOURNEY (Shelia Donald).
MCSET. Cat no: **CLT 1007**. Released on Candlelight, '88 by AVLS (Audio-Visual Library Services).

SISTER MARCH'S SECRET (Gwyneth Guthrie).
MCSET. Cat no: **CLT 1002**. Released on Candlelight, '88 by AVLS (Audio-Visual Library Services).

Lewis, Cecil Day

(see under Day Lewis, C

Lewis, C.S

CHRONICLES OF NARNIA SOUNDBOOK (Michael Hordern).
MCSET. Cat no: **9137/9138F.** Released on Travellers Tales, '91 by Travellers Tales. Note: 13 Cassettes.

MCSET. Cat no: **701.** Released on Caedmon (USA), '91 by Caedmon Records (USA), Bond Street Music.

CHRONICLES OF NARNIA, THE (Unknown narrator(s)).
MC. Cat no: **000104270 X.** Released on Collins-Caedmon, '88 by Collins Audio, Taylors, Bond Street Music.

HORSE AND HIS BOY, THE (Anthony Quayle).
MC. Cat no: **1655.** Released on Caedmon (USA), '88 by Caedmon Records (USA), Bond Street Music.

MC. Cat no: **0001034138.** Released on Harper Collins, '91 by Harper Collins. Note: Playing time: 59 mins.

HORSE AND HIS BOY, THE (Sir Michael Hordern).
Note: Michael Hordern with music composed and played by Marisa Robles on the harp.
2LP. Cat no: **SWD 353.** Released on ASV (Academy Sound & Vision), Apr '81 by Academy Sound & Vision Records **Deleted** '88.

MCSET. Cat no: **ZC SWD 353.** Released on ASV (Academy Sound & Vision), Apr '81 by Academy Sound & Vision Records.

MCSET. Cat no: **0001016180.** Released on Harper Collins, '91 by Harper Collins.

LAST BATTLE, THE (Sir Michael Hordern).
2LP. Cat no: **SWD 357.** Released on ASV (Academy Sound & Vision), Feb '82 by Academy Sound & Vision Records **Deleted** '88.

MCSET. Cat no: **ZC SWD 357.** Released on ASV (Academy Sound & Vision), Feb '82 by Academy Sound & Vision Records.

MCSET. Cat no: **0001016237.** Released on Harper Collins, '91 by Harper Collins.

LAST BATTLE, THE (Michael York).
MC. Cat no: **1674.** Released on Caedmon (USA), '88 by Caedmon Records (USA), Bond Street Music.

MC. Cat no: **0001034154.** Released on Harper Collins, '91 by Harper Collins.

LION, THE WITCH AND THE WARDROBE, THE (Various artists).
Note: Radio 4 Dramatisation.
MCSET. Cat no: **ZBBC 1110.** Released on BBC, Mar '90 by BBC Records, Taylors. Note: ISBN No: 0563 410256.

LION, THE WITCH AND THE WARDROBE, THE (Ian Richardson).
MC. Cat no: **1587.** Released on Caedmon (USA), '88 by Caedmon Records (USA), Bond Street Music.

MC. Cat no: **000103409X.** Released on Harper Collins, '91 by Harper Collins. Note: Playing time: 66 mins.

LION, THE WITCH AND THE WARDROBE, THE (Sir Michael Hordern).
2LP. Cat no: **SWD 352.** Released on ASV (Academy Sound & Vision), Sep '81 by Academy Sound & Vision Records **Deleted** '88.

MCSET. Cat no: **ZC SWD 352.** Released on ASV (Academy Sound & Vision), Mar '81 by Academy Sound & Vision Records.

CDSET. Cat no: **CD SWD 352.** Released on ASV (Academy Sound & Vision), Jun '88 by Academy Sound & Vision Records.

MCSET. Cat no: **0001016180.** Released on Harper Collins, '91 by Harper Collins.

MAGICIAN'S NEPHEW, THE (Various artists).
Note: Radio 4 Dramatisation.
MCSET. Cat no: **ZBBC 1109.** Released on BBC, Mar '90 by BBC Records, Taylors. Note: ISBN No: 0563 410248.

MAGICIAN'S NEPHEW, THE (Sir Michael Hordern).
2LP. Cat no: **SWD 351.** Released on ASV (Academy Sound & Vision), Mar '81 by Academy Sound & Vision Records **Deleted** '88.

MCSET. Cat no: **ZC SWD 351.** Released on ASV (Academy Sound & Vision), Mar '81 by Academy Sound & Vision Records.

MCSET. Cat no: **0001016199.** Released on Harper Collins, '91 by Harper Collins.

MAGICIAN'S NEPHEW, THE (Claire Bloom).
MC. Cat no: **1660.** Released on Caedmon (USA), '88 by Caedmon Records (USA), Bond Street Music.

MAGICIAN'S NEPHEW, THE (Ian Richardson).
MC. Cat no: **0001034146.** Released on Harper Collins, '91 by Harper Collins. Note: Playing time: 61 mins.

PRINCE CASPIAN (Claire Bloom).
MC. Cat no: **1603.** Released on Caedmon (USA), '88 by Caedmon Records (USA), Bond Street Music.

MC. Cat no: **0001034111.** Released on Harper Collins, '91 by Harper Collins. Note: Playing time: 64 mins.

PRINCE CASPIAN (Sir Michael Hordern).
2LP. Cat no: **SWD 354.** Released on ASV (Academy Sound & Vision), Sep '81 by Academy Sound & Vision Records **Deleted** '88.

MCSET. Cat no: **ZC SWD 354.** Released on ASV (Academy Sound & Vision), Sep '81 by Academy Sound & Vision Records.

MCSET. Cat no: **0001016180.** Released on Harper Collins, '91 by Harper Collins.

SCREWTAPE LETTERS, THE (John Cleese).
MCSET. Cat no: **HCA 38.** Released on Harper Collins, '92 by Harper Collins.

SILVER CHAIR, THE (Sir Michael Hordern).
2LP. Cat no: **SWD 356.** Released on ASV (Academy Sound & Vision), Dec '81 by Academy Sound & Vision Records **Deleted** '88.

MCSET. Cat no: **ZC SWD 356.** Released on ASV (Academy Sound & Vision), Dec '81 by Academy Sound & Vision Records.

MCSET. Cat no: **0001016210.** Released on Harper Collins, '91 by Harper Collins.

SILVER CHAIR, THE (Anthony Quayle).
MC. Cat no: **1631.** Released on Caedmon (USA), '88 by Caedmon Records (USA), Bond Street Music.

MC. Cat no: **000103412X.** Released on Harper Collins, '91 by Harper Collins. Note: Playing time: 1 hour.

VOYAGE OF THE DAWN TREADER, THE (Anthony Quayle).
MC. Cat no: **1615.** Released on Caedmon (USA), '88 by Caedmon Records (USA), Bond Street Music.

MC. Cat no: **009034103.** Released on Harper Collins, '91 by Harper Collins. Note: Playing time: 54 mins.

VOYAGE OF THE DAWN TREADER, THE (Sir Michael Hordern).
2LP. Cat no: **SWD 355.** Released on ASV (Academy Sound & Vision), Nov '81 by Academy Sound & Vision Records **Deleted** '88.

MCSET. Cat no: **ZC SWD 355.** Released on ASV (Academy Sound & Vision), Nov '81 by Academy Sound & Vision Records.

MCSET. Cat no: **009016156.** Released on Harper Collins, '91 by Harper Collins.

Lewis, Michael

LIAR'S POKER (Michael Lewis).
MCSET. Cat no: **ZBBC 1230.** Released on BBC, '91 by BBC Records, Taylors. Note: ISBN No: 0563 408030

Lewis, T.

JACK'S RETURN HOME (Ray Dunbobbin).
MCSET. Cat no: **1269T.** Released on Travellers Tales, '91 by Travellers Tales. Note: 5 Cassettes.

MCSET. Cat no: **1854961365.** Released on Bramhope, '91 by Ulverscroft Soundings. Note: 5 Cassettes.

Lindgren, Astrid

EMIL IN THE SOUP TUREEN (Tom Conti).
Note: For 4 to 8 year olds.
MC. Cat no: **A 003.** Released on Green Dragon, '91 by Green Dragon Audio Visual.

STORIES FROM PIPPI LONG-STOCKING (Jill Shilling).
MC. Cat no: **TS 351**. Released on Tellastory, Aug '92 by Random Century Audiobooks. Note: ISBN no. 1856560317

Lindsay, Eliza

ADVENTURES OF HEGGARTY HAGGERTY (George Cole).
LP. Cat no: **STMP 9033**. Released on Super Tempo, Aug '84 by Warwick Records, Taylors, Solomon & Peres, Sony Music Operations.
MC. Cat no: **STMP4 9033**. Released on Super Tempo, Aug '84 by Warwick Records, Taylors, Solomon & Peres, Sony Music Operations.

Ling & Ace

CROWN HOUSE (Various artists).
Note: 1988's major Radio 4 serial - a gripping family saga set in the twenties. By Peter Ling and Julie Ace.
MCSET. Cat no: **ZBBC 1045**. Released on BBC Radio Collection, Sep '88 by BBC Records. Note: ISBN No: 0563 225564

Lively, Penelope

ACCORDING TO MARK (Michael Williams).
MCSET. Cat no: **1094F**. Released on Travellers Tales, '91 by Travellers Tales. Note: 6 cassettes.

FANNY AND THE MONSTERS (Jan Francis).
MCSET. Cat no: **2CCA 3083**. Released on Chivers Audio Books, '91 by Chivers Audio Books, Green Dragon Audio Visual. Note: 2 Cassettes.
MCSET. Cat no: **9162F**. Released on Travellers Tales, '91 by Travellers Tales. Note: 2 cassettes.

GHOST OF THOMAS KEMPE, THE (Rosalind Adams).
MCSET. Cat no: **CC/040**. Released on Cover to Cover, '87 by Cover to Cover Cassettes.
MC. Cat no: **882154**. Released on Puffin Cover To Cover, '88, Green Dragon Audio Visual.
MCSET. Cat no: **9111F**. Released on Travellers Tales, '91 by Travellers Tales. Note: 3 Cassettes.

HOUSE INSIDE OUT, A (Sheila Mitchell).
MC. Cat no: **2CCA 3064**. Released on Chivers Audio Books, '88 by Chivers Audio Books, Green Dragon Audio Visual. Note: 2 Cassettes.
MCSET. Cat no: **9131F**. Released on Travellers Tales, '91 by Travellers Tales. Note: 2 Cassettes.

JUDGEMENT DAY (Sheila Mitchell).
MCSET. Cat no: **1320F**. Released on Travellers Tales, '91 by Travellers Tales. Note: 6 cassettes.
MCSET. Cat no: **CAB 324**. Released on Chivers Audio Books, '88 by Chivers Audio Books, Green Dragon Audio Visual. Note: 6 Cassettes.

MOON TIGER (Sheila Mitchell).
MCSET. Cat no: **1280F**. Released on Travellers Tales, '91 by Travellers Tales. Note: 6 cassettes.
MCSET. Cat no: **IAB 88012**. Released on Isis Audio Books, '91. Note: 6 Cassettes.

NEXT TO NATURE, ART (Gretel Davis).
MCSET. Cat no: **1417F**. Released on Travellers Tales, '91 by Travellers Tales. Note: 6 cassettes.
MCSET. Cat no: **OAS 89076**. Released on Oasis Audio Books, '91 by Isis Audio Books. Note: 6 Cassettes.

PASSING ON (Sheila Mitchell).
MCSET. Cat no: **1591F**. Released on Travellers Tales, '91 by Travellers Tales. Note: 7 cassettes.
MCSET. Cat no: **IAB 90071**. Released on Isis Audio Books, '91.

PERFECT HAPPINESS (Anne Dover).
MCSET. Cat no: **1162R**. Released on Travellers Tales, '91 by Travellers Tales. Note: 5 Cassettes.
MCSET. Cat no: **1854964216**. Released on Bramhope, '91 by Ulverscroft Soundings. Note: 5 Cassettes.

TREASURES OF TIME (Anne Dover).
MCSET. Cat no: **1159R**. Released on Travellers Tales, '91 by Travellers Tales. Note: 6 Cassettes.
MCSET. Cat no: **1854963791**. Released on Soundings, '91 by Soundings Records, Bond Street Music. Note: 6 Cassettes.

UNINVITED GHOSTS (Delia Lindsay).
MCSET. Cat no: **2CCA 3008**. Released on Chivers Audio Books, '91 by Chivers Audio Books, Green Dragon Audio Visual. Note: 2 Cassettes.
MCSET. Cat no: **9055F**. Released on Travellers Tales, '91 by Travellers Tales. Note: 2 Cassettes.
MCSET. Cat no: **086 222 0482**. Released on Chivers Calvacade, '91 by Chivers Audio Books, Green Dragon Audio Visual. Note: 2 Cassettes.

LLewellyn, Richard

HOW GREEN WAS MY VALLEY (Philip Madoc).
MCSET. Cat no: **CAB 650**. Released on Chivers Audio Books, Oct '91 by Chivers Audio Books, Green Dragon Audio Visual. Note: 12 Cassettes.

Llewellyn, Sam

BLOOD KNOT (Michael Jayston).
MCSET. Cat no: **CAB 635**. Released on Chivers Audio Books, Sep '91 by Chivers Audio Books, Green Dragon Audio Visual. Note: 8 Cassettes.

BLOOD ORANGE (Michael Jayston).
MCSET. Cat no: **1382T**. Released on Travellers Tales, '91 by Travellers Tales. Note: 8 Cassettes.

DEAD EYE (Christopher Kay).
MCSET. Cat no: **1741T**. Released on Travellers Tales, '91 by Travellers Tales. Note: 8 Cassettes.
MCSET. Cat no: **1854964283**. Released on Soundings, '91 by Soundings Records, Bond Street Music. Note: 8 Cassettes.

DEAD RECKONING (Gordon Griffin).
MCSET. Cat no: **1747T**. Released on Travellers Tales, '91 by Travellers Tales. Note: 4 Cassettes.
MCSET. Cat no: **1854964410**. Released on Bramhope, '91 by Ulverscroft Soundings. Note: 4 Cassettes.

DEATH ROLL (Michael Jayston).
MCSET. Cat no: **CAB 465**. Released on Chivers Audio Books, '91 by Chivers Audio Books, Green Dragon Audio Visual. Note: 8 Cassettes.
MCSET. Cat no: **1538T**. Released on Travellers Tales, '91 by Travellers Tales. Note: 8 Cassettes.

Lloyd, Jeremy

CAPTAIN BEAKY (The Woodland Gospels And Poems) (Unknown narrator(s)).
MCSET. Cat no: **LFP 7472**. Released on Listen For Pleasure, Jun '90 by EMI Records.
MCSET. Cat no: **DTO 10521**. Released on Ditto, '88 by Pickwick Records, Midland Records.

CAPTAIN BEAKY (Volumes 1 & 2) (Various artists).
2LP. Cat no: **2664483**. Released on Polydor, '83 by Polydor Ltd, Solomon & Peres **Deleted** '88.
LP. Cat no: **2383 588**. Released on Polydor, Jan '81 by Polydor Ltd, Solomon & Peres.

Lodge, David

NICE WORK (Geoffrey Matthews).
MCSET. Cat no: **1343F**. Released on Travellers Tales, '91 by Travellers Tales. Note: 8 cassettes.
MCSET. Cat no: **IAB 89032**. Released on Isis Audio Books, '91. Note: 8 Cassettes.

Lofts, Norah

CALF FOR VENUS, A (Roger Rees).
MCSET. Cat no: **1095F**. Released on Travellers Tales, '91 by Travellers Tales. Note: 6 cassettes.

MADSELIN (Rosalind Lloyd).
MCSET. Cat no: **COL 2018**. Released on Colophone, Sep '81 by AVLS (Audio-Visual Library Services).

London, Jack

CALL OF THE WILD, THE (Daniel Massey).
MCSET. Cat no: **ARGO 1205**. Released on Argo (EMI), May '90 by EMI Records. Note: 2 Cassettes.

CALL OF THE WILD, THE (Ed Begley).

MC. Cat no: **1219**. Released on Caedmon (USA), '88 by Caedmon Records (USA), Bond Street Music.

IRON HEEL, THE (Diana Olsson).
Note: Abridged version.
MCSET. Cat no: **1365F**. Released on Travellers Tales, '91 by Travellers Tales. Note: 4 cassettes
MCSET. Cat no: **SPF 525-2**. Released on Schiltron Audio Books, '91 by Schiltron Publishing. Note: 4 Cassettes. Playing time: 5 hours 30 minutes.

SEA WOLF, THE (Anthony Quayle).
Note: Chapters 17-19 of the robust narrative of suspense and seafaring adventure.
MC. Cat no: **CDL 51689**. Released on Caedmon (USA), '82 by Caedmon Records (USA), Bond Street Music.

SEA WOLF, THE (Arthur Boland).
MCSET. Cat no: **COL 2008**. Released on Colophone, Feb '81 by AVLS (Audio-Visual Library Services).

SEA WOLF, THE (Frank Muller).
MCSET. Cat no: **1347F**. Released on Travellers Tales, '91 by Travellers Tales. Note: 6 cassettes.
MCSET. Cat no: **IAB 89012**. Released on Isis Audio Books, '91. Note: 6 Cassettes.

WILDERNESS TALES (John Sheddon).
Note: Includes:- Love of Live, The Man With the Gash, The God of His Fathers, The League of Old Men.
MCSET. Cat no: **SPF 525-1**. Released on Schiltron Audio Books, '92 by Schiltron Publishing. Note: 2 Cassettes. Playing time 2 hours 30 minutes.

WORLD OF JACK LONDON, THE (A Collection of Stories) (Frank Muller).
Note: A collection of short stories.
MCSET. Cat no: **RB 80111**. Released on Recorded Books, '91 by Isis Audio Books. Note: 4 cassettes.

Long, Elliot

INCIDENT AT RYKER'S CREEK (John Chancer).
MCSET. Cat no: **185496593X**. Released on Trio, Apr '92 by EMI Records. Note: Playing time: 60 minutes.

Longden, Deric

DIANA'S STORY (Deric Longden).
MCSET. Cat no: **ZBBC 1112**. Released on BBC Radio Collection, 5 Mar '90 by BBC Records. Note: ISBN No: 0563 410280.

Longfellow, Pamela

CHINA BLUES (Liza Rose).
MCSET. Cat no: **1601/2F**. Released on Travellers Tales, '91 by Travellers Tales. Note: 10 cassettes.
MCSET. Cat no: **1854963996**. Released on Soundings, '91 by Soundings Records, Bond Street Music. Note: 10 Cassettes.

Loos, Anita

GENTLEMEN PREFER BLONDES (Lorelei's Diary) (Carol Channing).
MC. Cat no: **1148**. Released on Caedmon (USA), '88 by Caedmon Records (USA), Bond Street Music.

Lord Buckley

BLOWING HIS MIND AND YOURS TOO.
Note: Includes: Subconcious Mind, Fire Chief, Let It Down, Murder, The Grasser, Maharaja and Scrooge.
LP. Cat no: **VERB 3**. Released on Demon Verbals, Sep '84 by Demon Records.

MOST IMMACULATELY HIP ARISTOCRAT.
Note: Includes: Bad Rapping of the Marquis De Sade, The King of Bad Cats, Governor Slugwell, The Raven, The Train and The Hip Einie.
LP. Cat no: **VERB 8**. Released on Demon Verbals, Dec '89 by Demon Records.

Lovecraft H.P.

CALL OF CTHULHU, THE (Garrick Hagon).
MC. Cat no: **RSJ 5006**. Released on Landfall, '91.

LURKING FEAR, THE (David Healy).
MC. Cat no: **RSJ 5003**. Released on Landfall, '91.

REANIMATOR (Garrick Hagon).
MC. Cat no: **RSJ 5007**. Released on Landfall, '91.

THING ON THE DOORSTEP, THE (David Healy).
MC. Cat no: **RSJ 5004**. Released on Landfall, '91.

Lovesey, Peter

ABRACADAVER (A Sergeant Cribb Mystery) (John Kennedy Melling).
MCSET. Cat no: **1241T**. Released on Travellers Tales, '91 by Travellers Tales. Note: 6 Cassettes.
MCSET. Cat no: **CAB 294**. Released on Chivers Audio Books, Apr '88 by Chivers Audio Books, Green Dragon Audio Visual.

BERTIE AND THE SEVEN BODIES (Terrence Hardiman).
MCSET. Cat no: **CAB 623**. Released on Chivers Audio Books, Sep '91 by Chivers Audio Books, Green Dragon Audio Visual. Note: 6 Cassettes.

BERTIE AND THE TINMAN (From The Detective Memoirs of King Edward VII) (Terrence Hardiman).
MCSET. Cat no: **1631T**. Released on Travellers Tales, '91 by Travellers Tales. Note: 6 Cassettes.
MCSET. Cat no: **CAB 502**. Released on Chivers Audio Books, '91 by Chivers Audio Books, Green Dragon Audio Visual. Note: 6 Cassettes.

DETECTIVE WORE SILK DRAWERS, THE (John Kennedy Melling).
MC. Cat no: **CAB 338**. Released on Chivers Audio Books, '88 by Chivers Audio Books, Green Dragon Audio Visual. Note: 4 Cassettes.
MCSET. Cat no: **1365T**. Released on Travellers Tales, '91 by Travellers Tales. Note: 4 Cassettes.

ON THE EDGE (Stephen Thorne).
MCSET. Cat no: **1401F**. Released on Travellers Tales, '91 by Travellers Tales. Note: 6 cassettes.
MCSET. Cat no: **IAB 89103**. Released on Isis Audio Books, '91. Note: 6 Cassettes.

ROUGH CIDER (Stephen Thorne).
MCSET. Cat no: **1281F**. Released on Travellers Tales, '91 by Travellers Tales. Note: 6 cassettes.
MCSET. Cat no: **IAB 88022**. Released on Isis Audio Books, '91. Note: 6 Cassettes.

Lowe, S. & Ince, A.

LOSING CONTROL (Judith Porter).
Note: Authors are Shirley Lowe and Angela Ince.
MCSET. Cat no: **1854964682**. Released on Soundings, '91 by Soundings Records, Bond Street Music. Note: 6 cassettes.

SWAPPING (Judith Porter).
Note: Authors are Shirley Lowe and Angela Ince.
MCSET. Cat no: **1497F**. Released on Travellers Tales, '91 by Travellers Tales. Note: 7 cassettes.
MCSET. Cat no: **185496318X**. Released on Soundings, '91 by Soundings Records, Bond Street Music. Note: 7 Cassettes.

TAKING OVER (Judith Porter).
MCSET. Cat no: **1059H**. Released on Travellers Tales, '91 by Travellers Tales. Note: 8 cassettes.
MCSET. Cat no: **1854963678**. Released on Soundings, '91 by Soundings Records, Bond Street Music. Note: 8 cassettes.

Lowell, Robert

ROBERT LOWELL: A READING (Robert Lowell).
MC. Cat no: **1569**. Released on Caedmon (USA), '88 by Caedmon Records (USA), Bond Street Music.

Lucky Grills

TRUE BLUE COMEDY VOL 1 (Hard Up for Sex).
MCSET. Cat no: **PLAC 471**. Released on Prism, Sep '89 by Prism Records, Outlet Records, I & B Records.

TRUE BLUE COMEDY VOL 2 (Red Hot & Very Blue).
MCSET. Cat no: **PLAC 472**. Released on Prism, Sep '89 by Prism Records, Outlet Records, I & B Records.

TRUE BLUE COMEDY VOL 3 (True Blue Aussie).
MCSET. Cat no: **PLAC 473**. Released on Prism, Sep '89 by Prism Records,

Outlet Records, I & B Records.

Ludlum, Robert
BOURNE IDENTITY, THE (Darren McGavin).
MCSET. Cat no: **unknown**. Released on Hamlyn Books On Tape, Apr '88, Bond Street Music. Note: 2 cassette set.
BOURNE SUPREMACY, THE (Darren McGavin).
Note: Also available on hanging format, catalogue number:- 0001031295.
MCSET. Cat no: **HCA 1**. Released on Harper Collins, '92 by Harper Collins. Note: ISBN no. 0001072145. 2 cassettes.
CHANCELLOR MANUSCRIPT, THE (Michael Moriaty).
Note: Also available on hanging format, catalogue number:- 0001031287.
MCSET. Cat no: **HCA 3**. Released on Harper Collins, '92 by Harper Collins. Note: 2 cassettes. ISBN no. 0001072161
MATARESE CIRCLE, THE (Martin Balsam).
Note: Also available on hanging format, catalogue number:- 0001031309.
MCSET. Cat no: **HCA 21**. Released on Harper Collins, '92 by Harper Collins. Note: ISBN no. 0001072153. 2 cassettes.
ROAD TO OMAHA, THE (Martin Shaw).
MCSET. Cat no: **0001046527**. Released on Harper Collins, Mar '92 by Harper Collins.
SHORT STORIES (Various artists).
MCSET. Cat no: **1479T**. Released on Travellers Tales, '91 by Travellers Tales. Note: 6 Cassettes.
TREVAYNE (Philip Bosco).
MCSET. Cat no: **ZBBC 1233**. Released on BBC, '91 by BBC Records, Taylors. Note: ISBN No: 0563 408065

Luellen, Valentina
CASTLE OF THE MIST (Carole Boyd).
MCSET. Cat no: **PMB 022**. Released on Mills & Boon, '88. Note: 2 Cassettes

Lurtsema, Robert J.
CHRISTMAS STORIES (Unknown narrator(s)).
LP. Cat no: **PH 1078**. Released on Philo (USA), '88 by Rounder Records (USA), Roots Records, Projection, Topic Records, Jazz Music, Ross Records, Celtic Music, Impetus Records.
MC. Cat no: **PH 1078C**. Released on Philo (USA), '88 by Rounder Records (USA), Roots Records, Projection, Topic Records, Jazz Music, Ross Records, Celtic Music, Impetus Records.

Lyall, Gavin
CONDUCT OF MAJOR MAXIM, THE (Robin Browne).
MCSET. Cat no: **IAB 92062**. Released on Isis Audio Books, Jun '92. Note: 8 Cassettes. Playing time: 9 hours, 15 mins.
SECRET SERVANT, THE (John Graham).
MCSET. Cat no: **1230T**. Released on Travellers Tales, '91 by Travellers Tales. Note: 6 Cassettes.
UNCLE TARGET (John Graham).
MCSET. Cat no: **CAB 357**. Released on Chivers Audio Books, '91 by Chivers Audio Books, Green Dragon Audio Visual. Note: 8 cassettes
MCSET. Cat no: **1386T**. Released on Travellers Tales, '91 by Travellers Tales. Note: 8 Cassettes.

Lynch, Francis
IN THE HOUSE OF DARK MUSIC (Arthur Boland).
MCSET. Cat no: **COL 2011**. Released on Colophone, Sep '81 by AVLS (Audio-Visual Library Services).

Lyons, Mary
PASSIONATE DECEPTION (Carole Boyd).
MCSET. Cat no: **PMB 017**. Released on Mills & Boon, '88. Note: 2 Cassettes.
MC. Cat no: **0263 11503 8**. Released on Mills & Boon, 30 Jun '87

McBain, Ed
COP HATER (Peter Whitman).
MCSET. Cat no: **CAB 674**. Released on Chivers Audio Books, Feb '92 by Chivers Audio Books, Green Dragon Audio Visual. Note: 6 cassettes.
DOWN TOWN (Michael Ferrone).
MCSET. Cat no: **IAB 92087**. Released on Isis Audio Books, Aug '92. Note: 8 Cassettes. Playing time: 10 hours, 45 mins.
FUZZ (Don Fellows).
MCSET. Cat no: **1115T**. Released on Travellers Tales, '91 by Travellers Tales. Note: 6 Cassettes.
LADYKILLER (Steve Dunn).
MCSET. Cat no: **CAB 320**. Released on Chivers Audio Books, '91 by Chivers Audio Books, Green Dragon Audio Visual. Note: 4 Cassettes.
MCSET. Cat no: **1396T**. Released on Travellers Tales, '91 by Travellers Tales. Note: 4 Cassettes.
LULLABY (Peter Whitman).
MCSET. Cat no: **CAB 549**. Released on Chivers Audio Books, '91 by Chivers Audio Books, Green Dragon Audio Visual. Note: 8 Cassettes.
MCSET. Cat no: **1691T**. Released on Travellers Tales, '91 by Travellers Tales. Note: 8 Cassettes.
MUGGER, THE (Harry Crane).
MCSET. Cat no: **CAB 321**. Released on Chivers Audio Books, '91 by Chivers Audio Books, Green Dragon Audio Visual. Note: 4 Cassettes.
MCSET. Cat no: **1427T**. Released on Travellers Tales, '91 by Travellers Tales. Note: 4 Cassettes.
POISON (Joe Spano).
MCSET. Cat no: **0671641603**. Released on Simon & Schuster, '91 by Simon & Schuster Ltd. Note: 2 cassettes.
SNOW WHITE AND ROSE RED (Ed Bishop).
MCSET. Cat no: **CAB 162**. Released on Chivers Audio Books, '91 by Chivers Audio Books, Green Dragon Audio Visual. Note: 6 Cassettes.
MCSET. Cat no: **1116T**. Released on Travellers Tales, '91 by Travellers Tales. Note: 6 Cassettes.
TRICKS (Joe Spano).
MCSET. Cat no: **0671668382**. Released on Simon & Schuster, '91 by Simon & Schuster Ltd. Note: 2 cassettes.

McBratney, Sam
GHOSTS OF HUNGRY HOUSE LAND, THE (Christian Rodska).
MCSET. Cat no: **2CCA 3129**. Released on Chivers Audio Books, '91 by Chivers Audio Books, Green Dragon Audio Visual. Note: 2 Cassettes.

MacCaig, Norman
WAY I SAY IT, THE (Unknown narrator(s)).
LP. Cat no: **CCA 4**. Released on Claddagh (Ireland), Aug '88 by Claddagh Records (Ireland), Projection, Impetus Records, Jazz Music, Roots Records, C.M. Distribution, Outlet Records, Taylors.

McCall, Dina
WHITE ORCHID (Unknown narrator(s)).
MCSET. Cat no: **1854963856**. Released on Trio, '91 by EMI Records. Note: 3 Cassettes.

McCaughna, David
WINDCHILL (And Child's Play) (Various artists).
MC. Cat no: **NF 11**. Released on Nightfall Tapes, '89 by BMG Records (UK) Ltd..

McCloy, Helen
HE NEVER CAME BACK (Kate Harper).
MCSET. Cat no: **CAT 4060**. Released on Chivers Audio Books, '91 by Chivers Audio Books, Green Dragon Audio Visual. Note: 4 Cassettes.
MCSET. Cat no: **1632T**. Released on Travellers Tales, '91 by Travellers Tales. Note: 4 Cassettes.

McConnell, Jean
DOCTOR ON APPROVAL (Jean McConnell).
MCSET. Cat no: **SOUND 31**. Released on Soundings, Mar '85 by Soundings Records, Bond Street Music.
NINETY MINUTES OF SUSPENSE (Unknown narrator(s)).

MC. Cat no: **SOUND 38**. Released on Soundings, Feb '85 by Soundings Records, Bond Street Music.

McCullagh, Sheila

PUDDLE LANE (Fire In The Grass) (Unknown narrator(s)).
Note: Book and cassette.

MC. Cat no: **PLBP 241**. Released on Tell-A-Tale, '88 by Pickwick Records, Taylors, Clyde Factors.

PUDDLE LANE (The Gruffle) (Unknown narrator(s)).
Note: Book and cassette.

MC. Cat no: **PLBP 242**. Released on Tell-A-Tale, '88 by Pickwick Records, Taylors, Clyde Factors.

PUDDLE LANE (The Sandalwood Girl) (Unknown narrator(s)).
Note: Book and cassette.

MC. Cat no: **PLBP 243**. Released on Tell-A-Tale, '88 by Pickwick Records, Taylors, Clyde Factors.

PUDDLE LANE (The Gruffle In Puddle Lane) (Unknown narrator(s)).
Note: Book and cassette.

MC. Cat no: **PLBP 244**. Released on Tell-A-Tale, '88 by Pickwick Records, Taylors, Clyde Factors.

PUDDLE LANE (The Silver River) (Unknown narrator(s)).
Note: Book and cassette.

MC. Cat no: **PLBP 245**. Released on Tell-A-Tale, '88 by Pickwick Records, Taylors, Clyde Factors.

PUDDLE LANE (The Flying Saucer) (Unknown narrator(s)).
Note: Book and cassette.

MC. Cat no: **PLBP 246**. Released on Tell-A-Tale, '88 by Pickwick Records, Taylors, Clyde Factors.

PUDDLE LANE (The Dragon's Egg) (Unknown narrator(s)).
Note: Book and cassette.

MC. Cat no: **PLBP 247**. Released on Tell-A-Tale, '88 by Pickwick Records, Taylors, Clyde Factors.

PUDDLE LANE (On The Way To The Blue Mountain) (Unknown narrator(s)).
Note: Book and cassette.

MC. Cat no: **PLBP 248**. Released on Tell-A-Tale, '88 by Pickwick Records, Taylors, Clyde Factors.

PUDDLE LANE (The Clock Struck Thirteen) (Unknown narrator(s)).
Note: Book and cassette. For ages 3 - 6 years.

MC. Cat no: **PLBP 215**. Released on Tell-A-Tale, '88 by Pickwick Records, Taylors, Clyde Factors.

PUDDLE LANE (Hickory Mouse) (Unknown narrator(s)).
Note: Book and cassette. For ages 3 - 6 years.

MC. Cat no: **PLBP 218**. Released on Tell-A-Tale, '88 by Pickwick Records, Taylors, Clyde Factors.

PUDDLE LANE (The Little Monster) (Unknown narrator(s)).
Note: Book and cassette. For ages 3 - 6 years.

MC. Cat no: **PLBP 169**. Released on Tell-A-Tale, '88 by Pickwick Records, Taylors, Clyde Factors.

PUDDLE LANE (The Magic Penny) (Unknown narrator(s)).
Note: Book and cassette. For ages to 3 - 6 years.

MC. Cat no: **PLBP 217**. Released on Tell-A-Tale, '88 by Pickwick Records, Taylors, Clyde Factors.

PUDDLE LANE (The Magic Box) (Unknown narrator(s)).
Note: Book and cassette. For ages to 3-6 years.

MC. Cat no: **PLBP 162**. Released on Tell-A-Tale, '88 by Pickwick Records, Taylors, Clyde Factors.

PUDDLE LANE (Tim Catchmouse) (Unknown narrator(s)).
Note: Book and cassette. For ages up to 3 - 6 years.

MC. Cat no: **PLBP 161**. Released on Tell-A-Tale, '88 by Pickwick Records, Taylors, Clyde Factors.

PUDDLE LANE (The Magician's Party) (Unknown narrator(s)).
Note: Book and cassette. For ages up to 3 - 6 years.

MC. Cat no: **PLBP 216**. Released on Tell-A-Tale, '88 by Pickwick Records, Taylors, Clyde Factors.

PUDDLE LANE (Mrs Pitter Patter and The Magician) (Unknown narrator(s)).
Note: Book and cassette. For ages up to 3 - 6 years.

MC. Cat no: **PLBP 168**. Released on Tell-A-Tale, '88 by Pickwick Records, Taylors, Clyde Factors.

PUDDLE LANE (Old Mr Gotobed) (Unknown narrator(s)).
Note: Book and cassette. For ages up to 3 - 6 years.

MC. Cat no: **PLBP 221**. Released on Tell-A-Tale, '88 by Pickwick Records, Taylors, Clyde Factors.

PUDDLE LANE (Tessa And The Magician) (Unknown narrator(s)).
Note: Book and cassette. For ages to 3 - 6 years.

MC. Cat no: **PLBP 166**. Released on Tell-A-Tale, '88 by Pickwick Records, Taylors, Clyde Factors.

PUDDLE LANE (Tessa in Puddle Lane) (Unknown narrator(s)).
Note: Book and cassette. For ages up to 3 - 6 years.

MC. Cat no: **PLBP 219**. Released on Tell-A-Tale, '88 by Pickwick Records, Taylors, Clyde Factors.

PUDDLE LANE (When The Magic Stopped) (Unknown narrator(s)).
Note: Book and cassette. For ages up to 3 - 6 years.

MC. Cat no: **PLBP 170**. Released on Tell-A-Tale, '88 by Pickwick Records, Taylors, Clyde Factors.

PUDDLE LANE (Toby Spelldragon And The Magician) (Unknown narrator(s)).
Note: Book and cassette. For ages up to 3 - 6 years.

MC. Cat no: **PLBP 222**. Released on Tell-A-Tale, '88 by Pickwick Records, Taylors, Clyde Factors.

PUDDLE LANE (Vanishing Monster) (Unknown narrator(s)).
Note: Book and cassette. For ages up to 3 - 6 years.

MC. Cat no: **PLBP 163**. Released on Tell-A-Tale, '88 by Pickwick Records, Taylors, Clyde Factors.

PUDDLE LANE (Wideawake Mice Go To Market) (Unknown narrator(s)).
Note: Book and cassette.

MC. Cat no: **PLBP 220**. Released on Tell-A-Tale, '88 by Pickwick Records, Taylors, Clyde Factors.

PUDDLE LANE (Wideawake Mice) (Unknown narrator(s)).
Note: Book and cassette. For ages up to 3 - 6 years.

MC. Cat no: **PLBP 167**. Released on Tell-A-Tale, '88 by Pickwick Records, Taylors, Clyde Factors.

McCullough, Colleen

INDECENT OBSESSION, AN (Nigel Graham).
MCSET. Cat no: **IAB 91106**. Released on Isis Audio Books, Oct '91. Note: 8 Cassettes. Playing time 11 hours 20 minutes.

LADIES OF MISSALONGH, THE (Davina Porter).
Note: Abridged version.

MCSET. Cat no: **1349F**. Released on Travellers Tales, '91 by Travellers Tales. Note: 4 cassettes.

LADIES OF MISSALONGH, THE (Davina Porter).
MCSET. Cat no: **IAB 89013**. Released on Isis Audio Books, '91. Note: 4 Cassettes.

McCutchan, Philip

CAMERON ORDINARY SEAMAN (Joss Ackland).
MCSET. Cat no: **1119T**. Released on Travellers Tales, '91 by Travellers Tales. Note: 4 Cassettes.

CAMERON'S CONVOY (Christopher Kay).
MCSET. Cat no: **SOUND 11**. Released on Soundings, Mar '85 by Soundings Records, Bond Street Music.

MCSET. Cat no: **1118T**. Released on Travellers Tales, '91 by Travellers Tales. Note: 4 Cassettes.

CONVOY COMMODORE, THE (Clifford Norgate).
MCSET. Cat no: **1465F**. Released on Travellers Tales, '91 by Travellers Tales. Note: 6 cassettes.

MCSET. Cat no: **CAB 418**. Released on Chivers Audio Books, '91 by Chivers Audio Books, Green Dragon Audio Visual. Note: 6 cassettes.

MacDiarmid, Hugh

ASSESSMENT AND CHOICE (Volume 1) (Edwin Morgan & Sandy Rose).
MC. Cat no: **SSC 028**. Released on Scotsoun, '91 by Scotsoun Recordings, Morley Audio Services.

ASSESSMENT AND CHOICE (Volume 2) (Edwin Morgan & Sandy Rose).
MC. Cat no: **SSC 029**. Released on Scotsoun, '91 by Scotsoun Recordings, Morley Audio Services.

LANGHOLM MEMORIAL SCULPTURE (Unknown narrator(s)).
MC. Cat no: **SSC 079**. Released on Scotsoun, '91 by Scotsoun Recordings, Morley Audio Services.

SANGSCHAW (And Penny Wheep) (Various artists).
Tracks / Bonnie broukit bairn, The: *Various artists* / Watergaw, The: *Various artists* / Sauchs in the reuch heuch hauch, The: *Various artists* / I heard Christ sing: *Various artists* / Moonlight among the pines: *Various artists* / You know not who I am: *Various artists* / Overinziervar: *Various artists* / Ex vermibus: *Various artists* / Au clair de la lune: *Various artists* / In the hedgeback: *Various artists* / Reid e'en: *Various artists* / Crowdieknowe: *Various artists* / Eemis stane, The: *Various artists* / Scarlet woman, The: *Various artists* / Frightened bride, The: *Various artists* / Last trump, The: *Various artists* / Cophetua: *Various artists* / Wheelrig: *Various artists* / Country life: *Various artists* / O Jesu parvule: *Various artists* / Innumerable Christ, The: *Various artists* / God takes a rest: *Various artists* / In the pantry: *Various artists* / Farmer's death: *Various artists* / Diseased salmon, The: *Various artists* / Whip the world: *Various artists* / Ballad of the five senses: *Various artists* / In Glasgow: *Various artists* / La fourmiliere: *Various artists* / Trompe l'oeil: *Various artists* / Wheesht wheesht: *Various artists* / Ex ephemeride mare: *Various artists* / Blind man's luck: *Various artists* / Currant bush, The: *Various artists* / Cloudburst and soaring moon: *Various artists* / Ferry-o'-the-feet: *Various artists* / Somersault: *Various artists* / Song: *Various artists* / Love: *Various artists* / Sea serpent: *Various artists* / Locked: *Various artists* / Thunderstorm: *Various artists* / Hungry waters: *Various artists* / Tam: *Various artists* / Focherty: *Various artists* / Sabine: *Various artists* / Parley of beasts: *Various artists* / Lovesick lass, The: *Various artists* / Wild roses: *Various artists* / Widower, The: *Various artists* / Long black night, The: *Various artists* / To one who urges more ambitious flights: *Various artists* / Dead liebknecht, The: *Various artists* / In Mysie's bed: *Various artists* / Guid conceit: *Various artists* / Morning: *Various artists* / Under the greenwood tree: *Various artists* / Three fishes, The: *Various artists* / Robber, The: *Various artists* / Bombinations of a chimaera: *Various artists* / Scunner: *Various artists* / Servant girl's bed: *Various artists* / Jimsy: an idiot: *Various artists* / Empty vessel: *Various artists* / Fairmer's lass, The: *Various artists* / Bonnie lowe, The: *Various artists* / Sunny gale: *Various artists* / On the threshold: *Various artists* / Krang: *Various artists* / Supper to God: *Various artists* / Fairy tales: *Various artists* / Bubblyjock: *Various artists* / Herd of does, A: *Various artists* / U samago Moria: *Various artists* / Your immortal memory, burns: *Various artists*.

Note: This cassette celebrates the centenary of the birth of Hugh MacDiarmid and consists of all the early lyrics. Readers are Tom Fleming, Iain Cuthbertson, Eileen MacCallum, Alec Monteath and John Shedden. All poems are read in Scots, with the exception of In Glasgow (English), La Fourmiliere (French), A Herd of Does (English), U Samago Moria (English) and Your Immortal Memory, Burns (English).

MCSET. Cat no: **SSC 095**. Released on Scotsoun, Apr '92 by Scotsoun Recordings, Morley Audio Services.

MacDonald, Geoff

LIGHT PRINCESS, THE (Glynis Johns).
MC. Cat no: **1676**. Released on Caedmon (USA), Aug '83 by Caedmon Records (USA), Bond Street Music.

MacDonald, George

PRINCESS AND THE GOBLIN (Caroline Bliss).
MCSET. Cat no: **TS 362**. Released on Tellastory, May '92 by Random Century Audiobooks. Note: 2 cassettes. ISBN no. 1856560430

PRINCESS AND THE GOBLIN (Rose McBain).
MCSET. Cat no: **COL 3003**. Released on Colophone, Sep '81 by AVLS (Audio-Visual Library Services).
MCSET. Cat no: **9056F**. Released on Travellers Tales, '91 by Travellers Tales.

SIR GIBBIE (Tom Flemming).
MCSET. Cat no: **COL 2021**. Released on Colophone, Nov '81 by AVLS (Audio-Visual Library Services).

MacDonald, John

BARRIER ISLAND (Jeremiah Kissel).
MCSET. Cat no: **CAB 403**. Released on Chivers Audio Books, '91 by Chivers Audio Books, Green Dragon Audio Visual. Note: 6 Cassettes
MCSET. Cat no: **1590T**. Released on Travellers Tales, '91 by Travellers Tales. Note: 6 Cassettes.

MacDonald, William

WHEELS IN THE DUST (John Keyworth).
MCSET. Cat no: **1020W**. Released on Travellers Tales, '91 by Travellers Tales. Note: 2 Cassettes.

WHEELS IN THE DUST (Various artists).
MCSET. Cat no: **185496139X**. Released on Bramhope, '91 by Ulverscroft Soundings. Note: 4 cassettes.

McFadden, M

THAT FIRST SUMMER (Unknown narrator(s)).
MCSET. Cat no: **1854963813**. Released on Bramhope, '91 by Ulverscroft Soundings. Note: 5 Cassettes.

McGough, Roger

ESSENTIAL MCGOUGH, THE (Roger McGough).
Note: Advanced release.
MCSET. Cat no: **RC 80**. Released on Random Century, Aug '92 by Random Century Audiobooks, Conifer Records. Note: ISBN No. 1856861104

JELLY PIE (Roger McGough & Brian Patten).
MCSET. Cat no: **CC/042**. Released on Cover to Cover, '87 by Cover to Cover Cassettes.

MacInnes, Helen

ABOVE SUSPICION (Christine Dawe).
MCSET. Cat no: **1245T**. Released on Travellers Tales, '91 by Travellers Tales. Note: 6 Cassettes.
MCSET. Cat no: **1854961403**. Released on Soundings, '91 by Soundings Records, Bond Street Music. Note: 6 Cassettes.

ASSIGNMENT IN BRITTANY (Peter Wheeler).
MCSET. Cat no: **1271T**. Released on Travellers Tales, '91 by Travellers Tales. Note: 8 Cassettes.
MCSET. Cat no: **1854961411**. Released on Soundings, '91 by Soundings Records, Bond Street Music. Note: 8 Cassettes.

CLOAK OF DARKNESS (Rula Lenska).
MCSET. Cat no: **CAB 347**. Released on Chivers Audio Books, '91 by Chivers Audio Books, Green Dragon Audio Visual. Note: 8 Cassettes.
MCSET. Cat no: **1383T**. Released on Travellers Tales, '91 by Travellers Tales. Note: 8 Cassettes.

FRIENDS AND LOVERS (Unknown narrator(s)).
MCSET. Cat no: **185496142X**. Released on Soundings, '91 by Soundings Records, Bond Street Music. Note: 8 Cassettes.

HORIZON (Eric Collinson).
MCSET. Cat no: **1107T**. Released on Travellers Tales, '91 by Travellers Tales. Note: 4 Cassettes.
MCSET. Cat no: **1854961438**. Released on Bramhope,'91 by Ulverscroft Soundings. Note: 4 Cassettes.

NORTH FROM ROME (Rula Lenska).
MCSET. Cat no: **CAB 461**. Released

on Chivers Audio Books, '91 by Chivers Audio Books, Green Dragon Audio Visual. Note: 8 Cassettes.
MCSET. Cat no: **1539T**. Released on Travellers Tales, '91 by Travellers Tales. Note: 8 Cassettes.

PRAY FOR A BRAVE HEART (Bruce Montague).
MCSET. Cat no: **CAB 498**. Released on Chivers Audio Books, '91 by Chivers Audio Books, Green Dragon Audio Visual. Note: 8 Cassettes.
MCSET. Cat no: **1633T**. Released on Travellers Tales, '91 by Travellers Tales. Note: 8 Cassettes.

PRELUDE TO TERROR (William Roberts).
MCSET. Cat no: **CAB 690**. Released on Chivers Audio Books, Apr '92 by Chivers Audio Books, Green Dragon Audio Visual. Note: 10 Cassettes

RIDE A PALE HORSE (Rula Lenska).
MCSET. Cat no: **CAB 155**. Released on Chivers Audio Books, '91 by Chivers Audio Books, Green Dragon Audio Visual. Note: 8 Cassettes
MCSET. Cat no: **1108T**. Released on Travellers Tales, '91 by Travellers Tales. Note: 8 Cassettes.

SALZBURG CONNECTION, THE (Steven Pacey).
MCSET. Cat no: **CAB 645**. Released on Chivers Audio Books, Nov '91 by Chivers Audio Books, Green Dragon Audio Visual. Note: 12 cassettes

SNARE OF THE HUNTER, THE (Rula Lenska).
MCSET. Cat no: **CAB 419**. Released on Chivers Audio Books, '91 by Chivers Audio Books, Green Dragon Audio Visual. Note: 8 Cassettes.
MCSET. Cat no: **1480T**. Released on Travellers Tales, '91 by Travellers Tales. Note: 8 Cassettes.

UNCONQUERABLE, THE (Christopher Kay).
MCSET. Cat no: **1377/1378T**. Released on Travellers Tales, '91 by Travellers Tales. Note: 12 Cassettes.
MCSET. Cat no: **1854961446**. Released on Soundings, '91 by Soundings Records, Bond Street Music. Note: 12 Cassettes.

VENETIAN AFFAIR, THE (Rula Lenska).
MCSET. Cat no: **CAB 556**. Released on Chivers Audio Books, '91 by Chivers Audio Books, Green Dragon Audio Visual. Note: 10 Cassettes.
MCSET. Cat no: **1694/1695T**. Released on Travellers Tales, '91 by Travellers Tales. Note: 10 Cassettes.

Mack, William P.

SOUTH TO JAVA (War in the Pacific) (Nelson Runger).
Note: Authors are William P. Mack and William P. Mack Jr.
MCSET. Cat no: **RB 89650**. Released on Recorded Books, '91 by Isis Audio Books. Note: 10 cassettes.
MCSET. Cat no: **1629/30F**. Released on Travellers Tales, '91 by Travellers Tales. Note: 10 Cassettes.

MacKenzie, Compton

MONARCH OF THE GLEN, THE (Gabriel Woolf).
MCSET. Cat no: **OAS 20492**. Released on Oasis Audio Books, Apr '92 by Isis Audio Books. Note: 8 cassettes. Playing time 10hrs 45mins.

McKie, Anne

TOWN MOUSE AND THE COUNTRY MOUSE, THE (Well Loved Tales Up to Age 9) (Unknown narrator(s)).
Note: Book and cassette.
MC. Cat no: **PLB 66**. Released on Tell-A-Tale, '83 by Pickwick Records, Taylors, Clyde Factors.

MacKinlay, Leila

NO ROOM FOR LONELINESS (Angela Down).
MCSET. Cat no: **1854965727**. Released on Bramhope, Mar '92 by Ulverscroft Soundings. Note: Playing time: 60 minutes.

THIRD BOAT, THE (Anne Dover).
MCSET. Cat no: **1854965581**. Released on Bramhope, Feb '92 by Ulverscroft Soundings. Note: Playing time: 60 minutes.

MacLachlan, Patricia

SARAH, PLAIN AND TALL (Glenn Close).
MC. Cat no: **1793**. Released on Caedmon (USA), '88 by Caedmon Records (USA), Bond Street Music.

MacLaverty, Bernard

GREAT PROFUNDO, THE (And Other Stories) (Denys Hawthorne).
MCSET. Cat no: **1466F**. Released on Travellers Tales, '91 by Travellers Tales. Note: 5 cassettes.
MCSET. Cat no: **OAS 90046**. Released on Oasis Audio Books, '91 by Isis Audio Books. Note: 5 Cassettes.

MacLean, Alistair

ATHABASCA (Joss Ackland).
MCSET. Cat no: **CAB 090**. Released on Chivers Audio Books, '91 by Chivers Audio Books, Green Dragon Audio Visual. Note: 6 Cassettes.
MCSET. Cat no: **1109T**. Released on Travellers Tales, '91 by Travellers Tales. Note: 6 Cassettes.

BREAKHEART PASS (Ed Bishop).
MC. Cat no: **CAB 325**. Released on Chivers Audio Books, '88 by Chivers Audio Books, Green Dragon Audio Visual.
MCSET. Cat no: **1362T**. Released on Travellers Tales, '91 by Travellers Tales. Note: 4 Cassettes.
MCSET. Cat no: **0745128076**. Released on Word For Word, May '92 by Chivers Audio Books.

CARAVAN TO VACCARES (Francis Matthews).
MCSET. Cat no: **CAB 286**. Released on Chivers Audio Books, '91 by Chivers Audio Books, Green Dragon Audio Visual. Note: 6 Cassettes
MCSET. Cat no: **1235T**. Released on Travellers Tales, '91 by Travellers Tales. Note: 6 Cassettes.

CIRCUS (Simon Ward).
MCSET. Cat no: **CAB 047**. Released on Chivers Audio Books, '91 by Chivers Audio Books, Green Dragon Audio Visual. Note: 6 Cassettes.
MCSET. Cat no: **1110T**. Released on Travellers Tales, '91 by Travellers Tales. Note: 6 Cassettes.

FEAR IS THE KEY (Francis Matthews).
MCSET. Cat no: **CAB 548**. Released on Chivers Audio Books, '91 by Chivers Audio Books, Green Dragon Audio Visual. Note: 8 Cassettes.
MCSET. Cat no: **1682T**. Released on Travellers Tales, '91 by Travellers Tales. Note: 8 Cassettes.

GOLDEN RENDEZVOUS, THE (Francis Matthews).
MCSET. Cat no: **CAB 390**. Released on Chivers Audio Books, '91 by Chivers Audio Books, Green Dragon Audio Visual. Note: 8 Cassettes.
MCSET. Cat no: **1481T**. Released on Travellers Tales, '91 by Travellers Tales. Note: 8 Cassettes.

GOODBYE CALIFORNIA (Francis Matthews).
MCSET. Cat no: **CAB 478**. Released on Chivers Audio Books, '91 by Chivers Audio Books, Green Dragon Audio Visual. Note: 10 Cassettes.
MCSET. Cat no: **1540/1541T**. Released on Travellers Tales, '91 by Travellers Tales. Note: 10 Cassettes.

GUNS OF NAVARONE, THE (Patrick Allen).
MC. Cat no: **LFP 41 7150 5**. Released on Listen For Pleasure, May '84 by EMI Records.

H M S ULYSSES (Peter Joyce).
MCSET. Cat no: **1854963414**. Released on Soundings, '91 by Soundings Records, Bond Street Music. Note: 10 Cassettes.
MCSET. Cat no: **1502/3F**. Released on Travellers Tales, '91 by Travellers Tales. Note: 10 Cassettes.

ICE STATION ZEBRA (Steve Hodson).
MCSET. Cat no: **1446T**. Released on Travellers Tales, '91 by Travellers Tales. Note: 8 Cassettes.
MCSET. Cat no: **OAS 89065**. Released on Oasis Audio Books, '91 by Isis Audio Books. Note: 8 Cassettes.

PARTISANS (Francis Matthews).
MCSET. Cat no: **CAB 446**. Released on Chivers Audio Books, '91 by Chivers Audio Books, Green Dragon Audio Visual. Note: 6 Cassettes.
MCSET. Cat no: **1542T**. Released on

Travellers Tales, '91 by Travellers Tales. Note: 6 Cassettes.

PUPPET ON A CHAIN (Francis Matthews).
MCSET. Cat no: **CAB 206**. Released on Chivers Audio Books, '91 by Chivers Audio Books, Green Dragon Audio Visual. Note: 6 Cassettes.
MCSET. Cat no: **1150T**. Released on Travellers Tales, '91 by Travellers Tales. Note: 6 Cassettes.

RIVER OF DEATH (Gordon Griffin).
MCSET. Cat no: **1438T**. Released on Travellers Tales, '91 by Travellers Tales. Note: 4 Cassettes.
MCSET. Cat no: **1854962256**. Released on Bramhope, '91 by Ulverscroft Soundings. Note: 4 Cassettes.

SAN ANDREAS (Alistair Maydon).
MCSET. Cat no: **1634T**. Released on Travellers Tales, '91 by Travellers Tales. Note: 8 Cassettes.
MCSET. Cat no: **OAS 90073**. Released on Oasis Audio Books, '91 by Isis Audio Books. Note: 8 Cassettes.

SANTORINI (Francis Matthews).
MCSET. Cat no: **CAB 232**. Released on Chivers Audio Books, '91 by Chivers Audio Books, Green Dragon Audio Visual. Note: 6 Cassettes.
MCSET. Cat no: **1183T**. Released on Travellers Tales, '91 by Travellers Tales. Note: 6 Cassettes.

SATAN BUG, THE (Oliver Cotton).
MCSET. Cat no: **CAB 680**. Released on Chivers Audio Books, Mar '92 by Chivers Audio Books, Green Dragon Audio Visual. Note: 8 Cassettes.

WHEN EIGHT BELLS TOLL (Hugh Dickson).
MCSET. Cat no: **CAB 615**. Released on Chivers Audio Books, '91 by Chivers Audio Books, Green Dragon Audio Visual. Note: 8 Cassettes.

MacLean, Sorley

BARRAN AGUS ASBHUAIN (Unknown narrator(s)).
LP. Cat no: **CCA 3**. Released on Claddagh (Ireland), Aug '88 by Claddagh Records (Ireland), Projection, Impetus Records, Jazz Music, Roots Records, C.M. Distribution, Outlet Records, Taylors.

McMurty, Larry

BUFFALO GIRLS (Betty Buckley).
MCSET. Cat no: **1027W**. Released on Travellers Tales, '91 by Travellers Tales. Note: 8 Cassettes.
MCSET. Cat no: **0671727818**. Released on Simon & Schuster, '91 by Simon & Schuster Ltd.

LAST PICTURE SHOW, THE (John Randolph Jones).
MCSET. Cat no: **IAB 92036**. Released on Isis Audio Books, Mar '92. Note: 6 cassettes. Playing time 8hrs 45mins.

TERMS OF ENDEARMENT (Barbara Rosenblat).
MCSET. Cat no: **1526/7F**. Released on Travellers Tales, '91 by Travellers Tales. Note: 10 cassettes.
MCSET. Cat no: **IAB 90094**. Released on Isis Audio Books, '91. Note: 10 Cassettes.

McNab, Tom

FAST MEN, THE (John Randolph Jones).
MCSET. Cat no: **RB 89610**. Released on Recorded Books, '91 by Isis Audio Books. Note: 9 cassettes.

McNeile, H.C.

BULLDOG DRUMMOND (Richard Todd).
Note: Abridged version.
MCSET. Cat no: **1385F**. Released on Travellers Tales, '91 by Travellers Tales. Note: 2 cassettes.

BULLDOG DRUMMOND (Richard Todd).
MCSET. Cat no: **418 186-4**. Released on Argo (Polygram), Apr '88 by Poly-Gram Classics **Deleted** Jan '89.
MCSET. Cat no: **ARGO 1088**. Released on Argo (EMI), May '89 by EMI Records **Deleted** '91.

McPherson, Bunty

REEKIN' LUM, THE (And Other Stories) (Bunty McPherson).
Tracks / Introduction / Ailments / Slimming / Tiny's visit to the pictures / Drink and driving / Mains o' yavel's dook / Reekin' lum, The / Johnny at school / Sonia Schnell / Clockin' hen, The / Nod and a wink, A / Prunes / Affectation / Loo, The / John and Tibby's dispute / Parson's cure / Lass o' pairts / Corn, The / Cleaning oot my handbag / R.S.V.P. / Good old days / Auld man's thoughts, An / Something gaun aboot.
MC. Cat no: **CWGR 132**. Released on Ross (1), Oct '89 by Ross Records, Taylors, Celtic Music, Duncans, Record Merchandisers, Terry Blood Dist..

McWilliam, Candia

LITTLE STRANGER, A (Di Langford).
MCSET. Cat no: **1446F**. Released on Travellers Tales, '91 by Travellers Tales. Note: 4 cassettes.
MCSET. Cat no: **OAS 90014**. Released on Oasis Audio Books, '91 by Isis Audio Books. Note: 4 Cassettes.

Madden, Anne Wakefield

DARK OF MOON (Antonia Swinson).
MCSET. Cat no: **MRC 1026**. Released on Chivers Audio Books, '91 by Chivers Audio Books, Green Dragon Audio Visual. Note: 2 cassettes

Maddocks, Pete

JIMBO FLIES TO FRANCE (Peter Hawkins).
Note: Read by the Jimbo character. Book and cassette.
MC. Cat no: **00 1034537**. Released on Tempo, '88 by Warwick Records, Celtic Music, Henry Hadaway Organisation.

JIMBO FLIES TO SPAIN (Peter Hawkins).
Note: Read by the Jimbo character. Book and cassette.
MC. Cat no: **00 1034545**. Released on Tempo, '88 by Warwick Records, Celtic Music, Henry Hadaway Organisation.
Note: Book and tape set

Mahon, Derek

DEREK MAHON READS HIS OWN POETRY (Derek Mahon).
LP. Cat no: **CCT 11**. Released on Claddagh (Ireland), Aug '88 by Claddagh Records (Ireland), Projection, Impetus Records, Jazz Music, Roots Records, C.M. Distribution, Outlet Records, Taylors.

Mahy, Margaret

BIRTHDAY BURGLAR, THE (And a Very Wicked Headmistress) (Richard Mitchley).
MCSET. Cat no: **2CCA 3102**. Released on Chivers Audio Books, '91 by Chivers Audio Books, Green Dragon Audio Visual. Note: 2 Cassettes.
MCSET. Cat no: **9184F**. Released on Travellers Tales, '91 by Travellers Tales. Note: 2 Cassettes.

BLOOD-AND-THUNDER ADVENTURE ON HURRICANE PEAK, THE (Richard Mitchley).
MCSET. Cat no: **2CCA 2135**. Released on Chivers Audio Books, '91 by Chivers Audio Books, Green Dragon Audio Visual. Note: 2 Cassettes.

CHEWING GUM RESCUE, THE (And Other Stories) (Richard Mitchley).
MCSET. Cat no: **3CCA 3037**. Released on Chivers Audio Books, '91 by Chivers Audio Books, Green Dragon Audio Visual. Note: 3 Cassettes.
MCSET. Cat no: **9126F**. Released on Travellers Tales, '91 by Travellers Tales. Note: 3 Cassettes.

GREAT PIRATICAL RUMBUSTIFICATION, THE (Martin Jarvis).
MC. Cat no: **881 530**. Released on Puffin Cover To Cover, Apr '88, Green Dragon Audio Visual.

HAUNTING, THE (Richard Mitchley).
MCSET. Cat no: **3CCA 3010**. Released on Chivers Audio Books, '91 by Chivers Audio Books, Green Dragon Audio Visual. Note: 3 Cassettes.
MCSET. Cat no: **9057F**. Released on Travellers Tales, '91 by Travellers Tales. Note: 3 Cassettes

NONSTOP NONSENSE (Tony Robinson & Jane Asher).
MCSET. Cat no: **2CCA 3096**. Released on Chivers Audio Books, '91 by Chivers Audio Books, Green Dragon Audio Visual. Note: 2 Cassettes.
MCSET. Cat no: **9178F**. Released on Travellers Tales, '91 by Travellers Tales. Note: 2 Cassettes.

PIRATE UNCLE, THE (Richard Mitchley).

MCSET. Cat no: **2CCA 3153.** Released on Chivers Audio Books, '91 by Chivers Audio Books, Green Dragon Audio Visual. Note: 2 Cassettes.
PIRATES' MIXED-UP VOYAGE, THE (Richard Mitchley).
MCSET. Cat no: **3CCA 3079.** Released on Chivers Audio Books, '91 by Chivers Audio Books, Green Dragon Audio Visual. Note: 3 Cassettes.
MCSET. Cat no: **9140F.** Released on Travellers Tales, '91 by Travellers Tales. Note: 3 Cassettes
RAGING ROBOTS AND UNRULY UNCLES (Richard Mitchley).
MCSET. Cat no: **2CCA 3119.** Released on Chivers Audio Books, '91 by Chivers Audio Books, Green Dragon Audio Visual. Note: 2 Cassettes.

Mailer, Norman
ANCIENT EVENINGS (Unknown narrator(s)).
MC. Cat no: **2091.** Released on Caedmon (USA), '88 by Caedmon Records (USA), Bond Street Music.
HARLOT'S GHOST (Norman Mailer).
MCSET. Cat no: **RC 85.** Released on Random Century, Jun '92 by Random Century Audiobooks, Conifer Records. Note: ISBN no. 1856861058
NAKED AND THE DEAD (Unknown narrator(s)).
MC. Cat no: **CDL 51619.** Released on Caedmon (USA), '84 by Caedmon Records (USA), Bond Street Music.
MC. Cat no: **0001071521.** Released on Collins-Caedmon, '91 by Collins Audio, Taylors, Bond Street Music.

Maitland, William
HAIRST GAITHERINS (Various artists).
MC. Cat no: **SSC 090.** Released on Scotsoun, '91 by Scotsoun Recordings, Morley Audio Services.

Malcolm, Alix
FALCON'S LURE (Unknown narrator(s)).
MCSET. Cat no: **1854963554.** Released on Bramhope, '91 by Ulverscroft Soundings. Note: 4 Cassettes.

Malory, Sir Thomas
KASAM (HINDI) (Kishen Bhutani & Rekha Sahaya).
MCSET. Cat no: **SGX 001.** Released on Cover to Cover, '91 by Cover to Cover Cassettes. Note: 2 cassettes.
MORTE D'ARTHUR (Siobhan McKenna).
Note: Quests and adventures are interspersed with episodes of the story of Lancelot and Guinevere.
MC. Cat no: **1374.** Released on Caedmon (USA), '88 by Caedmon Records (USA), Bond Street Music.
MC. Cat no: **0001051903.** Released on Collins-Caedmon, '91 by Collins Audio, Taylors, Bond Street Music.

MORTE D'ARTHUR (Various artists).
MCSET. Cat no: **SAY 46.** Released on Argo (Polygram), Jun '88 by PolyGram Classics **Deleted** Jan '89.

Mandeville, A
BARBIE (Dream Glow Collection) (Unknown narrator(s)).
Note: For ages 7-12. Book and cassette.
MC. Cat no: **PLBB 192.** Released on Tell-A-Tale, '88 by Pickwick Records, Taylors, Clyde Factors.
BARBIE (Mountain Kidnap) (Unknown narrator(s)).
Note: For ages 7-12. Book and cassette.
MC. Cat no: **PLBB 208.** Released on Tell-A-Tale, '88 by Pickwick Records, Taylors, Clyde Factors.
BARBIE (Island Adventure) (Unknown narrator(s)).
Note: For ages 7-12. Book and cassette.
MC. Cat no: **PLBB 209.** Released on Tell-A-Tale, '88 by Pickwick Records, Taylors, Clyde Factors.
BARBIE (Girl with the Golden Hair) (Unknown narrator(s)).
Note: For ages 7-12. Book and cassette.
MC. Cat no: **PLBB 193.** Released on Tell-A-Tale, '88 by Pickwick Records, Taylors, Clyde Factors.

Mann, Jessica
DEATH BEYOND THE NILE (Frances Jeater).
MCSET. Cat no: **1706T.** Released on Travellers Tales, '91 by Travellers Tales. Note: 4 Cassettes.
MCSET. Cat no: **OAS 10591.** Released on Oasis Audio Books, '91 by Isis Audio Books. Note: 4 Cassettes.
GRAVE GOODS (Tammy Ustinov).
MCSET. Cat no: **1111T.** Released on Travellers Tales, '91 by Travellers Tales. Note: 4 Cassettes.
MCSET. Cat no: **OAT 4004.** Released on Chivers Audio Books, '91 by Chivers Audio Books, Green Dragon Audio Visual. Note: 4 cassettes
KIND OF HEALTHY GRAVE, A (Joe Dunlop).
MCSET. Cat no: **1543T.** Released on Travellers Tales, '91 by Travellers Tales. Note: 7 Cassettes.
MCSET. Cat no: **OAS 90034.** Released on Oasis Audio Books, '91 by Isis Audio Books. Note: 7 Cassettes.

Manning, Bernard
LIVE AT THE EMBASSY CLUB (Bernard Manning).
LP. Cat no: **PRX 1.** Released on President, May '77 by President Records, Jazz Music, Taylors, Spartan, Swift, Wellard Dist., Enterprise Distribution.

Manning, Rosemary
GREEN SMOKE (Stan Phillips).

MCSET. Cat no: **3CCA 3140.** Released on Chivers Audio Books, '91 by Chivers Audio Books, Green Dragon Audio Visual. Note: 3 Cassettes.

Manning-Sanders, Ruth
GOBLINS AT THE BATH HOUSE (And Calamander Chest) (Vincent Price).
MC. Cat no: **1574.** Released on Caedmon (USA), '88 by Caedmon Records (USA), Bond Street Music.

Mannix, Dan
MEMOIRS OF A SWORD SWALLOWER (Mickey Dolenz).
MCSET. Cat no: **ZBBC 1157.** Released on BBC Radio Collection, Jul '90 by BBC Records. Note: ISBN No: 0563 410833

Mansfield, Katherine
GARDEN PARTY, THE (Dame Peggy Ashcroft).
Note: Includes "Her First Ball", "The Singing Lesson", "The Daughters of the Late Colonel" and "The Stranger".
MCSET. Cat no: **CTC 004.** Released on Cover to Cover, Jun '85 by Cover to Cover Cassettes. Note: 2 cassettes. Playing time: 2 hrs 5 mins.
MCSET. Cat no: **1104F.** Released on Travellers Tales, '91 by Travellers Tales. Note: 2 cassettes.
GARDEN PARTY, THE (Dame Peggy Ashcroft).
MCSET. Cat no: **ZBBC 1265.** Released on BBC Radio Collection, Aug '91 by BBC Records. Note: ISBN No: 0563 365757

Mantell, Laurie
MURDER IN VAIN (John Hendry).
MCSET. Cat no: **1854964720.** Released on Bramhope, Jul '91 by Ulverscroft Soundings. Note: 5 Cassettes.

March, Stella
BARRIER TO LOVE.
MCSET. Cat no: **SOUND 35.** Released on Soundings, Feb '85 by Soundings Records, Bond Street Music.
BECAUSE OF YESTERDAY (Unknown narrator(s)).
MCSET. Cat no: **1854962264.** Released on Bramhope, '91 by Ulverscroft Soundings. Note: 4 Cassettes.
CARRIAGE FOR FIONA, A (Unknown narrator(s)).
MCSET. Cat no: **SOUND 21.** Released on Soundings, Mar '85 by Soundings Records, Bond Street Music.
CLOUD IN THE SKY, A (Judith Porter).
MCSET. Cat no: **1854965735.** Released on Bramhope, Mar '92 by Ulverscroft Soundings.
CONSULTANT IN LOVE (Unknown narrator(s)).
MCSET. Cat no: **1854962396.** Released on Bramhope, '91 by Ulverscroft

Soundings. Note: 4 cassettes.

DEAR PRETENDER (Unknown narrator(s)).
MCSET. Cat no: **1854961470**. Released on Soundings, '91 by Soundings Records, Bond Street Music. Note: 2 Cassettes.

FLICKERING FLAME, THE (Unknown narrator(s)).
MCSET. Cat no: **1854963627**. Released on Bramhope, '91 by Ulverscroft Soundings. Note: 4 cassettes.

FOR ALL BUT ONE (Margaret Holt).
MCSET. Cat no: **1854964119**. Released on Bramhope, '91 by Ulverscroft Soundings. Note: 5 Cassettes.

MCSET. Cat no: **1681F**. Released on Travellers Tales, '91 by Travellers Tales. Note: 5 Cassettes.

LOVE IN THE AIR (Unknown narrator(s)).
MCSET. Cat no: **1854963937**. Released on Bramhope, '91 by Ulverscroft Soundings. Note: 4 Cassettes.

LOVE WAS THE REASON (Unknown narrator(s)).
MCSET. Cat no: **1854963724**. Released on Bramhope, '91 by Ulverscroft Soundings. Note: 4 Cassettes.

LOVE WILL WAIT (Unknown narrator(s)).
MCSET. Cat no: **1854964038**. Released on Bramhope, '91 by Ulverscroft Soundings. Note: 4 Cassettes.

MISTRESS OF LAMBERLY GRANGE (Anne Cater).
MCSET. Cat no: **1854964828**. Released on Bramhope, Aug '91 by Ulverscroft Soundings. Note: 4 Cassettes.

OUT OF THE SHADOWS (Unknown narrator(s)).
MCSET. Cat no: **1854961489**. Released on Soundings, '91 by Soundings Records, Bond Street Music. Note: 2 Cassettes.

RUNAWAY HEIRESS, THE (Unknown narrator(s)).
MCSET. Cat no: **1854961497**. Released on Soundings, '91 by Soundings Records, Bond Street Music. Note: 2 Cassettes.

SCENT OF HEATHER, THE (Unknown narrator(s)).
MCSET. Cat no: **1854964348**. Released on Soundings, '91 by Soundings Records, Bond Street Music. Note: 4 Cassettes.

SENTIMENTAL JOURNEY (Unknown narrator(s)).
MCSET. Cat no: **1854961500**. Released on Soundings, '91 by Soundings Records, Bond Street Music. Note: 2 Cassettes.

SHADOW OF A DREAM, A (Unknown narrator(s)).
MCSET. Cat no: **1854964461**. Released on Trio, '91 by EMI Records. Note: 3 Cassettes.

SILK FOR MY LADY (Unknown narrator(s)).

MCSET. Cat no: **1854961519**. Released on Trio, '91 by EMI Records. Note: 3 Cassettes.

SING HIGH, SING LOW (Unknown narrator(s)).
MCSET. Cat no: **1854964941**. Released on Bramhope, '91 by Ulverscroft Soundings. Note: 4 Cassettes.

TO MYSELF A STRANGER (Margaret Holt).
MCSET. Cat no: **1854965883**. Released on Bramhope, Apr '92 by Ulverscroft Soundings. Note: Playing time: 60 minutes.

WRONG DOCTOR, THE (Unknown narrator(s)).
MCSET. Cat no: **1854961527**. Released on Soundings, '91 by Soundings Records, Bond Street Music. Note: 2 Cassettes.

Marchant, Catherine

FEN TIGER, THE (Anne Dover).
MCSET. Cat no: **1680F**. Released on Travellers Tales, '91 by Travellers Tales. Note: 8 cassettes.

MCSET. Cat no: **1854964127**. Released on Bramhope, '91 by Ulverscroft Soundings. Note: 8 cassettes.

HOUSE OF MEN (Geraldine Somerville).
MCSET. Cat no: **CAB 636**. Released on Chivers Audio Books, Oct '91 by Chivers Audio Books, Green Dragon Audio Visual. Note: 6 Cassettes.

MISS MARTHA MARY CRAWFORD (Anne Dover).
MCSET. Cat no: **1854965654**. Released on Soundings, Mar '92 by Soundings Records, Bond Street Music. Note: 7 cassettes.

SLOW AWAKENING, THE (Unknown narrator(s)).
MCSET. Cat no: **1854965247**. Released on Soundings, '91 by Soundings Records, Bond Street Music. Note: 5 Cassettes.

Mark, Jan

FRANKIE'S HAT (Judy Bennett).
MCSET. Cat no: **2CCA 3021**. Released on Chivers Audio Books, '91 by Chivers Audio Books, Green Dragon Audio Visual. Note: 2 Cassettes.

MCSET. Cat no: **9058F**. Released on Travellers Tales, '91 by Travellers Tales. Note: 2 Cassettes.

HAIRS IN THE PALM OF THE HAND (Tony Robinson).
MC. Cat no: **2CCA 3061**. Released on Chivers Audio Books, '88 by Chivers Audio Books, Green Dragon Audio Visual. Note: 2 Cassettes.

NOTHING TO BE AFRAID OF (Lynda Bellingham).
MCSET. Cat no: **2CCA 3097**. Released on Chivers Audio Books, '91 by Chivers Audio Books, Green Dragon Audio Visual. Note: 2 Cassettes.

MCSET. Cat no: **9179F**. Released on Travellers Tales, '91 by Travellers Tales. Note: 2 Cassettes.

THUNDER AND LIGHTNINGS (Andy Crane).
MCSET. Cat no: **3CCA 3138**. Released on Chivers Audio Books, '91 by Chivers Audio Books, Green Dragon Audio Visual. Note: 3 Cassettes.

Marlowe, Christopher

DOCTOR FAUSTUS (Peter Jeffrey & Timothy Bateson).
MCSET. Cat no: **LD 2**. Released on Green Dragon, '91 by Green Dragon Audio Visual. Note: 2 Cassettes.

DOCTOR FAUSTUS (Various artists).
MC. Cat no: **1033**. Released on Caedmon (USA), '88 by Caedmon Records (USA), Bond Street Music.

EDWARD II (Various artists).
Note: With Ian McKellan, Timothy West and others.
MCSET. Cat no: **SAY 82**. Released on Argo (Polygram), Oct '83 by PolyGram Classics **Deleted** Jan '89.
MCSET. Cat no: **1006P**. Released on Travellers Tales, '91 by Travellers Tales. Note: 2 Cassettes.

Marsh, Ngaio

CLUTCH OF CONSTABLES (James Saxon).
MCSET. Cat no: **CAB 355**. Released on Chivers Audio Books, '91 by Chivers Audio Books, Green Dragon Audio Visual. Note: 6 Cassettes.

MCSET. Cat no: **1387T**. Released on Travellers Tales, '91 by Travellers Tales. Note: 6 Cassettes.

DEAD WATER (James Saxon).
MCSET. Cat no: **CAB 280**. Released on Chivers Audio Books, '91 by Chivers Audio Books, Green Dragon Audio Visual. Note: 6 Cassettes.

MCSET. Cat no: **1231T**. Released on Travellers Tales, '91 by Travellers Tales. Note: 6 Cassettes.

DEATH IN ECSTASY (James Saxon).
MCSET. Cat no: **CAB 597**. Released on Chivers Audio Books, '91 by Chivers Audio Books, Green Dragon Audio Visual. Note: 8 Cassettes.

MCSET. Cat no: **1735T**. Released on Travellers Tales, '91 by Travellers Tales. Note: 8 Cassettes.

GRAVE MISTAKE (Jane Asher).
MCSET. Cat no: **CAB 144**. Released on Chivers Audio Books, '91 by Chivers Audio Books, Green Dragon Audio Visual. Note: 8 cassettes.

MCSET. Cat no: **1113T**. Released on Travellers Tales, '91 by Travellers Tales. Note: 8 Cassettes.

HAND IN GLOVE (Jeremy Sinden).
MCSET. Cat no: **CAB 196**. Released on Chivers Audio Books, '91 by Chivers Audio Books, Green Dragon Audio Visual. Note: 6 Cassettes.

MCSET. Cat no: **1156T**. Released on Travellers Tales, '91 by Travellers Tales. Note: 6 Cassettes.

NURSING HOME MURDER, THE (James Saxon).
MCSET. Cat no: **CAB 691.** Released on Chivers Audio Books, Apr '92 by Chivers Audio Books, Green Dragon Audio Visual. Note: 6 Cassettes.

OPENING NIGHT (James Saxon).
MCSET. Cat no: **CAB 530.** Released on Chivers Audio Books, '91 by Chivers Audio Books, Green Dragon Audio Visual. Note: 6 Cassettes.
MCSET. Cat no: **1648T.** Released on Travellers Tales, '91 by Travellers Tales. Note: 6 Cassettes.

SCALES OF JUSTICE (James Saxon).
MCSET. Cat no: **CAB 252.** Released on Chivers Audio Books, '91 by Chivers Audio Books, Green Dragon Audio Visual. Note: 6 Cassettes.
MCSET. Cat no: **1195T.** Released on Travellers Tales, '91 by Travellers Tales. Note: 6 Cassettes.

TIED UP IN TINSEL (James Saxon).
MCSET. Cat no: **CAB 412.** Released on Chivers Audio Books, '91 by Chivers Audio Books, Green Dragon Audio Visual. Note: 6 Cassettes.
MCSET. Cat no: **1482T.** Released on Travellers Tales, '91 by Travellers Tales. Note: 6 Cassettes.

WHEN IN ROME (James Saxon).
MCSET. Cat no: **CAB 466.** Released on Chivers Audio Books, '91 by Chivers Audio Books, Green Dragon Audio Visual. Note: 8 Cassettes.
MCSET. Cat no: **1544T.** Released on Travellers Tales, '91 by Travellers Tales. Note: 8 Cassettes.

Marshall, Catherine

MACCORMAC CONSPIRACY, THE (Alison Skilbeck).
MCSET. Cat no: **MRC 1059.** Released on Chivers Audio Books, '91 by Chivers Audio Books, Green Dragon Audio Visual. Note: 2 cassettes.

Martin, Steve

WILD AND CRAZY GUY (Steve Martin).
Tracks / Wild and crazy guy / I'm feelin' it / Philosophy/religion/college/language / Creativity in action / I'm in the mood for love / Charitable kind of guy / Expose / Cat handcuffs / You naive Americans / My real name / King Tut.
LP. Cat no: **K 56573.** Released on Warner Bros., Jun '80 by Warner Music International (WEA), Solomon & Peres **Deleted** '85.

Marx, Groucho

ON RADIO (Groucho Marx).
MC. Cat no: **CMR 1072.** Released on Derann Trax, Aug '91 by Pinnacle.
CD. Cat no: **CDMR 1072.** Released on Derann Trax, Aug '91 by Pinnacle.

Mason, A.E.W.

FOUR FEATHERS (Martin Heller).
MCSET. Cat no: **COL 4003.** Released on Colophone, Jun '81 by AVLS (Audio-Visual Library Services).
MCSET. Cat no: **1114T.** Released on Travellers Tales, '91 by Travellers Tales. Note: 4 Cassettes.

Mason, Jackie

BRAND NEW (Jackie Mason).
Tracks / Opening observations / Newscasters and personalities / Israelis, terrorists and Arabs / Jew's discussion in the lobby / Intermission / Health and sickness / Food fads and status / Gentiles and Jews / Difference, The.
MC. Cat no: **4692914.** Released on Columbia, Dec '91 by Sony Music.
CD. Cat no: **4692912.** Released on Columbia, Dec '91 by Sony Music.

I'M THE GREATEST COMEDIAN IN THE WORLD (Jackie Mason).
LP. Cat no: **839 675 1.** Released on Polydor, Jun '89 by Polydor Ltd, Solomon & Peres **Deleted** Sep '90.
MC. Cat no: **839 675 4.** Released on Polydor, Jun '89 by Polydor Ltd, Solomon & Peres.

Masters, John

BHOWANI JUNCTION (Various artists).
Note: Read by Patrick Tull, Neil Hunt and Jill Tanner.
MCSET. Cat no: **IAB 89083.** Released on Isis Audio Books, '91. Note: 12 Cassettes.

BHOWANI JUNCTION (Patrick Tull).
MCSET. Cat no: **1402/3F.** Released on Travellers Tales, '91 by Travellers Tales. Note: 12 cassettes.

BHOWANI JUNCTION (Various artists).
MCSET. Cat no: **ZBBC 1105.** Released on BBC Radio Collection, May '90 by BBC Records. Note: ISBN No: 0563 410027

BIT OF A DO, A (John Rowe).
MCSET. Cat no: **ZBBC 1132.** Released on BBC Audio Collection, Aug '90 by BBC Records. Note: ISBN No: 0563 410744.

DECEIVERS, THE (Patrick Tull).
MCSET. Cat no: **1607F.** Released on Travellers Tales, '91 by Travellers Tales. Note: 8 cassettes.
MCSET. Cat no: **RB 90084.** Released on Recorded Books, '91 by Isis Audio Books. Note: 8 Cassettes.

Masterton, Barbara

MRS MILSENT'S DAUGHTER (Anne Dover).
MCSET. Cat no: **1854965433.** Released on Bramhope, '92 by Ulverscroft Soundings.

Mather, Anne

FOR THE LOVE OF SARA (Georgina Melville).
MCSET. Cat no: **PMB 001.** Released on Mills & Boon, '88. Note: 2 cassettes.

Matthew, Christopher

DIARY OF A SOMEBODY (Christopher Matthew).
MCSET. Cat no: **ZBBC 1111.** Released on BBC, 5 Mar '90 by BBC Records, Taylors. Note: ISBN No: 0563 410272. 2 cassettes.

JUNKET MAN, THE (Martin Jarvis).
MCSET. Cat no: **1105F.** Released on Travellers Tales, '91 by Travellers Tales. Note: 6 cassettes.
MCSET. Cat no: **CAB 174.** Released on Chivers Audio Books, '91 by Chivers Audio Books, Green Dragon Audio Visual. Note: 6 cassettes.

Maugham, W. Somerset

ASHENDEN (British agent) (Neil Hunt).
MCSET. Cat no: **IAB 90104.** Released on Isis Audio Books, '91. Note: 8 Cassettes. Playing time 9hrs.
MCSET. Cat no: **1528F.** Released on Travellers Tales, '91 by Travellers Tales. Note: 8 cassettes.

CAKES AND ALE (James Saxon).
MCSET. Cat no: **CAB 202.** Released on Chivers Audio Books, '91 by Chivers Audio Books, Green Dragon Audio Visual. Note: 6 Cassettes.
MCSET. Cat no: **1185F.** Released on Travellers Tales, '91 by Travellers Tales. Note: 6 cassettes.

COLONEL'S LADY, THE (And Lord Mountdrago) (Hugh Burden).
MC. Cat no: **TTC/M10.** Released on Talking Tape Company, '88, Conifer Records.

FACTS OF LIFE, THE (Hugh Burden).
MC. Cat no: **TTC/WSM 4.** Released on Talking Tape Company, '84, Conifer Records.

GIGOLO AND GIGOLETTE (And The Facts Of Life) (Hugh Burden).
MC. Cat no: **TTC/WSM 1.** Released on Talking Tape Company, Sep '84, Conifer Records.

LORD MOUNTDRAGO (Hugh Burden).
MC. Cat no: **TTC/WSM 2.** Released on Talking Tape Company, '84, Conifer Records.

LOTUS EATER, THE (Alan Howard).
MC. Cat no: **CDL 51663.** Released on Caedmon (USA), May '82 by Caedmon Records (USA), Bond Street Music.

MOON AND SIXPENCE, THE (Robert Hardy).
MCSET. Cat no: **1111F.** Released on Travellers Tales, '91 by Travellers Tales. Note: 6 cassettes.

MOON AND SIXPENCE, THE (Frank Langella).
MCSET. Cat no: **2096.** Released on Caedmon (USA), '88 by Caedmon Records (USA), Bond Street Music.

POINT OF HONOUR, THE (Hugh Burden).
MC. Cat no: **TTC/WSM 3.** Released on

Talking Tape Company, '84, Conifer Records.

SHORT STORIES (Hugh Burden).
MCSET. Cat no: **LFP 7442**. Released on Listen For Pleasure, Oct '89 by EMI Records. Note: Playing time: 2 hours 30 minutes.
MCSET. Cat no: **1219F**. Released on Travellers Tales, '91 by Travellers Tales. Note: 6 cassettes.

SHORT STORIES (Volume 2) (Tony Britton & Hugh Burden).
Note: Running time: 3 hours approx.
MCSET. Cat no: **LFP 7466**. Released on Listen For Pleasure, Jun '90 by EMI Records.

THREE FAT WOMEN OF ANTIBES (Hugh Burden).
MC. Cat no: **TTCWSM 6**. Released on Talking Tape Company, '84, Conifer Records.

Maxwell, Gavin
RING OF BRIGHT WATER (David Rintoul).
MCSET. Cat no: **CAB 540**. Released on Chivers Audio Books, '91 by Chivers Audio Books, Green Dragon Audio Visual. Note: 6 Cassettes.
MCSET. Cat no: **1644F**. Released on Travellers Tales, '91 by Travellers Tales. Note: 6 cassettes.

Mayle, Peter
YEAR IN PROVENCE, A (Peter Mayle).
MCSET. Cat no: **ZBBC 1218**. Released on BBC Radio Collection, Jul '91 by BBC Records. Note: ISBN No: 0563 409886

Mayne, William
KELPIE (Siobhan Redmond).
MCSET. Cat no: **2CCA 3050**. Released on Chivers Audio Books, '91 by Chivers Audio Books, Green Dragon Audio Visual. Note: 2 Cassettes.
MCSET. Cat no: **9116F**. Released on Travellers Tales, '91 by Travellers Tales. Note: 2 Cassettes.

Melville, Herman
BILLY BUDD (George Rose).
MC. Cat no: **CDL 51653**. Released on Caedmon (USA), '81 by Caedmon Records (USA), Bond Street Music.

BILLY BUDD, FORETOPMAN (Frank Muller).
MCSET. Cat no: **RB 81030**. Released on Recorded Books, '91 by Isis Audio Books. Note: 3 cassettes. Playing time 3hrs.

MOBY DICK (Charlton Heston).
MC. Cat no: **2077**. Released on Caedmon (USA), '88 by Caedmon Records (USA), Bond Street Music.

MOBY DICK (George Kennedy).
MCSET. Cat no: **LFP 7240**. Released on Listen For Pleasure, Jul '86 by EMI Records.

MOBY DICK (Joss Ackland).
Note: For 8 to 16 year olds.

MC. Cat no: **C 003**. Released on Green Dragon, '91 by Green Dragon Audio Visual.

MOBY DICK (George Kennedy).
Note: Abridged version.
MCSET. Cat no: **1114F**. Released on Travellers Tales, '91 by Travellers Tales. Note: 2 cassettes.

Meynell, Laurence
HOOKY AND THE VILLAINOUS CHAFFEUR (Garard Green).
MCSET. Cat no: **IAB 91126**. Released on Isis Audio Books, Dec '91. Note: 7 Cassettes. Playing time: 7 hours

Mhac An Saoi, Maire
OMOS DO SCOIL DHUN CHAOIN (Unknown narrator(s)).
LP. Cat no: **CCT 8**. Released on Claddagh (Ireland), Aug '88 by Claddagh Records (Ireland), Projection, Impetus Records, C.M. Distribution, Outlet Records, Taylors.

Michaels, Barbara
BE BURIED IN THE RAIN (Pat Starr).
MCSET. Cat no: **1196T**. Released on Travellers Tales, '91 by Travellers Tales. Note: 8 Cassettes.
MCSET. Cat no: **CAB 249**. Released on Chivers Audio Books, '91 by Chivers Audio Books, Green Dragon Audio Visual. Note: 8 Cassettes.

BLACK RAINBOW (Barbara Rosenblat).
MCSET. Cat no: **IAB 92078**. Released on Isis Audio Books, Jul '92. Note: 8 Cassettes. Playing time: 10 hours, 15 mins

INTO THE DARKNESS (Pat Starr).
MCSET. Cat no: **CAB 692**. Released on Chivers Audio Books, Apr '92 by Chivers Audio Books, Green Dragon Audio Visual. Note: 10 Cassettes.

MASTER OF BLACKTOWER, THE (Phyllis Logan).
MCSET. Cat no: **CAB 300**. Released on Chivers Audio Books, '91 by Chivers Audio Books, Green Dragon Audio Visual. Note: 6 Cassettes.
MCSET. Cat no: **1135R**. Released on Travellers Tales, '91 by Travellers Tales. Note: 6 Cassettes.

SEARCH THE SHADOWS (Bonnie Hurren).
MCSET. Cat no: **CAB 531**. Released on Chivers Audio Books, '91 by Chivers Audio Books, Green Dragon Audio Visual. Note: 10 Cassettes.
MCSET. Cat no: **1539/40F**. Released on Travellers Tales, '91 by Travellers Tales. Note: 10 cassettes.

SHATTERED SILK (Pat Starr).
MCSET. Cat no: **CAB 375**. Released on Chivers Audio Books, '91 by Chivers Audio Books, Green Dragon Audio Visual. Note: 8 Cassettes.
MCSET. Cat no: **1141R**. Released on Travellers Tales, '91 by Travellers Tales. Note: 8 Cassettes.

SMOKE AND MIRRORS (Pat Starr).
MCSET. Cat no: **CAB 438**. Released on Chivers Audio Books, '91 by Chivers Audio Books, Green Dragon Audio Visual. Note: 10 cassettes.
MCSET. Cat no: **1595/1596T**. Released on Travellers Tales, '91 by Travellers Tales. Note: 10 Cassettes.

SONS OF THE WOLF (Ciaran Madden).
MCSET. Cat no: **CAB 479**. Released on Chivers Audio Books, '91 by Chivers Audio Books, Green Dragon Audio Visual. Note: 6 Cassettes.
MCSET. Cat no: **1546T**. Released on Travellers Tales, '91 by Travellers Tales. Note: 6 Cassettes.

Millay, Edna
MILLAY READING HER POETRY (Edna Millay).
Note: Including *Renascence, Recuerdo, This Beast That Rends Me, Love Is Not All, I Must Not Die of Pity, God's World.*
MC. Cat no: **1123**. Released on Caedmon (USA), '88 by Caedmon Records (USA), Bond Street Music.

Miller, Arthur
CRUCIBLE, THE (Various artists).
MCSET. Cat no: **0356**. Released on Caedmon (USA), '88 by Caedmon Records (USA), Bond Street Music. Note: 4 cassettes

DEATH OF A SALESMAN (Various artists).
MCSET. Cat no: **0310**. Released on Caedmon (USA), '88 by Caedmon Records (USA), Bond Street Music. Note: 2 cassettes

Miller, Max
ALL GOOD STUFF, MARY (Max Miller).
Tracks / Mary from the dairy / Woman improver / Ophelia / Down in the valley / Old oak tree / Put it down / I never thought that she'd do that to me / Let's all have a charabanc ride / Ain't love grand / Annie the farmer's daughter / She said she wouldn't / I'm the only bit of comfort that she's got / Every Sunday afternoon / Um-ta-ra-ra / I bought a horse / Does she still remember / Everything happens to me / At the bathing parade / She'll never be the same again / No, no, no.
LP. Cat no: **NTS 214**. Released on Note, Sep '80 by EMI Records **Deleted** Sep '85.

Milligan, Spike
COLLECTION OF SPIKES, A (Spike Milligan).
Tracks / Q 5 piano tune, The / Ning nang nong / Python, The / Silly old baboon / Call up / Purple aeroplane / Another lot / Sewers of the strand, The / Frank J. Itchikutchi / Brass band samba / My darling little baby / Nothing at all / I've got a photograph of you /

Postman's knock / Sex, food and a pig / Wormwood scrubs tango / Cougher royal / Morning in Puckoon / Tower bridge / Word power / You gotta go oww! / Escape / Fun, fun, fun / Wish I knew / Father Rudden / Silent night / Hit parade / RAF interview / Underneath it all / Good King Eccleslas / Q8 theme / Finale / Q8 theme reprise / Will I find my love today / After lights out / Ning nang nong / I'm walking out with a mountain / Woe is me / Puckoon flyer, The / My September love / Hippo rhinostricow / Power of licorice, The / Have they gone / Australia.
MCSET. Cat no: **ECC 11.** Released on EMI, Oct '90 by EMI Records.

EVENING WITH SPIKE MILLIGAN (Spike Milligan).
LP. Cat no: **MFP 50408.** Released on MFP, Jan '78 by EMI Records, Solomon & Peres **Deleted** '83.

MILLIGAN PRESERVED (Spike Milligan).
LP. Cat no: **PMC 1152.** Released on Parlophone, Nov '61 by EMI Records, Solomon & Peres **Deleted** Nov '66.

PUCKOON (And Adolf Hitler - My Part in his Downfall) (Spike Milligan). Tracks / Adolf Hitler - my part in his downfall / Puckoon - part one / Ah well Isobel (theme music) / Puckoon - part two.
Note: Puckoon also features T.P. McKenna, Dermot Kelly etc. Adolf Hitler - My Part In His Downfall also features John Wells, Graham Stark & Alan Clare.
MCSET. Cat no: **ECC 24.** Released on EMI, Feb '92 by EMI Records.

SNOW GOOSE, THE (Spike Milligan).
Tracks / Marshland theme, The / Rhayader's theme / Snow goose theme, The / Fritha's theme / Goose walk, The / Walking by the sea / Lonely man / Goose conversation / Sailing.
LP. Cat no: **RS 1088.** Released on RCA, Dec '76 by BMG Records (UK) Ltd., Solomon & Peres, Outlet Records **Deleted** Dec '81.

MC. Cat no: **PK 11765.** Released on RCA, Dec '76 by BMG Records (UK) Ltd., Solomon & Peres, Outlet Records **Deleted** Dec '81.

UNSPUN SOCKS FROM A CHICKENS LAUNDRY (Spike Milligan).
LP. Cat no: **SPIKE L1.** Released on Spike, Oct '82.
MC. Cat no: **SPIKE C1.** Released on Spike, Oct '82.

WOLVES, WITCHES AND GIANTS (Spike Milligan).
LP. Cat no: **MIL 2.** Released on Impression, Nov '84.
MC. Cat no: **TCMIL 2.** Released on Impression, Nov '84.

Milne, A.A.

HOUSE AT POOH CORNER (Part 1) (Unknown narrator(s)).
MCSET. Cat no: **DTO 10553.** Released on Ditto, '88 by Pickwick Records, Midland Records.
HOUSE AT POOH CORNER (Part 2) (Unknown narrator(s)).
MCSET. Cat no: **DTO 10554.** Released on Ditto, '88 by Pickwick Records, Midland Records.
HOUSE AT POOH CORNER (Lionel Jeffries).
MCSET. Cat no: **LFP 7079.** Released on Listen For Pleasure, Jan '84 by EMI Records.
MCSET. Cat no: **9059F.** Released on Travellers Tales, '91 by Travellers Tales. Note: 2 Cassettes.
HOUSE AT POOH CORNER (Norman Shelly).
MCSET. Cat no: **SAY 96.** Released on Argo (Polygram), Nov '83 by PolyGram Classics **Deleted** Jan '89.
MCSET. Cat no: **ARGO 1121.** Released on Argo (EMI), Sep '89 by EMI Records. Note: 2 Cassettes.
HOUSE AT POOH CORNER (Dame Judith Anderson).
MC. Cat no: **1670.** Released on Caedmon (USA), Sep '88 by Caedmon Records (USA), Bond Street Music.
NOW WE ARE SIX (Unknown narrator(s)).
MCSET. Cat no: **DTO 10563.** Released on Ditto, '88 by Pickwick Records, Midland Records.
WHEN WE WERE VERY YOUNG (Dame Judith Anderson).
MC. Cat no: **1356.** Released on Caedmon (USA), '88 by Caedmon Records (USA), Bond Street Music.
WHEN WE WERE VERY YOUNG (And Now We Are Six) (Norman Shelly).
MCSET. Cat no: **9060F.** Released on Travellers Tales, '91 by Travellers Tales. Note: 2 Cassettes
WHEN WE WERE VERY YOUNG (Norman Shelly).
MCSET. Cat no: **SAY 97.** Released on Argo (Polygram), Mar '84 by PolyGram Classics **Deleted** Jan '89.
WHEN WE WERE VERY YOUNG (Unknown narrator(s)).
MCSET. Cat no: **DTO 10560.** Released on Ditto, '88 by Pickwick Records, Midland Records.
WINNIE THE POOH (Super Soundbook) (Dame Judith Anderson).
MCSET. Cat no: **702.** Released on Caedmon (USA), Sep '88 by Caedmon Records (USA), Bond Street Music.
WINNIE THE POOH (Lionel Jeffries).
MCSET. Cat no: **LFP 7052.** Released on Listen For Pleasure, Jan '84 by EMI Records.
MCSET. Cat no: **9061F.** Released on Travellers Tales, '91 by Travellers Tales. Note: 2 Cassettes.
WINNIE THE POOH (Dame Judith Anderson).
MC. Cat no: **1408.** Released on Caedmon (USA), Sep '88 by Caedmon Records (USA), Bond Street Music.
WINNIE THE POOH (Alan Bennett).
LP. Cat no: **REC 528.** Released on BBC, Sep '84 by BBC Records, Taylors **Deleted** 31 Aug '88.
MC. Cat no: **ZCM 528.** Released on BBC, Sep '84 by BBC Records, Taylors **Deleted** 31 Aug '88.
WINNIE THE POOH (And The House At Pooh Corner) (Alan Bennett).
MCSET. Cat no: **ZBBC 1001.** Released on BBC, '88 by BBC Records, Taylors. Note: ISBN No: 0563 225521
WINNIE THE POOH (And Wind in the Willows) (Various artists).
MCSET. Cat no: **0563365889.** Released on BBC, Nov '91 by BBC Records, Taylors.
WINNIE THE POOH (Norman Shelly).
MCSET. Cat no: **SAY 95.** Released on Argo (Polygram), Oct '83 by PolyGram Classics **Deleted** Jan '89.
MCSET. Cat no: **ARGO 1055.** Released on Argo (EMI), May '89 by EMI Records. Note: 2 Cassettes.
WINNIE THE POOH (Part 1) (Unknown narrator(s)).
MCSET. Cat no: **DTO 10548.** Released on Ditto, '88 by Pickwick Records, Midland Records.
WINNIE THE POOH (Part 2) (Unknown narrator(s)).
MCSET. Cat no: **DTO 10549.** Released on Ditto, '88 by Pickwick Records, Midland Records.
WINNIE THE POOH (Selected Stories) (Norman Shelly).
MC. Cat no: **0600560864.** Released on Hamlyn Books On Tape, '88, Bond Street Music.
WINNIE THE POOH AND CHRISTOPHER ROBIN (Unknown narrator(s)).
MC. Cat no: **1743.** Released on Caedmon (USA), '84 by Caedmon Records (USA), Bond Street Music.
WINNIE THE POOH AND CHRISTOPHER ROBIN (Dame Judith Anderson).
MC. Cat no: **1744.** Released on Caedmon (USA), Sep '88 by Caedmon Records (USA), Bond Street Music.
WINNIE THE POOH AND EEYORE (Unknown narrator(s)).
MC. Cat no: **1747.** Released on Caedmon (USA), Sep '88 by Caedmon Records (USA), Bond Street Music.
WINNIE THE POOH AND KANGA AND ROO (Dame Judith Anderson).
MC. Cat no: **1685.** Released on Caedmon (USA), Sep '88 by Caedmon Records (USA), Bond Street Music.
WINNIE THE POOH AND THE BLUSTERY DAY (Unknown narrator(s)).
MC. Cat no: **DIS 007.** Released on Disney (Read-a-long), Jul '90 by Disneyland Records.

WINNIE THE POOH AND THE HONEY TREE (Various artists).
LP. Cat no: **D 313**. Released on Disneyland, Dec '82 by Disneyland-Vista Records (USA).
MC. Cat no: **D 21DC**. Released on Disneyland, Dec '82 by Disneyland-Vista Records (USA).

WINNIE THE POOH AND TIGGER (Unknown narrator(s)).
MC. Cat no: **CP 1696**. Released on Caedmon (USA), Sep '82 by Caedmon Records (USA), Bond Street Music.
MC. Cat no: **1696**. Released on Caedmon (USA), Sep '88 by Caedmon Records (USA), Bond Street Music.

WINNIE THE POOH AND TIGGER TOO (Various artists).
LP. Cat no: **D 366**. Released on Disneyland, Dec '82 by Disneyland-Vista Records (USA).
MC. Cat no: **D 10DC**. Released on Disneyland, Dec '82 by Disneyland-Vista Records (USA).

Milton, John

COMUS (And Samson Agonistes) (John Westbrook).
MCSET. Cat no: **OAS 89115**. Released on Oasis Audio Books, '91 by Isis Audio Books. Note: 3 cassettes. Playing time 3hrs 45mins.
MCSET. Cat no: **1034Y**. Released on Travellers Tales, '91 by Travellers Tales. Note: 3 Cassettes.

EXTRACTS FROM PARADISE LOST (Various artists).
Note: Read by Tony Church, Michael Redgrave and Prunella Scales.
MCSET. Cat no: **1012Y**. Released on Travellers Tales, '91 by Travellers Tales. Note: 2 cassettes.

PARADISE LOST (Various artists).
MCSET. Cat no: **414 736-4**. Released on Argo (Polygram), Apr '85 by PolyGram Classics **Deleted** Jan '89.

PARADISE LOST (Books 1-4) (Anthony Quayle).
MC. Cat no: **4004**. Released on Caedmon (USA), '88 by Caedmon Records (USA), Bond Street Music.

Ming, Sexton

MAN WHO CREATED HIMSELF, THE (Unknown narrator(s)).
LP. Cat no: **WORDUP 002**. Released on Hangman, Jun '88 by Hangman Records, Cartel.

Miscellaneous

CYCLE OF THE WEST (John Neilhardt).
MC. Cat no: **CDL 51665**. Released on Caedmon (USA), Oct '81 by Caedmon Records (USA), Bond Street Music.

DAWN OF LOVE, THE (John Carson).
MC. Cat no: **PTB 609**. Released on Pickwick Talking Books, '83 by Pickwick Records, Clyde Factors..

HANDS OFF (And the Monkey's Paw) (John Graham).
MC. Cat no: **NF 10**. Released on Nightfall Tapes, '89 by BMG Records (UK) Ltd..

JIVE BUNNY FINDS FAME (Unknown narrator(s)).
MC. Cat no: **JBM 001**. Released on Jive Bunny, Nov '90.

JIVE BUNNY SAVES THE DAY (Unknown narrator(s)).
MC. Cat no: **JBM 002**. Released on Jive Bunny, Nov '90.

MAPLE TOWN (The Lonely Eagle) (Unknown narrator(s)).
MC. Cat no: **STK 011**. Released on Stick-A-Tale, Jan '89 by Pickwick Records.

MAPLE TOWN (The Treasure Map) (Unknown narrator(s)).
MC. Cat no: **STK 012**. Released on Stick-A-Tale, Jan '89 by Pickwick Records.

PHANTOM OF THE LAKE (Various artists).
MC. Cat no: **TCFWM 1545494**. Released on Fun With Music, Jul '83 **Deleted** Jul '88.

SNITCHNOSE SWITCH (Various artists).
MC. Cat no: **STK 030**. Released on Stick-A-Tale, Jul '90 by Pickwick Records.

SPACE BOAT, THE (Unknown narrator(s)).
MC. Cat no: **RWM 004**. Released on Tell-A-Tale, Sep '90 by Pickwick Records, Taylors, Clyde Factors.

SPECIAL PRESENT, THE (Unknown narrator(s)).
MC. Cat no: **PLBG 286**. Released on Tell-A-Tale, Jul '90 by Pickwick Records, Taylors, Clyde Factors.

TIME FOR TEA (Miriam Margoyles).
MC. Cat no: **00 1021524**. Released on Tempo, '88 by Warwick Records, Celtic Music, Henry Hadaway Organisation.

WITCHES REVENGE, THE (Unknown narrator(s)).
MC. Cat no: **DTO 10567**. Released on Ditto, '88 by Pickwick Records, Midland Records.

WOOLLY RHINO, THE (Norman Shelly).
LP. Cat no: **ZDSW 729**. Released on Argo, Sep '79 by Decca International **Deleted** '84.

Mitchell, James

DEAD ERNEST (Peter Joyce).
MCSET. Cat no: **1572T**. Released on Travellers Tales, '91 by Travellers Tales. Note: 5 Cassettes.
MCSET. Cat no: **1854963139**. Released on Bramhope, '91 by Ulverscroft Soundings. Note: 5 Cassettes.

WHEN THE BOAT COMES IN (Christopher Kay).
MCSET. Cat no: **1117F**. Released on Travellers Tales, '91 by Travellers Tales. Note: 4 cassettes.
MCSET. Cat no: **1854961535**. Released on Bramhope, '91 by Ulverscroft Soundings. Note: 4 Cassettes.

Mitford, Nancy

HIGHLAND FLING (Carol Marsh).
MCSET. Cat no: **IAB 92075**. Released on Isis Audio Books, Jul '92. Note: 6 Cassettes. Playing time: 8 1/2 hours.

LOVE IN A COLD CLIMATE (Patricia Hodge).
MCSET. Cat no: **CAB 295**. Released on Chivers Audio Books, Apr '88 by Chivers Audio Books, Green Dragon Audio Visual. Note: 6 Cassettes.
MCSET. Cat no: **1292F**. Released on Travellers Tales, '91 by Travellers Tales.

PIGEON PIE (Rosalind Ayres).
MCSET. Cat no: **1091R**. Released on Travellers Tales, '91 by Travellers Tales. Note: 4 Cassettes.

PURSUIT OF LOVE, THE (Rosemary Davis).
MCSET. Cat no: **OAS 40891**. Released on Oasis Audio Books, '91 by Isis Audio Books. Note: 8 cassettes.

Moliere

DON JUAN (Edited By Jean B. Biard) (Unknown narrator(s)).
MC. Cat no: **F 7560**. Released on Exeter Tapes, '91 by Drakes Educational Associates.

L'AVARE (Edited By Jean B. Biard) (Unknown narrator(s)).
MC. Cat no: **F 7680**. Released on Exeter Tapes, '91 by Drakes Educational Associates.

LE MISANTHROPE (Edited By Jean B. Biard) (Unknown narrator(s)).
MC. Cat no: **F 7518**. Released on Exeter Tapes, '91 by Drakes Educational Associates.

L'ECOLE DES FEMMES (Edited By Jean B. Biard) (Unknown narrator(s)).
MC. Cat no: **F 7762**. Released on Exeter Tapes, '91 by Drakes Educational Associates.

LES FEMMES SAVANTES (Edited By Jean B. Biard) (Unknown narrator(s)).
MC. Cat no: **F 7568**. Released on Exeter Tapes, '91 by Drakes Educational Associates.

Monsarrat, Nicholas

CRUEL SEA, THE (Jack Hawkins).
MC. Cat no: **CDL 51604**. Released on Caedmon (USA), Oct '79 by Caedmon Records (USA), Bond Street Music.
MC. Cat no: **0001071378**. Released on Collins-Caedmon, '91 by Collins Audio, Taylors, Bond Street Music.

CRUEL SEA, THE (Various narrators).
MCSET. Cat no: **E60**. Released on Tutor Tape, '91 by Morley Audio Services. Note: 2 cassettes.

Montgomerie, Alexander

ALEXANDER MONTGOMERIE (1545-1611) (Various artists).

MC. Cat no: **SSC 060.** Released on Scotsoun, '91 by Scotsoun Recordings, Morley Audio Services.

Montgomery, L.M.

ANNE OF GREEN GABLES (Jermyn, Jane).
MCSET. Cat no: **SOUND 22.** Released on Soundings, Mar '85 by Soundings Records, Bond Street Music.
MCSET. Cat no: **1854961543.** Released on Bramhope, '91 by Ulverscroft Soundings. Note: 4 Cassettes.
MCSET. Cat no: **1056R.** Released on Travellers Tales, '91 by Travellers Tales. Note: 4 Cassettes.

ANNE OF GREEN GABLES (Kim Braden).
MCSET. Cat no: **LFP 7355.** Released on Listen For Pleasure, Sep '88 by EMI Records.

Monty Python

ANOTHER MONTY PYTHON RECORD.
Tracks / Trondheim hammer dance / Liberty bell / Fanfare opening / Formal presentation / Contesana padwana / Man of power / Gold lame / Southern breeze / Spam song / Man of power / Bahama parakeet / House of fashion / Circus tumble / Fanfare / Mystery drums, / Mystery place / Ode to Edward / In step with Johann / Knees up Mother Brown.
LP. Cat no: **CHC 79.** Released on Charisma, Apr '87 by Virgin Records. Note: (MM)
MC. Cat no: **CHCMC 79.** Released on Charisma, Apr '87 by Virgin Records. Note: (MM)
LP. Cat no: **CAS 1049.** Released on Charisma, Oct '71 by Virgin Records **Deleted** Oct '76.
CD. Cat no: **CASCD 1049.** Released on Charisma, Jan '90 by Virgin Records. Note: (MM)

CONTRACTUAL OBLIGATION.
Tracks / Henry Kissinger / Never be rude to an Arab / I like Chinese / Medical love song / Finland / I'm so worried / I bet you they won't play this song on the rad / Here comes another one / Do wot John / Muddy knees / Traffic lights / All things dull and ugly / Scottish farewell, A / Sing as we go / Polygon / Sportstrack / Decomposing composers.
LP. Cat no: **CAS 1152.** Released on Charisma, '83 by Virgin Records **Deleted** '88.
LP. Cat no: **CHC 34.** Released on Charisma, Apr '87 by Virgin Records. Note: (MM)
MC. Cat no: **CHCMC 34.** Released on Charisma, Apr '87 by Virgin Records. Note: (MM)
CD. Cat no: **CASCD 1152.** Released on Charisma, Nov '89 by Virgin Records. Note: (MM)

FINAL RIP OFF, THE (Highlights Compilation album).
Tracks / Introduction / Constitutional peasants / Fish licence / Eric the half bee / Finland song / Travel agent / Are you embarrassed easily? / Australian table wines / Argument / Henry Kissinger / Parrot (Oh not again) / I like Chinese / Spanish inquisition (parts 1/2/3) / Cheese soup / Cherry orchard / Architect's sketch / Spam / Comfy chair / Famous person quiz / You be the actor / Nudge nudge / Cannibalism / Spanish inquisition revisited / Sit on my face / Undertaker / Novel writing (Live from Wessex) / String / Bells / Traffic lights / Cocktail bar / Four Yorkshiremen / Election special / Lumberjack song / I bet you they won't play this song on the radio / Bruces / Do wot John / Rock notes / I'm so worried / Crocodile / French taunter / Marylin Monroe / Swamp castle / Last word, The / Bookshop / French taunter (part 2).
LP. Cat no: **MPD 1.** Released on Virgin, 21 Nov '87 by Virgin Records, Music Sales Records.
CD. Cat no: **CDMP 1.** Released on Virgin, '87 by Virgin Records, Music Sales Records.
MC. Cat no: **MPDC 1.** Released on Virgin, '87 by Virgin Records, Music Sales Records.

INSTANT RECORD COLLECTION.
Tracks / Introductions / Alastair Cooke / Nudge nudge / Mrs. Nigger Baiter / Constitutional peasants / Fish licence / Eric the half a bee / Australian table wines / Silly noises / Novel writing / Elephantoplasty / How to do it / Gumby cherry orchard / Oscar Wilde / Introduction / Argument / French taunter / Summarized Proust competition / Cheese emporium / Funerals at Prestatyn / Camelot / Word association / Bruces / Parrot / Monty Python.
LP. Cat no: **CAS 1134.** Released on Charisma, Apr '87 by Virgin Records.
MC. Cat no: **CASMC 1134.** Released on Charisma, Apr '87 by Virgin Records.
CD. Cat no: **CASCD 1134.** Released on Charisma, Nov '89 by Virgin Records. Note: (MM)

LIFE OF BRIAN (Film soundtrack).
LP. Cat no: **K 56751.** Released on WEA, Oct '79 by Warner Music International (WEA), Solomon & Peres, Outlet Records, Music Sales Records.
MC. Cat no: **K4 56751.** Released on WEA, Oct '79 by Warner Music International (WEA), Solomon & Peres, Outlet Records, Music Sales Records **Deleted** '84.

LIVE AT DRURY LANE.
Tracks / Introduction / Llamas / Gumby cherry orchard / Flower arranging / Secret service / Wrestling / Communist quiz / Idiot song / Albatross / Colonel / Nudge nudge / Cocktail bar / Travel agent / Spot the brain cell / Bruces / Argument / Four Yorkshiremen / Election special / Lumberjack song / Parrot sketch.
LP. Cat no: **CLASS 4.** Released on Charisma, Apr '87 by Virgin Records. Note: (BB)
LP. Cat no: **VVIP 104.** Released on Virgin V.I.P., Sep '89. Note: (BB)
MC. Cat no: **VVIPC 104.** Released on Virgin V.I.P., Sep '89. Note: (BB)
CD. Cat no: **VVIPD 104.** Released on Virgin V.I.P., Sep '89. Note: (BB)

MATCHING TIE AND HANDKERCHIEF.
LP. Cat no: **CHC 81.** Released on Charisma, Apr '87 by Virgin Records. Note: (MM)
MC. Cat no: **CHCMC 81.** Released on Charisma, Sep '83 by Virgin Records.
LP. Cat no: **CAS 1080.** Released on Charisma, Feb '74 by Virgin Records **Deleted** Feb '79.
CD. Cat no: **CASCD 1080.** Released on Charisma, Nov '89 by Virgin Records. Note: (MM)

MONTY PYTHON AND THE HOLY GRAIL (Film soundtrack).
Tracks / Jeunesse / Honours list / Big country / Homeward bound / God choir / Fanfare / Camelot song, The / Sunrise music / Magic finger / Sir Robin's song / In the shadows / Desperate moment / Knights of Ni / Circle of danger / Love theme / Magenta / Starlet in the starlight / Monk's chat / Promised land, The.
LP. Cat no: **CHC 17.** Released on Charisma, Mar '83 by Virgin Records. Note: (MM)
MC. Cat no: **CHCMC 17.** Released on Charisma, Mar '83 by Virgin Records. Note: (MM)
CD. Cat no: **CASCD 1103.** Released on Charisma, Nov '89 by Virgin Records. Note: (MM)

MONTY PYTHON'S FLYING CIRCUS.
Tracks / Flying sheep / Television interviews / Trades descriptions act / Nudge nudge / Mouse problem / Buying a bed / Interesting people / Barber, The / Interviews / More television interviews / Children's stories / Visitors, The / Cinema / North Minehead by-election / Me, doctor / Pet shop / Self defence.
LP. Cat no: **REB 73.** Released on BBC, '74 by BBC Records, Taylors **Deleted** May '91.
CD. Cat no: **BBCCD 73.** Released on BBC, Jun '85 by BBC Records, Taylors **Deleted** Jun '91.
MC. Cat no: **REMC 73.** Released on BBC, Jun '85 by BBC Records, Taylors **Deleted** Jun '91.

MONTY PYTHON'S MEANING OF LIFE (Film soundtrack).
MC. Cat no: **40 70239.** Released on CBS, Jun '83 by Sony Music, Solomon & Peres, Outlet Records **Deleted** Aug '87.

LP. Cat no: **CBS 70239.** Released on CBS, Jun '83 by Sony Music, Solomon & Peres, Outlet Records **Deleted** Aug '87.

PREVIOUS ALBUM.
Tracks / Fashion parade / Alla handel / Sporting news / Money song / Dennis Moore (Robin Hood theme) / Happy movement / Eric the half a bee / Holiday time / Beethoven's 5th / Comic giggles / Beachy head / Yangtse music / Medieval fanfares / Great adventure suite / Fairytale music / Ya de bucketty / Television tensions.
LP. Cat no: **CHC 80.** Released on Charisma, Apr '87 by Virgin Records. Note: (MM)
MC. Cat no: **CHCMC 80.** Released on Charisma, Sep '83 by Virgin Records. Note: (MM)
LP. Cat no: **CAS 1063.** Released on Charisma, Jan '73 by Virgin Records **Deleted** Jan '78.
CD. Cat no: **CASCD 1063.** Released on Charisma, Nov '89 by Virgin Records.

Moore, Brian
BLACK ROBE (Ian Craig).
MCSET. Cat no: **1483T.** Released on Travellers Tales, '91 by Travellers Tales. Note: 6 Cassetts.
MCSET. Cat no: **OAS 89094.** Released on Oasis Audio Books, '91 by Isis Audio Books. Note: 6 Cassettes.
COLD HEAVEN (Hugh Ross).
MCSET. Cat no: **1657T.** Released on Travellers Tales, '91 by Travellers Tales. Note: 7 Cassettes.
MCSET. Cat no: **OAS 90123.** Released on Oasis Audio Books, '91 by Isis Audio Books. Note: 7 Cassettes.
COLOUR OF BLOOD, THE (Derek Jacobi).
MCSET. Cat no: **CAB 343.** Released on Chivers Audio Books, '88 by Chivers Audio Books, Green Dragon Audio Visual.
MCSET. Cat no: **1369T.** Released on Travellers Tales, '91 by Travellers Tales. Note: 4 Cassettes.
LIES OF SILENCE (Dermot Crowley).
MCSET. Cat no: **CAB 532.** Released on Chivers Audio Books, '91 by Chivers Audio Books, Green Dragon Audio Visual. Note: 6 Cassettes
MCSET. Cat no: **1541F.** Released on Travellers Tales, '91 by Travellers Tales.

Moore, Dudley
AD NAUSEUM (See under Derek & Clive)
CLEAN TAPES (See under Cook, Peter.)
COME AGAIN (See under Derek & Clive)
ONCE MORE WITH COOK (See under Cook, Peter)
WORLD OF PETE & DUD (See under Cook, Peter).

Moore, Katherine
SUMMER AT THE HAVEN (Maggie Jones).
MCSET. Cat no: **1437F.** Released on Travellers Tales, '91 by Travellers Tales. Note: 5 cassettes
MCSET. Cat no: **OAS 90025.** Released on Oasis Audio Books, '91 by Isis Audio Books. Note: 5 cassettes

Moray Williams, Ursula
GRANDMA AND THE GHOWLIES (Gwen Watford).
MCSET. Cat no: **3CCA 3159.** Released on Chivers Audio Books, '91 by Chivers Audio Books, Green Dragon Audio Visual. Note: 3 Cassettes.
JEFFY, THE BURGLAR'S CAT (Geoffrey Matthews).
MC. Cat no: **3CCA 3066.** Released on Chivers Audio Books, '88 by Chivers Audio Books, Green Dragon Audio Visual. Note: 3 Cassettes.
MCSET. Cat no: **9129F.** Released on Travellers Tales, '91 by Travellers Tales. Note: 3 Cassettes.
SPID (Bill Oddie).
MCSET. Cat no: **2CCA 3126.** Released on Chivers Audio Books, '91 by Chivers Audio Books, Green Dragon Audio Visual. Note: 2 Cassettes.

Morecambe & Wise
WEEKEND SOUNDS.
Tracks / Here you are / Forty-five minutes of fun and laughter / Eric Morecambe, you'll do anything for a laugh / There's a lot of 'flu. about - 'flu's a nasty thing / Diamond ring in the window, The / Ern, you have got a magnificent body / Carry on, Ern / Visit from the police, A - are you Mrs. T. Potter? / Welcome to the show / I'm going to be Bob Hope's chief scriptwriter / And finale.
LP. Cat no: **REC 258.** Released on BBC, '82 by BBC Records, Taylors **Deleted** '87.

Morgan, Edwin
DOUBLE SCOTCH, A (Edwin Morgan & Alexander Scott).
LP. Cat no: **CCA 5.** Released on Claddagh (Ireland), Aug '88 by Claddagh Records (Ireland), Projection, Impetus Records, Jazz Music, Roots Records, C.M. Distribution, Outlet Records, Taylors.

Morgan, John
BLUEGRASS RANGE (Unknown narrator(s)).
MCSET. Cat no: **1854961551.** Released on Soundings, '91 by Soundings Records, Bond Street Music. Note: 3 Cassettes.

Morgan, Katie
WALLPAPER MAN, THE (Anne Rosenfield).
MCSET. Cat no: **MRC 1023.** Released on Chivers Audio Books, '91 by Chivers Audio Books, Green Dragon Audio Visual. Note: 2 cassettes.

Morice, Anne
DESIGN FOR DYING (Eve Karpf).
MCSET. Cat no: **CAT 4070.** Released on Chivers Audio Books, '91 by Chivers Audio Books, Green Dragon Audio Visual. Note: 4 Cassettes.

Morley, Adele
LAKELAND LOVE, A (Judy Bennett).
MCSET. Cat no: **MRC 1044.** Released on Chivers Moonlight Romances, Apr '88 by Chivers Audio Books, Green Dragon Audio Visual. Note: 2 cassettes

Morley, Sheridan
OTHER SIDE OF THE MOON, THE (Sheridan Morley).
Note: Also available on hanging format, cataglogue number:- 0001387472.
MCSET. Cat no: **0001386549.** Released on Harper Collins, '91 by Harper Collins. Note: 2 Cassettes.

Morpurgo, Michael
MY FRIEND WALTER (Barbara Ewing).
MCSET. Cat no: **3CCA 3156.** Released on Chivers Audio Books, '91 by Chivers Audio Books, Green Dragon Audio Visual. Note: 3 Cassettes.
WHY THE WHALES CAME (Michael Morpurgo).
MCSET. Cat no: **3CCA 3088.** Released on Chivers Audio Books, '91 by Chivers Audio Books, Green Dragon Audio Visual. Note: 3 Cassettes.
MCSET. Cat no: **9160F.** Released on Travellers Tales, '91 by Travellers Tales. Note: 3 Cassettes.

Morris, Dr. Desmond
SOCCER TRIBE, THE (Unknown narrator(s)).
MC. Cat no: **SS 130.** Released on Seminar Cassettes, Oct '81 by Seminar Cassettes.

Morris, James D
WHERE DOES THE NEWS COME FROM? (And Future Fear) (Unknown narrator(s)).
MC. Cat no: **NF 13.** Released on Nightfall Tapes, '89 by BMG Records (UK) Ltd..

Morrison, Toni
JAZZ (Toni Morrison).
MCSET. Cat no: **RC 86.** Released on Random Century, Apr '92 by Random Century Audiobooks, Conifer Records. Note: ISBN no. 1856861147

Mortimer, Carole
SAVAGE INTERLUDE (Carole Boyd).
MCSET. Cat no: **PMB 003.** Released on Mills & Boon, '90. Note: 2 cassettes.

Mortimer, John
CHARADE (Paul Shelley).
MC. Cat no: **CAB 268.** Released on Chivers Audio Thrillers, '88 by Chivers Audio Books, Green Dragon Audio Visual.

MCSET. Cat no: **1317F**. Released on Travellers Tales, '91 by Travellers Tales. Note: 4 cassettes.

PARADISE POSTPONED (Sir Michael Horden).
MCSET. Cat no: **LFP 7276**. Released on Listen For Pleasure, Nov '86 by EMI Records.
MCSET. Cat no: **1200F**. Released on Travellers Tales, '91 by Travellers Tales.

PARADISE POSTPONED (Paul Shelley).
MCSET. Cat no: **CAB 504**. Released on Chivers Audio Books, '91 by Chivers Audio Books, Green Dragon Audio Visual. Note: 10 Cassettes.
MCSET. Cat no: **1616/7F**. Released on Travellers Tales, '91 by Travellers Tales. Note: 10 cassettes.

RUMPOLE (Maurice Denham & Margot Boyd).
Note: Four plays.
MCSET. Cat no: **ZBBC 1022**. Released on BBC Records. Note: 2 cassettes. Starring Maurice Denham.
MCSET. Cat no: **1383F**. Released on Travellers Tales, '91 by Travellers Tales. Note: 2 cassettes.

RUMPOLE 2 (Various artists).
Note: Starring Maurice Denham.
MCSET. Cat no: **ZBBC 1219**. Released on BBC Radio Collection, Apr '91 by BBC Records. Note: ISBN No: 0563 40972X

RUMPOLE A LA CARTE (Rob Inglis).
MCSET. Cat no: **IAB 91082**. Released on Isis Audio Books, '91. Note: 8 Cassettes.

RUMPOLE AND THE GOLDEN THREAD (Patrick Tull).
MCSET. Cat no: **IAB 92016**. Released on Isis Audio Books, Jan '92. Note: 8 cassettes. Playing time 10hrs 30mins.

RUMPOLE FOR THE DEFENCE (Patrick Tull).
MCSET. Cat no: **1610F**. Released on Travellers Tales, '91 by Travellers Tales. Note: 5 cassettes.
MCSET. Cat no: **TE 858**. Released on Isis Audio Books, '91. Note: 5 cassettes.
MCSET. Cat no: **IAB 91024**. Released on Isis Audio Books, '91. Note: 5 Cassettes.

RUMPOLE OF THE BAILEY (Leo McKern).
MCSET. Cat no: **TC-LFP 7110**. Released on Listen For Pleasure, '83 by EMI Records.

RUMPOLE'S RETURN (Partrick Tull).
MCSET. Cat no: **IAB 91111**. Released on Isis Audio Books, Nov '91. Note: 5 Cassettes. Playing time 6 hours

SUMMER'S LEASE (Susan Fleetwood).
MCSET. Cat no: **ZBBC 1098**. Released on BBC Audio Collection, Oct '89 by BBC Records. Note: ISBN No: 0563 227265

SUMMER'S LEASE (Martin Jarvis).
MCSET. Cat no: **CAB 368**. Released on Chivers Audio Books, '91 by Chivers Audio Books, Green Dragon Audio Visual. Note: 8 cassettes
MCSET. Cat no: **1401T**. Released on Travellers Tales, '91 by Travellers Tales. Note: 8 Cassettes.

TITMUSS REGAINED (Paul Shelley).
MCSET. Cat no: **CAB 664**. Released on Chivers Audio Books, Jan '92 by Chivers Audio Books, Green Dragon Audio Visual. Note: 8 cassettes.

TRIALS OF RUMPOLE, THE (Leo McKern).
Note: Abridged version.
MCSET. Cat no: **1119F**. Released on Travellers Tales, '91 by Travellers Tales. Note: 2 cassettes.

TRIALS OF RUMPOLE, THE (Leo McKern).
MCSET. Cat no: **LFP 7200**. Released on Listen For Pleasure, Jul '85 by EMI Records.

Mosco, Maisie

ALMONDS AND RAISINS: CONSEQUENCES (Judeth Franklyn).
MCSET. Cat no: **1122F**. Released on Travellers Tales, '91 by Travellers Tales. Note: 4 cassettes.
MCSET. Cat no: **1854961586**. Released on Bramhope, '91 by Ulverscroft Soundings. Note: 4 Cassettes.

ALMONDS AND RAISINS: HOPES AND DREAMS (Judeth Franklyn).
MCSET. Cat no: **1120F**. Released on Travellers Tales, '91 by Travellers Tales. Note: 4 cassettes.
MCSET. Cat no: **185496156X**. Released on Soundings, '91 by Soundings Records, Bond Street Music. Note: 4 Cassettes.

ALMONDS AND RAISINS: REALITIES (Judeth Franklyn).
MCSET. Cat no: **1121F**. Released on Travellers Tales, '91 by Travellers Tales. Note: 4 cassettes.
MCSET. Cat no: **1854961578**. Released on Soundings, '91 by Soundings Records, Bond Street Music. Note: 4 Cassettes.

CHILDREN'S CHILDREN PART 1 (Judeth Franklyn).
MCSET. Cat no: **1310F**. Released on Travellers Tales, '91 by Travellers Tales. Note: 5 cassettes.
MCSET. Cat no: **1854961594**. Released on Bramhope, '91 by Ulverscroft Soundings. Note: 5 Cassettes.

CHILDREN'S CHILDREN PARTS 2 AND 3 (All That Glitters and Echoes From The Past) (Judeth Franklyn).
MCSET. Cat no: **1311F**. Released on Travellers Tales, '91 by Travellers Tales. Note: 8 cassettes.
MCSET. Cat no: **1854961608**. Released on Soundings, '91 by Soundings Records, Bond Street Music. Note: 8 Cassettes.

SCATTERED SEED: CORDS AND DISCORDS (Judeth Franklyn).
MCSET. Cat no: **1245F**. Released on Travellers Tales, '91 by Travellers Tales. Note: 4 Cassettes.
MCSET. Cat no: **1854961632**. Released on Bramhope, '91 by Ulverscroft Soundings. Note: 4 Cassettes.

SCATTERED SEED: RELATIVE VALUES (Judeth Franklyn).
MCSET. Cat no: **1204F**. Released on Travellers Tales, '91 by Travellers Tales. Note: 5 Cassettes.
MCSET. Cat no: **1854961616**. Released on Bramhope, '91 by Ulverscroft Soundings. Note: 5 Cassettes.

SCATTERED SEED: STICKS AND STONES (Judeth Franklyn).
MCSET. Cat no: **1205F**. Released on Travellers Tales, '91 by Travellers Tales. Note: 5 cassettes.
MCSET. Cat no: **1854961624**. Released on Bramhope, '91 by Ulverscroft Soundings. Note: 5 Cassettes.

Moyes, Patricia

MURDER FANTASTICAL (Clifford Norgate).
MCSET. Cat no: **CAT 4048**. Released on Chivers Audio Books, '91 by Chivers Audio Books, Green Dragon Audio Visual. Note: 6 Cassettes.
MCSET. Cat no: **1484T**. Released on Travellers Tales, '91 by Travellers Tales. Note: 6 Cassettes.

Muir, Frank

WONDERFUL WHAT A MESS (Unknown narrator(s)).
MC. Cat no: **TS 353**. Released on Tellastory, '88 by Random Century Audiobooks.

Munro, H.H.

ALL RECORDINGS (See Under Saki).

Munro, James

DIE RICH, DIE HAPPY (Gordon Griffin).
MCSET. Cat no: **1172T**. Released on Travellers Tales, '91 by Travellers Tales. Note: 4 Cassettes.
MCSET. Cat no: **1854961667**. Released on Bramhope, '91 by Ulverscroft Soundings. Note: 4 Cassettes.

MAN WHO SOLD DEATH, THE (Gordon Griffin).
MCSET. Cat no: **1173T**. Released on Travellers Tales, '91 by Travellers Tales. Note: 4 Cassettes.
MCSET. Cat no: **1854961675**. Released on Bramhope, '91 by Ulverscroft Soundings. Note: 4 Cassettes.

Munro, Neil

HURRICANE JACK OF THE VITAL SPARK (Robert Trotter).
Note: Part of the complete para handy stories.

MCSET. Cat no: **SPF 559-3**. Released on Schiltron Audio Books, '91 by Schiltron Publishing. Note: 4 Cassettes. Playing time 4 hours 21 minutes.

MCSET. Cat no: **1404F**. Released on Travellers Tales, '91 by Travellers Tales. Note: 4 cassettes.

IN HIGHLAND HARBOURS (Volume Two) (Robert Trotter).
Note: Part of the complete para handy stories.
MCSET. Cat no: **SPF 559-2**. Released on Schiltron Audio Books, '91 by Schiltron Publishing. Note: 4 Cassettes. Playing time 4 hours 10 minutes.

ISLE OF ILLUSION (And Other Stories) (Sheila Donald & Robert Trotter).
MCSET. Cat no: **SPF 599-4**. Released on Schiltron Audio Books, '91 by Schiltron Publishing. Note: 2 Cassettes. Playing time 2 hours 52 minutes.

VITAL SPARK, THE (Volume One) (Robert Trotter).
Note: Part of the complete para handy stories.
MCSET. Cat no: **SPF 559-1**. Released on Schiltron Audio Books, '91 by Schiltron Publishing. Note: 4 Cassettes. Playing time 4 hours 32 minutes.

MCSET. Cat no: **1369F**. Released on Travellers Tales, '91 by Travellers Tales. Note: 4 cassettes.

Murdoch, Iris

SEVERED HEAD, A (Derek Jacobi).
MCSET. Cat no: **1130F**. Released on Travellers Tales, '91 by Travellers Tales. Note: 6 cassettes.

Murphy, Eddie

COMEDIAN (Eddie Murphy).
Tracks / Faggots revisited / Sexual prime / Singers / Ice cream man / Shoe throwin' mothers / Modern women / Barbecue, The / Politics / Racism / Languages / TV.
LP. Cat no: **CBS 25760**. Released on CBS, Apr '84 by Sony Music, Solomon & Peres, Outlet Records **Deleted** Apr '89.
MC. Cat no: **40-25760**. Released on CBS, '91 by Sony Music, Solomon & Peres, Outlet Records.

Murphy, Jill

WORST WITCH, THE (Miriam Margoyles).
MCSET. Cat no: **CTC 012**. Released on Cover to Cover, '87 by Cover to Cover Cassettes.

Murphy, Richard

BATTLE OF AUGHRIM, THE (Unknown narrator(s)).
LP. Cat no: **CCT 7**. Released on Claddagh (Ireland), Aug '88 by Claddagh Records (Ireland), Projection, Impetus Records, Jazz Music, Roots Records, C.M. Distribution, Outlet Records, Taylors.

Murray, Charles

HAMEWITH (And Other Poems) (Various artists).
MC. Cat no: **SSC 056**. Released on Scotsoun, '91 by Scotsoun Recordings, Morley Audio Services.

Murray, Gordon K

TALES O A GAMIE (Various artists).
Note: Stories from the North East. Read by David Buchan, Flora Garry, Douglas Kynoch, Alexander Scott and the author.
MC. Cat no: **SSC 049**. Released on Scotsoun, '91 by Scotsoun Recordings, Morley Audio Services.

Murray, Jill

ARROW TO THE HEART (Nancy Mitchell).
MCSET. Cat no: **CLT 1012**. Released on Candlelight, '88 by AVLS (Audio-Visual Library Services).

Murray, William

DRAGON DEN, THE (Childrens Story Book) (Unknown narrator(s)).
MC. Cat no: **RWM 003**. Released on Tell-A-Tale, Sep '90 by Pickwick Records, Taylors, Clyde Factors.

Musman, Richard

HOUSE NEAR THE SEA, THE (And Other Stories) (Various narrators).
MC. Cat no: **0582790506**. Released on Longman/Pickwick, '91 by Pickwick Records.

Myers, Amy

MURDER AT PLUMS (John Hendry).
MCSET. Cat no: **1854965441**. Released on Bramhope, '92 by Ulverscroft Soundings.

MURDER IN THE LIMELIGHT (John Hendry).
MCSET. Cat no: **1854965891**. Released on Bramhope, Apr '92 by Ulverscroft Soundings. Note: Playing time: 60 minutes.

Mystery

CLASSIC DETECTIVE STORIES (Edward Hardwicke).
Note: Authors included are:- Conan Doyle, Sapper, Chesterton, Wallace.
MCSET. Cat no: **TTDMC 412**. Released on CSA Tell Tapes, Mar '92 by CSA Tell-Tapes. Note: 2 Cassettes. ISBN No: 1873859120

CLASSIC TALES OF MURDER (Christopher Lee).
Note: Authors are: London, Bennett, Sapper and Conan Doyle.
MCSET. Cat no: **TTDMC 413**. Released on CSA Tell-Tapes, '91 by CSA Tell-Tapes. Note: 2 Cassettes. ISBN No: 1873859139

DOGS OF WAR / SHALL WE TELL THE PRESIDENT/A SMALL TOWN IN GERMANY (Various artists).
MCSET. Cat no: **1220T**. Released on Travellers Tales, '91 by Travellers Tales. Note: 6 Cassettes.

THIRTEEN PROBLEMS, KISS KISS (And Tales of Suspense) (Various artists).
MCSET. Cat no: **1218T**. Released on Travellers Tales, '91 by Travellers Tales. Note: 6 Cassettes.

Nash, Ogden

PARENTS KEEP OUT (Unknown narrator(s)).
MC. Cat no: **1282**. Released on Caedmon (USA), '88 by Caedmon Records (USA), Bond Street Music.

Neels, Betty

WISH WITH THE CANDLES (Georgina Melville).
MCSET. Cat no: **PMB 006**. Released on Mills & Boon, '88. Note: 2 cassettes.

Neill, William

POEMS IN THE THRIE LEIDS O ALBA (Joy Hendry & Ian MacDonald).
MC. Cat no: **SSC 089**. Released on Scotsoun, '91 by Scotsoun Recordings, Morley Audio Services.

Nesbitt, Edith

BOOK OF DRAGONS, THE (Dame Judith Anderson).
MC. Cat no: **1427**. Released on Caedmon (USA), '88 by Caedmon Records (USA), Bond Street Music.

FIERY DRAGON, THE (And The Book Of Beasts) (Caroline Bliss & Peter Bartlett).
MC. Cat no: **TS 354**. Released on Tellastory, Apr '88 by Random Century Audiobooks.

FIVE CHILDREN AND IT (And Phoenix and The Carpet) (Sheila Donald & Gwyneth Gutherie).
Note: Abridged.
MCSET. Cat no: **COL 3002**. Released on Colophone, Sep '81 by AVLS (Audio-Visual Library Services).
MCSET. Cat no: **9063F**. Released on Travellers Tales, '91 by Travellers Tales. Note: 6 Cassettes.

FOUR DRAGON STORIES (Gwyneth Guthrie).
MCSET. Cat no: **COL 3008**. Released on Colophone, '88 by AVLS (Audio-Visual Library Services).

FROM THE DEAD (And Man-Size in Marble) (George Irving).
MC. Cat no: **RSJ 5008**. Released on Landfall, '91.

PHOENIX AND THE CARPET, THE (Sheila Donald).
MCSET. Cat no: **COL 3009**. Released on Colophone, '88 by AVLS (Audio-Visual Library Services).

RAILWAY CHILDREN, THE (Dinah Sheridan).
MCSET. Cat no: **LFP 7436**. Released on Listen For Pleasure, Oct '89 by EMI Records. Note: Playing time: 2 hours.

RAILWAY CHILDREN, THE (Un-

known narrator(s)).
Note: Book and cassette.
MC. Cat no: **PLBC 177.** Released on Tell-A-Tale, '88 by Pickwick Records, Taylors, Clyde Factors.

Neville, Anne
HOUSE OF THE CHESTNUT TREES, THE (Joanna Wake).
MCSET. Cat no: **MRC 1010.** Released on Chivers Audio Books, '91 by Chivers Audio Books, Green Dragon Audio Visual. Note: 2 cassettes.

Newhart, Bob
BEST OF BOB NEWHART (Bob Newhart).
Tracks / Introducing tobacco to civilisation / Edison's most famous inventions / Bus drivers' school / Kruschev landing rehearsal / Driving instructor, The / Defusing a bomb / Infinitive number of monkeys.
LP. Cat no: **K 46001.** Released on Warner Bros., Jan '74 by Warner Music International (WEA), Solomon & Peres.
MC. Cat no: **K4 46001.** Released on Warner Bros., Jan '74 by Warner Music International (WEA), Solomon & Peres.

BEST OF BOB NEWHART (2) (Bob Newhart).
Tracks / Driving instructor, The / Introducing tobacco to civilisation / Grace L. Ferguson air line, The / Cruise of the USS Codfish / Retirement party, The / Returning a gift / Ledge psychology.
MC. Cat no: **HSC 3288.** Released on Pickwick, Oct '89 by Pickwick Records, Clyde Factors, Taylors, Arabesque, Solomon & Peres, I & B Records, Prism Leisure, Outlet Records.
CD. Cat no: **PWKS 548.** Released on Pickwick, Oct '89 by Pickwick Records, Clyde Factors, Taylors, Arabesque, Solomon & Peres, I & B Records, Prism Leisure, Outlet Records.

BOB NEWHART (Bob Newhart).
Tracks / Driving instructor / Introducing tobacco to civilisation / Returning a gift / Retirement party / Grace L. Ferguson air line, The / Cruise of the USS Codfish / Ledge psychology.
LP. Cat no: **SSP 3079.** Released on Pickwick, Oct '80 by Pickwick Records, Clyde Factors, Taylors, Arabesque, Solomon & Peres, I & B Records, Prism Leisure, Outlet Records **Deleted** Oct '85.

Newton, William
RIO CONTRACT, THE (Unknown narrator(s)).
MCSET. Cat no: **1854964356.** Released on Trio, '91 by EMI Records. Note: 3 Cassettes.

SET UP, THE (Unknown narrator(s)).
MCSET. Cat no: **SOUND 6.** Released on Soundings, May '85 by Soundings Records, Bond Street Music.
MCSET. Cat no: **1120T.** Released on Travellers Tales, '91 by Travellers Tales.

SMELL OF MONEY, THE (Peter Joyce).
MCSET. Cat no: **1854964763.** Released on Trio, Jul '91 by EMI Records. Note: 3 Cassettes.

SOMEONE HAS TO TAKE THE FALL (Gordon Griffin).
MCSET. Cat no: **1854964550.** Released on Trio, May '91 by EMI Records. Note: 3 Cassettes.

Nichols, Grace
CONTEMPORARY LITERATURE READINGS (Grace Nichols & Samuel Selvon).
MC. Cat no: **NSA C4.** Released on National Sound Archive, Oct '87.

Nicol, Hector
HOBO SEXUAL, THE (Hector Nicol).
LP. Cat no: **KLP 24.** Released on Klub, Nov '80 by Klub Records, Musac (Scotland) Ltd., Ross Records, Gordon Duncan Distributions, Taylors.
MC. Cat no: **ZCKLP 24.** Released on Klub, Nov '80 by Klub Records, Musac (Scotland) Ltd., Ross Records, Gordon Duncan Distributions, Taylors.

LADY AND THE CHAMP, THE (Hector Nicol).
LP. Cat no: **KLP 03.** Released on Klub, May '79 by Klub Records, Musac (Scotland) Ltd., Ross Records, Gordon Duncan Distributions, Taylors.

SCOTCH AND FULL OF IT (Hector Nicol).
LP. Cat no: **KLP 07.** Released on Klub, May '79 by Klub Records, Musac (Scotland) Ltd., Ross Records, Gordon Duncan Distributions, Taylors.

Nicol, Jean
HOTEL REGINA (John Brand).
MCSET. Cat no: **1132F.** Released on Travellers Tales, '91 by Travellers Tales. Note: 4 cassettes.
MCSET. Cat no: **1854961691.** Released on Bramhope, '91 by Ulverscroft Soundings. Note: 4 Cassettes.

MEET ME AT THE SAVOY (Unknown narrator(s)).
MCSET. Cat no: **SOUND 24.** Released on Soundings, Mar '85 by Soundings Records, Bond Street Music.
MCSET. Cat no: **1013N.** Released on Travellers Tales, '91 by Travellers Tales. Note: 4 Cassettes.

Nicoll, Helen
MEG AND MOG (Maureen Lipman).
MCSET. Cat no: **CC/025-6.** Released on Cover to Cover, '87 by Cover to Cover Cassettes.

Nimmo, Jenny
CHESTNUT SOLDIER, THE (Nigel Lambert).
MCSET. Cat no: **4CCA 3150.** Released on Chivers Audio Books, '91 by Chivers Audio Books, Green Dragon Audio Visual. Note: 4 Cassettes.

EMLYN'S MOON (Sian Phillips).
MCSET. Cat no: **3CCA 3098.** Released on Chivers Audio Books, '91 by Chivers Audio Books, Green Dragon Audio Visual. Note: 3 Cassettes.
MCSET. Cat no: **9180F.** Released on Travellers Tales, '91 by Travellers Tales. Note: 3 Cassettes.

SNOW SPIDER, THE (Jane Asher).
MC. Cat no: **3CCA 3062.** Released on Chivers Audio Books, '88 by Chivers Audio Books, Green Dragon Audio Visual. Note: 3 Cassettes.
MCSET. Cat no: **9128F.** Released on Travellers Tales, '91 by Travellers Tales. Note: 3 Cassettes.

TATTY APPLE (Jane Asher).
MCSET. Cat no: **2CCA 3039.** Released on Chivers Audio Books, '91 by Chivers Audio Books, Green Dragon Audio Visual. Note: 2 Cassettes.
MCSET. Cat no: **9117F.** Released on Travellers Tales, '91 by Travellers Tales. Note: 2 Cassettes.

Niven, David
ENCHANTED ORCHESTRA, THE (David Niven & National Philharmonic Orchestra).
LP. Cat no: **MR 116.** Released on Maiden, Oct '79 by Maiden Records.
MC. Cat no: **MRC 116.** Released on Maiden, Oct '79 by Maiden Records.

Nobbs, David
BIT OF A DO, A (John Rowe).
MCSET. Cat no: **0563410744.** Released on BBC Radio Collection, '91 by BBC Records. Note: 2 cassettes.

Norton, Mary
BORROWERS AFIELD, THE (Rowena Cooper).
MCSET. Cat no: **4CCA 3143.** Released on Chivers Audio Books, '91 by Chivers Audio Books, Green Dragon Audio Visual. Note: 4 Cassettes.

BORROWERS, THE (Rowena Cooper).
MCSET. Cat no: **3CCA 3002.** Released on Chivers Audio Books, '91 by Chivers Audio Books, Green Dragon Audio Visual. Note: 3 Cassettes.
MCSET. Cat no: **9065F.** Released on Travellers Tales, '91 by Travellers Tales. Note: 3 Cassettes.

Not the Nine o'Clock
HEDGEHOG SANDWICH (TV soundtrack) (Various artists).
Tracks / Loyal apology: *Various artists* / News summary: *Various artists* / Constable Savage: *Various artists* / Baronet Ernold Oswald Mosley: *Various artists* / University challenge: *Various artists* / (I like) trucking: *Various artists* / Sir Robert Mark: *Various artists* / Hi-fi shop: *Various artists* / England my leotard: *Various artists* / Divorce: *Various artists* / Main points again, The: *Various artists* / Bad language: *Various artists* / Gift shop: *Various artists* / Hedgehog

apology: *Various artists* / Supa dupa: *Various artists* / Soccer violence: *Various artists* / (Because I'm) wet and lonely: *Various artists* / That's lies: *Various artists* / Creed (The new revised version): *Various artists* / I believe: *Various artists* / Aide, The: *Various artists* / Main points again, The: *Various artists* / Not the parrot sketch: *Various artists* / Open marriage: *Various artists* / Lager: *Various artists* / And finally: *Various artists*.
LP. Cat no: **REB 421.** Released on BBC, Oct '81 by BBC Records, Taylors **Deleted** 31 Aug '88.
MC. Cat no: **ZCF 421.** Released on BBC, Oct '81 by BBC Records, Taylors **Deleted** 31 Aug '88.

MEMORY KINDA LINGERS, THE/NOT IN FRONT OF THE AUDIENCE (TV soundtrack & Live at Drury Lane) (Various artists).
Tracks / Spy who came in from the cold, The: *Various artists* / News, The: *Various artists* / Budget: *Various artists* / Question: *Various artists* / Headbangers: *Various artists* / Rock interview: *Various artists* / Game for a laugh: *Various artists* / Typical bloody typical: *Various artists* / Well, Mr. Glossop: *Various artists* / Financial times: *Various artists* / Hey Bob: *Various artists* / New glea: *Various artists* / Holiday habits: *Various artists* / Pizza moment: *Various artists* / Failed in Wales: *Various artists* / Rinbley's pies: *Various artists* / Made from whales: *Various artists* / Brain death: *Various artists* / Swedish chemists: *Various artists* / Hey wow: *Various artists* / Nice video, shame about the song: *Various artists* / Jackanory: *Various artists* / Golf trousers: *Various artists* / News, The: *Various artists* / Two ninnies song: *Various artists* / Aussie pilot: *Various artists* / Does God exist: *Various artists* / Re-altered images: *Various artists* / McEnroe's breakfast: *Various artists* / Ah come in Rawlinson: *Various artists* / Ask the family: *Various artists* / Polish show: *Various artists* / Aleebee: *Various artists* / Main points again, The: *Various artists* / What a load of willies: *Various artists* / Kinda lingers, (The memory): *Various artists* / Grow up you bastards: *Various artists* / Confrontation song: *Various artists* / American improv: *Various artists* / Duke of Kent: *Various artists* / Alien: *Various artists* / Oh oh oh means I respect you: *Various artists* / Simon and Garfunkel: *Various artists* / Awards: *Various artists* / S.A.S.: *Various artists* / Prompt: *Various artists* / Barry Manilow: *Various artists* / Return of Constable Savage, The: *Various artists* / Gob on you: *Various artists* / The pope's visit: *Various artists*.
2LP. Cat no: **REF 453.** Released on BBC, Oct '82 by BBC Records, Taylors.
MC. Cat no: **ZCD 453.** Released on BBC, Oct '82 by BBC Records, Taylors.
NOT THE DOUBLE ALBUM (TV soundtrack) (Various artists).

LP. Cat no: **REH 516.** Released on BBC, Oct '84 by BBC Records, Taylors **Deleted** 31 Aug '88.
MC. Cat no: **ZCR 516.** Released on BBC, Oct '84 by BBC Records, Taylors **Deleted** 31 Aug '88.
NOT THE NINE O'CLOCK NEWS (TV soundtrack) (Various artists).
Tracks / Death of a princess (apology to the Saudis): *Rhys Jones, Griff* (With: "The News" - Pamela Stephenson and Mel Smith.) / Gorilla interview, The: *Atkinson, Rowan/Mel Smith/Pamela Stephenson* / Confrontation (song): *Smith, Mel* (Brewis) / Airline safety: *Stephenson, Pamela* (One word from Billy Connolly.) / National wealth beds: *Smith, Mel* / Simultaneous translation: *Atkinson, Rowan/Pamela Stephenson* (With "The News" (main points again)- Pamela Stephenson and Mel Smith.) / General synod's, The "Life of Monty Python": *Atkinson, Rowan/Mel Smith/Pamela Stephenson* / There's a man (in Iran)...: *Stephenson, Pamela* / Closedown: *Rhys Jones, Griff/Rowan Atkinson/Mel Smith/Pamela Stephenson* / Point of view: *Rhys Jones, Griff/Rowan Atkinson/Mel Smith/Pamela Stephenson* / Rowan's rant: *Rhys Jones, Griff/Rowan Atkinson/Mel Smith/Pamela Stephenson* / Stout life: *Rhys Jones, Griff/Rowan Atkinson/Mel Smith/Pamela Stephenson* / Gob on you: *Smith, Mel* (With: "The News" - Pamela Stephenson and Mel Smith (Chris Judge Smith)) / Gay Christian: *Smith, Mel* / Bouncin' (song): *Atkinson, Rowan & Sox* (With: "The main points of the news again" - Mel Smith & Pamela Stephenso) / Oh Bosanquet (song): *Stephenson, Pamela* / I believe: *Rhys Jones, Griff/Rowan Atkinson/Mel Smith/Pamela Stephenson*.
LP. Cat no: **MFP 5810.** Released on MFP, Oct '87 by EMI Records, Solomon & Peres **Deleted** '89.
MC. Cat no: **TCMFP 5810.** Released on MFP, Oct '87 by EMI Records, Solomon & Peres.
NOT THE NINE O'CLOCK NEWS (Original cast) (Various artists).
LP. Cat no: **REB 400.** Released on BBC, Oct '80 by BBC Records, Taylors **Deleted** '88.
MC. Cat no: **ZCF 400.** Released on BBC, Oct '80 by BBC Records, Taylors **Deleted** '88.
NOT THE NINE O'CLOCK NEWS (Various artists).
MCSET. Cat no: **ZBBC 1009.** Released on BBC, Mar '89 by BBC Records, Taylors. Note: 2 Cassettes. ISBN No: 0563 225483.

O Henry
(See under Henry, O.)

Oakley, Graham
CHURCH MOUSE AND CHURCH CAT (Baker, Tom).
MC. Cat no: **CDSC 2.** Released on Delyse, Oct '80.

O'Brian, Patrick
DESOLATION ISLAND (Unknown narrator(s)).
MCSET. Cat no: **1854965123.** Released on Soundings, '91 by Soundings Records, Bond Street Music. Note: 9 Cassettes.

O'Brien, Edna
COUNTRY GIRLS, THE (Edna O'Brien).
MCSET. Cat no: **CAB 306.** Released on Chivers Audio Books, Apr '88 by Chivers Audio Books, Green Dragon Audio Visual. Note: 6 cassette set
MCSET. Cat no: **SAY 19.** Released on Argo (Polygram), Jul '82 by PolyGram Classics **Deleted** Jan '89.
MCSET. Cat no: **ARGO 1256.** Released on Argo (EMI), Apr '91 by EMI Records.
COUNTRY GIRLS, THE (Edna O'Brien).
MCSET. Cat no: **1133F.** Released on Travellers Tales, '91 by Travellers Tales. Note: 2 cassettes.
GIRLS IN THEIR MARRIED BLISS (Edna O'Brien).
MCSET. Cat no: **CAB 380.** Released on Chivers Audio Books, '91 by Chivers Audio Books, Green Dragon Audio Visual. Note: 6 Cassettes
MCSET. Cat no: **1375F.** Released on Travellers Tales, '91 by Travellers Tales. Note: 6 cassettes.
LONELY GIRL (Edna O'Brien).
MCSET. Cat no: **CAB 348.** Released on Chivers Audio Books, '91 by Chivers Audio Books, Green Dragon Audio Visual. Note: 6 Cassettes.
MCSET. Cat no: **1341F.** Released on Travellers Tales, '91 by Travellers Tales. Note: 6 cassettes.
SOME IRISH LOVING (Edna O'Brien).
Tracks / Some Irish loving / What is love / Courtship of Etain / Dawning of the day / Young serving man / Poet loves from afar / Her Praise / Eleanor Alexander / He that's dead can do no hurt / Advice to lovers / Love among the Irish / Making of a chapter / Noble lay of Aillinn / Letter to Vanessa / My husband Queen Maeve / Light love / Aileen Aroon / Men improve with the year / Death and the lady / Once I was yellow haired / On the death of his wife / Red rose.
LP. Cat no: **ZDSW 728.** Released on Argo, '79 by Decca International **Deleted** '84.

O'Brien, Robert C
MRS FRISBY AND THE RATS OF NIMH (Gwen Watford).
MCSET. Cat no: **4CCA 3123.** Released on Chivers Audio Books, '91 by Chivers Audio Books, Green Dragon Audio Visual. Note: 4 Cassettes.

O'Casey, Sean
JUNO AND THE PAYCOCK (Various artists).
MCSET. Cat no: **0358**. Released on Caedmon (USA), '88 by Caedmon Records (USA), Bond Street Music. Note: 2 cassettes

O'Connor, Tom
LOOK AT LIFE, A (Tom O'Connor). Tracks / Let's look at life / Cash in your pocket / I'm coming back / Me and my gang / Comedy sketches.
LP. Cat no: **PRCV 140**. Released on President, Jun '90 by President Records, Jazz Music, Taylors, Spartan, Swift, Wellard Dist., Enterprise Distribution.
MC. Cat no: **TCPRCV 140**. Released on President, Jun '90 by President Records, Jazz Music, Taylors, Spartan, Swift, Wellard Dist., Enterprise Distribution.
CD. Cat no: **PRCD 140**. Released on President, Jun '90 by President Records, Jazz Music, Taylors, Spartan, Swift, Wellard Dist., Enterprise Distribution.

O'Kelly, Jeffrey
ADVENTURES OF DOCTOR SNUGGLES (John Craven).
MC. Cat no: **TBC 9507**. Released on Tempo Storytime, May '84 by Warwick Records, Celtic Music.

Oldfield, Pamela
ADVENTURES OF THE GUMBY GANG, THE (Jean Waggoner).
MCSET. Cat no: **2CCA 3040**. Released on Chivers Audio Books, '91 by Chivers Audio Books, Green Dragon Audio Visual. Note: 2 Cassettes.

GUMBY GANG AGAIN, THE (Jean Waggoner).
MCSET. Cat no: **2CCA 3084**. Released on Chivers Audio Books, '91 by Chivers Audio Books, Green Dragon Audio Visual. Note: 2 Cassettes.

MCSET. Cat no: **9163F**. Released on Travellers Tales, '91 by Travellers Tales. Note: 2 Cassettes.

GUMBY GANG ON HOLIDAY, THE (Jean Waggoner).
MCSET. Cat no: **2CCA 3124**. Released on Chivers Audio Books, '91 by Chivers Audio Books, Green Dragon Audio Visual. Note: 2 Cassettes.

GUMBY GANG STRIKES AGAIN, THE (Jean Waggoner).
MCSET. Cat no: **2CCA 3144**. Released on Chivers Audio Books, '91 by Chivers Audio Books, Green Dragon Audio Visual. Note: 2 Cassettes.

MORE ABOUT THE GUMBY GANG (Jean Waggoner).
MCSET. Cat no: **2CCA 3106**. Released on Chivers Audio Books, '91 by Chivers Audio Books, Green Dragon Audio Visual. Note: 2 Cassettes.

MCSET. Cat no: **9181F**. Released on Travellers Tales, '91 by Travellers Tales. Note: 2 Cassettes.

ONCE UPON A TIME (8 Favourite Children's Stories) (Penelope Keith).
Note: For children aged 3 - 9 years. Includes The Soldier Doll, The Really Dreadful Dragon, The Unwanted Giant, The Terribly Plain Princess, The Silver Key, The Lonely Mermaid, The Chancellor who Wouldn't Smile and Viola and the Ogre.
MC. Cat no: **OTC 001**. Released on VFM Cassettes, '85 by VFM Cassettes, Midland Records, Crusader Marketing Co., Taylors, Morley Audio Services. Note: Picture bag.

RETURN OF THE GUMBY GANG (Jean Waggoner).
MCSET. Cat no: **2CCA 3157**. Released on Chivers Audio Books, Sep '91 by Chivers Audio Books, Green Dragon Audio Visual. Note: 2 Cassettes.

STORYTIME TOP TEN (Volume 1) (Penelope Keith).
Note: Music by Major Records. Include The Really Dreadful Dragon, The Unwanted Giant and The Terribly Plain Princess. For children aged 4 - 8 years.
MC. Cat no: **VCA 055**. Released on VFM Cassettes, Jan '85 by VFM Cassettes, Midland Records, Crusader Marketing Co., Taylors, Morley Audio Services.

SWEET SALLY LUNN (Jane Asher).
MCSET. Cat no: **CAB 576**. Released on Chivers Audio Books, '91 by Chivers Audio Books, Green Dragon Audio Visual. Note: 10 cassettes

MCSET. Cat no: **1657/8F**. Released on Travellers Tales, '91 by Travellers Tales. Note: 10 cassettes.

TERRIBLY PLAIN PRINCESS, THE (Penelope Keith).
Note: For 4 to 8 year olds.
MC. Cat no: **B 003**. Released on Green Dragon, '91 by Green Dragon Audio Visual.

WILLERBY'S AND THE BANK ROBBERS, THE (Jean Waggoner).
MCSET. Cat no: **9066F**. Released on Travellers Tales, '91 by Travellers Tales. Note: 2 Cassettes.

O'Neill, Eugene
EMPEROR JONES, THE (Various artists).
MCSET. Cat no: **0341**. Released on Caedmon (USA), '88 by Caedmon Records (USA), Bond Street Music. Note: 2 cassettes

ICE MAN COMETH, THE (Various artists).
MCSET. Cat no: **0359**. Released on Caedmon (USA), '88 by Caedmon Records (USA), Bond Street Music. Note: 4 cassettes

LONG DAY'S JOURNEY INTO NIGHT (Various artists).
MCSET. Cat no: **0350**. Released on Caedmon (USA), '88 by Caedmon Records (USA), Bond Street Music. Note: 4 cassettes

Orwell, George
1984 (Derek Jacobi).
MCSET. Cat no: **TCLFP 417140 5**. Released on Listen For Pleasure, Jan '84 by EMI Records.

1984 (Frank Muller).
MCSET. Cat no: **RB 86650**. Released on Recorded Books, '91 by Isis Audio Books. Note: 7 cassette set. Playing time 9hrs 48mins

MCSET. Cat no: **1572F**. Released on Travellers Tales, '91 by Travellers Tales. Note: 7 cassettes.

ANIMAL FARM (Patrick Tull).
MC. Cat no: **LFP 41 7178 5**. Released on Listen For Pleasure, Oct '84 by EMI Records.

MCSET. Cat no: **1571F**. Released on Travellers Tales, '91 by Travellers Tales. Note: 3 cassettes.

MCSET. Cat no: **RB 87430**. Released on Recorded Books, '91 by Isis Audio Books. Note: 3 Cassettes. Playing time: 3 hours 15 minutes.

BURMESE DAYS (Margaret Hilton).
MCSET. Cat no: **RB 88440**. Released on Recorded Books, '91 by Isis Audio Books. Note: 8 cassettes. Playing time 11hrs 30mins

MCSET. Cat no: **1628F**. Released on Travellers Tales, '91 by Travellers Tales. Note: 8 cassettes

COMING UP FOR AIR (A Comedy) (Patrick Tull).
MCSET. Cat no: **RB 88130**. Released on Recorded Books, '91 by Isis Audio Books. Note: 6 cassettes. Playing time 7hrs 42mins.

MCSET. Cat no: **1631F**. Released on Travellers Tales, '91 by Travellers Tales. Note: 6 cassettes.

ROAD TO WIGAN PIER, THE (Patrick Tull).
MCSET. Cat no: **IAB 89091**. Released on Isis Audio Books, '91. Note: 6 cassette set. Playing time 7hrs 30mins.

MCSET. Cat no: **1070N**. Released on Travellers Tales, '91 by Travellers Tales. Note: 6 cassettes.

Osborne, John
LUTHER (Various artists).
MCSET. Cat no: **0363**. Released on Caedmon (USA), by Caedmon Records (USA), Bond Street Music. Note: 2 cassettes

Ovid
METAMORPHOSES (Edited By Alan Griffin) (Unknown narrator(s)).
Note: Ovid's greatest poem.
MC. Cat no: **L 7858**. Released on Exeter Tapes, '91 by Drakes Educational Associates.

Owen, Gareth
FINAL TEST, THE (Richard Mitchley).

MCSET. Cat no: **3CCA 3030**. Released on Chivers Audio Books, '91 by Chivers Audio Books, Green Dragon Audio Visual. Note: 3 Cassettes.
MCSET. Cat no: **9102F**. Released on Travellers Tales, '91 by Travellers Tales. Note: 3 Cassettes.

Oxenbury, Helen
HELEN OXENBURY'S NURSERY RHYMES (Helen Oxenbury).
MC. Cat no: **0 00 109032 1**. Released on Tempo, '88 by Warwick Records, Celtic Music, Henry Hadaway Organisation.
HELEN OXENBURY'S NURSERY STORIES (Helen Oxenbury).
MC. Cat no: **0 00 109031 3**. Released on Tempo, '88 by Warwick Records, Celtic Music, Henry Hadaway Organisation.

Packer, Joy
DARK CURTAIN, THE (Virginia McKenna).
MCSET. Cat no: **1121T**. Released on Travellers Tales, '91 by Travellers Tales. Note: 6 Cassettes.

Paige, Frances
DISTAFF SIDE, THE (Elizabeth Henry).
MCSET. Cat no: **1485/6F**. Released on Travellers Tales, '91 by Travellers Tales. Note: 10 cassettes.
MCSET. Cat no: **185496304X**. Released on Soundings, '91 by Soundings Records, Bond Street Music. Note: 10 Cassettes.
MAEVE'S DAUGHTER (Elizabeth Henry).
MCSET. Cat no: **1313F**. Released on Travellers Tales, '91 by Travellers Tales. Note: 8 cassettes.
MCSET. Cat no: **12854961721**. Released on Soundings, '91 by Soundings Records, Bond Street Music.
SHOLTIE BURN, THE (Elizabeth Henry).
MCSET. Cat no: **1297F**. Released on Travellers Tales, '91 by Travellers Tales. Note: 8 cassettes.
MCSET. Cat no: **185496173X**. Released on Soundings, '91 by Soundings Records, Bond Street Music.

Paine, Lauren
BORDERMEN, THE (Unknown narrator(s)).
MCSET. Cat no: **1854961748**. Released on Trio, '91 by EMI Records. Note: 3 Cassettes.
MEDICINE BOW, THE (Unknown narrator(s)).
MCSET. Cat no: **1854962477**. Released on Trio, '91 by EMI Records. Note: 3 cassettes.
THUNDER VALLEY (Unknown narrator(s)).
MCSET. Cat no: **1854961756**. Released on Trio, '91 by EMI Records. Note: 3 Cassettes.

TRAIL OF THE HAWKS, THE (Unknown narrator(s)).
MCSET. Cat no: **1854965093**. Released on Trio, '91 by EMI Records. Note: 3 Cassettes.

Paretsky, Sara
INDEMNITY ONLY (Kathy Bates).
MCSET. Cat no: **ZBBC 1232**. Released on BBC, '91 by BBC Records, Taylors. Note: ISBN No: 0563 408022

Parker, Dorothy
DOROTHY PARKER STORIES (Shirley Booth).
MC. Cat no: **1136**. Released on Caedmon (USA), by Caedmon Records (USA), Bond Street Music.

Parkinson, C.
JEEVES (A Gentleman's Personal Gentleman) (Gerald Harper & Others).
MCSET. Cat no: **SAY 20**. Released on Argo (Polygram), Jul '82 by PolyGram Classics **Deleted** Jan '89.
MCSET. Cat no: **ARGO 1133**. Released on Argo (EMI), Sep '89 by EMI Records. Note: 2 Cassettes.
MCSET. Cat no: **1136F**. Released on Travellers Tales, '91 by Travellers Tales. Note: ISBN No: 0563 410329

Parkinson, Robin
TWO STORIES FROM BUTTON MOON.
MC. Cat no: **ZCRDB 1152**. Released on Red Bus, Aug '85 by Red Bus Records.

Pasternak, Boris
DOCTOR ZHIVAGO (Paul Scofield).
MC. Cat no: **TC LFP 7054**. Released on Listen For Pleasure, Dec '79 by EMI Records.

Paterson, Cynthia
FOXWOOD TALES (Foxwood Kidnap) (Cynthia & Brian Paterson).
MC. Cat no: **0 00 102193 1**. Released on Tempo Storytime, '88 by Warwick Records, Celtic Music.
FOXWOOD TALES (Foxwood Regatta) (Cynthia & Brian Paterson).
MC. Cat no: **0 00 102194 X**. Released on Tempo Storytime, '88 by Warwick Records, Celtic Music.
FOXWOOD TALES (Foxwood Treasure) (Cynthia & Brian Paterson).
MC. Cat no: **0 00 102195 8**. Released on Tempo Storytime, '88 by Warwick Records, Celtic Music.
FOXWOOD TALES (Robbery At Foxwood) (Cynthia & Brian Paterson).
MC. Cat no: **0 00 102196 6**. Released on Tempo Storytime, '88 by Warwick Records, Celtic Music.

Paton, Alan
CRY, THE BELOVED COUNTRY (Ben Kingsley).
MCSET. Cat no: **LFP 7288**. Released on Listen For Pleasure, Apr '87 by EMI Records **Deleted** Oct '90. Note: Playing time: 2 hours.
MCSET. Cat no: **1206F**. Released on Travellers Tales, '91 by Travellers Tales.
CRY, THE BELOVED COUNTRY (Unknown narrator(s)).
MC. Cat no: **CDL 51605**. Released on Caedmon (USA), '79 by Caedmon Records (USA), Bond Street Music.
CRY, THE BELOVED COUNTRY (Alan Paton).
MCSET. Cat no: **0001071370**. Released on BBC Radio Collection, '91 by BBC Records.
TOO LATE THE PHALAROPE (John Cartwright).
MCSET. Cat no: **1405F**. Released on Travellers Tales, '91 by Travellers Tales. Note: 6 cassettes.
MCSET. Cat no: **OAS 89093**. Released on Oasis Audio Books, '91 by Isis Audio Books. Note: 6 Cassettes.

Paton Walsh, Jill
GAFFER SAMPSON'S LUCK (Richard Mitchley).
MCSET. Cat no: **3CCA 3024**. Released on Chivers Audio Books, '91 by Chivers Audio Books, Green Dragon Audio Visual. Note: 3 Cassettes.
MCSET. Cat no: **9067F**. Released on Travellers Tales, '91 by Travellers Tales. Note: 3 Cassettes.

Patten, Brian
BRIAN PATTEN READING HIS POEMS (Brian Patten).
MC. Cat no: **1300**. Released on Caedmon (USA), '88 by Caedmon Records (USA), Bond Street Music.

Pattinson, James
DEAD MEN NEVER RISE UP (David Telfer).
MCSET. Cat no: **1665T**. Released on Travellers Tales, '91 by Travellers Tales. Note: 4 Cassettes.
MCSET. Cat no: **1854963732**. Released on Bramhope, '91 by Ulverscroft Soundings. Note: 4 Cassettes.
FLIGHT TO THE SEA (Alan Dunbavin).
MCSET. Cat no: **SOUND 25**. Released on Soundings, Mar '85 by Soundings Records, Bond Street Music.
MCSET. Cat no: **1122T**. Released on Travellers Tales, '91 by Travellers Tales. Note: 4 Cassettes.
KILLER (Nicholas Lumley).
MCSET. Cat no: **1667T**. Released on Travellers Tales, '91 by Travellers Tales. Note: 4 Cassettes.
MCSET. Cat no: **1854963821**. Released on Bramhope, '91 by Ulverscroft Soundings.
LEGATEE (Unknown narrator(s)).
MCSET. Cat no: **1854962965**. Released on Bramhope, '91 by Ulverscroft Soundings. Note: 5 cassettes.

LETHAL ORDERS (Peter Joyce).
MCSET. Cat no: **1583T**. Released on Travellers Tales, '91 by Travellers Tales. Note: 4 Cassettes.
MCSET. Cat no: **1854963457**. Released on Bramhope, '91 by Ulverscroft Soundings. Note: 4 Cassettes.

PETRONOV PLAN, THE (Eric Collinson).
MCSET. Cat no: **1123T**. Released on Travellers Tales, '91 by Travellers Tales. Note: 4 Cassettes.
MCSET. Cat no: **1854961772**. Released on Bramhope, '91 by Ulverscroft Soundings. Note: 4 Cassettes.

Pattrick, William
MYSTERIOUS RAILWAY STORIES (Robert Hardy).
MCSET. Cat no: **1124T**. Released on Travellers Tales, '91 by Travellers Tales. Note: 6 Cassettes.
MCSET. Cat no: **CAB 097**. Released on Chivers Audio Books, '91 by Chivers Audio Books, Green Dragon Audio Visual. Note: 6 cassettes

Peake, Mervyn
TITUS GROAN AND GORMENGHAST (Various narrators).
Note: Starring Sting.
MCSET. Cat no: **ZBBC 1114**. Released on BBC Radio Collection, 5 Mar '90 by BBC Records. Note: ISBN No: 0563 410302

Pearce, Flora
ESSIE (Diana Bishop).
MCSET. Cat no: **OAS 20991**. Released on Oasis Audio Books, Sep '91 by Isis Audio Books. Note: 8 Cassettes. Playing time: 9 hrs 32 mins.

Pearce, Philippa
BATTLE OF THE BUBBLE AND SQUEAK (Judy Bennett).
MCSET. Cat no: **9068F**. Released on Travellers Tales, '91 by Travellers Tales. Note: 2 Cassettes.
MCSET. Cat no: **086 222 0490**. Released on Chivers Calvacade, '91 by Chivers Audio Books, Green Dragon Audio Visual. Note: 2 Cassettes.
MCSET. Cat no: **2CCA 3005**. Released on Chivers Audio Books, '91 by Chivers Audio Books, Green Dragon Audio Visual.

LION AT SCHOOL (And Other Stories) (Jan Francis).
MCSET. Cat no: **2CCA 3145**. Released on Chivers Audio Books, '91 by Chivers Audio Books, Green Dragon Audio Visual. Note: 2 Cassettes.

TOM'S MIDNIGHT GARDEN (Jan Francis).
MCSET. Cat no: **4CCA 3120**. Released on Chivers Audio Books, '91 by Chivers Audio Books, Green Dragon Audio Visual. Note: 4 Cassettes.

WHAT THE NEIGHBOURS DID (And Other Stories) (Judy Bennett).
MCSET. Cat no: **2CCA 3018**. Released on Chivers Audio Books, '91 by Chivers Audio Books, Green Dragon Audio Visual. Note: 2 Cassettes.
MCSET. Cat no: **9069F**. Released on Travellers Tales, '91 by Travellers Tales. Note: 2 Cassettes.

Peel, Colin D
FLAMEOUT (Unknown narrator(s)).
MCSET. Cat no: **1854964135**. Released on Bramhope, '91 by Ulverscroft Soundings. Note: 5 Cassettes.

FLAMEOUT (Peter Joyce).
MCSET. Cat no: **1737T**. Released on Travellers Tales, '91 by Travellers Tales. Note: 4 Cassettes.

NIGHT DIVE (Dave Wade).
MCSET. Cat no: **1584T**. Released on Travellers Tales, '91 by Travellers Tales. Note: 4 Cassettes.
MCSET. Cat no: **1854963465**. Released on Bramhope, '91 by Ulverscroft Soundings. Note: 4 Cassettes.

Peploe, Frances
MAGNETIC LOVE (Unknown narrator(s)).
MCSET. Cat no: **1854964364**. Released on Trio, '91 by EMI Records. Note: 3 Cassettes.

Peppe, Rodney
HUXLEY PIG AT THE CIRCUS (Unknown narrator(s)).
MC. Cat no: **39567**. Released on Tempo, Sep '89 by Warwick Records, Celtic Music, Henry Hadaway Organisation.

Perrault, Charles
LITTLE RED RIDING HOOD (Well Loved Tales Age Up To 9) (Unknown narrator(s)).
Note: Book and cassette.
MC. Cat no: **PLB 55**. Released on Tell-A-Tale, Feb '83 by Pickwick Records, Taylors, Clyde Factors.

LITTLE RED RIDING HOOD (Unknown narrator(s)).
MC. Cat no: **TS 305**. Released on Tellastory, Oct '79 by Random Century Audiobooks.
MC. Cat no: **STK 002**. Released on Stick-A-Tale, Jan '89 by Pickwick Records.

LITTLE RED RIDING HOOD (Various narrators).
MC. Cat no: **STC 006**. Released on VFM Cassettes, Jun '88 by VFM Cassettes, Midland Records, Crusader Marketing Co., Taylors, Morley Audio Services.

LITTLE RED RIDING HOOD (Claire Bloom).
MC. Cat no: **1331**. Released on Caedmon (USA), '88 by Caedmon Records (USA), Bond Street Music.

LITTLE RED RIDING HOOD (Unknown narrator(s)).
MC. Cat no: **FT 111**. Released on Cassettes For Young People, May '92 by Cassettes For Young People Lmd, DMS Dist.. Note: ISBN no. 1871449111. Playing time 20 minutes approx.

LITTLE RED RIDING HOOD (Michaela Strachan).
MC. Cat no: **STOR 1**. Released on Storytime Cassettes, Apr '92 by VFM Cassettes, Iona Records, Rio Communications.

RED RIDING HOOD (Various narrators).
MC. Cat no: **STC 302A**. Released on VFM Cassettes, '88 by VFM Cassettes, Midland Records, Crusader Marketing Co., Taylors, Morley Audio Services.

SLEEPING BEAUTY (Well Loved Tales Up to Age 9) (Unknown narrator(s)).
Note: Book and cassette.
MC. Cat no: **PLB 110**. Released on Tell-A-Tale, '88 by Pickwick Records, Taylors, Clyde Factors.

SLEEPING BEAUTY (Unknown narrator(s)).
MC. Cat no: **DIS 004**. Released on Disney (Read-a-long), Jul '90 by Disneyland Records.

SLEEPING BEAUTY (Denise Bryer).
MC. Cat no: **BKK 405**. Released on Kiddy Kassettes, Aug '77.

SLEEPING BEAUTY (Susan Hampshire).
MC. Cat no: **3600**. Released on Storytime Cassettes, Aug '83 by VFM Cassettes, Iona Records, Rio Communications.

SLEEPING BEAUTY (Unknown narrator(s)).
MC. Cat no: **TS 303**. Released on Tellastory, Oct '79 by Random Century Audiobooks.

SLEEPING BEAUTY (And Puss in Boots) (Dora Bryan).
MC. Cat no: **LP 302**. Released on Listen Productions, Nov '84.
MC. Cat no: **LPMC 302**. Released on Listen, '88, Cartel.

Perry, Anne
SILENCE IN HANOVER CLOSE (Peter Joyce).
MCSET. Cat no: **1662/1663T**. Released on Travellers Tales, '91 by Travellers Tales. Note: 9 Cassettes.
MCSET. Cat no: **1854963686**. Released on Soundings, '91 by Soundings Records, Bond Street Music. Note: 9 Cassettes.

Peters, Elizabeth
CROCODILE ON THE SANDBANK (Barbara Rosenblat).
MCSET. Cat no: **IAB 91124**. Released on Isis Audio Books, Dec '91. Note: 8 Cassettes. Playing time 10 hours.

CURSE OF THE PHARAOHS, THE (Barbara Rosenblat).
MCSET. Cat no: **IAB 91084**. Released on Isis Audio Books, '91. Note: 8 Cassettes

JACKAL'S HEAD, THE (Shirley Dixon).

211

MCSET. Cat no: **1125T**. Released on Travellers Tales, '91 by Travellers Tales. Note: 4 cassettes.
LAST CAMEL DIED AT NOON, THE (Barbara Rosenblat).
MCSET. Cat no: **IAB 92035**. Released on Isis Audio Books, Mar '92. Note: 10 cassettes. Playing time 15hrs 15mins.

Peters, Ellis

CITY OF GOLD AND SHADOWS (Simon Prebble).
MCSET. Cat no: **1677T**. Released on Travellers Tales, '91 by Travellers Tales. Note: 7 cassettes.
MCSET. Cat no: **IAB 91033**. Released on Isis Audio Books, '91. Note: 7 Cassettes.
DEATH AND THE JOYFUL WOMAN (Simon Prebble).
MCSET. Cat no: **IAB 92086**. Released on Isis Audio Books, Aug '92. Note: 6 Cassettes. Playing time: 7 hours, 45 mins.
DEATH MASK (Richard Owens).
MCSET. Cat no: **IAB 92041**. Released on Isis Audio Books, Apr '92. Note: 7 cassettes. Playing time 7hrs 12mins.
FALLEN INTO THE PIT (Simon Prebble).
MCSET. Cat no: **IAB 92025**. Released on Isis Audio Books, Feb '92. Note: 8 cassettes. Playing time 10hrs 25mins.
FUNERAL OF FIGARO (Sean Barrett).
MCSET. Cat no: **1174T**. Released on Travellers Tales, '91 by Travellers Tales. Note: 4 Cassettes.
LEPER OF SAINT GILES, THE (Stephen Thorne).
MCSET. Cat no: **CAB 587**. Released on Chivers Audio Books, '91 by Chivers Audio Books, Green Dragon Audio Visual. Note: 6 Cassettes
MCSET. Cat no: **1726t**. Released on Travellers Tales, '91 by Travellers Tales. Note: 6 Cassettes.
MONK'S HOOD (Stephen Thorne).
MCSET. Cat no: **CAB 524**. Released on Chivers Audio Books, '91 by Chivers Audio Books, Green Dragon Audio Visual. Note: 6 Cassettes.
MCSET. Cat no: **1635T**. Released on Travellers Tales, '91 by Travellers Tales. Note: 6 Cassettes.
MONK'S HOOD (Various narrators)..
MCSET. Cat no: **ZBBC 1209**. Released on BBC Radio Collection, Sep '91 by BBC Records. Note: ISBN No: 0563 409843
MORBID TASTE FOR BONES, A (Mediaeval Whodunnit) (Glyn Houston).
MCSET. Cat no: **LFP 7481**. Released on Listen For Pleasure, Oct '90 by EMI Records.
MORBID TASTE FOR BONES, A (Stephen Thorne).
MCSET. Cat no: **CAB 455**. Released on Chivers Audio Books, '91 by Chivers Audio Books, Green Dragon Audio Visual. Note: 6 Cassettes.
MCSET. Cat no: **1547T**. Released on Travellers Tales, '91 by Travellers Tales. Note: 6 Cassettes.
NEVER PICK UP HITCH-HIKERS (William Gaminara).
MCSET. Cat no: **CAT 4064**. Released on Chivers Audio Books, '91 by Chivers Audio Books, Green Dragon Audio Visual. Note: 6 Cassettes.
MCSET. Cat no: **1728T**. Released on Travellers Tales, '91 by Travellers Tales. Note: 6 Cassettes.
NICE DERANGEMENT OF EPITAPHS, A (Ian Hogg).
MCSET. Cat no: **1636T**. Released on Travellers Tales, '91 by Travellers Tales. Note: 6 Cassettes.
MCSET. Cat no: **IAB 90102**. Released on Isis Audio Books, '91. Note: 6 Cassettes.
ONE CORPSE TOO MANY (Stephen Thorne).
MCSET. Cat no: **CAB 488**. Released on Chivers Audio Books, '91 by Chivers Audio Books, Green Dragon Audio Visual. Note: 6 Cassettes.
MCSET. Cat no: **1567T**. Released on Travellers Tales, '91 by Travellers Tales. Note: 6 Cassettes.
ONE CORPSE TOO MANY (A Mediaeval Whodunnit) (Glyn Houston).
MCSET. Cat no: **LFP 7508**. Released on Listen For Pleasure, Apr '91 by EMI Records.
PIPER ON THE MOUNTAIN, THE (Simon Prebble).
MCSET. Cat no: **IAB 92067**. Released on Isis Audio Books, Jun '92. Note: 6 Cassettes. Playing Time: 7 hours, 10 mins.
RAINBOW'S END (Simon Prebble).
MCSET. Cat no: **1679T**. Released on Travellers Tales, '91 by Travellers Tales. Note: 6 Cassettes.
MCSET. Cat no: **IAB 91064**. Released on Isis Audio Books, '91. Note: 6 Cassettes.
SAINT PETERS FAIR (Stephen Thorne).
MCSET. Cat no: **CAB 550**. Released on Chivers Audio Books, '91 by Chivers Audio Books, Green Dragon Audio Visual. Note: 8 Cassettes.
MCSET. Cat no: **1692T**. Released on Travellers Tales, '91 by Travellers Tales. Note: 8 Cassettes.
SANCTUARY SPARROW, THE (Stephen Thorne).
MCSET. Cat no: **CAB 681**. Released on Chivers Audio Books, Mar '92 by Chivers Audio Books, Green Dragon Audio Visual. Note: 8 Cassettes.
VIRGIN IN THE ICE, THE (A Mediaeval Who Dunnit) (Stephen Thorne).
MCSET. Cat no: **CAB 624**. Released on Chivers Audio Books, Sep '91 by Chivers Audio Books, Green Dragon Audio Visual. Note: 8 Cassettes.

Peters, Maureen

ENGLAND'S MISTRESS (Judith Porter).
MCSET. Cat no: **1854965905**. Released on Bramhope, Apr '92 by Ulverscroft Soundings. Note: Playing time: 60 minutes.
LADY FOR A CHEVALIER (Unknown narrator(s)).
MCSET. Cat no: **1854963384**. Released on Bramhope, '91 by Ulverscroft Soundings. Note: 4 cassettes.
MUCH SUSPECTED OF ME (Judeth Franklyn).
MCSET. Cat no: **1854964739**. Released on Bramhope, Jul '91 by Ulverscroft Soundings. Note: 5 Cassettes.
PATCHWORK (Judith Porter).
MCSET. Cat no: **1504F**. Released on Travellers Tales, '91 by Travellers Tales. Note: 7 cassettes.
MCSET. Cat no: **1854963422**. Released on Soundings, '91 by Soundings Records, Bond Street Music. Note: 7 Cassettes.
PROUD BESS (Anne Dover).
MCSET. Cat no: **1854964534**. Released on Bramhope, May '91 by Ulverscroft Soundings. Note: ISBN No: 1 85496 453 4.
VINEGAR BLOSSOM, THE (Christine Dawe).
MCSET. Cat no: **1247F**. Released on Travellers Tales, '91 by Travellers Tales. Note: 4 cassettes.
MCSET. Cat no: **1854961780**. Released on Bramhope, '91 by Ulverscroft Soundings. Note: 4 Cassettes.
VINEGAR SEED, THE (Christine Dawe).
MCSET. Cat no: **1207F**. Released on Travellers Tales, '91 by Travellers Tales. Note: 4 cassettes.
MCSET. Cat no: **1854961799**. Released on Bramhope, '91 by Ulverscroft Soundings. Note: 4 Cassettes.
VINEGAR TREE, THE (Unknown narrator(s)).
MCSET. Cat no: **1854962515**. Released on Bramhope, '91 by Ulverscroft Soundings. Note: 5 cassettes.
WIFE IN WAITING (Unknown narrator(s)).
MCSET. Cat no: **1854965182**. Released on Bramhope, '91 by Ulverscroft Soundings. Note: 4 Cassettes.

Peyton, K.M.

GOING HOME (Nicolette McKenzie).
MCSET. Cat no: **2CCA 3009**. Released on Chivers Audio Books, '91 by Chivers Audio Books, Green Dragon Audio Visual. Note: 2 Cassettes.
MCSET. Cat no: **9028F**. Released on Travellers Tales, '91 by Travellers Tales. Note: 2 Cassettes.
MCSET. Cat no: **086 222 0504**. Released on Chivers Calvacade, Apr '88 by Chivers Audio Books, Green Dragon Audio Visual. Note: 2 Cassettes.

Pilcher, Rosamunde
ANOTHER VIEW (Unknown narrator(s)).
MCSET. Cat no: **ZBBC 1312**. Released on BBC, Apr '91 by BBC Records, Taylors. Note: 12" limited edition pic. bag

SEPTEMBER (Eve Karpf).
MCSET. Cat no: **CAB 625**. Released on Chivers Audio Books, Sep '91 by Chivers Audio Books, Green Dragon Audio Visual. Note: 16 Cassettes.

SEPTEMBER (Lynn Redgrave).
MCSET. Cat no: **ZBBC 1220**. Released on BBC, '91 by BBC Records, Taylors. Note: ISBN No: 0563 408014

SHELL SEEKERS, THE (Lynne Redgrave).
Note: Also available on hanging format, catalogue number:- 000103538X.
MCSET. Cat no: **HCA 40**. Released on Harper Collins, '92 by Harper Collins.

SHELL SEEKERS, THE (Barbara Rosenblat).
MCSET. Cat no: **IAB 92013**. Released on Isis Audio Books, Jan '92. Note: 15 cassettes. Playing time 23hrs.

VOICES IN SUMMER (Lindsay Duncan).
MCSET. Cat no: **CAB 675**. Released on Chivers Audio Books, Feb '92 by Chivers Audio Books, Green Dragon Audio Visual. Note: 8 cassettes.

Pinter, Harold
HOMECOMING, THE (Various narrators).
MCSET. Cat no: **0361**. Released on Caedmon (USA), by Caedmon Records (USA), Bond Street Music. Note: 2 cassettes

Plaidy, Jean
GOLDSMITH'S WIFE, THE (Rowena Cooper).
MCSET. Cat no: **CAB 588**. Released on Chivers Audio Books, '91 by Chivers Audio Books, Green Dragon Audio Visual. Note: 8 Cassettes

MCSET. Cat no: **1667F**. Released on Travellers Tales, '91 by Travellers Tales. Note: 8 cassettes.

SIXTH WIFE, THE (Marie Palmer).
MCSET. Cat no: **SOUND 29**. Released on Soundings, Mar '85 by Soundings Records, Bond Street Music.

MCSET. Cat no: **1854961802**. Released on Bramhope, '91 by Ulverscroft Soundings. Note: 4 Cassettes.

MCSET. Cat no: **1063R**. Released on Travellers Tales, '91 by Travellers Tales. Note: 4 Cassettes.

ST. THOMAS' EVE (Clifford Norgate).
MCSET. Cat no: **CAB 514**. Released on Chivers Audio Books, '91 by Chivers Audio Books, Green Dragon Audio Visual. Note: 8 Cassettes

MCSET. Cat no: **1590F**. Released on Travellers Tales, '91 by Travellers Tales. Note: 8 cassettes.

Plain, Belva
BLESSINGS (Bonnie Hurren).
MCSET. Cat no: **CAB 495**. Released on Chivers Audio Books, '91 by Chivers Audio Books, Green Dragon Audio Visual. Note: 8 Cassettes.

MCSET. Cat no: **1529F**. Released on Travellers Tales, '91 by Travellers Tales. Note: 8 cassettes.

CRESCENT CITY (Bonnie Hurren).
MCSET. Cat no: **CAB 665**. Released on Chivers Audio Books, Jan '92 by Chivers Audio Books, Green Dragon Audio Visual. Note: 12 cassettes.

Plater, Alan
BEIDERBECKE AFFAIR, THE (James Bolam) (Volume 1).
MCSET. Cat no: **LFP 7385**. Released on Listen For Pleasure, Mar '89 by EMI Records. Note: Playing time: 3 hours.

BEIDERBECKE TAPES, THE (James Bolam).(Volume 2).
MCSET. Cat no: **LFP 7439**. Released on Listen For Pleasure, Oct '89 by EMI Records. Note: Playing time: Approximately 3 hours.

BEIDERBECKE TAPES, THE (Arthur Blake).
MCSET. Cat no: **IAB 91125**. Released on Isis Audio Books, Dec '91. Note: 6 Cassettes. Playing time 5 hours 50 minutes.

Plays
CHARLEY'S AUNT (Various artists).
Note: The cast of this official centenary production feature Frank Windsor, Patrick Cargill, Mark Curry and Gabrielle Drake.
MCSET. Cat no: **TTC 2043**. Released on Talking Tape Company, Mar '92, Conifer Records. Note: 2 Cassettes.

SIX PLAYS (Various artists).
Note: Alan Bennet: Forty Years On and A Woman of No Importance. Terence Rattigan: The Browning Version and The Winslow Bay. Alan Bennet: Relatively Speaking and Season's Greetings.
MCSET. Cat no: **1052P**. Released on Travellers Tales, '91 by Travellers Tales. Note: 6 Cassettes.

SOUND OF CLASSICAL DRAMA, THE (Various artists).
Note: Chekov, Sheridan and Goldsmith
MCSET. Cat no: **1050P**. Released on Travellers Tales, '91 by Travellers Tales. Note: 6 cassettes.

SOUND OF MODERN DRAMA, THE (Various artists).
Note: Van Dranton, Hart, Yeats, Becket, Albee and Miller.
MCSET. Cat no: **1051P**. Released on Travellers Tales, '91 by Travellers Tales. Note: 6 cassettes.

Poe, Edgar Allan
ANTOLOGIA DI RACCONTI (Adriano Giraldi).
MCSET. Cat no: **1024L**. Released on Travellers Tales, '91 by Travellers Tales. Note: 4 cassettes.

BEST OF EDGAR ALLAN POE, THE (Edward Blake).
MCSET. Cat no: **1282F**. Released on Travellers Tales, '91 by Travellers Tales. Note: 6 cassettes.

FALL OF THE HOUSE OF USHER (Basil Rathbone).
MC. Cat no: **1195**. Released on Caedmon (USA), '88 by Caedmon Records (USA), Bond Street Music.

NARRATIVE OF GORDON PYM OF NANTUCKET, THE (Jamie Hanes).
MCSET. Cat no: **1579F**. Released on Travellers Tales, '91 by Travellers Tales. Note: 5 cassettes.

MCSET. Cat no: **RB 88390**. Released on Recorded Books, '91 by Isis Audio Books. Note: 5 Cassettes.

PIT AND THE PENDULUM (Bill Wallis).
Note: Also includes "The Facts in the Case of M. Valdemar", and "The Cask of Amontillado".
MC. Cat no: **RSJ 5001**. Released on Landfall, '91.

PIT AND THE PENDULUM (And Other Works) (Basil Rathbone).
MC. Cat no: **1115**. Released on Caedmon (USA), '88 by Caedmon Records (USA), Bond Street Music.

PURLOINED LETTER, THE (And Other Works) (Anthony Quayle).
MC. Cat no: **1288**. Released on Caedmon (USA), '88 by Caedmon Records (USA), Bond Street Music.

RAVEN, THE (And Other Works) (Basil Rathbone).
MC. Cat no: **1028**. Released on Caedmon (USA), '88 by Caedmon Records (USA), Bond Street Music.

SHORT STORIES (Volume 1) (Martin Donegan).
LP. Cat no: **PRCS 117**. Released on Peerless (USA), Jan '75 by Discos Latin International (USA).

TALES OF HORROR (Lee, Christopher).
MCSET. Cat no: **LFP 7454**. Released on Listen For Pleasure, Apr '90 by EMI Records.

TALES OF MYSTERY AND IMAGINATION (Bill Mitchell).
MCSET. Cat no: **SAY 54**. Released on Argo (Polygram), Jun '88 by PolyGram Classics **Deleted** Jan '89.

TALES OF TERROR (Jack Foreman).
Note: Contains the stories: The Tell Tale Heart, The Black Cat, The Cask of Amontillo, The Pit and The Pendulum, The Masque of the Red Death, The Facts in the Case of M. Valdemar, Hopfrog, The Fall of The House of Usher, The Murders in the Rue Morgue.
MCSET. Cat no: **RB 81330**. Released on Recorded Books, Sep '91 by Isis

Audio Books. Note: 4 cassettes. Playing time 5hrs.

TELL-TALE HEART, THE (Bill Wallis).
Note: Also includes "Hop-Frog" and "The Premature Burial".
MC. Cat no: **RSJ 5002**. Released on Landfall, '91.

TERROR TALES, THE (Edgar Lustgarten).
MCSET. Cat no: **LD 12**. Released on Green Dragon, '91 by Green Dragon Audio Visual.

Poetry

10 MEDIEVAL MAKARS (Alexander Scott).
Note: A selection from Barbour, James 1, Blin Harry, Douglas, Lindsay, Maitland, Scott, Montgomerie, Hume and Boyd.
MC. Cat no: **SSC 021**. Released on Scotsoun, '91 by Scotsoun Recordings, Morley Audio Services.

20TH CENTURY POETRY (Various artists).
Note: T.S Elliot, David Jones, Robert Graves and Philip Larkin reading their own works. Includes: Old Possum's Book of Practical Cats, In Parenthesis, Anathemata and High Windows.
MCSET. Cat no: **414 718-4**. Released on Argo (Polygram), Oct '84 by PolyGram Classics **Deleted** Jan '89.
MCSET. Cat no: **ARGO 1067**. Released on Argo (EMI), May '89 by EMI Records. Note: 2 Cassettes.
MCSET. Cat no: **1017Y**. Released on Travellers Tales, '91 by Travellers Tales. Note: 2 Cassettes.

ALLIGATOR PIE (And Other Poems) (Dennis Lee).
MC. Cat no: **1530**. Released on Caedmon (USA), '88 by Caedmon Records (USA), Bond Street Music.

ANOTHER ROUND OF POEMS AND PINTS (Unknown narrator(s)).
LP. Cat no: **NTS 150**. Released on Note, '88 by EMI Records.

ANTHOLOGY - POETRY READINGS (Richard Burton).
MCSET. Cat no: **SAY 47**. Released on Argo (Polygram), Jun '88 by PolyGram Classics **Deleted** Jan '89.
MCSET. Cat no: **ARGO 1046**. Released on Argo (EMI), May '89 by EMI Records.

ARGO TREASURY OF COMIC AND CURIOUS VERSE (Various artists).
MCSET. Cat no: **418 189-4**. Released on Argo (Polygram), Apr '88 by PolyGram Classics **Deleted** Jan '89.
MCSET. Cat no: **ARGO 1208**. Released on EMI, Jul '90 by EMI Records.
MCSET. Cat no: **1032Y**. Released on Travellers Tales, '91 by Travellers Tales.

ARGO TREASURY OF ENGLISH POETRY (VOLUME 1) (Chaucer to Shakespeare) (Various artists).

MCSET. Cat no: **417 931-4**. Released on Argo (Polygram), Jun '88 by PolyGram Classics **Deleted** Jan '89.

ARGO TREASURY OF ENGLISH POETRY (VOLUME 2) (Donne to Gray) (Various artists).
MCSET. Cat no: **417 934-4**. Released on Argo (Polygram), Jun '88 by PolyGram Classics **Deleted** Jan '89.
MCSET. Cat no: **1029Y**. Released on Travellers Tales, '91 by Travellers Tales.

ARGO TREASURY OF ENGLISH POETRY (VOLUME 3) (Hardy to Elliot) (Various artists).
MCSET. Cat no: **417 928-4**. Released on Argo (Polygram), Jun '88 by PolyGram Classics **Deleted** Jan '89.
MCSET. Cat no: **1030Y**. Released on Travellers Tales, '91 by Travellers Tales.

ARGO TREASURY OF LOVE POEMS (Various artists).
MCSET. Cat no: **418 216-4**. Released on Argo (Polygram), Apr '88 by PolyGram Classics **Deleted** Jan '89.
MCSET. Cat no: **ARGO 1280**. Released on Argo (EMI), Jul '91 by EMI Records.
MCSET. Cat no: **1033Y**. Released on Travellers Tales, '91 by Travellers Tales.

ARGO TREASURY OF READINGS FROM LONGER POEMS (Various artists).
MCSET. Cat no: **418 012-4**. Released on Argo (Polygram), Jun '88 by PolyGram Classics **Deleted** Jan '89.
MCSET. Cat no: **1022Y**. Released on Travellers Tales, '91 by Travellers Tales.

ARGO TREASURY OF RELIGIOUS VERSE (Various artists).
Note: Includes poems by John Donne, John Milton, William Blake, D.H.Lawrence & Rudyard Kipling. Read by Sir John Gielgud, Dame Wendy Hiller, David King, Peter Orr, Tim Piggot-Smith & Richard Pasco.
MCSET. Cat no: **418 195-4**. Released on Argo (Polygram), Apr '88 by PolyGram Classics **Deleted** Jan '89.
MCSET. Cat no: **1031Y**. Released on Travellers Tales, '91 by Travellers Tales.

ARGO TREASURY OF ROMANTIC VERSE (Various artists).
MCSET. Cat no: **418 015-4**. Released on Argo (Polygram), Jun '88 by PolyGram Classics **Deleted** Jan '89.
MCSET. Cat no: **ARGO 1169**. Released on Argo (EMI), Oct '89 by EMI Records.
MCSET. Cat no: **1021Y**. Released on Travellers Tales, '91 by Travellers Tales.

ARGO TREASURY OF VICTORIAN POETRY (Unknown narrator(s)).
MCSET. Cat no: **418 009-4**. Released on Argo (Polygram), Jun '88 by Poly-

Gram Classics **Deleted** Jan '89.
MCSET. Cat no: **ARGO 1115**. Released on Argo (EMI), Jun '89 by EMI Records.
MCSET. Cat no: **1023Y**. Released on Travellers Tales, '91 by Travellers Tales.

BEOWULF, THE BATTLE OF MALDEN (And Other Old English Poems) (Various artists).
Note: Read by Frank Duncan, Prunella Scales and others. Abridged.
MCSET. Cat no: **1001Y**. Released on Travellers Tales, '91 by Travellers Tales. Note: 2 Cassettes.

BEST LOVED VERSE (Gwen Watson & Richard Pasco).
MCSET. Cat no: **LFP 7520**. Released on Listen For Pleasure, Apr '91 by EMI Records. Note: Playing time: 2 1/4 hours.

CANTICO DEL SOLE, CANTO 99... (And Other Poems) (Unknown narrator(s)).
MC. Cat no: **2088**. Released on Caedmon (USA), '83 by Caedmon Records (USA), Bond Street Music.

CAUTIONARY VERSES (Various artists).
MC. Cat no: **ANV 628**. Released on Anvil Cassettes, Jan '81 by Anvil Cassettes, Chivers Audio Books.

COLLECTED POEMS (Various artists).
Note: Read and written by Louis Macneice, C. Day Lewis, Stephen Spender and W.H. Auden
MCSET. Cat no: **1015Y**. Released on Travellers Tales, '91 by Travellers Tales. Note: 2 Cassettes.

COME LOVE WITH ME (Various narrators).
MCSET. Cat no: **LD 5**. Released on Green Dragon, '91 by Green Dragon Audio Visual. Note: 2 Cassettes.

COMIC RHYMES (Rushton, Willie & Sheila Steafel).
MC. Cat no: **0600560899**. Released on Hamlyn Books On Tape, '88, Bond Street Music.

COMMENTARY AND SELECTION (Maurice Lindsay).
Note: Poets are Violet Jacob, Marion Angus, and Helen B Cruickshank.
MC. Cat no: **SSC 058**. Released on Scotsoun, '91 by Scotsoun Recordings, Morley Audio Services.

CURRIE FLAVOUR (Rev James Currie).
MC. Cat no: **SSC 003**. Released on Scotsoun, '91 by Scotsoun Recordings, Morley Audio Services.

EPIC POEMS (Robert Powell).
Tracks / How Horatius held the bridge / Elegy written in a country churchyard / John Gilpin / Hiawatha's wooing / Hiawatha's departure / Pied piper / Lepanto / Jackdaw of Rheims / Rime of the ancient mariner, The / Revenge-a ballad of the fleet / Armada - a fragment / Ballad of the East and West, The /

Sicilian's tale, King Robert / Morte d'Arthur.
Note: Robert Powell reads his own choice.
MCSET. Cat no: **ZBBC 1026.** Released on BBC Radio Collection, Sep '88 by BBC Records. Note: ISBN No: 0563 225750

FAVOURITE POEMS (Robert Donat).
MCSET. Cat no: **1016Y.** Released on Travellers Tales, '91 by Travellers Tales. Note: 2 Cassettes.

FIFTY PAWKY POEMS (Various artists).
MC. Cat no: **SSC 062.** Released on Scotsoun, '91 by Scotsoun Recordings, Morley Audio Services.

MATTER OF CHOICE (Sarah Churchill).
MC. Cat no: **ZSW 637.** Released on Argo, Apr '80 by Decca International **Deleted** '85.

MERVYN MOUSE (Rhyming Stories For The Very Young) (Unknown narrator(s)).
Note: Book and cassette.
MC. Cat no: **PLB 86.** Released on Tell-A-Tale, '88 by Pickwick Records, Taylors, Clyde Factors.

MORE FAVOURITE POEMS (Various artists).
Note: Read by Dame Peggy Ashcroft, Alan Bates, Sir John Gielgud, Sir Alec Guiness and others.
MCSET. Cat no: **SAY 80.** Released on Argo (Polygram), Jun '88 by PolyGram Classics **Deleted** Jan '89.
MCSET. Cat no: **1018Y.** Released on Travellers Tales, '91 by Travellers Tales. Note: 2 Cassettes.

NIGHTMARES (Poems To Trouble Your Sleep) (Jack Prelustksy).
MC. Cat no: **1705.** Released on Caedmon (USA), Aug '83 by Caedmon Records (USA), Bond Street Music.

NONSENSE POETRY (Various artists).
Note: Works by Edward Lear and Lewis Carroll etc. Read by John Gielgud, Derek Jacobi and Daniel Massey etc.
MCSET. Cat no: **418 168-4.** Released on Argo (Polygram), Jun '88 by PolyGram Classics **Deleted** Jan '89. Note: 2 cassette set
MCSET. Cat no: **ARGO 1079.** Released on Argo (EMI), May '89 by EMI Records. Note: 2 Cassettes.

POEMS (Various artists).
LP. Cat no: **CRELP 055.** Released on Creation, Oct '89 by Creation Records, Rough Trade GmbH Germany, Rough Trade BV (Holland).

POEMS IN SCOTS (Various artists).
MC. Cat no: **SSC 048.** Released on Scotsoun, '91 by Scotsoun Recordings, Morley Audio Services.

POEMS IN SCOTS AND GAELIC (Various artists).
MC. Cat no: **SSC 072.** Released on Scotsoun, '91 by Scotsoun Record-

ings, Morley Audio Services.
POEMS IN SCOTS AND GAELIC (Various artists).
MC. Cat no: **SSC 072.** Released on Scotsoun, '91 by Scotsoun Recordings, Morley Audio Services.

POEMS YOU LOVE (Various artists).
Note: Read by John Gielgud, Peter Jeffrey, Daniel Massey, Derek Jacobi, David King, Peter Orr and Imogen Stubbs.
MCSET. Cat no: **418 165-4.** Released on Argo (Polygram), Jun '88 by PolyGram Classics **Deleted** Jan '89. Note: 2 cassette set
MCSET. Cat no: **ARGO 1181.** Released on Argo (EMI), Mar '90 by EMI Records.

POET SPEAKS, THE (A Twentieth Century Anthology) (Various artists).
Note: Read by Auden, Betjeman, Day Lewis, Eliot, Graves and others.
MCSET. Cat no: **SAY 60.** Released on Argo (Polygram), Jun '88 by PolyGram Classics **Deleted** Jan '89.
MCSET. Cat no: **1019Y.** Released on Travellers Tales, '91 by Travellers Tales. Note: 2 Cassettes.
MCSET. Cat no: **ARGO 1313.** Released on Argo (EMI), Apr '92 by EMI Records.

POETRY FROM WORLD WAR I AND II (Various artists).
Note: Read by Robert Hardy, Martin Jarvis and others.
MCSET. Cat no: **1028Y.** Released on Travellers Tales, '91 by Travellers Tales. Note: 2 Cassettes.

POETRY IN MOTION (Alan Bennett).
Note: Includes works by Hardy, Auden, Betjeman and Larkin.
MCSET. Cat no: **ZBBC 1169.** Released on BBC Audio Collection, '91 by BBC Records. Note: ISBN No: 0563 410914

POETRY OF CATULLUS (James Mason).
MC. Cat no: **CDL 51611.** Released on Caedmon (USA), '79 by Caedmon Records (USA), Bond Street Music.

POETRY OLYMPICS (Volume 1) (Various artists).
LP. Cat no: **ARRLP 1.** Released on All Round Productions, Mar '82.

POETRY PLEASE (Various artists).
Note: Tim Piggot-Smith, Ronald Pickup, Andrew Sachs and Rosalind Shanks read favourite poems.
MCSET. Cat no: **ZBBC 1034.** Released on BBC, Sep '88 by BBC Records, Taylors. Note: ISBN No: 0563 225793

POETRY PLEASE (Volume 2) (Various artists).
Note: Over 90 poems are featured from the works of Robert Browning, Edward Lear, Steve Smith-Yeats and TS Elliot and many other poets.
MCSET. Cat no: **ZBBC 1241.** Re-

leased on BBC, Aug '91 by BBC Records, Taylors. Note: ISBN No: 0563 408499

POETRY PROSE AND PIANO (Various artists).
LP. Cat no: **KPM 7015.** Released on Unicorn-Kanchana, Jan '82 by Unicorn - Kanchana Records, Outlet Records **Deleted** Jan '87.

POET'S GOLD (David Ross).
Note: From Keats to Cummings, from Shelley to Shakespeare, a collection of favourite poems read by David Ross, who was awarded a gold medal for radio diction. This recording is a memorial to Ross from the Poetry Society of America.
MC. Cat no: **1741.** Released on Caedmon (USA), '84 by Caedmon Records (USA), Bond Street Music.

POETS OF THE WEST INDIES (Various artists).
Note: Edited by John Figueroa.
MC. Cat no: **1379.** Released on Caedmon (USA), '89 by Caedmon Records (USA), Bond Street Music.

PORTRAIT OF FOUR POETS IN PROSE AND POETRY, A (Various artists).
Note: Wilfred Owen, Herbert Read, Edward Thomas and Idris Davies. Read by Richard Johnson, Tony Church and Frank Duncan.
MCSET. Cat no: **414 757-4.** Released on Argo (Polygram), Jun '88 by PolyGram Classics **Deleted** Jan '89.
MCSET. Cat no: **ARGO 1250.** Released on Argo (EMI), Oct '90 by EMI Records. Note: 2 Cassettes.
MCSET. Cat no: **1002Y.** Released on Travellers Tales, '91 by Travellers Tales.

RAVENSWOOD POEMS (Richard Ryan).
LP. Cat no: **CCT 17.** Released on Claddagh (Ireland), Aug '88 by Claddagh Records (Ireland), Projection, Impetus Records, Jazz Music, Roots Records, C.M. Distribution, Outlet Records, Taylors.

RIME OF THE ANCIENT MARINER, THE (And Other Poems) (Richard Burton).
MCSET. Cat no: **1020Y.** Released on Travellers Tales, '91 by Travellers Tales. Note: 2 Cassettes.

SELECTION OF FAVOURITE POETRY, A (Peter Barkworth & Tim Pigott-Smith).
MCSET. Cat no: **LFP 7302.** Released on Listen For Pleasure, Oct '87 by EMI Records.

SONNETS FROM THE PORTUGUESE (Various artists).
Note: 19 sonnets and an excerpt from Bessier's autobiographical play.
MC. Cat no: **1071.** Released on Caedmon (USA), '88 by Caedmon Records (USA), Bond Street Music.

TAKE MY YOUTH (An Anthology Of Great War Poetry) (Robert Hardy &

Martin Jarvis).
MC. Cat no: **TTC 1012**. Released on Talking Tape Company, Apr '91, Conifer Records. Note: Playing time - 40 mins. ISBN no. 187252088X

MC. Cat no: **TTC/FWO 2**. Released on Talking Tape Company, '84, Conifer Records.

TEMPO FAVOURITE POEMS (Patrick Allen & Sarah Lawson).
MCSET. Cat no: **00 103 211 9**. Released on Tempo, Apr '88 by Warwick Records, Celtic Music, Henry Hadaway Organisation. Note: 2 cassette set.

TEN POETS OF THE 20TH CENTURY (Various artists).
MCSET. Cat no: **414 769-4**. Released on Argo (Polygram), Jun '88 by PolyGram Classics **Deleted** Jan '89.

TONY THE TURTLE (Comic And Curious Verse) (Various artists).
MC. Cat no: **ANV 610**. Released on Anvil Cassettes, Jan '81 by Anvil Cassettes, Chivers Audio Books.

TWA CHIELS AND A LASS (Various artists).
MC. Cat no: **SSC 054**. Released on Scotsoun, '91 by Scotsoun Recordings, Morley Audio Services.

TWELVE POETS OF THE 20TH CENTURY (Various artists).
MCSET. Cat no: **414 772-4**. Released on Argo (Polygram), Jun '88 by PolyGram Classics **Deleted** Jan '89.

VIRGIL, DANTE ET AL (Volume 1) (Various artists).
MC. Cat no: **SSC 087**. Released on Scotsoun, '91 by Scotsoun Recordings, Morley Audio Services.

VIRGIL, DANTE ET AL (Volume 2) (Various artists).
MC. Cat no: **SSC 088**. Released on Scotsoun, '91 by Scotsoun Recordings, Morley Audio Services.

W.H. AUDEN READING (W.H. Auden).
MC. Cat no: **1019**. Released on Caedmon (USA), '89 by Caedmon Records (USA), Bond Street Music.

YOUR FAVOURITE POEMS (Various artists).
Note: Read by Peggy Ashcroft, Richard Burton, John Gielgud, Alec Guinness, Derek Jacobi, Richard Johnson, Richard Pasco, Michael Redgrave, Prunella Scales and others.
MCSET. Cat no: **SAY 18**. Released on Argo (Polygram), Jul '82 by PolyGram Classics **Deleted** Jan '89.
MCSET. Cat no: **ARGO 1139**. Released on Argo (EMI), Sep '89 by EMI Records. Note: 2 Cassettes.
MCSET. Cat no: **1024Y**. Released on Travellers Tales, '91 by Travellers Tales.

Pooley, Sarah

DAY OF RHYMES, A (Various narrators).
MC. Cat no: **TS 374**. Released on Tellastory, '91 by Random Century Audiobooks. Note: ISBN no. 1856561054

Pope, Dudley

CONVOY (William Gaminara).
MCSET. Cat no: **CAB 604**. Released on Chivers Audio Books, '91 by Chivers Audio Books, Green Dragon Audio Visual. Note: 10 Cassettes.

RAMAGE (Steven Pacey).
MCSET. Cat no: **CAB 682**. Released on Chivers Audio Books, Mar '92 by Chivers Audio Books, Green Dragon Audio Visual. Note: 8 Cassettes

Potter, Beatrix

MOUSE TALES (Sir Michael Hordern).
MC. Cat no: **881662**. Released on Puffin Cover To Cover, '88, Green Dragon Audio Visual.

MRS TIGGY-WINKLE AND FRIENDS (Sir Michael Hordern).
MC. Cat no: **881751**. Released on Puffin Cover To Cover, '88, Green Dragon Audio Visual.

TAILOR OF GLOUCESTER, THE (And Other Stories) (Unknown narrator(s)).
Note: Includes: Tale of Mrs Tittlemouse and Tale of Mr Tod.
MC. Cat no: **TSP 405**. Released on Tellastory, Dec '86 by Random Century Audiobooks.

TALE OF BENJAMIN BUNNY (Unknown narrator(s)).
MC. Cat no: **TSP 404**. Released on Tellastory, Aug '81 by Random Century Audiobooks.
MC. Cat no: **BPO 004**. Released on Pickwick, '92 by Pickwick Records, Clyde Factors, Taylors, Arabesque, Solomon & Peres, I & B Records, Prism Leisure, Outlet Records.

TALE OF JEMIMA PUDDLE-DUCK (Unknown narrator(s)).
MC. Cat no: **PLBN 226**. Released on Tell-A-Tale, '89 by Pickwick Records, Taylors, Clyde Factors.

TALE OF JEMIMA PUDDLE-DUCK (And Other Stories) (Unknown narrator(s)).
Note: Includes: Tale of Samuel Whiskers and the Roly-Poly Pudding and Tale of the Pie and the Patty Pan.
MC. Cat no: **TSP 403**. Released on Tellastory, Aug '81 by Random Century Audiobooks.
MC. Cat no: **BPO 002**. Released on Pickwick, '92 by Pickwick Records, Clyde Factors, Taylors, Arabesque, Solomon & Peres, I & B Records, Prism Leisure, Outlet Records.

TALE OF MRS TIGGY-WINKLE, THE (Unknown narrator(s)).
MC. Cat no: **BPO 005**. Released on Pickwick, '92 by Pickwick Records, Clyde Factors, Taylors, Arabesque, Solomon & Peres, I & B Records, Prism Leisure, Outlet Records.

TALE OF PETER RABBIT, THE (And Other Stories) (Unknown narrator(s)).
Note: For ages up to 3+ years. Includes: Tale of the Flopsy Bunnies, Tale of Mrs Tiggywinkle, Appley Dapply's Nursery Rhymes, Tale of Two Bad Mice, Tale of Mr Jeremy Fisher, Tale of Ginger and Pickles and Tales of Peter Rabbit.
MC. Cat no: **TSP 401**. Released on Tellastory, Aug '81 by Random Century Audiobooks.
MC. Cat no: **TSP 411**. Released on Tellastory, Aug '81 by Random Century Audiobooks.
MC. Cat no: **PLBN 224**. Released on Tell-A-Tale, '88 by Pickwick Records, Taylors, Clyde Factors.
MC. Cat no: **BPO 001**. Released on Pickwick, '92 by Pickwick Records, Clyde Factors, Taylors, Arabesque, Solomon & Peres, I & B Records, Prism Leisure, Outlet Records.

TALE OF SQUIRREL NUTKIN, THE (Unknown narrator(s)).
Note: Book and cassette. For ages up to 3+.
MC. Cat no: **PLBN 225**. Released on Tell-A-Tale, '88 by Pickwick Records, Taylors, Clyde Factors.
MC. Cat no: **BPO 003**. Released on Pickwick, '92 by Pickwick Records, Clyde Factors, Taylors, Arabesque, Solomon & Peres, I & B Records, Prism Leisure, Outlet Records.

TALE OF TOM KITTEN (And Other Stories).
Note: Includes: Cecily Parsley's Nursery Rhymes, Tale of Timmy Tiptoes, Tale of JohnnyTown-Mouse, Tale of Squirrel Nutkin and Tale of Tom Kitten.
MC. Cat no: **TSP 402**. Released on Tellastory, Dec '86 by Random Century Audiobooks.

TALE OF TUPPENY (And Other Stories).
Note: Includes: Tale of the Faithful Dove, The Sly Old Cat and Tale of Tuppeny.
MC. Cat no: **TSP 412**. Released on Tellastory, Dec '86 by Random Century Audiobooks.

TALE OF TWO BAD MICE, THE (Unknown narrator(s)).
MC. Cat no: **BPO 006**. Released on Pickwick, '92 by Pickwick Records, Clyde Factors, Taylors, Arabesque, Solomon & Peres, I & B Records, Prism Leisure, Outlet Records.

YOURS AFFECTIONATELY PETER RABBIT (And Other Stories) (Unknown narrator(s)).
Note: Includes: Peter Rabbit's Correspondence, Squirrel Nutkin's Correspondence, Lucinda Doll's Correspondence, Mrs Tiggywinkle's Correspondence, Correspondence Concerning Jeremy Fisher, Mr Alderman PT Tortoise, Invitations, Ribby's Invitation, Mr Samuel Whisker's Correspondence, Sally Henny Penny's Invitations, Rebecca Puddleduck Invitations, Rebecca Puddleduck Correspondence, The Bird's Correspondence and Flopsy Bunnies Correspondence.

MC. Cat no: **TSP 413**. Released on Tellastory, Dec '86 by Random Century Audiobooks.

Potts, Jean

GO, LOVELY ROSE (Pat Starr).
MCSET. Cat no: **CAT 4041**. Released on Chivers Audio Books, '91 by Chivers Audio Books, Green Dragon Audio Visual. Note: 6 Cassettes.

MCSET. Cat no: **1432T**. Released on Travellers Tales, '91 by Travellers Tales. Note: 6 cassettes

Preston, Ivy

HEARTS DO NOT BREAK (Anne Cater).
MCSET. Cat no: **185496559X**. Released on Bramhope, Feb '92 by Ulverscroft Soundings. Note: Playing time: 60 minutes.

HOUSE ABOVE THE BAY, THE (Unknown narrator(s)).
MCSET. Cat no: **185496240X**. Released on Bramhope, '91 by Ulverscroft Soundings. Note: 4 cassettes.

ISLAND OF ENCHANTMENT (Carole Boyd).
MCSET. Cat no: **1854965743**. Released on Bramhope, Mar '92 by Ulverscroft Soundings.

RELEASE THE PAST (Judith Porter).
MCSET. Cat no: **1854965913**. Released on Bramhope, Apr '92 by Ulverscroft Soundings. Note: Playing time: 60 minutes.

Priess, B. & Stout, W.

LITTLE BLUE BRONTOSAURUS (Unknown narrator(s)).
Note: Adapted by George S Irving. Authors are Byron Priess and William Stout.
MC. Cat no: **CDL 51726**. Released on Caedmon (USA), '84 by Caedmon Records (USA), Bond Street Music.

Priestley, J.B.

ANGEL PAVEMENT (Anthony Homyer).
MCSET. Cat no: **TCL 15**. Released on Complete Listener, '91 by Complete Listener. Note: 14 Cassettes. (BB) Playing Time: 1,260 Minutes.

MCSET. Cat no: **1563/4F**. Released on Travellers Tales, '91 by Travellers Tales. Note: 14 cassettes.

FESTIVAL AT FARBRIDGE (Anthony Homyer).
MCSET. Cat no: **1565/6/7F**. Released on Travellers Tales, '91 by Travellers Tales. Note: 20 cassettes.

MCSET. Cat no: **TCL 16**. Released on Complete Listener, '91 by Complete Listener. Note: 20 Cassettes. Playing time: 1,800 minutes.

GOOD COMPANIONS, THE (Anthony Homyer).
MCSET. Cat no: **TCL 14**. Released on Complete Listener, '91 by Complete Listener. Note: 19 Cassettes. (BB)

Playing Time: 1,710 Minutes.
MCSET. Cat no: **1560/1/2F**. Released on Travellers Tales, '91 by Travellers Tales. Note: 19 cassettes.

Pritchett, V.S.

CARELESS WIDOW, A (And Other Stories) (Robin Browne & Frances Jeater).
Note: Stories include :- A Careless Widow, Cocky Olly, A Trip To Me Seaside, Things, A Change Of Policy and The Image Trade.
MCSET. Cat no: **OAS 10492**. Released on Oasis Audio Books, Apr '92 by Isis Audio Books. Note: 8 cassettes. Playing time 4hrs 40mins.

Prokofiev (composer)

PETER AND THE WOLF (Angela Rippon).
Note: Narrated by Angela Rippon. Also includes Saint-Saens' *Carnival of the Animals*. Music performed by the RPO, conducted by Owain Arwel Hughes.
LP. Cat no: **ACM 2005**. Released on ASV (Academy Sound & Vision), '86 by Academy Sound & Vision Records **Deleted** Feb '89.

MC. Cat no: **ZC ACM 2005**. Released on ASV (Academy Sound & Vision), '86 by Academy Sound & Vision Records **Deleted** Feb '89.

PETER AND THE WOLF (David Bowie).
CD. Cat no: **RD 82743**. Released on RCA, '86 by BMG Records (UK) Ltd., Solomon & Peres, Outlet Records. Note: AAD

LP. Cat no: **RL 82743**. Released on RCA, '86 by BMG Records (UK) Ltd., Solomon & Peres, Outlet Records **Deleted** Jul '90.

MC. Cat no: **RK 92743**. Released on RCA, '86 by BMG Records (UK) Ltd., Solomon & Peres, Outlet Records.

PETER AND THE WOLF (Carol Channing).
MC. Cat no: **CDL 51623**. Released on Caedmon (USA), May '80 by Caedmon Records (USA), Bond Street Music.

PETER AND THE WOLF & TUBBY THE TUBA (Carol Channing).
LP. Cat no: **TC 1623**. Released on Caedmon (USA), 1/81 by Caedmon Records (USA). Bond Street Music. Deleted '86.

Proust, Marcel

REMEMBRANCE OF THINGS PAST (Sir Ralph Richardson).
MCSET. Cat no: **2017**. Released on Caedmon (USA), '88 by Caedmon Records (USA), Bond Street Music.

Proysen, Alf

LITTLE OLD MRS. PEPPERPOT (Unknown narrator(s)).
MCSET. Cat no: **DTO 10558**. Released on Ditto, '88 by Pickwick Records, Midland Records.

MRS. PEPPERPOT STORIES (Patricia Gallimore).
Tracks / Mrs. Pepperpot tries to please her husband / Mrs. Pepperpot's penny watchman / Mrs. Pepperpot & the moose / Mrs. Pepperpot finds hidden treasure / Mr. Pepperpot.
MC. Cat no: **TS 345**. Released on Tellastory, Dec '86 by Random Century Audiobooks.

Pryor, Richard

IS IT SOMETHING I SAID (Richard Pryor).
Tracks / Eulogy / Shorter of white people / New niggers / Cocaine / Just us / Mudbone - intro / Mudbone - little feets / When your woman leaves you / Goodnight kiss, The / Women are beautiful / Our text for today.
LP. Cat no: **K 54052**. Released on Reprise, '88 by Warner Music International (WEA).

LIVE IN CONCERT - WANTED (Richard Pryor).
Tracks / Heart attacks / Ali / Keeping in shape / Leon Spinks / Nature / Things in the woods / Deer hunter / Chinese food / Being sensitive / Dogs and horses / Jim Brown / Monkeys / Kids / New Year's eve / White and black people / Black funerals / Discipline.
2LP. Cat no: **K 66091**. Released on WEA, Apr '80 by Warner Music International (WEA), Solomon & Peres, Outlet Records, Music Sales Records.

Pullein-Thompson, C.

PRINCE AT BLACK PONY INN (Unknown narrator(s)).
MCSET. Cat no: **DTO 10546**. Released on Ditto, '88 by Pickwick Records, Midland Records.

STRANGE RIDERS AT BLACK PONY INN (Unknown narrator(s)).
MCSET. Cat no: **DTO 10523**. Released on Ditto, '88 by Pickwick Records, Midland Records.

Purves, Libby

ONE SUMMERS GRACE (Libby Purves).
MCSET. Cat no: **ZBBC 1167**. Released on BBC Radio Collection, Aug '90 by BBC Records. Note: ISBN No: 0563 410892

Pyatt, Rosina

EAGER HEART, THE (Coralyn Sheldon).
MCSET. Cat no: **MRC 1014**. Released on Chivers Audio Books, '91 by Chivers Audio Books, Green Dragon Audio Visual. Note: 2 cassettes.

TO CATCH AN EARL (Georgina Melville).
MCSET. Cat no: **PMB 005**. Released on Mills & Boon, '88. Note: 2 cassettes.

TO LOVE AGAIN (Jan Carey).
MCSET. Cat no: **MRC 1050**. Released on Chivers Audio Books, '91 by Chivers

Audio Books, Green Dragon Audio Visual. Note: 2 cassettes.
UNLIKELY DOCTOR, THE (Lesley Seaward).
MCSET. Cat no: **MRC 1027.** Released on Chivers Audio Books, '91 by Chivers Audio Books, Green Dragon Audio Visual. Note: 2 cassettes

Pyle, Howard
MEN OF IRON (Ian Richardson).
MC. Cat no: **1704.** Released on Caedmon (USA), Apr '83 by Caedmon Records (USA), Bond Street Music.

Pym, Barbara
ACADEMIC QUESTION, AN (Angela Pleasance).
MCSET. Cat no: **CAB 208.** Released on Chivers Audio Books, '91 by Chivers Audio Books, Green Dragon Audio Visual. Note: 4 cassettes

MCSET. Cat no: **1186F.** Released on Travellers Tales, '91 by Travellers Tales. Note: 4 cassettes.

CRAMPTON HODNET (Angela Pleasance).
MCSET. Cat no: **1140F.** Released on Travellers Tales, '91 by Travellers Tales. Note: 4 cassettes.

FEW GREEN LEAVES, A (Elizabeth Proud).
MCSET. Cat no: **1623F.** Released on Travellers Tales, '91 by Travellers Tales. Note: 6 cassettes

NO FOND RETURN OF LOVE (Angela Pleasance).
MCSET. Cat no: **CAB 391.** Released on Chivers Audio Books, '91 by Chivers Audio Books, Green Dragon Audio Visual. Note: 6 Cassettes.

MCSET. Cat no: **1148R.** Released on Travellers Tales, '91 by Travellers Tales. Note: 6 Cassettes.

QUARTET IN AUTUMN (Elizabeth Stepha).
MCSET. Cat no: **IAB 91122.** Released on Isis Audio Books, Dec '91. Note: 6 Cassettes. Playing time approximately 7 hours.

UNSUITABLE ATTACHMENT, AN (Gretel Davis).
MCSET. Cat no: **1406F.** Released on Travellers Tales, '91 by Travellers Tales. Note: 7 cassettes.

MCSET. Cat no: **OAS 89116.** Released on Oasis Audio Books, '91 by Isis Audio Books. Note: 7 Cassettes.

UNSUITABLE ATTACHMENT, AN (Penelope Keith).
MCSET. Cat no: **ZBBC 1214.** Released on BBC Radio Collection, Jul '91 by BBC Records. Note: ISBN No: 0563 409711

Queen, Ellery
CALENDAR OF CRIME (Various narrators).
MCSET. Cat no: **1485T.** Released on Travellers Tales, '91 by Travellers Tales. Note: 8 cassettes.

DOOR BETWEEN, THE (Blain Fairman).
MCSET. Cat no: **CAB 431.** Released on Chivers Audio Books, '91 by Chivers Audio Books, Green Dragon Audio Visual. Note: 8 Cassettes

MCSET. Cat no: **1486T.** Released on Travellers Tales, '91 by Travellers Tales. Note: 8 cassettes.

DRAGON'S TEETH, THE (Blain Fairman).
MCSET. Cat no: **CAB 369.** Released on Chivers Audio Books, '91 by Chivers Audio Books, Green Dragon Audio Visual. Note: 8 Cassettes

MCSET. Cat no: **1402T.** Released on Travellers Tales, '91 by Travellers Tales. Note: 8 cassettes.

Quest, Erica
COLD COFFIN (Angela Down).
MCSET. Cat no: **1854964836.** Released on Bramhope, Aug '91 by Ulverscroft Soundings. Note: 5 Cassettes.

DEATH WALK (Unknown narrator(s)).
MCSET. Cat no: **1854965069.** Released on Bramhope, '91 by Ulverscroft Soundings. Note: 5 Cassettes.

MODEL MURDER (Carole Boyd).
MCSET. Cat no: **1854965603.** Released on Bramhope, Feb '92 by Ulverscroft Soundings. Note: Playing time: 60 minutes.

Quinnell, A.J.
MAN ON FIRE (Gordon Griffin).
MCSET. Cat no: **1127T.** Released on Travellers Tales, '91 by Travellers Tales. Note: 6 Cassettes.

MCSET. Cat no: **1854961837.** Released on Soundings, '91 by Soundings Records, Bond Street Music. Note: 6 Cassettes.

Racine, Jean
ATHALIE (Edited By Jean D. Biard) (Unknown narrator(s)).
Note: In French.
MC. Cat no: **F 7609.** Released on Exeter Tapes, '91 by Drakes Educational Associates.

BAJAZET (Edited By Jean D. Biard) (Unknown narrator(s)).
Note: In French.
MC. Cat no: **F 7963.** Released on Exeter Tapes, '91 by Drakes Educational Associates.

BERENICE (Edited By Jean B. Biard) (Unknown narrator(s)).
Note: In French.
MC. Cat no: **F 7531.** Released on Exeter Tapes, '91 by Drakes Educational Associates.

MITHRIDATE (Edited By Jean D. Biard) (Unknown narrator(s)).
Note: In French.
MC. Cat no: **F 7820.** Released on Exeter Tapes, '91 by Drakes Educational Associates.

Radio
AL READ SHOW (Al Read).

Note: Four classic shows.
MCSET. Cat no: **ZBBC 1012.** Released on BBC, Sep '88 by BBC Records, Taylors. Note: 2 Cassettes. ISBN No: 0563 225408.

ARCHERS - THE WEDDING, THE (Various artists).
Note: The courtship and Jack and Peggy's big day.
MCSET. Cat no: **ZBBC 1206.** Released on BBC Radio Collection, Jan '91 by BBC Records. Note: ISBN No: 0563 409010

BEACHCOMBER - BY THE WAY (Various artists).
MCSET. Cat no: **ZBBC 1101.** Released on BBC, Nov '89 by BBC Records, Taylors. Note: 2 Cassettes. ISBN No: 0536 227814.

BEYOND OUR KEN (Excerpts from BBC Radio) (Various artists).
LP. Cat no: **NTSM 195.** Released on Note April '92. Owned by EMI Records, distriubuted by EMI Distribution.

BEYOND OUR KEN (Various artists)
MCSET. Cat no: **ZBBC 1148.** Released on BBC April '92 by BBC Records, Taylors.

BEST OF ROUND THE HORNE (Various artists).
Note: With Kenneth Horne, Kenneth Williams, Hugh Paddick, Betty Marsden, Bill Pertwee, Douglas Smith.
LP. Cat no: **REH 193.** Released on BBC, Sep '75 by BBC Records, Taylors **Deleted** 31 Aug '88.
MC. Cat no: **RMC 4018.** Released on BBC, '79 by BBC Records, Taylors **Deleted** 31 Aug '88.

CHILDREN'S HOUR (Various artists).
Note: Includes two Toytown plays. Introduction by David Davis.
MCSET. Cat no: **ZBBC 1028.** Released on BBC, Sep '88 by BBC Records, Taylors. Note: ISBN No: 0563 225513.

CLITHEROE KID, THE (Various artists).
Note: Starring Jimmy Clitheroe.
MCSET. Cat no: **ZBBC 1104.** Released on BBC, May '90 by BBC Records, Taylors. Note: ISBN No: 0563 410019

DAN DARE (Various artists).
MCSET. Cat no: **ZBBC 1129.** Released on BBC, Mar '90 by BBC Records, Taylors.

DICK BARTON (Various artists).
MCSET. Cat no: **ZBBC 1063.** Released on BBC Radio Collection, Sep '89 by BBC Records. Note: ISBN No: 0563 226331

DOCTOR WHO (Various artists).
Note: The only radio production of Dr. Who.
MCSET. Cat no: **ZBBC 1020.** Released on BBC Radio Collection, Sep '88 by BBC Records. Note: ISBN No: 0563 225572

EMMA (Volume 1) (Various artists).
Note: Starring Angharad Rees
MCSET. Cat no: **ZBBC 1077.** Released on BBC Radio Collection, '90 by BBC Records. Note: 2 cassettes. ISBN (0563) 226625

EMMA (Volume 2) (Various artists.)
Note: Starring Angharad Rees.
MCSET. Cat no: **ZBBC 1079.** Released on BBC Radio Collection, '90 by BBC Records. Note: 2 cassettes. ISBN (0563)226633

FLYWHEEL, SHYSTER AND FLYWHEEL (Lost Radio Scripts) (Various artists).
MCSET. Cat no: **ZBBC 1225.** Released on BBC, Jul '91 by BBC Records, Taylors. Note: ISBN No: 0563 409975.

FUN AT ONE (Comedy from Radio 1) (Various artists).
LP. Cat no: **REB 371.** Released on BBC, '79 by BBC Records, Taylors **Deleted** '88.
MC. Cat no: **ZCF 371.** Released on BBC, Nov '79 by BBC Records, Taylors **Deleted** '88.

FUNNY COMMERCIALS AND OTHER RADIO FLUFFS (Various artists).
LP. Cat no: **LP 1901.** Released on Tandem, '78.

I'M SORRY I'LL READ THAT AGAIN (Various artists).
LP. Cat no: **REH 342.** Released on BBC, '78 by BBC Records, Taylors **Deleted** '88.
MC. Cat no: **ZCR 342.** Released on BBC, '78 by BBC Records, Taylors **Deleted** '87.

I'M SORRY I'LL READ THAT AGAIN (Various artists).
Note: Starring John Cleese, Tim Brooke Taylor, Graeme Garden and Bill Oddie.
MCSET. Cat no: **ZBBC 1100.** Released on BBC, Nov '89 by BBC Records, Taylors. Note: 2 Cassettes. ISBN No: 0563 227176.

I'M SORRY I'LL READ THAT AGAIN (Volume 2) (Various artists).
MCSET. Cat no: **ZBBC 1329.** Released on BBC, Feb '92 by BBC Records, Taylors.

I.T.M.A. (It's That Man Again) (Various artists).
MCSET. Cat no: **ZBBC 1011.** Released on BBC, Sep '88 by BBC Records, Taylors. Note: 2 Cassettes. ISBN No: 0563 225475

LAKE WOBEGON DAYS/LEAVING HOME (Various artists).
MCSET. Cat no: **0563365897.** Released on BBC, Nov '91 by BBC Records, Taylors.

LENIN OF THE ROVERS (Various artists).
Note: Starring Alexei Sayle
MCSET. Cat no: **ZBBC 1257.** Released on BBC, Nov '91 by BBC Records, Taylors. Note: 2 Cassettes.

ISBN No: 0563 365706.

LISTEN WITH MOTHER (Various artists).
LP. Cat no: **REC 525.** Released on BBC, Aug '84 by BBC Records, Taylors **Deleted** 31 Aug '88.
MC. Cat no: **ZCM 525.** Released on BBC, Aug '84 by BBC Records, Taylors **Deleted** 31 Aug '88.

MEMORIES OF GREAT WIRELESS COMEDY SHOWS (1939-41) (Various artists) See under Comedy

MORE FUN AT ONE (Various artists).
LP. Cat no: **REB 399.** Released on BBC, Nov '80 by BBC Records, Taylors **Deleted** '88.

MORE OF THE BEST OF ROUND THE HORNE (Various artists).
Note: With Kenneth Horne, Kenneth Williams, Hugh Paddick, Betty Marsden, Bill Pertwee, Douglas Smith.
LP. Cat no: **REH 240.** Released on BBC, Oct '76 by BBC Records, Taylors **Deleted** 31 Aug '88.
MC. Cat no: **RMC 4044.** Released on BBC, Oct '76 by BBC Records, Taylors **Deleted** 31 Aug '88.

MUCH BINDING IN THE MARSH (Various artists).
MCSET. Cat no: **ZBBC 1197.** Released on BBC, Feb '91 by BBC Records, Taylors. Note: 2 Cassettes. ISBN No: 0563 409037.

NAVY LARK, THE (Various artists).
MCSET. Cat no: **ZBBC 1096.** Released on BBC, Nov '89 by BBC Records, Taylors. Note: 2 Cassettes. ISBN No: 0563 227168.

NAVY LARK, THE (Volume 2) (Various artists).
MCSET. Cat no: **ZBBC 1173.** Released on BBC, Oct '90 by BBC Records, Taylors. Note: 2 Cassettes. ISBN No: 0563 411163.

NAVY LARK, THE (Volume 3) (Various artists).
MCSET. Cat no: **ZBBC 1250.** Released on BBC, Aug '91 by BBC Records, Taylors. Note: 2 Cassettes. ISBN No: 0563 36520X.

NAVY LARK, THE (Volume 4) (Various artists).
MCSET. Cat no: **ZBBC 1327.** Released on BBC, Mar '92 by Taylors.

NEW QUIZ, THE (Chaired By Barry Took) (Various artists).
MCSET. Cat no: **ZBBC 1271.** Released on BBC, Nov '91 by BBC Records, Taylors. Note: 2 Cassettes. ISBN No: 0563 36579X.

ROUND THE HORNE (Volume 1) (Various artists).
Note: Starring Kenneth Horne, Kenneth Williams, Hugh Paddick, Betty Marsden and Bill Pertwee.
MCSET. Cat no: **ZBBC 1010.** Released on BBC, Sep '88 by BBC Records, Taylors. Note: 2 Cassettes. ISBN No: 0563 225491

ROUND THE HORNE (Volume 2)

(Various artists).
MCSET. Cat no: **ZBBC 1092.** Released on BBC, Nov '89 by BBC Records, Taylors. Note: 2 Cassettes.

ROUND THE HORNE (Volume 3) (Various artists).
Note: With Kenneth Horne, Kenneth Williams, Hugh Paddick, Betty Marsden, Bill Pertwee, Douglas Smith.
LP. Cat no: **REH 296.** Released on BBC, Oct '77 by BBC Records, Taylors **Deleted** Apr '89.
MC. Cat no: **ZCF 296.** Released on BBC, Oct '77 by BBC Records, Taylors **Deleted** Apr '89.

ROUND THE HORNE (Volume 3)
MCSET. Cat no: **ZBBC 1093.** Released on BBC, Nov '89 by BBC Records, Taylors. Note: 2 Cassettes. ISBN No: 0563 409916.

ROUND THE HORNE (Volume 4) (Various artists).
MCSET. Cat no: **ZBBC 1222.** Released on BBC Radio Collection, Apr '91 by BBC Records.

STAR IS BORN, A (Radio Version 1942) (Various artists).
MC. Cat no: **CMR 1155.** Released on Radiola, July, '91 by Pinnacle.
CD. Cat no: **CDMR 1155.** Released on Radiola, Oct '90 by Pinnacle.

STEPTOE AND SON (Various artists).
MCSET. Cat no: **ZBBC 1145.** Released on BBC, Nov '90 by BBC Records, Taylors. Note: 2 Cassettes. ISBN No: 0563 411228

STEPTOE & SON (See also Steptoe & Son)

SYMPHONY OF THE BODY (Anthony Smith).
LP. Cat no: **REC 367.** Released on BBC, Oct '79 by BBC Records, Taylors **Deleted** '84.

TAKE IT FROM HERE (Various artists)
MCSET. Cat no: **ZBBC 1113.** Released on BBC, Mar '90 by BBC Records, Taylors.

TAKE IT FROM HERE (Volume 2) (Various artists)
MCSET. Cat no: **ZBBC 1217.** Released on BBC Radio Collection, April '91 by BBC Records, Taylors.

VINTAGE ARCHERS (Volume 1) (Various artists).
Note: Great moments from radio's longest running serial.
MCSET. Cat no: **ZBBC 1036.** Released on BBC Radio Collection, Sep '88 by BBC Records. Note: ISBN No: 0563 225866

VINTAGE ARCHERS (Volume 2) (Various artists).
MCSET. Cat no: **ZBBC 1080.** Released on BBC Radio Collection, Oct '89 by BBC Records. Note: ISBN No: 0563 227044

WINSTON (Peter Tinniswood).
MCSET. Cat no: **ZBBC 1298.** Released on BBC April '92 by BBC Re-

cords, Taylors.

WOMEN'S HOUR SHORT STORIES See under Romance (Various artists).

YES MINISTER (Volume 1) (Various artists).
MCSET. Cat no: **ZBBC 1147.** Released on BBC, Oct '90 by BBC Records, Taylors. Note: 2 Cassettes. ISBN No: 0563 412690.

YES MINISTER (Volume 2) (Various artists).
Note: Includes: 'Jobs For The Boys', 'The Right To Know', 'Doing The Honours' and 'The Devil You Know'.
MCSET. Cat no: **ZBBC 1177.** Released on BBC, Oct '90 by BBC Records, Taylors. Note: 2 Cassettes. ISBN No: 0563 412747.

YES MINISTER (Volume 3) (Various artists).
Note: Includes: 'The Quality of Life', 'The Whiskey Priest', 'The Death List' and 'The Moral Dimension'.
MCSET. Cat no: **ZBBC 1269.** Released on BBC, Sep '91 by BBC Records, Taylors. Note: 2 Cassettes. ISBN No: 0563 365773.

YES MINISTER (Volume 4) (Various artists).
MCSET. Cat no: **ZBBC 1277.** Released on BBC, Sep '91 by BBC Records, Taylors.

Radio Active
RADIO ACTIVE (Featuring Hee Bee Gee B) (Various artists).
Tracks: Police file and shipping forecast / Various artists / Commercial break / Various artists / Radiothon / Various artists / S.O.S. message / Various artists / Thought for the day / Various artists / Results service / Various artists.
LP. Cat no: **REH 471.** Released on BBC May ' 83 by BBC Records, Taylors. **Deleted** April '89.

MC. Cat no: **ZCR 471.** Released on BBC May '83 by BBC Records, Taylors. **Deleted** April '89.

Ramsay, Allan
ALLAN RAMSAY (Volume 1) (Various artists).
MC. Cat no: **SSC 051.** Released on Scotsoun, '91 by Scotsoun Recordings, Morley Audio Services.

ALLAN RAMSAY (Volume 2) (Various artists).
MC. Cat no: **SSC 052.** Released on Scotsoun, '91 by Scotsoun Recordings, Morley Audio Services.

Ramsay, Fay
MASTER'S WIFE (Diana Olsson).
MCSET. Cat no: **CLT 1009.** Released on Candlelight, '88 by AVLS (Audio-Visual Library Services).

Ransome, Arthur
SWALLOWS AND AMAZONS (Bernard Cribbins).

MCSET. Cat no: **LFP 7090.** Released on Listen For Pleasure, Jan '84 by EMI Records.

MCSET. Cat no: **9024F.** Released on Travellers Tales, '91 by Travellers Tales. Note: 2 Cassettes.

Raspe, Rudolf Erich
BARON MUNCHAUSEN TRULY TALL TALES (Peter Ustinov).
Note: 18 tales of the world's champion liar, which, like Swift's *Gulliver's Travels*, also contains scathing social comment.
MC. Cat no: **1409.** Released on Caedmon (USA), '88 by Caedmon Records (USA), Bond Street Music.

Rattigan, Terence
BROWNING VERSION, THE (Various artists).
MCSET. Cat no: **0370.** Released on Caedmon (USA), '88 by Caedmon Records (USA), Bond Street Music. Note: 2 cassettes

DOUBLE BILL (Nigel Stock & Michael Aldridge).
Note: Includes: The Browning Version and The Winslow Bay.
MCSET. Cat no: **ZBBC 1037.** Released on BBC Radio Collection, '91 by BBC Records. Note: 2 cassettes. ISBN No: 0563 225661

Rawlings, Marjorie
YEARLING, THE (David Wayne).
MCSET. Cat no: **2057.** Released on Caedmon (USA), '88 by Caedmon Records (USA), Bond Street Music.

Ray, Ted
RAY'S A LAUGH (Ted Ray).
MCSET. Cat no: **ZBBC 1117.** Released on BBC, Jun '90 by BBC Records, Taylors. Note: 2 Cassettes. ISBN No: 0563 410337.

Raymond, Alex
FLASH GORDON (Unknown narrator(s)).
MCSET. Cat no: **DTO 10522.** Released on Ditto, '88 by Pickwick Records, Midland Records.

Rayner, Claire
POSTSCRIPTS (Peter Whitman).
MCSET. Cat no: **CAB 637.** Released on Chivers Audio Books, Dec '91 by Chivers Audio Books, Green Dragon Audio Visual. Note: 10 cassettes.

REPRISE (Eileen Atkins).
MCSET. Cat no: **CAB 551.** Released on Chivers Audio Books, '91 by Chivers Audio Books, Green Dragon Audio Visual. Note: 8 Cassettes.

MCSET. Cat no: **1613F.** Released on Travellers Tales, '91 by Travellers Tales. Note: 8 cassettes.

STARCH OF APRONS, A (Unknown narrator(s)).
MCSET. Cat no: **1854964046.** Released on Bramhope, '91 by Ulverscroft Soundings. Note: 5 Cassettes.

Read, Giles
MUNCH BUNCH (Rory Rhubarb) (Nigel Pegram).
MC. Cat no: **TTS 9830.** Released on Tempo, Aug '84 by Warwick Records, Celtic Music, Henry Hadaway Organisation.

MUNCH BUNCH (Sally Strawberry) (Nigel Pegram).
MC. Cat no: **TTS 9829.** Released on Tempo, Aug '84 by Warwick Records, Celtic Music, Henry Hadaway Organisation.

MUNCH BUNCH (Scruff Gosseberry) (Nigel Pegram).
MC. Cat no: **TTS 9832.** Released on Tempo, Aug '84 by Warwick Records, Celtic Music, Henry Hadaway Organisation.

MUNCH BUNCH (Spud) (Nigel Pegram).
MC. Cat no: **TTS 9831.** Released on Tempo, Aug '84 by Warwick Records, Celtic Music, Henry Hadaway Organisation.

MUNCH BUNCH STORIES (Volume 1) (Matthew Kelly).
MC. Cat no: **TBC 9501.** Released on Tempo Storytime, May '84 by Warwick Records, Celtic Music.

MUNCH BUNCH STORIES (Volume 2) (Matthew Kelly).
MC. Cat no: **TBC 9502.** Released on Tempo Storytime, May '84 by Warwick Records, Celtic Music.

MUNCH BUNCH STORIES AND SONGS (Various artists).
Note: Narrators are: John Noakes, Peter Purves and Lesley Judd.
LP. Cat no: **STMP 9018.** Released on Super Tempo, May '84 by Warwick Records, Taylors, Solomon & Peres, Sony Music Operations.

Read, Miss
AFFAIRS AT THRUSH GREEN (Gwen Watford).
MCSET. Cat no: **CAB 083.** Released on Chivers Audio Books, '91 by Chivers Audio Books, Green Dragon Audio Visual. Note: 6 Cassettes.

MCSET. Cat no: **1142F.** Released on Travellers Tales, '91 by Travellers Tales. Note: 6 Cassettes.

AT HOME IN THRUSH GREEN (Gwen Watford).
MCSET. Cat no: **CAB 160.** Released on Chivers Audio Books, '91 by Chivers Audio Books, Green Dragon Audio Visual. Note: 6 Cassettes.

MCSET. Cat no: **1144F.** Released on Travellers Tales, '91 by Travellers Tales. Note: 6 cassettes.

BATTLES AT THRUSH GREEN (Gwen Watford).
MCSET. Cat no: **CAB 227.** Released on Chivers Audio Books, '91 by Chivers Audio Books, Green Dragon Audio Visual. Note: 6 Cassettes

MCSET. Cat no: **1208F.** Released on Travellers Tales, '91 by Travellers

CHRISTMAS MOUSE, THE (No Holly for Miss Quinn) (Gwen Watford).
MCSET. Cat no: **CAB 639.** Released on Chivers Audio Books, 1 Oct '91 by Chivers Audio Books, Green Dragon Audio Visual. Note: 6 cassettes

FRESH FROM THE COUNTRY (Gwen Watford).
MCSET. Cat no: **CAB 683.** Released on Chivers Audio Books, Mar '92 by Chivers Audio Books, Green Dragon Audio Visual. Note: 6 Cassettes

FRIENDS AT THRUSH GREEN (Gwen Watford).
MCSET. Cat no: **CAB 605.** Released on Chivers Audio Books, '91 by Chivers Audio Books, Green Dragon Audio Visual. Note: 8 Cassettes.

GOSSIP FROM THRUSH GREEN (Gwen Watford).
MCSET. Cat no: **CAB 046.** Released on Chivers Audio Books, '91 by Chivers Audio Books, Green Dragon Audio Visual. Note: 6 Cassettes

MCSET. Cat no: **1143F.** Released on Travellers Tales, '91 by Travellers Tales. Note: 6 cassettes.

MRS PRINGLE (Gwen Watford).
MCSET. Cat no: **CAB 462.** Released on Chivers Audio Books, '91 by Chivers Audio Books, Green Dragon Audio Visual. Note: 4 Cassettes.

MCSET. Cat no: **1467F.** Released on Travellers Tales, '91 by Travellers Tales. Note: 4 cassettes.

NEWS FROM THRUSH GREEN (Gwen Watford).
MCSET. Cat no: **CAB 505.** Released on Chivers Audio Books, '91 by Chivers Audio Books, Green Dragon Audio Visual. Note: 6 Cassettes.

MCSET. Cat no: **1530F.** Released on Travellers Tales, '91 by Travellers Tales. Note: 6 cassettes.

SCHOOL AT THRUSH GREEN, THE (Gwen Watford).
MCSET. Cat no: **CAB 363.** Released on Chivers Audio Books, '91 by Chivers Audio Books, Green Dragon Audio Visual. Note: 6 Cassettes.

MCSET. Cat no: **1345F.** Released on Travellers Tales, '91 by Travellers Tales. Note: 6 cassettes.

SUMMER AT FAIRACRE (Prunella Scales).
MCSET. Cat no: **CAB 139.** Released on Chivers Audio Books, '91 by Chivers Audio Books, Green Dragon Audio Visual. Note: 6 Cassettes.

MCSET. Cat no: **1145F.** Released on Travellers Tales, '91 by Travellers Tales. Note: 6 cassettes.

VILLAGE DIARY (Gwen Watford).
MCSET. Cat no: **CAB 558.** Released on Chivers Audio Books, '91 by Chivers Audio Books, Green Dragon Audio Visual. Note: 6 Cassettes.

MCSET. Cat no: **1620F.** Released on Travellers Tales, '91 by Travellers Tales. Note: 6 cassettes.

VILLAGE SCHOOL (Gwen Watford).
MCSET. Cat no: **CAB 009.** Released on Chivers Audio Books, '81 by Chivers Audio Books, Green Dragon Audio Visual.

MCSET. Cat no: **1146F.** Released on Travellers Tales, '91 by Travellers Tales. Note: 6 cassettes.

Reagan, Ronald

WIT AND WISDOM OF RONALD REAGAN (Ronald Reagan).
Note: This record is predictably blank.
LP. Cat no: **ABRA 1.** Released on Magic (1), Dec '80 by Submarine Records, Submarine Records, Swift, Wellard Dist., Celtic Music, Charly Records.

Redmayne, Ann

FUGITIVE YEAR, THE (Jean Waggoner).
MCSET. Cat no: **MRC 1036.** Released on Chivers Audio Books, '91 by Chivers Audio Books, Green Dragon Audio Visual. Note: 2 Cassettes.

HATE, AKIN TO LOVE (Eve Karpf).
MCSET. Cat no: **MRC 1055.** Released on Chivers Audio Books, '91 by Chivers Audio Books, Green Dragon Audio Visual. Note: 2 cassettes.

Reeman, Douglas

IN DANGER'S HOUR (David Rintoul).
MCSET. Cat no: **CAB 424.** Released on Chivers Audio Books, '91 by Chivers Audio Books, Green Dragon Audio Visual. Note: 8 Cassettes.

MCSET. Cat no: **1407F.** Released on Travellers Tales, '91 by Travellers Tales. Note: 8 cassettes.

IRON PIRATE, THE (Daniel Massey).
MCSET. Cat no: **LFP 7349.** Released on Listen For Pleasure, Aug '88 by EMI Records. Note: Playing time: 2 hours 30 minutes.

STRIKE FROM THE SEA (David Rintoul).
MCSET. Cat no: **CAB 525.** Released on Chivers Audio Books, '91 by Chivers Audio Books, Green Dragon Audio Visual. Note: 8 cassettes.

MCSET. Cat no: **1637T.** Released on Travellers Tales, '91 by Travellers Tales. Note: 8 cassettes.

TORPEDO RUN (David Rintoul).
MCSET. Cat no: **CAB 567.** Released on Chivers Audio Books, '91 by Chivers Audio Books, Green Dragon Audio Visual. Note: 8 cassettes.

MCSET. Cat no: **1652F.** Released on Travellers Tales, '91 by Travellers Tales. Note: 8 cassettes.

WHITE GUNS, THE (David Rintoul).
MCSET. Cat no: **CAB 467.** Released on Chivers Audio Books, '91 by Chivers Audio Books, Green Dragon Audio Visual. Note: 10 Cassettes.

MCSET. Cat no: **1475/6F.** Released on Travellers Tales, '91 by Travellers Tales. Note: 10 cassettes

Reeves, James

CASTLE OF THE GOLDEN SUN, THE (And Other Stories) (Georgina Melville).
MCSET. Cat no: **TTC/K 10.** Released on Talking Tape Company, '84, Conifer Records.

MCSET. Cat no: **TTC 2103.** Released on Talking Tape Company, Apr '91, Conifer Records. Note: 2 Cassettes

Reid Banks, Lynne

FAIRY REBEL, THE (Lynne Reid Banks).
MCSET. Cat no: **2CCA 3113.** Released on Chivers Audio Books, '91 by Chivers Audio Books, Green Dragon Audio Visual. Note: 2 Cassettes.

MCSET. Cat no: **9188F.** Released on Travellers Tales, '91 by Travellers Tales. Note: 2 Cassettes.

INDIAN IN THE CUPBOARD, THE (Lynne Reid Banks).
MCSET. Cat no: **3CCA 3075.** Released on Chivers Audio Books, '91 by Chivers Audio Books, Green Dragon Audio Visual. Note: 3 Cassettes.

MCSET. Cat no: **9185F.** Released on Travellers Tales, '91 by Travellers Tales. Note: 3 Cassettes.

RETURN OF THE INDIAN (Lynne Reid Banks).
MCSET. Cat no: **3CCA 3107.** Released on Chivers Audio Books, '91 by Chivers Audio Books, Green Dragon Audio Visual. Note: 3 Cassettes.

MCSET. Cat no: **9187F.** Released on Travellers Tales, '91 by Travellers Tales. Note: 3 Cassettes

SECRET OF THE INDIAN, THE (Lynne Reid Banks).
MCSET. Cat no: **3CCA 3131.** Released on Chivers Audio Books, '91 by Chivers Audio Books, Green Dragon Audio Visual. Note: 3 Cassettes.

Reid, George

STORIES GRANDAD TELLS ME (Andrew Cruickshank).
Note: Includes Nessie the Loch Ness Monster, Hamish the Sheep That Wanted to be a Human and Glug and Nip (the Explorers).
MC. Cat no: **VCA 099.** Released on VFM Cassettes, Jan '85 by VFM Cassettes, Midland Records, Crusader Marketing Co., Taylors, Morley Audio Services.

Reid, Mike

GOLDEN HOUR OF MIKE REID (Mike Reid).
CD. Cat no: **KGHCD 123.** Released on Knight, Sep '90 by Knight Records Ltd., BMG Distribution Operations **Deleted** Feb '92.

MC. Cat no: **KGHMC 123.** Released on Knight, Sep '90 by Knight Records Ltd., BMG Distribution Operations **Deleted** Feb '92.

Reid, P.R.

COLDITZ STORY, THE (Tim Woodward).
MCSET. Cat no: **CAB 577**. Released on Chivers Audio Books, '91 by Chivers Audio Books, Green Dragon Audio Visual. Note: 6 Cassettes

MCSET. Cat no: **1026W**. Released on Travellers Tales, '91 by Travellers Tales. Note: 6 Cassettes

COLDITZ STORY, THE (Patrick Allen).
MC. Cat no: **P 90018**. Released on Pinnacle, '79 by Pinnacle Records, Outlet Records, Music Sales Records.

Remarque, E.M.

ALL QUIET ON THE WESTERN FRONT (Unknown narrator(s)).
MCSET. Cat no: **1283F**. Released on Travellers Tales, '91 by Travellers Tales. Note: 6 cassettes.

Renault, Mary

BULL FROM THE SEA, THE (Jamie Hanes).
MCSET. Cat no: **RB 88680**. Released on Recorded Books, Nov '91 by Isis Audio Books. Note: 6 cassettes. Playing time 8hrs 30mins.

BULL FROM THE SEA, THE (Michael York).
Note: Also available on hanging fromat, catalogue number:- 000138709X.
MCSET. Cat no: **0001386476**. Released on Harper Collins, '91 by Harper Collins. Note: 2 Cassettes.

CHARIOTEER, THE (Davina Porter).
MCSET. Cat no: **1626/7F**. Released on Travellers Tales, '91 by Travellers Tales. Note: 10 cassettes.

MCSET. Cat no: **RB 88760**. Released on Recorded Books, '91 by Isis Audio Books. Note: 10 cassettes.

KING MUST DIE, THE (Walt McPherson).
MCSET. Cat no: **RB 82053**. Released on Recorded Books, Oct '91 by Isis Audio Books. Note: 9 cassettes. Playing time 13hrs.

KING MUST DIE, THE (Michael York).
Note: Also available on hanging format, catalogue number:- 0001387081
MCSET. Cat no: **0001386468**. Released on Harper Collins, '91 by Harper Collins. Note: 2 Cassettes.

LAST OF THE WINE, THE (George Wilson).
MCSET. Cat no: **RB 90061**. Released on Recorded Books, Apr '92 by Isis Audio Books. Note: 9 cassettes. Playing time 12hrs 15mins.

PERSIAN BOY, THE (Aviva Skell).
MCSET. Cat no: **RB 83060**. Released on Recorded Books, Jul '92 by Isis Audio Books. Note: 10 Cassettes. Playing time: 15 hours.

Rendell, Ruth

COPPER PEACOCK, THE (And Other Stories) (James Fox).
MCSET. Cat no: **RC 50**. Released on Random Century, Feb '92 by Random Century Audiobooks, Conifer Records. Note: ISBN no. 185686068X

FROM DOON WITH DEATH (George Baker).
MCSET. Cat no: **RC 24**. Released on Random Century, Aug '91 by Random Century Audiobooks, Conifer Records. Note: 2 cassettes. ISBN 1856860655. 3 hrs approx.

GOING WRONG (Dermot Crowley).
MCSET. Cat no: **CAB 684**. Released on Chivers Audio Books, Mar '92 by Chivers Audio Books, Green Dragon Audio Visual. Note: 8 Cassettes

HEARTSTONES (And Thornapple) (Geraldine James).
MCSET. Cat no: **ZC SWD 362**. Released on ASV (Academy Sound & Vision), Oct '89 by Academy Sound & Vision Records. Note: 2 Cassettes. Playing time: 2 hours 45 minutes.

INSPECTOR WEXFORD - MEANS OF EVIL (George Baker).
MCSET. Cat no: **LFP 7526**. Released on Listen For Pleasure, Apr '91 by EMI Records. Note: Playing time: 2 hours 15 minutes.

INSPECTOR WEXFORD ON HOLIDAY (George Baker).
MCSET. Cat no: **LFP 7499**. Released on Listen For Pleasure, Oct '90 by EMI Records.

JUDGEMENT IN STONE, A (Carole Hayman).
MCSET. Cat no: **CAB 215**. Released on Chivers Audio Books, '91 by Chivers Audio Books, Green Dragon Audio Visual. Note: 6 Cassettes

MCSET. Cat no: **1155T**. Released on Travellers Tales, '91 by Travellers Tales. Note: 6 cassettes

KINDNESS OF RAVENS, A (Michael Bryant).
MCSET. Cat no: **CAB 151**. Released on Chivers Audio Books, '91 by Chivers Audio Books, Green Dragon Audio Visual. Note: 6 Cassettes.

MCSET. Cat no: **1131T**. Released on Travellers Tales, '91 by Travellers Tales. Note: 6 cassettes.

KISSING THE GUNNER'S DAUGHTER (Christopher Ravenscroft).
MCSET. Cat no: **RC 92**. Released on Random Century, Jul '92 by Random Century Audiobooks, Conifer Records. Note: ISBN no. 1856861236

LAKE OF DARKNESS, THE (David Suchet).
MCSET. Cat no: **CAB 250**. Released on Chivers Audio Books, '91 by Chivers Audio Books, Green Dragon Audio Visual. Note: 6 Cassettes.

MCSET. Cat no: **1197T**. Released on Travellers Tales, '91 by Travellers Tales. Note: 6 cassettes.

LIVE FLESH (Ian Holm).
MCSET. Cat no: **CAB 187**. Released on Chivers Audio Books, '91 by Chivers Audio Books, Green Dragon Audio Visual. Note: 8 Cassettes.

MCSET. Cat no: **1128T**. Released on Travellers Tales, '91 by Travellers Tales. Note: 8 cassettes.

MASTER OF THE MOOR (Michael Bryant).
MCSET. Cat no: **CAB 061**. Released on Chivers Audio Books, '91 by Chivers Audio Books, Green Dragon Audio Visual. Note: 6 Cassettes

MCSET. Cat no: **1129T**. Released on Travellers Tales, '91 by Travellers Tales. Note: 6 cassettes.

SPEAKER OF MANDARIN, THE (Michael Bryant).
MCSET. Cat no: **CAB 108**. Released on Chivers Audio Books, '91 by Chivers Audio Books, Green Dragon Audio Visual. Note: 6 Cassettes

MCSET. Cat no: **1130T**. Released on Travellers Tales, '91 by Travellers Tales. Note: 6 cassettes.

TALKING TO STRANGE MEN (Christian Rodska).
MCSET. Cat no: **CAB 439**. Released on Chivers Audio Books, '91 by Chivers Audio Books, Green Dragon Audio Visual. Note: 8 Cassettes

MCSET. Cat no: **1592T**. Released on Travellers Tales, '91 by Travellers Tales. Note: 8 cassettes.

TREE OF HANDS, THE (Imelda Staunton).
MCSET. Cat no: **CAB 638**. Released on Chivers Audio Books, Oct '91 by Chivers Audio Books, Green Dragon Audio Visual. Note: 8 Cassettes.

VEILED ONE, THE (Andrew Sachs).
MCSET. Cat no: **1419T**. Released on Travellers Tales, '91 by Travellers Tales. Note: 8 cassettes.

VEILED ONE, THE (Robin Bailey).
MCSET. Cat no: **CAB 385**. Released on Chivers Audio Books, '91 by Chivers Audio Books, Green Dragon Audio Visual. Note: 8 Cassettes.

WOLF TO THE SLAUGHTER (Robin Bailey).
MCSET. Cat no: **CAB 541**. Released on Chivers Audio Books, '91 by Chivers Audio Books, Green Dragon Audio Visual. Note: 6 Cassettes.

MCSET. Cat no: **1711T**. Released on Travellers Tales, '91 by Travellers Tales. Note: 6 cassettes.

MCSET. Cat no: **074512805X**. Released on Word For Word, May '92 by Chivers Audio Books.

Rey, H.A.

CURIOUS GEORGE (Julie Harris).
MC. Cat no: **1420**. Released on Caedmon (USA), '88 by Caedmon Records (USA), Bond Street Music.

Rhodes, Elvi

OPAL (Jan Francis).
MCSET. Cat no: **CAB 646**. Released

on Chivers Audio Books, Nov '91 by Chivers Audio Books, Green Dragon Audio Visual. Note: 6 cassettes

Rice, A
WITCHING HOUR (Lindsay Crouse).
MCSET. Cat no: **RC 4**. Released on Random Century, '91 by Random Century Audiobooks, Conifer Records. Note: 2 cassettes. ISBN 1856860655. 3 hrs approx.

Rice, Nicky
RINGING THE CHANGES (And Lazarus Rising) (Various narrators).
MC. Cat no: **NF 12**. Released on Nightfall Tapes, '89 by BMG Records (UK) Ltd..

Richards, Frank
BILLY BUNTER GETS THE BOOT (Christopher Biggins).
MCSET. Cat no: **LFP 7490**. Released on Listen For Pleasure, Oct '90 by EMI Records.

Richardson, John
WITH A LITTLE HELP. (Unknown narrators).
MC. Cat no: **C 606**. Released on New World Cassettes, '88.

Rider Haggard, H
KING SOLOMON'S MINES (Miles Anderson).
MCSET. Cat no: **414 724-4**. Released on Argo (Polygram), Nov '84 by PolyGram Classics **Deleted** Jan '89.
MCSET. Cat no: **ARGO 1190**. Released by Argo (EMI), Mar '90 by EMI Records. Note: 2 Cassettes.
KING SOLOMON'S MINES (John Young).
MCSET. Cat no: **COL 2003**. Released on Colophone, Feb '81 by AVLS (Audio-Visual Library Services).
KING SOLOMON'S MINES (John Young).
Note: Abridged version.
MCSET. Cat no: **1065F**. Released on Travellers Tales, '91 by Travellers Tales. Note: 2 cassettes.
KING SOLOMON'S MINES (Anthony Homyer).
MCSET. Cat no: **TCL 30**. Released on Complete Listener, '91 by Complete Listener. Note: 14 Cassettes. (BB) Playing Time: 1,260 Minutes.
KING SOLOMON'S MINES (Michael Jayston).
MC. Cat no: **P 90039**. Released on Pinnacle, '79 by Pinnacle Records, Outlet Records, Music Sales Records.
SHE (Martin Heller).
Note: Abridged version.
MCSET. Cat no: **SPF 350-1**. Released on Schiltron Audio Books, '91 by Schiltron Publishing. Note: 4 Cassettes. Playing time 5 hours 30 minutes.
MCSET. Cat no: **1473F**. Released on Travellers Tales, '91 by Travellers Tales. Note: 4 cassettes.

Rieu, E.V.
SIR SMASHAM UPPE (Various narrators).
MC. Cat no: **ANV 611**. Released on Anvil Cassettes, Jan '81 by Anvil Cassettes, Chivers Audio Books.

Riley, Phil
PUFFALUMPS AND THE CAVES (Judy Buxton).
MC. Cat no: **0 00 102182 6**. Released on Tempo, '88 by Warwick Records, Celtic Music, Henry Hadaway Organisation.
PUFFALUMPS AND THE WIZARD, THE (Judy Buxton).
MC. Cat no: **0 00 102181 8**. Released on Tempo, '88 by Warwick Records, Celtic Music, Henry Hadaway Organisation.

Roach, Hal
BEST OF IRISH HUMOUR (Hal Roach).
LP. Cat no: **CAB 101**. Released on Cabaret, Jun '84.
MC. Cat no: **CCAB 101**. Released on Cabaret, Jun '84.

Roberts, Paddy
WORLD OF PADDY ROBERTS (Paddy Roberts).
LP. Cat no: **SPA 37**. Released on Decca, '69 by PolyGram Classics, Thames Distributors Ltd..

Robertson, Don
GREATEST THING SINCE SLICED BREAD (Tony Barbour).
MCSET. Cat no: **RB 80180**. Released on Recorded Books, May '92 by Isis Audio Books. Note: 6 Cassettes. Playing time: 8 hours.

Robins, Denise
INFATUATION (Sheila Latimer).
MCSET. Cat no: **CLT 1005**. Released on Candlelight, '88 by AVLS (Audio-Visual Library Services).
NEVER LOOK BACK (Victoria Kempton).
MCSET. Cat no: **CLT 1013**. Released on Candlelight, '91 by AVLS (Audio-Visual Library Services). Note: 2 cassettes.
STRANGE RAPTURE (Gwyneth Guthrie).
MCSET. Cat no: **CLT 1006**. Released on Candlelight, '88 by AVLS (Audio-Visual Library Services).

Robinson, T. & Curtis, R.
ODYSSEUS - THE GREATEST HERO OF THEM ALL (Tony Robinson).
Note: Authors are Tony Robinson and Richard Curtis
MCSET. Cat no: **2CCA 3121**. Released on Chivers Audio Books, '91 by Chivers Audio Books, Green Dragon Audio Visual. Note: 2 Cassettes.
MCSET. Cat no: **2CCA 3158**. Released on Chivers Audio Books, '91 by Chivers Audio Books, Green Dragon Audio Visual. Note: 2 Cassettes.

Robinson, Joan
BEST OF TEDDY ROBINSON.
Note: Includes: Teddy Robinson Goes To Hospital, Teddy Robinson Night Out and Teddy Robinson is put in a Book.
MC. Cat no: **TS 306**. Released on Tellastory, Jul '92 by Random Century Audiobooks. Note: ISBN no. 1856560007

Roethke, Theodore
THEODORE ROETHKE READS (Theodore Roethke).
MC. Cat no: **1351**. Released on Caedmon (USA), '88 by Caedmon Records (USA), Bond Street Music.

Romance
AFFAIRS OF THE HEART (Diana Olsson, Morag Hood, Robert Trotter & Michael Elder).
Note: Includes:- Dennis Haggarty's Wife by William Makepeace Thackeray, Malachi's Cove by Anthony Trollope, Genefer by S. Baring-Gould, The Lion's Share by Arnold Bennett, The Darlings by Anton Chekhov, A Young Girl's Diary, Wolf-Solange and Mademoiselle Heudier's Husband by Marcel Prevost, Her Turn by D H Lawrence, White Marriage by Jules Lemaitre and Cupids Arrow by Rudyard Kipling.
MCSET. Cat no: **SPF 981-1**. Released on Schiltron Audio Books, '91 by Schiltron Publishing. Note: 4 Cassettes. Playing time 4 hours 15 minutes.
CLASSIC LOVE STORIES (Rosalind Ayres & Martin Jarvis).
Note: Contains works by Dickens, Mansfield, Hardy and Alcott.
MCSET. Cat no: **TTDMC 402**. Released on CSA Tell Tapes, May '89 by CSA Tell-Tapes. Note: 2 Cassettes. ISBN No: 1873859023. Playing time: 3 hours.
WOMAN'S HOUR SHORT STORIES (Various artists).
Note: 12 short stories.
MCSET. Cat no: **ZBBC 1115**. Released on BBC, Mar '90 by BBC Records, Taylors. Note: ISBN No: 0563 410310

Romer, Jane
ROCK A BYE BABY (Various narrators).
MCSET. Cat no: **000184962X**. Released on Harper Collins, '91 by Harper Collins.

Roosevelt, Elliott
MURDER IN THE OVAL OFFICE (Nelson Runger).

MCSET. Cat no: **RB 89940.** Released on Recorded Books, Jan '92 by Isis Audio Books. Note: 5 cassettes. Playing time 7hrs 45mins.

RED AND THE BLACK, THE (Davina Porter).
MCSET. Cat no: **RB 88900.** Released on Recorded Books, '91 by Isis Audio Books. Note: 15 cassettes. Playing time 20hrs.

WHITE HOUSE PANTRY MURDER, THE (Nelson Runger).
MCSET. Cat no: **RB 88120.** Released on Recorded Books, Jul '92 by Isis Audio Books. Note: 5 Cassettes. Playing time: 7 hours.

Rorie, David

DAVID RORIE (Various artists).
MC. Cat no: **SSC 072.** Released on Scotsoun, '91 by Scotsoun Recordings, Morley Audio Services.

Ross, Jonathan

BLOOD RUNNING COLD, THE (Barry Cookson).
MCSET. Cat no: **1175T.** Released on Travellers Tales, '91 by Travellers Tales. Note: 6 cassettes.

MCSET. Cat no: **CAT 4021.** Released on Chivers Audio Books, '91 by Chivers Audio Books, Green Dragon Audio Visual. Note: 6 cassettes.

BURIAL DEFERRED (Unknown narrator(s)).
MCSET. Cat no: **1854962752.** Released on Soundings, '91 by Soundings Records, Bond Street Music. Note: 6 Cassettes.

BURNING OF BILLY TOOBER, THE (Peter Joyce).
MCSET. Cat no: **1854964224.** Released on Bramhope, '91 by Ulverscroft Soundings. Note: 5 Cassettes.

MCSET. Cat no: **1740T.** Released on Travellers Tales, '91 by Travellers Tales. Note: 5 Cassettes.

DEAD EYE (David Wade).
MCSET. Cat no: **1439T.** Released on Travellers Tales, '91 by Travellers Tales. Note: 5 Cassettes.

MCSET. Cat no: **1854962272.** Released on Bramhope, '91 by Ulverscroft Soundings. Note: 5 Cassettes.

DEADEST THING YOU EVER SAW, THE (Barrie Cookson).
MCSET. Cat no: **CAT 4054.** Released on Chivers Audio Books, '91 by Chivers Audio Books, Green Dragon Audio Visual. Note: 4 Cassettes.

MCSET. Cat no: **1549T.** Released on Travellers Tales, '91 by Travellers Tales. Note: 4 cassettes.

DROPPED DEAD (Clive Champney).
MCSET. Cat no: **1573T.** Released on Travellers Tales, '91 by Travellers Tales. Note: 4 Cassettes.

MCSET. Cat no: **1854963147.** Released on Bramhope, '91 by Ulverscroft Soundings. Note: 4 Cassettes

HERE LIES NANCY FRAIL (Clive Champney).
MCSET. Cat no: **1668T.** Released on Travellers Tales, '91 by Travellers Tales. Note: 5 Cassettes.

MCSET. Cat no: **185496383X.** Released on Bramhope, '91 by Ulverscroft Soundings.

SUDDEN DEPARTURES (Barrie Cookson).
MCSET. Cat no: **CAT 4065.** Released on Chivers Audio Books, '91 by Chivers Audio Books, Green Dragon Audio Visual. Note: 6 cassettes.

MCSET. Cat no: **1730T.** Released on Travellers Tales, '91 by Travellers Tales. Note: 6 Cassettes.

Ross, Stella

GIRL FROM NOWHERE, THE (Unknown narrator(s)).
MCSET. Cat no: **185496416X.** Released on Trio, '91 by EMI Records. Note: 3 Cassettes.

SHADOW OF THE PAST (Unknown narrator(s)).
MCSET. Cat no: **1854963767.** Released on Trio, '91 by EMI Records. Note: 3 Cassettes.

TREAD SOFTLY, MY HEART (Unknown narrator(s)).
MCSET. Cat no: **1854963864.** Released on Trio, '91 by EMI Records. Note: 3 Cassettes.

YESTERDAY'S LOVE (Unknown narrator(s)).
MCSET. Cat no: **1854964976.** Released on Trio, '91 by EMI Records. Note: 3 Cassettes.

Ross, Tony

TONY ROSS' FAIRY TALES (Sir Michael Horden).
MC. Cat no: **TS 399.** Released on Tellastory, Jan '92 by Random Century Audiobooks. Note: ISBN no. 185656178X

Rossner, Judith

HIS LITTLE WOMEN (Various narrators).
MCSET. Cat no: **0671662007.** Released on Simon & Schuster, '91 by Simon & Schuster Ltd. Note: 2 cassettes.

LOOKING FOR MR. GOODBAR (Susan Adams).
MCSET. Cat no: **1608F.** Released on Travellers Tales, '91 by Travellers Tales. Note: 7 cassettes.

MCSET. Cat no: **RB 80220.** Released on Recorded Books, '91 by Isis Audio Books. Note: 7 Cassettes.

Rostand, Edmund

CYRANO DE BERGERAC (Various artists).
MCSET. Cat no: **0306.** Released on Caedmon (USA), by Caedmon Records (USA), Bond Street Music. Note: 2 cassettes

Royce, Kenneth

BONES IN THE SAND (David Rintoul).
MCSET. Cat no: **CAT 4035.** Released on Chivers Audio Books, '88 by Chivers Audio Books, Green Dragon Audio Visual.

MCSET. Cat no: **1265T.** Released on Travellers Tales, '91 by Travellers Tales. Note: 4 Cassettes.

Runyon, Damon

BROADWAY STORIES, THE (Al Mancini).
MCSET. Cat no: **LD 7.** Released on Green Dragon, '91 by Green Dragon Audio Visual. Note: 2 Cassettes.

SNATCHING OF BOOKIE BOB, THE (Al Mancini).
MCSET. Cat no: **D 003.** Released on Green Dragon, '91 by Green Dragon Audio Visual.

Russell, Robert

GO ON I'M LISTENING (Geoffrey Banks).
MCSET. Cat no: **1256F.** Released on Travellers Tales, '91 by Travellers Tales. Note: 5 cassettes.

MCSET. Cat no: **1854961853.** Released on Bramhope, '91 by Ulverscroft Soundings. Note: 5 Cassettes.

WHILE YOU'RE HERE DOCTOR (Geoffrey Banks).
MCSET. Cat no: **1248F.** Released on Travellers Tales, '91 by Travellers Tales. Note: 5 cassettes.

MCSET. Cat no: **1854961861.** Released on Bramhope, '91 by Ulverscroft Soundings. Note: 5 Cassettes.

Russo, John A.

NIGHT OF THE LIVING DEAD (Unknown narrator(s)).
MCSET. Cat no: **0671662007.** Released on Simon & Schuster, '91 by Simon & Schuster Ltd.

Rutherford, Douglas

SKIN FOR SKIN (Michael Kitchen).
MCSET. Cat no: **CAT 4042.** Released on Chivers Audio Books, '91 by Chivers Audio Books, Green Dragon Audio Visual. Note: 4 Cassettes.

MCSET. Cat no: **1433T.** Released on Travellers Tales, '91 by Travellers Tales. Note: 4 Cassettes.

Rutherford, E

RUSSKA (Unknown narrator(s)).
MCSET. Cat no: **RC 12.** Released on Random Century, '91 by Random Century Audiobooks, Conifer Records. Note: 2 cassettes. ISBN 1856860124. 3 hrs approx.

Ryan, John

CAPTAIN PUGWASH (Peter Hawkins).
MCSET. Cat no: **CC 041.** Released on Cover to Cover, '87 by Cover to Cover Cassettes.

Sackville-West, Vita
ALL PASSION SPENT (Dame Wendy Hiller).
MCSET. Cat no: **CAB 233**. Released on Chivers Audio Books, '91 by Chivers Audio Books, Green Dragon Audio Visual. Note: 6 Cassettes.
MCSET. Cat no: **1212F**. Released on Travellers Tales, '91 by Travellers Tales. Note: 6 cassettes.

Sadowitz, Jerry
GOBSHITE (Jerry Sadowitz).
LP. Cat no: **GOBSHITE 01**. Released on Gobshite, Jan '88, Cartel.

Saki
BEST OF SAKI, THE (Hugh Burden).
MCSET. Cat no: **1220F**. Released on Travellers Tales, '91 by Travellers Tales. Note: 6 cassettes.

BROGUE (Hugh Burden).
MC. Cat no: **SA 6**. Released on Talking Tape Company, '88, Conifer Records.

BROGUE, TOBERMORY, THE (And Eight Other Stories) (Various narrators).
Note: Includes: The Brogue, Tobermory, The Byzantine Omelette, The Woman Who Always Told The Truth, The Interlopers, The Schartz Metterklume Method, The Philanthropist And The Happy Cat Laura. The Remoulding Of Groby Lington And The Lumber Room.
MCSET. Cat no: **TTC 2016**. Released on Talking Tape Company, '91, Conifer Records. Note: 2 cassettes. Playing time 2hrs 2mins. ISBN no. 1872520030

CLASSIC SAKI STORIES (Barbara Leigh-Hunt).
MCSET. Cat no: **TTDMC 411**. Released on CSA Tell Tapes, Mar '92 by CSA Tell-Tapes. Note: 2 cassettes. ISBN No: 1873859112

MRS. PACKLETIDE'S TIGER (And Nine Other Stories) (Unknown narrator(s)).
MCSET. Cat no: **TTC 2017**. Released on Talking Tape Company, Apr '91, Conifer Records. Note: 2 cassettes. Playing time 1hr. 52mins. ISBN no. 1872520049

MUSIC ON THE HILL, THE (Patrick Barlow).
Note: Also includes "The Cobwebs", "The Interlopers", and "The Hounds of Fate".
MC. Cat no: **RSJ 5009**. Released on Landfall, '91.

OPEN WINDOW, THE (And Other Stories) (Unknown narrator(s)).
Note: Includes: The Romancers, Sredni Vashtar, The Seventh Pullet and The Lumber Room.
MC. Cat no: **ANV 659**. Released on Anvil Cassettes, '85 by Anvil Cassettes, Chivers Audio Books.

QUAIL SEED (And Other Stories) (Unknown narrator(s)).
Note: Includes: Quail Seed, The She-Wolf, Story Teller, The Schartz-Metterklume Method and Talking out of Tarrington.
MC. Cat no: **ANV 660**. Released on Anvil Cassettes, '85 by Anvil Cassettes, Chivers Audio Books.

ROMANCERS, THE (And Eight Other Stories) (Hugh Burden).
Note: Includes: The Romancers, The She Wolf, The Music On The Hill, The Open Window, The Stalled Ox, The Forbidden Buzzards, The Hounds Of Fate, The Mouse and The Secret Sin Of Septimiss Brope.
MCSET. Cat no: **TTC 2015**. Released on Talking Tape Company, '91, Conifer Records. Note: 2 cassettes. Playing time - 1hr 48mins. ISBN no. 1872520022
MCSET. Cat no: **SA 5**. Released on Talking Tape Company, '91, Conifer Records.

SAKI (Volume 1) (Hugh Burden).
Note: Includes: Sredni Vashtar, The Story Teller and Morlvera.
MCSET. Cat no: **TTC/SA 01**. Released on Talking Tape Company, Sep '84, Conifer Records.

SHE WOLF (And Other Stories) (Hugh Burden).
MC. Cat no: **SA 2**. Released on Talking Tape Company, Aug '81, Conifer Records.

SHOCK TACTICS (And Other Stories) (Various artists).
Tracks / Shock tactics: *Various artists* / Stalled ox: *Various artists* / Chaplet, The: *Various artists* / Bull, The: *Various artists* / Mappined life, The: *Various artists* / Fate: *Various artists* / Gabriel-Ernest: *Various artists* / Holiday task, A: *Various artists* / Unrest-cure, The: *Various artists* / Louise: *Various artists* / Name-day, The: *Various artists*.
MC. Cat no: **418 048-4**. Released on Argo (Polygram), Jun '88 by PolyGram Classics.

TOBERMORY (And Other Stories) (Jonathan Newth).
MCSET. Cat no: **COL 2015**. Released on Colophone, Jun '81 by AVLS (Audio-Visual Library Services).
MCSET. Cat no: **4180244**. Released on Argo (Polygram), Jun '88 by Poly-Gram Classics.

WORLD OF SAKI, THE (Collected Stories) (Alexander Spencer).
Note: A collection of short stories.
MCSET. Cat no: **RB 83051**. Released on Recorded Books, '91 by Isis Audio Books. Note: 2 cassettes.

Sale, Charles
SPECIALIST, THE (And Other Stories) (John Sheddon).
Note: Also includes the Maysville Minstrel and the Golden Honeymoon by Ring Lardner.
MC. Cat no: **SPF 990-1A**. Released on Schiltron Audio Books, '91 by Schiltron Publishing.

Salgari, Emilio
I MISTERI DELLA GIUNGLA NERA (Adriano Giraldi).
MCSET. Cat no: **1017L**. Released on Travellers Tales, '91 by Travellers Tales. Note: 6 cassettes.

LA RIVINCITA DI TREMAL NAIK (Adriano Giraldi).
MCSET. Cat no: **1018L**. Released on Travellers Tales, '91 by Travellers Tales. Note: 6 cassettes.

Sallis, Susan
SUMMER VISITORS (Joanna David).
MCSET. Cat no: **CAB 598**. Released on Chivers Audio Books, '91 by Chivers Audio Books, Green Dragon Audio Visual. Note: 10 Cassettes.
MCSET. Cat no: **1692/3F**. Released on Travellers Tales, '91 by Travellers Tales. Note: 10 cassettes.

Salten, Felix
BAMBI (Unknown narrator(s)).
MC. Cat no: **TS 338**. Released on Tellastory, Dec '86 by Random Century Audiobooks.

BAMBI (Unknown narrator(s)).
MC. Cat no: **DIS 005**. Released on Disney (Read-a-long), Jul '90 by Disneyland Records.

BAMBI (Felicity Kendal).
MC. Cat no: **PTB 632**. Released on Pickwick, '83 by Pickwick Records, Clyde Factors, Taylors, Arabesque, Solomon & Peres, I & B Records, Prism Leisure, Outlet Records.

Sameer
DAULAT AUR MAMTA (HINDI) (Various narrators).
MCSET. Cat no: **94824**. Released on Sonex, '91. Note: 3 cassettes.

Sampson, Fay
JOSH'S PANTHER (Tony Robinson).
MCSET. Cat no: **2CCA 3051**. Released on Chivers Audio Books, '91 by Chivers Audio Books, Green Dragon Audio Visual. Note: 2 Cassettes.
MCSET. Cat no: **9119F**. Released on Travellers Tales, '91 by Travellers Tales. Note: 2 Cassettes.

Samuels, Arthur
FATAL EGGS, THE (And Harris and the Mare) (Unknown narrator(s)).
MC. Cat no: **NF 5**. Released on Nightfall Tapes, '89 by BMG Records (UK) Ltd..

REPOSSESSION, THE (And The Telltale Heart) (Unknown narrator(s)).
MC. Cat no: **NF 1**. Released on Nightfall Tapes, '89 by BMG Records (UK) Ltd. **Deleted** Feb '92.

Sanders, Lawrence
SULLIVAN'S STING (Victoria Garber).
MCSET. Cat no: **0671706519**. Re-

leased on Simon & Schuster, '91 by Simon & Schuster Ltd. Note: 2 cassettes.

Sartre, Jean-Paul
NO EXIT (Various artists).
MCSET. Cat no: **327.** Released on Caedmon (USA), '89 by Caedmon Records (USA), Bond Street Music. Note: 2 cassettes

Saunders, Jean
RAINBOW'S END (Emma Sutton).
MCSET. Cat no: **MRC 1064.** Released on Chivers Audio Books, '91 by Chivers Audio Books, Green Dragon Audio Visual. Note: 2 cassettes.

Savarin, Julian Jay
LYNX (Gordon Griffin).
MCSET. Cat no: **1854962418.** Released on Soundings, '91 by Soundings Records, Bond Street Music. Note: 6 cassettes.

MCSET. Cat no: **1445T.** Released on Travellers Tales, '91 by Travellers Tales. Note: 6 cassettes.

WATERHOLE (Gordon Griffin).
MCSET. Cat no: **1435/1436T.** Released on Travellers Tales, '91 by Travellers Tales. Note: 9 Cassettes.

MCSET. Cat no: **1854962221.** Released on Soundings, '91 by Soundings Records, Bond Street Music. Note: 9 Cassettes.

Saville, Andrew
BERGERAC AND THE FATAL WEAKNESS (John Nettles).
MCSET. Cat no: **CAB 420.** Released on Chivers Audio Books, '91 by Chivers Audio Books, Green Dragon Audio Visual. Note: 4 Cassettes.

MCSET. Cat no: **1487T.** Released on Travellers Tales, '91 by Travellers Tales. Note: 4 Cassettes.

BERGERAC AND THE MOVING FEVER (John Nettles).
MCSET. Cat no: **CAB 606.** Released on Chivers Audio Books, '91 by Chivers Audio Books, Green Dragon Audio Visual. Note: 6 Cassettes.

BERGERAC AND THE TRAITOR'S CHILD (John Nettles).
MCSET. Cat no: **CAB 381.** Released on Chivers Audio Books, '91 by Chivers Audio Books, Green Dragon Audio Visual. Note: 4 Cassettes.

MCSET. Cat no: **1425T.** Released on Travellers Tales, '91 by Travellers Tales. Note: 4 Cassettes.

Sayers, Dorothy L.
FIVE RED HERRINGS, THE (Patrick Malahide).
MCSET. Cat no: **CAB 607.** Released on Chivers Audio Books, '91 by Chivers Audio Books, Green Dragon Audio Visual. Note: 10 cassettes.

LORD PETER VIEWS THE BODY (Ian Carmichael).
MCSET. Cat no: **CAB 109.** Released on Chivers Audio Books, '91 by Chivers Audio Books, Green Dragon Audio Visual. Note: 6 cassettes.

MCSET. Cat no: **1132T.** Released on Travellers Tales, '91 by Travellers Tales. Note: 6 Cassettes.

MURDER MUST ADVERTISE (Ian Carmichael).
MCSET. Cat no: **ZBBC 1124.** Released on BBC Radio Collection, Aug '90 by BBC Records. Note: ISBN No: 0563 410604

MCSET. Cat no: **CAB 331.** Released on Chivers Audio Books, '91 by Chivers Audio Books, Green Dragon Audio Visual. Note: 10 cassettes.

MCSET. Cat no: **1410/1411T.** Released on Travellers Tales, '91 by Travellers Tales. Note: 10 Cassettes.

NINE TAILORS, THE (Ian Carmichael).
MCSET. Cat no: **CAB 203.** Released on Chivers Audio Books, '91 by Chivers Audio Books, Green Dragon Audio Visual. Note: 8 cassettes.

MCSET. Cat no: **1151T.** Released on Travellers Tales, '91 by Travellers Tales. Note: 8 Cassettes.

MCSET. Cat no: **ZBBC 1056.** Released on BBC Radio Collection, '91 by BBC Records. Note: 8 Cassettes.

STRONG POISON (Ian Carmichael).
MCSET. Cat no: **CAB 400.** Released on Chivers Audio Books, '91 by Chivers Audio Books, Green Dragon Audio Visual. Note: 6 Cassettes.

MCSET. Cat no: **1488T.** Released on Travellers Tales, '91 by Travellers Tales. Note: 6 Cassettes.

UNNATURAL DEATH (Ian Carmichael).
MCSET. Cat no: **CAB 496.** Released on Chivers Audio Books, '91 by Chivers Audio Books, Green Dragon Audio Visual. Note: 6 cassettes.

MCSET. Cat no: **1638T.** Released on Travellers Tales, '91 by Travellers Tales. Note: 6 Cassettes.

UNPLEASANTNESS AT THE BELLONA CLUB, THE (Ian Carmichael).
MCSET. Cat no: **CAB 448.** Released on Chivers Audio Books, '91 by Chivers Audio Books, Green Dragon Audio Visual. Note: 6 Cassettes.

MCSET. Cat no: **1550T.** Released on Travellers Tales, '91 by Travellers Tales. Note: 6 Cassettes.

MCSET. Cat no: **ZBBC 1210.** Released on BBC Radio Collection, '91 by BBC Records. Note: ISBN No: 0563 410345. 6 Cassettes.

WHOSE BODY? (Ian Carmichael).
MCSET. Cat no: **CAB 287.** Released on Chivers Audio Books, '91 by Chivers Audio Books, Green Dragon Audio Visual. Note: 6 cassettes.

MCSET. Cat no: **1236T.** Released on Travellers Tales, '91 by Travellers Tales. Note: 6 Cassettes

Scholefield, Alan
POINT OF HONOUR (Christopher Kay).
MCSET. Cat no: **185496562X.** Released on Bramhope, Feb '92 by Ulverscroft Soundings. Note: Playing time: 60 minutes.

Schultz, Charles
CHARLIE BROWN'S ALL STARS (Various artists).
MC. Cat no: **82DC 82.** Released on Polydor, Nov '80 by Polydor Ltd, Solomon & Peres.

HE'S YOUR DOG, CHARLIE BROWN (Various artists).
MC. Cat no: **83DC 83.** Released on Polydor, Nov '80 by Polydor Ltd, Solomon & Peres.

IT'S THE GREAT PUMPKIN, CHARLIE BROWN (Various artists).
MC. Cat no: **84DC 84.** Released on Polydor, Nov '80 by Polydor Ltd, Solomon & Peres.

YOU'RE IN LOVE, CHARLIE BROWN (Various artists).
MC. Cat no: **85DC 85.** Released on Polydor, Nov '80 by Polydor Ltd, Solomon & Peres.

Science Fiction
CLASSIC SCIENCE FICTION STORIES (Nicky Henson).
MCSET. Cat no: **TTDMC 406.** Released on CSA Tell Tapes, Jun '90 by CSA Tell-Tapes. Note: 2 Cassettes. ISBN No: 1873859066.

INSIDE STAR TREK (Various artists).
Tracks / Asimov's world of science fiction: *Various artists* / William Shatner meets Captain Kirk: *Various artists* / Origin of Spock: *Various artists* / Letter from a network censor: *Various artists* / Star Trek philosophy: *Various artists*.
LP. Cat no: **CBS 31765.** Released on CBS, Feb '80 by Sony Music, Solomon & Peres, Outlet Records **Deleted** '85.
MC. Cat no: **40 31765.** Released on CBS, Feb '80 by Sony Music, Solomon & Peres, Outlet Records **Deleted** '85.

RETURN OF THE JEDI (Various artists).
LP. Cat no: **D 455.** Released on Disneyland, Jul '83 by Disneyland-Vista Records (USA).
MC. Cat no: **D 155DC.** Released on Disneyland, Jul '83 by Disneyland-Vista Records (USA).

RETURN OF THE JEDI (The Ewoks Join The Fight) (Various artists).
LP. Cat no: **D 460.** Released on Disneyland, Jul '83 by Disneyland-Vista Records (USA).
MC. Cat no: **D 160DC.** Released on Disneyland, Jul '83 by Disneyland-Vista Records (USA).

SCIENCE FICTION ADVENTURES (Volume 1) (Unknown narrator(s)).
MCSET. Cat no: **DTO 10556.** Released on Ditto, '88 by Pickwick Re-

cords, Midland Records.
SCIENCE FICTION ADVENTURES (Volume 2) (Unknown narrator(s)).
MCSET. Cat no: **DTO 10557.** Released on Ditto, '88 by Pickwick Records, Midland Records.

SCIENCE FICTION SOUNDBOOK (William Shatner & Leonard Nimoy).
LPS. Cat no: **SBR 104.** Released on Caedmon (USA), Sep '80 by Caedmon Records (USA), Bond Street Music. Note: 4 album set.
MCSET. Cat no: **SBC 104.** Released on Caedmon (USA), Sep '80 by Caedmon Records (USA), Bond Street Music. Note: 4 cassette set

STAR TREK (The Kobayashi Maru) (James Doohan).
Note: Adapted by Julia Ecklar.
MC. Cat no: **0671708953.** Released on Simon & Schuster, '91 by Simon & Schuster Ltd.

STAR TREK (Strangers from the Sky) (Leonard Nimoy & George Takei).
Note: Adapted by Margaret W. Bonanno.
MCSET. Cat no: **0671647180.** Released on Simon & Schuster, '91 by Simon & Schuster Ltd. Note: 2 Cassettes.

STAR TREK (The Final Frontier) (Leonard Nimoy & James Doohan).
Note: Adapted by Diane Carey.
MCSET. Cat no: **0671670166.** Released on Simon & Schuster, '91 by Simon & Schuster Ltd. Note: 7 Cassette set.

STAR TREK (The Next Generation) (Various artists).
Note: Adapted by Jean Lorrah.
MCSET. Cat no: **0167170480X.** Released on Simon & Schuster, '91 by Simon & Schuster Ltd. Note: 2 cassettes.

STAR TREK (Enterprise, The First Adventure) (Leonard Nimoy & George Takei).
Note: Adapted by Vonda V. McIntyre.
MCSET. Cat no: **0671629514.** Released on Simon & Schuster, '91 by Simon & Schuster Ltd. Note: 2 cassettes.

STAR TREK (The Entropy Effect) (Leonard Nimoy & George Takei).
Note: Adapted by Vonda V. McIntyre.
MCSET. Cat no: **0671668641.** Released on Simon & Schuster, '91 by Simon & Schuster Ltd. Note: 2 cassettes.

STAR TREK (The Voyage Home) (Leonard Nimoy & George Takei).
Note: Adapted by Vonda V. McIntyre.
MCSET. Cat no: **067164629X.** Released on Simon & Schuster, '91 by Simon & Schuster Ltd. Note: 2 cassettes.

STAR TREK (Time For Yesterday) (Leonard Nimoy & James Doohan).
Note: Adapted by A.C. Crispin
MC. Cat no: **0671670174.** Released on Simon & Schuster, '91 by Simon & Schuster Ltd.

STAR TREK (Yesterday's Son) (Leonard Nimoy & James Doohan).
Note: Adapted By A.C. Crispin.
MCSET. Cat no: **067166865V.** Released on Simon & Schuster, '91 by Simon & Schuster Ltd. Note: 2 cassettes.

STAR TREK (The Final Frontier) (Leonard Nimoy & George Takei).
Note: Adapted by J.M. Dillard.
MCSET. Cat no: **0671685074.** Released on Simon & Schuster, '91 by Simon & Schuster Ltd. Note: 2 cassettes.

STAR TREK (Spock's World) (Leonard Nimoy & George Takei).
Note: Adapted By Diane Duane.
MCSET. Cat no: **0671679171.** Released on Simon & Schuster, '91 by Simon & Schuster Ltd. Note: 2 cassettes.

STAR TREK (The Next Generation: Contamination) (Unknown narrator(s)).
MCSET. Cat no: **0671740458.** Released on Simon & Schuster, '91 by Simon & Schuster Ltd.

STAR TREK (The Next Generation: Gulliver's Fugitives) (Unknown narrator(s)).
MCSET. Cat no: **0671723197.** Released on Simon & Schuster, '91 by Simon & Schuster Ltd.

STAR TREK (Various artists).
LP. Cat no: **D 461.** Released on Disneyland, Feb '84 by Disneyland-Vista Records (USA).
MC. Cat no: **D 461 DC.** Released on Disneyland, Feb '84 by Disneyland-Vista Records (USA).

STAR TREK (Lost Years) (Leonard Nimoy & George Takei).
MCSET. Cat no: **0671686321.** Released on Simon & Schuster, '91 by Simon & Schuster Ltd.

STAR TREK (Prime Directive) (Leonard Nimoy & George Takei).
MCSET. Cat no: **0671726315.** Released on Simon & Schuster, '91 by Simon & Schuster Ltd.

STAR TREK (The Next Generation: Vendetta) (Unknown narrator(s)).
MCSET. Cat no: **0671743414.** Released on Simon & Schuster, '91 by Simon & Schuster Ltd.

STORY OF STAR WARS (Various artists).
LP. Cat no: **D 62101.** Released on Disneyland, Jul '83 by Disneyland-Vista Records (USA).

STORY OF THE EMPIRE STRIKES BACK (Various artists).
LP. Cat no: **D 62102.** Released on Disneyland, Jul '83 by Disneyland-Vista Records (USA).

STORY OF THE RETURN OF THE JEDI (Various artists).
LP. Cat no: **D 62103.** Released on Disneyland, Jul '83 by Disneyland-Vista Records (USA).

Scofield, Alan
LION IN THE EVENING (Gordon Griffin).
MCSET. Cat no: **185496545X.** Released on Bramhope, '92 by Ulverscroft Soundings.

Scott, Alexander
ALEXANDER SCOTT (1515-1583) (Jack Aitken & David Murison).
MC. Cat no: **SSC 043.** Released on Scotsoun, '91 by Scotsoun Recordings, Morley Audio Services.
ALEXANDER SCOTT (1920-89) (Various artists).
MC. Cat no: **SSC 044.** Released on Scotsoun, '91 by Scotsoun Recordings, Morley Audio Services.
BONNIE FECHTER, A (Various artists).
MC. Cat no: **SSC 086.** Released on Scotsoun, '91 by Scotsoun Recordings, Morley Audio Services.

Scott, Dufton
ROBBIE SHEPHERD READS DUFTON SCOTT (Robbie Shepherd).
Tracks / Auction sale / Old bellman, The / Selling sewing machines / Hugh McCurrie's marriage / My communicative friend / Rural drive, A / Out of his element / Sandy on sousa / Examination of a witness / Drama in a barn.
MC. Cat no: **ACLMC 4.** Released on City Arts, Dec '90 by Aberdeen City Arts Department.

Scott, Sir Walter
HIGHLAND WIDOW, THE (And Other Stories) (Eileen McCallum & Robert Trotter).
Note: Includes:- The Highland Widow, The Two Drovers and Wandering Willies Tale.
MCSET. Cat no: **SPF 760-1.** Released on Schiltron Audio Books, '91 by Schiltron Publishing. Note: 4 Cassettes.
MCSET. Cat no: **1734T.** Released on Travellers Tales, '91 by Travellers Tales. Note: 4 Cassettes.

IVANHOE (Tim Pigott-Smith).
MCSET. Cat no: **418 000-4.** Released on Argo (Polygram), Jun '88 by PolyGram Classics **Deleted** Jan '89.
MCSET. Cat no: **ARGO 1076.** Released on Argo (EMI), May '89 by EMI Records **Deleted** '91. Note: 2 Cassettes.
MCSET. Cat no: **1046C.** Released on Travellers Tales, '91 by Travellers Tales. Note: 2 cassettes.

IVANHOE (Douglas Fairbanks Jnr).
2LP. Cat no: **TC 2076.** Released on Caedmon (USA), May '79 by Caedmon Records (USA), Bond Street Music.
MCSET. Cat no: **CDL 52076.** Released on Caedmon (USA), May '78 by Caedmon Records (USA), Bond Street Music.

IVANHOE (And the Rose of Persia) (Various artists).
LP. Cat no: **SHE 509.** Released on Pearl Records (USA), Jun '76 by Atlanta International (USA).

Secombe, Fred

CURATE FOR ALL SEASONS, A (Fred Secombe).
MCSET. Cat no: **1854964542.** Released on Bramhope, May '91 by Ulverscroft Soundings. Note: 5 Cassettes.

GOODBYE CURATE (Fred Secombe).
MCSET. Cat no: **1854965468.** Released on Bramhope, '92 by Ulverscroft Soundings.

HOW GREEN WAS MY CURATE (Fred Secombe).
MCSET. Cat no: **1682F.** Released on Travellers Tales, '91 by Travellers Tales. Note: 4 cassettes.
MCSET. Cat no: **1854964143.** Released on Bramhope, '91 by Ulverscroft Soundings. Note: 4 Cassettes.

Sefton, Catherine

EMMA DILEMMA, THE (Sarah Greene).
MCSET. Cat no: **2CCA 3041.** Released on Chivers Audio Books, '91 by Chivers Audio Books, Green Dragon Audio Visual. Note: 2 Cassettes.
MCSET. Cat no: **9120F.** Released on Travellers Tales, '91 by Travellers Tales. Note: 2 Cassettes.

EMMA'S GHOST (Carole Hayman).
MCSET. Cat no: **9132F.** Released on Travellers Tales, '91 by Travellers Tales. Note: 2 Cassettes.
MCSET. Cat no: **2CCA 3065.** Released on Travellers Tales, '91 by Travellers Tales. Note: 2 Cassettes.

GHOST AND BERTIE BOGGIN, THE (Judy Bennett).
MCSET. Cat no: **2CCA 3136.** Released on Chivers Audio Books, '91 by Chivers Audio Books, Green Dragon Audio Visual. Note: 2 Cassettes.

Sellers, Peter

BEST OF SELLERS (Peter Sellers). Tracks / Trumpet volunteer, The / Auntie Rotter / All the things you are / We need the money / I'm so ashamed / Party political speech / Balham, gateway to the south / Suddenly it's folk song.
LP. Cat no: **MRS 5157.** Released on Starline (EMI), Jun '73 by EMI Records **Deleted** Jun '91.
LP. Cat no: **PMD 1069.** Released on Parlophone, Feb '59 by EMI Records, Solomon & Peres **Deleted** Feb '64.

PETER SELLERS COLLECTION (Peter Sellers).
Tracks / Any old iron / Hards day's night, A / Common entrance (Not on CD.) / My old dutch (Not on CD.) / Can't buy me love (Not on CD.) / Thank heaven for little girls (Not on CD.) / All the things you are / We'll let you know (Not on CD.) / Wouldn't it be loverly (Not on CD.) / In a free state / Peter Sellers sings Rudolph Friml / Goodness gracious me / So little time / Puttin' on the smile (Not on CD.) / Trumpet volunteer, The / I'm so ashamed (Not on CD.) / She loves you (inspired by Dr. Strangelove) / Unchained melody / Peter Sellers sings George Gershwin / Dance with me, Henry / Critics, The (Not on CD.) / Why worry? (Not on CD.) / Grandpa's grave (Not on CD.) / Boiled bananas and carrots (Not on CD.) / We need the money (Not on CD.) / Never never land / Suddenly it's folk song / Auntie Rotter / Bangers and mash / Conversation No. 1 (a right bird) / Help (Not on CD.) / Singin' in the rain (Not on CD.) / Party political speech / House on the Rue Sichel ((Some voices inspired by the film 'Soft Beds, Hard bath') Not on CD.) / Dipso calypso / Face to face (Not on CD.) / Balham - gateway to the South / I haven't told her, she hasn't told me (Not on CD.).
MCSET. Cat no: **ECC 5.** Released on EMI, Jul '90 by EMI Records.
CD. Cat no: **CZ 323.** Released on EMI, Jul '90 by EMI Records.

SELLERS MARKET (Peter Sellers).
Tracks / All-England George Formby finals / Complete guide to accents of the British Isles.
LP. Cat no: **UAG 30266.** Released on United Artists, Nov '79 by EMI Records **Deleted** '84.

Sendak, Maurice

HIGGLETY PIGGLETY POP (Or There Must be More to Life) (Tammy Grimes).
MC. Cat no: **1519.** Released on Caedmon (USA), '88 by Caedmon Records (USA), Bond Street Music.

HORNBOOK FOR WITCHES, A (Vincent Price).
MC. Cat no: **1497.** Released on Caedmon (USA), '88 by Caedmon Records (USA), Bond Street Music.

KENNY'S WINDOW (Tammy Grimes).
LP. Cat no: **TC 51548.** Released on Caedmon (USA), '78 by Caedmon Records (USA), Bond Street Music.
MC. Cat no: **CDL 51548.** Released on Caedmon (USA), '78 by Caedmon Records (USA), Bond Street Music.

WHERE THE WILD THINGS ARE (And Other Stories) (Tammy Grimes).
LP. Cat no: **TC 1531.** Released on Caedmon (USA), '79 by Caedmon Records (USA), Bond Street Music.
MC. Cat no: **CDL 1531.** Released on Caedmon (USA), '79 by Caedmon Records (USA), Bond Street Music.

Serraillier, Ian

SILVER SWORD, THE (Sean Barrett).
MCSET. Cat no: **CTC 050.** Released on Cover to Cover, '90 by Cover to Cover Cassettes. Note: 3 cassettes. Playing time 4 hrs.

Sewell, Anna

ADVENTURES OF BLACK BEAUTY, THE (Stacy Dorning).
MCSET. Cat no: **TTC 2041.** Released on Talking Tape Company, '91, Conifer Records. Note: 2 cassettes. Playing time 3hrs ISBN no. 1872520359

BLACK BEAUTY (Angela Rippon).
MCSET. Cat no: **SAY 10.** Released on Argo (Polygram), Jul '82 by PolyGram Classics **Deleted** Jan '89.

BLACK BEAUTY (David Davis).
MC. Cat no: **P 90006.** Released on Pinnacle, '79 by Pinnacle Records, Outlet Records, Music Sales Records.

BLACK BEAUTY (Hayley Mills).
MCSET. Cat no: **LFP 7162.** Released on Listen For Pleasure, Jul '84 by EMI Records **Deleted** Apr '90.

BLACK BEAUTY (Unknown narrator(s)).
Note: Book and cassette.
MC. Cat no: **PLBC 197.** Released on Tell-A-Tale, '88 by Pickwick Records, Taylors, Clyde Factors.

BLACK BEAUTY (Unknown narrator(s)).
MCSET. Cat no: **DTO 10571.** Released on Ditto, '88 by Pickwick Records, Midland Records.
MC. Cat no: **CBB 1.** Released on Sierra, Dec '87 by Sierra Records.

BLACK BEAUTY (Hayley Mills).
Note: Abridged.
MCSET. Cat no: **9073F.** Released on Travellers Tales, '91 by Travellers Tales. Note: 2 Cassettes.

Seymour, Gerald

CONDITION BLACK (Peter Whitman).
MCSET. Cat no: **CAB 647.** Released on Chivers Audio Books, Nov '91 by Chivers Audio Books, Green Dragon Audio Visual. Note: 10 cassettes

CONTRACT, THE (Dermot Crowley).
MCSET. Cat no: **CAB 599.** Released on Chivers Audio Books, '91 by Chivers Audio Books, Green Dragon Audio Visual. Note: 10 Cassettes
MCSET. Cat no: **1713/1714T.** Released on Travellers Tales, '91 by Travellers Tales. Note: 10 Cassettes.

FIELD OF BLOOD (Dermot Crowley).
MCSET. Cat no: **CAB 693.** Released on Chivers Audio Books, Apr '92 by Chivers Audio Books, Green Dragon Audio Visual. Note: 8 Cassettes

GLORY BOYS, THE (Christian Rodska).
MCSET. Cat no: **CAB 542.** Released on Chivers Audio Books, '91 by Chivers Audio Books, Green Dragon Audio Visual. Note: 8 Cassettes.
MCSET. Cat no: **1712T.** Released on

Travellers Tales, '91 by Travellers Tales. Note: 8 Cassettes.

HARRY'S GAME (Ray Lonnen).
MCSET. Cat no: **CAB 288**. Released on Chivers Audio Books, '91 by Chivers Audio Books, Green Dragon Audio Visual. Note: 8 Cassettes.

MCSET. Cat no: **1237T**. Released on Travellers Tales, '91 by Travellers Tales. Note: 8 Cassettes.

HOME RUN (David Banks).
MCSET. Cat no: **IAB 92083**. Released on Isis Audio Books, Aug '92. Note: 10 Cassettes. Playing time: 13 hours, 32 mins.

JOURNEYMAN TAILOR, THE (Brian Cox).
MCSET. Cat no: **0001046543**. Released on Harper Collins, Mar '92 by Harper Collins.

RED FOX (Michael Kitchen).
MCSET. Cat no: **CAB 469**. Released on Chivers Audio Books, '91 by Chivers Audio Books, Green Dragon Audio Visual. Note: 10 Cassettes.

MCSET. Cat no: **1551/1552T**. Released on Travellers Tales, '91 by Travellers Tales. Note: 10 Cassettes.

SONG IN THE MORNING, A (David Calder).
MCSET. Cat no: **CAB 382**. Released on Chivers Audio Books, '91 by Chivers Audio Books, Green Dragon Audio Visual. Note: 8 Cassettes.

MCSET. Cat no: **1426T**. Released on Travellers Tales, '91 by Travellers Tales. Note: 8 Cassettes.

Shakespeare, William

AGES OF MAN (Sir John Gielgud).
Note: Speeches from:- As you like it , Merchant of Venice, Tempest , Romeo and Juliet, Measure for measure, Henry IV parts 1 & 2, Richard II, Richard III, Julius Caesar, Hamlet, King Lear and Sonnets 18, 71, 116, 130 and 138.
2LP. Cat no: **SRS 200**. Released on Caedmon (USA), Sep '79 by Caedmon Records (USA), Bond Street Music.

2LP. Cat no: **CBS 61830**. Released on CBS, Sep '79 by Sony Music, Solomon & Peres, Outlet Records.

AGES OF MAN (Sir John Gielgud).
Note: Also available on hanging format, cataglogue number:- 00013524X.
MCSET. Cat no: **HCA 53**. Released on Harper Collins, '92 by Harper Collins. Note: 2 Cassettes.

ALL'S WELL THAT ENDS WELL (Various artists).
Note: Starring Prunella Scales, Michael Hordern, Margaretta Scott, Patrick Wymark and The Marlow Dramatic Society.
MCSET. Cat no: **ARGO 1271**. Released on Argo (EMI), Jul '91 by EMI Records.

MCSET. Cat no: **SAY 105**. Released on Argo (Polygram), Jun '84 by PolyGram Classics **Deleted** Jan '89.

MCSET. Cat no: **212**. Released on Caedmon (USA), '88 by Caedmon Records (USA), Bond Street Music.

ANTHONY AND CLEOPATRA (Various artists).
Note: With Irene Worth, Richard Johnson, Diana Rigg and others.
MCSET. Cat no: **1008P**. Released on Travellers Tales, '91 by Travellers Tales. Note: 2 Cassettes.

ANTHONY AND CLEOPATRA (Marlowe Dramatic Society).
MCSET. Cat no: **SAY 63**. Released on Argo (Polygram), Jun '88 by PolyGram Classics **Deleted** Jan '89.

MCSET. Cat no: **235**. Released on Caedmon (USA), '91 by Caedmon Records (USA), Bond Street Music. Note: 3 Cassettes.

MCSET. Cat no: **ARGO 1307**. Released on Argo (EMI), Apr '92 by EMI Records.

AS YOU LIKE IT (Various artists).
Note: Starring Janet Suzman, John Stride and The Marlowe Dramatic Society.
MCSET. Cat no: **210**. Released on Caedmon (USA), by Caedmon Records (USA), Bond Street Music. Note: 3 cassettes

AS YOU LIKE IT (Janet Suzman & John Stride).
MCSET. Cat no: **SAY 22**. Released on Argo (Polygram), Jul '82 by PolyGram Classics **Deleted** Jan '89.

MCSET. Cat no: **1009P**. Released on Travellers Tales, '91 by Travellers Tales. Note: 2 Cassettes.

AS YOU LIKE IT (Various artists).
MCSET. Cat no: **ARGO 1028**. Released on Argo (EMI), May '89 by EMI Records. Note: 2 Cassettes. Playing time: 2 1/2 hours.

AS YOU LIKE IT (Vanessa Redgrave & Others).
MCSET. Cat no: **HCA 54**. Released on Harper Collins, '92 by Harper Collins. Note: 2 Cassettes.

COMEDY OF ERRORS, THE (Various artists).
MCSET. Cat no: **205**. Released on Caedmon (USA), '89 by Caedmon Records (USA), Bond Street Music. Note: 2 cassettes

COMEDY OF ERRORS, THE (Marlowe Dramatic Society).
MCSET. Cat no: **1056P**. Released on Travellers Tales, '91 by Travellers Tales. Note: 2 Cassettes.

COMEDY OF ERRORS, THE (A Lover's Complaint) (Various artists).
Note: Starring Michael Hordern, Prunella Scales and the Marlowe Dramatic Society.
MCSET. Cat no: **417 943-4**. Released on Argo (Polygram), Jun '88 by PolyGram Classics **Deleted** Jan '89.

MCSET. Cat no: **ARGO 1106**. Released on Argo (EMI), Jun '89 by EMI Records. Note: 2 Cassettes.

CORIOLANUS (Various artists).
MCSET. Cat no: **0226**. Released on Caedmon (USA), '88 by Caedmon Records (USA), Bond Street Music. Note: 3 cassettes

MCSET. Cat no: **417 946-4**. Released on Argo (Polygram), Jun '88 by PolyGram Classics **Deleted** Jan '89.

CORIOLANUS (Marlowe Dramatic Society).
MCSET. Cat no: **1057P**. Released on Travellers Tales, '91 by Travellers Tales. Note: 2 cassettes

CYMBELINE (Marlowe Dramatic Society).
MCSET. Cat no: **1054P**. Released on Travellers Tales, '91 by Travellers Tales. Note: 2 Cassettes.

CYMBELINE (Various artists).
MCSET. Cat no: **417 949-4**. Released on Argo (Polygram), Jun '88 by PolyGram Classics **Deleted** Jan '89.

ESSENTIAL SHAKESPEARE, THE (Various narrators).
Note: Advanced release.
MCSET. Cat no: **RC 57**. Released on Random Century, Aug '92 by Random Century Audiobooks, Conifer Records. Note: ISBN no. 1856860914

GREAT SHAKESPEAREANS (Various narrators).
Note: Performances by Edwin Booth, Sir Herbert Beerbohm Tree, Arthur Bourchier, Lewis Walker, Ben Greet, John Barrymore, Sir Johnston Forbes-Robertson, Henry Ainley, Maurice Evans and Sir John Gielgud.
CD. Cat no: **GEMM CD 9465**. Released on Pearl, Oct '90 by Pavilion Records, Harmonia Mundi (UK).

MC. Cat no: **GEMM 7465**. Released on Pearl, '91 by Pavilion Records, Harmonia Mundi (UK).

HAMLET (John Gielgud & The Old Vic Company).
MCSET. Cat no: **LFP 41 7218 5**. Released on Listen For Pleasure, Sep '85 by EMI Records.

MCSET. Cat no: **LFP 7218**. Released on Listen For Pleasure, Sep '85 by EMI Records.

HAMLET (Old Vic Company).
MCSET. Cat no: **1010P**. Released on Travellers Tales, '91 by Travellers Tales.

HAMLET (Various artists).
Note: Starring Ronald Pickup.
MCSET. Cat no: **ZBBC 1004**. Released by BBC Radio Collection, Sep '88 by BBC Records. Note: ISBN No: 0563 225599.

HAMLET (Various artists).
Note: Featuring Derek Jacobi, Timothy West and the Old Vic Company.
MCSET. Cat no: **SAY 35**. Released on Argo (Polygram), Jul '82 by PolyGram Classics **Deleted** Jan '89.

MCSET. Cat no: **TC LFP 7021**. Released on Listen For Pleasure, Nov '77 by EMI Records.

MCSET. Cat no: **ARGO 1127**. Released on Argo (EMI), Sep '89 by EMI

Records. Note: 2 Cassettes.

HAMLET (Derek Jacobi & The Old Vic Company).
LPS. Cat no: **D 158 D 3**. Released on Decca, '79 by PolyGram Classics, Thames Distributors Ltd. **Deleted** '84.

HAMLET (Various artists).
LP. Cat no: **CBS 72259**. Released on CBS, Dec '84 by Sony Music, Solomon & Peres, Outlet Records.

MCSET. Cat no: **232**. Released on Caedmon (USA), '89 by Caedmon Records (USA), Bond Street Music. Note: 4 Cassettes.

HAMLET (Renaissance Theatre Company).
Note: Cast includes Kenneth Brannagh, Dame Judi Dench, Derek Jacobi, Richard Briers, Emma Thompson, Sophie Thompson, Brian Blessed and Michael Williams. Directed by Kenneth Branagh and Glyn Dearman. Music by Patrick Doyle.

MCSET. Cat no: **RC 100**. Released on Random Century, Apr '92 by Random Century Audiobooks, Conifer Records. Note: ISBN no. 1856861287

CDSET. Cat no: **RC 101**. Released on Random Century, Apr '92 by Random Century Audiobooks, Conifer Records. Note: ISBN no. 1856861287

HAMLET (Paul Schofield & Others). Note: Also starring Ronald Pickup.
MCSET. Cat no: **HCA 55**. Released on Harper Collins, '92 by Harper Collins. Note: 4 Cassettes.

HENRY IV (Part 1) (Various artists).
Note: With Paul Scofield, and Marlowe Dramatic Society.
MCSET. Cat no: **SAY 88**. Released on Argo (Polygram), Oct '83 by PolyGram Classics **Deleted** Jan '89.

MCSET. Cat no: **1012P**. Released on Travellers Tales, '91 by Travellers Tales. Note: 2 cassettes

HENRY IV (Part 2) (Various artists).
Note: With Ian McKellen and The Marlowe Dramatic Society.
MCSET. Cat no: **SAY 89**. Released on Argo (Polygram), Nov '83 by PolyGram Classics **Deleted** Jan '89.

MCSET. Cat no: **1013P**. Released on Travellers Tales, '91 by Travellers Tales. Note: 2 Cassettes

HENRY IV (Part 1) (Various artists).
MCSET. Cat no: **217**. Released on Caedmon (USA), by Caedmon Records (USA), Bond Street Music. Note: 2 cassettes

HENRY IV (Part 2) (Various artists).
MCSET. Cat no: **218**. Released on Caedmon (USA), by Caedmon Records (USA), Bond Street Music. Note: 4 cassettes

HENRY IV (Part 1) (Harry Andrews & Others).
MCSET. Cat no: **HCA 56**. Released on Harper Collins, '92 by Harper Collins. Note: 2 Cassettes.

HENRY V (Ian Holm & Others).

MCSET. Cat no: **HCA 57**. Released on Harper Collins, Jan '92 by Harper Collins. Note: 4 cassettes.

HENRY V (Various artists).
Note: With Fay Wilson and The Marlowe Dramatic Society.
MCSET. Cat no: **SAY 103**. Released on Argo (Polygram), Mar '84 by PolyGram Classics **Deleted** Jan '89.

MCSET. Cat no: **1014P**. Released on Travellers Tales, '91 by Travellers Tales. Note: 2 Cassettes.

MCSET. Cat no: **219**. Released on Caedmon (USA), May '88 by Caedmon Records (USA), Bond Street Music.

HENRY V (John Rye).
MC. Cat no: **TS 3**. Released on Green Dragon, '91 by Green Dragon Audio Visual.

HENRY VI (Part I) (Marlowe Dramatic Society).
MCSET. Cat no: **1015P**. Released on Travellers Tales, '91 by Travellers Tales. Note: 2 Cassettes.

HENRY VI (Part II) (Marlowe Dramatic Society).
MCSET. Cat no: **1016P**. Released on Travellers Tales, '91 by Travellers Tales. Note: 2 Cassettes.

HENRY VI (Part III) (Marlowe Dramatic Society).
MCSET. Cat no: **1017P**. Released on Travellers Tales, '91 by Travellers Tales. Note: 2 Cassettes.

HENRY VI (Part 1) (Various artists).
MCSET. Cat no: **418 027-4**. Released on Argo (Polygram), Jun '88 by PolyGram Classics **Deleted** Jan '89.

HENRY VI (Part 2) (Various artists).
MCSET. Cat no: **418 030-4**. Released on Argo (Polygram), Jun '88 by PolyGram Classics **Deleted** Jan '89.

HENRY VI (Part 3) (Various artists).
MCSET. Cat no: **418 033-4**. Released on Argo (Polygram), Jun '88 by PolyGram Classics **Deleted** Jan '89.

HOW PLEASANT TO KNOW MR. LEAR (Richard Pasco & Barbara Leigh Hunt).
MC. Cat no: **THE 604**. Released on Pearl, '91 by Pavilion Records, Harmonia Mundi (UK).

JULIUS CAESAR (Various narrators).
Note: Narrators are John Rye, William Squire and Stephen Murray.
MC. Cat no: **TS 1**. Released on Green Dragon, '91 by Green Dragon Audio Visual.

JULIUS CAESAR (Sir Ralph Richardson & Others).
MCSET. Cat no: **HCA 58**. Released on Harper Collins, Jan '92 by Harper Collins. Note: 2 cassettes.

JULIUS CAESAR (Various artists).
MCSET. Cat no: **SAY 40**. Released on Argo (Polygram), Nov '82 by PolyGram Classics **Deleted** Jan '89.

MCSET. Cat no: **ARGO 1043**. Released on Argo (EMI), May '89 by EMI

Records. Note: 2 Cassettes.
MCSET. Cat no: **0230**. Released on Caedmon (USA), '90 by Caedmon Records (USA), Bond Street Music.

JULIUS CAESAR (Various artists).
Note: Featuring Richard Johnson and Marlowe Dramatic Society.
MCSET. Cat no: **1018P**. Released on Travellers Tales, '91 by Travellers Tales. Note: 2 Cassettes.

KING HENRY VIII (Various artists).
MCSET. Cat no: **418 036-4**. Released on Argo (Polygram), Jun '88 by PolyGram Classics **Deleted** Jan '89.

KING JOHN (Various artists).
Note: With Sir Michael Hordern and The Marlowe Dramatic Society.
MCSET. Cat no: **414 742-4**. Released on Argo (Polygram), Oct '85 by PolyGram Classics **Deleted** Jan '89.

MCSET. Cat no: **1019P**. Released on Travellers Tales, '91 by Travellers Tales. Note: 2 Cassettes.

KING LEAR (Various artists).
MCSET. Cat no: **SAY 67**. Released on Argo (Polygram), Mar '83 by PolyGram Classics **Deleted** Jan '89.

KING LEAR (And The Duchess of Malfi) (Dylan Thomas).
MC. Cat no: **1158**. Released on Caedmon (USA), '89 by Caedmon Records (USA), Bond Street Music.

KING LEAR (Various artists).
Note: With William Devlin and Marlowe Dramatic Society.
MCSET. Cat no: **1020P**. Released on Travellers Tales, '91 by Travellers Tales. Note: 2 Cassettes

KING LEAR (Various artists).
Note: Starring Sir Alec Guinness.
MCSET. Cat no: **0233**. Released on Caedmon (USA), May '88 by Caedmon Records (USA), Bond Street Music. Note: 4 cassettes

MCSET. Cat no: **ZBBC 1002**. Released on BBC, Sep '88 by BBC Records, Taylors. Note: ISBN No: 0563 225629

KING LEAR (Paul Scofield & Others).
MCSET. Cat no: **HCA 59**. Released on Harper Collins, Jan '92 by Harper Collins. Note: 4 cassettes.

LOVE'S LABOUR'S LOST (Various artists).
MCSET. Cat no: **SAY 106**. Released on Argo (Polygram), Sep '84 by PolyGram Classics **Deleted** Jan '89.

MCSET. Cat no: **207**. Released on Caedmon (USA), '88 by Caedmon Records (USA), Bond Street Music. Note: 2 cassettes

LOVE'S LABOUR'S LOST (Various artists).
Note: With Diana Rigg and The Marlowe Dramatic Society.
MCSET. Cat no: **1021P**. Released on Travellers Tales, '91 by Travellers Tales. Note: 2 Cassettes.

MACBETH (Various artists).

MCSET. Cat no: **1022P.** Released on Travellers Tales, '91 by Travellers Tales. Note: 2 Cassettes.

MCSET. Cat no: **TS 4.** Released on Green Dragon, '91 by Green Dragon Audio Visual.

MACBETH (Sir Alec Guiness & The Old Vic Company).
MCSET. Cat no: **LFP 7228.** Released on Listen For Pleasure, Aug '88 by EMI Records.

MACBETH (Various artists).
Note: Starring Dennis Quilley and Hannah Gordon.
MCSET. Cat no: **ZBBC 1005.** Released on BBC, Sep '88 by BBC Records, Taylors. Note: ISBN No: 0563 225637

MACBETH (Marlowe Dramatic Society).
MCSET. Cat no: **SAY 21.** Released on Argo (Polygram), Jun '88 by PolyGram Classics **Deleted** Jan '89.
MCSET. Cat no: **ARGO 1025.** Released on Argo (EMI), May '89 by EMI Records. Note: 2 Cassettes.
MCSET. Cat no: **231.** Released on Caedmon (USA), '89 by Caedmon Records (USA), Bond Street Music. Note: 2 Cassettes.

MEASURE FOR MEASURE (Various artists).
Note: With Sir John Gielgud, Ralph Richardson and Margaret Leighton.
MCSET. Cat no: **1060P.** Released on Travellers Tales, '91 by Travellers Tales. Note: 3 Cassettes.

MEASURE FOR MEASURE (Various artists).
MCSET. Cat no: **204.** Released on Caedmon (USA), by Caedmon Records (USA), Bond Street Music. Note: 3 cassettes
MCSET. Cat no: **418 051-4.** Released on Argo (Polygram), Jun '88 by PolyGram Classics **Deleted** Jan '89. Note: 2 Cassettes.

MERCHANT OF VENICE, THE (Various artists).
MCSET. Cat no: **209.** Released on Caedmon (USA), '89 by Caedmon Records (USA), Bond Street Music. Note: 3 cassettes

MERCHANT OF VENICE, THE (Marlowe Dramatic Society).
Note: Performed by Tony Church, Margaretta Scott, Gary Watson and The Marlowe Dramatic Society.
MCSET. Cat no: **SAY 83.** Released on Argo (Polygram), Jun '88 by PolyGram Classics **Deleted** Jan '89.
MCSET. Cat no: **ARGO 1199.** Released on Argo (EMI), May '90 by EMI Records. Note: 2 Cassettes.
MCSET. Cat no: **1024P.** Released on Travellers Tales, '91 by Travellers Tales. Note: 2 Cassettes.

MERCHANT OF VENICE, THE (Lee Montague & Barbara Jefford).
MC. Cat no: **TS 8.** Released on Green Dragon, '91 by Green Dragon Audio Visual.

MERCHANT OF VENICE, THE (Dorothy Tutin, Anthony Andrews & Others).
Note: Also available on hanging format, catalogue number:- 0001389904.
MCSET. Cat no: **HCA 60.** Released on Harper Collins, Jan '92 by Harper Collins. Note: 2 cassettes.

MERRY WIVES OF WINDSOR, THE (Various artists).
MCSET. Cat no: **203.** Released on Caedmon (USA), '88 by Caedmon Records (USA), Bond Street Music. Note: 3 Cassettes
MCSET. Cat no: **1025P.** Released on Travellers Tales, '91 by Travellers Tales. Note: 3 Cassettes

MERRY WIVES OF WINDSOR, THE (Sir Anthony Quayle & Others).
Note: Also available on hanging format, catalogue number:- 000135223.
MCSET. Cat no: **HCA 61.** Released on Harper Collins, Jan '92 by Harper Collins. Note: 2 cassettes.

MERRY WIVES OF WINDSOR, THE (Various artists).
Note: Starring Angela Baddeley, Geraldine McEwan, Patrick Wymark, Roy Dotrice and The Marlowe Dramatic Society.
MCSET. Cat no: **414 733-4.** Released on Argo (Polygram), Apr '85 by PolyGram Classics **Deleted** Jan '89.
MCSET. Cat no: **ARGO 1211.** Released on Argo (EMI), Jul '90 by EMI Records. Note: 2 Cassettes.

MIDSUMMER NIGHT'S DREAM, A (Robert Helpman & The Old Vic Company).
MCSET. Cat no: **LFP 7266.** Released on Listen For Pleasure, Sep '86 by EMI Records.

MIDSUMMER NIGHTS DREAM, A (Various artists).
Note: Narrators are Sarah Badel, Lynn Farleigh and John Turner.
MC. Cat no: **TS 7.** Released on Green Dragon, '91 by Green Dragon Audio Visual.

MIDSUMMER NIGHT'S DREAM, A (Prunella Scales & Ian McKellen).
Note: With The Marlowe Dramatic Society.
MCSET. Cat no: **208.** Released on Caedmon (USA), by Caedmon Records (USA), Bond Street Music. Note: 2 cassettes

MIDSUMMER NIGHTS DREAM, A (Paul Scofield & Others).
MCSET. Cat no: **HCA 62.** Released on Harper Collins, Jan '92 by Harper Collins. Note: 2 cassettes.

MIDSUMMER NIGHT'S DREAM, A (Various artists).
MCSET. Cat no: **SAY 38.** Released on Argo (Polygram), Jun '88 by PolyGram Classics **Deleted** Jan '89.
MCSET. Cat no: **ARGO 1040.** Released on Argo (EMI), May '89 by EMI Records. Note: 2 Cassettes.

MCSET. Cat no: **1026P.** Released on Travellers Tales, '91 by Travellers Tales. Note: 2 Cassettes.

MUCH ADO ABOUT NOTHING (Rex Harrison & Others).
MCSET. Cat no: **HCA 63.** Released on Harper Collins, Jan '92 by Harper Collins. Note: 2 cassettes.

MUCH ADO ABOUT NOTHING (Various artists).
MCSET. Cat no: **SAY 36.** Released on Argo (Polygram), Jul '82 by PolyGram Classics **Deleted** Jan '89.
MCSET. Cat no: **ARGO 1034.** Released on Argo (EMI), May '89 by EMI Records. Note: 2 Cassettes.

MUCH ADO ABOUT NOTHING (Various artists).
Note: With Sir John Gielgud and The Marlowe Dramatic Society.
MCSET. Cat no: **1027P.** Released on Travellers Tales, '91 by Travellers Tales. Note: 2 Cassettes.

MUCH ADO ABOUT NOTHING (Marlowe Dramatic Society).
MCSET. Cat no: **206.** Released on Caedmon (USA), by Caedmon Records (USA), Bond Street Music. Note: 3 cassettes

OTHELLO (John Turner & Maureen O'Brien).
MC. Cat no: **TS 5.** Released on Green Dragon, '91 by Green Dragon Audio Visual.

OTHELLO (Various artists).
MCSET. Cat no: **0225.** Released on Caedmon (USA), '89 by Caedmon Records (USA), Bond Street Music. Note: 3 cassettes

OTHELLO (Various artists).
Note: Starring Paul Scofield.
MCSET. Cat no: **ZBBC 1003.** Released on BBC, Sep '88 by BBC Records, Taylors. Note: ISBN No: 0563 225653

OTHELLO (Various artists).
Note: Featuring Ian Holm, Peggy Ashcroft and the Marlowe Dramatic Society.
MCSET. Cat no: **SAY 64.** Released on Argo (Polygram), Jul '83 by PolyGram Classics **Deleted** Jan '89.
MCSET. Cat no: **ARGO 1157.** Released on Argo (EMI), Oct '89 by EMI Records. Note: 2 Cassettes.
MCSET. Cat no: **1028P.** Released on Travellers Tales, '91 by Travellers Tales. Note: 2 Cassettes.

PERICLES (Marlowe Dramatic Society).
MCSET. Cat no: **1058P.** Released on Travellers Tales, '91 by Travellers Tales. Note: 2 Cassettes.

PERICLES (Various artists).
MCSET. Cat no: **418 039-4.** Released on Argo (Polygram), Jun '88 by PolyGram Classics **Deleted** Jan '89.

RICHARD II (Various artists).
MCSET. Cat no: **216.** Released on Caedmon (USA), '88 by Caedmon Re-

cords (USA), Bond Street Music. Note: 2 cassettes

MCSET. Cat no: **SAY 66.** Released on Argo (Polygram), May '83 by PolyGram Classics **Deleted** Jan '89. Note: 2 Cassettes.

RICHARD II (Various artists).
Note: Wtih Richard Pasco and The Marlowe Dramatic Society.
MCSET. Cat no: **1029P.** Released on Travellers Tales, '91 by Travellers Tales. Note: 2 Cassettes.

RICHARD II (Sir John Gielgud).
MCSET. Cat no: **HCA 64.** Released on Harper Collins, Jan '92 by Harper Collins. Note: 2 cassettes.

RICHARD III (Various artists).
MCSET. Cat no: **0223.** Released on Caedmon (USA), '88 by Caedmon Records (USA), Bond Street Music. Note: 4 cassettes

MCSET. Cat no: **1030P.** Released on Travellers Tales, '91 by Travellers Tales. Note: 4 cassettes

RICHARD III (Dame Peggy Ashcroft, Robert Stephens & Others).
MCSET. Cat no: **HCA 65.** Released on Harper Collins, Jan '92 by Harper Collins. Note: 4 cassettes.

RICHARD III (Various artists).
Note: With Patrick Wymark and The Marlowe Dramatic Society.
MCSET. Cat no: **1030P.** Released on Travellers Tales, '91 by Travellers Tales. Note: 2 Cassettes.

ROMEO AND JULIET (John Rye & Barbara Jefford).
MC. Cat no: **TS 6.** Released on Green Dragon, '91 by Green Dragon Audio Visual.

ROMEO AND JULIET (Various artists).
Note: With Richard Marguard, Janette Richard and Others.
MCSET. Cat no: **1031P.** Released on Travellers Tales, '91 by Travellers Tales. Note: 2 Cassettes.

ROMEO AND JULIET (Marlowe Dramatic Society).
MCSET. Cat no: **ARGO 1229.** Released on Argo (EMI), Oct '90 by EMI Records. Note: 2 Cassettes.

ROMEO AND JULIET (Various artists).
MCSET. Cat no: **0228.** Released on Caedmon (USA), '89 by Caedmon Records (USA), Bond Street Music. Note: 3 cassettes

MCSET. Cat no: **SAY 37.** Released on Argo (Polygram), Jun '88 by PolyGram Classics **Deleted** Jan '89.

ROMEO AND JULIET (Various artists).
Note: Featuring Alan Badel, Claire Bloom, Peter Finch, Athene Seyler and the Old Vic Company.
MCSET. Cat no: **LFP 7296.** Released on Listen For Pleasure, Jun '87 by EMI Records. Note: Playing time: 2 1/2 hours.

ROMEO AND JULIET (Claire Bloom & Others).
MCSET. Cat no: **HCA 66.** Released on Harper Collins, Jan '92 by Harper Collins. Note: 2 cassettes.

SHAKESPEARE SONNETS-1 (Sonnets 1-77) (Jack Edward).
MCSET. Cat no: **KH 88021.** Released on Helios, '91 by Hyperion Records, Gamut Distribution.

SHAKESPEARE SONNETS-2 (Sonnets 78 To 154) (Jack Edward).
MCSET. Cat no: **KH 88022.** Released on Helios, '91 by Hyperion Records, Gamut Distribution.

SONNETS (Sir John Gielgud).
MCSET. Cat no: **HCA 67.** Released on Harper Collins, Jan '92 by Harper Collins. Note: 2 cassettes.

SONNETS (Various artists).
MCSET. Cat no: **241.** Released on Caedmon (USA), '89 by Caedmon Records (USA), Bond Street Music. Note: 2 cassettes

SONNETS (Richard Pasco).
MCSET. Cat no: **SAY 114.** Released on Argo (Polygram), Oct '84 by PolyGram Classics **Deleted** Jan '89.

MCSET. Cat no: **1032P.** Released on Travellers Tales, '91 by Travellers Tales. Note: 2 Cassettes.

TAMING OF THE SHREW (Various artists).
MCSET. Cat no: **211.** Released on Caedmon (USA), by Caedmon Records (USA), Bond Street Music. Note: 3 cassettes

TAMING OF THE SHREW (Various artists).
Note: Featuring Peggy Ashcroft and The Marlowe Dramatic Society.
MCSET. Cat no: **SAY 65.** Released on Argo (Polygram), May '83 by PolyGram Classics **Deleted** Jan '89.

MCSET. Cat no: **ARGO 1160.** Released on Argo (EMI), Oct '89 by EMI Records. Note: 2 Cassettes.

MCSET. Cat no: **1033P.** Released on Travellers Tales, '91 by Travellers Tales. Note: 2 Cassettes.

TAMING OF THE SHREW (Trevor Hollard, Margaret Leighton & Others).
MCSET. Cat no: **HCA 68.** Released on Harper Collins, Jan '92 by Harper Collins. Note: 2 cassettes.

TEMPEST, THE (Various artists).
Note: With Sir Michael Hordern and The Marlowe Dramatic Society.
MCSET. Cat no: **1034P.** Released on Travellers Tales, '91 by Travellers Tales. Note: 2 Cassettes.

MCSET. Cat no: **201.** Released on Caedmon (USA), by Caedmon Records (USA), Bond Street Music. Note: 2 cassettes

TEMPEST, THE (Sir Michael Redgrave & Others).
MCSET. Cat no: **HCA 69.** Released on Harper Collins, Jan '92 by Harper Collins. Note: 2 cassettes.

TEMPEST, THE (Various artists).
MCSET. Cat no: **SAY 69.** Released on Argo (Polygram), Jun '88 by PolyGram Classics **Deleted** Jan '89.

MCSET. Cat no: **ARGO 1103.** Released on Argo (EMI), Jun '89 by EMI Records. Note: 2 Cassettes.

TIMON OF ATHENS (Various artists).
Note: With William Squire, Peter Woodthorpe, John Wood and the Marlowe Dramatic Society.
MCSET. Cat no: **414 739-4.** Released on Argo (Polygram), Jun '88 by PolyGram Classics **Deleted** Jan '89.

MCSET. Cat no: **1035P.** Released on Travellers Tales, '91 by Travellers Tales. Note: 2 Cassettes.

TITUS AND ANDRONICUS (Various artists).
Note: With Jill Balcon and The Marlowe Dramatic Society.
MCSET. Cat no: **414 703-4.** Released on Argo (Polygram), Apr '85 by PolyGram Classics **Deleted** Jan '89.

MCSET. Cat no: **1036P.** Released on Travellers Tales, '91 by Travellers Tales. Note: 2 Cassettes.

TRAGEDY OF RICHARD III, THE (Marlowe Dramatic Society).
MCSET. Cat no: **ARGO 1262.** Released on Argo (EMI), May '91 by EMI Records.

TROILUS AND CRESSIDA (Various artists).
MCSET. Cat no: **417 937-4.** Released on Argo (Polygram), Jun '88 by PolyGram Classics **Deleted** Jan '89.

TWELFTH NIGHT (Old Vic Company).
LPS. Cat no: **D 159 D 3.** Released on Argo, Dec '79 by Decca International **Deleted** '84.

TWELFTH NIGHT (Various narrators).
Note: Narrators are Stephen Murray, Barbara Jefford and Marius Goring.
MC. Cat no: **TS 2.** Released on Green Dragon, '91 by Green Dragon Audio Visual.

TWELFTH NIGHT (Various artists).
MCSET. Cat no: **213.** Released on Caedmon (USA), by Caedmon Records (USA), Bond Street Music. Note: 2 cassettes

TWELFTH NIGHT (Siobhan McKenna & Others).
MCSET. Cat no: **HCA 70.** Released on Harper Collins, Jan '92 by Harper Collins. Note: 2 cassettes.

TWELFTH NIGHT (Various artists).
Note: Featuring Eileen Atkins, Michael Denison and the Old Vic Company.
MCSET. Cat no: **SAY 39.** Released on Argo (Polygram), Jun '88 by PolyGram Classics **Deleted** Jan '89.

MCSET. Cat no: **ARGO 1130.** Released on Argo (EMI), Sep '89 by EMI Records. Note: 2 Cassettes.

MCSET. Cat no: **1037P.** Released on

Travellers Tales, '91 by Travellers Tales. Note: 2 Cassettes.

TWO GENTLEMEN OF VERONA (Marlowe Dramatic Society).
MCSET. Cat no: **1055P**. Released on Travellers Tales, '91 by Travellers Tales. Note: 2 Cassettes.
MCSET. Cat no: **4179404**. Released on Argo (Polygram), '91 by PolyGram Classics.

VENUS AND ADONIS (And The Rape of Lucrece) (Various artists).
Note: With Dame Peggy Ashcroft, Tony Church and Irene Worth.
MCSET. Cat no: **414 745-4**. Released on Argo (Polygram), Dec '85 by Poly-Gram Classics **Deleted** Jan '89.
MCSET. Cat no: **1038P**. Released on Travellers Tales, '91 by Travellers Tales. Note: 2 Cassettes.

WINTER'S TALE, THE (Marlowe Dramatic Society).
MCSET. Cat no: **SAY 81**. Released on Argo (Polygram), Nov '83 by PolyGram Classics **Deleted** Jan '89. Note: Playing time: 2 1/2 hours.
MCSET. Cat no: **ARGO 1193**. Released on Argo (EMI), Mar '90 by EMI Records. Note: 2 Cassettes.

WINTER'S TALE, THE (Various artists).
Note: With William Squire and The Marlowe Dramatic Society.
MCSET. Cat no: **214**. Released on Caedmon (USA), '88 by Caedmon Records (USA), Bond Street Music. Note: 3 cassettes
MCSET. Cat no: **1039P**. Released on Travellers Tales, '91 by Travellers Tales. Note: 3 Cassettes.

WINTER'S TALE, THE (Sir John Gielgud & Others).
MCSET. Cat no: **HCA 71**. Released on Harper Collins, Jan '92 by Harper Collins. Note: 2 cassettes.

WORLD OF SHAKESPEARE, THE (Various artists).
Note: With Sir John Gielgud, Dame Peggy Ashcroft and others. Excerpts from Ricard II, Henry IV, Henry V, Julius Caeser, Macbeth, Twelfth Night, King Lear, Othello, Anthony and Cleopatra, Tempest and Sonnets.
MCSET. Cat no: **SAY 41**. Released on Argo (Polygram), Jun '88 by PolyGram Classics **Deleted** Jan '89.
LP. Cat no: **SPA 558**. Released on Decca, Oct '79 by PolyGram Classics, Thames Distributors Ltd. **Deleted** '84.
MCSET. Cat no: **1040P**. Released on Travellers Tales, '91 by Travellers Tales. Note: 2 Cassettes.

Sharpe, Tom

ANCESTRAL VICES (Griff Rhys Jones).
MCSET. Cat no: **CAB 617**. Released on Chivers Audio Books, Mar '92 by Chivers Audio Books, Green Dragon Audio Visual. Note: 8 Cassettes.

PORTERHOUSE BLUE (David Jason).
MCSET. Cat no: **060055855X**. Released on Hamlyn Books On Tape, Apr '88, Bond Street Music. Note: 2 cassette set

PORTERHOUSE BLUE (Griff Rhys Jones).
MCSET. Cat no: **1063H**. Released on Travellers Tales, '91 by Travellers Tales. Note: 6 cassettes.
MCSET. Cat no: **CAB 269**. Released on Chivers Audio Books, '91 by Chivers Audio Books, Green Dragon Audio Visual. Note: 6 Cassettes.

THROWBACK, THE (Geoffrey Matthews).
MCSET. Cat no: **1054H**. Released on Travellers Tales, '91 by Travellers Tales. Note: 6 cassettes.
MCSET. Cat no: **IAB 90072**. Released on Isis Audio Books, '91. Note: 6 Cassettes.

VINTAGE STUFF (Stephen Fry).
MCSET. Cat no: **1034H**. Released on Travellers Tales, '91 by Travellers Tales. Note: 6 cassettes.
MCSET. Cat no: **IAB 88042**. Released on Isis Audio Books, '91. Note: 6 cassettes.

Shaw Gardner, Craig

BATMAN (Funhouse of Fear) (Unknown narrator(s)).
MC. Cat no: **PLBB 265**. Released on Tell-A-Tale, '89 by Pickwick Records, Taylors, Clyde Factors.

BATMAN (The Warhawk) (Unknown narrator(s)).
MC. Cat no: **PLBB 264**. Released on Tell-A-Tale, '89 by Pickwick Records, Taylors, Clyde Factors.

BATMAN (Roddy McDowall).
Note: Also available on hanging format, catalogue number:- 0001388436.
MC. Cat no: **0001388428**. Released on Harper Collins, '91 by Harper Collins.
MC. Cat no: **38843**. Released on Tempo, Sep '89 by Warwick Records, Celtic Music, Henry Hadaway Organisation.

BATMAN IN RHYMES, RIDDLES AND RIOTS (Various artists).
Note: From the Super Heroes series.
MC. Cat no: **415 716-4**. Released on MFP, Oct '85 by EMI Records, Solomon & Peres.

Shaw, George Bernard

CAESAR AND CLEOPATRA (Various artists).
MCSET. Cat no: **0304**. Released on Caedmon (USA), '89 by Caedmon Records (USA), Bond Street Music. Note: 2 cassettes

HEARTBREAK HOUSE (Various artists).
MCSET. Cat no: **0335**. Released on Caedmon (USA), '89 by Caedmon Records (USA), Bond Street Music. Note: 3 cassettes

JOHN BULL'S OTHER ISLAND (Various artists).
MCSET. Cat no: **0346**. Released on Caedmon (USA), '89 by Caedmon Records (USA), Bond Street Music. Note: 4 cassettes

MAJOR BARBARA (Various artists).
MCSET. Cat no: **0319**. Released on Caedmon (USA), '88 by Caedmon Records (USA), Bond Street Music. Note: 4 cassettes.

MISALLIANCE (Various artists).
MCSET. Cat no: **0365**. Released on Caedmon (USA), '89 by Caedmon Records (USA), Bond Street Music. Note: 3 cassettes

PYGMALION (Alec McCowen & Diana Rigg).
MCSET. Cat no: **SAY 28**. Released on Argo (Polygram), Jul '82 by PolyGram Classics **Deleted** Jan '89.
MCSET. Cat no: **1042P**. Released on Travellers Tales, '91 by Travellers Tales. Note: 2 Cassettes.

PYGMALION (Various artists).
MCSET. Cat no: **0354**. Released on Caedmon (USA), May '88 by Caedmon Records (USA), Bond Street Music. Note: 2 cassettes

SAINT JOAN (Various artists).
MCSET. Cat no: **0311**. Released on Caedmon (USA), '89 by Caedmon Records (USA), Bond Street Music. Note: 4 cassettes
MCSET. Cat no: **SAY 42**. Released on Argo (Polygram), Jun '88 by PolyGram Classics **Deleted** Jan '89.

SAINT JOAN (Various artists).
Note: Starring with Barbara Jefford, Alex McCowen, Max Adrian and Cast.
MCSET. Cat no: **ARGO 1253**. Released on Argo (EMI), Apr '91 by EMI Records.
MCSET. Cat no: **1043P**. Released on Travellers Tales, '91 by Travellers Tales. Note: 2 Cassettes.

Shelburne, A.V.

MELODY OF THE MOON (Nicolette McKenzie).
MCSET. Cat no: **MRC 1019**. Released on Chivers Audio Books, '91 by Chivers Audio Books, Green Dragon Audio Visual. Note: 2 cassettes.

Sheldon, Sidney

IF TOMORROW COMES (Roger Moore).
Note: Also available on hanging format, catalogue number:- 0001031317.
MCSET. Cat no: **0001072838**. Released on Harper Collins, '91 by Harper Collins. Note: 2 Cassettes.

MASTER OF THE GAME (Roddy McDowall).
Note: Also available on hanging format, catalogue number:- 0001387065.
MCSET. Cat no: **000138645X**. Released on Harper Collins, '91 by Harper Collins. Note: 2 Cassettes.

NAKED FACE, THE (Roger Moore).
MCSET. Cat no: **0001387812**. Released on Harper Collins, '91 by Harper Collins.

OTHER SIDE OF MIDNIGHT, THE (Jenny Agutter).
Note: Also available on hanging format, catalogue number:- 0001388215.
MCSET. Cat no: **0001388010**. Released on Harper Collins, '91 by Harper Collins. Note: 2 Cassettes.

RAGE OF ANGELS, A (Susannah York).
Note: Also available on hanging format, catalogue number:- 0001387073
MCSET. Cat no: **0001386441**. Released on Harper Collins, '91 by Harper Collins. Note: 2 Cassettes.

SANDS OF TIME, THE (Sidney Sheldon).
Note: Also available on hanging format, catalogue number:- 0001388231.
MCSET. Cat no: **0001388037**. Released on Harper Collins, '91 by Harper Collins. Note: 2 Cassettes.

SHORT STORIES (Roger Moore & Lee Remick).
MCSET. Cat no: **1489T**. Released on Travellers Tales, '91 by Travellers Tales. Note: 8 Cassettes.

WINDMILLS OF THE GODS (Lee Remick).
Note: Also available on hanging format, catalogue number:- 0001031325.
MCSET. Cat no: **0001072845**. Released on Harper Collins, '91 by Harper Collins. Note: 2 Cassettes.

Shelley, Mary

FRANKENSTEIN (Or the Modern Prometheus) (Robert Trotter).
MCSET. Cat no: **SPF 765-1**. Released on Schiltron Audio Books, '91 by Schiltron Publishing. Note: 6 Cassettes. Playing time 7 hours 30 minutes.
MCSET. Cat no: **1031S**. Released on Travellers Tales, '91 by Travellers Tales.

FRANKENSTEIN (James Mason).
LP. Cat no: **TC 1541**. Released on Caedmon (USA), '79 by Caedmon Records (USA), Bond Street Music.
MC. Cat no: **CDL 51541**. Released on Caedmon (USA), '79 by Caedmon Records (USA), Bond Street Music.

FRANKENSTEIN (Unknown narrator(s)).
Note: Book and cassette. Ages up to 7 - 12 years.
MC. Cat no: **PLB 126**. Released on Tell-A-Tale, '88 by Pickwick Records, Taylors, Clyde Factors.

Sheridan, Paula

DARK MENACE (Jill Shilling).
MCSET. Cat no: **MRC 1028**. Released on Chivers Audio Books, '91 by Chivers Audio Books, Green Dragon Audio Visual. Note: 2 cassettes.

Short, Luke

MAN COULD GET KILLED, A (Jack Clancy).
MCSET. Cat no: **CAB 258**. Released on Chivers Audio Books, Apr '88 by Chivers Audio Books, Green Dragon Audio Visual. Note: 6 Cassettes.
MCSET. Cat no: **1266T**. Released on Travellers Tales, '91 by Travellers Tales. Note: 6 Cassettes.

Short Stories

CLASSIC SHORT STORIES (Volume 1) (Various artists).
Note: Readers are: Martin Jarvis, Rosalind Ayres, Robin Bailey, Richard Pasco, Iain Cuthbertson and Nicky Henson. Authors include Dickens, Hardy, Conan Doyle, Poe, Saki and Mansfield. 27 Stories.
MCSET. Cat no: **TTDMC 501**. Released on CSA Tell Tapes, Mar '92 by CSA Tell-Tapes. Note: 6 Cassettes. ISBN No: 1873859996

CLASSIC SHORT STORIES (Volume 2) (Various artists).
Note: Readers include: Martin Jarvis, Rosalind Ayres, Robin Bailey, Richard Pasco, Iain Cuthbertson and Nicky Henson. Authors include: Dickens, Hardy, Conan Doyle, Poe, Saki, Mansfield, Wilde and many more. 25 stories.
MCSET. Cat no: **TTDMC 502**. Released on CSA Tell Tapes, Mar '92 by CSA Tell-Tapes. Note: 6 Cassettes. ISBN No: 1873859988

HEROES AND VILLAINS (Various narrators).
MCSET. Cat no: **LD 6**. Released on Green Dragon, '91 by Green Dragon Audio Visual. Note: 2 Cassettes.

IN PRAISE OF CATS (Joanna Morris & Clive Champaney).
Note: Includes authors:- Leigh Hunt, Barbara Wood, Thomas Hardy and Richard Church.
MC. Cat no: **GCS 1**. Released on Schiltron Audio Books, '91 by Schiltron Publishing.

MODERN SHORT STORIES (Volume 1) (Various narrators).
MC. Cat no: **E 107A**. Released on Tutor Tape, '91 by Morley Audio Services.

MODERN SHORT STORIES (Volume 2) (Various narrators).
MC. Cat no: **E 107B**. Released on Tutor Tape, '91 by Morley Audio Services.

MODERN SHORT STORIES (Volume 3) (Various artists).
MC. Cat no: **E 107C**. Released on Tutor Tape, '91 by Morley Audio Services.

Shute, Nevil

FAR COUNTRY, THE (Robin Bailey).
MCSET. Cat no: **CAB 421**. Released on Chivers Audio Books, '91 by Chivers Audio Books, Green Dragon Audio Visual. Note: 8 Cassettes.
MCSET. Cat no: **1408F**. Released on Travellers Tales, '91 by Travellers Tales. Note: 8 cassettes.

LONELY ROAD (Robin Bailey).
MCSET. Cat no: **CAB 559**. Released on Chivers Audio Books, '91 by Chivers Audio Books, Green Dragon Audio Visual. Note: 8 Cassettes.
MCSET. Cat no: **1619F**. Released on Travellers Tales, '91 by Travellers Tales. Note: 8 cassettes.

NO HIGHWAY (Robin Bailey).
MCSET. Cat no: **CAB 281**. Released on Chivers Audio Books, '91 by Chivers Audio Books, Green Dragon Audio Visual. Note: 8 Cassettes.
MCSET. Cat no: **1284F**. Released on Travellers Tales, '91 by Travellers Tales. Note: 8 cassettes.

ON THE BEACH (Sam Neill).
MCSET. Cat no: **LFP 7220**. Released on Listen For Pleasure, Oct '85 by EMI Records.

ON THE BEACH (James Smilie).
MCSET. Cat no: **CAB 376**. Released on Chivers Audio Books, '91 by Chivers Audio Books, Green Dragon Audio Visual. Note: 8 Cassettes.

ON THE BEACH (Sam Neill).
Note: Abridged version.
MCSET. Cat no: **1148F**. Released on Travellers Tales, '91 by Travellers Tales. Note: 2 cassettes.

PASTORAL (Nicholas Farrell).
MCSET. Cat no: **1147F**. Released on Travellers Tales, '91 by Travellers Tales. Note: 8 cassettes.
MCSET. Cat no: **CAB 156**. Released on Chivers Audio Books, '91 by Chivers Audio Books, Green Dragon Audio Visual.

PIED PIPER (Robin Bailey).
MCSET. Cat no: **CAB 220**. Released on Chivers Audio Books, '91 by Chivers Audio Books, Green Dragon Audio Visual. Note: 8 cassettes.
MCSET. Cat no: **1209F**. Released on Travellers Tales, '91 by Travellers Tales. Note: 8 cassettes.

RAINBOW AND THE ROSE, THE (Robin Bailey).
MCSET. Cat no: **1482F**. Released on Travellers Tales, '91 by Travellers Tales. Note: 6 Cassettes.
MCSET. Cat no: **CAB 489**. Released on Chivers Audio Books, '91 by Chivers Audio Books, Green Dragon Audio Visual. Note: 6 cassettes.

REQUIEM FOR A WREN (Stephen Thorne).
MCSET. Cat no: **CAB 694**. Released on Chivers Audio Books, Apr '92 by Chivers Audio Books, Green Dragon Audio Visual. Note: 8 Cassettes

RUINED CITY (Robin Bailey).
MCSET. Cat no: **CAB 648**. Released on Chivers Audio Books, Dec '91 by Chivers Audio Books, Green Dragon Audio Visual. Note: 6 cassettes

TOWN LIKE ALICE, A (Leo McKern).

Note: Abridged version.
MCSET. Cat no: **1314F.** Released on Travellers Tales, '91 by Travellers Tales. Note: 2 cassettes.

TOWN LIKE ALICE, A (Robin Bailey).
MCSET Cat no: **CAB 339.** Released on Chivers Audio Books, '88 by Chivers Audio Books, Green Dragon Audio Visual.

MCSET. Cat no: **1323F.** Released on Travellers Tales, '91 by Travellers Tales. Note: 8 cassettes.

TOWN LIKE ALICE, A (Leo McKern).
MCSET. Cat no: **LFP 7330.** Released on Listen For Pleasure, Apr '88 by EMI Records.

Sibley, Raymond

MUMMY, THE (Horror Classics For Ages 7-12) (Unknown narrator(s)). Note: Book and cassette.
MC. Cat no: **PLBC 175.** Released on Tell-A-Tale, '88 by Pickwick Records, Taylors, Clyde Factors.

Sillitoe, Alan

BIKE, THE (And On Saturday Afternoon) (Various narrators).
MC. Cat no: **0582240824.** Released on Longman/Pickwick, '91 by Pickwick Records.

DOWN FROM THE HILL (Richard Earthy).
MCSET. Cat no: **OAS 90104.** Released on Oasis Audio Books, '91 by Isis Audio Books. Note: 5 cassettes.

Simenon, Georges

MAIGRET (Various artists).
MCSET. Cat no: **ZBBC 1221.** Released on BBC Radio Collection, '91 by BBC Records. Note: ISBN No: 0563409908

MAIGRET AND THE KILLER (Andrew Sachs).
MCSET. Cat no: **CAB 600.** Released on Chivers Audio Books, '91 by Chivers Audio Books, Green Dragon Audio Visual. Note: 4 Cassettes.

MCSET. Cat no: **1754T.** Released on Travellers Tales, '91 by Travellers Tales. Note: 4 Cassettes.

MAIGRET AND THE TOY VILLAGE (Andrew Sachs).
MCSET. Cat no: **CAB 666.** Released on Chivers Audio Books, Jan '92 by Chivers Audio Books, Green Dragon Audio Visual. Note: 4 cassettes.

Simple, Lee J.

PHANTOM OF THE SOAP OPERA (Lee J Simple).
LP. Cat no: **RIV 89001.** Released on Silverword, 31 Jul '89 by Silverword Records.

Simpson, Dorothy

DEAD BY MORNING (Terrence Hardiman).
MCSET. Cat no: **CAB 440.** Released on Chivers Audio Books, '91 by Chivers Audio Books, Green Dragon Audio Visual. Note: 6 Cassettes.

MCSET. Cat no: **1593T.** Released on Travellers Tales, '91 by Travellers Tales. Note: 6 Cassettes.

DEAD ON ARRIVAL (Terrence Hardiman).
MCSET. Cat no: **1176T.** Released on Travellers Tales, '91 by Travellers Tales. Note: 6 Cassettes.

HARBINGERS OF FEAR (Eve Karpf).
MCSET. Cat no: **1177T.** Released on Travellers Tales, '91 by Travellers Tales. Note: 6 Cassettes.

MCSET. Cat no: **CAT 4022.** Released on Chivers Audio Books, '91 by Chivers Audio Books, Green Dragon Audio Visual. Note: 6 cassettes.

LAST SEEN ALIVE (Terrence Hardiman).
MCSET. Cat no: **CAB 515.** Released on Chivers Audio Books, '91 by Chivers Audio Books, Green Dragon Audio Visual. Note: 6 Cassettes.

MCSET. Cat no: **1639T.** Released on Travellers Tales, '91 by Travellers Tales. Note: 6 Cassettes.

NIGHT SHE DIED, THE (Bruce Montague).
MCSET. Cat no: **IAB 91115.** Released on Isis Audio Books, Nov '91. Note: 8 Cassettes. Playing time 7 hours 30 minutes.

SUSPICIOUS DEATH (Terrence Hardiman).
MCSET. Cat no: **1388T.** Released on Travellers Tales, '91 by Travellers Tales. Note: 8 Cassettes.

MCSET. Cat no: **CAB 356.** Released on Chivers Audio Books, '91 by Chivers Audio Books, Green Dragon Audio Visual. Note: 8 Cassettes.

Sinclair, Clover

LALLIE (Unknown narrator(s)).
MCSET. Cat no: **185496531X.** Released on Bramhope, '91 by Ulverscroft Soundings. Note: 4 Cassettes.

VENETIAN ROMANCE (Hazel Temperley).
MCSET. Cat no: **1854964658.** Released on Trio, Jun '91 by EMI Records. Note: 3 Cassettes.

Sinclair, Olga

BITTER SWEET SUMMER (Unknown narrator(s)).
MCSET. Cat no: **1854964437.** Released on Bramhope, '91 by Ulverscroft Soundings. Note: 4 Cassettes.

MASTER OF MELTHORPE (Unknown narrator(s)).
MCSET. Cat no: **1854965077.** Released on Bramhope, '91 by Ulverscroft Soundings. Note: 4 Cassettes.

MY DEAR FUGITIVE (Judith Porter).
MCSET. Cat no: **185496464X.** Released on Bramhope, Jun '91 by Ulverscroft Soundings. Note: 4 Cassettes.

NEVER FALL IN LOVE (Unknown narrator(s)).
MCSET. Cat no: **1854965190.** Released on Soundings, '91 by Soundings Records, Bond Street Music. Note: 4 Cassettes.

ORCHIDS FROM THE ORIENT (Elizabeth Henry).
MCSET. Cat no: **1854964860.** Released on Soundings, Aug '91 by Soundings Records, Bond Street Music. Note: 3 Cassettes.

Sitwell, Dame Edith

DYLAN THOMAS AND EDITH SITWELL READ HER POEMS (Edith Sitwell & Dylan Thomas).
MC. Cat no: **1343.** Released on Caedmon (USA), '89 by Caedmon Records (USA), Bond Street Music.

EDITH SITWELL READING HER POEMS (Dame Edith Sitwell).
MC. Cat no: **1016.** Released on Caedmon (USA), '89 by Caedmon Records (USA), Bond Street Music.

Slataper, Scipio

IL MIO CARSO (Adriano Giraldi). Note: Written by Scipio Slataper. In Italian.
MCSET. Cat no: **1021L.** Released on Travellers Tales, '91 by Travellers Tales. Note: 4 cassettes.

Slater, Elizabeth

LOVES LAST CHANCE (Rowena Cooper).
MCSET. Cat no: **MRC 1015.** Released on Chivers Audio Books, '91 by Chivers Audio Books, Green Dragon Audio Visual. Note: 2 cassettes

MAGIC OF INNOCENCE (Delia Lindsay).
MCSET. Cat no: **MRC 1012.** Released on Chivers Audio Books, '91 by Chivers Audio Books, Green Dragon Audio Visual. Note: 2 cassettes

MAN OF HONOUR, A (Emma Sutton).
MCSET. Cat no: **MRC 1056.** Released on Chivers Audio Books, '91 by Chivers Audio Books, Green Dragon Audio Visual. Note: 2 cassettes.

TENDER LOVING, A (Francis Jeater).
MCSET. Cat no: **MRC 1020.** Released on Chivers Audio Books, '91 by Chivers Audio Books, Green Dragon Audio Visual. Note: 2 cassettes.

Smith, Dodie

GIRL FROM THE CANDLE-LIT BATH (Prunella Scales).
MCSET. Cat no: **CAB 016.** Released on Chivers Audio Books, '81 by Chivers Audio Books, Green Dragon Audio Visual.

MCSET. Cat no: **1133T.** Released on Travellers Tales, '91 by Travellers Tales. Note: 4 Cassettes.

I CAPTURE THE CASTLE.
MCSET. Cat no: **CTC 049.** Released on Cover to Cover, '90 by Cover to Cover Cassettes. Note: 9 cassettes.

Playing time: 13 hrs 55 mins.

ONE HUNDRED AND ONE DALMATIANS (Joanna Lumley).
MCSET. Cat no: **LFP 7132**. Released on Listen For Pleasure, '83 by EMI Records **Deleted** '89.

ONE HUNDRED AND ONE DALMATIANS (Anton Rodgers).
MC. Cat no: **Unknown**. Released on Whinfrey Strachan, Jan '85 **Deleted** '86.

STARLIGHT BARKING, THE (Delia Corrie).
MCSET. Cat no: **3CCA 3006**. Released on Chivers Audio Books, '91 by Chivers Audio Books, Green Dragon Audio Visual. Note: 3 Cassettes.

MCSET. Cat no: **9075F**. Released on Travellers Tales, '91 by Travellers Tales. Note: 3 Cassettes.

Smith, Frederick E.

633 SQUADRON (Simon Ward).
MCSET. Cat no: **LFP 41 7144 5**. Released on Listen For Pleasure, May '84 by EMI Records.

Smith & Jones
(Mel Smith & Griff Rhys Jones)

ALAS SMITH AND JONES (From the TV series).
LP. Cat no: **REB 527**. Released on BBC, Nov '85 by BBC Records, Taylors **Deleted** May '91.

MC. Cat no: **ZCF 527**. Released on BBC, Nov '85 by BBC Records, Taylors.

BITTER AND TWISTED.
LP. Cat no: **DIX 79**. Released on Ten, Nov '88 by 10 Records.

MC. Cat no: **CDIX 79**. Released on Ten, Nov '88 by 10 Records.

CD. Cat no: **DIXCD 79**. Released on Ten, Nov '88 by 10 Records **Deleted** Mar '91.

SCRATCH 'N' SNIFF.
Tracks / I spy / Antiques roadshow / Hooligans / Drugs / Video nasties / Meryl Streep / Autumn / Richard Branson / Christmas / Bob Geldof / V.D. / Mia Farrow / Aids / Taboos / Perverts / Animals / Senior citizens / Rigor mortis / Marvellous marvellous / Sex.
LP. Cat no: **DIX 51**. Released on Ten, Nov '86 by 10 Records **Deleted** Mar '91.

MC. Cat no: **CDIX 51**. Released on Ten, '87 by 10 Records.

Smith, Sydney Goodsir

DEVIL'S WALTZ, THE (Unknown narrator(s)).
LP. Cat no: **CCA 8**. Released on Claddagh (Ireland), Aug '88 by Claddagh Records (Ireland), Projection, Impetus Records, Jazz Music, Roots Records, C.M. Distribution, Outlet Records, Taylors.

Smith, Wilbur

BURNING SHORE, THE (Gabrielle Drake).
MCSET. Cat no: **LFP 7310**. Released on Listen For Pleasure, Oct '87 by EMI Records.

CRY WOLF (Nigel Davenport).
MCSET. Cat no: **CAB 560**. Released on Chivers Audio Books, '91 by Chivers Audio Books, Green Dragon Audio Visual. Note: 12 Cassettes.

MCSET. Cat no: **1696/1697T**. Released on Travellers Tales, '91 by Travellers Tales. Note: 12 Cassettes.

DARK OF THE SUN, THE (Nigel Davenport).
MCSET. Cat no: **CAB 301**. Released on Chivers Audio Books, Apr '88 by Chivers Audio Books, Green Dragon Audio Visual. Note: 8 cassettes

MCSET. Cat no: **1267T**. Released on Travellers Tales, '91 by Travellers Tales. Note: 8 Cassettes.

DIAMOND HUNTERS, THE (Roy Marsden).
MCSET. Cat no: **CAB 053**. Released on Chivers Audio Books, '91 by Chivers Audio Books, Green Dragon Audio Visual. Note: 6 Cassettes

MCSET. Cat no: **1134T**. Released on Travellers Tales, '91 by Travellers Tales. Note: 8 Cassettes.

MCSET. Cat no: **0745128084**. Released on Word For Word, May '92 by Chivers Audio Books.

EAGLE IN THE SKY (Nigel Davenport).
MCSET. Cat no: **CAB 209**. Released on Chivers Audio Books, '91 by Chivers Audio Books, Green Dragon Audio Visual. Note: 8 Cassettes

MCSET. Cat no: **1152T**. Released on Travellers Tales, '91 by Travellers Tales. Note: 8 Cassettes.

ELEPHANT SONG (Unknown narrator(s)).
MCSET. Cat no: **1856861031**. Released on Random Century, '91 by Random Century Audiobooks, Conifer Records.

EYE OF THE TIGER, THE (Nigel Davenport).
MCSET. Cat no: **CAB 157**. Released on Chivers Audio Books, '91 by Chivers Audio Books, Green Dragon Audio Visual. Note: 8 Cassettes

MCSET. Cat no: **1135T**. Released on Travellers Tales, '91 by Travellers Tales. Note: 8 Cassettes.

GOLD MINE (Roy Marsden).
MCSET. Cat no: **CAB 084**. Released on Chivers Audio Books, '91 by Chivers Audio Books, Green Dragon Audio Visual. Note: 6 Cassettes

MCSET. Cat no: **1136T**. Released on Travellers Tales, '91 by Travellers Tales. Note: 6 Cassettes

HUNGRY AS THE SEA (Nigel Davenport).
MCSET. Cat no: **CAB 480**. Released on Chivers Audio Books, '91 by Chivers Audio Books, Green Dragon Audio Visual. Note: 12 Cassettes.

MCSET. Cat no: **1553/1554T**. Released on Travellers Tales, '91 by Travellers Tales. Note: 12 Cassettes.

LEOPARD HUNTS IN DARKNESS, THE (Edward Woodward).
MCSET. Cat no: **LFP 7194**. Released on Listen For Pleasure, May '85 by EMI Records.

MCSET. Cat no: **1137T**. Released on Travellers Tales, '91 by Travellers Tales. Note: 2 Cassettes.

POWER OF THE SWORD (Gabrielle Drake).
MCSET. Cat no: **LFP 7316**. Released on Listen For Pleasure, Oct '87 by EMI Records.

RAGE (Gabrielle Drake).
MCSET. Cat no: **LFP 7332**. Released on Listen For Pleasure, Apr '88 by EMI Records.

SHOUT AT THE DEVIL (Nigel Davenport).
MCSET. Cat no: **CAB 386**. Released on Chivers Audio Books, '91 by Chivers Audio Books, Green Dragon Audio Visual. Note: 10 Cassettes.

MCSET. Cat no: **1421/1422T**. Released on Travellers Tales, '91 by Travellers Tales. Note: 10 Cassettes.

TIME TO DIE, A (Anthony Valentine).
MCSET. Cat no: **LFP 7496**. Released on Listen For Pleasure, Oct '90 by EMI Records.

WILD JUSTICE (Nigel Davenport).
MCSET. Cat no: **CAB 447**. Released on Chivers Audio Books, '91 by Chivers Audio Books, Green Dragon Audio Visual. Note: 12 Cassettes.

MCSET. Cat no: **1660/1661T**. Released on Travellers Tales, '91 by Travellers Tales. Note: 12 Cassettes.

WILD JUSTICE (The Power of the Sword, The Burning Shore and The Rage) (Various artists).
MCSET. Cat no: **1232T**. Released on Travellers Tales, '91 by Travellers Tales. Note: 8 Cassettes.

Somerset Maugham, W

(See under Maugham, W. Somerset).

Sophocles

ANTIGONE (Various artists).
MCSET. Cat no: **0320**. Released on Caedmon (USA), by Caedmon Records (USA), Bond Street Music. Note: 2 cassettes

OEDIPUS REX (Various artists).
MCSET. Cat no: **2012**. Released on Caedmon (USA), by Caedmon Records (USA), Bond Street Music. Note: 2 cassettes

Soutar, William

MERRY MATANZIE (Alex McCrindle).
MC. Cat no: **SSC 083**. Released on Scotsoun, '91 by Scotsoun Recordings, Morley Audio Services.

POEMS, RIDDLES AND SONGS

(Various artists).
MC. Cat no: **SSC 033**. Released on Scotsoun, '91 by Scotsoun Recordings, Morley Audio Services.

SCOTS POEMS (Alexander Scott).
MC. Cat no: **SSC 026**. Released on Scotsoun, '91 by Scotsoun Recordings, Morley Audio Services.

Southgate, Vera

LITTLE RED HEN, THE (Well Loved Tales Up To Age 9) (Unknown narrator(s)).
Note: Book and cassette.
MC. Cat no: **PLB 91**. Released on Tell-A-Tale, '88 by Pickwick Records, Taylors, Clyde Factors.

SLY FOX AND THE LITTLE RED HEN (Well Loved Tales Up To Age 9) (Unknown narrator(s)).
Note: Book and cassette.
MC. Cat no: **PLB 92**. Released on Tell-A-Tale, '88 by Pickwick Records, Taylors, Clyde Factors

Spark, Muriel

FAR CRY FROM KENSINGTON, A (Eleanor Bron).
MCSET. Cat no: **IAB 90022**. Released on Isis Audio Books, '91. Note: 5 cassette set. Playing time 5hrs 50mins.
MCSET. Cat no: **1422F**. Released on Travellers Tales, '91 by Travellers Tales. Note: 5 cassettes.

PRIME OF MISS JEAN BRODIE (And the Girls of Slender Means) (Geraldine McEwan).
MCSET. Cat no: **IAB 88062**. Released on Isis Audio Books, '91. Note: 6 cassette set. Playing time 7hrs 40mins.
MCSET. Cat no: **1306F**. Released on Travellers Tales, '91 by Travellers Tales. Note: 6 cassettes.
MCSET. Cat no: **TE 861**. Released on Isis Audio Books, '91. Note: 6 cassettes.

STORIES OF MURIEL SPARK, THE (Part 1) (Eleanor Bron).
MCSET. Cat no: **1637F**. Released on Travellers Tales, '91 by Travellers Tales. Note: 6 cassettes.
MCSET. Cat no: **IAB 91054**. Released on Isis Audio Books, '91. Note: 6 Cassettes.

STORIES OF MURIEL SPARK, THE (Volume 2) (Derek Jacobi).
Note: Short stories include The Ormolu Clock, The Dark Glasses, A Member of the Family, The House of the Famous Poet, The Father's Daughter, Alice Long's Dachshunds, The First Year of my Life, The Gentile Jewesses, The Executor, The Fortune-Teller, Another Pair of Hands, and The Dragon.
MCSET. Cat no: **IAB 91073**. Released on Isis Audio Books, '91. Note: 6 cassettes.

TERRITORIAL RIGHTS (Nigel Hawthorne).
MCSET. Cat no: **1150F**. Released on Travellers Tales, '91 by Travellers Tales. Note: 6 cassettes.

Spender, Stephen

READING HIS POETRY (Stephen Spender).
MC. Cat no: **1084**. Released on Caedmon (USA), '89 by Caedmon Records (USA), Bond Street Music.

Spenser, Edmund

FAERIE QUEEN (And Ephithalamion) (Micheal MacLiammoir).
MC. Cat no: **1126**. Released on Caedmon (USA), '89 by Caedmon Records (USA), Bond Street Music.

Spillane, Mickey

BIG KILL (Unknown narrator(s)).
MCSET. Cat no: **0671704230**. Released on Simon & Schuster, '91 by Simon & Schuster Ltd.

KILLING MAN, THE (Stacy Keach).
MC. Cat no: **0671691937**. Released on Simon & Schuster, '91 by Simon & Schuster Ltd.

KISS ME DEADLY (Unknown narrator(s)).
MCSET. Cat no: **0671725718**. Released on Simon & Schuster, '91 by Simon & Schuster Ltd.

MY GUN IS QUICK (Unknown narrator(s)).
MCSET. Cat no: **0671704249**. Released on Simon & Schuster, '91 by Simon & Schuster Ltd.

ONE LONELY NIGHT (Unknown narrator(s)).
MCSET. Cat no: **0671726086**. Released on Simon & Schuster, '91 by Simon & Schuster Ltd.

VENGEANCE IS MINE (Unknown narrator(s)).
MCSET. Cat no: **0671704222**. Released on Simon & Schuster, '91 by Simon & Schuster Ltd.

Spitting Image

SPIT IN YOUR EAR (TV Soundtrack)(Spitting Image Caste) (Various artists).
Tracks / Spitting Image sig tune: Various artists / Ronnie and Maggie goodbye: Various artists / Royal singalong: Various artists / Weather forecast: Various artists / Coleman peaks: Various artists / We've got beards: Various artists (ZZ Top) / Second coming: Various artists / Someone famous has died: Various artists / Tea at Johnnies: Various artists / Trendy Kinnock: Various artists / Do do run Ron: Various artists / Ronnie's birthday: Various artists / One man and his bitch: Various artists / Special relationship: Various artists / Clean rugby songs: Various artists / O'Toole's night out: Various artists / Spock the actor: Various artists / Line of celebrities: Various artists / Price is right, The: Various artists / Botha tells the truth: Various artists / I've never met a nice South African: Various artists / End announcement: Various artists / Andy and Fergie: Various artists / Pete Townsend appeals: Various artists / Our generation (The Who): Various artists / Three Davids, The: Various artists / Party system, The: Various artists / Hello you must be going: Various artists / Naming the Royal baby: Various artists / Bruno and Ruthless: Various artists / South Bank show on Ronnie Hazelhurst: Various artists / Bernard Manning newsflash: Various artists / Juan Carlos meets the Queen: Various artists / Chicken song, The (celebrity megamix): Various artists / Lawson goes bonkers: Various artists / Talk bollocks: Various artists / Snooker games: Various artists / Good old British bloke: Various artists / Black moustache: Various artists (Prince.) / Uranus: Various artists / Dennis Thatcher's pacemaker: Various artists / John And Tatum - the young marrieds: Various artists / We're scared of Bob: Various artists / Trooping the colour: Various artists / Night thoughts: Various artists.
LP. Cat no: **OVED 227**. Released on Virgin, Oct '86 by Virgin Records, Music Sales Records **Deleted** May '90. Note: Track details not advised
MC. Cat no: **OVEDC 227**. Released on Virgin, Oct '86 by Virgin Records, Music Sales Records.
LP. Cat no: **V 2403**. Released on Virgin, Oct '86 by Virgin Records, Music Sales Records.
MC. Cat no: **TCV 2403**. Released on Virgin, Oct '86 by Virgin Records, Music Sales Records.
MC. Cat no: **VVIPC 110**. Released on Virgin V.I.P., Nov '90.
CD. Cat no: **VVIPD 110**. Released on Virgin V.I.P., Nov '90.

Spurgeon, Maureen

GHOSTBUSTER OF THE YEAR (Unknown narrator(s)).
MC. Cat no: **39579**. Released on Tempo, Sep '89 by Warwick Records, Celtic Music, Henry Hadaway Organisation.

Spyri, Johanna

HEIDI (Susan Sheridan).
MC. Cat no: **TS 325**. Released on Tellastory, '91 by Random Century Audiobooks. Note: ISBN no. 1856561143

HEIDI (Claire Bloom).
MC. Cat no: **1292**. Released on Caedmon (USA), '89 by Caedmon Records (USA), Bond Street Music.

HEIDI (Judi Dench).
MCSET. Cat no: **SAY 11**. Released on Argo (Polygram), Jul '82 by PolyGram Classics **Deleted** Jan '89.

HEIDI (Petula Clark).
MCSET. Cat no: **LFP 7109**. Released on Listen For Pleasure, Oct '82 by EMI Records.

HEIDI (Unknown narrator(s)).
MC. Cat no: **1856561143**. Released on Random Century, '91 by Random Century Audiobooks, Conifer Records.
MCSET. Cat no: **DTO 10577**. Released on Ditto, '91 by Pickwick Re-

cords, Midland Records.

St. Clair, Joy
LOVE'S TANGLED WEB (Angela Down).
MCSET. Cat no: **1854965611.** Released on Bramhope, Feb '92 by Ulverscroft Soundings. Note: Playing time: 60 minutes.

Stacey, Kathryn
GOVERNESS, THE (Unknown narrator(s)).
MCSET. Cat no: **1854963740.** Released on Soundings, '91 by Soundings Records, Bond Street Music. Note: 4 Cassettes.

Standiford, Natalie
ADVENTURES OF THE SPACE DOG, THE (Griff Rhys Jones).
MCSET. Cat no: **TS 406.** Released on Tellastory, Apr '92 by Random Century Audiobooks. Note: 2 cassettes. ISBN no. 1856561879

Standish, Buck
HARDIN COUNTY (Unknown narrator(s)).
MCSET. Cat no: **1854965344.** Released on Trio, '91 by EMI Records. Note: 3 Cassettes.

Stanshall, Vivian
SIR HENRY AT RAWLINSON END (Unknown narrator(s)).
Tracks / Aunt Florrie's walk / Interlewd / Wheelbarrow / Socks / Rub, The / Nice'n'tidy / Pigs 'ere purse / 6/8 hoodoo / Smeeton / Fool and bladder endroar / Jungle bunny / Beasht inshide, The / Rawlinsons and Maynards / Papadumb.
LP. Cat no: **CAS 1139.** Released on Charisma, '78 by Virgin Records **Deleted** '88.
CD. Cat no: **CASCD 1139.** Released on Charisma, 17 Apr '89 by Virgin Records. Note: (MM)
LP. Cat no: **CHC 83.** Released on Charisma, '89 by Virgin Records **Deleted** Jun '91.
MC. Cat no: **CHCMC 83.** Released on Charisma, '89 by Virgin Records **Deleted** Jun '91. Note: (MM)

Stapleton, Maureen
SUMMER PEOPLE, THE (Unknown narrator(s)).
LP. Cat no: **TC 1498.** Released on Caedmon (USA), Sep '77 by Caedmon Records (USA), Bond Street Music.
MC. Cat no: **CDL 51498.** Released on Caedmon (USA), Sep '77 by Caedmon Records (USA), Bond Street Music.

Steig, William
DOCTOR DE SOTO (And Other Stories) (Unknown narrator(s)).
MC. Cat no: **1751.** Released on Caedmon (USA), Apr '85 by Caedmon Records (USA), Bond Street Music.
ROLAND, THE MINSTREL PIG (And Other Stories) (Carol Channing).
MC. Cat no: **1305.** Released on Caedmon (USA), '89 by Caedmon Records (USA), Bond Street Music.

Steinbeck, John
CANNERY ROW (Jerry Farden).
MCSET. Cat no: **1570F.** Released on Travellers Tales, '91 by Travellers Tales. Note: 4 cassettes.
MCSET. Cat no: **RB 89390.** Released on Recorded Books, '91 by Isis Audio Books. Note: 4 cassettes.
GRAPES OF WRATH (Unknown narrator(s)).
LP. Cat no: **TC 1570.** Released on Caedmon (USA), '79 by Caedmon Records (USA), Bond Street Music.
MC. Cat no: **CDL 51570.** Released on Caedmon (USA), '78 by Caedmon Records (USA), Bond Street Music.
GRAPES OF WRATH, THE (Henry Fonda).
MCSET. Cat no: **0001071467.** Released on Collins-Caedmon, '91 by Collins Audio, Taylors, Bond Street Music. Note: 2 Cassettes.
SWEET THURSDAY (Jerry Farden).
MCSET. Cat no: **IAB 91093.** Released on Isis Audio Books, Sep '91. Note: 7 cassette set. Playing time 9hrs

Steptoe & Son
MORE JUNK (Harry H. Corbett & Wilfred Brambell).
LP. Cat no: **NPL 18090.** Released on Pye, Mar '64 **Deleted** '69.
STEPTOE & SON (Harry H Corbett & Wilfred Brambell).
LP. Cat no: **HMA 238.** Released on Hallmark, '72 by Pickwick Records, Outlet Records **Deleted** '88.
LP. Cat no: **NPL 18081.** Released on Pye, Mar '63 **Deleted** '68.
LP. Cat no: **MAL 1160.** Released on Marble Arch, '69.
STEPTOE & SON (Volume 2) (Harry H. Corbett & Wilfred Brambell).
LP. Cat no: **GGL 0217.** Released on Golden Guinea, Mar '64 **Deleted** '69
STEPTOE & SON (See under Radio)

Sterne, Laurence
SENTIMENTAL JOURNEY, A (Donald Sinden).
MCSET. Cat no: **SAY 14.** Released on Argo (Polygram), Jul '82 by PolyGram Classics **Deleted** Jan '89.
MCSET. Cat no: **ARGO 1019.** Released on Argo (EMI), May '89 by EMI Records. Note: 2 Cassettes.
SENTIMENTAL JOURNEY, A (Donald Sinden).
Note: Abridged version.
MCSET. Cat no: **1152F.** Released on Travellers Tales, '91 by Travellers Tales. Note: 2 cassettes.

Stevens, Wallace
WALLACE STEVENS READING (Wallace Stevens).
MC. Cat no: **1068.** Released on Caedmon (USA), '89 by Caedmon Records (USA), Bond Street Music.

Stevenson, Robert L.
BODY SNATCHERS, THE (John Sheddon).
MCSET. Cat no: **COL 2009.** Released on Colophone, Feb '81 by AVLS (Audio-Visual Library Services).
MCSET. Cat no: **RB 81280.** Released on Recorded Books, '91 by Isis Audio Books. Note: 2 cassettes.
BOTTLE IMP, THE (And Other Stories) (Alexander Spencer).
MCSET. Cat no: **RB 81281.** Released on Recorded Books, '91 by Isis Audio Books. Note: 3 cassettes.
CHILD'S GARDEN OF VERSES, A (Dame Judith Anderson).
MC. Cat no: **1077.** Released on Caedmon (USA), '89 by Caedmon Records (USA), Bond Street Music.
CHILD'S GARDEN OF VERSES, A (Harriet Buchan & John Sheddon).
MC. Cat no: **0001010417.** Released on Harper Collins, '91 by Harper Collins.
DR. JEKYLL AND MR. HYDE (Alex Spencer).
MCSET. Cat no: **RB 80050.** Released on Recorded Books, '91 by Isis Audio Books. Note: 2 cassettes.
KIDNAPPED (Douglas Fairbanks Jnr).
LP. Cat no: **TC 1636.** Released on Caedmon (USA), Sep '80 by Caedmon Records (USA), Bond Street Music.
MC. Cat no: **CDL 51636.** Released on Caedmon (USA), Sep '80 by Caedmon Records (USA), Bond Street Music.
KIDNAPPED (Jon Pertwee).
MC. Cat no: **P 90014.** Released on Pinnacle, Jan '79 by Pinnacle Records, Outlet Records, Music Sales Records.
KIDNAPPED (Various artists).
MCSET. Cat no: **ZBBC 1060.** Released on BBC Radio Collection, Mar '89 by BBC Records. Note: ISBN No: 0563 209844.
KIDNAPPED (Unknown narrator(s)).
MC. Cat no: **PLBC 176.** Released on Tell-A-Tale, '88 by Pickwick Records, Taylors, Clyde Factors.
LOVE AND THE LONELY DIE (And the Body Snatchers) (John Graham).
MC. Cat no: **NF 3.** Released on Nightfall Tapes, '89 by BMG Records (UK) Ltd..
MASTER OF BALLANTRAE (Tom Watson).
MCSET. Cat no: **COL 4005.** Released on Colophone, '88 by AVLS (Audio-Visual Library Services).
MCSET. Cat no: **1048C.** Released on Travellers Tales, '91 by Travellers

Tales. Note: 4 cassettes.

SHORT STORIES (Volume One) (Robert Trotter).
MCSET. Cat no: **SPF 780-1**. Released on Schiltron Audio Books, '91 by Schiltron Publishing. Note: 4 Cassettes. Playing time 3 hours 40 minutes.

MCSET. Cat no: **1030S**. Released on Travellers Tales, '91 by Travellers Tales. Note: 4 Cassetess

SHORT STORIES (Volume 2) (Robert Trotter).
MCSET. Cat no: **SPF 780-2**. Released on Schiltron Audio Books, Feb '92 by Schiltron Publishing. Note: 4 cassettes. Playing time 4hrs 28mins

STRANGE CASE OF DR. JEKYLL AND MR. HYDE (Tom Baker).
MCSET. Cat no: **SAY 12**. Released on Argo (Polygram), Jul '82 by PolyGram Classics **Deleted** Jan '89.

MCSET. Cat no: **ARGO 1013**. Released on Argo (EMI), May '89 by EMI Records **Deleted** '91. Note: 2 Cassettes.

2LP. Cat no: **ZDSW 722/3**. Released on Argo, '79 by Decca International.

STRANGE CASE OF DR. JEKYLL AND MR. HYDE (John Hurt).
MC. Cat no: **PTB 619**. Released on Pickwick Talking Books, '83 by Pickwick Records, Clyde Factors.

STRANGE CASE OF DR. JEKYLL AND MR. HYDE (Horror Classics for Ages 7-12) (Unknown narrator(s)).
Note: Book and cassette.

MC. Cat no: **PLBC 196**. Released on Tell-A-Tale, '88 by Pickwick Records, Taylors, Clyde Factors.

STRANGE CASE OF DR. JEKYLL AND MR. HYDE (Anthony Quayle).
MC. Cat no: **1283**. Released on Caedmon (USA), '89 by Caedmon Records (USA), Bond Street Music.

STRANGE CASE OF DR. JEKYLL AND MR. HYDE, THE (Tom Baker).
Note: Abridged version.

MCSET. Cat no: **1154F**. Released on Travellers Tales, '91 by Travellers Tales. Note: 2 cassettes.

TREASURE ISLAND (Anthony Bate).
MCSET. Cat no: **TC LFP 7018**. Released on Listen For Pleasure, '77 by EMI Records **Deleted** '85.

MCSET. Cat no: **LFP 7170**. Released on Listen For Pleasure, Sep '84 by EMI Records.

TREASURE ISLAND (Ian Richardson).
MCSET. Cat no: **2075**. Released on Caedmon (USA), Sep '88 by Caedmon Records (USA), Bond Street Music.

TREASURE ISLAND (Anthony Bate).
Note: Abridged.

MCSET. Cat no: **9079F**. Released on Travellers Tales, '91 by Travellers Tales. Note: 2 Cassettes.

TREASURE ISLAND (Paul Daneman).

MC. Cat no: **BKK 414**. Released on Kiddy Kassettes, Feb '81.

TREASURE ISLAND (Children's Classics) (Unknown narrator(s)).
Note: Book and cassette.

MC. Cat no: **PLBC 74**. Released on Tell-A-Tale, '88 by Pickwick Records, Taylors, Clyde Factors.

TREASURE ISLAND (Jon Pertwee).
MC. Cat no: **P 90008**. Released on Storyteller Cassettes, '79.

TREASURE ISLAND (Unknown narrator(s)).
MCSET. Cat no: **DTO 10576**. Released on Ditto, '88 by Pickwick Records, Midland Records.

TREASURE ISLAND (David Buck).
MCSET. Cat no: **CTC 013**. Released on Cover to Cover, Jun '85 by Cover to Cover Cassettes. Note: 6 cassettes. Playing time: 7 hrs 30 mins.

Stewart, J.I.M.

VILLA IN FRANCE, A (Maria Aitken).
MCSET. Cat no: **1155F**. Released on Travellers Tales, '91 by Travellers Tales. Note: 6 cassettes.

Stewart, Mary

AIRS ABOVE THE GROUND (Jane Asher).
MCSET. Cat no: **CAB 608**. Released on Chivers Audio Books, '91 by Chivers Audio Books, Green Dragon Audio Visual. Note: 8 Cassettes.

CRYSTAL CAVE, THE (Stephen Thorne).
MCSET. Cat no: **CAB 676**. Released on Chivers Audio Books, Feb '92 by Chivers Audio Books, Green Dragon Audio Visual. Note: 12 cassettes.

GABRIEL HOUNDS, THE (Davina Porter).
MCSET. Cat no: **1751T**. Released on Travellers Tales, '91 by Travellers Tales. Note: 8 Cassettes.

MCSET. Cat no: **IAB 91042**. Released on Isis Audio Books, '91. Note: 8 Cassettes.

IVY TREE, THE (Jane Asher).
MCSET. Cat no: **CAB 533**. Released on Chivers Audio Books, '91 by Chivers Audio Books, Green Dragon Audio Visual. Note: 10 Cassettes.

MCSET. Cat no: **1542/3F**. Released on Travellers Tales, '91 by Travellers Tales. Note: 10 cassettes.

LITTLE BROOMSTICK, THE (Valerie Singleton).
Note: For 6 to 8 years olds.

MCSET. Cat no: **A 002A/B**. Released on Green Dragon, '91 by Green Dragon Audio Visual. Note: 2 Cassettes.

LUDO AND THE STAR HORSE.
Note: For 8 to 16 year olds.

MCSET. Cat no: **C 001A/B**. Released on Green Dragon, '91 by Green Dragon Audio Visual.

MADAM, WILL YOU TALK (Nyree Dawn Porter).
MCSET. Cat no: **CAB 103**. Released on Chivers Audio Books, '91 by Chivers Audio Books, Green Dragon Audio Visual. Note: 6 Cassettes.

MCSET. Cat no: **1156F**. Released on Travellers Tales, '91 by Travellers Tales. Note: 6 cassettes.

MOON-SPINNERS, THE (Nyree Dawn Porter).
MCSET. Cat no: **CAB 197**. Released on Chivers Audio Books, '91 by Chivers Audio Books, Green Dragon Audio Visual. Note: 8 Cassettes.

MCSET. Cat no: **1191F**. Released on Travellers Tales, '91 by Travellers Tales. Note: 8 Cassettes.

MY BROTHER MICHAEL (Jane Asher).
MCSET. Cat no: **CAB 432**. Released on Chivers Audio Books, '91 by Chivers Audio Books, Green Dragon Audio Visual. Note: 8 Cassettes.

MCSET. Cat no: **1490T**. Released on Travellers Tales, '91 by Travellers Tales. Note: 8 Cassettes.

NINE COACHES WAITING (Davina Porter).
MCSET. Cat no: **IAB 91101**. Released on Isis Audio Books, Oct '91. Note: 8 Cassettes. Playing time approximately 11 hrs

THIS ROUGH MAGIC (Jane Asher).
MCSET. Cat no: **CAB 276**. Released on Chivers Audio Books, '91 by Chivers Audio Books, Green Dragon Audio Visual. Note: 8 Cassettes

MCSET. Cat no: **1285F**. Released on Travellers Tales, '91 by Travellers Tales. Note: 8 cassettes.

THORNYHOLD (Jane Asher).
MCSET. Cat no: **CAB 392**. Released on Chivers Audio Books, '91 by Chivers Audio Books, Green Dragon Audio Visual. Note: 6 Cassettes.

MCSET. Cat no: **1409F**. Released on Travellers Tales, '91 by Travellers Tales. Note: 6 Cassettes.

THUNDER ON THE RIGHT (Harriet Walter).
MCSET. Cat no: **CAB 318**. Released on Chivers Audio Thrillers, '88 by Chivers Audio Books, Green Dragon Audio Visual. Note: 8 Cassettes.

MCSET. Cat no: **1359T**. Released on Travellers Tales, '91 by Travellers Tales. Note: 8 Cassettes.

TOUCH NOT THE CAT (Davina Porter).
MCSET. Cat no: **IAB 91074**. Released on Isis Audio Books, '91. Note: 8 cassette set.

WILDFIRE AT MIDNIGHT (Jane Asher).
MCSET. Cat no: **CAB 470**. Released on Chivers Audio Books, '91 by Chivers Audio Books, Green Dragon Audio Visual. Note: 6 Cassettes.

MCSET. Cat no: **1555T**. Released on Travellers Tales, '91 by Travellers Tales. Note: 6 Cassettes.

Stimson, Joan
STORYTIME FOR 2 YEAR OLDS (Unknown narrator(s)).
MC. Cat no: **PLB 284**. Released on Tell-A-Tale, '89 by Pickwick Records, Taylors, Clyde Factors.

STORYTIME FOR 3 YEAR OLDS (Unknown narrator(s)).
MC. Cat no: **PLB 253**. Released on Tell-A-Tale, Jan '89 by Pickwick Records, Taylors, Clyde Factors.

STORYTIME FOR 4 YEAR OLDS (Unknown narrator(s)).
MC. Cat no: **PLB 267**. Released on Tell-A-Tale, '89 by Pickwick Records, Taylors, Clyde Factors.

STORYTIME FOR 5 YEAR OLDS (Unknown narrator(s)).
MC. Cat no: **PLB 254**. Released on Tell-A-Tale, Jan '89 by Pickwick Records, Taylors, Clyde Factors.

STORYTIME FOR 6 YEAR OLDS (Unknown narrator(s)).
MC. Cat no: **PLB 268**. Released on Tell-A-Tale, '89 by Pickwick Records, Taylors, Clyde Factors.

Stirling, Jessica
ASKING PRICE, THE (Kara Wilson).
MCSET. Cat no: **1621F**. Released on Travellers Tales, '91 by Travellers Tales. Note: 8 cassettes.

BELOVED SINNER (Delia Corrie).
MCSET. Cat no: **1140R**. Released on Travellers Tales, '91 by Travellers Tales. Note: 8 Cassettes.

MCSET. Cat no: **CAB 349**. Released on Chivers Audio Books, '91 by Chivers Audio Books, Green Dragon Audio Visual. Note: 8 cassettes.

GOOD PROVIDER, THE (Kara Wilson).
MCSET. Cat no: **1531/2F**. Released on Travellers Tales, '91 by Travellers Tales. Note: 10 cassettes.

MCSET. Cat no: **CAB 483**. Released on Chivers Audio Books, '91 by Chivers Audio Books, Green Dragon Audio Visual. Note: 10 cassettes.

Stoker, Bram
DRACULA (Various artists).
Note: Read by Robert Eddison, Angela Scaular and cast. Abridged.
MCSET. Cat no: **SAY 104**. Released on Argo (Polygram), Mar '84 by Poly-Gram Classics **Deleted** Jan '89.

MCSET. Cat no: **ARGO 1223**. Released on Argo (EMI), Oct '89 by EMI Records **Deleted** '91. Note: 2 Cassettes.

MCSET. Cat no: **1019S**. Released on Travellers Tales, '91 by Travellers Tales. Note: 2 Cassettes.

DRACULA (Anthony Valentine).
MCSET. Cat no: **PTB 631**. Released on Pickwick Talking Books, '83 by Pickwick Records, Clyde Factors.

MCSET. Cat no: **1033/1034S**. Released on Travellers Tales, '91 by Trav-ellers Tales. Note: 12 Cassettes.

DRACULA (David McCallum & Carole Shelley).
MC. Cat no: **1468**. Released on Caedmon (USA), '89 by Caedmon Records (USA), Bond Street Music.

DRACULA (Sir Michael Horden).
MC. Cat no: **0600560554**. Released on Hamlyn Books On Tape, '88, Bond Street Music.

DRACULA (Horror Classics For Ages 7-12) (Unknown narrator(s)).
Note: Book and cassette.
MC. Cat no: **PLB 120**. Released on Tell-A-Tale, '88 by Pickwick Records, Taylors, Clyde Factors.

DRACULA (Anthony Homyer).
Note: This recording includes an opening chapter left out on publication and issued later as a short story, 'Dracula's Guest'.
MCSET. Cat no: **TCL 19**. Released on Complete Listener, '91 by Complete Listener. Note: 12 Cassettes. (BB) Playing Time: 1080 Minutes.

DRACULA (Christopher Lee).
LP. Cat no: **NTS 186**. Released on Note, Nov '79 by EMI Records **Deleted** '84.

Stokoe, E.G.
ONCE A MARINE (Christopher Kay).
MCSET. Cat no: **1854964747**. Released on Soundings, Jul '91 by Soundings Records, Bond Street Music. Note: 4 Cassettes.

SHOWDOWN AT MESA (John Chancer).
MCSET. Cat no: **1854964666**. Released on Trio, Jun '91 by EMI Records. Note: 3 Cassettes.

Stoppard, Tom
ROSENCRANTZ AND GUILDENSTERN ARE DEAD (Various artists).
MCSET. Cat no: **ZBBC 1058**. Released on BBC Radio Collection, Mar '89 by BBC Records. Note: ISBN No: 0563 226102

Storr, Catherine
CLEVER POLLY AND THE STUPID WOLF (Derek Griffiths).
MCSET. Cat no: **CC 024**. Released on Cover to Cover, Sep '86 by Cover to Cover Cassettes.

Straub, Peter
GHOST STORY (Unknown narrator(s)).
MCSET. Cat no: **0671725882**. Released on Simon & Schuster, '91 by Simon & Schuster Ltd.

HOUSES WITHOUT DOORS (Unknown narrator(s)).
MCSET. Cat no: **0671725920**. Released on Simon & Schuster, '91 by Simon & Schuster Ltd.

KOKO (James Wood).
MCSET. Cat no: **0671652397**. Released on Simon & Schuster, '91 by Simon & Schuster Ltd. Note: 2 Cassettes

MRS. GOD (Unknown narrator(s)).
MCSET. Cat no: **0671748793**. Released on Simon & Schuster, '91 by Simon & Schuster Ltd.

MYSTERY (Unknown narrator(s)).
MCSET. Cat no: **0671692682**. Released on Simon & Schuster, '91 by Simon & Schuster Ltd.

Streatfield, Noel
BALLET SHOES (Jan Francis).
MCSET. Cat no: **LFP 7286**. Released on Listen For Pleasure, Apr '87 by EMI Records. Note: Playing time: 3 Hours

BALLET SHOES (Moira Shearer).
MCSET. Cat no: **SAY 110**. Released on Argo (Polygram), Apr '84 by Poly-Gram Classics **Deleted** Jan '89.

LPS. Cat no: **ZDSW 715/7**. Released on Argo, '79 by Decca International **Deleted** '84.

BALLET SHOES (Moira Shearer).
Note: Abridged.
MCSET. Cat no: **9081F**. Released on Travellers Tales, '91 by Travellers Tales. Note: 2 Cassettes.

Street, Pamela
BENEFICIARIES, THE (Anne Dover).
MCSET. Cat no: **1498F**. Released on Travellers Tales, '91 by Travellers Tales. Note: 5 Cassettes.

MCSET. Cat no: **1854963155**. Released on Bramhope, '91 by Ulverscroft Soundings. Note: 5 Cassettes.

DOUBTFUL COMPANY (Anne Dover).
MCSET. Cat no: **1505F**. Released on Travellers Tales, '91 by Travellers Tales. Note: 4 Cassettes.

MCSET. Cat no: **1854963473**. Released on Bramhope, '91 by Ulverscroft Soundings. Note: 4 Cassettes.

GUILTY PARTIES (Unknown narrator(s)).
MCSET. Cat no: **185496495X**. Released on Bramhope, '91 by Ulverscroft Soundings. Note: 4 Cassettes.

LIGHT OF EVENING (Unknown narrator(s)).
MCSET. Cat no: **1854962531**. Released on Bramhope, '91 by Ulverscroft Soundings. Note: 4 Cassettes.

MANY WATERS: PART 3 (Jane Jermyn).
MCSET. Cat no: **1160F**. Released on Travellers Tales, '91 by Travellers Tales. Note: 4 cassettes.

MCSET. Cat no: **185496187X**. Released on Bramhope, '91 by Ulverscroft Soundings. Note: 4 Cassettes.

MILL RACE, THE (Unknown narrator(s)).
MCSET. Cat no: **SOUND 36**. Released on Soundings, Feb '85 by Soundings Records, Bond Street Music.

MCSET. Cat no: **1158F**. Released on Travellers Tales, '91 by Travellers Tales. Note: 4 Cassettes.
MORNING GLORY (Unknown narrator(s)).
MCSET. Cat no: **1854962892**. Released on Bramhope, '91 by Ulverscroft Soundings. Note: 5 Cassettes.
PERSONAL RELATIONS (Unknown narrator(s)).
MCSET. Cat no: **185496271X**. Released on Bramhope, '91 by Ulverscroft Soundings. Note: 5 Cassettes.
PORTRAIT OF A ROSE (Jane Jermyn).
MCSET. Cat no: **1210F**. Released on Travellers Tales, '91 by Travellers Tales. Note: 4 cassettes.
MCSET. Cat no: **1854961896**. Released on Bramhope, '91 by Ulverscroft Soundings. Note: 4 cassettes.
STEPSISTERS, THE (Judith Porter).
MCSET. Cat no: **1489F**. Released on Travellers Tales, '91 by Travellers Tales. Note: 4 cassettes.
MCSET. Cat no: **1854963015**. Released on Bramhope, '91 by Ulverscroft Soundings. Note: 4 Cassettes.
TIMELESS MOMENT, THE (Unknown narrator(s)).
MCSET. Cat no: **1854962345**. Released on Bramhope, '91 by Ulverscroft Soundings. Note: 5 Cassettes.
UNTO THE FOURTH GENERATION: PART 4 (Jane Jermyn).
MCSET. Cat no: **1161F**. Released on Travellers Tales, '91 by Travellers Tales. Note: 4 cassettes.
MCSET. Cat no: **185496190X**. Released on Bramhope, '91 by Ulverscroft Soundings. Note: 4 Cassettes.
WAY OF THE RIVER, THE: PART 2 (Jane Jermyn).
MCSET. Cat no: **1159F**. Released on Travellers Tales, '91 by Travellers Tales. Note: 4 cassettes
MCSET. Cat no: **1854981918**. Released on Bramhope, '91 by Ulverscroft Soundings. Note: 4 Cassettes.

Streiber, Whitley
MAJESTIC (William Windom & Chris Saradon).
MC. Cat no: **0671693425**. Released on Simon & Schuster, '91 by Simon & Schuster Ltd.
COMMUNION (Roddy McDowall). Note: Also available on hanging format, catalogue number:- 0001031864.
MCSET Cat no: **0001072900**. Released on Harper Collins, '91 by Harper Collins. Note: 2 Cassettes.
TRANSFORMATION (Roddy McDowall).
Note: Also available on hanging format, catalogue number:- 0001388312.
MCSET. Cat no: **0001388118**. Released on Harper Collins, '91 by Harper Collins. Note: 2 Cassettes.

Strong, Patience
REFLECTIONS: A MISCELLANY OF WORDS AND MUSIC (Patience Strong).
MC. Cat no: **GCS 2**. Released on Schiltron Audio Books, Feb '92 by Schiltron Publishing. Note: Playing time: 1hr.

Struther, Jan
MRS. MINIVER (Bridget Forsyth).
MCSET. Cat no: **1675F**. Released on Travellers Tales, '91 by Travellers Tales. Note: 4 Cassettes.
MCSET. Cat no: **OAS 20391**. Released on Oasis Audio Books, '91 by Isis Audio Books. Note: 4 Cassettes.

Stuart, Alex
CAPTAIN'S TABLE, THE (Unknown narrator(s)).
MCSET. Cat no: **1854961926**. Released on Bramhope, '91 by Ulverscroft Soundings. Note: 4 Cassettes.
DOCTOR MARY COURAGE (Margaret Holt).
MCSET. Cat no: **1102R**. Released on Travellers Tales, '91 by Travellers Tales. Note: 4 Cassettes.
MCSET. Cat no: **1854961934**. Released on Bramhope, '91 by Ulverscroft Soundings. Note: 4 Cassettes.
DOCTOR ON HORSEBACK (Margaret Holt).
MCSET. Cat no: **1854965751**. Released on Bramhope, Mar '92 by Ulverscroft Soundings. Note: Playing time: 60 minutes.
GARRISON HOSPITAL (Unknown narrator(s)).
MCSET. Cat no: **1854963392**. Released on Bramhope, '91 by Ulverscroft Soundings. Note: 5 Cassettes.
LIFE IS THE DESTINY (Margaret Marsh).
MCSET. Cat no: **1077R**. Released on Travellers Tales, '91 by Travellers Tales. Note: 4 Cassettes.
MCSET. Cat no: **1854961942**. Released on Bramhope, '91 by Ulverscroft Soundings.
MAIDEN VOYAGE (Unknown narrator(s)).
MCSET. Cat no: **1854963023**. Released on Bramhope, '91 by Ulverscroft Soundings. Note: 5 Cassettes.
QUEEN'S COUNSEL (Unknown narrator(s)).
MCSET. Cat no: **1854963236**. Released on Bramhope, '91 by Ulverscroft Soundings. Note: 5 Cassettes.
RANDOM ISLAND (Unknown narrator(s)).
MCSET. Cat no: **1854961950**. Released on Bramhope, '91 by Ulverscroft Soundings. Note: 4 Cassettes.
SPENCER'S HOSPITAL (Unknown narrator(s)).
MCSET. Cat no: **1854965328**. Released on Bramhope, '91 by Ulverscroft Soundings. Note: 5 Cassettes.
THERE BUT FOR FORTUNE (Unknown narrator(s)).
MCSET. Cat no: **1854961969**. Released on Bramhope, '91 by Ulverscroft Soundings. Note: 5 Cassettes.
VALIANT SAILORS, THE (Unknown narrator(s)).
MCSET. Cat no: **1854961977**. Released on Bramhope, '91 by Ulverscroft Soundings. Note: 4 Cassettes.
YOUNG DOCTOR MASON (Tracy Shaw).
MCSET. Cat no: **1078R**. Released on Travellers Tales, '91 by Travellers Tales. Note: 4 Cassettes.
MCSET. Cat no: **1854961985**. Released on Bramhope, '91 by Ulverscroft Soundings.

Stuart, Francis
ALTERNATIVE GOVERNMENT (Francis Stuart).
MC. Cat no: **4CCT 18**. Released on Claddagh (Ireland), Aug '88 by Claddagh Records (Ireland), Projection, Impetus Records, Jazz Music, Roots Records, C.M. Distribution, Outlet Records, Taylors.
LP. Cat no: **CCT 18**. Released on Claddagh (Ireland), Aug '88 by Claddagh Records (Ireland), Projection, Impetus Records, Jazz Music, Roots Records, C.M. Distribution, Outlet Records, Taylors.

Stuart, Vivian
SUMMER'S FLOWER, THE (Unknown narrator(s)).
MCSET. Cat no: **1854963635**. Released on Bramhope, '91 by Ulverscroft Soundings. Note: 5 Cassettes.

Stubbs, Jean
LASTING SPRING, A (Joanna David).
MCSET. Cat no: **CAB 685**. Released on Chivers Audio Books, Mar '92 by Chivers Audio Books, Green Dragon Audio Visual. Note: 12 Cassettes

Summers, Judith
DEAR SISTER (Melissa Jane Sinden).
MCSET. Cat no: **1487F**. Released on Travellers Tales, '91 by Travellers Tales. Note: 7 Cassettes.
MCSET. Cat no: **1854963058**. Released on Soundings, '91 by Soundings Records, Bond Street Music. Note: 7 Cassettes.
I, GLORIA GOLD (Unknown narrator(s)).
MCSET. Cat no: **1854962280**. Released on Bramhope, '91 by Ulverscroft Soundings. Note: 5 Cassettes.

Superman
DOUBLE TROUBLE (Unknown narrator(s)).
MC. Cat no: **PLBS 278**. Released on Tell-A-Tale, '89 by Pickwick Records, Taylors, Clyde Factors.
STORY, THE (Unknown narrator(s)).

241

MC. Cat no: **PLBS 277.** Released on Tell-A-Tale, '89 by Pickwick Records, Taylors, Clyde Factors.

Susann, Jacqueline
ONCE IS NOT ENOUGH (Genie Francis).
Note: Also available on hanging format, catalogue number:- 0001031503.
MCSET. Cat no: **0001072889.** Released on Harper Collins, '91 by Harper Collins. Note: 2 Cassettes.
VALLEY OF THE DOLLS (Juliet Mills).
Note: Also available on hanging format, catalogue number:- 0001031511
MCSET. Cat no: **0001072870.** Released on Harper Collins, '91 by Harper Collins. Note: 2 Cassettes.

Suskind, Patrick
PERFUME: THE STORY OF A MURDERER (Sean Barrett).
MCSET. Cat no: **1252T.** Released on Travellers Tales, '91 by Travellers Tales. Note: 8 Cassettes.
MCSET. Cat no: **IAB 88072.** Released on Isis Audio Books, '91. Note: 8 Cassettes.

Sutcliff, Rosemary
DRAGON SLAYER (Sean Barrett).
MCSET. Cat no: **2CCA 3014.** Released on Chivers Audio Books, '91 by Chivers Audio Books, Green Dragon Audio Visual. Note: 2 Cassettes.
MCSET. Cat no: **9082F.** Released on Travellers Tales, '91 by Travellers Tales. Note: 2 Cassettes.

Sutton, June
PENREATH GIRL, THE (Margaret Holt).
MCSET. Cat no: **1854965794.** Released on Trio, Mar '92 by EMI Records.

Sutton, Lee
BEST OF LEE SUTTON: UNCENSORED (Lee Sutton).
LP. Cat no: **NTS 163.** Released on Note, Feb '79 by EMI Records **Deleted** Feb '84.

Swift, Jonathan
GULLIVER'S TRAVELS (Michael Hordern).
MCSET. Cat no: **1162F.** Released on Travellers Tales, '91 by Travellers Tales. Note: 2 cassettes.
GULLIVER'S TRAVELS (Children's Classics).
Note: Book and cassette.
MC. Cat no: **PLBC 80.** Released on Tell-A-Tale, '88 by Pickwick Records, Taylors, Clyde Factors.
GULLIVER'S TRAVELS (Anthony Hyde).
MC. Cat no: **TS 320.** Released on Tellastory, '91 by Random Century Audiobooks. Note: ISBN no. 1856560104

GULLIVER'S TRAVELS (Derek Hart).
MC. Cat no: **BKK 404.** Released on Kiddy Kassettes, '77.
GULLIVER'S TRAVELS (Anton Rodgers).
MCSET. Cat no: **LFP 7451.** Released on Listen For Pleasure, Apr '90 by EMI Records.
GULLIVER'S TRAVELS (And Other Favourite Children's Stories) (Unknown narrator(s)).
Note: Includes Gulliver's Travels, Gulliver in Laputa, Gulliver on the Adventure and The Seventh Voyage of Sinbad. For Ages 5 - 9.
MC. Cat no: **VCA 612.** Released on VFM Cassettes, Jul '85 by VFM Cassettes, Midland Records, Crusader Marketing Co., Taylors, Morley Audio Services.
GULLIVER'S TRAVELS (Michael Hordern).
MCSET. Cat no: **4147304.** Released on Argo (Polygram), Jun '88 by PolyGram Classics **Deleted** Jan '89. Note: 5 cassettes.
GULLIVER'S TRAVELS (The Houyhnhnms) (Sir Michael Redgrave).
MC. Cat no: **1099.** Released on Caedmon (USA), '88 by Caedmon Records (USA), Bond Street Music.
GULLIVERS' TRAVELS (Gulliver in Lilliput) (Frank Duncan).
MC. Cat no: **P 90034.** Released on Pinnacle, '79 by Pinnacle Records, Outlet Records, Music Sales Records.
MODEST PROPOSAL, A (Patrick Magee).
MC. Cat no: **1383.** Released on Caedmon (USA), '91 by Caedmon Records (USA), Bond Street Music.
MC. Cat no: **0001051881.** Released on Collins-Caedmon, '91 by Collins Audio, Taylors, Bond Street Music.

Symge, John
PLAYBOY OF THE WESTERN WORLD, THE (Unknown narrator(s)).
MCSET. Cat no: **0348.** Released on Caedmon (USA), '89 by Caedmon Records (USA), Bond Street Music. Note: 2 cassettes

Symons, Julian
CRIMINAL COMEDY OF THE CONTENTED COUPLE, THE (Hugh Ross).
MCSET. Cat no: **1641T.** Released on Travellers Tales, '91 by Travellers Tales. Note: 6 Cassettes.
MCSET. Cat no: **OAS 90072.** Released on Oasis Audio Books, '91 by Isis Audio Books.
DEATH'S DARKEST FACE (Edward De Souza).
MCSET. Cat no: **CAB 543.** Released on Chivers Audio Books, '91 by Chivers Audio Books, Green Dragon Audio Visual. Note: 8 Cassettes.

MCSET. Cat no: **1645F.** Released on Travellers Tales, '91 by Travellers Tales. Note: 8 Cassettes.
GIGANTIC SHADOW, THE (Nicholas Ball).
MCSET. Cat no: **CAT 4036.** Released on Chivers Audio Books, '88 by Chivers Audio Books, Green Dragon Audio Visual.
MCSET. Cat no: **1268T.** Released on Travellers Tales, '91 by Travellers Tales. Note: 4 Cassettes.
KENTISH MANOR MURDERS, THE (George Hagan).
MCSET. Cat no: **1658T.** Released on Travellers Tales, '91 by Travellers Tales. Note: 6 cassettes.
MCSET. Cat no: **OAS 90124.** Released on Oasis Audio Books, '91 by Isis Audio Books. Note: 6 Cassettes.
TALES OF THINGS THAT GO BUMP IN THE NIGHT (Various narrators).
MCSET. Cat no: **1026S.** Released on Travellers Tales, '91 by Travellers Tales. Note: 6 Cassettes.
MCSET. Cat no: **CSL 018.** Released on Chivers Audio Books, '91 by Chivers Audio Books, Green Dragon Audio Visual. Note: 6 Cassettes.

Taylor, Andrew
CAROLINE MINUSCULE (Martin Jarvis).
MCSET. Cat no: **ZBBC 1158.** Released on BBC, Jul '90 by BBC Records, Taylors. Note: ISBN No: 0563 410787
OUR FATHER'S LIES (Christopher Kay).
MCSET. Cat no: **1379T.** Released on Travellers Tales, '91 by Travellers Tales.
MCSET. Cat no: **1854962000.** Released on Bramhope, '91 by Ulverscroft Soundings. Note: 5 Cassettes.

Taylor, Elizabeth
IN A SUMMER SEASON (Gretel Davis).
MCSET. Cat no: **1468F.** Released on Travellers Tales, '91 by Travellers Tales. Note: 7 Cassettes.
MCSET. Cat no: **OAS 90033.** Released on Oasis Audio Books, '91 by Isis Audio Books. Note: 7 Cassettes.

Taylor, Susan
DEAREST ENEMY (Jill Shilling).
MCSET. Cat no: **MRC 1024.** Released on Chivers Audio Books, '91 by Chivers Audio Books, Green Dragon Audio Visual. Note: 2 cassettes.

Television
ACTION FORCE (Flint's Holiday) (Unknown narrator(s)).
Note: Book and cassette. For ages 7 to 12.
MC. Cat no: **PLBA 226.** Released on Tell-A-Tale, '88 by Pickwick Records, Taylors, Clyde Factors.

ACTION FORCE (Return of the Dinosaurs) (Unknown narrator(s)).
Note: Book and cassette. For ages 7 to 12.
MC. Cat no: **PLBA 227**. Released on Tell-A-Tale, '88 by Pickwick Records, Taylors, Clyde Factors.

'ALLO 'ALLO (The War Diaries of Rene Artois) (Various artists).
Note: Adapted from the television programme.
MCSET. Cat no: **ZBBC 1094**. Released on BBC, Nov '89 by BBC Records, Taylors. Note: 2 Cassettes. ISBN No: 0563 227052

BANGERS AND MASH (Eggs is Eggs) (Various artists).
MC. Cat no: **PLBM 273**. Released on Tell-A-Tale, '89 by Pickwick Records, Taylors, Clyde Factors.

BANGERS AND MASH (Chimps at Work) (Various artists).
MC. Cat no: **STK 029**. Released on Stick-A-Tale, Jul '90 by Pickwick Records.

BERTHA (Roy Kinnear & Sheila Walker).
MC. Cat no: **00 103457 X**. Released on Tempo, '88 by Warwick Records, Celtic Music, Henry Hadaway Organisation.

BERTHA (Children's TV Series) (Various artists).
Tracks / Bertha: *Various artists* / Mrs. Tupp: *Various artists* / Packing and stacking: *Various artists* / Flying bear, The: *Various artists* / Mr. Duncan: *Various artists* / Turning wheels: *Various artists* / Tom the robot: *Various artists* / Isn't it nice: *Various artists* / Mr. Willmake: *Various artists* / Tracy's robot song: *Various artists* / Spottiswood march: *Various artists* / Roy the apprentice: *Various artists*.
LP. Cat no: **REH 585**. Released on BBC, Oct '85 by BBC Records, Taylors **Deleted** Apr '89.
MC. Cat no: **ZCR 585**. Released on BBC, Oct '85 by BBC Records, Taylors **Deleted** Apr '89.

BRAVESTARR (The Moonstone Crisis) (Unknown narrator(s)).
Note: Read by the Bravestarr character.
MC. Cat no: **0 00 102155 9**. Released on Tempo, '88 by Warwick Records, Celtic Music, Henry Hadaway Organisation.

BRAVESTARR (Water Fever) (Unknown narrator(s)).
Note: Read by the Bravestarr character.
MC. Cat no: **0 00 102156 7**. Released on Tempo, '88 by Warwick Records, Celtic Music, Henry Hadaway Organisation.

BRONTONAPPERS, THE (Unknown narrator(s)).
MC. Cat no: **PLBF 282**. Released on Tell-A-Tale, '89 by Pickwick Records, Taylors, Clyde Factors.

CHILDREN'S HOUR (Wendy Craig).
LP. Cat no: **MMT LP 105**. Released on Multi-Media, Jul '81.

CHIP 'N' DALE (Unknown narrator(s)).
MC. Cat no: **DIS 021**. Released on Disney (Read-a-long), Sep '90 by Disneyland Records.

COUNT DUCKULA (Vampire Vacation) (Unknown narrator(s)).
Note: Read by the Count Duckula character.
MC. Cat no: **0 00 109019 4**. Released on Tempo, '88 by Warwick Records, Celtic Music, Henry Hadaway Organisation.

COUNT DUCKULA (No Sax Please We're Eygptian) (Unknown narrator(s)).
Note: Read by the Count Duckula character.
MC. Cat no: **0 00 109021 6**. Released on Tempo, '88 by Warwick Records, Celtic Music, Henry Hadaway Organisation.

COUNT DUCKULA (The Mystic Saxophone) (David Jason).
MC. Cat no: **0411375687**. Released on Harper Collins, '91 by Harper Collins.

COUNT DUCKULA (Vampire Vacation) (David Jason).
MC. Cat no: **0411375695**. Released on Harper Collins, '91 by Harper Collins.

COUNT DUCKULA (The Ghost of Castle Duckula) (David Jason).
Note: Read by the Count Duckula character.
MC. Cat no: **0 00 109018 6**. Released on Tempo, '88 by Warwick Records, Celtic Music, Henry Hadaway Organisation.

MC. Cat no: **0411375709**. Released on Harper Collins, '91 by Harper Collins.

COUNT DUCKULA (Restoration Comedy) (David Jason).
Note: Read by the Count Duckula character.
MC. Cat no: **0 00 109020 8**. Released on Tempo, '88 by Warwick Records, Celtic Music, Henry Hadaway Organisation.

MC. Cat no: **0411375679**. Released on Harper Collins, '91 by Harper Collins.

DAD'S ARMY (Various artists).
Note: Includes: When Did You Last See Your Money?, Time on my Hands, A Jumbo Sized Problem and Ten Seconds From Now.
MCSET. Cat no: **ZBBC 1140**. Released on BBC, Nov '90 by BBC Records, Taylors. Note: ISBN No: 0563 411201.

DAD'S ARMY (Volume 2) (Various artists).
MCSET. Cat no: **ZBBC 1272**. Released on BBC, Nov '91 by BBC Records, Taylors. Note: ISBN No: 0563 365803.

DANGERMOUSE AND PUBLIC ENEMY NO.1 (Various artists).
MC. Cat no: **TTS 9807**. Released on Tempo, Aug '84 by Warwick Records, Celtic Music, Henry Hadaway Organisation.

DOCTOR WHO (State of Decay) (Various artists).
MCSET. Cat no: **DTO 10517**. Released on Ditto, '88 by Pickwick Records, Midland Records.

DOCTOR WHO (Genesis of the Daleks) (Various artists).
LP. Cat no: **REH 364**. Released on BBC, '78 by BBC Records, Taylors.
MC. Cat no: **ZCR 364**. Released on BBC, Sep '79 by BBC Records, Taylors.

DOCTOR WHO AND THE PESCATONS (Unknown narrator(s)).
LP. Cat no: **4144591**. Released on Argo (Polygram), Apr '85 by PolyGram Classics.
MC. Cat no: **4144594**. Released on Argo (Polygram), Apr '85 by PolyGram Classics.

FAWLTY TOWERS (Various artists).
Note: Includes: Mrs Richards, Hotel Inspectors, Basil the Rat, The Builders.
MCSET. Cat no: **ZBBC 1006**. Released on BBC, Sep '88 by BBC Records, Taylors. Note: 2 Cassettes. ISBN No: 0563 225416.

FAWLTY TOWERS (Second Sitting) (Various artists).
LP. Cat no: **REB 405**. Released on BBC, Jan '81 by BBC Records, Taylors **Deleted** 31 Aug '88.
MC. Cat no: **ZCF 405**. Released on BBC, Jan '81 by BBC Records, Taylors **Deleted** 31 Aug '88.

FAWLTY TOWERS (Volume 2) (Various artists).
Note: Includes: The Kipper, The Corpse, The Germans, Waldorf Salad and Gourmet Night.
MCSET. Cat no: **ZBBC 1015**. Released on BBC, Sep '88 by BBC Records, Taylors. Note: 2 Cassettes. ISBN No: 0563 225424.

FRED THE FISHERMAN (Unknown narrator(s)).
MC. Cat no: **PLBF 283**. Released on Tell-A-Tale, '89 by Pickwick Records, Taylors, Clyde Factors.

HENRY'S CAT (The Outlaws) (Unknown narrator(s)).
MC. Cat no: **STK 010**. Released on Stick-A-Tale, Jan '89 by Pickwick Records.

HENRY'S CAT (Volume 1) (Unknown narrator(s)).
MCSET. Cat no: **DTO 10555**. Released on Ditto, '88 by Pickwick Records, Midland Records.

HENRY'S CAT (Volume 2) (Unknown narrator(s)).
MCSET. Cat no: **DTO 10582**. Re-

leased on Ditto, '88 by Pickwick Records, Midland Records.

HENRY'S CAT BECOMES PRIME MINISTER (Unknown narrator(s)).
MC. Cat no: **STK 009.** Released on Stick-A-Tale, Jan '89 by Pickwick Records.

IT AIN'T HALF HOT MUM (Various artists).
LP. Cat no: **EMC 3074.** Released on EMI, Apr '75 by EMI Records **Deleted** '79.

IVOR THE ENGINE (Stories from the BBC TV Childrens Series) (Various artists).
Tracks / Railway, The: *Various artists* / Egg, The: *Various artists* / Proper container, The: *Various artists* / Alarm, The: *Various artists* / Retreat, The: *Various artists* / Unidentified objects: *Various artists* / Gold?: *Various artists* / Mrs. Porty: *Various artists* / Cold: *Various artists* / Endowment, The: *Various artists*.
LP. Cat no: **REC 517.** Released on BBC, Jul '84 by BBC Records, Taylors **Deleted** Apr '89.
MC. Cat no: **ZCM 517.** Released on BBC, Jul '84 by BBC Records, Taylors.

MASTERS OF THE UNIVERSE (Trap for He-Man) (Unknown narrator(s)).
Note: Book and cassette. For ages up to 5-10 years.
MC. Cat no: **PLBM 122.** Released on Tell-A-Tale, '88 by Pickwick Records, Taylors, Clyde Factors.

MASTERS OF THE UNIVERSE (He-Man - The Iron Master) (Unknown narrator(s)).
Note: Book and cassette. For ages up to 5-10 years.
MC. Cat no: **PLBM 123.** Released on Tell-A-Tale, '88 by Pickwick Records, Taylors, Clyde Factors.

MASTERS OF THE UNIVERSE (He-man Meets the Beast) (Unknown narrator(s)).
Note: Book and cassette. For ages up to 5-10 years.
MC. Cat no: **PLBM 153.** Released on Tell-A-Tale, '88 by Pickwick Records, Taylors, Clyde Factors.

MASTERS OF THE UNIVERSE (He-Man and the Masters of the Universe) (Unknown narrator(s)).
MCSET. Cat no: **DTO 10561.** Released on Ditto, '88 by Pickwick Records, Midland Records.

MASTERS OF THE UNIVERSE (Unknown narrator(s)).
LP. Cat no: **SPR 8552.** Released on Spot, May '84 by Pickwick Records.
MC. Cat no: **SPC 8552.** Released on Spot, May '84 by Pickwick Records.

MASTERS OF THE UNIVERSE (He-man and the Asteroid of Doom) (Unknown narrator(s)).
Note: Book and cassette. For ages up to 5-10 years.
MC. Cat no: **PLBM 187.** Released on Tell-A-Tale, '88 by Pickwick Records, Taylors, Clyde Factors.

MASTERS OF THE UNIVERSE (He-man - The Wings Of Doom) (Unknown narrator(s)).
Note: Book and cassette. For ages up to 5-10 years.
MC. Cat no: **PLBM 146.** Released on Tell-A-Tale, Oct '84 by Pickwick Records, Taylors, Clyde Factors.

MASTERS OF THE UNIVERSE (He-Man and the Lost Dragon) (Unknown narrator(s)).
Note: Book and cassette. For ages up to 5-10 years.
MC. Cat no: **PLBM 188.** Released on Tell-A-Tale, '88 by Pickwick Records, Taylors, Clyde Factors.

MASTERS OF THE UNIVERSE (He-Man - Castle Grayskull Under Attack) (Unknown narrator(s)).
Note: Book and cassette. For ages up to 5 - 10 years.
MC. Cat no: **PLBM 124.** Released on Tell-A-Tale, '88 by Pickwick Records, Taylors, Clyde Factors.

MASTERS OF THE UNIVERSE (He-Man - Skeltor's Ice Attack) (Unknown narrator(s)).
Note: Book and cassette. For ages up to 5-10 years.
MC. Cat no: **PLBM 147.** Released on Tell-A-Tale, '88 by Pickwick Records, Taylors, Clyde Factors.

MOP AND SMIFF (Various artists).
Tracks / Two of a kind: *Various artists* / Happy birthday Mop and Smiff: *Various artists* / Special day: *Various artists* / Big top travelling show: *Various artists* / Sniffin': *Various artists* / Trackin' through the bracken: *Various artists* / Wooly friends: *Various artists* / Flower floats and beauty queens: *Various artists* / With the May Queen: *Various artists* / Down by the lakeside: *Various artists* / Bumpity bang: *Various artists* / Fluttering by: *Various artists* / Home for gnomes, A: *Various artists* / Mop's no Sherlock Holmes: *Various artists* / Painting song, The: *Various artists*.
Note: From the BBC children's TV programme.
LP. Cat no: **REC 558.** Released on BBC, May '85 by BBC Records, Taylors **Deleted** Apr '89.
MC. Cat no: **ZCM 558.** Released on BBC, May '85 by BBC Records, Taylors **Deleted** Apr '89.

MOP AND SMIFF GO TO SCHOOL (Various artists).
MC. Cat no: **BBM 109.** Released on Bibi (Budget Cassettes), Oct '81.

MOP AND SMIFF IN SEARCH OF A PEDIGREE (Various artists).
MC. Cat no: **BBM 108.** Released on Bibi (Budget Cassettes), Oct '81.

MOP AND SMIFF ON BUNNY HILL (Various artists).
MC. Cat no: **BBM 106.** Released on Bibi (Budget Cassettes), Oct '81.

MOP AND SMIFF'S DAY SUN-

NYSEAS (Various artists).
MC. Cat no: **BBM 107.** Released on Bibi (Budget Cassettes), Oct '81.

MORE WILLO THE WISP STORIES (Kenneth Williams).
LP. Cat no: **REC 473.** Released on BBC, Jul '83 by BBC Records, Taylors **Deleted** 31 Aug '88.
MC. Cat no: **ZCM 473.** Released on BBC, Jul '83 by BBC Records, Taylors **Deleted** 31 Aug '88.

PORRIDGE (With Original Cast) (Various artists).
MC. Cat no: **ZCF 270.** Released on BBC, Apr '77 by BBC Records, Taylors **Deleted** '88.
LP. Cat no: **REB 270.** Released on BBC, Oct '79 by BBC Records, Taylors **Deleted** '84.

RAINBOW - THE SQUARE (Unknown narrator(s)).
CD. Cat no: **38H 38.** Released on CBS, '88 by Sony Music, Solomon & Peres, Outlet Records. Note: Import.

SHE-RA (Shadow Weaver's Magic Mirror) (Unknown narrator(s)).
Note: Book and cassette. For ages 5 to 10.
MC. Cat no: **PLBS 172.** Released on Tell-A-Tale, '88 by Pickwick Records, Taylors, Clyde Factors.

SHE-RA (She-Ra and the Surprise Party) (Unknown narrator(s)).
Note: Book and cassette. For ages 5 to 10.
MC. Cat no: **PLBS 182.** Released on Tell-A-Tale, '88 by Pickwick Records, Taylors, Clyde Factors.

SHE-RA (She-Ra and the Golden Goose) (Unknown narrator(s)).
Note: Book and cassette. For ages 5 to 10.
MC. Cat no: **PLBS 199.** Released on Tell-A-Tale, '88 by Pickwick Records, Taylors, Clyde Factors.

SHE-RA (The Secret of the Sword) (Unknown narrator(s)).
Note: Book and cassette. For ages 5 to 10.
MC. Cat no: **PLBS 173.** Released on Tell-A-Tale, '88 by Pickwick Records, Taylors, Clyde Factors.

SHE-RA (She-Ra and the Dark Pool) (Unknown narrator(s)).
Note: Book and cassette. For ages 5 to 10.
MC. Cat no: **PLBS 171.** Released on Tell-A-Tale, '88 by Pickwick Records, Taylors, Clyde Factors.

SHE-RA (Spirit is Kidnapped) (Unknown narrator(s)).
Note: Book and cassette. For ages 5 to 10.
MC. Cat no: **PLBS 181.** Released on Tell-A-Tale, '88 by Pickwick Records, Taylors, Clyde Factors.

SHE-RA (Catra's Ice Palace) (Unknown narrator(s)).
Note: Book and cassette. For ages 5 to 10.
MC. Cat no: **PLBS 200.** Released on Tell-A-Tale, '88 by Pickwick Records,

Taylors, Clyde Factors.

SILVER JACKANORY (Various narrators).
Note: Ten stories featuring such writers and readers as Dick King-Smith, Bernard Cribbins and Griff Rhys-Jones.
MCSET. Cat no: **ZBBC 1204**. Released on BBC Audio Collection, '91 by BBC Records. Note: ISBN No: 0563 40910X.

SILVERHAWKS (The Origin) (Unknown narrator(s)).
Note: Read by Silverhawks characters.
MC. Cat no: **0 00 109012 7**. Released on Tempo, '88 by Warwick Records, Celtic Music, Henry Hadaway Organisation.

SILVERHAWKS (The Planet Eater) (Unknown narrator(s)).
Note: Read by the Silverhawks characters.
MC. Cat no: **0 00 109013 5**. Released on Tempo, '88 by Warwick Records, Celtic Music, Henry Hadaway Organisation.

SUPERTED AND BUBBLES THE CLOWN (Unknown narrator(s)).
MC. Cat no: **0001010182**. Released on Harper Collins, '91 by Harper Collins.

SUPERTED AND THE LUMBERJACKS (Peter Hawkins).
MC. Cat no: **0 00 109009 7**. Released on Tempo, '88 by Warwick Records, Celtic Music, Henry Hadaway Organisation.

SUPERTED AND THE SPACE BEAVERS (Unknown narrator(s)).
MC. Cat no: **0001010190**. Released on Harper Collins, '91 by Harper Collins.

SUPERTED IN SUPERTED'S DREAM (Peter Hawkins).
MC. Cat no: **0 00 109010 0**. Released on Tempo, '88 by Warwick Records, Celtic Music, Henry Hadaway Organisation.

TEENAGE MUTANT HERO TURTLES (Splinter No More) (Unknown narrator(s)).
MC. Cat no: **0411396178**. Released on Harper Collins, '91 by Harper Collins.

TEENAGE MUTANT HERO TURTLES (Return of the Technodrome) (Unknown narrator(s)).
CDSET. Cat no: **0411396188**. Released on Harper Collins, '91 by Harper Collins.

TEENAGE MUTANT HERO TURTLES (Undercover Heroes) (Unknown narrator(s)).
MC. Cat no: **0001010514**. Released on Harper Collins, '91 by Harper Collins.

TEENAGE MUTANT HERO TURTLES (Attack of the Time Spiders) (Unknown narrator(s)).
MC. Cat no: **0001010506**. Released on Harper Collins, '91 by Harper Collins.

TEENAGE MUTANT HERO TURTLES (Krang's Space Raid) (Unknown narrator(s)).
MC. Cat no: **0001010522**. Released on Harper Collins, '91 by Harper Collins.

TEENAGE MUTANT HERO TURTLES (Enter the Rat King) (Unknown narrator(s)).
MC. Cat no: **0411396218**. Released on Harper Collins, '91 by Harper Collins.

TEENAGE MUTANT HERO TURTLES (Follow My Leader) (Unknown narrator(s)).
MC. Cat no: **041139620X**. Released on Harper Collins, '91 by Harper Collins.

TEENAGE MUTANT HERO TURTLES (Unknown narrator(s)).
Note: Three stories:- Undercover Heroes, Krang's Space Radio and Shredder's Invisible Maze.
MCSET. Cat no: **000192591**. Released on Harper Collins, '91 by Harper Collins.

TEENAGE MUTANT HERO TURTLES (Shredder's Invisible Maze) (Unknown narrator(s)).
MC. Cat no: **0001010530**. Released on Harper Collins, '91 by Harper Collins.

THREE OF A KIND (Various artists).
LP. Cat no: **REB 480**. Released on BBC, Sep '83 by BBC Records, Taylors
Deleted 31 Aug '88.
MC. Cat no: **ZCF 480**. Released on BBC, Sep '83 by BBC Records, Taylors
Deleted 31 Aug '88.

THUNDERCATS (Ho - The Movie) (Various artists).
Note: Read by Thundercats characters.
MC. Cat no: **0 00 102149 4**. Released on Tempo, '88 by Warwick Records, Celtic Music, Henry Hadaway Organisation.

THUNDERCATS (Quest for the Magic Crystal) (Various artists).
Note: Read by Thundercats characters.
MC. Cat no: **0 00 102148 6**. Released on Tempo, '88 by Warwick Records, Celtic Music, Henry Hadaway Organisation.

THUNDERCATS (Various artists).
Note: Read by Thundercats characters.
MC. Cat no: **0 00 102213 X**. Released on Tempo, '88 by Warwick Records, Celtic Music, Henry Hadaway Organisation.

TOM AND JERRY (Magical Cat) (Unknown narrator(s)).
MC. Cat no: **0411396102**. Released on Harper Collins, '91 by Harper Collins.

TOM AND JERRY (Fat Free Cat) (Unknown narrator(s)).
MC. Cat no: **0411396099**. Released on Harper Collins, '91 by Harper Collins.

TRANSFORMERS (Galvatron's Air Attack) (Unknown narrator(s)).
Note: Book and cassette. For ages 5 to 10.
MC. Cat no: **PLBT 185**. Released on Tell-A-Tale, '88 by Pickwick Records, Taylors, Clyde Factors.

TRANSFORMERS (Battle for Planet Earth) (Unknown narrator(s)).
MCSET. Cat no: **DTO 10537**. Released on Ditto, '88 by Pickwick Records, Midland Records.

TRANSFORMERS (Megatron's Fight for Power) (Unknown narrator(s)).
Note: Book and cassette. For ages 5 to 10
MC. Cat no: **PLBT 164**. Released on Tell-A-Tale, '88 by Pickwick Records, Taylors, Clyde Factors.

TRANSFORMERS (Laserbeak's Fury) (Unknown narrator(s)).
Note: Book and cassette. For ages 5 to 10.
MC. Cat no: **PLBT 174**. Released on Tell-A-Tale, '88 by Pickwick Records, Taylors, Clyde Factors.

TRANSFORMERS (Autobots Strike Oil) (Unknown artist(s)).
MC. Cat no: **PLBT 236**. Released on Tell-A-Tale, Jan '89 by Pickwick Records, Taylors, Clyde Factors.

TRANSFORMERS (Decepticons at the Pole) (Unknown narrator(s)).
Note: Book and cassette. For ages 5 to 10.
MC. Cat no: **PLBT 235**. Released on Tell-A-Tale, Jan '89 by Pickwick Records, Taylors, Clyde Factors.

TRANSFORMERS (Autobot Hostage) (Unknown narrator(s)).
MC. Cat no: **PLBT 251**. Released on Tell-A-Tale, Jan '89 by Pickwick Records, Taylors, Clyde Factors.

TRANSFORMERS (The Movie) (Unknown narrator(s)).
Note: Book and cassette. For ages 5 to 10.
MC. Cat no: **PLBT 201**. Released on Tell-A-Tale, '88 by Pickwick Records, Taylors, Clyde Factors.

TRANSFORMERS (Decepticon Hide Out) (Unknown narrator(s)).
Note: Book and cassette. For ages 5 to 10.
MC. Cat no: **PLBT 186**. Released on Tell-A-Tale, '88 by Pickwick Records, Taylors, Clyde Factors.

TRANSFORMERS (Autobots Fight Back) (Unknown narrator(s)).
Note: Book and cassette. For ages 5 to 10.
MC. Cat no: **PLBT 165**. Released on Tell-A-Tale, '88 by Pickwick Records, Taylors, Clyde Factors.

TRANSFORMERS (Autobots' Lighting Strike) (Unknown narrator(s)).
Note: Book and cassette. For ages 5 to 10.
MC. Cat no: **PLBT 154**. Released on

Tell-A-Tale, '88 by Pickwick Records, Taylors, Clyde Factors.

TRANSFORMERS (Decepticon's Under-Ground) (Unknown narrator(s)).
Note: Book and cassette. For ages 5 to 10.
MC. Cat no: **PLBT 252.** Released on Tell-A-Tale, Jan '89 by Pickwick Records, Taylors, Clyde Factors.

VISIONARIES (The Age of Magic Begins) (Unknown narrator(s)).
Note: Read by the Visionaries characters.
MC. Cat no: **00 102163 X.** Released on Tempo, '88 by Warwick Records, Celtic Music, Henry Hadaway Organisation.

VISIONARIES (The Dark Hand of Treachery) (Unknown narrator(s)).
Note: Read by the Visionaries characters.
MC. Cat no: **00 102164 8.** Released on Tempo, '88 by Warwick Records, Celtic Music, Henry Hadaway Organisation.

WILL O' THE WISP (Games With Edna) (Various artists).
MC. Cat no: **LL 41 8001 4.** Released on Listen For Pleasure, Jun '84 by EMI Records.

WILL O' THE WISP (The Chrysalis) (Various artists).
MC. Cat no: **LL 41 8002 4.** Released on Listen For Pleasure, Jun '84 by EMI Records.

WILL O' THE WISP (Kenneth Williams).
Tracks / Bridegroom, The / Food for thought / You know what, The / Chrysalis, The / Flight of Mavis, The / Holidays / Hot hot day, The / Gnome, The / Beauty contents, The / Midas touch, The / Beanstalk, The / Christmas box.
LP. Cat no: **REC 427.** Released on BBC, Oct '81 by BBC Records, Taylors **Deleted** 31 Aug '88.
MC. Cat no: **ZCM 427.** Released on BBC, Oct '81 by BBC Records, Taylors **Deleted** 31 Aug '88.

WILL O' THE WISP (The Joys of Spring) (Various artists).
MC. Cat no: **LL 41 8005 4.** Released on Listen For Pleasure, Jun '84 by EMI Records.

WILL O' THE WISP (The Wishbone) (Various artists).
MC. Cat no: **LL 41 8003 4.** Released on Listen For Pleasure, Jun '84 by EMI Records.

WILL O' THE WISP (Magic Golf) (Various artists).
MC. Cat no: **LL 41 8004 4.** Released on Listen For Pleasure, Jun '84 by EMI Records.

WILL O' THE WISP (The Beanstalk) (Various artists).
MC. Cat no: **LL 41 8006 4.** Released on Listen For Pleasure, Jun '84 by EMI Records.

Tennyson, Jesse F.

PIN TO SEE THE PEEPSHOW, A (Judith Whale).
MCSET. Cat no: **1414/5F.** Released on Travellers Tales, '91 by Travellers Tales. Note: 12 Cassettes.
MCSET. Cat no: **OAS 89113.** Released on Oasis Audio Books, '91 by Isis Audio Books. Note: 12 Cassettes.

Tevis, Walter

QUEEN'S GAMBIT, THE (Alexandra O'Karma).
MCSET. Cat no: **RB 87870.** Released on Recorded Books, Feb '92 by Isis Audio Books. Note: 7 cassettes. Playing time 10hrs 30mins

Tey, Josephine

BRAT FARRAR (Carole Boyd).
MCSET. Cat no: **CAB 499.** Released on Chivers Audio Books, '91 by Chivers Audio Books, Green Dragon Audio Visual. Note: 8 Cassettes.
MCSET. Cat no: **1533F.** Released on Travellers Tales, '91 by Travellers Tales. Note: 8 Cassettes.

DAUGHTER OF TIME, THE (Derek Jacobi).
MCSET. Cat no: **CAB 092.** Released on Chivers Audio Books, '91 by Chivers Audio Books, Green Dragon Audio Visual. Note: 6 cassettes.
MCSET. Cat no: **1138T.** Released on Travellers Tales, '91 by Travellers Tales. Note: 6 Cassettes.

FRANCHISE AFFAIR, THE (Edward Petherbridge).
MCSET. Cat no: **ZBBC 1183.** Released on BBC Radio Collection, Apr '91 by BBC Records. Note: ISBN No: 0563 409932

FRANCHISE AFFAIR, THE (Carole Boyd).
MCSET. Cat no: **CAB 578.** Released on Chivers Audio Books, '91 by Chivers Audio Books, Green Dragon Audio Visual. Note: 8 cassettes.
MCSET. Cat no: **1659F.** Released on Travellers Tales, '91 by Travellers Tales.

MISS. PYM DISPOSES (Carole Boyd).
MCSET. Cat no: **CAB 649.** Released on Chivers Audio Books, Nov '91 by Chivers Audio Books, Green Dragon Audio Visual. Note: 6 Cassettes.

SINGING SANDS, THE (Stephen Thorne).
MCSET. Cat no: **CAB 401.** Released on Chivers Audio Books, '91 by Chivers Audio Books, Green Dragon Audio Visual. Note: 6 Cassettes.
MCSET. Cat no: **1556T.** Released on Travellers Tales, '91 by Travellers Tales. Note: 6 Cassettes,

Thackeray, William

MEMOIRS OF BARRY LYNDON (Volume 1) (Arthur Boland).
MCSET. Cat no: **COL 2006.** Released on Colophone, Feb '81 by AVLS (Audio-Visual Library Services).

VANITY FAIR (Claire Bloom).
MC. Cat no: **1669.** Released on Caedmon (USA), '89 by Caedmon Records (USA), Bond Street Music.

Thane, Elswyth

YANKEE STRANGER (Pat Starr).
MCSET. Cat no: **1151/1152R.** Released on Travellers Tales, '91 by Travellers Tales. Note: 12 Cassettes.
MCSET. Cat no: **OAS 90054.** Released on Oasis Audio Books, '91 by Isis Audio Books. Note: 12 cassettes.
MCSET. Cat no: **OAS 91014.** Released on Oasis Audio Books, '91 by Isis Audio Books. Note: 12 Cassettes.

Theroux, Paul

CONSUL'S FILE, THE (Ed Bishop).
MCSET. Cat no: **1290F.** Released on Travellers Tales, '91 by Travellers Tales. Note: 6 cassettes.
MCSET. Cat no: **CAB 285.** Released on Chivers Audio Books, '91 by Chivers Audio Books, Green Dragon Audio Visual. Note: 6 cassettes.

HALF MOON STREET (Davina Porter & Norman Dietz).
MCSET. Cat no: **1669F.** Released on Travellers Tales, '91 by Travellers Tales. Note: 4 Cassettes.
MCSET. Cat no: **RB 87210.** Released on Recorded Books, '91 by Isis Audio Books. Note: 4 Cassettes.

LONDON EMBASSY, THE (Ed Bishop).
MCSET. Cat no: **1165F.** Released on Travellers Tales, '91 by Travellers Tales. Note: 6 Cassettes.

LONDON SNOW (Stephen Thorne).
MCSET. Cat no: **2CCA 3052.** Released on Chivers Audio Books, '91 by Chivers Audio Books, Green Dragon Audio Visual. Note: 2 Cassettes.
MCSET. Cat no: **9122F.** Released on Travellers Tales, '91 by Travellers Tales. Note: 2 Cassettes.

Theydon, Jean

FATEFUL DECISION (Deidre Edwards).
MCSET. Cat no: **MRC 1051.** Released on Chivers Audio Books, '91 by Chivers Audio Books, Green Dragon Audio Visual. Note: 2 cassettes.

Thomas, Craig

ALL THE GREY CATS (Stephen Thorne).
MCSET. Cat no: **CAB 516.** Released on Chivers Audio Books, '91 by Chivers Audio Books, Green Dragon Audio Visual. Note: 12 Cassettes
MCSET. Cat no: **1642/1643T.** Released on Travellers Tales, '91 by Travellers Tales. Note: 12 Cassettes.

Thomas, Dylan

ADVENTURES IN THE SKIN TRADE (Unknown narrator(s)).

MCSET. Cat no: **2078**. Released on Caedmon (USA), '89 by Caedmon Records (USA), Bond Street Music.

AND DEATH SHALL HAVE NO DOMINATION (Unknown narrator(s)).
MC. Cat no: **1018**. Released on Caedmon (USA), '89 by Caedmon Records (USA), Bond Street Music.

CHILD'S CHRISTMAS IN WALES, A (Dylan Thomas).
Note: Also available on hanging format, Cat. No: 000103555X.
MC. Cat no: **1002**. Released on Caedmon (USA), '88 by Caedmon Records (USA), Bond Street Music.
MCSET. Cat no: **HCA 4**. Released on Harper Collins, '92 by Harper Collins.
MC. Cat no: **0001035568**. Released on Harper Collins, '91 by Harper Collins.

DYLAN THOMAS READING HIS POETRY (Dylan Thomas).
MC. Cat no: **001042467**. Released on Collins-Caedmon, '88 by Collins Audio, Taylors, Bond Street Music.
MC. Cat no: **1342**. Released on Caedmon (USA), '89 by Caedmon Records (USA), Bond Street Music.

DYLAN THOMAS READS A PERSONAL ANTHOLOGY (Dylan Thomas).
MC. Cat no: **1294**. Released on Caedmon (USA), '89 by Caedmon Records (USA), Bond Street Music.

IN COUNTRY HEAVEN (The Evolution of a Poem) (Unknown narrator(s)).
MC. Cat no: **1281**. Released on Caedmon (USA), '89 by Caedmon Records (USA), Bond Street Music.

MAN BE MY METAPHOR (A Tribute To Dylan Thomas) (Unknown narrator(s)).
MC. Cat no: **TTC 1009**. Released on Talking Tape Company, Apr '91, Conifer Records. Note: Playing time- 1hr 6mins. ISBN no. 187252091X

OVER SIR JOHN'S HILL (Unknown narrator(s)).
MC. Cat no: **1043**. Released on Caedmon (USA), '89 by Caedmon Records (USA), Bond Street Music.

QUITE EARLY ONE MORNING (Unknown narrator(s)).
MC. Cat no: **1132**. Released on Caedmon (USA), '89 by Caedmon Records (USA), Bond Street Music.

UNDER MILK WOOD (Various narrators).
Note: Read by Richard Burton and the original cast.
MCSET. Cat no: **SAY 13**. Released on Argo (Polygram), Jun '82 by PolyGram Classics **Deleted** Jan '89.
MCSET. Cat no: **ARGO 1016**. Released on Argo (EMI), '91 by EMI Records. Note: 2 cassettes.
MCSET. Cat no: **2005**. Released on Caedmon (USA), '88 by Caedmon Records (USA), Bond Street Music.
MCSET. Cat no: **HCA 46**. Released on Harper Collins, '91 by Harper Collins.
MCSET. Cat no: **1044P**. Released on Travellers Tales, '91 by Travellers Tales. Note: 2 Cassettes.

UNDER MILK WOOD - A PLAY FOR VOICES (Various artists).
Tracks / Main theme: *Various artists* / Johnnie Crack and Flossie Snail: *Various artists* / I loved a man: *Various artists* / Love duet: *Various artists* / Evening prayer, An: *Various artists* / Come and sweep my chimney (Mr. Waldo): *Various artists*.
Note: Starring Anthony Hopkins as First Voice with Freddie Jones, Jonathon Pryce, Nerys Hughes, Windsor Davies, Sian Phillips, Sir Geraint Evans, Ruth Madoc, Gemma Jones, Sir Harry Secombe and many more. And featuring specially written musical numbers sung by: Mary Hopkin, Bonnie Tyler and Tom Jones. Produced by George Martin. The first recording for 35 years.
CDSET. Cat no: **CDS 791 232 2**. Released on Columbia (EMI), Nov '88 by EMI Records.
2LP. Cat no: **SCXD 6715**. Released on Columbia (EMI), Nov '88 by EMI Records **Deleted** Mar '92.
MCSET. Cat no: **TCSCXD 6715**. Released on Columbia (EMI), Nov '88 by EMI Records. Note: Double cassette set.
CDSET. Cat no: **CDSCXD 6715**. Released on Columbia (EMI), Nov '88 by EMI Records.

VISIT TO AMERICA, A (Unknown narrator(s)).
MC. Cat no: **1061**. Released on Caedmon (USA), '89 by Caedmon Records (USA), Bond Street Music.

Thomas, Edward

TALYLLYN NON STOP - ENGINE NO.4 (Unknown narrator(s)).
LP. Cat no: **RESM 016**. Released on Response, Feb '81 by Priority Records, Taylors.

Thomas, Leslie

ADVENTURES OF GOODNIGHT AND LOVING, THE (Keith Barron).
MC. Cat no: **0600560546**. Released on Hamlyn Books On Tape, '88, Bond Street Music.

DANGEROUS DAVIES, THE LAST DETECTIVE (Bernard Cribbins).
MC. Cat no: **CAB 344**. Released on Chivers Audio Books, '91 by Chivers Audio Books, Green Dragon Audio Visual. Note: 6 cassettes.
MCSET. Cat no: **1061H**. Released on Travellers Tales, '91 by Travellers Tales. Note: 6 cassettes.

DANGEROUS IN LOVE (Bernard Cribbins).
MCSET. Cat no: **CAB 282**. Released on Chivers Audio Books, '91 by Chivers Audio Books, Green Dragon Audio Visual. Note: 6 cassettes.
MCSET. Cat no: **1062H**. Released on Travellers Tales, '91 by Travellers Tales. Note: 6 cassettes.

IN MY WILDEST DREAMS (Hywel Bennett).
MCSET. Cat no: **ZBBC 1216**. Released on BBC Radio Collection, Jul '91 by BBC Records. Note: ISBN No: 0563 409681

VIRGIN SOLDIERS, THE (Hywel Bennett).
MCSET. Cat no: **ZC SWD 360**. Released on ASV (Academy Sound & Vision), Oct '89 by Academy Sound & Vision Records. Note: 2 cassettes. Playing time: 2 3/4 hours.

Thomas, Ross

EIGHTH DWARF, THE (Frank Muller).
MCSET. Cat no: **RB 84120**. Released on Recorded Books, Jun '92 by Isis Audio Books. Note: 6 Cassettes. Playing time: 8 hours.

Thomas, Ruth

RUNAWAYS, THE (Judi Dench).
MCSET. Cat no: **TS 428**. Released on Tellastory, Jul '92 by Random Century Audiobooks. Note: 2 cassettes. ISBN no. 1856561941

Thompson, Estelle

HUNTER IN THE DARK (Peter Joyce).
MCSET. Cat no: **1748T**. Released on Travellers Tales, '91 by Travellers Tales. Note: 4 Cassettes.
MCSET. Cat no: **1854964445**. Released on Bramhope, '91 by Ulverscroft Soundings. Note: 4 Cassettes.

THREE WOMEN IN THE HOUSE (Judith Porter).
MCSET. Cat no: **1672T**. Released on Travellers Tales, '91 by Travellers Tales. Note: 4 Cassettes.
MCSET. Cat no: **1854963945**. Released on Bramhope, '91 by Ulverscroft Soundings. Note: 5 Cassettes.

TO CATCH A RAINBOW (Unknown narrator(s)).
MCSET. Cat no: **1854964232**. Released on Bramhope, '91 by Ulverscroft Soundings. Note: 4 Cassettes.

TOAST TO COUSIN JULIAN, A (Unknown narrator(s)).
MCSET. Cat no: **1854962728**. Released on Bramhope, '91 by Ulverscroft Soundings. Note: 5 Cassettes.

Thompson, E.V.

GOD'S HIGHLANDER (David Rintoul).
MCSET. Cat no: **CAB 618**. Released on Chivers Audio Books, '91 by Chivers Audio Books, Green Dragon Audio Visual. Note: 12 Cassettes.

SINGING SPEARS (Jon Cartwright).
MCSET. Cat no: **1469/70F**. Released on Travellers Tales, '91 by Travellers Tales. Note: 12 Cassettes.
MCSET. Cat no: **OAS 90036**. Re-

leased on Oasis Audio Books, '91 by Isis Audio Books. Note: 12 Cassettes.

Thomson, Daisy
FROM SOLITUDE WITH LOVE (Unknown narrator(s)).
MCSET. Cat no: **1854962736**. Released on Bramhope, '91 by Ulverscroft Soundings. Note: 4 Cassettes.

IN LOVE IN VIENNA (Unknown narrator(s)).
MCSET. Cat no: **1854962353**. Released on Bramhope, '91 by Ulverscroft Soundings. Note: 4 Cassettes.

Thoreau, Henry David
CIVIL DISOBEDIENCE (Archibald MacLeish).
MC. Cat no: **1263**. Released on Caedmon (USA), '89 by Caedmon Records (USA), Bond Street Music.

THOREAU'S WORLD (Unknown narrator(s)).
MCSET. Cat no: **2052**. Released on Caedmon (USA), '89 by Caedmon Records (USA), Bond Street Music. Note: 2 cassettes

WALDEN (Archibald MacLeish).
MC. Cat no: **1261**. Released on Caedmon (USA), '89 by Caedmon Records (USA), Bond Street Music.

Thorne, Nerina
AMSTERDAM AFFAIR (Margaret Holt).
MCSET. Cat no: **1854965948**. Released on Trio, Apr '93 by EMI Records. Note: Playing time: 60 minutes.

Thorpe, Kay
NOT WANTED ON VOYAGE (Georgina Melville).
MCSET. Cat no: **PMB 008**. Released on Mills & Boon, '88. Note: 2 cassettes.

Thubron, Colin
FALLING (Ian Craig).
MCSET. Cat no: **IAB 92063**. Released on Isis Audio Books, Jun '92. Note: 5 Cassettes. Playing time: 5 hours, 19 mins.

Thurber, James
CURB IN THE SKY (And Other Thurber Stories) (Peter Ustinov).
LP. Cat no: **TC 1641**. Released on Caedmon (USA), Sep '80 by Caedmon Records (USA), Bond Street Music.
MC. Cat no: **CP 1641**. Released on Caedmon (USA), Feb '81 by Caedmon Records (USA), Bond Street Music.

THIRTEEN CLOCKS, THE (Peter Ustinov).
MCSET. Cat no: **2089**. Released on Caedmon (USA), '89 by Caedmon Records (USA), Bond Street Music.

UNICORN IN THE GARDEN, THE (Peter Ustinov).
MC. Cat no: **1398**. Released on Caedmon (USA), '89 by Caedmon Records (USA), Bond Street Music.

Tilbury, Quenna
PRISONER OF A PROMISE (Isobel Spouse).
MCSET. Cat no: **CLT 1011**. Released on Candlelight, '88 by AVLS (Audio-Visual Library Services).

Timperley, Rosemary
THAT YEAR AT THE OFFICE (Jane Jermyn).
MCSET. Cat no: **1081R**. Released on Travellers Tales, '91 by Travellers Tales. Note: 4 Cassettes.
MCSET. Cat no: **1854962019**. Released on Bramhope, '91 by Ulverscroft Soundings. Note: 4 Cassettes.

Timpson, John
PAPER TRAIL (John Timpson).
MCSET. Cat no: **CAB 627**. Released on Chivers Audio Books, Sep '91 by Chivers Audio Books, Green Dragon Audio Visual. Note: 8 cassettes

Tinniswood, Peter
MORE TALES FROM A LONG ROOM (Robin Bailey).
MC. Cat no: **TCLFP 417117-5**. Released on Listen For Pleasure, '83 by EMI Records.

TALES FROM A LONG ROOM (Volume 1 and 2) (Robin Bailey).
MCSET. Cat no: **LISF 0001/0002**. Released on Listen Productions, Nov '84.

TALES FROM A LONG ROOM (Robin Bailey).
MCSET. Cat no: **ZBBC 1021**. Released on BBC, Sep '88 by BBC Records, Taylors. Note: ISBN No: 0563 225815

UNCLE MORT'S NORTH COUNTRY (Various artists).
Note: Includes: My Friend Dornford and other stories. With Peter Skellern as Carter.
MCSET. Cat no: **ZBBC 1103**. Released on BBC Radio Collection, May '90 by BBC Records. Note: ISBN No: 0563 410000.

UNCLE MORT'S SOUTH COUNTRY (Various artists).
MCSET. Cat no: **ZBBC 1176**. Released on BBC Radio Collection, Oct '90 by BBC Records. Note: ISBN No: 0563 412798.

Todd, Barbara
WORZEL GUMMIDGE See under Waterhouse, Keith

Todd, H.E.
STORYTIME TOP TEN (Volume 6) (H. E. Todd).
Note: Music by Major Records. Includes Silly Shoes, The Sick Cow, A Funny Thing Happened and The Walking Pyjamas. For children aged 3 - 5 years old.
MC. Cat no: **VCA 060**. Released on VFM Cassettes, Jan '85 by VFM Cassettes, Midland Records, Crusader Marketing Co., Taylors, Morley Audio Services.

STORYTIME TOP TEN (Volume 8) (Ronnie Stevens).
Note: For children aged 3 - 7 years. With music by Major Records and De Wolfe. Includes The Man who Knew Better, Spoon on Holiday and Cuckoo Clock.
MC. Cat no: **VCA 062**. Released on VFM Cassettes, Jan '85 by VFM Cassettes, Midland Records, Crusader Marketing Co., Taylors, Morley Audio Services.

Tolkien, J.R.R.
HOBBIT (And the Fellowship of the Ring) (Unknown narrator(s)).
Note: Poems and prose from the first volume of *The Lord of the Rings*.
MC. Cat no: **1477**. Released on Caedmon (USA), '89 by Caedmon Records (USA), Bond Street Music.

HOBBIT, THE (Unknown narrator(s)).
LP. Cat no: **TC 1477**. Released on Caedmon (USA), Jul '77 by Caedmon Records (USA), Bond Street Music.
MC. Cat no: **CP 1477**. Released on Caedmon (USA), Jul '77 by Caedmon Records (USA), Bond Street Music.
MC. Cat no: **0600560570**. Released on Hamlyn Books On Tape, '88, Bond Street Music.
MCSET. Cat no: **MCFR 105/7**. Released on Conifer, '88 by Conifer Records, Jazz Music.

HOBBIT, THE (Nicol Williamson).
MCSET. Cat no: **9083F**. Released on Travellers Tales, '91 by Travellers Tales. Note: 3 Cassettes.

HOBBIT, THE (Various artists).
MCSET. Cat no: **ZBBC 1038**. Released on BBC Radio Collection, Sep '91 by BBC Records. Note: ISBN No: 0563 225610. 4 Cassettes.
MCSET. Cat no: **9168F**. Released on Travellers Tales, '91 by Travellers Tales. Note: 4 Cassettes.

J.R.R. TOLKIEN COLLECTION, THE (J.R.R. Tolkien).
Note: Read by the Author and includes excerpts from The Hobbit, The Lord Of The Rings, Poems & Songs Of The Middle Earth and also features the Silmarillion "Of Beren and Luthien".
MC. Cat no: **0001042734**. Released on Collins-Caedmon, '88 by Collins Audio, Taylors, Bond Street Music.

LORD OF THE RINGS (Two Towers & the Return of the King) (Unknown narrator(s)).
MC. Cat no: **1478**. Released on Caedmon (USA), '88 by Caedmon Records (USA), Bond Street Music.

LORD OF THE RINGS (Various artists).
Note: Radio 4 production starring Michael Hordern, Ian Holm, Robert Stephens and Peter Woodthorpe.
LPS. Cat no: **RINGS 1**. Released on BBC, Oct '87 by BBC Records, Taylors. Note: 13 hour-long tapes.

LORD OF THE RINGS (Unknown

narrator(s)).
LP. Cat no: **REH 415.** Released on BBC, Jul '81 by BBC Records, Taylors. Note: 13 hour-long tapes.

MC. Cat no: **ZCR 415.** Released on BBC, Jun '91 by BBC Records, Taylors. Note: 13 hour-long tapes.

LP. Cat no: **TC 1478.** Released on Caedmon (USA), Jul '77 by Caedmon Records (USA), Bond Street Music. Note: 13 hour-long tapes.

MC. Cat no: **CP 1478.** Released on Caedmon (USA), Jul '77 by Caedmon Records (USA), Bond Street Music. Note: 13 hour-long tapes.

MCSET. Cat no: **ZBBC 1050.** Released on BBC Radio Collection, '91 by BBC Records. Note: 13 Cassettes.

MCSET. Cat no: **9070/9071F.** Released on Travellers Tales, '91 by Travellers Tales. Note: 13 Cassettes.

LORD OF THE RINGS, PART 1 (The Fellowship of the Ring) (Rob Inglis).
MCSET. Cat no: **1581/2F.** Released on Travellers Tales, '91 by Travellers Tales. Note: 14 Cassettes.

MCSET. Cat no: **IAB 90121.** Released on Isis Audio Books, '91. Note: 14 Cassettes.

LORD OF THE RINGS, PART 2 (The Two Towers) (Rob Inglis).
MCSET. Cat no: **1583/4F.** Released on Travellers Tales, '91 by Travellers Tales. Note: 12 Cassettes.

MCSET. Cat no: **IAB 90122.** Released on Isis Audio Books, '91. Note: 12 Cassettes.

LORD OF THE RINGS, PART 3 (The Return of the King) (Rob Inglis).
MCSET. Cat no: **1585/6F.** Released on Travellers Tales, '91 by Travellers Tales. Note: 12 Cassettes.

MCSET. Cat no: **IAB 90123.** Released on Isis Audio Books, '91. Note: 12 Cassettes.

POEMS AND SONGS OF MIDDLE EARTH (Unknown narrator(s)).
LP. Cat no: **TC 1231.** Released on Caedmon (USA), Jul '77 by Caedmon Records (USA), Bond Street Music.

MC. Cat no: **CP 1231.** Released on Caedmon (USA), Jul '77 by Caedmon Records (USA), Bond Street Music.

SILMARILLION, THE (Of Beren and Luthien) (Unknown narrator(s)).
LP. Cat no: **TC 1564.** Released on Caedmon (USA), Nov '77 by Caedmon Records (USA), Bond Street Music.

MC. Cat no: **CDL 51564.** Released on Caedmon (USA), Nov '77 by Caedmon Records (USA), Bond Street Music.

SILMARILLION, THE (Of the Darkening of Valinor etc.) (Unknown narrator(s)).
LP. Cat no: **TC 1579.** Released on Caedmon (USA), Jul '79 by Caedmon Records (USA), Bond Street Music.

MC. Cat no: **CDL 51579.** Released on Caedmon (USA), Jul '79 by Caedmon Records (USA), Bond Street Music.

TOLKIEN GIFT SET (J R R & Christoper Tolkien).
MCSET. Cat no: **HCA 81.** Released on Harper Collins, '92 by Harper Collins.

TOLKIEN SOUNDBOOK (Various artists).
MCSET. Cat no: **101.** Released on Caedmon (USA), Sep '88 by Caedmon Records (USA), Bond Street Music.

Tolstoy, Leo
ANNA KARENINA (Irene Worth).
LP. Cat no: **TC 1571.** Released on Caedmon (USA), '79 by Caedmon Records (USA), Bond Street Music.

MC. Cat no: **CDL 1571.** Released on Caedmon (USA), '78 by Caedmon Records (USA), Bond Street Music.

Tomlinson, Jill
OWL WHO WAS AFRAID OF THE DARK, THE (Maureen Lipman).
MCSET. Cat no: **CTC 007.** Released on Cover to Cover, Sep '86 by Cover to Cover Cassettes.

Toole, John Kennedy
(See under Kennedy Toole, John)

Townsend, Sue
GROWING PAINS OF ADRIAN MOLE, THE (Simon Schatzberger).
MCSET. Cat no: **LFP 7184.** Released on Listen For Pleasure, Mar '85 by EMI Records.

MC. Cat no: **1166F.** Released on Travellers Tales, '91 by Travellers Tales. Note: 2 Cassettes.

SECRET DIARY OF ADRIAN MOLE (Alex Lowe).
MC. Cat no: **TTC/K 02.** Released on Talking Tape Company, '84, Conifer Records.

MCSET. Cat no: **TTC 2014.** Released on Talking Tape Company, Apr '9, Conifer Records. Note: 2 Cassettes. Playing time: 2 hours. ISBN No: 87250014.

SECRET DIARY OF ADRIAN MOLE (Part 1) (Alex Lowe).
MC. Cat no: **TTC/K 01.** Released on Talking Tape Company, '84, Conifer Records.

SECRET DIARY OF ADRIAN MOLE AGED 13 & 3/4 (Unknown narrator(s)).
MC. Cat no: **TTC/K 11.** Released on Talking Tape Company, '88, Conifer Records.

Townshend Bickers, R.
CAULDRON, THE (John Hendry).
MCSET. Cat no: **1742T.** Released on Travellers Tales, '91 by Travellers Tales. Note: 4 Cassettes.

MCSET. Cat no: **1854964313.** Released on Bramhope, '91 by Ulverscroft Soundings. Note: 4 Cassettes.

GINGER LACEY - FIGHTER PILOT (John Hendry).
MCSET. Cat no: **1854964593.** Released on Bramhope, Jun '91 by Ulverscroft Soundings. Note: ISBN No: 1 85496 459 3.

Tozzi, Federico
CON GLI OCCHI CHIUSI.
MCSET. Cat no: **1020L.** Released on Travellers Tales, '91 by Travellers Tales. Note: 4 cassettes.

Traditional
ADVENTURES OF ROBIN HOOD, THE (Anthony Quayle).
Note: Adapted by Paul Cresick.
MC. Cat no: **109.** Released on Caedmon (USA), '88 by Caedmon Records (USA), Bond Street Music.

ADVENTURES OF ROBIN HOOD, THE (Keith Barron).
Note: Abridged. Adapted by Patricia Leitch.
MCSET. Cat no: **LFP 7426.** Released on Listen For Pleasure, '88 by EMI Records.

ADVENTURES OF ROBIN HOOD, THE (Various authors).
Note: Adapted by Patricia Leitch.
MC. Cat no: **SBC 109.** Released on Caedmon (USA), '81 by Caedmon Records (USA), Bond Street Music.

ADVENTURES OF ROBIN HOOD, THE (Keith Barron).
Note: Adapted by Patricia Leitch.
MCSET. Cat no: **9052F.** Released on Travellers Tales, '91 by Travellers Tales. Note: 2 Cassettes.

ADVENTURES OF SINBAD THE SAILOR (Volume 1 - Voyages 1-4) (Terry Jones).
Note: Adapted by Jean Adamson.
MC. Cat no: **MCLIS 105.** Released on Listen, '91, Cartel. Note: 60 minutes.

ADVENTURES OF SINBAD THE SAILOR (Peter Bartlett).
Note: Adapted by Jean Adamson.
MC. Cat no: **TS 312.** Released on Bartlett Bliss, '91 by Bartlett Bliss Productions Ltd..

ADVENTURES OF SINBAD THE SAILOR (Volume 2 - Voyages 5-7) (Terry Jones).
Note: Adapted by Jean Adamson.
MC. Cat no: **MCLIS 106.** Released on Listen, '91, Cartel. Note: 40 mins.

ALADDIN (Unknown narrator(s)).
MC. Cat no: **PLB 129.** Released on Tell-A-Tale, Oct '84 by Pickwick Records, Taylors, Clyde Factors.

ALADDIN (Pantomine Cassettes) (Various artists).
MC. Cat no: **ST 410.** Released on Cassettes For Young People, Nov '91 by Cassettes For Young People Lmd, DMS Dist..

ALADDIN AND ALI BABA (John Graham).
MC. Cat no: **TS 326.** Released on Tellastory, Apr '92 by Random Century Audiobooks. Note: ISBN no, 1856560155

ALADDIN AND HIS LAMP (Various artists).
Note: Tales from Arabia. Includes:

Deer and the Jaguar, The Beef Tongue of Orula, Uncle Bookie, The Balsam Tree and The Soupstone.
MC. Cat no: **ANV 653.** Released on Anvil Cassettes, '85 by Anvil Cassettes, Chivers Audio Books.

ALADDIN AND HIS LAMP (Dennis Lee).
MC. Cat no: **1250.** Released on Caedmon (USA), '89 by Caedmon Records (USA), Bond Street Music.

ALADDIN AND HIS MAGIC LAMP (And Other Favourite Stories for Children) (Peter Whitbread & Gillian Blake).
Note: Includes Aladdin and his Magic Lamp, The Little Match Seller, The Fifth Voyage of Sinbad and The Sixth Voyage of Sinbad. For ages 5 - 9.
MC. Cat no: **VCA 611.** Released on VFM Cassettes, Jul '85 by VFM Cassettes, Midland Records, Crusader Marketing Co., Taylors, Morley Audio Services.

ALADDIN AND THE WONDERFUL LAMP (Terry Jones).
MC. Cat no: **LP 214.** Released on Listen Productions, Nov '84.

ALEXANDER THE GREAT (Various artists).
Note: Includes: The Turkish Magician.
MC. Cat no: **ANV 617.** Released on Anvil Cassettes, '81 by Anvil Cassettes, Chivers Audio Books.

ALI BABA (Unknown narrator(s)).
MC. Cat no: **HA 5.** Released on Happy Learning, Aug '91 by Happy Learning Co.Ltd., Castle Sales & Marketing.

ALI BABA AND THE FORTY THIEVES (Classic Tales) (Unknown narrator(s)).
Note: Book and cassette.
MC. Cat no: **PLBC 139.** Released on Tell-A-Tale, '84 by Pickwick Records, Taylors, Clyde Factors.

ALI BABA AND THE FORTY THIEVES (And Other Favourite Stories) (Peter Whitbread & Gillian Blake).
Note: Includes Ali Baba and the Forty Thieves, The First Voyage of Sinbad, The Thief of Baghdad and The Second Voyage of Sinbad. For ages 5 - 9.
MC. Cat no: **VCA 609.** Released on VFM Cassettes, '85 by VFM Cassettes, Midland Records, Crusader Marketing Co., Taylors, Morley Audio Services.

ALI BABA AND THE FORTY THIEVES (Dennis Lee).
MC. Cat no: **1251.** Released on Caedmon (USA), '89 by Caedmon Records (USA), Bond Street Music.

ALI BABA AND THE FORTY THIEVES (Unknown narrator(s)).
Note: Tales from Arabia. Includes: Not Yours to Yours, The Camlet Flower, Judgement of Karakoush, King John and the Abbot of Canterbury, The Snake and the Dreams, The King's Tower and Why the Parrot Repeats Men's Words.

MC. Cat no: **ANV 654.** Released on Anvil Cassettes, '85 by Anvil Cassettes, Chivers Audio Books.

ARABIAN NIGHTS: ALADDIN (Terry Jones).
MC. Cat no: **LPMC 214.** Released on Listen, '88, Cartel.

ARABIAN TALES, LEGENDS AND ROMANCES (Unknown narrator(s)).
MC. Cat no: **A 7961.** Released on Exeter Tapes, '91 by Drakes Educational Associates.

BLACK FAIRY TALES (Claudia McNeil).
Note: Gathered from the Bantu-speaking tribes of Africa, these tales of the Swazis and Shangani are resplendent with customs and lore. Adapted by Terry Berger.
MC. Cat no: **1425.** Released on Caedmon (USA), '90 by Caedmon Records (USA), Bond Street Music.

BOOK OF MERLYN, THE (King Arthur and Merlin's Animal Council) (Christopher Plummer).
Note: Adapted by T.H. White.
MC. Cat no: **0001051644.** Released on Collins-Caedmon, '91 by Collins Audio, Taylors, Bond Street Music.

BOOK OF MERLYN, THE (Christopher Plummer).
Note: Adapted by T.H. White.
LP. Cat no: **TC 1852.** Released on Caedmon (USA), Jul '79 by Caedmon Records (USA), Bond Street Music.
MC. Cat no: **CDL 51852.** Released on Caedmon (USA), Jul '79 by Caedmon Records (USA), Bond Street Music.

CINDERELLA (Various artists).
MC. Cat no: **STC 304A.** Released on VFM Cassettes, '88 by VFM Cassettes, Midland Records, Crusader Marketing Co., Taylors, Morley Audio Services.

CINDERELLA (Unknown narrator(s)).
MC. Cat no: **STK 003.** Released on Stick-A-Tale, Jan '89 by Pickwick Records.

MC. Cat no: **DIS 027.** Released on Pickwick, Jun '91 by Pickwick Records, Clyde Factors, Taylors, Arabesque, Solomon & Peres, I & B Records, Prism Leisure, Outlet Records.

CINDERELLA (Well Loved Tales age up to 9) (Unknown narrator(s)).
MC. Cat no: **TS 301.** Released on Tellastory, Oct '79 by Random Century Audiobooks.

MC. Cat no: **D 6DC.** Released on Disneyland, Dec '82 by Disneyland-Vista Records (USA).

MC. Cat no: **PLB 61.** Released on Tell-A-Tale, '83 by Pickwick Records, Taylors, Clyde Factors.

CINDERELLA (And Other Fairy Tales) (Claire Bloom).
MC. Cat no: **1330.** Released on Caedmon (USA), '88 by Caedmon Records (USA), Bond Street Music.

CINDERELLA (And Babes In The Wood) (Leslie Crowther).
MC. Cat no: **LPMC 300.** Released on Listen, '88, Cartel.

MC. Cat no: **MCLIS 104.** Released on Listen, '91, Cartel.

CINDERELLA (Well Loved Tales age up to 9) (Unknown narrator(s)).
MLP. Cat no: **D 308.** Released on Disneyland, Dec '82 by Disneyland-Vista Records (USA).
LP. Cat no: **D 3908.** Released on Disneyland, Dec '82 by Disneyland-Vista Records (USA).

CINDERELLA (And Other Stories) (Unknown narrator(s)).
Note: Book and cassettes. Adapted by Buddy Childers. Includes: The Four Clever Brothers, Bright Brownie, Fire on the Mountain, The Brave Tailor and The Fibbers.
MC. Cat no: **ANV 661.** Released on Anvil Cassettes, '85 by Anvil Cassettes, Chivers Audio Books.

CINDERELLA (Pantomine Cassettes) (Various artists).
MC. Cat no: **ST 411.** Released on Cassettes For Young People, Nov '91 by Cassettes For Young People Lmd, DMS Dist..

CINDERELLA (Well Loved Tales age up to 9) (Unknown narrator(s)).
7"**PD.** Cat no: **D 3107.** Released on Disneyland, Dec '82 by Disneyland-Vista Records (USA).

COMING OF ARTHUR, THE (Various artists).
Note: Adapted by Alfred Tennyson. Includes: Balin and Balan.
MC. Cat no: **ANV 605.** Released on Anvil Cassettes, Jan '81 by Anvil Cassettes, Chivers Audio Books.

DICK WHITTINGTON (Gyles Brandreth).
MC. Cat no: **LPMC 301.** Released on Listen, '88, Cartel.

DICK WHITTINGTON AND HIS CAT (And Other Tales) (Claire Bloom).
MC. Cat no: **1091.** Released on Caedmon (USA), '88 by Caedmon Records (USA), Bond Street Music.

DICK WHITTINGTON AND HIS CAT (Well Loved Tales Up To Age 9) (Unknown narrator(s)).
MC. Cat no: **PLB 56.** Released on Tell-A-Tale, '88 by Pickwick Records, Taylors, Clyde Factors.

DON'T KNOW BOY, THE (Various artists).
Tracks / Don't know boy, The: Various artists / Comorre the accursed: Various artists / North-West wind, The: Various artists / Foster brother, The: Various artists / King's godson, The: Various artists / Tristram and Ysondeḋ: Various artists.
Note: Tales from France.
MC. Cat no: **ANV 656.** Released on Anvil Cassettes, '85 by Anvil Cassettes, Chivers Audio Books.

EMPEROR AND THE NIGHTIN-

GALE, THE (And Other Stories) (Unknown narrator(s)).
Note: Includes: The Master Thief, The Three Oranges and The Three Musicians.
MC. Cat no: **ANV 650.** Released on Anvil Cassettes, Jul '82 by Anvil Cassettes, Chivers Audio Books.

EMPEROR AND THE NIGHTINGALE, THE (Unknown narrator(s)).
Note: Book and cassette.
MC. Cat no: **PLB 238.** Released on Tell-A-Tale, '88 by Pickwick Records, Taylors, Clyde Factors.

FABLES OF INDIA (Zia Mohyeddin).
MC. Cat no: **1168.** Released on Caedmon (USA), '89 by Caedmon Records (USA), Bond Street Music.

FAIRY TALES (Philip Schofield & Tony Robinson).
Note: Puss in Boots, Cinderella, Jack and the Beanstalk, Goldilocks and the Three Bears.
CD. Cat no: **CDMFP 5951.** Released on MFP, Dec '91 by EMI Records, Solomon & Peres.
MC. Cat no: **TCMFP 5951.** Released on MFP, Dec '91 by EMI Records, Solomon & Peres.

FAIRY TALES (Unknown narrator(s)).
Note: Includes: The Corn Dooly, The Silly King, The Wonderful Cake Horse, The Fly-By-Night, Three Raindrops, The Butterfly Who Sang, Jack One-Step, The Glass Cupboard, Katy-Make-Sure, The Wooden City, The Ship of Bones, Simple Peter's Mirror, Brave Molly, The Sea Tiger, The Wind Ghosts, The Big Noses, Fish of the World, Tim O'Leary, Witch and the Rainbow Cat, The Monster Tree, The Snuff-Box, The Man Who Owned the Earth, Why Birds Sing in the Morning, The Key, The Wine of Li-Po, Island of Purple Fruits, The Beast with a Thousand Teeth, Faraway Castle, Doctor Bonocolus's Devil and The Boat That Went Nowhere.
MCSET. Cat no: **414 760-4.** Released on Argo (Polygram), Oct '85 by PolyGram Classics **Deleted** Jan '89.

FAIRY TALES FOR YOU (Unknown narrator(s)).
MCSET. Cat no: **DTO 10533.** Released on Ditto, '88 by Pickwick Records, Midland Records.

FAVOURITE EUROPEAN TALES (Katherine Hepburn).
Note: Includes: Jack and the Beanstalk, The Nightingale, The Musicians of Bremen, Tattercoats, The Emperor's New Clothes and Beauty and the Beast.
MC. Cat no: **LFP 41 7180 5.** Released on Listen For Pleasure, Oct '84 by EMI Records. Note: Playing time: 1 1/4 hours.

FAVOURITE FAIRY STORIES (Sally James).

Note: Book and cassette.
LP. Cat no: **STMP 9019.** Released on Super Tempo, May '84 by Warwick Records, Taylors, Solomon & Peres, Sony Music Operations.
MC. Cat no: **STMP4 9019.** Released on Super Tempo, May '84 by Warwick Records, Taylors, Solomon & Peres, Sony Music Operations.
MC. Cat no: **TBC 9304.** Released on Tempo Storytime, May '84 by Warwick Records, Celtic Music.

FAVOURITE FAIRY TALES (Volume 1) (Various artists).
Note: For children aged 3 - 9 years. Includes Sleeping Beauty, The Adventures of Little Peachling, The Foxes Wedding and Cut Sparrow.
LP. Cat no: **SPR 8520.** Released on Spot, Feb '83 by Pickwick Records.
MC. Cat no: **SPC 8520.** Released on Spot, Feb '83 by Pickwick Records.
MC. Cat no: **VCA 106.** Released on VFM Cassettes, Jan '85 by VFM Cassettes, Midland Records, Crusader Marketing Co., Taylors, Morley Audio Services.

FIRST ANANSI STORY, THE (Various artists).
Note: Tales from The West Indies. Includes: How Bear Learned to Swim, How Anansi got his Limp, How Crab got his Shell, Only Birds May Fly, Tiger's Stew and Anansi's Birthday.
MC. Cat no: **ANV 632.** Released on Anvil Cassettes, Jan '81 by Anvil Cassettes, Chivers Audio Books.

FOLK TALES FROM AROUND THE WORLD (Ronnie Stevens).
Note: For 4 to 8 year olds. Adapted by Lelia Berg.
MC. Cat no: **A 004.** Released on Green Dragon, '91 by Green Dragon Audio Visual.

FOLK TALES OF THE TRIBES OF AFRICA (Eartha Kitt).
MC. Cat no: **1267.** Released on Caedmon (USA), '88 by Caedmon Records (USA), Bond Street Music.

FOUR TRADITIONAL FAIRY TALES (Various artists).
LP. Cat no: **TMP 9005.** Released on Tempo, Nov '79 by Warwick Records, Celtic Music, Henry Hadaway Organisation.
MC. Cat no: **TMP4 9005.** Released on Tempo, Nov '79 by Warwick Records, Celtic Music, Henry Hadaway Organisation.

GAWAIN AND THE GREEN KNIGHT (Various artists).
Note: Includes: Lancelot on the Quest.
MC. Cat no: **ANV 606.** Released on Anvil Cassettes, Jan '81 by Anvil Cassettes, Chivers Audio Books.

GAWAIN AND THE GREEN KNIGHT AND THE PEARL (Various artists).
Note: In Middle English
MC. Cat no: **1192.** Released on Caedmon (USA), '88 by Caedmon Records (USA), Bond Street Music.

GINGERBREAD MAN, THE (Susan Hampshire).
MC. Cat no: **3605.** Released on Storytime Cassettes, Aug '83 by VFM Cassettes, Iona Records, Rio Communications.

GIRL OF THE GREAT MOUNTAIN, THE (Unknown narrator(s)).
Note: Includes: Bear Woman and the Little Navaho, Black Bull and the Magic Drum, Magic Bag of Golden Eagle, Sleeper of the Cave of Darkness and Three Brothers.
MC. Cat no: **ANV 635.** Released on Anvil Cassettes, '81 by Anvil Cassettes, Chivers Audio Books.

GOLDILOCKS (Unknown narrator(s)).
MC. Cat no: **STC 008.** Released on VFM Cassettes, Jun '88 by VFM Cassettes, Midland Records, Crusader Marketing Co., Taylors, Morley Audio Services.
MC. Cat no: **STC 304C.** Released on VFM Cassettes, '88 by VFM Cassettes, Midland Records, Crusader Marketing Co., Taylors, Morley Audio Services.

GOLDILOCKS AND THE THREE BEARS (Well Loved Tales Age Up To 9) (Unknown narrator(s)).
Note: Book & cassette
MC. Cat no: **PLB 53.** Released on Tell-A-Tale, Feb '83 by Pickwick Records, Taylors, Clyde Factors.

GOLDILOCKS AND THE THREE BEARS (Unknown narrator(s)).
MC. Cat no: **FT 112.** Released on Cassettes For Young People, May '92 by Cassettes For Young People Lmd, DMS Dist.. Note: ISBN no. 187144912X. 20 mins approx.
MC. Cat no: **STK 006.** Released on Stick-A-Tale, Jan '89 by Pickwick Records.

GOLDILOCKS AND THE THREE BEARS (And Other Stories) (Unknown narrator(s)).
Note: Stories include: Goldilocks and the Three Bears - Read by Dorit Wells, Sleeping Beauty - Read by Peter Barlett, Cock the mouse and the Little Red Hen - Read by Barbara Bliss, Hansel and Gretel - Read by Barbara Bliss and Little Red Riding Hodd - Read by Barabara Bliss.
MC. Cat no: **TS 339.** Released on Tellastory, Dec '86 by Random Century Audiobooks.

GOLDILOCKS AND THE THREE BEARS (Claire Bloom).
MC. Cat no: **1392.** Released on Caedmon (USA), Jul '88 by Caedmon Records (USA), Bond Street Music.
MC. Cat no: **000184525X.** Released on Harper Collins, '91 by Harper Collins. Note: Playing time: 46 mins.

GREAT FAIRY TALES OF THE WORLD (Unknown narrator(s)).
MCSET. Cat no: **DTO 10578.** Released on Ditto, '88 by Pickwick Records, Midland Records.

HOUR OF FAIRY STORIES, AN (Various artists).
Note: Includes: Cincderella, Goldilocks and the Three Bars, Little Red Riding Hood, Jack and the Beanstalk, Rumpelstiltskin and Sleeping Beauty.
MC. Cat no: **HR 8169.** Released on Hour Of Pleasure, Sep '88 by EMI Records.

HOW ROBIN BECAME AN OUTLAW (Anthony Quayle).
Note: Adapted by Paul Cresick.
MC. Cat no: **1369.** Released on Caedmon (USA), '88 by Caedmon Records (USA), Bond Street Music.

HOW TIGER GOT HIS STRIPES (Various artists).
Note: Includes: Postman Snake, Candlefly and Mancrow, The Perfect Little Gentleman, Ma ncrow's Crow, Rubber Man and The Wives in the Sky.
MC. Cat no: **ANV 668.** Released on Anvil Cassettes, '85 by Anvil Cassettes, Chivers Audio Books.

JACK AND THE BEANSTALK (And Dick Whittington) (Gyles Brandreth).
MC. Cat no: **MCLIS 103.** Released on Listen, '91, Cartel. Note: 60 mins.

JACK AND THE BEANSTALK (Well Loved Tales Age Up To 9) (Unknown narrator(s)).
Note: Book and cassette. Includes: The Spindle, the Shuttle and the Needle, Teh Stork Caliph, The Fisherman and his Wife and The Ninepence and the Norka.
MC. Cat no: **ANV 652.** Released on Anvil Cassettes, Jul '82 by Anvil Cassettes, Chivers Audio Books.
MC. Cat no: **PLB 60.** Released on Tell-A-Tale, Feb '83 by Pickwick Records, Taylors, Clyde Factors.

JACK AND THE BEANSTALK (Unknown narrator(s)).
MC. Cat no: **STK 020.** Released on Stick-A-Tale, Jan '89 by Pickwick Records.

KING ARTHUR (Freddie Jones).
MC. Cat no: **SQRL 12.** Released on Squirrel, Nov '81.

KING ARTHUR (Unknown narrator(s)).
MC. Cat no: **185656021X.** Released on Random Century, '91 by Random Century Audiobooks, Conifer Records. Note: Playing time: 60 Minutes.

KING ARTHUR (Christopher Plummer).
MC. Cat no: **CDL 51629.** Released on Caedmon (USA), '81 by Caedmon Records (USA), Bond Street Music.

KING ARTHUR AND HIS KNIGHTS (Anthony Hyde).
Note: Adapted by Alan Haines.
MC. Cat no: **TS 334.** Released on Tellastory, '91 by Random Century Audiobooks. Note: ISBN no. 185656021X

KING ARTHUR AND MERLIN'S ANIMAL COUNCIL (Christopher Plummer).
MC. Cat no: **1630.** Released on Caedmon (USA), '88 by Caedmon Records (USA), Bond Street Music.

KING ARTHUR - EXCALIBUR (Tales of King Arthur & his Knights) (Howard Pyle).
MC. Cat no: **1462.** Released on Caedmon (USA), '88 by Caedmon Records (USA), Bond Street Music.

LEGENDS OF THE CLANS (Various artists).
Note: Includes: Seal King's Daughter, The Glaistig, Raven's Rock and Dunvegan Banner.
MC. Cat no: **ANV 616.** Released on Anvil Cassettes, Jan '81 by Anvil Cassettes, Chivers Audio Books.

MAGIC QUERN, THE (Stories from Barra in Gaelic & English) (Unknown narrator(s)).
MC. Cat no: **30-463.** Released on Folktracks Cassettes, Nov '79, Roots Records.

MAGIC SWORD, THE (Various artists).
Note: Tales from Japan. Includes: Inchling, The Invisible Man, The Old Man and the Sparrow, Urashima and the Turtle, The Mouse's Husbund and The Farmer and his Dog.
MC. Cat no: **ANV 633.** Released on Anvil Cassettes, Jan '81 by Anvil Cassettes, Chivers Audio Books.

MARRIAGE OF GAWAIN, THE (Various artists).
Note: Stories of King Arthur.
MC. Cat no: **ANV 613.** Released on Anvil Cassettes, Jan '81 by Anvil Cassettes, Chivers Audio Books.

MERLIN AND PERCEVAL (Various artists).
MC. Cat no: **ANV 607.** Released on Anvil Cassettes, Jan '81 by Anvil Cassettes, Chivers Audio Books.

MOON PRINCESS, THE (Various artists).
Note: Tales from Japan. Includes: The Luck of the Sea and the Luck of the Mountains, Peach Boy and The Badger Kettle.
MC. Cat no: **ANV 666.** Released on Anvil Cassettes, '85 by Anvil Cassettes, Chivers Audio Books.

MOTHER GOOSE (Various artists).
MC. Cat no: **1091.** Released on Caedmon (USA), '88 by Caedmon Records (USA), Bond Street Music.

MY FAVOURITE FAIRY STORIES (Various artists).
Note: Read by Nanette Newman, Richard Norman, Judi Dench and Pete Murray.
MC. Cat no: **TC-LFP 7003.** Released on Listen For Pleasure, Nov '77 by EMI Records **Deleted** '88.

NUTCRACKER (Christopher Plummer).
MCSET. Cat no: **128.** Released on Caedmon (USA), '88 by Caedmon Records (USA), Bond Street Music.

ONCE UPON A TIME (Volume 2) (Various artists).
Note: Featuring Arthur Mullard, Una Stubbs, and Henry Cooper. Includes: Dick Whittington and his Cat, Lavender Blue, Sleeping Beauty, This Old Man, The Three Billy Goats Gruff, Oh Dear, What can the Matter Be?, Pease Pudding Hot, Emperor's New Clothes, The Spider and the Fly, Goldilocks and the Three Bears, Girls and Boys Come out to Play, Snow White and the Seven Dwarfs, Nursery Rhymes Medley and Times Talbes.
LP. Cat no: **CBR 1044.** Released on Premier (Sony), '89 by Premier Records, Spartan, Pinnacle.
MC. Cat no: **KCBR 1044.** Released on Premier (Sony), '89 by Premier Records, Spartan, Pinnacle.

ONCE UPON A TIME (Volume 3) (Various artists).
Note: Featuring Ed Stewart, Una Stubbs and Penelope Keith. Includes: The Three Little Pigs, Little Tin Soldier, The Ugly Duckling, Little Red Riding Hood, Rumpelstiltskin, Hansel and Gretel and Thumbelina
LP. Cat no: **CBR 1045.** Released on Premier (Sony), '89 by Premier Records, Spartan, Pinnacle.
MC. Cat no: **KCBR 1045.** Released on Premier (Sony), '89 by Premier Records, Spartan, Pinnacle.

ONCE UPON A TIME (Volume 1) (Various artists).
Note: Featuring Barbara Windsor, Jon Pertwee, and Penelope Keith. Includes: Cinderella, When the Boat Comes in, Aladdin and his Lamp, Ding Dong Bell, The Little Gingerbread Boy, Beauty and the Beast, Cockles and Mussels, Pied Piper, Who Killed Cock Robin?, Tom Thumb and Polly Wolly Doodle.
LP. Cat no: **CBR 1032.** Released on Premier (Sony), '89 by Premier Records, Spartan, Pinnacle.
MC. Cat no: **KCBR 1032.** Released on Premier (Sony), '89 by Premier Records, Spartan, Pinnacle.

OUTLAW BAND OF SHERWOOD FOREST, THE (Anthony Quayle).
Note: Adapted by Paul Cresick.
MC. Cat no: **1370.** Released on Caedmon (USA), '88 by Caedmon Records (USA), Bond Street Music.

PEARL OF BABAR SHAH, THE (Various artists).
Note: Includes: Elephant, The Bird Who Told Lies, Queen Precious Pearl, The clever Jackal and The Man Who Loved Horses.
MC. Cat no: **ANV 638.** Released on Anvil Cassettes, Apr '80 by Anvil Cassettes, Chivers Audio Books.

PRINCE IVAN AND THE FROG PRINCESS (Natalia Makarova).
MC. Cat no: **13491 6003 4.** Released on Delos, Dec '90.

PRINCESS AND THE FROG (well

loved Tales Age Up To 9) (Unknown narrator(s)).
Note: Book and cassette.
MC. Cat no: **PLB 64**. Released on Tell-A-Tale, '83 by Pickwick Records, Taylors, Clyde Factors.

PRINCESS FEROZSHAH AND THE HORSE PRINCE (Various artists).
Note: Includes: The Weaver and the Devh, The Water Carrier and the Three Walnuts, Rustum and the Iron Fortress, The Shah's Ring and The Magnificent Slippers.
MC. Cat no: **ANV 602**. Released on Anvil Cassettes, Jan '81 by Anvil Cassettes, Chivers Audio Books.

PUSS IN BOOTS (And Jack In the Beanstalks) (J Graham).
MC. Cat no: **TS 330**. Released on Tellastory, Jan '87 by Random Century Audiobooks.

PUSS IN BOOTS (Also See under Charles Perrault) (Unknown narrator(s)).

PUSS IN BOOTS (And Sleeping Beauty) (Dora Bryan).
MC. Cat no: **MCLIS 102**. Released on Listen, '91, Cartel. Note: 55 mins.

PUSS IN BOOTS (Various artists).
MC. Cat no: **ST 412**. Released on Cassettes For Young People, Nov '91 by Cassettes For Young People Lmd, DMS Dist..

PUSS IN BOOTS (Well Loved Tales Age Up To 9) (Unknown narrator(s)).
Note: Book and cassette. Includes: Bearskin, One Eye, Two Eyes and Three Eyes, Cinderella and The Little Farmer.
MC. Cat no: **ANV 621**. Released on Anvil Cassettes, Jan '81 by Anvil Cassettes, Chivers Audio Books.
MC. Cat no: **PLB 54**. Released on Tell-A-Tale, Feb '83 by Pickwick Records, Taylors, Clyde Factors.

RED RIDING HOOD (And Goldilocks) (Meg Ryan).
CD. Cat no: **WD 0718**. Released on Windham Hill, Jan '92 by Windham Hill Records (USA), New Note.
MC. Cat no: **WT 0718**. Released on Windham Hill, Jan '92 by Windham Hill Records (USA), New Note.

ROBIN AND HIS MERRY MEN (Anthony Quayle).
Note: Adapted by Paul Cresick.
MC. Cat no: **1372**. Released on Caedmon (USA), '88 by Caedmon Records (USA), Bond Street Music.

ROBIN HOOD (Unknown narrator(s)).
Note: Book and cassette.
MC. Cat no: **PLBC 178**. Released on Tell-A-Tale, '88 by Pickwick Records, Taylors, Clyde Factors.

ROBIN HOOD (Unknown narrator(s)).
MCSET. Cat no: **1856561127**. Released on Random Century, '91 by Random Century Audiobooks, Conifer Records. Note: Playing time: 42 minutes.

ROBIN HOOD (Anthony Hyde).
Note: Adapted by Roger Lancelyn Green.
MC. Cat no: **TS 327**. Released on Tellastory, '91 by Random Century Audiobooks. Note: ISBN no. 1856561127

ROBIN HOOD (Unknown narrator(s)).
Note: Ages up to 7 - 12 years.
MC. Cat no: **DIS 008**. Released on Disney (Read-a-long), Jul '90 by Disneyland Records.

ROBIN HOOD (Martin Jarvis).
MC. Cat no: **P 90038**. Released on Pinnacle, '79 by Pinnacle Records, Outlet Records, Music Sales Records.

ROBIN HOOD (Gabriel Woolf & David Brierly).
MC. Cat no: **SQRL 13**. Released on Squirrel, Nov '81.

ROBIN HOOD (And Other Favourite Stories) (Peter Whitbread & Gillian Blake).
Note: Includes Robin Hood, King Arthur and Excalibur, King Arthur's Dream and King Midas (the King Who Loved Gold). For ages 5 - 9.
MC. Cat no: **VCA 604**. Released on VFM Cassettes, Jul '85 by VFM Cassettes, Midland Records, Crusader Marketing Co., Taylors, Morley Audio Services.

ROBIN HOOD (Various artists).
MC. Cat no: **STC 301B**. Released on VFM Cassettes, '88 by VFM Cassettes, Midland Records, Crusader Marketing Co., Taylors, Morley Audio Services.

ROBIN HOOD (Various artists).
Note: Includes: Childe Roland, Young Bekie, Thomas the Rhymer and Little Lord Lorn.
MC. Cat no: **ANV 662**. Released on Anvil Cassettes, '85 by Anvil Cassettes, Chivers Audio Books.

ROBIN'S ADVENTURES WITH LITTLE JOHN (Anthony Quayle).
MC. Cat no: **1371**. Released on Caedmon (USA), '88 by Caedmon Records (USA), Bond Street Music.

ROBINSON CRUSOE (And Other Favourite Stories for Children) (Peter Whitbread & Gillian Blake).
Note: Includes Robinson Crusoe, The Third Voyage of Sinbad, The Fourth Voyage of Sinbad and Achmed and the Sultan's Daughter. For ages 5 - 9.
MC. Cat no: **VCA 610**. Released on VFM Cassettes, Jul '85 by VFM Cassettes, Midland Records, Crusader Marketing Co., Taylors, Morley Audio Services.

ROLAND AND OLIVER (Various artists).
Note: Tales from France. Includes: The Bell of Atri, King Robert and the Angel and Sir Huon the Brave.
MC. Cat no: **ANV 645**. Released on Anvil Cassettes, Jul '82 by Anvil Cassettes, Chivers Audio Books.

ROMANY TALES (Various artists).
Note: Includes: Carrot Top, Black Lopez, The Mayfly, The Magic Peg-Basket, The Bird Woman and The Roman who Talked to Animals.
MC. Cat no: **ANV 639**. Released on Anvil Cassettes, Jan '81 by Anvil Cassettes, Chivers Audio Books.

SEAL BOY, THE (Various artists).
Note: Tales from Lapland. Includes: The Advice Merchant, The Boy Who Know Where the Winds Came From, The Reindeer Fur Coat, The Blacksmith's Son and Footsteps and the Three Reindeers.
MC. Cat no: **ANV 648**. Released on Anvil Cassettes, Jul '82 by Anvil Cassettes, Chivers Audio Books.

SINBAD THE SAILOR (Various artists).
Note: Tales from Arabia. Includes: Maruf the Cobbler and The Lives of Sultan Mahmud.
MC. Cat no: **ANV 663**. Released on Anvil Cassettes, '85 by Anvil Cassettes, Chivers Audio Books.

SINBAD THE SAILOR (Peter Bartlett & Barbara Bliss).
MC. Cat no: **TS 312**. Released on Tellastory, Jun '92 by Random Century Audiobooks. Note: ISBN no. 1856560058

SINBAD THE SAILOR (Dennis Lee).
MC. Cat no: **1245**. Released on Caedmon (USA), '89 by Caedmon Records (USA), Bond Street Music.

SINGING STONES, THE (And Other Stories) (Various artists).
Tracks / Singing stones, The: *Various artists* / Yellow bird and the pipe of peace: *Various artists* / Pontiac and the sixty chiefs: *Various artists* / Dog and the bear, The: *Various artists* / Fair Mohican, The: *Various artists* / Trail to the west, The: *Various artists*.
Note: Tales of North America.
MC. Cat no: **ANV 636**. Released on Anvil Cassettes, '81 by Anvil Cassettes, Chivers Audio Books.

SIX FOLK TALES (David Purves).
MC. Cat no: **SSC 074**. Released on Scotsoun, '91 by Scotsoun Recordings, Morley Audio Services.

SNOWBIRD AND THE SUNBIRD (Grace Kelly).
LP. Cat no: **ALB 6004**. Released on Conifer, Jan '83 by Conifer Records, Jazz Music.

SOLDIER'S TALE, THE (Igor Stravinsky) (Sting/Vanessa Redgrave).
LP. Cat no: **461048 1**. Released on Pangaea, Nov '88 **Deleted** Jan '90.
MC. Cat no: **461048 4**. Released on Pangaea, Nov '88.
CD. Cat no: **461048 2**. Released on Pangaea, Nov '88 **Deleted** Oct '90.

SORIA MORIA CASTLE (Various artists).

Note: Tales from Norway. Includes: Changeling, Peter and the Troll, The Troll and Smoky Joe and Dapplegrim.
MC. Cat no: **ANV 640**. Released on Anvil Cassettes, Apr '80 by Anvil Cassettes, Chivers Audio Books.

STORY OF HATIM TAI, THE (Various artists).
Note: Tales from Arabia. Includes: Princess, the Vizier and the Ape, The Deaf Brother and the Blind Brother, The Sultan's Emissary and the Leopard and The Faithfull Gazelle.
MC. Cat no: **ANV 601**. Released on Anvil Cassettes, Jan '81 by Anvil Cassettes, Chivers Audio Books.

STORY OF SIR GALAHAD, THE (Tales of King Arthur & his Knights) (Howard Pyle).
MC. Cat no: **1625**. Released on Caedmon (USA), '88 by Caedmon Records (USA), Bond Street Music.

STORY OF SIR GALAHAD, THE (Ian Richardson).
LP. Cat no: **TC 1625**. Released on Caedmon (USA), May '80 by Caedmon Records (USA), Bond Street Music.
MC. Cat no: **CDL 51625**. Released on Caedmon (USA), May '80 by Caedmon Records (USA), Bond Street Music.

STORY OF SIR LANCELOT, THE (Tales of King Arthur and his Knights) (Howard Pyle).
MC. Cat no: **1609**. Released on Caedmon (USA), '88 by Caedmon Records (USA), Bond Street Music.

STORY OF SWAN LAKE (Claire Bloom).
MC. Cat no: **1673**. Released on Caedmon (USA), '89 by Caedmon Records (USA), Bond Street Music.

STORY OF SWAN LAKE (Adapted by Ward Botsford) (Various artists).
MC. Cat no: **CDL 51673**. Released on Caedmon (USA), '82 by Caedmon Records (USA), Bond Street Music.

STORY OF THE NUTCRACKER (Claire Bloom).
LP. Cat no: **TC 1524**. Released on Caedmon (USA), '88 by Caedmon Records (USA), Bond Street Music.
MC. Cat no: **CDL 51524**. Released on Caedmon (USA), Jan '78 by Caedmon Records (USA), Bond Street Music.

STORY OF THE TAJ MAHAL, THE (Various artists).
Note: Tales from India. Includes: The Story of Taj Mahal, The Man Who Made Gold, The Young Ant, The Mister and the Generous Man, The Koh-i-noor, The King Who Had Everything, The Meatball's Fate and The Emerald Scorpion.
MC. Cat no: **ANV 637**. Released on Anvil Cassettes, Apr '80 by Anvil Cassettes, Chivers Audio Books.

SWORD IN THE ANVIL, THE (Tales of King Arthur & His Knights) (Howard Pyle).
MC. Cat no: **1465**. Released on Caedmon (USA), '88 by Caedmon Records

(USA), Bond Street Music.

TALE OF SCHEHEREZADE (Dennis Lee).
MC. Cat no: **1373**. Released on Caedmon (USA), '89 by Caedmon Records (USA), Bond Street Music.

TALES FROM THE ARABIAN NIGHTS (Various artists).
Note: Tales from Arabia. Includes: Tales from the Arbian Nights, The Three Sisters, The Three Dervishes Tales and The Dib-dib.
MC. Cat no: **ANV 655**. Released on Anvil Cassettes, '85 by Anvil Cassettes, Chivers Audio Books.

TALES OF KING ARTHUR (Ian Richardson).
MC. Cat no: **CDL 51609**. Released on Caedmon (USA), Oct '79 by Caedmon Records (USA), Bond Street Music.

TALES OF THE DESERT (Omar Sharif).
LP. Cat no: **TC 1590**. Released on Caedmon (USA), '79 by Caedmon Records (USA), Bond Street Music.
MC. Cat no: **CDL 51590**. Released on Caedmon (USA), '79 by Caedmon Records (USA), Bond Street Music.

TALKING BIRD, THE (And Other Stories) (Various artists).
Note: Tales from Arabia. Includes: The Talking Bird, The Little Dwarf, Zaid the Roper, The Barber and the Dyer, The Inescapable Shoes and Olives and Gold.
MC. Cat no: **ANV 664**. Released on Anvil Cassettes, '85 by Anvil Cassettes, Chivers Audio Books.

TEN SCOTTISH BALLADS (Matthew P McDiarmid).
MC. Cat no: **SSC 073**. Released on Scotsoun, '91 by Scotsoun Recordings, Morley Audio Services.

THREE BEARS, THE (Various artists).
MC. Cat no: **TS 302**. Released on Tellastory, Oct '79 by Random Century Audiobooks.

THREE BILLY GOATS GRUFF (And The Three Little Pigs) (Holly Hunter).
CD. Cat no: **WD 0713**. Released on Windham Hill, Jan '92 by Windham Hill Records (USA), New Note.
MC. Cat no: **WT 0713**. Released on Windham Hill, Jan '92 by Windham Hill Records (USA), New Note.

THREE BILLY GOATS GRUFF (Well Loved Tales up to Age 9) (Unknown narrator(s)).
Note: Book and cassette.
MC. Cat no: **PLB 93**. Released on Tell-A-Tale, '88 by Pickwick Records, Taylors, Clyde Factors.

THREE BILLY GOATS GRUFF (And Other Favourite Stories) (Peter Whitbread & Gillian Blake).
Note: For children aged 3-7 years. Includes The Three Billy Goats Gruff, The Tortoise and the Hare, The Ugly Duckling and The Princess and the Pea.

MC. Cat no: **VCA 607**. Released on VFM Cassettes, Jul '85 by VFM Cassettes, Midland Records, Crusader Marketing Co., Taylors, Morley Audio Services.

THREE LITTLE PIGS (Michaela Strachan).
MC. Cat no: **STOR 2**. Released on Storytime Cassettes, Apr '92 by VFM Cassettes, Iona Records, Rio Communications.

THREE LITTLE PIGS (Unknown narrator(s)).
MLP. Cat no: **D 303**. Released on Disneyland, Apr '81 by Disneyland-Vista Records (USA). Note: 7"LP with book
MC. Cat no: **FT 110**. Released on Cassettes For Young People, May '92 by Cassettes For Young People Lmd, DMS Dist. Note: ISBN No: 1871449103. Playing time: 20 minutes.

THREE LITTLE PIGS (Maiden Theatre Co./Group).
MC. Cat no: **ZCPTE 7**. Released on PRT, Nov '77 by Castle Communications PLC.

THREE LITTLE PIGS (Well Loved Tales up to Age 9) (Unknown narrator(s)).
Note: Book and cassette.
LP. Cat no: **ST 3963**. Released on Disneyland, Dec '78 by Disneyland-Vista Records (USA).
MC. Cat no: **PLB 51**. Released on Tell-A-Tale, Feb '83 by Pickwick Records, Taylors, Clyde Factors.
MC. Cat no: **STC 302C**. Released on VFM Cassettes, '88 by VFM Cassettes, Midland Records, Crusader Marketing Co., Taylors, Morley Audio Services.
MC. Cat no: **STK 004**. Released on Stick-A-Tale, Jan '89 by Pickwick Records.

TINY LIFEBOAT, THE (Various artists).
Note: Stories from The Holy Land. Includes: The Tiny Lifeboat, A General's Concern, The Orphan who became Queen, Friends Indeed, A Change of Heart and A Rich Man's Faith in a Poor Man.
MC. Cat no: **ANV 634**. Released on Anvil Cassettes, Jan '81 by Anvil Cassettes, Chivers Audio Books.

TOM THUMB (And Other Fairy Stories) (Unknown narrator(s)).
MC. Cat no: **1062**. Released on Caedmon (USA), Jul '88 by Caedmon Records (USA), Bond Street Music.

TOM THUMB (Susan Hampshire).
MC. Cat no: **3602**. Released on Storytime Cassettes, Aug '83 by VFM Cassettes, Iona Records, Rio Communications.

TOM THUMB (Well Loved Tales Up to Age 9) (Unknown narrator(s)).
Note: Book and cassette.
MC. Cat no: **PLB 59**. Released on Tell-A-Tale, Feb '83 by Pickwick Records, Taylors, Clyde Factors.

TOP BRAIN ANANSI (Various artists).
Note: Tales from The West Indies. Includes: Top Brain Anansi, The First Web, The Fancy Dress Party, The Old Witch, The Tortoise Race, How the Hare Lost his Tail, The Treasure Hunt, How Anansi got his Waist and Rainbow's End.
MC. Cat no: **ANV 658**. Released on Anvil Cassettes, '85 by Anvil Cassettes, Chivers Audio Books.

TRADITIONAL STORIES COLLECTION (Volume 10) (Shireen Shah).
Note: Stories include :- The Emperor's New Clothes and Snow White And Red Rose.
MCSET. Cat no: **TTC 1028**. Released on Talking Tape Company, Apr '91, Conifer Records. Note: ISBN no. 1872520855

TRADITIONAL STORY COLLECTION (Volume 6) (Shireen Shah).
Note: Stories include :- Snow White And The Seven Dwarfs and The Frog Prince.
MCSET. Cat no: **TTC 1024**. Released on Talking Tape Company, Apr '91, Conifer Records. Note: ISBN no. 1872520812

TRADITIONAL STORY COLLECTION (Volume 2) (Shireen Shah).
Note: Stories include :- Puss In Boots and Beauty And The Beast.
MCSET. Cat no: **TTC 1020**. Released on Talking Tape Company, Apr '91, Conifer Records. Note: ISBN no.1872520774

TRADITIONAL STORY COLLECTION (Volume 3) (Unknown narrator(s)).
Note: Stories include :- Jack And The Beanstalk and Rapunzel.
MCSET. Cat no: **TTC 1021**. Released on Talking Tape Company, Apr '91, Conifer Records. Note: ISBN no. 1872520780

TRADITIONAL STORY COLLECTION (Volume 1) (Shireen Shah).
Note: Stories include :- The Three Little Pigs and Cinderella.
MCSET. Cat no: **TTC 1019**. Released on Talking Tape Company, Apr '91, Conifer Records. Note: ISBN no. 1872520766

TRADITIONAL STORY COLLECTION (Volume 5) (Shireen Shah).
Note: Stories include :- Hansel And Gretel and Thumbelina.
MCSET. Cat no: **TTC 1023**. Released on Talking Tape Company, Apr '91, Conifer Records. Note: ISBN no. 1872520804

TRADITIONAL STORY COLLECTION (Volume 9) (Shireen Shah).
Note: Stories include:- Rumplestiltskin and Tom Thumb.
MCSET. Cat no: **TTC 1027**. Released on Talking Tape Company, Apr '91, Conifer Records. Note: ISBN no.

1872520847

TRADITIONAL STORY COLLECTION (Volume 8) (Shireen Shah).
Note: Stories include :- The Tinderbox and The Golden Goose.
MCSET. Cat no: **TTC 1026**. Released on Talking Tape Company, Apr '91, Conifer Records. Note: ISBN no. 1872520839

TRADITIONAL STORY COLLECTION (Volume 7) (Shireen Shah).
Note: Stories include:- Sleeping Beauty and The Ugly Duckling.
MCSET. Cat no: **TTC 1025**. Released on Talking Tape Company, Apr '91, Conifer Records. Note: ISBN no.1872520820

TRADITIONAL STORY COLLECTION (Volume 4) (Unknown narrator(s)).
Note: Stories include:- Little Red Riding Hood and The Elves and the Shoe Maker.
MCSET. Cat no: **TTC 1022**. Released on Talking Tape Company, Apr '91, Conifer Records. Note: ISBN no. 1872520790

TREASURY OF FAIRY TALES (Chapters 3 and 4) (June Whitfield & Jenny Hanley).
2LP. Cat no: **2668 023**. Released on Polydor, Feb '81 by Polydor Ltd, Solomon & Peres **Deleted** '86.

TREASURY OF FAIRY TALES (Chapter One) (Wendy Craig & Lesley Judd).
Note: Includes: Snow White and the Seven Dwarfs, Hansel and Gretel, Babes in the Wood, The Frog Prince, Pied Piper, Puss 'n' Boots, Tom Thumb and The Wild Swan.
2LP. Cat no: **2668 017**. Released on Polydor, Dec '80 by Polydor Ltd, Solomon & Peres.

TWO BROTHERS, THE (Various artists).
Note: Includes: The Two Brothers, The Fox and the Geese, The Farmer's Daughter, Iron Man and The Cock, Tfhe Hen and the Brindled Cow
MC. Cat no: **ANV 622**. Released on Anvil Cassettes, Jan '81 by Anvil Cassettes, Chivers Audio Books.

VASSILI LACKLUCK (Various artists).
Note: Tales from Russia. Includes: Vassili Lackluck, Semyon the Speedy, The Frog Princess and The Miller's Son.
MC. Cat no: **ANV 667**. Released on Anvil Cassettes, '85 by Anvil Cassettes, Chivers Audio Books.

VOYAGES OF SINBAD (Volumes I to III) (Terry Jones).
MC. Cat no: **LPMC 212**. Released on Listen, '88, Cartel.

VOYAGES OF SINBAD (Volumes IV to VI) (Terry Jones).
MC. Cat no: **LPMC 213**. Released on Listen, '88, Cartel.

WU AND THE DRAGON (Various artists).
Note: Tales from China. Wu and the Dragon, The Ambassador from Tibet, The Eels and Gold, The Wonderful Tapestry, The Priest and the Pear Tree and The Heavenly Bowman.
MC. Cat no: **ANV 665**. Released on Anvil Cassettes, '85 by Anvil Cassettes, Chivers Audio Books.

YOUR FAVOURITE FAIRY STORIES (Wendy Craig).
Note: Includes: Babes in the Wood, The Frog Princess, Snow White and the Seven Dwarfs and Hansel and Gretel.
LP. Cat no: **SPR 8541**. Released on Spot, Feb '84 by Pickwick Records.
MC. Cat no: **SPC 8541**. Released on Spot, Feb '84 by Pickwick Records.

YOUR FAVOURITE FAIRY STORIES (Wendy Craig & Richard Briers).
Note: Adapted and produced by Richard Baldwyn. Includes: Cinderella, Three Little Pigs, Rapunzel, Goldilocks and the Three Bears, Snow White and the Seven Dwarfs, Jack and the Beanstalk, Gingerbread Man, Dick Whittington, Beauty and the Beast, Hansel and Gretel, Little Red Riding Hood, Rumpelstiltskin, Hard and the Hedgehog and Sleeping Beauty.
MCSET. Cat no: **LFP 7262**. Released on Listen For Pleasure, Sep '86 by EMI Records.
MCSET. Cat no: **9093F**. Released on Travellers Tales, '91 by Travellers Tales. Note: 2 Cassettes.

ZADIG, MAN OF DESTINY (Various artists).
MC. Cat no: **ANV 631**. Released on Anvil Cassettes, Apr '80 by Anvil Cassettes, Chivers Audio Books.

Travers, P.L.

MARY POPPINS (Maggie Smith).
MC. Cat no: **1246**. Released on Caedmon (USA), '89 by Caedmon Records (USA), Bond Street Music.

MARY POPPINS (Unknown narrator(s)).
MC. Cat no: **DIS 015**. Released on Disney (Read-a-long), Apr '91 by Disneyland Records.

MARY POPPINS AND THE BANKS FAMILY (Maggie Smith).
MC. Cat no: **1270**. Released on Caedmon (USA), '89 by Caedmon Records (USA), Bond Street Music.

MARY POPPINS COMES BACK (Maggie Smith).
MC. Cat no: **1269**. Released on Caedmon (USA), '89 by Caedmon Records (USA), Bond Street Music.

MARY POPPINS OPENS THE DOOR (Maggie Smith).
MC. Cat no: **1271**. Released on Caedmon (USA), '89 by Caedmon Records (USA), Bond Street Music.

MARY POPPINS / THE JUNGLE BOOK) (Unknown narrator(s)).
MCSET. Cat no: **DTO 10510**. Released on Ditto, '88 by Pickwick Re-

cords, Midland Records.

Treece, Henry
DREAM-TIME, SPLINTERED SWORD (And War Dog) (Various artists).
MCSET. Cat no: **9086F.** Released on Travellers Tales, '91 by Travellers Tales. Note: 6 Cassettes.

DREAM-TIME, THE (Tim Bentinck).
MCSET. Cat no: **2CCA 3023.** Released on Chivers Audio Books, '91 by Chivers Audio Books, Green Dragon Audio Visual. Note: 2 Cassettes.

SPLINTERED SWORD (John Sheddon).
MCSET. Cat no: **COL 3004.** Released on Colophone, Nov '81 by AVLS (Audio-Visual Library Services).

WAR DOG (David Steuart).
MCSET. Cat no: **COL 3005.** Released on Colophone, Sep '81 by AVLS (Audio-Visual Library Services).

Trelford, Donald
SNOOKERED (Robert Powell).
MCSET. Cat no: **LFP 7270.** Released on Listen For Pleasure, Nov '86 by EMI Records.

Trenhaile, John
KRYSALIS (Gordon Griffin).
MCSET. Cat no: **1574/1575T.** Released on Travellers Tales, '91 by Travellers Tales. Note: 10 Cassettes.

MCSET. Cat no: **1854963252.** Released on Soundings, '91 by Soundings Records, Bond Street Music. Note: 10 Cassettes.

MAN CALLED KYRIL, THE (Christian Rodska).
MC. Cat no: **CAB 326.** Released on Chivers Audio Books, '88 by Chivers Audio Books, Green Dragon Audio Visual.

MCSET. Cat no: **1370T.** Released on Travellers Tales, '91 by Travellers Tales. Note: 8 Cassetes.

Treves, Kathleen
FOURTH FOLLY (Rose McBain).
MCSET. Cat no: **CLT 1004.** Released on Candlelight, Jun '81 by AVLS (Audio-Visual Library Services).

MONK'S HARTWELL (Isabelle Amyes).
MCSET. Cat no: **CLT 1015.** Released on Candlelight, '91 by AVLS (Audio-Visual Library Services). Note: 2 cassettes.

Tripathi, Gouardhanram
SARASNATICHANDRA (GUJARATI) (Harish Bhimanui & Rekha Bhimani).
MCSET. Cat no: **SGX 002.** Released on Sonex, '91. Note: 4 cassettes.

Tritten, Charles
HEIDI GROWS UP (Jan Francis).
MCSET. Cat no: **LFP 7268.** Released on Listen For Pleasure, Sep '86 by EMI Records **Deleted** Aug '89.

HEIDI GROWS UP (Jan Francis).
Note: Abridged.
MCSET. Cat no: **9088F.** Released on Travellers Tales, '91 by Travellers Tales. Note: 2 Cassettes.

Trollope, Anthony
BARCHESTER TOWERS (Nigel Hawthorne).
Note: Abridged version.
MCSET. Cat no: **1068C.** Released on Travellers Tales, '91 by Travellers Tales. Note: 2 cassettes.

BARCHESTER TOWERS (Timothy West).
MCSET. Cat no: **CTC 035.** Released on Cover to Cover, Apr '87 by Cover to Cover Cassettes. Note: 14 cassettes. Playing time: 19 hrs 5 mins.

MCSET. Cat no: **1051/1052C.** Released on Travellers Tales, '91 by Travellers Tales. Note: 14 cassettes.

BARCHESTER TOWERS (Nigel Hawthorne).
MCSET. Cat no: **SAY 92.** Released on Argo (Polygram), Oct '83 by PolyGram Classics **Deleted** Jan '89.

MCSET. Cat no: **ARGO 1265.** Released on Argo (EMI), May '91 by EMI Records.

DOCTOR THORNE (Timothy West).
MCSET. Cat no: **CTC 051.** Released on Cover to Cover, Jun '88 by Cover to Cover Cassettes. Note: 15 cassettes. Playing time: 20 hrs 40 mins.

MCSET. Cat no: **1077/1078C.** Released on Travellers Tales, '91 by Travellers Tales. Note: 15 Cassettes.

FRAMLEY PARSONAGE (Timothy West).
MCSET. Cat no: **CTC 057.** Released on Cover to Cover, '90 by Cover to Cover Cassettes. Note: 15 cassettes. Playing time: 19 hrs 40 mins.

SMALL HOUSE AT ALLINGTON, THE (Timothy West).
MCSET. Cat no: **CTC 058.** Released on Cover to Cover, '90 by Cover to Cover Cassettes. Note: 18 cassettes.

WARDEN, THE (Irene Sutcliffe).
MCSET. Cat no: **CTC 015.** Released on Cover to Cover, Jun '85 by Cover to Cover Cassettes. Note: 6 cassettes. Playing time: 7 hrs 50 mins.

MCSET. Cat no: **ZBBC 1213.** Released on BBC Radio Collection, May '91 by BBC Records. Note: ISBN No: 0563 409703

MCSET. Cat no: **1049C.** Released on Travellers Tales, '91 by Travellers Tales. Note: 6 cassettes.

WARDEN, THE (Nigel Hawthorne).
MCSET. Cat no: **1065C.** Released on Travellers Tales, '91 by Travellers Tales. Note: 6 cassettes.

Trower, Terry
FOLLOW ME TO THE SEASIDE (Unknown narrator(s)).
Note: Authors are Terry Trower and Aubrey Woods.

MC. Cat no: **1856561100.** Released on Random Century, '91 by Random Century Audiobooks, Conifer Records.

FOLLOW ME TO THE SEASIDE (Various narrators).
Note: Authors are Terry Trower and Aubrey Woods.
MC. Cat no: **TS 363.** Released on Tellastory, '91 by Random Century Audiobooks. Note: ISBN no. 1856561135

Truman, Margaret
MURDER IN GEORGETOWN (E.C. Kelly).
MCSET. Cat no: **CAB 404.** Released on Chivers Audio Books, '91 by Chivers Audio Books, Green Dragon Audio Visual. Note: 6 Cassettes.

MCSET. Cat no: **1594T.** Released on Travellers Tales, '91 by Travellers Tales. Note: 6 Cassettes.

Turow, Scott
BURDEN OF PROOF (Unknown narrator(s)).
MCSET. Cat no: **0671707434.** Released on Simon & Schuster, '91 by Simon & Schuster Ltd.

PRESUMED INNOCENT (John Herd).
MC. Cat no: **0600560538.** Released on Hamlyn Books On Tape, '88, Bond Street Music.

Twain, Mark
ADVENTURES OF HUCKLEBERRY FINN (Alfred Gingold).
MCSET. Cat no: **1578F.** Released on Travellers Tales, '91 by Travellers Tales. Note: 7 Cassettes.

MCSET. Cat no: **RB 80150.** Released on Recorded Books, '91 by Isis Audio Books. Note: 7 Cassettes.

ADVENTURES OF TOM SAWYER (Unknown narrator(s)).
MCSET. Cat no: **RB 87350.** Released on Recorded Books, '91 by Isis Audio Books.

ADVENTURES OF TOM SAWYER (Bing Crosby).
MCSET. Cat no: **SAY 31.** Released on Argo (Polygram), Jul '82 by PolyGram Classics **Deleted** Jan '89.

MCSET. Cat no: **ARGO 1166.** Released on Argo (EMI), Oct '89 by EMI Records. Note: 2 Cassettes.

ADVENTURES OF TOM SAWYER, THE (Bing Crosby).
Note: Abridged.
MCSET. Cat no: **9089F.** Released on Travellers Tales, '91 by Travellers Tales. Note: 2 Cassettes.

ADVENTURES OF TOM SAWYER, THE (Norman Dietz).
MCSET. Cat no: **RB 86890.** Released on Recorded Books, '91 by Isis Audio Books. Note: 5 cassettes. Playing time 7hrs.

HUCKLEBERRY FINN (Kerry

Shale).
MC. Cat no: **LFP 41 7206 5.** Released on Listen For Pleasure, Aug '85 by EMI Records.

HUCKLEBERRY FINN (Kerry Shale).
Note: Abridged.
MCSET. Cat no: **9090F.** Released on Travellers Tales, '91 by Travellers Tales. Note: 2 Cassettes.

HUCKLEBERRY FINN (Ed Begley).
MC. Cat no: **2038.** Released on Caedmon (USA), '89 by Caedmon Records (USA), Bond Street Music.

HUCKLEBERRY FINN (Bob Sherman).
MC. Cat no: **P 90020.** Released on Pinnacle, '79 by Pinnacle Records, Outlet Records, Music Sales Records.

PRINCE AND THE PAUPER THE (Unknown narrator(s)).
LP. Cat no: **TC 1542.** Released on Caedmon (USA), Jan '79 by Caedmon Records (USA), Bond Street Music.
MC. Cat no: **CDL 51542.** Released on Caedmon (USA), Jan '79 by Caedmon Records (USA), Bond Street Music.
MCSET. Cat no: **DTO 10580.** Released on Ditto, '88 by Pickwick Records, Midland Records. Note: 4 Cassettes.

TOM SAWYER (Adventures with Injun Joe) (Ed Begley).
MC. Cat no: **1165.** Released on Caedmon (USA), by Caedmon Records (USA), Bond Street Music.

TOM SAWYER (Children's Classics) (Unknown narrator(s)).
Note: Book and cassette.
MC. Cat no: **PLBC 214.** Released on Tell-A-Tale, '88 by Pickwick Records, Taylors, Clyde Factors.

TOM SAWYER (Bob Sherman).
MC. Cat no: **P 90013.** Released on Pinnacle, '79 by Pinnacle Records, Outlet Records, Music Sales Records.

TOM SAWYER (The Glorious Whitewasher) (Ed Begley).
MC. Cat no: **1205.** Released on Caedmon (USA), '89 by Caedmon Records (USA), Bond Street Music.

TWAIN SOUNDBOOK (Various artists).
MC. Cat no: **SBC 119.** Released on Caedmon (USA), '81 by Caedmon Records (USA), Bond Street Music.

Two Ronnies
TWO RONNIES.
LP. Cat no: **RED 257.** Released on BBC, Oct '76 by BBC Records, Taylors Deleted '88.
MC. Cat no: **RMC 4054.** Released on BBC, Oct '76 by BBC Records, Taylors Deleted '88.

TWO RONNIES (Volume 2).
LP. Cat no: **REB 300.** Released on BBC, Nov '77 by BBC Records, Taylors Deleted '87.
MC. Cat no: **ZCF 300.** Released on BBC, Nov '77 by BBC Records, Taylors Deleted '85.

VERY BEST OF ME AND THE VERY BEST OF HIM, THE.
Tracks / But first the news / Plain speaking / Mark my words / Train of events / British Rail / Night night / Limerick writers / Complete book, The / Restaurant, The / Castaway, The / Language barrier, The / Cheers / Late news, The.
LP. Cat no: **REC 514.** Released on BBC, Oct '84 by BBC Records, Taylors.
MC. Cat no: **ZCM 514.** Released on BBC, Oct '84 by BBC Records, Taylors Deleted Jun '91.

Tyler, Anne
ACCIDENTAL TOURIST, THE (George Guidall).
MCSET. Cat no: **IAB 92077.** Released on Isis Audio Books, Jul '92. Note: 10 Cassettes. Playing time: 13 hours, 15 mins.

SAINT MAYBE (John Lithgow).
MCSET. Cat no: **RC 31.** Released on Random Century, '91 by Random Century Audiobooks, Conifer Records. Note: 2 cassettes. ISBN 185686040X. 3 hrs approx.

Uncle Remus
BRER RABBIT (Danny Glover & Taj Mahal).
CD. Cat no: **WD 0716.** Released on Windham Hill, Jan '92 by Windham Hill Records (USA), New Note.
MC. Cat no: **WT 0716.** Released on Windham Hill, Jan '92 by Windham Hill Records (USA), New Note.

Underwood, Michael
CAUSE OF DEATH (Stephen Thorne).
MCSET. Cat no: **1178T.** Released on Travellers Tales, '91 by Travellers Tales. Note: 6 Cassettes.

CLEAR CASE OF SUICIDE, A (Unknown narrator(s)).
MCSET. Cat no: **1854965085.** Released on Bramhope, '91 by Ulverscroft Soundings. Note: 5 Cassettes.

COMPELLING CASE, A (Judyth Franklyn).
MCSET. Cat no: **1854965921.** Released on Bramhope, Apr '92 by Ulverscroft Soundings. Note: Playing time: 60 minutes.

DEATH IN CAMERA (Stephen Thorne).
MCSET. Cat no: **1139T.** Released on Travellers Tales, '91 by Travellers Tales. Note: 4 Cassettes.

DOUBLE JEOPARDY (Unknown narrator(s)).
MCSET. Cat no: **1854964968.** Released on Bramhope, '91 by Ulverscroft Soundings. Note: 5 Cassettes.

DUAL ENGIMA (Judith Franklyn).
MCSET. Cat no: **185496576X.** Released on Bramhope, Mar '92 by Ulverscroft Soundings. Note: Playing time: 60 minutes.

GIRL FOUND DEAD (Stephen Thorne).
MCSET. Cat no: **CAT 4066.** Released on Chivers Audio Books, '91 by Chivers Audio Books, Green Dragon Audio Visual. Note: 6 cassettes.
MCSET. Cat no: **1732T.** Released on Travellers Tales, '91 by Travellers Tales. Note: 6 Cassettes.

HIDDEN MAN, THE (Judith Franklyn).
MCSET. Cat no: **1854965476.** Released on Bramhope, '92 by Ulverscroft Soundings.

Untermeyer, Louis
DISCOVERING RHYTHM & RHYME IN POETRY (Julie Harris).
MC. Cat no: **1156.** Released on Caedmon (USA), '89 by Caedmon Records (USA), Bond Street Music.

Updike, John
COUPLES (And Pigeon Feathers) (Unknown narrator(s)).
MC. Cat no: **1276.** Released on Caedmon (USA), '89 by Caedmon Records (USA), Bond Street Music.

Upshall, Helen
CANDLES FOR THE SURGEON (Carole Boyd).
MCSET. Cat no: **PMB 018.** Released on Mills & Boon, '88. Note: 2 Cassettes

Ustinov, Peter
GRAND PRIX OF GIBRALTAR (Peter Ustinov).
MC. Cat no: **RLPC 833.** Released on Riverside (USA), Aug '91 by Ace Records, Ace Records, Cadillac Music, Jazz Music, Hot Shot, Crusader Marketing Co..

Uttley, Alison
LITTLE GREY RABBIT COLLECTION, THE (Nanette Newman).
Note: Includes four books.
MC. Cat no: **00 104 132 2.** Released on Tempo, Apr '88 by Warwick Records, Celtic Music, Henry Hadaway Organisation.

LITTLE GREY RABBIT STORIES (June Whitfield).
MC. Cat no: **P 90003.** Released on Pinnacle, '79 by Pinnacle Records, Outlet Records, Music Sales Records.

LITTLE GREY RABBIT, THE (Fuzzy Peg Goes to School) (Nanette Newman).
MC. Cat no: **00 102150 8.** Released on Tempo, '88 by Warwick Records, Celtic Music, Henry Hadaway Organisation.

LITTLE GREY RABBIT, THE (Nicolette McKenzie).
MC. Cat no: **00 102218 0.** Released on Tempo, '88 by Warwick Records, Celtic Music, Henry Hadaway Organisation.

LITTLE RED FOX BOOK (And

Brown Mouse Book) (Prunella Scales).
MCSET. Cat no: **LFP 7373.** Released on Listen For Pleasure, Nov '88 by EMI Records **Deleted** Apr '90.

MORE LITTLE GREY RABBIT STORIES (June Whitfield).
MC. Cat no: **P 90015.** Released on Pinnacle, '79 by Pinnacle Records, Outlet Records, Music Sales Records.

TALES FROM LAVENDER SHOES (Jill Shilling).
MCSET. Cat no: **TS 405.** Released on Tellastory, Mar '92 by Random Century Audiobooks. Note: 2 cassettes. ISBN no. 1856561712

Valentine, Anthony

GOLDEN FOX (Unknown narrator(s)).
MCSET. Cat no: **LFP 7529.** Released on Listen For Pleasure, Apr '91 by EMI Records. Note: Playing time: 3 hours.

Van Der Zee, Karen

SECRET SORROW, A (Lesley Seaward).
MCSET. Cat no: **PMB 016.** Released on Mills & Boon, '88. Note: 2 Cassettes

Van Gelder, Dora

REAL FAIRIES (Unknown narrator(s)).
MCSET. Cat no: **DTO 10570.** Released on Ditto, '88 by Pickwick Records, Midland Records.

Van Gulik, Robert

CELEBRATED CASES OF JUDGE DEE (Norman Dietz).
MCSET. Cat no: **RB 89560.** Released on Recorded Books, Jul '92 by Isis Audio Books. Note: 6 Cassettes. Playing time: 8 hours, 30 mins

Van Lustbader, Eric

ZERO (James Keach).
MCSET. Cat no: **0671663437.** Released on Simon & Schuster, '91 by Simon & Schuster Ltd.

Van Tilbury Clark

OX-BOW INCIDENT (Henry Fonda).
MC. Cat no: **CDL 51620.** Released on Caedmon (USA), May '80 by Caedmon Records (USA), Bond Street Music.
LP. Cat no: **TC 1620.** Released on Caedmon (USA), Oct '82 by Caedmon Records (USA), Bond Street Music **Deleted** Oct '87.

Venables, Terry

HAZELL: THREE CARD TRICK (B.P. Yuill).
MC. Cat no: **PTB 610.** Released on Pickwick Talking Books, '83 by Pickwick Records, Clyde Factors.

Verga, Giovanni

RACCOLTA DI NOVELLE (Adriano Giraldi).
MCSET. Cat no: **1022L.** Released on Travellers Tales, '91 by Travellers Tales. Note: 4 cassettes.

Verne, Jules

20,000 LEAGUES UNDER THE SEA (James Mason).
MC. Cat no: **1472.** Released on Caedmon (USA), '89 by Caedmon Records (USA), Bond Street Music.

20,000 LEAGUES UNDER THE SEA (Norman Dietz).
MCSET. Cat no: **RB 89880.** Released on Recorded Books, Mar '92 by Isis Audio Books. Note: 14 cassettes. Playing time 14hrs 30mins

AROUND THE WORLD IN 80 DAYS (Tim Pigott-Smith).
MCSET. Cat no: **ARGO 1310.** Released on Argo (EMI), Apr '92 by EMI Records.

AROUND THE WORLD IN 80 DAYS (Children's Classics) (Unknown narrator(s)).
Note: Book and cassette.
MC. Cat no: **PLBC 84.** Released on Tell-A-Tale, '88 by Pickwick Records, Taylors, Clyde Factors.

AROUND THE WORLD IN 80 DAYS (Christopher Plummer).
LP. Cat no: **TC 1553.** Released on Caedmon (USA), Jul '78 by Caedmon Records (USA), Bond Street Music.
MC. Cat no: **1553.** Released on Caedmon (USA), Jul '78 by Caedmon Records (USA), Bond Street Music.

AROUND THE WORLD IN 80 DAYS (Patrick Tull).
MCSET. Cat no: **1624F.** Released on Travellers Tales, '91 by Travellers Tales. Note: 5 Cassettes.
MCSET. Cat no: **RB 86460.** Released on Recorded Books, '91 by Isis Audio Books. Note: 5 Cassettes.

JOURNEY TO THE CENTRE OF THE EARTH (Jon Pertwee).
MC. Cat no: **P 90028.** Released on Pinnacle, '79 by Pinnacle Records, Outlet Records, Music Sales Records.

JOURNEY TO THE CENTRE OF THE EARTH (Nigel Lambert).
MC. Cat no: **C 002.** Released on Green Dragon, '91 by Green Dragon Audio Visual.

JOURNEY TO THE CENTRE OF THE EARTH (Tom Baker).
MCSET. Cat no: **1172F.** Released on Travellers Tales, '91 by Travellers Tales. Note: 2 Cassettes.
MCSET. Cat no: **SAY 53.** Released on Argo (Polygram), Jun '88 by PolyGram Classics **Deleted** Jan '89.
MCSET. Cat no: **ARGO 1241.** Released on Argo (EMI), Oct '90 by EMI Records. Note: 2 Cassettes.

JOURNEY TO THE CENTRE OF THE EARTH (James Mason).
MC. Cat no: **1581.** Released on Caedmon (USA), '88 by Caedmon Records (USA), Bond Street Music.

JOURNEY TO THE CENTRE OF THE EARTH (Unknown narrator(s)).

Note: Book and cassette.
MC. Cat no: **PLBC 77.** Released on Tell-A-Tale, '88 by Pickwick Records, Taylors, Clyde Factors.

JOURNEY TO THE CENTRE OF THE EARTH (Norman Dietz).
MCSET. Cat no: **RB 88490.** Released on Recorded Books, Jun '92 by Isis Audio Books. Note: 8 Cassettes. Playing time: 10 hours.

JOURNEY TO THE CENTRE OF THE EARTH (Unknown narrator(s)).
MC. Cat no: **CDL 51581.** Released on Caedmon (USA), Jul '79 by Caedmon Records (USA), Bond Street Music.

Vincent, Monica

GIRL AGAINST THE JUNGLE (Unknown narrator(s)).
MC. Cat no: **0582526795.** Released on Longman Books, '91 by Longman Books. Note: 14 cassettes. Playing time 14hrs 30mins

Vine, Barbara

DARK-ADAPTED EYE, A (Harriet Walter).
MCSET. Cat no: **CAB 456.** Released on Chivers Audio Books, '91 by Chivers Audio Books, Green Dragon Audio Visual. Note: 10 cassettes.
MCSET. Cat no: **1557/1558T.** Released on Travellers Tales, '91 by Travellers Tales. Note: 10 Cassettes.

FATAL INVERSION, A (William Gaminara).
MCSET. Cat no: **CAB 413.** Released on Chivers Audio Books, '91 by Chivers Audio Books, Green Dragon Audio Visual. Note: 8 Cassettes.
MCSET. Cat no: **1494T.** Released on Travellers Tales, '91 by Travellers Tales. Note: 8 Cassettes.

FATAL INVERSION, A (Unknown narrator(s)).
MCSET. Cat no: **ZBBC 1297.** Released on BBC Radio Collection, '91 by BBC Records.

GALLOWGLASS (Dermot Crowley).
MCSET. Cat no: **CAB 568.** Released on Chivers Audio Books, '91 by Chivers Audio Books, Green Dragon Audio Visual. Note: 8 Cassettes
MCSET. Cat no: **1717T.** Released on Travellers Tales, '91 by Travellers Tales. Note: 8 Cassetes.

HOUSE OF STAIRS, THE (Jane Asher).
MCSET. Cat no: **CAB 506.** Released on Chivers Audio Books, '91 by Chivers Audio Books, Green Dragon Audio Visual. Note: 8 Cassettes.
MCSET. Cat no: **1534F.** Released on Travellers Tales, '91 by Travellers Tales. Note: 8 Cassettes.

KING SOLOMON'S CARPET (Davina Porter).
MCSET. Cat no: **IAB 92057.** Released on Isis Audio Books, May '92. Note: 10

Cassettes. Playing time: 13 hours.

Viorst, Judith
ALEXANDER AND THE TERRIBLE, HORRIBLE, NO GOOD VERY BAD DAY (Blythe Danner).
MC. Cat no: **1722**. Released on Caedmon (USA), '89 by Caedmon Records (USA), Bond Street Music.

Voltaire
CANDIDE (Mimmo Lo Vecchio).
MCSET. Cat no: **1023L**. Released on Travellers Tales, '91 by Travellers Tales. Note: 4 cassettes.

Von Armin, Elizabeth
ENCHANTED APRIL, THE (Josie Lawrence).
MCSET. Cat no: **RC 78**. Released on Random Century, Mar '92 by Random Century Audiobooks, Conifer Records. Note: ISBN no. 1856861120

Vonnegut, Kurt
BREAKFAST OF CHAMPIONS (Unknown narrator(s)).
MC. Cat no: **CDL 51602**. Released on Caedmon (USA), Oct '79 by Caedmon Records (USA), Bond Street Music.

CAT'S CRADLE (Kurt Vonnegut).
MC. Cat no: **1346**. Released on Caedmon (USA), '91 by Caedmon Records (USA), Bond Street Music.

GALAPAGOS (Alan Arkin).
MCSET. Cat no: **0671629948**. Released on Simon & Schuster, '91 by Simon & Schuster Ltd. Note: ISBN No: 0563 227044

SLAUGHTERHOUSE FIVE (Kurt Vonnegut).
MC. Cat no: **1376**. Released on Caedmon (USA), '91 by Caedmon Records (USA), Bond Street Music.

Waggoner, Jean
PATTERN OF SHADOWS, A (Unknown narrator(s)).
MCSET. Cat no: **MRC 1029**. Released on Moonlight Romance, Jun '87.

Wakefield, Tom
VARIETY ARTISTES, THE (Unknown narrator(s)).
MCSET. Cat no: **1854962043**. Released on Bramhope, '91 by Ulverscroft Soundings. Note: 7 Cassettes.

VARIETY ARTISTES, THE (Margaret Holt).
MCSET. Cat no: **1338F**. Released on Travellers Tales, '91 by Travellers Tales. Note: 5 Cassettes.

Walker, Alice
TEMPLE OF MY FAMILIAR (Alice Walker).
MCSET. Cat no: **0671688332**. Released on Simon & Schuster, '91 by Simon & Schuster Ltd.

Wallace, Edgar
CLUE OF THE TWISTED CANDLE, THE (Robert Trotter).
MCSET. Cat no: **SPF 905-1**. Released on Schiltron Audio Books, '91 by Schiltron Publishing. Note: 4 Cassettes. Playing time 5 hours 30 minutes.

MCSET. Cat no: **1491T**. Released on Travellers Tales, '91 by Travellers Tales. Note: 4 Cassettes.

FOUR JUST MEN (Michael Elder).
MCSET. Cat no: **SPF 905-2**. Released on Schiltron Audio Books, '91 by Schiltron Publishing. Note: 4 Cassettes. Playing time 4 hours 8 minutes.

MCSET. Cat no: **1417T**. Released on Travellers Tales, '91 by Travellers Tales. Note: 4 Cassettes.

MIND OF MR. J.G. REEDER, THE (Timothy West).
Tracks / Poetical policeman, The / Treasure hunt, The / Troupe, The / Stealer of marble, The.
MCSET. Cat no: **SAY 116**. Released on Argo (Polygram), Sep '84 by PolyGram Classics **Deleted** Jan '89.

MIND OF MR. J.G. REEDER, THE (John Thaw).
MCSET. Cat no: **1140T**. Released on Travellers Tales, '91 by Travellers Tales. Note: 4 Cassettes.

MCSET. Cat no: **CAT 4005**. Released on Chivers Audio Books, '91 by Chivers Audio Books, Green Dragon Audio Visual.

SANDERS OF THE RIVER (Martin Heller).
MCSET. Cat no: **SPF 905-4**. Released on Schiltron Audio Books, Jun '91 by Schiltron Publishing. Note: 4 Cassettes. Playing time 5 hours.

MCSET. Cat no: **1755T**. Released on Travellers Tales, '91 by Travellers Tales. Note: 4 Cassettes.

SHEER MELODRAMA (And Other Stories) (Timothy West).
Note: Includes: Sheer Meolodrama, The Green Mamba, The Strange Case and The Investors.
MCSET. Cat no: **SAY 117**. Released on Argo (Polygram), Nov '81 by PolyGram Classics **Deleted** Jan '89.

THREE OAK MYSTERY, THE (Michael Elder).
Note: Abridged.
MCSET. Cat no: **SPF 905-3**. Released on Schiltron Audio Books, '91 by Schiltron Publishing. Note: 4 Cassettes. Playing time 5 hours.

MCSET. Cat no: **1656T**. Released on Travellers Tales, '91 by Travellers Tales. Note: 4 Cassettes.

Wallace, Irving
GUEST OF HONOUR (Roddy McDowall).
Note: Also available on hanging format, catalogue number:- 0001388274
MCSET. Cat no: **000138807X**. Released on Harper Collins, '91 by Harper Collins. Note: 2 Cassettes.

GUEST OF HONOUR (And Carmilla) (Unknown narrator(s)).
MC. Cat no: **NF 9**. Released on Nightfall Tapes, '89 by BMG Records (UK) Ltd..

PRIZE, THE (Joseph Campanella).
MCSET. Cat no: **0001072854**. Released on Harper Collins, '91 by Harper Collins. Note: 2 Cassettes.

SEVENTH SECRET, THE (Paul Scofield).
Note: Also available on hanging format, catalogue number:- 000103149X.
MCSET. Cat no: **0001072862**. Released on Harper Collins, '91 by Harper Collins. Note: 2 Cassettes.

SHORT STORIES (Various artists).
MCSET. Cat no: **1492T**. Released on Travellers Tales, '91 by Travellers Tales. Note: 4 Cassettes.

Wallington, Mark
FIVE HUNDRED MILE WALKIES (Bill Oddie).
MCSET. Cat no: **LFP 7324**. Released on Listen For Pleasure, Feb '88 by EMI Records **Deleted** Apr '90.

Walsh, Maurice
GREEN RUSHES (The Quiet Man) (Peter Adair).
MCSET. Cat no: **COL 2004**. Released on Colophone, Feb '81 by AVLS (Audio-Visual Library Services) **Deleted** '88.

Warner, Jack
ORDINARY COPPER, AN (Jack Warner).
Tracks / Ordinary copper, An / My bruvver in the life guards / Walking hup and dahn the rawlway laines / You can't help laughing / Sea lions and seals / Bunger up o' rat 'oles / Fumper and a flattener of fevvers / Caster up of alabaster plaster / Claude and his sword / Turkish bath attendant / If I'd only put an X instead / Thank you my lady / Frank and his tank / I didn't orter a'ett it.
LP. Cat no: **OU 2237**. Released on One-Up, Aug '81 by EMI Records **Deleted** Aug '86.

Warren, Robert Penn
ROBERT PENN WARREN READS (Robert Penn Warren).
MC. Cat no: **1654**. Released on Caedmon (USA), '89 by Caedmon Records (USA), Bond Street Music.

SELECTED POEMS (Robert Penn Warren).
MC. Cat no: **UNKNOWN.** Released on Caedmon (USA), '81 by Caedmon Records (USA), Bond Street Music.

Waterhouse, Keith
ADVENTURES OF WORZEL GUMMIDGE, THE (Pertwee, Jon).
MC. Cat no: **PTB 604**. Released on Pickwick Talking Books, Jan '83 by Pickwick Records, Clyde Factors.

BILLY LIAR (Keith Barron).
MCSET. Cat no: **1291F**. Released on Travellers Tales, '91 by Travellers Tales. Note: 6 Cassettes.

WORZEL GIVES A LECTURE (And Worzel's Wedding) (Jon Pertwee).
MC. Cat no: **KC 006**. Released on

Kidstuff, Nov '80.
WORZEL GUMMIDGE (Jon Pertwee).
Note: Includes Worzel Gummidge at the Village Fete and New Friends for Worzel.
MCSET. Cat no: **KC 001**. Released on Cover to Cover, Nov '86 by Cover to Cover Cassettes.

WORZEL GUMMIDGE (And His Nephew) (Jon Pertwee).
MC. Cat no: **TTS 9839**. Released on Tempo, Aug '84 by Warwick Records, Celtic Music, Henry Hadaway Organisation.

WORZEL GUMMIDGE (And Muvvers Day) (Jon Pertwee).
MC. Cat no: **TTS 9837**. Released on Tempo, Aug '84 by Warwick Records, Celtic Music, Henry Hadaway Organisation.

WORZEL GUMMIDGE (Fire Drill) (Jon Pertwee).
MC. Cat no: **TTS 9838**. Released on Tempo, Aug '84 by Warwick Records, Celtic Music, Henry Hadaway Organisation.

WORZEL GUMMIDGE (The Trial) (Jon Pertwee).
MC. Cat no: **TTS 9840**. Released on Tempo, Aug '84 by Warwick Records, Celtic Music, Henry Hadaway Organisation.

WORZEL GUMMIDGE (Volume 1) (Jon Pertwee).
Note: Includes the stories Scarecrow Hop and The Tea Party.
MCSET. Cat no: **KC 002**. Released on Cover to Cover, Nov '86 by Cover to Cover Cassettes.

WORZEL GUMMIDGE (Volume 2) (Jon Pertwee).
Note: Includes the stories Saucy Nancy and Worzel's 'Ansome 'Head.
MCSET. Cat no: **KC 003**. Released on Cover to Cover, Nov '86 by Cover to Cover Cassettes.

WORZEL GUMMIDGE (Volume 3) (Jon Pertwee).
Note: Includes the stories A Fair Old Pullover and A Little Learning.
MCSET. Cat no: **KC 004**. Released on Cover to Cover, Nov '86 by Cover to Cover Cassettes.

WORZEL GUMMIDGE (Volume 4) (Jon Pertwee).
Note: Includes the stories Worzels Nephew and The Trial of Worzel.
MCSET. Cat no: **KC 005**. Released on Cover to Cover, Nov '86 by Cover to Cover Cassettes.

WORZEL GUMMIDGE (Volume 5) (Jon Pertwee).
Note: Includes the stories Worzel Gives a Lecture and Worzel's Wedding.
MCSET. Cat no: **KC 006**. Released on Cover to Cover, Nov '86 by Cover to Cover Cassettes.

WORZEL GUMMIDGE (Unknown narrator(s)).
MCSET. Cat no: **DTO 10520**. Released on Ditto, '88 by Pickwick Records, Midland Records.

Watson, Colin
COFFIN SCARCELY USED (Joe Dunlop).
MCSET. Cat no: **1644T**. Released on Travellers Tales, '91 by Travellers Tales. Note: 6 Cassettes.

MCSET. Cat no: **OAS 90093**. Released on Oasis Audio Books, '91 by Isis Audio Books. Note: 6 Cassettes.

LONELY HEART 4122 (Geoffrey Palmer).
MCSET. Cat no: **1179T**. Released on Travellers Tales, '91 by Travellers Tales. Note: 4 Cassettes.

Watson, Jonathan
ONLY A WORLD CUP EXCUSE (Jonathan Watson & Tony Roper).
MC. Cat no: **ZCF 779**. Released on BBC, Apr '90 by BBC Records, Taylors.

ONLY AN EXCUSE (Real History of Scottish Football) (Jonathan Watson & Tony Roper).
Note: From the Naked Radio team, the hilarious history of Scottish football. A must for football fans everywhere.
MC. Cat no: **ZCM 722**. Released on BBC, Dec '88 by BBC Records, Taylors.

ONLY ANOTHER EXCUSE (Jonathan Watson & Tony Roper).
MC. Cat no: **ZCR 752**. Released on BBC, Oct '89 by BBC Records, Taylors.

Waugh, Evelyn
BRIDESHEAD REVISITED (Sir John Gielgud).
MCSET. Cat no: **SAY 1**. Released on Argo (Polygram), Jul '82 by PolyGram Classics **Deleted** Jan '89. Note: Playing time: 2 hours 30 minutes.

MCSET. Cat no: **ARGO 1001**. Released on Argo (EMI), May '89 by EMI Records. Note: 2 Cassettes.

MCSET. Cat no: **1175F**. Released on Travellers Tales, '91 by Travellers Tales. Note: 2 Cassettes.

BRIDESHEAD REVISITED (Jeremy Irons).
MCSET. Cat no: **CAB 350**. Released on Chivers Audio Books, '91 by Chivers Audio Books, Green Dragon Audio Visual. Note: 10 Cassettes.

MCSET. Cat no: **1356/7F**. Released on Travellers Tales, '91 by Travellers Tales. Note: 10 Cassettes.

SCOOP (Simon Cadell).
MCSET. Cat no: **CTC 023**. Released on Cover to Cover, '87 by Cover to Cover Cassettes. Note: 6 cassettes. Playing time: 8 hrs.

MCSET. Cat no: **1019H**. Released on Travellers Tales, '91 by Travellers Tales. Note: 6 cassettes.

VILE BODIES (Robert Hardy).
MCSET. Cat no: **1008H**. Released on Travellers Tales, '91 by Travellers Tales. Note: 6 cassettes.

Webster, Jan
BLUEBELL BLUE (Unknown narrator(s)).
MCSET. Cat no: **1854965204**. Released on Bramhope, '91 by Ulverscroft Soundings. Note: 5 cassettes.

COLLIERS ROW (Elizabeth Henry).
MCSET. Cat no: **1501F**. Released on Travellers Tales, '91 by Travellers Tales. Note: 8 Cassettes.

MCSET. Cat no: **1854963260**. Released on Soundings, '91 by Soundings Records, Bond Street Music. Note: 8 Cassettes.

DIFFERENT WOMAN, A (Anne Dover).
MCSET. Cat no: **1593F**. Released on Travellers Tales, '91 by Travellers Tales. Note: 6 Cassettes.

MCSET. Cat no: **1854963694**. Released on Soundings, '91 by Soundings Records, Bond Street Music. Note: 6 Cassettes.

I ONLY CAN DANCE WITH YOU (Unknown narrator(s)).
MCSET. Cat no: **1854964240**. Released on Bramhope, '91 by Ulverscroft Soundings. Note: 5 Cassettes.

MUCKLE ANNIE (Linda St Claire).
MCSET. Cat no: **1177F**. Released on Travellers Tales, '91 by Travellers Tales. Note: 6 Cassettes.

MCSET. Cat no: **1854962051**. Released on Soundings, '91 by Soundings Records, Bond Street Music. Note: 6 Cassettes.

ONE LITTLE ROOM (Unknown narrator(s)).
MCSET. Cat no: **185496206X**. Released on Bramhope, '91 by Ulverscroft Soundings. Note: 4 Cassettes.

RAGS OF TIME, THE (Unknown narrator(s)).
MCSET. Cat no: **1854962078**. Released on Trio, '91 by EMI Records. Note: 3 Cassettes.

SATURDAY CITY (Elizabeth Henry).
MCSET. Cat no: **1834965662**. Released on Soundings, Mar '92 by Soundings Records, Bond Street Music. Note: 9 cassettes.

Webster, Jean
DADDY-LONG-LEGS (Morag Hood).
MCSET. Cat no: **SPF 912-1**. Released on Schiltron Audio Books, '91 by Schiltron Publishing. Note: 2 Cassettes. Playing time 2 hours

DEAR ENEMY (Morag Hood).
MCSET. Cat no: **SPF 912-2**. Released on Schiltron Audio Books, '91 by Schiltron Publishing. Note: 2 Cassettes. Playing time 3 hours.

Webster, John
DUCHESS OF MALFI, THE (Vari-

ous artists).
MCSET. Cat no: **0334**. Released on Caedmon (USA), '89 by Caedmon Records (USA), Bond Street Music.

Wechsberg, Joseph

LOOKING FOR A BLUEBIRD (Peter Jones).
MCSET. Cat no: **ZBBC 1136**. Released on BBC Radio Collection, Jul '90 by BBC Records. Note: ISBN No: 0563 410839

Weigh, Audrey

SOMEONE TO CARE (Unknown narrator(s)).
MCSET. Cat no: **1854964062**. Released on Trio, '91 by EMI Records. Note: 3 Cassettes.

Weis & Hickman

DRAGONLANCE CHRONICLES VOL.1 (Dragons Of Autumn Twilight) (Peter MacNicol).
Note: Authors are:- Margaret Weis and Tracy Hickman.
MCSET. Cat no: **RC 49**. Released on Random Century, May '92 by Random Century Audiobooks, Conifer Records. Note: ISBN no. 1856860957

Weldon, Fay

BOTTOM LINE (& The Sharp End) (Julie Christie).
MCSET. Cat no: **TTDMC 414**. Released on CSA Tell Tapes, Mar '92 by CSA Tell-Tapes. Note: 2 Cassettes. ISBN No: 1873859147

DARCY'S UTOPIA (Tamara Ustinov).
MCSET. Cat no: **IAB 91112**. Released on Isis Audio Books, '91. Note: 7 Cassettes. Playing time approximately 7 hours 50 minutes.

HEART OF THE COUNTRY (Jacqueline Tong).
MCSET. Cat no: **CAB 239**. Released on Chivers Audio Books, '91 by Chivers Audio Books, Green Dragon Audio Visual. Note: 6 Cassettes.
MCSET. Cat no: **1106R**. Released on Travellers Tales, '91 by Travellers Tales. Note: 6 Cassettes.

LIFE AND LOVES OF A SHE DEVIL, THE (Davina Porter).
MCSET. Cat no: **1348F**. Released on Travellers Tales, '91 by Travellers Tales. Note: 5 cassettes
MCSET. Cat no: **IAB 89022**. Released on Isis Audio Books, '91. Note: 5 Cassettes.

SHRAPNEL ACADEMY, THE (Davina Porter).
MCSET. Cat no: **1604F**. Released on Travellers Tales, '91 by Travellers Tales. Note: 5 Cassettes.
MCSET. Cat no: **IAB 90112**. Released on Isis Audio Books, '91. Note: 5 Cassettes.

WATCHING YOU, WATCHING ME (Patricia Hodge).
MCSET. Cat no: **060055972X**. Released on Hamlyn Books On Tape, Apr '88, Bond Street Music. Note: 2 cassettes.

Wells, H.G.

COUNTRY OF THE BLIND (Various artists).
MC. Cat no: **E 31**. Released on Tutor Tape, '91 by Morley Audio Services.

HISTORY OF MR. POLLY, THE (Peter Jeffrey).
MCSET. Cat no: **418 159-4**. Released on Argo (Polygram), Jun '88 by PolyGram Classics **Deleted** Jan '89.
MCSET. Cat no: **ARGO 1085**. Released on Argo (EMI), May '89 by EMI Records. Note: 2 Cassettes.

MAGIC SHOP AND THE RED ROOM, THE (Peter Bartlett).
MC. Cat no: **TS 352**. Released on Tellastory, '88 by Random Century Audiobooks.

MAN WHO COULD WORK MIRACLES, THE (Hugh Dickson).
MC. Cat no: **TS 357**. Released on Tellastory, '88 by Random Century Audiobooks.

TIME MACHINE, THE (Robert Hardy).
MC. Cat no: **TC LFP 7044**. Released on Listen For Pleasure, Apr '79 by EMI Records.

TIME MACHINE, THE (And War of the Worlds) (Kim Grant & Jonathan Scott).
MCSET. Cat no: **E 54**. Released on Tutor Tape, '91 by Morley Audio Services.

TIME MACHINE, THE (James Mason).
MC. Cat no: **1678**. Released on Caedmon (USA), '89 by Caedmon Records (USA), Bond Street Music.
MC. Cat no: **0001051997**. Released on Collins-Caedmon, '91 by Collins Audio, Taylors, Bond Street Music.

WAR OF THE WORLDS (Robert Hardy).
MCSET. Cat no: **LFP 7502**. Released on Listen For Pleasure, Oct '90 by EMI Records.
MCSET. Cat no: **TC-LFP 7020**. Released on Listen For Pleasure, Nov '77 by EMI Records.

Wesker, Arnold

DRAMATIST SPEAKS, THE (John Arden).
Note: With John Arnold.
MCSET. Cat no: **SAY 58**. Released on Argo (Polygram), Jul '83 by PolyGram Classics **Deleted** Jan '89.
MCSET. Cat no: **1045P**. Released on Travellers Tales, '91 by Travellers Tales. Note: 2 Cassettes.

Wesley, Mary

CAMOMILE LAWN, THE (Sian Phillips).
MCSET. Cat no: **ZBBC 1090**. Released on BBC Audio Collection, Oct '89 by BBC Records. Note: ISBN No: 0563 227222

CAMOMILE LAWN, THE (Carole Boyd).
MCSET. Cat no: **CAB 433**. Released on Chivers Audio Books, '91 by Chivers Audio Books, Green Dragon Audio Visual. Note: 8 Cassettes.
MCSET. Cat no: **1421F**. Released on Travellers Tales, '91 by Travellers Tales. Note: 8 Cassettes.

HAPHAZARD HOUSE (Jane Asher).
MCSET. Cat no: **IAB 91072**. Released on Isis Audio Books, '91. Note: 5 cassettes.

HARNESSING PEACOCKS (Carole Boyd).
MCSET. Cat no: **1690F**. Released on Travellers Tales, '91 by Travellers Tales. Note: 7 Cassettes.
MCSET. Cat no: **IAB 91041**. Released on Isis Audio Books, '91. Note: 7 Cassettes.

JUMPING THE QUEUE (Anna Massey).
MCSET. Cat no: **CAB 471**. Released on Chivers Audio Books, '91 by Chivers Audio Books, Green Dragon Audio Visual. Note: 6 Cassettes.
MCSET. Cat no: **1471F**. Released on Travellers Tales, '91 by Travellers Tales. Note: 6 Cassettes.

NOT THAT SORT OF GIRL (Hazel Temperley).
MCSET. Cat no: **1377F**. Released on Travellers Tales, '91 by Travellers Tales. Note: 8 Cassettes.

SECOND FIDDLE (Anna Massey).
MCSET. Cat no: **1544F**. Released on Travellers Tales, '91 by Travellers Tales. Note: 6 Cassettes.

SENSIBLE LIFE, A (Eleanor Bron).
MCSET. Cat no: **1535/6F**. Released on Travellers Tales, '91 by Travellers Tales. Note: 6 Cassettes.
MCSET. Cat no: **IAB 90114**. Released on Isis Audio Books, '91. Note: 10 Cassettes.

SIXTH SEAL, THE (Carole Boyd).
MCSET. Cat no: **IAB 91102**. Released on Isis Audio Books, Oct '91. Note: 5 Cassettes, Playing time 6 hours 10 minutes.

VACILLATIONS OF POPPY CAREW (Carole Boyd).
MCSET. Cat no: **1636F**. Released on Travellers Tales, '91 by Travellers Tales. Note: 10 Cassettes.
MCSET. Cat no: **IAB 91023**. Released on Isis Audio Books, '92. Note: 10 Cassettes.

West, Morris

MASTERCLASS (Peter Whitman).
MCSET. Cat no: **CAB 485**. Released on Chivers Audio Books, '91 by Chivers Audio Books, Green Dragon Audio Visual. Note: 10 Cassettes.
MCSET. Cat no: **1480/1F**. Released on Travellers Tales, '91 by Travellers Tales. Note: 10 Cassettes.

NAKED COUNTRY, THE (Patrick Malahide).

MCSET. Cat no: **CAB 657**. Released on Chivers Audio Books, Dec '91 by Chivers Audio Books, Green Dragon Audio Visual. Note: 6 cassettes.

SHOES OF THE FISHERMAN, THE (Dermot Crowley).
Note: Also available on hanging format, catalogue number:- 0001388266.
MCSET. Cat no: **CAB 579**. Released on Chivers Audio Books, '91 by Chivers Audio Books, Green Dragon Audio Visual. Note: 8 Cassettes.
MCSET. Cat no: **1660F**. Released on Travellers Tales, '91 by Travellers Tales. Note: 8 Cassettes.

SHOES OF THE FISHERMAN, THE (Roddy McDowall).
MCSET. Cat no: **0001388061**. Released on Harper Collins, '91 by Harper Collins. Note: 2 Cassettes.

West, Sarah
GAME OF CONSEQUENCES, A (Unknown narrator(s)).
MCSET. Cat no: **1854965107**. Released on Trio, '91 by EMI Records. Note: 3 Cassettes.

TO GIVE AND TO HOLD (Unknown narrator(s)).
MCSET. Cat no: **1854964984**. Released on Soundings, '91 by Soundings Records, Bond Street Music. Note: 3 Cassettes.

Westall, Robert
BLITZCAT (Alistair Maydon).
MCSET. Cat no: **1639F**. Released on Travellers Tales, '91 by Travellers Tales. Note: 6 Cassettes.
MCSET. Cat no: **OAS 20591**. Released on Oasis Audio Books, '91 by Isis Audio Books. Note: 6 Cassettes.

Westhall, Robert
MACHINE GUNNERS, THE (James Bolam).
MCSET. Cat no: **CTC 034**. Released on Cover to Cover, '87 by Cover to Cover Cassettes. Note: 4 cassettes. Playing time 5 hrs 10 mins.
MCSET. Cat no: **9095F**. Released on Travellers Tales, '91 by Travellers Tales. Note: 4 Cassettes.

Whalley, Peter
OLD MURDERS (Gordon Griffin).
MCSET. Cat no: **1141T**. Released on Travellers Tales, '91 by Travellers Tales. Note: 4 Cassettes.
MCSET. Cat no: **1854962086**. Released on Bramhope, '91 by Ulverscroft Soundings. Note: 4 Cassettes.

Wharton, Edith
HOUSE OF MIRTH, THE (Eleanor Bron).
MCSET. Cat no: **CTC 053**. Released on Cover to Cover, Oct '88 by Cover to Cover Cassettes. Note: 9 cassettes. 12 hrs.
MCSET. Cat no: **1371/2F**. Released on Travellers Tales, '91 by Travellers Tales. Note: 9 Cassettes.

Wheatley, Dennis
DEVIL RIDES OUT, THE (Anton Rodgers).
MC. Cat no: **TC-LFP 7111**. Released on Listen For Pleasure, '83 by EMI Records.

DEVIL RIDES OUT, THE (Clifford Norgate).
MCSET. Cat no: **CAB 695**. Released on Chivers Audio Books, Apr '92 by Chivers Audio Books, Green Dragon Audio Visual. Note: 10 Cassettes.

White, Antonia
FROST IN MAY (Gretel Davis).
MCSET. Cat no: **OAS 10292**. Released on Oasis Audio Books, Feb '92 by Isis Audio Books. Note: 7 Cassettes. Playing time: 7hrs 30mins.

White, Kenneth
18 POEMS FROM THE BIRD PATH (And 41 Poems from Handbook for the Diamond (Kenneth White).
Tracks / Scotia deserta / Early morning light on Loch Sunart / Letter from Harris / Craw meditation text / Holderlin in Bordeaux / Remembering Gourgounel / In Aquitania / Reading Han Shan in the Pyrenees / Mountain study / Labrador / In the Nashvak night / Brandan's last voyage / Melville in Arrowhead / Ocean way, The / House at the head of the tide, The / Chaoticist manifesto, The / Winter ceremony, The / Late August on the coast.
MC. Cat no: **SSC 092**. Released on Scotsoun, Mar '92 by Scotsoun Recordings, Morley Audio Services. Note: NNYunused

41 POEMS FROM HANDBOOK FOR THE DIAMOND COUNTRY (Kenneth White).
Tracks / Report to Erigena / Morning walk / Chant / New moon / Territory, The / McTaggart / Crab nebula / Near point of Stoer / Most difficult area, The / Sun yoga / In a cafe at Largs / Letter to an old calligrapher / Late December by the sound of Jura / Walls / Round North again / Strathclyde / Late summer journey / Ludaig jetty / Last page of a notebook / High blue day on Scalpay, A / Xephones of Kolophon / Found on the shores of the Black Sea / Europe in the fall / Last days of the academy, The / Theory / Morning's work, A / Fragment of yellow silk, A / Raw blue morning in Antwerp, A / Letter from Amsterdam / Joseph Martin's report / West labrador / Ungava / Achawakamik / Autumn afternoon / South-west corner news / Prose for the Col de Marie-Blanque / Blue thistle sermon / Old seachapel at Paimpol, The / Letter from Wisconsin, A / On the quay at Lannion / Meditant.
MC. Cat no: **SSC 093**. Released on Scotsoun, Apr '92 by Scotsoun Recordings, Morley Audio Services. Note: NNYunused

Whitman, Peter
TRICKS (Ed Bishop).
MCSET. Cat no: **CAB 616**. Released on Chivers Audio Books, '91 by Chivers Audio Books, Green Dragon Audio Visual. Note: 6 Cassettes.

Whitman, Walt
CROSSING BROOKLYN FERRY (Ed Begley).
MC. Cat no: **1233**. Released on Caedmon (USA), '89 by Caedmon Records (USA), Bond Street Music.

I HEAR AMERICA SINGING (Leaves of Grass) (Ed Begley).
MC. Cat no: **1037**. Released on Caedmon (USA), '89 by Caedmon Records (USA), Bond Street Music.

SONG OF THE OPEN ROAD (Leaves of Grass) (Ed Begley).
MC. Cat no: **1154**. Released on Caedmon (USA), '89 by Caedmon Records (USA), Bond Street Music.

Whitney, Phyllis A
BLACK AMBER (Kate Harper).
MCSET. Cat no: **CAB 507**. Released on Chivers Audio Books, '91 by Chivers Audio Books, Green Dragon Audio Visual. Note: 8 Cassettes
MCSET. Cat no: **1645T**. Released on Travellers Tales, '91 by Travellers Tales. Note: 8 Cassettes.

DREAM OF ORCHIDS (Kate Harper).
MCSET. Cat no: **CAB 422**. Released on Chivers Audio Books, '91 by Chivers Audio Books, Green Dragon Audio Visual. Note: 8 Cassettes
MCSET. Cat no: **1493T**. Released on Travellers Tales, '91 by Travellers Tales. Note: 8 Cassettes.

FEATHER ON THE MOON (Kate Harper).
MCSET. Cat no: **CAB 383**. Released on Chivers Audio Books, '91 by Chivers Audio Books, Green Dragon Audio Visual. Note: 8 Cassettes.

FLAMING TREE, THE (Kate Harper).
MCSET. Cat no: **CAB 264**. Released on Chivers Audio Books, '91 by Chivers Audio Books, Green Dragon Audio Visual. Note: 8 Cassettes.
MCSET. Cat no: **1234T**. Released on Travellers Tales, '91 by Travellers Tales. Note: 8 Cassettes.

RAINBOW IN THE MIST (Kate Harper).
MCSET. Cat no: **CAB 457**. Released on Chivers Audio Books, '91 by Chivers Audio Books, Green Dragon Audio Visual. Note: 8 Cassettes.
MCSET. Cat no: **1559T**. Released on Travellers Tales, '91 by Travellers Tales. Note: 8 Cassettes.

RAINSONG (Helen Horton).
MCSET. Cat no: **CAB 145**. Released on Chivers Audio Books, '91 by Chivers Audio Books, Green Dragon Audio Visual. Note: 8 Cassettes.

MCSET. Cat no: **1179F**. Released on Travellers Tales, '91 by Travellers Tales. Note: 8 Cassettes.

SILVERWORD (Kate Harper).
MCSET. Cat no: **CAB 332**. Released on Chivers Audio Books, '91 by Chivers Audio Books, Green Dragon Audio Visual. Note: 8 Cassettes.

MCSET. Cat no: **1384T**. Released on Travellers Tales, '91 by Travellers Tales. Note: 8 Cassettes.

SINGING STONES, THE (Kate Harper).
MCSET. Cat no: **CAB 569**. Released on Chivers Audio Books, '91 by Chivers Audio Books, Green Dragon Audio Visual. Note: 8 Cassettes.

MCSET. Cat no: **1651F**. Released on Travellers Tales, '91 by Travellers Tales. Note: 8 Cassettes.

Whybrow, Ian

SNIFF STORIES, THE (Tony Robinson).
MCSET. Cat no: **3CCA 3125**. Released on Chivers Audio Books, '91 by Chivers Audio Books, Green Dragon Audio Visual. Note: 3 Cassettes.

Widdicombe, Susan

EMPTY MOON, THE (Anna Bentinck).
MCSET. Cat no: **MRC 1052**. Released on Chivers Audio Books, '91 by Chivers Audio Books, Green Dragon Audio Visual.

Wiggin, Kate

See under Douglas Wiggin, Kate

Wilbur, Richard

READING HIS POETRY (Richard Wilbur).
MC. Cat no: **1248**. Released on Caedmon (USA), '89 by Caedmon Records (USA), Bond Street Music.

Wilde, Oscar

BALLAD OF READING GAOL (James Mason).
MC. Cat no: **1473**. Released on Caedmon (USA), '90 by Caedmon Records (USA), Bond Street Music.

CANTERVILLE GHOST, THE (Unknown narrator(s)).
MC. Cat no: **TTC/OWO2**. Released on Talking Tape Company, '84, Conifer Records.
MC. Cat no: **TS 350**. Released on Tellastory, '88 by Random Century Audiobooks.
MC. Cat no: **2051**. Released on Caedmon (USA), '88 by Caedmon Records (USA), Bond Street Music.

HAPPY PRINCE, THE (And Other Stories) (Peter Bartlett & Barbara Bliss).
MC. Cat no: **TS 308**. Released on Tellastory, '91 by Random Century Audiobooks. Note: ISBN no.1856561135

HAPPY PRINCE, THE (Unknown narrator(s)).

Note: Book and cassette.
MC. Cat no: **PLBC 113**. Released on Tell-A-Tale, '88 by Pickwick Records, Taylors, Clyde Factors.

MC. Cat no: **TTCOWO 3**. Released on Talking Tape Company, '84, Conifer Records.

HAPPY PRINCE, THE (Unknown narrator(s)).
MC. Cat no: **1856561135**. Released on Random Century, '91 by Random Century Audiobooks, Conifer Records.

HAPPY PRINCE, THE (Part 2) (Sir John Gielgud).
Tracks / Devoted friend, The / Remarkable rocket, The.
Note: Incidental music by Ravel: Laideronette, Imperatrice; and Shostakovich preludes No. 9 and No. 10. Playing time: 54.59.
CD. Cat no: **NIM 5037**. Released on Nimbus, '88 by Nimbus Records, Taylors, Nimbus Records.

HAPPY PRINCE, THE (Part One) (Sir John Gielgud).
Tracks / Happy prince, The / Rose and the nightingale / Selfish giant, The.
Note: Incidental music by Vaughan Williams: Fantasia on Greensleeves, Sarabande from Concerto Grosso, and Granados 'Oriental'. Playing time: 56:49.
CD. Cat no: **NIM 5036**. Released on Nimbus, '88 by Nimbus Records, Taylors, Nimbus Records.

HAPPY PRINCE, THE (And Other Fairy Tales) (Basil Rathbone).
MC. Cat no: **1044**. Released on Caedmon (USA), '88 by Caedmon Records (USA), Bond Street Music.

IMPORTANCE OF BEING EARNEST, THE (Various artists).
MCSET. Cat no: **0329**. Released on Caedmon (USA), '89 by Caedmon Records (USA), Bond Street Music. Note: 2 cassettes

IMPORTANCE OF BEING EARNEST, THE (Sir John Gielgud & Dame Edith Evans).
Note: Cast includes: John Worthing - Sir John Gielgud, Algernon Moncrieff - Roland Culver, Lady Bracknell - Dame Edith Evans, Hon. Gwendolen Fairfax - Pamela Brown, Cecily Cardew - C lia Johnson, Miss Prism - Jean Cadell, Rev. Canon Chausuble - Aubrey Mather, Merriman - Brewster Mason, Lane - Peter Sallis.
MCSET. Cat no: **LFP 7242**. Released on Listen For Pleasure, May '86 by EMI Records.

MCSET. Cat no: **1049P**. Released on Travellers Tales, '91 by Travellers Tales. Note: 2 Cassettes.

LORD ARTHUR SAVILE'S CRIME (And The Canterville Ghost) (John Standing).
MCSET. Cat no: **TTC 2018**. Released on Talking Tape Company, Apr '91, Conifer Records. Note: 2 cassettes. Playing time 1hr 35 mins. ISBN No. 187252011

MCSET. Cat no: **TTC 025**. Released on Talking Tape Company, '91, Conifer Records.

PICTURE OF DORIAN GRAY, THE (Anthony Homyer).
MCSET. Cat no: **TCL 18**. Released on Complete Listener, '91 by Complete Listener. Note: 6 Cassettes. Playing Time: 540 Minutes.

PICTURE OF DORIAN GRAY, THE (Hurd Hatfield).
MC. Cat no: **1095**. Released on Caedmon (USA), '88 by Caedmon Records (USA), Bond Street Music.

STORIES FOR CHILDREN (Robert Morley).
Note: Includes: The Happy Prince, The Starchild, The Selfish Giant, The Nightingale and the Rose and The Young King.
MCSET. Cat no: **SAY 72**. Released on Argo (Polygram), Jun '88 by PolyGram Classics **Deleted** Jan '89.

MCSET. Cat no: **9097F**. Released on Travellers Tales, '91 by Travellers Tales. Note: 2 Cassettes.

Willard, Barbara

SPELL ME A WITCH (Rula Lenska).
MCSET. Cat no: **3CCA 3154**. Released on Chivers Audio Books, '91 by Chivers Audio Books, Green Dragon Audio Visual. Note: 3 Cassettes.

Williams, David

ADVERTISE FOR TREASURE (William Franklyn).
MCSET. Cat no: **CAT 4071**. Released on Chivers Audio Books, '91 by Chivers Audio Books, Green Dragon Audio Visual. Note: 6 cassettes.

Williams, Eric

WOODEN HORSE (Sheila Hancock).
MC. Cat no: **TCLFP 417 122 5**. Released on Listen For Pleasure, '83 by EMI Records.

Williams, Margery

VELVETEEN RABBIT, THE (Unknown narrator(s)).

MC. Cat no: **00 102219 9**. Released on Tempo, '88 by Warwick Records, Celtic Music, Henry Hadaway Organisation.

Williams, Tennessee

GLASS MENAGERIE, THE (Various artists).
MCSET. Cat no: **301**. Released on Caedmon (USA), '88 by Caedmon Records (USA), Bond Street Music. Note: 2 cassettes

ROSE TATTOO, THE (Various artists).
MCSET. Cat no: **0324**. Released on Caedmon (USA), '89 by Caedmon Records (USA), Bond Street Music. Note: 3 cassettes

STREETCAR NAMED DESIRE, A (Various artists).
MCSET. Cat no: **0357**. Released on Caedmon (USA), May '88 by Caedmon

Records (USA), Bond Street Music. Note: 2 cassettes

Williamson, Henry

TARKA THE OTTER (Richard Attenborough).
MCSET. Cat no: **1183F**. Released on Travellers Tales, '91 by Travellers Tales. Note: 2 Cassettes.

TARKA THE OTTER (David Attenborough).
MCSET. Cat no: **LFP 7034**. Released on Listen For Pleasure, Jan '84 by EMI Records.

Wilmer, Diane

ADVENTURES OF FIREMAN SAM, THE (John Alderton).
MC. Cat no: **00 1041339**. Released on Tempo, '88 by Warwick Records, Celtic Music, Henry Hadaway Organisation. Note: 1 cassette & 4 books

FIREMAN SAM (Unknown narrator(s)).
Tracks / Fireman Sam / Pontpandy bus, The / Person in charge is Officer Steele, The / Bella and her cat, Rosa / Elvis cooks the lunch / Dilys always knows / Sarah and James / Naughty Norman Price / Inventing shed, The / Snow Business suite, The / Snowy morning - here comes Trevor, A / Elvis helps out / Great sledge race, The / Jupiter to the rescue / Four steps to safety / Another mince pie / Christmas tree / Lights out.
MCSET. Cat no: **HSC 654**. Released on Pickwick, May '89 by Pickwick Records, Clyde Factors, Taylors, Arabesque, Solomon & Peres, I & B Records, Prism Leisure, Outlet Records.

FIREMAN SAM (Norman's Spooky Night) (Victor Spinetti).
MCSET. Cat no: **0411396129**. Released on Harper Collins, '91 by Harper Collins.

FIREMAN SAM (Bad Day For Dilys) (Victor Spinetti).
MC. Cat no: **0001010077**. Released on Harper Collins, '91 by Harper Collins.

FIREMAN SAM (Bella And The Bird's Nest) (Victor Spinetti).
MC. Cat no: **0001010085**. Released on Harper Collins, '91 by Harper Collins.

FIREMAN SAM (Jeremy Bullock). Note: Also available on hanging format, Cat. No: 0411381024.
MC. Cat no: **0411400525**. Released on Harper Collins, '91 by Harper Collins. Note: Playing time: 68 minutes.

FIREMAN SAM (Trevor's Trial Run) (Victor Spinetti).
MC. Cat no: **0411396110**. Released on Harper Collins, '91 by Harper Collins.

SAM SMELLS A RAT (John Alderton).
MC. Cat no: **00 103455 3**. Released on Tempo, '88 by Warwick Records, Celtic Music, Henry Hadaway Organisation. Note: Book and tape set

SAM TO THE RESCUE (Unknown narrator(s)).
MC. Cat no: **RWM 005**. Released on Tell-A-Tale, Sep '90 by Pickwick Records, Taylors, Clyde Factors.

SAM'S BUMPER JUMPER (John Alderton).
MC. Cat no: **0 00 102180 X**. Released on Tempo, '88 by Warwick Records, Celtic Music, Henry Hadaway Organisation.

SAM'S NIGHT WATCH (John Alderton).
MC. Cat no: **00 1034561**. Released on Tempo, '88 by Warwick Records, Celtic Music, Henry Hadaway Organisation. Note: Book and ttape set

SAM'S RABBIT RESCUE (John Alderton).
MC. Cat no: **0 00 102179 6**. Released on Tempo, '88 by Warwick Records, Celtic Music, Henry Hadaway Organisation.

Wilson, A. & N.

GENTLEMEN IN ENGLAND (Michael Barnes).
MCSET. Cat no: **1423/4F**. Released on Travellers Tales, '91 by Travellers Tales. Note: 12 cassettes.

MCSET. Cat no: **OAS 90016**. Released on Oasis Audio Books, '91 by Isis Audio Books.

Wilson, Bob

STANLEY BAGSHAW (Bob Wilson).
MC. Cat no: **881654**. Released on Puffin Cover To Cover, '88, Green Dragon Audio Visual.

Wilson, David Henry

THERE'S A WOLF IN MY PUDDING (Tony Robinson).
MCSET. Cat no: **2CCA 3110**. Released on Chivers Audio Books, '91 by Chivers Audio Books, Green Dragon Audio Visual. Note: 2 Cassettes.
MCSET. Cat no: **9200F**. Released on Travellers Tales, '91 by Travellers Tales. Note: 2 Cassettes.

Wilson, Des

COSTA DEL SOL (Gordon Griffin).
MC. Cat no: **1854965670**. Released on Soundings, Mar '92 by Soundings Records, Bond Street Music. Note: 9 cassettes

Wilson, Forrest

SUPER GRAN (Gudrun Ure).
MCSET. Cat no: **3CCA 3137**. Released on Chivers Audio Books, '91 by Chivers Audio Books, Green Dragon Audio Visual. Note: 3 Cassettes.

Wimpole Village

FIRE ON THE FARM.
MC. Cat no: **39570**. Released on Tempo, Sep '89 by Warwick Records, Celtic Music, Henry Hadaway Organisation.

Winchester, Kay

STADDLECOMBE (Hilary Thomson).
MCSET. Cat no: **CLT 1010**. Released on Candlelight, '88 by AVLS (Audio-Visual Library Services).

Winterson, Jeanette

ORANGES ARE NOT THE ONLY FRUIT (Charlotte Coleman).
MCSET. Cat no: **ZBBC 1152**. Released on BBC Audio Collection, Mar '90 by BBC Records. Note: ISBN No: 0563 410701

Wodehouse, P.G.

BLANDINGS CASTLE (Martin Jarvis).
MCSET. Cat no: **RC 71**. Released on Random Century, Jun '92 by Random Century Audiobooks, Conifer Records. Note: ISBN no. 1856860752

CARRY ON JEEVES (Jonathan Cecil).
MCSET. Cat no: **CAB 570**. Released on Chivers Audio Books, '91 by Chivers Audio Books, Green Dragon Audio Visual. Note: 8 Cassettes.
MCSET. Cat no: **1060H**. Released on Travellers Tales, '91 by Travellers Tales. Note: 8 cassettes.

CODE OF THE WOOSTERS, THE (Jonathan Cecil).
MCSET. Cat no: **CAB 497**. Released on Chivers Audio Books, '91 by Chivers Audio Books, Green Dragon Audio Visual. Note: 6 Cassettes.
MCSET. Cat no: **1057H**. Released on Travellers Tales, '91 by Travellers Tales. Note: 6 Cassettes.

FULL MOON (Jeremy Sinden).
MCSET. Cat no: **CAB 696**. Released on Chivers Audio Books, Apr '92 by Chivers Audio Books, Green Dragon Audio Visual. Note: 6 Cassettes

GALAHAD AT BLANDINGS (Unknown narrator(s)).
MCSET. Cat no: **ZBBC 1308**. Released on BBC Radio Collection, '91 by BBC Records.

GOLF OMNIBUS, THE (Simon Cadell).
MCSET. Cat no: **ZBBC 1160**. Released on BBC Radio Collection, Jul '90 by BBC Records. Note: ISBN No: 0563 410841

HEAVY WEATHER (Martin Jarvis).
MCSET. Cat no: **RC 54**. Released on Random Century, May '92 by Random Century Audiobooks, Conifer Records. Note: ISBN no. 1856860639

INIMITABLE JEEVES, THE (Jonathon Cecil).
MCSET. Cat no: **1014H**. Released on Travellers Tales, '91 by Travellers Tales. Note: 6 cassettes.

JEEVES (Various artists).
MC. Cat no: **1137**. Released on Caedmon (USA), '89 by Caedmon Records (USA), Bond Street Music.

JEEVES AND THE FEUDAL SPIRIT (Michael Horden & Richard Briers).
Note: Starring Richard Briers as Bertie

Wooster and Michael Hordern as Jeeves.
MCSET. Cat no: ZBBC 1116. Released on BBC Radio Collection, Apr '90 by BBC Records. Note: ISBN No: 0563 410329

JEEVES AND THE YULETIDE SPIRIT (And The Clicking Of Cuthbert) (Timothy Carlton).
MCSET. Cat no: TTC 2033. Released on Talking Tape Company, Apr '91, Conifer Records. Note: 2 cassettes. Playing time 1hr. 28mins. ISBN no.187252009X

MCSET. Cat no: TTCW 14. Released on Talking Tape Company, '91, Conifer Records. Note: 6 cassettes

JEEVES AND THE YULETIDE SPIRIT (Unknown narrator(s)).
MC. Cat no: **TTC/PGW 2.** Released on Talking Tape Company, '84, Conifer Records.

JEEVES IN THE OFFING (Ian Carmichael).
MCSET. Cat no: 1013H. Released on Travellers Tales, '91 by Travellers Tales. Note: 6 cassettes

JEEVES STORIES (Unknown narrator(s)).
MC. Cat no: **PTB 620.** Released on Pickwick, '83 by Pickwick Records, Clyde Factors, Taylors, Arabesque, Solomon & Peres, I & B Records, Prism Leisure, Outlet Records.

JOY IN THE MORNING (Jonathan Cecil).
MCSET. Cat no: CAB 628. Released on Chivers Audio Books, '91 by Chivers Audio Books, Green Dragon Audio Visual. Note: 8 Cassettes.

LEAVE IT TO PSMITH (Martin Jarvis).
Note: From the Blandings Castle series.
MCSET. Cat no: RC 19. Released on Random Century, '91 by Random Century Audiobooks, Conifer Records. Note: 2 cassettes. ISBN 1856860469. 3 hrs approx.

LORD EMSWORTH (And Others) (Martin Jarvis).
Note: From The Blandings Castle series.
MCSET. Cat no: RC 39. Released on Random Century, '91 by Random Century Audiobooks, Conifer Records. Note: 2 cassettes. ISBN 1856860671. 3 hrs approx.

LORD EMSWORTH AND THE GIRLFRIEND (And Mulliners-U-Uppo) (Timothy Carlton).
MCSET. Cat no: TTC 2034. Released on Talking Tape Company, Apr '91, Conifer Records. Note: 2 cassettes. Playing time 1hr. 20mins. ISBN no.1872520103

MCSET. Cat no: TTCW 15. Released on Talking Tape Company, '91, Conifer Records.

MAN UPSTAIRS, THE (And Other Stories) (Robin Browne).

MCSET. Cat no: IAB 92042. Released on Isis Audio Books, Apr '92. Note: 8 cassettes. Playing time 11hrs. 45mins.

MATING SEASON, THE (Jonathan Cecil).
MCSET. Cat no: CAB 667. Released on Chivers Audio Books, Jan '92 by Chivers Audio Books, Green Dragon Audio Visual. Note: 8 cassettes.

MUCH OBLIGED, JEEVES (Dinsdale Landen).
MCSET. Cat no: 1016H. Released on Travellers Tales, '91 by Travellers Tales. Note: 4 cassettes.

PELICAN AT BLANDINGS (Unknown narrator(s)).
MCSET. Cat no: RC 64. Released on Random Century, '91 by Random Century Audiobooks, Conifer Records.

PIGS HAVE WINGS (Martin Jarvis).
MCSET. Cat no: RC 53. Released on Random Century, May '92 by Random Century Audiobooks, Conifer Records. Note: ISBN no. 1856860760

RIGHT HO, JEEVES (Jonathan Cecil).
MCSET. Cat no: CAB 414. Released on Chivers Audio Books, '91 by Chivers Audio Books, Green Dragon Audio Visual. Note: 6 Cassettes.

MCSET. Cat no: 1050H. Released on Travellers Tales, '91 by Travellers Tales. Note: 6 cassettes.

RIGHT HO, JEEVES (Ian Carmichael).
MCSET. Cat no: 0563225807. Released on BBC, '91 by BBC Records, Taylors.

SHORT STORIES (Timothy Carlton).
MCSET. Cat no: 1021H. Released on Travellers Tales, '91 by Travellers Tales. Note: 6 cassettes.

SOMETHING FRESH (Peter Barker).
MCSET. Cat no: 1056H. Released on Travellers Tales, '91 by Travellers Tales. Note: 8 cassettes.

MCSET. Cat no: OAS 90101. Released on Oasis Audio Books, '91 by Isis Audio Books. Note: 8 Cassettes.

SUMMER LIGHTNING (Ian Carmichael).
MCSET. Cat no: ZBBC 1044. Released on BBC Radio Collection, Sep '88 by BBC Records. Note: ISBN No: 0563 225807

THANK YOU, JEEVES (Al Spencer).
MCSET. Cat no: 1058H. Released on Travellers Tales, '91 by Travellers Tales. Note: 4 cassettes.

MCSET. Cat no: RB 84130. Released on Recorded Books, '91 by Isis Audio Books.

UKRIDGE'S ACCIDENT SYNDICATE (And Anselm Gets His Chance) (Timothy Carlton).
MCSET. Cat no: TTC 2032. Released on Talking Tape Company, '91, Conifer Records. Note: 2 cassettes. Playing

time 1hr-40mins. ISBN no.187252081
MCSET. Cat no: TTCW 13. Released on Talking Tape Company, '91, Conifer Records. Note: 2 cassettes. Playing time 1hr-40mins. ISBN no.187252081

UNCLE FRED IN THE SPRINGTIME (Martin Jarvis).
Note: From the Blandings Castle series.
MCSET. Cat no: RC 20. Released on Random Century, '91 by Random Century Audiobooks, Conifer Records. Note: 2 cassettes. ISBN 1856860477. 3 hrs approx.

VERY GOOD JEEVES (Martin Jarvis).
MCSET. Cat no: 0600560767. Released on Hamlyn Books On Tape, Apr '88, Bond Street Music. Note: 2 Cassettes.

Wold, Gary K

WHO FRAMED ROGER RABBIT? (Unknown narrator(s)).
MC. Cat no: **DIS 009.** Released on Disney (Read-a-long), Jul '90 by Disneyland Records.

Wolfe, Tom

BONFIRE OF THE VANITIES (John Lithgow).
MCSET. Cat no: RC 5. Released on Random Century, '91 by Random Century Audiobooks, Conifer Records. Note: 2 cassettes. ISBN 1856860043. 3 hrs approx.

Wonzencraft, Kim

RUSH (Unknown narrator(s)).
MCSET. Cat no: 0671704508. Released on Simon & Schuster, '91 by Simon & Schuster Ltd.

Wood, Margaret

LAMPLIGHT OVER THE LAKE (Anne Cater).
MCSET. Cat no: 1854965778. Released on Bramhope, Mar '92 by Ulverscroft Soundings. Note: Playing time: 60 minutes.

Wood, Victoria

VICTORIA WOOD (Victoria Wood).
MCSET. Cat no: ZBBC 1263. Released on BBC, Nov '91 by BBC Records, Taylors.

Woodman, Richard

CORVETTE, THE (A Nathaniel Drinkwater Adventure) (Jeremy Sinden).
MCSET. Cat no: **IAB 92068.** Released on Isis Audio Books, Jun '92. Note: 8 Cassettes. Playing time: 11 1/2 hours

Woolf, Virginia

MRS. DALLOWAY (And to the Lighthouse) (Celia Johnson).
MC. Cat no: **1105.** Released on Caedmon (USA), '89 by Caedmon Records (USA), Bond Street Music.
MC. Cat no: **00010725601.** Released on Collins-Caedmon, '91 by Collins Audio, Taylors, Bond Street Music.

ROOM OF ONE'S OWN, A (Claire Bloom).
MC. Cat no: **1718.** Released on Caedmon (USA), Aug '83 by Caedmon Records (USA), Bond Street Music.
MC. Cat no: **0001071556.** Released on Collins-Caedmon, '91 by Collins Audio, Taylors, Bond Street Music.

Wordsworth, William
POETRY OF WORDSWORTH, THE (Sir Cedric Hardwick).
Note: Includes *The Prelude*, *Tintern Abbey*, *Intimations of immortality*.
MC. Cat no: **1026.** Released on Caedmon (USA), '89 by Caedmon Records (USA), Bond Street Music.

Wright, Daphne
LONGEST WINTER, THE (Judith Porter).
MCSET. Cat no: **185496478X.** Released on Soundings, Aug '91 by Soundings Records, Bond Street Music. Note: 9 Cassettes.

PARROT CAGE, THE (Anne Dover).
MCSET. Cat no: **1854965522.** Released on Soundings, Feb '92 by Soundings Records, Bond Street Music. Note: 10 cassettes.

Wright, Katrina
DANGEROUS LOVE (Unknown narrator(s)).
MCSET. Cat no: **1854962094.** Released on Soundings, '91 by Soundings Records, Bond Street Music. Note: 2 Cassettes.

LOVE IN THE SPOTLIGHT (Elizabeth Henry).
MCSET. Cat no: **1854964569.** Released on Trio, May '91 by EMI Records. Note: 3 Cassettes.

LOVE ON A DARK ISLAND (Unknown narrator(s)).
MCSET. Cat no: **1854962108.** Released on Soundings, '91 by Soundings Records, Bond Street Music. Note: 2 Cassettes.

LOVE ON THE NILE (Unknown narrator(s)).
MCSET. Cat no: **1854962116.** Released on Soundings, '91 by Soundings Records, Bond Street Music. Note: 2 Cassettes.

MASKED LOVE (Unknown narrator(s)).
MCSET. Cat no: **1854962124.** Released on Soundings, '91 by Soundings Records, Bond Street Music. Note: 2 Cassettes.

SHADOW OF CLORINDA (Unknown narrator(s)).
MCSET. Cat no: **1854962132.** Released on Soundings, '91 by Soundings Records, Bond Street Music. Note: 2 Cassettes.

SPY IN PETTICOATS, THE (Unknown narrator(s)).
MCSET. Cat no: **1854962140.** Released on Soundings, '91 by Soundings Records, Bond Street Music. Note: 2 Cassettes.

SUSANNAH'S SECRET (Unknown narrator(s)).
MCSET. Cat no: **SOUND 19.** Released on Soundings, Mar '85 by Soundings Records, Bond Street Music.

MCSET. Cat no: **1854962159.** Released on Soundings, '91 by Soundings Records, Bond Street Music. Note: 2 Cassettes.

Wright, Richard
BLACK BOY (Brock Peters).
MCSET. Cat no: **2030.** Released on Caedmon (USA), '89 by Caedmon Records (USA), Bond Street Music.

NATIVE SON (James Earl Jones).
MC. Cat no: **2068.** Released on Caedmon (USA), '89 by Caedmon Records (USA), Bond Street Music.

Wynd, Oswald
GINGER TREE, THE (Simon Cadell).
MCSET. Cat no: **ZBBC 1130.** Released on BBC Radio Collection, Mar '90 by BBC Records. Note: ISBN No: 0563 410663

GINGER TREE, THE (Hannah Gordon).
MCSET. Cat no: **1477F.** Released on Travellers Tales, '91 by Travellers Tales. Note: 8 cassettes

MCSET. Cat no: **OAS 90062.** Released on Oasis Audio Books, '91 by Isis Audio Books. Note: 8 Cassettes.

Wyndham, John
CHRYSALIDS, THE (Robert Powell).
MCSET. Cat no: **1012S.** Released on Travellers Tales, '91 by Travellers Tales. Note: 6 Cassettes.

DAY OF THE TRIFFIDS, THE (Robert Powell).
Note: Abridged.
MCSET. Cat no: **LFP 7298.** Released on Listen For Pleasure, Jun '87 by EMI Records.

MCSET. Cat no: **1016S.** Released on Travellers Tales, '91 by Travellers Tales. Note: 2 Cassettes.

Wynne-Jones, Tim
THINKING ROOM, THE (And The Jogger) (Various artists).
MC. Cat no: **NF 14.** Released on Nightfall Tapes, '89 by BMG Records (UK) Ltd..

Wyss, Johann
SWISS FAMILY ROBINSON (Anthony Quayle).
MC. Cat no: **1485.** Released on Caedmon (USA), '89 by Caedmon Records (USA), Bond Street Music.

SWISS FAMILY ROBINSON (Children's Classics) (Unknown narrator(s)).
Note: Book and cassette.

MC. Cat no: **PLBC 75.** Released on Tell-A-Tale, '88 by Pickwick Records, Taylors, Clyde Factors.

SWISS FAMILY ROBINSON (Ray Dunbobbin).
MCSET. Cat no: **1334F.** Released on Travellers Tales, '91 by Travellers Tales. Note: 8 cassettes

MCSET. Cat no: **1854962167.** Released on Soundings, '91 by Soundings Records, Bond Street Music. Note: 8 Cassettes.

Yates, Dornford
BLIND CORNER (Alan Rickman).
MCSET. Cat no: **1142T.** Released on Travellers Tales, '91 by Travellers Tales. Note: 6 Cassettes.

Yeats, W.B.
FIVE ONE-ACT PLAYS (Various artists).
MCSET. Cat no: **0315.** Released on Caedmon (USA), '89 by Caedmon Records (USA), Bond Street Music. Note: 3 cassettes

POETRY OF WILLIAM BUTLER YEATS, THE (Various artists).
Note: Includes *Sailing to Byzantium*, *The Second Coming*
MC. Cat no: **1081.** Released on Caedmon (USA), '89 by Caedmon Records (USA), Bond Street Music.

Yeoman, John
HERMIT AND THE BEAR, THE (Tony Robinson).
MCSET. Cat no: **2CCA 3093.** Released on Chivers Audio Books, '91 by Chivers Audio Books, Green Dragon Audio Visual. Note: 2 Cassettes.

MCSET. Cat no: **9154F.** Released on Travellers Tales, '91 by Travellers Tales. Note: 2 Cassettes.

York, Susannah
LARK'S CASTLE (Susannah York).
Note: For 6 to 8 year olds.

MC. Cat no: **B 005.** Released on Green Dragon, '91 by Green Dragon Audio Visual.

Yorke, Margaret
CHINA DOLL, THE (Jan Carey).
MCSET. Cat no: **CAT 4072.** Released on Chivers Audio Books, '91 by Chivers Audio Books, Green Dragon Audio Visual. Note: 4 cassettes.

DEAD IN THE MORNING (Carole Hayman).
MCSET. Cat no: **1143T.** Released on Travellers Tales, '91 by Travellers Tales. Note: 4 cassettes.

DEATH ON ACCOUNT (Carole Hayman).
MCSET. Cat no: **1180T.** Released on Travellers Tales, '91 by Travellers Tales. Note: 4 cassettes.

NO MEDALS FOR THE MAJOR (Carole Hayman).
MCSET. Cat no: **CAT 4030.** Released on Chivers Audio Books, '91 by Chivers

Audio Books, Green Dragon Audio Visual. Note: 4 cassettes.
MCSET. Cat no: **1253T.** Released on Travellers Tales, '91 by Travellers Tales. Note: 4 cassettes.

Young, Rose
SECRET OF ABBEY PLACE (Delia Corrie).
MCSET. Cat no: **MRC 1048.** Released on Chivers Moonlight Romances, Apr '88 by Chivers Audio Books, Green Dragon Audio Visual. Note: 2 cassette set.

Young, Vivien
JENNI (Unknown narrator(s)).
MCSET. Cat no: **SOUND 12.** Released on Soundings, Mar '85 by Soundings Records, Bond Street Music.

SECOND HONEYMOON (Elizabeth Henry).
MCSET. Cat no: **1854965646.** Released on Trio, Feb '92 by EMI Records.

Zabel, Jennifer
ADVENTURES OF CREAMCAKE AND COMPANY (Una Stubbs).
MC. Cat no: **TBC 9509.** Released on Tempo Storytime, May '84 by Warwick Records, Celtic Music.

MORE ADVENTURES OF MY LITTLE PONY (Antonia Swinson).
MC. Cat no: **00 103460X.** Released on Tempo, '88 by Warwick Records, Celtic Music, Henry Hadaway Organisation.

MY LITTLE PONY (Gusty And Genie) (Antonia Swinson).
MC. Cat no: **00 102119 2.** Released on Tempo, '88 by Warwick Records, Celtic Music, Henry Hadaway Organisation.

MY LITTLE PONY (Little Ponies & The Pixie Sea Pirates) (Antonia Swinson).
MC. Cat no: **0 00 102121 4.** Released on Tempo, '88 by Warwick Records, Celtic Music, Henry Hadaway Organisation.

MY LITTLE PONY (The Little Magic Nut Tree) (Antonia Swinson).
MC. Cat no: **0 00 102122 2.** Released on Tempo, '88 by Warwick Records, Celtic Music, Henry Hadaway Organisation.

MY LITTLE PONY (Dancing & Bad Tempered Butterflies) (Antonia Swinson).
MC. Cat no: **0 00 102123 0.** Released on Tempo, '88 by Warwick Records, Celtic Music, Henry Hadaway Organisation.

MY LITTLE PONY (Baby Quackers & The Sad Quolly) (Antonia Swinson).
MC. Cat no: **0 00 102124 9.** Released on Tempo, '88 by Warwick Records, Celtic Music, Henry Hadaway Organisation.

MY LITTLE PONY (The Grand Pony Parade) (Antonia Swinson).
MC. Cat no: **00 102120 6.** Released on Tempo, '88 by Warwick Records, Celtic Music, Henry Hadaway Organisation.

Zola, Emile
CONTES A NINON (Various narrators).
Note: French narration for practice linguists.
MCSET. Cat no: **EAC 04D.** Released on European Audio Classics, '91 by Unknown. Note: 2 cassettes - ISBN no. 1873256159

NANA (Irene Worth).
MC. Cat no: **000105192X.** Released on Collins-Caedmon, '91 by Collins Audio, Taylors, Bond Street Music.

NON-FICTION SECTION

Adams, Douglas
LAST CHANCE TO SEE (Unknown narrator(s)).
Note: Authors are Douglas Adams and Mark Carwardine.
MCSET. Cat no: **RC 6.** Released on Random Century, '91 by Random Century Audiobooks, Conifer Records. Note: 2 cassettes. ISBN no.1856860051. Playing time 3hrs approx.

Adamson, Joy
BORN FREE (Virginia McKenna).
Note: Abridged version.
MCSET. Cat no: **1018N.** Released on Travellers Tales, '91 by Travellers Tales. Note: 2 cassettes.
BORN FREE (Virginia McKenna).
MCSET. Cat no: **LFP 7258.** Released on Listen For Pleasure, Aug '86 by EMI Records **Deleted** Apr '90. Note: 2 Cassettes. Playing time: 2 hours.

Africa
AFRICAN FORESTS AND SAVANNAHS (See under Environmental Sounds) (Various).
BLACK AFRICA: YESTERDAY AND TODAY (Unknown narrator(s)).
MC. Cat no: **HB 13.** Released on Sussex Tapes, '91 by Sussex Publications Ltd..

African
AFRIKAANS (Language Learn) (Unknown narrator(s)).
MCSET. Cat no: **LL01.** Released on Sussex Tapes, '91 by Sussex Publications Ltd.. Note: Playing time: 6 hours. 4 Cassettes.
FSI BASIC AMHARIC (Volume 1) (Unknown narrator(s)).
MCSET. Cat no: **AM 10.** Released on Audio Forum (Language courses), '91. Note: 26 cassettes
FULA BASIC COURSE (Unknown narrator(s)).
MCSET. Cat no: **FU 10.** Released on Audio Forum (Language courses), '91. Note: 29 Cassettes
HAUSA BASIC COURSE (Unknown narrator(s)).
MCSET. Cat no: **HA 1.** Released on Audio Forum (Language courses), '91. Note: 15 Cassettes
SHONA BASIC COURSE (Unknown narrator(s)).
MCSET. Cat no: **SH 10.** Released on Audio Forum (Language courses), '91. Note: 10 Cassettes
SWAHILI, ACTIVE INTRODUCTION (And General Conversation) (Unknown narrator(s)).
MCSET. Cat no: **W 300.** Released on Audio Forum (Language courses), '91. Note: 2 Cassettes
SWAHILI BASIC COURSE (Unknown narrator(s)).
MCSET. Cat no: **W 426.** Released on Audio Forum (Language courses), '91. Note: 20 Cassettes
TWI BASIC COURSE (Unknown narrator(s)).
MCSET. Cat no: **TW 1.** Released on Audio Forum (Language courses), '91. Note: 9 Cassettes
YORUBA BASIC COURSE (Unknown narrator(s)).
MCSET. Cat no: **YR 1.** Released on Audio Forum (Language courses), '91. Note: 36 Cassettes
ZULU (Language Courses) (Unknown narrator(s)).
MCSET. Cat no: **LL02.** Released on Sussex Tapes, '91 by Sussex Publications Ltd.. Note: Playing time: 6 hours. 4 Cassettes

A-Level
ANTHONY AND CLEOPATRA (And Coriolanus) (John Goode & Dr. Terry Eagleton).
MCSET. Cat no: **ELA 030.** Released on AVP, '91 by AVP Publishing.
ART OF THE GENERAL PROLOGUE, THE (Art, Order and Justice in the Knight's Tale) (Dr. Martin Coyle & William O'Evans).
MCSET. Cat no: **ELA 082.** Released on AVP, '91 by AVP Publishing.
AS YOU LIKE IT (The Pastoral World: The Play of Attitudes) (Dr. Michael Hattaway & Ann Thompson).
MCSET. Cat no: **ELA 020.** Released on AVP, '91 by AVP Publishing.
D H LAWRENCE: SONS AND LOVERS (Angus Easson & Terence Wright).
MCSET. Cat no: **ELA 034.** Released on AVP, '91 by AVP Publishing.
D H LAWRENCE: THE RAINBOW (Angus Easson & Terence Wright).
MCSET. Cat no: **ELA 041.** Released on AVP, '91 by AVP Publishing.
DEVELOPMENT OF JANE AUSTEN'S COMIC ART, THE (Dr W A Craik & B C Southam).
MCSET. Cat no: **ELA 007.** Released on AVP, '91 by AVP Publishing.
F SCOTT FITZGERALD (Edward Gallafent & Iain Bruce).
MCSET. Cat no: **ELA 111.** Released on AVP, '91 by AVP Publishing.
FAR FROM THE MADDING CROWD (C G Martin & Barbara Hardy).
MCSET. Cat no: **ELA 029.** Released on AVP, '91 by AVP Publishing.
FIRST WORLD WAR POETS: WILFRED OWEN AND ISAAC ROSENBURG (Dr. Paul Lawley & Dr. Andrew Nicholson).
MCSET. Cat no: **ELA 102.** Released on AVP, '91 by AVP Publishing.
GERARD MANLEY HOPKINS: THE WRECK OF THE DEUTSCHLAND (John Wain & A C Harvey).
MCSET. Cat no: **ELA 015.** Released on AVP, '91 by AVP Publishing.
HAMLET AS PLAY OF REVENGE (The 'Play' of Hamlet) (Moelwyn Merchant & Dr. Terence Hawkes).
MCSET. Cat no: **ELA 004.** Released on AVP, '91 by AVP Publishing.
HAMLET: BOOK OR PLAY? (Hamlet and the Popular Dramatic Tradition) (Dr. Terence Hawkes & Proffessor Maurice Charney).
MCSET. Cat no: **ELA 023.** Released on AVP, '91 by AVP Publishing.
HARDY'S TRAGIC FICTION (Ronald Draper & Roger Gilmour).
MCSET. Cat no: **ELA 043.** Released on AVP, '91 by AVP Publishing.
HARDY'S WESSEX NOVELS (And Tess of the D'Urbervilles) (John Goode & Joan Skidmore).
MCSET. Cat no: **ELA 016.** Released on AVP, '91 by AVP Publishing.
HAROLD PINTER: THE CARETAKER (Katharine Worth & Richard Cave).
MCSET. Cat no: **ELA 108.** Released on AVP, '91 by AVP Publishing.
JUDE THE OBSCURE (John Goode & Dr. Terry Eagleton).
MCSET. Cat no: **ELA 028.** Released on AVP, '91 by AVP Publishing.
KING LEAR (Issues and Resolutions) (R.A. Foakes & Mark Kinhead-Weekes).
MCSET. Cat no: **ELA 005.** Released on AVP, '91 by AVP Publishing.
KING LEAR (Primitivism and the Family/Justice) (Michael Quinn & Martin Coyle).
MCSET. Cat no: **ELA 075.** Released on AVP, '91 by AVP Publishing.
LIFE IN CHAUCER'S ENGLAND (And Courtly Love) (N.F. Blake & J.D. Burnley).
MCSET. Cat no: **ELA 085.** Released on AVP, '91 by AVP Publishing.
LORD OF THE FLIES (And The Spire) (Stephen Metcalfe & John S Whitley).
MCSET. Cat no: **ELA 110.** Released on AVP, '91 by AVP Publishing.
MACBETH AS A TRAGEDY (Macbeth as a Drama) (A R Humphreys & Roger Warren).
MCSET. Cat no: **ELA 025.** Released on AVP, '91 by AVP Publishing.
MANSFIELD PARK: THE SYMBOL OF THE HOUSE (Tone and Meaning in Mansfield Park) (Dr. Stephen Fender & Dr. John Sutherland).
MCSET. Cat no: **ELA 006.** Released on AVP, '91 by AVP Publishing.
MARRIAGE GROUP, THE (Dr. Martin Coyle & William O'Evans).
Note: Includes: The Wife of Bath;s Tale, The Clerk's Tale, The Merchant's Tale and The Franklin's Tale.
MCSET. Cat no: **ELA 081.** Released on AVP, '91 by AVP Publishing.
MEASURE FOR MEASURE (Kenneth Muir & Ann Thompson).
MCSET. Cat no: **ELA 078.** Released on AVP, '91 by AVP Publishing.
MUCH ADO ABOUT NOTHING (Plot & Characters/The Society and its Problems) (Dr. Juliet Dusinberre & Dr. Michael Hattaway).
MCSET. Cat no: **ELA 021.** Released on AVP, '91 by AVP Publishing.
NATURE AND STRUCTURE OF SHAKESPEAREAN COMEDY (Comedy in Elizabethan Theatre) (Peter Davison & Dr. Michael Hattaway).

MCSET. Cat no: **ELA 071**. Released on AVP, '91 by AVP Publishing.
NATURE OF KEATS' GREAT ODES, THE (On a Grecian Urn; To Autumn) (R.A. Foakes & Mark Kinhead-Weekes).
MCSET. Cat no: **ELA 010**. Released on AVP, '91 by AVP Publishing.
NUN'S PRIEST'S TALE, THE (And The Pardoner's Tale) (Dr. Derek Brewer & A.C.Spearing).
MCSET. Cat no: **ELA 019**. Released on AVP, '91 by AVP Publishing.
OTHELLO (The Structure & Organisation of the Play) (Dr D J Palmer & P W Thompson).
MCSET. Cat no: **ELA 024**. Released on AVP, '91 by AVP Publishing.
PARADISE LOST (Gordon Campbell & Brian Nellist).
MCSET. Cat no: **ELA 088**. Released on AVP, '91 by AVP Publishing.
PHILIP LARKIN AND TED HUGHES (Blake Morrison & Craig Raine).
MCSET. Cat no: **ELA 065**. Released on AVP, '91 by AVP Publishing.
POETRY OF GEORGE HERBERT AND ANDREW MARVELL, THE (Dr. Paulina Palmer & Paul Merchant).
MCSET. Cat no: **ELA 093**. Released on AVP, '91 by AVP Publishing.
PRACTICAL CRITCISM: POETRY (Dr. Martin Coyle & John Peck).
MCSET. Cat no: **ELA 083**. Released on AVP, '91 by AVP Publishing.
PRACTICAL CRITICISM: PROSE (Dr. Martin Coyle & John Peck).
MCSET. Cat no: **ELA 084**. Released on AVP, '91 by AVP Publishing.
PRIDE AND PREJUDICE (People and Events - Moral Intelligence) (Dr. W A Craik & A J Smith).
MCSET. Cat no: **EAL 049**. Released on AVP, '91 by AVP Publishing.
RAPE OF THE LOCK, THE (Heroi-Comic and from War to Sex War) (J C Hilson & J S Cunningham).
MCSET. Cat no: **ELA 057**. Released on AVP, '91 by AVP Publishing.
RICHARD II (Dr. Martin Coyle & Michael Quinn).
MCSET. Cat no: **ELA 076**. Released on AVP, '91 by AVP Publishing.
SHAKESPEARE'S WOMEN (Revolution and Submission - Shrews and Victims) (Barbara Hardy & Dr. John Sutherland).
MCSET. Cat no: **ELA 069**. Released on AVP, '91 by AVP Publishing.
SILAS MARNER (Dr. Stephen Fender & Dr. John Sutherland).
MCSET. Cat no: **ELA 054**. Released on AVP, '91 by AVP Publishing.
T S ELLIOT: PRUFROCK, PORTRAIT OF A LADY AND THE WASTELAND (John Chalker & Edward Neil).
MCSET. Cat no: **ELA 035**. Released on AVP, '91 by AVP Publishing.
TEMPEST: UNITY (Elements and Occasions?) (Ronald Knowles & Dr J Pilling).
MCSET. Cat no: **ELA 033**. Released on AVP, '91 by AVP Publishing.
TROILUS AND CRESSIDA (The Play and it's Critics; The Unity of the Play) (Kenneth Muir & Ann Thompson).
MCSET. Cat no: **ELA 079**. Released on AVP, '91 by AVP Publishing.
W B YEATS AND THE ROMANTIC TRADITION (C J Rawson & Marjorie Perloff).
MCSET. Cat no: **ELA 026**. Released on AVP, '91 by AVP Publishing.
W B YEATS: POET OF LOVE, POLITICS AND THE OTHER (Yeats' Interest in Politics, the Paranormal and (Desiree Hirst & Dr G M Matthews).
MCSET. Cat no: **ELA 080**. Released on AVP, '91 by AVP Publishing.
W B YEATS: THE NATURAL AND THE SUPERNATURAL (J A Berthoud & A J Smith).
MCSET. Cat no: **ELA 059**. Released on AVP, '91 by AVP Publishing.
WEBSTER: THE WHITE DEVIL (The Duchess of Malfi) (John Russell Brown & Inga-Stina Ewbank).
MCSET. Cat no: **ELA 036**. Released on AVP, '91 by AVP Publishing.
WORDSWORTH: THE LYRICAL BALLADS (The Lyrical Ballads - Intentions and Themes) (Angus Easson & Terence Wright).
MCSET. Cat no: **ELA 063**. Released on AVP, '91 by AVP Publishing.
WORDSWORTH'S 'THE PRELUDE' (The Growth of the Poet's Mind; Spots of Time) (Angus Easson & Terence Wright).
MCSET. Cat no: **ELA 066**. Released on AVP, '91 by AVP Publishing.

Alexander the Great
ALEXANDER THE GREAT (History for Ages 8+) (Unknown narrator(s)). Note: Book and cassette.
MC. Cat no: **PLBH 98**. Released on Tell-A-Tale, '84 by Pickwick Records, Taylors, Clyde Factors.

Allison, William
MONOCLED MUTINEER, THE (Raymond Sawyer).
Note: Authors: William Allison & John Fairley.
MCSET. Cat no: **OAS 91012**. Released on Oasis Audio Books, '91 by Isis Audio Books. Note: 6 cassettes.
MCSET. Cat no: **1634F**. Released on Travellers Tales, '91 by Travellers Tales. Note: 6 Cassettes.

American...
AMERICAN FORESTS AND LAKES (See under Environmental Sounds for details) (Various).
IDEA OF THE FRONTIER, THE (H C Allen & Dr. C W E Bigsby).
MCSET. Cat no: **HAA 001**. Released on AVP, '91 by AVP Publishing.
THOMAS JEFFERSON (P S Haffenden & Dr. G E Watson).
MCSET. Cat no: **HAA 002**. Released on AVP, '91 by AVP Publishing.
WAR OF 1812, THE (C Bonwick & Martin Crawford).
MCSET. Cat no: **HAA 003**. Released on AVP, '91 by AVP Publishing.
WESTWARD EXPANSION (R A Burchell & P D Marshall).
MCSET. Cat no: **HAA 018**. Released on AVP, '91 by AVP Publishing.

Ancient Greek
PRONUNCIATION AND READING OF ANCIENT GREEK, THE (Unknown narrator(s)).
Note: Includes booklet and selections from Homer and Plato.
MCSET. Cat no: **23660**. Released on Sussex Tapes, '91 by Sussex Publications Ltd..
RECITAL OF ANCIENT GREEK POETRY, A (Unknown narrator(s)).
Note: Includes selections from Homer, Sappho, Pindar, Euripides and Aristophanes.
MCSET. Cat no: **23600**. Released on Sussex Tapes, '91 by Sussex Publications Ltd..

Angelou, Maya
I KNOW WHY THE CAGED BIRD SINGS (Maya Angelou).
Note: From the 'Virago' collection.
MCSET. Cat no: **RC 18**. Released on Random Century, '91 by Random Century Audiobooks, Conifer Records. Note: 2 cassettes. ISBN no. 1856860482. Playing time 3hrs approx.

Anouilh, J
ANTIGONE (Edited By Jacqueline Fox) (Unknown narrator(s)).
Note: A review of the different interpretations this play by J. Anouilh has been given. In French.
MC. Cat no: **F 7558**. Released on Exeter Tapes, '91 by Drakes Educational Associates.
BECKET (Edited By Gerard Poulet) (Unknown narrator(s)).
Note: An evaluation of the historical and purely theatrical dimension of this work by Anouilh. In French.
MC. Cat no: **F 7557**. Released on Exeter Tapes, '91 by Drakes Educational Associates.

Arabic
ARABIC CASSETTE COURSE (Unknown narrator(s)).
Note: Includes a book and an instruction leaflet.
MCSET. Cat no: **852851588**. Released on Hugo Languages, '92 by Hugo Language Books Limited. Note: 4 cassettes. Playing time 4hrs.
ARABIC TRAVEL PACK (Unknown narrator(s)).
Note: Contains a Hugo phrase book.
MC. Cat no: **852851456**. Released on Hugo Languages, '92 by Hugo Language Books Limited. Note: 4 cassettes.
BASIC SAUDI ARABIC (Unknown narrator(s)).

MCSET. Cat no: **A 234.** Released on Audio Forum (Language courses), '91. Note: 10 Cassettes

EASTERN ARABIC (Unknown narrator(s)).
MCSET. Cat no: **A 450.** Released on Audio Forum (Language courses), '91. Note: 9 Cassettes

GET BY ARABIC (Language Courses) (Unknown narrator(s)).
Note: Each book contains phrases and conversations.
MCSET. Cat no: **PTT 281.** Released on BBC Publications, '91. Note : 2 Cassettes.

GET BY TRAVEL PACKS (Language Courses) (Unknown narrator(s)).
MCSET. Cat no: **PACK 2281.** Released on BBC Publications, '91. Note : 2 Cassettes.

INTRODUCING THE ARABIC LANGUAGE (J.R. Smart).
Note: With special reference to the learning problems facing European students of the language.
MC. Cat no: **A 7827.** Released on Exeter Tapes, '91 by Drakes Educational Associates.

LANGUAGE COURSE - ARABIC (MODERN STANDARD) (Unknown narrator(s)).
LPS. Cat no: **074730176 X.** Released on Linguaphone, Apr '82 by Linguaphone Institute, Taylors, Century Records (USA), Bond Street Music.

LEVANTINE ARABIC PRONOUNCIATION (Unknown narrator(s)).
MCSET. Cat no: **A 244.** Released on Audio Forum (Language courses), '91. Note: 10 Cassettes

MODERN WRITTEN ARABIC (Volume 1) (Unknown narrator(s)).
MCSET. Cat no: **A 269.** Released on Audio Forum (Language courses), '91. Note: 8 Cassettes

MODERN WRITTEN ARABIC (Volume 2) (Unknown narrator(s)).
MCSET. Cat no: **A 320.** Released on Audio Forum (Language courses), '91. Note: 8 Cassettes

MOROCCAN ARABIC (Unknown narrator(s)).
MCSET. Cat no: **A 300.** Released on Audio Forum (Language courses), '91. Note: 16 Cassettes

SOUNDS OF ARABIC, THE - PART 1 (Edited by T.F. Mitchell) (Unknown narrator(s)).
Note: Introductory account of the pronunciation of Egyptian colloquial Arabic (Cairo)
MC. Cat no: **A 7861.** Released on Exeter Tapes, '91 by Drakes Educational Associates.

SOUNDS OF ARABIC, THE - PART 2 (Edited by T.F. Mitchell) (Unknown narrator(s)).
Note: With emphasis on Arabic vowel sounds, elision and accentuation.
MC. Cat no: **A 7862.** Released on Exeter Tapes, '91 by Drakes Educational Associates.

tional Associates.
SPOKEN EGYPTIAN ARABIC (Unknown narrator(s)).
MCSET. Cat no: **A 400.** Released on Audio Forum (Language courses), '91. Note: 2 Cassettes

SYRIAN ARABIC (Phonology and Reference Grammar) (Unknown narrator(s)).
MCSET. Cat no: **A 470.** Released on Audio Forum (Language courses), '91. Note: 3 Cassettes

Ariosto, L

ORLANDO FURIOSO (Edited By Luisa Quartermaine) (Unknown narrator(s)).
Note: A brief outline of the main themes in this poetry by Ariosto. It's success and universal appeal are examined. In Italian.
MC. Cat no: **I 7576.** Released on Exeter Tapes, '91 by Drakes Educational Associates.

Arthursson, Elizabeth

EWES AND I (Beryl Dixon).
MCSET. Cat no: **1106N.** Released on Travellers Tales, '91 by Travellers Tales. Note: 4 cassettes.
MCSET. Cat no: **1854964305.** Released on Bramhope, '91 by Ulverscroft Soundings. Note: 4 Cassettes.

Ashcroft, Peggy

WORLD OF, THE (Dame Peggy Ashcroft & Sir John Geilgud).
LP. Cat no: **SPA 573.** Released on Decca, Apr '80 by PolyGram Classics, Thames Distributors Ltd. **Deleted** '88.

Astaire, Fred

TRIBUTE TO FRED ASTAIRE (See under Carrick, Peter) (Christopher Kay).

Astrology

AQUARIUS (Linda Goodman's Star Signs) (Martin Jarvis & Jan Francis).
MC. Cat no: **0600559769.** Released on Hamlyn Books On Tape, Apr '88, Bond Street Music.

ARIES (Linda Goodman's Star Signs) (Martin Jarvis & Jan Francis).
MC. Cat no: **0600559742.** Released on Hamlyn Books On Tape, Apr '88, Bond Street Music.

CANCER (Linda Goodman's Star Signs) (Martin Jarvis & Jan Francis).
MC. Cat no: **0600559661.** Released on Hamlyn Books On Tape, Apr '88, Bond Street Music.

CAPRICORN (Linda Goodman's Star Signs) (Martin Jarvis & Jan Francis).
MC. Cat no: **060055967X.** Released on Hamlyn Books On Tape, Apr '88, Bond Street Music.

GEMINI (Linda Goodman's Star Signs) (Martin Jarvis & Jan Francis).
MC. Cat no: **060055970X.** Released on Hamlyn Books On Tape, Apr '88, Bond Street Music.

LEO (Linda Goodman's Star Signs)

(Martin Jarvis & Jan Francis).
MC. Cat no: **0600559688.** Released on Hamlyn Books On Tape, Apr '88, Bond Street Music.

LIBRA (Linda Goodman's Star Signs) (Martin Jarvis & Jan Francis).
MC. Cat no: **0600559750.** Released on Hamlyn Books On Tape, Apr '88, Bond Street Music.

PISCES (Linda Goodman's Star Signs) (Martin Jarvis & Jan Francis).
MC. Cat no: **0600559769.** Released on Hamlyn Books On Tape, Apr '88, Bond Street Music.

SAGITTARIUS (Linda Goodman's Star Signs) (Martin Jarvis & Jan Francis).
MC. Cat no: **0600559718.** Released on Hamlyn Books On Tape, Apr '88, Bond Street Music.

SCORPIO (Linda Goodman's Star Signs) (Martin Jarvis & Jan Francis).
MC. Cat no: **0600559726.** Released on Hamlyn Books On Tape, Apr '88, Bond Street Music.

TAURUS (Linda Goodman's Star Signs) (Martin Jarvis & Jan Francis).
MC. Cat no: **0600559696.** Released on Hamlyn Books On Tape, Apr '88, Bond Street Music.

VIRGO (Linda Goodman's Star Signs) (Martin Jarvis & Jan Francis).
MC. Cat no: **0600559734.** Released on Hamlyn Books On Tape, Apr '88, Bond Street Music.

Astronomy

NIGHT SKY, THE (Patrick Moore).
Note: A guide to the heavens by Patrick Moore. A layman's guide to astronomy throughout changing seasons of the year.
MC. Cat no: **AC 150.** Released on Audicord, '91 by Audicord Cassettes.

Attenborough, David

TRIALS OF LIFE, THE (A Natural History of Animal Behaviour) (David Attenborough).
MCSET. Cat no: **IAB 92017.** Released on Isis Audio Books, Mar '92. Note : 8 Cassettes. Playing time: 8 hours 48 mins.

Auden, W.H.

POETRY OF W.H. AUDEN, THE (W.H. Auden).
Note: Author reads his work and discusses his formative influences.
MC. Cat no: **AS 02.** Released on Sussex Tapes, '91 by Sussex Publications Ltd..

SOMETHING ABOUT POETRY (W.H. Auden).
MC. Cat no: **23154.** Released on Sussex Tapes, '91 by Sussex Publications Ltd.

Austen, Jane

JANE AUSTEN (David Daiches & Barbara Hardy).
Note: Pre-recorded discussion which show literary criticism as a living, evolving interchange.
MC. Cat no: **A5.** Released on Sussex

Aviation

AVIATORS, THE (Various artists).
Tracks / Air battle over the English Channel 1940: *Various artists* / Amelia Earhart: Women in flying: *Various artists* / Grahame White: The first night flight: *Various artists* / Hon. Mrs Bruce's flight around the world: *Various artists* / Dornier Do. X's transatlantic flight: *Various artists* / Alan Cobham's England to Australia flight: *Various artists* / Condor Legion's 'bomber march': *Various artists* / Kaiser in a Zeppelin, The: *Various artists* / Amy Johnson's flight: *Various artists* / W/Cdr. Charles Kinsford-Smith: *Various artists* / Graf von Zeppelin: *Various artists* / Lindbergh's speech to President Coolidge: *Various artists* / Chamberlin/Levine's transatlantic flight: *Various artists* / Maryse bastie on aviation: *Various artists* / Condor Legion's 'parade' march: *Various artists* / Hindenburg disaster (in full), The: *Various artists*.
CD. Cat no: **PASTCD 9760.** Released on Pearl, Aug '91 by Pavilion Records, Harmonia Mundi (UK).
MC. Cat no: **PAST 7760.** Released on Pearl, Sep '91 by Pavilion Records, Harmonia Mundi (UK).

GREAT BRITISH AIRCRAFT (Various narrators).
Note: Historic recordings, some from World War II, of the aircraft that won the war in the sky over Britain. Also featured are post war jet fighters and bombers.
MC. Cat no: **AC 115.** Released on Audicord, '91 by Audicord Cassettes.

WINGS OF HISTORY VOL. 1 (Sounds at Shuttleworth 1909-42) (Various artists).
LP. Cat no: **AFP 01.** Released on Flightstream, Jun '83.
MC. Cat no: **AFP 01T.** Released on Flightstream, Jun '83.

WINGS OF HISTORY VOL. 2 (Return to Shuttleworth) (Various artists).
LP. Cat no: **AFP 02.** Released on Flightstream, Jun '83.
MC. Cat no: **AFP 02T.** Released on Flightstream, Jun '83.

WINGS OF HISTORY VOL. 3 (Rendezvous - Shuttleworth) (Various artists).
LP. Cat no: **AFP 03.** Released on Flightstream, Jun '83.
MC. Cat no: **AFP 03T.** Released on Flightstream, Jun '83.

WINGS OF HISTORY VOL. 4 (Power in the Sky) (Various artists).
MC. Cat no: **AFP 04T.** Released on Flightstream, Jun '83.

Babel, Isaak

RASSKAZY (Edited By Arnold B. McMillin) (Unknown narrator(s)).
Note: A discussion of the work of Isaak Babel.
MC. Cat no: **R 7698.** Released on Tapes, '91 by Sussex Publications Ltd..

Bach, J.S. (composer)

JOHANN SEBASTIAN BACH (Biography) (John Ringham).
MC. Cat no: **GC 2.** Released on Green Dragon, '91 by Green Dragon Audio Visual.

JOHANN SEBASTIAN BACH 1685 - 1750 (Biography) (Unknown narrator(s)).
MC. Cat no: **DFC 5.** Released on Sussex Tapes, '91 by Sussex Publications Ltd..

Baker Eddy, Mary

MARY BAKER EDDY (Biography) (Ed Bishop).
MC. Cat no: **FW 8.** Released on Green Dragon, '91 by Green Dragon Audio Visual.

Baldursson

MELODY OF LIFE (Baldursson, Hurdle and Ricotti).
MC. Cat no: **C 104.** Released on New World Cassettes, '88.

Baldwin, James

ARTISTS STRUGGLE FOR INTEGRITY, THE (James Baldwin).
Note: Author reads his work and discusses his formative influences.
MC. Cat no: **AS 03.** Released on Sussex Tapes, '91 by Sussex Publications Ltd..

Baldwin, Monica

I LEAP OVER THE WALL (Biography) (Fleur Chandler).
MCSET. Cat no: **OAS 89125.** Released on Oasis Audio Books, '91 by Isis Audio Books. Note: 8 cassettes.

Bardot, Brigitte

CHILD ALONE, A (Biography) (Robin Browne).
MCSET. Cat no: **OAS 90022.** Released on Oasis Audio Books, '91 by Isis Audio Books. Note: 5 cassettes.

Barrymore, John

JOHN BARRYMORE: FROM MATINEE IDOL TO BUFFOON (John Barrymore).
MC. Cat no: **FACET 8112.** Released on Facet (USA), Sep '90.
CD. Cat no: **FCD 8112.** Released on Facet (USA), Sep '90.

Bassini, G

IL GIARDINO DEI FINZI-CONTINI (Edited By Clive Griffiths And Luisa Quartermain (Unknown narrator(s)).
Note: An introduction to fascist Italy as historical background to Bassini's novel. Quotations from interviews with Bassini. In English and Italian.
MC. Cat no: **I 7848.** Released on Exeter Tapes, '91 by Drakes Educational Associates.

Baudelaire

LES FLEURS DU MAL (Edited By Anthony Kelly) (Unknown narrator(s)).
Note: Baudelaire's theory of imagination is discussed. 'La Cloche Felee' is analysed.
MC. Cat no: **F 7561.** Released on Exeter Tapes, '91 by Drakes Educational Associates.

BBC...

BBC-READINGS BY: (Various artists).
Note: Memoirs read by: Maureen Lipman, John Mortimer, & Arthur Marshall.
MCSET. Cat no: **1079A.** Released on Travellers Tales, '91 by Travellers Tales. Note: 6 cassettes.

Beaumarchais

LE BARBIER DE SEVILLE (Edited By Jean D. Biard) (Unknown narrator(s)).
Note: Beaumarchais' play is assessed. A commentary on act 1, scenes 1 and 2 is included. In French.
MC. Cat no: **F 7514.** Released on Exeter Tapes, '91 by Drakes Educational Associates.

LE MARIAGE DE FIGARO (Edited By Philip Thody) (Unknown narrator(s)).
Note: A study of Beaumarchais' play as a comedy and as a socially significant work of literature.
MC. Cat no: **F 7776.** Released on Exeter Tapes, '91 by Drakes Educational Associates.

Beckett, Samuel

SAMUEL BECKETT (Cyril Cussack).
MC. Cat no: **1169.** Released on Caedmon (USA), '88 by Caedmon Records (USA), Bond Street Music.

WAITING FOR GODOT (Edited By Philip Thody) (Unknown narrator(s)).
Note: A study of this play by Samuel Beckett relating it to the modern and traditional theatre and modern sensibility.
MC. Cat no: **F 7970.** Released on Exeter Tapes, '91 by Drakes Educational Associates.

Beethoven (composer)

LUDWIG VAN BEETHOVEN 1770-1827 (Biography) (Richard Mayes).
MC. Cat no: **DFC 1.** Released on Sussex Tapes, '91 by Sussex Publications Ltd..

Biafra, Jello

NO MORE COCOONS (Jello Biafra).
LP. Cat no: **VIRUS 59.** Released on Alternative Tentacles, Nov '87 by Alternative Tentacles Records, Pinnacle.

Bible

ACTS (PART 1) (New International Version) (Tenniel Evans).
MC. Cat no: **0340515481.** Released on Hodder & Stoughton, '91 by Hodder & Stoughton.

ACTS (PART 2) (New International Version) (Tenniel Evans).
MC. Cat no: **034051549X.** Released

on Hodder & Stoughton, '91 by Hodder & Stoughton.

BIBLE STORIES (Various narrators). Note: 10 stories from the Bible read for children. Stories include: The Good Samaritan, The Great Flood and Joseph's Coat.
MC. Cat no: **AC 110**. Released on Audicord, May '83 by Audicord Cassettes.

BIBLE STORIES (David Kossoff).
MCSET. Cat no: **LFP 7433**. Released on Listen For Pleasure, Oct '89 by EMI Records. Note: Playing time: 2 hours 45 minutes.

BOYS FROM BEERSHEBA, THE (Various artists).
Tracks / Boys from Beersheba, The: *Various artists* / Boy Jesus, The: *Various artists* / Joha the silly boy: *Various artists* / Hannah and the patriarch: *Various artists* / St. George: *Various artists* / Selim and the frog: *Various artists* / Fisherman: *Various artists* / Slave king, The: *Various artists* / Prince's robe, The: *Various artists* / Jesus and the dog: *Various artists*.
Note: Stories from The Holy Land.
MC. Cat no: **ANV 657**. Released on Anvil Cassettes, '85 by Anvil Cassettes, Chivers Audio Books.

BRING US TOGETHER (Elaine Storkey).
MC. Cat no: **SU 404C**. Released on Sound & Vision (2), '91 by Scripture Union. Note:

CHANGES THE WORLD (Garth Hewitt).
MC. Cat no: **SV 404C**. Released on Sound & Vision (2), '91 by Scripture Union. Note:

CHILDREN'S BIBLE IN 365 STORIES, THE (New Testament 4) (Various narrators).
Note: Adapted by Mary Batchelor.
MCSET. Cat no: **TS 384**. Released on Tellastory, Apr '92 by Random Century Audiobooks. Note: 2 cassettes. ISBN no, 1856561577

CHILDREN'S BIBLE IN 365 STORIES, THE (Old Testament 4) (Various narrators).
Note: Adapted by Mary Batchelor.
MCSET. Cat no: **TS 380**. Released on Tellastory, Apr '92 by Random Century Audiobooks. Note: 2 cassettes. ISBN no. 1856561569

CHILDREN'S BIBLE IN 365 STORIES, THE (Old Testament 2) (Unknown narrator(s)).
Note: Adapted By Mary Batchelor.
MCSET. Cat no: **TS 378**. Released on Tellastory, Oct '91 by Random Century Audiobooks. Note: 2 cassettes. ISBN no. 1856561526

CHILDREN'S BIBLE IN 365 STORIES, THE (New Testament 2) (Unknown narrator(s)).
Note: Adapted By Mary Batchelor.
MCSET. Cat no: **TS 382**. Released on Tellastory, Oct '91 by Random Century Audiobooks. Note: 2 cassettes. ISBN no. 1856561534

CHILDREN'S BIBLE IN 365 STORIES, THE (Old Testament 3) (Peter Wickham & Stephen Thorne).
Note: Adapted by Mary Batchelor.
MCSET. Cat no: **TS 379**. Released on Tellastory, Jan '92 by Random Century Audiobooks. Note: 2 cassettes. ISBN no. 1856561542

CHILDREN'S BIBLE IN 365 STORIES, THE (New Testament 3) (Sam Dastor).
Note: Adapted by Mary Batchelor.
MCSET. Cat no: **TS 383**. Released on Tellastory, Jan '92 by Random Century Audiobooks. Note: 2 cassettes. ISBN no. 1856561550

CHILDREN'S BIBLE IN 365 STORIES, THE (New Testament 1) (Various narrators).
Note: Adapted by Mary Batchelor.
MCSET. Cat no: **TS 381**. Released on Tellastory, '91 by Random Century Audiobooks. Note: 2 cassettes. ISBN no. 1856561518

CHILDREN'S BIBLE IN 365 STORIES, THE (Old Testament 1) (Various narrators).
Note: Adapted By Mary Batchelor
MCSET. Cat no: **TS 377**. Released on Tellastory, '91 by Random Century Audiobooks. Note: 2 cassettes. ISBN no. 185656150X

CORINTHIANS (New International Version) (Michael Haughey).
MC. Cat no: **0340515511**. Released on Hodder & Stoughton, '91 by Hodder & Stoughton.

CROSS, THE (David Watson).
MC. Cat no: **SV 047C**. Released on Sound & Vision (2), '91 by Scripture Union.

FIRST STORY IN THE WORLD, THE (Various artists).
Tracks / First story in the world: *Various artists* / Four men: *Various artists* / Building of the temple, The: *Various artists* / Coloured coat, The: *Various artists* / Tables are turned, The: *Various artists*.
Note: Stories from The Holy Land
MC. Cat no: **ANV 608**. Released on Anvil Cassettes, Jan '81 by Anvil Cassettes, Chivers Audio Books.

FOLLOWING JESUS (David Watson).
MC. Cat no: **SV 048C**. Released on Sound & Vision (2), '91 by Scripture Union.

GALATIANS TO THESSALONIANS (New International Version) (Michael Haughey).
MC. Cat no: **0340515528**. Released on Hodder & Stoughton, '91 by Hodder & Stoughton.

GIVES US THE FUTURE (David Cohen).
MC. Cat no: **SV 405C**. Released on Sound & Vision (2), '91 by Scripture Union. Note:

HOLY BIBLE, THE (Various artists).
MC. Cat no: **HB 1-15**. Released on Signal, Nov '86, Prism Leisure, Pinnacle. Note: 60 Cassettes.

HOLY SPIRIT (David Watson).
MC. Cat no: **SV 049C**. Released on Sound & Vision (2), '91 by Scripture Union.

JAMES TO JUDE (New International Version) (Sarah Finch).
MC. Cat no: **0340515546**. Released on Hodder & Stoughton, '91 by Hodder & Stoughton.

JESUS (David Watson).
MC. Cat no: **SV 050C**. Released on Sound & Vision (2), '91 by Scripture Union.

JOHN (New International Version) (Timothy Bateson).
MC. Cat no: **030419168**. Released on Hodder & Stoughton, '91 by Hodder & Stoughton.

JOHN (PART 1) (New International Version) (Michael Haughey).
MC. Cat no: **0340515465**. Released on Hodder & Stoughton, '91 by Hodder & Stoughton.

JOHN (PART 2) (New International Version) (Michael Haughey).
MC. Cat no: **0340515473**. Released on Hodder & Stoughton, '91 by Hodder & Stoughton.

LION CHILDREN'S BIBLE, THE (The New Testament) (Paul Jones).
MCSET. Cat no: **2CCA 3161**. Released on Chivers Audio Books, Sep '91 by Chivers Audio Books, Green Dragon Audio Visual. Note: 2 Cassettes.

LION CHILDREN'S BIBLE, THE (The Old Testament) (Paul Jones).
MCSET. Cat no: **3CCA 3160**. Released on Chivers Audio Books, Sep '91 by Chivers Audio Books, Green Dragon Audio Visual. Note: 3 Cassettes.

LUKE (New International Version) (Timothy Bateson).
MC. Cat no: **0340419156**. Released on Hodder & Stoughton, '91 by Hodder & Stoughton.

LUKE (PART 1) (New International Version) (Tenniel Evans).
MC. Cat no: **0340515449**. Released on Hodder & Stoughton, '91 by Hodder & Stoughton.

LUKE (PART 2) (Tenniel Evans).
MC. Cat no: **0340515457**. Released on Hodder & Stoughton, '91 by Hodder & Stoughton.

MAKES ALL THE DIFFERENCE (Selwyn Hughes).
MC. Cat no: **SV 401C**. Released on Sound & Vision (2), '91 by Scripture Union. Note:

MAKES US USEFUL (Pip Luilson).
MC. Cat no: **SV 403C**. Released on Sound & Vision (2), '91 by Scripture Union.

MARK (New International Version) (Timothy Bateson).
MC. Cat no: **0340419148**. Released

on Hodder & Stoughton, '91 by Hodder & Stoughton. Note: 2 Cassettes

MARK (New International Version) (Sarah Finch).
MC. Cat no: **0340515430**. Released on Hodder & Stoughton, '91 by Hodder & Stoughton.

MATTER OF LIFE AND DEATH, A (Various narrators).
MC. Cat no: **SV 107C**. Released on Sound & Vision (2), '91 by Scripture Union.

MATTHEW (Part 1) (Timothy Bateson).
MC. Cat no: **0340515414**. Released on Hodder & Stoughton, '91 by Hodder & Stoughton.

MATTHEW (New International Version) (Timothy Bateson).
MCSET. Cat no: **0340417803**. Released on Hodder & Stoughton, '91 by Hodder & Stoughton. Note: 2 Cassettes

MATTHEW (Part 2) (Timothy Bateson).
MC. Cat no: **0340515422**. Released on Hodder & Stoughton, '91 by Hodder & Stoughton. Note: 2 Cassettes.

NEW TESTAMENT (New International Version) (Timothy Bateson & Others).
MCSET. Cat no: **0340504900**. Released on Hodder & Stoughton, '91 by Hodder & Stoughton. Note: 15 Cassettes.

NEW TESTAMENT IN SCOTS (Passages from) (Robert Lorimer).
MC. Cat no: **SSC 070**. Released on Scotsoun, '91 by Scotsoun Recordings, Morley Audio Services.

NEW TESTAMENT - VOL.12 (Matthew c1 v1 to Mark c16 v20) (Unknown narrator(s)).
MCSET. Cat no: **1012B**. Released on Travellers Tales, '91 by Travellers Tales. Note: 4 cassettes.

NEW TESTAMENT - VOL.13 (Luke c1 v1 to John c21 v25) (Unknown narrator(s)).
MCSET. Cat no: **1013B**. Released on Travellers Tales, '91 by Travellers Tales. Note: 4 cassettes.

NEW TESTAMENT - VOL.14 (Acts c1 v1 to Corinthians c14 v14) (Unknown narrator(s)).
MCSET. Cat no: **1014B**. Released on Travellers Tales, '91 by Travellers Tales. Note: 4 cassettes.

NEW TESTAMENT - VOL.15 (Galations c1 v1 to Revelations c22 c21) (Unknown narrator(s)).
MCSET. Cat no: **1015B**. Released on Travellers Tales, '91 by Travellers Tales. Note: 4 cassettes.

NIGHT ON'T TOWN, A (Various narrators).
MC. Cat no: **SV 105C**. Released on Sound & Vision (2), '91 by Scripture Union.

NORMAL PROCEDURE (Various narrators).
MC. Cat no: **SV 104C**. Released on Sound & Vision (2), '91 by Scripture Union.

OLD TESTAMENT (Psalms 131 to Isaiah c41 v9) (Unknown narrator(s)).
MCSET. Cat no: **1008B**. Released on Travellers Tales, '91 by Travellers Tales. Note: 4 cassettes.

OLD TESTAMENT (Readings from the psalms) (Various narrators).
Note: Narrators include:- Sir John Gielgud, Barbara Leigh Hunt.
MCSET. Cat no: **418 006-4**. Released on Argo (Polygram), Jun '88 by Polygram Classics **Deleted** Jan '89.
MCSET. Cat no: **1017B**. Released on Travellers Tales, '91 by Travellers Tales. Note: 2 cassettes.

OLD TESTAMENT (Isaiah c41 v10 to Jeremiah c52 v23) (Unknown narrator(s)).
MCSET. Cat no: **1009B**. Released on Travellers Tales, '91 by Travellers Tales. Note: 4 cassettes.

OLD TESTAMENT - THE AUTHORISED VERSION (Readings from the Bible) (Various narrators).
Note: Narrators include:- Brian Glover, Wendy Hiller and Michael Hordern.
MCSET. Cat no: **SAY 85**. Released on Argo (Polygram), Nov '83 by PolyGram Classics **Deleted** Jan '89.
MCSET. Cat no: **1016 B**. Released on Travellers Tales, '91 by Travellers Tales. Note: 2 cassettes.

OLD TESTAMENT - VOL.1 (Genesis c1 v1 to Exodus c29 v27) (Unknown narrator(s)).
MCSET. Cat no: **1001B**. Released on Travellers Tales, '91 by Travellers Tales. Note: 4 cassettes

OLD TESTAMENT - VOL.2 (Exodus c29 v28 to Numbers c31 v54) (Unknown narrator(s)).
MCSET. Cat no: **1002B**. Released on Travellers Tales, '91 by Travellers Tales. Note: 4 cassettes

OLD TESTAMENT - VOL.3 (Numbers c32 v1 to Judges c10 v3) (Unknown narrator(s)).
MCSET. Cat no: **1003B**. Released on Travellers Tales, '91 by Travellers Tales. Note: 4 cassettes.

OLD TESTAMENT - VOL.4 (Judges c10 v4 to 1 Kings c5 v12) (Unknown narrator(s)).
MCSET. Cat no: **1004B**. Released on Travellers Tales, '91 by Travellers Tales. Note: 4 cassettes.

OLD TESTAMENT - VOL.5 (1 Kings c5 v13 to 1 Chronicles c26 v22) (Unknown narrator(s)).
MCSET. Cat no: **1005B**. Released on Travellers Tales, '91 by Travellers Tales. Note: 4 cassettes.

OLD TESTAMENT - VOL.6 (1 Chronicles c26 v23 to Job c15 v24) (Unknown narrator(s)).
MCSET. Cat no: **1006B**. Released on Travellers Tales, '91 by Travellers Tales. Note: 4 cassettes.

OLD TESTAMENT - VOL.7 (Job c15 v25 to Psalms 130) (Unknown narrator(s)).
MCSET. Cat no: **1007B**. Released on Travellers Tales, '91 by Travellers Tales. Note: 4 cassettes.

OLD TESTAMENT - VOL.10 (Jeremiah c52 v24 to Daniel c8 v2) (Unknown narrator(s)).
MCSET. Cat no: **1010B**. Released on Travellers Tales, '91 by Travellers Tales. Note: 4 cassettes.

OLD TESTAMENT - VOL.11 (Daniel c8 v3 to Malachi c4 v5) (Unknown narrator(s)).
MCSET. Cat no: **1011B**. Released on Travellers Tales, '91 by Travellers Tales. Note: 4 cassettes.

ONCE UPON A WORLD (Bible Bedtime Stories) (John Le Mesurier).
Note: Adapted by Robert Duncan.
MCSET. Cat no: **9031F**. Released on Travellers Tales, '91 by Travellers Tales. Note: 2 Cassettes.

REVELATION (New International Version) (Sarah Finch).
MC. Cat no: **0340515554**. Released on Hodder & Stoughton, '91 by Hodder & Stoughton.

ROMANS (New International Version) (Michael Haughey).
MC. Cat no: **0340515503**. Released on Hodder & Stoughton, '91 by Hodder & Stoughton.

SOMETIMES HURTS (Joyce Huggett).
MC. Cat no: **SV 400C**. Released on Sound & Vision (2), '91 by Scripture Union.

START THE DAY WITH COLOSSIANS (Vic Jackopson).
MC. Cat no: **SV 034C**. Released on Sound & Vision (2), '91 by Scripture Union.

START THE DAY WITH EPHESIANS (David Watson).
MC. Cat no: **SV 032C**. Released on Sound & Vision (2), '91 by Scripture Union.

START THE DAY WITH EXODUS (Richard Belves).
MC. Cat no: **SV 020C**. Released on Sound & Vision (2), '91 by Scripture Union.

START THE DAY WITH GALATIANS (Morris Stuart).
MC. Cat no: **SV 031C**. Released on Sound & Vision (2), '91 by Scripture Union.

START THE DAY WITH HEBREWS (John Allan).
MC. Cat no: **SV 036C**. Released on Sound & Vision (2), '91 by Scripture Union.

START THE DAY WITH ISAIAH (David Sheppard).
MC. Cat no: **SV 024C**. Released on Sound & Vision (2), '91 by Scripture Union.

START THE DAY WITH JAMES (George Hoffman).
MC. Cat no: **SV 037C**. Released on Sound & Vision (2), '91 by Scripture Union.

START THE DAY WITH JOB (Martin Goldsmith).

MC. Cat no: **SV 021C.** Released on Sound & Vision (2), '91 by Scripture Union.

START THE DAY WITH JOHN (Billy Strachan).
MC. Cat no: **SV 028C.** Released on Sound & Vision (2), '91 by Scripture Union.

START THE DAY WITH LUKE (Garth Hewitt).
MC. Cat no: **SV 027C.** Released on Sound & Vision (2), '91 by Scripture Union.

START THE DAY WITH MARK (Ian Barclay).
MC. Cat no: **SV 026C.** Released on Sound & Vision (2), '91 by Scripture Union.

START THE DAY WITH MATTHEW (Martin Goldsmith).
MC. Cat no: **SV 025C.** Released on Sound & Vision (2), '91 by Scripture Union.

START THE DAY WITH PHILIPPIANS (Jean Darnell).
MC. Cat no: **SV 033C.** Released on Sound & Vision (2), '91 by Scripture Union.

START THE DAY WITH PSALMS (David Watson).
MC. Cat no: **SV 022C.** Released on Sound & Vision (2), '91 by Scripture Union.

START THE DAY WITH ROMANS (Roger Forster).
MC. Cat no: **SV 030C.** Released on Sound & Vision (2), '91 by Scripture Union.

START THE DAY WITH TIMOTHY (Gavin Reid).
MC. Cat no: **SV 035C.** Released on Sound & Vision (2), '91 by Scripture Union.

STORY BOX (Various narrators).
MC. Cat no: **SV 084C.** Released on Sound & Vision (2), '91 by Scripture Union.

STORY BOX 2 (Various narrators).
MC. Cat no: **SV 085C.** Released on Sound & Vision (2), '91 by Scripture Union.

STORY BOX 3 (Various narrators).
MC. Cat no: **SV 086C.** Released on Sound & Vision (2), '91 by Scripture Union.

STORY BOX 4 (Various narrators).
MC. Cat no: **SV 087C.** Released on Sound & Vision (2), '91 by Scripture Union.

STORY OF THE THREE KINGS (George Rose).
Note: Re-written by John of Hildesheim.
MC. Cat no: **CDL 51724.** Released on Caedmon (USA), '84 by Caedmon Records (USA), Bond Street Music.

TIMOTHY TO HEBREWS (New International Version) (Michael Haughley & Sarah Finch).
MC. Cat no: **0340515538.** Released on Hodder & Stoughton, '91 by Hodder & Stoughton.

Bird Songs

ALL THE BIRD SONGS OF BRITAIN & EUROPE (Various).
Note: A sound guide to the songs and calls of 396 breeding and migrant birds of Britain and Western Europe in systematic order. Descriptive booklet with each CD. Average length 75 mins each. CD's available as full set or separately.
CDSET. Cat no: **02963.** Released on Sittelle, Feb '92 by Sittelle Records (France).
MCSET. Cat no: **000911.** Released on Sittelle, Feb '92 by Sittelle Records (France).

ALL THE BIRD SONGS OF EUROPE VOL.2 (Gamebirds to Sandgrouse) (Various).
CD. Cat no: **200809.** Released on Sittelle, Feb '92 by Sittelle Records (France).

ALL THE BIRD SONGS OF EUROPE VOL.1 (Divers to Birds of Prey) (Various).
CD. Cat no: **100802.** Released on Sittelle, Feb '92 by Sittelle Records (France).

ALL THE BIRD SONGS OF EUROPE VOL.3 (Cuckoos to Hippolais Warblers) (Various).
CD. Cat no: **300806.** Released on Sittelle, Feb '92 by Sittelle Records (France).

ALL THE BIRD SONGS OF EUROPE VOL.4 (Sylvia Warblers to Buntings) (Various).
CD. Cat no: **400803.** Released on Sittelle, Feb '92 by Sittelle Records (France).

BIRD SONGS VOLUME 1 (Various).
Note: Red-throated Diver, Black-throated Diver, Great Northern Diver, White-billed Diver, Little Grebe, Black-necked Grebe, Slavonian Grebe, Red-necked Grebe, Great Crested Grebe, Fulmar, Cory's Shearwater, Great Shearwater, Sooty Shearwater, Manx Shearwater, Storm Petrel, Wilson's Petrel, Leach's Petrel, White Pelican, Dalmation Pelican, Gannet, Cormorant, Shag, Pygmy Cormorant, Bittern, American bittern, Little Bittern, Night Heron, Squacco Heron, Cattle Egret, Great White Heron, Little Egret, Heron, Purple Heron, White Stork, Black Stork, Spoonbill, Glossy Ibis, Greater Flamingo, Canada Goose, Barnacle Goose, Brent Goose, Red-breasted Goose, Grey Lag Goose, White-fronted Goose, Lesser White-fronted Goose, Bean Goose, Pink-footed Goose, Snow Goose, Mute Swan, Whooper Swan, Bewick's Swan.
LP. Cat no: **RFLP 5001.** Released on BBC-Swedish Radio(Import), Jul '82.
MCSET. Cat no: **SRMK 5021/4.** Released on BBC-Swedish Radio(Import), Jul '82. Note: 4 cassette box set.

BIRD SONGS VOLUME 2 (Various).
Note: Ruddy Shelduck, Shelduck, Mallard, Teal, Blue Winged Teal, Baikal Teal, Gadwall, Wigeon, American Wigeon, Pintail, Garganey, Shoveler, Marbled Teal, Red-crested Pochard, Pochard, Ferruginous Duck, Tufted Duck, Scaup, Mandarin, Levant Sparrow Hawk, Eider, King Eider, Stellers' Eider, Common Scoter, Velvet Scoter, Surf Scoter, Harlequin, Long-tailed Duck, Goldeneye, Barrow's Goldeneye, Smew, Red-breasted Merganser, Goosander, White-headed Duck, Oprey, Black-winged Kite, Honey Buzzard, Long-legged Buzzard, Buzzard, Booted Eagle, Bonellis' Eagle, Tawny Eagle, Spotted Eagle, Imperial Eagle, Golden Eagle, White-tailed eagle, Short-toed Eagle, Hen Harrier, Pallid Harrier, Montagu's Harrier, Egyptian Vulture, Bearded Vulture, Black Vulture, Griffon Vulture, Gyr Falcon, Saker Lanner, Peregrine, Hobby, Eleonoras' Falcon, Merlin, Red-footed Falcon, Lesser Kestrel, Kestrel.
LP. Cat no: **RFLP 5002.** Released on BBC-Swedish Radio(Import), Jul '82.
MCSET. Cat no: **SRMK 5025/8.** Released on BBC-Swedish Radio(Import), Jul '82. Note: 4 cassette box set.

BIRD SONGS VOLUME 3 (Various).
Note: Oystercatcher, Ringed Plover, Little Ringed Plover, Kentish Plover, Dotterei, Golden Plover, Lesser Golden Plover, Grey Plover, Killdeer, Sociable Plover, Lapwing, Spur-winged Plover, Turnstone, Little Stint, Temminck's Stint, White-rumped Sandpiper, Pectoral Sandpiper, Purple Sandpiper, Dunlin, Curlew, Sandpiper, Knot, Sanderling, Knot, Sanderling, Ruff, Broad-billed Sandpiper, Willow Grouse/Red Grouse, Ptarmigan, Hazel Grouse, Black Grouse, Capercaillie, Rock Partridge, Chuckar, Barbary Partridge, Red-legged Partridge, Partridge, Quail, Pheasant, Crane, Demoiselle Crane, Water Rail, Spotted Crake, Little Crake, Baillon's Crake, Corncrake, Moorhen, Purple Gallinule, Coot, Crested Coot, Great Bustard, Little Bustard, Parsley Frog.
LP. Cat no: **RFLP 5003.** Released on BBC-Swedish Radio(Import), Jul '82.

BIRD SONGS VOLUME 4 (Various).
Note: Grey Phalarope, Red-necked Phalarope, Wilson's Phalarope, Stone Curlew, Cream-coloured Courser, Pratincole, Black-winged Pratincole, Great Skua, Pomarine Skua, Arctic Skua, Long-tailed Skua, Mediterranean Gull, Bonapart's Gull, Little Gull, Black-headed Gull, Slender-billed Gull, Lesser Black-backed Gull, Herring Gull, Glaucous Gull, Black-backed Gull, Audouin's Gull, Sabine's Gull, Kittiwake, Ivory Gull, Spotted Redshank, Redshank, Marsh Sandpiper, Greenshank, Greater Yellowlegs, Lesser Yellowlegs, Green Sandpiper, Common Sandpiper, Terek Sandpiper, Black-tailed Godwit, Curlew, Whimbrel, Upland Sandpiper, Woodcock, Snipe, Great Snipe, Jack Snipe, Black-winged Stilt, Avocet.

LP. Cat no: **RFLP 5004**. Released on BBC-Swedish Radio(Import), Jul '82.
MCSET. Cat no: **SRMK 5033/6**. Released on BBC-Swedish Radio(Import), Jul '82. Note: 4 cassette box set.
BIRD SONGS VOLUME 5 (Various).
Note: Cuckoo, Great Spotted Cuckoo, Yellow-billed Cuckoo, Barn Owl, Snowy Owl, Eagle Owl, Long-eared Owl, Short-eared Owl, Scowl Owl, Midwife Toad, Tengmain's Owl, Little Owl, Pigmy Owl, Hawk Owl, Tawny owl, Ural Owl, Great Grey Owl, Tern, Caspian Tern, Whiskered Tern, Gull-billed Tern, White-winged Black Tern, Sandwich Tern, Common Tern, Arctic Tern, Roseate Tern, Sooty Tern, Little Tern, Little Auk, Razorbill, Guillemot, Brunnich's Guillemot, Black Guillemot, Puffin, Black-bellied Sandgrouse, Pintailed Sandgrouse, Wood Pigeon, Stock Dove, Rock Dove, Collared Dove, Palm Dove, Turtle Dove.

LP. Cat no: **RFLP 5005**. Released on BBC-Swedish Radio(Import), Jul '82.
BIRD SONGS VOLUME 6 (Various).
Note: Dupont's Lark, Short-toed Lark, Lesser Short-toed Lark, Calandra Lark, Shore Lark, Thekea Lark, Wood Lark, Sky Lark, Nightjar, Mole Cricket, Red-necked Nightjar, Egyptian Nightjar, Pallid Swift, Swift, Alpine Swift, Kingfisher, Bee-eater, Roller, Hoope, Wryneck Green Woodpecker, Grey-headed Woodpecker, Black Woodpecker, Great Spotted Woodpecker, Syrian Woodpecker, Middle Spotted Woodpecker, White-backed Woodpecker, Lesser Spotted Woodpecker, Three-toed Woodpecker.

LP. Cat no: **RFLP 5006**. Released on BBC-Swedish Radio(Import), Jul '82.
MCSET. Cat no: **SRMK 5029/32**. Released on BBC-Swedish Radio(Import), Jul '82. Note: 4 cassette box set.
BIRD SONGS VOLUME 7 (Various).
Note: Sand Martin, Crag Martin, Swallow, Red-rumped Swallow, House Martin, Richard's Pipit, Tawny Pipit, Tree Pipit, Meadow Pipit, Red-throated Pipit, Rock Pipit, Yellow Wagtail, Grey Wagtail, White Wagtail, Red-backed Shrike, Woodchat Shrike, Lesser Grey Shrike, Great Grey Shrike, Waxwing, Dipper, Wren, ALpine Accentor, Dunnock, Cett's Warbler, Pallas's Grasshopper, Warbler, Savi's Warbler, River Warbler, Grasshopper Warbler, Lanceolated Warbler.

LP. Cat no: **RFLP 5007**. Released on BBC-Swedish Radio(Import), Jul '82.
BIRD SONGS VOLUME 8 (Various).
Note: Moustached Warbler, Aquatic Warbler, Sedge Warbler, Blyth's Reed Warbler, Marsh Warbler, Reed Warbler, Great Reed Warbler, Icterine Warbler, Melodious Warbler, Olive Tree Warbler, Olivaceous Warbler, Barred Warbler, Orphean Warbler, Garden Warbler, Blackcap Svarthatta, Whitethroat Tornsgangare, Lesser Whitethroat, Ruppell's Warbler, Sardinian Warbler, Subalpine Warbler, Spectacled Warbler, Dartford Warbler, Marmora's Warbler, Willow Warbler, Chiffchaff Gransangare, Bonelli's, Wood Warbler, Yellow-browed Warbler, Palla's Warbler, Arctic Warbler, Greenish Warbler.

LP. Cat no: **RFLP 5008**. Released on BBC-Swedish Radio(Import), Jul '82.
BIRD SONGS VOLUME 9 (Various).
Note: Rufous Bush Cat, Rock Thrush, Blue Rock Thrush, Black Redstart, Redstart, Robin, White-throated Robin, Nightingale, Thrush Nightingale, Bluethroat, red-flanked Bluetail, Goldcrest, Firecrest, Fan-tailed Warbler, Pied Flycatcher, Collared Flycatcher, Red-breasted Flycatcher, Spotted Flycatcher, Whinchat, Stonechat, Wheatear, Pied Wheatear, Black-eared Wheatear, Desert Wheatear, Isabelline Wheatear, Black Wheatear.

LP. Cat no: **RFLP 5009**. Released on BBC-Swedish Radio(Import), Jul '82.
BIRD SONGS VOLUME 10 (Various).
Note: Olive-backed Thrush, Dusky Thrush, Nuamann' Thrush, Fieldfare, Ring Ouzel, American Robin, Blackbird, Siberian Thrush, Redwing, Song Thrush, Mistle Thrush, White's Thrush, Bearded Reading (Tit), Long-tailed Tit, Marsh Tit, Willow Tit, Sombre Tit, Siberian Tit, Crested Tit, Coal Tit, Blue Tit, Great Tit, Penduline Tit, Nuthatch, Corsican Nuthatch, Rock Nuthatch, Wall Creeper, Tree Creeper, Short-tailed Creeper.

LP. Cat no: **RFLP 5010**. Released on BBC-Swedish Radio(Import), Jul '82.
BIRD SONGS VOLUME 11 (Various).
Note: Corn Bunting, Yellowhammer, Rock Bunting, Cinerous Bunting, Ortolan Bunting, Cretzschmar's Bunting, Ciri Bunting, Little Bunting, Rustic Bunting, Yellow-breasted Bunting, Black-headed Bunting, Reed Bunting, Lapland Bunting, Snow Bunting, Chaffinch, Brambling, Citril Finch, Serin, Greenfinch, Siskin, Goldfinch, Twite, Linnet, Redpoll, Arctic Redpoll, Trumpeter Bullfinch, Scarlet Rosefinch.

LP. Cat no: **RFLP 5011**. Released on BBC-Swedish Radio(Import), Jul '82.
BIRD SONGS VOLUME 12 (Various).
Note: Pine Grosbeak, Parrot Crossbill, Two-barred Crossbill, Bullfinch, Hawfinch, House Sparrow, Spanish Sparrow, Tree Sparrow, Rock Sparrow, Snow Finch, Starling, Spotless Starling, Golden Oriole, Siberian Jay, Jay, Azure-winged Magpie, Magpie, Nutcracker, Chough, Alpine Chough, Jackdaw, Rook, Carrion Crow, Hooded Crow, Raven.

LP. Cat no: **RFLP 5012**. Released on BBC-Swedish Radio(Import), Jul '82.
BIRD SONGS VOLUME 13 (Various).
Note: Pied-billed Grebe, Wandering Albatross, Black-browed Albatross, Yellow-nosed Albatross, Grey-headed Albatross, Light-mantled Sooty Albatross, Cape Pigeon (Pintado Petrel), Bulwer's Petrel, Little Shearwater, Frigate Petrel, Medeiran Petrel, Magnificent Frigate-Bird, Bald Ibis, Ring-necked duck, Dark Chanting Goshawk, American Kestrel, Asiatic White Crane, Sora Rail, American Purple Gallinule, Green-backed Gallinule, Allen's Gallinule, Western Sandpiper, Semi-palmated Sandpiper, Least Sandpiper, Baird's Sandpiper, Stilt Sandpiper, Short-billed Dowditcher, Solitary Sandpiper, Spotted Sandpiper, Laughing Gull, Royal Tern, Forster's Tern, Noddy, Chestnut-bellied Sandgrouse, Rufous Turtle Dover, Black-billed Cuckoo, African Marsh Owl, American Nighthawk.

LP. Cat no: **RFLP 5013**. Released on BBC-Swedish Radio(Import), Jul '82.
BIRD SONGS VOLUME 14 (Various).
Note: Neddle-tailed Swift, Little Swift (White-rumped Swift), White-rumped Swift, Pied Kingfisher, Belted Kingfisher, Blue-cheeked Bee-eater, Yellow-bellied Sap Sucker, Desert Lark, Bar-tailed Desert Lark, Hoopoe Lark, Indian Tree Pipit, Common Bulbul, Catbird, Gray's Grasshopper Warbler, Thick-billed Warbler, Booted Warbler, Radde's Warbler, White-crowned Black Wheatear, Moussier's Redstart, Siberian Rubythroat, Hermit Thrush, Grey-cheeked Thrush, Pine Bunting, Siverian Meadow Bunting, Red-headed Bunting, Back-faced Bunting, Song Sparrow, Fox Sparrow, White-throated Sparrow, Slate-coloured Junco, Rose-breasted Grosbeak, Indigo Bunting, Summer Tanager, Black-and-white Warbler, Tennessee Warbler, Parula Warbler, Myrtle Warbler, Black-throated Green Warbler, Northern Waterthrush, Common Yellowthroat, American Restart, Red-eyed Vireo, Bobolink, Yellow-headed Blackbird, Baltimore Oriole, Daurian Jackdaw.

LP. Cat no: **RFLP 5014**. Released on BBC-Swedish Radio(Import), Jul '82.
BIRD SONGS VOLUME 15 (Various).
Note: White-throated Robin, Isabelline Shrike, Brown Thrasher, Siberian Accentor, Paddyfield Warbler, Thick-billed Warbler, Booted Warbler, Menetries' Warbler, Dusky Warbler, Brown Flycatcher, Finsch's Wheatear, Wood Thrush, Veery, Tickell's Thrush, Red-breasted Nuthatch, Yellow-browed Bunting, Chestnut Bunting, Whit-crowned Sparrow, Rufous-sided Towhee, Scarlet Tanager, Yellow Warbler, Blackpoll Warbler, Hooded Warblerl, Evening Grosbeak, Daurian Jackdaw, White-headed Duck, Levant Sparrowhawk, Black Vulture, Buff-breasted Sandpiper, Long-billed Dowditcher, Ross's Gull, Pallas's Sandgrouse, Pechora Pipit, Yellow-browed Warbler, Eye-browed Thrush, Kruper's Nuthatch, Rose-coloured Starling, Green

heron, Lesser Flamingo, Egyptian Goose, Bufflehead, Hooded Merganser, Ruddy Duck, Sandhill Crane, White-tailed Plover, Great Black-headed Gull, Crested Auklet, Parakeet Auklet, White-breasted Kingfisher, Acadian Flycatcher, Birmaculated Lark, Citrine Wagtail.

LP. Cat no: **RFLP 5015.** Released on BBC-Swedish Radio(Import), Jul '82.

BIRD SPOT (British wild birds) (Various).
Tracks / Some large birds in the woods / Collared dove and owls / Woodpeckers, The / Swallow tribe and skylark, The / Farm crows / Some small birds of the woods / Thrushers of the woods and farms / Nightingale and warblers / Two hole nesters / Finch tribe.

LP. Cat no: **REC 438.** Released on BBC, Apr '82 by BBC Records, Taylors **Deleted** Jun '91.

MC. Cat no: **ZCM 438.** Released on BBC, Apr '82 by BBC Records, Taylors.

BIRDS AWAKENING (Spring Dawn Chorus in the Alpine Foothills) (Various).

CD. Cat no: **034114.** Released on Sittelle, Feb '92 by Sittelle Records (France).

CD. Cat no: **222207.** Released on Sittelle, Feb '92 by Sittelle Records (France).

BRITISH BIRD SONGS AND CALLS (Various).

MCSET. Cat no: **NSA C5/6.** Released on National Sound Archive, Oct '87.

BRITISH WILD BIRDS IN STEREO (Various).

MC. Cat no: **RMC 4008.** Released on BBC, Jun '88 by BBC Records, Taylors.

LP. Cat no: **REC 197.** Released on BBC, Jan '75 by BBC Records, Taylors **Deleted** Jun '91.

LARGER THRUSHES (Various).

CD. Cat no: **242809.** Released on Sittelle, Feb '92 by Sittelle Records (France).

MC. Cat no: **042713.** Released on Sittelle, Feb '92 by Sittelle Records (France).

LARKS ASCENDING (Various).

CD. Cat no: **242403.** Released on Sittelle, Feb '92 by Sittelle Records (France).

MC. Cat no: **042317.** Released on Sittelle, Feb '92 by Sittelle Records (France).

NOCTURNAL AND DIURNAL BIRDS OF PREY (From Eagles to Falcons and Owls of Europe) (Various).

MC. Cat no: **035012.** Released on Sittelle, Feb '92 by Sittelle Records (France).

NOCTURNE OF NIGHTINGALES (Various).

CD. Cat no: **243608.** Released on Sittelle, Feb '92 by Sittelle Records (France).

MC. Cat no: **043512.** Released on Sittelle, Feb '92 by Sittelle Records (France).

OUR FAVOURITE GARDEN BIRDS (Various).

CD. Cat no: **204708.** Released on Sittelle, Feb '92 by Sittelle Records (France).

SOUND GUIDE TO BRITISH WADERS (Various).

LP. Cat no: **REC 545.** Released on BBC, Nov '84 by BBC Records, Taylors **Deleted** Jun '91.

MC. Cat no: **ZCM 545.** Released on BBC, Nov '84 by BBC Records, Taylors.

WARBLERS (Various).

CD. Cat no: **242205.** Released on Sittelle, Feb '92 by Sittelle Records (France).

MC. Cat no: **042119.** Released on Sittelle, Feb '92 by Sittelle Records (France).

WOODLAND AND GARDEN BIRDS (Various).

2LP. Cat no: **REF 235.** Released on BBC, Oct '76 by BBC Records, Taylors **Deleted** Jun '91.

MC. Cat no: **HRMC 235.** Released on BBC, Oct '76 by BBC Records, Taylors.

WORLD'S BEST BIRD SONGS (24 of the World's Finest) (Various).

MC. Cat no: **035111.** Released on Sittelle, Feb '92 by Sittelle Records (France).

YOUR FAVOURITE BIRD SONGS (Various).

LP. Cat no: **REC 511.** Released on BBC, Apr '84 by BBC Records, Taylors **Deleted** Jun '91.

MC. Cat no: **ZCM 511.** Released on BBC, Apr '84 by BBC Records, Taylors.

Blake, Dorothy

MEMORIES OF OSBORNE (Dorothy Blake).
Note: Miss Blake reminesces about her childhood at Osborne House (Isle of Wight), and of Queen Victoria, the Royal family, Royal Christmas, tea in the Royal nursery, etc.

LP. Cat no: **SDL 285.** Released on Saydisc, Jun '78 by Amon Ra Records, Taylors, C.M. Distribution, Gamut Distribution **Deleted** '89.

MC. Cat no: **CSDL 285.** Released on Saydisc, Jun '78 by Amon Ra Records, Taylors, C.M. Distribution, Gamut Distribution. Note: Playing time: 34 minutes.

Blake, William

WILLIAM BLAKE (David Bindman & Michael Mason).
Note: Pre-recorded discussions which show literary criticism as a living, evolving interchange.

MC. Cat no: **A26.** Released on Sussex Tapes, '91 by Sussex Publications Ltd..

Blixen, Karen

OUT OF AFRICA (Geraldine James).
MCSET. Cat no: **LFP 7272.** Released on Listen For Pleasure, Nov '86 by EMI Records.

MCSET. Cat no: **1023A.** Released on Travellers Tales, '91 by Travellers Tales.

Bloch, Michael

WALLIS AND EDWARD (The Personal Correspondence 1931-1937) (Neil Hunt & Betty Harris).
MCSET. Cat no: **1046A.** Released on Travellers Tales, '91 by Travellers Tales. Note: 8 cassettes.

MCSET. Cat no: **IAB 90021.** Released on Isis Audio Books, '91.

Bogarde, Dirk

BACKCLOTH (Dirk Bogarde).
MCSET. Cat no: **IAB 92053.** Released on Isis Audio Books, May '92. Note : 8 Cassettes. Playing time: 10 hours, 43 mins.

ORDERLY MAN, AN (Dirk Bogarde)
MCSET. Cat no: **1078A.** Released on Travellers Tales, '91 by Travellers Tales.

MCSET. Cat no: **OAS 40391.** Released on Oasis Audio Books, '91.

PARTICULAR FRIENDSHIP, A (Dirk Bogarde)
MCSET. Cat no: **1073A.** Released on Travellers Tales, '91 by Travellers Tales.

MCSET. Cat no: **OAS 10691.** Released on Oasis Audio Books, '91

Boll, Heinrich

ANSICHTEN EINES CLOWNS (Edited By William P. Hanson) (Unknown narrator(s)).
Note: A discussion of the importance of this title.

MC. Cat no: **G 7966.** Released on Exeter Tapes, '91 by Drakes Educational Associates.

DAS BROT DER FRUHEN JAHRE (Edited By William P. Hanson) (Unknown narrator(s)).
Note: A sketch of Heinrich Boll's early stories, their themes and attitudes.

MC. Cat no: **G 7554.** Released on Exeter Tapes, '91 by Drakes Educational Associates.

DIE VERLORENE EHRE DER KATHARINA BLUM (Edited By William P. Hanson) (Unknown narrator(s)).
Note: Deals with the political and social aspects of Heinrich Boll's most controversial novel.

MC. Cat no: **G 7997.** Released on Exeter Tapes, '91 by Drakes Educational Associates.

Bonnie Prince Charlie

BONNIE PRINCE CHARLIE (History for Ages 8+) (Unknown narrator(s)).
Note: Book and cassette.

MC. Cat no: **PLBH 148.** Released on Tell-A-Tale, '88 by Pickwick Records, Taylors, Clyde Factors.

Borchert, W

DRAUSSEN VOR DER TUR (Edited By Keith A. Dickson) (Unknown narrator(s)).
Note: The reasons for the theme of war

dominating German literature after World War II is explored.
MC. Cat no: **G 7541**. Released on Exeter Tapes, '91 by Drakes Educational Associates.

Border, Allan
ALLAN BORDER: AN AUTOBIOGRAPHY (Richie Benaud).
MCSET. Cat no: **TTC 2037**. Released on Talking Tape Company, Apr '91, Conifer Records. Note: 2 cassettes. Playing time 3hrs. ISBN no.1872520723

Borland, Hal
HIGH, WIDE AND LONESOME (Robert Gorman).
MCSET. Cat no: **RB 88890**. Released on Recorded Books, Jan '92 by Isis Audio Books. Note: 6 cassettes. Playing time 9hrs

Bosco, H
BARBOCHE (Edited By Gerard Poulet) (Unknown narrator(s)).
Note: A study of the theme of childhood as well as the use of the 'merveilleux' in Bosco's novel. In French
MC. Cat no: **F 7777**. Released on Exeter Tapes, '91 by Drakes Educational Associates.

Brassens, Georges
SONGS OF GEORGES BRASSENS, THE (Edited By W.J. Perry) (Unknown narrator(s)).
Note: A general commentary on his work together with observations on each of the selected songs. Accompanying booklet available.
MC. Cat no: **F 7775**. Released on Exeter Tapes, '91 by Drakes Educational Associates.

Brecht, Bertolt
BRECHT AND THE ACTOR (Edited By Peter Thomson) (Unknown narrator(s)).
Note: An examination of Brecht's theories about acting and the ways in which these theories illuminate his plays and poems.
MC. Cat no: **G 7325**. Released on Exeter Tapes, '91 by Drakes Educational Associates.

DER GUTE MENSCH VON SEZUAN (Edited By Keith A. Dickson) (Unknown narrator(s)).
Note: The play's dramatic, lyric and epic elements are discussed.
MC. Cat no: **G 7542**. Released on Exeter Tapes, '91 by Drakes Educational Associates.

KALENDERGESCHICHTEN (Edited By Keith A. Dickson) (Unknown narrator(s)).
Note: Provides factual detail and a critical analysis of this miscellany of prose and verse.
MC. Cat no: **G 7814**. Released on Exeter Tapes, '91 by Drakes Educational Associates.

MUTTER COURAGE UND IHRE KIN- **DER** (Edited By Keith A. Dickson) (Unknown narrator(s)).
Note: The historical dramatic and 'epic' dimensions of this play by Bertolt Brecht are explored.
MC. Cat no: **G 7617**. Released on Exeter Tapes, '91 by Drakes Educational Associates.

Brel, Jacques
A TRAVERS SIS CHANSONS (Edited By Gerard Poulet) (Unknown narrator(s)).
Note: A study of Jacques Brel.
MC. Cat no: **F 7731**. Released on Exeter Tapes, '91 by Drakes Educational Associates.

Brickhill, Paul
DAMBUSTERS, THE GREAT ESCAPE (And Reach For The Sky) (Richard Todd & Tony Britton).
Note: Abridged.
MCSET. Cat no: **1022W**. Released on Travellers Tales, '91 by Travellers Tales. Note: 6 Cassettes.

GREAT ESCAPE, THE (Richard Todd).
MCSET. Cat no: **LFP 7148**. Released on Listen For Pleasure, May '84 by EMI Records **Deleted** Aug '89.

REACH FOR THE SKY (Robert Hardy).
MCSET. Cat no: **CAB 633**. Released on Chivers Audio Books, Oct '91 by Chivers Audio Books, Green Dragon Audio Visual. Note: 12 Cassettes.

REACH FOR THE SKY (Tony Britton).
MCSET. Cat no: **LFP 7146**. Released on Listen For Pleasure, May '84 by EMI Records.

Briggs, Ted
FLAGSHIP HOOD (Christopher Kay).
MCSET. Cat no: **1042N**. Released on Travellers Tales, '91 by Travellers Tales. Note: 6 cassettes.
MCSET. Cat no: **1854960334**. Released on Soundings, '91 by Soundings Records, Bond Street Music. Note: 6 Cassettes.

Brittain, Vera
TESTAMENT OF FRIENDSHIP (Gretel Davis).
MCSET. Cat no: **OAS 90023**. Released on Oasis Audio Books, '91 by Isis Audio Books. Note: 12 cassette set. Playing time 18hrs.
MCSET. Cat no: **1038/1039A**. Released on Travellers Tales, '91 by Travellers Tales.

Bronte, Charlotte
JANE EYRE BY CHARLOTTE BRONTE (Joseph Prescott).
MC. Cat no: **23079**. Released on Sussex Tapes, '91 by Sussex Publications Ltd.

Bronte, Emily
EMILY BRONTE (Miriam Allott & Barbara Hardy).
Note: Pre-recorded discussions which show literary criticism as a living, evolving interchange.
MC. Cat no: **IA35**. Released on Sussex Tapes, '91 by Sussex Publications Ltd.. Note: Single-sided disc

Brown, Fred
GRASS IS GREENER, THE (Unknown narrator(s)).
MCSET. Cat no: **1854962442**. Released on Bramhope, '91 by Ulverscroft Soundings. Note: 5 Cassettes.

HAPPY (Unknown narrator(s)).
MCSET. Cat no: **1854962663**. Released on Soundings, '91 by Soundings Records, Bond Street Music. Note: 6 Cassettes.

Browning, Robert
ROBERT BROWNING (Laurence Lerner).
Note: Pre-recorded discussions which show literary criticism as a living, evolving interchange.
MC. Cat no: **A48**. Released on Sussex Tapes, '91 by Sussex Publications Ltd..

Buchner, G
DANTONS TOD (Edited By Mary Garland) (Unknown narrator(s)).
Note: Buchner's personal and political background is outlined and the historical background explained, hence creating the conditions which prompted the writing of the play. In German.
MC. Cat no: **G 7796**. Released on Exeter Tapes, '91 by Drakes Educational Associates.

WOYZECK (Edited By Mary Garland) (Unknown narrator(s)).
Note: The discussion aims at a comprehensive introduction to Buchner's play. The reading is based on Professor Lehmann's arrangement of 1967.
MC. Cat no: **G 7797**. Released on Exeter Tapes, '91 by Drakes Educational Associates.

Bulgakov, M
DNI TURBINYKH (Unknown narrator(s)).
Note: This play by Bulgakov is analysed and examined against the background of ideological demands made on the Soviet theatre in the mid to late 1920's.
MC. Cat no: **R 7781**. Released on Exeter Tapes, '91 by Drakes Educational Associates.

Bunin, I
GRAMMATIKA LYUBVI (Edited By D. Richards) (Unknown narrator(s)).
Note: A general review of Bunin's literary career and a close analysis of one highly typical short story.
MC. Cat no: **R 7782**. Released on Exeter Tapes, '91 by Drakes Educational Associates.

Burgess, Anthony
PROSE READINGS (Anthony Burgess).

Note: Author reads their works and discuss their formative influences.
MC. Cat no: **AS 09**. Released on Sussex Tapes, '91 by Sussex Publications Ltd..

Burns, George
GRACIE (Unknown narrator(s)).
MCSET. Cat no: **0671689282**. Released on Simon & Schuster, '91 by Simon & Schuster Ltd. Note: 2 cassettes.

Burns, Robert
STORY OF ROBERT BURNS (John Cairney).
2LP. Cat no: **REL 448**. Released on BBC, May '79 by BBC Records, Taylors.

Business
BEWARE THE NAKED MAN WHO OFFERS HIS SHIRT (Unknown narrator(s)).
MCSET. Cat no: **0671703700**. Released on Simon & Schuster, '91 by Simon & Schuster Ltd.

BIAS FOR ACTION (Unknown narrator(s)).
MCSET. Cat no: **1555253407**. Released on Simon & Schuster, '91 by Simon & Schuster Ltd.

BIG DEAL, THE (An Essential Course in Business English) (Unknown narrator(s)).
MCSET. Cat no: **VEB 7**. Released on Sussex Tapes, '91 by Sussex Publications Ltd.

BUSINESS TRADING ETHICS (UNESCO Reports) (Unknown narrator(s)).
MC. Cat no: **IR 104**. Released on International Report, Oct '81 by Seminar Cassettes.

CALL ME ROGER (Unknown narrator(s)).
MCSET. Cat no: **155525196X**. Released on Simon & Schuster, '91 by Simon & Schuster Ltd.

CHANGING THE GAME: THE NEW WAY TO SELL (Unknown narrator(s)).
MCSET. Cat no: **1555251846**. Released on Simon & Schuster, '91 by Simon & Schuster Ltd.

COPING WITH DIFFICULT PEOPLE (Robert Bramson).
MC. Cat no: **0671617850**. Released on Simon & Schuster, '91 by Simon & Schuster Ltd.

CREATING WEALTH (Unknown narrator(s)).
MCSET. Cat no: **0671622943**. Released on Simon & Schuster, '91 by Simon & Schuster Ltd. Note: ISBN No: 0563 227044

DINOSAUR BRAINS (Unknown narrator(s)).
MCSET. Cat no: **1555253717**. Released on Simon & Schuster, '91 by Simon & Schuster Ltd.

DOING IT NOW (Edwin C. Bliss).
MC. Cat no: **0671629956**. Released on Simon & Schuster, '91 by Simon & Schuster Ltd.

DO'S AND DON'T'S OF DELEGATION (Unknown narrator(s)).
MCSET. Cat no: **0671662546**. Released on Simon & Schuster, '91 by Simon & Schuster Ltd.

EXCELLENCE IN ORGANIZATION (Unknown narrator(s)).
MCSET. Cat no: **1555252265**. Released on Simon & Schuster, '91 by Simon & Schuster Ltd.

EXECUTIVE ESP (Unknown narrator(s)).
MCSET. Cat no: **0671684647**. Released on Simon & Schuster, '91 by Simon & Schuster Ltd.

FINANCIAL SELF DEFENCE (Unknown narrator(s)).
MCSET. Cat no: **0671728164**. Released on Simon & Schuster, '91 by Simon & Schuster Ltd.

FIVE STEPS TO SUCCESSFUL SELLING (Unknown narrator(s)).
MCSET. Cat no: **1555252761**. Released on Simon & Schuster, '91 by Simon & Schuster Ltd. Note: 10 Cassettes.

FRIENDLY PERSUASION (Unknown narrator(s)).
MCSET. Cat no: **1555253970**. Released on Simon & Schuster, '91 by Simon & Schuster Ltd.

FRONTIERS OF MANAGEMENT (Unknown narrator(s)).
MCSET. Cat no: **0671641107**. Released on Simon & Schuster, '91 by Simon & Schuster Ltd. Note: 2 Cassettes.

GETTING ORGANISED (Stephanie Winston).
MC. Cat no: **0671618695**. Released on Simon & Schuster, '91 by Simon & Schuster Ltd.

GETTING TO YES (Roger Fisher).
MC. Cat no: **0671634062**. Released on Simon & Schuster, '91 by Simon & Schuster Ltd.

GOOD WORK (Unknown narrator(s)).
MCSET. Cat no: **0555254276**. Released on Simon & Schuster, '91 by Simon & Schuster Ltd.

GREATEST MANAGEMENT PRINCIPLE IN THE WORLD (Unknown narrator(s)).
MCSET. Cat no: **1555252303**. Released on Simon & Schuster, '91 by Simon & Schuster Ltd.

HARDBALL (Unknown narrator(s)).
MCSET. Cat no: **1555253881**. Released on Simon & Schuster, '91 by Simon & Schuster Ltd. Note: 6 Cassettes,

HOW TO BE A WINNER (Unknown narrator(s)).
MCSET. Cat no: **1555253830**. Released on Simon & Schuster, '91 by Simon & Schuster Ltd.

HOW TO BE THE D.I.R.E.C.T.O.R OF YOUR LIFE (Unknown narrator(s)).
MCSET. Cat no: **0671662538**. Released on Simon & Schuster, '91 by Simon & Schuster Ltd.

HOW TO PUT MORE TIME INTO YOUR LIFE (Unknown narrator(s)).
MCSET. Cat no: **1555251803**. Released on Simon & Schuster, '91 by Simon & Schuster Ltd.

HOW TO PUT YOUR POINT ACROSS IN 30 SECONDS (Milo O. Frank).
MC. Cat no: **0671602470**. Released on Simon & Schuster, '91 by Simon & Schuster Ltd.

HOW TO RUN A SUCCESSFUL MEETING IN HALF THE TIME (Unknown narrator(s)).
MCSET. Cat no: **0671677861**. Released on Simon & Schuster, '91 by Simon & Schuster Ltd. Note: 2 cassettes.

HOW TO TURN AN INTERVIEW INTO A JOB (Unknown narrator(s)).
MCSET. Cat no: **0671602489**. Released on Simon & Schuster, '91 by Simon & Schuster Ltd.

IF YOU HAVEN'T GOT THE TIME TO DO IT RIGHT (When Will You Find Time To Do It) (Unknown narrator(s)).
MCSET. Cat no: **0671702720**. Released on Simon & Schuster, '91 by Simon & Schuster Ltd. Note: 2 cassettes.

IMPROVE YOUR TYPING (Intermediate Course) (Unknown narrator(s)).
MCSET. Cat no: **S 17060**. Released on Sussex Tapes, '91 by Sussex Publications Ltd.. Note: 2 Cassettes.

INDUSTRIAL ESPIONAGE (New York, Tokyo, Bonn, London, UNESCO Reports) (Unknown narrator(s)).
MC. Cat no: **IR 111**. Released on International Report, Oct '81 by Seminar Cassettes.

INNER MANAGEMENT (Unknown narrator(s)).
MCSET. Cat no: **1555252826**. Released on Simon & Schuster, '91 by Simon & Schuster Ltd. Note: 6 Cassettes,

INNOVATIVE SECRETS OF SUCCESS (Unknown narrator(s)).
MCSET. Cat no: **1555252834**. Released on Simon & Schuster, '91 by Simon & Schuster Ltd. Note: 10 Cassettes.

IT'S ALWAYS SOMETHING (Unknown narrator(s)).
MCSET. Cat no: **0671683616**. Released on Simon & Schuster, '91 by Simon & Schuster Ltd.

IT'S NOT MY DEPARTMENT (Unknown narrator(s)).
MCSET. Cat no: **0671730150**. Released on Simon & Schuster, '91 by Simon & Schuster Ltd.

LEADERSHIP SECRETS OF ATTILA THE HUN (Unknown narrator(s)).
MCSET. Cat no: **1555252818**. Released on Simon & Schuster, '91 by Simon & Schuster Ltd.

LEARNING TO TOUCH TYPE (Basic Course) (Unknown narrator(s)).
MCSET. Cat no: **S 17055**. Released on Sussex Tapes, '91 by Sussex Publications Ltd.. Note: 3 Cassettes.

LIGHT TOUCH, THE (Unknown narrator(s)).
MCSET. Cat no: **0671725300**. Released on Simon & Schuster, '91 by Simon & Schuster Ltd. Note: 2 Cassettes.

MANAGING THE FUTURE (Unknown narrator(s)).
MCSET. Cat no: **155525389X**. Released on Simon & Schuster, '91 by Simon & Schuster Ltd.

MASTERTHINKER (Unknown narrator(s)).
MCSET. Cat no: **0671668927**. Released on Simon & Schuster, '91 by Simon & Schuster Ltd. Note: 2 cassettes.

MEGA TRENDS (Unknown narrator(s)).
MCSET. Cat no: **1555252923**. Released on Simon & Schuster, '91 by Simon & Schuster Ltd.

MENTALLY TOUGH (Unknown narrator(s)).
MCSET. Cat no: **1555254039**. Released on Simon & Schuster, '91 by Simon & Schuster Ltd.

NEW TIME MANAGEMENT (Unknown narrator(s)).
MCSET. Cat no: **1555252400**. Released on Simon & Schuster, '91 by Simon & Schuster Ltd. Note: 10 Cassettes.

NOTHING DOWN (Unknown narrator(s)).
MCSET. Cat no: **0671618555**. Released on Simon & Schuster, '91 by Simon & Schuster Ltd. Note: ISBN No: 0563 227044

ON BECOMING A LEADER (Unknown narrator(s)).
MCSET. Cat no: **1555254160**. Released on Simon & Schuster, '91 by Simon & Schuster Ltd. Note: 10 Cassettes.

ONE MINUTE MANAGER (Unknown narrator(s)).
MCSET. Cat no: **1555252931**. Released on Simon & Schuster, '91 by Simon & Schuster Ltd. Note: 6 Cassettes.

ONE MINUTE MANAGER GETS FIT (Unknown narrator(s)).
MCSET. Cat no: **1555252699**. Released on Simon & Schuster, '91 by Simon & Schuster Ltd.

ONE MINUTE MANAGER MEETS THE MONKEY (Unknown narrator(s)).
MCSET. Cat no: **0671660772**. Released on Simon & Schuster, '91 by Simon & Schuster Ltd.

ONE MINUTE MANAGER & PUTTING THE ONE MINUTE MANAGER TO WORK (Unknown narrator(s)).
MCSET. Cat no: **1555252435**. Released on Simon & Schuster, '91 by Simon & Schuster Ltd.

ONE MINUTE SALES (Unknown narrator(s)).
MCSET. Cat no: **1555252710**. Released on Simon & Schuster, '92 by Simon & Schuster Ltd.

ONLY OTHER INVESTMENT GUIDE YOU'LL EVER NEED (Unknown narrator(s)).
MCSET. Cat no: **0671647237**. Released on Simon & Schuster, '91 by Simon & Schuster Ltd. Note: ISBN No: 0563 227044

ORGANISED EXECUTIVE, THE (Stephanie Winston).
MC. Cat no: **0671625683**. Released on Simon & Schuster, '91 by Simon & Schuster Ltd.

PEOPLE MANAGEMENT (Unknown narrator(s)).
MCSET. Cat no: **1555253199**. Released on Simon & Schuster, '91 by Simon & Schuster Ltd. Note: 6 Cassettes.

PERFECT SALES PRESENTATION, THE (Secrets of Success Series) (Robert L. Shook).
MC. Cat no: **0600560643**. Released on Hamlyn Books On Tape, '88, Bond Street Music.

PHONE POWER: HOW TO GET WHATEVER YOU WANT ON THE TELEPHONE (Unknown narrator(s)).
MCSET. Cat no: **0671625691**. Released on Simon & Schuster, '91 by Simon & Schuster Ltd.

POWER OF BUSINESS RAPPORT (Unknown narrator(s)).
MCSET. Cat no: **1555254225**. Released on Simon & Schuster, '91 by Simon & Schuster Ltd.

POWER OF MONEY DYNAMICS (Unknown narrator(s)).
MCSET. Cat no: **1555252567**. Released on Simon & Schuster, '91 by Simon & Schuster Ltd. Note: 6 Cassettes,

POWER TALKING (Unknown narrator(s)).
MCSET. Cat no: **1555254179**. Released on Simon & Schuster, '91 by Simon & Schuster Ltd. Note: 10 Cassettes.

POWERSPEAK (Unknown narrator(s)).
MCSET. Cat no: **1555252982**. Released on Simon & Schuster, '91 by Simon & Schuster Ltd.

PSYCHOLOGY OF SELLING (Unknown narrator(s)).
MCSET. Cat no: **1555252427**. Released on Simon & Schuster, '91 by Simon & Schuster Ltd. Note: 6 Cassettes,

PUTTING THE ONE MINUTE MANAGER TO WORK (Unknown narrator(s)).
MCSET. Cat no: **155525294X**. Released on Simon & Schuster, '91 by Simon & Schuster Ltd.

SECRETS OF POWER NEGOTIATING (Unknown narrator(s)).
MCSET. Cat no: **1555253849**. Released on Simon & Schuster, '91 by Simon & Schuster Ltd. Note: 6 Cassettes,

SECRETS OF SUCCESS (Unknown narrator(s)).

Note: Includes:- The Perfect Sales Presentation, The One Minute Manager, The Psychology Of Negotiating and In Search Of Excellence.
MCSET. Cat no: **1001M**. Released on Travellers Tales, '91 by Travellers Tales. Note: 4 cassettes.

SEE YOURSELF SUCCEED (Unknown narrator(s)).
MCSET. Cat no: **1555252745**. Released on Simon & Schuster, '91 by Simon & Schuster Ltd.

SELL YOUR WAY TO THE TOP (Unknown narrator(s)).
MCSET. Cat no: **1555252141**. Released on Simon & Schuster, '91 by Simon & Schuster Ltd.

SELLING IN THE 90'S (Unknown narrator(s)).
MCSET. Cat no: **1555253393**. Released on Simon & Schuster, '91 by Simon & Schuster Ltd. Note: 10 Cassettes.

SILICON CHIPS - THEIR IMPACT (UNESCO Reports) (Unknown narrator(s)).
MC. Cat no: **IR 119**. Released on International Report, Oct '81 by Seminar Cassettes.

SILICON CHIPS - THEIR USES (UNESCO Reports) (Unknown narrator(s)).
MC. Cat no: **IR 118**. Released on International Report, Oct '81 by Seminar Cassettes.

SKILLS FOR SUCCESS (Unknown narrator(s)).
MCSET. Cat no: **1555253164**. Released on Simon & Schuster, '91 by Simon & Schuster Ltd.

SOUND SELLING (Issue 9) (Unknown narrator(s)).
MCSET. Cat no: **1555253857**. Released on Simon & Schuster, '91 by Simon & Schuster Ltd.

SOUND SELLING (Issue 10) (Unknown narrator(s)).
MCSET. Cat no: **1555253989**. Released on Simon & Schuster, '91 by Simon & Schuster Ltd.

SOUND SELLING (Issue 11) (Unknown narrator(s)).
MCSET. Cat no: **155525408X**. Released on Simon & Schuster, '91 by Simon & Schuster Ltd.

SPEAK TO WIN (Unknown narrator(s)).
MCSET. Cat no: **1555252133**. Released on Simon & Schuster, '91 by Simon & Schuster Ltd. Note: 6 Cassettes,

STILL FURTHER UP THE ORGANISATION (Unknown narrator(s)).
MCSET. Cat no: **1555253121**. Released on Simon & Schuster, '91 by Simon & Schuster Ltd. Note: 10 Cassettes.

STRATEGY OF MEETINGS (Unknown narrator(s)).
MCSET. Cat no: **0671667777**. Released on Simon & Schuster, '91 by Simon & Schuster Ltd. Note: 7 Cassette set.

STRESS FOR SUCCESS (Unknown narrator(s)).
MCSET. Cat no: **1555252990**. Released on Simon & Schuster, '91 by Simon & Schuster Ltd.

SUBTEXT (Unknown narrator(s)).
MCSET. Cat no: **155525280X**. Released on Simon & Schuster, '91 by Simon & Schuster Ltd.

SUCCESS AND THE SELF-IMAGE (Unknown narrator(s)).
MCSET. Cat no: **1555253091**. Released on Simon & Schuster, '91 by Simon & Schuster Ltd.

SUCCESS PROFILE (Unknown narrator(s)).
MCSET. Cat no: **0671682628**. Released on Simon & Schuster, '91 by Simon & Schuster Ltd. Note: 2 Cassettes.

SUCCESS THROUGH A POSITIVE MENTAL ATTITUDE (Unknown narrator(s)).
MCSET. Cat no: **1555252702**. Released on Simon & Schuster, '91 by Simon & Schuster Ltd. Note: 10 Cassettes.

THINK YOUR WAY TO SUCCESS (Lilyan Wilder).
MC. Cat no: **067162993X**. Released on Simon & Schuster, '91 by Simon & Schuster Ltd.

WHAT EVERYONE IN BUSINESS BETTER KNOW ABOUT THE LAW (Unknown narrator(s)).
MCSET. Cat no: **0671646311**. Released on Simon & Schuster, '91 by Simon & Schuster Ltd. Note: 2 cassettes.

WINNING MOVES: THE BODY LANGUAGE OF SELLING (Unknown narrator(s)).
MCSET. Cat no: **1555252575**. Released on Simon & Schuster, '91 by Simon & Schuster Ltd. Note: 6 Cassettes.

WIN-WIN NEGOTIATOR (Unknown narrator(s)).
MCSET. Cat no: **1555252338**. Released on Simon & Schuster, '91 by Simon & Schuster Ltd. Note: 10 Cassettes.

WORDBANK (Unknown narrator(s)).
MCSET. Cat no: **0671668935**. Released on Simon & Schuster, '91 by Simon & Schuster Ltd. Note: 2 Cassettes

WORKING SMARTER (Unknown narrator(s)).
MCSET. Cat no: **1555253105**. Released on Simon & Schuster, '91 by Simon & Schuster Ltd.

WORKING WITH JERKS (Unknown narrator(s)).
MCSET. Cat no: **0671658360**. Released on Simon & Schuster, '91 by Simon & Schuster Ltd.

YOU ARE THE MESSAGE (Unknown narrator(s)).
MCSET. Cat no: **0671662244**. Released on Simon & Schuster, '91 by Simon & Schuster Ltd.

YOU CAN GET ANYTHING YOU WANT (Unknown narrator(s)).
MCSET. Cat no: **155525215X**. Released on Simon & Schuster, '91 by Simon & Schuster Ltd. Note: 6 Cassettes,

Butor, M

LA MODIFICATION (Edited By J.B. Howitt) (Unknown narrator(s)).
Note: Explores how Butor's work can be read initially as a rather different psychological novel.
MC. Cat no: **F 7562**. Released on Exeter Tapes, '91 by Drakes Educational Associates.

Caesar, Julius

JULIUS CAESAR (Biography) (Robert Rietty).
MC. Cat no: **L 1**. Released on Green Dragon, '91 by Green Dragon Audio Visual.
MC. Cat no: **DHM 9**. Released on Sussex Tapes, '91 by Sussex Publications Ltd..

JULIUS CAESAR (History for ages 8+) (Unknown narrator(s)).
Note: Book & cassette.
MC. Cat no: **PLBH 102**. Released on Tell-A-Tale, Mar '84 by Pickwick Records, Taylors, Clyde Factors.

Caldwell, Erskine

NATURALISM AND THE AMERICAN NOVEL (Erskine Caldwell).
Note: Author reads their works and discuss their formative influences.
MCSET. Cat no: **AS 10**. Released on Sussex Tapes, '91 by Sussex Publications Ltd..

Calvino

FIRST TWENTY YEARS, THE (Edited By J.R. Woodhouse) (Unknown narrator(s)).
Note: The first twenty years of Galvino, from 1945.
MC. Cat no: **I 7869**. Released on Exeter Tapes, '91 by Drakes Educational Associates. Note: 4 Cassettes.

Camus, A

CALIGULA (Edited By Ray Davison) (Unknown narrator(s)).
Note: An analysis of Camus's conception of tragedy and of this, his first play, which explores the concept of nihilism.
MC. Cat no: **F 7676**. Released on Exeter Tapes, '91 by Drakes Educational Associates.

LA CHUTE (Edited By Philip Thody) (Unknown narrator(s)).
Note: A study of the text in the context of Camus's ideas on christianity and on politics with some reference to his personal life and intellectual development.
MC. Cat no: **F 7655**. Released on Exeter Tapes, '91 by Drakes Educational Associates.

L'ETRANGER (Edited By Ray Davison) (Unknown narrator(s)).
Note: The problems of interpretation posed by 'L'etranger' capital punishment and the character of Mersaut are explored in this approach to Camus' novel.
MC. Cat no: **F 7504**. Released on Exeter Tapes, '91 by Drakes Educational Associates.

L'EXIL ET LE ROYAUME (Edited By Philip Thody) (Unknown narrator(s)).
Note: A study of the six stories in the volume in the context of Camus' work and its relationship to his native Algeria.
MC. Cat no: **F 7308**. Released on Exeter Tapes, '91 by Drakes Educational Associates.

Canals

RECOLLECTIONS NO. 2: LIFE ON THE CANAL (Frank Richards).
Note: A look back to life between the great wars of life on the Black Country canals. Related by Frank Richards who spent over 50 years with Birmingham canal and navigation.
MC. Cat no: **AC 149**. Released on Audicord, '91 by Audicord Cassettes.

STEAM AND HARNESS (See under Trains).

Carpozi, George Jnr.

JOHN WAYNE STORY, THE (Peter Wheeler).
MCSET. Cat no: **1026N**. Released on Travellers Tales, '91 by Travellers Tales. Note: 4 cassettes.
MCSET. Cat no: **1854960369**. Released on Bramhope, '91 by Ulverscroft Soundings. Note: 4 Cassettes.

Carrick, Peter

THANKS FOR THE MEMORY (A Tribute To Bob Hope) (Garrick Hagon).
MCSET. Cat no: **1101N**. Released on Travellers Tales, '91 by Travellers Tales. Note: 4 cassettes
MCSET. Cat no: **1854963910**. Released on Bramhope, '91 by Ulverscroft Soundings. Note: 4 cassettes

TRIBUTE TO FRED ASTAIRE, A (Christopher Kay).
MCSET. Cat no: **1030N**. Released on Travellers Tales, '91 by Travellers Tales. Note: 5 cassettes.
MCSET. Cat no: **1854963104**. Released on Bramhope, '91 by Ulverscroft Soundings. Note: 5 cassettes.

Castaneda, Carlos

DON JUAN: THE SORCERER (Carlos Casteanada).
Note: Author reads their works and discuss their formative influences.
MC. Cat no: **AS 11**. Released on Sussex Tapes, '91 by Sussex Publications Ltd..

CB Radio

OFFICIAL GUIDE TO CB RADIO (Various artists).
MC. Cat no: **SP 101**. Released on Stage One, Mar '81.

Celtic

CELTIC LANGUAGE, THE (Edited By Ian Press) (Unknown narrator(s)).
MC. Cat no: **CL 7804**. Released on Exeter Tapes, '91 by Drakes Educational Associates.

Cezanne

CEZANNE (Edited By David Kinmont) (Unknown narrator(s)).
Note: An introduction to the painter's background and family and the influences on and development of his work.
MC. Cat no: **F 7978**. Released on Exeter Tapes, '91 by Drakes Educational Associates.

Chatterbox

CHATTERBOX CLASSICS 1 (Various).
MC. Cat no: **CBX 102**. Released on Chatterbox, Jun '82 by BMG Records (UK) Ltd..

CHATTERBOX HUMOUR 1 (Various).
MC. Cat no: **CBX 103**. Released on Chatterbox, Jun '82 by BMG Records (UK) Ltd..

CHATTERBOX MIXED BAG 1 (Various).
MC. Cat no: **CBX 104**. Released on Chatterbox, Jun '82 by BMG Records (UK) Ltd..

CHATTERBOX POPS 1 (Various).
MC. Cat no: **CBX 101**. Released on Chatterbox, Jun '82 by BMG Records (UK) Ltd..

Chekhov, Anton

DAMA'S SOBACHKOI (Edited By Roger Cockrell) (Unknown narrator(s)).
Note: A discussion of some of the more important ideas and themes of Anton Chekhov's later stories, with particular reference to 'Dama's Sobachkoi'.
MC. Cat no: **R 7622**. Released on Exeter Tapes, '91 by Drakes Educational Associates.

VISHNYOVYI SAD (Edited By Patricia Cockrell) (Unknown narrator(s)).
Note: A discussion of Chekhov's play, 'The Cherry Orchard'.
MC. Cat no: **R 7623**. Released on Exeter Tapes, '91 by Drakes Educational Associates.

China

REVOLUTIONARY CHINA (Malcolm Caldwell & William Jenner).
MC. Cat no: **HB 6**. Released on Sussex Tapes, '91 by Sussex Publications Ltd..

Chinese

BASIC CANTONESE (Volume 1) (Unknown narrator(s)).
MCSET. Cat no: **C 131**. Released on New World Cassettes, '91.

BASIC CANTONESE (Volume 2) (Unknown narrator(s)).
MCSET. Cat no: **C140**. Released on Sussex Tapes, '91 by Sussex Publications Ltd..

CHINESE CASSETTE COURSE (Unknown narrator(s)).
Note: Includes:- 3 months' book and an instruction leaflet.
MCSET. Cat no: **852851847**. Released on Hugo Languages, '92 by Hugo Language Books Limited. Note: 4 cassettes. Playing time 4hrs.

CHINESE - ENGLISH DICTIONARIES AND HOW TO USE THEM (Unknown narrator(s)).
MC. Cat no: **C 7768**. Released on Exeter Tapes, '91 by Drakes Educational Associates.

CHINESE TRAVEL PACK (Unknown narrator(s)).
Note: Contains a Hugo phrase book.
MC. Cat no: **852851561**. Released on Hugo Languages, '92 by Hugo Language Books Limited.

GET BY IN CHINESE (Language Courses) (Unknown narrator(s)).
Note: Each book contains phrases and conversations.
MCSET. Cat no: **PTT 300**. Released on BBC Publications, '91. Note : 2 Cassettes.

GET BY TRAVEL PACKS (Language Courses) (Unknown narrator(s)).
MCSET. Cat no: **PACK 2300**. Released on BBC Publications, '91. Note : 2 Cassettes.

SPEAKING CHINESE IN CHINA (Unknown narrator(s)).
MCSET. Cat no: **M320**. Released on Sussex Tapes, '91 by Sussex Publications Ltd.

Churchill, Sir Winston

25 YEARS OF HIS SPEECHES (1918-1943, Volume 2) (Sir Winston Churchill).
MCSET. Cat no: **ARGO 1232**. Released on Argo (EMI), Oct '90 by EMI Records. Note: 2 Cassettes.

SELECTION OF HIS WARTIME SPEECHES (1939-1945) (Sir Winston Churchill).
MCSET. Cat no: **SAY 79**. Released on Argo (Polygram), Jun '88 by PolyGram Classics **Deleted** Jan '89.

MCSET. Cat no: **ARGO 1118**. Released on Argo (EMI), Jun '89 by EMI Records.

MCSET. Cat no: **1002N**. Released on Travellers Tales, '91 by Travellers Tales. Note: 2 cassettes.

STATE FUNERAL OF SIR WINSTON CHURCHILL,K.G.,OM,C (Unknown narrator(s)).
2LP. Cat no: **WCF 101**. Released on Decca, Feb '65 by PolyGram Classics, Thames Distributors Ltd. **Deleted** '88.

VOICE OF CHURCHILL, THE (Sir Winston Churchill).
LP. Cat no: **LXT 6200**. Released on Unknown, Feb '65 **Deleted** Feb '70.

WINSTON CHURCHILL (A Brief Life) (Timothy West).
Note: Written by Piers Brandon.
MCSET. Cat no: **1027A**. Released on Travellers Tales, '91 by Travellers Tales. Note: 6 cassettes.
MCSET. Cat no: **IAB 87114**. Released on Isis Audio Books, '91. Note : 6 Cassettes.

Ciardi, John

POETRY OF JOHN CIARDI, THE (John Ciardi).
Note: Author reads their works and discuss their formative influences.
MC. Cat no: **AS 13**. Released on Sussex Tapes, '91 by Sussex Publications Ltd..

Cinema

RECOLLECTIONS NO. 3: SILENT DAYS OF THE CINEMA (Tom Mellor).
Note: Stories from behind the screen recalling the rise and decline of 'going to the flicks' recalled by Tom Mellor, who started as a 13 year old page boy in 1914 through to retirement in 1966 after over 50 years in the operating box.
MC. Cat no: **AC 147**. Released on Audicord, '91 by Audicord Cassettes.

Cleghorn Gaskell, Elizabeth

LIFE OF CHARLOTTE BRONTE, THE (Anthony Homyer).
MCSET. Cat no: **1070/1071A**. Released on Travellers Tales, '91 by Travellers Tales. Note: 12 Cassettes.
MCSET. Cat no: **TCL 20**. Released on Complete Listener, '91 by Complete Listener. Note: 12 Cassettes, Playing time: 18 hours.

Cocteau, Jean

LA MACHINE INFERNALE (Edited By Jacqueline Fox) (Unknown narrator(s)).
Note: A discussion of this play by Jean Cocteau. Reference is made to Cocteau's own remarks and the effect of outside influences on the play. In French.
MC. Cat no: **F 7934**. Released on Exeter Tapes, '91 by Drakes Educational Associates.

Colette

LE BLE EN HERBE (Edited By Odile Cook) (Unknown narrator(s)).
Note: Studies the theme of adolescence in the novel with an introduction to Colette's sources of inspiration.
MC. Cat no: **F 7866**. Released on Exeter Tapes, '91 by Drakes Educational Associates.

Columbus, Christopher

CHRISTOPHER COLUMBUS (Biography) (Clifford Rose).
MC. Cat no: **EP 1**. Released on Green Dragon, '91 by Green Dragon Audio Visual.
MC. Cat no: **DHM 10**. Released on Sussex Tapes, '91 by Sussex Publications Ltd.

CHRISTOPHER COLUMBUS (History for Ages 8+) (Unknown narrator(s)).
MC. Cat no: **PLBH 104**. Released on

Tell-A-Tale, Apr '84 by Pickwick Records, Taylors, Clyde Factors.

Computing

HISTORY AND HARDWARE OF COMPUTERS (Peter Leblond).
MCSET. Cat no: **0055701MC1**. Released on Sussex Tapes, '91 by Sussex Publications Ltd.. Note: 2 Cassettes.

INTRODUCTION TO COMPUTING, AN (Edited by Ernest Jones) (Ernest Jones).
MCSET. Cat no: **0034177MT7**. Released on Mobile Training, '91 by Mobile Training Records. Note: 2 Cassettes.

Conrad, Joseph

CONRAD (Laurence Lerner).
Note: Pre-recorded discussions which show literary criticism as a living, evolving interchange.
MC. Cat no: **A14**. Released on Sussex Tapes, '91 by Sussex Publications Ltd.. Note: 4 Cassettes.

Cookson, Catherine

OUR KATE (Elizabeth Henry).
MCSET. Cat no: **1093N**. Released on Travellers Tales, '91 by Travellers Tales. Note: 8 Cassettes.
MCSET. Cat no: **185496349X**. Released on Soundings, '91 by Soundings Records, Bond Street Music. Note: 8 Cassettes.

Cooper, Jilly

COMMON YEARS, THE (Norma West).
MCSET. Cat no: **1072A**. Released on Travellers Tales, '91 by Travellers Tales. Note: 7 Cassettes.
MCSET. Cat no: **OAS 20691**. Released on Oasis Audio Books, '91 by Isis Audio Books. Note: 7 Cassettes.

Corneille, P

LE CID (Edited By Christopher J. Gossip) (Unknown narrator(s)).
MC. Cat no: **F 7855**. Released on Exeter Tapes, '91 by Drakes Educational Associates.

Cotswolds

COTSWOLD CHARACTERS (Various narrators).
Tracks / Shepherd Tidmarsh: *Archer, Fred* / Life as a roadsweeper: *Cook, Amy*.
Note: 45 minutes. Life on the Cotswolds remembered with humour and the occasional song.
LP. Cat no: **SDL 222**. Released on Saydisc, by Amon Ra Records, Taylors, C.M. Distribution, Gamut Distribution **Deleted** '89.
MC. Cat no: **CSDL 222**. Released on Saydisc, by Amon Ra Records, Taylors, C.M. Distribution, Gamut Distribution **Deleted** '89.

COTSWOLD CRAFTSMEN (Various narrators).
Note: 47 minutes. Recollections of thatching, cider-making, wheel-wrighting, hurdle-making, working with oxen, Gloucester cheese, and the Cotswold roof, wall, and sheep.
MC. Cat no: **CSDL 247**. Released on Saydisc, Apr '81 by Amon Ra Records, Taylors, C.M. Distribution, Gamut Distribution **Deleted** '89.

COTSWOLD VOICES (Various narrators).
Note: 46 minutes. George & Dorcas Juggins on snuff-taking & their courting days, Bert Butler on bath nights and 'oss muckin', plus ...
MC. Cat no: **CSDL 267**. Released on Saydisc, Apr '81 by Amon Ra Records, Taylors, C.M. Distribution, Gamut Distribution **Deleted** '89.

WHILE I WORK I WHISTLE.
Tracks / Granny's old armchair / Nettle tea.
Note: 44 minutes. Songs and humour of the Cotswolds.
LP. Cat no: **SDL 300**. Released on Saydisc, Nov '79 by Amon Ra Records, Taylors, C.M. Distribution, Gamut Distribution **Deleted** '84.
MC. Cat no: **CSDL 300**. Released on Saydisc, Oct '79 by Amon Ra Records, Taylors, C.M. Distribution, Gamut Distribution **Deleted** '89.

Crawley, Aidan

ESCAPE FROM GERMANY (Gene Ford).
MCSET. Cat no: **1076/7N**. Released on Travellers Tales, '91 by Travellers Tales. Note: 12 Cassettes.
MCSET. Cat no: **OAS 89121**. Released on Oasis Audio Books, '91 by Isis Audio Books. Note: 12 Cassettes.

Cricket

ASHES 1948-1981, THE (Bradman to Botham) (Various narrators).
Note: Commentaries from the BBC Sound Archives.
MCSET. Cat no: **ZBBC 1172**. Released on BBC Radio Collection, Nov '90 by BBC Records. Note: ISBN No: 0563 411171

AUSTRALIA'S GREATEST CRICKET CHARACTERS (Greg Matthews).
MC. Cat no: **TTC 2036**. Released on Talking Tape Company, Apr '91, Conifer Records. Note: 2 Cassettes. Playing time 3hrs. ISBN no. 1872520715

BRADMAN - THE DON DECLARES (Donald Bradman).
Note: The world's greatest cricketer looks back.
MCSET. Cat no: **ZBBC 1089**. Released on BBC Radio Collection, Jul '89 by BBC Records. Note: ISBN No: 0563 226765

ENGLAND V THE WEST INDIES (1950 - 1976) (Various narrators).
Note: Commentaries from the BBC Sound Archives.
MCSET. Cat no: **ZBBC 1174**. Released on BBC Radio Collection, '91 by BBC Records. Note: ISBN No: 0563 41118X

GOLDEN AGE, THE (Various narrators).
Note: Highlights from W.G.Grace up to the end of the thirties.
MCSET. Cat no: **ZBBC 1027**. Released on BBC Radio Collection, Sep '88 by BBC Records. Note: ISBN No: 0563 225823

GREAT CRICKET MATCHES (Various narrators).
Tracks / England V Australia 1948: *Various artists* / England V West Indies 1950: *Various artists* / England V Australia 1953: *Various artists* / England V Australia 1956: *Various artists* / England V West Indies 1957: *Various artists* / England V West Indies 1963: *Various artists* / England V Australia 1968: *Various artists* / Australia V West Indies 1975: *Various artists*.
MCSET. Cat no: **ZBBC 1181**. Released on BBC Radio Collection, Nov '90 by BBC Records. Note: ISBN No: 0563 41149X

LILLEE: OVER AND OUT (Biography) (Richie Benaud).
MCSET. Cat no: **TTC 2038**. Released on Talking Tape Company, Apr '91, Conifer Records. Note: 2 Cassettes. Playing time 3hrs. ISBN No.1872520731

LORD'S THE HOME OF CRICKET (E.W. Swanton).
MCSET. Cat no: **ZBBC 1235**. Released on BBC Radio Collection, May '91 by BBC Records. Note: ISBN No: 0563 408391

VIEW FROM THE BOUNDARY (Brian Johnston).
Note: Star interviews - talking cricket with Brian Johnston.
MCSET. Cat no: **ZBBC 1162**. Released on BBC Radio Collection, Nov '90 by BBC Records. Note: ISBN No: 0563 411236

VOICE OF CRICKET, THE (John Arlott).
Note: The highlights of his commentating career from 1946 to 1980.
MCSET. Cat no: **ZBBC 1108**. Released on BBC Radio Collection, Apr '90 by BBC Records. Note: ISBN No: 0563 410213

Crisp, Quentin

EVENING WITH QUENTIN CRISP, AN (Quentin Crisp).
2LP. Cat no: **S2L 5188**. Released on DRG (USA), '88 by DRG Records (USA), Silva Screen, Conifer Records.
MC. Cat no: **S2LC 5188**. Released on DRG (USA), '88 by DRG Records (USA), Silva Screen, Conifer Records.
2LP. Cat no: **DRED 2**. Released on Cherry Red, '81 by Cherry Red Records.

Croall, James
FOURTEEN MINUTES: THE SINKING OF THE EMPRESS OF IRELAND (Gordon Griffin).
MCSET. Cat no: **1022N**. Released on Travellers Tales, '91 by Travellers Tales. Note: 4 Cassettes.
MCSET. Cat no: **1854960644**. Released on Bramhope, '91 by Ulverscroft Soundings. Note: 4 Cassettes.

Cromwell, Oliver
OLIVER CROMWELL (History for Ages 8+) (Unknown narrator(s)).
Note: Book & cassette
MC. Cat no: **PLBH 103**. Released on Tell-A-Tale, Mar '84 by Pickwick Records, Taylors, Clyde Factors.

Cronin, Vincent
WISE MAN FROM THE WEST, THE (Tom Crowe).
MCSET. Cat no: **1040A**. Released on Travellers Tales, '91 by Travellers Tales. Note: 8 Cassettes.
MCSET. Cat no: **OAS 89124**. Released on Oasis Audio Books, '91 by Isis Audio Books. Note: 8 Cassettes.

Cunningham Graham, R.B.
SCOTTISH SKETCHES (Robert Trotter).
MCSET. Cat no: **SPF 148-1**. Released on Schiltron Audio Books, Feb '92 by Schiltron Publishing. Note: 2 Cassettes. Playing time 2hrs

Curling
ROARIN' GAME, THE (Unknown narrator(s)).
Note: History and development of curling in Scotland with sound effects.
MC. Cat no: **SSC 501**. Released on Scotsoun, '91 by Scotsoun Recordings, Morley Audio Services.

Cushing, Peter
AUTOBIOGRAPHY, AN (Peter Cushing).
MCSET. Cat no: **IAB 89021**. Released on Isis Audio Books, '91. Note : 6 Cassette set.
MCSET. Cat no: **1030A**. Released on Travellers Tales, '91 by Travellers Tales. Note: 6 Cassettes.
MEMOIRS OF THE HAMMER YEARS (Peter Cushing).
MCSET. Cat no: **1031A**. Released on Travellers Tales, '91 by Travellers Tales. Note: 3 Cassettes.
PAST FORGETTING (Peter Cushing).
MCSET. Cat no: **IAB 89111**. Released on Isis Audio Books, '91. Note : 3 Cassette set

Czech
CONTEMPORARY CZECH (Language Courses) (Unknown narrator(s)).
MCSET. Cat no: **CZ10**. Released on Sussex Tapes, '91 by Sussex Publications Ltd.
CZECH PHONOLOGY - PART 1 (Edited By Derek J. Hunns) (Unknown narrator(s)).
MC. Cat no: **CZ 7650**. Released on Exeter Tapes, '91 by Drakes Educational Associates.
CZECH PHONOLOGY - PART 2 (Edited By Derek J. Hunns) (Unknown narrator(s)).
MC. Cat no: **CZ 7651**. Released on Exeter Tapes, '91 by Drakes Educational Associates.
CZECH TRAVEL PACK (Unknown narrator(s)).
Note: Contains a Hugo phrase book.
MC. Cat no: **852851677**. Released on Hugo Languages, '92 by Hugo Language Books Limited.
SOUNDS AND ALPHABET OF CZECH, THE (Edited By Derek J. Hunns) (Unknown narrator(s)).
MC. Cat no: **CZ 7647**. Released on Exeter Tapes, '91 by Drakes Educational Associates.

Daneski, Gavin
ANIMAL MAN, THE (Unknown narrator(s)).
MCSET. Cat no: **1854965026**. Released on Bramhope, '91 by Ulverscroft Soundings. Note: 5 Cassettes.

Daniels, Paul
PAUL DANIELS MAGIC SHOW (Paul Daniels Explains Some of his Magic Tricks) (Paul Daniels).
LP. Cat no: **REB 434**. Released on BBC, Jan '82 by BBC Records, Taylors
Deleted Jan '87.

Danish
DANISH CASSETTE COURSE (Unknown narrator(s)).
Note: Includes:- 3 months' book and an instruction leaflet.
MCSET. Cat no: **852851707**. Released on Hugo Languages, '92 by Hugo Language Books Limited. Note: 4 Cassettes. Playing time 4hrs.
DANISH TRAVEL PACK (Unknown narrator(s)).
Note: Contains a Hugo phrase book.
MC. Cat no: **85285143X**. Released on Hugo Languages, '92 by Hugo Language Books Limited. Note: 4 Cassettes.
LANGUAGE COURSE - DANISH (Unknown narrator(s)).
LPS. Cat no: **0747301816**. Released on Linguaphone, Apr '82 by Linguaphone Institute, Taylors, Century Records (USA), Bond Street Music.
LEARN TO SPEAK DANISH (Unknown narrator(s)).
MCSET. Cat no: **DA 40**. Released on Audio Forum (Language courses), '91. Note: 6 Cassettes. 7 hours.

Dante
LA DIVINA COMMEDIA (Edited By M. Constable) (Unknown narrator(s)).
Note: Deals with the value that Dante attributes to Virgil and to his role as a co-ordinating figure in the overall message of the 'divine comedy'.
MC. Cat no: **I 7577**. Released on Exeter Tapes, '91 by Drakes Educational Associates.
PURGATORIO (Edited By John Barnes) (Unknown narrator(s)).
Note: An examination of Dante's moral philosophy as articulated in 'Purgatorio'.
MC. Cat no: **I 7965**. Released on Exeter Tapes, '91 by Drakes Educational Associates.

Darwin, Charles
CHARLES DARWIN (Biography) (Paul Eddington).
MC. Cat no: **SI 2**. Released on Green Dragon, '91 by Green Dragon Audio Visual.
MC. Cat no: **DHM 20**. Released on Sussex Tapes, '91 by Sussex Publications Ltd.. Note: 3 Cassettes. Playing time 3hrs 30mins.

Dawkins, Richard
SELFISH GENE (Richard Dawkins).
MC. Cat no: **PT 22**. Released on Psychology Today (USA), Oct '81 by Seminar Cassettes.

De Balzac, Honore
LE COLONEL CHABERT: GOBSECK (Edited By J.B. Howitt) (Unknown narrator(s)).
Note: Discusses Honore De Balzac's narrative technique. Includes an analysis of the theme of money in his work.
MC. Cat no: **F 7748**. Released on Exeter Tapes, '91 by Drakes Educational Associates.
LE CURE DE TOURS (Edited By Anthony Kelly) (Unknown narrator(s)).
Note: Honore De Balzac's description of human behaviour is examined.
MC. Cat no: **F 7523**. Released on Exeter Tapes, '91 by Drakes Educational Associates.
LE PERE GORIOT (Edited By Donald Haggis) (Unknown narrator(s)).
Note: Examines Honore De Balzac's novel with reference to the complex character of Vautrin, discussing the relation between him and Balzac himself.
MC. Cat no: **F 7503**. Released on Exeter Tapes, '91 by Drakes Educational Associates.

De Gaulle, Charles
DE GAULLE AND THE FRENCH POLITICAL SCENE (Edited By A Julian Petrie) (Unknown narrator(s)).
MC. Cat no: **F 7773**. Released on Exeter Tapes, '91 by Drakes Educational Associates.

De La Fontaine, Jean
FABLES (Edited By Jean D. Biard) (Unknown narrator(s)).
Note: An approach to J. De La Fontaine's complexity of style including his use of language for humorous and poetic effects includes a literary com-

mentary on 'Le Chat', 'La Belette' and 'Le Petit Lapin'. In French.
MC. Cat no: **F 7517**. Released on Exeter Tapes, '91 by Drakes Educational Associates.

De Maupassant, Guy
PIERRE ET JEAN (Edited By Dorothy Steer) (Unknown narrator(s)).
Note: A general survey of Maupassant the novelist includes a special exploration of the novel as seen from Pierre's point of view.
MC. Cat no: **F 7864**. Released on Exeter Tapes, '91 by Drakes Educational Associates.
SCENES DE LA VIE DE PROVINCE (Edited By Dorothy Steer) (Unknown narrator(s)).
Note: A wide - ranging examination of Maupassant's fictional technique in relation to his personal philosphy.
MC. Cat no: **F 7779**. Released on Exeter Tapes, '91 by Drakes Educational Associates.

De Medici, Catherine
CATHERINE DE MEDICI (Biography) (Joss Ackland).
MC. Cat no: **FW 2**. Released on Green Dragon, '91 by Green Dragon Audio Visual.
MC. Cat no: **DHM 1**. Released on Sussex Tapes, '91 by Sussex Publications Ltd..

De Montherlant, H
LA REINE MORTE (Edited By Patricia O'Flaherty) (Unknown narrator(s)).
Note: A general commentary on the themes of the play, the characterisation and an analysis of the genesis of the work, relating it to Montherlant's novels and other plays. Talk in English with French version.
MC. Cat no: **F 7338**. Released on Exeter Tapes, '91 by Drakes Educational Associates.
LE MAITRE DE SANTIAGO (Edited By Gerard Poulet) (Unknown narrator(s)).
Note: A study of the religious inspiration as well as the dramatic technique of this play by De Montherlant. In French.
MC. Cat no: **F 7607**. Released on Exeter Tapes, '91 by Drakes Educational Associates.

De Musset, A
ON NE BADINE PAS AVEC L'AMOUR (Edited By Jean D. Biard) (Unknown narrator(s)).
Note: This play by A. De Musset has its environment, variety of style and unity of tone explored in French.
MC. Cat no: **F 7303**. Released on Exeter Tapes, '91 by Drakes Educational Associates.

De Saint-Exupery
TERRE DES HOMMES (Edited By Jean D Biard) (Unknown narrator(s)).
Note: The scope of the text from the early days of flying to the didactic and ethical values implied in the narrative is examed in this work by A. De Saint Exupery. In French.
MC. Cat no: **F 7882**. Released on Exeter Tapes, '91 by Drakes Educational Associates.

De Sica, Vittorio
LADRI DE BICICLETTE (Edited By Christopher Wagstaff) (Unknown narrator(s)).
Note: This work by Vittorio De Sica is discussed, showing the goals that the film makers were pursuing and how they achieved them.
MC. Cat no: **I 7924**. Released on Exeter Tapes, '91 by Drakes Educational Associates.

De Souza, Edward
MYSTERY OF BORLEY RECTORY, THE (Edward De Souza).
MC. Cat no: **00115304210**. Released on Drake, '91 by Morley Audio Services.

De Tocqueville, Alexis
DEMOCRACY IN AMERICA (Anthony Quayle).
MC. Cat no: **2039**. Released on Caedmon (USA), '88 by Caedmon Records (USA), Bond Street Music.

De Tormes, Lazarillo
UNEXPECTED MASTERPIECE, THE (Edited By Richard Hitchcock) (Unknown narrator(s)).
Note: The claim that this work by Lazarillo De Tormes was 'The best novel of the sixteenth century' is examined.
MC. Cat no: **S 7711**. Released on Exeter Tapes, '91 by Drakes Educational Associates.

De Valois, Dame
PATH OF MORNING, THE (Moira Shearer).
Note: Dame Ninette de Valois recalls her childhood in Ireland. Sketches and short stories.
MCSET. Cat no: **ZC SWD 364**. Released on ASV (Academy Sound & Vision), '89 by Academy Sound & Vision Records.

De Vega Carpio, Lope
EL CABALLERO DE OLMEDO (Edited By William F. Hunter) (Unknown narrator(s)).
Note: An examination of this play by Lope Vega Carpio.
MC. Cat no: **S 7713**. Released on Exeter Tapes, '91 by Drakes Educational Associates.

Defoe, Daniel
DANIEL DEFOE (Colin Brooks & Angus Ross).
Note: Pre-recorded discussions which show literary criticism as a living, evolving interchange.
MC. Cat no: **A34**. Released on Sussex Tapes, '91 by Sussex Publications Ltd..

Dessau, Joanna
AMAZING GRACE (Elizabeth Henry).
MCSET. Cat no: **SOUND 1**. Released on Soundings, Mar '85 by Soundings Records, Bond Street Music.
MCSET. Cat no: **1003N**. Released on Travellers Tales, '91 by Travellers Tales. Note: 4 Cassettes.

Dickens, Charles
CHARLES DICKENS (Angus Wilson).
MC. Cat no: **23075**. Released on Sussex Tapes, '91 by Sussex Publications Ltd..
DICKENS (A E Dyson & Angus Wilson).
Note: Pre-recorded discussions which show literary criticism as a living, evolving interchange.
MC. Cat no: **A6**. Released on Sussex Tapes, '91 by Sussex Publications Ltd..
STORY OF CHARLES DICKENS, THE (Biography) (John Ringham).
MCSET. Cat no: **LD 4**. Released on Green Dragon, '91 by Green Dragon Audio Visual. Note: 2 Cassettes.

Dickens, Monica
MY TURN TO MAKE THE TEA (Biography) (Hannah Gordon).
MCSET. Cat no: **1001A**. Released on Travellers Tales, '91 by Travellers Tales. Note: 6 Cassettes.
ONE PAIR OF FEET (Biography) (Hannah Gordon).
MCSET. Cat no: **1002A**. Released on Travellers Tales, '91 by Travellers Tales. Note: 6 cassettes.
ONE PAIR OF HANDS (Biography) (Hannah Gordon).
MCSET. Cat no: **1003A**. Released on Travellers Tales, '91 by Travellers Tales. Note: 6 Cassettes.

Dimbleby, Richard
VOICE OF RICHARD DIMBLEBY (Richard Dimbleby).
LP. Cat no: **1087**. Released on MFP, Jun '66 by EMI Records, Solomon & Peres **Deleted** '71.

Dos Passos, John
JOHN DOS PASSOS READS HIS POETRY (John Dos Passos).
Note: Author reads his works and discuss their formative influences.
MC. Cat no: **AS 16**. Released on Sussex Tapes, '91 by Sussex Publications Ltd..

Dostoyevsky, Fyodor
ZAPISKI IZ PODPOL'YA (Edited By Malcolm V. Jones) (Unknown narrator(s)).
Note: A discussion of one of Fyodor Dostoyevsky's most influential works, 'Notes From Underground'.
MC. Cat no: **R 7624**. Released on Exeter Tapes, '91 by Drakes Educational Associates.

Drake, Sir Francis
FRANCIS DRAKE (Biography) (Tony Britton).
MC. Cat no: **EP 2**. Released on Green Dragon, '91 by Green Dragon Audio Visual.
MC. Cat no: **DHM 11**. Released on Sussex Tapes, '91 by Sussex Publications Ltd..
SIR FRANCIS DRAKE (History for Ages 8+) (Unknown narrator(s)).
Note: Book & cassette
MC. Cat no: **PLBH 105**. Released on Tell-A-Tale, Mar '84 by Pickwick Records, Taylors, Clyde Factors.

Driving...
IMPROVE YOUR DRIVING (Various artists).
MC. Cat no: **TC 044**. Released on Times Cassettes, Jan '79.

Duff, David
GEORGE AND ELIZABETH (A Royal Marriage) (Frances Jeater).
MCSET. Cat no: **1025A**. Released on Travellers Tales, '91 by Travellers Tales. Note: 8 Cassettes.
MCSET. Cat no: **IAB 88011**. Released on Isis Audio Books, '91. Note : 8 Cassettes.

Duhamel, G
LE NOTAIRE DU HAVRE (Edited By Gerard Poulet) (Unknown narrator(s)).
Note: A study of Duhamel's craftsmanship in re-creating a child's experience of life in Paris at the turn of the century. In French.
MC. Cat no: **F 7778**. Released on Exeter Tapes, '91 by Drakes Educational Associates.

Duke Of Edinburgh
QUESTION OF BALANCE, A (Biography) (H.R.H. The Duke of Edinburgh).
MCSET. Cat no: **LFP 7164**. Released on Listen For Pleasure, Jul '84 by EMI Records.
MCSET. Cat no: **1015A**. Released on Travellers Tales, '91 by Travellers Tales. Note: 2 Cassettes.

Duncan, Alex
IT'S A VET'S LIFE (Stephen Martin).
MCSET. Cat no: **SOUND 4**. Released on Soundings, Mar '85 by Soundings Records, Bond Street Music.
CDSET. Cat no: **1005N**. Released on Travellers Tales, '91 by Travellers Tales. Note: 4 Cassettes.
TO BE A COUNTRY DOCTOR (John Kay).
MCSET. Cat no: **SOUND 8**. Released on Soundings, Mar '85 by Soundings Records, Bond Street Music.
MCSET. Cat no: **1004N**. Released on Travellers Tales, '91 by Travellers Tales. Note: 4 Cassettes.

Duras, Marguerite
L'AMANTE ANGLAISE (Edited By J.B. Howitt) (Unknown narrator(s)).
Note: The importance of dialogue and the techniques of presenting character are analysed in this New Novel by Duras, together with a study of the major and minor characters.
MC. Cat no: **F 7644**. Released on Exeter Tapes, '91 by Drakes Educational Associates.
MODERATO CANTABILE (Edited By J.B. Howitt) (Unknown narrator(s)).
Note: An outline of the characteristics of the New Novel class struggle in Duras's work is also considered.
MC. Cat no: **F 7580**. Released on Exeter Tapes, '91 by Drakes Educational Associates.
WAR: A MEMOIR
MCSET. Cat no: **RB 90023**. Released on Recorded Books, Mar '92 by Isis Audio Books. Note: 4 Cassettes. Playing time 6hrs.

Durrell, Gerald
MY FAMILY AND OTHER ANIMALS (Gerald Harper).
MCSET. Cat no: **LFP 7318**. Released on Listen For Pleasure, Oct '87 by EMI Records.

Durrenmatt, Friedrich
DER BESUCH DER ALTEN DAME (Edited By Keith A. Dickson) (Unknown narrator(s)).
Note: A discussion of the novel and an analysis of Durrenmatt's new approach to tragedy.
MC. Cat no: **G 7535**. Released on Exeter Tapes, '91 by Drakes Educational Associates.
DER RICHTER UND SEIN HENKER UND DIE TRADITION DE (Edited By Schoschana Maitek) (Unknown narrator(s)).
Note: A comparison of Durrenmatt's techniques with those of 'pulp' novelists. In German.
MC. Cat no: **G 7839**. Released on Exeter Tapes, '91 by Drakes Educational Associates.

Dutch
DUTCH CASSETTE COURSE (Unknown narrator(s)).
MCSET. Cat no: **852850735**. Released on Hugo Languages, '92 by Hugo Language Books Limited. Note: 4 Cassettes. Playing time 4 hrs.
DUTCH FOR TRAVEL (Unknown narrator(s)).
MC. Cat no: **BCP 003**. Released on Berlitz Language Courses, '88, Conifer Records.
DUTCH LANGUAGE BASICS (Unknown narrator(s)).
MC. Cat no: **BMC 004**. Released on Berlitz Language Courses, '88, Conifer Records.
DUTCH TRAVEL PACK (Unknown narrator(s)).
Note: Contains a Hugo phrase book.
MC. Cat no: **852851146**. Released on Hugo Languages, '92 by Hugo Language Books Limited.
INTRODUCING THE DUTCH LANGUAGE (Edited By Peter King) (Unknown narrator(s)).
Note: Accompanying booklet
MC. Cat no: **D 7764**. Released on Exeter Tapes, '91 by Drakes Educational Associates.
SPEAK DUTCH TODAY (Conversational Courses) (Various narrators).
Note: Consists of a book and a 75-90 minute cassette.
MC. Cat no: **852851324**. Released on Hugo Languages, '92 by Hugo Language Books Limited. Note: 4 Cassettes.

Early Learning
ABC (ALPHABET) (Various artists).
MC. Cat no: **DIS 014**. Released on Disney (Read-a-long), Apr '91 by Disneyland Records.
ABC RHYMES (Various artists).
MC. Cat no: **PLB 258**. Released on Tell-A-Tale, '89 by Pickwick Records, Taylors, Clyde Factors.
ABC (THE ALPHABET HUNT) (Various artists).
MC. Cat no: **STK 023**. Released on Stick-A-Tale, Jan '89 by Pickwick Records.
ADD ON ... TAKE AWAY (Various artists).
Note: Includes: Introduction, Add on, 1 to 9, Add on 10, Takeaway and 1 to 10.
MC. Cat no: **CC 007**. Released on Start Early, Apr '90.
ALPHABET, THE (Floella Benjamin).
Tracks / World of ABC song, The / Introduction / Alphabet, The A-Z / Test singalong / My friends from A to Z / Happy birthday party singalong / Alphabet countdown, The / General test.
MC. Cat no: **CC 005**. Released on Start Early, Apr '90.
ANIMAL MAGIC (Catrine O'Neil).
Tracks / Introduction / Hello to the world of animals / Magic / Lazy cat, The / Tips on pet care / Trip to the zoo, A / Meet some wild animals / Duggy the dog / Sing a theme / More tips of pet care / Magic frog / Animal sounds / Yellow canary, The / Mr & Mrs Mouse / Test time.
MC. Cat no: **CC 011**. Released on Start Early, Apr '90.
CALENDAR, THE (Catrine O'Neil).
Tracks / Introduction / Calendar song, The / 7 days of the week, The / Test - The week / How many days in each month ? / Test - The months / Four seasons, the / Test - The seasons / Special days in the calendar / Test - The calendar.
MC. Cat no: **CC 004**. Released on Start Early, Apr '90.
CHILDRENS NUMBER SONGS AND STORIES (19 Favourite Songs and Stories) (Various artists).
MC. Cat no: **BBM 150**. Released on Bibi (Budget Cassettes), Sep '83.

CLOCK, THE (Catrine O'Neil).
Tracks / Introduction to the clock / Minutes, The - Long hand / Hours and minutes, The (up to 5-30) / Up to twelve o'clock / Hours and minutes continued, The / Test - What's the time?.
MC. Cat no: **CC 002**. Released on Start Early, Apr '90.

COLOURS (Catrine O'Neil).
Tracks / Introduction / Rainbow song, The / Talking colours / Red song, The / Primary colours / Green song, The / Test time / Mixing colours / Yellow song, The / Black and white world / Blue song, The / Test time.
MC. Cat no: **CC 009**. Released on Start Early, Apr '90.

COLOURS (Various artists).
MC. Cat no: **PLB 275**. Released on Tell-A-Tale, '89 by Pickwick Records, Taylors, Clyde Factors.

COLOURS (THE RAINBOW SHIP) (Various artists).
MC. Cat no: **STK 016**. Released on Stick-A-Tale, Jan '89 by Pickwick Records.

COUNTDOWN (Floella Benjamin).
Tracks / Song - simple as 1 2 3 / From 1 to 10 / Fruit bowl, The / 1 to 10 singalong / Shopping with Mum / Eleven plus - 11-20 / Test - 11-20 / Counting.
MC. Cat no: **CC 006**. Released on Start Early, Apr '90.

COUNTING IS FUN (Unknown narrator(s)).
MC. Cat no: **DIS 013**. Released on Disney (Read-a-long), Apr '91 by Disneyland Records.

COUNTING SONGS (Various artists).
MC. Cat no: **HSC 202**. Released on VFM Cassettes, '92 by VFM Cassettes, Midland Records, Crusader Marketing Co., Taylors, Morley Audio Services.

DAY AT THE ZOO, A (Unknown narrator(s)).
MCSET. Cat no: **DTO 10524**. Released on Ditto, '88 by Pickwick Records, Midland Records.

DINOSAURS (Catrine O'Neil).
MC. Cat no: **HL 014**. Released on Happy Learning, Dec '90 by Happy Learning Co.Ltd., Castle Sales & Marketing.

FIRST WORDS (Unknown narrator(s)).
MC. Cat no: **RWM 001**. Released on Tell-A-Tale, Sep '90 by Pickwick Records, Taylors, Clyde Factors.

I CAN COUNT (Various artists).
MC. Cat no: **ST 3634**. Released on Invicta, Jul '84 by Audio-Visual Library Services.

JENNY AND JAMES LEARN TO COUNT (Unknown narrator(s)).
MC. Cat no: **STK 034**. Released on Stick-A-Tale, Sep '90 by Pickwick Records.

LEARN THE ALPHABET (Unknown narrator(s)).
MC. Cat no: **PE 305**. Released on Cassettes For Young People, '91 by Cassettes For Young People Lmd, DMS Dist.. Note: ISBN no. 1871449448. Playing time 40 mins.

LEARN TO COUNT (Various narrators).
Tracks / Can you count from 1 to 5 / Can you count from 1 to 10 / Echo count / Ten is ? / Can you count in 2's to 10 / Cecil was a caterpillar / Chook chook / 10 little pigs / Enormous number chants / One man went to mow / Ten in a bed.
Note: Songs written by Ken Bolam. Sung by Lisa Abbott, Anthony Corriette and the Bolam children. Presented by Lisa Abbott and Anthony Corriette.
MC. Cat no: **PE 306**. Released on Cassettes For Young People, Aug '90 by Cassettes For Young People Lmd, DMS Dist.. Note: ISBN no. 1871449456. Playing time 40 mins.

LEARNING COLOURS (Various artists).
MC. Cat no: **HSC 206**. Released on VFM Cassettes, '92 by VFM Cassettes, Midland Records, Crusader Marketing Co., Taylors, Morley Audio Services.

LEARNING THE ALPHABET (Unknown narrator(s)).
MC. Cat no: **HSC 201**. Released on VFM Cassettes, '92 by VFM Cassettes, Midland Records, Crusader Marketing Co., Taylors, Morley Audio Services.

LEARNING THE ALPHABET AND LEARNING TO COUNT (Dame Judi Dench).
CD. Cat no: **CDMFP 5954**. Released on MFP, Dec '91 by EMI Records, Solomon & Peres.
MC. Cat no: **TCMFP 5954**. Released on MFP, Dec '91 by EMI Records, Solomon & Peres.

LEARNING TO SPELL (Various artists).
MC. Cat no: **HSC 208**. Released on VFM Cassettes, '92 by VFM Cassettes, Midland Records, Crusader Marketing Co., Taylors, Morley Audio Services.

LEARNING YOUR TABLES (Various artists).
MC. Cat no: **HSC 204**. Released on VFM Cassettes, '92 by VFM Cassettes, Midland Records, Crusader Marketing Co., Taylors, Morley Audio Services.

MULTIPLICATION (Floella Benjamin).
Tracks / Introduction to the tables / Tables 2 to 7 / Test / Tables 8 to 12 / Test.
MC. Cat no: **CC 001**. Released on Start Early, Apr '90.

MUSICAL SOUNDS (Catrine O'Neil).
Tracks / Introduction / Beat on the bass drum / I love a snare drum / Explaining the rhythm / Instruments / Tambourine, The / Let's play / String bass, The / Trumpet on parade / Explaining the melody / Instruments / Toot on your flute / I am a keyboard / Meet the guitar / Altogether.
MC. Cat no: **CC 012**. Released on Start Early, Apr '90.

MUSICAL SUMS (Various narrators).
Tracks / Simple sums song / Adding song / Take away song / Adding test / Take away test / Add and take away test / Ten green bottles / Five little monkeys / 10 little pussy cats.
Note: Sung by Dave Wall and Lisa Abbott. Presented by Lisa Abbott and Anthony Corriette.
MC. Cat no: **PE 307**. Released on Cassettes For Young People, '91 by Cassettes For Young People Lmd, DMS Dist.. Note: ISBN no. 1871449464. Playing time 40 mins.

MUSICAL TIMES TABLES (Various narrators).
Note: All songs written and performed by Dave Wall. Presented by Lisa Abbott and Anthony Corriette.
MC. Cat no: **PE 301**. Released on Cassettes For Young People, Aug '90 by Cassettes For Young People Lmd, DMS Dist.. Note: ISBN no. 1871449405. Playing time 40 mins.

MY BOOK OF PETS (Various artists).
MC. Cat no: **ST 3635**. Released on Invicta, Jul '84 by Audio-Visual Library Services.

MY BOOK OF WORDS (Various artists).
MC. Cat no: **ST 3634**. Released on Invicta, Jul '84 by Audio-Visual Library Services.

NUMBERS (Various artists).
MC. Cat no: **PLB 259**. Released on Pickwick, '89 by Pickwick Records, Clyde Factors, Taylors, Arabesque, Solomon & Peres, I & B Records, Prism Leisure, Outlet Records.

NUMBERS (Bluey Learns To Count) (Unknown narrator(s)).
MC. Cat no: **STK 022**. Released on Stick-A-Tale, Jan '89 by Pickwick Records.

OPPOSITES (Catrine O'Neil).
MC. Cat no: **HL 013**. Released on Happy Learning, Dec '90 by Happy Learning Co.Ltd., Castle Sales & Marketing.

OPPOSITES (Various artists).
MC. Cat no: **PLB 274**. Released on Tell-A-Tale, '89 by Pickwick Records, Taylors, Clyde Factors.

PLAY LISTEN AND LEARN WITH RONALD MCDONALD (Various artists).
LP. Cat no: **SPR 8549**. Released on Spot, May '84 by Pickwick Records.
MC. Cat no: **SPC 8549**. Released on Spot, May '84 by Pickwick Records.

PRIMARY FRENCH (Anne-Marie Pumphrey).
Tracks / Introduction / Frere Jacques / Simple words / Counting un, deux, trois / Colours / Test time / Sur le pont d'avignon / Simple phrases / Je suis un petit garcon / Alouette / Questions and answers / Au clair de la lune / Wolf story, The / Premenons nous dans le bois / Shopping / Test time / Il court il furet.
MC. Cat no: **CC 008**. Released on Start Early, Apr '90.

PRIMARY GERMAN (Unknown narrator(s)).
MC. Cat no: **PE 311.** Released on Cassettes For Young People, May '92 by Cassettes For Young People Lmd, DMS Dist.. Note: ISBN no. 1871449952. Playing time 40 mins.

PRIMARY SCIENCE (Various narrators).
MC. Cat no: **PE 309.** Released on Cassettes For Young People, Apr '91 by Cassettes For Young People Lmd, DMS Dist.. Note: ISBN no. 1871449480. Playing time 40 mins.

RHYMING WORDS (Various artists).
Tracks / Introduction: *Various artists* / Explanation of phonetical vowels: *Various artists* / A sound test, The: *Various artists* / E sound test, The: *Various artists* / I sound test, The: *Various artists* / O sound test, The: *Various artists* / U sound test, The: *Various artists*.
MC. Cat no: **CC 010.** Released on Start Early, Apr '90.

SIMPLE ADDING SUMS (Various artists).
MC. Cat no: **HSC 205.** Released on VFM Cassettes, '92 by VFM Cassettes, Midland Records, Crusader Marketing Co., Taylors, Morley Audio Services.

SIMPLE SPELLING (Unknown narrator(s)).
MC. Cat no: **PE 312.** Released on Cassettes For Young People, May '92 by Cassettes For Young People Lmd, DMS Dist.. Note: ISBN no. 1871449960. Playing time 40mins.

SIMPLE TAKE-AWAY SONGS (Various artists).
MC. Cat no: **HSC 207.** Released on VFM Cassettes, '92 by VFM Cassettes, Midland Records, Crusader Marketing Co., Taylors, Morley Audio Services.

SOUNDS OF MUSIC (Various narrators).
Tracks / Arpeggio / Music music / If I was a drummer / Double bass / Melody, melody / When you play / This is how it sounds / If you're happy making music.
Note: All songs written and performed by Dave Wall. Presented by Lisa Abbott and Anthony Corriette.
MC. Cat no: **PE 303.** Released on Cassettes For Young People, '91 by Cassettes For Young People Lmd, DMS Dist.. Note: ISBN no. 187449421. Playing time 40 mins.

STARTING SCHOOL (Unknown narrator(s)).
MC. Cat no: **PLB 257.** Released on Tell-A-Tale, Jan '89 by Pickwick Records, Taylors, Clyde Factors.

STREETWISE (Road Safety Tape) (Various artists).
Tracks / Streetwise theme: *Various artists* / Green cross code: *Various artists* / Road safety song: *Various artists* / Road is not a playground, A: *Various artists* / Do not play with danger: *Various artists* / Never talk to strangers: *Various artists* / Police are your friends,

The: *Various artists* / What to do in an emergency: *Various artists*.
MC. Cat no: **CC 003.** Released on Start Early, Apr '90.

TELLING THE TIME (Various artists).
MC. Cat no: **HSC 203.** Released on VFM Cassettes, '92 by VFM Cassettes, Midland Records, Crusader Marketing Co., Taylors, Morley Audio Services.

WHAT'S THE TIME ? (Various narrators).
Tracks / Ticky tock / Sixty minutes / Hour song / Minute song / Hours test / Minutes test / AM/PM song / Grandfather clock / Chuck it in the bucket (alarm clock song).
Note: All songs written and performed by Dave Wall. Presented by Lisa Abbott and Anthony Corriette.
MC. Cat no: **PE 302.** Released on Cassettes For Young People, Aug '90 by Cassettes For Young People Lmd, DMS Dist.. Note: ISBN no. 1871449413. Playing time 40 mins.

WORLD OF COLOURS, THE (Unknown narrator(s)).
MC. Cat no: **PE 304.** Released on Cassettes For Young People, Aug '90 by Cassettes For Young People Lmd, DMS Dist.. Note: ISBN no. 187144943X. Playing time 40mins.

YOUR FIRST ANIMAL BOOK AND SAFETY FIRST AT HOME (Bill Oddie/Philip Schofield).
CD. Cat no: **CDMFP 5953.** Released on MFP, Dec '91 by EMI Records, Solomon & Peres.
MC. Cat no: **TCMFP 5953.** Released on MFP, Dec '91 by EMI Records, Solomon & Peres.

Ebdon, John

EBDON'S ENGLAND (John Westbrook).
MCSET. Cat no: **1046H.** Released on Travellers Tales, '91 by Travellers Tales. Note: 5 Cassettes.
MCSET. Cat no: **OAS 89095.** Released on Oasis Audio Books, '91 by Isis Audio Books. Note: 5 Cassettes.

EBDON'S ODYSSEY (Peter Barker).
MCSET. Cat no: **IAB 92082.** Released on Isis Audio Books, Aug '92. Note : 6 Cassettes. Playing time: 6 hours, 45 mins

Edison, Thomas Alva

THOMAS ALVA EDISON (Biography) (Stephen Thorne).
MC. Cat no: **SI 3.** Released on Green Dragon, '91 by Green Dragon Audio Visual.
MC. Cat no: **DHM 23.** Released on Sussex Tapes, '91 by Sussex Publications Ltd..

Edwards, Bernard

GREY WIDOW MAKER, THE (Twenty Four Disasters At Sea) (John Hendry).
MCSET. Cat no: **1854964526.** Released on Bramhope, '91 by Ulverscroft Soundings. Note: 5 Cassettes.

Eichendorff

AUS DEM LEBEN EINES TAUGENICHTS (Edited By Keith A. Dickson) (Unknown narrator(s)).
Note: The reasons for the enduring appeal of this story for Eichendorff are investigated and some of its intricacies revealed.
MC. Cat no: **G 7544.** Released on Exeter Tapes, '91 by Drakes Educational Associates.

Einstein, Albert

ALBERT EINSTEIN (Biography) (Guy Thomas).
MC. Cat no: **SI 5.** Released on Green Dragon, '91 by Green Dragon Audio Visual.
MC. Cat no: **DHM 25.** Released on Sussex Tapes, '91 by Sussex Publications Ltd..

Ekland, Britt

TRUE BRITT (Biography) (Britt Ekland).
MCSET. Cat no: **SAY 3.** Released on Argo (Polygram), Jul '82 by PolyGram Classics **Deleted** Jan '89.
MCSET. Cat no: **1004A.** Released on Travellers Tales, '91 by Travellers Tales. Note: 2 Cassettes.

Elizabeth 1

ELIZABETH 1 (Biography) (Robert Vahey).
MC. Cat no: **FW 1.** Released on Green Dragon, '91 by Green Dragon Audio Visual.
MC. Cat no: **DHM 4.** Released on Sussex Tapes, '91 by Sussex Publications Ltd..

FIRST QUEEN ELIZABETH (History For Ages 8+) (Unknown narrator(s)).
Note: Book and cassette.
MC. Cat no: **PLBH 101.** Released on Tell-A-Tale, May '84 by Pickwick Records, Taylors, Clyde Factors.

Elliot, Emily

DOWN TO EARTH (Emily Elliot).
LP. Cat no: **SDL 301.** Released on Saydisc, Nov '79 by Amon Ra Records, Taylors, C.M. Distribution, Gamut Distribution **Deleted** '84. Note : Playing time: 53 minutes.
MC. Cat no: **CSDL 301.** Released on Saydisc, Oct '79 by Amon Ra Records, Taylors, C.M. Distribution, Gamut Distribution **Deleted** '89.

Elliot, George

GEORGE ELLIOT (David Daiches & Barbara Hardy).
Note: Pre-recorded discussions which show literary criticism as a living, evolving interchange.
MC. Cat no: **A11.** Released on Sussex Tapes, '91 by Sussex Publications Ltd..

England

SAILOR'S HORSE, THE (May Day: Minehead Documentary of Somerset) (Unknown narrator(s)).

MC. Cat no: 60216. Released on Folktracks Cassettes, Nov '79, Roots Records.

English

EL INGLES SIMPLIFICADO (English For Foreign Students) (Unknown narrator(s)).
MCSET. Cat no: 852851197. Released on Hugo Languages, '92 by Hugo Language Books Limited. Note: 2 Cassettes.

EL INGLES SIMPLIFICADO CASSETTE COURSE (English For Foreign Students) (Unknown narrator(s)).
MCSET. Cat no: 852851219. Released on Hugo Languages, '92 by Hugo Language Books Limited.

ENGLISH CASSETTE COURSE (English For Foreign Students) (Unknown narrator(s)).
MCSET. Cat no: 85285126X. Released on Hugo Languages, '92 by Hugo Language Books Limited. Note: 4 Cassettes.

ENGLISH SIMPLIFIED (Unknown narrator(s)).
MCSET. Cat no: 852851251. Released on Hugo Languages, '92 by Hugo Language Books Limited. Note: 2 Cassettes.

ENGLISH WITH A DIALECT (Unknown narrator(s)).
LP. Cat no: REC 173. Released on BBC, '74 by BBC Records, Taylors.
MC. Cat no: ZCM 173. Released on BBC, Jan '79 by BBC Records, Taylors.

ENGLISH WITH AN ACCENT (Unknown narrator(s)).
LP. Cat no: REC 166. Released on BBC, '74 by BBC Records, Taylors **Deleted** Apr '89.
MC. Cat no: ZCM 166. Released on BBC, Jan '79 by BBC Records, Taylors.

IMPROVE YOUR ENGLISH (English For Foreign Students) (Unknown narrator(s)).
MCSET. Cat no: 852851030. Released on Hugo Languages, '92 by Hugo Language Books Limited. Note: 2 Cassettes.

IMPROVE YOUR WORD POWER (English For Foreign Students) (Unknown narrator(s)).
MCSET. Cat no: 852851278. Released on Hugo Languages, '92 by Hugo Language Books Limited. Note: 2 Cassettes.

L'ANGLAIS SIMPLIFIE (English For Foreign Students) (Unknown narrator(s)).
MCSET. Cat no: 852851103. Released on Hugo Languages, '92 by Hugo Language Books Limited. Note: 2 Cassettes.

L'ANGLAIS SIMPLIFIE CASSETTE COURSE (Unknown narrator(s)).
MCSET. Cat no: 852851200. Released on Hugo Languages, '92 by Hugo Language Books Limited.

LANGUAGE COURSE - ENGLISH ('Audio Active' Course) (Unknown narrator(s)).

LPS. Cat no: 0747301891. Released on Linguaphone, Apr '82 by Linguaphone Institute, Taylors, Century Records (USA), Bond Street Music. Note: 9 Cassettes

SPEAK ENGLISH TODAY (English For Foreign Students) (Various narrators).
MCSET. Cat no: 852851855. Released on Hugo Languages, '92 by Hugo Language Books Limited. Note: 2 Cassettes.

English Literature

APPROACH TO POETRY CRITICISM (Laurence Lerner).
Note: Pre-recorded discussions which show literary criticism as a living, evolving interchange.
MC. Cat no: A9. Released on Sussex Tapes, '91 by Sussex Publications Ltd..

APPROACH TO THE NINETEENTH CENTURY NOVEL (Laurence Lerner & Barry Supple).
Note: Pre-recorded discussions which show literary criticism as a living, evolving interchange.
MC. Cat no: A7. Released on Sussex Tapes, '91 by Sussex Publications Ltd..

BEOWULF (Julian Glover).
MC. Cat no: A49. Released on Sussex Tapes, '91 by Sussex Publications Ltd..

BYRON'S RHETORIC (G Wilson Knight).
MC. Cat no: 23068. Released on Sussex Tapes, '91 by Sussex Publications Ltd..

ENGLISH NOVEL TODAY: FROM DICKENS TO SNOW, THE (Angus Wilson).
MC. Cat no: 23074. Released on Sussex Tapes, '91 by Sussex Publications Ltd..

FIRST WORLD WAR POETS (John Stallworthy).
Note: Pre-recorded discussions which show literary criticism as a living, evolving interchange.
MC. Cat no: A30. Released on Sussex Tapes, '91 by Sussex Publications Ltd..

FOUR MODERN POETS (Laurence Lerner).
Note: Pre-recorded discussions which show literary criticism as a living, evolving interchange.
MC. Cat no: A12. Released on Sussex Tapes, '91 by Sussex Publications Ltd..

HEROIC VILLAINS, THE (G.H. Hunter & Martin Wright).
MC. Cat no: S20. Released on Sussex Tapes, '91 by Sussex Publications Ltd.

LANGUAGE OF POETRY, THE (Alan Sinfield & Peter Wilson).
MC. Cat no: A23. Released on Sussex Tapes, '91 by Sussex Publications Ltd..

LITERATURE AND SOCIETY IN THE 1930'S (Various narrators).
Note: Narrators are: Stephen Spender, Arnold Kettle, David Daiches, Cyril Connolly, Laurence Lerner and Tom Harrison.

MC. Cat no: A16. Released on Sussex Tapes, '91 by Sussex Publications Ltd..

MODERN POETRY (Ted Walker & John Wain).
Note: Pre-recorded discussion which show literary criticism as a living, evolving interchange.
MC. Cat no: A10. Released on Sussex Tapes, '91 by Sussex Publications Ltd..

NECESSARY TREASON, A (The Poet and the Translater) (George Steiner).
MC. Cat no: 23148. Released on Sussex Tapes, '91 by Sussex Publications Ltd..

OBSCURE BEAUTY: DIFFICULTY IN POETRY, THE (I A Richards).
MC. Cat no: 23155. Released on Sussex Tapes, '91 by Sussex Publications Ltd..

POET AS A TRANSLATOR, THE (George Steiner).
MC. Cat no: 23149. Released on Sussex Tapes, '91 by Sussex Publications Ltd..

POETIC VISION AND MODERN LITERATURE (Stephen Spender).
MC. Cat no: 23001. Released on Sussex Tapes, '91 by Sussex Publications Ltd..

POPE AND AUGUSTAN POETRY (Jack Pembroke & Richard Luckett).
Note: Pre-recorded discussions which show literary criticism as a living, evolving interchange.
MC. Cat no: A21. Released on Sussex Tapes, '91 by Sussex Publications Ltd..

PROSE AND POETRY (Stephen Spender).
MC. Cat no: 23083. Released on Sussex Tapes, '91 by Sussex Publications Ltd..

PROSE APPRECIATION (Peter Hollindale).
Note: Pre-recorded discussions which who literary criticism as a living, evolving interchange.
MC. Cat no: A32. Released on Sussex Tapes, '91 by Sussex Publications Ltd..

READING DIFFICULT POETRY (Laurence Lerner).
Note: Pre-recorded discussions which show literary criticism as a living, evolving interchange.
MC. Cat no: A18. Released on Sussex Tapes, '91 by Sussex Publications Ltd..

ROLE OF PERSONALITY IN SCIENCE, THE (C P Snow).
MC. Cat no: 23011. Released on Sussex Tapes, '91 by Sussex Publications Ltd..

ROMANTICS, THE (Christopher Salvesen & William Walsh).
Note: Pre-recorded discussions which show literary criticism as a living, evolving interchange.
MC. Cat no: A4. Released on Sussex Tapes, '91 by Sussex Publications Ltd..

SEVENTEENTH CENTURY LITERATURE (Frank Kermode & A.J. Smith).
Note: Pre-recorded discussions which show literary criticism as a living, evolving interchange.

MC. Cat no: **AS**. Released on Sussex Tapes, '91 by Sussex Publications Ltd..

SOCIETY AND LITERATURE IN THE 1930'S FOR SCHOOLS (Various narrators).
Note: Pre-recorded discussions which show literary criticism as a living, evolving interchange. Narrators are: Stephen Spender, Cyril Connolly, Arnold Kettle and David Daiches.
MC. Cat no: **A15**. Released on Sussex Tapes, '91 by Sussex Publications Ltd..

SOME PROBLEMS IN READING CANTERBURY TALES (Peter Brown & Derek Pearsall).
Note: Pre-recorded discussions which show literary criticism as a living, evolving interchange.
MC. Cat no: **A42**. Released on Sussex Tapes, '91 by Sussex Publications Ltd..

SOUNDS OF POETRY, THE (Edward Lee & Edwin Webb).
Note: Pre-recorded discussions which show literary criticism as a living, evolving interchange.
MC. Cat no: **A51**. Released on Sussex Tapes, '91 by Sussex Publications Ltd..

Environmental Sounds

AFRICAN FORESTS AND SAVANNAHS (Wilderness recordings from Senegal/Cameroon/Kenya) (Various).
CD. Cat no: **222306**. Released on Sittelle, Feb '92 by Sittelle Records (France).
MC. Cat no: **034213**. Released on Sittelle, Feb '92 by Sittelle Records (France).

AMERICAN FORESTS AND LAKES (Wilderness recordings from Canada, Martinique) (Various).
CD. Cat no: **222405**. Released on Sittelle, Feb '92 by Sittelle Records (France).
MC. Cat no: **034312**. Released on Sittelle, Feb '92 by Sittelle Records (France).

BABBLING BROOK (Atmosphere collection) (Various).
CD. Cat no: **RCD 30015**. Released on Rykodisc (Holland), Apr '92 by Pinnacle.

BABBLING BROOK / SUMMER RAIN (Various).
MCSET. Cat no: **RACS 0015/0017**. Released on Rykodisc (Holland), Apr '92 by Pinnacle.

DAWN AT JOSIAH'S BAY (In the absence of man) (Various).
CD. Cat no: **CD 2001**. Released on Daring (USA), '88 by Roots Records.

EARLY CAPE MORNING / SUNSET SURF (Various).
MCSET. Cat no: **RACS 0012/0016**. Released on Rykodisc (Holland), Apr '92 by Pinnacle.

ENVIRONMENTAL ATMOSPHERES: AUSTRALIA (Various).
CD. Cat no: **223907**. Released on Sittelle, Feb '92 by Sittelle Records (France).
MC. Cat no: **023811**. Released on Sittelle, Feb '92 by Sittelle Records (France).

FORESTS AND MOUNTAINS OF ASIA (Wilderness recordings from China/Nepal/Malaysia) (Various).
CD. Cat no: **222702**. Released on Sittelle, Feb '92 by Sittelle Records (France).
MC. Cat no: **024411**. Released on Sittelle, Feb '92 by Sittelle Records (France).

FORESTS OF THE AMAZON (Various).
CD. Cat no: **223105**. Released on Sittelle, Feb '92 by Sittelle Records (France).
MC. Cat no: **023019**. Released on Sittelle, Feb '92 by Sittelle Records (France).

FROGS AND TOADS (Calls of 20 Species of Frogs & Toads of Europe) (Various).
MC. Cat no: **034619**. Released on Sittelle, Feb '92 by Sittelle Records (France).

MARSH MELODIES (Various).
CD. Cat no: **223709**. Released on Sittelle, Feb '92 by Sittelle Records (France).
MC. Cat no: **023613**. Released on Sittelle, Feb '92 by Sittelle Records (France).

MID-DAY ON JOST VAN DYKE (In the Absence of Man) (Various artists).
CD. Cat no: **CD 2002**. Released on Daring (USA), '88 by Rounder Records (USA), Topic Records, Jazz Music, Duncans, Impetus Records.

MOUNTAIN MEDLEY (Atmosphere recordings from the Alps) (Various).
CD. Cat no: **023501**. Released on Sittelle, Feb '92 by Sittelle Records (France).
MC. Cat no: **023415**. Released on Sittelle, Feb '92 by Sittelle Records (France).

SONGS FROM THE DEEP (See under Whales).

SUMMER RAIN (Various).
CD. Cat no: **RCD 30017**. Released on Rykodisc (Holland), Apr '92 by Pinnacle.

SUNSET SURF (Various).
CD. Cat no: **RCD 30016**. Released on Rykodisc (Holland), Apr '92 by Pinnacle.

WILD ANIMALS (EUROPE) (Birds, Mammals, Amphibians and Insects) (Various).
MC. Cat no: **035210**. Released on Sittelle, Feb '92 by Sittelle Records (France).

Etcherelli, Claire

ELISE OU LA VRAIE VIE (Edited By Margaret Atack) (Unknown narrator(s)).
Note: An analysis of the novel by Claire Etcherelli which looks at the social and political aspects of the textans and the themes associated with it.
MC. Cat no: **F 7331**. Released on Exeter Tapes, '91 by Drakes Educational Associates.

Eysenck, H.J.

GENETICS OF ENVIRONMENT (Prof. H J Eysenck).
MC. Cat no: **PT 33**. Released on Psychology Today (USA), Oct '81 by Seminar Cassettes.

Fermor, Patrick Leigh

TIME OF GIFTS, A (Garard Green).
MCSET. Cat no: **1084/5N**. Released on Travellers Tales, '91 by Travellers Tales. Note: 10 Cassettes.
MCSET. Cat no: **IAB 90041**. Released on Isis Audio Books, '91. Note : 10 Cassettes.

Ferre, Leo

LEO FERRE (Edited By Peter Hawkins) (Unknown narrator(s)).
Note: An illustrated introduction to his works.
MC. Cat no: **F 7332**. Released on Exeter Tapes, '91 by Drakes Educational Associates.

Fielding, Henry

HENRY FIELDING (Colin Brooks & Angus Ross).
Note: Pre-recorded discussions which show literary criticism as a living, evolving interchange.
MC. Cat no: **A41**. Released on Sussex Tapes, '91 by Sussex Publications Ltd..

Fields, Gracie

OUR GRACIE (Unknown narrator(s)).
MCSET. Cat no: **1854961659**. Released on Bramhope, '91 by Ulverscroft Soundings. Note: 4 Cassettes.

Films

BEHIND THE SCENES AT WIZARD OF OZ (Complete NBC Maxwell House Good News Broadcast) (Various artists).
LP. Cat no: **JASS 17**. Released on Jass, '88, Jazz Music, Swift.
CD. Cat no: **JCD 629**. Released on Jass, Feb '91, Jazz Music, Swift.

Finnish

FINNISH FOR FOREIGNERS (Volume 1) (Unknown narrator(s)).
MCSET. Cat no: **FN 01**. Released on Audio Forum (Language courses), '91. Note: 8 Cassettes.

FINNISH FOR FOREIGNERS (Volume 2) (Unknown narrator(s)).
MCSET. Cat no: **FN 25**. Released on Audio Forum (Language courses), '91. Note: 3 Cassettes

KORVA TARKKANA (Listen Attentively) (Unknown narrator(s)).
MC. Cat no: **FN 20**. Released on Audio Forum (Language courses), '91.

LANGUAGE COURSE - FINNISH (Unknown narrator(s)).
LPS. Cat no: **0747303126**. Released on Linguaphone, Apr '82 by Linguaphone Institute, Taylors, Century Records (USA), Bond Street Music.

Fisher, Graham
MONARCH: LIFE AND TIMES OF ELIZABETH II (With Heather Fisher) (Jane Jermyn).
MCSET. Cat no: **1007N.** Released on Travellers Tales, '91 by Travellers Tales. Note: 6 Cassettes.
MCSET. Cat no: **185496089X.** Released on Soundings, '91 by Soundings Records, Bond Street Music. Note: 6 Cassettes.
QUEEN'S TRAVELS, THE (With Heather Fisher) (Gordon Griffin).
MCSET. Cat no: **1043N.** Released on Travellers Tales, '91 by Travellers Tales. Note: 6 Cassettes.
MCSET. Cat no: **1854960903.** Released on Soundings, '91 by Soundings Records, Bond Street Music. Note: 6 Cassettes.

Flaubert, Gustave
MADAME BOVARY (Edited By Martin Sorrell) (Unknown narrator(s)).
Note: An account of Gustave Flaubert's description of real mid 19th century Provincial France.
MC. Cat no: **F 7574.** Released on Exeter Tapes, '91 by Drakes Educational Associates.
TROIS CONTES (Edited By Timothy A. Unwin) (Unknown narrator(s)).
Note: A critical introduction to this work, assessing its place in Flaubert's work and examining the artistic problems it posed Flaubert.
MC. Cat no: **F 7750.** Released on Exeter Tapes, '91 by Drakes Educational Associates.

Fleming, Alexander
ALEXANDER FLEMING (Biography) (Tony Britton).
MC. Cat no: **SI 6.** Released on Green Dragon, '91 by Green Dragon Audio Visual.
MC. Cat no: **DHM 27.** Released on Sussex Tapes, '91 by Sussex Publications Ltd..

Fletcher, Cyril
LIFE IN THE COUNTRY, A (Biography) (John Westbrook).
MCSET. Cat no: **1048A.** Released on Travellers Tales, '91 by Travellers Tales. Note: 6 Cassettes.
MCSET. Cat no: **OAS 89103.** Released on Oasis Audio Books, '91 by Isis Audio Books.
NICE ONE, CYRIL (Cyril Fletcher).
MCSET. Cat no: **1065A.** Released on Travellers Tales, '91 by Travellers Tales. Note: 8 Cassettes.

Foley, Winifred
BACK TO THE FOREST (Part 2) (Sian Phillips).
MCSET. Cat no: **1005A.** Released on Travellers Tales, '91 by Travellers Tales. Note: 6 cassettes.
CHILD IN THE FOREST, A (Part 1) (Sian Phillips).
MCSET. Cat no: **1006A.** Released on Travellers Tales, '91 by Travellers Tales. Note: 6 Cassettes.
MCSET. Cat no: **CAB 003.** Released on Chivers Audio Books, '91 by Chivers Audio Books, Green Dragon Audio Visual.

Fonda, Jane
ALL JANE FONDA WORKOUT RECORDS (See under Health & Fitness).

Fontaine, T.H.
EFFI BRIEST (Edited By H.B. Garland) (Unknown narrator(s)).
Note: This work by T.H. Fontaine is considered from various standpoints as a remarkable and subtle novel of martial infidelity.
MC. Cat no: **G 7618.** Released on Exeter Tapes, '91 by Drakes Educational Associates.
FRAU JENNY TREIBEL (Edited By H.B. Garland) (Unknown artist(s)).
Note: An exploration of T.H. Fontane's novel, considered in terms of an ironic comedy of manners.
MC. Cat no: **G 7549.** Released on Exeter Tapes, '91 by Drakes Educational Associates.

Fonteyn, Dame Margot
DAME MARGOT FONTEYN (Biography) (Dame Margot Fonteyn).
MCSET. Cat no: **1007A.** Released on Travellers Tales, '91 by Travellers Tales. Note: 2 Cassettes.

Fonvizin, D
FONVIZIN - HIS LIFE AND LITERARY CAREER (Edited By Ruth Sobel) (Unknown narrator(s)).
Note: Includes analyses of 'The Brigadier' and 'The Minor'.
MC. Cat no: **R 7788.** Released on Exeter Tapes, '91 by Drakes Educational Associates.

Football
EUROPEAN CUP FINAL-1968 (Manchester United v Benfica).
LP. Cat no: **QP 12/73.** Released on Quality, Oct '81 by Quality Recordings.
EUROPEAN CUP FINAL-1977 (Liverpool v Borrusia MGB).
LP. Cat no: **QP 24/77.** Released on Quality, Oct '81 by Quality Recordings.
EUROPEAN CUP FINAL-1978 (Liverpool v Bruges).
LP. Cat no: **QP 27/78.** Released on Quality, Oct '81 by Quality Recordings.
EUROPEAN CUP FINAL-1981 (Liverpool v Real Madrid).
LP. Cat no: **QP 37/81.** Released on Quality, Oct '81 by Quality Recordings.
EUROPEAN CUP FINAL-1982 (Villa-The Champions of Europe).
LP. Cat no: **QP 39/82.** Released on Quality, Oct '82 by Quality Recordings.
EUROPEAN CUP FINALS-1979 AND 1980 (Nottingham Forest's double).
LP. Cat no: **QP 33/80.** Released on Quality, Oct '81 by Quality Recordings.
F.A. CUP FINAL-1972 (Arsenal v Leeds).
LP. Cat no: **REC 122.** Released on BBC, Oct '81 by BBC Records, Taylors **Deleted** '88.
LEAGUE CUP FINAL-1981 (Liverpool v West Ham).
LP. Cat no: **QP 34/81.** Released on Quality, Oct '81 by Quality Recordings.
LEAGUE CUP FINAL-1982 (Liverpool v Tottenham Hotspur).
LP. Cat no: **QP 38/82.** Released on Quality, Jul '82 by Quality Recordings.
SCOTTISH CUP-1976 (Rangers v Hearts).
LP. Cat no: **QP 20/76.** Released on Quality, Oct '81 by Quality Recordings.
SO YOU THINK YOU KNOW ABOUT FOOTBALL (Bill Shankly).
LP. Cat no: **PPLP 001.** Released on Personality Promotions, Jan '90.
MC. Cat no: **PPMC 001.** Released on Personality Promotions, Jan '90.
UEFA CUP-1976 (Liverpool v Bruges).
LP. Cat no: **QP 21/76.** Released on Quality, Oct '81 by Quality Recordings.

Ford, Henry
HENRY FORD (Biography) (Stephen Thorne).
MC. Cat no: **EP 5.** Released on Green Dragon, '91 by Green Dragon Audio Visual.
MC. Cat no: **DHM 26.** Released on Sussex Tapes, '91 by Sussex Publications Ltd..

Forrester, Helen
BY THE WATERS OF LIVERPOOL (Part 3 - Biography) (Christine Dawe).
MCSET. Cat no: **1010A.** Released on Travellers Tales, '91 by Travellers Tales. Note: 6 Cassettes.
MCSET. Cat no: **1854960911.** Released on Soundings, '91 by Soundings Records, Bond Street Music. Note: 6 Cassettes.
LIME STREET AT TWO (Biography) (Christine Dawe).
MCSET. Cat no: **1008N.** Released on Travellers Tales, '91 by Travellers Tales. Note: 4 Cassettes.
MCSET. Cat no: **185496092X.** Released on Soundings, '91 by Soundings Records, Bond Street Music. Note: 4 Cassettes.
MINERVA'S STEPCHILD (Part 2 - Biography) (Christine Dawe).
MCSET. Cat no: **1009A.** Released on Travellers Tales, '91 by Travellers Tales. Note: 4 Cassettes.
MCSET. Cat no: **1854960946.** Released on Soundings, '91 by Soundings Records, Bond Street Music. Note: 4 Cassettes.
TWOPENCE TO CROSS THE MERSEY (Part 1 - Biography) (Christine Dawe).
MCSET. Cat no: **1008A.** Released on Travellers Tales, '91 by Travellers Tales. Note: 4 Cassettes.
MCSET. Cat no: **1854960970.** Released on Bramhope, '91 by Ulverscroft Soundings. Note: 4 Cassettes.

Forster, E.M.

E M FORSTER (Arnold Kettle & Richard Hoggart).
Note: Pre-recorded discussions which show literary criticism as a living, evolving interchange.
MC. Cat no: **A 38.** Released on Sussex Tapes, '91 by Sussex Publications Ltd..

Fournier, Alain

LE GRAND MEAULNES (Edited By Martin Sorrell) (Unknown narrator(s)).
Note: This early 20th century work by Alain Fournier is examined with particular reference to the role of Francois Seurel and the theme of initiation and quest.
MC. Cat no: **F 7501.** Released on Exeter Tapes, '91 by Drakes Educational Associates.

Fox, James

WHITE MISCHIEF (Neil Hunt).
MCSET. Cat no: **1104N.** Released on Travellers Tales, '91 by Travellers Tales. Note: 7 Cassettes.
MCSET. Cat no: **RB 89660.** Released on Recorded Books, '91 by Isis Audio Books. Note: 7 Cassettes.

France

17TH CENTURY FRANCE; CONTINUITY AND CHANGE (John Shennan & Dr. David Parker).
MCSET. Cat no: **HUA 023.** Released on AVP, '91 by AVP Publishing.

BOURGES AND BERRY (Edited By Valerie Howard) (Unknown narrator(s)).
Note: A description of present and past aspects of Berry and its provincial capital Bourges. With various points being illustrated by its inhabitants.
MC. Cat no: **F 7946.** Released on Exeter Tapes, '91 by Drakes Educational Associates.

CHARLES V (H.G. Koenigsberger & Geoffrey Parker).
MC. Cat no: **HE 26.** Released on Sussex Tapes, '91 by Sussex Publications Ltd..

CONTINUITY OF CONFLICT IN FRENCH SOCIETY (Douglas Johnson & Dr. Nicholas Richardson).
MCSET. Cat no: **HUA 002.** Released on AVP, '91 by AVP Publishing.

DECOLONIZATION (Edited By Philip Thody) (Unknown narrator(s)).
Note: A controversial study of decolonization from the 18th to the 20th century.
MC. Cat no: **F 7972.** Released on Exeter Tapes, '91 by Drakes Educational Associates.

DEFENCE IN THE FIFTH REPUBLIC (Edited By Anthony Kelly) (Unknown narrator(s)).
Note: An examination of the defence policy of the socialist government of Mitterand.
MC. Cat no: **F 7971.** Released on Exeter Tapes, '91 by Drakes Educational Associates.

EMPEROR CHARLES V, THE (Dr. Henry J Cohn & Dr. Henry Kamen).
MCSET. Cat no: **HUA 049.** Released on AVP, '91 by AVP Publishing.

FRENCH LOCAL GOVERNMENT (Edited By H.D. Lewis) (Unknown narrator(s)).
MC. Cat no: **F 7800.** Released on Exeter Tapes, '91 by Drakes Educational Associates.

FRENCH POLITICAL PARTIES - PART 2 (Edited By H.D. Lewis) (Unknown narrator(s)).
Note: The development of the major French political parties of the centre and right from the beginning of the fifth republic to the 1978 election.
MC. Cat no: **F 7746.** Released on Exeter Tapes, '91 by Drakes Educational Associates.

FRENCH POLITICAL PARTIES - PART 1 (Edited By H.D. Lewis) (Unknown narrator(s)).
Note: An analysis of the development of political parties of the left, from the beginning of the fifth republic to the general election of 1978.
MC. Cat no: **F 7745.** Released on Exeter Tapes, '91 by Drakes Educational Associates.

FRENCH PRESS, THE (Edited By Philip Thody) (Unknown narrator(s)).
Note: A general account of the press in 1979.
MC. Cat no: **F 7824.** Released on Exeter Tapes, '91 by Drakes Educational Associates.

FRENCH REVOLUTION AND THE PEASANTS, THE (The French Revolution - Leaders and Leadership) (Maurice Hutt & George Rude).
MCSET. Cat no: **HUA 038.** Released on AVP, '91 by AVP Publishing.

FRENCH REVOLUTION, THE (Richard Cobb & Norman Hampson).
MC. Cat no: **HE 12.** Released on Sussex Tapes, '91 by Sussex Publications Ltd..

FRENCH YOUTH AND ITS PROBLEMS (Edited By Anthony E. Greaves) (Unknown narrator(s)).
MC. Cat no: **F 7774.** Released on Exeter Tapes, '91 by Drakes Educational Associates.

HENRY IV OF FRANCE (R J Knecht & Mark Greengrass).
MCSET. Cat no: **HUA 046.** Released on AVP, '91 by AVP Publishing.

INDUSTRIAL RELATIONS IN FRANCE (Edited By Jeff Bridgford) (Unknown narrator(s)).
Note: Includes reference to collective bargaining workplace representation, industrial conflict and May 1968.
MC. Cat no: **F 7904.** Released on Exeter Tapes, '91 by Drakes Educational Associates.

INTRODUCTION TO BRITTANY, AN (Edited By H.D. Lewis) (Unknown narrator(s)).
MC. Cat no: **F 7712.** Released on Exeter Tapes, '91 by Drakes Educational Associates.

JEAN CALVIN (T.H.L. Parker & Rev. R. Buick).
MC. Cat no: **HE 27.** Released on Sussex Tapes, '91 by Sussex Publications Ltd..

LA FRANCE SOUS MITTERRAND, 1981-1988 (Edited By Alan Pedley) (Unknown narrator(s)).
MC. Cat no: **F 7329.** Released on Exeter Tapes, '91 by Drakes Educational Associates.

LA POLITIQUE FRANCAISE DU TEMPS LIBRE (Edited By Nicole Pakenham) (Unknown narrator(s)).
Note: A wide ranging study of leisure from the middle ages to the fifth republic under Mitterrand. In French.
MC. Cat no: **F 7883.** Released on Exeter Tapes, '91 by Drakes Educational Associates.

LA PROVENCE - PART 1 (Edited By W.J. Perry) (Unknown narrator(s)).
Note: An introduction to the history and geography of Provence and to the economic life of the region. Agriculture, industry and tourism are covered. In French.
MC. Cat no: **F 7916.** Released on Exeter Tapes, '91 by Drakes Educational Associates.

LA PROVENCE - PART 2 (Edited By W.J. Perry) (Unknown narrator(s)).
Note: Follows part 1 in discussing the region, but with particular attention to the cultural heritage, artistic life and literature of Provence. In French.
MC. Cat no: **F 7917.** Released on Exeter Tapes, '91 by Drakes Educational Associates.

LE CINEMA FRANCAIS DEPUIS 1945 (Edited By Jean Pascal) (Unknown narrator(s)).
MC. Cat no: **F 7310.** Released on Exeter Tapes, '91 by Drakes Educational Associates.

LE MASSIF CENTRAL (Edited By Mark Cleary) (Unknown narrator(s)).
Note: A discussion of the economic and geographical background to the recent development of the region.
MC. Cat no: **F 7942.** Released on Exeter Tapes, '91 by Drakes Educational Associates.

LE MONDE DES ANNEES 80 - PART 2 (By Various Editors) (Various narrators).
Note: Edited by K.C. Cameron, M.E. Cameron and C.Jones, Isabelle Rodrigues and Jean Paul Martial. A selection of passages from 'Le Monde' recorded by two native French speakers.
MC. Cat no: **F 7312.** Released on Exeter Tapes, '91 by Drakes Educational Associates.

LE MONDE DES ANNEES 80 - PART 1 (By Various Editors) (Various narrators).
Note: Edited by K.C. Cameron, M.E. Cameron and C. Jones, Isabelle Rodrigues and Jean Paul Martial. A selection of passages from 'Le Monde' recorded by two native French speakers.

MC. Cat no: **F 7311**. Released on Exeter Tapes, '91 by Drakes Educational Associates.
LES RELATIONS ENTRE LA FRANCE ET L'ALGERIE (1830 A Nos Jours)(Edited By Hamid Lefleurier) (Unknown narrator(s)).
Note: The war of independence. In French
MC. Cat no: **F 7977**. Released on Exeter Tapes, '91 by Drakes Educational Associates.
L'ESPACE FRANCAIS: RURAL FRANCE (Edited By M.C. Cleary) (Unknown narrator(s)).
Note: Transformations that have taken place since 1890.
MC. Cat no: **F 7887**. Released on Exeter Tapes, '91 by Drakes Educational Associates.
L'ESPRIT FRANCAIS (Edited By Jean D. Biard) (Unknown narrator(s)).
Note: With examples of the various comic devices and forms used from the middle ages to the present in French.
MC. Cat no: **F 7831**. Released on Exeter Tapes, '91 by Drakes Educational Associates.
L'IMMIGRATION EN FRANCE (Edited By Nicole Pakenham) (Unknown narrator(s)).
Note: A historical survey from 1850 to the present day.
MC. Cat no: **F 7905**. Released on Exeter Tapes, '91 by Drakes Educational Associates.
LOUIS XIV (Ragnhild Hatton & J.H. Shennan).
MC. Cat no: **HE 1**. Released on Sussex Tapes, '91 by Sussex Publications Ltd..
NAPOLEON BONAPARTE (J P T Bury).
MCSET. Cat no: **HUA 003**. Released on AVP, '91 by AVP Publishing.
NAPOLEON II (JPT. Bury & Douglas Johnson).
MC. Cat no: **HE 22**. Released on Sussex Tapes, '91 by Sussex Publications Ltd..
NAPOLEON III (Dr. Vincent Wright & Roger Price).
MCSET. Cat no: **HUA 027**. Released on AVP, '91 by AVP Publishing.
ORIGINS AND DEVELOPMENT OF THE FRENCH REVOLUTION (Douglas Johnson & Maurice Hutt).
MCSET. Cat no: **HUA 001**. Released on AVP, '91 by AVP Publishing.
OVERVIEW OF TRANSPORT IN FRANCE (Edited By H.D. Lewis) (Unknown narrator(s)).
Note: Concentrates on the last twenty years and the situation in the early to middle eighties.
MC. Cat no: **F 7941**. Released on Exeter Tapes, '91 by Drakes Educational Associates.
PARLIAMENTARY MONARCHY IN FRANCE 1815-1848 (Irene Collins & Douglas Johnson).
MCSET. Cat no: **HUA 051**. Released on AVP, '91 by AVP Publishing.
REGIONALISM IN FRANCE (Edited by Peter Wagstaff) (Unknown narrator(s)).
MC. Cat no: **F 7809**. Released on Exeter Tapes, '91 by Drakes Educational Associates.
REVOLUTIONS OF 1848 IN FRANCE AND CENTRAL EUROPE (Dr Ernst Wangermann & Roger Price).
MCSET. Cat no: **HUA 024**. Released on AVP, '91 by AVP Publishing.
SIXTEENTH CENTURY FRANCE (RJ. Knecht & Nicola Sutherland).
MC. Cat no: **HE 15**. Released on Sussex Tapes, '91 by Sussex Publications Ltd..
TRADE UNIONS IN FRANCE (Edited By Jeff Bridgford) (Unknown narrator(s)).
MC. Cat no: **F 7856**. Released on Exeter Tapes, '91 by Drakes Educational Associates.

France, Anatole
L'AFFAIRE DREYFUS (Edited by Odile Cook) (Unknown narrator(s)).
Note: A study of the historical facts of the 'Affaire' and Anatole France's reactions to it, plus an analysis of his novel 'Monsieur Bergeret a Paris'. In French.
MC. Cat no: **F 7952**. Released on Exeter Tapes, '91 by Drakes Educational Associates.
L'ILE DES PINGOUINS (Edited By Jean D. Biard) (Unknown narrator(s)).
Note: An attempt to bring out the complexity of the satirical aspect of Anatole France's novel. In French.
MC. Cat no: **F 7322**. Released on Exeter Tapes, '91 by Drakes Educational Associates.

Frances, Edmond
ANOTHER BLOODY TOUR (Unknown narrator(s)).
MCSET. Cat no: **0600558479**. Released on Hamlyn Books On Tape, Apr '88, Bond Street Music. Note: 2 Cassette set

Francia, Paul
MORTAR FIRE - NORMANDY TO GERMANY 1944-45 (John Hosken).
MCSET. Cat no: **STD 001**. Released on Isis Audio Books, '91. Note : 2 Cassettes.

Frank, Anne
DIARY OF ANNE FRANK, THE (Claire Bloom).
MC. Cat no: **CDL 51522**. Released on Caedmon (USA), Aug '79 by Caedmon Records (USA), Bond Street Music.

French
A VOUS LA FRANCE (Language Courses) (Unknown narrator(s)).
Note: Available with cassette are: Tutor's Notes, Work-Book and a Book.
MC. Cat no: **PTT 272**. Released on BBC Publications, '91. Note : 2 Cassettes.
A VOUS LA FRANCE (2) (Language Courses) (Unknown narrator(s)).
Note: Available with cassette are: Tutor's Notes, Work-Book and a Book.
MC. Cat no: **PTT 273**. Released on BBC Publications, '91.
BASIC FRENCH (PART A) (Unknown narrator(s)).
MC. Cat no: **F 170**. Released on Audio Forum (Language courses), '91. Note: 12 Cassettes. Playing time: 15 hours.
BASIC FRENCH (PART A) (Advanced Level) (Unknown narrator(s)).
MC. Cat no: **F 260**. Released on Audio Forum (Language courses), '91. Note: 18 Cassettes.
BASIC FRENCH (PART B) (Unknown narrator(s)).
MC. Cat no: **F 181**. Released on Audio Forum (Language courses), '91. Note: 18 Cassettes.
BASIC FRENCH (PART B) (Advanced Level) (Unknown narrator(s)).
MC. Cat no: **F 290**. Released on Audio Forum (Language courses), '91. Note: 18 Cassettes.
BRANCHE ENTRE NOUS (Unknown narrator(s)).
Note: Comprehension programme designed to introduce students of French to the informal idioms used everyday by French speakers of all ages.
MC. Cat no: **FR 0624**. Released on Audio Forum (Language courses), '91.
CARMEN (Various narrators).
Note: French narration for practice linguists. By Prosper Merimee.
MCSET. Cat no: **EAC 03C**. Released on European Audio Classics, '91 by Unknown. Note: 2 Cassettes - ISBN no. 1873256051
CONTES A NINON (Various narrators)
Note: French narration for practice linguists.
MCSET. Cat no: **EAC 04D**. Released on European Audio Classics, '91 by Unknown. Note: 2 Cassettes - ISBN 1873256159
CONTES DE LA BECASSE (Various narrators).
Note: French narration for practice linguists a selection of short stories set in Normandy.
MCSET. Cat no: **EAC 02B**. Released on European Audio Classics, '91 by Unknown. Note: 2 Cassettes - ISBN 1873256051
DECOLLAGE (Bridge Material From GCSE to A-Level) (Unknown narrator(s)).
MCSET. Cat no: **0748700609**. Released on Stanley Thornes, '90 by Stanley Thornes.
ENGLISH CHILD IN FRANCE, AN (Language Courses) (Unknown narrator(s)).
MC. Cat no: **AECIFC**. Released on Beuret Language Courses, Aug '83.
ENTRE NOUS (Unknown narrator(s)).
Note: Programmes recorded live in Paris. You can hear French spoken as the French speak it.

MCSET. Cat no: **FR 622.** Released on Audio Forum (Language courses), '91. Note: 2 Cassettes and 2 books.

FABLES (Various narrators).
Note: French narration for practice linguists. An anthology of 35 of the more famous fables, including The Tortoise And The Hare and The Hen Who Laid Golden Eggs. ByJean La Fontaine and Aesop.

MCSET. Cat no: **EAC 01A.** Released on European Audio Classics, '91 by Unknown. Note: 2 Cassettes - ISBN 1873256000

FRANC PARLER (Language Courses) (Unknown narrator(s)).
MCSET. Cat no: **PTT 288.** Released on BBC Publications, '91.

FRANCE TRAVEL KIT (Unknown narrator(s)).
MC. Cat no: **BTK 003.** Released on Berlitz Language Courses, '88, Conifer Records.

FRENCH AT THE WHEEL (Unknown narrator(s)).
Note: Includes:- sixteen information cards.
MCSET. Cat no: **852850980.** Released on Hugo Languages, '92 by Hugo Language Books Limited. Note: 4 Cassettes.

FRENCH BUSINESS CASSETTE COURSE (Unknown narrator(s)).
MC. Cat no: **852851510.** Released on Hugo Languages, '92 by Hugo Language Books Limited.

FRENCH CASSETTE COURSE (Unknown narrator(s)).
Note: Includes:- Three months book and an instruction leaflet.
MCSET. Cat no: **852851014.** Released on Hugo Languages, '92 by Hugo Language Books Limited. Note: 4 Cassettes. Playing time 4hrs.

FRENCH EXTRA (Language Courses) (Unknown narrator(s)).
Note: Tutor's Notes available with cassette.
MCSET. Cat no: **PTT 278.** Released on BBC Publications, '91. Note : 3 Cassettes.

FRENCH FOR BUSINESS (Unknown narrator(s)).
Note: Book and four cassettes.
MC. Cat no: **852851502.** Released on Hugo Languages, '92 by Hugo Language Books Limited.

FRENCH FOR BUSINESS (Unknown narrator(s)).
Note: Contains 11 lessons, plus appendices, tips and tactics, reading your customer's letter, abbreviations, review grammar and glossary.
MCSET. Cat no: **SE 225.** Released on Audio Forum (Language courses), '91. Note: 8 Cassettes

FRENCH FOR TRAVEL (Unknown narrator(s)).
MC. Cat no: **BCP 004.** Released on Berlitz Language Courses, '88, Conifer Records.

FRENCH LANGUAGE BASICS (Unknown narrator(s)).
MC. Cat no: **BMC 005.** Released on Berlitz Language Courses, '88, Conifer Records.

FRENCH LEGAL AND COMMERCIAL PROFESSIONS (Unknown narrator(s)).
Note: The course assumes at least 'A' Level standard French and is the perfect supplement to a higher education course in French with Law or Business. The course is in two parts, and contains vocabulary excercises.
MCSET. Cat no: **BPA 1.** Released on Audio Forum (Language courses), '91. Note: 5 Cassettes.

FRENCH OUTSIDE FRANCE: FRENCH SPEAKING SWITZERLAND (Edited By Donald R. Haggis & Marie Jose Piguet) (Unknown narrator(s)).
MC. Cat no: **F 7826.** Released on Exeter Tapes, '91 by Drakes Educational Associates.

FRENCH OUTSIDE FRANCE: LE FRANCAIS DU QUEBEC (Edited By Louis Mignault) (Unknown narrator(s)).
Note: In French.
MC. Cat no: **F 7954.** Released on Exeter Tapes, '91 by Drakes Educational Associates.

FRENCH PHONOLOGY (Unknown narrator(s)).
Note: Perfect way to pronounce French like a native.
MC. Cat no: **F 250.** Released on Audio Forum (Language courses), '91. Note: 8 Cassettes.

FRENCH TRAVEL PACKS.
Note: Contains a Hugo phrase book.
MC. Cat no: **852850867.** Released on Hugo Languages, '92 by Hugo Language Books Limited. Note: 4 cassettes. Playing time 4hrs.

GET BY IN FRENCH (Language Courses) (Unknown narrator(s)).
Note: Each book contains phrases and conversations.
MC. Cat no: **PTT 232/3.** Released on BBC Publications, Jun '83. Note : 2 Cassettes.

GET BY TRAVEL PACKS (Language Courses) (Unknown narrator(s)).
MCSET. Cat no: **PACK 2232.** Released on BBC Publications, '91. Note : 2 Cassettes.

IMPROVE YOUR FRENCH (Language Courses) (Unknown narrator(s)).
LPS. Cat no: **HIYFC.** Released on Harrap Languages, Apr '83. Note : 4 Cassettes.

INTERVIEWS IN FRENCH (Politician, Engineer & Executive) (Unknown narrator(s)).
Note: Intermediate/Advanced level taped conversations with three contemporary French women. A listener's guide and vocabulary list accompany each cassette.
MC. Cat no: **F 400.** Released on Audio Forum (Language courses), '91. Note: 3 Cassettes.

INTERVIEWS IN FRENCH (Dentist, Secretary & Nurse) (Unknown narrator(s)).
MC. Cat no: **F 405.** Released on Audio Forum (Language courses), '91. Note: 3 Cassettes

LANGUAGE COURSE - ENSEMBLE (Help Yourself GCSE French) (Unknown narrator(s)).
2LP. Cat no: **OP 216/7.** Released on BBC Publications, Jun '83. Note : French course in 2 volumes.
MCSET. Cat no: **PTT 216/7.** Released on BBC Publications, Jun '83. Note : French course in 2 volumes.

LANGUAGE COURSE - FRENCH (Travel Pack) (Unknown narrator(s)).
LPS. Cat no: **0747305978.** Released on Linguaphone, Apr '82 by Linguaphone Institute, Taylors, Century Records (USA), Bond Street Music.

LANGUAGE COURSE - FRENCH (Unknown narrator(s)).
LPS. Cat no: **07473021446.** Released on Linguaphone, Apr '82 by Linguaphone Institute, Taylors, Century Records (USA), Bond Street Music.

LANGUAGE COURSE - FRENCH AT HOME (Harraps) (Unknown narrator(s)).
LPS. Cat no: **HFAHC.** Released on Harrap Languages, Apr '83.

LANGUAGE COURSE - MAKE SENTENCES IN FRENCH 1 (Language Courses) (Unknown narrator(s)).
MC. Cat no: **MSIFC 1.** Released on Beuret Language Courses, Aug '83.

LINGUAPHONE FRENCH TRAVELLERS (Language Courses) (Unknown narrator(s)).
MC. Cat no: **0747306826.** Released on Linguaphone, '91 by Linguaphone Institute, Taylors, Century Records (USA), Bond Street Music.

MAKE SENTENCES IN FRENCH 2 (Language Courses) (Unknown narrator(s)).
MC. Cat no: **MSIFC 2.** Released on Beuret Language Courses, Aug '83.

SPEAK FRENCH TODAY (Conversational Courses) (Unknown narrator(s)).
Note: Consists of a book and a 75-90 minute cassette.
MC. Cat no: **852851154.** Released on Hugo Languages, '92 by Hugo Language Books Limited.

SURE LE VIF (Language Courses) (Unknown narrator(s)).
2LP. Cat no: **OP 222/3.** Released on BBC Publications, Jun '83. Note : Second stage French course in 2 volumes.
MCSET. Cat no: **PPT 222/3.** Released on BBC Publications, Jun '83. Note : Second stage French course in 2 volumes.

WHEN IN FRANCE (Language Courses) (Unknown narrator(s)).
Note: Also available with cassette is a Travel Pack and a Book.
MC. Cat no: **PTT 329.** Released on BBC Publications, '91.

French Literature

FRENCH ALEXANDRINE AND THE SONNET, THE (Edited By Steven Dodd And Lucile Ducroquet) (Unknown narrator(s)).
Note: With illustrations from the works of such writers such as Racine, Hugo, Verlaine and Baudelaine.
MC. Cat no: **F 7600**. Released on Exeter Tapes, '91 by Drakes Educational Associates.

FRENCHNESS OF FRENCH LITERATURE, THE (Edited By Donald Haggs) (Unknown narrator(s)).
MC. Cat no: **F 7923**. Released on Exeter Tapes, '91 by Drakes Educational Associates.

HOW FRENCH POETRY WORKS (Edited By Steven Dodd And Lucile Ducroquet) (Unknown narrator(s)).
MC. Cat no: **F 7599**. Released on Exeter Tapes, '91 by Drakes Educational Associates.

PHONETIC TRANSCRIPTION (Edited By Steven Dodd And Lucile Ducroquet) (Unknown narrator(s)).
Note: A seven unit course. Includes transcription exercises, drills and examples in French. Accompanying booklet available. Cat no. F 7659B
MC. Cat no: **F 7659**. Released on Exeter Tapes, '91 by Drakes Educational Associates.

POETRY AND AUDIENCE (Edited By Philip Thody) (Unknown narrator(s)).
Note: An approach to analysing poetry. Accompanying notes available cat. no. F 7823B.
MC. Cat no: **F 7823**. Released on Exeter Tapes, '91 by Drakes Educational Associates.

ROMANTIC HERO, THE (Edited By Timothy A. Unwin) (Unknown narrator(s)).
Note: An analysis of the phenomenon of romanticism in French literature.
MC. Cat no: **F 7805**. Released on Exeter Tapes, '91 by Drakes Educational Associates.

Freud, Sigmund

SIGMUND FREUD (Biography) (Clifford Rose).
MC. Cat no: **EP 4**. Released on Green Dragon, '91 by Green Dragon Audio Visual.

Frisch, Max

ANDORRA (Edited By Keith A. Dickson) (Unknown narrator(s)).
Note: A study of Frisch's contribution to the war theme and the question of guilt in 'Andorra'; Frisch and the theatre of confrontation.
MC. Cat no: **G 7537**. Released on Exeter Tapes, '91 by Drakes Educational Associates.

BIEDERMANN UND DIE BRANDSTIFTER (Edited By Keith A. Dickson) (Unknown narrator(s)).
Note: Max Frisch in the context of epic theatre with a preliminary discussion of Brecht's views.
MC. Cat no: **G 7545**. Released on Exeter Tapes, '91 by Drakes Educational Associates.

Frost, Robert

ROBERT FROST READS HIS POEMS (Robert Frost).
Note: Author reads his works and discuss their formative influences.
MC. Cat no: **AS 20**. Released on Sussex Tapes, '91 by Sussex Publications Ltd..

Fulop-Miller, Rene

RASPUTIN (The Holy Devil) (Anthony Homyer).
MCSET. Cat no: **TCL 34**. Released on Complete Listener, '91 by Complete Listener. Note: 12 Cassettes.

Gaelic

CANSEO (Language Courses) (Unknown narrator(s)).
MCSET. Cat no: **PTT 236**. Released on BBC Publications, '91.

Galica, Divina

PREHISTORIC SCANDINAVIA (Divina Galica).
LP. Cat no: **136 1031**. Released on EMI (Sweden), '88 by EMI Records.

Gandhi

GANDHI (His Life And Philosophy) (Unknown narrator(s)).
LP. Cat no: **REH 466**. Released on BBC, '82 by BBC Records, Taylors **Deleted** Apr '89.
MC. Cat no: **ZCR 466**. Released on BBC, '82 by BBC Records, Taylors **Deleted** Apr '89.

WORDS OF GANDHI, THE (Ben Kingsley).
MC. Cat no: **1740**. Released on Caedmon (USA), '84 by Caedmon Records (USA), Bond Street Music.

Gautier, T.H

POESIES (Edited By Gerard Poulet) (Unknown narrator(s)).
Note: The originality of Gautier's first 'romantic' poetical writing is explored includes a detailed comparative commentary on two poems with the same subject matter. In French.
MC. Cat no: **F 7677**. Released on Exeter Tapes, '91 by Drakes Educational Associates.

G.C.E. O Level...

ENGLISH LANGUAGE (Study Guide) (Unknown narrator(s)).
Note: Study pack consists of a 90 minute tape and course book providing a transcript of the tape with additional exercises for the student to work on.
MC. Cat no: **TD 03**. Released on Real Revision, Jan '84 by Tap-ed Cassettes Ltd.. Note: ISBN No:0946060002

ENGLISH LITERATURE (Henry IV Part 1) (Unknown narrator(s)).
Note: Study pack consists of a 90 minute tape and course book providing a transcript of the tape and additional exercises for the student to work on.
MC. Cat no: **TD 01**. Released on Real Revision, Jan '84 by Tap-ed Cassettes Ltd..

ENGLISH LITERATURE (Macbeth) (Unknown narrator(s)).
Note: Study packs consist of: 90 minute Dolby cassette plus a closely related course book, containing additional exercises for the student to work on.
MC. Cat no: **TD 05**. Released on Real Revision, Jan '84 by Tap-ed Cassettes Ltd..

ENGLISH LITERATURE (Romeo and Juliet) (Unknown narrator(s)).
Note: Study packs consist of: 90 minute Dolby cassette plus a closely related course book containing additional exercises for the student to work on.
MC. Cat no: **TD 07**. Released on Real Revision, Jan '84 by Tap-ed Cassettes Ltd..

G.C.S.E.

ART AND DESIGN (Unknown narrator(s)).
Note: Book & tape set written by G.C.S.E. examiners with specimen questions & answers & revision planners.
MC. Cat no: **PASS 11**. Released on Longman/Pickwick, '88 by Pickwick Records.

BIOLOGY (COURSE) (Unknown narrator(s)).
Note: Book & tape set written by G.C.S.E. examiners with specimen question & answers & revision planners.
MCSET. Cat no: **PASS 10**. Released on Longman/Pickwick, Apr '88 by Pickwick Records. Note: 1 tape & 1 book set

BUSINESS STUDIES (COURSE) (Unknown narrator(s)).
Note: Book & tape set written by G.C.S.E. examiners with specimen questions & answers & revision planners.
MCSET. Cat no: **PASS 01**. Released on Longman/Pickwick, Apr '88 by Pickwick Records. Note: 1 book & 1 tape set.

CHEMISTRY (COURSE) (Unknown narrator(s)).
Note: Book & tape set written by G.C.S.E. examiners with specimen question & answers & revision planners.
MC. Cat no: **PASS 06**. Released on Longman/Pickwick, Apr '88 by Pickwick Records.

COMPUTER STUDIES (Unknown narrator(s)).
Note: Book & tape set written by G.C.S.E. examiners with specimen questions & answers & revision planner.
MC. Cat no: **PASS 13**. Released on Longman/Pickwick, '88 by Pickwick Records.

CRAFT, DESIGN AND TECHNOLOGY (Unknown narrator(s)).
Note: Book & tape set written by G.C.S.E. examiners with specimen questions & answers & revision planner.
MC. Cat no: **PASS 15.** Released on Longman/Pickwick, '88 by Pickwick Records.

ECONOMICS (Unknown narrator(s)).
Note: Book & tape set written by G.C.S.E. examiners with specimen questions & answers & revision planner.
MC. Cat no: **PASS 20.** Released on Longman/Pickwick, '88 by Pickwick Records.

ENGLISH (COURSE) (Unknown narrator(s)).
Note: Book & tape set written by G.C.S.E. examiners with specimen question & answers & revision planners.
MC. Cat no: **PASS 07.** Released on Longman/Pickwick, Apr '88 by Pickwick Records.

ENGLISH LITERATURE (COURSE) (Unknown narrator(s)).
Note: Book & tape set written by C.C.S.E. examiners with specimen question & answers & revision planners.
MC. Cat no: **PASS 05.** Released on Longman/Pickwick, Apr '88 by Pickwick Records.

FRENCH (COURSE) (Unknown narrator(s)).
Note: Book & tape set written by G.C.S.E. examiners with specimen questions & answers & a revision planner.
MC. Cat no: **PASS 04.** Released on Longman/Pickwick, Apr '88 by Pickwick Records.

GEOGRAPHY (COURSE) (Unknown narrator(s)).
Note: Book & tape set written by G.C.S.E. examiners with specimen question & answers & revision planners.
MC. Cat no: **PASS 03.** Released on Longman/Pickwick, Apr '88 by Pickwick Records.

HOME ECONOMICS (COURSE) (Unknown narrator(s)).
Note: Book & tape set written by G.C.S.E. examiners with specimen question & answers & revision planners.
MC. Cat no: **PASS 09.** Released on Longman/Pickwick, Apr '88 by Pickwick Records.

HUMAN BIOLOGY (Unknown narrator(s)).
Note: Book & tape set written by G.C.S.E. examiners with specimen questions & answers & revision planner.
MC. Cat no: **PASS 19.** Released on Longman/Pickwick, '88 by Pickwick Records.

MATHEMATICS (COURSE) (Unknown narrator(s)).

Note: Book & tape set written by G.C.S.E. examiners with specimen question & answers & revision planners.
MC. Cat no: **PASS 08.** Released on Longman/Pickwick, Apr '88 by Pickwick Records.

PHYSICS (COURSE) (Unknown narrator(s)).
Note: Book & tape set written by G.C.S.E. examiners with specimen question & answers & revision planners.
MC. Cat no: **PASS 02.** Released on Longman/Pickwick, Apr '88 by Pickwick Records.

RELIGIOUS STUDIES (Unknown narrator(s)).
Note: Book & tape set written by G.C.S.E. examiners with specimen questions & answers & revision planner.
MC. Cat no: **PASS 17.** Released on Longman/Pickwick, '88 by Pickwick Records.

SCIENCE (Unknown narrator(s)).
Note: Book & tape set written by G.C.S.E. Examiners with specimen questions & answers & revision planner.
MC. Cat no: **PASS 16.** Released on Longman/Pickwick, '88 by Pickwick Records.

SOCIAL AND ECONOMIC HISTORY (Unknown narrator(s)).
Note: Book & tape set written by G.C.S.E. examiners with specimen questions & answers & revision planner.
MC. Cat no: **PASS 14.** Released on Longman/Pickwick, '88 by Pickwick Records.

TYPEWRITING (Unknown narrator(s)).
Note: Book & tape set written by G.C.S.E. examiners with specimen questions & answers & revision planner.
MC. Cat no: **PASS 18.** Released on Longman/Pickwick, '88 by Pickwick Records.

WORLD HISTORY (Unknown narrator(s)).
Note: Book & tape set written by G.C.S.E. examiners with specimen questions & answers & revision planner.
MC. Cat no: **PASS 12.** Released on Longman/Pickwick, '88 by Pickwick Records.

Genova, Jackie
WORK THAT BODY (See Under Health & Fitness) (Jackie Genova).
WORK THAT BODY INTO SKI SHAPE (See Under Health & Fitness) (Jackie Genova).

German
BASIC GERMAN (Volume 1) (Unknown narrator(s)).
MCSET. Cat no: **G 141.** Released on Audio Forum (Language courses), '91.

BASIC GERMAN ADVANCED LEVEL (Unknown narrator(s)).
MC. Cat no: **G 160.** Released on Audio Forum (Language courses), '91.

BASIC GERMAN INTERMEDIATE (Unknown narrator(s)).
MCSET. Cat no: **G 151.** Released on Audio Forum (Language courses), '91.

DAS FRAULEIN VON SCUDERI (Unknown narrator(s)).
Note: German narration for practice linguists, a tale of murder and mystery set in Paris of Louis XIV.
MCSET. Cat no: **EAC 05E.** Released on European Audio Classics, '91 by Unknown. Note: 2 Cassettes - ISBN no. 1873256205

DECLENSION OF ADJECTIVES, THE (Edited By Hilda Swinburne) (Unknown narrator(s)).
MC. Cat no: **G 7857.** Released on Exeter Tapes, '91 by Drakes Educational Associates.

DECLENSION OF NOUNS, THE (Edited By Hilda Sunburne) (Unknown narrator(s)).
MC. Cat no: **G 7715.** Released on Exeter Tapes, '91 by Drakes Educational Associates.

DEUTSCH DIREKT (Language Courses) (Unknown narrator(s)).
Note: An introduction to simple everyday German. Also available with cassette are Tutor's Notes, Work-book and a Book.
MC. Cat no: **PTT 275.** Released on BBC Publications, '91.

DEUTSCH DIREKT (2) (Language Courses) (Unknown narrator(s)).
Note: An introduction to simple everyday German. Also available with cassette are Tutor's Notes, Work-book and a Book.
MC. Cat no: **PTT 276.** Released on BBC Publications, '91.

DEUTSCH DIREKT (3) (Language Courses) (Unknown narrator(s)).
Note: An introduction to simple everyday German. Also available with cassette are Tutor's Notes, Work-book and a Book.
MC. Cat no: **PTT 277.** Released on BBC Publications, '91.

DEUTSCH EXPRESS (Language Courses) (Unknown narrator(s)).
Note: Available with Cassette are Tutor's Notes.
MCSET. Cat no: **PTT 285.** Released on BBC Publications, '91. Note : 3 Cassettes.

DEVELOPMENT OF THE GERMAN LANGUAGE, THE (Edited By Hilda Swinburne) (Unknown narrator(s)).
MC. Cat no: **G 7630.** Released on Exeter Tapes, '91 by Drakes Educational Associates.

DIE MARQUISE VON O AND DAS (Various narrators).
Note: German narration for practice linguists. Two historical romances. By Heinrich Kleist.

MCSET. Cat no: **EAC 06F.** Released on European Audio Classics, '91 by Unknown. Note: 2 cassettes - ISBN no. 1873256256

GANZ SPONTAN (Language Courses) (Unknown narrator(s)).
Note: Includes a book.
MCSET. Cat no: **PTT 298.** Released on BBC Publications, '91. Note : 2 Cassettes.

GENDER OF NOUNS, THE (Edited By Hilda Swinburne) (Unknown narrator(s)).
MC. Cat no: **G 7821.** Released on Exeter Tapes, '91 by Drakes Educational Associates.

GERMAN AT THE WHEEL (Unknown narrator(s)).
Note: Includes:- sixteen information cards.
MCSET. Cat no: **852851499.** Released on Hugo Languages, '92 by Hugo Language Books Limited. Note: 4 cassettes.

GERMAN BUSINESS CASSETTE COURSE (Unknown narrator(s)).
MC. Cat no: **852851731.** Released on Hugo Languages, '92 by Hugo Language Books Limited.

GERMAN CASSETTE COURSE (Unknown narrator(s)).
Note: Includes:- Three months' book and an instruction leaflet.
MCSET. Cat no: **852851618.** Released on Hugo Languages, '92 by Hugo Language Books Limited. Note: 4 cassettes. Playing time 4hrs.

GERMAN FOR BUSINESS (Unknown narrator(s)).
Note: Book and four cassettes.
MC. Cat no: **852851723.** Released on Hugo Languages, '92 by Hugo Language Books Limited.

GERMAN FOR TRAVEL (Unknown narrator(s)).
MC. Cat no: **BCP 005.** Released on Berlitz Language Courses, '88, Conifer Records.

GERMAN LANGUAGE BASICS (Unknown narrator(s)).
MC. Cat no: **BMC 003.** Released on Berlitz Language Courses, '88, Conifer Records.

GERMAN TRAVEL PACKS (Unknown narrator(s)).
Note: Contains a Hugo phrase book.
MC. Cat no: **852850875.** Released on Hugo Languages, '92 by Hugo Language Books Limited. Note: 4 Cassettes. Playing time 4hrs.

GERMAN-ENGLISH DICTIONARIES AND HOW TO USE THEM (Edited By Howard Jackson) (Unknown narrator(s)).
MC. Cat no: **G 7771.** Released on Exeter Tapes, '91 by Drakes Educational Associates.

GERMAN TRAVEL KIT (Unknown narrator(s)).
MC. Cat no: **BTK 004.** Released on Berlitz Language Courses, '88, Conifer Records.

GET BY IN GERMAN (Language Courses) (Unknown narrator(s)).
Note: Each book contains phrases and conversations.
MCSET. Cat no: **PTT 252.** Released on BBC Publications, '91. Note : 2 Cassettes.

GET BY TRAVEL PACKS (Language Courses) (Unknown narrator(s)).
MCSET. Cat no: **PACK 2252.** Released on BBC Publications, '91. Note : 2 Cassettes.

IMMENSEE (Various narrators).
Note: By Theodor Storm. German narration for practice linguists. A semi-autobiographical account set in Storms native Schleswig-Holstein.
MCSET. Cat no: **EAC 07G.** Released on European Audio Classics, '91 by Unknown. Note: 2 cassettes - ISBN no. 1873256302

KEIN PROBLEM (Language Courses) (Unknown narrator(s)).
2LP. Cat no: **OP 234/5.** Released on BBC Publications, Jun '83.
MCSET. Cat no: **PTT 234/5.** Released on BBC Publications, Jun '83. Note : A third year German course in 2 volumes.

LANGUAGE COURSE - GERMAN VOL. 1 (Travel Pack) (Unknown narrator(s)).
LPS. Cat no: **0747305986.** Released on Linguaphone, Apr '82 by Linguaphone Institute, Taylors, Century Records (USA), Bond Street Music.

LANGUAGE COURSE - GERMAN VOL. 2 (Unknown narrator(s)).
LPS. Cat no: **0747303649.** Released on Linguaphone, Apr '82 by Linguaphone Institute, Taylors, Century Records (USA), Bond Street Music.

LAWYERS AND INDUSTRY IN GERMANY (Unknown narrator(s)).
Note: At least 'A' Level German is required for this course.
MC. Cat no: **BPA 2.** Released on Audio Forum (Language courses), '91.
Note: 5 Cassettes

LINGUAPHONE GERMAN TRAVELLERS (Language Courses) (Unknown narrator(s)).
MC. Cat no: **0747306834.** Released on Linguaphone, '91 by Linguaphone Institute, Taylors, Century Records (USA), Bond Street Music.

MAKING SENSE OF THE VERB (Edited By Howard Jackson) (Unknown narrator(s)).
MC. Cat no: **G 7843.** Released on Exeter Tapes, '91 by Drakes Educational Associates.

MODAL AUXILIARY VERBS, THE (Edited By Hilda Swinburne) (Unknown narrator(s)).
MC. Cat no: **G 7833.** Released on Exeter Tapes, '91 by Drakes Educational Associates.

PREPOSITIONS AND THE CASES WHICH THEY GOVERN (Edited By Hilda Swinburne) (Unknown narrator(s)).
MC. Cat no: **G 7808.** Released on Exeter Tapes, '91 by Drakes Educational Associates.

SEPARABLE AND INSEPARABLE VERBS, THE (Edited By Hilda Swinburne) (Unknown narrator(s)).
MC. Cat no: **G 7849.** Released on Exeter Tapes, '91 by Drakes Educational Associates.

SPEAK GERMAN TODAY (Conversational Courses) (Unknown narrator(s)).
Note: Consists of a book and a 75-90 minute cassette.
MC. Cat no: **852851189.** Released on Hugo Languages, '92 by Hugo Language Books Limited.

WHEN IN GERMANY (Language Courses) (Unknown narrator(s)).
MC. Cat no: **PTT 360.** Released on BBC Publications, '91.

German Literature

GERMAN POETRY SINCE 1945 (Edited By Keith A. Dickson) (Unknown narrator(s)).
MC. Cat no: **G 7619.** Released on Exeter Tapes, '91 by Drakes Educational Associates.

Germany

BISMARCK AND THE GERMAN PROBLEM (Michael Sturmer & B J Williams).
MCSET. Cat no: **HUA 028.** Released on AVP, '91 by AVP Publishing.

BISMARK AND GERMANY (Geoffrey Barraclough & AJP Taylor).
MC. Cat no: **HE 6.** Released on Sussex Tapes, '91 by Sussex Publications Ltd..

DAS GETEILTE DEUTSCHLAND: GESCHICHTE UND GEGENWA (Edited By J. Schlosser) (Unknown narrator(s)).
Note: A discussion of German history from the beginning of the 19th century until 1945.
MC. Cat no: **G 7989.** Released on Exeter Tapes, '91 by Drakes Educational Associates.

DECLINE OF THE HABSBURG MONARCHY, THE (Norman Stone & Joe Lee).
MCSET. Cat no: **HUA 015.** Released on AVP, '91 by AVP Publishing.

EDUCATION IN THE FEDERAL REPUBLIC OF GERMANY (Edited By E.J. Neather) (Unknown narrator(s)).
MC. Cat no: **G 7931.** Released on Exeter Tapes, '91 by Drakes Educational Associates.

GERMANY 1914-1945 (V. Berghahn & LJCG. Rohl).
MC. Cat no: **HB 2.** Released on Sussex Tapes, '91 by Sussex Publications Ltd.

HAPSBURG AND OTTOMAN EMPIRES, THE (Dr VJ Parry & Michael Kitch).
MC. Cat no: **HE 10.** Released on Sussex Tapes, '91 by Sussex Publications Ltd..

HITLER'S WORLD POLICY (Hitler's War?) (Hugh Trevor-Roper & Alan Milward).

MCSET. Cat no: **HUA 009.** Released on AVP, '91 by AVP Publishing.

INTRODUCTION TO THE GERMAN DEMOCRATIC REPUBLIC (Edited By Derek Lewis) (Unknown narrator(s)).
MC. Cat no: **G 7333.** Released on Exeter Tapes, '91 by Drakes Educational Associates.

KAISER'S GERMANY, THE (1890-1918) (David Blackbourn & J.C.G. Rohl).
MC. Cat no: **HE 25.** Released on Sussex Tapes, '91 by Sussex Publications Ltd..

KOLN - EIN HORBILD (Edited By Schoschana Maitek) (Unknown narrator(s)).
Note: An introduction to the varied history of Cologne and to the many facets of its thriving life today.
MC. Cat no: **G 7906.** Released on Exeter Tapes, '91 by Drakes Educational Associates.

NEW IMPERIALISM 1870 - 1914, THE (Eric Stokes & Dr, David Gillard).
MCSET. Cat no: **HUA 029.** Released on AVP, '91 by AVP Publishing.

PARTY POLITICS, THE (And Economy of Whilhelmine Germany) (Norman Stone & Joe Lee).
MCSET. Cat no: **HUA 016.** Released on AVP, '91 by AVP Publishing.

PRESS IN THE GERMAN - SPEAKING COUNTRIES, THE (Edited By John Sandford) (Unknown narrator(s)).
MC. Cat no: **G 7795.** Released on Exeter Tapes, '91 by Drakes Educational Associates.

ROAD TO MUNICH, THE (From Munich to the Fall of France) (John Grenville & David Dilks).
MCSET. Cat no: **HUA 020.** Released on AVP, '91 by AVP Publishing.

SOUNDS OF GERMANY, THE - PARTS 1 AND 2 (Edited By Wilfried Gunther) (Unknown narrator(s)).
MC. Cat no: **G 7605.** Released on Exeter Tapes, '91 by Drakes Educational Associates.

THIRD REICH - A SOCIAL REVOLUTION? (National Socialism and Capitalism) (Alan Milward & Dr. Ian Kershaw).
MCSET. Cat no: **HUA 052.** Released on AVP, '91 by AVP Publishing.

WEIMAR REPUBLIC, THE (Edited By John MacKenzie) (Unknown narrator(s)).
MC. Cat no: **G 7615.** Released on Exeter Tapes, '91 by Drakes Educational Associates.

Gershwin (Composer)

GEORGE GERSHWIN REMEMBERED (Various artists).
CD. Cat no: **FCD 8100.** Released on Freedom, Jan '89, Jazz Music, Swift, W.R.P.M., Wellard Dist., Cadillac Music, Koch International.

Ghost Stories

EXORCISM OF BROTHER SIMEON, THE (Valentine Dyall).
MCSET. Cat no: **D 002.** Released on Green Dragon, '91 by Green Dragon Audio Visual.

FLYING SAUCER MYSTERY, THE (Ed Bishop).
MCSET. Cat no: **D 005.** Released on Green Dragon, '91 by Green Dragon Audio Visual.

HAUNTINGS AT BORLEY RECTORY, THE (Edward De Souza).
MCSET. Cat no: **D 001.** Released on Green Dragon, '91 by Green Dragon Audio Visual.

TRUE STORIES OF THE SUPERNATURAL (Valentine Dyall).
MCSET. Cat no: **BS 17/20.** Released on Chiron Cassettes, Apr '82.

Gibran, Khalil

PROPHET , THE (And The Garden of The Prophet) (Garard Green).
MCSET. Cat no: **1059N.** Released on Travellers Tales, '91 by Travellers Tales. Note: 3 Cassettes.
MCSET. Cat no: **OAS 89111.** Released on Oasis Audio Books, '91 by Isis Audio Books. Note: 3 Cassettes.

Gibson, Charles

DEATH OF A PHANTOM RAIDER (Garard Green).
MCSET. Cat no: **1024N.** Released on Travellers Tales, '91 by Travellers Tales. Note: 6 Cassettes
MCSET. Cat no: **1854961047.** Released on Soundings, '91 by Soundings Records, Bond Street Music. Note: 6 Cassettes

Gide, Andre

BACKGROUND TO GIDE (Edited By Ray Davison) (Unknown narrator(s)).
Note: An analysis of Gide's ideas on self-liberation and of his theory of fiction.
MC. Cat no: **F 7678.** Released on Exeter Tapes, '91 by Drakes Educational Associates.

LA PORTE ETROITE (Edited By Gerard Poulet) (Unknown narrator(s)).
Note: An analysis of Gide's art through the study of his narrative technique. In French.
MC. Cat no: **F 7556.** Released on Exeter Tapes, '91 by Drakes Educational Associates.

Gielgud, Sir John

EARLY STAGES (Biography) (Sir John Gielgud).
MCSET. Cat no: **1047N.** Released on Travellers Tales, '91 by Travellers Tales. Note: 7 cassettes.
MCSET. Cat no: **IAB 89121.** Released on Isis Audio Books, '91. Note : 7 Cassettes.

Gingold, Hermione

HOW TO GROW OLD GRACEFULLY (Biography) (Gretel Davis).
MCSET. Cat no: **1077N.** Released on Travellers Tales, '91 by Travellers Tales. Note: 7 Cassettes.

MCSET. Cat no: **OAS 91021.** Released on Oasis Audio Books, '91 by Isis Audio Books. Note: 7 Cassettes.

Ginzburg, Natalia

FIVE EXAMPLES OF SENSE AND SENSIBILITY IN MODERN... (Edited By Alan Bullock) (Unknown narrator(s)).
Note: Examines Natalia Ginzburg's attitude to various problems implicit in human relationships as exemplified in her work.
MC. Cat no: **I 7953.** Released on Exeter Tapes, '91 by Drakes Educational Associates.

Giono, J

REGAIN (Edited By Gerard Poulet) (Unknown narrator(s)).
Note: An analysis of the mythological dimension of the book, followed by a case study of Giono's writing technique. In French.
MC. Cat no: **F 7515.** Released on Exeter Tapes, '91 by Drakes Educational Associates.

Giraudoux, Jean

LA GUERRE DE TROIE (Edited By Jacqueline Fox) (Unknown narrator(s)).
Note: Examines two special episodes which throw light on the theme of love, beauty and death in this play by J. Giraudoux.
MC. Cat no: **F 7516.** Released on Exeter Tapes, '91 by Drakes Educational Associates.

Glasser, Ralph

GROWING UP IN THE GORBALS (Biography) (Joe Dunlop).
MCSET. Cat no: **1049A.** Released on Travellers Tales, '91 by Travellers Tales. Note: 8 Cassettes.
MCSET. Cat no: **OAS 89071.** Released on Oasis Audio Books, '91 by Isis Audio Books. Note: 8 Cassettes.

Godfrey, L

CARY GRANT, THE LIGHT TOUCH (Christopher Kay).
MCSET. Cat no: **1038N.** Released on Travellers Tales, '91 by Travellers Tales. Note: 6 Cassettes.
MCSET. Cat no: **1854961055.** Released on Soundings, '91 by Soundings Records, Bond Street Music. Note: 6 Cassettes.

Goethe, J.W.
(See under Von Goethe, J.W.)

Gogol, Nikolai

POVEST'O TOM KAK POSSORILSYA IVAN IVANOVICH S IV (Edited By R.A. Peace) (Unknown narrator(s)).
Note: Full title:- Povest'o tom kak possorilsya Ivan Ivanovich s ivanom nikiforovichem. An examination of Gogol's comic story.
MC. Cat no: **R 7699.** Released on Exeter Tapes, '91 by Drakes Educational Associates.

SHINEL (Edited By R.A. Peace) (Unknown narrator(s)).
Note: A critique of 'The Overcoat', Gogol's most famous short story.
MC. Cat no: **R 7625**. Released on Exeter Tapes, '91 by Drakes Educational Associates.

Golding, William

WILLIAM GOLDING (Bernard Bergonzi & J S Whitely).
Note: Pre-recorded discussions which show literary criticism as a living, evolving interchange.
MC. Cat no: **A20**. Released on Sussex Tapes, '91 by Sussex Publications Ltd..
WILLIAM GOLDING (A-Level Certification) (Stephen Metcalfe & John S Whitley).
MCSET. Cat no: **ELA 019**. Released on AVP, '91 by AVP Publishing.

Golf

GOLF COURSES AT TURNBERRY, THE (Various narrators).
Note: Souvenir with historical comment and notes on the nomenclature of the game and course (with sound effects).
MC. Cat no: **SSC 038**. Released on Scotsoun, '91 by Scotsoun Recordings, Morley Audio Services.
STRAIGHT DOWN THE MIDDLE (Great Moments In Golf) (Various narrators).
LP. Cat no: **HAV 1025**. Released on Haven, Nov '86 by MCA Records **Deleted** '87.
MC. Cat no: **HAVC1025**. Released on Haven, Nov '86 by MCA Records **Deleted** '87.

Golka, F.W.

PROTESTANT CHURCH IN GERMANY, THE (Unknown narrator(s)).
MC. Cat no: **G 7847**. Released on Exeter Tapes, '91 by Drakes Educational Associates.

Goncharov, I.A

OBLOMOV (Edited By David J. Richards) (Unknown narrator(s)).
Note: A discussion of the shape and the import of Goncharov's mid-nineteenth century novel.
MC. Cat no: **R 7990**. Released on Exeter Tapes, '91 by Drakes Educational Associates.

Gordy Singleton, Raynoma

BERRY, ME AND MOTOWN (Biography) (Raynoma Gordy Singleton).
MCSET. Cat no: **TTC 2040**. Released on Talking Tape Company, '91, Conifer Records. Note: 2 Cassettes. Playing time 3hrs ISBN no. 1872520707

Grahame, Laurie

PARENT'S SURVIVAL GUIDE (Maggie Steed).
MCSET. Cat no: **ZBBC 1070**. Released on BBC Radio Collection, Oct '89 by BBC Records. Note: ISBN No: 0563 226412

Grant, Elizabeth

MEMORIES OF HIGHLAND LADY (1877 - 1927) (Morag Hood).
MCSET. Cat no: **SPN 334-1**. Released on Schiltron Audio Books, '91 by Schiltron Publishing. Note: 6 Cassettes. Playing time 8 hours 30 minutes.

Grass, Gunther

KATZ UND MAUS (Edited By William P. Hanson) (Unknown narrator(s)).
Note: Offers some general approaches to Gunther Grass's work, including his main preoccupations and aspects of his narrative technique.
MC. Cat no: **G 7579**. Released on Exeter Tapes, '91 by Drakes Educational Associates.

Graves, Robert

POET AMONG SCIENTISTS, A (Robert Graves).
MC. Cat no: **23021**. Released on Sussex Tapes, '91 by Sussex Publications Ltd..
SERGEANT LAMB'S AMERICA (Ron Keith).
MCSET. Cat no: **RB 90104**. Released on Recorded Books, Apr '92 by Isis Audio Books. Note: 10 Cassettes. Playing time 14hrs 30mins.

Greek

DISCUSSION OF MODERN GREEK POETRY (Kimon Friar).
Note: Kimon Friar discusses and reads selection from the work of one of the greatest and most celebrated of modern Greek poets, Konstantinos Kavaphes.
MC. Cat no: **C 23163**. Released on Sussex Tapes, '91 by Sussex Publications Ltd..
GET BY IN GREEK (Language Courses) (Unknown narrator(s)).
Note: Each book contains phrases and conversations.
MC. Cat no: **PTT 264/5**. Released on BBC Publications, Jun '83.
GET BY TRAVEL PACKS (Language Courses) (Unknown narrator(s)).
MCSET. Cat no: **PACK 2264**. Released on BBC Publications, '91. Note : 2 Cassettes.
GREEK CASSETTE COURSE (Unknown narrator(s)).
Note: Includes :- 3 months' book and an instruction leaflet.
MCSET. Cat no: **852851316**. Released on Hugo Languages, '92 by Hugo Language Books Limited. Note: 4 Cassettes. Playing time 4hrs.
GREEK FOR TRAVEL (Unknown narrator(s)).
MC. Cat no: **BCP 006**. Released on Berlitz Language Courses, '88, Conifer Records.
GREEK LANGUAGE AND PEOPLE (Language Courses) (Unknown narrator(s)).
Note: An introduction to modern Greek for beginners. Plus book.
MCSET. Cat no: **PTT 269**. Released on BBC Publications, '91. Note : 2 Cassettes.
GREEK LANGUAGE BASICS (Unknown narrator(s)).
MC. Cat no: **BMC 006**. Released on Berlitz Language Courses, '88, Conifer Records.
GREEK TRAVEL PACK (Unknown narrator(s)).
Note: Contains a Hugo phrase book.
MC. Cat no: **85285112X**. Released on Hugo Languages, '92 by Hugo Language Books Limited.
INTRODUCING ANCIENT GREEK (Edited By N.E. Collinge) (Unknown narrator(s)).
MC. Cat no: **GK 7818**. Released on Exeter Tapes, '91 by Drakes Educational Associates.
LINGUAPHONE GREEK TRAVELLERS (Language Courses) (Unknown narrator(s)).
MC. Cat no: **0747306982**. Released on Linguaphone, '91 by Linguaphone Institute, Taylors, Century Records (USA), Bond Street Music.
MODERN GREEK BASIC COURSE (Volume 1) (Unknown narrator(s)).
MCSET. Cat no: **R 301**. Released on Audio Forum (Language courses), '91. Note: 12 Cassettes
MODERN GREEK BASIC COURSE (Volume 2) (Unknown narrator(s)).
MCSET. Cat no: **R 318**. Released on Audio Forum (Language courses), '91. Note: 12 Cassettes
MODERN GREEK BASIC COURSE (Volume 3) (Unknown narrator(s)).
MCSET. Cat no: **R 338**. Released on Audio Forum (Language courses), '91. Note: 6 Cassettes
OUTSTANDING GREEK MODERN POETRY (Unknown narrator(s)).
Note: Includes poetry by Solomos, Plamas, Karyotakis, Cavafy, Kazantzikis, Ritsos, Seferis, Elytis and others.
MC. Cat no: **SFR 401**. Released on Sussex Tapes, '91 by Sussex Publications Ltd..
SPEAK GREEK TODAY (Conversational Courses) (Unknown narrator(s)).
Note: Consists of a book and a 75-90 minute cassette.
MC. Cat no: **852851332**. Released on Hugo, '92, Bond Street Music, Taylors.

Greene, Graham

NOVELS OF GRAHAM GREENE, THE (Ian Gregor & David Lodge).
Note: Pre-recorded discussions which show literary criticism as a living, evolving interchange.
MC. Cat no: **A19**. Released on Sussex Tapes, '91 by Sussex Publications Ltd..

Grenfell & Moore

INVISIBLE FRIENDSHIP (Biography) (Patricia Hughes).
Note: Authors are Joyce Grenfell and Katherine Moore.

MCSET. Cat no: **1053/1054A.** Released on Travellers Tales, '91 by Travellers Tales.

MCSET. Cat no: **OAS 89102.** Released on Oasis Audio Books, '91 by Isis Audio Books. Note: 12 Cassettes.

Griboedov, A
GORE OT UMA (Edited By D. Offord) (Unknown narrator(s)).
Note: An account of the literary and historical background to Griboedov's play and a discussion of its form and content
MC. Cat no: **R 7897.** Released on Exeter Tapes, '91 by Drakes Educational Associates.

Grillparzer, F
KONIG OTTOKARS GLUCK UND ENDE (Edited By Mary Garland) (Unknown narrator(s)).
Note: The play is Grillparzer's first venture into the genre of historical drama. In German.
MC. Cat no: **G 7752.** Released on Exeter Tapes, '91 by Drakes Educational Associates.

Guerolt, Denis
J R R TOLKIEN (Denis Guerolt).
Note: Author reads their work and discuss their formative influences.
MC. Cat no: **AS 08.** Released on Sussex Tapes, '91 by Sussex Publications Ltd..

Hamilton, Emma
EMMA HAMILTON (Biography) (Nigel Lambert).
MC. Cat no: **FW 6.** Released on Green Dragon, '91 by Green Dragon Audio Visual.

Handel (composer)
GEORGE FREDERIC HANDEL (Biography) (John Ringham).
MC. Cat no: **DFC 2.** Released on Sussex Tapes, '91 by Sussex Publications Ltd..

Handy, C
AGE OF UNREASON (Unknown narrator(s)).
MCSET. Cat no: **RC 8.** Released on Random Century, '91 by Random Century Audiobooks, Conifer Records. Note: 2 cassettes. ISBN no.1856860078. 3hrs approx.

Harding, Mike
FOOTLOOSE IN THE HIMALAYAS (Mike Harding).
MCSET. Cat no: **CAB 679.** Released on Chivers Audio Books, Mar '92 by Chivers Audio Books, Green Dragon Audio Visual. Note: 8 Cassettes.

ROCHDALE COWBOY RIDES AGAIN, THE (Volume 2) (Mike Harding).
LP. Cat no: **RUB 016.** Released on Rubber, Jun '88 by Mawson & Wareham Music, Roots Records, Projection, Celtic Music, Jazz Music, Pinnacle.

MC. Cat no: **RUBC 016.** Released on Rubber, Jun '88 by Mawson & Wareham Music, Roots Records, Projection, Celtic Music, Jazz Music, Pinnacle.

Hardy, Thomas
HARDY AND MANCHILD (Benjamin Demott).
MC. Cat no: **23069.** Released on Sussex Tapes, '91 by Sussex Publications Ltd..

THOMAS HARDY 1 (Ian Gregor & David Lodge).
Note: Pre-recorded discussions which show literary criticism as a living, evolving interchange.
MC. Cat no: **A13.** Released on Sussex Tapes, '91 by Sussex Publications Ltd..

Harvey-Jones, John
MAKING IT HAPPEN (John Harvey Jones).
MCSET. Cat no: **RC 36.** Released on Random Century, '91 by Random Century Audiobooks, Conifer Records. Note: 2 Cassettes. ISBN no. 1856860701. Playing time 3hrs approx.

Hauxwell, Hannah
DAUGHTER OF THE DALES (Biography) (Unknown narrator(s)).
MCSET. Cat no: **1854964208.** Released on Soundings, '91 by Soundings Records, Bond Street Music. Note: 4 Cassettes.

DAUGHTER OF THE DALES (Biography) (Unknown narrator(s)).
Note: Adapted by Barry Cockcroft
MCSET. Cat no: **RC 25.** Released on Random Century, '91 by Random Century Audiobooks, Conifer Records. Note: 2 Cassettes. ISBN no. 1856860531. Playing time 3 hrs approx.

DAUGHTER OF THE DALES (Biography) (Elizabeth Henry).
MCSET. Cat no: **1105N.** Released on Travellers Tales, '91 by Travellers Tales. Note: 4 Cassettes.

INNOCENT ABROAD, AN (Biography) (Hannah Hauxwell).
Note: Adapted by Barry Cockcroft.
MCSET. Cat no: **RC 38.** Released on Random Century, '91 by Random Century Audiobooks, Conifer Records. Note: 2 Cassettes. ISBN no. 1856860574. Playing time 3hrs approx.

MCSET. Cat no: **1854965425.** Released on Bramhope, '92 by Ulverscroft Soundings. Note: 6 Cassettes.

SEASONS OF MY LIFE (Biography) (Hannah Hauxwell).
Note: Adapted By Barry Cockcroft.
MCSET. Cat no: **1854963716.** Released on Bramhope, '91 by Ulverscroft Soundings. Note: 4 Cassettes.

SEASONS OF MY LIFE (Biography) (Unknown narrator(s)).
MCSET. Cat no: **1856860140.** Released on Random Century, '91 by Random Century Audiobooks, Conifer Records. Note: 5 Cassettes.

SEASONS OF MY LIFE (Biography) (H. Hauxwell & C. Kay).
MCSET. Cat no: **1099N.** Released on Travellers Tales, '91 by Travellers Tales. Note: 4 Cassettes.

SEASONS OF MY LIFE (Biography) (Hannah Hauxwell).
MC. Cat no: **RC 15.** Released on Random Century, '91 by Random Century Audiobooks, Conifer Records. Note: 2 cassettes. IBSN no. 1856860140. Playing time 3hrs approx.

Hawking, Stephen
BRIEF HISTORY IN TIME, A (Michael Jackson).
MCSET. Cat no: **1082N.** Released on Travellers Tales, '91 by Travellers Tales. Note: 4 Cassettes.

Haydn (composer)
FRANZ JOSEPH HAYDN 1732 -1809 (Biography) (Michael Burrell).
MC. Cat no: **DFC 3.** Released on Sussex Tapes, '91 by Sussex Publications Ltd..

Health & Fitness
AEROBIC EXERCISE MUSIC (With Subliminal Suggestions) (Various artists).
MC. Cat no: **C 308.** Released on New World Cassettes, '88.

AEROBICISE (The California Exercise Craze) (Various artists).
LP. Cat no: **RTL 2092.** Released on Ronco, May '83.
MC. Cat no: **4 CRTL 2092.** Released on Ronco, May '83.

AIDS - THE FACTS (Dr. Richard Tedder).
Note: Aids - How much of a threat is it to you - Find out the facts. 50 of your questions answered - 70 minutes playing time. A proportion of the proceeds from the sales of this cassette will go to Dr. Richard Tedder's laboratory in London to develop educational and research facilities for AIDS control
MC. Cat no: **AIDS 3.** Released on CBS, Feb '88 by Sony Music, Solomon & Peres, Outlet Records.

ARNOLD SCHWARZENEGGER'S TOTAL BODY WORKOUT (Various artists).
LP. Cat no: **CBS 26022.** Released on CBS, Oct '84 by Sony Music, Solomon & Peres, Outlet Records.

AS YOUNG AS YOU FEEL WITH EILEEN FOWLER (Various artists).
Note: Gentle exercises at an easy pace by Eileen Fowler, to favourite old tunes and also specially composed music by Helen Shields. Based on Eileen's popular 'stay young' spot on BBC TV's '60, 70, 80. This disc is for the 'not so young' and side 2 is devoted to those who prefer to, or have to sit.
LP. Cat no: **REC 195.** Released on BBC, Jun '78 by BBC Records, Taylors **Deleted** '88.

MC. Cat no: **MRMC 007**. Released on BBC, '79 by BBC Records, Taylors.

BABY SOOTHER TAPE (Various artists).
MC. Cat no: **ZCLUL 1**. Released on Conifer, Oct '86 by Conifer Records, Jazz Music.

CALLANETICS FOR YOUR BACK (Edited by Callan Pinckey) (Unknown narrator(s)).
MCSET. Cat no: **0671681990**. Released on Simon & Schuster, '91 by Simon & Schuster Ltd. Note: 2 Cassettes.

COMPLETE FITNESS COURSE, THE (With Simon Ward & Al Murray) (Various artists).
LP. Cat no: **LEG 11**. Released on Lifestyle, '83 by Jive Records.
MC. Cat no: **LEGC 11**. Released on Lifestyle, '83 by Jive Records.

COMPLETE YOGA (Volume 2) (Lyn Marshall).
MC. Cat no: **TCT 50394**. Released on Sunset (Liberty), Sep '76 by EMI Records **Deleted** '83.

DANCE KEEP FIT & SLIM TO MUSIC (With Eileen Fowler) (Various artists).
Tracks / Warm-up: *Various artists* / Tangotime: *Various artists* / Ragtime swing: *Various artists* / Criss cross: *Various artists* / Beguine: *Various artists*.
LP. Cat no: **REC 382**. Released on BBC, May '80 by BBC Records, Taylors **Deleted** Apr '89.
MC. Cat no: **ZCM 382**. Released on BBC, May '80 by BBC Records, Taylors **Deleted** Apr '89.

ENJOY YOUR SLIMMING WITH EILEEN FOWLER (Various artists).
Note: Eileen Fowler special exercises to music for men and women. With advice on sensible eating by Silhouette Slimming Club in a special slimming leaflet enclosed in the sleeve.
LP. Cat no: **REC 284**. Released on BBC, Oct '77 by BBC Records, Taylors **Deleted** '87.
MC. Cat no: **ZCM 284**. Released on BBC, Oct '77 by BBC Records, Taylors **Deleted** '88.

EVERYDAY YOGA (Lyn Marshall).
Note: Includes: Complete Breath, Standing Stretch Into The Refresher, Triangle, Leg Grip, Front Push Up, Cat, Fish, Coil, Back Push Up, Slow Motion Firming and Leg Over Into Deep Relaxation.
LP. Cat no: **REH 461**. Released on BBC, Feb '83 by BBC Records, Taylors **Deleted** Apr '89.
MC. Cat no: **ZCR 461**. Released on BBC, Feb '83 by BBC Records, Taylors.

EX 'N' DANS (Various artists).
MC. Cat no: **TDS 012**. Released on Dansan, Jul '82 by Spartan, Taylors.

EXPECTANT FATHER (Edited by Betty Parsons) (Richard O'Sullivan).
LP. Cat no: **LEG 5**. Released on Lifestyle, Nov '82 by Jive Records.

EXPECTANT MOTHER (Edited by Betty Parsons) (Esther Rantzen).
LP. Cat no: **LEG 4**. Released on Lifestyle, Nov '82 by Jive Records.

FAMILY KEEP FIT WITH EILEEN FOWLER (Various artists).
Note: This third Eileen Fowler disc has been introduced with all the family in mind based on the radio 4 "Today" Family Keep Fit series. Ideal for home or class.
LP. Cat no: **REC 174**. Released on BBC, Jun '78 by BBC Records, Taylors **Deleted** '83.

FIT TO SKI (Divina Galica).
MC. Cat no: **MCFR 103**. Released on Conifer, '88 by Conifer Records, Jazz Music.

GET FIT WITH THE GREEN GODDESS (Diana Moran).
Tracks / Introduction - Breakfast time / Morning dance (Legs and ankles.) / Wake up everybody (the great stretch) / Chi Mai (Neck and shoulders) / Hill Street blues / I heard it through the grapevine (Boobs, Chest & Underarms) / (They long to be) close to you / Daybreak (Hips) / I'm not in love (Back.) / Rise / Whiter shade of pale, A / Green goddess, The / In the Summertime (exercises for legs) / Who pays the ferryman? ((back and leg exercises)) / Relax.
LP. Cat no: **REH 479**. Released on BBC, '83 by BBC Records, Taylors **Deleted** Apr '89.
MC. Cat no: **ZCR 479**. Released on BBC, '83 by BBC Records, Taylors **Deleted** Jun '91.

GET INTO SHAPE AFTER CHILDBIRTH (Gillian Fletcher).
Note: Produced by the National Childbirth Trust.
MCSET. Cat no: **RC 73**. Released on Random Century, Mar '93 by Random Century Audiobooks, Conifer Records. Note: ISBN no. 1856861015

HIP AND THIGH WORKOUT (Rosemary Conley).
MCSET. Cat no: **RC 7**. Released on Random Century, '91 by Random Century Audiobooks, Conifer Records. Note: ISBN no. 185686006X. 40 mins approx.

INCH LOSS PLAN (Rosemary Conley).
MCSET. Cat no: **RC 14**. Released on Random Century, '91 by Random Century Audiobooks, Conifer Records. Note: 2 Cassettes. ISBN no. 185686023X. 2hrs. approx.

JANE FONDA WORKOUT (Various artists).
Tracks / Warm-up: *Various artists* / Biceps curls: *Various artists* / Push ups: *Various artists* / Standing stretches: *Various artists* / Buttocks extension: *Various artists* / Lower body stretches: *Various artists* / Upright rows: *Various artists* / Lateral raises: *Various artists* / Aerobics: *Various artists* / Lunges, quad stretch: *Various artists* / Abdominals: *Various artists*.
LP. Cat no: **K 925851 1**. Released on Atlantic, Mar '89 by Warner Music International (WEA) **Deleted** Jul '90.
MC. Cat no: **K 925851 4**. Released on Atlantic, Mar '89 by Warner Music International (WEA).
CD. Cat no: **K 925851 2**. Released on Atlantic, Mar '89 by Warner Music International (WEA).

JANE FONDA'S WORKOUT RECORD (Various artists).
Tracks / Can you feel it?: *Various artists* / In your letter: *Various artists* / Stomp: *Various artists* / Bridge over troubled water: *Various artists* / Night (feel like getting down): *Various artists* / Bricklayer's beautiful daughter, The: *Various artists*.
LP. Cat no: **CBS 88581**. Released on CBS, Jul '82 by Sony Music, Solomon & Peres, Outlet Records **Deleted** Jan '90.
MC. Cat no: **40 88581**. Released on CBS, Jul '82 by Sony Music, Solomon & Peres, Outlet Records.

JANE FONDA'S WORKOUT RECORD FOR PREGNANCY, BIRTH (Various artists).
Tracks / On posture: *Fonda, Jane* / Breathing: *Fonda, Jane* / Warm-up: *Fonda, Jane* / Daily exercise routine: *Fonda, Jane* / Pregnancy workout, The: *Fonda, Jane*.
2LP. Cat no: **CBS 88620**. Released on CBS, Jun '83 by Sony Music, Solomon & Peres, Outlet Records **Deleted** '85.
MCSET. Cat no: **40 88620**. Released on CBS, Jun '83 by Sony Music, Solomon & Peres, Outlet Records.

KEEP IN SHAPE SYSTEM (Arlene Phillips) (Various artists).
LP. Cat no: **SUP 1**. Released on Ferroway, Aug '82.
MC. Cat no: **ZCSUPS 1**. Released on Ferroway, Aug '82.

KEEP IN SHAPE, VOL.2 (Arlene Phillips) (Various artists).
LP. Cat no: **SUP 2**. Released on Ferroway, Nov '83.
MC. Cat no: **ZCSUP 2**. Released on Ferroway, Nov '83.

LOTTE BERK EXERCISE RECORD - GET PHYSICAL (Lotte Berk).
LP. Cat no: **WW 5122**. Released on Warwick, '82 by Warwick Records, Solomon & Peres, Taylors, Henry Hadaway Organisation, Multiple Sound Distributors.
MC. Cat no: **WW 4 5122**. Released on Warwick, '82 by Warwick Records, Solomon & Peres, Taylors, Henry Hadaway Organisation, Multiple Sound Distributors.

MIND-BODY TEMPO (60 Beats a Minute Music) (Janalea Hoffman).
MC. Cat no: **C 190**. Released on New World Cassettes, '88.

MUSIC 'N' MOTION (Christina Gregg).
LP. Cat no: **WW 5041**. Released on Warwick, May '78 by Warwick Rec-

ords, Solomon & Peres, Taylors, Henry Hadaway Organisation, Multiple Sound Distributors **Deleted** '83.

NATURAL WAY TO ALLEVIATE STRESS (Hypnostress) (Henry Milton).
MC. Cat no: **HMH 05**. Released on Schiltron Audio Books, '91 by Schiltron Publishing.

NATURAL WAY TO CONTROL AGORAPHOBIA (Henry Milton).
MC. Cat no: **HMH 08**. Released on Schiltron Audio Books, '91 by Schiltron Publishing.

NATURAL WAY TO CONTROL NAIL BITING (Henry Milton).
MC. Cat no: **HMH 11**. Released on Schiltron Audio Books, '91 by Schiltron Publishing.

NATURAL WAY TO INCREASE CONFIDENCE (Henry Milton).
MC. Cat no: **HMH 06**. Released on Schiltron Audio Books, '91 by Schiltron Publishing.

NATURAL WAY TO LEARN SELF HYPNOSIS AND RELAX DEEPLY (Henry Milton).
MC. Cat no: **HMH 03**. Released on Schiltron Audio Books, '91 by Schiltron Publishing.

NATURAL WAY TO OVERCOME FEAR OF FLYING (Henry Milton).
MC. Cat no: **HMH 10**. Released on Schiltron Audio Books, '91 by Schiltron Publishing.

NATURAL WAY TO OVERCOME INSOMNIA (Hypnosleep) (Henry Milton).
MC. Cat no: **HMH 07**. Released on Schiltron Audio Books, '91 by Schiltron Publishing.

NATURAL WAY TO REDUCE DRIVING TEST NERVES (Henry Milton).
MC. Cat no: **HMH 09**. Released on Schiltron Audio Books, '91 by Schiltron Publishing.

NATURAL WAY TO REDUCE EXAM NERVES (And Improve Revision and Recall) (Henry Milton).
MC. Cat no: **HMH 04**. Released on Schiltron Audio Books, '91 by Schiltron Publishing.

NATURAL WAY TO SLIM, THE (Hypnoslim) (Henry Milton).
MC. Cat no: **HMH 01**. Released on Schiltron Audio Books, '91 by Schiltron Publishing.

NATURAL WAY TO STOP SMOKING (Hypnosmoke) (Henry Milton).
MC. Cat no: **HMH 02**. Released on Schiltron Audio Books, '91 by Schiltron Publishing.

PRIME TIME WORKOUT WITH JANE FONDA (Various artists).
LP. Cat no: **9603821**. Released on Elektra, '89 by Warner Music International (WEA).

SHAPE UP AND DANCE (Volume 1) (Felicity Kendal).
Note: Tracks include: Isn't She Lovely, Dancing Queen, YMCA, I Will Survive, Making Your Mind Up and Being With You.
LP. Cat no: **LEG 1**. Released on Lifestyle, '83 by Jive Records **Deleted** Mar '90.
MC. Cat no: **LEGC 1**. Released on Lifestyle, '83 by Jive Records **Deleted** Jul '90.

SHAPE UP FOR MOTHERHOOD (Various artists).
LP. Cat no: **LEG 6**. Released on Lifestyle, '83 by Jive Records.
MC. Cat no: **LEGC 6**. Released on Lifestyle, '83 by Jive Records.

SLIM TO RHYTHM WITH EILEEN FOWLER (Various artists).
Note: Eileen Fowler presents her second disc for BBC records, this time based on slimming exercises broadcast in BBC radio's today programme, with gay, specially composed music by Helen Shields played by a rhythm group.
LP. Cat no: **REC 132**. Released on BBC, Jun '78 by BBC Records, Taylors **Deleted** '88.

TECHNIQUES FOR GREATER BEAUTY & GREATER VITALITY (Unknown narrator(s)).
MCSET. Cat no: **0671684205**. Released on Simon & Schuster, '92 by Simon & Schuster Ltd. Note: 2 Cassettes

TECHNIQUES FOR GREATER ENERGY AND VITALITY (Unknown narrator(s)).
MCSET. Cat no: **0671678191**. Released on Simon & Schuster, '91 by Simon & Schuster Ltd.

TECHNIQUES FOR PMS RELIEF AND GREATER VITALITY (Unknown narrator(s)).
MCSET. Cat no: **0671684310**. Released on Simon & Schuster, '91 by Simon & Schuster Ltd. Note: 2 Cassettes

TECHNIQUES FOR WEIGHT LOSS AND GREATER VITALITY (Unknown narrator(s)).
MCSET. Cat no: **0671684302**. Released on Simon & Schuster, '91 by Simon & Schuster Ltd.

TRANSCENDENTAL MEDITATION (Various narrators).
MC. Cat no: **SV 078C**. Released on Sound & Vision (2), '91 by Scripture Union.

WORK THAT BODY (Jackie Genova).
LP. Cat no: **ILPS 9732**. Released on Island, May '83 by Island Records, Outlet Records, Solomon & Peres, Projection, Jetstar **Deleted** '87.
MC. Cat no: **ICT 9732**. Released on Island, May '83 by Island Records, Outlet Records, Solomon & Peres, Projection, Jetstar **Deleted** '87.

WORK THAT BODY INTO SKI SHAPE (Jackie Genova).
Tracks / Warm up / Aerobics for skiers / Strengthening and fatigue-resisting exercises / Cool down.
MC. Cat no: **ICT 4749**. Released on Island, Nov '83 by Island Records, Outlet Records, Solomon & Peres, Projection, Jetstar.

WORKOUT RECORD NEW AND IMPROVED (Various artists).
Tracks / Wanna be startin' something: *Jackson, Michael* / Keep the fire burning: *REO Speedwagon* / Rhythm, part 1: *Correa, Dean* / Dance for me: *Correa, Dean* / Megatron man: *Cowley, Patrick* / Do you wanna funk: *Sylvester* / One hundred ways: *Jones, Quincy & James Ingram* / X-cit-mental: *Correa, Dean*.
2LP. Cat no: **CBS 88640**. Released on CBS, Sep '84 by Sony Music, Solomon & Peres, Outlet Records **Deleted** Jan '90.
MCSET. Cat no: **40 88640**. Released on CBS, Sep '84 by Sony Music, Solomon & Peres, Outlet Records.

Heaney, Seamus

O, THE NORTHERN MUSE (Biography) (Seamus Heaney & John Montague).
LP. Cat no: **CCT 4**. Released on Claddagh (Ireland), Aug '88 by Claddagh Records (Ireland), Projection, Impetus Records, Jazz Music, Roots Records, C.M. Distribution, Outlet Records, Taylors.

Hebbel, F

AGNES BERNAUER (Edited By Mary Garland) (Unknown narrator(s)).
Note: Hebbel's attempt to accommodate two seperate themes in the play is considered. In German.
MC. Cat no: **G 7842**. Released on Exeter Tapes, '91 by Drakes Educational Associates.

JUDITH (Edited By Mary Garland) (Unknown narrator(s)).
Note: Hebbel's views on the apocryphal story and his adaption of the source material for his first tragedy are considered.
MC. Cat no: **G 7841**. Released on Exeter Tapes, '91 by Drakes Educational Associates.

Hebrew

HEBREW TRAVEL PACK (Unknown narrator(s)).
Note: Contains a Hugo phrase book.
MC. Cat no: **852851820**. Released on Hugo Languages, '92 by Hugo Language Books Limited.

LANGUAGE COURSE - HEBREW (MODERN) (Unknown narrator(s)).
LPS. Cat no: **0747302480**. Released on Linguaphone, Apr '82 by Linguaphone Institute, Taylors, Century Records (USA), Bond Street Music.

Heinlein, Robert

FORRESTAL LECTURE AT THE U.S. NAVAL ACADEMY (Robert Heinlein).
Note: Author reads their works and discuss their formative influences.
MC. Cat no: **AS 23**. Released on Sussex Tapes, '91 by Sussex Publications Ltd..

Hellman, Lillian

INTERVIEW WITH LILLIAN HELLMAN, AN (Liilan Hellman).
Note: Author reads their works and dis-

cuss their formative influences.
MC. Cat no: **AS 24.** Released on Sussex Tapes, '91 by Sussex Publications Ltd..

Henderson, Hamish
FREEDOM COME ALL YE (Biography).
LP. Cat no: **CCA 7.** Released on Claddagh (Ireland), Aug '88 by Claddagh Records (Ireland), Projection, Impetus Records, Jazz Music, Roots Records, C.M. Distribution, Outlet Records, Taylors.

Henry VIII
HENRY VIII (History for ages 8+) (Unknown narrator(s)).
Note: Book and cassette.
MC. Cat no: **PLBH 100.** Released on Tell-A-Tale, Mar '84 by Pickwick Records, Taylors, Clyde Factors.

Hepburn, Katherine
ME (Katherine Hepburn).
MCSET. Cat no: **RC 32.** Released on Random Century, '91 by Random Century Audiobooks, Conifer Records.
Note: 2 Cassettes. ISBN no. 1856860418. Playing time 3hrs approx.

Heyerdahl, Thor
ACHIEVEMENT (Unknown narrator(s)).
MC. Cat no: **SS 126.** Released on Seminar Cassettes, Oct '81 by Seminar Cassettes.
KON-TIKI EXPEDITION (Tim Pigott-Smith).
MCSET. Cat no: **LFP 7282.** Released on Listen For Pleasure, Feb '87 by EMI Records.
KON-TIKI EXPEDITION (Tim Pigott-Smith).
Note: Abridged version.
MCSET. Cat no: **1019N.** Released on Travellers Tales, '91 by Travellers Tales. Note: 2 Cassettes.

Hill, Susan
MAGIC APPLE TREE, THE (Delia Corrie).
MCSET. Cat no: **1009N.** Released on Travellers Tales, '91 by Travellers Tales. Note: 6 Cassettes.
MCSET. Cat no: **1854961179.** Released on Soundings, '91 by Soundings Records, Bond Street Music. Note: 6 Cassettes.

Hillaby, John
JOURNEY THROUGH BRITAIN (John Hillaby).
MCSET. Cat no: **1027N.** Released on Travellers Tales, '91 by Travellers Tales.
MCSET. Cat no: **IAB 87121.** Released on Isis Audio Books, '91. Note : 8 Cassettes.
JOURNEY TO THE JADE SEA (John Hillaby).
MCSET. Cat no: **1060N.** Released on Travellers Tales, '91 by Travellers

Tales. Note: 6 Cassettes.
MCSET. Cat no: **IAB 89071.** Released on Travellers Tales, '91 by Travellers Tales. Note: 6 Cassettes.

Hindi
BOL CHAAL (Hindi/Urdu Language Courses) (Unknown narrator(s)).
MCSET. Cat no: **PTT 326.** Released on BBC Publications, '91. Note : 2 Cassettes.
GET BY IN HINDI (Language Courses) (Unknown narrator(s)).
Note: Each book contains phrases and conversations.
MCSET. Cat no: **PTT 324.** Released on BBC Publications, '91.
LANGUAGE COURSE - HINDI (Unknown narrator(s)).
LPS. Cat no: **0747302502.** Released on Linguaphone, Apr '82 by Linguaphone Institute, Taylors, Century Records (USA), Bond Street Music.

Hiscock, E
AROUND THE WORLD IN WANDERER III (Unknown narrator(s)).
MCSET. Cat no: **1854961209.** Released on Soundings, '91 by Soundings Records, Bond Street Music. Note: 6 Cassettes.

History
16TH CENTURY SCOTLAND (Gordon Donaldson & Lady Antonia Fraser).
MC. Cat no: **H 9.** Released on Sussex Tapes, '91 by Sussex Publications Ltd..
AGE OF APPEASEMENT IN EUROPE 1918-1929, THE (Donald Watt & Geoffrey Warner).
MCSET. Cat no: **HUA 044.** Released on AVP, '91 by AVP Publishing.
AGRICULTURE IN ENGLAND (1650-1900) (E. Collins & Eric Jones).
MC. Cat no: **H 8.** Released on Sussex Tapes, '91 by Sussex Publications Ltd..
CENTRE AND THE PROVINCES, THE (1603-1640) (John Morrill & Kevin Sharpe).
MC. Cat no: **H 22.** Released on Sussex Tapes, '91 by Sussex Publications Ltd..
CHARLES 1 AND PURITANISM (G.E. Aylmer & William Lamont).
MC. Cat no: **H 4.** Released on Sussex Tapes, '91 by Sussex Publications Ltd..
CHARLES II (Lady Antonia Fraser & Richard Ollard).
MC. Cat no: **H 21.** Released on Sussex Tapes, '91 by Sussex Publications Ltd..
CHARTISM (John Breuilly).
MCSET. Cat no: **HEA 019.** Released on AVP, '91 by AVP Publishing.
CHINA - REVOLUTION AND FOREIGN POLICY (China - Ideolgy and Power) (Dr. Coral Bell & Michael Yahuda).
MCSET. Cat no: **HMA 003.** Released on AVP, '91 by AVP Publishing.
CHURCH OF ENGLAND (The Eli-

zabethan Settlement, and after) (Claire Cross & P. Collinson).
MC. Cat no: **H 28.** Released on Sussex Tapes, '91 by Sussex Publications Ltd..
COLD WAR IN EUROPE 1945-1950, THE (The Cold War Worldwide) (Robert L Frazier & Peter Boyle).
MCSET. Cat no: **HUA 060.** Released on AVP, '91 by AVP Publishing.
COURT AND KINGDOM (Felicity Heal & David Starkey).
MC. Cat no: **H 24.** Released on Sussex Tapes, '91 by Sussex Publications Ltd..
CROMWELL, SCIENCE AND SOCIETY (Christopher Hill & Donald Pennington).
MC. Cat no: **H 3.** Released on Sussex Tapes, '91 by Sussex Publications Ltd..
DARWIN AND UTILITARIANISM (J.W. Burrow & W.E.S. Thomas).
MC. Cat no: **HA 5.** Released on Sussex Tapes, '91 by Sussex Publications Ltd..
DEVELOPMENT OF INDIA, THE (Up to and Since 1900) (Dr. Clive Dewey & Dr. Peter Robb).
MCSET. Cat no: **HMA 006.** Released on AVP, '91 by AVP Publishing.
DISRAELI (Lord Blake & Derek Beales).
MC. Cat no: **HA 7.** Released on Sussex Tapes, '91 by Sussex Publications Ltd.
ELIZABETH I (Joel Hurstfield & Dr. Penny Williams).
MCSET. Cat no: **HEAL 002.** Released on AVP, '91 by AVP Publishing.
ELIZABETHAN ENGLAND (Jole Hurtsfield & A.G.R. Smith).
MC. Cat no: **H 2.** Released on Sussex Tapes, '91 by Sussex Publications Ltd..
ENGLISH AND DUTCH TRADE (1500-1700) (Ralph Davis & F.J. Fisher).
MC. Cat no: **H 5.** Released on Sussex Tapes, '91 by Sussex Publications Ltd..
ENGLISH MONARCHS (Line of Succession) (Unknown narrator(s)).
MC. Cat no: **WHC 004.** Released on Sound Fact, Jul '81 by Sound Fact Records, Sound Fact Records.
GEORGE III (Unknown narrator(s)).
MC. Cat no: **HA 12.** Released on Sussex Tapes, '91 by Sussex Publications Ltd..
GERMAN FOREIGN POLICY 1918-1970 (Donald Watt & A J Ryder).
MCSET. Cat no: **HUA 042.** Released on AVP, '91 by AVP Publishing.
GLADSTONE AND THE LIBERAL PARTY (M D R Foot & Dr R T D Shannon).
MCSET. Cat no: **HEA 014.** Released on AVP, '91 by AVP Publishing.
HENRY VII (S.B. Chrimes & R.L. Storey).
MC. Cat no: **H 11.** Released on Sussex Tapes, '91 by Sussex Publications Ltd..
HENRY VIII (Geoffrey Elton & J.J. Scarisbrick).

MC. Cat no: **H 1**. Released on Sussex Tapes, '91 by Sussex Publications Ltd..
HISTORIAN ON HISTORY, A (Lord Bullock).
MC. Cat no: **PH 1**. Released on Sussex Tapes, '91 by Sussex Publications Ltd..
HISTORY REFLECTED, ELIZABETH 1, THE ARMADA 1588 (Various narrators).
MCSET. Cat no: **414 712-4**. Released on Argo (Polygram), Oct '84 by PolyGram Classics **Deleted** Jan '89.
JAMES I (Robert Ashton & William Lamont).
MC. Cat no: **H 16**. Released on Sussex Tapes, '91 by Sussex Publications Ltd..
KINGS AND QUEENS OF ENGLAND (1,000 years of English Monarchy) (Unknown narrator(s)).
MC. Cat no: **WHC 006**. Released on Sound Fact, Jul '81 by Sound Fact Records, Sound Fact Records.
KINGS AND QUEENS OF ENGLAND (Book 1) (Unknown narrator(s)).
Note: Book and cassette. History for ages 8+.
MC. Cat no: **PLBH 108**. Released on Tell-A-Tale, Mar '84 by Pickwick Records, Taylors, Clyde Factors.
KINGS AND QUEENS OF ENGLAND (Book 2) (Unknown narrator(s)).
Note: Book and cassette. History for ages 8+
MC. Cat no: **PLBH 109**. Released on Tell-A-Tale, Mar '84 by Pickwick Records, Taylors, Clyde Factors.
LEAGUE OF NATIONS, THE (Frank Hardie & M Robertson).
MCSET. Cat no: **HUA 039**. Released on AVP, '91 by AVP Publishing.
MARY TUDOR (Christopher Haigh & David Loades).
MC. Cat no: **H 29**. Released on Sussex Tapes, '91 by Sussex Publications Ltd..
PLANNING FOR PEACE 1914-1918 (The Inconclusive Peace Settlement 1919-1920) (Keith Robbins & Zara Steiner).
MCSET. Cat no: **HUA 007**. Released on AVP, '91 by AVP Publishing.
POST-WAR DIVISION IN EUROPE, THE (The Post-War Intergration of Western Europe) (Max Beloff & James Joll. Stevenson).
MCSET. Cat no: **HUA 010**. Released on AVP, '91 by AVP Publishing.
REFORMATION IN ENGLAND, THE (C S L Davies & Jennifer Loach).
MCSET. Cat no: **HEA 031**. Released on AVP, '91 by AVP Publishing.
REIGN OF EDWARD VI, THE (M.L. Bush & C.S.L. Davies).
MC. Cat no: **H 25**. Released on Sussex Tapes, '91 by Sussex Publications Ltd..
RESTORATION, THE (G.E. Aylmer & J.R. Jones).
MC. Cat no: **H 12**. Released on Sussex Tapes, '91 by Sussex Publications Ltd..
RISE OF THE NAZI PARTY, THE (The Nazi Sizure of Power) (Dr. Tim Mason & Dr. Jeremy Noakes).
MCSET. Cat no: **HUA 008**. Released on AVP, '91 by AVP Publishing.
ROBERT CECIL, LORD SALISBURY (Joel Hurtsfield & Peter Wilson).
MC. Cat no: **H 17**. Released on Sussex Tapes, '91 by Sussex Publications Ltd..
SAMUEL PEPYS (R.C. Latham & Richard Ollard).
MC. Cat no: **H 23**. Released on Sussex Tapes, '91 by Sussex Publications Ltd..
SIR ROBERT PEEL (Norman Gash & Dr Norman McCord).
MCSET. Cat no: **HEA 008**. Released on AVP, '91 by AVP Publishing.
SOVIET POLITICAL SYSTEM, THE (Archie Brown & Alex Pravda).
MCSET. Cat no: **HUA 053**. Released on AVP, '91 by AVP Publishing.
TEN KITTLE QUIRKS IN SCOTTISH HISTORY (Adapted by Nigel Tranter) (Unknown narrator(s)).
Note: Includes Stone of Destiny, Knighting of William Wallace and Queen Mary.
MC. Cat no: **SSC 027**. Released on Scotsoun, '91 by Scotsoun Recordings, Morley Audio Services.
THOMAS WOLSEY (J.J. Scarisbrick & Peter Gwyn).
MC. Cat no: **H 26**. Released on Sussex Tapes, '91 by Sussex Publications Ltd..
VICTORIAN ENGLAND (Dr Peter Clarke & O Anderson).
MCSET. Cat no: **HEA 045**. Released on AVP, '91 by AVP Publishing.
VIETNAM - THE HISTORY OF AMERICAN INVOLVEMENT (Vietnam - The Crossroads of American Foreign) (Dr. Peter Lyon & Dr. Michael Leifer).
MCSET. Cat no: **HMA 002**. Released on AVP, '91 by AVP Publishing.
WILLIAM CECIL, LORD BURGHLEY (Joel Hurtsfield & Peter Wilson).
MC. Cat no: **H 15**. Released on Sussex Tapes, '91 by Sussex Publications Ltd..

Hitler, Adolf
ADOLF HITLER (Biography) (Stephen Thorne).
MC. Cat no: **L 6**. Released on Green Dragon, '91 by Green Dragon Audio Visual.
MC. Cat no: **DHM 17**. Released on Sussex Tapes, '91 by Sussex Publications Ltd..

Hocken, Sheila
EMMA AND CO. (Biography) (Rosemary Davies).
Note: A biography of Sheila Hocken and her guide dog Emma.
MCSET. Cat no: **OAS 90032**. Released on Oasis Audio Books, '91 by Isis Audio Books. Note: 5 Cassettes.
MCSET. Cat no: **1083N**. Released on Travellers Tales, '91 by Travellers Tales. Note: 5 Cassettes.

Hodgson, David
LETTERS FROM A BOMBER PILOT (Biography) (Robin Browne).
Note: A biography of Bob Hodgson, compiled from his letters sent to family and friends during World War II, a war from which he never returned.
MCSET. Cat no: **OAS 90012**. Released on Oasis Audio Books, '91 by Isis Audio Books. Note: 3 Cassette set.
MCSET. Cat no: **1041A**. Released on Travellers Tales, '91 by Travellers Tales. Note: 3 Cassettes.

Hoey, Brian
ANNE: THE PRINCESS ROYAL (Her Life and Work) (Ronald Markham).
MCSET. Cat no: **OAS 10391**. Released on Oasis Audio Books, '91 by Isis Audio Books. Note: 6 Cassettes.
MCSET. Cat no: **1074A**. Released on Travellers Tales, '91 by Travellers Tales. Note: 6 Cassettes.

Holden, Edith
COUNTRY DIARY OF AN EDWARDIAN LADY (Francesca Annis).
LPS. Cat no: **WW 5077**. Released on Warwick, Nov '79 by Warwick Records, Solomon & Peres, Taylors, Henry Hadaway Organisation, Multiple Sound Distributors.
MC. Cat no: **WW 4 5077**. Released on Warwick, Nov '81 by Warwick Records, Solomon & Peres, Taylors, Henry Hadaway Organisation, Multiple Sound Distributors.

Holland
RISE AND FALL OF THE DUTCH REPUBLIC, THE (Geoffrey Parker & Charles Wilson).
MC. Cat no: **HE 16**. Released on Sussex Tapes, '91 by Sussex Publications Ltd..

Hope, Bob
THANKS FOR THE MEMORY (See under Carrick, Peter) (Garrick Hagon).

Hopkins, Gerald Manley
GERARD MANLEY HOPKINS (Graham Storey & Father A. Thomas).
Note: Pre-recorded discussions which show literary criticism as a living, evolving interchange.
MC. Cat no: **A29**. Released on Sussex Tapes, '9 by Sussex Publications Ltd..

Horse Racing
FIVE GRAND NATIONALS 1973-1977 (Various artists).
LP. Cat no: **REP 1**. Released on Unknown, '77 **Deleted** '82.

Hugo, Victor
LE LEGENDE DES SIECLES (Edited By Jean D. Biard) (Unknown narrator(s)).
Note: An assessment of the imaginitive, poetic and epic value of this work by Victor Hugo with close reference to the text. In French.
MC. Cat no: **F 7634.** Released on Exeter Tapes, '91 by Drakes Educational Associates.

Hungarian
BASIC HUNGARIAN (Volume 1) (Unknown narrator(s)).
MCSET. Cat no: **U 500.** Released on Audio Forum (Language courses), '91. Note: 12 Cassettes
BASIC HUNGARIAN (Volume 2) (Unknown narrator(s)).
MCSET. Cat no: **U 550.** Released on Audio Forum (Language courses), '91. Note: 26 Cassettes
HUNGARIAN TRAVEL PACK (Unknown narrator(s)).
Note: Contains a Hugo phrase book.
MC. Cat no: **852851685.** Released on Hugo Languages, '92 by Hugo Language Books Limited.

Icelandic
LANGUAGE COURSE - ICELANDIC (Unknown narrator(s)).
LPS. Cat no: **0747303231.** Released on Linguaphone, Apr '82 by Linguaphone Institute, Taylors, Century Records (USA), Bond Street Music.

Indian
LANGUAGES OF INDIA - PART 1 INDO-EUROPEAN (Edited By G. James) (Unknown narrator(s)).
MC. Cat no: **IN 7850.** Released on Exeter Tapes, '91 by Drakes Educational Associates.
LANGUAGES OF INDIA - PART 2 NON-INDO EUROPEAN (Edited By G.James) (Unknown narrator(s)).
MC. Cat no: **IN 7851.** Released on Exeter Tapes, '91 by Drakes Educational Associates.

Ionesco, E
RHINOCEROS (Edited By H.D. Lewis) (Unknown narrator(s)).
Note: An analysis of the play and its place in the development of Ionesco's theatre as a whole.
MC. Cat no: **F 7637.** Released on Exeter Tapes, '91 by Drakes Educational Associates.
TUEUR SANS GAGES (Edited By Philip Thody) (Unknown narrator(s)).
Note: An account of the play showing Ionesco as a playwright of the absurd. An examination of the play's anti-realism stance and the problems this poses for a producer.
MC. Cat no: **F 7928.** Released on Exeter Tapes, '91 by Drakes Educational Associates.

Irish...
IRISH-ENGLISH DICTIONARIES AND HOW TO USE THEM (Edited By Tomas De Bhaldraithe) (Unknown narrator(s)).
MC. Cat no: **IR 7930.** Released on Exeter Tapes, '91 by Drakes Educational Associates.
LANGUAGE COURSE - IRISH (Unknown narrator(s)).
LPS. Cat no: **0747302510.** Released on Linguaphone, Apr '82 by Linguaphone Institute, Taylors, Century Records (USA), Bond Street Music.

Isabella
ISABELLA OF CASTILE & LEON (Biography) (Valentine Palmer).
MC. Cat no: **FW 5.** Released on Green Dragon, '91 by Green Dragon Audio Visual.
MC. Cat no: **DHM 2.** Released on Sussex Tapes, '91 by Sussex Publications Ltd..

Italian
BUONGIORNO ITALIA (Language Courses) (Unknown narrator(s)).
LPS. Cat no: **OP 260/61/62.** Released on BBC Publications, Jun '83.
MCSET. Cat no: **PTT 260/61/62.** Released on BBC Publications, Jun '83.
GET BY IN ITALIAN (Language Courses) (Unknown narrator(s)).
Note: Each book contains phrases and conversations.
MC. Cat no: **PTT 254/5.** Released on BBC Publications, Jun '83.
GET BY TRAVEL PACKS (Language Courses) (Unknown narrator(s)).
MCSET. Cat no: **PACK 2254.** Released on BBC Publications, '91. Note: 2 Cassettes.
IL PROBLEMA DELL' UNIFICAZIONE LINGUISTICA ITALI (Edited By Luciano Giannelli) (Unknown narrator(s)).
Note: An account of the linguistic situation in nineteenth century Italy and of contemporary opinions on language unification. In Italian.
MC. Cat no: **I 7937.** Released on Exeter Tapes, '91 by Drakes Educational Associates.
ITALIA, ANNI '80: CORSO DI LINGUA E CULTURA (Edited By Noemi Messora and Luisa Quartermaine) (Unknown narrator(s)).
Note: Course for students with a basic knowledge of Italian, arranged as 6 units.
MC. Cat no: **I 7860.** Released on Exeter Tapes, '91 by Drakes Educational Associates.
ITALIAN AT THE WHEEL (Unknown narrator(s)).
Note: Includes:- sixteen information cards.
MCSET. Cat no: **852851715.** Released on Hugo Languages, '92 by Hugo Language Books Limited. Note: 4 Cassettes.

ITALIAN BETWEEN PAST AND PRESENT (Edited By Diego Zancani) (Unknown narrator(s)).
Note: Talk in English with Italian version.
MC. Cat no: **I 7335.** Released on Exeter Tapes, '91 by Drakes Educational Associates.
ITALIAN CASSETTE COURSE (Unknown narrator(s)).
Note: Includes:- Three months book and an instruction leaflet.
MCSET. Cat no: **852851758.** Released on Hugo Languages, '92 by Hugo Language Books Limited. Note: 4 Cassettes. Playing time 4hrs.
ITALIAN FOR TRAVEL (Unknown narrator(s)).
MC. Cat no: **BCP 012.** Released on Berlitz Language Courses, '88, Conifer Records.
ITALIAN LANGUAGE BASICS (Unknown narrator(s)).
MC. Cat no: **BMC 008.** Released on Berlitz Language Courses, '88, Conifer Records.
ITALIAN TRAVEL PACK (Unknown narrator(s)).
Note: Contains a Hugo phrase book.
MC. Cat no: **852850891.** Released on Hugo Languages, '92 by Hugo Language Books Limited.
ITALY TRAVEL KIT (Unknown narrator(s)).
MC. Cat no: **BTK 007.** Released on Berlitz Language Courses, '88, Conifer Records.
LA QUESTIONE DELLA LINGUA NEL RINASCIMENTS (Edited By Franco Musarra) (Unknown narrator(s)).
Note: Traces the development of the Italian language since the renaissance. In Italian.
MC. Cat no: **I 7922.** Released on Exeter Tapes, '91 by Drakes Educational Associates.
LANGUAGE COURSE - ITALIAN VOL. 1 (Unknown narrator(s)).
LPS. Cat no: **0747302553.** Released on Linguaphone, Apr '82 by Linguaphone Institute, Taylors, Century Records (USA), Bond Street Music.
LANGUAGE COURSE - ITALIAN VOL. 2 (Travel Pack) (Unknown narrator(s)).
LPS. Cat no: **0747306001.** Released on Linguaphone, Apr '82 by Linguaphone Institute, Taylors, Century Records (USA), Bond Street Music.
LINGUAPHONE ITALIAN TRAVELLERS (Language Courses) (Unknown narrator(s)).
MC. Cat no: **0747306842.** Released on Linguaphone, '91 by Linguaphone Institute, Taylors, Century Records (USA), Bond Street Music.
L'ITALIA DAL VIVO (Language Courses) (Unknown narrator(s)).
LPS. Cat no: **OP 266/8.** Released on BBC Publications, Jun '83.

MCSET. Cat no: **PTT 266/8.** Released on BBC Publications, Jun '83. Note : A second stage Italian course (cassette version).

MODERN SPOKEN ITALIAN (Part A) (Unknown narrator(s)).
MCSET. Cat no: **Z 501.** Released on Audio Forum (Language courses), '91. Note: 8 Cassettes

MODERN SPOKEN ITALIAN (Part B) (Unknown narrator(s)).
MCSET. Cat no: **Z 551.** Released on Audio Forum (Language courses), '91. Note: 8 Cassettes

SENILITA (Adriano Giraldi).
Note: Written by Italo Svevo. In Italian.
MCSET. Cat no: **1019L.** Released on Travellers Tales, '91 by Travellers Tales. Note: 6 Cassettes.

SPEAK ITALIAN TODAY (Conversational Courses) (Unknown narrator(s)).
Note: Consists of a book and a 75-90 minute cassette.
MC. Cat no: **852851189.** Released on Hugo Languages, '92 by Hugo Language Books Limited.

WHEN IN ITALY (Language Courses) (Unknown narrator(s)).
Note: Includes a C60 cassette and phrase book with a 5000 word mini-dictionary.
MC. Cat no: **PTT 314.** Released on BBC Publications, '91.

Italy

CINEMA E LETTERATURA IN ITALIA 1945-1965 (Edited By Luciano Giannelli) (Unknown narrator(s)).
Note: The birth of neo-realism, Italian cinema and society from 1945 to 1965; Rossellini, De Sica, Pasolini, Visconti. In Italian.
MC. Cat no: **I 7981.** Released on Exeter Tapes, '91 by Drakes Educational Associates.

CLASSICAL REVOLUTION IN ITALIAN THEATRE 1500-152 (Edited By Richard Andrews) (Unknown narrator(s)).
MC. Cat no: **I 7959.** Released on Exeter Tapes, '91 by Drakes Educational Associates.

FASCISM IN ITALY 1919-1945 (Edited By Doug Thompson) (Unknown narrator(s)).
MC. Cat no: **I 7913.** Released on Exeter Tapes, '91 by Drakes Educational Associates.

I SUONI DELL ITALIANO E LE VARAINTI REGIONALI (Edited By Luciano Giannelli) (Unknown narrator(s)).
Note: The sounds of standard Italian and comments on the most important regional variations. In Italian.
MC. Cat no: **I 7936.** Released on Exeter Tapes, '91 by Drakes Educational Associates.

IL CINEMA ITALIANO DURANTE IL FASCISMO (Edited By Luisa Quartermaine) (Unknown narrator(s)).
Note: The Italian film production is looked at after the introduction of sound in 1930. The cinema industry is studied against the historical background of fascism. In Italian.
MC. Cat no: **I 7306.** Released on Exeter Tapes, '91 by Drakes Educational Associates.

IL FUTURISMO IN ITALIA (Edited By Aldo Nemesio) (Unknown narrator(s)).
Note: The origin, background and manifesto of the futurist movement in Italy and its social and political implications. In Italian.
MC. Cat no: **I 7853.** Released on Exeter Tapes, '91 by Drakes Educational Associates.

ITALIAN POLITICS SINCE WORLD WAR II - PART 1 (Edited By Martin Slater) (Unknown narrator(s)).
MC. Cat no: **I 7925.** Released on Exeter Tapes, '91 by Drakes Educational Associates.

ITALIAN POLITICS SINCE WORLD WAR II - PART 2 (Edited By Martin Slater) (Unknown narrator(s)).
MC. Cat no: **I 7926.** Released on Exeter Tapes, '91 by Drakes Educational Associates.

ITALIAN RISORGIMENTO, THE (Derek Beales & Dennis Mack Smith).
MC. Cat no: **HE 7.** Released on Sussex Tapes, '91 by Sussex Publications Ltd..

MODERN ITALIAN CINEMA (Edited By Luisa Quartermaine) (Unknown narrator(s)).
Note: In Italian.
MC. Cat no: **I 7687.** Released on Exeter Tapes, '91 by Drakes Educational Associates.

MUSSOLINI (Dennis Mack Smith & Adrian Lyttleton).
MCSET. Cat no: **HUA 019.** Released on AVP, '91 by AVP Publishing.

POLITICS IN POST-WAR ITALY: AN ASSESSMENT (Edited By L. Sponza) (Unknown narrator(s)).
Note: In Italian.
MC. Cat no: **I 7880.** Released on Exeter Tapes, '91 by Drakes Educational Associates.

ROLE OF THE CHURCH IN MODERN ITALIAN HISTORY, THE (Edited By John Pollard) (Unknown narrator(s)).
MC. Cat no: **I 7980.** Released on Exeter Tapes, '91 by Drakes Educational Associates.

UNIFICATION OF ITALY, THE (The Italian Revolutions of 1848 - 1849) (Harry Hearder & Dr. Stuart Woolf).
MCSET. Cat no: **HUA 025.** Released on AVP, '91 by AVP Publishing.

WOMAN WRITERS IN ITALY 1943-1956 (Edited By Ann Caeser) (Unknown narrator(s)).
MC. Cat no: **I 7321.** Released on Exeter Tapes, '91 by Drakes Educational Associates.

Jackson, Arthur

FURTHER TALES FROM A COUNTRY PRACTICE (David Telfer).
MCSET. Cat no: **1102N.** Released on Travellers Tales, '91 by Travellers Tales. Note: 4 Cassettes.
MCSET. Cat no: **185496402X.** Released on Bramhope, '91 by Ulverscroft Soundings. Note: 4 Cassettes.

MORE TALES FROM A COUNTRY PRACTICE (Unknown narrator(s)).
MCSET. Cat no: **1854963651.** Released on Soundings, '91 by Soundings Records, Bond Street Music. Note: 6 Cassettes.
MCSET. Cat no: **1095N.** Released on Travellers Tales, '91 by Travellers Tales. Note: 4 Cassettes.

TALES FROM A COUNTRY PRACTICE (Nigel Carrington).
MCSET. Cat no: **1092N.** Released on Travellers Tales, '91 by Travellers Tales. Note: 7 Cassettes.
MCSET. Cat no: **1854963406.** Released on Soundings, '91 by Soundings Records, Bond Street Music. Note: 7 Cassettes.

James, Clive

FALLING TOWARDS ENGLAND (Clive James).
MCSET. Cat no: **LFP 7364.** Released on Listen For Pleasure, Nov '88 by EMI Records.

UNRELIABLE MEMOIRS (Clive James).
MCSET. Cat no: **LFP 7304.** Released on Listen For Pleasure, Sep '87 by EMI Records.

Japan

INTRODUCTION TO NO DRAMA, AN (Unknown narrator(s)).
MC. Cat no: **J 7767.** Released on Exeter Tapes, '91 by Drakes Educational Associates.

Japanese

BEGINNING JAPANESE (Part 1) (Unknown narrator(s)).
MCSET. Cat no: **J 401.** Released on Audio Forum (Language courses), '91. Note: 8 Cassettes and book.

BEGINNING JAPANESE (Part 2) (Unknown narrator(s)).
MC. Cat no: **J 409.** Released on Audio Forum (Language courses), '91. Note: 16 Cassettes

DOING BUSINESS IN JAPAN (Unknown narrator(s)).
Note: Thirty informative and interesting articles based on the experience of foreign born businessmen and journalists who have lived and worked in Japan. Recorded in English.
MCSET. Cat no: **JA 02.** Released on Audio Forum (Language courses), '91. Note: 3 Cassettes

EXECUTIVE JAPANESE (Volume 1) (Unknown narrator(s)).
MCSET. Cat no: **J 510.** Released on Audio Forum (Language courses), '91. Note: 2 Cassettes

EXECUTIVE JAPANESE (Volume 2) (Unknown narrator(s)).
MCSET. Cat no: **J 520.** Released on

Audio Forum (Language courses), '91. Note: 2 Cassettes

EXECUTIVE JAPANESE (Volume 3) (Unknown narrator(s)).
MCSET. Cat no: **J 530.** Released on Audio Forum (Language courses), '91. Note: 2 Cassettes

GET BY IN JAPANESE (Language Courses) (Unknown narrator(s)).
Note: Each book contains phrases and conversations.
MCSET. Cat no: **PTT 295.** Released on BBC Publications, '91. Note : 2 Cassettes.

GET BY TRAVEL PACKS (Language Courses) (Unknown narrator(s)).
MCSET. Cat no: **PACK 2295.** Released on BBC Publications, '92. Note : 2 Cassettes.

HOW TO END A JAPANESE SENTENCE (Edited By Satoshi Okano) (Unknown artist(s)).
MC. Cat no: **J 7798.** Released on Exeter Tapes, '91 by Drakes Educational Associates.

INTRODUCING THE JAPANESE LANGUAGE (Edited By Christopher Seeley) (Unknown narrator(s)).
MC. Cat no: **J 7763.** Released on Exeter Tapes, '91 by Drakes Educational Associates.

JAPANESE CASSETTE COURSE (Unknown narrator(s)).
Note: Includes:- 3 months' book and an instruction leaflet.
MCSET. Cat no: **852851049.** Released on Hugo Languages, '92 by Hugo Language Books Limited. Note: 4 Cassettes. Playing time 4hrs.

JAPANESE LANGUAGE AND PEOPLE (Language Courses) (Unknown narrator(s)).
Note: Comprehensive course on the language and culture of Japan. Plus book.
MCSET. Cat no: **PTT 371.** Released on BBC Publications, '91. Note : 5 Cassettes.

JAPANESE TRAVEL PACK (Unknown narrator(s)).
Note: Contains a Hugo phrase book.
MC. Cat no: **852851235.** Released on Hugo Languages, '92 by Hugo Language Books Limited. Note: 4 Cassettes. Playing time 4hrs.

LANGUAGE COURSE - JAPANESE (Unknown narrator(s)).
LPS. Cat no: **0747303266.** Released on Linguaphone, Apr '82 by Linguaphone Institute, Taylors, Century Records (USA), Bond Street Music.

READING JAPANESE (Unknown narrator(s)).
Note: This course is designed to introduce adult foreigners to written Japanese. The terminology, romanization and special symbols used in the Beginning Japanese courses are retained in this reader.
MCSET. Cat no: **J 450.** Released on Audio Forum (Language courses), '91. Note: 17 Cassettes

Jarry, A

UBU ROI (Edited By Jim Cutshall) (Unknown narrator(s)).
Note: Jarry's life and work is briefly surveyed with details of 'Ubu Roi's' publication and performance. The significance of the play in the history of the theatre.
MC. Cat no: **F 7328.** Released on Exeter Tapes, '91 by Drakes Educational Associates.

Joan Of Arc

JOAN OF ARC (Biography) (Valentine Palmer).
MC. Cat no: **FW 3.** Released on Green Dragon, '91 by Green Dragon Audio Visual.
MC. Cat no: **DHM 3.** Released on Sussex Tapes, '91 by Sussex Publications Ltd..
JOAN OF ARC (History for ages 8+) (Unknown narrator(s)).
Note: Book & cassette.
MC. Cat no: **PLBH 99.** Released on Tell-A-Tale, Mar '84 by Pickwick Records, Taylors, Clyde Factors.

Johnson, Amy

AMY JOHNSON (Biography) (Nigel Lambert).
MC. Cat no: **FW 7.** Released on Green Dragon, '91 by Green Dragon Audio Visual.
MC. Cat no: **DHM 21.** Released on Sussex Tapes, '91 by Sussex Publications Ltd..

Johnson & Boswell

JOURNEY TO THE WESTERN ISLES, A (Patrick Tull & Alexander Spencer).
Note: Excerpts. Authors are Samuel Johnson and James Boswell.
MCSET. Cat no: **1061N.** Released on Travellers Tales, '91 by Travellers Tales. Note: 4 Cassettes.
MCSET. Cat no: **IAB 89092.** Released on Isis Audio Books, '91. Note : Playing time: 4 hours 30 minutes. 4 Cassettes.

Johnson, Stanley

ANTARCTICA (Gordon Dulieu).
MCSET. Cat no: **1057N.** Released on Travellers Tales, '91 by Travellers Tales. Note: 8 Cassettes.
MCSET. Cat no: **OAS 89061.** Released on Oasis Audio Books, '91 by Isis Audio Books. Note: 8 Cassettes.

Joyce, James

JAMES JOYCE (Richard Ellman, Joyce Scholar & George Whitmore).
Note: Pre-recorded discussions which show literary criticism as a living, evolving interchange.
MC. Cat no: **A47.** Released on Sussex Tapes, '91 by Sussex Publications Ltd..
JAMES JOYCE STEPHEN HERO (Joseph Prescott).
MC. Cat no: **23070.** Released on Sussex Tapes, '91 by Sussex Publications Ltd..

JAMES JOYCE (Brendan Behan).
MC. Cat no: **23071.** Released on Sussex Tapes, '91 by Sussex Publications Ltd..
LAWRENCE AND JOYCE (See under Lawrence, D.H.) (Ian Gregor & Mark Kinhead-Weekes).

Kafka, Franz

DER PROZESS (Edited By William P. Hanson) (Unknown narrator(s)).
Note: A general introduction to some of the critical approaches to Franz Kafka's work.
MC. Cat no: **G 7564.** Released on Exeter Tapes, '91 by Drakes Educational Associates.
DIE VERWANDLING (Edited By William P. Hanson) (Unknown narrator(s)).
Note: A close textual commentary on the opening section of Franz Kafka's 'Die Verwandlung'.
MC. Cat no: **G 7573.** Released on Exeter Tapes, '91 by Drakes Educational Associates.

Kane, Charlotte

WELCOME TO THE PEACH TREE COTTAGE (Biography) (Judith Porter).
MCSET. Cat no: **1854965492.** Released on Trio, '92 by EMI Records.

Kataev, V

BELEET PARUS ODINOKII (Edited By R. Russell) (Unknown narrator(s)).
Note: A brief general introduction to Kataev, followed by a detailed examination of the work and its place in Soviet literature of the 1930's.
MC. Cat no: **R 7700.** Released on Exeter Tapes, '91 by Drakes Educational Associates.
VREMYA VPERYOD (Edited By Olive Stevens) (Unknown narrator(s)).
Note: A consideration of 'Time, Forward', showing Kataev's development as a writer and his own position in the idealistic period after the Russian revolution.
MC. Cat no: **R 7895.** Released on Exeter Tapes, '91 by Drakes Educational Associates.

Kazakov, Yu

SELECTED STORIES (Edited By M. Pursglove) (Unknown narrator(s)).
Note: An examination of Yu Kazakov's role in the history of post-Stalinist literature, concentrating on 'The Smell Of Bread', 'The Plain Girl' and 'Arcturus The Hound'.
MC. Cat no: **R 7315.** Released on Exeter Tapes, '91 by Drakes Educational Associates.

Keats

KEATS (Robert Gittings & Roger Sharrock).
Note: Pre-recorded discussions which show literary criticism as a living, evolving interchange.
MC. Cat no: **A28.** Released on Sussex

Tapes, '91 by Sussex Publications Ltd..

Kelly, Kitty
ELIZABETH TAYLOR (The Last Star) (Susan Stasberg).
Note: Also available on hanging format, catalogue number:- 0001387480.
MCSET. Cat no: **0001386557**. Released on Harper Collins, '91 by Harper Collins. Note: 2 Cassettes.

NANCY REAGAN (Unknown narrator(s)).
MCSET. Cat no: **0671739557**. Released on Simon & Schuster, '91 by Simon & Schuster Ltd.

Keneally, Thomas
SCHINDLER'S ARK (Gordon Dulieu).
MCSET. Cat no: **1062/3N**. Released on Travellers Tales, '91 by Travellers Tales.
MCSET. Cat no: **OAS 89092**. Released on Oasis Audio Books, '91 by Isis Audio Books. Note: 12 Cassettes.

Kermack, Mary
LANG SYNE IN THE EAST NEUK O FIFE (Unknown narrator(s)).
MC. Cat no: **SSC 069**. Released on Scotsoun, '91 by Scotsoun Recordings, Morley Audio Services.

Khayyam, Omar
RUBAIYAT OF OMAR KHAYYAM, THE (The Fourth Translation) (Alfred Drake).
MC. Cat no: **1023**. Released on Caedmon (USA), '88 by Caedmon Records (USA), Bond Street Music.

Kilvert, Rev. Francis
HE BEING DEAD YET SPEAKETH (Biography) (Timothy Davies).
2LP. Cat no: **SDX 309**. Released on Saydisc, Nov '80 by Amon Ra Records, Taylors, C.M. Distribution, Gamut Distribution **Deleted** '89.
MC. Cat no: **CSDX 309**. Released on Saydisc, Nov '80 by Amon Ra Records, Taylors, C.M. Distribution, Gamut Distribution.

King, Dr. Alexander
TECHNOLOGY TWO EDGED SWORD (Unknown narrator(s)).
MC. Cat no: **SS 112**. Released on Seminar Cassettes, Oct '81 by Seminar Cassettes.

WORLD AND MEN (Dr. Alexander King).
MC. Cat no: **SS 108**. Released on Seminar Cassettes, Oct '81 by Seminar Cassettes.

King, Martin Luther
MARTIN LUTHER KING (Biography) (Geoffrey Hinsliff).
MC. Cat no: **L 2**. Released on Green Dragon, '91 by Green Dragon Audio Visual.
MC. Cat no: **DHM 13**. Released on Sussex Tapes, '91 by Sussex Publications Ltd..

Kingston Platt, J
J KINGSTON PLATT (Memoirs of a Theatrical Colossus) (Peter Jones).
MCSET. Cat no: **ZBBC 1246**. Released on BBC Radio Collection, Jul '91 by BBC Records. Note: ISBN No: 0563 365137

Koestler, Arthur
UNCONSCIOUS FACTORS IN CREATIVITY (Arthur Koestler).
Note: Author reads their works and discuss their formative influences.
MC. Cat no: **AS 26**. Released on Sussex Tapes, '91 by Sussex Publications Ltd..

Kray, Reg & Ron
OUR STORY (With Fred Dinenage) (Roger Blake & Jim McManus).
MCSET. Cat no: **LFP 7445**. Released on Listen For Pleasure, Oct '89 by EMI Records. Note: Playing time: 2 hours 30 mins.

Krushchev, Nikita
NIKITA KHRUSHCHEV (Biography) (Stephen Thorne).
MC. Cat no: **L 8**. Released on Green Dragon, '91 by Green Dragon Audio Visual.
MC. Cat no: **DHM 18**. Released on Sussex Tapes, '91 by Sussex Publications Ltd..

Laclos, P
LES LIAISONS DANGEREUSES (Edited By Philip Thody) (Unknown narrator(s)).
Note: An analysis of P. Laclos' novel as a highly moral denunciation of the sexual immorality of the 18th century French aristocracy.
MC. Cat no: **F 7679**. Released on Exeter Tapes, '91 by Drakes Educational Associates.

Laine, Pascal
LA DENTELLIERE (Edited By Adrienne Mason) (Unknown narrator(s)).
Note: An analysis of Pascal Laine's views on the nature of fictional discourse and its application in La Dentelliere. With French quotations.
MC. Cat no: **F 7314**. Released on Exeter Tapes, '91 by Drakes Educational Associates.

Laing, R.D.
SCHIZOPHRENIA - A VIEWPOINT (R D Laing).
MC. Cat no: **PT 34**. Released on Psychology Today (USA), Oct '81 by Seminar Cassettes.

Lasgarn, Hugh
VET FOR ALL SEASONS (Ray Dunbobbin).
MCSET. Cat no: **1031N**. Released on Travellers Tales, '91 by Travellers Tales. Note: 5 Cassettes.
MCSET. Cat no: **1854961276**. Released on Bramhope, '91 by Ulverscroft Soundings. Note: 5 Cassettes.

VET IN A STORM (Ray Dunbobbin).
MCSET. Cat no: **1037N**. Released on Travellers Tales, '91 by Travellers Tales. Note: 5 Cassettes.
MCSET. Cat no: **1854961292**. Released on Bramhope, '91 by Ulverscroft Soundings. Note: 5 Cassettes.

VET IN A VILLAGE (Peter Joyce).
MCSET. Cat no: **1090N**. Released on Travellers Tales, '91 by Travellers Tales. Note: 5 Cassettes.
MCSET. Cat no: **1854963309**. Released on Bramhope, '91 by Ulverscroft Soundings. Note: 5 cassettes.

VET IN GREEN PASTURES (Peter Wheeler).
MCSET. Cat no: **1023N**. Released on Travellers Tales, '91 by Travellers Tales. Note: 5 Cassettes.
MCSET. Cat no: **1854961284**. Released on Bramhope, '91 by Ulverscroft Soundings. Note: 5 Cassettes.

Latin
PRONUNCIATION AND READING OF CLASSICAL LATIN (Unknown narrator(s)).
MCSET. Cat no: **23675**. Released on Sussex Tapes, '91 by Sussex Publications Ltd.

SELECTIONS FROM THE GREEK ORATORS (Unknown narrator(s)).
MC. Cat no: **S 23800**. Released on Sussex Tapes, '91 by Sussex Publications Ltd..

SELECTIONS FROM VIRGIL (Robert P. Sonkowsky).
MCSET. Cat no: **23685**. Released on Sussex Tapes, '91 by Sussex Publications Ltd..

SOUNDS OF CLASSICAL LATIN, THE (Edited By A.J. Baird) (Unknown narrator(s)).
MC. Cat no: **L 7911**. Released on Exeter Tapes, '91 by Drakes Educational Associates.

Lawrence, D.H.
D H LAWRENCE (Garnini Salgado & Jeff Hernstedt).
Note: Pre-recorded discussions which show literary criticism as a living, evolving interchange.
MC. Cat no: **A36**. Released on Sussex Tapes, '91 by Sussex Publications Ltd..
Note: 8 Cassettes.

LAWRENCE AND JOYCE (Ian Gregor & Mark Kinhead-Weekes).
Note: Authors are D H Lawrence and James Joyce. Pre-recorded discussions which show literary criticism as a living, evolving interchange.
MC. Cat no: **A8**. Released on Sussex Tapes, '91 by Sussex Publications Ltd..

Lee, Laurie
AS I WALKED OUT ONE MIDSUMMER MORNING (Laurie Lee).
MCSET. Cat no: **IAB 88051**. Released on Isis Audio Books, '91. Note : 7 Cassette set. Playing time 7hrs 50mins.

MCSET. Cat no: **1035N**. Released on Travellers Tales, '91 by Travellers Tales. Note: 7 Cassettes.

CIDER WITH ROSIE (Laurie Lee).
Note: Abridged version.
MCSET. Cat no: **1016A**. Released on Travellers Tales, '91 by Travellers Tales. Note: 2 Cassettes.
MCSET. Cat no: **TE 859**. Released on Isis Audio Books, '91. Note : 6 Cassettes.

CIDER WITH ROSIE (Laurie Lee).
MCSET. Cat no: **IAB 88121**. Released on Isis Audio Books, '91. Note : 8 Cassette set. Playing time 7hrs 55mins.
MCSET. Cat no: **1029A**. Released on Travellers Tales, '91 by Travellers Tales.

CIDER WITH ROSIE (Unknown narrator(s)).
MCSET. Cat no: **SAY 55**. Released on Argo (Polygram), '82 by PolyGram Classics **Deleted** Jan '89.
MCSET. Cat no: **ARGO 1094**. Released on Argo (EMI), Jun '89 by EMI Records. Note: 2 Cassettes.

I CAN'T STAY LONG (Laurie Lee).
MCSET. Cat no: **IAB 88081**. Released on Isis Audio Books, '91. Note : 8 Cassette set. Playing time 9hrs 30mins.
MCSET. Cat no: **1041N**. Released on Travellers Tales, '91 by Travellers Tales. Note: 8 Cassettes

MOMENT OF WAR, A (Martin Jarvis).
MCSET. Cat no: **IAB 92051**. Released on Isis Audio Books, May '92. Note: 4 Cassettes. Playing time: 4 hours, 35 mins.

Lenin

LENIN (Biography) (Clifford Rose).
MC. Cat no: **L 5**. Released on Green Dragon, '91 by Green Dragon Audio Visual.

MC. Cat no: **DHM 16**. Released on Sussex Tapes, '91 by Sussex Publications Ltd..

Lenz, S

DAS WRACK AND OTHER STORIES (Edited By William P. Hanson) (Unknown narrator(s)).
Note: A general introduction to Lenz's short stories as a whole.
MC. Cat no: **G 7546**. Released on Exeter Tapes, '91 by Drakes Educational Associates.

Leopardi, Giacomo

CANTI (Edited By Madeleine Constable) (Unknown narrator(s)).
Note: Leopardi's poetry as an example of romantic subjectivity turning to deep pessimism. In Italian.
MC. Cat no: **I 7521**. Released on Exeter Tapes, '91 by Drakes Educational Associates. Note: 4 Cassettes.

Lermontov, M

DEMON (Edited By Robert Reid) (Unknown narrator(s)).

Note: A balanced criticism of Lemontov's major poetical work.
MC. Cat no: **R 7783**. Released on Exeter Tapes, '91 by Drakes Educational Associates.

Lessing, Doris

ANCIENT WAYS TO NEW FREEDOM (Unknown narrator(s)).
MC. Cat no: **SS 102**. Released on Seminar Cassettes, Oct '81 by Seminar Cassettes.

Lessing G.E.

EMILIA GALOTTI (Edited By Keith A. Dickson) (Unknown narrator(s)).
Note: The tape defines Lessing's view of middle class tragedy, and examines how he puts theory into practice in this work.
MC. Cat no: **G 7720**. Released on Exeter Tapes, '91 by Drakes Educational Associates.

Levin, Bernard

TAKING SIDES, SPEAKING UP (Bernard Levin).
Note: Abridged version.
MCSET. Cat no: **1010N**. Released on Travellers Tales, '91 by Travellers Tales. Note: 2 cassettes.

Lewis, Cecil Day

SAGITTARIUS RISING (Alistair Maydon).
MCSET. Cat no: **1054N**. Released on Travellers Tales, '91 by Travellers Tales. Note: 8 Cassettes.
MCSET. Cat no: **OAS 89063**. Released on Oasis Audio Books, '91 by Isis Audio Books. Note: 8 Cassettes.

Lipman, Maureen

HOW WAS IT FOR YOU? (Biography) (Maureen Lipman).
MCSET. Cat no: **ZBBC 1025**. Released on BBC Radio Collection, Sep '88 by BBC Records. Note: ISBN No: 0563 225769

SOMETHING TO FALL BACK ON (Maureen Lipman).
MCSET. Cat no: **CAB 354**. Released on Chivers Audio Books, '91 by Chivers Audio Books, Green Dragon Audio Visual. Note: 6 Cassettes.
MCSET. Cat no: **1040H**. Released on Travellers Tales, '91 by Travellers Tales. Note: 6 Cassettes.

Locke, Angela

SEARCH DOG (Margaret Holt).
MCSET. Cat no: **1078N**. Released on Travellers Tales, '91 by Travellers Tales. Note: 5 Cassettes.
MCSET. Cat no: **1854962655**. Released on Bramhope, '91 by Ulverscroft Soundings. Note: 5 Cassettes.

Lorca, F. Garcia

BODAS DE SANGRE (Edited By Dr. Anderson) (Unknown narrator(s)).
Note: A general literary-critical study of probably the most popular play of Lorca.

MC. Cat no: **S 7838**. Released on Exeter Tapes, '91 by Drakes Educational Associates.

Lord Mountbatten

LIFE AND TIMES OF LORD MOUNTBATTEN, THE (Various artists).
LPS. Cat no: **LM 101**. Released on Pye, Oct '79. Note: 3 LP set.

Lowell, Robert

POETRY OF ROBERT LOWELL, THE (Robert Lowell).
Note: Author reads their works and discuss their formative influences.
MC. Cat no: **AS 29**. Released on Sussex Tapes, '91 by Sussex Publications Ltd..

Lumley, Joanna

STARE BACK AND SMILE (Joanna Lumley).
MCSET. Cat no: **IAB 92056**. Released on Isis Audio Books, May '92. Note : 7 Cassettes. Playing time: 7 hours, 10 mins.

Lustgarten, Edgar

BRIDES IN THE BATH CASE & THE PENGE MYSTERY, THE (Famous Trials) (Edgar Lustgarten).
MC. Cat no: **FT 4**. Released on Green Dragon, '91 by Green Dragon Audio Visual.

BRIGHTON TRUNK CASE & THE BLAZING CAR CASE, THE (Famous Trials) (Edgar Lustgarten).
MC. Cat no: **FT 3**. Released on Green Dragon, '91 by Green Dragon Audio Visual.

LIZZIE BORDEN TOOK AN AXE (Famous Trials) (Edgar Lustgarten).
MC. Cat no: **FT 8**. Released on Green Dragon, '91 by Green Dragon Audio Visual.

MONKEYVILLE CASE, THE (Famous Trials) (Edgar Lustgarten).
MC. Cat no: **FT 7**. Released on Green Dragon, '91 by Green Dragon Audio Visual.

MRS MAYBRICK & MRS MERRYFIELD (Famous Trials) (Edgar Lustgarten).
MC. Cat no: **FT 1**. Released on Green Dragon, '91 by Green Dragon Audio Visual.

MURDER AT THE FOLLIES (Famous Trials) (Edgar Lustgarten).
MC. Cat no: **FT 5**. Released on Green Dragon, '91 by Green Dragon Audio Visual.

NEWCASTLE TRAIN MURDER & DEATH ON THE CRUMBLE (Famous Trials) (Edgar Lustgarten).
MC. Cat no: **FT 2**. Released on Green Dragon, '91 by Green Dragon Audio Visual.

UNDER THE CRAB APPLE TREE (Famous Trials) (Edgar Lustgarten).
MC. Cat no: **FT 6**. Released on Green Dragon, '91 by Green Dragon Audio Visual.

Lynn, Vera
WE'LL MEET AGAIN (Biography) (Carol Marsh).
Note: Written with Robin Cross and Jenny De Gex.
MCSET. Cat no: **IAB 92031**. Released on Isis Audio Books, Mar '92. Note : 7 Cassettes. Playing time 7hrs 47mins.

McCormack, Mark
110% SOLUTION, THE (Mark H. McCormack).
MC. Cat no: **RC 35**. Released on Random Century, '91 by Random Century Audiobooks, Conifer Records. Note: ISBN no. 1856860523. Playing time 80 mins approx.

SUCCESS SECRETS (Mark McCormack).
MCSET. Cat no: **HCA 43**. Released on Harper Collins, '92 by Harper Collins.

MacDiarmid, Hugh
DRUNK MAN LOOKS AT THE THISTLE, A (Unknown narrator(s)).
2LP. Cat no: **CCA 1/2**. Released on Claddagh (Ireland), Aug '88 by Claddagh Records (Ireland), Projection, Impetus Records, Jazz Music, Roots Records, C.M. Distribution, Outlet Records, Taylors.

HUGH MACDIARMID (Unknown narrator(s)).
LP. Cat no: **CCT 5**. Released on Claddagh (Ireland), Aug '88 by Claddagh Records (Ireland), Projection, Impetus Records, Jazz Music, Roots Records, C.M. Distribution, Outlet Records, Taylors.

MacDonald, Finlay J
CROWDIE AND CREAM (Memoirs of a Hebridean Childhood) (Finlay J MacDonald).
MCSET. Cat no: **ZBBC 1212**. Released on BBC Radio Collection, Apr '91 by BBC Records. Note: ISBN No: 0563 409673

Machiavelli
ETHNIC PRINCE (Edited By John Gatt-Rutter) (Unknown narrator(s)).
Note: A discussion of this work by Machiavelli. It's 'scientific' approach to politics.
MC. Cat no: **I 7892**. Released on Exeter Tapes, '91 by Drakes Educational Associates.

MACHIAVELLI AND THE MEDICI (Edited By Brian Richardson) (Unknown narrator(s)).
MC. Cat no: **I 7870**. Released on Exeter Tapes, '91 by Drakes Educational Associates.

McLellan, Robert
FOUR LINMILL STORIES (Robert McLellan).
MC. Cat no: **SSC 050**. Released on Scotsoun, '91 by Scotsoun Recordings, Morley Audio Services.

McMullen, Jeanine
MY SMALL COUNTRY LIVING (Biography) (Jeanine McMullen).
MCSET. Cat no: **1033A**. Released on Travellers Tales, '91 by Travellers Tales. Note: 7 Cassettes.
MCSET. Cat no: **IAB 89081**. Released on Isis Audio Books, '91. Note : 7 Cassettes.

Mailer, Norman
EXISTENTIALIST WRITING (Norman Mailer).
Note: Authors read their works and discuss their formative influences.
MC. Cat no: **AS 30**. Released on Sussex Tapes, '91 by Sussex Publications Ltd..

Malay
LANGUAGE COURSE - MALAY (BAHASA MALAYSIA) (Unknown narrator(s)).
LPS. Cat no: **0747303304**. Released on Linguaphone, Apr '82 by Linguaphone Institute, Taylors, Century Records (USA), Bond Street Music.

Malraux, Andre
LA CONDITION HUMAINE (Edited By Malcolm Cook) (Unknown narrator(s)).
Note: A study of Malraux' philosophical meaning of the text, also questions the political interpretations.
MC. Cat no: **F 7960**. Released on Exeter Tapes, '91 by Drakes Educational Associates.

Mandeville, John
TRAVELS OF SIR JOHN MANDEVILLE (Various narrators).
MC. Cat no: **ANV 629**. Released on Anvil Cassettes, Jan '81 by Anvil Cassettes, Chivers Audio Books.

Mann, Thomas
DER TOD IN VENEDIG (Edited By John McKenzie) (Unknown narrator(s)).
MC. Cat no: **G 7572**. Released on Exeter Tapes, '91 by Drakes Educational Associates.

TONIO KROGER (Edited By John McKenzie) (Unknown narrator(s)).
Note: Thomas Mann's fusion of a story of unrequited love with an exploration of the central conflict.
MC. Cat no: **G 7538**. Released on Exeter Tapes, '91 by Drakes Educational Associates.

Manzoni, Alessandro
I PROMESSI SPOSI (Edited By Madeleine Constable) (Unknown narrator(s)).
Note: A discussion of Manzoni's only novel.
MC. Cat no: **I 7522**. Released on Exeter Tapes, '91 by Drakes Educational Associates. Note: 4 Cassettes.

Mao Tse-Tung
MAO TSE-TUNG (Biography) (John Ringham).
MC. Cat no: **L 7**. Released on Green Dragon, '91 by Green Dragon Audio Visual.
MC. Cat no: **DHM 19**. Released on Sussex Tapes, '91 by Sussex Publications Ltd..

Marconi, Guglielmo
GUGLIELMO MARCONI (Biography) (Stephen Thorne).
MC. Cat no: **SI 4**. Released on Green Dragon, '91 by Green Dragon Audio Visual.

Marivaux
LE JEU DE L'AMOUR ET DU HASARD (Edited By Peter Wagstaff) (Unknown narrator(s)).
Note: Peter Wagstaff looks at Marivaux' classical play.
MC. Cat no: **F 7318**. Released on Exeter Tapes, '91 by Drakes Educational Associates.

LES FAUSSES CONFIDENCES (Edited By Derek Connon) (Unknown narrator(s)).
Note: A study of Marivaux' play looking at its place in theatrical history as well as its artistic importance.
MC. Cat no: **F 7317**. Released on Exeter Tapes, '91 by Drakes Educational Associates.

Marshall, Arthur
LIFE'S RICH PAGEANT (Arthur Marshall).
MCSET. Cat no: **ZBBC 1024**. Released on BBC Radio Collection, Sep '88 by BBC Records. Note: ISBN No: 0563 225777

WHIMPERING IN THE RHODODENDRONS (Biography) (Arthur Marshall).
MCSET. Cat no: **1064N**. Released on Travellers Tales, '91 by Travellers Tales. Note: 4 Cassettes.
MCSET. Cat no: **OAS 89106**. Released on Oasis Audio Books, '91 by Isis Audio Books. Note: 4 Cassettes.

Marx, Karl
MARX AND THE MATERIAL CONCEPT OF HISTORY (Marx and the Theory of Revolution in the State) (Chimen Abramsky & Dr. David McLellan).
MCSET. Cat no: **HUA 026**. Released on AVP, '91 by AVP Publishing.

Mason, James
ODD MAN OUT (Edited by Sheridan Morley) (John Rye).
MCSET. Cat no: **OAS 10991**. Released on Oasis Audio Books, Sep '91 by Isis Audio Books. Note: 7 Cassettes. Playing time: 7 hours.

Mauriac, F
THERESE DESQUEYROUX (Edited By Dorothy Steer) (Unknown narrator(s)).
Note: An assessment of Mauriac's art as a novelist.
MC. Cat no: **F 7636**. Released on Exeter Tapes, '91 by Drakes Educational Associates.

Mawer, R.K.
TALES FROM A PALM COURT (Clive Champney).

MCSET. Cat no: **1091N.** Released on Travellers Tales, '91 by Travellers Tales. Note: 5 Cassettes.
MCSET. Cat no: **1854963317.** Released on Bramhope, '91 by Ulverscroft Soundings. Note: 5 Cassettes.

Mean, Margaret
HOW PEOPLE CHANGE (Margaret Mean).
MC. Cat no: **AS 31.** Released on Sussex Tapes, '91 by Sussex Publications Ltd..

Meegan, George
LONGEST WALK, THE (Graeme Malcom).
MCSET. Cat no: **RB 90017.** Released on Recorded Books, Feb '92 by Isis Audio Books. Note: 11 Cassettes. Playing time 15hrs 15mins.

Mehta, Ved
LEDGE BETWEEN THE STREAMS, THE (Garard Green).
MCSET. Cat no: **OAS 10891.** Released on Oasis Audio Books, '91 by Isis Audio Books. Note: 12 Cassettes.
MCSET. Cat no: **1061/1062A.** Released on Travellers Tales, '91 by Travellers Tales. Note: 12 Cassettes.

Merimee, Prosper
COLOMBA (Edited By Anthony Kelly) (Unknown narrator(s)).
Note: P. Merimee's Columba is examined as a character who does not conform to the traditional 'feminine' role.
MC. Cat no: **F 7506.** Released on Exeter Tapes, '91 by Drakes Educational Associates.

MG Cars
MG JUST FOR THE RECORD (Volume 1) (Various narrator(s)).
LP. Cat no: **WES 88000.** Released on West 4, Aug '80 by West 4 Records & Tapes.

Michelmore, Cliff
TWO-WAY STORY (Cliff Michelmore & Jean Metcalfe).
MCSET. Cat no: **OAS 90122.** Released on Oasis Audio Books, '91 by Isis Audio Books. Note: 8 Cassettes.
MCSET. Cat no: **1064A.** Released on Travellers Tales, '91 by Travellers Tales.

Middle East
ARAB CULTURE AND THE WEST (Norman Daniel).
Note: The interaction, influence and relations between Arab culture and the West are traced and studied from the beginnings to the present day.
MC. Cat no: **A 7962.** Released on Exeter Tapes, '91 by Drakes Educational Associates.

ARAB - ISRAELI CONFLICT, THE (Part 1) (Timothy Niblock).
Note: Examines the reasons for and development of the conflict from the first Jewish settlement in Palestine to the establishment of the state of Israel.
MC. Cat no: **A 7828.** Released on Exeter Tapes, '91 by Drakes Educational Associates.

ARAB - ISRAELI CONFLICT, THE (Part 2) (Timothy Niblock).
Note: Arab/Israeli policies from 1948 to the 1967 war.
MC. Cat no: **A 7830.** Released on Exeter Tapes, '91 by Drakes Educational Associates.

IBN KHALDUN - HIS LIFE. HIS WORKS AND HIS SOURCE (Edited by H.T. Norris) (Unknown narrator(s)).
MC. Cat no: **A 7898.** Released on Exeter Tapes, '91 by Drakes Educational Associates.

INTRODUCING THE ARAB WORLD (Ian Netton).
Note: The culture of the near and Middle East with reference to Islam, Muslim architecture and literature and the development of Arab civilisation.
MC. Cat no: **A 7772.** Released on Exeter Tapes, '91 by Drakes Educational Associates.

IRANIAN REVOLUTION, THE (Sir Anthony Parsons).
Note: An analysis of the causes, the principle elements involved and its future.
MC. Cat no: **A 7323.** Released on Exeter Tapes, '91 by Drakes Educational Associates.

REAPPRAISAL OF WHAT WENT WRONG IN PALESTINE, A (Michael Adams).
Note: An account of the Arab-Israeli conflict over Palestine, stressing the international aspect and the failure to implement existing commitments.
MC. Cat no: **A 7324.** Released on Exeter Tapes, '91 by Drakes Educational Associates.

Military History
ATTITUDES TO WAR IN ENGLAND BEFORE 1914 (Z Steiner & Dr. Paul Kennedy).
MCSET. Cat no: **HEA 043.** Released on AVP, '91 by AVP Publishing.

BATTLE OF BRITAIN (Various narrators).
2LP. Cat no: **AFP 131.** Released on Flightstream, Jun '83.
MCSET. Cat no: **AFP 131T.** Released on Flightstream, Jun '83.

BATTLE OF BRITAIN, THE (Stephen Murray).
MC. Cat no: **W6.** Released on Green Dragon, '91 by Green Dragon Audio Visual.

BATTLE OF JUTLAND, THE (Nigel Lambert).
MC. Cat no: **W4.** Released on Green Dragon, '91 by Green Dragon Audio Visual.

BATTLE OF MIDWAY, THE (Stephen Thorne).

MC. Cat no: **W3.** Released on Green Dragon, '91 by Green Dragon Audio Visual.

BATTLE OF WATERLOO (Nigel Lambert).
MC. Cat no: **W7.** Released on Green Dragon, '91 by Green Dragon Audio Visual.

D-DAY DESPATCHES (War Correspondents Reports) (Various narrators).
LP. Cat no: **REC 522.** Released on BBC, '84 by BBC Records, Taylors.
MC. Cat no: **ZCM 522.** Released on BBC, '84 by BBC Records, Taylors.

D-DAY DESPATCHES (And Victory In Europe) (Various narrators).
Note: Original recordings from the BBC Sound Archives, June 1944 and Spring 1945.
MCSET. Cat no: **ZBBC 1084.** Released on BBC Radio Collection, May '90 by BBC Records. Note: ISBN No: 0563 226684

HINDENBURG DISASTER, THE (Nigel Lambert).
MC. Cat no: **W2.** Released on Green Dragon, '91 by Green Dragon Audio Visual.

LAST GUNBOAT BLOCKADE, THE (Stephen Murray).
MCSET. Cat no: **W5.** Released on Green Dragon, '91 by Green Dragon Audio Visual.

METTERNICH AND THE NAPOLEONIC WARS 1809-1815 (The Metternich System, 1815-1848) (Paul W Shroeder & Dr. Francis Bridge).
MCSET. Cat no: **HUA 022.** Released on AVP, '91 by AVP Publishing.

ORIGINS OF THE FIRST WORLD WAR, THE (Dr. Hartmut Pogge Von Strandmann & Prof. Volker Berghahn).
MCSET. Cat no: **HUA 005.** Released on AVP, '91 by AVP Publishing.

PATH TO WORLD WAR II, THE (AJP. Taylor & Christopher Thorne).
MC. Cat no: **HB 4.** Released on Sussex Tapes, '91 by Sussex Publications Ltd.

SECOND WORLD WAR (June 1944 and Spring 1945) (Various artists).
Note: Original recordings from the BBC Sound Archives.
MCSET. Cat no: **ZBBC 1081.** Released on BBC Radio Collection, Oct '89 by BBC Records. Note: ISBN No: 0563 226668.

SINKING OF THE LUSITANIA (John Graham).
MC. Cat no: **W1.** Released on Green Dragon, '91 by Green Dragon Audio Visual.

SPANISH ARMADA, THE (Edward De Souza).
MC. Cat no: **W8.** Released on Green Dragon, '91 by Green Dragon Audio Visual.

THIRTY YEARS WAR, THE (Michael Hughes & Henry Kamen).
MC. Cat no: **HE 17.** Released on Sussex Tapes, '91 by Sussex Publications Ltd..

VICTORY IN EUROPE (Archive Sound Recordings) (Various artists).
LP. Cat no: **REC 562**. Released on BBC, May '85 by BBC Records, Taylors.
MC. Cat no: **ZCM 562**. Released on BBC, May '85 by BBC Records, Taylors.
WORLD WAR II (The Early Years) (Unknown narrator(s)).
Note: Tells the story of the important events of World War II, narrated by well known actors. Titles include: Dunkirk, North Africa, Desert Victory and the Battle of Britain.
MCSET. Cat no: **HWS 1**. Released on Sussex Tapes, '91 by Sussex Publications Ltd.. Note: 8 Cassettes.
WORLD WARS 1914/1939 (Military History) (Various narrator(s)).
MCSET. Cat no: **SAY 101**. Released on Argo (Polygram), Mar '84 by PolyGram Classics **Deleted** Jan '89.

Miller, Henry
TROPIC OF CANCER (Martin Balsam).
MCSET. Cat no: **LFP 7236**. Released on Listen For Pleasure, Feb '86 by EMI Records.
MCSET. Cat no: **1115F**. Released on Travellers Tales, '91 by Travellers Tales.

Milligan, Spike
ADOLF HITLER: MY PART IN HIS DOWNFALL / ROMMEL? GUNNER WHO? (Spike Milligan).
MCSET. Cat no: **TE 857**. Released on Isis Audio Books, '91. Note : 6 Cassettes.
ADOLPH HITLER: MY PART IN HIS DOWNFALL (Spike Milligan).
LP. Cat no: **SCX 6636**. Released on Columbia (EMI), Apr '81 by EMI Records.
MCSET. Cat no: **1033H**. Released on Travellers Tales, '91 by Travellers Tales. Note: 3 Cassettes.
MCSET. Cat no: **IAB 88031**. Released on Isis Audio Books, '91. Note : 3 Cassettes.
MUSSOLINI: HIS PART IN MY DOWNFALL (Spike Milligan).
MCSET. Cat no: **1036H**. Released on Travellers Tales, '91 by Travellers Tales. Note: 8 Cassettes.
MCSET. Cat no: **IAB 88091**. Released on Isis Audio Books, '91. Note : 8 Cassettes.
ROMMEL? GUNNER WHO? (and Monty: His Part in my Victory) (Spike Milligan).
MCSET. Cat no: **IAB 88061**. Released on Isis Audio Books, '88. Note : 6 Cassettes.
MCSET. Cat no: **1032H**. Released on Travellers Tales, '91 by Travellers Tales. Note: 6 Cassettes.
WHERE HAVE ALL THE BULLETS GONE? (Spike Milligan).
MCSET. Cat no: **IAB 89031**. Released on Isis Audio Books, '91. Note : 6 Cassettes.
MCSET. Cat no: **1041H**. Released on Travellers Tales, '91 by Travellers Tales.

Mitchell, W.R.
DALESMAN'S DIARY, A (W.R. Mitchell).
MCSET. Cat no: **1089N**. Released on Travellers Tales, '91 by Travellers Tales. Note: 5 Cassettes.
MCSET. Cat no: **1854963007**. Released on Bramhope, '91 by Ulverscroft Soundings. Note: 5 Cassettes.

Mitford, Mary Russell
OUR VILLAGE (Rosemary Davis).
MCSET. Cat no: **OAS 89104**. Released on Oasis Audio Books, '91 by Isis Audio Books. Note: 4 Cassette set. Playing time 5hrs.
MCSET. Cat no: **1065N**. Released on Travellers Tales, '91 by Travellers Tales. Note: 4 Cassettes.

Moliere
LE BOURGEOIS GENTIL HOMME (Edited By Jean D. Biard And Gerard Poulet) (Unknown narrator(s)).
Note: The origins of comedie - ballet are traced, showing how Moliere created a new type of comedy by integrating musical and choreographic entertainment in his plays. In French.
MC. Cat no: **F 7519**. Released on Exeter Tapes, '91 by Drakes Educational Associates.
LE MALADE IMAGINAIRE (Edited By Jean D. Biard) (Unknown narrator(s)).
Note: An insight into the dramatic and comic mechanism of Moliere's play as well as an examination of its contemporary social and historical background. In French.
MC. Cat no: **F 7559**. Released on Exeter Tapes, '91 by Drakes Educational Associates.
TARTUFFE (Edited By Jean D. Biard) (Unknown narrator(s)).
Note: An analysis of the main themes of Moliere's play. In French.
MC. Cat no: **F 7575**. Released on Exeter Tapes, '91 by Drakes Educational Associates.

Moore, Ray
TOMORROW IS TOO LATE (Biography) (David Ryder).
MCSET. Cat no: **1060A**. Released on Travellers Tales, '91 by Travellers Tales. Note: 6 Cassettes.
MCSET. Cat no: **OAS 90063**. Released on Oasis Audio Books, '91 by Isis Audio Books. Note: 6 Cassettes.

Moorehead, Alan
BLUE NILE, THE (Patrick Tull).
MCSET. Cat no: **1050N**. Released on Travellers Tales, '91 by Travellers Tales. Note: 8 Cassettes.
MCSET. Cat no: **IAB 89041**. Released on Isis Audio Books, '91. Note : 8 Cassettes.

COOPER'S CREEK (The Opening Of Australia) (Nelson Runger).
MCSET. Cat no: **1098N**. Released on Travellers Tales, '91 by Travellers Tales. Note: 6 Cassettes.
MCSET. Cat no: **RB 89393**. Released on Recorded Books, '91 by Isis Audio Books. Note: 6 Cassettes.
WHITE NILE, THE (Patrick Tull).
MCSET. Cat no: **1066/7N**. Released on Travellers Tales, '91 by Travellers Tales. Note: 12 Cassettes.
MCSET. Cat no: **IAB 89112**. Released on Isis Audio Books, '91. Note : 12 Cassettes.

Morike, E
GEDICHTE (Edited By W.E. Yates) (Unknown narrator(s)).
Note: An introduction to Morike's poetry, considering it in the context of his wider literary development.
MC. Cat no: **G 7754**. Released on Exeter Tapes, '91 by Drakes Educational Associates.

Morris, Johnny
THERE'S LOVELY (Johnny Morris).
MCSET. Cat no: **OAS 20192**. Released on Oasis Audio Books, Jan '92 by Isis Audio Books. Note: 8 Cassettes. Playing time: 9 hrs 10 mins.

Mortimer, John
CLINGING TO THE WRECKAGE (John Mortimer).
Note: Extracts from his autobiography.
MCSET. Cat no: **ZBBC 1019**. Released on BBC, Sep '88 by BBC Records, Taylors. Note: ISBN No: 0563 225726

Moss, W. Stanley
I'LL MET BY MOONLIGHT (Unknown narrator(s)).
MCSET. Cat no: **SOUND 18**. Released on Soundings, Mar '85 by Soundings Records, Bond Street Music.
MCSET. Cat no: **1011N**. Released on Travellers Tales, '91 by Travellers Tales. Note: 4 Cassettes.

Motorcycling
CLASSIC MOTORCYCLES (Unknown narrator(s)).
Note: Recordings of motorcycles built in the period when Britain led the world. Including road and racing models.
MC. Cat no: **AC 145**. Released on Audicord, '91 by Audicord Cassettes.
ISLE OF MAN TT RACES, 1967 (Various artists).
2LP. Cat no: **SSD 577 578**. Released on Taylors, Jul '77 by H.R. Taylor Records.
MC. Cat no: **CSS 577 578**. Released on Taylors, Jul '77 by H.R. Taylor Records.
RECOLLECTIONS NO. 5: BRITISH MOTORCYCLE INDUSTRY (Edward Turner & Val Page).
Note: Recalled by Edward Turner and Val Page. Two of the leading designers during the years between the wars.

MC. Cat no: **AC 146.** Released on Audicord, '91 by Audicord Cassettes.
TT HIGHLIGHTS (1957-64 Volume 1) (Various).
LP. Cat no: **BLP 702.** Released on Sound Stories, Feb '80 by H.R. Taylor Records.
TT HIGHLIGHTS (1965-8 Volume 2) (Various).
LP. Cat no: **BLP 703.** Released on Sound Stories, Feb '80 by H.R. Taylor Records.

Mountbatten
LIFE AND TIMES OF LORD MOUNTBATTEN, THE (See Under Lord Mountbatten) (Various narrators).

Mountford, G
WHY SAVE WILD ANIMALS (G.Mountford/G.Durrell).
MC. Cat no: **SS 111.** Released on Seminar Cassettes, Oct '81 by Seminar Cassettes.

Mozart (composer)
WOLFGANG AMADEUS MOZART (Biography) (Richard Mayes).
MC. Cat no: **GC 8.** Released on Green Dragon, '91 by Green Dragon Audio Visual.
WOLFGANG AMADEUS MOZART 1756-1791 (Biography) (Unknown narrator(s)).
MC. Cat no: **DFC 6.** Released on Sussex Tapes, '91 by Sussex Publications Ltd..

Muggeridge, Malcolm
ON THE SIDE OF LAUGHTER (Formative Influences on Writers) (Malcolm Muggeridge).
Note: Author reads their works and discuss their formative influences.
MC. Cat no: **AS 34.** Released on Sussex Tapes, '91 by Sussex Publications Ltd.

Murphy, Devia
EIGHT FEET IN THE ANDES (Kate Binchy).
MCSET. Cat no: **1046/7N.** Released on Travellers Tales, '91 by Travellers Tales. Note: 12 Cassettes.
MCSET. Cat no: **IAB 89011.** Released on Isis Audio Books, '91. Note : 12 Cassettes.
FULL TILT - IRELAND TO INDIA WITH A BICYCLE (Kate Binchy).
MCSET. Cat no: **1028N.** Released on Travellers Tales, '91 by Travellers Tales. Note: 8 Cassettes.
MCSET. Cat no: **IAB 87111.** Released on Isis Audio Books, '91. Note : 8 Cassettes.

Napoleon
NAPOLEON (history for ages 8+) (Unknown narrator(s)).
Note: Book and cassette.
MC. Cat no: **PLBH 106.** Released on Tell-A-Tale, Mar '84 by Pickwick Records, Taylors, Clyde Factors.

NAPOLEON BONAPARTE (Edward De Souza).
MC. Cat no: **L 3.** Released on Green Dragon, '91 by Green Dragon Audio Visual.
MC. Cat no: **DHM 14.** Released on Sussex Tapes, '91 by Sussex Publications Ltd.

Nekrasov, V
KIRA GEORGIEVNA (Edited By Olive Stevens) (Unknown narrator(s)).
Note: A discussion of a story by Nekrasov that was controversially greeted in the U.S.S.R. of the 50's.
MC. Cat no: **R 7701.** Released on Exeter Tapes, '91 by Drakes Educational Associates.

Nelson
HORATIO NELSON (Biography) (John Graham).
MC. Cat no: **L 4.** Released on Green Dragon, '91 by Green Dragon Audio Visual.
MC. Cat no: **DHM 15.** Released on Sussex Tapes, '91 by Sussex Publications Ltd..
NELSON (History for Ages 8+) (Unknown narrator(s)).
Note: Book and cassette.
MC. Cat no: **PLB 107.** Released on Tell-A-Tale, Mar '84 by Pickwick Records, Taylors, Clyde Factors.

Netherlands
DUTCH REPUBLIC IN THE 17TH CENTURY, THE (J L Price & C R Emery).
MCSET. Cat no: **HUA 035.** Released on AVP, '91 by AVP Publishing.

Newby, Eric
LAST GRAIN RACE, THE (Michael Sinclair).
MCSET. Cat no: **IAB 92046.** Released on Isis Audio Books, Apr '92. Note : 8 Cassettes. Playing time 10hrs.
LOVE AND WAR IN THE APENNINES (Biography) (Richard Mitchley).
MCSET. Cat no: **1053N.** Released on Travellers Tales, '91 by Travellers Tales. Note: 7 Cassettes.
MCSET. Cat no: **IAB 89061.** Released on Isis Audio Books, '91. Note : 8 Cassettes.
SHORT WALK IN THE HINDU KUSH, A (Richard Mitchley).
MCSET. Cat no: **1029N.** Released on Travellers Tales, '91 by Travellers Tales. Note: 8 Cassettes.
MCSET. Cat no: **IAB 88021.** Released on Isis Audio Books, '91. Note : 8 Cassettes.

Newton, Isaac
ISAAC NEWTON (Biography) (Clifford Rose).
MC. Cat no: **SI 1.** Released on Green Dragon, '91 by Green Dragon Audio Visual.
MC. Cat no: **DHM 24.** Released on Sussex Tapes, '91 by Sussex Publications Ltd..
ISAAC NEWTON (History Makers 1642-1727) (Unknown narrator(s)).
MC. Cat no: **HM 002.** Released on History Makers, Apr '82.

Ngor, Haing
SURVIVING THE KILLING FIELDS (Biography) (Crawford Logan).
MCSET. Cat no: **1058/1059A.** Released on Travellers Tales, '91 by Travellers Tales. Note: 12 Cassettes.
MCSET. Cat no: **OAS 90041.** Released on Oasis Audio Books, '91 by Isis Audio Books. Note: 12 Cassettes.

Nicholson, Michael
ACROSS THE LIMPOPO (Ian Craig).
MCSET. Cat no: **1086N.** Released on Travellers Tales, '91 by Travellers Tales. Note: 6 Cassettes.
MCSET. Cat no: **OAS 90042.** Released on Oasis Audio Books, '91 by Isis Audio Books. Note: 6 Cassettes.

Nightingale, Florence
FLORENCE NIGHTINGALE (Biography) (Valentine Palmer).
MC. Cat no: **FW 4.** Released on Green Dragon, '91 by Green Dragon Audio Visual.
MC. Cat no: **DHM 5.** Released on Sussex Tapes, '91 by Sussex Publications Ltd..

Niven, David
BRING ON THE EMPTY HORSES (Biography) (David Niven).
MC. Cat no: **TC LFP 7067.** Released on Listen For Pleasure, Oct '80 by EMI Records.
MOON'S A BALLOON, THE (Biography) (Unknown narrator(s)).
MCSET. Cat no: **LFP 7010.** Released on Listen For Pleasure, Oct '85 by EMI Records.
MCSET. Cat no: **1017A.** Released on Travellers Tales, '91 by Travellers Tales. Note: 2 Cassettes. Playing time 2 hours 5 minutes.

Nolan, Christopher
UNDER THE EYE OF THE CLOCK (Biography) (Colm Hefferon).
MCSET. Cat no: **1028A.** Released on Travellers Tales, '91 by Travellers Tales.
MCSET. Cat no: **IAB 88111.** Released on Isis Audio Books, '91. Note : 6 Cassettes.

Norwegian
LANGUAGE COURSE - NORWEGIAN (Unknown narrator(s)).
LPS. Cat no: **0747303320.** Released on Linguaphone, Apr '82 by Linguaphone Institute, Taylors, Century Records (USA), Bond Street Music.
NORSK FONETIKK FOR UTLENDINGER (Unknown narrator(s)).
MCSET. Cat no: **NW 98.** Released on Audio Forum (Language courses), '91. Note: 4 Cassettes

NORSK FOR UTLENDINGER (Volume 1) (Unknown narrator(s)).
MCSET. Cat no: **NW 1.** Released on Audio Forum (Language courses), '91. Note: 6 Cassettes

NORSK FOR UTLENDINGER (Volume 2) (Unknown narrator(s)).
MCSET. Cat no: **NW 20.** Released on Audio Forum (Language courses), '91. Note: 4 Cassettes

NORWEGIAN CASSETTE COURSE (Unknown narrator(s)).
Note: Includes:- 3 months' book and an instruction leaflet.
MCSET. Cat no: **852851472.** Released on Hugo Languages, '92 by Hugo Language Books Limited. Note: 4 Cassettes. Playing time 4hrs.

NORWEGIAN TRAVEL PACK (Unknown narrator(s)).
Note: Contains a Hugo phrase book.
MC. Cat no: **852851804.** Released on Hugo Languages, '92 by Hugo Language Books Limited.

Nostradamus
PROPHECIES OF NOSTRADAMUS, THE (Valentine Dyall).
MCSET. Cat no: **D 006.** Released on Green Dragon, '91 by Green Dragon Audio Visual.

O'Hanlon, Redmond
IN TROUBLE AGAIN (Richard Mitchley).
MCSET. Cat no: **IAB 89051.** Released on Isis Audio Books, '91. Note : 8 Cassettes.

IN TROUBLE AGAIN (A Journey From The Orinoco To The Amazon) (Redmond O'Hanlon).
MCSET. Cat no: **1058N.** Released on Travellers Tales, '91 by Travellers Tales. Note: 8 Cassettes.

Olesha, Yu
ZAVIST (Edited By Neil Cornwell) (Unknown narrator(s)).
Note: An analysis of one of the most interesting texts of the NEP period of Soviet literature.
MC. Cat no: **R 7756.** Released on Exeter Tapes, '91 by Drakes Educational Associates.

Orwell, George
CHARLES DICKENS (And Other Essays) (Patrick Tull).
MCSET. Cat no: **RB 89170.** Released on Recorded Books, '91 by Isis Audio Books. Note: 3 Cassettes. Playing time 3hrs 30mins.
MCSET. Cat no: **1097N.** Released on Travellers Tales, '91 by Travellers Tales. Note: 3 Cassettes.

DOWN AND OUT IN PARIS AND LONDON (Biography) (Patrick Tull).
MCSET. Cat no: **IAB 90011.** Released on Isis Audio Books, '91. Note : 5 Cassette set. Playing time 6hrs 30mins.
MCSET. Cat no: **1045A.** Released on Travellers Tales, '91 by Travellers Tales. Note: 5 Cassettes.

GEORGE ORWELL (Bernard Crick & Dr. Patrick Parringer).
Note: Pre-recorded discussions which show literary criticism as a living, evolving interchange.
MC. Cat no: **A46.** Released on Sussex Tapes, '91 by Sussex Publications Ltd..

HOMAGE TO CATALONIA (Fighting the Spanish Civil War) (Patrick Tull).
MCSET. Cat no: **RB 89398.** Released on Recorded Books, '91 by Isis Audio Books. Note: 6 Cassettes. Playing time 8hrs.
MCSET. Cat no: **1063A.** Released on Travellers Tales, '91 by Travellers Tales. Note: 6 Cassettes.

NINETEEN EIGHTY-FOUR, GEORGE ORWELL (Julian Glover).
Note: Pre-recored discussions which show literary criticism as a living, evolving interchange.
MC. Cat no: **A50.** Released on Sussex Tapes, '91 by Sussex Publications Ltd..

O'Sullevan, Peter
PETER O'SULLEVAN TALKS TURF (Peter O'Sullevan).
LP. Cat no: **CAS 1160.** Released on Charisma, May '83 by Virgin Records **Deleted** '88.
MC. Cat no: **CASMC 1160.** Released on Charisma, May '83 by Virgin Records **Deleted** May '88.

Owen, Robert Dale
ROBERT OWEN & NEW LANARK (Biography) (John Sheddon).
MCSET. Cat no: **SPN 670-1.** Released on Schiltron Audio Books, '91 by Schiltron Publishing. Note: 2 Cassettes. Playing time 2 hours 36 minutes.

Pagnol, M
LA GLOIRE DE MON PERE (Edited By Nicole Pakenham) (Unknown narrator(s)).
Note: Treats the relationship between certain themes in the book and Pagnol's own upbringing and examines the authenticity of Pagnol's description of the 'Marseillais'. In French.
MC. Cat no: **F 7569.** Released on Exeter Tapes, '91 by Drakes Educational Associates.

LE CHATEAU DE MA MERE (Edited By P.M. Thody) (Unknown narrator(s)).
Note: A discussion of this work by Pagnol linking it to French society in the late 19th and early 20th centuries as well as to the world of a child.
MC. Cat no: **F 7819.** Released on Exeter Tapes, '91 by Drakes Educational Associates.

Pardo Bazan, E
LOS PAZOS DE ULLOA (Edited By M. Hemingway) (Unknown narrator(s)).
Note: A study of point and view and psychological analysis.

MC. Cat no: **S 7710.** Released on Exeter Tapes, '91 by Drakes Educational Associates.

Parkman, Francis
OREGON TRAIL, THE (Adrian Cronauer).
MCSET. Cat no: **RB 86570.** Released on Recorded Books, Oct '91 by Isis Audio Books. Note: 8 Cassettes. Playing time 11hrs 30mins.

Pasternak, Boris
POETRY OF BORIS PASTERNAK, THE (Lydia Pasternak Slater).
Note: Pre-recored discussions which show literary criticism as a living, evolving interchange.
MC. Cat no: **GS 1.** Released on Sussex Tapes, '91 by Sussex Publications Ltd..

Pavese, C
LA LUNA E I FALO (Edited By Luisa Quartermaine) (Unknown narrator(s)).
Note: A wide interpretation of Pavese's work. In Italian.
MC. Cat no: **I 7688.** Released on Exeter Tapes, '91 by Drakes Educational Associates.

Penn, Margaret
FOOLISH VIRGIN, THE (Elizabeth Proud).
MCSET. Cat no: **OAS 10192.** Released on Oasis Audio Books, Jan '92 by Isis Audio Books. Note: 8 Cassettes. Playing time: 8hrs 35mins.

MANCHESTER FOURTEEN MILES (Elizabeth Proud).
MCSET. Cat no: **OAS 21191.** Released on Oasis Audio Books, Nov '91 by Isis Audio Books. Note: 8 Cassettes. Playing time 8hrs 30mins.

YOUNG MRS. BURTON, THE (Elizabeth Proud).
MCSET. Cat no: **OAS 10392.** Released on Oasis Audio Books, Mar '92 by Isis Audio Books. Note: 8 Cassettes. Playing time: 8hrs 45mins.

Pepys, Samuel
DIARY OF SAMUEL PEPYS (Ian Richardson).
MC. Cat no: **1464.** Released on Caedmon (USA), '88 by Caedmon Records (USA), Bond Street Music.

Pern, Stephen
GREAT DIVIDE, THE (Christopher Kay).
MCSET. Cat no: **1096N.** Released on Travellers Tales, '91 by Travellers Tales. Note: 9 Cassettes.
MCSET. Cat no: **185496366X.** Released on Soundings, '91 by Soundings Records, Bond Street Music. Note: 9 Cassettes.

Peters, Thomas. J.
IN SEARCH OF EXCELLENCE (Secrets of Success series) (Unknown narrator(s)).
MC. Cat no: **0600560678.** Released

on Hamlyn Books On Tape, '88, Bond Street Music.

Peters, Tom
BEYOND HIERARCHY (Tom Peters). MCSET. Cat no: **RC 56.** Released on Random Century, Jul '92 by Random Century Audiobooks, Conifer Records. Note: ISBN no. 1856860507

THRIVING ON CHAOS (Tom Peters). MC. Cat no: **RC 33.** Released on Random Century, '91 by Random Century Audiobooks, Conifer Records. Note: ISBN no. 1856860647. Playing time 90 mins approx.

Petrarch
INTRODUCTION TO PETRARCH'S SELECTED POEMS (Edited By Mark Davie) (Unknown narrator(s)). MC. Cat no: **I 7996.** Released on Exeter Tapes, '91 by Drakes Educational Associates.

Picasso & Rouault
EXPRESSIONISM (Edited By David Kinmont) (Unknown narrators). Note: Includes a discussion of the works of Rouault and Picasso. MC. Cat no: **F 7979.** Released on Exeter Tapes, '91 by Drakes Educational Associates.

Pirandello, Luigi
ENRICO IV - TWO TRAGIC HUMORISTS (Edited By Susan Bassnett) (Unknown narrator(s)). Note: Deals with Luigi Pirandello's concept of humour, with particular reference to this, one of his best known parts. MC. Cat no: **I 7947.** Released on Exeter Tapes, '91 by Drakes Educational Associates. Note: 4 Cassette set.

PIRANDELLO'S THEATRE (Edited By Madeleine Constable) (Unknown narrator(s)). MC. Cat no: **I 7578.** Released on Exeter Tapes, '91 by Drakes Educational Associates.

Pithers & Greene
WE CAN SAY NO (Sarah Greene). Note: Authors are David Pithers and Sarah Greene.

MC. Cat no: **TS 398.** Released on Tellastory, Jan '92 by Random Century Audiobooks. Note: ISBN no. 1856561909

Poland
INTRODUCTION TO POLISH HISTORY, AN (Edited By Aubert Zawadzki) (Unknown narrator(s)). MC. Cat no: **PL 7766.** Released on Exeter Tapes, '91 by Drakes Educational Associates.

Polish
CONVERSATIONAL POLISH: A BEGINNERS COURSE (Unknown narrator(s)). MCSET. Cat no: **P 500.** Released on Audio Forum (Language courses), '91. Note: 8 Cassettes

LANGUAGE COURSE - POLISH (Unknown narrator(s)). LPS. Cat no: **0747302634.** Released on Linguaphone, Apr '82 by Linguaphone Institute, Taylors, Century Records (USA), Bond Street Music.

POLISH TRAVEL PACK (Unknown narrator(s)). Note: Contains a Hugo phrase book. MC. Cat no: **852851669.** Released on Hugo Languages, '92 by Hugo Language Books Limited.

SOUNDS AND ALPHABET OF POLISH, THE (Edited By Derek J. Hunns) (Unknown narrator(s)). MC. Cat no: **PL 7652.** Released on Exeter Tapes, '91 by Drakes Educational Associates.

Pope John-Paul II
HIS HOLINESS POPE JOHN PAUL II. Note: The official ILR recording of the Pope's visit to the UK 1982. LP. Cat no: **POPE 11.** Released on Phonogram, Jul '82 by Phonogram Ltd Deleted Jul '87.

JOHN PAUL II (The visit of the Pope to Ireland) (Unknown narrator(s)). MC. Cat no: **CIRL 1979.** Released on Outlet, Jan '80 by Outlet Records, Duncans, Outlet Records, Celtic Music, Prism Leisure, I & B Records, Record Services, Ross Records.

PILGRIM POPE, THE. Note: Highlights of the Pope's 1982 visit to Britain from BBC recordings. Introduced by Gerald Priestland, it features the Pope's speeches and addresses, together with a selection of the music, choirs and masses. LP. Cat no: **REB 445.** Released on BBC, Jun '82 by BBC Records, Taylors Deleted 31 Aug '88.

MC. Cat no: **ZCF 445.** Released on BBC, Jun '82 by BBC Records, Taylors Deleted 31 Aug '88.

Portuguese
DISCOVERING PORTUGUESE (Language Courses) (Unknown narrator(s)). Note: An introduction to simple everyday Portuguese.

MCSET. Cat no: **PTT 293.** Released on BBC Publications, '91. Note : 2 Cassettes.

GET BY IN PORTUGUESE (Language Courses) (Unknown narrator(s)). Note: Each book contains phrases and conversations. MC. Cat no: **PTT 258/9.** Released on BBC Publications, Jun '83. Note : 2 Cassettes.

GET BY TRAVEL PACKS (Language Courses) (Unknown narrator(s)). MCSET. Cat no: **PACK 2258.** Released on BBC Publications, '91. Note : 2 Cassettes.

LANGUAGE COURSE - PORTUGUESE (Unknown narrator(s)). LPS. Cat no: **0747303371.** Released on Linguaphone, Apr '82 by Linguaphone Institute, Taylors, Century Records (USA), Bond Street Music.

LINGUAPHONE PORTUGUESE TRAVELLERS (Language Courses) (Unknown narrator(s)). MC. Cat no: **0747306974.** Released on Linguaphone, '91 by Linguaphone Institute, Taylors, Century Records (USA), Bond Street Music.

PORTUGUESE CASSETTE COURSE (Unknown narrator(s)). Note: Includes three months' book and an instruction leaflet. MCSET. Cat no: **852850727.** Released on Hugo Languages, '92 by Hugo Language Books Limited. Note: 4 cassettes. Playing time 4hrs.

PORTUGUESE FOR TRAVEL (Unknown narrator(s)). MC. Cat no: **BCP 011.** Released on Berlitz Language Courses, '88, Conifer Records.

PORTUGUESE LANGUAGE BASICS (Unknown narrator(s)). MC. Cat no: **BMC 011.** Released on Berlitz Language Courses, '88, Conifer Records.

PORTUGUESE TRAVEL PACK (Unknown narrator(s)). Note: Contains a Hugo phrase book. MC. Cat no: **852851138.** Released on Hugo Languages, '92 by Hugo Language Books Limited. Note: 4 Cassettes. Playing time 4hrs.

PROGRAMMATIC PORTUGUESE (Volume 1) (Unknown narrator(s)). MCSET. Cat no: **P 151.** Released on Audio Forum (Language courses), '91. Note: 16 Cassettes

PROGRAMMATIC PORTUGUESE (Volume 2) (Unknown narrator(s)). MCSET. Cat no: **P 180.** Released on Audio Forum (Language courses), '91. Note: 22 Cassettes

SPEAK PORTUGUESE TODAY (Conversational Courses) (Unknown narrator(s)). Note: Consists of a book and a 75-90 minute cassette. MC. Cat no: **852851111.** Released on Hugo Languages, '92 by Hugo Language Books Limited.

Powell, Margaret
BELOW STAIRS (Christine Dawe). MCSET. Cat no: **1312F.** Released on Travellers Tales, '91 by Travellers Tales. Note: 4 Cassettes

MCSET. Cat no: **1854961810.** Released on Bramhope, '91 by Ulverscroft Soundings. Note: 4 Cassettes.

BUTLER'S REVENGE, THE (Nanette Newman). MCSET. Cat no: **1138F.** Released on Travellers Tales, '91 by Travellers Tales. Note: 6 Cassettes.

CLIMBING THE STAIRS (Anne Cater). MCSET. Cat no: **1416F.** Released on Travellers Tales, '91 by Travellers

Tales. Note: 5 Cassettes.
MCSET. Cat no: **1854962523.** Released on Bramhope, '91 by Ulverscroft Soundings. Note: 5 Cassettes.
MAIDS AND MISTRESSES (Nanette Newman).
MCSET. Cat no: **1139F.** Released on Travellers Tales, '91 by Travellers Tales. Note: 6 Cassettes.
TREASURE UPSTAIRS, THE (Unknown narrator(s)).
MCSET. Cat no: **1854962841.** Released on Soundings, '91 by Soundings Records, Bond Street Music. Note: 6 Cassettes.

Powell, Sandy
CAN YOU HEAR ME, MOTHER? (Sandy Powell).
Tracks / Lost policeman, The / Sandy the shopwalker / Sandy the windowcleaner / Sandy joins the nudists / Gracie's and Sandy's party / Sandy plays in the test match / Sandy's own Labour exchange / Sandy the dirt track rider / Night on the Embankment, A / Sandy the barber / Sandy's Irish sweepstake song / Return of the lost poilceman, The.
CD. Cat no: **PAST CD 9731.** Released on Flapper, '90 by Pavilion Records, Taylors, Pinnacle.

Prebble, John
CULLODEN - THE LAST JACOBITE RISING (Davina Porter).
MCSET. Cat no: **1003G.** Released on Travellers Tales, '91 by Travellers Tales. Note: 8 Cassettes
MCSET. Cat no: **IAB 89082.** Released on Isis Audio Books, '91.
GLENCOE (Donal Donnelly).
MCSET. Cat no: **RB 86830.** Released on Recorded Books, Apr '92 by Isis Audio Books. Note: 4 Cassettes. Playing time 10hrs 30mins.

Prevert, Jacques
PAROLES (Edited By Martin Sorrell) (Unknown narrator(s)).
Note: An evaluation of Prevert's work.
MC. Cat no: **F 7527.** Released on Exeter Tapes, '91 by Drakes Educational Associates.

Prevost, Abbe
MANON LESCAUT (Edited By Simon Davies) (Unknown narrator(s)).
Note: A discussion of the two main characters in Abbe Prevosts novel.
MC. Cat no: **F 7508.** Released on Exeter Tapes, '91 by Drakes Educational Associates.

Pushkin, Alexander S.
LYRICS (Edited By Peter Scorer) (Unknown narrator(s)).
Note: A general introduction to the poetry of Pushkin and Lemontov, followed by a reading in Russian of a selection of the poems. With commentary.

MC. Cat no: **R 7628.** Released on Exeter Tapes, '91 by Drakes Educational Associates.
MEDNYI VSADNIK (Edited By A.D. Briggs) (Unknown narrator(s)).
Note: The themes of Pushkin's narrative poem are discussed.
MC. Cat no: **R 7627.** Released on Exeter Tapes, '91 by Drakes Educational Associates.
MOZART I SALIERI (Edited By T.E. Little) (Unknown narrator(s)).
Note: An analysis of the form and content of the work and its relationship with Pushkin's work and thought.
MC. Cat no: **R 7702.** Released on Exeter Tapes, '91 by Drakes Educational Associates.
PIKOVAYA DAMA (Edited By W.J. Leatherspoon) (Unknown narrator(s)).
Note: A detailed examination of the significance of the work among Pushkin's prose writings.
MC. Cat no: **R 7703.** Released on Exeter Tapes, '91 by Drakes Educational Associates.

Queffelec, H
UN RECTEUR DE L'ILE DE SEIN (Edited By Philip Thody) (Unknown narrator(s)).
Note: The mixture of primitive superstition and traditional catholic doctrine as aspects of Queffelec's novel are all examined.
MC. Cat no: **F 7608.** Released on Exeter Tapes, '91 by Drakes Educational Associates.

Race, Steve
TWO WORLDS OF JOSEPH RACE (Gordon Griffin).
MCSET. Cat no: **1051N.** Released on Travellers Tales, '91 by Travellers Tales. Note: 4 Cassettes.
MCSET. Cat no: **1854962213.** Released on Bramhope, '91 by Ulverscroft Soundings. Note: 4 Cassettes.

Racine, Jean
ANDROMAQUE (Edited By Anthony Greaves) (Unknown narrator(s)).
MC. Cat no: **F 7563.** Released on Exeter Tapes, '91 by Drakes Educational Associates.
BRITANNICUS (Edited By Roger Pensom and Anthony Kelly) (Unknown narrator(s)).
Note:
A discussion of J. Racine's notion of tragedy against the background of classical drama and contemporary French theatre.
MC. Cat no: **F 7510.** Released on Exeter Tapes, '91 by Drakes Educational Associates.
PHEDRE (Edited By Jean D. Biard) (Unknown narrator(s)).
Note:
An introduction to J. Racine's tragedy. The poetry of the play is also explored. In French.

MC. Cat no: **F 7681.** Released on Exeter Tapes, '91 by Drakes Educational Associates.

Rackham, Neil
PSYCHOLOGY OF NEGOTIATING, THE (Secrets of Success Series) (Neil Rakham).
MC. Cat no: **060056066X.** Released on Hamlyn Books On Tape, '88, Bond Street Music.

Radio
50 YEARS OF ROYAL BROADCASTS (Various narrators).
2LP. Cat no: **REJ 187.** Released on BBC, '74 by BBC Records, Taylors **Deleted** '88.
MC. Cat no: **HRMC 187.** Released on BBC, '74 by BBC Records, Taylors.
PLAIN TALES FROM THE RAJ (Various narrators).
Note: The story of the British Raj at first hand.
MCSET. Cat no: **ZBBC 1017.** Released on BBC Radio Collection, Sep '88 by BBC Records. Note: ISBN No: 0563 225858

Ratushinskaya, Irina
GREY IS THE COLOUR OF HOPE (Gretel Davis).
MCSET. Cat no: **1042/1043A.** Released on Travellers Tales, '91 by Travellers Tales. Note: 12 Cassettes.
MCSET. Cat no: **OAS 90011.** Released on Oasis Audio Books, '91 by Isis Audio Books.

Read, Miss
FORTUNATE GRANDCHILD, A (And Time Remembered).
MCSET. Cat no: **CAB 283.** Released on Chivers Audio Books, '91 by Chivers Audio Books, Green Dragon Audio Visual. Note: 4 Cassettes.
MCSET. Cat no: **1026A.** Released on Travellers Tales, '91 by Travellers Tales. Note: 4 Cassettes.

Reagan, Ronald
RONALD REAGAN: AN AMERICAN LIFE (Unknown narrator(s)).
MCSET. Cat no: **0671726307.** Released on Simon & Schuster, '91 by Simon & Schuster Ltd.

Religious
BUDDHIST CHANTS AND MUSIC FROM SRI LANKA (Various artists).
MCSET. Cat no: **BC 5.** Released on Sussex Tapes, '91 by Sussex Publications Ltd.. Note: 2 Cassettes
CENTURIES (Edited by Harold Kushner) (John Westbrook).
MCSET. Cat no: **OAS 90013.** Released on Oasis Audio Books, '91 by Isis Audio Books. Note: 8 Cassettes.
CHURCH OF ENGLAND AND THE ENGLISH REFORMATION (Claire Cross & P. Collinson).
MC. Cat no: **H 28.** Released on Sussex Tapes, '91 by Sussex Publications Ltd.

EVANGELICAL RELIGION AND SOCIETY FROM 1789-1859 (David Thompson & Dr I Bradley).
MCSET. Cat no: **HEA 024.** Released on AVP, '91 by AVP Publishing.

EVENSONG AT EXETER CATHEDRAL (Exeter Cathedral Choir).
Tracks / Locus Iste / Versicles and responses / Christ is made the sure foundation (Plainsong.) / Psalm 84 / First lesson / Magnificat / Nunc dimittis in D / Second lesson / Creed / Lesser litany / Lord's prayer, The / Responses and collects / Blessed city, heavenly Salem (Anthem.) / Prayers / Ye watchers and ye holy ones / Flourish for an occasion.
Note: Exeter Cathedral Choir, director Lucian Nethsingha.
LP. Cat no: **ACA 544.** Released on Alpha, '85 by Abbey Recording Co.Ltd., Gamut Distribution, Abbey Recording Co.Ltd..
MC. Cat no: **CACA 544.** Released on Alpha, '85 by Abbey Recording Co.Ltd., Gamut Distribution, Abbey Recording Co.Ltd..

HINDU CHANTS AND TEMPLE MUSIC (Various artists).
MCSET. Cat no: **HB 3.** Released on Sussex Tapes, '91 by Sussex Publications Ltd.. Note: 2 Cassettes.

IN PRAISE OF BUDDHA (Various artists).
MCSET. Cat no: **HB 5.** Released on Sussex Tapes, '91 by Sussex Publications Ltd.. Note: 2 Cassettes

JEHOVAH'S WITNESSES (Various narrators).
MC. Cat no: **SV 075C.** Released on Sound & Vision (2), '91 by Scripture Union.

MISSION ENGLAND VOL.2 (Various artists).
LP. Cat no: **WST 9661.** Released on Word (UK), '1 by Word Records (UK), Sony Music Operations, Outlet Records, Taylors **Deleted** '88.
MC. Cat no: **WC 9661.** Released on Word (UK), '1 by Word Records (UK), Sony Music Operations, Outlet Records, Taylors.

MOONIES, THE (Various narrators).
MC. Cat no: **SV 076C.** Released on Sound & Vision (2), '91 by Scripture Union.

MORMONS (Various narrators).
MC. Cat no: **SV 077C.** Released on Sound & Vision (2), '91 by Scripture Union.

MUEZZIN'S CALL AND ISLAMIC CHANTS (Various artists).
MCSET. Cat no: **B 12.** Released on Sussex Tapes, '91 by Sussex Publications Ltd.. Note: 2 Cassettes.

OUT OF THE BLUE (Lionel Blue).
MC. Cat no: **7201.** Released on Bridge Studios, '91 by Bridge Studios.

TEACH US TO PRAY (Joyce Huggett).
MC. Cat no: **0340539291.** Released on Hodder & Stoughton, '91 by Hodder & Stoughton.

WHO NEEDS GOD? (Harold Kushner).
MC. Cat no: **0671689037.** Released on Simon & Schuster, '91 by Simon & Schuster Ltd.

Rhea, Nicholas

CONSTABLE AROUND THE VILLAGE (Christopher Kay).
MCSET. Cat no: **1107N.** Released on Travellers Tales, '91 by Travellers Tales. Note: 5 Cassettes.
MCSET. Cat no: **1854964429.** Released on Bramhope, '91 by Ulverscroft Soundings. Note: 5 Cassettes.

CONSTABLE ON THE HILL (Christopher Kay).
MCSET. Cat no: **1094N.** Released on Travellers Tales, '91 by Travellers Tales. Note: 6 Cassettes.
MCSET. Cat no: **1854963503.** Released on Soundings, '91 by Soundings Records, Bond Street Music. Note: 6 Cassettes.

CONSTABLE ON THE PROWL (Christopher Kay).
MCSET. Cat no: **1854964844.** Released on Bramhope, '91 by Ulverscroft Soundings. Note: 5 Cassettes.

Richardson, Anthony

ONE MAN AND HIS DOG (Ray Dunbobbin).
MCSET. Cat no: **1021N.** Released on Travellers Tales, '91 by Travellers Tales. Note: 4 Cassettes.
MCSET. Cat no: **1854961845.** Released on Bramhope, '91 by Ulverscroft Soundings. Note: 4 Cassettes.

Rilke

SIX ANALYSES (Edited By Keith A. Dickson) (Unknown narrator(s)).
Note: Six of Rilke's poems are analysed.
MC. Cat no: **G 7686.** Released on Exeter Tapes, '91 by Drakes Educational Associates.

Rix, Sir Brian

FARCE ABOUT FACE (Biography) (Sir Brian Rix).
MCSET. Cat no: **OAS 90114.** Released on Oasis Audio Books, '91 by Isis Audio Books. Note: 8 Cassettes.
MCSET. Cat no: **1066A.** Released on Travellers Tales, '91 by Travellers Tales.

Roathke, Theodore

POETRY OF THEODORE ROATHKE, THE (Theodore Roathke).
Note: Author reads their work and discuss their formative influences.
MC. Cat no: **AS 38.** Released on Sussex Tapes, '91 by Sussex Publications Ltd..

Robbe-Grillet, Alain

LES GOMMES (Edited By J.B. Howitt) (Unknown narrator(s)).
Note: A discussion of the narrative technique of this novel by Alain Robbe - Grillet.
MC. Cat no: **F 7570.** Released on Exeter Tapes, '91 by Drakes Educational Associates.

Robert The Bruce

ROBERT THE BRUCE (History for ages 8+) (Unknown narrator(s)).
Note: Book and cassette.
MC. Cat no: **PLBH 149.** Released on Tell-A-Tale, '88 by Pickwick Records, Taylors, Clyde Factors.

Rochefort, C

LES PETITS ENFANTS DU SIECLE (Edited By Philip Thody) (Unknown narrator(s)).
Note: An account of Rochefort's realistic novel which deals with the impact of family allowances and other social factors on a French working class family.
MC. Cat no: **F 7786.** Released on Exeter Tapes, '91 by Drakes Educational Associates.

Rogers, Jim

TUNNELLING INTO COLDITZ (Christopher Kay).
MCSET. Cat no: **1025N.** Released on Travellers Tales, '91 by Travellers Tales. Note: 5 Cassettes.
MCSET. Cat no: **1854961829.** Released on Bramhope, '91 by Ulverscroft Soundings. Note: 5 Cassettes.

Romains, J

KNOCK (Edited By Jean D. Biard) (Unknown narrator(s)).
Note: An examination of the implications, structure and intensity of this play by Romains with a detailed analysis of the principal character. In French.
MC. Cat no: **F 7532.** Released on Exeter Tapes, '91 by Drakes Educational Associates.

Romance Languages

ROMANCE LANGUAGES, THE (Edited By Ian Press) (Unknown narrator(s)).
MC. Cat no: **RL 7907.** Released on Exeter Tapes, '91 by Drakes Educational Associates.

Romanian

INTRODUCING THE ROMANIAN LANGUAGE (Edited By Graham Mallinson) (Unknown narrator(s)).
MC. Cat no: **RM 7816.** Released on Exeter Tapes, '91 by Drakes Educational Associates.

SOUNDS AND ALPHABET OF ROMANIAN (Edited By Graham Mallinson) (Unknown narrator(s)).
MC. Cat no: **RM 7932.** Released on Exeter Tapes, '91 by Drakes Educational Associates.

SPOKEN ROMANIAN (Unknown narrator(s)).
MCSET. Cat no: **RM 10.** Released on Audio Forum (Language courses), '91.

Rubik's Cube

HOW TO SOLVE THE RUBIK CUBE (Unknown narrator(s)).

MC. Cat no: NEVC 96. Released on Nevis, Nov '81.

Rugby Union

HISTORY AND THE HUMOUR, THE (Cliff Morgan).
Note: Memories of great teams, matches and tries with Cliff Morgan.
MCSET. Cat no: ZBBC 1251. Released on BBC, Aug '91 by BBC Records, Taylors. Note: ISBN NO: 0563 365234.

Russia

19TH CENTURY RUSSIA (The Challenge to the Autocracy) (Dr. Lionel Kochan & Michael Pushkin).
MCSET. Cat no: HUA 014. Released on AVP, '91 by AVP Publishing.
ARCHPRIEST AVVAKUM AND THE RUSSIAN CHURCH SCHISM (Edited By Alan Wood) (Unknown narrator(s)).
MC. Cat no: R 7790. Released on Exeter Tapes, '91 by Drakes Educational Associates.
DECEMBRISTS, THE (Edited By P.J. O'Meary) (Unknown narrator(s)).
Note: An account of the first attempt in Russian history to overthrow Russian Tsarism and replace it with a constitutional form of government, in December 1825.
MC. Cat no: R 7671. Released on Exeter Tapes, '91 by Drakes Educational Associates.
EARLY SOVIET CINEMA (The Revolution In Techniques And Human Values) (Unknown narrator(s)).
MC. Cat no: R 7844. Released on Exeter Tapes, '91 by Drakes Educational Associates.
END OF ROMANOV RUSSIA, THE (Edited By Peter Morris) (Unknown narrator(s)).
MC. Cat no: R 7738. Released on Exeter Tapes, '91 by Drakes Educational Associates.
FORMATION OF THE RUSSIAN STATE, THE (Edited By Derek J. Hunns) (Unknown narrator(s)).
MC. Cat no: R 7690. Released on Exeter Tapes, '91 by Drakes Educational Associates.
FROM REVOLUTION TO INDUSTRIALISATION (The Soviet Economy 1917-1928) (Unknown narrator(s)).
MC. Cat no: R 7876. Released on Exeter Tapes, '91 by Drakes Educational Associates.
GEROI NASHEGO VREMENI (Edited By David J. Richards) (Unknown narrator(s)).
Note: An examination of two of the most striking features of Lermontov's novel, the design of the work and the character of the hero.
MC. Cat no: R 7626. Released on Exeter Tapes, '91 by Drakes Educational Associates.
KRUSCHEV AND EASTERN EUROPE (Harry Hanak & Hugh Seton-Watson).
MC. Cat no: HB 7. Released on Sussex Tapes, '91 by Sussex Publications Ltd..
LENIN (Alec Nove & Dr. Tibor Szamuely).
MCSET. Cat no: HUA 006. Released on AVP, '91 by AVP Publishing.
LENIN AND LENINISM (Edited By William Tupman) (Unknown narrator(s)).
MC. Cat no: R 7873. Released on Exeter Tapes, '91 by Drakes Educational Associates.
MARX AND MARXISM (Edited By Iain Hampsher-Monk) (Unknown narrator(s)).
MC. Cat no: R 7872. Released on Exeter Tapes, '91 by Drakes Educational Associates.
MODERN SOVIET CINEMA (Edited By Frank Beardon) (Unknown narrator(s)).
MC. Cat no: R 7829. Released on Exeter Tapes, '91 by Drakes Educational Associates.
NEP AND SOVIET INDUSTRIALISATION, THE (R.W. Davies & M. Lewin).
MC. Cat no: HB 3. Released on Sussex Tapes, '91 by Sussex Publications Ltd.. Note: AAD
NINETEENTH CENTURY RUSSIA (Norman Stone & Harry Willets).
MC. Cat no: HE 23. Released on Sussex Tapes, '91 by Sussex Publications Ltd..
OUTLINE OF RUSSIAN MUSIC, AN (Edited By Gerald Seaman) (Unknown narrator(s)).
MC. Cat no: R 7736. Released on Exeter Tapes, '91 by Drakes Educational Associates.
OUTLINE OF SOVIET MUSIC, AN (Edited By Gerald Seaman) (Unknown narrator(s)).
MC. Cat no: R 7737. Released on Exeter Tapes, '91 by Drakes Educational Associates.
PEOPLES OF THE U.S.S.R., THE (Edited By Derek J. Hunns) (Unknown narrator(s)).
MC. Cat no: R 7691. Released on Exeter Tapes, '91 by Drakes Educational Associates.
PETER THE GREAT AND CATHERINE THE GREAT (Isabel De Maderiaza & Roger Bartlett).
MC. Cat no: HE 24. Released on Sussex Tapes, '91 by Sussex Publications Ltd..
REIGN OF CATHERINE THE GREAT, 1762-1796, THE (Edited By Janet Hartley) (Unknown narrator(s)).
MC. Cat no: R 7867. Released on Exeter Tapes, '91 by Drakes Educational Associates.
RELIGION IN THE SOVIET UNION (Edited By Derek J. Hunns) (Unknown narrator(s)).
MC. Cat no: R 7692. Released on Exeter Tapes, '91 by Drakes Educational Associates.
ROOTS OF MARXISM-LENINISM, THE (Edited By William Tupman) (Unknown narrator(s)).
MC. Cat no: R 7717. Released on Exeter Tapes, '91 by Drakes Educational Associates.
RUSSIA 1917: YEAR OF REVOLUTION (Edited By Peter Morris) (Unknown narrator(s)).
MC. Cat no: R 7868. Released on Exeter Tapes, '91 by Drakes Educational Associates.
RUSSIAN CLASSICISM (Edited By W.G. Jones) (Unknown narrator(s)).
MC. Cat no: R 7802. Released on Exeter Tapes, '91 by Drakes Educational Associates.
RUSSIAN FOLK THEATRE, THE (Edited By Elizabeth Warner) (Unknown narrator(s)).
MC. Cat no: R 7801. Released on Exeter Tapes, '91 by Drakes Educational Associates.
RUSSIAN ICONS (Edited By Marilyn Minto) (Unknown narrator(s)).
MC. Cat no: R 7815. Released on Exeter Tapes, '91 by Drakes Educational Associates.
RUSSIAN REVOLUTION, THE (Alec Nove & Dr. Tibor Szamuely).
MCSET. Cat no: HUA 004. Released on AVP, '91 by AVP Publishing.
SOVIET ECONOMIC DEVELOPMENT 1917-1953 (Alec Nove & Dr. Olga Crisp).
MCSET. Cat no: HUA 070. Released on AVP, '91 by AVP Publishing.
SOVIET ECONOMY: THE BREZHNEV ERA (Edited By Robert Lewis) (Unknown narrator(s)).
MC. Cat no: R 7879. Released on Exeter Tapes, '91 by Drakes Educational Associates.
SOVIET ECONOMY UNDER KHRUSHCHEV, THE (Edited By Robert Lewis) (Unknown narrator(s)).
MC. Cat no: R 7878. Released on Exeter Tapes, '91 by Drakes Educational Associates.
SOVIET JEWS (Edited By Derek J. Hunns) (Unknown narrator(s)).
MC. Cat no: R 7693. Released on Exeter Tapes, '91 by Drakes Educational Associates.
SOVIET UNION'S GEOGRAPHICAL PROBLEMS, THE (Edited By Derek J. Hunns) (Unknown narrator(s)).
MC. Cat no: R 7951. Released on Exeter Tapes, '91 by Drakes Educational Associates.
SPORT IN SOVIET SOCIETY (Edited By James Riordan) (Unknown narrator(s)).
MC. Cat no: R 7944. Released on Exeter Tapes, '91 by Drakes Educational Associates.
STALIN (Angus Walker & David Shapiro).
MCSET. Cat no: HUA 031. Released on AVP, '91 by AVP Publishing.
STALIN AND SOVIET ECONOMIC DEVELOPMENT (Edited By Robert Lewis) (Unknown narrator(s)).
MC. Cat no: R 7877. Released on Exeter Tapes, '91 by Drakes Educational Associates.
STALIN AND STALINISM (Edited By

William Tupman) (Unknown narrator(s)).
MC. Cat no: **R 7874**. Released on Exeter Tapes, '91 by Drakes Educational Associates.

TROTSKY AND TROTSKYISM (Edited By William Tupman) (Unknown narrator(s)).
MC. Cat no: **R 7875**. Released on Exeter Tapes, '91 by Drakes Educational Associates.

USSR AND COMECON, THE (Edited By A.R. Layton) (Unknown narrator(s)).
MC. Cat no: **R 7789**. Released on Exeter Tapes, '91 by Drakes Educational Associates.

Russian

ASPECTS OF RUSSIAN GRAMMAR (Unknown narrator(s)).
MC. Cat no: **R 7695**. Released on Exeter Tapes, '91 by Drakes Educational Associates.

CHURCH SLAVONICISMS IN RUSSIAN (Edited By Ian Press) (Unknown narrator(s)).
MC. Cat no: **R 7696**. Released on Exeter Tapes, '91 by Drakes Educational Associates.

COLLOQUIAL RUSSIAN (Edited By Aidan Cahill) (Unknown narrator(s)).
MC. Cat no: **R 7672**. Released on Exeter Tapes, '91 by Drakes Educational Associates.

DEVELOPMENT OF THE RUSSIAN LANGUAGE, THE (Edited By Derek J. Hunns) (Unknown narrator(s)).
MC. Cat no: **R 7643**. Released on Exeter Tapes, '91 by Drakes Educational Associates.

GENDER IN RUSSIAN (Edited By Aidan Cahill) (Unknown narrator(s)).
MC. Cat no: **R 7938**. Released on Exeter Tapes, '91 by Drakes Educational Associates.

GET BY IN RUSSIAN (Language Courses) (Unknown narrator(s)).
Note: Each book contains phrases and conversations.
MCSET. Cat no: **PTT 321**. Released on BBC Publications, '91.

GET BY TRAVEL PACKS (Language Courses) (Unknown narrator(s)).
MCSET. Cat no: **PACK 2321**. Released on BBC Publications, '91. Note : 2 Cassettes.

LANGUAGE COURSE - RUSSIAN (Unknown narrator(s)).
LPS. Cat no: **0747302650**. Released on Linguaphone, Apr '82 by Linguaphone Institute, Taylors, Century Records (USA), Bond Street Music.

MODERN RUSSIAN (Volume 1) (Unknown narrator(s)).
MCSET. Cat no: **B 101**. Released on Audio Forum (Language courses), '91. Note: 24 Cassettes.

MODERN RUSSIAN (Volume 2) (Unknown narrator(s)).
MCSET. Cat no: **B 125**. Released on Audio Forum (Language courses), '91. Note: 24 Cassettes

PENGUIN BASIC RUSSIAN - PART 1 (Edited By Derek J. Hunns) (Unknown narrator(s)).
MC. Cat no: **R 7739**. Released on Exeter Tapes, '91 by Drakes Educational Associates.

PENGUIN BASIC RUSSIAN - PART 2 (Edited By J. Hunns) (Unknown narrator(s)).
MC. Cat no: **R 7740**. Released on Exeter Tapes, '91 by Drakes Educational Associates.

PENGUIN BASIC RUSSIAN - PART 3 (Edited By Derek J. Hunns) (Unknown narrator(s)).
MC. Cat no: **R 7741**. Released on Exeter Tapes, '91 by Drakes Educational Associates.

PENGUIN BASIC RUSSIAN - PART 4 (Edited By Derek J. Hunns) (Unknown narrator(s)).
MC. Cat no: **R 7742**. Released on Exeter Tapes, Feb '91 by Drakes Educational Associates.

RUSSIAN AND THE LANGUAGES OF THE U.S.S.R. (Edited By Ian Press) (Unknown narrator(s)).
MC. Cat no: **R 7716**. Released on Exeter Tapes, '91 by Drakes Educational Associates.

RUSSIAN CASSETTE COURSE (Unknown narrator(s)).
Note: Includes:- 3 months' book and an instruction leaflet.
MCSET. Cat no: **852851294**. Released on Hugo Languages, '92 by Hugo Language Books Limited. Note: 4 Cassettes. Playing time 4hrs.

RUSSIAN DIALECTS (Edited By John Dunn) (Unknown narrator(s)).
MC. Cat no: **R 7732**. Released on Exeter Tapes, '91 by Drakes Educational Associates.

RUSSIAN LANGUAGE AND PEOPLE (Language Courses) (Unknown narrator(s)).
2LP. Cat no: **OP 248/3**. Released on BBC Publications, Jun '83.
MCSET. Cat no: **PTT 248/3**. Released on BBC Publications, Jun '83.

RUSSIAN LISTENING COMPREHENSION - PART 1 (Edited By J.G. Devereux) (Unknown narrator(s)).
Note: Accompanying booklet available. Cat no: R 7722B
MC. Cat no: **R 7722**. Released on Exeter Tapes, '91 by Drakes Educational Associates.

RUSSIAN LISTENING COMPREHENSION - PART 2 (Edited By J.G. Devereux) (Unknown narrator(s)).
Note: Accompany booklet available . Cat. no. R 7722B
MC. Cat no: **R 7723**. Released on Exeter Tapes, '91 by Drakes Educational Associates.

RUSSIAN STRESS (Edited By Aidan Cahill) (Unknown narrator(s)).
MC. Cat no: **R 7939**. Released on Exeter Tapes, '91 by Drakes Educational Associates.

RUSSIAN TRAVEL PACK (Unknown narrator(s)).
Note: Contains a Hugo phrase book.
MC. Cat no: **852851553**. Released on Hugo Languages, '92 by Hugo Language Books Limited.

SOUNDS AND ALPHABET OF RUSSIAN, THE (Edited By Derek J. Hunns) (Unknown narrator(s)).
Note: With accompanying notes.
MC. Cat no: **R 7648**. Released on Exeter Tapes, '91 by Drakes Educational Associates.

USE OF CASES IN RUSSIAN, THE (Edited By Aidan Cahill) (Unknown narrator(s)).
MC. Cat no: **R 7791**. Released on Exeter Tapes, '91 by Drakes Educational Associates.

VERBS OF MOTION (Edited By Aidan Cahill) (Unknown narrator(s)).
MC. Cat no: **R 7694**. Released on Exeter Tapes, '91 by Drakes Educational Associates.

Russian Literature

LEXIS OF RUSSIAN, THE (Edited By Aidan Cahill) (Unknown narrator(s)).
MC. Cat no: **R 7697**. Released on Exeter Tapes, '91 by Drakes Educational Associates.

RUSSIAN APPROACH TO LITERATURE, THE (Edited By David J. Richards) (Unknown narrator(s)).
MC. Cat no: **R 7708**. Released on Exeter Tapes, '91 by Drakes Educational Associates.

RUSSIAN REVOLUTIONARY NOVEL, THE (Edited By Richard Freeborn) (Unknown narrator(s)).
MC. Cat no: **R 7835**. Released on Exeter Tapes, '91 by Drakes Educational Associates.

Sabatier, R

LES ALLUMETTES SUEDOISES (Edited By Andrew Rothwell) (Unknown narrator(s)).
Note: A critical analysis centred on the problem of realism in this novel by R. Sabatier.
MC. Cat no: **F 7327**. Released on Exeter Tapes, '91 by Drakes Educational Associates.

Sagan, Francoise

BONJOUR TRISTESSE (Edited By Andrew Rothwell) (Unknown narrator(s)).
Note: A literary and contextual study of this best selling French cult novel of 1954.
MC. Cat no: **F 7319**. Released on Exeter Tapes, '91 by Drakes Educational Associates.

Salacrou, A

BOULEVARD DURAND (Edited By David Looseley) (Unknown narrator(s)).
Note: The play's concern with the problem of commitment is detailed. It is discussed in relation to Salacrou's work as a whole.
MC. Cat no: **F 7896**. Released on

Exeter Tapes, '91 by Drakes Educational Associates.

Sartre, Jean-Paul
BACKGROUND TO JEAN PAUL SARTRE (Edited By Ray Davison) (Unknown narrator(s)).
Note: Includes an analysis of the principal features of Jean Paul Sartre's existentialism and the development of his political philosophy.
MC. Cat no: **F 7566.** Released on Exeter Tapes, '91 by Drakes Educational Associates.
LES JEUX SONT FAITS (Edited By Philip Thody) (Unknown narrator(s)).
Note: Sartre's early philosophy considered with particular reference to the misleading nature of the work as a guide to his central teaching.
MC. Cat no: **F 7682.** Released on Exeter Tapes, '91 by Drakes Educational Associates.
LES MAINS SALES (Edited By Jeremy Whistle) (Unknown narrator(s)).
Note: Aims to situate the play within the framework of Sartre's 'engagement' showing to what extent the author's views on literature and politics are reflected in it.
MC. Cat no: **F 7511.** Released on Exeter Tapes, '91 by Drakes Educational Associates.
LES SEQUESTRES D'ALTONA (Edited By Philip Thody) (Unknown narrator(s)).
Note: An analysis of the play in the context of Sartre's own work and in his attitude to the problem of Algeria.
MC. Cat no: **F 7307.** Released on Exeter Tapes, '91 by Drakes Educational Associates.

Sassoon, Siegfried
DIARIES 1915-1918, THE (John Westbrook).
MCSET. Cat no: **OAS 89091.** Released on Oasis Audio Books, '91 by Isis Audio Books. Note: 12 Cassette set. Playing time 12hrs.
MCSET. Cat no: **1051/1052A.** Released on Travellers Tales, '91 by Travellers Tales. Note: 12 Cassette set.

Schiller, Franz
(See under Von Schiller, Franz)

Sciascia
IL CONTESTO (Edited By Judith Kelly) (Unknown narrator(s)).
Note: A study of Sciascia's novel of political corruption.
MC. Cat no: **I 7339.** Released on Exeter Tapes, '91 by Drakes Educational Associates.

Science Fiction
SCIENCE FICTION (Dr. Patrick Parrinder & David Ketterer).
Note: Pre-recorded discussions which show literary criticism as a living, evolving interchange.
MCSET. Cat no: **SF 1.** Released on Sussex Tapes, '91 by Sussex Publications Ltd.. Note: 2 Cassette set

Scipion, M
LE CLOS DU ROI (Edited By Philip Thody) (Unknown narrator(s)).
Note: An examination of the social and geographical information provided in this novel by M. Scipion.
MC. Cat no: **F 7921.** Released on Exeter Tapes, '91 by Drakes Educational Associates.

Scotland
BRUCE MEMORIAL WINDOW (Unknown narrator(s)).
Note: Story of stained glass windows installed in North Transept of Dunfermline Abbey.
MC. Cat no: **SSC 025.** Released on Scotsoun, '91 by Scotsoun Recordings, Morley Audio Services.
BURNS NICHT AT LUGTON (Unknown narrator(s)).
MC. Cat no: **SSC 002.** Released on Scotsoun, '91 by Scotsoun Recordings, Morley Audio Services.
LALLANS (Unknown narrator(s)).
MC. Cat no: **SSC 005.** Released on Scotsoun, '91 by Scotsoun Recordings, Morley Audio Services.
NEEPS AND TATTIES (Alex Mair & Sid Robertson).
Note: Guide to growing vegetables in the Scottish climate.
MC. Cat no: **SSC 010.** Released on Scotsoun, '91 by Scotsoun Recordings, Morley Audio Services.

Scott, Mary
FORGETTING'S NO EXCUSE (D. Langford).
MCSET. Cat no: **OAS 11191.** Released on Oasis Audio Books, Nov '91 by Isis Audio Books.

Scottish
GLEG (Learning Scots) (Unknown narrator(s)).
MC. Cat no: **SSC 084.** Released on Scotsoun, '91 by Scotsoun Recordings, Morley Audio Services.
TWA LEIDS AND DA CHANAN (Unknown narrator(s)).
Note: This cassette brings together Scots and Gaelic poems of note with worthy translations in the alternative language.
MC. Cat no: **SSC 080.** Released on Scotsoun, '91 by Scotsoun Recordings, Morley Audio Services.

Self Improvement
5-00 REFRESHER, THE (Unknown narrator(s)).
MC. Cat no: **067168115X.** Released on Simon & Schuster, '91 by Simon & Schuster Ltd.
ACCELERATED (HIGH-SPEED) LEARNING (Dick Sutphen).
MC. Cat no: **RX 105.** Released on Valley Of The Sun, '88.
ALTERNATIVES TO MARRIAGE (Edited by Carol Rogers) (Unknown narrator(s)).
MC. Cat no: **PT 28.** Released on Psychology Today (USA), Oct '81 by Seminar Cassettes.
AMERICAN CANCER SOCIETY'S "FRESHSTART" (21 Days to Stop Smoking) (Unknown narrator(s)).
MCSET. Cat no: **0671617834.** Released on Simon & Schuster, '91 by Simon & Schuster Ltd. Note: 2 Cassettes.
ANGER WORKOUT (Unknown narrator(s)).
MCSET. Cat no: **1555253180.** Released on Simon & Schuster, '91 by Simon & Schuster Ltd. Note: 6 Cassettes,
AQUARIAN CONSPIRACY: TOOLS FOR CHANGE (Unknown narrator(s)).
MCSET. Cat no: **0671668390.** Released on Simon & Schuster, '91 by Simon & Schuster Ltd. Note: 7 Cassette set.
ATTRACTING PERFECT LOVE (Dick Sutphen).
MC. Cat no: **RX 102.** Released on Valley Of The Sun, '88.
AWAKENED LIFE (Unknown narrator(s)).
MCSET. Cat no: **1555253792.** Released on Simon & Schuster, '91 by Simon & Schuster Ltd.
BANISH PAIN - MIND POWER AND PAIN RELIEF (Dick Sutphen).
MC. Cat no: **RX 121.** Released on Valley Of The Sun, '88.
BE A CONFIDENT WINNER (Unknown narrator(s)).
MCSET. Cat no: **155525277X.** Released on Simon & Schuster, '91 by Simon & Schuster Ltd.
BE HAPPY ATTITUDES (Unknown narrator(s)).
MCSET. Cat no: **1555252796.** Released on Simon & Schuster, '91 by Simon & Schuster Ltd.
BE POSITIVE (Unknown narrator(s)).
MCSET. Cat no: **155525411X.** Released on Simon & Schuster, '91 by Simon & Schuster Ltd.
BECOME A NEW PERSON (Dick Sutphen).
MC. Cat no: **RX 114.** Released on Valley Of The Sun, '88.
BEING THE BEST (Unknown narrator(s)).
MCSET. Cat no: **1555252222.** Released on Simon & Schuster, '91 by Simon & Schuster Ltd. Note: 6 Cassettes,
BELIEVE AND BE HAPPY (Unknown narrator(s)).
MCSET. Cat no: **0671626620.** Released on Simon & Schuster, '91 by Simon & Schuster Ltd.
BETWEEN THE WORDS (Hidden Meanings in What People Say) (Unknown narrator(s)).
MCSET. Cat no: **067160662X.** Released on Simon & Schuster, '91 by

BIO-FEEDBACK (Jo Kamiya & Robert Ornstein).
MC. Cat no: **SS 120**. Released on Drake, '91 by Morley Audio Services.

BREATHE, RELAX AND IMAGINE (Paul Lambillion).
MC. Cat no: **C 10841**. Released on Jacobeus, '91 by Jacobeus Records.

CALM AND PEACEFUL MIND, A (Dick Sutphen).
MC. Cat no: **RX 103**. Released on Valley Of The Sun, '88.

CASE AGAINST IT (Unknown narrator(s)).
MC. Cat no: **SS 118**. Released on Seminar Cassettes, Oct '81 by Seminar Cassettes.

CHARISMA - DRAWING PEOPLE TO YOU (Dick Sutphen).
MC. Cat no: **RX 134**. Released on Valley Of The Sun, '88.

CHOICES (Unknown narrator(s)).
MCSET. Cat no: **0671693433**. Released on Simon & Schuster, '91 by Simon & Schuster Ltd.

CHOOSING YOUR OWN GREATNESS (Unknown narrator(s)).
MCSET. Cat no: **1555252184**. Released on Simon & Schuster, '91 by Simon & Schuster Ltd.

CO-DEPENDENTS GUIDE TO THE TWELVE STEPS (Unknown narrator(s)).
MCSET. Cat no: **0671726064**. Released on Simon & Schuster, '91 by Simon & Schuster Ltd.

CONCENTRATION - POWER PLUS (Dick Sutphen).
MC. Cat no: **RX 126**. Released on Valley Of The Sun, '88.

CONSTRUCTIVE ANGER (George Bach).
MC. Cat no: **PT 25**. Released on Psychology Today (USA), Oct '81 by Seminar Cassettes.

CONTROL FREAKS (Unknown narrator(s)).
MCSET. Cat no: **1555254209**. Released on Simon & Schuster, '91 by Simon & Schuster Ltd. Note: 10 Cassettes.

CONTROL YOUR WEIGHT (Paul Lambillion).
MC. Cat no: **C 02861**. Released on Jacobeus, '91 by Jacobeus Records.

CREATE WEALTH - POWER PROGRAMMING (Dick Sutphen).
MC. Cat no: **RX 115**. Released on Valley Of The Sun, '88.

CREATING POSITIVE RELATIONSHIPS (Unknown narrator(s)).
MCSET. Cat no: **1555253385**. Released on Simon & Schuster, '91 by Simon & Schuster Ltd.

CURING DEPRESSION (Nathan S Kline).
MC. Cat no: **PT 42**. Released on Psychology Today (USA), Oct '81 by Seminar Cassettes.

Simon & Schuster Ltd. Note: 2 Cassettes.

DIFFERENT DRUM, THE (M Scott Peck).
MC. Cat no: **0671646338**. Released on Simon & Schuster, '91 by Simon & Schuster Ltd.

DISCOVER INNER ENERGY AND OVERCOME STRESS (Unknown narrator(s)).
MCSET. Cat no: **1555252311**. Released on Simon & Schuster, '91 by Simon & Schuster Ltd.

DISCOVER WHAT YOU'RE BEST AT (Unknown narrator(s)).
MCSET. Cat no: **0671602462**. Released on Simon & Schuster, '91 by Simon & Schuster Ltd. Note: ISBN No: 0563 227044

DO MORE IN LESS TIME (Dick Sutphen).
MC. Cat no: **RX 135**. Released on Valley Of The Sun, '88.

DREAM SOLUTIONS-FIND YOUR ANSWERS IN YOUR DREAMS (Dick Sutphen).
MC. Cat no: **RX 106**. Released on Valley Of The Sun, '88.

DREAMS AND DREAMING (Dr Christopher Evans).
MC. Cat no: **SS 107**. Released on Seminar Cassettes, Oct '81 by Seminar Cassettes.

EMOTIONS AND CANCER (Lawrence Leshan).
MC. Cat no: **PT 29**. Released on Psychology Today (USA), Oct '81 by Seminar Cassettes.

ESP IS ALIVE AND WELL (Stanley Krippner).
MC. Cat no: **PT 30**. Released on Psychology Today (USA), Oct '81 by Seminar Cassettes.

EVERYDAY HEROICS OF LIVING AND DYING (Ernest Becker).
MC. Cat no: **PT 41**. Released on Psychology Today (USA), Oct '81 by Seminar Cassettes.

EXPERIENCE HIGH SELF-ESTEEM (Nathaniel Branden).
MC. Cat no: **0671663887**. Released on Simon & Schuster, '91 by Simon & Schuster Ltd.

FEEL SECURE NOW (Dick Sutphen).
MC. Cat no: **RX 119**. Released on Valley Of The Sun, '88.

FEEL THE FEAR AND DO IT ANYWAY (Unknown narrator(s)).
MCSET. Cat no: **155525182X**. Released on Simon & Schuster, '91 by Simon & Schuster Ltd. Note: 6 Cassettes.

FIND YOUR INNER HAPPINESS (Jack Boland).
MC. Cat no: **T 77**. Released on Listen (UK), '91 by Listen (UK).

FIVE DAYS TO AN ORGANIZED LIFE (Unknown narrator(s)).
MCSET. Cat no: **1555253725**. Released on Simon & Schuster, '91 by Simon & Schuster Ltd.

FURTHER ALONG THE ROAD LESS TRAVELLED (Togetherness and Seperateness in Marriage) (M Scott Peck).
MC. Cat no: **0671658085**. Released

on Simon & Schuster, '91 by Simon & Schuster Ltd.

FURTHER ALONG THE ROAD LESS TRAVELLED (Self Love Versus Self Esteem) (M Scott Peck).
MC. Cat no: **0671663445**. Released on Simon & Schuster, '91 by Simon & Schuster Ltd.

FURTHER ALONG THE ROAD LESS TRAVELLED (Sexuality and Spirituality) (M Scott Peck).
MC. Cat no: **0671668919**. Released on Simon & Schuster, '91 by Simon & Schuster Ltd.

GARDEN OF PEACE (Paul Lambillion).
MC. Cat no: **C 05851**. Released on Jacobeus, '91 by Jacobeus Records.

GENTLY AND DEEPLY (Paul Lambillion).
MC. Cat no: **C 09871**. Released on Jacobeus, '91 by Jacobeus Records.

GET IT DONE NOW (Unknown narrator(s)).
MCSET. Cat no: **1555254101**. Released on Simon & Schuster, '91 by Simon & Schuster Ltd. Note: 6 Cassettes.

GETTING UNSTUCK: BREAKING THROUGH THE BARRIERS OF CHANGE (Unknown narrator(s)).
MCSET. Cat no: **1555252648**. Released on Simon & Schuster, '91 by Simon & Schuster Ltd.

GIFTS OF LEGENDS (Michael Ayrton).
MC. Cat no: **SS 115**. Released on Seminar Cassettes, Oct '81 by Seminar Cassettes.

GOAL SETTING (Barrie Konicov).
MC. Cat no: **3727**. Released on Potential Unlimited, '91 by Potential Unlimited.

GOALS (Unknown narrator(s)).
MCSET. Cat no: **15552520404**. Released on Simon & Schuster, '91 by Simon & Schuster Ltd.

GOOD LIFE, THE - HEALTH, WEALTH AND HAPPINESS (Dick Sutphen).
MC. Cat no: **RX 104**. Released on Valley Of The Sun, '88.

GREAT MEMORY, A (Dick Sutphen).
MC. Cat no: **RX 131**. Released on Valley Of The Sun, '88.

GREATEST OF THESE IS LOVE (Unknown narrator(s)).
MCSET. Cat no: **0671677861**. Released on Simon & Schuster, '91 by Simon & Schuster Ltd.

GURDJIEFF THE MAN (J G Bennett).
MC. Cat no: **SS 124**. Released on Seminar Cassettes, '81 by Seminar Cassettes.

GURUS DISCIPLES AND ASHRAMS (Peter Brent).
MC. Cat no: **SS 122**. Released on Seminar Cassettes, '81 by Seminar Cassettes.

HEALING FORCE - USING YOUR MIND TO HELP HEAL (Dick Sutphen).

323

MC. Cat no: **RX 117**. Released on Valley Of The Sun, '88.

HOW TO BE A NO-LIMIT PERSON (Unknown narrator(s)).
MCSET. Cat no: **1555252214**. Released on Simon & Schuster, '91 by Simon & Schuster Ltd.

HOW TO CHANGE IDEAS (Ted De Bono).
MC. Cat no: **SS 106**. Released on Seminar Cassettes, Oct '81 by Seminar Cassettes.

HOW TO DECIDE EXACTLY WHAT YOU WANT (Dick Sutphen).
MC. Cat no: **RX 125**. Released on Valley Of The Sun, '88.

HOW TO DEVELOP YOUR ESP POWER (Jane Roberts).
MC. Cat no: **0671621483**. Released on Simon & Schuster, '91 by Simon & Schuster Ltd.

HOW TO GET WHATEVER YOU WANT OUT OF LIFE (Unknown narrator(s)).
MCSET. Cat no: **0671605151**. Released on Simon & Schuster, '91 by Simon & Schuster Ltd.

HOW TO IMPROVE YOUR MEMORY (Arthur Bornstein).
MC. Cat no: **T 18**. Released on Listen (UK), '91 by Listen (UK).

HOW TO MAKE LOVE TO A MAN (Unknown narrator(s)).
MCSET. Cat no: **0671606603**. Released on Simon & Schuster, '91 by Simon & Schuster Ltd.

HOW TO TURN A FRIENDSHIP INTO A LOVE AFFAIR (Unknown narrator(s)).
MCSET. Cat no: **0671617877**. Released on Simon & Schuster, '91 by Simon & Schuster Ltd.

HUSBANDS AND WIVES (Melvyn Kinder & Connell Coweh).
MCSET. Cat no: **0671687980**. Released on Simon & Schuster, '91 by Simon & Schuster Ltd. Note: 2 Cassettes

I NEVER KNOW WHAT TO SAY (How to Help Your Family and Friends Cope With Tragedy) (Nina H. Donnelly).
MC. Cat no: **0671663909**. Released on Simon & Schuster, '91 by Simon & Schuster Ltd.

IMAGINEERING (Unknown narrator(s)).
MCSET. Cat no: **0671624911**. Released on Simon & Schuster, '91 by Simon & Schuster Ltd. Note: 2 Cassettes.

INCREDIBLE SELF-CONFIDENCE (Dick Sutphen).
MC. Cat no: **RX 127**. Released on Valley Of The Sun, '88.

INFLIGHT RELAXATION (Unknown narrator(s)).
MCSET. Cat no: **1555253113**. Released on Simon & Schuster, '91 by Simon & Schuster Ltd.

INTENSIFY CREATIVE ABILITY (Dick Sutphen).
MC. Cat no: **RX 128**. Released on Valley Of The Sun, '88.

KRESKIN ON MIND POWER (Amazing Kreskin).
MC. Cat no: **T 81**. Released on Listen (UK), '91 by Listen (UK).

LEARNING AND MEMORY (Toney Buzan).
MC. Cat no: **PT 21**. Released on Psychology Today (USA), Oct '81 by Seminar Cassettes.

LEARNING TO CONTROL PAIN (David Bresler).
MC. Cat no: **PT 31**. Released on Psychology Today (USA), Nov '81 by Seminar Cassettes.

LIFESPRING (Unknown narrator(s)).
MCSET. Cat no: **067168498**. Released on Simon & Schuster, '91 by Simon & Schuster Ltd.

LIVING WITHOUT LIMITS (Unknown narrator(s)).
MCSET. Cat no: **1555252869**. Released on Simon & Schuster, '91 by Simon & Schuster Ltd.

LOVE MYSELF - SELF-ESTEEM PROGRAMMING (Dick Sutphen).
MC. Cat no: **RX 122**. Released on Valley Of The Sun, '88.

MAGIC OF BELIEVING (Claude Bristol).
MC. Cat no: **0671605194**. Released on Simon & Schuster, '91 by Simon & Schuster Ltd.

MAGIC OF THINKING BIG, THE (David J Schwartz).
MC. Cat no: **6671618601**. Released on Simon & Schuster, '91 by Simon & Schuster Ltd.

MAKING RELATIONSHIPS LAST (Denise Dudley).
MC. Cat no: **0671662554**. Released on Simon & Schuster, '91 by Simon & Schuster Ltd.

MANWATCHING (Dr. Desmond Morris).
MC. Cat no: **PT 23**. Released on Psychology Today (USA), Oct '81 by Seminar Cassettes.

MEDICINE THE HUMAN ASPECT (Various narrators).
MC. Cat no: **SS/128/129**. Released on Seminar Cassettes, Oct '81 by Seminar Cassettes.

MEDITATION (Daniel, Goleman).
MC. Cat no: **PT 32**. Released on Psychology Today (USA), Oct '81 by Seminar Cassettes.

MEDITATIONS FOR PERSONAL HARMONY (Unknown narrator(s)).
MCSET. Cat no: **155525327X**. Released on Simon & Schuster, '91 by Simon & Schuster Ltd.

MENTAL STRESS AND PHYSICAL FITNESS (Kenneth R Pelletier).
MC. Cat no: **PT 37**. Released on Psychology Today (USA), Oct '81 by Seminar Cassettes.

MIND OVER ILLNESS (Unknown narrator(s)).
MCSET. Cat no: **155525425X**. Released on Simon & Schuster, '91 by Simon & Schuster Ltd.

NEVER BE NERVOUS AGAIN (Unknown narrator(s)).

MCSET. Cat no: **0671675672**. Released on Simon & Schuster, '91 by Simon & Schuster Ltd.

NEW LOOK AT PSYCHOLOGISTS (Prof. Liam Hudson).
MC. Cat no: **PT 35**. Released on Psychology Today (USA), Oct '81 by Seminar Cassettes.

OVERCOMING FEARFUL FLYING (Unknown narrator(s)).
MCSET. Cat no: **0671628445**. Released on Simon & Schuster, '91 by Simon & Schuster Ltd.

OVERCOMING SHYNESS (Philip Zimbardo).
MC. Cat no: **PT 36**. Released on Psychology Today (USA), Oct '81 by Seminar Cassettes.

PATHWAY TO HEALING, A (Paul Lambillion).
MC. Cat no: **C 02851**. Released on Jacobeus, '91 by Jacobeus Records.

PEACE OF MIND (Barrie Konicov).
MC. Cat no: **3740**. Released on Potential Unlimited, '91 by Potential Unlimited.

PERFECT HEALTH (Unknown narrator(s)).
MCSET. Cat no: **1555254098**. Released on Simon & Schuster, '91 by Simon & Schuster Ltd.

PERFECT WEIGHT - PERFECT BODY (Dick Sutphen).
MC. Cat no: **RX 111**. Released on Valley Of The Sun, '88.

PICTURE YOURSELF RELAXED (Paul Lambillion).
MC. Cat no: **C 08841**. Released on Jacobeus, '91 by Jacobeus Records.

POWER AND SUCCESS - GET IT, KEEP IT, USE IT (Dick Sutphen).
MC. Cat no: **RX 132**. Released on Valley Of The Sun, '88.

POWER OF PERSISTENCE, THE (Dick Sutphen).
MC. Cat no: **RX 129**. Released on Valley Of The Sun, '88.

POWER OF POSITIVE THINKING, THE (Norman Vincent).
MC. Cat no: **0671635301**. Released on Simon & Schuster, '91 by Simon & Schuster Ltd.

POWER OF SELF TALK (Unknown narrator(s)).
MCSET. Cat no: **1555253733**. Released on Simon & Schuster, '91 by Simon & Schuster Ltd.

POWER OF YOUR OWN VOICE (Unknown narrator(s)).
MCSET. Cat no: **0671676946**. Released on Simon & Schuster, '91 by Simon & Schuster Ltd. Note: 2 Cassettes.

POWER WORDS (Unknown narrator(s)).
MCSET. Cat no: **1555253156**. Released on Simon & Schuster, '91 by Simon & Schuster Ltd.

POWERFUL PERSON - PROGRAMMING (Dick Sutphen).
MC. Cat no: **RX 101**. Released on

Valley Of The Sun, '88.

PSYCHOLOGY OF ACHIEVEMENT (Unknown narrator(s)).
MCSET. Cat no: **1555253148**. Released on Simon & Schuster, '91 by Simon & Schuster Ltd. Note: 10 Cassettes.

PSYCHOLOGY OF WINNING (Unknown narrator(s)).
MCSET. Cat no: **1555252273**. Released on Simon & Schuster, '91 by Simon & Schuster Ltd. Note: 6 Cassettes.

RADIANT HEALTH AND A STRONG IMMUNE SYSTEM (Dick Sutphen).
MC. Cat no: **RX 116**. Released on Valley Of The Sun, '88.

RATIONAL AND THE INTUITIVE BRAIN (C B Fry).
MC. Cat no: **SS 105**. Released on Seminar Cassettes, '91 by Seminar Cassettes.

RATIONAL AND THE INTUITIVE BRAIN (D. Galin & Rbt. Omstein).
MC. Cat no: **SS 119**. Released on Seminar Cassettes, Oct '81 by Seminar Cassettes.

RATIONAL EMOTIVE THERAPY (Albert Ellis).
MC. Cat no: **PT 26**. Released on Psychology Today (USA), Oct '81 by Seminar Cassettes.

RELIEVE STRESS AND ANXIETY (Barrie Konicov).
MC. Cat no: **3728**. Released on Potential Unlimited, '91 by Potential Unlimited.

RIGHT-BRAIN SOLUTIONS (Programming to Find Creative Answers Within) (Dick Sutphen).
MC. Cat no: **RX 118**. Released on Valley Of The Sun, '88.

ROAD LESS TRAVELLED, THE (Part 1: Discipline) (M Scott Peck).
MC. Cat no: **0671621378**. Released on Simon & Schuster, '91 by Simon & Schuster Ltd.

ROAD LESS TRAVELLED, THE (Part 2: Love) (M Scott Peck).
MC. Cat no: **0671627015**. Released on Simon & Schuster, '91 by Simon & Schuster Ltd.

ROAD LESS TRAVELLED, THE (Part 3: Religion and Grace) (M Scott Peck).
MC. Cat no: **0671634682**. Released on Simon & Schuster, '91 by Simon & Schuster Ltd.

SATISFACTION AND HAPPINESS (Dick Sutphen).
MC. Cat no: **RX 110**. Released on Valley Of The Sun, '88.

SCIENTIFIC VIEW OF MEDITATION, A (Proffessor Robert Ornstein).
MC. Cat no: **SS 123**. Released on Seminar Cassettes, Oct '81 by Seminar Cassettes.

SELF DEFEATING BEHAVIOURS (Unknown narrator(s)).
MCSET. Cat no: **1555254217**. Released on Simon & Schuster, '91 by Simon & Schuster Ltd.

SETH: THE VOICE AND THE MESSAGE (Unknown narrator(s)).
MCSET. Cat no: **0671684140**. Released on Simon & Schuster, '91 by Simon & Schuster Ltd. Note: 2 Cassettes.

SEVEN HABITS OF HIGHLY EFFECTIVE PEOPLE (Unknown narrator(s)).
MCSET. Cat no: **0671687964**. Released on Simon & Schuster, '91 by Simon & Schuster Ltd.

SILVA MIND CONTROL METHOD OF MENTAL DYNAMICS (Burt Goldman).
MC. Cat no: **0671673521**. Released on Simon & Schuster, '91 by Simon & Schuster Ltd.

SIX THINKING HATS (Edward De Bono).
MC. Cat no: **0001046209**. Released on Collins-Caedmon, '91 by Collins Audio, Taylors, Bond Street Music.

SLEEP LIKE A BABY (Dick Sutphen).
MC. Cat no: **RX 112**. Released on Valley Of The Sun, '88.

SLEEP PEACEFULLY (Paul Lambillion).
MC. Cat no: **C 07851**. Released on Jacobeus, '91 by Jacobeus Records.

SLEEPING EASY (Unknown narrator(s)).
MCSET. Cat no: **1555252443**. Released on Simon & Schuster, '91 by Simon & Schuster Ltd.

SPEAK UP - SAY WHAT YOU WANT TO SAY (Dick Sutphen).
MC. Cat no: **RX 123**. Released on Valley Of The Sun, '88.

SPEED READING (Dick Sutphen).
MC. Cat no: **RX 133**. Released on Valley Of The Sun, '88.

SPEND YOUR LIFE IN SLENDER (Unknown narrator(s)).
MCSET. Cat no: **1555252060**. Released on Simon & Schuster, '91 by Simon & Schuster Ltd.

STAYING ON TOP WHEN YOUR WORLD TURNS UPSIDE DOWN (Unknown narrator(s)).
MCSET. Cat no: **1555253784**. Released on Simon & Schuster, '91 by Simon & Schuster Ltd.

STRATEGIES FOR STRESS FREE LIVING (Unknown narrator(s)).
MCSET. Cat no: **155525232X**. Released on Simon & Schuster, '91 by Simon & Schuster Ltd. Note: 6 Cassettes.

STRENGTHEN YOUR EGO (Nathaniel Branden).
MC. Cat no: **0671666754**. Released on Simon & Schuster, '91 by Simon & Schuster Ltd.

STRESS PROOF CHILD (Unknown narrator(s)).
MCSET. Cat no: **1555252419**. Released on Simon & Schuster, '91 by Simon & Schuster Ltd.

SUCCESS AND EXCELLENCE (High Performance and Goal Accomplishment) (Dick Sutphen).
MC. Cat no: **RX 107**. Released on Valley Of The Sun, '88.

SUCCESSFUL INDEPENDENT LIFESTYLE (Dick Sutphen).
MC. Cat no: **RX 120**. Released on Valley Of The Sun, '88.

SUPER LEARNING (Optimal Weight) (Lynn Schroeder).
MC. Cat no: **0671663860**. Released on Simon & Schuster, '91 by Simon & Schuster Ltd.

SUPER LEARNING (Maximise Your Memory) (Lynn Schroeder).
MC. Cat no: **0671663917**. Released on Simon & Schuster, '91 by Simon & Schuster Ltd.

SURVIVING LOSS (Unknown narrator(s)).
MCSET. Cat no: **1555252907**. Released on Simon & Schuster, '91 by Simon & Schuster Ltd.

TAKE CONTROL OF YOUR LIFE (Dick Sutphen).
MC. Cat no: **RX 109**. Released on Valley Of The Sun, '88.

TEENAGERS AND SEXUALITY (John Coleman).
MCSET. Cat no: **1871504023**. Released on Tapewise, '91 by Tapewise. Note : 2 Cassettes

TEENAGERS UNDER STRESS (John Coleman).
MCSET. Cat no: **1871504015**. Released on Tapewise, '91 by Tapewise. Note : 2 Cassettes

THRIVING SELF (Unknown narrator(s)).
MCSET. Cat no: **1555252915**. Released on Simon & Schuster, '91 by Simon & Schuster Ltd.

TOUGH TIMES NEVER LAST BUT TOUGH PEOPLE DO (Unknown narrator(s)).
MCSET. Cat no: **155525229X**. Released on Simon & Schuster, '91 by Simon & Schuster Ltd.

TRANSFORMATION: THE NEXT STEP FOR THE NO-LIMIT PERSON (Unknown narrator(s)).
MCSET. Cat no: **1555252389**. Released on Simon & Schuster, '91 by Simon & Schuster Ltd.

TRAVELLER'S REFRESHER, THE (Unknown narrator(s)).
MC. Cat no: **0671681133**. Released on Simon & Schuster, '91 by Simon & Schuster Ltd.

TURNING YOUR STRESS INTO HIGH ENERGY PERFORMANCE (Unknown narrator(s)).
MCSET. Cat no: **0671623311**. Released on Simon & Schuster, '91 by Simon & Schuster Ltd.

ULTIMATE RELAXATION (Dick Sutphen).
MC. Cat no: **RX 136**. Released on Valley Of The Sun, '88.

ULTIMATE SECRET TO GETTING ABSOLUTELY EVERYTHING YOU WANT (Unknown narrator(s)).
MCSET. Cat no: **1555251773**. Released on Simon & Schuster, '91 by Simon & Schuster Ltd.

UNDERSTANDING AND COPING

WITH ANXIETY (Rollo May).
MC. Cat no: **PT 38.** Released on Psychology Today (USA), '81 by Seminar Cassettes.

UNDERSTANDING AND MANAGING JEALOUSY (Gordon Clanton).
MC. Cat no: **PT 40.** Released on Psychology Today (USA), '81 by Seminar Cassettes.

UNDERSTANDING AND OVERCOMING LONELINESS (L A Peplau).
MC. Cat no: **PT 39.** Released on Psychology Today (USA), '81 by Seminar Cassettes.

UNLIMITED POWER (Anthony Robbins).
MC. Cat no: **0671621467.** Released on Simon & Schuster, '91 by Simon & Schuster Ltd.

UPPER HAND, THE (Quick Thinking and Fast Action) (Dick Sutphen).
MC. Cat no: **RX 113.** Released on Valley Of The Sun, '88.

VALUABLE AS YOU ARE (Unknown narrator(s)).
MCSET. Cat no: **0671748777.** Released on Simon & Schuster, '91 by Simon & Schuster Ltd.

WAKE-UP REFRESHER, THE (Unknown narrator(s)).
MC. Cat no: **0671681168.** Released on Simon & Schuster, '91 by Simon & Schuster Ltd.

WATERS OF THE WORLD (Dr. T Heyerdahl & Dr. D. George).
MC. Cat no: **SS 110.** Released on Seminar Cassettes, '81 by Seminar Cassettes.

WEIGHT LOST (Dick Sutphen).
MC. Cat no: **RX 124.** Released on Valley Of The Sun, '88.

WHEN ALL YOU'VE EVER WANTED ISN'T ENOUGH (Unknown narrator(s)).
MCSET. Cat no: **067163402X.** Released on Simon & Schuster, '91 by Simon & Schuster Ltd. Note: 2 Cassettes

WHEN I SAY NO, I FEEL GUILTY (Unknown narrator(s)).
MCSET. Cat no: **0671647253.** Released on Simon & Schuster, '91 by Simon & Schuster Ltd.

WOULDA, SHOULDA, COULDA (Unknown narrator(s)).
MCSET. Cat no: **1555253245.** Released on Simon & Schuster, '91 by Simon & Schuster Ltd.

YOU ARE THE POWER (Triumph Over Fear and Depression) (Paul Lambillion).
MC. Cat no: **C 05852.** Released on Jacobeus, '91 by Jacobeus Records.

YOU CAN BECOME THE PERSON YOU WANT TO BE (Unknown narrator(s)).
MCSET. Cat no: **0671634844.** Released on Simon & Schuster, '91 by Simon & Schuster Ltd. Note: 2 Cassettes.

YOU CAN DO IT (Stop Worrying) (Paul Lambillion).
MC. Cat no: **C 10851.** Released on Jacobeus, '91 by Jacobeus Records.

YOU CAN IF YOU THINK YOU CAN (Norman Vincent).
MC. Cat no: **0671660721.** Released on Simon & Schuster, '91 by Simon & Schuster Ltd.

YOUR LAST CIGARETTE - NO EXCEPTIONS! (Dick Sutphen).
MC. Cat no: **RX 108.** Released on Valley Of The Sun, '88.

Serbo Croat

SERBO CROAT (Language Courses) (Unknown narrator(s)).
LPS. Cat no: **0747302758.** Released on Linguaphone, Apr '82 by Linguaphone Institute, Taylors, Century Records (USA), Bond Street Music.

SOUNDS AND ALPHABET OF SERBO CROATIAN, THE (Edited By Derek J. Hunns) (Unknown narrator(s)).
MC. Cat no: **SC 7649.** Released on Exeter Tapes, '91 by Drakes Educational Associates.

Severin, Tim

JASON VOYAGE, THE (Ian Craig)
MCSET. Cat no: **1068 N.** Released on Travellers Tales, '91 by Travellers Tales. Note: 8 Cassettes.

MCSET. Cat no: **OAS 89082.** Released on Oasis Audio Books, '91 by Isis Audio Books. Note: 8 Cassettes.

SINBAD VOYAGE, THE (Gordon Dulieu)
MCSET. Cat no: **IAB 92011.** Released on Isis Audio Books, '91. Note : 8 Cassettes. Playing time 10hrs 30 mins.

Sexton, Anne

POETRY OF ANNE SEXTON, THE (Anne Sexton).
MC. Cat no: **AS 41.** Released on Sussex Tapes, '91 by Sussex Publications Ltd..

Shackleton, Sir Ernest

SOUTH (Sean Barrett).
MCSET. Cat no: **1069N.** Released on Travellers Tales, '91 by Travellers Tales. Note: 8 Cassettes.

MCSET. Cat no: **IAB 89101.** Released on Isis Audio Books, '91. Note : 8 Cassettes.

Shakespeare, William

ANTHONY AND CLEOPATRA (F A Foakes & A R Humphreys).
MC. Cat no: **S6.** Released on Sussex Tapes, '91 by Sussex Publications Ltd.

AS YOU LIKE IT (Terence Hawkes & Moelwyn Merchant).
MC. Cat no: **S16.** Released on Sussex Tapes, '91 by Sussex Publications Ltd.

BACKGROUND TO HAMLET (Moelwyn Merchant & Brian Morris).
MC. Cat no: **S15.** Released on Sussex Tapes, '91 by Sussex Publications Ltd.

CORIOLANUS (A R Humphreys & Anthony Nuttal).
MC. Cat no: **S1.** Released on Sussex Tapes, '91 by Sussex Publications Ltd.

CYMBELINE (Stanley Wells & John Wilders).

MC. Cat no: **S23.** Released on Sussex Tapes, '91 by Sussex Publications Ltd.

HAMLET (David Daiches & L.C. Knights).
MC. Cat no: **S2.** Released on Sussex Tapes, '91 by Sussex Publications Ltd.

HENRY IV (Part I) Peter Hollindale & Gareth Lloyd Evans).
MC. Cat no: **S18.** Released on Sussex Tapes, '91 by Sussex Publications Ltd.

HENRY IV (Part II) (Peter Hollindale & Gareth Lloyd Evans).
MC. Cat no: **S19.** Released on Sussex Tapes, '91 by Sussex Publications Ltd.

JULIUS CAESAR (Joel Hurstfield & A G R Smith).
MC. Cat no: **S12.** Released on Sussex Tapes, '91 by Sussex Publications Ltd.

KING LEAR (Gareth Lloyd Evans & Brian Morris).
MC. Cat no: **S7.** Released on Sussex Tapes, '91 by Sussex Publications Ltd.

MACBETH (R A Foakes & Kenneth Muir).
MC. Cat no: **S3.** Released on Sussex Tapes, '91 by Sussex Publications Ltd.

MEASURE FOR MEASURE (Gareth Lloyd Evans & Brian Morris).
MC. Cat no: **S9.** Released on Sussex Tapes, '91 by Sussex Publications Ltd.

MERCHANT OF VENICE, THE (Moelwyn Merchant & Brian Morris).
MC. Cat no: **S14** Released on Sussex Tapes, '91 by Sussex Publications Ltd.

OTHELLO (R A Foakes & Kenneth Muir).
MC. Cat no: **S4.** Released on Sussex Tapes, '91 by Sussex Publications Ltd.

RICHARD II (Moelwyn Merchant & Brian Morris).
MC. Cat no: **S13.** Released on Sussex Tapes, '91 by Sussex Publications Ltd.

RICHARD III (Moelwyn Merchant & Brian Morris).
MC. Cat no: **S17.** Released on Sussex Tapes, '91 by Sussex Publications Ltd.

ROMEO AND JULIET (Nigel Alexander & Nicholas Brooke).
MC. Cat no: **S11.** Released on Sussex Tapes, '91 by Sussex Publications Ltd.

STORY OF WILLIAM SHAKESPEARE, THE (Clifford Rose)
MCSET. Cat no: **LD 1.** Released on Green dragon, '91 by Green Dragon Audio Visual. Note: 2 Cassettes.

TEMPEST, THE (David Dalches & L C Knights).
MC. Cat no: **S5.** Released on Sussex Tapes, '91' by Sussex Publications Ltd.

TROILUS AND CRESSIDA (Stanley Wells & John Wilders).
MC. Cat no: **S22.** Released on Sussex Tapes, '91 by Sussex Publications.

TWELFTH NIGHT (E A J Honizman & John Dixon).
MC. Cat no: **S8.** Released on Sussex Tapes, '91 by Sussex Publications Ltd.

WINTER'S TALE, THE (Gareth Lloyd Evans & Brian Morris).
MC. Cat no: **S10.** Released on Sussex Tapes, '91 by Sussex Publications Ltd.

WORLD OF KING LEAR, THE (Philip Brockbank & Alan Sinfield).
MC. Cat no: **S21.** Released on Sussex

Tapes, '91 by Sussex Publications Ltd.

Shand, Mark
TRAVELS ON MY ELEPHANT (Mark Shand).
MCSET. Cat no: **RC 51**. Released on Random Century, Mar '92 by Random Century Audiobooks, Conifer Records. Note: ISBN no. 1856860949

Sholokhov, Michael
SUD'BA CHELOVEKA (Edited By Michael Savage) (Unknown narrator(s)). Note: A discussion of the short story 'The Fate Of A Man' by Sholokhov, analysing both its narrative style and characterisation
MC. Cat no: **R 7955**. Released on Exeter Tapes, '91 by Drakes Educational Associates.

Shooting Times
RANDOM SHOTS (Correspondence From The Shooting Times) (Michael Aldridge & Paul Eddington).
MCSET. Cat no: **ZBBC 1159**. Released on BBC Radio Collection, Jul '90 by BBC Records. Note: ISBN No: 0563 410817.

Silone
THREE NOVELS (Edited By M. McLaughlin) (Unknown narrator(s)). Note: A critical analysis of Silone's 'Fontamara', 'Vino E Pane' and 'Una Manciata Di More'.
MC. Cat no: **I 7993**. Released on Exeter Tapes, '91 by Drakes Educational Associates. Note: 4 cassette set.

Silone & Levi
TWO VIEWS OF ITALIAN RURAL SOCIETY (Edited By Brian Moloney) (Unknown narrator(s)).
Note: Explores the accuracy with which these two writers, Silone and Levi, presented their very different views of rural peasant life in the fascist period.
MC. Cat no: **I 7914**. Released on Exeter Tapes, '91 by Drakes Educational Associates.

Simpson, Joe
TOUCHING THE VOID (Gene Ford).
MCSET. Cat no: **1072N**. Released on Travellers Tales, '91 by Travellers Tales. Note: 5 Cassettes.
MCSET. Cat no: **IAB 90012**. Released on Isis Audio Books, '91. Note : 5 Cassettes.

Singer, Isaac Bashevis
REB MOISHE BABBA (Isaac B Singer).
MC. Cat no: **AS 43**. Released on Sussex Tapes, '91 by Sussex Publications Ltd.

Skynner, Dr Robin
FAMILIES AND HOW TO SURVIVE (Dr Robin Skynner & John Cleese).
MCSET. Cat no: **ZBBC 1244**. Released on BBC Radio Collection, Aug '91 by BBC Records. Note: ISBN No: 0563 365196

Slavonic
INTRODUCING THE BYELORUSSIAN LANGUAGE (Edited By P.J. Mayo) (Unknown narrator(s)).
MC. Cat no: **BY 7837**. Released on Exeter Tapes, '91 by Drakes Educational Associates.
SLAVONIC LANGUAGE, THE (Edited By Derek J. Hunns) (Unknown narrator(s)).
MC. Cat no: **SL 7793**. Released on Exeter Tapes, '91 by Drakes Educational Associates.
YUGOSLAV TRAVEL PACK (Unknown narrator(s)).
Note: Contains a Hugo phrase book.
MC. Cat no: **852851448**. Released on Hugo Languages, '92 by Hugo Language Books Limited.

Slocum, Joshua
SAILING ALONE AROUND THE WORLD (Nelson Runger).
MCSET. Cat no: **1668F**. Released on Travellers Tales, '91 by Travellers Tales. Note: 5 Cassettes.
MCSET. Cat no: **RB 88700**. Released on Recorded Books, '91 by Isis Audio Books.

Social Sciences
19TH AND 20TH CENTURY BRITISH TRADE UNIONISM (Dr J M Winter & J F C Harrison).
MCSET. Cat no: **HEA 033**. Released on AVP, '91 by AVP Publishing.
ASQUITH (Stephen Koss & Dr. Peter Clarke).
MCSET. Cat no: **HEA 006**. Released on AVP, '91 by AVP Publishing.
BRITAIN BETWEEN THE WARS (David Marquand & Robert Skidelsky).
MC. Cat no: **HB 1**. Released on Sussex Tapes, '91 by Sussex Publications Ltd.
BRITISH APPEASEMENT (Robert Skidelsky & Dr. David Carleton).
MCSET. Cat no: **HEA 044**. Released on AVP, '91 by AVP Publishing.
BRITISH POLITICAL ECONOMY 1919-1939, THE (Dr. Robert Skidelsky & Donald Winch).
MCSET. Cat no: **HEA 038**. Released on AVP, '91 by AVP Publishing.
BURDEN OF POPULATION (Peking, Tokyo, Unesco) (Unknown narrator(s)).
MC. Cat no: **IR 113**. Released on International Report, Oct '81 by Seminar Cassettes.
CHAMBERLAIN (David Hammer & John Spiers).
MC. Cat no: **HA 4**. Released on Sussex Tapes, '91 by Sussex Publications Ltd..
CHAMBERLAIN (David Dilks & Keith Roberts).
MCSET. Cat no: **HEA 036**. Released on AVP, '91 by AVP Publishing.
CHARTISM AND THE 1870 EDUCATION ACT (Asa Briggs).
MCSET. Cat no: **HA 6**. Released on Sussex Tapes, '91 by Sussex Publications Ltd.. Note: 2 Cassettes
CONFLICT IN EUROPE (1783-1815) (A. Goodwin & Felix Markham).
MC. Cat no: **HE 5**. Released on Sussex Tapes, '91 by Sussex Publications Ltd..
CONSERVATIVE PARTY FROM PEEL TO GLADSTONE (Dr A Warren & Ian Bradley).
MCSET. Cat no: **HEA 015**. Released on AVP, '91 by AVP Publishing.
DEVELOPMENT OF BRITISH SOCIETY - 1914-1945, THE (Roderick Floud & Pat Thane).
MCSET. Cat no: **HEA 018**. Released on AVP, '91 by AVP Publishing. Note : 2 Cassettes
DISRAELI (Vernon Bogdanor & Paul Smith).
MCSET. Cat no: **HEA 020**. Released on AVP, '91 by AVP Publishing.
DREYFUS AFFAIR, THE (Douglas Johnson & Maurice Hutt).
MC. Cat no: **HE 19**. Released on Sussex Tapes, '91 by Sussex Publications Ltd..
EMPIRE TO COMMONWEALTH (Donald Watt).
MC. Cat no: **HA 16**. Released on Sussex Tapes, '91 by Sussex Publications Ltd
ENGLISH PARLIAMENTS IN PERSPECTIVE (G.E. Aylmer & Conrad Russell).
MC. Cat no: **H 13**. Released on Sussex Tapes, '91 by Sussex Publications Ltd..
ENLIGHTENMENT, THE (Norman Hampson & Jack Lively).
MC. Cat no: **HE 4**. Released on Sussex Tapes, '91 by Sussex Publications Ltd..
EUROPEAN SOCIALISM IN THE 19TH CENTURY (Ralph Miliband).
MCSET. Cat no: **HE 8**. Released on Sussex Tapes, '91 by Sussex Publications Ltd.. Note: 2 Cassettes
FASCISM (H.R. Kedward).
MCSET. Cat no: **HB 5**. Released on Sussex Tapes, '91 by Sussex Publications Ltd.. Note: 2 Cassettes
FIRST INDUSTRIAL REVOLUTION, THE (1760-1830) (Unknown narrator(s)).
MCSET. Cat no: **OLH 2**. Released on Sussex Tapes, '91 by Sussex Publications Ltd.. Note: 2 Cassettes
FOOD FOR MILLIONS (China, USA, Third World, UK, UNESCO Books) (Unknown narrator(s)).
MC. Cat no: **IR 120**. Released on International Report, Oct '81 by Seminar Cassettes.
FRAMEWORK FOR NEW KNOWLEDGE (Idres Shah).
MC. Cat no: **SS 101**. Released on Seminar Cassettes, Oct '81 by Seminar Cassettes.
GENERAL STRIKE, THE (And Unemployment Between the Wars) (Unknown narrator(s)).

MCSET. Cat no: **OLH 7**. Released on Sussex Tapes, '91 by Sussex Publications Ltd.. Note: 2 Cassettes

GLADSTONE (M.R.D. Foot & R.T. Shannon).
MC. Cat no: **HA 3**. Released on Sussex Tapes, '91 by Sussex Publications Ltd..

GOVERNMENT AND SCIENCE IN BRITAIN, USA & USSR (Margaret Gowing & David Holloway).
MC. Cat no: **HB 10**. Released on Sussex Tapes, '91 by Sussex Publications Ltd..

GREAT DEPRESSION OF 1990, THE (Edited by Ravi Batra) (John Hockenberry).
MCSET. Cat no: **0671660756**. Released on Simon & Schuster, '91 by Simon & Schuster Ltd. Note: 2 Cassettes

GREAT SLUMP, THE (Origins and Causes) (John G rule & Adrian Vinson).
MCSET. Cat no: **HEA 059**. Released on AVP, '91 by AVP Publishing.

HISTORICAL DEMOGRAPHY (1450-1700) (Peter Laslett & E.A. Wrigley).
MCSET. Cat no: **H 6**. Released on Sussex Tapes, '91 by Sussex Publications Ltd.. Note: 2 Cassettes

HUMAN GEOGRAPHY (Peter Toyne & Peter Whiteley).
MC. Cat no: **T2**. Released on Sussex Tapes, '91 by Sussex Publications Ltd..

INDUSTRIAL AND AGRARIAN CHANGE IN THE 18TH CENTURY ENGLAND (T C Barker & G E Mingay).
MCSET. Cat no: **HEA 005**. Released on AVP, '91 by AVP Publishing.

INDUSTRIAL REVOLUTION, THE (Norman Hampson & Jack Lively).
MC. Cat no: **HA 1**. Released on Sussex Tapes, '91 by Sussex Publications Ltd..

INTERNATIONAL RELATIONS BETWEEN THE WARS (FH. Hinsley & Donald Watt).
MC. Cat no: **HB 8**. Released on Sussex Tapes, '91 by Sussex Publications Ltd..

IRISH QUESTION 1800-1922, THE (Angus Macintyre & Philip Waller).
MCSET. Cat no: **HEA 017**. Released on AVP, '91 by AVP Publishing.

JOB SATISFACTION (Stockholm, Tokyo, New York, London, UNESCO) (Unknown narrator(s)).
MC. Cat no: **IR 103**. Released on International Report, Oct '81 by Seminar Cassettes.

LABOUR GOVERNMENT, THE (1945-1951) (Kenneth O Morgan & Ross McKibblin).
MC. Cat no: **HB 11**. Released on Sussex Tapes, '91 by Sussex Publications Ltd..

LIBERALS IN THE 20TH CENTURY, THE (Cameron Hazlehurst & Kenneth O Morgan).
MC. Cat no: **HA 8**. Released on Sussex Tapes, '91 by Sussex Publications Ltd.

LLOYD GEORGE (Dr Ian Bradley & Peter Rowland).

MCSET. Cat no: **HEA 035**. Released on AVP, '91 by AVP Publishing.

LLOYD GEORGE TO BEVERIDGE (Unknown narrator(s)).
MCSET. Cat no: **OLH 8**. Released on Sussex Tapes, '91 by Sussex Publications Ltd.. Note: 2 Cassettes

MERCANTILISM (DC. Coleman & Charles Wilson).
MC. Cat no: **HE 11**. Released on Sussex Tapes, '91 by Sussex Publications Ltd..

MORALITY OF STRIKES (UNESCO Reports) (Unknown narrator(s)).
MC. Cat no: **IR 108**. Released on International Report, Oct '81 by Seminar Cassettes.

NEW ALIGNMENTS, THE (Peter Calvocoressi & Philip Windsor).
MC. Cat no: **HB 9**. Released on Sussex Tapes, '91 by Sussex Publications Ltd..

NINETEENTH CENTURY IMPERIALISM (DK. Fieldhouse & Paul Kennedy).
MC. Cat no: **HE 18**. Released on Sussex Tapes, '91 by Sussex Publications Ltd..

OIL A WORLD CRISIS (Beirut, Washington, London, UNESCO Reports) (Unknown narrator(s)).
MC. Cat no: **IR 101**. Released on International Report, Oct '81 by Seminar Cassettes.

ONE MAN'S WAR (1914-1918) (Bernard Martin).
MC. Cat no: **HA 17**. Released on Sussex Tapes, '91 by Sussex Publications Ltd.

PALMERSTON (Dr. Donald Southgate & Dr. Christopher Barlett).
MCSET. Cat no: **HEA 013**. Released on AVP, '91 by AVP Publishing.

PARTY POLITICS BETWEEN THE WARS (Michael Bentley & Maurice Cowling).
MC. Cat no: **HA 9**. Released on Sussex Tapes, '91 by Sussex Publications Ltd.

PEACEFUL REVOLUTION (Laurens Van Der Post).
MC. Cat no: **SS 117**. Released on Seminar Cassettes, Oct '81 by Seminar Cassettes.

PEEL (G. Kitson Clark & Derek Fraser).
MC. Cat no: **HA 2**. Released on Sussex Tapes, '91 by Sussex Publications Ltd..

PERFECT INTERVIEW, THE (And The Perfect CV) (Max Eggert).
MCSET. Cat no: **RC 40**. Released on Random Century, Jul '92 by Random Century Audiobooks, Conifer Records. Note: ISBN no. 1856861163

PETROL AND POLLUTION (Coventry, Brussels, New York, UNESCO Reports) (Unknown narrator(s)).
MC. Cat no: **IR 105**. Released on International Report, Oct '81 by Seminar Cassettes.

POLITICAL PARTIES AND WALPOLE (Geoffrey Holmes & J.P. Kenyon).

MC. Cat no: **H 7**. Released on Sussex Tapes, '91 by Sussex Publications Ltd..

POLLUTION AND INDUSTRY (UNESCO Reports) (Unknown narrator(s)).
MC. Cat no: **IR 102**. Released on International Report, Oct '81 by Seminar Cassettes.

POPULATION (A Delicate Balance) (David Glass & Others).
MC. Cat no: **SS 109**. Released on Drake, '91 by Morley Audio Services.

POPULATION (Dr. Michael Morgan & Peter Whiteley).
MCSET. Cat no: **T 1**. Released on Sussex Tapes, '91 by Sussex Publications Ltd.. Note: 2 Cassettes

POSITION OF WOMEN IN 20TH CENTURY BRITAIN, THE (Pat Thane & Dr. Peter Clarke).
MCSET. Cat no: **HEA 030**. Released on AVP, '91 by AVP Publishing.

PRE-EMINENCE AND COMPETITION (1830-1914) (Unknown narrator(s)).
MCSET. Cat no: **OLH 6**. Released on Sussex Tapes, '91 by Sussex Publications Ltd.. Note: 2 Cassettes

PREMIERSHIP OF STANLEY BALDWIN, THE (John Mackintosh & Keith Middlemas).
MCSET. Cat no: **HEA 041**. Released on AVP, '91 by AVP Publishing.

QUESTIONS AND ANSWERS (Idres Shah).
MC. Cat no: **SS 103**. Released on Seminar Cassettes, '91 by Seminar Cassettes.

REFORMATION, THE (A.G. Dickens & Geoffrey Elton).
MC. Cat no: **HE 2**. Released on Sussex Tapes, '91 by Sussex Publications Ltd..

RENAISSANCE, THE (JR. Hale & Denys Hay).
MC. Cat no: **HE 9**. Released on Sussex Tapes, '91 by Sussex Publications Ltd..

REVOLUTION OF 1848, THE (Eric Hobsbawm & R.F. Leslie).
MC. Cat no: **HE 13**. Released on Sussex Tapes, '91 by Sussex Publications Ltd..

RISE OF THE LABOUR PARTY 1885-1906, THE (The Decline of the Liberal Party) (Dr Henry Pelling & Dr Peter Clarke).
MCSET. Cat no: **HAE 009**. Released on AVP, '91 by AVP Publishing.

ROOTS OF INFLATION (Bonn, New York, London, Buenos Aires, UNESCO) (Unknown narrator(s)).
MC. Cat no: **IR 106**. Released on International Report, Oct '81 by Seminar Cassettes.

SCIENTISTS AND RESPONSIBILITY (Professor Linus Pauling).
MC. Cat no: **SS 127**. Released on Seminar Cassettes, Oct '81 by Seminar Cassettes.

SOCIAL CHANGE (Norman Long).
MCSET. Cat no: **0056048**. Released on Sussex Tapes, '91 by Sussex Pub-

lications Ltd.. Note: 2 Cassettes.

SOCIAL CHANGE IN THE SIXTEENTH CENTURY (Peter Burke, Michael Hawkins & Malcolm Kitch).
MC. Cat no: **H 10**. Released on Sussex Tapes, '91 by Sussex Publications Ltd..

SOCIAL IMPACT OF THE INDUSTRIAL REVOLUTION (Unknown narrator(s)).
MCSET. Cat no: **OLH 3**. Released on Sussex Tapes, '91 by Sussex Publications Ltd.. Note: 2 Cassettes

SOURCES OF ENERGY (England, New York, Tel Aviv, UNESCO Reports) (Unknown narrator(s)).
MC. Cat no: **IR 109**. Released on International Report, Oct '81 by Seminar Cassettes.

SPORT AND POLITICS (Controversies in World Sport, UNESCO Reports) (Unknown narrator(s)).
MC. Cat no: **IR 107**. Released on International Report, Oct '81 by Seminar Cassettes.

SURVIVING THE GREAT DEPRESSION OF 1990 (Ravi Batra).
MCSET. Cat no: **0671674056**. Released on Simon & Schuster, '91 by Simon & Schuster Ltd. Note: 2 Cassettes.

TEENAGERS IN THE FAMILY (John Coleman).
MCSET. Cat no: **1871504007**. Released on Tapewise, '91 by Tapewise. Note : 2 Cassettes

TO BE A SLAVE (Julius Lester & Others).
MCSET. Cat no: **2066**. Released on Caedmon (USA), '91 by Caedmon Records (USA), Bond Street Music.
MCSET. Cat no: **000107167X**. Released on Sussex Tapes, '91 by Sussex Publications Ltd.. Note: 2 Cassettes

TRADE UNION MOVEMENT AND THE GENERAL STRIKE (Christopher Farman & Henry Pelling).
MC. Cat no: **HA 14**. Released on Sussex Tapes, '91 by Sussex Publications Ltd.

TRAFFIC CONTROL (Bonn, Tokyo, London, UNESCO Reports) (Unknown narrator(s)).
MC. Cat no: **IR 115**. Released on International Report, Oct '81 by Seminar Cassettes.

TRANSPORT REVOLUTION, THE (T.C. Barker & Peter Mathias).
MC. Cat no: **HA 11**. Released on Sussex Tapes, '91 by Sussex Publications Ltd.

TUDOR FOREIGN POLICY (P.S. Crowson & Malcolm Robinson).
MC. Cat no: **H 14**. Released on Sussex Tapes, '91 by Sussex Publications Ltd..

TUDOR REGIME RECONSIDERED, THE (Geoffrey Elton & Christopher Haigh).
MC. Cat no: **H 20**. Released on Sussex Tapes, '91 by Sussex Publications Ltd..

UNWILLING TO SCHOOL (Los Angeles, Paris, Moscow, London, UNESCO) (Unknown narrator(s)).
MC. Cat no: **IR 112**. Released on International Report, Oct '81 by Seminar Cassettes.

URBAN GEOGRAPHY (Peter Hall & Peter Whiteley).
MCSET. Cat no: **T 4**. Released on Sussex Tapes, '91 by Sussex Publications Ltd.. Note: 2 Cassettes

VEIL: THE SECRET WARS OF THE CIA (1981-1987) (Robert Woodward).
MCSET. Cat no: **0671658433**. Released on Simon & Schuster, '91 by Simon & Schuster Ltd. Note: 2 Cassettes

WALPOLE, PITT AND FOREIGN POLICY (Paul Langford & Malcolm Robinson).
MC. Cat no: **H 18**. Released on Sussex Tapes, '91 by Sussex Publications Ltd..

WAR AND SOCIETY FROM 1914 (Arthur Marwick & Henry Pelling).
MC. Cat no: **HA 10**. Released on Sussex Tapes, '91 by Sussex Publications Ltd.. Note: AAD

WHY OVERTIME? (Moscow, New York, London, UNESCO Reports) (Unknown narrator(s)).
MC. Cat no: **IR 110**. Released on International Report, Oct '81 by Seminar Cassettes.

WORLD DEVELOPMENT AND EUROPE'S LONG-TERM RISE (Michael Havinden & Eric Jones).
MC. Cat no: **HB 12**. Released on Sussex Tapes, '91 by Sussex Publications Ltd..

ZEN: THE ETERNAL NOW (Alan Watts).
MC. Cat no: **SS 121**. Released on Seminar Cassettes, Oct '81 by Seminar Cassettes.

Solzhentizyn, A

MATRYONIN DVOR (Edited By Robert Porter) (Unknown narrator(s)).
Note: An examination of one of the few works of Solzhenitsyn to be officially published in the U.S.S.R.
MC. Cat no: **R 7757**. Released on Exeter Tapes, '91 by Drakes Educational Associates.

Somerville-Large

TO THE NAVEL OF THE WORLD (Garard Green).
MCSET. Cat no: **OAS 40591**. Released on Oasis Audio Books, '91 by Isis Audio Books. Note: 8 Cassettes.
MCSET. Cat no: **1103N**. Released on Travellers Tales, '91 by Travellers Tales.

Sound Effects

COURAGE THE GUARD DOG
Note: Alsatian dog barking ferociously for use as a security device against intruders.
MC. Cat no: **WIV 4-001**. Released on West 4, Aug '82 by West 4 Records & Tapes.

ESSENTIAL COMBAT AND DISASTER SOUND EFFECTS (Various).
CD. Cat no: **BBCCD 839**. Released on BBC, Feb '91 by BBC Records, Taylors.

ESSENTIAL DEATH AND HORROR 1 (Various artists).
CD. Cat no: **BBCCD 822**. Released on BBC, Oct '90 by BBC Records, Taylors.

ESSENTIAL DEATH AND HORROR 2 (Various artists).
CD. Cat no: **BBCCD 823**. Released on BBC, Oct '90 by BBC Records, Taylors.

ESSENTIAL HI-TECH (Various artists).
CD. Cat no: **BBCCD 856**. Released on BBC, Apr '91 by BBC Records, Taylors.

ESSENTIAL HOME VIDEO SOUND EFFECTS (Various artists).
CD. Cat no: **BBCCD 953**. Released on BBC, May '91 by BBC Records, Taylors.

ESSENTIAL SCIENCE FICTION (Volume 2) (Various narrator(s)).
CD. Cat no: **BBCCD 855**. Released on BBC, Apr '91 by BBC Records, Taylors.

ESSENTIAL SOUND EFFECTS (Various artists).
Note: Sound Effects are:- Water, Horses, Farmyard, Sports, Space, Zoo, Air Travel, Trains, Motor Traffic, Boats, Disaster, Weather, Interior Atmospheres, Bells and Music for Silent Movies.
LP. Cat no: **REFX 448**. Released on BBC, Aug '82 by BBC Records, Taylors **Deleted** Jun '91.

ESSENTIAL SOUND EFFECTS (2) (Various artists).
MC. Cat no: **ZCF 792**. Released on BBC, Sep '90 by BBC Records, Taylors.
CD. Cat no: **BBCCD 792**. Released on BBC, Sep '90 by BBC Records, Taylors.

LONDON LIVE (Effects of London) (Various).
Note: An audio souvenir of London life and sounds. Robin Lumley & Peter Willsher take you across London by sound, visiting the many fascinating aspects of life in the capital. This album, recorded entirely on location, gives a picture of London life in sound.
LP. Cat no: **ALA 3008**. Released on ASV (Academy Sound & Vision), 1 Jul '87 by Academy Sound & Vision Records.
MC. Cat no: **ZC ALA 3008**. Released on ASV (Academy Sound & Vision), 1 Jul '87 by Academy Sound & Vision Records.

MID-DAY ON JOST VAN DYKE (In the Absence of Man) (Various artists).
CD. Cat no: **CD 2002**. Released on Daring (USA), '88 by Rounder Records (USA), Topic Records, Jazz Music, Duncans, Impetus Records.

MUSIC AND SOUND LIBRARY VOLS.1 & 2 (Various).
2LP. Cat no: **MSL 12**. Released on

PRT, Nov '85 by Castle Communications PLC.

SCI-FI AND FUTURISTIC (Various).
CD. Cat no: **BBCCD 847.** Released on BBC, Apr '91 by BBC Records, Taylors.

SOUND EFFECTS AND LINDRUM FILLS.
Tracks / Drum fills and cowbell tracks / Scratching / Satellite signals / Asteroids / Lazer gun / Earthquake / Explosion / Space invaders.
LP. Cat no: **XTLP 2.** Released on Ecstasy, Dec '83 by Creole Records **Deleted** '88.

SOUND EFFECTS NO.1 (Various artists).
LP. Cat no: **RED 47.** Released on BBC, Dec '81 by BBC Records, Taylors.
MC. Cat no: **ZCM 47.** Released on BBC, Dec '81 by BBC Records, Taylors.

SOUND EFFECTS NO.2 (Various artists).
LP. Cat no: **RED 76.** Released on BBC, Dec '81 by BBC Records, Taylors **Deleted** Jun '91.
MC. Cat no: **ZCM 76.** Released on BBC, Dec '81 by BBC Records, Taylors.

SOUND EFFECTS NO.3 (Various artists).
LP. Cat no: **RED 102.** Released on BBC, Dec '81 by BBC Records, Taylors.
MC. Cat no: **ZCM 102.** Released on BBC, Dec '81 by BBC Records, Taylors.

SOUND EFFECTS NO.4 (Various artists).
LP. Cat no: **RED 104.** Released on BBC, Dec '81 by BBC Records, Taylors.
MC. Cat no: **ZCM 104.** Released on BBC, Dec '81 by BBC Records, Taylors.

SOUND EFFECTS NO.5 (Various artists).
LP. Cat no: **RED 105.** Released on BBC, Dec '81 by BBC Records, Taylors **Deleted** Jun '91.
MC. Cat no: **ZCM 105.** Released on BBC, Dec '81 by BBC Records, Taylors.

SOUND EFFECTS NO.6 (Various artists).
LP. Cat no: **RED 106.** Released on BBC, Dec '81 by BBC Records, Taylors **Deleted** Jun '91.
MC. Cat no: **ZCM 106.** Released on BBC, Dec '81 by BBC Records, Taylors.

SOUND EFFECTS NO.7 (Various artists).
LP. Cat no: **RED 113.** Released on BBC, Dec '81 by BBC Records, Taylors **Deleted** Jun '91.
MC. Cat no: **ZCM 113.** Released on BBC, Dec '81 by BBC Records, Taylors.

SOUND EFFECTS NO.8 (Various artists).
LP. Cat no: **RED 126.** Released on BBC, Dec '81 by BBC Records, Taylors **Deleted** Jun '91.
MC. Cat no: **ZCM 126.** Released on BBC, Dec '81 by BBC Records, Taylors.

SOUND EFFECTS NO.9 (Various artists).
LP. Cat no: **RED 164.** Released on BBC, Dec '81 by BBC Records, Taylors **Deleted** Jun '91.
MC. Cat no: **ZCM 164.** Released on BBC, Dec '81 by BBC Records, Taylors.

SOUND EFFECTS NO.10 (Music and Effects for Home Movies) (Various artists).
LP. Cat no: **RED 120.** Released on BBC, Dec '81 by BBC Records, Taylors **Deleted** Jun '91.
MC. Cat no: **ZCM 120.** Released on BBC, Dec '81 by BBC Records, Taylors.

SOUND EFFECTS NO.11 (Off Beat Sound Effects) (Various artists).
LP. Cat no: **REC 198.** Released on BBC, Dec '81 by BBC Records, Taylors **Deleted** Jun '91.
MC. Cat no: **RMC 4013.** Released on BBC, Dec '81 by BBC Records, Taylors.

SOUND EFFECTS NO.12 (Out of This World) (Various artists).
LP. Cat no: **REC 225.** Released on BBC, Dec '81 by BBC Records, Taylors **Deleted** Jun '91.
MC. Cat no: **MRMC 040.** Released on BBC, Dec '81 by BBC Records, Taylors.

SOUND EFFECTS NO.13 (Death and Horror) (Various artists).
LP. Cat no: **REC 269.** Released on BBC, Dec '81 by BBC Records, Taylors **Deleted** Jun '91.
MC. Cat no: **ZCM 269.** Released on BBC, Dec '81 by BBC Records, Taylors.

SOUND EFFECTS NO.14 (Steam Trains in Stereo) (Various artists).
LP. Cat no: **REC 220.** Released on BBC, Dec '81 by BBC Records, Taylors **Deleted** Jun '91.

SOUND EFFECTS NO.15 (Vanishing Sounds in Britain) (Various artists).
LP. Cat no: **REC 227.** Released on BBC, Dec '81 by BBC Records, Taylors **Deleted** Jun '91.
MC. Cat no: **MRMC 041.** Released on BBC, Dec '81 by BBC Records, Taylors **Deleted** Jun '91.

SOUND EFFECTS NO.16 (Disasters) (Various artists).
LP. Cat no: **REC 295.** Released on BBC, Dec '81 by BBC Records, Taylors **Deleted** Jun '91.
MC. Cat no: **ZCM 295.** Released on BBC, Dec '81 by BBC Records, Taylors.

SOUND EFFECTS NO.17 (Birds and Other Sounds of the Countryside) (Various artists).
LP. Cat no: **REC 299.** Released on BBC, Dec '81 by BBC Records, Taylors **Deleted** Jun '91.
MC. Cat no: **ZCM 299.** Released on BBC, Dec '81 by BBC Records, Taylors.

SOUND EFFECTS NO.18 (Holiday Sound Effects) (Various artists).
LP. Cat no: **REC 301.** Released on BBC, Dec '81 by BBC Records, Taylors **Deleted** Jun '91.
MC. Cat no: **ZCM 301.** Released on BBC, Dec '81 by BBC Records, Taylors.

SOUND EFFECTS NO.19 (Doctor Who Sound Effects from TV Series) (Various artists).
LP. Cat no: **REC 316.** Released on BBC, Dec '81 by BBC Records, Taylors **Deleted** Jun '91.
MC. Cat no: **ZCM 316.** Released on BBC, Dec '81 by BBC Records, Taylors.

SOUND EFFECTS NO.20 (Sporting Sound Effects) (Various artists).
LP. Cat no: **REC 322.** Released on BBC, Dec '81 by BBC Records, Taylors **Deleted** Jun '91.
MC. Cat no: **ZCM 322.** Released on BBC, Dec '81 by BBC Records, Taylors.

SOUND EFFECTS NO.21 (Death and Horror Vol.2) (Various artists).
LP. Cat no: **REC 340.** Released on BBC, Dec '81 by BBC Records, Taylors **Deleted** Jun '91.
MC. Cat no: **ZCM 340.** Released on BBC, Dec '81 by BBC Records, Taylors.

SOUND EFFECTS NO.22 (Music for Silent Movies) (Various artists).
LP. Cat no: **REC 347.** Released on BBC, Dec '81 by BBC Records, Taylors **Deleted** Jun '91.
MC. Cat no: **ZCM 347.** Released on BBC, Dec '81 by BBC Records, Taylors.

SOUND EFFECTS NO.23 (Relaxing Sounds) (Various artists).
Tracks: Country stream / Ariel currents / Garden in springtime / Seashore / Forest adagio / Rain.
LP. Cat no: **REC 360.** Released on BBC, Dec '81 by BBC Records, Taylors **Deleted** Jun '91.
MC. Cat no: **ZCM 360.** Released on BBC, Dec '81 by BBC Records, Taylors.

SOUND EFFECTS NO.24 (Combat) (Various artists).
LP. Cat no: **REC 383.** Released on BBC, Dec '81 by BBC Records, Taylors **Deleted** Jun '91.
MC. Cat no: **ZCM 383.** Released on BBC, Dec '81 by BBC Records, Taylors.

SOUND EFFECTS NO.25 (Sounds of Speed) (Various artists).

LP. Cat no: **REC 390.** Released on BBC, Dec '81 by BBC Records, Taylors **Deleted** Jun '91.

MC. Cat no: **ZCM 390.** Released on BBC, Dec '81 by BBC Records, Taylors.

SOUND EFFECTS NO.26 (Science Fiction) (Various artists).
LP. Cat no: **REC 420.** Released on BBC, Dec '81 by BBC Records, Taylors **Deleted** Jun '91.

MC. Cat no: **ZCM 420.** Released on BBC, Dec '81 by BBC Records, Taylors.

MC. Cat no: **ZCM 420.** Released on BBC, Dec '81 by BBC Records, Taylors.

SOUND EFFECTS NO.27 (Even more Death and Horror)
Tracks / Staking a vampire - three mallet blows (Band 1 - Intentional death) / Two throat cuts (Band 1 - Intentional death) / Gas chamber (cyanide tablets into acid) (Band 1 - Intentional death) / Wrists cut - the blood drips into the bucket (Band 1 - Intentional death) / Assorted stabbing (Band 1 - Intentional death) / Drilling into the head - enough said (Band 1 - Intentional death) / Body put into the acid bath (Band 1 - Intentional death) / Self immolation (Band 1 - Intentional death) / Silencer (pistol) (Band 1 - Intentional death Vocal, Synth, Mechanical) / Electric fire thrown into the bath (Band 1 - Intentional death) / Boiling oil - poured off the castle wall (Band 1 - Intentional death) / Tongue pulled out (Band 2 - Torture) / Fingernails pulled out (Band 2 - Torture) / Fingers chopped off (Band 2 - Torture) / Trial by ordeal (picking ring from deep pot of (Band 2 - Torture contd - if burns healed quickly then innocent - some c) / Whipping V (Band 2 - Torture) / Torture lab AD 2500 (Band 2 - Torture) / Lift falling (with passengers) (Band 3 - Accidental? death) / Female falling from a height (ladies first!) (Band 3 - Accidental? death) / Male falling from a height (Band 3 - Accidental? death) / Reaction (to previous sounds) (Band 4) / Werewolf - transformation from human to beast (Side 2 - Nasty animals and birds) / Giant killer bees (no honey from these) (Side 2 - Nasty animals and birds) / Sleeping dragon - don't wake it up (Side 2 - Nasty animals and birds) / Dragon moving through bushes - occasional flame (Side 2 - Nasty animals and birds) / Dragon kill - the death of the monster (Side 2 - Nasty animals and birds) / Pterodactyl flying - with squawks (Side 2 - Nasty animals and birds) / Vultures feeding - if you lie around long enough Various artists (Side 2 - Nasty animals and birds) / Piranha fish feeding - don't go for a swim (Side 2 - Nasty animals and birds) / Birds attack a feed (Side 2 - Nasty animals and birds) / Triffids - sting, talking (Side 2 - Nasty animals and birds).

LP. Cat no: **REC 452.** Released on BBC, Oct '82 by BBC Records, Taylors **Deleted** Jun '91.

MC. Cat no: **ZCM 452.** Released on BBC, Oct '82 by BBC Records, Taylors.

SOUND EFFECTS NO.28 (Comedy) (Various artists).
Tracks / Human / Fights / Footsteps / Crashes / Laughter and applause / Animals / Bizarre / Birds / Impacts / Space age
Note: Another addition to the BBC Sound Effects Catalogue. Essential for all those making comedy films, vidos or stage productions.
LP. Cat no: **REC 478.** Released on BBC, Aug '83 by BBC Records, Taylors.

MC. Cat no: **ZCM 478.** Released on BBC, Aug '83 by BBC Records, Taylors.

SOUND EFFECTS NO.29 (Hi-Tech FX) (Various artists).
Tracks / Computer bleeps / Disk drive / Drive activity / Printers / Video games / Stings / Heavier stings / Whooshes and zings / Computer background fax / Singularly Simon / Computer rant / Computer waltz / Invaders rock / Arcadea / JDC background / Fanfare / Purple space and white coronas / Ascending asteroids / Pulsar patterns / Through the black hole / Force of the universe / "43".
LP. Cat no: **REC 531.** Released on BBC, Sep '84 by BBC Records, Taylors **Deleted** Jun '91.

MC. Cat no: **ZCM 531.** Released on BBC, Sep '84 by BBC Records, Taylors.

SOUNDS FOR WARGAMES (Various artists).
Note: Authentic sound affects for period and modern war games. Compiled to add realism and atmosphere to battle scenes, including cavalry, beach landings and artillery.
MC. Cat no: **AC 114.** Released on Audicord, May '83 by Audicord Cassettes.

SPECTACULAR SOUND EFFECTS VOL. 1 (Various artists).
Note: Featuring:- The Seaside, Weather, Wedding Organ Playing, Street Noises, Road Transport, Emergency, Crowds, Gatherings, Animals (Dogs, cats and horses), Air Raid Effects, Clocks, Doors-Gates-Stairs-Squeaks & Creaks, Ghosts, Tree Felling, Sports, Footsteps, Farmyard Effects.
CD. Cat no: **CZ 350.** Released on EMI, Sep '90 by EMI Records.

LP. Cat no: **THIS 34.** Released on EMI, Jun '81 by EMI Records **Deleted** May '91.

MC. Cat no: **TCTHIS 34.** Released on EMI, Jun '81 by EMI Records **Deleted** Nov '88.

SPECTACULAR SOUND EFFECTS VOL. II (Various artists).
Note: Featuring: Space Ships, Steam Trains, Diesel Trains, Underground Train, Gun & Pistol Shots, Country Sounds, Demolition, Hammering, Glass, Telephone Bell, Children & Baby, Applause, Laughter, Murmur, Birds, Cars, Shipping, Aircraft, Fanfares For Shakespearian & Other Plays.
CD. Cat no: **CZ 351.** Released on EMI, Sep '90 by EMI Records.

LP. Cat no: **THIS 35.** Released on EMI, Jun '81 by EMI Records **Deleted** Feb '92.

MC. Cat no: **TCTHIS 35.** Released on EMI, Jun '81 by EMI Records **Deleted** Feb '91.

STAR TREK - SOUND EFFECTS: THE TV SERIES (Various artists).
Note: Sound effects from the original TV series.
LP. Cat no: **GNPS 8010.** Released on GNP Crescendo, Jan '89 by GNP Crescendo Records (USA), Silva Screen, Flexitron Ltd..

MC. Cat no: **GNP5 8010.** Released on GNP Crescendo, Jan '89 by GNP Crescendo Records (USA), Silva Screen, Flexitron Ltd..

CD. Cat no: **GNPD 8010.** Released on GNP Crescendo, Jan '89 by GNP Crescendo Records (USA), Silva Screen, Flexitron Ltd..

VERMONT HEARTH (In the Absence of Man) (Various artists).
CD. Cat no: **CD 2004.** Released on Daring (USA), '88 by Rounder Records (USA), Topic Records, Jazz Music, Duncans, Impetus Records.

VERMONT STREAM (In the Absence of Man) (Various artists).
CD. Cat no: **CD 2003.** Released on Daring (USA), '88 by Rounder Records (USA), Topic Records, Jazz Music, Duncans, Impetus Records.

Spain...

ORIGINS AND POLITICS OF THE SPANISH CIVIL WAR (Raymond Carr & Hugh Thomas).
MCSET. Cat no: **HUA 030**. Released on AVP, '91 by AVP Publishing.

ANDALUSINS, THE (Edited By Michael T. Newton) (Unknown narrator(s)).
MC. Cat no: **S 7903**. Released on Exeter Tapes, '91 by Drakes Educational Associates.

BASQUES, THE (Edited By Michael T. Newton) (Unknown narrator(s)).
MC. Cat no: **BA 7901**. Released on Exeter Tapes, '91 by Drakes Educational Associates.

CATALANS, THE (Edited By Michael T. Newton) (Unknown narrator(s)).
MC. Cat no: **CA 7902**. Released on Exeter Tapes, '91 by Drakes Educational Associates.

FRANCO: THE MAN AND THE RULER (Spain under Franco) (Dr. Paul Preston & Dr. R A H Robinson).
MCSET. Cat no: **HUA 067**. Released on AVP, '91 by AVP Publishing.

RISE OF THE SPANISH EMPIRE, THE (The Decline of Spain as a Great Power) (Dr. Peter Lineham & Dr. Geoffrey Parker).
MCSET. Cat no: **HUA 036**. Released on AVP, '91 by AVP Publishing.

SPAIN (1494-1659) (John Elliot & Henry Kamen).
MC. Cat no: **HE 3**. Released on Sussex Tapes, '91 by Sussex Publications Ltd..

Spanish

ARTICULOS (Various narrators).
Note: Spanish narration for practice linguists.
MCSET. Cat no: **EAC 10J**. Released on European Audio Classics, '91 by Unknown. Note: 2 cassettes - ISBN no. 1873256353

BASIC SPANISH (ADVANCED LEVEL) (Part A) (Unknown narrator(s)).
MCSET. Cat no: **S 153**. Released on Audio Forum (Language courses), '91. Note: 12 Cassettes

BASIC SPANISH (BEGINNERS) (Volume 1) (Unknown narrator(s)).
MCSET. Cat no: **S 101**. Released on Audio Forum (Language courses), '91. Note: 12 Cassettes.

BASIC SPANISH (ADVANCED LEVEL) (Part B) (Unknown narrator(s)).
MCSET. Cat no: **S 170**. Released on Audio Forum (Language courses), '91. Note: 12 Cassettes.

BASIC SPANISH (INTERMEDIATE) (Unknown narrator(s)).
MCSET. Cat no: **S 121**. Released on Audio Forum (Language courses), '91. Note: 8 Cassettes.

BUSINESS SPANISH (Unknown narrator(s)).
Note: Provides dialogues, exercises and specialised vocabulary used in a wide range of business situations. The course is also self testing.
MCSET. Cat no: **S 24300**. Released on Audio Forum (Language courses), '91. Note: 6 Cassettes and book.

DIGAME (Language Courses) (Unknown narrator(s)).
2LP. Cat no: **OP 230/31**. Released on BBC Publications, Jun '83. Note : A beginners course in Spanish (volumes 1 & 2).

MCSET. Cat no: **PTT 230/31**. Released on BBC Publications, Jun '83. Note: A beginners course in Spanish (volumes 1 & 2).

DIGAME (Language Courses) (Unknown narrator(s)).
LP. Cat no: **OP 251**. Released on BBC Publications, Jun '83. Note : A beginners course in Spanish (volume 3).
MC. Cat no: **PTT 251**. Released on BBC Publications, Jun '83. Note : A beginners course in Spanish (volume 3).

ESPANA VIVA (Language Courses) (Unknown narrator(s)).
Note: Includes: Book, Tutor's Notes and Work-Book.
MC. Cat no: **PTT 291**. Released on BBC Publications, '91.

ESPANA VIVA (2) (Language Courses) (Unknown narrator(s)).
Note: Includes:- Book, Tutor's Notes and Work-Book.
MCSET. Cat no: **PTT 292**. Released on BBC Publications, '91.

FOUR SPANISH SHORT STORIES (Various narrators).
Note: Spanish narration for practice linguists. The short stories and the authors are:- Clarin - Adios, Cordera: Emilia Pardo Bazan - Viernes Santo: Fernan Caballero - La Maldicion Paterna and Pedro Antonio De Alarcon.
MCSET. Cat no: **EAC 091**. Relases on European Audio Classics, '91 by Unknown. Note: 2 Cassettes - ISBN no. 1873256450

GET BY IN SPANISH (Language Coures) (Unknown narrator(s)).
Note: Each book contains phrases and conversations.
MCSET. Cat no: **PTT 227/8**. Released on BBC Publications, Jun '83. Note : 2 Cassettes.

GET BY TRAVEL PACKS (Language Courses) (Unknown narrator(s)).
MCSET. Cat no: **PACK 2227**. Released on BBC Publications, '91. Note : 2 Cassettes.

LANGUAGE COURSE - SPANISH (Travel Pack) (Unknown narrator(s)).
LPS. Cat no: **0747305994**. Released on Linguaphone, Apr '82 by Linguaphone Institute, Taylors, Century Records (USA), Bond Street Music.

LANGUAGE COURSE - SPANISH (CASTILIAN) (Unknown narrator(s)).
LPS. Cat no: **0747302804**. Released on Linguaphone, Apr '82 by Linguaphone Institute, Taylors, Century Records (USA), Bond Street Music.

LANGUAGE COURSE - SPANISH (LATIN-AMERICAN) (Unknown narrator(s)).
LPS. Cat no: **0747303940**. Released on Linguaphone, Apr '82 by Linguaphone Institute, Taylors, Century Records (USA), Bond Street Music.

LEYENDAS (Various narrators).
Note: Spanish narration for practice linguists. Four tales which reveal the lyrical quality of Bequers prose.
MCSET. Cat no: **EAC 08H**. Released on European Audio Classics, '91 by Unknown. Note: 2 Cassettes - ISBN no. 187325640X

LINGUAPHONE SPANISH TRAVELLERS (Language Courses) (Unknown narrator(s)).
MCSET. Cat no: **0747306850**. Released on Linguaphone, '91 by Linguaphone Institute, Taylors, Century Records (USA), Bond Street Music.

MEXICO VIVO (Language Courses) (Unknown narrator(s)).
Note: Book and cassette.
MC. Cat no: **PTT 344**. Released on BBC Publications, '91.

PASO DOBLE (Language Courses) (Unknown narrator(s)).
Note: Includes a book.
MCSET. Cat no: **PTT 308**. Released on BBC Publications, '91.

POR AQUI (Language Courses) (Unknown narrator(s)).
Note: Book and cassette.
MC. Cat no: **PTT 238**. Released on BBC Publications, '91.

POR AQUI (2) (Language Courses) (Unknown narrator(s)).
Note: Book and cassette.
MC. Cat no: **PTT 239**. Released on BBC Publications, '91.

POR AQUI (3) (Language Courses) (Unknown narrator(s)).
Note: Book and cassette.
MC. Cat no: **PTT 256**. Released on BBC Publications, '91.

SOUNDS AND ALPHABET OF SPANISH, THE (Edited By Steven Dodd) (Unknown narrator(s)).
MC. Cat no: **S 7657**. Released on Exeter Tapes, '91 by Drakes Educational Associates.

SOUNDS OF SPANISH, THE (Edited By Steven Dodd) (Unknown narrator(s)).
Note: In Spanish.
MC. Cat no: **S 7629**. Released on Exeter Tapes, '91 by Drakes Educational Associates.

SPANISH AT THE WHEEL (Unknown narrator(s)).
Note: Includes:- sixteen information cards.
MCSET. Cat no: **852451480**. Released on Hugo Languages, '92 by Hugo Language Books Limited. Note: 4 Cassettes.

SPANISH CASSETTE COURSE (Unknown narrator(s)).

Note: Includes:- Three months' book and an instruction leaflet.
MCSET. Cat no: **852850700.** Released on Hugo Languages, '92 by Hugo Language Books Limited. Note: 4 cassettes. Playing time 4hrs.

SPANISH FOR TRAVEL (Unknown narrator(s)).
MC. Cat no: **BCP 013.** Released on Berlitz Language Courses, '88, Conifer Records.

SPANISH LANGUAGE BASICS (Unknown narrator(s)).
MC. Cat no: **BMC 009.** Released on Berlitz Language Courses, '88, Conifer Records.

SPANISH LANGUAGE IN AMERICA, THE (Edited By Ian Press) (Unknown narrator(s)).
MC. Cat no: **S 7834.** Released on Exeter Tapes, '91 by Drakes Educational Associates.

SPAIN TRAVEL KIT (Unknown narrator(s)).
MC. Cat no: **BTK 010.** Released on Berlitz Language, '88 by Conifer Records.

SPANISH TRAVEL PACK (Unknown narrator(s)).
Note: Contains a Hugo phrase book.
MC. Cat no: **852850883.** Released on Hugo Languages, '92 by Hugo Language Books Limited.

SPEAK SPANISH TODAY (Conversational Courses) (Unknown narrator(s)).
Note: Consists of a book and a 75-90 minute cassette.
MC. Cat no: **852851170.** Released on Hugo Languages, '92 by Hugo Language Books Limited.

WHEN IN SPAIN (Language Courses) (Unknown narrator(s)).
Note: Available with cassette is a Travel Pack and a Book.
MC. Cat no: **PTT 290.** Released on BBC Publications, '91.

Spanish Literature

HOW SPANISH POETRY WORKS (Edited By Steven Dodd) (Unknown narrator(s)).
MC. Cat no: **S 7658.** Released on Exeter Tapes, '91 by Drakes Educational Associates. Note: Accompanying booklet - cat no. S 7658B

Spector, Ronnie

BE MY BABY (Ronnie Spector).
Note: Written by Ronnie Spector and Vince Waldron.
MCSET. Cat no: **TTC 2039.** Released on Talking Tape Company, Apr '91, Conifer Records. Note: 2 Cassettes. Playing time 3hrs. ISBN no. 1872520693

Spender, Stephen

POETRY OF STEPHEN SPENDER, THE (Stephen Spender).
MC. Cat no: **AS 44.** Released on Sussex Tapes, '91 by Sussex Publications Ltd..

Stafford, Jean

JEAN STAFFORD READS ONE OF HER SHORT STORIES (Jean Stafford).
MC. Cat no: **AS 45.** Released on Sussex Tapes, '91 by Sussex Publications Ltd..

Stalker, John

STALKER (John Stalker).
MCSET. Cat no: **LFP 7352.** Released on Listen For Pleasure, Sep '88 by EMI Records. Note: Playing time: 3 hours.

Stamp, Terence

COMING ATTRACTIONS (Terence Stamp).
MCSET. Cat no: **OAS 10791.** Released on Oasis Audio Books, '91 by Isis Audio Books. Note: 8 Cassette set.

DOUBLE FEATURE (Biography) (Terence Stamp).
Note: The conclusion of his autobiography.
MCSET. Cat no: **IAB 91096.** Released on Isis Audio Books, Sep '91. Note : 8 cassette set. Playing time 10hrs 40mins.

STAMP ALBUM (Terence Stamp).
MCSET. Cat no: **OAS 91011.** Released on Oasis Audio Books, '91 by Isis Audio Books. Note: 5 Cassette set.
MCSET. Cat no: **1076A.** Released on Travellers Tales, '91 by Travellers Tales. Note: 5 Cassettes.

Stark, Freya

DUST IN THE LION'S PAW (Biography) (Rosemary Davis).
MCSET. Cat no: **1036/1037A.** Released on Travellers Tales, '91 by Travellers Tales. Note: 12 Cassettes.
MCSET. Cat no: **OAS 89081.** Released on Oasis Audio Books, '91 by Isis Audio Books. Note: 12 Cassettes.

Stendhal

LE ROUGE ET LE NOIR (Edited By Donald Haggis) (Unknown narrator(s)).
Note: The character of Julien Sorel and the paradox of ambition are explored in this novel by Stendhal.
MC. Cat no: **F 7684.** Released on Exeter Tapes, '91 by Drakes Educational Associates.

Stevenson, Robert

AMATEUR EMIGRANT, THE (Donal Donnelly).
MCSET. Cat no: **RB 88460.** Released on Recorded Books, Sep '91 by Isis Audio Books. Note: 3 Cassettes. Playing time 4hrs 30mins.

Storm, Theodor

DER SCHIMMELREITER (Edited By Gerald Opie) (Unknown narrator(s)).
Note: The tape sets this late work of Storm in the context of his literary 'oeuvre' as a whole and considers the nature of the writer's realism.
MC. Cat no: **G 7539.** Released on Exeter Tapes, '91 by Drakes Educational Associates.

DREI NOVELLEN (Edited By Gerald Opie) (Unknown narrator(s)).
Note: Demonstrates the development of Storm's narrative style from post-romantic sentimentality to a sterner social realism.
MC. Cat no: **G 7540.** Released on Exeter Tapes, '91 by Drakes Educational Associates.

Strachey, Lytton

FLORENCE NIGHTINGALE (Biography) (Anthony Homyer).
MCSET. Cat no: **TCL 31.** Released on Complete Listener, '91 by Complete Listener. Note: 6 Cassettes.

LAST DAYS OF GENERAL GORDON (Biography) (Anthony Homyer).
MCSET. Cat no: **TCL 32.** Released on Complete Listener, '91 by Complete Listener. Note: 6 Cassettes.

Strauss, Johann

JOHANN STRAUSS 1825-1899 (Biography) (Unknown narrator(s)).
MC. Cat no: **DFC 7.** Released on Sussex Tapes, '91 by Sussex Publications Ltd..

JOHANN STRAUSS THE YOUNGER (Biography) (Richard Mayes).
MC. Cat no: **GC 6.** Released on Green Dragon, '91 by Green Dragon Audio Visual.

Styron, William

WILLIAM STYRON READS HIS WORK (William Styron).
MC. Cat no: **AS 46.** Released on Sussex Tapes, '91 by Sussex Publications Ltd..

Swanton, E.W.

LORD'S - THE HOME OF CRICKET (See Under Cricket) (E.W. Swanton).

Sweden

RISE AND FALL OF SWEDEN, THE (1500-1721) (Ragnhild Hatton & Stewart Oakley).
MC. Cat no: **HE 14.** Released on Sussex Tapes, '91 by Sussex Publications Ltd..

Swedish

FSI SWEDISH BASIC COURSE (Unknown narrator(s)).
MCSET. Cat no: **K 501.** Released on Audio Forum (Language courses), '91. Note: 8 Cassettes

LANGUAGE COURSE - SWEDISH (Unknown narrator(s)).
LPS. Cat no: **0747302898.** Released on Linguaphone, Apr '82 by Linguaphone Institute, Taylors, Century Records (USA), Bond Street Music.

SWEDISH CASSETTE COURSE (Unknown narrator(s)).
Note: Includes:- 3 months' book and an instruction leaflet.
MCSET. Cat no: **852850743.** Released on Hugo Languages, '92 by Hugo Language Books Limited. Note: 4 Cassettes. Playing time 4hrs.

SWEDISH TRAVEL PACK (Unknown narrator(s)).

Note: Contains a Hugo phrase book
MC. Cat no: **852851421.** Released on Hugo Languages, '92 by Hugo Language Books Limited. Note: 4 Cassettes.

Swift, Jonathan
JONATHAN SWIFT (Colin Brooks & Angus Ross).
Note: Pre-recorded discussions which show literary criticism as a living, evolving interchange.
MC. Cat no: **A33.** Released on Sussex Tapes, '91 by Sussex Publications Ltd..

Switzerland...
SWITZERLAND IN QUESTION (Edited By Clive H. Church) (Unknown narrator(s)).
Note: Includes an analysis of the unusual nature of Switzerland's domestic structures and diplomatic stance.
MC. Cat no: **F 7969.** Released on Exeter Tapes, '91 by Drakes Educational Associates.

Szasz, Thomas S.
MYTHS OF MENTAL ILLNESS (Unknown narrator(s)).
MC. Cat no: **PT 24.** Released on Psychology Today (USA), Oct '81 by Seminar Cassettes.

Tangye, Derek
EVENING GULL, THE (Peter Joyce).
MCSET. Cat no: **1100N.** Released on Travellers Tales, '91 by Travellers Tales. Note: 5 Cassettes.

MCSET. Cat no: **1854963848.** Released on Bramhope, '91 by Ulverscroft Soundings. Note: 5 Cassettes.

GULL ON THE ROOF (Christopher Kay).
MCSET. Cat no: **1032N.** Released on Travellers Tales, '91 by Travellers Tales. Note: 5 Cassettes.

MCSET. Cat no: **1854961993.** Released on Bramhope, '91 by Ulverscroft Soundings. Note: 5 Cassettes.

JEANNIE (Unknown narrator(s)).
MCSET. Cat no: **1854962973.** Released on Bramhope, '91 by Ulverscroft Soundings. Note: 4 Cassettes.

LAMA (Biography) (Paul Eddington).
MCSET. Cat no: **1019A.** Released on Travellers Tales, '91 by Travellers Tales. Note: 4 Cassettes.

WORLD OF MINACK, THE (Peter Joyce).
MCSET. Cat no: **1854965824.** Released on Soundings, Apr '92 by Soundings Records, Bond Street Music. Note: 6 Cassettes

Tchaikovsky (composer)
PETER ILYICH TCHAIKOVSKY (Biography) (Richard Mayes).
MC. Cat no: **GC 7.** Released on Green Dragon, '91 by Green Dragon Audio Visual.

PETER ILYICH TCHAIKOVSKY 1840 - 1893 (Biography) (Unknown narrator(s)).

MC. Cat no: **DFC 4.** Released on Sussex Tapes, '91 by Sussex Publications Ltd.

Tennis
TENNIS: CONCENTRATION, TIMING, STROKES & STRATEGY (Dick Sutphen).
MC. Cat no: **RX 130.** Released on Valley Of The Sun, '88.

Tennyson, Alfred Lord
ALFRED LORD TENNYSON (John Dixon-Hunt & David Palmer).
Note: Pre-recorded discussions which show literary criticism as a living, evolving interchange.
MC. Cat no: **A22.** Released on Sussex Tapes, '91 by Sussex Publications Ltd..

Terkel, Studs
HARD TIMES (The Story of the Depression) (Unknown narrator(s)).
MCSET. Cat no: **2048.** Released on Caedmon (USA), '89 by Caedmon Records (USA), Bond Street Music.

Teyte, Dame Maggie
HER LIFE AND ART (Unknown narrator(s)).
LP. Cat no: **REGL 369.** Released on BBC, Oct '79 by BBC Records, Taylors **Deleted** 31 Aug '88.

MC. Cat no: **ZCF 369.** Released on BBC, Oct '79 by BBC Records, Taylors **Deleted** 31 Aug '88.

Thai
THAI TRAVEL PACK (Unknown narrator(s)).
Note: Contains a Hugo phrase book.
MC. Cat no: **85285157X.** Released on Hugo Languages, '92 by Hugo Language Books Limited.

Theroux, Paul
GREAT RAILWAY BAZAAR BY TRAIN THROUGH ASIA (Frank Muller).
MCSET. Cat no: **IAB 88071.** Released on Isis Audio Books, '88.

MCSET. Cat no: **1036N.** Released on Travellers Tales, '91 by Travellers Tales. Note: 8 cassettes.

KINGDOM BY THE SEA, THE (Ron Keith).
MCSET. Cat no: **1108/9N.** Released on Travellers Tales, '91 by Travellers Tales. Note: 10 Cassettes

MCSET. Cat no: **IAB 91043.** Released on Isis Audio Books, '91.

OLD PATAGONIAN EXPRESS, THE (Norman Dietz).
MCSET. Cat no: **1048/9N.** Released on Travellers Tales, '91 by Travellers Tales. Note: 12 Cassettes.

MCSET. Cat no: **IAB 88123.** Released on Isis Audio Books, '91. Note : 12 Cassettes.

Thomas, Dylan
BOY GROWING UP, A (Biography) (Emlyn Williams).
MCSET. Cat no: **1020A.** Released on Travellers Tales, '91 by Travellers Tales. Note: 2 Cassettes.

MCSET. Cat no: **SAY 48.** Released on Argo (Polygram), Mar '83 by PolyGram Classics **Deleted** Jan '89.

POETRY OF DYLAN THOMAS, THE (John Wain).
Note: Pre-recorded discussions which show literary criticism as a living, evolving interchange.
MC. Cat no: **A24.** Released on Sussex Tapes, '91 by Sussex Publications Ltd..

Thompson, John Cargill
UNCOOKING OLD SHERRY (A Portrait of Richard Brinsley Sheridan) (Martin Heller).
MC. Cat no: **SPN 825-1.** Released on Schiltron Audio Books, '91 by Schiltron Publishing. Note: Playing time 85 minutes.

Thrower, Percy
GUIDE TO GOOD GARDENING (Percy Thrower).
LP. Cat no: **RES 002.** Released on Response, Jan '77 by Priority Records, Taylors **Deleted** '80.

Thubron, Colin
AMONG THE RUSSIANS (Frank Duncan).
MCSET. Cat no: **1071N.** Released on Travellers Tales, '91 by Travellers Tales. Note: 8 Cassettes.

MCSET. Cat no: **OAS 89072.** Released on Oasis Audio Books, '91 by Isis Audio Books. Note: 8 Cassettes.

BEHIND THE WALL (A Journey Through China) (Garard Green).
MCSET. Cat no: **IAB 92021.** Released on Isis Audio Books, Feb '92. Note : 12 Cassettes. Playing time 15hrs 30mins.

Tolstoy, Leo
ANNA KARENINA (Edited By M. Pursglove) (Unknown narrator(s)).
Note: A general introduction to this work by Tolstoy.
MC. Cat no: **R 7330.** Released on Exeter Tapes, '91 by Drakes Educational Associates.

DETSTVO (Edited By Olive Stevens) (Unknown artist(s)).
Note: An analysis of Leo Tolstoy's first publishing work, concentrating on its autobiographical features.
MC. Cat no: **R 7956.** Released on Exeter Tapes, '91 by Drakes Educational Associates.

SMERT' IVANA IL'ICHA (Edited By Olive Stevens) (Unknown narrator(s)).
Note: A consideration of 'The Death Of Ivan Il'ich', in the context of Tolstoy's attitude to death.
MC. Cat no: **R 7759.** Released on Exeter Tapes, '91 by Drakes Educational Associates.

VOINA I MIR (Edited By Roger Cockrell And David Richards) (Unknown narrator(s)).
Note: A general introduction to the work

focusing on some of its main themes, including Tolstoy's philosophy of history.
MC. Cat no: **R 7704**. Released on Exeter Tapes, '91 by Drakes Educational Associates.

Tomkies, Mike

MOOBLI (Joe Dunlop).
MCSET. Cat no: **1088N**. Released on Travellers Tales, '91 by Travellers Tales. Note: 8 Cassettes.
MCSET. Cat no: **OAS 91022**. Released on Oasis Audio Books, '91 by Isis Audio Books. Note: 8 Cassettes.

Townsend, Peter

DUEL IN THE DARK, A (Christopher Kay).
MCSET. Cat no: **1044N**. Released on Travellers Tales, '91 by Travellers Tales. Note: 6 Cassettes.
MCSET. Cat no: **1854962027**. Released on Soundings, '91 by Soundings Records, Bond Street Music. Note: 6 Cassettes.

Trains...

AGAINST THE GRADE (Various).
Note: Steam at work in the 1960s at Shap, Ais Gill, Lickey, Standedge, and on the Waverley Route (Carlisle to Edinburgh). Including classes A4, 8F, 4F, 9F, Britannia, Jubilee, and LMS class 5.
MC. Cat no: **AC 160**. Released on Audicord, '88 by Audicord Cassettes.

AGE OF STEAM, THE (Various).
Note: Steam locomotives at work, by day and night, at various locations on British Railways between 1959 and 1961, and in 1982 in Zimbabwe. On the Lickey Incline at Bromsgrove & near Blackwell, on the Settle-Carlisle line at Ribblehead, at Basingstoke, at Princes Risborough Station, on the 'Waverley' route, at Grantham Station; Steam hauled passenger train in Zimbabwe.
CD. Cat no: **CD ATR 7037**. Released on ASV-Transacord, 1 Sep '87 by Academy Sound & Vision Records, Taylors, Wellard Dist.

ALL IN A DIESEL DAY (Various).
Note: Themed on a 'typical' 24-hour period on British Rail. Features 14 classes of motive power past and present at various stations and lineside locations.
MC. Cat no: **AC 154**. Released on Audicord, by Audicord Cassettes.
LP. Cat no: **ADL 154**. Released on Audicord, by Audicord Cassettes.

BIG FOUR, THE (Various).
Note: Recordings of SR, GWR, LMSR, and LNER locomotives at work between 1959 and 1967.
MC. Cat no: **AC 125**. Released on Audicord, May '83 by Audicord Cassettes.

BLACK FIVES (Various).

Note: Former LMSR class 5 4-6-0 locomotives at locations throughout Britain.
MC. Cat no: **AC 101**. Released on Audicord, May '83 by Audicord Cassettes.

BRITISH RAILWAYS STANDARD LOCOMOTIVES (Various).
Note: BR standard locomotives hauling freight and passenger trains throughout mainland Great Britain.
MC. Cat no: **AC 105**. Released on Audicord, May '83 by Audicord Cassettes.

BUILT SWINDON (Various).
Note: Former GWR locomotives recorded between 1958 and 1965. Classes include Castle, King, Hall, Grange, 2-6-0, 2-6-2T.
MC. Cat no: **AC 102**. Released on Audicord, May '83 by Audicord Cassettes.

CASTLES AND KINGS (Various).
Note: G.W.R 'Castle' class and 'King' class 4-6-0 steam locos at work on British Railways between 1956 and 1967.
LP. Cat no: **ATR 7015**. Released on ASV-Transacord, Oct '81 by Academy Sound & Vision Records, Taylors, Wellard Dist..
MC. Cat no: **ZC ATR 7015**. Released on ASV-Transacord, Apr '85 by Academy Sound & Vision Records, Taylors, Wellard Dist..

CHANGING TRAINS (Various).
Note: Steam and diesel locomotives at work on British Railways between 1957 and 1966, and a journey in the cab of a High Speed Train during a 125mph test run, in February 1975.
LP. Cat no: **ATR 7018**. Released on ASV-Transacord, Mar '82 by Academy Sound & Vision Records, Taylors, Wellard Dist..
MC. Cat no: **ZC ATR 7018**. Released on ASV-Transacord, Mar '82 by Academy Sound & Vision Records, Taylors, Wellard Dist..

COPPER CAPPED ENGINES (Various).
Note: Ex-Great Western Railway steam locos at work at Princes Risborough, Evershot Tunnel, Gresford Station, Llanvihangel Station, Basingstoke Station and Talerddig summit.
LP. Cat no: **ATR 7008**. Released on ASV-Transacord, May '81 by Academy Sound & Vision Records, Taylors, Wellard Dist..
MC. Cat no: **ZC ATR 7008**. Released on ASV-Transacord, May '81 by Academy Sound & Vision Records, Taylors, Wellard Dist..

DELTIC DUTIES (Various).
Note: Britain's most powerful diesel locomotives until shortly before their withdrawal, class 55 with their revolutionary Napier 'Deltic' engines, at work on the East Coast Main Line.
MC. Cat no: **AC 131**. Released on

Audicord, May '83 by Audicord Cassettes.

DIESELS ON DAINTON (Various).
Note: Diesel locomotives working between Newton Abbot and Totnes, Devon, featuring the formidable climb over Dainton Incline.
MC. Cat no: **AC 138**. Released on Audicord, May '83 by Audicord Cassettes.

DIESELS ON THE LICKEY INCLINE (Various).
Note: Diesel locomotives on Britain's steepest main-line gradient. Including classes 20, 31, 37, 40, 45, 47, 50, 55, and InterCity 125 units.
MC. Cat no: **AC 142**. Released on Audicord, May '83 by Audicord Cassettes.

DOUBLE HEAD OF STEAM (Various).
Note: Steam locomotives at work with passenger and goods trains, mostly double-headed, at various locations on British Railways between 1956 and 1966 and on the KWVR in 1977.
LP. Cat no: **ATR 7024**. Released on ASV-Transacord, Mar '83 by Academy Sound & Vision Records, Taylors, Wellard Dist..
MC. Cat no: **ZC ATR 7024**. Released on ASV-Transacord, Mar '83 by Academy Sound & Vision Records, Taylors, Wellard Dist..

DYNAMIC DIESELS (Various).
Note: Featuring British Rail classes 31, 40, 46, 47, 55 and InterCity 125 units.
MC. Cat no: **AC 130**. Released on Audicord, May '83 by Audicord Cassettes.

EARLY 60'S STEAM (Are You Going to Get the Sound of it Coming In) (Various).
Note: Early 60's steam from a personal collection featuring steam train recordings taken from a personal collection and featuring the following railway locations:- Ludlow - Wooferton / Tenbury Wells / Kidderminster (B.R.) / Aberystwyth / Weymouth Harbour / Bewdley (B.R.) / Worcester and Leominster.
This cassette is available direct from GLTK Recordings, 20 Church Walk, Kidderminster, Worcestershire.
MC. Cat no: **GLTK 1**. Released on GLTK, Jun '87.

ECHOES OF ENGINES (Various).
Note: Re-edited stereo version. GWR and BR locomotives at Gresford, on the climb from Chester, evening, night and morning in 1964. GWR SR and BR engines at Evershot Tunnel, on the climb from Yeovil towards Weymouth, in 1961. LMS black fives at Scout Green on the climb to Shap summit in 1960. LNER class C15 and B1 at Arrochar (West Highland line), winter 1958. LNER class A3 leaving Montrose with a passenger train in 1959, and with a freight on the Waverley route

335

in 1961, also LNER V2 class with a Waverley route passenger train, 1961.
LP. Cat no: **ATR 7034**. Released on ASV-Transacord, Jul '86 by Academy Sound & Vision Records, Taylors, Wellard Dist..
MC. Cat no: **ZC ATR 7034**. Released on ASV-Transacord, Jul '86 by Academy Sound & Vision Records, Taylors, Wellard Dist..

ENGINES FROM DERBY AND CREWE (Various).
Note: The original mono recording.
LP. Cat no: **ATR 7032**. Released on ASV-Transacord, Sep '85 by Academy Sound & Vision Records, Taylors, Wellard Dist..
MC. Cat no: **ZC ATR 7032**. Released on ASV-Transacord, Sep '85 by Academy Sound & Vision Records, Taylors, Wellard Dist..

ENGINES WITH ACCENTS (Various).
Note: Steam locomotives at work on European railways. A 181-ton Garratt and other locomotives with freight and passenger trains on the 5' 6" gauge RENFE in Spain in 1968. Italian locomotives with freight and passenger trains on the FS in Italy 1973. DB and DR Pacific locomotives and a 38 class 4-6-0 with passenger trains on the DB in West Germany 1970-73. On the SNCF (France), a Pacific with a Brussels-Paris express in 1959, 141R locomotives with freight trains in 1965 and a 141TA with a freight train in 1966. Various locomotives, including an Austrian-designed 2-8-4, with passenger and freight trains on the CFR in Romania in 1971. An Austrian-built 0-10-0 marshalling a freight train on the JZ in Yugoslavia, on a night in the Istrian mountains in 1970.
LP. Cat no: **ATR 7036**. Released on ASV-Transacord, May '87 by Academy Sound & Vision Records, Taylors, Wellard Dist..
MC. Cat no: **ZC ATR 7036**. Released on ASV-Transacord, May '87 by Academy Sound & Vision Records, Taylors, Wellard Dist..

FAREWELL TO STEAM (Various).
Note: Recordings from the final days of steam on British Rail during August 1968. Featuring the SLS and LCGB double-headed specials, plus the Fifteen Guinea special at Liverpool Lime Street, Ais Gill, and Manchester.
LP. Cat no: **RMPL 1007**. Released on Amberlee, Nov '81 by Amberlee Records.
MC. Cat no: **AC 193**. Released on Audicord, by Audicord Cassettes.

FAREWELL TO THE DELTICS (Various).
Note: The final years of the class 55 Deltic locomotives, working between London Kings Cross and Newcastle. Lineside and on-board recordings.
MC. Cat no: **AC 135**. Released on Audicord, May '83 by Audicord Cassettes.

LP. Cat no: **ADL 135**. Released on Audicord, '82 by Audicord Cassettes.

FAREWELL TO THE FORTIES (Various).
Note: One of British Rail's longest-serving classes of diesel locomotives, the 'dinosaur' class 40, first introduced in 1958, recorded at the lineside and on-board.
MC. Cat no: **AC 155**. Released on Audicord, by Audicord Cassettes.

FLYING SCOTSMAN AND OTHER LOCOMOTIVES (Various).
LP. Cat no: **PSP 8**. Released on President Special Projects, Nov '81 by President Records, Spartan, Taylors.

FROM THE FOOTPLATE (Various).
Note: Rare recordings from locomotive cabs, including a Gresley A4 reaching 100 MPH descending Stoke Bank.
MC. Cat no: **AC 124**. Released on Audicord, May '83 by Audicord Cassettes.

GONE WITH REGRET (Various).
Note: Ex-GWR locomotives working over former Great Western lines, including King, Grange, Hall, Manor and Castle classes, also nos. 3863, 9773, 6106, 6126, 6110, 1453 and 1458.
LP. Cat no: **RMPL 1006**. Released on Amberlee, Nov '81 by Amberlee Records.
MC. Cat no: **AC 191**. Released on Audicord, by Audicord Cassettes.

GREAT LITTLE TRAINS OF ENGLAND (Various).
Note: English narrow-gauge railways including Sittingbourne & Kemsley Light Railway, Romney, Hythe and Dymchurch Railway, Whipsnade and Umfolozi Railway (Whipsnade Zoo!), and lines at Wellingborough and Leighton Buzzard.
MC. Cat no: **AC 120**. Released on Audicord, May '83 by Audicord Cassettes.

GREAT NORTHERN FOR THE NORTH (Various).
Note: Former Great Northern Railway locomotives at work both on British Railways and preserved railways including 4744, 4472 Flying Scotsman, 68933, 1247, 64253, 990 Henry Oakley, 63985, and Stirling single-driver no. 1.
MC. Cat no: **AC 139**. Released on Audicord, May '83 by Audicord Cassettes.

GREAT TRAIN RECORD, THE (Various).
MC. Cat no: **AFP 142**. Released on Flightstream, Jan '82.

GREAT WESTERN IN GLOUCESTERSHIRE (Various).
Note: 52 minutes. 1961-5 recordings on the Coleford branch (Severn and Wye section) from trackside and cab, and recordings in the Cheltenham area.
LP. Cat no: **SDLB 220**. Released on Saydisc, Nov '80 by Amon Ra Records, Taylors, C.M. Distribution, Gamut Distribution **Deleted** '89.
MC. Cat no: **CSDLB 220**. Released on Saydisc, Nov '80 by Amon Ra Records,

Taylors, C.M. Distribution, Gamut Distribution **Deleted** '89.

GREAT WESTERN, THE (Various).
Note: A new version, electronically processed for stereo, of the original 1966 release (some sequences changed). Kings at Hatton. 2-6-2 Tank Engine on the Minehead Line at Dunster. New recordings of Halls, Castles and Kings at Princes Risborough. An 0-4-2 Tank Engine with a push and pull train at Chalford. Freight and passenger trains at Abergavenny Junction. The slip coach operations at Princes Risborough in 1956. Castle and King on the climb to Dainton Tunnel from Totnes. A busy summer Saturday in 1958 at Exeter St. David's Station. The Bristol-Weymouth boat train on the climb to Evershot tunnel.
LP. Cat no: **ATR 7031**. Released on ASV-Transacord, Apr '85 by Academy Sound & Vision Records, Taylors, Wellard Dist..
MC. Cat no: **ZC ATR 7031**. Released on ASV-Transacord, Apr '85 by Academy Sound & Vision Records, Taylors, Wellard Dist..

GRESLEY BEAT, THE (Various).
Note: Locomotives designed by Sir Nigel Gresley, including classes A3, A4, D49, J39, J50, K4 and V2 with a footplate recording on Mallard heading the Elizabethan express down Stoke Bank.
MC. Cat no: **AC 192**. Released on Audicord, by Audicord Cassettes.
LP. Cat no: **RMPL 1008**. Released on Amberlee, Nov '81 by Amberlee Records.

G.W.R. (Various).
Note: Ex-GWR steam locomotives, at work on British Railways between 1955 and 1963.
LP. Cat no: **ATR 7011**. Released on ASV-Transacord, Aug '81 by Academy Sound & Vision Records, Taylors, Wellard Dist..
MC. Cat no: **ZC ATR 7011**. Released on ASV-Transacord, Aug '81 by Academy Sound & Vision Records, Taylors, Wellard Dist..

HST 125 & DMU (Various).
Note: The modern age of British Rail highlighting the use of rapid transit.
MC. Cat no: **AC 141**. Released on Audicord, May '83 by Audicord Cassettes.

IRON-ORE STEAMERS (Various).
Note: 40 minutes. Industrial steam on the Storefield Quarry line, Northamptonshire, with Andrew Barclay engines and 'Caerphilly'.
LP. Cat no: **SDLB 311**. Released on Saydisc, Jul '81 by Amon Ra Records, Taylors, C.M. Distribution, Gamut Distribution **Deleted** '89.
MC. Cat no: **CSDLB 311**. Released on Saydisc, Jul '81 by Amon Ra Records, Taylors, C.M. Distribution, Gamut Distribution **Deleted** '89.

LAST TRAIN TO RYDE (Various).

Note: Adams class O2 0-4-4T locomotives on the Isle of Wight. Lineside and on-board recordings, including the island's last steam train.
LP. Cat no: **RMPL 1004.** Released on Amberlee, Nov '81 by Amberlee Records.
MC. Cat no: **AC 194.** Released on Audicord, by Audicord Cassettes.

LITTLE TRAINS OF WALES, THE (Various).
Note: Recordings between 1963 & 1977 of Welsh narrow-gauge railways.
MC. Cat no: **AC 116.** Released on Audicord, May '83 by Audicord Cassettes.

L.M.S. (Various).
Note: L.M.S steam locomotives at work on British Railways including Euston station in 1955, on board the 'Aberdeen Flyer' hauled by 'Pacific' no. 46201 'Princess Elizabeth' and the climb to Shap Summit.
LP. Cat no: **ATR 7004.** Released on ASV-Transacord, May '81 by Academy Sound & Vision Records, Taylors, Wellard Dist..
MC. Cat no: **ZC ATR 7004.** Released on ASV-Transacord, May '81 by Academy Sound & Vision Records, Taylors, Wellard Dist..

L.N.E.R. (Various).
Note: Steam trains of the London and North Eastern Railway, at work on British Railways between 1956 and 1961.
LP. Cat no: **ATR 7010.** Released on ASV-Transacord, Jul '81 by Academy Sound & Vision Records, Taylors, Wellard Dist..
MC. Cat no: **ZC ATR 7010.** Released on ASV-Transacord, Jul '81 by Academy Sound & Vision Records, Taylors, Wellard Dist..

LOCOMOTIVES FROM LEEDS (Various).
Note: Recordings of steam locomotives built by the six builders within the city of Leeds.
MC. Cat no: **AC 137.** Released on Audicord, May '83 by Audicord Cassettes.

MAGNIFICENT SEVERN, THE (Various).
Note: Sounds from the Severn Valley Railway, including locomotives 2857, 3205, 5164, 5764, 6960, 7819, 43106, (4)5000, and (4)5690.
MC. Cat no: **AC 133.** Released on Audicord, May '83 by Audicord Cassettes.

MAIN LINE STEAM SPECIALS (Various).
LP. Cat no: **SSLP 804.** Released on Sound Stories, Nov '81 by H.R. Taylor Records.

MIDLAND AND NORTH WESTERN (Various).
Note: Steam locomotives of the Midland, L.& N.W. and L.M.S. Railways at work on B.R. between 1955 and 1975.
LP. Cat no: **ATR 7021.** Released on ASV-Transacord, Sep '82 by Academy Sound & Vision Records, Taylors, Wellard Dist..
MC. Cat no: **ZC ATR 7021.** Released on ASV-Transacord, Sep '82 by Academy Sound & Vision Records, Taylors, Wellard Dist..

MOTIVE POWER VOL.1 (English Electric) (Various).
Note: English Electric engines working trains, including classes 20, 31, 37, 40 and 50.
MC. Cat no: **AC 153.** Released on Audicord, by Audicord Cassettes.

MOTIVE POWER VOL.2 (Sulzers and Shunters) (Various).
Note: The distinctive Sulzer roar of British Rail classes 26, 27, 33, 45 and 47 plus the bustle of class 03 and 08 shunters.
MC. Cat no: **AC 128.** Released on Audicord, by Audicord Cassettes.

MOTIVE POWER VOL. 3 (American Diesels) (Various).
Note: Featuring the present-day American diesel scene with AMTRAK.
MC. Cat no: **AC 158.** Released on Audicord, by Audicord Cassettes.

MOTIVE POWER VOL.4 (Diesels in Ireland) (Various).
Note: The sounds of CIE diesel engines, recorded lineside and on-board. Locations include Cork, Dublin, and Sligo.
MC. Cat no: **AC 159.** Released on Audicord, by Audicord Cassettes.

NOCTURNAL STEAM (Various).
Note: 49 minutes. 1967/8 recordings: including Flying Scotsman at Warrington, Liverpool-Crewe line, Leeds-Bradford line, Grand Junction Railway bridge.
LP. Cat no: **SDLB 306.** Released on Saydisc, by Amon Ra Records, Taylors, C.M. Distribution, Gamut Distribution **Deleted** '89.
MC. Cat no: **CSDLB 306.** Released on Saydisc, by Amon Ra Records, Taylors, C.M. Distribution, Gamut Distribution **Deleted** '89.

NORTH OF KINGS CROSS (Various).
Note: Steam locomotives of the former LNER at work; on the East Coast mainline in the 1950's and on the Carlisle-Edinburgh line in 1961. The sleeve boasts a fine picture of an A4 class Pacific No.60015, 'Quicksilver'.
LP. Cat no: **ATR7029.** Released on ASV-Transacord, Sep '84 by Academy Sound & Vision Records, Taylors, Wellard Dist..
MC. Cat no: **ZC ATR 7029.** Released on ASV-Transacord, Sep '84 by Academy Sound & Vision Records, Taylors, Wellard Dist..

PACIFIC POWER (Various).
Note: 'Pacific' (4-6-2) steam locomotives at work on British Railways, in France and West Germany.
LP. Cat no: **ATR 7022.** Released on ASV-Transacord, Jul '85 by Academy Sound & Vision Records, Taylors, Wellard Dist..
MC. Cat no: **ZC ATR 7022.** Released on ASV-Transacord, Jul '85 by Academy Sound & Vision Records, Taylors, Wellard Dist..
LP. Cat no: **SPA 563.** Released on Decca, Oct '79 by PolyGram Classics, Thames Distributors Ltd. **Deleted** '84.

PASSENGERS NO MORE (Various).
Note: Light-hearted sounds of the final trains on lines being closed. Includes Llanfyllin, Woodburn, Evercreech, Robin Hoods Bay, Midhurst, Musselburgh, and others.
MC. Cat no: **AC 106.** Released on Audicord, May '83 by Audicord Cassettes.

POWER OF STEAM, THE (Various).
Note: V2 locomotives on the Waverley route by day and night, at Steele Road and Stobs. Glen class 4-4-0's double-heading a passenger train on the West Highland line at Ardlui. Princess class Pacific on the 'Royal Scot' and a Jubilee 4-6-0 with a banked freight train at Scout Green on the climb to Shap. N.Z.R. Garratt locomotive with a heavy freight train on the climb to Heany Junction in Zimbabwe. Passenger trains to Bromsgrove and near Blackwell on the Lickey incline. An 8F 2-8-0 travelling flat out past Dent Signal Box on the Settle-Carlisle line, much to the annoyance of the signalman. At Basingstoke Station on a busy Saturday in Summer 1959.
LP. Cat no: **ATR 7028.** Released on ASV-Transacord, May '84 by Academy Sound & Vision Records, Taylors, Wellard Dist..
MC. Cat no: **ZC ATR 7028.** Released on ASV-Transacord, May '84 by Academy Sound & Vision Records, Taylors, Wellard Dist..

RAILWAY RHYTHMS (Various).
Note: Steam locomotives at work in Britain between 1955 and 1961 including: Express trains at Tring and Princes Risborough, freight trains on the 'Waverley' route, leaving Bromsgrove climbing the Lickey incline, and at Evershot tunnel.
LP. Cat no: **ATR 7002.** Released on ASV-Transacord, May '81 by Academy Sound & Vision Records, Taylors, Wellard Dist..
MC. Cat no: **ZC ATR 7002.** Released on ASV-Transacord, May '81 by Academy Sound & Vision Records, Taylors, Wellard Dist..

RAILWAY TO RICCARTON (Various).
Note: The famous 'Waverley' route northward to Edinburgh or south to Carlisle provided some of the steepest gradients in Great Britain. Here ex-LNER locomotives are heard between Steele Road and Riccarton Junction, And at Stobs and Hawick, in the spring of 1961.
LP. Cat no: **ATR 7013.** Released on ASV-Transacord, Sep '81 by Academy Sound & Vision Records, Taylors, Wellard Dist..
MC. Cat no: **ZC ATR 7013.** Released

on ASV-Transacord, Sep '81 by Academy Sound & Vision Records, Taylors, Wellard Dist.

RAILWAYS RECALLED (Various).
Note: Steam trains at work between 1959 and 1966, with passengers and freight; on the Central Wales line; the West Highland line; the Somerset and Dorset line; the Lickey Incline; the Settle-Carlisle line; the East Coast main line; the Carlisle-Edinburgh 'Waverley' route and on the climb to Shap summit.
LP. Cat no: **ATR 7017**. Released on ASV-Transacord, Jan '82 by Academy Sound & Vision Records, Taylors, Wellard Dist..
MC. Cat no: **ZC ATR 7017**. Released on ASV-Transacord, Jan '82 by Academy Sound & Vision Records, Taylors, Wellard Dist..

RAILWAYS ROUND THE CLOCK (Various).
Note: Steam locomotives at work, by day and night, on British Railways. At Gresford, Templecombe, Ribblehead Station, Barkston, Scout Green and on the footplate of a 'Britannia' Pacific between Ayr and Stranraer.
LP. Cat no: **ATR 7005**. Released on ASV-Transacord, May '81 by Academy Sound & Vision Records, Taylors, Wellard Dist..
MC. Cat no: **ZC ATR 7005**. Released on ASV-Transacord, May '81 by Academy Sound & Vision Records, Taylors, Wellard Dist..

RAINHILL REMEMBERED (Various).
Note: Recorded at the parade of locomotives at the 'Rocket 150' celebrations marking 150 years since the Rainhill locomotive trials of 1929.
MC. Cat no: **AC 134**. Released on Audicord, May '83 by Audicord Cassettes.

REAL DAYS OF STEAM (Various).
LP. Cat no: **PSP 2**. Released on President Special Projects, Nov '81 by President Records, Spartan, Taylors.

RECOLLECTIONS NO. 1: A RAILWAY GUARD (Unknown narrator(s)).
Note: The story of Al Lovell's working life from humble beginnings with the L.M.S. in the 20's to chief inspector at Birmingham New Street.
MC. Cat no: **AC 148**. Released on Audicord, '91 by Audicord Cassettes.

RECOLLECTIONS NO. 4: FOOT PLATE DAYS (Unknown narrator(s)).
Note: Features the life of an ex GNR driver beginning in 1914 at Copley Hill, Leeds and up through the links to New England in the 60's via Ardsley, Doncaster, Hull and Grantham. Wonderful stories about Sir Nigel Gresley and some uncomplimentary ones about Edward Thompson.
MC. Cat no: **AC 151**. Released on Audicord, '91 by Audicord Cassettes.

REGIONAL ROUND NO. 1 EASTERN (Various).
Note: Former LNER locomotives at Doncaster, Peterborough, Welwyn, Beamish, Aberdeen, Perth, and elsewhere, featuring classes A3, A4, B1, J6, J37, J39, O4, Q6 and V2.
MC. Cat no: **AC 104**. Released on Audicord, May '83 by Audicord Cassettes.

REGIONAL ROUND NO. 2 SOUTHERN (Various).
Note: Locomotives built for the Southern Railway, LSWR, and SECR including Bulleid 4-6-2s, and classes S15, Q, U, D1, C, M7, N, and P2.
MC. Cat no: **AC 118**. Released on Audicord, May '83 by Audicord Cassettes.

SEVERN VALLEY STEAM (Various).
LP. Cat no: **SSLP 802**. Released on Sound Stories, Nov '81 by H.R. Taylor Records.

SHAP (Various).
Note: Steam locomotives at work on the West Coast Main Line of the former LMSR, between Tebay and Shap Summit, in 1958-60 before the motorway arrived. Britannia pacifics, Patriot, Royal Scot, and Stanier 2-6-0s with passenger and freight trains at Tebay, inside Scout Green Signalbox, passenger and freight trains at Shap Summit, Patriot class climbing towards Scout Green, Jubilee class and 8F with banker at Greenholme, Coronation pacific and Jubilee on an evening and night at Shap Wells. This record includes some recordings from the original 'Shap' mono record and some previously unissued recordings. It has been entirely re-edited and processed for stereo.
LP. Cat no: **ATR 7035**. Released on ASV-Transacord, Feb '87 by Academy Sound & Vision Records, Taylors, Wellard Dist..
MC. Cat no: **ZC ATR 7035**. Released on ASV-Transacord, Feb '87 by Academy Sound & Vision Records, Taylors, Wellard Dist..

SHUNTING THE YARD (Various).
Note: Steam at work at wayside stations and busy marshalling yards.
MC. Cat no: **AC 136**. Released on Audicord, May '83 by Audicord Cassettes.

SOMERSET AND DORSET, THE (Various).
Note: Steam locomotives at work in 1956, between Bath and Templecombe on the now long-closed Somerset and Dorset Joint line: the journey over the 1 in 50 grades between Bath and Evercreech, on board the double-headed 'Pines Express'; the unique S&D 2-8-0's; double-headed trains climbing to Winsor Hill Tunnel and leaving Evercreech Junction; local trains at Evercreech; and an addition not on the original 1961 mono LP, the unusual two-engine workings at Templecombe Station.
LP. Cat no: **ATR 7030**. Released on ASV-Transacord, Jan '85 by Academy Sound & Vision Records, Taylors, Wellard Dist..

MC. Cat no: **ZC ATR 7030**. Released on ASV-Transacord, Jan '85 by Academy Sound & Vision Records, Taylors, Wellard Dist..

SOMERSET & DORSET (Various).
Note: Recordings at Highbridge, Shepton Mallet, Radstock, Evercreech Junction, and Chilcompton, with locomotives from the SDJR, SR, LMSR, and BR.
MC. Cat no: **AC 103**. Released on Audicord, May '83 by Audicord Cassettes.

SOUND EFFECTS NO.14 (Steam Trains in Stereo) (See under Sound Effects) (Various)

SOUNDS OF SEVERN VALLEY RAILWAY (Various).
LP. Cat no: **RESM 020**. Released on Response, Feb '81 by Priority Records, Taylors.

SOUTHERN STEAM (Various).
Note: Southern Railway steam locomotives at work on British Railways at Exeter St. David's, Victoria and Tonbridge stations, a journey from Victoria to Chatham with 4-4-0 no. 31019, a 'Terrier' tank engine, LBSC 'Atlantic' and 'Merchant Navy' Pacific, etc.
LP. Cat no: **ATR 7006**. Released on ASV-Transacord, May '81 by Academy Sound & Vision Records, Taylors, Wellard Dist..
MC. Cat no: **ZC ATR 7006**. Released on ASV-Transacord, May '81 by Academy Sound & Vision Records, Taylors, Wellard Dist..

SPECIALS IN STEAM (Various).
Note: Recordings from railtours of the 1960s, which often brought passenger trains and unusual classes of engine to remote railway backwaters.
MC. Cat no: **AC 121**. Released on Audicord, May '83 by Audicord Cassettes.

STEAM AND HARNESS (Various).
Note: 45 minutes. Recollections of working with shire horses, steam threshing with traction engines, railway building, life on & by the canal, the carrier and the 'passenger lorry'.
LP. Cat no: **SDL 284**. Released on Saydisc, by Amon Ra Records, Taylors, C.M. Distribution, Gamut Distribution **Deleted** '89.
MC. Cat no: **CSDL 284**. Released on Saydisc, by Amon Ra Records, Taylors, C.M. Distribution, Gamut Distribution **Deleted** '89.

STEAM FROM A TO V (Various).
Note: Ex-LNER steam locomotives working on British Railways 1957-60, reprocessed for stereo.
LP. Cat no: **ATR 7038**. Released on ASV-Transacord, Jul '89 by Academy Sound & Vision Records, Taylors, Wellard Dist..
MC. Cat no: **ZC ATR 7038**. Released on ASV-Transacord, Jul '89 by Academy Sound & Vision Records, Taylors, Wellard Dist..

STEAM HAULED BY A STANIER BLACK 5 (Various).
LP. Cat no: **PSP 9**. Released on Presi-

dent Special Projects, Nov '81 by President Records, Spartan, Taylors.

STEAM IN ALL DIRECTIONS (Various).
Note: Steam locomotives at work on railways in England, Scotland, Wales, Germany, Italy, Romania and Yugoslavia.
LP. Cat no: **ATR 7012.** Released on ASV-Transacord, Aug '81 by Academy Sound & Vision Records, Taylors, Wellard Dist..
MC. Cat no: **ZC ATR 7012.** Released on ASV-Transacord, Aug '81 by Academy Sound & Vision Records, Taylors, Wellard Dist..

STEAM IN SCOTLAND (Various).
Note: Steam locomotives at work on railways in Scotland between 1957 and 1965, including 'Gordon Highlander', HR no. 103, NBR 'Glens', 4-4-2T.
LP. Cat no: **ATR 7003.** Released on ASV-Transacord, May '81 by Academy Sound & Vision Records, Taylors, Wellard Dist..
MC. Cat no: **ZC ATR 7003.** Released on ASV-Transacord, May '81 by Academy Sound & Vision Records, Taylors, Wellard Dist..

STEAM IN THE FIFTIES (Various).
Note: Steam locomotives of the four main lines, at work on British Railways in the 1950's. At Templecombe Station, Tebay, Abergavenny Junction, Tyne Docks, Grantham Station, etc.
LP. Cat no: **ATR 7001.** Released on ASV-Transacord, May '81 by Academy Sound & Vision Records, Taylors, Wellard Dist..
MC. Cat no: **ZC ATR 7001.** Released on ASV-Transacord, May '81 by Academy Sound & Vision Records, Taylors, Wellard Dist..

STEAM IN THE SEVENTIES (Various).
Note: Recordings from the 'Return to steam' special trains on British Rail between 1974 & 1978. Includes Sir Nigel Gresley, Pendennis Castle, and King George V.
MC. Cat no: **AC 126.** Released on Audicord, May '83 by Audicord Cassettes.

STEAM IN TWILIGHT (Various).
LP. Cat no: **SSLP 803.** Released on Sound Stories, Nov '81 by H.R. Taylor Records.

STEAM LOCOMOTIVES ON THE GRADIENT (Various).
LP. Cat no: **PSP 6.** Released on President Special Projects, Nov '81 by President Records, Spartan, Taylors.

STEAM ON THE LICKEY INCLINE (Various).
Note: Steam locomotives on the Bristol-Birmingham line of the former Midland Railway climbing from Bromsgrove on a gradient of 1 in 37 3/4 for slightly over 2 miles, to the summit of the Lickey incline.
LP. Cat no: **ATR 7026.** Released on ASV-Transacord, Sep '83 by Academy Sound & Vision Records, Taylors, Wellard Dist..
MC. Cat no: **ZC ATR 7026.** Released on ASV-Transacord, Sep '83 by Academy Sound & Vision Records, Taylors, Wellard Dist..

STEAM OVER THE PENNINES (Various).
Note: A selection of preserved locomotives featured at Chinley, Hexham, Settle, Garsdale, Wennington, Hellifield, Appleby, etc. Included are LMSR 6115 Scots Guardsman, 46229, 4767, LNER 2005, 4498, 4472 Flying Scotsman, SR 35028 Clan Line, 777 Sir Lamiel, 850 Lord Nelson, 34092 City of Wells, plus LNWR, S&DJR, and BR classes.
MC. Cat no: **AC 152.** Released on Audicord, '88 by Audicord Cassettes.

STEAM RAILWAY MISCELLANY, A (Various).
LP. Cat no: **PSP 4.** Released on President Special Projects, Nov '81 by President Records, Spartan, Taylors.

STEAM SPECIALS OF THE 70S (Various).
LP. Cat no: **SSLP 801.** Released on Sound Stories, Nov '81 by H.R. Taylor Records.

STEAM THROUGH ALL SEASONS (Various).
Note: Steam locomotives at work in spring, summer, autumn and winter. On the Carlisle-Edinburgh line, Hereford-Abergavenny line, Central Wales line etc, and in the Italian Dolomites, Danube Valley in Romania and on the Schiefe Ebene in W.Germany.
LP. Cat no: **ATR 7007.** Released on ASV-Transacord, May '81 by Academy Sound & Vision Records, Taylors, Wellard Dist..
MC. Cat no: **ZC ATR 7007.** Released on ASV-Transacord, May '81 by Academy Sound & Vision Records, Taylors, Wellard Dist..

STEAM WEEKEND, A (Various).
LP. Cat no: **PSP 5.** Released on President Special Projects, Nov '81 by President Records, Spartan, Taylors.

STEAM'S FINAL HOURS (Various).
Note: 45 minutes. 1968 recordings from Halewood-Alntree, Preston-Blackburn, Manchester-Southport, Liverpool-Carlisle lines and at Kirkby, Burnley, etc.
LP. Cat no: **SDLB 305.** Released on Saydisc, Nov '80 by Amon Ra Records, Taylors, C.M. Distribution, Gamut Distribution **Deleted** '86.
MC. Cat no: **CSDLB 305.** Released on Saydisc, by Amon Ra Records, Taylors, C.M. Distribution, Gamut Distribution **Deleted** '89.

STOREFIELD IN THE RAIN (Various).
LP. Cat no: **PSP 3.** Released on President Special Projects, Nov '81 by President Records, Spartan, Taylors.

STOREFIELD STORY (Steam locomotives of the Storefield line) (Various).
LP. Cat no: **PSP 1.** Released on President Special Projects, Nov '81 by President Records, Spartan, Taylors.

SUNSET OF STEAM (Various).
Note: Recordings from the Republic of South Africa, of passenger and freight trains. Includes classes 12AR, 15AR, 15CB, 19D, 25NC, GMAM, and also narrow-gauge locos.
MC. Cat no: **AC 127.** Released on Audicord, '88 by Audicord Cassettes.

THIS IS YORK (Various).
Note: 'This is York' recaptures the sounds of this great station, with steam in the late 50's, and into the centenary year, 1977, with diesels.
LP. Cat no: **ATR 7014.** Released on ASV-Transacord, Sep '81 by Academy Sound & Vision Records, Taylors, Wellard Dist..
MC. Cat no: **ZC ATR 7014.** Released on ASV-Transacord, Sep '81 by Academy Sound & Vision Records, Taylors, Wellard Dist..

TRAINS IN THE HILLS (Various).
Note: Steam locomotives at work on some of the steepest gradients in the British Isles full of great evocative sounds of the steam age. Shap and Blea Moor, the Lickey Incline near Bromsgrove and the Monmouthshire hills near Abergavenny.
LP. Cat no: **ATR 7019.** Released on ASV-Transacord, May '82 by Academy Sound & Vision Records, Taylors, Wellard Dist..
MC. Cat no: **ZC ATR 7019.** Released on ASV-Transacord, May '82 by Academy Sound & Vision Records, Taylors, Wellard Dist..

TRAINS IN THE NIGHT (Various).
Note: At Bromsgrove, at the foot of the Lickey incline, on a summer evening in 1959. On winter nights, in frost, fog and snow, in the Chiltern Hills, on the GW & GC Joint Line. On the Central Wales line on a summer night and during the night and at dawn on the long climb to Whitrope Summit towards Riccarton Junction, on the Carlisle-Edinburgh 'Waverley' route in the spring of 1962. Locomotives featured include: 9F 2-10-0, 'Crab' 2-6-0, 8F 2-8-0, K3 2-6-0, 'King' and 'Castle' 4-6-0s and V2 2-6-2. A new re-edited master of the LP first issued in 1962 (by Argo).
LP. Cat no: **ATR 7020.** Released on ASV-Transacord, Aug '82 by Academy Sound & Vision Records, Taylors, Wellard Dist..
MC. Cat no: **ZC ATR 7020.** Released on ASV-Transacord, Aug '82 by Academy Sound & Vision Records, Taylors, Wellard Dist..

TRAINS IN TROUBLE (Various).
Note: Various steam locomotives in difficulties with passenger and freight trains. 0-6-0 Saddle Tank at Wissington; on board a Somerset and Dorset line train; 2-10-0 with a freight train in Yugoslavia; the last train from Watlington; 'V2' at Usan; 'B16' at Malton and 'V2' at Grantham; Caledonian 0-6-0 at Beattock; Stanier 'Black Five' at Bar-

gany; Austrian 2-10-0 at Rosenbach Tunnel.
LP. Cat no: **ATR 7016**. Released on ASV-Transacord, Nov '81 by Academy Sound & Vision Records, Taylors, Wellard Dist..
MC. Cat no: **ZC ATR 7016**. Released on ASV-Transacord, Nov '81 by Academy Sound & Vision Records, Taylors, Wellard Dist..

TRAINS TO REMEMBER (Various).
Note: Trains remembered are: 'Cambrian Coast Express' at Talerddig Station, goods trains in the night at Grantham Station, a passenger train and a goods train at Llangunllo Station, 'Pines Express' on the Lickey Incline, 'Whitby Moors' special train at Ravenscar and Goathland, 'Northern Irishman' passing Killochan.
LP. Cat no: **ATR 7025**. Released on ASV-Transacord, May '83 by Academy Sound & Vision Records, Taylors, Wellard Dist..
MC. Cat no: **ZC ATR 7025**. Released on ASV-Transacord, May '87 by Academy Sound & Vision Records, Taylors, Wellard Dist..

TRIUMPH OF AN A4 PACIFIC, THE (Various).
Note: The special run organised for the jubilee of the Stephenson Locomotive Society. A4 Pacific no. 60007, 'Sir Nigel Gresley', driven by Bill Hoole, made a distinguished run, on several occasions during the recording reaching speeds of well over 100mph.
LP. Cat no: **ATR 7009**. Released on ASV-Transacord, Jul '81 by Academy Sound & Vision Records, Taylors, Wellard Dist..
MC. Cat no: **ZC ATR 7009**. Released on ASV-Transacord, Jul '81 by Academy Sound & Vision Records, Taylors, Wellard Dist..

WEST OF EXETER (Various).
Note: Steam-hauled trains on the Exeter-Plymouth main line of the former Great Western Railway in 1957 and 1958 at: Dainton, Tigley Signal Box, Exeter St. David's West Signal Box and Exeter St. David's Station.
LP. Cat no: **ATR 7027**. Released on ASV-Transacord, Jan '84 by Academy Sound & Vision Records, Taylors, Wellard Dist..
MC. Cat no: **ZC ATR 7027**. Released on ASV-Transacord, Jan '84 by Academy Sound & Vision Records, Taylors, Wellard Dist..

WEST SOMERSET RAILWAY (Sounds of) (Various).
LP. Cat no: **RESM 018**. Released on Response, Feb '81 by Priority Records, Taylors.

WESTERN STEAM IN THE MIDLANDS (Various).
Note: Memories of Birmingham Snow Hill, Dudley, Tipton, etc. in the early 1960s. Classes include Castle, Grange, Manor, County, King, 2-8-0, 2-6-2T, and 0-6-0PT.
MC. Cat no: **AC 117**. Released on Audicord, May '83 by Audicord Cassettes.

WESTERN WAYS (Various).
Note: Western Region's Western, Warship, and Beyer-Peacock 'Hymek' classes working on British Rail, and preserved working on the Torbay Steam Railway, Severn Valley Railway, and North Yorkshire Moors Railway.
MC. Cat no: **AC 143**. Released on Audicord, May '83 by Audicord Cassettes.

WORKING ON THE FOOTPLATE (Various).
Note: Recordings made on the footplate of four different types of locomotive, of the varied sounds heard from the cabs of engines at work on passenger and goods trains. 5MT class 4-6-0 at work between Llandovery and Sugar Loaf Summit. V2 class 2-6-2 at work between Kinross Junction and Milnathort and crossing the Tay Bridge to Dundee; 8F class 2-8-0 at work between Knighton and Llangunllo; A4 class Pacific, running light between between St. Rollox and Buchanan Street, Glasgow and taking an Aberdeen-Glasgow express out of Stonehaven.
LP. Cat no: **ATR 7023**. Released on ASV-Transacord, Jan '83 by Academy Sound & Vision Records, Taylors, Wellard Dist..
MC. Cat no: **ZC ATR 7023**. Released on ASV-Transacord, Dec '87 by Academy Sound & Vision Records, Taylors, Wellard Dist..

WORLD OF RAILWAYS (Various).
LP. Cat no: **SPA 557**. Released on Decca, Sep '79 by PolyGram Classics, Thames Distributors Ltd. **Deleted** '84.

WORLD OF STEAM VOL 1 (Various).
Note: Includes recordings from India, Turkey, Austria, Poland, East Germany, and Czechoslovakia.
MC. Cat no: **AC 144**. Released on Audicord, '88 by Audicord Cassettes.

WORLD OF STEAM VOL 2 (American Steam) (Various).
Note: Recordings from some of the preserved railways in the USA.
MC. Cat no: **AC 156**. Released on Audicord, '88 by Audicord Cassettes.

YORK COLLECTION, THE (Various).
Note: Locomotives owned by the National Railway Museum, York. Includes Evening Star, Mallard, Sir Lamiel, and Cheltenham.
MC. Cat no: **AC 123**. Released on Audicord, May '83 by Audicord Cassettes.

Trevor, William

READING TURGENEV (Sinead Cusack).
MCSET. Cat no: **RC 90**. Released on Random Century, Jun '92 by Random Century Audiobooks, Conifer Records. Note: ISBN no. 1856861201

Troyat, H

LA NEIGE EN DEVIL (Edited By Philip Thody) (Unknown narrator(s)).
Note: An account of this popular text by Troyat which highlights the importance of the title.
MC. Cat no: **F 7613**. Released on Exeter Tapes, '91 by Drakes Educational Associates.

Turgel, Gena

I LIGHT A CANDLE (Jyll Craddick).
MCSET. Cat no: **1052N**. Released on Travellers Tales, '91 by Travellers Tales. Note: 4 Cassettes.
MCSET. Cat no: **1854962299**. Released on Bramhope, '91 by Ulverscroft Soundings. Note: 4 Cassettes.

Turgenev, Ivan

ASYA/ PERVAYA LYUBOV (Edited By Lesley Chamberlain) (Unknown narrator(s)).
Note: Turgenev's pessimism and his narrative style exemplified in this work.
MC. Cat no: **R 7705**. Released on Exeter Tapes, '91 by Drakes Educational Associates.

MESYATS V DEREVNE (Edited By A.D. Briggs) (Unknown narrator(s)).
Note: A general introduction to Turgenev as a dramatist together with a detailed analysis of his longest and best known play.
MC. Cat no: **R 7784**. Released on Exeter Tapes, '91 by Drakes Educational Associates.

OTTSY I DETI (Edited By A.D. Briggs) (Unknown narrator(s)).
Note: An analysis of Turgenev's fourth and best-known novel.
MC. Cat no: **R 7706**. Released on Exeter Tapes, '91 by Drakes Educational Associates.

Turkish

BASIC TURKISH (Volume 1) (Unknown narrator(s)).
MCSET. Cat no: **T 700**. Released on Audio Forum (Language courses), '91. Note: 12 Cassettes

BASIC TURKISH (Volume 2) (Unknown narrator(s)).
MCSET. Cat no: **T 750**. Released on Audio Forum (Language courses), '91. Note: 13 Cassettes

GET BY IN TURKISH (Language Courses) (Unknown narrator(s)).
Note: Each book contains phrases and conversations.
MCSET. Cat no: **PTT 306**. Released on BBC Publications, '91. Note : 2 Cassettes.

GET BY TRAVEL PACKS (Language Courses) (Unknown narrator(s)).
MCSET. Cat no: **PACK 2306**. Released on BBC Publications, '91. Note : 2 Cassettes.

INTRODUCING THE TURKISH LANGUAGE (Edited By Gul Durmusoglu) (Unknown narrator(s)).
MC. Cat no: **TU 7836**. Released on

Exeter Tapes, '91 by Drakes Educational Associates.

TURKISH CASSETTE COURSE (Unknown narrator(s)).
Note: Includes:- 3 months' book and an instruction leaflet.
MCSET. Cat no: **852851375.** Released on Hugo Languages, '92 by Hugo Language Books Limited. Note: 4 Cassettes. Playing time 4hrs.

TURKISH FOR TRAVEL (Unknown narrator(s)).
MC. Cat no: **BCP 015.** Released on Berlitz Language Courses, '88, Conifer Records.

TURKISH LANGUAGE BASICS (Unknown narrator(s)).
MC. Cat no: **BMC 014.** Released on Berlitz Language Courses, '88, Conifer Records.

TURKISH TRAVEL PACK (Unknown narrator(s)).
Note: Contains a Hugo phrase book.
MCSET. Cat no: **852851243.** Released on Hugo Languages, '92 by Hugo Language Books Limited. Note: 4 Cassettes. Playing time 4hrs.

Turner, Don
KIRIAKOS (Christopher Kay).
MCSET. Cat no: **1014N.** Released on Travellers Tales, '91 by Travellers Tales. Note: 4 Cassettes.
MCSET. Cat no: **1854962035.** Released on Bramhope, '91 by Ulverscroft Soundings. Note: 4 Cassettes.

Twain, Mark
LIFE ON THE MISSISSIPPI (Norman Dietz).
MCSET. Cat no: **RB 86930.** Released on Recorded Books, Oct '91 by Isis Audio Books. Note: 12 Cassettes. Playing time 14hrs 30mins.

Updike, John
PROSE AND POETRY OF JOHN UPDIKE, THE (John Updike).
MC. Cat no: **AS 47.** Released on Sussex Tapes, '91 by Sussex Publications Ltd..

Utley, Robert M.
BILLY THE KID (Nelson Runger).
MCSET. Cat no: **RB 90079.** Released on Recorded Books, Nov '91 by Isis Audio Books. Note: 6 Cassettes. Playing time 8hrs 15mins.

Vailland, R
325,000 FRANCS (Edited By J.E. Flower) (Unknown narrator(s)).
Note: A survey of Vailland's life and work followed by a detailed examination of the novel.
MC. Cat no: **F 7751.** Released on Exeter Tapes, '91 by Drakes Educational Associates.

Valle-Inclan, R
SONATA DE OTONO (Edited By Jose M. Alberich) (Unknown narrator(s)).
Note: A study of the main themes of this work by Valle-Inclan.
MC. Cat no: **S 7709.** Released on Exeter Tapes, '91 by Drakes Educational Associates.

Van Der Post, Laurens
LOST WORLD OF THE KALAHARI, THE (John Nettleton).
MCSET. Cat no: **1034N.** Released on Travellers Tales, '91 by Travellers Tales. Note: 8 Cassettes.
MCSET. Cat no: **IAB 88041.** Released on Isis Audio Books, '91. Note : 8 Cassettes.

Vercours
LE SILENCE DE LA MER (Edited By Jeanine Picard And Ted Freeman) (Unknown narrator(s)).
Note: A study of the famous short story by Vercours. A popular A level text. In French.
MC. Cat no: **F 7313.** Released on Exeter Tapes, '91 by Drakes Educational Associates.

Verdi (composer)
GIUSEPPE VERDI 1813-1901 (Biography) (Unknown narrator(s)).
MC. Cat no: **DFC 8.** Released on Sussex Tapes, '91 by Sussex Publications Ltd..
GUISEPPE VERDI (Biography) (Richard Mayes).
MC. Cat no: **GC 5.** Released on Green Dragon, '91 by Green Dragon Audio Visual.

Verga, Giovanni
SICILIAN WORLD (Edited By Madeleine Constable) (Unknown narrator(s)).
Note: Verga's portrayal of a society of which he was an eye-witness in the second half of the 19th century.
MC. Cat no: **I 7871.** Released on Exeter Tapes, '91 by Drakes Educational Associates.

Verlaine, Paul
POEMES (Edited by Martin Sorrell) (Unknown narrator(s)).
Note: Discusses Verlaine both as a sophisticated technician and as an early exponent of some aspects of modernism.
MC. Cat no: **F 7513.** Released on Exeter Tapes, '91 by Drakes Educational Associates.

Voltaire
BACKGROUND (Edited By Malcolm Cook) (Unknown narrator(s)).
Note: A critical analysis of the background to Voltaire's 'Contes". Includes an examination of Voltaire's own attitudes.
MC. Cat no: **F 7943.** Released on Exeter Tapes, '91 by Drakes Educational Associates.
CANDIDE (Edited By P. Pay) (Unknown narrator(s)).
Note: An approach to Voltaire as anti-historian and his use of irony and satire.
MC. Cat no: **F 7512.** Released on Exeter Tapes, '91 by Drakes Educational Associates.
ROMANS ET CONTES (Edited By G. Poulet) (Unknown narrator(s)).
Note: A general introduction to the medium and message of Voltaire in this work. In French.
MC. Cat no: **F 7888.** Released on Exeter Tapes, '91 by Drakes Educational Associates.

Von Droste-Hulshoff, Annette
DIE JUDENBUCHE (Edited By Mary Garland) (Unknown narrator(s)).
Note: Introduces both aspects of this story by Annette Von Droste - Hulshoff as an outstanding example of the German novelle and as a notable work of crime fiction. In German.
MC. Cat no: **G 7822.** Released on Exeter Tapes, '91 by Drakes Educational Associates.

Von Goethe, J.W.
DIE LEIDEN DES JUNGEN WERTHER (Edited By W.E. Yates) (Unknown narrator(s)).
Note: Goethe's best selling novel is introduced as an example of and comment on the 'Sturm' und 'Drang' movement.
MC. Cat no: **G 7552.** Released on Exeter Tapes, '91 by Drakes Educational Associates.
EGMONT (Edited By Keith A. Dickson) (Unknown narrator(s)).
Note: An analysis of Goethe's 'Egmont' which presents an outstanding figure of history whose life and death were closely and tragically related to the age in which he lived.
MC. Cat no: **G 7718.** Released on Exeter Tapes, '91 by Drakes Educational Associates.
IPHIGENIE AUF TAURIS (Edited By Keith A. Dickson) (Unknown narrator(s)).
Note: How J.W. Von Goethe's play deals with the ideas of crime and punishment underlying the myth of Tantalus and his descendants.
MC. Cat no: **G 7734.** Released on Exeter Tapes, '91 by Drakes Educational Associates.

Von Kleist, H
PRINZ FRIEDRICH VON HOMBURG (Edited By Mary Garland) (Unknown narrator(s)).
Note: A discussion of basic aspects of Kleist's last play. In German.
MC. Cat no: **G 7550.** Released on Exeter Tapes, '91 by Drakes Educational Associates.

Von Schiller, Franz
DON CARLOS (Edited By Lesley Sharpe) (Unknown narrator(s)).
Note: 'Don Carlos' is examined as a vital transitional work in Schiller's development as a dramatist.
MC. Cat no: **G 7840.** Released on

Exeter Tapes, '91 by Drakes Educational Associates.
KABALE UND LIEBE (Edited By Gerald Opie) (Unknown narrator(s)).
Note: The tape deals with this work by Schiller as one of the earliest German social dramas.
MC. Cat no: **G 7548**. Released on Exeter Tapes, '91 by Drakes Educational Associates.
WILHELM TELL (Edited By Gerald Opie) (Unknown narrator(s)).
Note: An attempt to convey some of the complexity involved in the interpretation of this play by Schiller.
MC. Cat no: **G 7755**. Released on Exeter Tapes, '91 by Drakes Educational Associates.

Wainwright, A
PENNINE JOURNEY, A (Unknown narrator(s)).
MCSET. Cat no: **1854962760**. Released on Soundings, '91 by Soundings Records, Bond Street Music.
Note: 7 Cassettes.

Wales...
WRITER IN WALES TODAY, THE (Edited By Ceridwen Lloyd-Morgan) (Unknown narrator(s)).
MC. Cat no: **W 7769**. Released on Exeter Tapes, '91 by Drakes Educational Associates.

Walker, Ted
RECENT POETRY (Ted Walker).
Note: Pre-recorded discussions which show literary criticism as a living, evolving interchange.
MC. Cat no: **A31**. Released on Sussex Tapes, '91 by Sussex Publications Ltd..

Wallace, Ian
NOTHING QUITE LIKE IT (Ian Wallace).
MCSET. Cat no: **1021A**. Released on Travellers Tales, '91 by Travellers Tales

Walton, Izaak
COMPLEAT ANGLER, THE (Gabriel Woolf).
MCSET. Cat no: **1087N**. Released on Travellers Tales, '91 by Travellers Tales. Note: 6 Cassettes.
MCSET. Cat no: **OAS 90031**. Released on Oasis Audio Books, '91 by Isis Audio Books. Note: 6 Cassettes.

Washington, George
GEORGE WASHINGTON (Biography) (John Ringham).
MC. Cat no: **L 9**. Released on Green Dragon, '91 by Green Dragon Audio Visual.
MC. Cat no: **DHM 12**. Released on Sussex Tapes, '91 by Sussex Publications Ltd..

Watkins-Pitchford
CHILD ALONE, A - MEMOIRS (Robin Browne).

MCSET. Cat no: **1044A**. Released on Travellers Tales, '91 by Travellers Tales. Note: 5 Cassettes.

Waugh, Evelyn
EVELYN WAUGH (Malcolm Bradbury & Martin Fagg).
Note: Pre-recorded discussions which show literary criticism as a living, evolving interchange.
MC. Cat no: **A39**. Released on Sussex Tapes, '91 by Sussex Publications Ltd..

Webb, Edwin
GIVING A TALK (Edward Lee & Edwin Webb).
MC. Cat no: **AB 2**. Released on Sussex Tapes, '91 by Sussex Publications Ltd..
HEAR ALL ABOUT IT - WHAT MAKES NEWS? (Edward Lee & Edwin Webb).
MC. Cat no: **CS 1**. Released on Sussex Tapes, '91 by Sussex Publications Ltd..
INTERVIEWS AND INTERVIEWING (Edward Lee & Edwin Webb).
MC. Cat no: **AB 3**. Released on Sussex Tapes, '91 by Sussex Publications Ltd..
LISTENING AND UNDERSTANDING (Edward Lee & Edwin Webb).
MCSET. Cat no: **AB 1**. Released on Sussex Tapes, '91 by Sussex Publications Ltd..
MEETING, THE (Edward Lee & Edwin Webb).
MC. Cat no: **AB 5**. Released on Sussex Tapes, '91 by Sussex Publications Ltd..
PEOPLE AND COMMUNICATIONS IN BUSINESS (Edward Lee & Edwin Webb).
MC. Cat no: **AB 4**. Released on Sussex Tapes, '91 by Sussex Publications Ltd..

Wedekind, Franz
FRUHLINGS ERWACHEN (Edited By Keith A. Dickson) (Unknown narrator(s)).
Note: Franz Wedekind's play is shown to have much in common with the drama of naturalism and also to foreshadow later developments in the theatre.
MC. Cat no: **G 7735**. Released on Exeter Tapes, '91 by Drakes Educational Associates.

Weir, Molly
SHOES WERE FOR SUNDAY (Biography) (Molly Weir).
MC. Cat no: **CAB 001**. Released on Chivers Audio Books, '81 by Chivers Audio Books, Green Dragon Audio Visual.
MCSET. Cat no: **1022 A**. Released on Travellers Tales, '91 by Travellers Tales. Note: 4 Cassettes.
TENEMENT TALES (Unknown narrator(s)).
MC. Cat no: **SSC 017**. Released on Scotsoun, '91 by Scotsoun Recordings, Morley Audio Services.

Welsh
LANGUAGE COURSE - WELSH (Unknown narrator(s)).
LPS. Cat no: **0747302936**. Released on Linguaphone, Apr '82 by Linguaphone Institute, Taylors, Century Records (USA), Bond Street Music.
SOUNDS AND ALPHABET OF WELSH, THE (Edited By Steven Dodd) (Unknown narrator(s)).
MC. Cat no: **W 7865**. Released on Exeter Tapes, '91 by Drakes Educational Associates.

Welty, Eudora
LEARNING TO WRITE FICTION (Eurdora Welty).
MC. Cat no: **AS 49**. Released on Sussex Tapes, '91 by Sussex Publications Ltd..

Weston, Simon
WALKING TALL (Biography) (Gareth Armstrong).
MCSET. Cat no: **OAS 10491**. Released on Oasis Audio Books, '91 by Isis Audio Books. Note: 6 Cassettes.
MCSET. Cat no: **1075A**. Released on Oasis Audio Books, '91 by Isis Audio Books. Note: 6 Cassettes.

Whales
SONGS FROM THE DEEP (Various).
CD. Cat no: **248207**. Released on Sittelle, Feb '92 by Sittelle Records (France).
MC. Cat no: **048111**. Released on Sittelle, Feb '92 by Sittelle Records (France).
SONGS OF THE HUMPBACK WHALE (Various).
Tracks / Solo whale / Slowed-down solo whale / Tower whale / Distant whale / Three whale trip.
CD. Cat no: **LD 0021**. Released on Living Music, Mar '92, Pinnacle.
MC. Cat no: **LC 0021**. Released on Living Music, Mar '92, Pinnacle.
WHALE SONGS (Various).
CD. Cat no: **JSL 009**. Released on JSL Green, Jul '91 by JSL Green Records.

Wilde, Oscar
OSCAR WILDE (His Life And Confessions) (Anthony Homyer).
Note: Written by Frank Harris.
MCSET. Cat no: **TCL 33**. Released on Complete Listener, '91 by Complete Listener. Note: 14 Cassettes.

Wildlife (natural)
GLOUCESTERSHIRE WILDLIFE TAPESTRY (Various).
LP. Cat no: **SDL 304**. Released on Saydisc, Oct '79 by Amon Ra Records, Taylors, C.M. Distribution, Gamut Distribution **Deleted** '86. Note : Playing time: 58 minutes.
MC. Cat no: **CSDL 304**. Released on Saydisc, Oct '79 by Amon Ra Records, Taylors, C.M. Distribution, Gamut Distribution.

SOUTH ATLANTIC ISLANDS (Various).
Note: A portrait of Falkland Islands wildlife including Paraguayan Snipe; Grass Wren; Guanaco; Sealion; Southern Elephant Seal; Magellan, King, Gentoo and Rockhopper Penguins; Steamer Ducks.
LP. Cat no: **SDL 299**. Released on Saydisc, Oct '79 by Amon Ra Records, Taylors, C.M. Distribution, Gamut Distribution **Deleted** '89. Note : Playing time: 50 minutes.
MC. Cat no: **CSDL 299**. Released on Saydisc, Oct '79 by Amon Ra Records, Taylors, C.M. Distribution, Gamut Distribution **Deleted** '89.

Williams, Kenneth
JUST WILLIAMS (Biography) (Kenneth Williams).
MCSET. Cat no: **ZBBC 1046**. Released on BBC Radio Collection, Oct '88 by BBC Records. Note: ISBN No: 0563 225971

Wings Of History
WINGS OF HISTORY VOLS 1-4 (See under Aviation) (Various).

Wise, Ernie
STILL ON MY WAY TO HOLLYWOOD (Ernie Wise).
MCSET. Cat no: **IAB 92015**. Released on Isis Audio Books, Jan '92. Note : 5 Cassettes. Playing time 5hrs 30mins.

Wood, Michael
IN SEARCH OF THE TROJAN WAR (Gordon Dulieu).
MCSET. Cat no: **1075N**. Released on Travellers Tales, '91 by Travellers Tales. Note: 8 Cassettes.
MCSET. Cat no: **OAS 89123**. Released on Oasis Audio Books, '91 by Isis Audio Books. Note: 8 Cassettes.

Woolf, Virginia
VIRGINIA WOOLF (Hermione Lee & Stella McNichol).
Note: Pre-recorded discussions which show literary crticism as a living, evovling interchange.
MC. Cat no: **A43**. Released on Sussex Tapes, '91 by Sussex Publications Ltd..

Wordsworth, William
WORDSWORTH (Stephen Gill & Mary Jacobs).
Note: Pre-recorded discussions which show literary criticism as a living, evolving interchange.
MC. Cat no: **A27**. Released on Sussex Tapes, '91 by Sussex Publications Ltd..

Wright Brothers
WILBUR AND ORVILLE WRIGHT (Biography) (Ed Bishop).
MC. Cat no: **EP 3**. Released on Green Dragon, '91 by Green Dragon Audio Visual.
WRIGHT BROTHERS (Biography) (Unknown narrator(s)).
MC. Cat no: **ZCHM 00022**. Released on Ice Berg, May '78.

Wynne, Greville
MAN FROM ODESSA, THE (Biography) (Joe Dunlop).
MCSET. Cat no: **OAS 90121**. Released on Oasis Audio Books, '91 by Isis Audio Books. Note: 8 Cassettes.
MCSET. Cat no: **1069A**. Released on Travellers Tales, '91 by Travellers Tales. Note: 8 Cassettes.

Yeats, W.B.
W B YEATS (Richard Ellmann).
Note: Pre-recorded discussions which show literary criticism as a living, evolving interchange.
MC. Cat no: **A17**. Released on Sussex Tapes, '91 by Sussex Publications Ltd..

Yesenin, S
BACKGROUND (Edited By Robert Porter And Galina Ransome) (Unknown narrator(s)).
Note: A brief discussion of Yesenin's writing, including working verse translations of two well-known poems.
MC. Cat no: **R 7813**. Released on Exeter Tapes, '91 by Drakes Educational Associates.

Young, Gavin
SLOW BOATS HOME (Ian Craig).
MCSET. Cat no: **1055/6N**. Released on Travellers Tales, '91 by Travellers Tales. Note: 12 Cassettes

MCSET. Cat no: **OAS 89062**. Released on Oasis Audio Books, '91 by Isis Audio Books. Note: 12 Cassettes.

Zamyatin, Evgeny
MY (Edited By R. Russell) (Unknown narrator(s)).
Note: A brief general introduction to Evgeny Zamyatin, followed by a discussion of his novel 'My'.
MC. Cat no: **R 7803**. Released on Exeter Tapes, '91 by Drakes Educational Associates.

Zola, Emile
GERMINAL (Edited By Philip Thody) (Unknown narrator(s)).
Note: Studies the novel as an illustration of Emile Zola's ideas on heredity and environment.
MC. Cat no: **F 7910**. Released on Exeter Tapes, '91 by Drakes Educational Associates.
LE BETE HUMAINE (Edited By Philip Thody) (Unknown narrator(s)).
Note: A discussion of Emile Zola's novel. Looks at Zola's philosophical views on determinism and political hostility to 19th century middle class society.
MC. Cat no: **F 7780**. Released on Exeter Tapes, '91 by Drakes Educational Associates.

Zoshchenko, M
LYUDI (Edited By Olive Stevens) (Unknown narrator(s)).
Note: A description of Zoshchenko's work in general and an analysis of this story.
MC. Cat no: **R 7654**. Released on Exeter Tapes, '91 by Drakes Educational Associates.

Zuckmayer, Carl
DES TEUFELS GENERAL (Edited By A.T. Robertshaw) (Unknown narrator(s)).
Note: By Carl Zuckmayer, the treatment of the central character, General Harras and his moral position as the 'Devil's General' are focussed upon.
MC. Cat no: **G 7940**. Released on Exeter Tapes, '91 by Drakes Educational Associates.

TITLE INDEX

TITLES INDEX

TITLE	HEADING	SECTION
3 Hours Of Favourite Children's Stories	Children's Stories..	Fiction
6 Children's Classics	Andersen, Hans Christian	Fiction
10 Medieval Makars	Poetry	Fiction
15 Minute Tales	Blyton, Enid	Fiction
16th Century Scotland	History	Non-Fiction
17th Century France; Continuity And Change	France	Non-Fiction
18 Poems From The Bird Path	White, Kenneth	Fiction
19th And 20th Century British Trade Unionism	Social Sciences	Non-Fiction
19th Century Russia	Russia	Non-Fiction
20th Century Poetry	Poetry	Fiction
25 Years Of His Speeches	Churchill, Sir Winston	Non-Fiction
41 Poems From Handbook For The Diamond Country	White, Kenneth	Fiction
50 Years Of Royal Broadcasts	Radio	Non-Fiction
52 Pick-up	Leonard, Elmore	Fiction
101 Dalmatians	Disney	Fiction
101 Dalmatians	Films	Fiction
101 Dalmatians	Smith, Dodie	Fiction
110% Solution, The	McCormack, Mark	Non-Fiction
4.50 From Paddington	Christie, Agatha	Fiction
5-00 Refresher, The	Self Improvement	Non-Fiction
633 Squadron	Smith, Frederick E.	Fiction
1001 Gelignites	Bates, Blaster	Fiction
1984	Orwell, George	Fiction
2001: A Space Odyssey	Clarke, Arthur C	Fiction
2010: Odyssey Two	Clarke, Arthur C	Fiction
20,000 Leagues Under The Sea	Verne, Jules	Fiction
325,000 Francs	Vailland, R	Non-Fiction
A Travers Sis Chansons	Brel, Jacques	Non-Fiction
A Vous La France (1 + 2)	French	Non-Fiction
ABC (Alphabet)	Early Learning	Non-Fiction
ABC Murders, The	Christie, Agatha	Fiction
ABC Rhymes	Early Learning	Non-Fiction
ABC (the Alphabet Hunt)	Early Learning	Non-Fiction
Above Suspicion	MacInnes, Helen	Fiction
Abracadaver	Lovesey, Peter	Fiction
Academic Question, An	Pym, Barbara	Fiction
Accelerated (High-Speed) Learning	Self Improvement	Non-Fiction
Accidental Tourist, The	Tyler, Anne	Fiction
According To Mark	Lively, Penelope	Fiction
Accounting For Murder	Lathen, Emma	Fiction
Ace	King-Smith, Dick	Fiction
Achievement	Heyerdahl, Thor	Non-Fiction
Across The Limpopo	Nicholson, Michael	Non-Fiction
Action Force	Television	Fiction
Acts (parts 1 & 2)	Bible	Non-Fiction
Ad Nauseam	Derek & Clive	Fiction
Add On ... Take Away	Early Learning	Non-Fiction
Adhocra Arman (Gujarati)	Brahmabhatti, Prahiad	Fiction
Adolf Hitler	Hitler, Adolf	Non-Fiction
Adolf Hitler: My Part In His Downfall	Milligan, Spike	Non-Fiction
Adolphe	Constant, B	Fiction
Adventurers, The	Hodge, Jane Aiken	Fiction
Adventures In The Skin Trade	Thomas, Dylan	Fiction
Adventures Of Black Beauty, The	Sewell, Anna	Fiction
Adventures Of Creamcake And Company	Zabel, Jennifer	Fiction
Adventures Of Doctor Snuggles	O'Kelly, Jeffrey	Fiction
Adventures Of Dusty And The Dinosaurs	Croft, Mike	Fiction
Adventures Of Fireman Sam, The	Wilmer, Diane	Fiction

TITLES INDEX

Title	Author	Category
Adventures Of Goodnight And Loving, The	Thomas, Leslie	Fiction
Adventures Of Heggarty Haggerty	Lindsay, Eliza	Fiction
Adventures Of Huckleberry Finn	Twain, Mark	Fiction
Adventures Of Mary Mouse	Blyton, Enid	Fiction
Adventures Of Mask	Jackson, Steve	Fiction
Adventures Of Milly-molly-mandy	Lankester Brisley	Fiction
Adventures Of Mr. Chatterbox	Hargreaves, Roger	Fiction
Adventures Of Mr. Greedy	Hargreaves, Roger	Fiction
Adventures Of Mr. Messy	Hargreaves, Roger	Fiction
Adventures Of Mr. Noisy	Hargreaves, Roger	Fiction
Adventures Of Mr. Pinkwhistle	Blyton, Enid	Fiction
Adventures Of Mr. Silly	Hargreaves, Roger	Fiction
Adventures Of Mr. Small	Hargreaves, Roger	Fiction
Adventures Of Mr. Sneeze	Hargreaves, Roger	Fiction
Adventures Of Mr. Tickle	Hargreaves, Roger	Fiction
Adventures Of Naughty Amelia Jane	Blyton, Enid	Fiction
Adventures Of Orlando	Hale, Kathleen	Fiction
Adventures Of Portland Bill	Armitage, David	Fiction
Adventures Of Postman Pat, The	Cunliffe, John	Fiction
Adventures Of Robin Hood, The	Traditional	Fiction
Adventures Of Roger And The Rotten Trolls, The	Children's Stories..	Fiction
Adventures Of Rupert Bear	Bestall, Alfred	Fiction
Adventures Of Sherlock Holmes, The	Conan Doyle, Arthur	Fiction
Adventures Of Sinbad The Sailor	Traditional	Fiction
Adventures Of Snuffy Steam Train	Adamson, Jean	Fiction
Adventures Of Space Dog, The	Standiford, Natalie	Fiction
Adventures Of The Gumby Gang, The	Oldfield, Pamela	Fiction
Adventures Of The Secret Seven	Blyton, Enid	Fiction
Adventures Of Tom Sawyer, The	Twain, Mark	Fiction
Adventures Of Topsy And Tim	Adamson, Jean	Fiction
Adventures Of Victoria Plum	Hyks, Veronika	Fiction
Adventures Of Worzel Gummidge, The	Waterhouse, Keith	Fiction
Adventures, The	Aiken Hodge, Jane	Fiction
Adventurous Four, The	Blyton, Enid	Fiction
Advertise For Treasure	Williams, David	Fiction
Aerobic Exercise Music	Health & Fitness	Non-Fiction
Aerobicise	Health & Fitness	Non-Fiction
Aesop In Fableland	Aesop	Fiction
Aesop's Fables	Aesop	Fiction
Aesop's Fables Books (1 + 2)	Aesop	Fiction
Affacombe Affair, The	Lemarchand, Elizabeth	Fiction
Affairs At Thrush Green	Read, Miss	Fiction
Affairs Of The Heart	Romance	Fiction
African Forests And Savannahs	Environmental Sounds	Non-Fiction
African Queen, The	Forester, C.S.	Fiction
African Village Folktales	Kaula, Edna Mason	Fiction
Afrikaans	African...	Non-Fiction
After Henry	Brett, Simon	Fiction
Afternoon For Lizards	Eden, Dorothy	Fiction
Against The Grade	Trains...	Non-Fiction
Age Of Appeasement In Europe 1918-1929, The	History	Non-Fiction
Age Of Steam, The	Trains...	Non-Fiction
Age Of Unreason	Handy, C	Non-Fiction
Ages Of Man	Shakespeare, William	Fiction
Agnes Bernauer	Hebbel, F	Non-Fiction
Agnes Grey	Bronte, Anne	Fiction
Agriculture In England	History	Non-Fiction
Ah, Sweet Mystery Of Life	Dahl, Roald	Fiction
Aids - The Facts	Health & Fitness	Non-Fiction
Aimer Gates	Garner, Alan	Fiction
Aince For Pleasure And Twice For Joy	Annand, JK	Fiction
Airs Above The Ground	Stewart, Mary	Fiction
Al Read Show	Radio	Fiction
Aladdin	Traditional	Fiction
Aladdin And Ali Baba	Traditional	Fiction
Aladdin And His Lamp	Traditional	Fiction
Aladdin And His Magic Lamp	Traditional	Fiction

TITLES INDEX

Title	Author	Type
Aladdin And The Wonderful Lamp	Traditional	Fiction
Alas Smith And Jones	Smith & Jones	Fiction
Albatross	Anthony, Evelyn	Fiction
Albert Einstein	Einstein, Albert	Non-Fiction
Albert Funnel	Children's Stories..	Fiction
Alex And The Raynhams	Bromige, Iris	Fiction
Alexander And The Terrible, Horrible, No Good...	Viorst, Judith	Fiction
Alexander Fleming	Fleming, Alexander	Non-Fiction
Alexander Montgomerie	Montgomerie, Alexander	Fiction
Alexander Scott	Scott, Alexander	Fiction
Alexander The Great	Alexander The Great	Non-Fiction
Alexander The Great	Traditional	Fiction
Alfie Gives A Hand	Hughes, Shirley	Fiction
Alfie's Feet	Hughes, Shirley	Fiction
Alfred Lord Tennyson	Tennyson, Alfred Lord	Non-Fiction
Ali Baba	Traditional	Fiction
Ali Baba And The Forty Thieves	Traditional	Fiction
Alibi Of Guilt	Daniels, Philip	Fiction
Alice In Wonderland	Carroll, Lewis	Fiction
Alice Through The Looking Glass	Carroll, Lewis	Fiction
Alice's Adventures In Wonderland	Carroll, Lewis	Fiction
Alien Earth, The	Elder, Michael	Fiction
All About Aura	Benhala, Zouina	Fiction
All About My Naughty Little Sister	Edwards, Dorothy	Fiction
All Creatures Great And Small	Herriot, James	Fiction
All Good Stuff, Mary	Miller, Max	Fiction
All In A Diesel Day	Trains...	Non-Fiction
All Jane Fonda Workout Records	Fonda, Jane	Non-Fiction
All Join In And Other Nonsense	Blake, Quentin	Fiction
All Our Tomorrows	Allbeury, Ted	Fiction
All Over The Town	Delderfield, R.F.	Fiction
All Passion Spent	Sackville-West, Vita	Fiction
All Quiet On The Western Front	Remarque, E.M.	Fiction
All The Bird Songs Of Britain & Europe	Bird Songs	Non-Fiction
All The Bird Songs Of Europe Vols 1 - 4	Bird Songs	Non-Fiction
All The Grey Cats	Thomas, Craig	Fiction
All Things Wise And Wonderful	Herriot, James	Fiction
Allan Border: An Autobiography	Border, Allan	Non-Fiction
Allan Ramsay	Ramsay, Allan	Fiction
Alligator Pie	Poetry	Fiction
'Allo 'Allo	Television	Fiction
All's Well That Ends Well	Shakespeare, William	Fiction
Almonds And Raisins: Consequences	Mosco, Maisie	Fiction
Almonds And Raisins: Hopes And Dreams	Mosco, Maisie	Fiction
Almonds And Raisins: Realities	Mosco, Maisie	Fiction
Almost Everything	Kavanagh, Patrick	Fiction
Alpha List, The	Allbeury, Ted	Fiction
Alphabet, The	Early Learning	Non-Fiction
Alternative Government	Stuart, Francis	Fiction
Alternatives To Marriage	Self Improvement	Non-Fiction
Always Say Die	Ferrars, Elizabeth	Fiction
Amateur Emigrant, The	Stevenson, Robert Louis	Non-Fiction
Amazing Grace	Dessau, Joanna	Non-Fiction
Amazing Monsters	Fisher, Robert	Fiction
Amazing Mrs. Pollifax, The	Gilman, Dorothy	Fiction
Amelia	Fielding, Henry	Fiction
American Cancer Society's "Freshstart"	Self Improvement	Non-Fiction
American Forests And Lakes	Environmental Sounds	Non-Fiction
American Heiress, The	Eden, Dorothy	Fiction
Among The Russians	Thubron, Colin	Non-Fiction
Amsterdam Affair	Thorne, Nerina	Fiction
Amy Johnson	Johnson, Amy	Non-Fiction
Anastasia Syndrome, The	Higgins Clark, Mary	Fiction
Ancestral Vices	Sharpe, Tom	Fiction
Ancient Evenings	Mailer, Norman	Fiction
Ancient Ways To New Freedom	Lessing, Doris	Non-Fiction
And Death Shall Have No Domination	Thomas, Dylan	Fiction

TITLES INDEX

And So To Murder	Dickson, Carter	Fiction
And Then There Were None	Christie, Agatha	Fiction
Andalusins, The	Spain...	Non-Fiction
Andorra	Frisch, Max	Non-Fiction
Andromaque	Racine, Jean	Non-Fiction
Andy Pandy And Teddy At The Zoo	Bird, Maria	Fiction
Andy Pandy And The Badger	Bird, Maria	Fiction
Andy Pandy And The Dovecot	Bird, Maria	Fiction
Andy Pandy And The Ducklings	Bird, Maria	Fiction
Andy Pandy And The Red Motor Car	Bird, Maria	Fiction
Andy Pandy And The Spotted Cow	Bird, Maria	Fiction
Andy Pandy And The Willow Tree	Bird, Maria	Fiction
Angel And The Soldier Boy, The	Films	Fiction
Angel Pavement	Priestley, J.B.	Fiction
Anger Workout	Self Improvement	Non-Fiction
Angry Mountain, The	Innes, Hammond	Fiction
Animal Alphabet, The	Craig, Bobbie	Fiction
Animal Fairyland	Children's Stories..	Fiction
Animal Farm	Orwell, George	Fiction
Animal Magic	Early Learning	Non-Fiction
Animal Man, The	Daneski, Gavin	Non-Fiction
Animals Of Farthing Wood	Dann, Colin	Fiction
Animals Went In Two By Two, The	Children's Stories..	Fiction
Anna Karenina	Tolstoy, Leo	Fiction
Anna Karenina	Tolstoy, Leo	Non-Fiction
Anna Of The Five Towns	Bennett, Arnold	Fiction
Annals Of The Parish	Galt, John	Fiction
Anne Of Green Gables	Montgomery, LM.	Fiction
Anne: The Princess Royal	Hoey, Brian	Non-Fiction
Anodyne Necklace, The	Grimes, Martha	Fiction
Another Bloody Tour	Frances, Edmond	Non-Fiction
Another Monty Python Record	Monty Python	Fiction
Another Round Of Poems And Pints	Poetry	Fiction
Another View	Pilcher, Rosamunde	Fiction
Ansichten Eines Clowns	Boll, Heinrich	Non-Fiction
Antarctica	Johnson, Stanley	Non-Fiction
Antelope Company Ashore, The	Hall, Willis	Fiction
Antelope Company At Large, The	Hall, Willis	Fiction
Anthology - Poetry Readings	Poetry	Fiction
Anthony And Cleopatra	A-Level	Non-Fiction
Anthony And Cleopatra	Shakespeare, William	Fiction
Antigone	Anouilh, J	Non-Fiction
Antigone	Sophocles	Fiction
Antologia Di Racconti	Poe, Edgar Allan	Fiction
Apache Moon	Durham, John	Fiction
Aphrodite Cargo, The	Fullerton, Alexander	Fiction
Appleby File, The	Innes, Michael	Fiction
Approach To Poetry Criticism	English Literature	Non-Fiction
Approach To The Nineteenth Century Novel	English Literature	Non-Fiction
April Morning	Fast, Howard	Fiction
April's Grave	Howatch, Susan	Fiction
Aquarian Conspiracy: Tools For Change	Self Improvement	Non-Fiction
Aquarius	Astrology	Non-Fiction
Arab Culture And The West	Middle East	Non-Fiction
Arab - Israeli Conflict, The	Middle East	Non-Fiction
Arabian Nights: Aladdin	Traditional	Fiction
Arabian Tales, Legends And Romances	Traditional	Fiction
Arabic Cassette Course	Arabic	Non-Fiction
Arabic Travel Pack	Arabic	Non-Fiction
Archers - The Wedding, The	Radio	Fiction
Archpriest Avvakum And The Russian Church Schism	Russia	Non-Fiction
Are You There God? it Is Me, Margaret	Blume, Judy	Fiction
Argo Treasury Of Comic And Curious Verse	Poetry	Fiction
Argo Treasury Of English Poetry (Volumes1, 2, & 3)	Poetry	Fiction
Argo Treasury Of Love Poems	Poetry	Fiction
Argo Treasury Of Readings From Longer Poems	Poetry	Fiction
Argo Treasury Of Religious Verse	Poetry	Fiction

TITLES INDEX

Argo Treasury Of Romantic Verse	Poetry	Fiction
Argo Treasury Of Victorian Poetry	Poetry	Fiction
Aries	Astrology	Non-Fiction
Aristocats	Disney	Fiction
Arminta The Pink Cat	Arkle, Phyllis	Fiction
Arnold Schwarzenegger's Total Body Workout	Health & Fitness	Non-Fiction
Around The World In 80 Days	Verne, Jules	Fiction
Around The World In Wanderer 3	Hiscock, E	Non-Fiction
Arrow To The Heart	Murray, Jill	Fiction
Arsenic And Old Lace	Christie, Agatha	Fiction
Art And Design	G.C.S.E.	Non-Fiction
Art Of The General Prologue, The	A-Level	Non-Fiction
Arthur And The Belly Button Diamond	Coren, Alan	Fiction
Articulos	Spanish	Non-Fiction
Artist's Struggle For Integrity, The	Baldwin, James	Non-Fiction
As I Walked Out One Midsummer Morning	Lee, Laurie	Non-Fiction
As The Crow Flies	Archer, Jeffrey	Fiction
As You Like It	A-Level	Non-Fiction
As You Like It	Shakespeare, William	Fiction
As You Like It	Shakespeare, William	Non-Fiction
As Young As You Feel With Eileen Fowler	Health & Fitness	Non-Fiction
Ashenden	Maugham, W. Somerset	Fiction
Ashes 1948-1981, The	Cricket	Non-Fiction
Asking Price, The	Stirling, Jessica	Fiction
Aspects Of Russian Grammar	Russian	Non-Fiction
Aspern Papers, The	James, Henry	Fiction
Asquith	Social Sciences	Non-Fiction
Assassin, The	Anthony, Evelyn	Fiction
Assassination Run	Gerson, Jack	Fiction
Assessment And Choice	Macdiarmid, Hugh	Fiction
Assessment And Selection	Burns, Robert	Fiction
Assignment In Brittany	Macinnes, Helen	Fiction
Asterix And The Gladiator	Goscinny & Uderzo	Fiction
Asterix And The Magic Carpet	Goscinny & Uderzo	Fiction
Asterix In Britain	Goscinny & Uderzo	Fiction
Asterix The Gaul	Goscinny & Uderzo	Fiction
Asya/ Pervaya Lyubov	Turgenev, Ivan	Non-Fiction
At Bertram's Hotel	Christie, Agatha	Fiction
At Death's Door	Barnard, Robert	Fiction
At High Risk	Harcourt, Palma	Fiction
At His Best Entertaining The Troops	Hope, Bob	Fiction
At Home In Thrush Green	Read, Miss	Fiction
At Home With German	German	Non-Fiction
At The Oxford Union	Hoffnung, Gerard	Fiction
Athabasca	Maclean, Alistair	Fiction
Athalie	Racine, Jean	Fiction
Atlantic Bridge	Connolly, Billy	Fiction
Atlantic Fury	Innes, Hammond	Fiction
Attitudes To War In England Before 1914	Military History	Non-Fiction
Attracting Perfect Love	Self Improvement	Non-Fiction
Aus Dem Leben Eines Taugenichts	Eichendorff	Non-Fiction
Australia's Greatest Cricket Characters	Cricket	Non-Fiction
Autobiography, An	Cushing, Peter	Non-Fiction
Avalanche Express	Forbes, Colin	Fiction
Aviators, The	Aviation	Non-Fiction
Awaken The Giant	Self Improvement	Non-Fiction
Awakened Life	Self Improvement	Non-Fiction
B Movie	Barstow, Stan	Fiction
Baa Baa Black Sheep	Children's Stories..	Fiction
Bab Ballads And Cautionary Verses, The	Gilbert, W.S.	Fiction
Babar And Father Christmas	De Brunhoff, Jean	Fiction
Babar At Home	De Brunhoff, Jean	Fiction
Babar The Elephant	De Brunhoff, Jean	Fiction
Babar The King	De Brunhoff, Jean	Fiction
Babar's Choice	De Brunhoff, Jean	Fiction
Babar's First Step	De Brunhoff, Jean	Fiction
Babar's Mystery	De Brunhoff, Jean	Fiction

TITLES INDEX

Baby Soother Tape	Health & Fitness	Non-Fiction
Back Of The Tiger, The	Gerson, Jack	Fiction
Back To The Forest	Foley, Winifred	Non-Fiction
Backcloth	Bogarde, Dirk	Non-Fiction
Background	Voltaire	Non-Fiction
Background	Yesenin, S	Non-Fiction
Background To Gide	Gide, Andre	Non-Fiction
Background To Hamlet	English Literature	Fiction
Background To Jean Paul Sartre	Sartre, Jean Paul	Non-Fiction
Backlash	Gosling, Paula	Fiction
Bafut Beagles, The	Durrell, Gerald	Fiction
Bag Of Moonshine, A	Garner, Alan	Fiction
Bahama Crisis	Bagley, Desmond	Fiction
Bailtean (Villages)	Campbell, Myles	Fiction
Bajazet	Racine, Jean	Fiction
Balcony, The	Genet, Jean	Fiction
Ballad Of Reading Gaol	Wilde, Oscar	Fiction
Ballet Shoes	Streatfield, Noel	Fiction
Bambi	Salten, Felix	Fiction
Banana Blush	Betjeman, Sir John	Fiction
Bangers And Mash	Television	Fiction
Banish Pain - Mind Power And Pain Relief	Self Improvement	Non-Fiction
Barbara Of The House Of Grebe	Hardy, Thomas	Fiction
Barbie	Mandeville, A	Fiction
Barboche	Bosco, H	Non-Fiction
Barchester Towers	Trollope, Anthony	Fiction
Bargain For Frances, A	Hoban, Russell	Fiction
Baron Munchausen Truly Tall Tales	Raspe, Rudolf Erich	Fiction
Barran Agus Asbhuain	Maclean, Sorley	Fiction
Barrier Island	Macdonald, John	Fiction
Barrier To Love	March, Stella	Fiction
Basic Cantonese	Chinese	Non-Fiction
Basic French (Parts A & B)	French	Non-Fiction
Basic German	German	Non-Fiction
Basic German Advanced Level	German	Non-Fiction
Basic German Intermediate	German	Non-Fiction
Basic Hungarian	Hungarian	Non-Fiction
Basic Saudi Arabic	Arabic	Non-Fiction
Basic Spanish (Advanced Level)	Spanish	Non-Fiction
Basic Spanish (Beginners)	Spanish	Non-Fiction
Basic Spanish (Intermediate)	Spanish	Non-Fiction
Basic Turkish	Turkish	Non-Fiction
Basques, The	Spain...	Non-Fiction
Batman	Shaw Gardner, Craig	Fiction
Batman In Rhymes, Riddles And Riots	Shaw Gardner, Craig	Fiction
Battle Of Aughrim, The	Murphy, Richard	Fiction
Battle Of Britain, The	Military History	Non-Fiction
Battle Of Dune	Herbert, Frank	Fiction
Battle Of Jutland, The	Military History	Non-Fiction
Battle Of Midway, The	Military History	Non-Fiction
Battle Of Newton Road	Dunkling, Leslie	Fiction
Battle Of The Bubble And Squeak	Pearce, Philippa	Fiction
Battle Of Villa Fiorita, The	Godden, Rumer	Fiction
Battle Of Waterloo	Military History	Non-Fiction
Battles At Thrush Green	Read, Miss	Fiction
Bavarian Overture	Dracup, Angela	Fiction
BBC - Readings By:	BBC...	Non-Fiction
Be A Confident Winner	Self Improvement	Non-Fiction
Be Buried In The Rain	Michaels, Barbara	Fiction
Be Happy Attitudes	Self Improvement	Non-Fiction
Be My Baby	Spector, Ronnie	Non-Fiction
Be Positive	Self Improvement	Non-Fiction
Beachcomber - By The Way	Radio	Fiction
Bean Bag	Bean, Billy	Fiction
Bear Called Paddington, A	Bond, Michael	Fiction
Bears' Christmas	Berenstain, Stan & Jan	Fiction
Bears' Picnic, The	Berenstain, Stan & Jan	Fiction

TITLES INDEX

Title	Author	Category
Beast, The	Benchley, Peter	Fiction
Beasts In My Belfry	Durrell, Gerald	Fiction
Beauty And The Beast	Grimm	Fiction
Beaver Towers	Hinton, Nigel	Fiction
Because Of Yesterday	March, Stella	Fiction
Becket	Anouilh, J	Non-Fiction
Become A New Person	Self Improvement	Non-Fiction
Bedtime Fairy Stories	Children's Stories..	Fiction
Bedtime For Frances	Hoban, Russell	Fiction
Bedtime Stories	Children's Stories..	Fiction
Beezus And Ramona	Cleary, Beverly	Fiction
Beginning Japanese	Japanese...	Non-Fiction
Behind The Scenes At Wizard Of Oz	Films	Non-Fiction
Behind The Wall	Thubron, Colin	Non-Fiction
Behold, Here's Poison	Heyer, Georgette	Fiction
Beiderbecke Affair, The	Plater, Alan	Fiction
Beiderbecke Tapes, The	Plater, Alan	Fiction
Being The Best	Self Improvement	Non-Fiction
Beleet Parus Odinokii	Kataev, V	Non-Fiction
Belgravia	Bingham, Charlotte	Fiction
Believe And Be Happy	Self Improvement	Non-Fiction
Bella	Eden, Dorothy	Fiction
Beloved Emma	Dessau, Joanna	Fiction
Beloved Sinner	Stirling, Jessica	Fiction
Below Stairs	Powell, Margaret	Non-Fiction
Beneficiaries, The	Street, Pamela	Fiction
Bengali Nursery Rhymes	Nursery Rhymes	Fiction
Bennygoak	Garry, Flora	Fiction
Beowulf	English Literature	Non-Fiction
Beowulf, The Battle Of Malden	Poetry	Fiction
Berenice	Racine, Jean	Fiction
Bergerac And The Fatal Weakness	Saville, Andrew	Fiction
Bergerac And The Moving Fever	Saville, Andrew	Fiction
Bergerac And The Traitor's Child	Saville, Andrew	Fiction
Berkeley Concert	Bruce, Lenny	Fiction
Berlin Game	Deighton, Len	Fiction
Berry, Me And Motown	Gordy Singleton, Raynoma	Non-Fiction
Bertha	Television	Fiction
Bertie And The Seven Bodies	Lovesey, Peter	Fiction
Bertie And The Tinman	Lovesey, Peter	Fiction
Best Loved Verse	Poetry	Fiction
Best Of Bob Newhart	Newhart, Bob	Fiction
Best Of Edgar Allan Poe, The	Poe, Edgar Allan	Fiction
Best Of Hysteria 3	Comedy...	Fiction
Best Of Irish Humour	Roach, Hal	Fiction
Best Of Jimmy Jones	Jones, Jimmy	Fiction
Best Of Lee Sutton: Uncensored	Sutton, Lee	Fiction
Best Of Mike Harding, The	Harding, Mike	Fiction
Best Of Milly Molly Mandy	Lankester Brisley	Fiction
Best Of Round The Horne	Radio	Fiction
Best Of Roy Chubby Brown	Brown, Roy 'Chubby'	Fiction
Best Of Saki, The	Saki	Fiction
Best Of Sellers	Sellers, Peter	Fiction
Best Of Teddy Robinson	Robinson, Joan	Fiction
Best Of The Goon Shows	Goons	Fiction
Best Science Fiction Of Brian Aldiss, The	Aldiss, Brian W.	Fiction
Betjeman Reads Betjeman	Betjeman, Sir John	Fiction
Betjeman's Britain	Betjeman, Sir John	Fiction
Betrayed	Chard, Judy	Fiction
Better Sleep	Self Improvement	Non-Fiction
Better World Than This, A	Joseph, Marie	Fiction
Between The Woods And The Waterfront	Fermor, Patrick Leigh	Fiction
Between The Words	Self Improvement	Non-Fiction
Beware The Naked Man Who Offers His Shirt	Business	Non-Fiction
Beyond Hierarchy	Peters, Tom	Non-Fiction
Beyond Our Ken	Radio	Fiction
Beyond The Fringe	Comedy...	Fiction

TITLES INDEX

Title	Author	Category
Beyond The Pale	Clarke, Austin	Fiction
B.F.G, The	Dahl, Roald	Fiction
Bhowani Junction	Masters, John	Fiction
Bias For Action	Business	Non-Fiction
Bible Stories	Bible	Non-Fiction
Biedermann Und Die Brandstifter	Frisch, Max	Non-Fiction
Big Alfie And Annie	Hughes, Shirley	Fiction
Big Alfie Out Of Doors Storybook, The	Hughes, Shirley	Fiction
Big Deal, The	Business	Non-Fiction
Big Four, The	Trains...	Non-Fiction
Big Kill	Spillane, Mickey	Fiction
Big Pancake, The	Children's Stories..	Fiction
Big Sleep, The	Chandler, Raymond	Fiction
Big Yin Double Helping, A	Connolly, Billy	Fiction
Biggles	Johns, Capt. W.E.	Fiction
Biggles Defies The Swastika	Johns, Capt. W.E.	Fiction
Biggles Flies East	Johns, Capt. W.E.	Fiction
Bike, The	Sillitoe, Alan	Fiction
Bill Bailey	Cookson, Catherine	Fiction
Bill Bailey's Daughter	Cookson, Catherine	Fiction
Bill Bailey's Lot	Cookson, Catherine	Fiction
Bill The Minder	Forder, Timothy	Fiction
Bills Best Friend	Cosby, Bill	Fiction
Bill's New Frock	Fine, Anne	Fiction
Billy And Albert	Connolly, Billy	Fiction
Billy And Blaze	Anderson, C.W.	Fiction
Billy Budd	Melville, Herman	Fiction
Billy Budd, Foretopman	Melville, Herman	Fiction
Billy Bunter Gets The Boot	Richards, Frank	Fiction
Billy Liar	Waterhouse, Keith	Fiction
Billy The Kid	Utley, Robert M.	Non-Fiction
Bio- Feedback	Self Improvement	Non-Fiction
Biology (Course)	G.C.S.E.	Non-Fiction
Bird Songs Volumes 1 - 15	Bird Songs	Non-Fiction
Bird Spot	Bird Songs	Non-Fiction
Birds Awakening	Bird Songs	Non-Fiction
Birds, Beasts And Relatives	Durrell, Gerald	Fiction
Birthday Burglar, The	Mahy, Margaret	Fiction
Birthday Treat, A	Bond, Michael	Fiction
Bismarck And The German Problem	Germany	Non-Fiction
Bismark And Germany	Germany	Non-Fiction
Bit Of A Do, A	Nobbs, David	Fiction
Bitter And Twisted	Smith & Jones	Fiction
Bitter Sweet Summer	Sinclair, Olga	Fiction
Black Africa: Yesterday And Today	Africa	Non-Fiction
Black Amber	Whitney, Phyllis A	Fiction
Black Beauty	Children's Stories..	Fiction
Black Beauty	Sewell, Anna	Fiction
Black Boy	Wright, Richard	Fiction
Black Candle, The	Cookson, Catherine	Fiction
Black Fairy Tales	Traditional	Fiction
Black Fives	Trains...	Non-Fiction
Black Gunsmoke	Floren, Lee	Fiction
Black Moth, The	Heyer, Georgette	Fiction
Black Narcissus	Godden, Rumer	Fiction
Black Rainbow	Michaels, Barbara	Fiction
Black Robe	Moore, Brian	Fiction
Black Stage, The	Gilbert, Anthony	Fiction
Black Tower, The	James, P.D.	Fiction
Black Tulip, The	Dumas, Alexandre	Fiction
Black Velvet Gown, The	Cookson, Catherine	Fiction
Blackground	Aiken, Joan	Fiction
Blackjack	Brand, Max	Fiction
Blackmore By The Stour	Barnes, William	Fiction
Blacksignal	Brand, Max	Fiction
Blake's Reach	Gaskin, Catherine	Fiction
Blandings Castle	Wodehouse, P.G.	Fiction

TITLES INDEX

Title	Author	Type
Blastermind	Bates, Blaster	Fiction
Blazing Ocean, The	Abraham, Cyril	Fiction
Bleak House	Dickens, Charles	Fiction
Bless Me Father	Boyd, Neil	Fiction
Blessing Way, The	Hillerman, Tony	Fiction
Blessings	Plain, Belva	Fiction
Blind Corner	Yates, Dornford	Fiction
Blindman's Bluff	Carr, Margaret	Fiction
Blitzcat	Westall, Robert	Fiction
Blood And Judgement	Gilbert, Michael	Fiction
Blood Donor	Hancock, Tony	Fiction
Blood Knot	Fugard, Athol	Fiction
Blood Knot	Llewellyn, Sam	Fiction
Blood Orange	Llewellyn, Sam	Fiction
Blood Running Cold, The	Ross, Jonathan	Fiction
Blood-And-Thunder Adventure On Hurricane Peak	Mahy, Margaret	Fiction
Bloodsport	Francis, Dick	Fiction
Bloodstained Bokhara, The	Gault, William Campbell	Fiction
Blossoms And The Green Phantom	Byars, Betsy	Fiction
Blossoms Meet The Vulture Lady	Byars, Betsy	Fiction
Blowing His Mind And Yours Too	Lord Buckley	Fiction
Blue Beard	Traditional	Fiction
Blue Geranium	Christie, Agatha	Fiction
Blue Ice, The	Innes, Hammond	Fiction
Blue Nile, The	Moorehead, Alan	Non-Fiction
Bluebell Blue	Webster, Jan	Fiction
Bluegrass Range	Morgan, John	Fiction
Blunderer, The	Highsmith, Patricia	Fiction
Blunt Instrument, A	Heyer, Georgette	Fiction
Bob Newhart	Newhart, Bob	Fiction
Bodas De Sangre	Lorca, F. Garcia	Non-Fiction
Bodies	Barnard, Robert	Fiction
Body In The Billiard Room, The	Keating, H.R.F.	Fiction
Body In The Library, The	Christie, Agatha	Fiction
Body Politic, The	Barker, Clive	Fiction
Body Snatchers, The	Stevenson, Robert Louis	Fiction
Bol Chaal	Hindi	Non-Fiction
Bolt	Francis, Dick	Fiction
Bone Crack	Francis, Dick	Fiction
Bones In The Sand	Royce, Kenneth	Fiction
Bonfire Of The Vanities	Wolfe, Tom	Fiction
Bonjour Tristesse	Sagan, Francoise	Non-Fiction
Bonkers Clocks	Fisk, Nicholas	Fiction
Bonnie Fechter, A	Scott, Alexander	Fiction
Bonnie Prince Charlie	Bonnie Prince Charlie	Non-Fiction
Book Of Dragons, The	Nesbitt, Edith	Fiction
Book Of Merlyn, The	Traditional	Fiction
Bordermen, The	Paine, Lauren	Fiction
Born Free	Adamson, Joy	Non-Fiction
Borrowers Afield, The	Norton, Mary	Fiction
Borrowers, The	Norton, Mary	Fiction
Bottle Imp, The	Stevenson, Robert Louis	Fiction
Bottom Line	Weldon, Fay	Fiction
Boule De Suif	De Maupassant, Guy	Fiction
Boulevard Durand	Salacrou, A	Non-Fiction
Bourges And Berry	France	Non-Fiction
Bourne Identity, The	Ludlum, Robert	Fiction
Bourne Supremacy, The	Ludlum, Robert	Fiction
Box Of Nothing, A	Dickinson, Peter	Fiction
Boy Growing Up, A	Thomas, Dylan	Non-Fiction
Boys From Beersheba, The	Bible	Non-Fiction
Boys From The Blackstuff	Bleasdale, Alan	Fiction
Bradman - The Don Declares	Cricket	Non-Fiction
Bradshaws Vol. 1	Bradshaws	Fiction
Bradshaws Vol. 2	Bradshaws	Fiction
Bradshaws Vol. 3	Bradshaws	Fiction
Brambly Hedge	Barklem, Jill	Fiction

TITLES INDEX

Branche Entre Nous	French	Non-Fiction
Brand New	Mason, Jackie	Fiction
Brat Farrar	Tey, Josephine	Fiction
Brave Little Tailor	Children's Stories..	Fiction
Bravestarr	Television	Fiction
Break In	Francis, Dick	Fiction
Breakfast At Tiffany's	Capote, Truman	Fiction
Breakfast Of Champions	Vonnegut, Kurt	Fiction
Breakheart Pass	Maclean, Alistair	Fiction
Breakthrough In Grey Room	Burroughs, William S.	Fiction
Breathe, Relax And Imagine	Self Improvement	Non-Fiction
Brecht And The Actor	Brecht, Bertolt	Non-Fiction
Brer Rabbit	Uncle Remus	Fiction
Brian Patten Reading His Poems	Patten, Brian	Fiction
Brides In The Bath Case & The Penge Mystery, The	Lustgarten, Edgar	Non-Fiction
Brideshead Revisited	Waugh, Evelyn	Fiction
Bridge On The River Kwai	Boulle, Pierre	Fiction
Brief History In Time, A	Hawking, Stephen	Non-Fiction
Brief Lives	Aubrey, John	Fiction
Brief Lives	Brookner, Anita	Fiction
Brighton Trunk Case & The Blazing Car Case, The	Lustgarten, Edgar	Non-Fiction
Bring On The Empty Horses	Niven, David	Non-Fiction
Bring Us Together	Bible	Non-Fiction
Britain Between The Wars	Social Sciences	Non-Fiction
Britannicus	Racine, Jean	Non-Fiction
British Appeasement	Social Sciences	Non-Fiction
British Bird Songs And Calls	Bird Songs	Non-Fiction
British Comedy Classics	Comedy...	Fiction
British Political Economy 1919-1939, The	Social Sciences	Non-Fiction
British Railways Standard Locomotives	Trains...	Non-Fiction
British Wild Birds In Stereo	Bird Songs	Non-Fiction
Broadway Stories, The	Runyon, Damon	Fiction
Brogue	Saki	Fiction
Brogue, The / Tobermory	Saki	Fiction
Brontonappers, The	Television	Fiction
Brownie Of The Black Haggs	Hogg, James	Fiction
Browning Version, The	Rattigan, Terence	Fiction
Bruce Memorial Window	Scotland	Non-Fiction
Buddhist Chants And Music From Sri Lanka	Religious	Non-Fiction
Buffalo Girls	McMurty, Larry	Fiction
Building Of Jalna, The	De La Roche, Mazo	Fiction
Built Swindon	Trains...	Non-Fiction
Bull From The Sea, The	Renault, Mary	Fiction
Bulldog Drummond	McNeile, H.C.	Fiction
Bullet In The Ballet	Brahms & Simon	Fiction
Bundle For The Toff, A	Creasey, John	Fiction
Bunnicula	Howe, Deborah & James	Fiction
Buongiorno Italia	Italian	Non-Fiction
Burden Of Population	Social Sciences	Non-Fiction
Burden Of Proof	Turow, Scott	Fiction
Burglar Bill	Ahlberg, Janet	Fiction
Burial Deferred	Ross, Jonathan	Fiction
Burmese Days	Orwell, George	Fiction
Burning Of Billy Toober, The	Ross, Jonathan	Fiction
Burning Shore, The	Smith, Wilbur	Fiction
Burns Cottage Selection	Burns, Robert	Fiction
Burns Nicht At Lugton	Scotland	Non-Fiction
Burns Supper, A	Christmas	Non-Fiction
Bus Stop	Inge, William	Fiction
Business Spanish	Spanish	Non-Fiction
Business Studies (course)	G.C.S.E.	Non-Fiction
Business Trading Ethics	Business	Non-Fiction
Butler's Revenge, The	Powell, Margaret	Non-Fiction
Butley	Gray, Simon	Fiction
By Hook Or By Crook	Lathen, Emma	Fiction
By Sandymount Strand	Iremonger, Valentin	Fiction
By The Waters Of Liverpool	Forrester, Helen	Non-Fiction

TITLES INDEX

Title	Author	Category
Byron's Rhetoric	English Literature	Non-Fiction
C. Day Lewis Reads C. Day Lewis	Day Lewis, C	Fiction
Caesar And Cleopatra	Shaw, George Bernard	Fiction
Cakes And Ale	Maugham, W. Somerset	Fiction
Calendar, The	Early Learning	Non-Fiction
Calendar Of Crime	Queen, Ellery	Fiction
Calf For Venus, A	Lofts, Norah	Fiction
Caligula	Camus, A	Non-Fiction
Call For The Dead	Le Carre, John	Fiction
Call In The Night	Howatch, Susan	Fiction
Call Me Roger	Business	Non-Fiction
Call Of Cthulhu, The	Lovecraft H.P.	Fiction
Call Of The Canyon	Grey, Zane	Fiction
Call Of The Wild, The	London, Jack	Fiction
Callanetics For Your Back	Health & Fitness	Non-Fiction
Calling Mr Callaghan	Cheyney, Peter	Fiction
Calm And Peaceful Mind, A	Self Improvement	Non-Fiction
Cameo	Graham, Winston	Fiction
Cameron Ordinary Seaman	McCutchan, Philip	Fiction
Cameron's Convoy	McCutchan, Philip	Fiction
Camomile Lawn, The	Wesley, Mary	Fiction
Campbell's Kingdom	Innes, Hammond	Fiction
Campion	Allingham, Margery	Fiction
Can You Hear Me, Mother?	Powell, Sandy	Non-Fiction
Cancer	Astrology	Non-Fiction
Candide	Voltaire	Non-Fiction
Candide	Voltaire	Fiction
Candles For The Surgeon	Upshall, Helen	Fiction
Cannery Row	Steinbeck, John	Fiction
Canseo	Gaelic	Non-Fiction
Canterbury Tales, The	Chaucer, Geoffrey	Fiction
Canterville Ghost, The	Wilde, Oscar	Fiction
Canti	Leopardi, Giacomo	Non-Fiction
Cantico Del Sole, Canto 99...	Poetry	Fiction
Capricorn	Astrology	Non-Fiction
Capricorn Stone, The	Brent, Madeleine	Fiction
Captain And The Enemy, The	Greene, Graham	Fiction
Captain Beaky	Lloyd, Jeremy	Fiction
Captain Kremmen	Everett, Kenny	Fiction
Captain Paralytic And The Brown Ale Cowboy	Harding, Mike	Fiction
Captain Pugwash	Ryan, John	Fiction
Captain's Table, The	Stuart, Alex	Fiction
Captive, The	Holt, Victoria	Fiction
Car Wars	Jackson, Steve	Fiction
Caravan To Vaccares	Maclean, Alistair	Fiction
Careless Widow, A	Pritchett, V.S.	Fiction
Caribbean Encounter	John, Phillipa	Fiction
Caribbean Mystery, A	Christie, Agatha	Fiction
Carmen	French	Non-Fiction
Caroline Minuscule	Taylor, Andrew	Fiction
Carriage For Fiona, A	March, Stella	Fiction
Carrie's War	Bawden, Nina	Fiction
Carrotts Condensed Classics	Carrott, Jasper	Fiction
Carry On Jeeves	Wodehouse, P.G.	Fiction
Cary Grant, The Light Touch	Godfrey, L	Non-Fiction
Case Against It	Self Improvement	Non-Fiction
Case Book Of Sherlock Holmes, The	Conan Doyle, Arthur	Fiction
Casino Royale	Fleming, Ian	Fiction
Cast, In Order Of Disappearance	Brett, Simon	Fiction
Cast Iron Man, The	Legat, Michael	Fiction
Castle Of Adventure, The	Blyton, Enid	Fiction
Castle Of Eagles	Heaven, Constance	Fiction
Castle Of The Golden Sun, The	Reeves, James	Fiction
Castle Of The Mist	Luellen, Valentina	Fiction
Castle Of Yew, The	Boston, Lucy M.	Fiction
Castles And Kings	Trains...	Non-Fiction
Cat Ate My Gymsuit, The	Danziger, Paula	Fiction

TITLES INDEX

Cat Who Ate Danish Modern, The	Jackson Braun, Lilian	Fiction
Cat Who Could Read Backwards, The	Jackson Braun, Lilian	Fiction
Cat Who Knew Shakespeare, The	Jackson Braun, Lilian	Fiction
Cat Who Saw Red, The	Jackson Braun, Lilian	Fiction
Cat Who Walks Through Walls, The	Heinlein, Robert	Fiction
Catalans, The	Spain...	Non-Fiction
Catch 22	Heller, Joseph	Fiction
Catch, The	Boland, John	Fiction
Catherine De Medici	De Medici, Catherine	Non-Fiction
Cat's Cradle	Vonnegut, Kurt	Fiction
Cat's Eye	Atwood, Margaret	Fiction
Cauldron, The	Townshend Bickers	Fiction
Cause Of Death	Underwood, Michael	Fiction
Cautionary Verses	Poetry	Fiction
Cavalier Case, The	Fraser, Antonia	Fiction
Celebrated Cases Of Judge Dee	Van Gulik, Robert	Fiction
Celtic Language, The	Celtic	Non-Fiction
Centre And The Provinces, The	History	Non-Fiction
Centuries	Religious	Non-Fiction
Cezanne	Cezanne	Non-Fiction
Challenge In The Dark	Leeson, Robert	Fiction
Chamberlain	Social Sciences	Non-Fiction
Chancellor Manuscript, The	Ludlum, Robert	Fiction
Chances	Collins, Jackie	Fiction
Change Is As Good As A Rest, A	Connolly, Billy	Fiction
Changes The World	Bible	Non-Fiction
Changing The Game: The New Way To Sell	Business	Non-Fiction
Changing Trains	Trains...	Non-Fiction
Chant Village Stories	Children's Stories..	Fiction
Charade	Mortimer, John	Fiction
Charioteer, The	Renault, Mary	Fiction
Charisma - Drawing People To You	Self Improvement	Non-Fiction
Charles 1 And Puritanism	History	Non-Fiction
Charles Darwin	Darwin, Charles	Non-Fiction
Charles Dickens	Dickens, Charles	Non-Fiction
Charles Dickens	Orwell, George	Non-Fiction
Charles II	History	Non-Fiction
Charles V	France	Non-Fiction
Charley's Aunt	Plays	Fiction
Charlie And The Chocolate Factory	Dahl, Roald	Fiction
Charlie And The Great Glass Elevator	Dahl, Roald	Fiction
Charlie Brown's All Stars	Schultz, Charles	Fiction
Charlie Lewis Plays For Time	Kemp, Gene	Fiction
Charlie Moon And The Big Bonanza Bust-up	Hughes, Shirley	Fiction
Chartism	History	Non-Fiction
Chartism And The 1870 Education Act	Social Sciences	Non-Fiction
Chatterbox Classics 1	Chatterbox	Non-Fiction
Chatterbox Humour 1	Chatterbox	Non-Fiction
Chatterbox Mixed Bag 1	Chatterbox	Non-Fiction
Chatterbox Pops 1	Chatterbox	Non-Fiction
Chemistry (Course)	G.C.S.E.	Non-Fiction
Chequered Silence, A	Gilbert, Jacqueline	Fiction
Chestnut Soldier, The	Nimmo, Jenny	Fiction
Chewing Gum Rescue, The	Mahy, Margaret	Fiction
Cheyenne Dawn	Brennan, Will	Fiction
Chicken Licken	Children's Stories..	Fiction
Child Alone, A	Bardot, Brigitte	Non-Fiction
Child Alone, A - Memoirs	Watkins-Pitchford	Non-Fiction
Child In The Forest, A	Foley, Winifred	Non-Fiction
Children Of Green Knowe, The	Boston, Lucy M.	Fiction
Children Of Tender Years	Allbeury, Ted	Fiction
Children's Bible In 365 Stories, The	Bible	Non-Fiction
Children's Children Parts 1, 2 & 3	Mosco, Maisie	Fiction
Children's Hour	Radio	Fiction
Children's Hour	Television	Fiction
Childrens Number Songs And Stories	Early Learning	Non-Fiction
Children's Stories	Children's Stories..	Fiction

TITLES INDEX

Children's Tales From Around The World	Children's Stories..	Fiction
Child's Christmas In Wales, A	Thomas, Dylan	Fiction
Child's Garden Of Verses, A	Stevenson, Robert Louis	Fiction
China Blues	Longfellow, Pamela	Fiction
China Doll, The	Yorke, Margaret	Fiction
China - Revolution And Foreign Policy	History	Non-Fiction
Chinese Cassette Course	Chinese	Non-Fiction
Chinese Travel Pack	Chinese	Non-Fiction
Chip 'n' Dale	Television	Fiction
Chiragh Ke Zakham	Chawla, Harcharan	Fiction
Chitty Chitty Bang Bang	Fleming, Ian	Fiction
Chocolate War, The	Cormier, Robert	Fiction
Choice And Commentary	Garioch, Robert	Fiction
Choice Of Enemies, A	Allbeury, Ted	Fiction
Choice, The	Allbeury, Ted	Fiction
Choices	Self Improvement	Non-Fiction
Choosing	Farr, Diana	Fiction
Choosing Your Own Greatness	Self Improvement	Non-Fiction
Christmas Activity Box	Christmas	Fiction
Christmas Books, The	Dickens, Charles	Fiction
Christmas Carol, A	Dickens, Charles	Fiction
Christmas Mouse, The	Read, Miss	Fiction
Christmas Stories	Lurtsema, Robert J.	Fiction
Christopher Columbus	Columbus, Christopher	Non-Fiction
Chronicles Of Narnia Soundbook	Lewis, C.S.	Fiction
Chronicles Of Narnia, The	Lewis, C.S.	Fiction
Chrysalids, The	Wyndham, John	Fiction
Church Mouse And Church Cat	Oakley, Graham	Fiction
Church Of England	History	Non-Fiction
Church Of England And The English Reformation	Religious	Non-Fiction
Church Slavonicisms In Russian	Russian	Non-Fiction
Cider With Rosie	Lee, Laurie	Non-Fiction
Cinder Path, The	Cookson, Catherine	Fiction
Cinderella	Traditional	Fiction
Cinderella Spy	Daniels, Philip	Fiction
Cinema E Letteratura In Italia 1945-1965	Italy	Non-Fiction
Cinna	Corneille, P	Fiction
Circle Of Friends	Binchy, Maeve	Fiction
Circles Of Deceit	Bawden, Nina	Fiction
Circus	Maclean, Alistair	Fiction
Circus Of Adventure, The	Blyton, Enid	Fiction
City Of Gold And Shadows	Peters, Ellis	Fiction
City Of Strangers, A	Barnard, Robert	Fiction
City Primeval	Leonard, Elmore	Fiction
Civil Disobedience	Thoreau, Henry David	Fiction
Clash Of Loyalties	Harcourt, Palma	Fiction
Class	Cooper, Jilly	Fiction
Classic Detective Stories	Mystery	Fiction
Classic Ghost Stories	Ghost Stories	Fiction
Classic Love Stories	Romance	Fiction
Classic Motorcycles	Motorcycling	Non-Fiction
Classic Saki Stories	Saki	Fiction
Classic Science Fiction Stories	Science Fiction	Fiction
Classic Short Stories	Short Stories	Fiction
Classic Tales Of Murder	Mystery	Fiction
Classic Tales Of Mystery And The Supernatural	Ghost Stories	Fiction
Classical Revolution In Italian Theatre 1500-152	Italy	Non-Fiction
Claudius The God	Graves, Robert	Fiction
Clean Tapes	Cook, Peter	Fiction
Clear Case Of Suicide, A	Underwood, Michael	Fiction
Clever Polly And The Stupid Wolf	Storr, Catherine	Fiction
Climate For Conspiracy	Harcourt, Palma	Fiction
Climbing The Stairs	Powell, Margaret	Non-Fiction
Clinging To The Wreckage	Mortimer, John	Non-Fiction
Clitheroe Kid, The	Radio	Fiction
Cloak Of Darkness	MacInnes, Helen	Fiction
Clock, The	Early Learning	Non-Fiction

TITLES INDEX

Title	Author	Category
Clock Tower Ghost, The	Kemp, Gene	Fiction
Clocks, The	Christie, Agatha	Fiction
Clockwork Orange, A	Burgess, Anthony	Fiction
Clogger's Child, The	Joseph, Marie	Fiction
Close Quarters	Golding, William	Fiction
Closed At Dusk	Dickens, Monica	Fiction
Closing Of The American Mind, The	Social Sciences	Non-Fiction
Cloud Howe	Gibbon, Lewis Grassic	Fiction
Cloud In The Sky, A	March, Stella	Fiction
Cloud Over Malverton	Buckingham, Nancy	Fiction
Clue Of The Twisted Candle, The	Wallace, Edgar	Fiction
Clutch Of Constables	Marsh, Ngaio	Fiction
Code Of The Woosters, The	Wodehouse, P.G.	Fiction
Co-Dependents Guide To The Twelve Steps	Self Improvement	Non-Fiction
Codeword Cromwell	Allbeury, Ted	Fiction
Coffin From The Past, A	Butler, Gwendoline	Fiction
Coffin In Malta	Butler, Gwendoline	Fiction
Coffin In The Black Museum	Butler, Gwendoline	Fiction
Coffin Scarcely Used	Watson, Colin	Fiction
Cold Coffin	Quest, Erica	Fiction
Cold Comfort Farm	Gibbons, Stella	Fiction
Cold Harbour	Higgins, Jack	Fiction
Cold Heaven	Moore, Brian	Fiction
Cold War In Europe 1945-1950, The	History	Non-Fiction
Colditz Story, The	Reid, P.R.	Fiction
Colin Campbell's Local Radio	Campbell, Colin	Fiction
Collected Poems	Poetry	Fiction
Collected Stories From Europe	Children's Stories..	Fiction
Collection: Joyce Grenfell	Grenfell, Joyce	Fiction
Collection Of Spikes, A	Milligan, Spike	Fiction
Colliers Row	Webster, Jan	Fiction
Colloquial Russian	Russian	Non-Fiction
Colomba	Merimee, Prosper	Non-Fiction
Colonel's Lady, The	Maugham, W. Somerset	Fiction
Colour Of Blood, The	Moore, Brian	Fiction
Colours	Early Learning	Non-Fiction
Colours (The Rainbow Ship)	Early Learning	Non-Fiction
Comanche Gold	Basker, Joe	Fiction
Come Again	Derek & Clive	Fiction
Come Back	Francis, Dick	Fiction
Come Home Charlie And Face Them	Delderfield, R.F.	Fiction
Come Love With Me	Poetry	Fiction
Comedian	Murphy, Eddie	Fiction
Comedian Dies, A	Brett, Simon	Fiction
Comedy Countdown	Kelly, Frank	Fiction
Comedy Of Errors, The	Shakespeare, William	Fiction
Comedy Spectacular	Comedy...	Fiction
Comic Rhymes	Poetry	Fiction
Comic Strip	Comedy...	Fiction
Comical Cuts	Comedy...	Fiction
Coming Attractions	Stamp, Terence	Non-Fiction
Coming From Behind	Jacobson, Howard	Fiction
Coming Home	Fraser, Alison	Fiction
Coming Of Arthur, The	Traditional	Fiction
Coming Up For Air	Orwell, George	Fiction
Commentary And Choice	Barbour, John	Fiction
Commentary And Choice	Douglas, Gavin	Fiction
Commentary And Selection	Poetry	Fiction
Commercial Road	Digance, Richard	Fiction
Common Years, The	Cooper, Jilly	Non-Fiction
Communion	Streiber, Whitley	Non-Fiction
Companions In A Death Boat	Childish, Wild Billy	Fiction
Company Of Saints, The	Anthony, Evelyn	Fiction
Compelling Case, A	Underwood, Michael	Fiction
Compleat Angler, The	Walton, Izaak	Non-Fiction
Complete Alice In Wonderland, The	Carroll, Lewis	Fiction
Complete Fitness Course, The	Health & Fitness	Non-Fiction

TITLES INDEX

Complete Steel, The	Aird, Catherine	Fiction
Complete Yoga	Health & Fitness	Non-Fiction
Computer Studies	G.C.S.E.	Non-Fiction
Comus	Milton, John	Fiction
Con Gli Occhi Chiusi	Tozzi, Federico	Fiction
Concentration - Power Plus	Self Improvement	Non-Fiction
Condition Black	Seymour, Gerald	Fiction
Conduct Of Major Maxim, The	Lyall, Gavin	Fiction
Confederacy Of Dunces	Kennedy Toole, John	Fiction
Confidential Agent, The	Greene, Graham	Fiction
Conflict In Europe	Social Sciences	Non-Fiction
Conflict Of Interests, A	Egleton, Clive	Fiction
Conrad	Conrad, Joseph	Non-Fiction
Consequences Of War, The	Burton, Betty	Fiction
Conservative Party From Peel To Gladstone	Social Sciences	Non-Fiction
Constable Around The Village	Rhea, Nicholas	Non-Fiction
Constable On The Hill	Rhea, Nicholas	Non-Fiction
Constable On The Prowl	Rhea, Nicholas	Non-Fiction
Constructive Anger	Self Improvement	Non-Fiction
Consul's File, The	Theroux, Paul	Fiction
Consultant In Love	March, Stella	Fiction
Contemporary Czech	Czech	Non-Fiction
Contemporary Literature Readings	Nichols, Grace	Fiction
Contes A Ninon	Zola, Emile	Fiction
Contes De La Becasse	French	Non-Fiction
Continuity Of Conflict In French Society	France	Non-Fiction
Contract, The	Seymour, Gerald	Fiction
Contractual Obligation	Monty Python	Fiction
Control Freaks	Self Improvement	Non-Fiction
Control Your Weight	Self Improvement	Non-Fiction
Conversational Polish: A Beginners Course	Polish	Non-Fiction
Conversations With Doctor X	Childish, Wild Billy	Fiction
Convoy	Pope, Dudley	Fiction
Convoy Commodore, The	McCutchan, Philip	Fiction
Cool Repentance	Fraser, Antonia	Fiction
Cooper's Creek	Moorehead, Alan	Non-Fiction
Cop Hater	McBain, Ed	Fiction
Cop Yer Whack Of This	Connolly, Billy	Fiction
Coping With Difficult People	Business	Non-Fiction
Copper Capped Engines	Trains...	Non-Fiction
Copper Peacock, The	Rendell, Ruth	Fiction
Cops And Robbers	Ahlberg, Janet & Allan	Fiction
Coral Island	Ballantyne, R.M.	Fiction
Corinthian, The	Heyer, Georgette	Fiction
Corinthians	Bible	Non-Fiction
Coriolanus	Shakespeare, William	Fiction
Coroner's Pidgin	Allingham, Margery	Fiction
Corvette, The	Woodman, Richard	Fiction
Cosmic Carrot	Carrott, Jasper	Fiction
Costa Del Sol	Wilson, Des	Fiction
Cotswold Characters	Cotswolds	Non-Fiction
Cotswold Craftsmen	Cotswolds	Non-Fiction
Cotswold Voices	Cotswolds	Non-Fiction
Count Duckula	Television	Fiction
Count Of Monte Cristo, The	Dumas, Alexandre	Fiction
Count To Ten With Mr. Men	Hargreaves, Roger	Fiction
Countdown	Early Learning	Non-Fiction
Counting Is Fun	Early Learning	Non-Fiction
Counting Songs	Early Learning	Non-Fiction
Country Comedy Time - Lonzo And Oscar	Comedy...	Fiction
Country Diary Of An Edwardian Lady	Holden, Edith	Non-Fiction
Country Girls, The	O'Brien, Edna	Fiction
Country Of The Blind	Wells, H.G.	Fiction
Couples	Updike, John	Fiction
Courage The Guard Dog	Sound Effects	Non-Fiction
Court And Kingdom	History	Non-Fiction
Courtesans And Fallen Women	Cornwell, Bernard	Fiction

TITLES INDEX

Title	Author	Category
Cousin Kate	Heyer, Georgette	Fiction
Cousin Phyllis	Gaskell, Elizabeth	Fiction
Cover For A Traitor	Harcourt, Palma	Fiction
Cover Her Face	James, P.D.	Fiction
Cover Story	Forbes, Colin	Fiction
Crack, The	Connolly, Billy	Fiction
Crackdown	Cornwell, Bernard	Fiction
Cracker Jackson	Byars, Betsy	Fiction
Craft, Design And Technology	G.C.S.E.	Non-Fiction
Crampton Hodnet	Pym, Barbara	Fiction
Cranford	Gaskell, Elizabeth	Fiction
Create Wealth - Power Programming	Self Improvement	Non-Fiction
Creating Positive Relationships	Self Improvement	Non-Fiction
Creating Wealth	Business	Non-Fiction
Crescent City	Plain, Belva	Fiction
Crime And Punishment	Dostoevsky, Fyodor	Fiction
Crime At Black Dudley, The	Allingham, Margery	Fiction
Crime Without Passion	Grayson, Richard	Fiction
Criminal Comedy Of The Contented Couple, The	Symons, Julian	Fiction
Crocodile On The Sandbank	Peters, Elizabeth	Fiction
Cromwell, Science And Society	History	Non-Fiction
Cross, The	Bible	Non-Fiction
Crossing Brooklyn Ferry	Whitman, Walt	Fiction
Crossing, The	Allbeury, Ted	Fiction
Crow	Hughes, Ted	Fiction
Crow And Wodwo	Hughes, Ted	Fiction
Crowdie And Cream	Macdonald, Finlay J.	Non-Fiction
Crown House	Ling & Ace	Fiction
Crucible, The	Miller, Arthur	Fiction
Cruel Count, The	Cartland, Barbara	Fiction
Cruel Sea, The	Monsarrat, Nicholas	Fiction
Cry, The Beloved Country	Paton, Alan	Fiction
Cry Wolf	Smith, Wilbur	Fiction
Crystal Cave, The	Stewart, Mary	Fiction
Crystal Gull, The	Andrews, Lucilla	Fiction
Crystal World, The	Ballard, J.G.	Fiction
Cuckoo Sister, The	Alcock, Vivien	Fiction
Culloden - The Last Jacobite Rising	Prebble, John	Non-Fiction
Cultured Handmaiden, The	Cookson, Catherine	Fiction
Curate For All Seasons, A	Secombe, Fred	Fiction
Curb In The Sky	Thurber, James	Fiction
Curing Depression	Self Improvement	Non-Fiction
Curious George	Rey, H.A.	Fiction
Currie Flavour	Poetry	Fiction
Curse Of The Pharaohs, The	Peters, Elizabeth	Fiction
Cycle Of The West	Miscellaneous	Fiction
Cymbeline	Shakespeare, William	Fiction
Cyrano De Bergerac	Rostand, Edmund	Fiction
Cyril Bonhamy	Gathorne-Hardy, Jonathan	Fiction
Czech Phonology - Parts 1 & 2	Czech	Non-Fiction
Czech Travel Pack	Czech	Non-Fiction
D H Lawrence	Lawrence, D.H.	Non-Fiction
D H Lawrence: Sons And Lovers	A-Level	Non-Fiction
D H Lawrence: The Rainbow	A-Level	Non-Fiction
Daddy-Long-Legs	Webster, Jean	Fiction
Dad's Army	Television	Fiction
Daggers Drawn	Carr, Margaret	Fiction
Dalesman's Diary, A	Mitchell, W.R.	Non-Fiction
Damage	Hart, Josephine	Fiction
Dama's Sobachkoi	Chekhov, Anton	Non-Fiction
Dambusters, The Great Escape	Brickhill, Paul	Non-Fiction
Dame Margot Fonteyn	Fonteyn, Dame Margot	Non-Fiction
Dan Dare	Radio	Fiction
Dance For Diplomats	Harcourt, Palma	Fiction
Dance Keep Fit & Slim To Music	Health & Fitness	Non-Fiction
Dances With Wolves	Blake, Michael	Fiction
Dancing Granny, The	Bryan, Ashley	Fiction

TITLES INDEX

Dandelion Seed, The	Kennedy, Lena	Fiction
Danger, The	Francis, Dick	Fiction
Dangermouse And Public Enemy No.1	Television	Fiction
Dangerous Curves	Cheyney, Peter	Fiction
Dangerous Davies, The Last Detective	Thomas, Leslie	Fiction
Dangerous In Love	Thomas, Leslie	Fiction
Dangerous Love	Wright, Katrina	Fiction
Daniel Defoe	Defoe, Daniel	Non-Fiction
Danish Cassette Course	Danish	Non-Fiction
Danish Travel Pack	Danish	Non-Fiction
Danny, The Champion Of The World	Dahl, Roald	Fiction
Dantons Tod	Buchner, G	Non-Fiction
Darcy's Utopia	Weldon, Fay	Fiction
Dark Curtain, The	Packer, Joy	Fiction
Dark Menace	Sheridan, Paula	Fiction
Dark Of Moon	Madden, Anne Wakefield	Fiction
Dark Of The Sun, The	Smith, Wilbur	Fiction
Dark Shore, The	Howatch, Susan	Fiction
Dark Side Of The Goons	Goons	Fiction
Dark Star, The	Gater, Dilys	Fiction
Dark Summer, The	Buckingham, Nancy	Fiction
Dark Tower, The	King, Stephen	Fiction
Dark-Adapted Eye, A	Vine, Barbara	Fiction
Darkness At Noon	Koestler, Arthur	Fiction
Darling Buds Of May, The	Bates, H.E.	Fiction
Darwin And Utilitarianism	History	Non-Fiction
Das Brot Der Fruhen Jahre	Boll, Heinrich	Non-Fiction
Das Fraulein Von Scuderi	German	Non-Fiction
Das Geteilte Deutschland: Geschichte Und Gegenwa	Germany	Non-Fiction
Das Wrack And Other Stories	Lenz, S	Non-Fiction
Daughter Of The Dales	Hauxwell, Hannah	Non-Fiction
Daughter Of The House	Gaskin, Catherine	Fiction
Daughter Of Time, The	Tey, Josephine	Fiction
Daughters Of The Prince	Barber, Noel	Fiction
Daulat Aur Mamta (Hindi)	Sameer	Fiction
David Copperfield	Dickens, Charles	Fiction
David Rorie	Rorie, David	Fiction
Dawn At Josiah's Bay	Environmental Sounds	Non-Fiction
Dawn Of Love, The	Miscellaneous	Fiction
Day At The Zoo, A	Early Learning	Non-Fiction
Day Of Rhymes, A	Pooley, Sarah	Fiction
Day Of The Jackal, The	Forsyth, Frederick	Fiction
Day Of The Sardine	Chaplin, Sid	Fiction
Day Of The Triffids, The	Wyndham, John	Fiction
Daylight Dig, The	Miscellaneous	Fiction
D-Day Despatches	Military History	Non-Fiction
De Gaulle And The French Political Scene	De Gaulle, Charles	Non-Fiction
Dead And Alive	Innes, Hammond	Fiction
Dead By Morning	Simpson, Dorothy	Fiction
Dead Cert	Francis, Dick	Fiction
Dead City Radio	Burroughs, William S.	Fiction
Dead Ernest	Mitchell, James	Fiction
Dead Eye	Llewellyn, Sam	Fiction
Dead Eye	Ross, Jonathan	Fiction
Dead In The Morning	Yorke, Margaret	Fiction
Dead Liberty, A	Aird, Catherine	Fiction
Dead Man's Folly	Christie, Agatha	Fiction
Dead Men Never Rise Up	Pattinson, James	Fiction
Dead Of Jericho, The	Dexter, Colin	Fiction
Dead On Arrival	Simpson, Dorothy	Fiction
Dead Reckoning	Llewellyn, Sam	Fiction
Dead, The	Joyce, James	Fiction
Dead Water	Marsh, Ngaio	Fiction
Deadest Thing You Ever Saw, The	Ross, Jonathan	Fiction
Deadly Developments	Ezrin, Arlene	Fiction
Deadly Draw	Floren, Lee	Fiction
Deadly Travellers, The	Eden, Dorothy	Fiction

TITLES INDEX

Title	Author	Type
Deadwood Stage, The	Kilgore, John	Fiction
Dear Enemy	Webster, Jean	Fiction
Dear Pretender	March, Stella	Fiction
Dear Sister	Summers, Judith	Fiction
Dearest Enemy	Taylor, Susan	Fiction
Death And The Joyful Woman	Peters, Ellis	Fiction
Death And The Pregnant Virgin	Haymon, S.T.	Fiction
Death At The Wedding	Duke, Madelaine	Fiction
Death Beyond The Nile	Mann, Jessica	Fiction
Death In Berlin	Kaye, M.M.	Fiction
Death In Camera	Underwood, Michael	Fiction
Death In Cyprus	Kaye, M.M.	Fiction
Death In Ectasy	Marsh, Ngaio	Fiction
Death In Fashion	Babson, Marian	Fiction
Death In High Heels	Brand, Christianna	Fiction
Death In Kashmir	Kaye, M.M.	Fiction
Death In Kenya	Kaye, M.M.	Fiction
Death In The Andamans	Kaye, M.M.	Fiction
Death In Verona	Harley Lewis, Roy	Fiction
Death In Willow Pattern	Burley, W.J.	Fiction
Death In Zanzibar	Kaye, M.M.	Fiction
Death Is A Red Rose	Eden, Dorothy	Fiction
Death Mask	Peters, Ellis	Fiction
Death Of A Con Man	Bell, Josephine	Fiction
Death Of A Dandie Dinmont	Duke, Madelaine	Fiction
Death Of A Ghost	Allingham, Margery	Fiction
Death Of A Good Woman	Eccles, Marjorie	Fiction
Death Of A Holy Murderer	Duke, Madelaine	Fiction
Death Of A Phantom Raider	Gibson, Charles	Non-Fiction
Death Of A Salesman	Miller, Arthur	Fiction
Death Of Abbe Didier, The	Grayson, Richard	Fiction
Death Of An Alderman	Hilton, John Buxton	Fiction
Death Of An Expert Witness	James, P.D.	Fiction
Death Of Jezebel	Brand, Christianna	Fiction
Death On A Quiet Beach	Challis, Simon	Fiction
Death On Account	Yorke, Margaret	Fiction
Death On The Nile	Christie, Agatha	Fiction
Death Roll	Llewellyn, Sam	Fiction
Death Speaks Softly	Fraser, Anthea	Fiction
Death Walk	Quest, Erica	Fiction
Death's Darkest Face	Symons, Julian	Fiction
Decameron, The	Boccaccio, Giovanni	Fiction
Deceiver, The	Forsyth, Frederick	Fiction
Deceivers, The	Masters, John	Fiction
Decembrists, The	Russia	Non-Fiction
Declension Of Adjectives, The	German	Non-Fiction
Declension Of Nouns, The	German	Non-Fiction
Decline Of The Habsburg Monarchy, The	Germany	Non-Fiction
Decollage	French	Non-Fiction
Decolonization	France	Non-Fiction
Deenie	Blume, Judy	Fiction
Deep Purple	Allbeury, Ted	Fiction
Defence In The Fifth Republic	France	Non-Fiction
Delicate Balance, A	Albee, Edward	Fiction
Delight	De La Roche, Mazo	Fiction
Deltic Duties	Trains...	Non-Fiction
Democracy In America	De Tocqueville, Alexis	Non-Fiction
Demolished Man, The	Bester, Alfred	Fiction
Demon	Lermontov, M	Non-Fiction
Demon Bike Rider, The	Leeson, Robert	Fiction
Demon Headmaster, The	Cross, Gillian	Fiction
Der Besuch Der Alten Dame	Durrenmatt, Friedrich	Non-Fiction
Der Gute Mensch Von Sezuan	Brecht, Bertolt	Non-Fiction
Der Prozess	Kafka, Franz	Non-Fiction
Der Richter Und Sein Henker Und Die Tradition De...	Durrenmatt, Friedrich	Non-Fiction
Der Schimmelreiter	Storm, Theodor	Non-Fiction
Der Tod In Venedig	Mann, Thomas	Non-Fiction

TITLES INDEX

Derek And Clive Come Again	Derek & Clive	Fiction
Derek Mahon Reads His Own Poetry	Mahon, Derek	Fiction
Des Teufels General	Zuckmayer, Carl	Non-Fiction
Design For Dying	Morice, Anne	Fiction
Desolation Island	O'Brian, Patrick	Fiction
Detective Wore Silk Drawers, The	Lovesey, Peter	Fiction
Detstvo	Tolstoy, Leo	Non-Fiction
Deutsch Direkt (1, 2, & 3)	German	Non-Fiction
Deutsch Express	German	Non-Fiction
Development Of British Society - 1914-1945, The	Social Sciences	Non-Fiction
Development Of India, The	History	Non-Fiction
Development Of Jane Austen's Comic Art, The	A-Level	Non-Fiction
Development Of The German Language, The	German	Non-Fiction
Development Of The Russian Language, The	Russian	Non-Fiction
Deviance	Social Sciences	Non-Fiction
Devices And Desires	James, P.D.	Fiction
Devil And Daniel Webster, The	Benet, Stephen Vincent	Fiction
Devil And Mary Ann	Cookson, Catherine	Fiction
Devil On Horseback, The	Holt, Victoria	Fiction
Devil On Lamas Night, The	Howatch, Susan	Fiction
Devil Rides Out, The	Wheatley, Dennis	Fiction
Devil's Alternative, The	Forsyth, Frederick	Fiction
Devil's Own, The	Edwards, Olwen	Fiction
Devil's Waltz, The	Smith, Sydney Goodsir	Fiction
Diamond As Big As The Ritz, The	Fitzgerald, F. Scott	Fiction
Diamond Hunters, The	Smith, Wilbur	Fiction
Diamonds Are Forever	Fleming, Ian	Fiction
Diana's Story	Longden, Deric	Fiction
Diaries 1915-1918, The	Sassoon, Siegfried	Non-Fiction
Diary Of A Country Doctor	Duncan, Alex	Fiction
Diary Of A Nobody, The	Grossmith, G & W	Fiction
Diary Of A Provincial Lady, The	Delafield, E.M.	Fiction
Diary Of A Somebody	Matthew, Christopher	Fiction
Diary Of Anne Frank, The	Frank, Anne	Non-Fiction
Diary Of Samuel Pepys	Pepys, Samuel	Non-Fiction
Dice	Dice Clay, Andrew	Fiction
Dick Barton	Radio	Fiction
Dick Tracy	Gould, Chester	Fiction
Dick Whittington	Children's Stories..	Fiction
Dick Whittington	Traditional	Fiction
Dick Whittington And His Cat	Traditional	Fiction
Dickens	Dickens, Charles	Non-Fiction
Diddakoi, The	Godden, Rumer	Fiction
Die Judenbuche	Von Droste-Hulshoff	Non-Fiction
Die Leiden Des Jungen Werther	Von Goethe, J.W.	Non-Fiction
Die Marquise Von O And Das	German	Non-Fiction
Die Rich, Die Happy	Munro, James	Fiction
Die Verlorene Ehre Der Katharina Blum	Boll, Heinrich	Non-Fiction
Die Verwandlung	Kafka, Franz	Non-Fiction
Diesels On Dainton	Trains...	Non-Fiction
Diesels On The Lickey Incline	Trains...	Non-Fiction
Different Drum, The	Self Improvement	Non-Fiction
Different Drummer, A	Egleton, Clive	Fiction
Different Woman, A	Webster, Jan	Fiction
Digame	Spanish	Non-Fiction
Digby	Hill, Pamela	Fiction
Dinosaur Brains	Business	Non-Fiction
Dinosaurs	Early Learning	Non-Fiction
Dirty Beasts	Dahl, Roald	Fiction
Disaster With The Fiend	Lavelle, Sheila	Fiction
Discover Inner Energy And Overcome Stress	Self Improvement	Non-Fiction
Discover What You're Best At	Self Improvement	Non-Fiction
Discovering Portuguese	Portuguese	Non-Fiction
Discovering Rhythm & Rhyme In Poetry	Untermeyer, Louis	Fiction
Discussion Of Modern Greek Poetry	Greek	Non-Fiction
Disorderly Elements	Cook, Bob	Fiction
Disraeli	History	Non-Fiction

TITLES INDEX

Title	Author	Category
Disraeli	Social Sciences	Non-Fiction
Distaff Side, The	Paige, Frances	Fiction
Distant Strangers, The	Harcourt, Palma	Fiction
Divine Comedy, The	Dante	Fiction
Dni Turbinykh	Bulgakov, M	Non-Fiction
Do More In Less Time	Self Improvement	Non-Fiction
Doctor At Large	Gordon, Richard	Fiction
Doctor Brent's Broken Journey	Lester, Jane	Fiction
Doctor David	Allan, Margaret	Fiction
Doctor De Soto	Steig, William	Fiction
Doctor Faustus	Marlowe, Christopher	Fiction
Doctor Is On The Market, The	Burroughs, William S.	Fiction
Doctor Mary Courage	Stuart, Alex	Fiction
Doctor On Approval	Mcconnell, Jean	Fiction
Doctor On Horseback	Stuart, Alex	Fiction
Doctor On The Boil	Gordon, Richard	Fiction
Doctor Thorne	Trollope, Anthony	Fiction
Doctor Who	Radio	Fiction
Doctor Who And The Pescatons	Television	Fiction
Doctor Zhivago	Pasternak, Boris	Fiction
Doctor's Affairs All Told, The	Duncan, Alex	Fiction
Dod And Davie	Busch, Wilhelm	Fiction
Dodos Are Forever	King-Smith, Dick	Fiction
Dog Crusoe, The	Ballantyne, R.M.	Fiction
Dogmatic	Barker, Les	Fiction
Dogs Of War / Shall We Tell The President...	Mystery	Fiction
Doing Business In Japan	Japanese...	Non-Fiction
Doing It Now	Business	Non-Fiction
Doll's House, A	Ibsen, Henrik	Fiction
Domino Principle, The	Kennedy, Adam	Fiction
Domino Vendetta, The	Kennedy, Adam	Fiction
Don Carlos	Von Schiller, F	Non-Fiction
Don Juan	Moliere	Fiction
Don Juan: The Sorcerer	Casteneda, Carlos	Non-Fiction
Don Quixote	De Cervantes, Miguel	Fiction
Donald's Pooch Parlour	Disney	Fiction
Donkey Cabbages, The	Children's Stories..	Fiction
Don't Bother To Knock	Chambers, Peter	Fiction
Don't Crush That Dwarf, Hand Me The Pliers	Firesign Theatre	Fiction
Don't Know Boy, The	Traditional	Fiction
Don't Look Now, The Birds	Du Maurier, Daphne	Fiction
Don't Run From Love	Hagar, Judith	Fiction
Doomed Oasis, The	Innes, Hammond	Fiction
Door Between, The	Queen, Ellery	Fiction
Dorian Gray	Wilde, Oscar	Fiction
Dorothy Parker Stories	Parker, Dorothy	Fiction
Do's And Don't's Of Delegation	Business	Non-Fiction
Double Bill	Ayckbourn, Alan	Fiction
Double Bill	Coward, Noel	Fiction
Double Bill	Rattigan, Terence	Fiction
Double Deceit	Harcourt, Palma	Fiction
Double Double Oil And Trouble	Lathen, Emma	Fiction
Double Feature	Stamp, Terence	Non-Fiction
Double Head Of Steam	Trains...	Non-Fiction
Double Indemnity	Cain, James M	Fiction
Double Jeopardy	Forbes, Colin	Fiction
Double Jeopardy	Underwood, Michael	Fiction
Double Scotch, A	Morgan, Edwin	Fiction
Double Trouble	Superman	Fiction
Double Vision	Higgins Clark, Mary	Fiction
Doubtful Company	Street, Pamela	Fiction
Down And Out In Paris And London	Orwell, George	Non-Fiction
Down From The Hill	Sillitoe, Alan	Fiction
Down Our Street	Kennedy, Lena	Fiction
Down To Earth	Elliot, Emily	Non-Fiction
Down Town	McBain, Ed	Fiction
Dr. Jekyll And Mr. Hyde	Stevenson, Robert Louis	Fiction

TITLES INDEX

Title	Author	Category
Dr. No	Fleming, Ian	Fiction
Dr Sam: Johnson, Detector	De La Torre, Lilian	Fiction
Dracula	Stoker, Bram	Fiction
Dracula Murders, The	Daniels, Philip	Fiction
Dragon Den, The	Murray, William	Fiction
Dragon Slayer	Sutcliff, Rosemary	Fiction
Dragonlance Chronicles Vol.1	Weis & Hickman	Fiction
Dragon's Teeth, The	Queen, Ellery	Fiction
Dramatist Speaks, The	Wesker, Arnold	Fiction
Draussen Vor Der Tur	Borchert, W	Non-Fiction
Dream Of A Strange Land	Greene, Graham	Fiction
Dream Of Orchids	Whitney, Phyllis A	Fiction
Dream Solutions-find Your Answers In Your Dreams	Self Improvement	Non-Fiction
Dreams And Dreaming	Self Improvement	Non-Fiction
Dream-Time, Splintered Sword	Treece, Henry	Fiction
Dream-Time, The	Treece, Henry	Fiction
Drei Novellen	Storm, Theodor	Non-Fiction
Dreyfus Affair, The	Social Sciences	Non-Fiction
Dropped Dead	Ross, Jonathan	Fiction
Drowned World, The	Ballard, J.G.	Fiction
Drunk Man Looks At The Thistle, A	MacDiarmid, Hugh	Non-Fiction
Dual Engima	Underwood, Michael	Fiction
Dublin 4	Binchy, Maeve	Fiction
Duchess Of Duke Street, The	Hardwick, Mollie	Fiction
Duchess Of Malfi, The	Webster, John	Fiction
Duchess, The	Deveraux, Jude	Fiction
Ducktails	Disney	Fiction
Duel In The Dark, A	Townsend, Peter	Non-Fiction
Dumbo	Disney	Fiction
Dune Trilogy Soundbook	Herbert, Frank	Fiction
Duplicate Death	Heyer, Georgette	Fiction
Dust In The Lion's Paw	Stark, Freya	Non-Fiction
Dutch Cassette Course	Dutch	Non-Fiction
Dutch For Travel	Dutch	Non-Fiction
Dutch Language Basics	Dutch	Non-Fiction
Dutch Republic In The 17th Century, The	Netherlands	Non-Fiction
Dutch Travel Pack	Dutch	Non-Fiction
Dying To Meet You	Gill, B.M.	Fiction
Dylan Thomas And Edith Sitwell Read Her Poems	Sitwell, Dame Edith	Fiction
Dylan Thomas Reading His Poetry	Thomas, Dylan	Fiction
Dylan Thomas Reads A Personal Anthology	Thomas, Dylan	Fiction
Dynamic Diesels	Trains...	Non-Fiction
E M Forster	Forster, E.M.	Non-Fiction
Eager Heart, The	Pyatt, Rosina	Fiction
Eagle Has Flown	Higgins, Jack	Fiction
Eagle Has Landed, The	Higgins, Jack	Fiction
Eagle In The Sky	Smith, Wilbur	Fiction
Eagle Trail	Howard, Troy	Fiction
Early 60's Steam	Trains...	Non-Fiction
Early Soviet Cinema	Russia	Non-Fiction
Early Stages	Gielgud, Sir John	Non-Fiction
East Of Desolation	Higgins, Jack	Fiction
Eastern Arabic	Arabic	Non-Fiction
Eavesdropper	Francombe, John	Fiction
Ebdon's England	Ebdon, John	Non-Fiction
Ebdon's Odyssey	Ebdon, John	Non-Fiction
Echoes From The Macabre	Dyall, Valentine	Fiction
Echoes Of Engines	Trains...	Non-Fiction
Economics	G.C.S.E.	Non-Fiction
Ecstasy Of Angus, The	Flaherty, Liam	Fiction
Edge Of Glass	Gaskin, Catherine	Fiction
Edge, The	Francis, Dick	Fiction
Edinburgh Calendar, The	Fergusson, Robert	Fiction
Edinburgh Excursion	Andrews, Lucilla	Fiction
Edith Sitwell Reading Her Poems	Sitwell, Dame Edith	Fiction
Education	Social Sciences	Non-Fiction
Education In The Federal Republic Of Germany	Germany	Non-Fiction

TITLES INDEX

Title	Author	Category
Edward Gets The Hiccups	Cole, Michael	Fiction
Edward, Gordon And Henry	Awdry, Rev. W.	Fiction
Edward II	Marlowe, Christopher	Fiction
Edward Joins The Band	Cole, Michael	Fiction
Edward Lear's Nonsense Rhymes	Lear, Edward	Fiction
E.E. Cummings Reading	Cummings, E.E.	Fiction
E.E. Cummings Reads His Poetry	Cummings, E.E.	Fiction
Effi Briest	Fontaine, T.H.	Non-Fiction
Egmont	Von Goethe, J.W.	Non-Fiction
Eight Feet In The Andes	Murphy, Devia	Non-Fiction
Eighteenth Emergency, The	Byars, Betsy	Fiction
Eighth Dwarf, The	Thomas, Ross	Fiction
El Caballero De Olmedo	De Vega Carpio, Lope	Non-Fiction
El Ingles Simplificado	English	Non-Fiction
Elephant Song	Smith, W	Fiction
Elephant's Child, The	Kipling, Rudyard	Fiction
Elise Ou La Vraie Vie	Etcherelli, Claire	Non-Fiction
Elizabeth I	Elizabeth I	Non-Fiction
Elizabeth I	History	Non-Fiction
Elizabeth Taylor	Kelly, Kitty	Non-Fiction
Elizabethan England	History	Non-Fiction
Ellie And The Hagwitch	Cresswell, Helen	Fiction
Elusive Mrs. Pollifax, The	Gilman, Dorothy	Fiction
Elves And The Shoemaker, The	Children's Stories..	Fiction
Elves And The Shoemaker, The	Grimm	Fiction
Emil In The Soup Tureen	Lindgren, Astrid	Fiction
Emilia Galotti	Lessing G.E.	Non-Fiction
Emily	Cooper, Jilly	Fiction
Emily	Gater, Dilys	Fiction
Emily Bronte	Bronte, Emily	Non-Fiction
Emlyn's Moon	Nimmo, Jenny	Fiction
Emma	Austen, Jane	Fiction
Emma	Radio	Fiction
Emma And Co.	Hocken, Sheila	Non-Fiction
Emma Dilemma, The	Sefton, Catherine	Fiction
Emma Hamilton	Hamilton, Emma	Non-Fiction
Emma Sparrow	Joseph, Marie	Fiction
Emma's Ghost	Sefton, Catherine	Fiction
Emotions And Cancer	Self Improvement	Non-Fiction
Emperor And The Nightingale, The	Traditional	Fiction
Emperor Charles V, The	France	Non-Fiction
Emperor Jones, The	O'Neill, Eugene	Fiction
Emperor's New Clothes, The	Andersen, Hans Christian	Fiction
Empire Of The Sun	Ballard, J.G.	Fiction
Empire To Commonwealth	Social Sciences	Non-Fiction
Empty Moon, The	Widdicombe, Susan	Fiction
Empty Nest, The	Cadell, Elizabeth	Fiction
Emu's Pink Windmill Adventures	Hull, Rod & Emu	Fiction
Enchanted April, The	Von Armin, Elizabeth	Fiction
Enchanted Orchestra, The	Niven, David	Fiction
Enchanted Wood, The	Blyton, Enid	Fiction
Enchantment	Chard, Judy	Fiction
Enchantment	Dickens, Monica	Fiction
End Of Romanov Russia, The	Russia	Non-Fiction
End Of The Affair, The	Greene, Graham	Fiction
End Of The Tale, The	Corbett, W.J.	Fiction
End Of The Tether, The	Conrad, Joseph	Fiction
Endless Game, The	Forbes, Bryan	Fiction
Enemy, The	Bagley, Desmond	Fiction
Engines From Derby And Crewe	Trains...	Non-Fiction
Engines With Accents	Trains...	Non-Fiction
England V The West Indies	Cricket	Non-Fiction
England's Mistress	Peters, Maureen	Fiction
English And Dutch Trade	History	Non-Fiction
English Cassette Course	English	Non-Fiction
English Child In France, An	French	Non-Fiction
English (Course)	G.C.S.E.	Non-Fiction

TITLES INDEX

English Girl, The	Driver, Grace	Fiction
English In A Week Pack	English	Non-Fiction
English Language	G.C.E.. O Level...	Non-Fiction
English Literature	G.C.E. O Level...	Non-Fiction
English Monarchs	History	Non-Fiction
English Novel Today: From Dickens To Snow, The	English Literature	Non-Fiction
English Parliaments In Perspective	Social Sciences	Non-Fiction
English Simplified	English	Non-Fiction
English With A Dialect	English	Non-Fiction
English With An Accent	English	Non-Fiction
Enjoy Your Slimming With Eileen Fowler	Health & Fitness	Non-Fiction
Enlightenment, The	Social Sciences	Non-Fiction
Enormous Crocodile, The	Dahl, Roald	Fiction
Enquiry	Francis, Dick	Fiction
Enrico IV - Two Tragic Humourists	Pirandello, Luigo	Non-Fiction
Entre Nous	French	Non-Fiction
Environmental Atmospheres: Australia	Environmental Sounds	Non-Fiction
Epic Poems	Poetry	Fiction
Episode At Toledo, The	Bridge, Ann	Fiction
Epitaph For A Spy	Ambler, Eric	Fiction
Equality Of Love	Edwards, Dorothy	Fiction
Escape From Germany	Crawley, Aidan	Non-Fiction
ESP Is Alive And Well	Self Improvement	Non-Fiction
Espana Viva (1 & 2)	Spanish	Non-Fiction
Essential Combat And Disaster Sound Effects	Sound Effects	Non-Fiction
Essential Death And Horror (1 & 2)	Sound Effects	Non-Fiction
Essential Hi-Tech	Sound Effects	Non-Fiction
Essential Home Video Sound Effects	Sound Effects	Non-Fiction
Essential McGough, The	McGough, Roger	Fiction
Essential Science Fiction	Sound Effects	Non-Fiction
Essential Shakespeare, The	Shakespeare, William	Fiction
Essential Sound Effects (1 & 2)	Sound Effects	Non-Fiction
Essie	Pearce, Flora	Fiction
E.T. The Extra Terrestrial	Films	Fiction
Ethnic Prince	Machiavelli	Non-Fiction
European Cup Final-1968	Football	Non-Fiction
European Cup Final-1977	Football	Non-Fiction
European Cup Final-1978	Football	Non-Fiction
European Cup Final-1981	Football	Non-Fiction
European Cup Final-1982	Football	Non-Fiction
European Cup Finals-1979 And 1980	Football	Non-Fiction
European Socialism In The 19th Century	Social Sciences	Non-Fiction
Evangelical Religion And Society From 1789-1859	Religious	Non-Fiction
Eve Of St. Venus	Burgess, Anthony	Fiction
Evelyn Waugh	Waugh, Evelyn	Non-Fiction
Evening At Alfie's, An	Hughes, Shirley	Fiction
Evening Gull, The	Tangye, Derek	Non-Fiction
Evening News, The	Hailey, Arthur	Fiction
Evening Wasted With Tom Lehrer, An	Lehrer, Tom	Fiction
Evening With Quentin Crisp, An	Crisp, Quentin	Non-Fiction
Evening With Spike Milligan	Milligan, Spike	Fiction
Evening With Wally Londo, An	Carlin, George	Fiction
Evensong At Exeter Cathedral	Religious	Non-Fiction
Everyday Heroics Of Living And Dying	Self Improvement	Non-Fiction
Everyday Stories	Children's Stories..	Fiction
Everyday Yoga	Health & Fitness	Non-Fiction
Everyman-Visions From Piers Plowman	Langland, William	Fiction
Everything Comes Up Blank	Gould, Chester	Fiction
Eve's Apples	Kennedy, Lena	Fiction
Ewes And I	Arthursson, Elizabeth	Non-Fiction
Ex 'n' Dans	Health & Fitness	Non-Fiction
Excellence In Organization	Business	Non-Fiction
Excerpts From Christmas Stories	Dickens, Charles	Fiction
Executive ESP	Business	Non-Fiction
Executive Japanese	Japanese...	Non-Fiction
Existentialist Writing	Mailer, Norman	Non-Fiction
Exocet	Higgins, Jack	Fiction

TITLES INDEX

Exorcism Of Brother Simeon, The	Ghost Stories	Non-Fiction
Expectant Father	Health & Fitness	Non-Fiction
Expectant Mother	Health & Fitness	Non-Fiction
Experience High Self-Esteem	Self Improvement	Non-Fiction
Exploits Of Brigadier Gerard	Conan Doyle, Arthur	Fiction
Exploits Of Don Quixote	De Cervantes, Miguel	Fiction
Expressionism	Picasso & Rouault	Non-Fiction
Extracts From Paradise Lost	Milton, John	Fiction
Eye Of The Needle	Follett, Ken	Fiction
Eye Of The Tiger, The	Smith, Wilbur	Fiction
F Scott Fitzgerald	A-Level	Non-Fiction
F.A. Cup Final-1972	Football	Non-Fiction
Fables	De La Fontaine, J	Non-Fiction
Fables	French	Non-Fiction
Fables Of Aesop, The	Aesop	Fiction
Fables Of India	Traditional	Fiction
Face Of Death, The	Grant-Adamson, Lesley	Fiction
Facts Of Life, The	Maugham, W. Somerset	Fiction
Faerie Queen	Spenser, Edmund	Fiction
Fair Eleanor, Christ Thee Save	Kinsella, Thomas	Fiction
Fair Prisoner	Bromige, Iris	Fiction
Fair Stood The Wind For France	Bates, H.E.	Fiction
Fairy Rebel, The	Reid Banks, Lynne	Fiction
Fairy Tales	Traditional	Fiction
Fairy Tales For You	Traditional	Fiction
Falcon For A Queen, A	Gaskin, Catherine	Fiction
Falcon's Lure	Malcolm, Alix	Fiction
Falklands War, The	Military History	Non-Fiction
Fall Of An Eagle, The	Cleary, Jon	Fiction
Fall Of The House Of Usher	Poe, Edgar Allan	Fiction
Fallen Into The Pit	Peters, Ellis	Fiction
Falling	Thubron, Colin	Fiction
Falling Towards England	James, Clive	Non-Fiction
Families And How To Survive	Skynner, Dr Robin	Non-Fiction
Family Gathering	Cadell, Elizabeth	Fiction
Family Keep Fit With Eileen Fowler	Health & Fitness	Non-Fiction
Family Madness, A	Keneally, Thomas	Fiction
Family Reunion	Eliot, T.S.	Fiction
Famous Cases Of Sherlock Holmes	Conan Doyle, Arthur	Fiction
Fanny And The Monsters	Lively, Penelope	Fiction
Fanny Hill	Cleland, John	Fiction
Fanny McBride	Cookson, Catherine	Fiction
Fanso And Granny Flo	Berry, James	Fiction
Fantastic Mr. Fox	Dahl, Roald	Fiction
Fantastic Tales	Bradbury, Ray	Fiction
Far Country, The	Shute, Nevil	Fiction
Far Cry From Kensington, A	Spark, Muriel	Fiction
Far From The Madding Crowd	A-Level	Non-Fiction
Far From The Madding Crowd	Hardy, Thomas	Fiction
Farce About Face	Rix, Sir Brian	Non-Fiction
Farewell To Steam	Trains...	Non-Fiction
Farewell To The Deltics	Trains...	Non-Fiction
Farewell To The Forties	Trains...	Non-Fiction
Farewell To The North Enclosure	Boyce, Max	Fiction
Farmer's Ingle And Other Poems, The	Fergusson, Robert	Fiction
Farthest Shore	Le Guin, Ursula	Fiction
Fascism	Social Sciences	Non-Fiction
Fascism In Italy 1919-1945	Italy	Non-Fiction
Fashion In Shrouds, The	Allingham, Margery	Fiction
Fast Men, The	McNab, Tom	Fiction
Fatal Eggs, The	Samuels, Arthur	Fiction
Fatal Inversion, A	Vine, Barbara	Fiction
Fateful Decision	Theydon, Jean	Fiction
Father Brown	Chesterton, G.K.	Fiction
Favourite European Tales	Traditional	Fiction
Favourite Fairy Stories	Traditional	Fiction
Favourite Fairy Tales	Traditional	Fiction

TITLES INDEX

Favourite Poems	Poetry	Fiction
Favourite Rupert Bear Stories	Bestall, Alfred	Fiction
Favourite Rupert Stories	Bestall, Alfred	Fiction
Fawlty Towers	Television	Fiction
Fear Is The Key	MacLean, Alistair	Fiction
Feather On The Moon	Whitney, Phyllis A	Fiction
Feel Secure Now	Self Improvement	Non-Fiction
Feel The Fear And Do It Anyway	Self Improvement	Non-Fiction
Female Handle With Care	Chambers, Peter	Fiction
Fen Tiger, The	Marchant, Catherine	Fiction
Fenwick Houses	Cookson, Catherine	Fiction
Festival At Farbridge	Priestley, J.B.	Fiction
Few Green Leaves, A	Pym, Barbara	Fiction
Fiddler Of The Reels	Hardy, Thomas	Fiction
Field Of Blood	Seymour, Gerald	Fiction
Fiend Next Door, The	Lavelle, Sheila	Fiction
Fiery Dragon, The	Nesbitt, Edith	Fiction
Fifteen Streets, The	Cookson, Catherine	Fiction
Fifth Child, The	Lessing, Doris	Fiction
Fifty Pawky Poems	Poetry	Fiction
File On Devlin, The	Gaskin, Catherine	Fiction
Fillets Of Plaice	Durrell, Gerald	Fiction
Final Rip Off, The	Monty Python	Fiction
Final Test, The	Owen, Gareth	Fiction
Financial Self Defence	Business	Non-Fiction
Find Your Inner Happiness	Self Improvement	Non-Fiction
Fine Night For Dying, A	Higgins, Jack	Fiction
Finnish For Foreigners	Finnish	Non-Fiction
Fiona	Gaskin, Catherine	Fiction
Fire Down Below	Golding, William	Fiction
Fire On The Farm	Wimpole Village	Fiction
Firebird, The	Children's Stories..	Fiction
Fireman Sam	Wilmer, Diane	Fiction
First Among Equals	Archer, Jeffrey	Fiction
First Anansi Story, The	Traditional	Fiction
First Class	Gray, Caroline	Fiction
First Industrial Revolution, The	Social Sciences	Non-Fiction
First Queen Elizabeth	Elizabeth 1	Non-Fiction
First Story In The World, The	Bible	Non-Fiction
First Term At Malory Towers	Blyton, Enid	Fiction
First Twenty Years, The	Calvino	Non-Fiction
First Words	Early Learning	Non-Fiction
First World War Poets	English Literature	Non-Fiction
First World War Poets: Owen & Rosenburg	A-Level	Non-Fiction
Fisherman And His Wife, The	Children's Stories..	Fiction
Fit To Ski	Health & Fitness	Non-Fiction
Five Children And It	Nesbitt, Edith	Fiction
Five Days To An Organized Life	Self Improvement	Non-Fiction
Five Examples Of Sense And Sensibility In Modern...	Ginzburg, Natalia	Non-Fiction
Five Get Into A Fix	Blyton, Enid	Fiction
Five Get Into Trouble	Blyton, Enid	Fiction
Five Go Adventuring Again	Blyton, Enid	Fiction
Five Go Off In A Caravan	Blyton, Enid	Fiction
Five Go Off To Camp	Blyton, Enid	Fiction
Five Go To Billycock Hill	Blyton, Enid	Fiction
Five Go To Demon's Rock	Blyton, Enid	Fiction
Five Go To Mystery Moor	Blyton, Enid	Fiction
Five Grand Nationals 1973-1977	Horse Racing	Non-Fiction
Five Have A Mystery To Solve	Blyton, Enid	Fiction
Five Have A Wonderful Time	Blyton, Enid	Fiction
Five Have Plenty Of Fun	Blyton, Enid	Fiction
Five Hundred Mile Walkies	Wallington, Mark	Fiction
Five On A Hike Together	Blyton, Enid	Fiction
Five On A Secret Trail	Blyton, Enid	Fiction
Five On A Treasure Island	Blyton, Enid	Fiction
Five On Finniston Farm	Blyton, Enid	Fiction
Five On Kirrin Island Again	Blyton, Enid	Fiction

TITLES INDEX

Title	Author	Category
Five One-Act Plays	Yeats, W.B.	Fiction
Five Passengers From Lisbon	Eberhart, Mignon G	Fiction
Five Red Herrings, The	Sayers, Dorothy L.	Fiction
Five Steps To Successful Selling	Business	Non-Fiction
Five Tales Of The Brothers Grimm	Grimm	Fiction
Flagship Hood	Briggs, Ted	Non-Fiction
Flame Of Diablo	Craven, Sara	Fiction
Flameout	Peel, Colin D	Fiction
Flaming Tree, The	Whitney, Phyllis A	Fiction
Flash Gordon	Raymond, Alex	Fiction
Flat Stanley	Brown, Jeff	Fiction
Flaubert's Parrot	Barnes, Julian	Fiction
Fledgling Spy, The	Le Carre, John	Fiction
Flickering Flame, The	March, Stella	Fiction
Flight Into Danger	Hailey, John	Fiction
Flight Of The Intruder, The	Coonts, Stephen	Fiction
Flight To The Sea	Pattinson, James	Fiction
Floating Prison, The	Leroux, Gaston	Fiction
Florence Nightingale	Nightingale, Florence	Non-Fiction
Florence Nightingale	Strachey, Lytton	Non-Fiction
Flossie Teacake - Again	Davies, Hunter	Fiction
Flossie Teacake Strikes Back	Davies, Hunter	Fiction
Flossie Teacake's Fur Coat	Davies, Hunter	Fiction
Flotsam And Jetsam	Flotsam & Jetsam	Fiction
Flowers For The God Of Love	Cartland, Barbara	Fiction
Flowers From The Doctor	Andrews, Lucilla	Fiction
Flowers In The Attic	Andrews, Virginia	Fiction
Flyaway	Bagley, Desmond	Fiction
Flying Finish	Francis, Dick	Fiction
Flying Hero Class	Keneally, Thomas	Fiction
Flying Saucer Mystery, The	Ghost Stories	Non-Fiction
Flying Scotsman And Other Locomotives	Trains...	Non-Fiction
Flywheel, Shyster And Flywheel	Radio	Fiction
Folk Of The Faraway Tree, The	Blyton, Enid	Fiction
Folk Tales From Around The World	Traditional	Fiction
Folk Tales Of The Tribes Of Africa	Traditional	Fiction
Follow Me To The Seaside	Trower, Terry	Fiction
Following Jesus	Bible	Non-Fiction
Fonvizin - His Life And Literary Career	Fonvizin, D	Non-Fiction
Foo Foo Shufflewick And Her Exotic Banana	Harding, Mike	Fiction
Food For Millions	Social Sciences	Non-Fiction
Fool Britannia	Comedy...	Fiction
Foolish Virgin, The	Penn, Margaret	Non-Fiction
Footloose In The Himalaya	Harding, Mike	Non-Fiction
Footsteps In The Dark	Heyer, Georgette	Fiction
For Adults Only	Cosby, Bill	Fiction
For All But One	March, Stella	Fiction
For Kicks	Francis, Dick	Fiction
For Special Services	Gardner, John	Fiction
For The Love Of Sara	Mather, Anne	Fiction
Forests And Mountains Of Asia	Environmental Sounds	Non-Fiction
Forests Of The Amazon	Environmental Sounds	Non-Fiction
Forfeit	Francis, Dick	Fiction
Forgetting's No Excuse	Scott, Mary	Non-Fiction
Forgiving Heart	Baxter, Olive	Fiction
Forgotten Heritage, A	Aitken, Hannah	Fiction
Forgotten Story, The	Graham, Winston	Fiction
Formation Of The Russian State, The	Russia	Non-Fiction
Forrestal Lecture At The U.S. Naval Academy	Heinlein, Robert	Non-Fiction
Forsaken	Gibbon, Lewis Grassic	Fiction
Forsyte Saga, The (parts 1 - 6)	Galsworthy, John	Fiction
Fortunate Grandchild, A	Read, Miss	Non-Fiction
Fortune Is A Woman	Graham, Winston	Fiction
Fortunes Of Love, The	Courtney, Caroline	Fiction
Forty Years On	Bennett, Alan	Fiction
Foundation And Empire	Asimov, Isaac	Fiction
Foundation: The Psychohistorians	Asimov, Isaac	Fiction

TITLES INDEX

Foundation Trilogy, The	Asimov, Isaac	Fiction
Foundations Edge	Asimov, Isaac	Fiction
Fountains Of Paradise	Clarke, Arthur C	Fiction
Four Abridged Stories	Higgins, Jack	Fiction
Four Classic Stories	Children's Stories..	Fiction
Four Dragon Stories	Nesbitt, Edith	Fiction
Four Faces Of Chubby Brown, The	Brown, Roy 'Chubby'	Fiction
Four Feathers	Mason, A.E.W.	Fiction
Four Just Men	Wallace, Edgar	Fiction
Four Linmill Stories	McLellan, Robert	Non-Fiction
Four Modern Poets	English Literature	Non-Fiction
Four Of Your Favourite Stories From Grimm	Grimm	Fiction
Four Sherlock Holmes Stories	Conan Doyle, Arthur	Fiction
Four Short Stories	Gaskell, Elizabeth	Fiction
Four Spanish Short Stories	Spain...	Fiction
Four Stories	Grimm	Fiction
Four Traditional Fairy Tales	Traditional	Fiction
Four Twentieth Century Poets	Poetry	Fiction
Fourteen Minutes: The Sinking Of The Empress ...	Croall, James	Non-Fiction
Fourth Folly	Treves, Kathleen	Fiction
Fourth Protocol, The	Forsyth, Frederick	Fiction
Fox Busters, The	King-Smith, Dick	Fiction
Fox, The	Lawrence, D.H.	Fiction
Foxwood Tales	Paterson, Cynthia	Fiction
Fragile Peace, A	Crane, Teresa	Fiction
Fragment Of Time, A	Graham, Margaret	Fiction
Framework For New Knowledge	Social Sciences	Non-Fiction
Framley Parsonage	Trollope, Anthony	Fiction
Franc Parler	French	Non-Fiction
France Travel Kit	French	Non-Fiction
Frances	Hoban, Russell	Fiction
Franchise Affair, The	Tey, Josephine	Fiction
Francis Drake	Drake, Sir Francis	Non-Fiction
Franco: The Man And The Ruler	Spain...	Non-Fiction
Frankenstein	Shelley, Mary	Fiction
Frankie's Hat	Mark, Jan	Fiction
Franz Joseph Haydn 1732 -1809	Haydn (Composer)	Non-Fiction
Frau Jenny Treibel	Fontaine, T.H.	Non-Fiction
Fred The Fisherman	Television	Fiction
Freddy The Detective	Brooks, Walter R.	Fiction
Freedom Come All Ye	Henderson, Hamish	Non-Fiction
Freedom Road	Fast, Howard	Fiction
Freedom Trap, The	Bagley, Desmond	Fiction
French Alexandrine And The Sonnet, The	French Literature	Non-Fiction
French At The Wheel	French	Non-Fiction
French Business Cassette Course	French	Non-Fiction
French Cassette Course	French	Non-Fiction
French (Course)	G.C.S.E..	Non-Fiction
French Extra	French	Non-Fiction
French For Business	French	Non-Fiction
French For Travel	French	Non-Fiction
French Language Basics	French	Non-Fiction
French Legal And Commercial Professions	French	Non-Fiction
French Lieutenant's Woman, The	Fowles, John	Fiction
French Local Government	France	Non-Fiction
French Outside France: French Speaking Switzerland	French	Non-Fiction
French Outside France: Le Francais Du Quebec	French	Non-Fiction
French Phonology	French	Non-Fiction
French Political Parties - Part 1	France	Non-Fiction
French Political Parties - Part 2	France	Non-Fiction
French Press, The	France	Non-Fiction
French Revolution And The Peasants, The	France	Non-Fiction
French Revolution, The	France	Non-Fiction
French Travel Packs	French	Non-Fiction
French Youth And Its Problems	France	Non-Fiction
Frenchman's Creek	Du Maurier, Daphne	Fiction
Frenchness Of French Literature, The	French Literature	Non-Fiction

TITLES INDEX

Title	Author	Category
Fresh From The Country	Read, Miss	Fiction
Fried Green Tomatoes At The Whistle Stop Cafe	Flagg, Fannie	Fiction
Friend From England, A	Bruckner, Anita	Fiction
Friendly Persuasion	Business	Non-Fiction
Friends And Lovers	MacInnes, Helen	Fiction
Friends At Thrush Green	Read, Miss	Fiction
Frogs And Toads	Environmental Sounds	Non-Fiction
From Doon With Death	Rendell, Ruth	Fiction
From Greece With Love	Fielding, Lucy	Fiction
From Inside The Helmet	Brown, Roy 'Chubby'	Fiction
From Revolution To Industrialisation	Russia	Non-Fiction
From Solitude With Love	Thomson, Daisy	Fiction
From The Dead	Nesbitt, Edith	Fiction
From The Footplate	Trains...	Non-Fiction
Front Page, The	Hecht, Ben	Fiction
Frontiers Of Management	Business	Non-Fiction
Frost In May	White, Antonia	Fiction
Fruhlings Erwachen	Wedekind, Franz	Non-Fiction
Fsi Basic Amharic	African...	Non-Fiction
Fsi Swedish Basic Course	Swedish	Non-Fiction
Fugitive From Love	Ashwell, Julia	Fiction
Fugitive Year, The	Redmayne, Ann	Fiction
Fula Basic Course	African...	Non-Fiction
Full Moon	Wodehouse, P.G.	Fiction
Full Tilt - Ireland To India With A Bicycle	Murphy, Devia	Non-Fiction
Fun And Games With Postman Pat	Cunliffe, John	Fiction
Fun At One	Radio	Fiction
Fun For The Secret Seven	Blyton, Enid	Fiction
Fundamental Frolics	Comedy...	Fiction
Funeral In Berlin	Deighton, Len	Fiction
Funeral Of Figaro	Peters, Ellis	Fiction
Funny Bones	Ahlberg, Janet & Allan	Fiction
Funny Commercials And Other Radio Fluffs	Radio	Fiction
Further Adventures Of Spot, The	Hill, Eric	Fiction
Further Along The Road Less Travelled	Self Improvement	Non-Fiction
Further Railway Stories	Awdry, Rev. W.	Fiction
Further Tales From A Country Practice	Jackson, Arthur	Non-Fiction
Future Is Ours, The	Graham, Margaret	Fiction
Fuzz	McBain, Ed	Fiction
Gabriel Hounds, The	Stewart, Mary	Fiction
Gaffer Sampson's Luck	Paton Walsh, Jill	Fiction
Gala Week	Clarke, Roy	Fiction
Galahad At Blandings	Wodehouse, P.G.	Fiction
Galapagos	Vonnegut, Kurt	Fiction
Galatians To Thessalonians	Bible	Non-Fiction
Gallowglass	Vine, Barbara	Fiction
Gambling Man, The	Cookson, Catherine	Fiction
Game Of Consequences, A	West, Sarah	Fiction
Gamekeeper, The	Hines, Barry	Fiction
Gandhi	Gandhi	Non-Fiction
Ganz Spontan	German	Non-Fiction
Garden Of Peace	Self Improvement	Non-Fiction
Garden Of The Gods, The	Durrell, Gerald	Fiction
Garden Party, The	Mansfield, Katherine	Fiction
Garment, The	Cookson, Catherine	Fiction
Garrick Year, The	Drabble, Margaret	Fiction
Garrison Hospital	Stuart, Alex	Fiction
Gawain And The Green Knight	Traditional	Fiction
Gawain And The Green Knight And The Pearl	Traditional	Fiction
Gedichte	Morike, E	Non-Fiction
Gellybabe	Bates, Blaster	Fiction
Gemini	Astrology	Non-Fiction
Gender In Russian	Russian	Non-Fiction
Gender Of Nouns, The	German	Non-Fiction
General Prologue From The Canterbury Tales, The	Chaucer, Geoffrey	Fiction
General Strike, The	Social Sciences	Non-Fiction
Genetics Of Environment	Medical	Non-Fiction

TITLES INDEX

Genteel Little Murder, A	Daniels, Philip	Fiction
Gentlemen In England	Wilson, A. & N.	Fiction
Gentlemen Prefer Blondes	Loos, Anita	Fiction
Gently And Deeply	Self Improvement	Non-Fiction
Geography (Course)	G.C.S.E..	Non-Fiction
George And Elizabeth	Duff, David	Non-Fiction
George Elliot	Elliot, George	Non-Fiction
George Frederic Handel	Handel (Composer)	Non-Fiction
George Gershwin Remembered	Gershwin (Composer)	Non-Fiction
George III	History	Non-Fiction
George Orwell	Orwell, George	Non-Fiction
George Washington	Washington, George	Non-Fiction
George's Marvellous Medicine	Dahl, Roald	Fiction
Gerald McBoing Boing	Children's Stories..	Fiction
Gerard Manley Hopkins	Hopkins, Gerard Manley	Non-Fiction
Gerard Manley Hopkins: Modern Or Victorian Poet?	A-Level	Non-Fiction
Gerard Manley Hopkins: The Wreck Of The ...	A-Level	Non-Fiction
German At The Wheel	German	Non-Fiction
German Business Cassette Course	German	Non-Fiction
German Cassette Course	German	Non-Fiction
German For Business	German	Non-Fiction
German For Travel	German	Non-Fiction
German Foreign Policy 1918-1970	History	Non-Fiction
German Language Basics	German	Non-Fiction
German Poetry Since 1945	German Literature	Non-Fiction
German Travel Packs	German	Non-Fiction
German-English Dictionaries And How To Use Them	German	Non-Fiction
Germany 1914-1945	Germany	Non-Fiction
Germany Travel Kit	German	Non-Fiction
Germinal	Zola, Emile	Non-Fiction
Geroi Nashego Vremeni	Russia	Non-Fiction
Gertrude Gooseberry And Belinda Blackcurrent	Garden Gang	Fiction
Get By In Arabic	Arabic	Non-Fiction
Get By In Chinese	Chinese	Non-Fiction
Get By In French	French	Non-Fiction
Get By In German	German	Non-Fiction
Get By In Greek	Greek	Non-Fiction
Get By In Hindi	Hindi	Non-Fiction
Get By In Italian	Italian	Non-Fiction
Get By In Japanese	Japanese...	Non-Fiction
Get By In Portuguese	Portuguese	Non-Fiction
Get By In Russian	Russian...	Non-Fiction
Get By In Spanish	Spanish	Non-Fiction
Get By In Turkish	Turkish	Non-Fiction
Get By Travel Packs	Greek	Non-Fiction
Get By Travel Packs	Japanese...	Non-Fiction
Get By Travel Packs	Arabic	Non-Fiction
Get By Travel Packs	Chinese	Non-Fiction
Get By Travel Packs	French	Non-Fiction
Get By Travel Packs	German	Non-Fiction
Get By Travel Packs	Italian	Non-Fiction
Get By Travel Packs	Portuguese	Non-Fiction
Get By Travel Packs	Russian...	Non-Fiction
Get By Travel Packs	Spanish	Non-Fiction
Get By Travel Packs	Turkish	Non-Fiction
Get Fit With The Green Goddess	Health & Fitness	Non-Fiction
Get Into Shape After Childbirth	Health & Fitness	Non-Fiction
Get It Done Now	Self Improvement	Non-Fiction
Get Right Intae Him	Connolly, Billy	Fiction
Getting On In English	English	Non-Fiction
Getting Organised	Business	Non-Fiction
Getting To Know The General	Greene, Graham	Fiction
Getting To Yes	Business	Non-Fiction
Getting Unstuck: Breaking Through ...	Self Improvement	Non-Fiction
Ghost And Bertie Boggin, The	Sefton, Catherine	Fiction
Ghost Boast	Ghost Stories	Fiction
Ghost Downstairs, The	Garfield, Leon	Fiction

TITLES INDEX

Title	Author	Category
Ghost Of Blacklake, The	Ghost Stories	Fiction
Ghost Of Thomas Kempe, The	Lively, Penelope	Fiction
Ghost Stories	James, M.R.	Fiction
Ghost Story	Straub, Peter	Fiction
Ghostbuster Of The Year	Spurgeon, Maureen	Fiction
Ghostly Companions	Alcock, Vivien	Fiction
Ghosts Of Hungry House Land, The	McBratney, Sam	Fiction
Giants, Gods, Gold And Greece	Greek Mythology	Fiction
Gift Of Fire, The	Hill, David	Fiction
Gift Of The Gods	Cartland, Barbara	Fiction
Gift Of The Magi, The	Henry, O	Fiction
Gifts Of Legends	Self Improvement	Non-Fiction
Gigantic Shadow, The	Symons, Julian	Fiction
Gigolo And Gigolette	Maugham, W. Somerset	Fiction
Gillyvors, The	Cookson, Catherine	Fiction
Ginger Lacey - Fighter Pilot	Townshend Bickers	Fiction
Ginger Tree, The	Wynd, Oswald	Fiction
Gingerbread Boy, The	Children's Stories..	Fiction
Gingerbread Man, The	Traditional	Fiction
Gingerbread Rabbit, The	Jarrell, Randall	Fiction
Giraffe, The Pelley And Me, The	Dahl, Roald	Fiction
Girl Against The Jungle	Vincent, Monica	Fiction
Girl Found Dead	Underwood, Michael	Fiction
Girl From Addis, The	Allbeury, Ted	Fiction
Girl From Nowhere, The	Ross, Stella	Fiction
Girl From The Candle-Lit Bath	Smith, Dodie	Fiction
Girl Like Wigan, A	Leeming, John F.	Fiction
Girl Of The Great Mountain, The	Traditional	Fiction
Girl Of The Sea Of Cortez, The	Benchley, Peter	Fiction
Girl With The Crystal Dove	Hardwick, Mollie	Fiction
Girls In Their Married Bliss	O'Brien, Edna	Fiction
Giuseppe Verdi 1813-1901	Verdi (Composer)	Non-Fiction
Gives Us The Future	Bible	Non-Fiction
Giving A Talk	Webb, Edwin	Non-Fiction
Gladstone	Social Sciences	Non-Fiction
Gladstone And The Liberal Party	History	Non-Fiction
Glamorous Powers	Howatch, Susan	Fiction
Glass Menagerie, The	Williams, Tennessee	Fiction
Glass Virgin, The	Cookson, Catherine	Fiction
Gleg	Scottish	Non-Fiction
Glencoe	Prebble, John	Non-Fiction
Glenda Jackson Reads From Her Storybook	Jackson, Glenda	Fiction
Glenmutchkin Railway, The	Edmonstoune Aytoun, William	Fiction
Glimpse Of Sion's Glory, A	Colegate, Isabel	Fiction
Glittering Images	Howatch, Susan	Fiction
Glo Bug	Children's Stories	Fiction
Glo Butterfly	Children's Stories	Fiction
Glo Cricket	Children's Stories	Fiction
Glo Worm	Children's Stories	Fiction
Glory Boys, The	Seymour, Gerald	Fiction
Glory Of The Garden, The	Chaucer, Geoffrey	Fiction
Gloucestershire Wildlife Tapestry	Wildlife (Natural)	Non-Fiction
Go, Lovely Rose	Potts, Jean	Fiction
Go On I'm Listening	Russell, Robert	Fiction
Go West, Inspector Ghote	Keating, H.R.F.	Fiction
Goal Setting	Self Improvement	Non-Fiction
Goals	Self Improvement	Non-Fiction
Go-Between, The	Hartley, L.P.	Fiction
Goblins At The Bath House	Manning-Sanders, Ruth	Fiction
Gobshite	Sadowitz, Jerry	Fiction
God And The Doctor	Duncan, Alex	Fiction
God's Highlander	Thompson, E.V.	Fiction
God's Own Drunk	Harding, Mike	Fiction
Going Home	Peyton, K.M.	Fiction
Going To The Zoo	Children's Stories..	Fiction
Going Wrong	Rendell, Ruth	Fiction
Gold Mine	Smith, Wilbur	Fiction

TITLES INDEX

Title	Author	Category
Golden Age, The	Cricket	Non-Fiction
Golden Fox	Smith, Wilbur	Fiction
Golden Goose, The	Grimm	Fiction
Golden Hour Of Comedy, A	Comedy...	Fiction
Golden Hour Of Mike Reid	Reid, Mike	Fiction
Golden Hour Of Tony Hancock	Hancock, Tony	Fiction
Golden Keel, The	Bagley, Desmond	Fiction
Golden Rendezvous, The	Maclean, Alistair	Fiction
Golden Slumbers	Gilbert, W.S.	Fiction
Goldilocks	Traditional	Fiction
Goldilocks And The Three Bears	Children's Stories..	Fiction
Goldilocks And The Three Bears	Traditional	Fiction
Goldmine London W1	Daniels, Philip	Fiction
Goldsmith's Wife, The	Plaidy, Jean	Fiction
Golf Courses At Turnberry, The	Golf	Non-Fiction
Golf Omnibus, The	Wodehouse, P.G.	Fiction
Gone With Regret	Trains...	Non-Fiction
Good Behaviour	Keane, Molly	Fiction
Good Companions, The	Priestley, J.B.	Fiction
Good Daughters	Hocking, Mary	Fiction
Good Friday	Holt, Victoria	Fiction
Good Life, The - Health, Wealth And Happiness	Self Improvement	Non-Fiction
Good Provider, The	Stirling, Jessica	Fiction
Good Work	Business	Non-Fiction
Good Work Secret Seven	Blyton, Enid	Fiction
Goodbye California	MaClean, Alistair	Fiction
Goodbye Curate	Secombe, Fred	Fiction
Goodbye Hamilton	Cookson, Catherine	Fiction
Goodbye Mr. Chips	Hilton, James	Fiction
Goodbye To All That	Graves, Robert	Fiction
Goodbye To Berlin	Isherwood, Christopher	Fiction
Goodey's Last Stand	Alverson, Charles	Fiction
Goodnight Stories	Children's Stories..	Fiction
Goon Show Classics	Goons	Fiction
Goon Show Greats	Goons	Fiction
Goon Show, The	Goons	Fiction
Goose Girl, The	Children's Stories..	Fiction
Gore Ot Uma	Griboedov, A	Non-Fiction
Gorky Park	Cruz Smith, Martin	Fiction
Gossip From Thrush Green	Read, Miss	Fiction
Governess, The	Stacey, Kathryn	Fiction
Government And Science In Britain, USA & USSR	Social Sciences	Non-Fiction
Gowie Corby Plays Chicken	Kemp, Gene	Fiction
Gracie	Burns, George	Non-Fiction
Grammatika Lyubvi	Bunin, I	Non-Fiction
Grand Man, A	Cookson, Catherine	Fiction
Grand Prix Of Gibraltar	Ustinov, Peter	Fiction
Grand Sophy, The	Heyer, Georgette	Fiction
Grandma And The Ghowlies	Moray Williams, Ursula	Fiction
Granny Reardun	Garner, Alan	Fiction
Granny Was A Buffer Girl	Doherty, Berlie	Fiction
Granny's Button Box	Everill, Joyce	Fiction
Grapes Of Wrath, The	Steinbeck, John	Fiction
Grass Is Greener, The	Brown, Fred	Non-Fiction
Grave Goods	Mann, Jessica	Fiction
Grave Mistake	Marsh, Ngaio	Fiction
Grave Of Truth, The	Anthony, Evelyn	Fiction
Great British Aircraft	Aviation	Non-Fiction
Great Cricket Matches	Cricket	Non-Fiction
Great Deliverance, A	George, Elizabeth	Fiction
Great Depression Of 1990, The	Social Sciences	Non-Fiction
Great Divide, The	Pern, Stephen	Non-Fiction
Great Escape, The	Brickhill, Paul	Non-Fiction
Great European Short Stories	Short Stories	Fiction
Great Expectations	Dickens, Charles	Fiction
Great Fairy Tales Of The World	Traditional	Fiction
Great Fire Of London, The	Ackroyd, Peter	Fiction

TITLES INDEX

Title	Author	Category
Great Gatsby, The	Fitzgerald, F. Scott	Fiction
Great Little Trains Of England	Trains...	Non-Fiction
Great Memory, A	Self Improvement	Non-Fiction
Great Northern For The North	Trains...	Non-Fiction
Great Piratical Rumbustification, The	Mahy, Margaret	Fiction
Great Profundo, The	MacLaverty, Bernard	Fiction
Great Railway Bazaar By Train Through Asia	Theroux, Paul	Non-Fiction
Great Shakespeareans	Shakespeare, William	Fiction
Great Slump, The	Social Sciences	Non-Fiction
Great Stone Face, The	Hawthorne, Nathaniel	Fiction
Great Switcheroo, The	Dahl, Roald	Fiction
Great Train Record, The	Trains...	Non-Fiction
Great Western In Gloucestershire	Trains...	Non-Fiction
Great Western, The	Trains...	Non-Fiction
Great Women Writers Read Their Work	Short Stories	Fiction
Greatest Management Principle In The World	Business	Non-Fiction
Greatest Of These Is Love	Self Improvement	Non-Fiction
Greatest Thing Since Sliced Bread	Robertson, Don	Fiction
Greek Cassette Course	Greek	Non-Fiction
Greek Fire	Graham, Winston	Fiction
Greek For Travel	Greek	Non-Fiction
Greek Language And People	Greek	Non-Fiction
Greek Language Basics	Greek	Non-Fiction
Greek Travel Pack	Greek	Non-Fiction
Green Empress, The	Cadell, Elizabeth	Fiction
Green Helmet, The	Cleary, Jon	Fiction
Green Hills Of Earth	Heinlein, Robert	Fiction
Green Mansions	Hudson, William H.	Fiction
Green Rushes	Walsh, Maurice	Fiction
Green Smoke	Manning, Rosemary	Fiction
Greengage Summer, The	Godden, Rumer	Fiction
Greenmantle	Buchan, John	Fiction
Green-Sailed Vessel, The	Graves, Robert	Fiction
Gresley Beat, The	Trains...	Non-Fiction
Grey Areas	Davidson, Peter	Fiction
Grey Goose, The	Dessau, Joanna	Fiction
Grey Granite	Gibbon, Lewis Grassic	Fiction
Grey Is The Colour Of Hope	Ratushinskaya, Irina	Non-Fiction
Grey Widow Maker, The	Edwards, Bernard	Non-Fiction
Grim Tales From The Scots	Ghost Stories	Fiction
Grimm Brothers Fairy Tales	Grimm	Fiction
Grimms Fairy Tales	Grimm	Fiction
Grinny	Fisk, Nicholas	Fiction
Growing Pains Of Adrian Mole, The	Townsend, Sue	Fiction
Growing Up In The Gorbals	Glasser, Ralph	Non-Fiction
Guest Of Honour	Wallace, Irving	Fiction
Guglielmo Marconi	Marconi, Guglielmo	Non-Fiction
Guide To Good Gardening	Thrower, Percy	Non-Fiction
Guilty Parties	Street, Pamela	Fiction
Guiseppe Verdi	Verdi (Composer)	Non-Fiction
Gull On The Roof	Tangye, Derek	Non-Fiction
Gullivers's Travels	Swift, Jonathan	Fiction
Gumby Gang Again, The	Oldfield, Pamela	Fiction
Gumby Gang On Holiday, The	Oldfield, Pamela	Fiction
Gumby Gang Strikes Again, The	Oldfield, Pamela	Fiction
Gumdrop	Biro, Val	Fiction
Gun For Sale, A	Greene, Graham	Fiction
Gunga Din	Kipling, Rudyard	Fiction
Guns Of Navarone, The	MacLean, Alistair	Fiction
Gurdjieff The Man	Self Improvement	Non-Fiction
Gurus Disciples And Ashrams	Self Improvement	Non-Fiction
Gwilam's Harp And Intracom	Le Guin, Ursula	Fiction
G.W.R.	Trains...	Non-Fiction
H M S Ulysses	MacLean, Alistair	Fiction
Hairs In The Palm Of The Hand	Mark, Jan	Fiction
Hairst Gaitherins	Maitland, William	Fiction
Half Moon Street	Theroux, Paul	Fiction

TITLES INDEX

Title	Author	Category
Hamewith	Murray, Charles	Fiction
Hamilton	Cookson, Catherine	Fiction
Hamlet	Shakespeare, William	Fiction
Hamlet As Play Of Revenge	A-Level	Non-Fiction
Hamlet: Book Or Play?	A-Level	Non-Fiction
Hammersleigh	Ellerbeck, R	Fiction
Hancock	Hancock, Tony	Fiction
Hancock's Half Hour	Hancock, Tony	Fiction
Hand In Glove	Marsh, Ngaio	Fiction
Hand Rhymes	Brown, Marc	Fiction
Handmaid's Tale, The	Atwood, Margaret	Fiction
Hands Off	Miscellaneous	Fiction
Hannah Massey	Cookson, Catherine	Fiction
Hans Andersen	Andersen, Hans Christian	Fiction
Hans Andersen Stories	Andersen, Hans Christian	Fiction
Hans C. Andersen Fairy Tales	Andersen, Hans Christian	Fiction
Hans Christian Andersen	Andersen, Hans Christian	Fiction
Hans Christian Andersen Fairy Tales	Andersen, Hans Christian	Fiction
Hansel And Gretel	Children's Stories..	Fiction
Hansel And Gretel	Grimm	Fiction
Haphazard House	Wesley, Mary	Fiction
Happy	Brown, Fred	Non-Fiction
Happy Adventure Tales	Children's Stories..	Fiction
Happy Birthday Bini	Bhatia, Mamta	Fiction
Happy Families	Ahlberg, Allan	Fiction
Happy Families Stories	Children's Stories..	Fiction
Happy Prince, The	Wilde, Oscar	Fiction
Happy Prisoner, The	Dickens, Monica	Fiction
Hapsburg And Ottoman Empires, The	Germany	Non-Fiction
Harbingers Of Fear	Simpson, Dorothy	Fiction
Hard Times	Dickens, Charles	Fiction
Hard Times	Terkel, Studs	Non-Fiction
Hardball	Business	Non-Fiction
Hardin County	Standish, Buck	Fiction
Hardy And Manchild	Hardy, Thomas	Non-Fiction
Hardy's Tragic Fiction	ALlevel	Non-Fiction
Hardy's Wessex Novels	A-Level	Non-Fiction
Hare Sitting Up	Innes, Michael	Fiction
Harlot's Ghost	Mailer, Norman	Fiction
Harnessing Peacocks	Wesley, Mary	Fiction
Harold	Cookson, Catherine	Fiction
Harold Pinter: The Caretaker	A-Level	Non-Fiction
Harriet	Cooper, Jilly	Fiction
Harrogate Secret, The	Cookson, Catherine	Fiction
Harry's Game	Seymour, Gerald	Fiction
Harry's Mad	King-Smith, Dick	Fiction
Hate, Akin To Love	Redmayne, Ann	Fiction
Haunting, The	Mahy, Margaret	Fiction
Hauntings At Borley Rectory, The	Ghost Stories	Non-Fiction
Hausa Basic Course	African...	Non-Fiction
Hazell: Three Card Trick	Venables, Terry	Fiction
He Being Dead Yet Speaketh	Kilvert, Rev. Francis	Non-Fiction
He Never Came Back	McCloy, Helen	Fiction
Healing Force - Using Your Mind To Help Heal	Self Improvement	Non-Fiction
Hear All About It - What Makes News?	Webb, Edwin	Non-Fiction
Heart Of Darkness	Conrad, Joseph	Fiction
Heart Of The Country	Weldon, Fay	Fiction
Heartbreak House	Shaw, George Bernard	Fiction
Hearts Do Not Break	Preston, Ivy	Fiction
Heartstones	Rendell, Ruth	Fiction
Heavy Weather	Wodehouse, P.G.	Fiction
Hebrew Travel Pack	Hebrew	Non-Fiction
Hedgehog Sandwich	Not The Nine O'Clock News	Fiction
Heidi	Spyri, Johanna	Fiction
Heidi Grows Up	Tritten, Charles	Fiction
Heights Of Rimring, The	Hart-Davis, Duff	Fiction
Heights Of Zervos, The	Forbes, Colin	Fiction

TITLES INDEX

Helen Oxenbury's Nursery Rhymes	Oxenbury, Helen	Fiction
Helen Oxenbury's Nursery Stories	Oxenbury, Helen	Fiction
Hell Is Always Today	Higgins, Jack	Fiction
Help Yourself Gcse English	English	Non-Fiction
Henrietta Who?	Aird, Catherine	Fiction
Henry Fielding	Fielding, Henry	Non-Fiction
Henry Ford	Ford, Henry	Non-Fiction
Henry IV	Shakespeare, William	Fiction
Henry IV Of France	France	Non-Fiction
Henry V	Shakespeare, William	Fiction
Henry VI	Shakespeare, William	Fiction
Henry VII	History	Non-Fiction
Henry VIII	Henry VIII	Non-Fiction
Henry VIII	History	Non-Fiction
Henry's Cat	Television	Fiction
Henry's Cat Becomes Prime Minister	Television	Fiction
Her Life And Art	Teyte, Dame Maggie	Non-Fiction
Herb Of Death	Christie, Agatha	Fiction
Herbert The Hedgehog	Kelham, John	Fiction
Here Comes A Candle	Hodge, Jane Aiken	Fiction
Here Comes Charlie Moon	Hughes, Shirley	Fiction
Here Comes The Judge	Cook, Peter	Fiction
Here Lies Nancy Frail	Ross, Jonathan	Fiction
Heretics Of Dune	Herbert, Frank	Fiction
Heritage Of Shadows, A	Brent, Madeleine	Fiction
Hermit And The Bear, The	Yeoman, John	Fiction
Heroes And Villains	Short Stories	Fiction
Heroic Villains, The	English Literature	Fiction
Herzog	Bellow, Saul	Fiction
He's Your Dog, Charlie Brown	Schultz, Charles	Fiction
Hidden Man, The	Underwood, Michael	Fiction
Hide My Eyes	Allingham, Margery	Fiction
Higglety Pigglety Pop	Sendak, Maurice	Fiction
High Citadel	Bagley, Desmond	Fiction
High Commissioner, The	Cleary, Jon	Fiction
High Stakes	Francis, Dick	Fiction
High Stand	Innes, Hammond	Fiction
High, Wide And Lonesome	Borland, Hal	Non-Fiction
High Wind In Jamaica	Hughes, Richard	Fiction
High Window, The	Chandler, Raymond	Fiction
Highland Fling	Mitford, Nancy	Fiction
Highland Interlude	Andrews, Lucilla	Fiction
Highland Widow, The	Scott, Sir Walter	Fiction
Hindenburg Disaster, The	Military History	Non-Fiction
Hindsight	Dickinson, Peter	Fiction
Hindu Chants And Temple Music	Religious	Non-Fiction
Hinge And Bracket In Concert	Hinge & Bracket	Fiction
Hip And Thigh Workout	Health & Fitness	Non-Fiction
Hired Man, The	Bragg, Melvin	Fiction
His Greatest Roles	Gielgud, Sir John	Fiction
His Holiness Pope John Paul II	Pope John-Paul II	Non-Fiction
His Little Women	Rossner, Judith	Fiction
Historian On History, A	History	Non-Fiction
Historical Demography	Social Sciences	Non-Fiction
Histories Of Gargantua & Pantagruel	Rabelais, Francois	Non-Fiction
History And Hardware Of Computers	Computing	Non-Fiction
History And The Humour, The	Rugby Union	Non-Fiction
History Of Mr. Polly, The	Wells, H.G.	Fiction
History Of The World In Ten And A Half Chapters, A	Barnes, Julian	Fiction
History Reflected, Elizabeth 1, The Armada 1588	History	Non-Fiction
Hit Them Where It Hurts	Chase, James Hadley	Fiction
Hitch-Hiker's 1	Adams, Douglas	Fiction
Hitch-Hiker's Guide To The Galaxy	Adams, Douglas	Fiction
Hitler's World Policy	Germany	Non-Fiction
Hobbit, The	Tolkien, J.R.R.	Fiction
Hobo Sexual, The	Nicol, Hector	Fiction
Hoffnung - A Last Encore	Hoffnung, Gerard	Fiction

TITLES INDEX

Title	Author	Category
Holiday With The Fiend	Lavelle, Sheila	Fiction
Holmes Collection, The	Conan Doyle, Arthur	Fiction
Holy Bible, The	Bible	Non-Fiction
Holy Spirit	Bible	Non-Fiction
Homage To Catalonia	Orwell, George	Non-Fiction
Home Economics (Course)	G.C.S.E.	Non-Fiction
Home Run	Seymour, Gerald	Fiction
Home Sweet Home	Grahame, Kenneth	Fiction
Homecoming, The	Pinter, Harold	Fiction
Homework	Digance, Richard	Fiction
Honour This Day	Kent, Alexander	Fiction
Hooky And The Villainous Chauffeur	Meynell, Laurence	Fiction
Horace	Corneille, P	Fiction
Horatio Nelson	Nelson	Non-Fiction
Horizon	MacInnes, Helen	Fiction
Hornbook For Witches, A	Sendak, Maurice	Fiction
Horse And His Boy, The	Lewis, C.S.	Fiction
Hospital Circles	Andrews, Lucilla	Fiction
Hospital Summer	Andrews, Lucilla	Fiction
Hot Money	Francis, Dick	Fiction
Hot Money Caper, The	Chambers, Peter	Fiction
Hotel Du Lac	Brookner, Anita	Fiction
Hotel Regina	Nicol, Jean	Fiction
Hound Of The Baskervilles, The	Conan Doyle, Arthur	Fiction
Hour Of Fairy Stories, An	Traditional	Fiction
Hour With O Henry, An	Henry, O	Fiction
Hour-Glass, The	Brennan, Will	Fiction
House Above The Bay, The	Preston, Ivy	Fiction
House At Pooh Corner	Milne, A.A.	Fiction
House For Sister Mary	Andrews, Lucilla	Fiction
House Inside Out, A	Lively, Penelope	Fiction
House Near The Sea, The	Musman, Richard	Fiction
House Of Cards	Dobbs, Michael	Fiction
House Of Care, The	Burley, W.J.	Fiction
House Of Men	Marchant, Catherine	Fiction
House Of Mirth, The	Wharton, Edith	Fiction
House Of Stairs, The	Vine, Barbara	Fiction
House Of The Chestnut Trees, The	Neville, Anne	Fiction
House Of The Seven Flies	Canning, Victor	Fiction
House Of Vandekar, The	Anthony, Evelyn	Fiction
House Of Women, A	Bates, H.E.	Fiction
House With The Green Shutters	Douglas, George	Fiction
Houses Without Doors	Straub, Peter	Fiction
Housewife Superstar	Humphries, Barry	Fiction
How French Poetry Works	French Literature	Non-Fiction
How Green Was My Curate	Secombe, Fred	Fiction
How Green Was My Valley	Llewellyn, Richard	Fiction
How People Change	Mean, Margaret	Non-Fiction
How Pleasant To Know Mr. Lear	Shakespeare, William	Fiction
How Robin Became An Outlaw	Traditional	Fiction
How Spanish Poetry Works	Spanish Literature	Non-Fiction
How The Leopard Got His Spots	Kipling, Rudyard	Fiction
How The Rhinoceros Got His Skin	Kipling, Rudyard	Fiction
How The Tiger Got His Stripes	Traditional	Fiction
How To Be A No-Limit Person	Self Improvement	Non-Fiction
How To Be A Winner	Business	Non-Fiction
How To Be The D.I.R.E.C.T.O.R. Of Your Life	Business	Non-Fiction
How To Change Ideas	Self Improvement	Non-Fiction
How To Decide Exactly What You Want	Self Improvement	Non-Fiction
How To Develop Your ESP Power	Self Improvement	Non-Fiction
How To End A Japanese Sentence	Japanese...	Non-Fiction
How To Get Whatever You Want Out Of Life	Self Improvement	Non-Fiction
How To Grow Old Gracefully	Gingold, Hermione	Non-Fiction
How To Improve Your Memory	Self Improvement	Non-Fiction
How To Make Love To A Man	Self Improvement	Non-Fiction
How To Put More Time Into Your Life	Business	Non-Fiction
How To Put Your Point Across In 30 Seconds	Business	Non-Fiction

TITLES INDEX

Title	Author/Subject	Category
How To Run A Successful Meeting In Half The Time	Business	Non-Fiction
How To Solve The Rubik Cube	Rubik's Cube	Non-Fiction
How To Turn A Friendship Into A Love Affair	Self Improvement	Non-Fiction
How To Turn An Interview Into A Job	Business	Non-Fiction
How To Win An Election	Goons	Fiction
How Was It For You?	Lipman, Maureen	Non-Fiction
HST 125 & Dmu	Trains...	Non-Fiction
Huckleberry Finn	Twain, Mark	Fiction
Hugh Macdiarmid	Macdiarmid, Hugh	Non-Fiction
Human Biology	G.C.S.E..	Non-Fiction
Human Factor, The	Greene, Graham	Fiction
Human Geography	Social Sciences	Non-Fiction
Human Voice, The	Cocteau, Jean	Fiction
Hungarian Travel Pack	Hungarian	Non-Fiction
Hungry As The Sea	Smith, Wilbur	Fiction
Hunt For Red October, The	Clancy, Tom	Fiction
Hunter In The Dark	Thompson, Estelle	Fiction
Hunting And Shooting Stories	Bates, Blaster	Fiction
Hunting Of The Snark, The	Carroll, Lewis	Fiction
Hunting Tower	Buchan, John	Fiction
Hurricane Jack Of The Vital Spark	Munro, Neil	Fiction
Husbands And Wives	Self Improvement	Non-Fiction
Huxley Pig At The Circus	Peppe, Rodney	Fiction
I Am The Doorway	King, Stephen	Fiction
I Can Count	Early Learning	Non-Fiction
I Can't Stay Long	Lee, Laurie	Non-Fiction
I Capture The Castle	Smith, Dodie	Fiction
I Claudius	Graves, Robert	Fiction
I, Gloria Gold	Summers, Judith	Fiction
I Hear America Singing	Whitman, Walt	Fiction
I Heard The Owl Call My Name	Craven, Margaret	Fiction
I, Judas	Caldwell & Stearn	Fiction
I Know Cos I Was There	Boyce, Max	Fiction
I Know Why The Caged Bird Sings	Angelou, Maya	Non-Fiction
I Leap Over The Wall	Baldwin, Monica	Non-Fiction
I Light A Candle	Turgel, Gena	Non-Fiction
I Misteri Della Giungla Nera	Salgari, Emilio	Fiction
I Never Know What To Say	Self Improvement	Non-Fiction
I Only Can Dance With You	Webster, Jan	Fiction
I Promessi Sposi	Manzoni, Alessandro	Non-Fiction
I Remember, I Remember	Duce, Joan	Fiction
I Suoni Dell Italiano E Le Varainti Regionali	Italy	Non-Fiction
Ibn Khaldun - His Life. His Works And His Source	Middle East	Non-Fiction
Ice House, The	Bawden, Nina	Fiction
Ice Man Cometh, The	O'Neill, Eugene	Fiction
Ice Station Zebra	MacLean, Alistair	Fiction
Idea Of The Frontier, The	American...	Non-Fiction
If Only They Could Talk	Herriot, James	Fiction
If Tomorrow Comes	Sheldon, Sidney	Fiction
If You Haven't Got The Time To Do It Right	Business	Non-Fiction
Iggie's House	Blume, Judy	Fiction
Il Cinema Italiano Durante Il Fascismo	Italy	Non-Fiction
Il Contesto	Sciascia	Non-Fiction
Il Futurismo In Italia	Italy	Non-Fiction
Il Giardino Dei Finzi-Contini	Bassini, G	Non-Fiction
Il Mio Carso	Slataper, Scipio	Fiction
Il Problema Dell' Unificazione Linguistica Itali	Italian	Non-Fiction
Iliad, The	Homer	Fiction
Ill Met By Moonlight	Moss, W. Stanley	Non-Fiction
Illusions	Bach, Richard	Fiction
Illustrated Man, The	Bradbury, Ray	Fiction
I'm Sorry I'll Read That Again	Radio	Fiction
I'm The Greatest Comedian In The World	Mason, Jackie	Fiction
Imaginative Woman, An	Hardy, Thomas	Fiction
Imagineering	Self Improvement	Non-Fiction
Imajica	Barker, Clive	Fiction
Inimitable Jeeves, The	Wodehouse, P.G.	Fiction

TITLES INDEX

Title	Author/Category	Type
Immensee	German	Non-Fiction
Imogen	Cooper, Jilly	Fiction
Importance Of Being Earnest, The	Wilde, Oscar	Fiction
Improve Your Driving	Driving...	Non-Fiction
Improve Your English	English	Non-Fiction
Improve Your French	French	Non-Fiction
Improve Your Typing	Business	Non-Fiction
Improve Your Word Power	English	Non-Fiction
In A Summer Season	Taylor, Elizabeth	Fiction
In Country Heaven	Thomas, Dylan	Fiction
In Custody	Desai, Anita	Fiction
In Danger's Hour	Reeman, Douglas	Fiction
In Highland Harbours	Munro, Neil	Fiction
In Love In Vienna	Thomson, Daisy	Fiction
In Mind O A Makar	Garioch, Robert	Fiction
In My Wildest Dreams	Thomas, Leslie	Fiction
In Pale Battalions	Goddard, Robert	Fiction
In Praise Of Buddha	Religious	Non-Fiction
In Praise Of Cats	Short Stories	Fiction
In Search Of Excellence	Peters, Thomas. J.	Non-Fiction
In Search Of The Trojan War	Wood, Michael	Non-Fiction
In Storm And In Calm	Andrews, Lucilla	Fiction
In The Company Of Eagles	Gann, Ernest K.	Fiction
In The Frame	Francis, Dick	Fiction
In The Heart Of The Country	Coetzee, J.m.	Fiction
In The Hour Before Midnight	Higgins, Jack	Fiction
In The House Of Dark Music	Lynch, Francis	Fiction
In Trouble Again	O'Hanlon, Redmond	Non-Fiction
Inch Loss Plan	Health & Fitness	Non-Fiction
Incident At Ryker's Creek	Long, Elliot	Fiction
Inconvenient Corpse, The	Daniels, Philip	Fiction
Incredible Plan, The	Boyce, Max	Fiction
Incredible Self-confidence	Self Improvement	Non-Fiction
Indecent Obsession, An	McCullough, Colleen	Fiction
Indemnity Only	Paretsky, Sara	Fiction
India Fan, The	Holt, Victoria	Fiction
Indian In The Cupboard, The	Reid Banks, Lynne	Fiction
Indian Summer, An	Cameron, James	Fiction
Indian Summer Of Dry Valley Johnson	Henry, O	Fiction
Industrial And Agrarian Change In 18th Ctry...	Social Sciences	Non-Fiction
Industrial Espionage	Business	Non-Fiction
Industrial Relations In France	France	Non-Fiction
Industrial Revolution, The	Social Sciences	Non-Fiction
Infatuation	Robins, Denise	Fiction
Inflight Relaxation	Self Improvement	Non-Fiction
Inn On The Marsh, The	Kennedy, Lena	Fiction
Inner Management	Business	Non-Fiction
Innocence Of Father Brown, The	Chesterton, G.K.	Fiction
Innocent Abroad	Hauxwell, Hannah	Non-Fiction
Innocent Anthropologist, The	Barley, Nigel	Fiction
Innocent Blood	James, P.D.	Fiction
Innovative Secrets Of Success	Business	Non-Fiction
Inshore Squadron, The	Kent, Alexander	Fiction
Inside Shelley Berman	Berman, Shelley	Fiction
Inside Star Trek	Science Fiction	Fiction
Inspector Ghote Draws A Line	Keating, H.R.F.	Fiction
Inspector Thackery Arrives	James, Kenneth	Fiction
Inspector West Cries Wolf	Creasey, John	Fiction
Inspector Wexford - Means Of Evil	Rendell, Ruth	Fiction
Inspector Wexford On Holiday	Rendell, Ruth	Fiction
Instant Record Collection	Monty Python	Fiction
Intensify Creative Ability	Self Improvement	Non-Fiction
International Relations Between The Wars	Social Sciences	Non-Fiction
Interview With Lillian Hellman, An	Hellman, Lillian	Non-Fiction
Interviews And Interviewing	Webb & Lee	Non-Fiction
Interviews In French	French	Non-Fiction
Into The Darkness	Michaels, Barbara	Fiction

Title	Author/Subject	Category
Introducing Ancient Greek	Greek	Non-Fiction
Introducing The Arab World	Middle East	Non-Fiction
Introducing The Arabic Language	Arabic	Non-Fiction
Introducing The Byelorussian Language	Slavonic	Non-Fiction
Introducing The Dutch Language	Dutch	Non-Fiction
Introducing The Japanese Language	Japanese...	Non-Fiction
Introducing The Romanian Language	Romanian	Non-Fiction
Introducing The Turkish Language	Turkish	Non-Fiction
Introduction To Brittany, An	France	Non-Fiction
Introduction To Computing, An	Computing	Non-Fiction
Introduction To No Drama, An	Japan	Non-Fiction
Introduction To Petrarch's Selected Poems	Petrarch	Non-Fiction
Introduction To Polish History, An	Poland	Non-Fiction
Introduction To The German Democratic Republic	Germany	Non-Fiction
Invisible Chord, The	Cookson, Catherine	Fiction
Invisible Friendship	Grenfell & Moore	Non-Fiction
Invitation, The	Cookson, Catherine	Fiction
Invitation To The Waltz	Lehmann, Rosamund	Fiction
Ipcress File, The	Deighton, Len	Fiction
Iphigenie Auf Tauris	Von Goethe, J.W.	Non-Fiction
Iranian Revolution, The	Middle East	Non-Fiction
Irish Question 1800-1922, The	Social Sciences	Non-Fiction
Irish-English Dictionaries And How To Use Them	Irish...	Non-Fiction
Iron Heel, The	London, Jack	Fiction
Iron Man, The	Hughes, Ted	Fiction
Iron Pirate, The	Reeman, Douglas	Fiction
Iron Tiger, The	Higgins, Jack	Fiction
Iron-Ore Steamers	Trains...	Non-Fiction
Irresistible Force, An	Charlton, Ann	Fiction
Is It Something I Said	Pryor, Richard	Fiction
Isaac Newton	Newton, Isaac	Non-Fiction
Isabella Of Castile & Leon	Isabella	Non-Fiction
Island Magic	Edwards, Rowan	Fiction
Island Of Adventure	Blyton, Enid	Fiction
Island Of Enchantment	Preston, Ivy	Fiction
Isle Of Illusion	Munro, Neil	Fiction
Isle Of Man TT Races, 1967	Motorcycling	Non-Fiction
It Ain't Half Hot Mum	Television	Fiction
It Always Rains In Rome	Leeming, John F.	Fiction
It Couldn't Matter Less	Cheyney, Peter	Fiction
Italia, Anni '80: Corso Di Lingua E Cultura	Italian	Non-Fiction
Italian Assets	Allbeury, Ted	Fiction
Italian At The Wheel	Italian	Non-Fiction
Italian Between Past And Present	Italian	Non-Fiction
Italian Cassette Course	Italian	Non-Fiction
Italian For Travel	Italian	Non-Fiction
Italian Language Basics	Italian	Non-Fiction
Italian Politics Since World War II - Parts 1 & 2	Italy	Non-Fiction
Italian Risorgimento, The	Italy	Non-Fiction
Italian Summer	Goodwin, Grace	Fiction
Italian Travel Pack	Italian	Non-Fiction
Italy Travel Kit	Italian	Non-Fiction
I.T.M.A.	Radio	Fiction
It's A Children's World	Children's Stories..	Fiction
It's A Vet's Life	Duncan, Alex	Non-Fiction
It's Always Something	Business	Non-Fiction
It's Not My Department	Business	Non-Fiction
It's The Great Pumpkin, Charlie Brown	Schultz, Charles	Fiction
It's Too Frightening For Me!	Hughes, Shirley	Fiction
Ivanhoe	Scott, Sir Walter	Fiction
Ivor The Engine	Television	Fiction
Ivy Tree, The	Stewart, Mary	Fiction
J Kingston Platt	Kingston Platt, J	Non-Fiction
J R R Tolkien	Guerolt, Denis	Non-Fiction
Jack And The Beanstalk	Children's Stories..	Fiction
Jackal's Head, The	Peters, Elizabeth	Fiction
Jack's Return Home	Lewis, T.	Fiction

TITLES INDEX

Jamaica Inn	Du Maurier, Daphne	Fiction
James And The Giant Peach	Dahl, Roald	Fiction
James I	History	Non-Fiction
James Joyce	Joyce, James	Non-Fiction
James Joyce Stephen Hero	Joyce, James	Non-Fiction
James To Jude	Bible	Non-Fiction
Jane Austen	Austen, Jane	Non-Fiction
Jane Eyre	Bronte, Charlotte	Fiction
Jane Eyre By Charlotte Bronte	Bronte, Charlotte	Non-Fiction
Jane Fonda's Workout	Health & Fitness	Non-Fiction
Jane Fonda's Workout Record For Pregnancy, Birth	Health & Fitness	Non-Fiction
Janus Man	Forbes, Colin	Fiction
Japanese Cassette Course	Japanese...	Non-Fiction
Japanese Language And People	Japanese...	Non-Fiction
Japanese Travel Pack	Japanese...	Non-Fiction
Jason And The Golden Fleece	Greek Mythology	Fiction
Jason Bodger And The Priory Ghost	Kemp, Gene	Fiction
Jason Voyage, The	Severin, Tim	Non-Fiction
Jazz	Morrison, Toni	Fiction
Jean Calvin	France	Non-Fiction
Jean Stafford Reads One Of Her Short Stories	Stafford, Jean	Non-Fiction
Jeannie	Tangye, Derek	Non-Fiction
Jeannie Urquhart	Hill, Pamela	Fiction
Jeeves	Parkinson, C. Northcote	Fiction
Jeeves	Wodehouse, P.G.	Fiction
Jeeves And The Feudal Spirit	Wodehouse, P.G.	Fiction
Jeeves And The Yuletide Spirit	Wodehouse, P.G.	Fiction
Jeeves In The Offing	Wodehouse, P.G.	Fiction
Jeeves Stories	Wodehouse, P.G.	Fiction
Jeffy, The Burglar's Cat	Moray Williams, Ursula	Fiction
Jehovah's Witnesses	Religious	Non-Fiction
Jelly Pie	McGough, Roger	Fiction
Jemima Shore's First Case	Fraser, Antonia	Fiction
Jenni	Young, Vivien	Fiction
Jennings Goes To School	Buckeridge, Anthony	Fiction
Jenny And James Learn To Count	Early Learning	Non-Fiction
Jenny And James Start School	Children's Stories	Fiction
Jenny And The Cat Club	Averill, Esther	Fiction
Jeremiah In The Dark Woods	Ahlberg, Janet & Allan	Fiction
Jessie Gray	Blair, Emma	Fiction
Jesus	Bible	Non-Fiction
Jim At The Corner	Farjeon, Eleanor	Fiction
Jimbo Flies To France	Maddocks, Pete	Fiction
Jimbo Flies To Spain	Maddocks, Pete	Fiction
Jimmy's Golden Mile	Cammell, Jim	Fiction
Jive Bunny Finds Fame	Miscellaneous	Fiction
Jive Bunny Saves The Day	Miscellaneous	Fiction
Joan Of Arc	Joan Of Arc	Non-Fiction
Job: A Comedy Of Justice	Heinlein, Robert	Fiction
Job Satisfaction	Social Sciences	Non-Fiction
Johann Sebastian Bach	Bach, J. S. (Composer)	Non-Fiction
Johann Sebastian Bach 1685 - 1750	Bach, J.S. (Composer)	Non-Fiction
Johann Strauss 1825-1899	Strauss, J. (Composer)	Non-Fiction
Johann Strauss The Younger	Strauss, J. (Composer)	Non-Fiction
John	Bible	Non-Fiction
John Barrymore: From Matinee Idol To Buffoon	Barrymore, John	Non-Fiction
John Betjeman Reads John Betjeman	Betjeman, Sir John	Fiction
John Bull's Other Island	Shaw, George Bernard	Fiction
John Dos Passos Reads His Poetry	Dos Passos, John	Non-Fiction
John (Parts 1 & 2)	Bible	Non-Fiction
John Paul Ii	Pope John-Paul II	Non-Fiction
John Wayne Story, The	Carpozi, George Jnr.	Non-Fiction
Johnny Tomorrow	Bear, Carolyn	Fiction
Jolly Postman, The	Ahlberg, Janet & Allan	Fiction
Jolly Tall	Hissey, Jane	Fiction
Jonathan Livingstone Seagull	Bach, Richard	Fiction
Jonathan Swift	Swift, Jonathan	Non-Fiction

Title	Author	Category
Jonathan Wild	Fielding, Henry	Fiction
Joseph Andrews	Fielding, Henry	Fiction
Josh Lawton	Bragg, Melvin	Fiction
Josh's Panther	Sampson, Fay	Fiction
Journey Into Fear	Ambler, Eric	Fiction
Journey Into Space	Chilton, Charles	Fiction
Journey Man Tailor, The	Seymour, Gerald	Fiction
Journey Through Britain	Hillaby, John	Non-Fiction
Journey To The Centre Of The Earth	Verne, Jules	Fiction
Journey To The Jade Sea	Hillaby, John	Non-Fiction
Journey To The Western Isles, A	Johnson & Boswell	Non-Fiction
Joy In The Morning	Wodehouse, P.G.	Fiction
Joyce Grenfell Requests The Pleasure	Grenfell, Joyce	Fiction
J.R.R. Tolkien Collection, The	Tolkien, J. R. R.	Fiction
Judas Factor, The	Allbeury, Ted	Fiction
Judas Tree, The	Cronin, A.J.	Fiction
Jude The Obscure	A-Level	Non-Fiction
Jude The Obscure	Hardy, Thomas	Fiction
Judgement Day	Lively, Penelope	Fiction
Judgement In Stone, A	Rendell, Ruth	Fiction
Judith	Hebbel, F	Non-Fiction
Juggernaut	Bagley, Desmond	Fiction
Julie Of The Wolves	Craighead, Jean-George	Fiction
Julius Caesar	Caesar, Julius	Non-Fiction
Julius Caesar	Shakespeare, William	Fiction
Jumping The Queue	Wesley, Mary	Fiction
Jungle Book Stories	Kipling, Rudyard	Fiction
Jungle Book Stories (Vols.1 - 4), The	Kipling, Rudyard	Fiction
Jungle Book, The	Kipling, Rudyard	Fiction
Juniper: A Mystery	Kemp, Gene	Fiction
Junket Man, The	Matthew, Christopher	Fiction
Juno And The Paycock	O'Casey, Sean	Fiction
Jurassic Park	Crichton, M	Fiction
Just So Stories	Kipling, Rudyard	Fiction
Just William	Crompton, Richmal	Fiction
Just William Stories	Crompton, Richmal	Fiction
Just Williams	Williams, Kenneth	Non-Fiction
Just You Wait And See	Barstow, Stan	Fiction
Justin Bayard	Cleary, Jon	Fiction
Kabale Und Liebe	Von Schiller, F	Non-Fiction
Kaiser's Germany, The	Germany	Non-Fiction
Kalendergeschichten	Brecht, Bertolt	Non-Fiction
Kasam (Hindi)	Malory, Sir Thomas	Fiction
Kate Hannigan	Cookson, Catherine	Fiction
Katz Und Maus	Grass, Gunther	Non-Fiction
Keats	Keats	Non-Fiction
Keep In Shape System	Health & Fitness	Non-Fiction
Keep In Shape, Vol.2	Health & Fitness	Non-Fiction
Keepsake	Grenfell, Joyce	Fiction
Kein Problem	German	Non-Fiction
Kelpie	Mayne, William	Fiction
Kenny's Window	Sendak, Maurice	Fiction
Kentish Manor Murders, The	Symons, Julian	Fiction
Kept In The Dark	Bawden, Nina	Fiction
Kes	Hines, Barry	Fiction
Key To Rebecca, The	Follett, Ken	Fiction
Keys Of The Kingdom	Cronin, A.J.	Fiction
Kidnapped	Stevenson, Robert Louis	Fiction
Killer	Pattinson, James	Fiction
Killer Mine, The	Innes, Hammond	Fiction
Killing Man, The	Spillane, Mickey	Fiction
Killshot	Leonard, Elmore	Fiction
Kim	Kipling, Rudyard	Fiction
Kind Of Healthy Grave, A	Mann, Jessica	Fiction
Kind Of Loving, A	Barstow, Stan	Fiction
Kindness Of Ravens, A	Rendell, Ruth	Fiction
Kindness Of Women, The	Ballard, J.G.	Fiction

TITLES INDEX

King Arthur	Traditional	Fiction
King Arthur And Excalibur	Children's Stories..	Fiction
King Arthur And His Knights	Traditional	Fiction
King Arthur And Merlyn's Animal Council	Traditional	Fiction
King Arthur - Excalibur	Traditional	Fiction
King Henry VIII	Shakespeare, William	Fiction
King In Love, A	Cartland, Barbara	Fiction
King John	Shakespeare, William	Fiction
King Lear	A-Level	Non-Fiction
King Lear	Shakespeare, William	Fiction
King Must Die, The	Renault, Mary	Fiction
King Of The Castle, The	Holt, Victoria	Fiction
King Richard The Lionheart	Children's Stories..	Fiction
King Solomon's Carpet	Vine, Barbara	Fiction
King Solomon's Mines	Rider Haggard, H	Fiction
Kingdom By The Sea, The	Theroux, Paul	Non-Fiction
Kingdom Under The Sea, The	Aiken, Joan	Fiction
Kingfisher's Catch Fire	Godden, Rumer	Fiction
Kings And Queens Of England	History	Non-Fiction
Kira Georgievna	Nekrasov, V	Non-Fiction
Kirby's Changeling	Brent, Madeleine	Fiction
Kiriakos	Turner, Don	Non-Fiction
Kirkland Revels	Holt, Victoria	Fiction
Kiss Me Deadly	Spillane, Mickey	Fiction
Kiss Yesterday Goodbye	Allan, Stella	Fiction
Kisses And Ha'pennies	Kingston, Beryl	Fiction
Kissing The Gunner's Daughter	Rendell, Ruth	Fiction
Kitchen Warriors, The	Aiken, Joan	Fiction
Knight In Shining Armour	Deveraux, Jude	Fiction
Knight's Tale, The	Chaucer, Geoffrey	Fiction
Knock	Romains, J	Non-Fiction
Knock Down	Francis, Dick	Fiction
Knox The Fox	Harvey, Richard	Fiction
Koko	Straub, Peter	Fiction
Koln - Ein Horbild	Germany	Non-Fiction
Komic Kutz	Harding, Mike	Fiction
Konig Ottokars Gluck Und Ende	Grillparzer, F	Non-Fiction
Kon-Tiki Expedition	Heyerdahl, Thor	Non-Fiction
Korva Tarkkana	Finnish	Non-Fiction
Kremmen The Movie	Everett, Kenny	Fiction
Kreskin On Mind Power	Self Improvement	Non-Fiction
Kruschev And Eastern Europe	Russia	Non-Fiction
Krysalis	Trenhaile, John	Fiction
La Chute	Camus, A	Non-Fiction
La Condition Humaine	Malraux, Andre	Non-Fiction
La Dentelliere	Laine, Pascal	Non-Fiction
La Divina Commedia	Dante	Non-Fiction
La France Sous Mitterrand, 1981-1988	France	Non-Fiction
La Gloire De Mon Pere	Pagnol, M	Non-Fiction
La Guerre De Troie	Giraudoux, Jean	Non-Fiction
La Luna E I Falo	Pavese, C	Non-Fiction
La Machine Infernale	Cocteau, Jean	Non-Fiction
La Modification	Butor, M	Non-Fiction
La Neige En Devil	Troyat, H	Non-Fiction
La Politique Francaise Du Temps Libre	France	Non-Fiction
La Porte Etroite	Gide, Andre	Non-Fiction
La Provence - Parts 1 & 2	France	Non-Fiction
La Questione Della Lingua Nel Rinasciments	Italian	Non-Fiction
La Reine Morte	De Montherlant, H	Non-Fiction
La Rivincita Di Tremal Naik	Salgari, Emilio	Fiction
Labour Government, The	Social Sciences	Non-Fiction
Labours Of Heracles, The	Greek Mythology	Fiction
Labours Of Hercules, The	Christie, Agatha	Fiction
Ladies Of Missalongh, The	McCullough, Colleen	Fiction
Ladri De Biciclette	De Sica, Vittorio	Non-Fiction
Lady And The Champ, The	Nicol, Hector	Fiction
Lady And The Tramp	Disney	Fiction

TITLES INDEX

Title	Author	Type
Lady Boss	Collins, Jackie	Fiction
Lady Chatterley's Lover	Lawrence, D.H.	Fiction
Lady For A Chevalier	Peters, Maureen	Fiction
Lady In The Lake, The	Chandler, Raymond	Fiction
Lady Of The Quinta	Driver, Grace	Fiction
Lady Penelope	Kennedy, Lena	Fiction
Lady With Carnations	Cronin, A.J.	Fiction
Ladykiller	McBain, Ed	Fiction
L'Affaire Dreyfus	France, Anatole	Non-Fiction
Laguna Heat	Jefferson Parker, T	Fiction
Lake Of Darkness, The	Rendell, Ruth	Fiction
Lake Wobegon Days	Keillor, Garrison	Fiction
Lake Wobegon Days/leaving Home	Radio	Fiction
Lakeland Love, A	Morley, Adele	Fiction
Lallans	Scotland	Non-Fiction
Lallie	Sinclair, Clover	Fiction
Lama	Tangye, Derek	Non-Fiction
L'Amante Anglaise	Duras, Marguerite	Non-Fiction
Lamb To The Slaughter	Eden, Dorothy	Fiction
Lamplight Over The Lake	Wood, Margaret	Fiction
Land God Gave To Cain, The	Innes, Hammond	Fiction
Land Of Green Ginger	Holtby, Winifred	Fiction
Land Of Make Believe	Children's Stories..	Fiction
Land Of Oz, The	Baum, L. Frank	Fiction
Landslide	Bagley, Desmond	Fiction
Lang Syne In The East Neuk O Fife	Kermack, Mary	Non-Fiction
Langholm Memorial Sculpture	MacDiarmid, Hugh	Fiction
L'anglais Simplifie	English	Non-Fiction
Language Course - Arabic (Modern Standard)	Arabic	Non-Fiction
Language Course - Chinese (Mandarin)	Chinese	Non-Fiction
Language Course - Danish	Danish	Non-Fiction
Language Course - Dutch	Dutch	Non-Fiction
Language Course - English	English	Non-Fiction
Language Course - Ensemble	French	Non-Fiction
Language Course - Finnish	Finnish	Non-Fiction
Language Course - French	French	Non-Fiction
Language Course - French At Home	French	Non-Fiction
Language Course - German	German	Non-Fiction
Language Course - Greek (Modern)	Greek	Non-Fiction
Language Course - Hebrew (Modern)	Hebrew	Non-Fiction
Language Course - Hindi	Hindi	Non-Fiction
Language Course - Icelandic	Icelandic	Non-Fiction
Language Course - Irish	Irish...	Non-Fiction
Language Course - Italian	Italian	Non-Fiction
Language Course - Japanese	Japanese...	Non-Fiction
Language Course - Malay (Bahasa Malaysia)	Malay	Non-Fiction
Language Course - Norwegian	Norwegian	Non-Fiction
Language Course - Polish	Polish	Non-Fiction
Language Course - Portuguese	Portuguese	Non-Fiction
Language Course - Russian	Russian...	Non-Fiction
Language Course - Spanish	Spanish	Non-Fiction
Language Course - Spanish (Castilian)	Spanish	Non-Fiction
Language Course - Spanish (Latin-American)	Spanish	Non-Fiction
Language Course - Swedish	Swedish	Non-Fiction
Language Of Poetry, The	English Literature	Non-Fiction
Language Of The Heart	Cadell, Elizabeth	Fiction
Languages Of India - Part 1 Indo-European	Indian	Non-Fiction
Languages Of India - Part 2 Non-Indo European	Indian	Non-Fiction
Lantern Network, The	Allbeury, Ted	Fiction
Larger Thrushes	Bird Songs	Non-Fiction
Larks Ascending	Bird Songs	Non-Fiction
Lark's Castle	York, Susannah	Fiction
Last Battle, The	Lewis, C.S	Fiction
Last Camel Died At Noon, The	Peters, Elizabeth	Fiction
Last Chance To See	Adams, Douglas	Non-Fiction
Last Days Of General Gordon	Strachey, Lytton	Non-Fiction
Last Goon Show Of All	Goons	Fiction

TITLES INDEX

Title	Author/Category	Type
Last Grain Race, The	Newby, Eric	Non-Fiction
Last Gunboat Blockade, The	Military History	Non-Fiction
Last Night Of The Poms	Everage, Dame Edna	Fiction
Last Of The Mohicans, The	Cooper, James Fenimore	Fiction
Last Of The Wine, The	Renault, Mary	Fiction
Last Picture Show, The	McMurty, Larry	Fiction
Last Seen Alive	Simpson, Dorothy	Fiction
Last Slice Of The Rainbow, The	Aiken, Joan	Fiction
Last Stage To Sunset Creek	Lee, Jesse	Fiction
Last Train To Ryde	Trains...	Non-Fiction
Last Vampire, The	Hall, Willis	Fiction
Last Vanity, The	Howard, Hartley	Fiction
Last Voyage, The	Innes, Hammond	Fiction
Last Year When I Was Young	Dickens, Monica	Fiction
Lasting Spring, A	Stubbs, Jean	Fiction
Latchkey Kid, The	Forrester, Helen	Fiction
Late Flowering Love	Betjeman, Sir John	Fiction
Late Phoenix, A	Aird, Catherine	Fiction
Late Special	Bomphray, Clint	Fiction
Latecomers	Brookner, Anita	Fiction
Laughing Stock Of The BBC	Comedy...	Fiction
Laughter With A Bang	Bates, Blaster	Fiction
Laurel And Hardy	Laurel & Hardy	Fiction
Laurel And Hardy On The Air	Laurel & Hardy	Fiction
L'Avare	Moliere	Fiction
Lawrence And Joyce	Lawrence & Joyce	Non-Fiction
Lawyers And Industry In Germany	German	Non-Fiction
Le Barbier De Seville	Beaumarchais	Non-Fiction
Le Bete Humaine	Zola, Emile	Non-Fiction
Le Ble En Herbe	Colette	Non-Fiction
Le Bourgeois Gentil Homme	Moliere	Non-Fiction
Le Chateau De Ma Mere	Pagnol, M	Non-Fiction
Le Cid	Corneille, P	Non-Fiction
Le Cinema Francais Depuis 1945	France	Non-Fiction
Le Clos Du Roi	Scipion, M	Non-Fiction
Le Colonel Chabert: Gobseck	De Balzac, Honore	Non-Fiction
Le Cure De Tours	De Balzac, Honore	Non-Fiction
Le Grand Meaulnes	Fournier, Alain	Non-Fiction
Le Jeu De L'amour Et Du Hasard	Marivaux	Non-Fiction
Le Legende Des Siecles	Hugo, Victor	Non-Fiction
Le Maitre De Santiago	De Montherlant, H	Non-Fiction
Le Malade Imaginaire	Moliere	Non-Fiction
Le Mariage De Figaro	Beaumarchais	Non-Fiction
Le Massif Central	France	Non-Fiction
Le Misanthrope	Moliere	Fiction
Le Monde Des Annees 80 - Parts 1 & 2	France	Non-Fiction
Le Notaire Du Havre	Duhamel, G	Non-Fiction
Le Pere Goriot	De Balzac, Honore	Non-Fiction
Le Rouge Et Le Noir	Stendhal	Non-Fiction
Le Silence De La Mer	Vercours	Non-Fiction
Leadership Secrets Of Attila The Hun	Business	Non-Fiction
League Cup Final-1981	Football	Non-Fiction
League Cup Final-1982	Football	Non-Fiction
League Of Nations, The	History	Non-Fiction
Learn The Alphabet	Early Learning	Non-Fiction
Learn To Count	Early Learning	Non-Fiction
Learn To Speak Danish	Danish	Non-Fiction
Learning And Memory	Self Improvement	Non-Fiction
Learning Colours	Early Learning	Non-Fiction
Learning The Alphabet	Early Learning	Non-Fiction
Learning The Alphabet And Learning To Count	Early Learning	Non-Fiction
Learning To Control Pain	Self Improvement	Non-Fiction
Learning To Spell	Early Learning	Non-Fiction
Learning To Touch Type	Business	Non-Fiction
Learning To Write Fiction	Welty, Eudora	Non-Fiction
Learning Your Tables	Early Learning	Non-Fiction
Leave It To Psmith	Wodehouse, P.G.	Fiction

Title	Author	Category
Leaving Home	Keillor, Garrison	Fiction
L'Ecole Des Femmes	Moliere	Fiction
Ledge Between The Streams, The	Metha, Ved	Non-Fiction
Legatee	Pattinson, James	Fiction
Legend Of Sleepy Hollow	Irving, Washington	Fiction
Legend Of The Seventh Virgin	Holt, Victoria	Fiction
Legends Of The Clans	Traditional	Fiction
Lemon Tree, The	Forrester, Helen	Fiction
Lenin	Lenin	Non-Fiction
Lenin	Russia	Non-Fiction
Lenin And Leninism	Russia	Non-Fiction
Lenin Of The Rovers	Radio	Fiction
Leo	Astrology	Non-Fiction
Leo Ferre	Ferre, Leo	Non-Fiction
Leopard Hunts In Darkness, The	Smith, Wilbur	Fiction
Leopard, The	De Lampedusa, Giuseppe	Fiction
Leper Of Saint Giles, The	Peters, Ellis	Fiction
Les Allumettes Suedoises	Sabatier, R	Non-Fiction
Les Fausses Confidences	Marivaux	Non-Fiction
Les Femmes Savantes	Moliere	Fiction
Les Fleurs Du Mal	Baudelaire	Non-Fiction
Les Gommes	Robbe-Grillet, Alain	Non-Fiction
Les Jeux Sont Faits	Sartre, Jean-Paul	Non-Fiction
Les Liasons Dangereuses	Laclos, P	Non-Fiction
Les Mains Sales	Sartre, Jean-Paul	Non-Fiction
Les Miserables	Hugo, Victor	Fiction
Les Petits Enfants Du Siecle	Rochefort, C	Non-Fiction
Les Relations Entre La France Et L'Algerie	France	Non-Fiction
Les Sequestres D'Altona	Sartre, Jean-Paul	Non-Fiction
L'Espace Francais: Rural France	France	Non-Fiction
L'Esprit Francais	France	Non-Fiction
Let Us Now Praise Famous Men	Agee, James	Fiction
Lethal Orders	Pattinson, James	Fiction
L'Etranger	Camus, A	Non-Fiction
Let's Listen	Aesop	Fiction
Let's Play	Children's Stories..	Fiction
Letters From A Bomber Pilot	Hodgson, David	Non-Fiction
Letters From America	Cooke, Alistair	Fiction
Letters From Constance	Hocking, Mary	Fiction
Letters From My Father	Allsop, Kenneth	Fiction
Levantine Arabic Pronounciation	Arabic	Non-Fiction
Level Five	Hart-Davis, Duff	Fiction
Levkas Man	Innes, Hammond	Fiction
Lewis Percy	Brookner, Anita	Fiction
L'Exil Et Le Royaume	Camus, A	Non-Fiction
Lexis Of Russian, The	Russian	Non-Fiction
Leyendas	Spanish	Non-Fiction
Liar, The	Fry, Stephen	Fiction
Liar's Poker	Lewis, Michael	Fiction
Liberals In The 20th Century, The	Social Sciences	Non-Fiction
Libertine In Love	Courtney, Caroline	Fiction
Libra	Astrology	Non-Fiction
Licence To Kill	Gardner, John	Fiction
Lies Of Silence	Moore, Brian	Fiction
Life And Loves Of A She Devil, The	Weldon, Fay	Fiction
Life And Mary Ann	Cookson, Catherine	Fiction
Life And Times Of Lord Mountbatten, The	Lord Mountbatten	Non-Fiction
Life In Chaucer's England	A-Level	Non-Fiction
Life In The Country, A	Fletcher, Cyril	Non-Fiction
Life Is The Destiny	Stuart, Alex	Fiction
Life Of Brian	Monty Python	Fiction
Life Of Charlotte Bronte, The	Cleghorn Gaskell, E	Non-Fiction
Life On The Mississippi	Twain, Mark	Non-Fiction
Life, The Universe And Everything	Adams, Douglas	Fiction
Life To Share, A	Kingston, Edna	Fiction
Life's Rich Pageant	Marshall, Arthur	Non-Fiction
Lifespring	Self Improvement	Non-Fiction

TITLES INDEX

Title	Author	Category
Lift Off	Bates, Blaster	Fiction
Lift, The	Hancock, Tony	Fiction
Light A Penny Candle	Binchy, Maeve	Fiction
Light In The Ward, The	Andrews, Lucilla	Fiction
Light Of Evening	Street, Pamela	Fiction
Light Princess, The	MacDonald, Geoff	Fiction
Light Touch, The	Business	Non-Fiction
Light Within, A	Francis, Helen	Fiction
Lighthouse Circle 1, The	Antek, Chris	Fiction
Lighthouse, The	Bates, H.E.	Fiction
Lightning	Koontz, Dean R.	Fiction
Lilac Bus, The	Binchy, Maeve	Fiction
L'Ile Des Pingouins	France, Anatole	Non-Fiction
Lillee: Over And Out	Cricket	Non-Fiction
Lime Street At Two	Forrester, Helen	Non-Fiction
Limited Options	Harcourt, Palma	Fiction
L'Immigration En France	France	Non-Fiction
Linguaphone French Travellers	French	Non-Fiction
Linguaphone German Travellers	German	Non-Fiction
Linguaphone Greek Travellers	Greek	Non-Fiction
Linguaphone Italian Travellers	Italian	Non-Fiction
Linguaphone Portuguese Travellers	Portuguese	Non-Fiction
Linguaphone Spanish Travellers	Spanish	Non-Fiction
Lion At School	Pearce, Philippa	Fiction
Lion Children's Bible, The	Bible	Non-Fiction
Lion In The Evening	Scofield, Alan	Fiction
Lion, The Witch And The Wardrobe, The	Lewis, C.S.	Fiction
Lionel's Car	Cole, Michael	Fiction
Lionel's Party	Cole, Michael	Fiction
Lisa Logan	Joseph, Marie	Fiction
Listen To This	Cecil, Laura	Fiction
Listen With Mother	Radio	Fiction
Listening And Understanding	Webb, Edwin	Non-Fiction
Listening Silence, The	Joseph, Marie	Fiction
Listening Woman	Hillerman, Tony	Fiction
L'italia Dal Vivo	Italian	Non-Fiction
Literature And Society In The 1930's For Universities	English Literature	Non-Fiction
Little Bear Lost	Hissey, Jane	Fiction
Little Blue Brontosaurus	Priess & Stout	Fiction
Little Bo Peep	Children's Stories..	Fiction
Little Broomstick, The	Stewart, Mary	Fiction
Little Drummer Girl, The	Le Carre, John	Fiction
Little Gingerbread Man, The	Children's Stories..	Fiction
Little Grey Rabbit Collection, The	Uttley, Alison	Fiction
Little Grey Rabbit Stories	Uttley, Alison	Fiction
Little Grey Rabbit, The	Uttley, Alison	Fiction
Little Match Girl, The	Andersen, Hans Christian	Fiction
Little Mermaid, The	Andersen, Hans Christian	Fiction
Little Miss Stories	Hargreaves, Roger	Fiction
Little Old Mrs. Pepperpot	Proysen, Alf	Fiction
Little Oz Stories	Baum, L. Frank	Fiction
Little Prince, The	De Saint-Exupery	Fiction
Little Princess, A	Hodgson Burnett, F.	Fiction
Little Red Fox Book	Uttley, Alison	Fiction
Little Red Hen, The	Southgate, Vera	Fiction
Little Red Riding Hood	Children's Stories..	Fiction
Little Red Riding Hood	Perrault, Charles	Fiction
Little Sister, The	Chandler, Raymond	Fiction
Little Stranger, A	McWilliam, Candia	Fiction
Little Tim And The Brave Sea Captain	Ardizzone, Edward	Fiction
Little Tin Soldier, The	Children's Stories..	Fiction
Little Toot Stories	Gramatsky, Hardie	Fiction
Little Trains Of Wales, The	Trains...	Non-Fiction
Little White Doves Of Love	Cartland, Barbara	Fiction
Little Women	Alcott, Louisa May	Fiction
Live And Let Die	Fleming, Ian	Fiction
Live And Unleashed	Henry, Lenny	Fiction

TITLES INDEX

Title	Author	Category
Live At Drury Lane	Monty Python	Fiction
Live At Jongleurs	Comedy...	Fiction
Live At The Embassy Club	Manning, Bernard	Fiction
Live At The Morgue	Bednarczyk, Stefan	Fiction
Live At The Talk Of East Anglia	Jones, Jimmy	Fiction
Live At Treorchy	Boyce, Max	Fiction
Live Flesh	Rendell, Ruth	Fiction
Live In America	Carrott, Jasper	Fiction
Live In Belfast	Atkinson, Rowan	Fiction
Live In Concert - Wanted	Pryor, Richard	Fiction
Liverpool Daisy	Forrester, Helen	Fiction
Living Ghosts	Kennelly, Brendan	Fiction
Living Without Limits	Self Improvement	Non-Fiction
Lizzie	Kennedy, Lena	Fiction
Lizzie Borden Took An Axe	Lustgarten, Edgar	Non-Fiction
Lizzie Dripping	Cresswell, Helen	Fiction
Lloyd George	Social Sciences	Non-Fiction
Lloyd George To Beveridge	Social Sciences	Non-Fiction
LM.S.	Trains...	Non-Fiction
L.N.E.R.	Trains...	Non-Fiction
Lobo Valley	Floren, Lee	Fiction
Locomotives From Leeds	Trains...	Non-Fiction
London Embassy, The	Theroux, Paul	Fiction
London Live	Sound Effects	Non-Fiction
London Snow	Theroux, Paul	Fiction
London Transports	Binchy, Maeve	Fiction
Lone Star Ranger, The	Grey, Zane	Fiction
Lone Wolf	Dever, Joe	Fiction
Lonely Girl	O'Brien, Edna	Fiction
Lonely Heart 4122	Watson, Colin	Fiction
Lonely Hearts	Harvey, John	Fiction
Lonely Margins, The	Allbeury, Ted	Fiction
Lonely Road	Shute, Nevil	Fiction
Lonely Skier, The	Innes, Hammond	Fiction
Long Corridor, The	Cookson, Catherine	Fiction
Long Day's Journey Into Night	O'Neill, Eugene	Fiction
Long Goodbye, The	Chandler, Raymond	Fiction
Long Masquerade, The	Brent, Madeleine	Fiction
Long Pursuit	Cleary, Jon	Fiction
Long Shadows	Jacob, Naomi	Fiction
Long Time Dead, A	Chambers, Peter	Fiction
Longest Walk, The	Meegan, George	Non-Fiction
Longest Winter, The	Wright, Daphne	Fiction
Look At Life, A	O'Connor, Tom	Fiction
Look At Me	Brookner, Anita	Fiction
Look To The Lady	Allingham, Margery	Fiction
Looking For A Bluebird	Wechsberg, Joseph	Fiction
Looking For Mr. Goodbar	Rossner, Judith	Fiction
Looking Glass, The	Coffman, Virginia	Fiction
Looking Glass War, The	Le Carre, John	Fiction
Loophole, The	Archer, Jeffrey	Fiction
Lord And Mary Ann, The	Cookson, Catherine	Fiction
Lord Arthur Savile's Crime	Wilde, Oscar	Fiction
Lord Emsworth	Wodehouse, P.G.	Fiction
Lord Emsworth And The Girlfriend	Wodehouse, P.G.	Fiction
Lord God Made Them All, The	Herriot, James	Fiction
Lord Jim	Conrad, Joseph	Fiction
Lord Mountdrago	Maugham, W. Somerset	Fiction
Lord Mullion's Secret	Innes, Michael	Fiction
Lord Of The Flies	A-Level	Non-Fiction
Lord Of The Flies	Golding, William	Fiction
Lord Of The Rings	Tolkien, J.R.R.	Fiction
Lord Peter Views The Body	Sayers, Dorothy L.	Fiction
Lord's The Home Of Cricket	Cricket	Non-Fiction
Lorna Doone	Blackmore, R.D.	Fiction
Los Pazos De Ulloa	Pardo Bazan, E	Non-Fiction
Losing Control	Lowe & Ince	Fiction

TITLES INDEX

Title	Author	Category
Lost Angel	Higgins Clark, Mary	Fiction
Lost Horizon	Hilton, James	Fiction
Lost World Of The Kalahari, The	Van Der Post, Laurens	Non-Fiction
Lost World, The	Conan Doyle, Arthur	Fiction
Lotte Berk Exercise Record - Get Physical	Health & Fitness	Non-Fiction
Lotus Eater, The	Maugham, W. Somerset	Fiction
Louis XIV	France	Non-Fiction
Love Among The Haystacks	Lawrence, D.H.	Fiction
Love And Desire And Hate	Collins, Joan	Fiction
Love And Friendship	Austen, Jane	Fiction
Love And Mary Ann	Cookson, Catherine	Fiction
Love And The Lonely Die	Stevenson, Robert Louis	Fiction
Love And War In The Apennines	Newby, Eric	Non-Fiction
Love For Lydia	Bates, H.E.	Fiction
Love In A Cold Climate	Mitford, Nancy	Fiction
Love In The Air	March, Stella	Fiction
Love In The Spotlight	Wright, Katrina	Fiction
Love Is The Key	Goodwin, Grace	Fiction
Love Locked In	Cartland, Barbara	Fiction
Love, Lords And Ladybirds	Cartland, Barbara	Fiction
Love Myself - Self-Esteem Programming	Self Improvement	Non-Fiction
Love On A Dark Island	Wright, Katrina	Fiction
Love On The Nile	Wright, Katrina	Fiction
Love Poems Of John Donne, The	Donne, John	Fiction
Love Song Of J. Alfred Prufrock, The	Eliot, T.S.	Fiction
Love Unmasked	Courtney, Caroline	Fiction
Love Was The Reason	March, Stella	Fiction
Love Will Wait	March, Stella	Fiction
Lover, The	Duras, Marguerite	Fiction
Lovers In Paradise	Cartland, Barbara	Fiction
Love's Labour's Lost	Shakespeare, William	Fiction
Loves Last Chance	Slater, Elizabeth	Fiction
Loves Music, Loves To Dance	Higgins Clark, Mary	Fiction
Love's Tangled Web	St. Clair, Joy	Fiction
Loving And Giving	Keane, Molly	Fiction
Lucia In London	Benson, E.F	Fiction
Luciano's Luck	Higgins, Jack	Fiction
Lucia's Progress	Benson, E.F	Fiction
Lucky	Collins, Jackie	Fiction
Lucky Jim	Amis, Kingsley	Fiction
Lucy And The Big Bad Wolf	Jungman, Ann	Fiction
Lucy And The Wolf In Sheep's Clothing	Jungman, Ann	Fiction
Ludo And The Star Horse	Stewart, Mary	Fiction
Ludwig Van Beethoven 1770-1827	Beethoven (composer)	Non-Fiction
Luke	Bible	Non-Fiction
Lullaby	McBain, Ed	Fiction
Lurking Fear, The	Lovecraft H.P.	Fiction
Luther	Osborne, John	Fiction
Lydlinch Bells	Barnes, William	Fiction
Lynx	Savarin, Julian Jay	Fiction
Lyrics	Pushkin & Lermontov	Non-Fiction
Lyudi	Zoshchenko, M	Non-Fiction
Macbeth	Shakespeare, William	Fiction
Macbeth As A Tragedy	A-Level	Non-Fiction
Maccormac Conspiracy, The	Marshall, Catherine	Fiction
Macgowran Speaking Beckett	Beckett, Samuel	Fiction
Machiavelli And The Medici	Machiavelli	Non-Fiction
Machine Gunners, The	Westhall, Robert	Fiction
Madam, Will You Talk	Stewart, Mary	Fiction
Madame Bovary	Flaubert, Gustave	Fiction
Madame Bovary	Flaubert, Gustave	Non-Fiction
Made In Germany 1	Antek, Chris	Fiction
Madselin	Lofts, Norah	Fiction
Maeve's Daughter	Paige, Frances	Fiction
Maggie	Kennedy, Lena	Fiction
Maggie - A Girl Of The Streets	Crane, Stephen	Fiction
Maggie Craig	Joseph, Marie	Fiction

TITLES INDEX

Title	Author	Category
Maggie Jordan	Blair, Emma	Fiction
Maggie Rowan	Cookson, Catherine	Fiction
Magic Apple Tree, The	Hill, Susan	Non-Fiction
Magic Faraway Tree, The	Blyton, Enid	Fiction
Magic Finger, The	Dahl, Roald	Fiction
Magic Of Believing	Self Improvement	Non-Fiction
Magic Of Innocence	Slater, Elizabeth	Fiction
Magic Of Thinking Big, The	Self Improvement	Non-Fiction
Magic Quern, The	Traditional	Fiction
Magic Shop And The Red Room, The	Wells, H.G.	Fiction
Magic Sword, The	Traditional	Fiction
Magician's Nephew, The	Lewis, C.S	Fiction
Magnetic Love	Peploe, Frances	Fiction
Magnificent Severn, The	Trains...	Non-Fiction
Magnus Powermouse	King-Smith, Dick	Fiction
Maiden Voyage	Stuart, Alex	Fiction
Maids And Mistresses	Powell, Margaret	Non-Fiction
Maigret	Simenon, Georges	Fiction
Maigret And The Killer	Simenon, Georges	Fiction
Maigret And The Toy Village	Simenon, Georges	Fiction
Main Line Steam Specials	Trains...	Non-Fiction
Majestic	Streiber, Whitley	Fiction
Major Barbara	Shaw, George Bernard	Fiction
Make Sentences In French 1 & 2	French	Non-Fiction
Makes All The Difference	Bible	Non-Fiction
Makes Us Useful	Bible	Non-Fiction
Making It Happen	Harvey-Jones, John	Non-Fiction
Making Relationships Last	Self Improvement	Non-Fiction
Making Sense Of The Verb	German	Non-Fiction
Malaspiga Exit, The	Anthony, Evelyn	Fiction
Malibu	Booth, Pat	Fiction
Malice Domestic	Hardwick, Mollie	Fiction
Mallen Girl, The	Cookson, Catherine	Fiction
Mallen Litter, The	Cookson, Catherine	Fiction
Mallen Streak, The	Cookson, Catherine	Fiction
Man Be My Metaphor	Thomas, Dylan	Fiction
Man Called Kyril, The	Trenhaile, John	Fiction
Man Could Get Killed, A	Short, Luke	Fiction
Man From Odessa, The	Wynne, Greville	Non-Fiction
Man From St. Petersburg, The	Follett, Ken	Fiction
Man In Her Life, The	Ayres, Ruby M.	Fiction
Man Of Honour, A	Holland, Lys	Fiction
Man Of Honour, A	Slater, Elizabeth	Fiction
Man On Fire	Quinnell, A.J.	Fiction
Man Upstairs, The	Wodehouse, P.J.	Fiction
Man Who Broke The Bank At Monte Carlo, The	Butterworth, Michael	Fiction
Man Who Could Work Miracles, The	Wells, H.G.	Fiction
Man Who Created Himself, The	Ming, Sexton	Fiction
Man Who Cried, The	Cookson, Catherine	Fiction
Man Who Sold Death, The	Munro, James	Fiction
Man Who Would Be King, The	Kipling, Rudyard	Fiction
Man With The Golden Gun, The	Fleming, Ian	Fiction
Managing The Future	Business	Non-Fiction
Manchester Fourteen Miles	Penn, Margaret	Non-Fiction
Mandeville Talent, The	Higgins, George	Fiction
Manhattan Magic	Davidson, Jean	Fiction
Manon Lescaut	Prevost, Abbe	Non-Fiction
Mansfield Park	Austen, Jane	Fiction
Mansfield Park: The Symbol Of The House	A-Level	Non-Fiction
Manwatching	Self Improvement	Non-Fiction
Many Waters: Part 3	Street, Pamela	Fiction
Mao Tse-Tung	Mao Tse-Tung	Non-Fiction
Maple Town	Miscellaneous	Fiction
Mapp And Lucia	Benson, E.F	Fiction
March Hare Murders, The	Ferrars, Elizabeth	Fiction
Mariana	Dickens, Monica	Fiction
Mark	Bible	Non-Fiction

TITLES INDEX

Title	Author	Category
Marmaduke The Lorry Goes To Italy	Chapman, Elizabeth	Fiction
Marriage And Mary Ann	Cookson, Catherine	Fiction
Marriage Chest, The	Eden, Dorothy	Fiction
Marriage Group, The	A-Level	Non-Fiction
Marriage Of Gawain, The	Traditional	Fiction
Marsh Melodies	Environmental Sounds	Non-Fiction
Martian Chronicles, The	Bradbury, Ray	Fiction
Martin Luther King	Luther King, Martin	Non-Fiction
Martin's Mice	King-Smith, Dick	Fiction
Marx And Marxism	Marx, Karl	Non-Fiction
Marx And The Material Concept Of History	Germany	Non-Fiction
Mary Ann And Bill	Cookson, Catherine	Fiction
Mary Ann's Angels	Cookson, Catherine	Fiction
Mary Baker Eddy	Baker Eddy, Mary	Non-Fiction
Mary Poppins	Travers, P.L.	Fiction
Mary Poppins	Travers, P.L.	Fiction
Mary Poppins And The Banks Family	Travers, P.L.	Fiction
Mary Poppins Comes Back	Travers, P.L.	Fiction
Mary Poppins Opens The Door	Travers, P.L.	Fiction
Mary Tudor	History	Non-Fiction
Mary Wakefield	De La Roche, Mazo	Fiction
Mask	Jackson, Steve	Fiction
Mask Of The Andes	Cleary, Jon	Fiction
Mask, The	Ghost Stories	Fiction
Mask-A-Raid	Jackson, Steve	Fiction
Masked Love	Wright, Katrina	Fiction
Masquerade	Dailey, Janet	Fiction
Masqueraders, The	Heyer, Georgette	Fiction
Master Builder, The	Ibsen, Henrik	Fiction
Master Of Ballantrae	Stevenson, Robert Louis	Fiction
Master Of Blacktower, The	Michaels, Barbara	Fiction
Master Of Melthorpe	Sinclair, Olga	Fiction
Master Of The Game	Sheldon, Sidney	Fiction
Master Of The Moor	Rendell, Ruth	Fiction
Masterclass	West, Morris	Fiction
Mastering English As A Foreign Language	English	Non-Fiction
Masters Of The Universe	Television	Fiction
Master's Wife	Ramsay, Fay	Fiction
Masterthinker	Business	Non-Fiction
Matanzas	Custer, Clint	Fiction
Matarese Circle, The	Ludlum, Robert	Fiction
Matching Tie And Handkerchief	Monty Python	Fiction
Mathematics (Course)	G.C.S.E..	Non-Fiction
Mathilde Mouse	Gillico, Paul	Fiction
Matilda	Dahl, Roald	Fiction
Mating Season, The	Wodehouse, P.G.	Fiction
Matryonin Dvor	Solzhentizyn, Alexander	Non-Fiction
Matter Of Choice	Poetry	Fiction
Matter Of Conscience, A	Harcourt, Palma	Fiction
Matter Of Honour, A	Archer, Jeffrey	Fiction
Matter Of Life And Death, A	Bible	Non-Fiction
Matthew	Bible	Non-Fiction
Maturing Sun, The	Edwards, Rowan	Fiction
Max Brand's Best Western Stories	Brand, Max	Fiction
Maximising Examination Performance	Self Improvement	Non-Fiction
Mayor Of Casterbridge	Hardy, Thomas	Fiction
Me	Hepburn, Katherine	Non-Fiction
Me And Billy Williams	Boyce, Max	Fiction
Measure For Measure	A-Level	Non-Fiction
Measure For Measure	Shakespeare, William	Fiction
Measure Of Peace, A	Graham, Margaret	Fiction
Medea	Euripides	Fiction
Medicine Bow, The	Paine, Lauren	Fiction
Medicine The Human Aspect	Self Improvement	Non-Fiction
Meditation	Self Improvement	Non-Fiction
Meditations For Personal Harmony	Self Improvement	Non-Fiction
Mednyi Vsadnik	Pushkin, Alexander S.	Non-Fiction

TITLES INDEX

Title	Author	Category
Medusa	Innes, Hammond	Fiction
Meet Me At The Savoy	Nicol, Jean	Fiction
Meet Posy Bates	Cresswell, Helen	Fiction
Meeting, The	Webb, Edwin	Non-Fiction
Meg And Mog	Nicoll, Helen	Fiction
Mega Trends	Business	Non-Fiction
Melancholy Hussar, The	Hardy, Thomas	Fiction
Melody Of Life	Baldursson	Non-Fiction
Melody Of The Moon	Shelburne, A.V.	Fiction
Melting Heart, The	Jameson, Claudia	Fiction
Memoirs Of A Sword Swallower	Mannix, Dan	Fiction
Memoirs Of Barry Lyndon	Thackeray, William Makepeace	Fiction
Memoirs Of Sherlock Holmes	Conan Doyle, Arthur	Fiction
Memoirs Of The Hammer Years	Cushing, Peter	Non-Fiction
Memories Of Great Wireless Comedy Shows	Comedy...	Fiction
Memories Of A Highland Lady	Grant, Elizabeth	Non-Fiction
Memories Of Osborne	Blake, Dorothy	Non-Fiction
Memory Kinda Lingers, The/Not In Front Of The...	Not The Nine O'clock News	Fiction
Men Of Iron	Pyle, Howard	Fiction
Menagerie, The	Cookson, Catherine	Fiction
Menfreya	Holt, Victoria	Fiction
Mental Stress And Physical Fitness	Self Improvement	Non-Fiction
Mentally Tough	Business	Non-Fiction
Mercantilism	Social Sciences	Non-Fiction
Merchant Of Venice, The	Shakespeare, William	Fiction
Merlin And Perceval	Traditional	Fiction
Merlin's Keep	Brent, Madeleine	Fiction
Merry Matanzie	Soutar, William	Fiction
Merry Wives Of Windsor, The	Shakespeare, William	Fiction
Mervyn Mouse	Poetry	Fiction
Mesyats V Derevne	Turgenev, Ivan	Non-Fiction
Metamorphoses	Ovid	Fiction
Metamorphosis, The	Kafka, Franz	Fiction
Metternich And The Napoleonic Wars 1809-1815	Military History	Non-Fiction
Mexico Set	Deighton, Len	Fiction
Mexico Vivo	Spanish	Non-Fiction
MG Just For The Record	MG Cars	Non-Fiction
Mid-day On Jost Van Dyke	Environmental Sounds	Non-Fiction
Midland And North Western	Trains...	Non-Fiction
Midsummer Night's Dream, A	Shakespeare, William	Fiction
Miffy	Bruna, Dick	Fiction
Miffy Stories	Bruna, Dick	Fiction
Mill On The Floss, The	Eliot, George	Fiction
Mill Race, The	Street, Pamela	Fiction
Millay Reading Her Poetry	Millay, Edna	Fiction
Milligan Preserved	Milligan, Spike	Fiction
Millionaire's Daughter	Eden, Dorothy	Fiction
Milly Molly Mandy	Lankester Brisley J.	Fiction
Milly Molly Mandy Stories	Lankester Brisley J.	Fiction
Minature Murder Mystery	Chambers, Peter	Fiction
Mind Of Mr. J.G. Reeder, The	Wallace, Edgar	Fiction
Mind Over Illness	Self Improvement	Non-Fiction
Mind To Murder, A	James, P.D.	Fiction
Mind-Body Tempo	Health & Fitness	Non-Fiction
Minerva's Stepchild	Forrester, Helen	Non-Fiction
Minpins, The	Dahl, Roald	Fiction
Minstrel Boy, The	Cronin, A.J.	Fiction
Misalliance	Shaw, George Bernard	Fiction
Misalliance, The	Brookner, Anita	Fiction
Miss Mapp	Benson, E.F	Fiction
Miss Martha Mary Crawford	Marchant, Catherine	Fiction
Miss. Pym Disposes	Tey, Josephine	Fiction
Missing Ambassador, The	Children's Stories	Fiction
Mission England Vol.2	Religious	Non-Fiction
Mistress Of Lamberly Grange	March, Stella	Fiction
Mistress Of Mellyn	Holt, Victoria	Fiction
Mithridate	Racine, Jean	Fiction

TITLES INDEX

Title	Author/Subject	Category
Moby Dick	Melville, Herman	Fiction
Modal Auxiliary Verbs, The	German	Non-Fiction
Model Murder	Quest, Erica	Fiction
Moderato Cantabile	Duras, Marguerite	Non-Fiction
Modern Greek Basic Course	Greek	Non-Fiction
Modern Italian Cinema	Italy	Non-Fiction
Modern Poetry	English Literature	Non-Fiction
Modern Russian	Russian...	Non-Fiction
Modern Short Stories	Short Stories	Fiction
Modern Soviet Cinema	Russia	Non-Fiction
Modern Spoken Italian	Italian	Non-Fiction
Modern Written Arabic	Arabic	Non-Fiction
Modest Proposal, A	Swift, Jonathan	Fiction
Modigliani Scandal, The	Follett, Ken	Fiction
Mogg's Christmas	Kerr, Judith	Fiction
Moll Flanders	Defoe, Daniel	Fiction
Molloy Malone Dies	Beckett, Samuel	Fiction
Mom, The Wolfman And Me	Klein, Norma	Fiction
Moment In Time, A	Bates, H.E.	Fiction
Moment Of War, A	Lee, Laurie	Non-Fiction
Monarch: Life And Times Of Elizabeth II	Fisher, Graham	Non-Fiction
Monarch Of The Glen, The	MacKenzie, Compton	Fiction
Moneylender Of Shahpur, The	Forrester, Helen	Fiction
Monkey Puzzle	Gosling, Paula	Fiction
Monkeyville Case, The	Lustgarten, Edgar	Non-Fiction
Monk's Hartwell	Treves, Kathleen	Fiction
Monk's Hood	Peters, Ellis	Fiction
Monocled Mutineer, The	Allison & Fairley	Non-Fiction
Monsieur Pamplemousse	Bond, Michael	Fiction
Monsieur Pamplemousse Investigates	Bond, Michael	Fiction
Monsignor Quixote	Greene, Graham	Fiction
Monster Maker	Fisk, Nicholas	Fiction
Monsters Of The Earth	Ghost Stories	Fiction
Montmarter Murders, The	Grayson, Richard	Fiction
Monty Python And The Holy Grail	Monty Python	Fiction
Monty Python's Flying Circus	Monty Python	Fiction
Monty Python's Meaning Of Life	Monty Python	Fiction
Moobli	Tomkies, Mike	Non-Fiction
Moon	Herbert, James	Fiction
Moon And Sixpence, The	Maugham, W. Somerset	Fiction
Moon Princess, The	Traditional	Fiction
Moon Tiger	Lively, Penelope	Fiction
Moonbather, The	Clarke, Roy	Fiction
Moonies, The	Religious	Non-Fiction
Moonlit Way, The	Dwyer-Joyce, Alice	Fiction
Moonraker	Fleming, Ian	Fiction
Moonraker's Bride	Brent, Madeleine	Fiction
Moon's A Balloon, The	Niven, David	Non-Fiction
Moon's Gibbet	Ghost Stories	Fiction
Moon-Spinners, The	Stewart, Mary	Fiction
Moonstone, The	Collins, Wilkie	Fiction
Mop And Smiff	Television	Fiction
Mop And Smiff Go To School	Television	Fiction
Mop And Smiff In Search Of A Pedigree	Television	Fiction
Mop And Smiff On Bunny Hill	Television	Fiction
Mop And Smiff's Day Sunnyseas	Television	Fiction
Morality Of Strikes	Social Sciences	Non-Fiction
Morbid Taste For Bones, A	Peters, Ellis	Fiction
More About Paddington Bear	Bond, Michael	Fiction
More About The Gumby Gang	Oldfield, Pamela	Fiction
More Adventures Of My Little Pony	Zabel, Jennifer	Fiction
More Deadly Than The Male	Chase, James Hadley	Fiction
More Father Brown Stories	Chesterton, G.K.	Fiction
More Favourite Poems	Poetry	Fiction
More From Ten In A Bed	Ahlberg, Allan	Fiction
More Fun At One	Radio	Fiction
More Ghost Stories	James, M.R.	Fiction

397

TITLES INDEX

Title	Author	Category
More Grimm's Fairy Tales	Grimm	Fiction
More Jungle Book Stories	Kipling, Rudyard	Fiction
More Junk	Steptoe & Son	Fiction
More Little Grey Rabbit Stories	Uttley, Alison	Fiction
More Monologues And Songs	Holloway, Stanley	Fiction
More Naughty Little Sister Stories	Edwards, Dorothy	Fiction
More Of The Best Of Round The Horne	Radio	Fiction
More Postman Pat Stories	Cunliffe, John	Fiction
More Railway Stories (1 & 2)	Awdry, Rev. W.	Fiction
More Sherlock Holmes Stories	Conan Doyle, Arthur	Fiction
More Tales From A Country Practice	Jackson, Arthur	Non-Fiction
More Tales From A Long Room	Tinniswood, Peter	Fiction
More Tales From Ten In A Bed	Ahlberg, Allan	Fiction
More William Stories	Crompton, Richmal	Fiction
More Will O' The Wisp Stories	Television	Fiction
More Work For The Undertaker	Allingham, Margery	Fiction
Mormons	Religious	Non-Fiction
Morning At Jalna	De La Roche, Mazo	Fiction
Morning Glory	Street, Pamela	Fiction
Moroccan Arabic	Arabic	Non-Fiction
Mortar Fire - Normandy To Germany 1944-45	Francia, Paul	Non-Fiction
Morte D'Arthur	Malory, Sir Thomas	Fiction
Mortimer Says Nothing	Aiken, Joan	Fiction
Mortimer's Cross	Aiken, Joan	Fiction
Moscow Quadrille	Allbeury, Ted	Fiction
Most Immaculately Hip Aristocrat	Lord Buckley	Fiction
Moth, The	Cookson, Catherine	Fiction
Mother And Daughter	Lawrence, D.H.	Fiction
Mother Goose	Traditional	Fiction
Motive Power Vols.1 - 4	Trains...	Non-Fiction
Motormouth	Elton, Ben	Fiction
Motorvation	Elton, Ben	Fiction
Mountain Laurel	Deveraux, Jude	Fiction
Mountain Medley	Environmental Sounds	Non-Fiction
Mountain Of Adventure	Blyton, Enid	Fiction
Mouse And His Child	Hoban, Russell	Fiction
Mouse Butcher, The	King-Smith, Dick	Fiction
Mouse Tales	Potter, Beatrix	Fiction
Mouth Organ Boys, The	Berry, James	Fiction
Mozart I Salieri	Pushkin, Alexander S.	Non-Fiction
Mr. Bridge	Connell, Evan S.	Fiction
Mr. Grumpy's Outing	Burningham, John	Fiction
Mr. Majeika	Carpenter, Humphrey	Fiction
Mr. Men And Little Miss	Hargreaves, Roger	Fiction
Mr. Men Ride Again, The	Hargreaves, Roger	Fiction
Mr. Men Stories	Hargreaves, Roger	Fiction
Mr. Midshipman Hornblower	Forester, C.S.	Fiction
Mr. Plod And Little Noddy	Blyton, Enid	Fiction
Mrs. Bridge	Connell, Evan S.	Fiction
Mrs. Craggs	Keating, H.R.F.	Fiction
Mrs. Dalloway	Woolf, Virginia	Fiction
Mrs. Frisby And The Rats Of Nimh	O'Brien, Robert C	Fiction
Mrs. God	Straub, Peter	Fiction
Mrs. Maybrick & Mrs Merryfield	Lustgarten, Edgar	Non-Fiction
Mrs. Milsent's Daughter	Masterton, Barbara	Fiction
Mrs. Miniver	Struther, Jan	Fiction
Mrs. Packletide's Tiger	Saki	Fiction
Mrs. Pargeter's Package	Brett, Simon	Fiction
Mrs. Pepperpot Stories	Proysen, Alf	Fiction
Mrs. Pollifax On The China Station	Gilman, Dorothy	Fiction
Mrs. Presumed Dead	Brett, Simon	Fiction
Mrs Pringle	Read, Miss	Fiction
Mrs Tiggy-Winkle And Friends	Potter, Beatrix	Fiction
Mrs.'Ardin's Kid	Harding, Mike	Fiction
Much Ado About Nothing	A-Level	Non-Fiction
Much Ado About Nothing	Shakespeare, William	Fiction
Much Binding In The Marsh	Radio	Fiction

TITLES INDEX

Much Obliged, Jeeves	Wodehouse, P.G.	Fiction
Much Suspected Of Me	Peters, Maureen	Fiction
Muckle Annie	Webster, Jan	Fiction
Muezzin's Call And Islamic Chants	Religious	Non-Fiction
Mugger, The	McBain, Ed	Fiction
Mule, The	Asimov, Isaac	Fiction
Multi National Firms	Social Sciences	Non-Fiction
Multiplication	Early Learning	Non-Fiction
Mummy, The	Sibley, Raymond	Fiction
Munch Bunch	Read, Giles	Fiction
Munch Bunch Stories	Read, Giles	Fiction
Munch Bunch Stories And Songs	Read, Giles	Fiction
Murder At Government House	Huxley, Elspeth	Fiction
Murder At Plums	Myers, Amy	Fiction
Murder At The Follies	Lustgarten, Edgar	Non-Fiction
Murder At The Vicarage, The	Christie, Agatha	Fiction
Murder Fantastical	Moyes, Patricia	Fiction
Murder In Georgetown	Truman, Margaret	Fiction
Murder In Mesopotamia	Christie, Agatha	Fiction
Murder In The Cathedral	Eliot, T.S.	Fiction
Murder In The Limelight	Myers, Amy	Fiction
Murder In The Mews	Christie, Agatha	Fiction
Murder In The Oval Office	Roosevelt, Elliott	Fiction
Murder In Vain	Mantell, Laurie	Fiction
Murder Is Announced, A	Christie, Agatha	Fiction
Murder Is For Keeps	Chambers, Peter	Fiction
Murder Must Advertise	Sayers, Dorothy L.	Fiction
Murder Of Quality, A	Le Carre, John	Fiction
Murder Of Roger Ackroyd	Christie, Agatha	Fiction
Murder Of The Maharajah, The	Keating, H.R.F.	Fiction
Murder On Safari	Huxley, Elspeth	Fiction
Murder On The Orient Express	Christie, Agatha	Fiction
Murder Too Many, A	Ferrars, Elizabeth	Fiction
Murder Unprompted	Brett, Simon	Fiction
Murder Without Icing	Lathen, Emma	Fiction
Music And Sound Library Vols.1 & 2	Sound Effects	Non-Fiction
Music 'n' Motion	Health & Fitness	Non-Fiction
Music On The Hill, The	Saki	Fiction
Musical Sounds	Early Learning	Non-Fiction
Musical Sums	Early Learning	Non-Fiction
Musical Times Tables	Early Learning	Non-Fiction
Musicians Of Bremen, The	Grimm	Fiction
Mussolini	Italy	Non-Fiction
Mussolini: His Part In My Downfall	Milligan, Spike	Non-Fiction
Mutter Courage Und Ihre Kinder	Brecht, Bertolt	Non-Fiction
My	Zamyatin, Evgeny	Non-Fiction
My Beloved Son	Cookson, Catherine	Fiction
My Book Of Pets	Early Learning	Non-Fiction
My Book Of Words	Early Learning	Non-Fiction
My Brother Michael	Stewart, Mary	Fiction
My Cousin Rachel	Du Maurier, Daphne	Fiction
My Dear Fugitive	Sinclair, Olga	Fiction
My Family And Other Animals	Durrell, Gerald	Non-Fiction
My Favourite Fairy Stories	Traditional	Fiction
My Friend The Professor	Andrews, Lucilla	Fiction
My Friend Walter	Morpurgo, Michael	Fiction
My Girl In Skin Tight Jeans	Boyd, William	Fiction
My Gorgeous Life	Everage, Dame Edna	Fiction
My Grandfather	Constanduros, Denis	Fiction
My Gun Is Quick	Spillane, Mickey	Fiction
My Last Duchess	Browning, Robert	Fiction
My Little Pony	Zabel, Jennifer	Fiction
My Old Chap	Goodland, Norman	Fiction
My Small Country Living	McMullen, Jeanine	Non-Fiction
My Turn To Make The Tea	Dickens, Monica	Non-Fiction
My Uncle Silas	Bates, H.E.	Fiction
Mysterious Mr Quin, The	Christie, Agatha	Fiction

TITLES INDEX

Title	Author	Category
Mysterious Railway Stories	Pattrick, William	Fiction
Mystery	Straub, Peter	Fiction
Mystery Mile	Allingham, Margery	Fiction
Mystery Of Borley Rectory, The	De Souza, Edward	Non-Fiction
Mystery Of Tally-Ho Cottage, The	Blyton, Enid	Fiction
Mystery Of The Burnt Cottage, The	Blyton, Enid	Fiction
Mystery Of The Secret Room, The	Blyton, Enid	Fiction
Myths Of Mental Illness	Szasz, Thomas S.	Non-Fiction
N Or M ?	Christie, Agatha	Fiction
Naked And The Dead	Mailer, Norman	Fiction
Naked Country, The	West, Morris	Fiction
Naked Face, The	Sheldon, Sidney	Fiction
Nana	Zola, Emile	Fiction
Nancy Regan	Kelly, Kitty	Non-Fiction
Napoleon	Napoleon	Non-Fiction
Napoleon Bonaparte	Bonaparte, Napoleon	Non-Fiction
Napoleon Bonaparte	France	Non-Fiction
Napoleon II	France	Non-Fiction
Napoleon III	France	Non-Fiction
Napoleon Of Nottinghill, The	Chesterton, G.K.	Fiction
Narrative Of Gordon Pym Of Nantucket, The	Poe, Edgar Allan	Fiction
Native Son	Wright, Richard	Fiction
Natural Way To Alleviate Stress	Health & Fitness	Non-Fiction
Natural Way To Control Agoraphobia	Health & Fitness	Non-Fiction
Natural Way To Control Nail Biting	Health & Fitness	Non-Fiction
Natural Way To Increase Confidence	Health & Fitness	Non-Fiction
Natural Way To Learn Self Hypnosis And ...	Health & Fitness	Non-Fiction
Natural Way To Overcome Fear Of Flying	Health & Fitness	Non-Fiction
Natural Way To Overcome Insomnia	Health & Fitness	Non-Fiction
Natural Way To Reduce Driving Test Nerves	Health & Fitness	Non-Fiction
Natural Way To Reduce Exam Nerves	Health & Fitness	Non-Fiction
Natural Way To Slim, The	Health & Fitness	Non-Fiction
Natural Way To Stop Smoking	Health & Fitness	Non-Fiction
Naturalism And The American Novel	Caldwell, Erskine	Non-Fiction
Nature And Structure Of Shakespearean Comedy	ALlevel	Non-Fiction
Nature Of Keats' Great Odes, The	A-Level	Non-Fiction
Nature Of The Beast	Howker, Janni	Fiction
Navy Lark, The	Radio	Fiction
Necessary Treason, A	English Literature	Non-Fiction
Necklace Of Raindrops, A	Aiken, Joan	Fiction
Neeps And Tatties	Scotland	Non-Fiction
Negotiator, The	Forsyth, Frederick	Fiction
Nellie The Elephant	Children's Stories..	Fiction
Nelly Kelly	Kennedy, Lena	Fiction
Nelson	Nelson	Non-Fiction
Nemesis	Asimov, Isaac	Fiction
Nemesis	Christie, Agatha	Fiction
Nep And Soviet Industrialisation, The	Russia	Non-Fiction
Nerve	Francis, Dick	Fiction
Never Be Nervous Again	Self Improvement	Non-Fiction
Never Fall In Love	Sinclair, Olga	Fiction
Never Look Back	Robins, Denise	Fiction
Never Pick Up Hitch-Hikers	Peters, Ellis	Fiction
Never Smile At A Crocodile	Children's Stories..	Fiction
New Alignments, The	Social Sciences	Non-Fiction
New Collected Short Stories, The	Forster, E.M.	Fiction
New Imperialism 1870 - 1914, The	Germany	Non-Fiction
New Life For Joanna, A	Bromige, Iris	Fiction
New Look At Psychologists	Self Improvement	Non-Fiction
New Theatre Sister, The	Andrews, Lucilla	Fiction
New Testament	Bible	Non-Fiction
New Testament In Scots	Bible	Non-Fiction
New Testament - Vols.12, 13,14, 15	Bible	Non-Fiction
New Time Management	Business	Non-Fiction
New York Stories, The	Henry, O	Fiction
Newcastle Train Murder & Death On The Crumbles	Lustgarten, Edgar	Non-Fiction
News From Lake Wobegon	Keillor, Garrison	Fiction

TITLES INDEX

Title	Author	Category
News From Thrush Green	Read, Miss	Fiction
News Quiz, The	Radio	Non-Fiction
Next To Nature, Art	Lively, Penelope	Fiction
Nice Bloke, The	Cookson, Catherine	Fiction
Nice Class Of Corpse, A	Brett, Simon	Fiction
Nice Derangement Of Epitaphs, A	Peters, Ellis	Fiction
Nice Knight For Murder	Daniels, Philip	Fiction
Nice One, Cyril	Fletcher, Cyril	Non-Fiction
Nice Work	Lodge, David	Fiction
Nicholas Nickleby	Dickens, Charles	Fiction
Nickums, The	Bell, J.J.	Fiction
Night Before Christmas, The	Children's Stories..	Fiction
Night Bright Shiners, The	Fraser, Anthea	Fiction
Night Dive	Peel, Colin D	Fiction
Night Journey	Graham, Winston	Fiction
Night Judgement At Sinos	Higgins, Jack	Fiction
Night Of Error	Bagley, Desmond	Fiction
Night Of The Fox	Higgins, Jack	Fiction
Night Of The Generals	Kirst, H.H.	Fiction
Night Of The Living Dead	Russo, John A.	Fiction
Night Of The Party, The	Bromige, Iris	Fiction
Night Of Wenceslas	Davidson, Lionel	Fiction
Night On't Town, A	Bible	Non-Fiction
Night She Died, The	Simpson, Dorothy	Fiction
Night Sky, The	Astronomy	Non-Fiction
Nightclub Years (1964-1968)	Allen, Woody	Fiction
Nightingale, The	Children's Stories..	Fiction
Nightmares	Poetry	Fiction
Night-Watchmen, The	Cresswell, Helen	Fiction
Nikita Khrushchev	Krushchev, Nikita	Non-Fiction
Nine Coaches Waiting	Stewart, Mary	Fiction
Nine Tailors, The	Sayers, Dorothy L.	Fiction
Nineteen Eighty-Four, George Orwell	Orwell, George	Non-Fiction
Nineteenth Century Imperialism	Social Sciences	Non-Fiction
Nineteenth Century Russia	Russia	Non-Fiction
Ninety Minutes Of Suspense	McConnell, Jean	Fiction
No Admitance, No Exit	Bailey, Don	Fiction
No Case For The Police	Clinton-Baddeley, U.C.	Fiction
No Comebacks	Forsyth, Frederick	Fiction
No Enemy But Time	Anthony, Evelyn	Fiction
No Exit	Sartre, Jean-Paul	Fiction
No Fond Return Of Love	Pym, Barbara	Fiction
No Gold When You Go	Chambers, Peter	Fiction
No Highway	Shute, Nevil	Fiction
No Medals For The Major	Yorke, Margaret	Fiction
No More Cocoons	Biafra, Jello	Non-Fiction
No Place Like	Kemp, Gene	Fiction
No Place To Hide	Allbeury, Ted	Fiction
No Room For Loneliness	MacKinlay, Leila	Fiction
Nocturnal And Diurnal Birds Of Prey	Bird Songs	Non-Fiction
Nocturnal Steam	Trains...	Non-Fiction
Nocturne Of Nightingales	Bird Songs	Non-Fiction
Noddy And The Magic Boots	Blyton, Enid	Fiction
Noddy And The Tootles	Blyton, Enid	Fiction
Noddy Goes To Sea	Blyton, Enid	Fiction
Noddy Has An Adventure	Blyton, Enid	Fiction
Noddy Makes Everyone Cross	Blyton, Enid	Fiction
Noddy Stories	Blyton, Enid	Fiction
Noddy's Big Balloon	Blyton, Enid	Fiction
Noddy's Unlucky Day	Blyton, Enid	Fiction
Noel Coward And Gertrude Lawrence	Coward, Noel	Fiction
Noel Coward Reading	Coward, Noel	Fiction
Noel's Funny Phone Calls	Edmonds, Noel	Fiction
Nonsense Poems	Lear, Edward	Fiction
Nonsense Poetry	Poetry	Fiction
Nonsense Verse	Carroll, Lewis	Fiction
Nonstop Nonsense	Mahy, Margaret	Fiction

Title	Author/Subject	Category
Normal Procedure	Bible	Non-Fiction
Norsk Fonetikk For Utlendinger	Norwegian	Non-Fiction
Norsk For Utlendinger	Norwegian	Non-Fiction
North From Rome	MacInnes, Helen	Fiction
North Of Kings Cross	Trains...	Non-Fiction
Northanger Abbey	Austen, Jane	Fiction
Norwegian Cassette Course	Norwegian	Non-Fiction
Norwegian Travel Pack	Norwegian	Non-Fiction
Norwood Builder, The	Conan Doyle, Arthur	Fiction
Nostroma	Conrad, Joseph	Fiction
Not A Penny More, Not A Penny Less	Archer, Jeffrey	Fiction
Not As Far As Velma	Freeling, Nicolas	Fiction
Not Just A Pretty Face	Atkinson, Rowan	Fiction
Not Just A Pretty Face	Cool, Phil	Fiction
Not That I'm Biased	Boyce, Max	Fiction
Not That Sort Of Girl	Wesley, Mary	Fiction
Not The Double Album	Not The Nine O'Clock News	Fiction
Not The Nine O'clock News	Not The Nine O'Clock News	Fiction
Not Wanted On Voyage	Thorpe, Kay	Fiction
Nothing Down	Business	Non-Fiction
Nothing Quite Like It	Wallace, Ian	Non-Fiction
Nothing To Be Afraid Of	Mark, Jan	Fiction
Not-just-anybody Family, The	Byars, Betsy	Fiction
Novels Of Graham Greene, The	Greene, Graham	Non-Fiction
Now We Are Six	Milne, A.A.	Fiction
Nowhere On Earth	Elder, Michael	Fiction
Number 13	James, M.R.	Fiction
Numbers	Early Learning	Non-Fiction
Nun's Priest's Tale, The	A-Level	Non-Fiction
Nurse At Radleigh	Goodwin, Grace	Fiction
Nurse Errant	Andrews, Lucilla	Fiction
Nurse In The Valley	Goodwin, Grace	Fiction
Nursing Home Murder, The	Marsh, Ngaio	Fiction
Nutcracker	Traditional	Fiction
O Henry Favourites	Henry, O	Fiction
O Pioneers	Cather, Willa	Fiction
O, The Northern Muse	Heaney, Seamus	Non-Fiction
Oblomov	Goncharov, L.A.	Non-Fiction
Obscure Beauty: Difficulty In Poetry, The	English Literature	Non-Fiction
Obsession	Lamb, Charlotte	Fiction
Occurence At Owl Creek Bridge, An	Bierce, Ambrose	Fiction
Octavia	Cooper, Jilly	Fiction
Odd Flamingo, The	Bawden, Nina	Fiction
Odd Job Man, The	Crisp, N.J.	Fiction
Odd Man Out	Mason, James	Non-Fiction
Odds Against	Francis, Dick	Fiction
Odessa File, The	Forsyth, Frederick	Fiction
Odysseus - The Greatest Hero Of Them All	Robinson, T. & Curtis, R.	Fiction
Odyssey, The	Homer	Fiction
Oedipus Rex	Sophocles	Fiction
Official Guide To CB Radio	CB Radio	Non-Fiction
Oh Baby	Cosby, Bill	Fiction
Oi, Get Off Our Train	Burningham, John	Fiction
Oil, A World Crisis	Social Sciences	Non-Fiction
Old Bear	Hissey, Jane	Fiction
Old MacDonald	Children's Stories..	Fiction
Old MacDonald Had A Farm	Children's Stories..	Fiction
Old Man And The Sea, The	Hemingway, Ernest	Fiction
Old Man Of Lochnagar	H.R.H. Prince Of Wales	Fiction
Old Murders	Whalley, Peter	Fiction
Old Patagonian Express, The	Theroux, Paul	Non-Fiction
Old Possum's Book Of Practical Cats	Eliot, T.S.	Fiction
Old Testament	Bible	Non-Fiction
Old Testament - The Authorised Version	Bible	Non-Fiction
Old Testament - Vols. 1,2,3,4,5,6,7,10,11	Bible	Non-Fiction
Old Wive's Tale, The	Bennett, Arnold	Fiction
Oliver And Company	Disney	Fiction

TITLES INDEX

Title	Author	Category
Oliver Cromwell	Cromwell, Oliver	Non-Fiction
Omos Do Scoil Dhun Chaoin	Mhac An Saoi, Maire	Fiction
On Becoming A Leader	Business	Non-Fiction
On Her Majesty's Secret Service	Fleming, Ian	Fiction
On Ne Badine Pas Avec L'Amour	De Musset, A	Non-Fiction
On Radio	Marx, Groucho	Fiction
On The Air	Dean, James	Fiction
On The Beach	Shute, Nevil	Fiction
On The Edge	Lovesey, Peter	Fiction
On The Side Of Laughter	Muggeridge, Malcolm	Non-Fiction
On Tour With The Big Yin	Connolly, Billy	Fiction
Once A Marine	Stokoe, E.G.	Fiction
Once In Austria	Duke, Madelaine	Fiction
Once Is Not Enough	Susann, Jacqueline	Fiction
Once More With Cook	Cook, Peter	Fiction
Once Upon A Time	Biro, Val	Fiction
Once Upon A Time	Children's Stories..	Fiction
Once Upon A Time	Oldfield, Pamela	Fiction
Once Upon A Time	Traditional	Fiction
Once Upon A World	Bible	Non-Fiction
One And Last Love	Braine, John	Fiction
One Corpse Too Many	Peters, Ellis	Fiction
One Flew Over The Cuckoo's Nest	Kesey, Ken	Fiction
One Hundred Comedy Inserts	Comedy...	Fiction
One Little Room	Webster, Jan	Fiction
One Lonely Night	Spillane, Mickey	Fiction
One Man And His Dog	Richardson, Anthony	Non-Fiction
One Man's War	Social Sciences	Non-Fiction
One Minute Manager	Business	Non-Fiction
One Minute Manager Gets Fit	Business	Non-Fiction
One Minute Manager Meets The Monkey	Business	Non-Fiction
One Minute Manager & Putting The One ...	Business	Non-Fiction
One Minute Sales	Business	Non-Fiction
One Night In London	Andrews, Lucilla	Fiction
One Pair Of Feet	Dickens, Monica	Non-Fiction
One Pair Of Hands	Dickens, Monica	Non-Fiction
One Summers Grace	Purves, Libby	Fiction
One, Two, Buckle My Shoe	Christie, Agatha	Fiction
Onedin Line: Iron Ships	Abraham, Cyril	Fiction
Onedin Line: The High Seas	Abraham, Cyril	Fiction
Onedin Line: The Shipmaster	Abraham, Cyril	Fiction
Onedin Line: The White Ships	Abraham, Cyril	Fiction
Onedin Line: Trade Winds	Abraham, Cyril	Fiction
Only A Matter Of Time	Clinton-Baddeley, U.C.	Fiction
Only A World Cup Excuse	Watson, Jonathan	Fiction
Only An Excuse	Watson, Jonathan	Fiction
Only Another Excuse	Watson, Jonathan	Fiction
Only Good German, The	Allbeury, Ted	Fiction
Only Other Investment Guide You'll Ever Need	Business	Non-Fiction
Only The Wind Is Free	Graham, Margaret	Fiction
Only Victor, The	Kent, Alexander	Fiction
Opal	Rhodes, Elvi	Fiction
Open Road, The	Grahame, Kenneth	Fiction
Open Window, The	Saki	Fiction
Opening Night	Marsh, Ngaio	Fiction
Operation Heartbreak	Cooper, Duff	Fiction
Operation Janus	Alexander, L.G.	Fiction
Opposites	Early Learning	Non-Fiction
Oranges Are Not The Only Fruit	Winterson, Jeanette	Fiction
Orchid Tree, The	Coffman, Virginia	Fiction
Orchids From The Orient	Sinclair, Olga	Fiction
Ordeal By Innocence	Christie, Agatha	Fiction
Orderly Man, An	Bogarde, Dirk	Non-Fiction
Ordinary Copper, An	Warner, Jack	Fiction
Ordinary People	Guest, Judith	Fiction
Ordinary Princess, The	Kaye, M.M.	Fiction
Oregon Trail, The	Parkman, Francis	Non-Fiction

Title	Author/Subject	Category
Organised Executive, The	Business	Non-Fiction
Origins And Development Of The French Revolution	France	Non-Fiction
Origins And Politics Of The Spanish Civil War	Spain...	Non-Fiction
Origins Of The First World War, The	Military History	Non-Fiction
Orlando Furioso	Ariosto, L	Non-Fiction
Orville And Cuddles	Harris, Keith	Fiction
Oscar And Lucinda	Carey, Peter	Fiction
Oscar Wilde	Wilde, Oscar	Non-Fiction
Othello	A-Level	Non-Fiction
Othello	Shakespeare, William	Fiction
Other Ghost Stories	James, M.R.	Fiction
Other Kinds Of Treason	Allbeury, Ted	Fiction
Other Side Of Midnight, The	Sheldon, Sidney	Fiction
Other Side Of Silence	Allbeury, Ted	Fiction
Other Side Of The Moon, The	Morley, Sheridan	Fiction
Ottsy I Deti	Turgenev, Ivan	Non-Fiction
Our Father's Lies	Taylor, Andrew	Fiction
Our Favourite Garden Birds	Bird Songs	Non-Fiction
Our Gracie	Fields, Gracie	Non-Fiction
Our Kate	Cookson, Catherine	Non-Fiction
Our Kate	Cookson, Catherine	Fiction
Our Man In Havana	Greene, Graham	Fiction
Our Story	Kray, Reg & Ron	Non-Fiction
Our Village	Mitford, Mary Russel	Non-Fiction
Out Of Africa	Blixen, Karen	Non-Fiction
Out Of The Blue	Religious	Non-Fiction
Out Of The Rain	Cadell, Elizabeth	Fiction
Out Of The Shadows	March, Stella	Fiction
Outlaw Band Of Sherwood Forest, The	Traditional	Fiction
Outline Of Russian Music, An	Russia	Non-Fiction
Outline Of Soviet Music, An	Russia	Non-Fiction
Outsiders, The	Hinton, S.E.	Fiction
Outstanding Greek Modern Poetry	Greek	Non-Fiction
Over Sir John's Hill	Thomas, Dylan	Fiction
Overcoming Fearful Flying	Self Improvement	Non-Fiction
Overcoming Shyness	Self Improvement	Non-Fiction
Overview Of Transport In France	France	Non-Fiction
Owl Who Was Afraid Of The Dark, The	Tomlinson, Jill	Fiction
Ox-bow Incident	Van Tilbury Clark	Fiction
Oxford Blood	Fraser, Antonia	Fiction
Oxford Marmalade	Hayes, Lesley	Fiction
Oxyoke, The	Bosworth, Frank	Fiction
Pacific Power	Trains...	Non-Fiction
Paddington	Bond, Michael	Fiction
Paddington Abroad	Bond, Michael	Fiction
Paddington And Pantomine Time	Bond, Michael	Fiction
Paddington And The Disappearing Trick	Bond, Michael	Fiction
Paddington At Large	Bond, Michael	Fiction
Paddington At The Station	Bond, Michael	Fiction
Paddington Bear	Bond, Michael	Fiction
Paddington Does It Himself	Bond, Michael	Fiction
Paddington Goes To The Sales	Bond, Michael	Fiction
Paddington Goes To Town	Bond, Michael	Fiction
Paddington Helps Out	Bond, Michael	Fiction
Paddington Hits Out	Bond, Michael	Fiction
Paddington Marches On	Bond, Michael	Fiction
Paddington On The River	Bond, Michael	Fiction
Paddington Takes A Bath	Bond, Michael	Fiction
Paddington's Birthday Party	Bond, Michael	Fiction
Paddington's Golden Record	Bond, Michael	Fiction
Paddington's New Room	Bond, Michael	Fiction
Palermo Ambush, The	Forbes, Colin	Fiction
Palmerston	Social Sciences	Non-Fiction
Palomino Blonde	Allbeury, Ted	Fiction
Pam Parsnip And Lawrence Lemon	Garden Gang	Fiction
Panic Of '89, The	Erdman, Paul	Fiction
Paper Money	Follett, Ken	Fiction

# TITLES INDEX

Paper Trail	Timpson, John	Fiction
Paradise Lost	A-Level	Non-Fiction
Paradise Lost	Milton, John	Fiction
Paradise Postponed	Mortimer, John	Fiction
Parents Keep Out	Nash, Ogden	Fiction
Parent's Survival Guide	Grahame, Laurie	Non-Fiction
Parliamentary Monarchy In France 1815-1848	France	Non-Fiction
Paroles	Prevert, Jacques	Non-Fiction
Parrot Cage, The	Wright, Daphne	Fiction
Parson's Daughter, The	Cookson, Catherine	Fiction
Parson's Pleasure	Hardwick, Mollie	Fiction
Particular Friendship, A	Bogarde, Dirk	Non-Fiction
Partisans	MacLean, Alistair	Fiction
Party Politics Between The Wars	Social Sciences	Non-Fiction
Party Politics, The	Germany	Non-Fiction
Paso Doble	Spanish	Non-Fiction
Passage By Night	Higgins, Jack	Fiction
Passage To India	Forster, E.M.	Fiction
Passengers No More	Trains...	Non-Fiction
Passing On	Lively, Penelope	Fiction
Passion And The Flower, The	Cartland, Barbara	Fiction
Passionate Deception	Lyons, Mary	Fiction
Past Eight O'Clock	Aiken, Joan	Fiction
Past Forgetting	Cushing, Peter	Non-Fiction
Pastoral	Shute, Nevil	Fiction
Patchwork	Peters, Maureen	Fiction
Path Of Morning, The	De Valois, Dame Ninette	Non-Fiction
Path To World War II, The	Military History	Non-Fiction
Pathway To Healing, A	Self Improvement	Non-Fiction
Patrick Pear And Colin Cucumber	Garden Gang	Fiction
Pattern Of Shadows, A	Waggoner, Jean	Fiction
Patterns In The Dust	Grant-Adamson, Lesley	Fiction
Paul Bunyan	Children's Stories..	Fiction
Paul Daniels Magic Show	Daniels, Paul	Non-Fiction
Paul Temple And The Conrad Case	Durbridge, Francis	Fiction
Pay Any Price	Allbeury, Ted	Fiction
Payment In Blood	George, Elizabeth	Fiction
Peace Of Mind	Self Improvement	Non-Fiction
Peaceful Revolution	Social Sciences	Non-Fiction
Pearl Of Babar Shah, The	Traditional	Fiction
Pecos Bill	Children's Stories..	Fiction
Pedro Pepper And The Cherry Twins	Garden Gang	Fiction
Peel	Social Sciences	Non-Fiction
Pegasus The Winged Horse	Greek Mythology	Fiction
Pelican At Blandings	Wodehouse, P.G.	Fiction
Pengara Summer	Goring, Anne	Fiction
Penguin Basic Russian - Parts 1 - 4	Russian	Non-Fiction
Pennine Journey, A	Wainwright, A	Non-Fiction
Penreath Girl, The	Sutton, June	Fiction
People And Communications In Business	Webb, Edwin	Non-Fiction
People And Places	Fergusson, Robert	Fiction
People Management	Business	Non-Fiction
Peoples Of The U.S.S.R., The	Russia	Non-Fiction
Peppermint Pig, The	Bawden, Nina	Fiction
Percival Pea And Polly Pomegranate	Garden Gang	Fiction
Percy And Harold	Awdry, Rev. W.	Fiction
Percy Runs Away	Awdry, Rev. W.	Fiction
Percy The Pigeon	Harvey, Roger	Fiction
Percy's Predicament	Awdry, Rev. W.	Fiction
Perfect Gallows	Dickinson, Peter	Fiction
Perfect Happiness	Lively, Penelope	Fiction
Perfect Health	Self Improvement	Non-Fiction
Perfect Interview, The	Social Sciences	Non-Fiction
Perfect Murder, A	Archer, Jeffrey	Fiction
Perfect Murder, The	Keating, H.R.F.	Fiction
Perfect Sales Presentation, The	Business	Non-Fiction
Perfect Spy, A	Le Carre, John	Fiction

405

TITLES INDEX

Title	Author	Category
Perfect Weight - Perfect Body	Self Improvement	Non-Fiction
Perfume: The Story Of A Murderer	Suskind, Patrick	Fiction
Pericles	Shakespeare, William	Fiction
Persian Boy, The	Renault, Mary	Fiction
Personal Relations	Street, Pamela	Fiction
Persuasion	Austen, Jane	Fiction
Petals On The Wind	Andrews, Virginia	Fiction
Peter And The Wolf	Children's Stories..	Fiction
Peter And The Wolf	Prokofiev (Composer)	Fiction
Peter And The Wolf And Tubby The Tuba	Children's Stories..	Fiction
Peter Ilyich Tchaikovsky	Tchaikovsky (Composer)	Non-Fiction
Peter Ilyich Tchaikovsky 1840 - 1893	Tchaikovsky (Composer)	Non-Fiction
Peter O'Sullevan Talks Turf	O'Sullevan, Peter	Non-Fiction
Peter Pan	Barrie, J.M.	Fiction
Peter Potato And Alice Apple	Garden Gang	Fiction
Peter Sellers Collection	Sellers, Peter	Fiction
Peter The Great And Catherine The Great	Russia	Non-Fiction
Peter's Pence	Cleary, Jon	Fiction
Petrol And Pollution	Social Sciences	Non-Fiction
Petronov Plan, The	Pattinson, James	Fiction
Phantom Of The Opera	Leroux, Gaston	Fiction
Phantom Of The Soap Opera	Simple, Lee J.	Fiction
Phantom Ship And Mr Midshipman Easy, The	Captain Marryat	Fiction
Phedre	Racine, Jean	Non-Fiction
Philip Larkin And Ted Hughes	A-Level	Non-Fiction
Phoenix And The Carpet, The	Nesbitt, Edith	Fiction
Phoenix Syndrome, The	Andrews, Lucilla	Fiction
Phone Power: How To Get Whatever ...	Business	Non-Fiction
Phonetic Transcription	French Literature	Non-Fiction
Physics (Course)	G.C.S.E..	Non-Fiction
Piano Players, The	Burgess, Anthony	Fiction
Pick Of Billy Connolly, The	Connolly, Billy	Fiction
Pickwick Papers	Dickens, Charles	Fiction
Picnic And Suchlike Pandemonium, The	Durrell, Gerald	Fiction
Picture Of Dorian Gray, The	Wilde, Oscar	Fiction
Picture Yourself Relaxed	Self Improvement	Non-Fiction
Pieces Of Hancock	Hancock, Tony	Fiction
Pied Piper	Shute, Nevil	Fiction
Pied Piper Of Hamelin	Browning & Andersen	Fiction
Pied Piper Of Hamelin	Browning, Robert	Fiction
Pied Piper Of Hamelin	Poetry	Fiction
Piemakers, The	Cresswell, Helen	Fiction
Pierre Et Jean	De Maupassant, Guy	Non-Fiction
Pigeon Pie	Mitford, Nancy	Fiction
Piggo	Ayres, Pam	Fiction
Pigs Have Wings	Wodehouse, P.G.	Fiction
Pigwig Papers	Harvey, Richard	Fiction
Pikovaya Dama	Pushkin, Alexander S.	Non-Fiction
Pilgrim Pope, The	Pope John-Paul	Non-Fiction
Pilgrim's Progress, The	Bunyan, John	Fiction
Pillars Of The Earth, The	Follett, Ken	Fiction
Pin To See The Peepshow, A	Tennyson, Jesse F.	Fiction
Pincher Martin	Golding, William	Fiction
Pink Medicine Album	Beetles, Chris	Fiction
Pinocchio	Collodi, Carlo	Fiction
Piper On The Mountain, The	Peters, Ellis	Fiction
Pirandello's Theatre	Pirandello, Luigi	Non-Fiction
Pirate Uncle, The	Mahy, Margaret	Fiction
Pirates' Mixed-Up Voyage, The	Mahy, Margaret	Fiction
Pisces	Astrology	Non-Fiction
Pistachio Prescription, The	Danziger, Paula	Fiction
Pistol For Two	Heyer, Georgette	Fiction
Pit And The Pendulum	Poe, Edgar Allan	Fiction
Place Of Happiness, The	Hagar, Judith	Fiction
Plain Tales From The Hills	Kipling, Rudyard	Fiction
Plain Tales From The Raj	Radio	Non-Fiction
Plain Tales Of The Afghan Border	Bowen, John	Fiction

TITLES INDEX

Plains Of Passage, The	Auel, Jean	Fiction
Planet Of The Elves, The	Children's Stories	Fiction
Planning For Peace 1914-1918	History	Non-Fiction
Play Listen And Learn With Ronald McDonald	Early Learning	Non-Fiction
Playboy Of The Western World, The	Symge, John	Fiction
Pocket Full Of Rye, A	Christie, Agatha	Fiction
Poemes	Verlaine, Paul	Non-Fiction
Poems	Poetry	Fiction
Poems And Letters	Dickinson, Emily	Fiction
Poems And Songs Of Middle Earth	Tolkien, J.R.R.	Fiction
Poems Chiefly In The Scottish Dialect	Burns, Robert	Fiction
Poems From Black Africa	Jones, James Earl	Fiction
Poems From The Barrier Block	Childish, Wild Billy	Fiction
Poems In Scots	Poetry	Fiction
Poems In Scots And Gaelic	Poetry	Fiction
Poems In The Thrie Leids O Alba	Neill, William	Fiction
Poems Of Laughter And Violence	Childish, Wild Billy	Fiction
Poems Of Thomas Hardy, The	Hardy, Thomas	Fiction
Poems, Riddles And Songs	Soutar, William	Fiction
Poems Without Rhyme	Childish, Wild Billy	Fiction
Poems You Love	Poetry	Fiction
Poesies	Gautier, T.H	Non-Fiction
Poet Among Scientists, A	Graves, Robert	Non-Fiction
Poet As A Translator, The	English Literature	Non-Fiction
Poet Speaks, The	Poetry	Fiction
Poetic Vision And Modern Literature	English Literature	Non-Fiction
Poetry And Audience	French Literature	Non-Fiction
Poetry And Voice Of Margaret Atwood	Atwood, Margaret	Fiction
Poetry From World War I And II	Poetry	Fiction
Poetry In Motion	Poetry	Fiction
Poetry Of Anne Sexton, The	Sexton, Anne	Non-Fiction
Poetry Of Boris Pasternak, The	Pasternak, Boris	Non-Fiction
Poetry Of Browning, The	Browning, Robert	Fiction
Poetry Of Catullus	Poetry	Fiction
Poetry Of Coleridge, The	Coleridge, Samuel Taylor	Fiction
Poetry Of Dylan Thomas, The	Thomas, Dylan	Non-Fiction
Poetry Of George Herbert And Andrew Marvell, The	A-Level	Non-Fiction
Poetry Of Gerard Manley Hopkins	Hopkins, Gerard Manley	Fiction
Poetry Of John Ciardi, The	Ciardi, John	Non-Fiction
Poetry Of Keats	Keats	Fiction
Poetry Of Robert Burns, The	Burns, Robert	Fiction
Poetry Of Robert Lowell, The	Lowell, Robert	Non-Fiction
Poetry Of Stephen Spender, The	Spender, Stephen	Non-Fiction
Poetry Of Theodore Roathke, The	Roathke, Theodore	Non-Fiction
Poetry Of W.h. Auden, The	Auden, W.H.	Non-Fiction
Poetry Of William Blake	Blake, William	Fiction
Poetry Of William Butler Yeats, The	Yeats, W.B.	Fiction
Poetry Of Wordsworth, The	Wordsworth, William	Fiction
Poetry Olympics	Poetry	Fiction
Poetry Please	Poetry	Fiction
Poetry Prose And Piano	Poetry	Fiction
Poetry Selection	Day Lewis, C	Fiction
Poet's Gold	Poetry	Fiction
Poets Of The West Indies	Poetry	Fiction
Point Of Honour	Scholefield, Alan	Fiction
Point Of Honour, The	Maugham, W. Somerset	Fiction
Poirot	Christie, Agatha	Fiction
Poirot Investigates	Christie, Agatha	Fiction
Poison	McBain, Ed	Fiction
Polar Star	Cruz Smith, Martin	Fiction
Police At The Funeral	Allingham, Margery	Fiction
Polish Travel Pack	Polish	Non-Fiction
Political Parties And Walpole	Social Sciences	Non-Fiction
Political Suicide	Barnard, Robert	Fiction
Politics In Post-War Italy: An Assessment	Italy	Non-Fiction
Pollution And Industry	Social Sciences	Non-Fiction
Polly Put The Kettle On	Children's Stories..	Fiction

TITLES INDEX

Pollypilgrim	Joseph, Marie	Fiction
Polyeucte	Corneille, P.	Fiction
Poor Caroline	Holtby, Winifred	Fiction
Pop Goes The Diesel	Awdry, Rev. W.	Fiction
Pope And Augustan Poetry	English Literature	Non-Fiction
Population	Social Sciences	Non-Fiction
Por Aqui (1, 2 & 3)	Spanish	Non-Fiction
Porridge	Television	Fiction
Porterhouse Blue	Sharpe, Tom	Fiction
Portland Bill	Armitage, David	Fiction
Portland Bill And The Storm	Armitage, David	Fiction
Portland Bill's Busy Day	Armitage, David	Fiction
Portland Bill's Important Message	Armitage, David	Fiction
Portrait Of A Rose	Street, Pamela	Fiction
Portrait Of Four Poets In Prose And Poetry, A	Poetry	Fiction
Portrait Of The Artist As A Young Man, A	Joyce, James	Fiction
Portrait, The	Connolly, Billy	Fiction
Portuguese Cassette Course	Portuguese	Non-Fiction
Portuguese For Travel	Portuguese	Non-Fiction
Portuguese Language Basics	Portuguese	Non-Fiction
Portuguese Travel Pack	Portuguese	Non-Fiction
Position Of Women In 20th Century Britain, The	Social Sciences	Non-Fiction
Possession	Byatt, A.S.	Fiction
Post Mortem	Cullingford, Guy	Fiction
Postman Pat	Cunliffe, John	Fiction
Postman Pat And The Christmas Pudding	Cunliffe, John	Fiction
Postman Pat And The Dinosaur Bones	Cunliffe, John	Fiction
Postman Pat And The Greendale Ghost	Cunliffe, John	Fiction
Postman Pat And The Letter Puzzle	Cunliffe, John	Fiction
Postman Pat Goes On Safari	Cunliffe, John	Fiction
Postman Pat Makes A Splash	Cunliffe, John	Fiction
Postman Pat - More Stories	Cunliffe, John	Fiction
Postman Pat Plays For Greendale	Cunliffe, John	Fiction
Postman Pat Stories, The	Cunliffe, John	Fiction
Postman Pat Takes A Message	Cunliffe, John	Fiction
Postman Pat's 123 Story	Cunliffe, John	Fiction
Postman Pat's ABC Story	Cunliffe, John	Fiction
Postman Pat's Bedtime Stories	Cunliffe, John	Fiction
Postman Pat's Breezy Day	Cunliffe, John	Fiction
Postman Pat's Day In Bed	Cunliffe, John	Fiction
Postman Pat's Messy Day	Cunliffe, John	Fiction
Postman Pat's Parcel Of Fun	Cunliffe, John	Fiction
Postman Pat's Secret	Cunliffe, John	Fiction
Postman Pat's Treasure Hunt	Cunliffe, John	Fiction
Postman Pat's Wet Day	Cunliffe, John	Fiction
Postscripts	Rayner, Claire	Fiction
Post-War Division In Europe, The	History	Non-Fiction
Poverty And Welfare	Social Sciences	Non-Fiction
Povest'o Tom Kak Possorilsya Ivan Ivanovich...	Gogol, Nikolai Vasilievich	Non-Fiction
Power And Success - Get It, Keep It, Use It	Self Improvement	Non-Fiction
Power Of Business Rapport	Business	Non-Fiction
Power Of Money Dynamics	Business	Non-Fiction
Power Of Persistence, The	Self Improvement	Non-Fiction
Power Of Positive Thinking, The	Self Improvement	Non-Fiction
Power Of Self Talk	Self Improvement	Non-Fiction
Power Of Steam, The	Trains...	Non-Fiction
Power Of The Sword	Smith, Wilbur	Fiction
Power Of Your Own Voice	Self Improvement	Non-Fiction
Power Talking	Business	Non-Fiction
Power Words	Self Improvement	Non-Fiction
Powerful Person - Programming	Self Improvement	Non-Fiction
Powerspeak	Business	Non-Fiction
Practical Critcism: Poetry	A-Level	Non-Fiction
Practical Criticism: Prose	A-Level	Non-Fiction
Pratigva (Hindi)	Chand, Prem	Fiction
Pray For A Brave Heart	MacInnes, Helen	Fiction
Prayer For The Dying	Higgins, Jack	Fiction

TITLES INDEX

Title	Author	Category
Pre-Eminence And Competition	Social Sciences	Non-Fiction
Prehistoric Scandinavia	Galica, Divina	Non-Fiction
Prejudiced Witness	Gater, Dilys	Fiction
Prelude To Foundation	Asimov, Isaac	Fiction
Prelude To Terror	MacInnes, Helen	Fiction
Premiership Of Stanley Baldwin, The	Social Sciences	Non-Fiction
Prepositions And The Cases Which They Govern	German	Non-Fiction
Present And The Past, The	Compton-Burnett, Ivy	Fiction
Present Laughter	Coward, Noel	Fiction
Press In The German - Speaking Countries, The	Germany	Non-Fiction
Pressure Point	Copper, Basil	Fiction
Presumed Innocent	Turow, Scott	Fiction
Pretty Lady, The	Bennett, Arnold	Fiction
Previous Album	Monty Python	Fiction
Price Of Fear, The	Ghost Stories	Fiction
Pride And Prejudice	A-Level	Non-Fiction
Pride And Prejudice	Austen, Jane	Fiction
Pride Of The Peacock, The	Holt, Victoria	Fiction
Primary French	Early Learning	Non-Fiction
Primary German	Early Learning	Non-Fiction
Primary Science	Early Learning	Non-Fiction
Prime Of Miss Jean Brodie	Spark, Muriel	Fiction
Prime Time Workout With Jane Fonda	Health & Fitness	Non-Fiction
Prince And The Pauper The	Twain, Mark	Fiction
Prince And The Pekinese, The	Cartland, Barbara	Fiction
Prince At Black Pony Inn	Pullein-Thompson, Christine	Fiction
Prince Caspian	Lewis, C.S	Fiction
Prince Ivan And The Frog Princess	Traditional	Fiction
Princess And The Frog	Traditional	Fiction
Princess And The Goblin	MacDonald, George	Fiction
Princess And The Pea	Andersen, Hans Christian	Fiction
Princess Bride, The	Goldman, William	Fiction
Princess Ferozshah And The Horse Prince	Traditional	Fiction
Princess, The	Lawrence, D.H.	Fiction
Print Petticoat, The	Andrews, Lucilla	Fiction
Prinz Friedrich Von Homburg	Von Kleist, H	Non-Fiction
Prisoner Of A Promise	Tilbury, Quenna	Fiction
Prisoner Of Zenda, The	Hope, Sir Anthony	Fiction
Private Eye Golden Satiricals	Comedy...	Fiction
Private Lives	Coward, Noel	Fiction
Private Memories And Confessions Of A Justified Sinner	Hogg, James	Fiction
Prize, The	Wallace, Irving	Fiction
Professor, The	Bronte, Charlotte	Fiction
Profile	Andi, Su	Fiction
Programmatic Portuguese	Portuguese	Non-Fiction
Promise Of The Morning	Goodwin, Grace	Fiction
Pronunciation And Reading Of Ancient Greek, The	Ancient Greek	Non-Fiction
Pronunciation And Reading Of Classical Latin	Latin...	Non-Fiction
Proof	Francis, Dick	Fiction
Prophecy For A Queen	Gater, Dilys	Fiction
Prophesis Of Nostradamus, The	Nostradamus	Non-Fiction
Prophet , The	Gibran, Khalil	Non-Fiction
Prose And Poetry	English Literature	Non-Fiction
Prose And Poetry Of John Updike, The	Updike, John	Non-Fiction
Prose Appreciation	English Literature	Non-Fiction
Prose Readings	Burgess, Anthony	Non-Fiction
Protestant Church In Germany, The	Golka, F.W.	Non-Fiction
Proud Bess	Peters, Maureen	Fiction
Providence	Brookner, Anita	Fiction
Prussian Officer, The	Lawrence, D.H.	Fiction
Psycho	Bloch, Robert	Fiction
Psychology Of Achievement	Self Improvement	Non-Fiction
Psychology Of Negotiating, The	Rackham, Neil	Non-Fiction
Psychology Of Selling	Business	Non-Fiction
Psychology Of Winning	Self Improvement	Non-Fiction
Puckoon	Milligan, Spike	Fiction
Puddle Lane	McCullagh, Sheila	Fiction

TITLES INDEX

Title	Author	Category
Puff The Magic Dragon	Children's Stories..	Fiction
Puffalumps And The Caves	Riley, Phil	Fiction
Puffalumps And The Wizard, The	Riley, Phil	Fiction
Puppet On A Chain	Maclean, Alistair	Fiction
Purgatorio	Dante	Non-Fiction
Purloined Letter, The	Poe, Edgar Allan	Fiction
Purple Plain, The	Bates, H.E.	Fiction
Pursuit Of Love, The	Mitford, Nancy	Fiction
Puss In Boots	Traditional	Fiction
Putting The One Minute Manager To Work	Business	Non-Fiction
Pygmalion	Shaw, George Bernard	Fiction
Q - Clearance	Benchley, Peter	Fiction
Quail Seed	Saki	Fiction
Quartet In Autumn	Pym, Barbara	Fiction
Queen Lucia	Benson, E.F	Fiction
Queen's Counsel	Stuart, Alex	Fiction
Queen's Gambit, The	Tevis, Walter	Fiction
Queen's Nose, The	King-Smith, Dick	Fiction
Queen's Travels, The	Fisher, Graham	Non-Fiction
Quest For Alexis	Buckingham, Nancy	Fiction
Question Of Balance, A	H.R.H. The Duke Of Edinburgh	Non-Fiction
Question Of Guilt, A	Fyfield, Frances	Fiction
Questions And Answers	Social Sciences	Non-Fiction
Quiet American, The	Greene, Graham	Fiction
Quiet As A Nun	Fraser, Antonia	Fiction
Quiet Wards, The	Andrews, Lucilla	Fiction
Quite Early One Morning	Thomas, Dylan	Fiction
Quiver Full Of Arrows, A	Archer, Jeffrey	Fiction
Rabbi Stories, The	Kossoff, David	Fiction
Rabbits On And On And On...	Carrott, Jasper	Fiction
Raccolta Di Novelle	Verga, Giovanni	Fiction
Radiant Health And A Strong Immune System	Self Improvement	Non-Fiction
Radio Active	Radio Active	Fiction
Raffles	Hornung, E.W.	Fiction
Raffles: A Thief In The Night	Hornung, E.W.	Fiction
Raffles - Amateur Cracksman	Hornung, E.W.	Fiction
Raffles - Black Mask	Hornung, E.W.	Fiction
Rage	Smith, Wilbur	Fiction
Rage Of Angels, A	Sheldon, Sidney	Fiction
Raging Robots And Unruly Uncles	Mahy, Margaret	Fiction
Rags Of Time, The	Webster, Jan	Fiction
Railway Cat, The	Arkle, Phyllis	Fiction
Railway Children, The	Nesbitt, Edith	Fiction
Railway Rhythms	Trains...	Non-Fiction
Railway Stories	Awdry, Rev. W.	Fiction
Ailway To Riccarton	Trains...	Non-Fiction
Railways Recalled	Trains...	Non-Fiction
Railways Round The Clock	Trains...	Non-Fiction
Rainbow And The Rose, The	Shute, Nevil	Fiction
Rainbow In The Mist	Whitney, Phyllis A	Fiction
Rainbow - The Square	Television	Fiction
Rainbow's End	Peters, Ellis	Fiction
Rainbow's End	Saunders, Jean	Fiction
Rainhill Remembered	Trains...	Non-Fiction
Rainsong	Whitney, Phyllis A	Fiction
Rampage	Pope, Dudley	Fiction
Ramona And Her Mother	Cleary, Beverly	Fiction
Ramona Forever	Cleary, Beverly	Fiction
Ramona Quimby, Age 8	Cleary, Beverly	Fiction
Ramona The Pest	Cleary, Beverly	Fiction
Randall Jarrell Reads Poems Against War	Jarrell, Randall	Fiction
Random Island	Stuart, Alex	Fiction
Random Shots	Shooting Times	Non-Fiction
Rape Of The Fair Country	Cordell, Alexander	Fiction
Rape Of The Lock, The	A-Level	Non-Fiction
Rapid Learn Yiddish	Yiddish	Non-Fiction
Rapunzel	Grimm	Fiction

TITLES INDEX

Title	Author/Subject	Type
Rasputin	Fulop-Miller, Rene	Non-Fiction
Rasskazy	Babel, Isaak	Non-Fiction
Rat Race	Francis, Dick	Fiction
Rational And The Intuitive Brain	Self Improvement	Non-Fiction
Rational Emotive Therapy	Self Improvement	Non-Fiction
Ratking	Dibdin, Michael	Fiction
Raven, The	Poe, Edgar Allan	Fiction
Ravenswood Poems	Poetry	Fiction
Raw Meat For The Balcony	Connolly, Billy	Fiction
Ray's A Laugh	Ray, Ted	Fiction
Reach For The Sky	Brickhill, Paul	Non-Fiction
Reading Difficult Poetry	English Literature	Non-Fiction
Reading His Poetry	Betjeman, Sir John	Fiction
Reading His Poetry	Spender, Stephen	Fiction
Reading His Poetry	Wilbur, Richard	Fiction
Reading Japanese	Japanese...	Non-Fiction
Reading Turgenev	Trevor, William	Non-Fiction
Real Days Of Steam	Trains...	Non-Fiction
Real Fairies	Van Gelder, Dora	Fiction
Reanimator	Lovecraft H.P.	Fiction
Reappraisal Of What Went Wrong In Palestine, A	Middle East	Non-Fiction
Reb Moishe Babba	Singer, Isaac B.	Non-Fiction
Rebecca	Du Maurier, Daphne	Fiction
Rebecca Of Sunnybrook Farm	Wiggin, Kate	Fiction
Recent Poetry	Walker, Ted	Non-Fiction
Recital Of Ancient Greek Poetry, A	Ancient Greek	Non-Fiction
Recollections No. 1: A Railway Guard	Trains...	Non-Fiction
Recollections No. 2: Life On The Canal	Canals	Non-Fiction
Recollections No. 3: Silent Days Of The Cinema	Cinema	Non-Fiction
Recollections No. 4: Foot Plate Days	Trains...	Non-Fiction
Recollections No. 5: British Motorcycle Industry	Motorcycling	Non-Fiction
Record Size Willy	Humour	Fiction
Red And The Black, The	Roosevelt, Elliott	Fiction
Red Badge Of Courage, The	Crane, Stephen	Fiction
Red Dog	Kipling, Rudyard	Fiction
Red Fox	Seymour, Gerald	Fiction
Red Fox, The	Hyde, Anthony	Fiction
Red Riding Hood	Perrault, Charles	Fiction
Red Riding Hood	Traditional	Fiction
Red Wind	Chandler, Raymond	Fiction
Redback	Jacobson, Howard	Fiction
Reekin' Lum, The	McPherson, Bunty	Fiction
Reel Murder	Babson, Marian	Fiction
Reflections: A Miscellany Of Words And Music	Strong, Patience	Fiction
Reflex	Francis, Dick	Fiction
Reformation In England, The	History	Non-Fiction
Reformation, The	Social Sciences	Non-Fiction
Regain	Giono, J	Non-Fiction
Regional Round No. 1 Eastern	Trains...	Non-Fiction
Regional Round No. 2 Southern	Trains...	Non-Fiction
Regionalism In France	France	Non-Fiction
Reign Of Catherine The Great, 1762-1796, The	Russia	Non-Fiction
Reign Of Edward VI, The	History	Non-Fiction
Re-Joyce	Grenfell, Joyce	Fiction
Release The Past	Preston, Ivy	Fiction
Relieve Stress And Anxiety	Self Improvement	Non-Fiction
Religion In The Soviet Union	Russia	Non-Fiction
Religious Body, The	Aird, Catherine	Fiction
Religious Studies	G.C.S.E.	Non-Fiction
Reluctant Dragon, The	Grahame, Kenneth	Fiction
Reluctant Paragon	George, Catherine	Fiction
Remember	Bradford, B. Taylor	Fiction
Remembrance Of Things Past	Proust, Marcel	Fiction
Remove The Bodies	Ferrars, Elizabeth	Fiction
Renaissance, The	Social Sciences	Non-Fiction
Rendezvouz, The	Du Maurier, Daphne	Fiction
Repossession, The	Samuels, Arthur	Fiction

Reprise	Rayner, Claire	Fiction
Requiem For A Wren	Shute, Nevil	Fiction
Requiem For The Living	Day Lewis, C	Fiction
Rescuers, The	Disney	Fiction
Restaurant At The End Of The Universe	Adams, Douglas	Fiction
Restoration, The	History	Non-Fiction
Return Journey	Ayres, Ruby M.	Fiction
Return Of Sherlock Holmes, The	Conan Doyle, Arthur	Fiction
Return Of The Antelope, The	Hall, Willis	Fiction
Return Of The Gumby Gang	Oldfield, Pamela	Fiction
Return Of The Indian	Reid Banks, Lynne	Fiction
Return Of The Jedi	Science Fiction	Fiction
Return Of The Mr. Men, The	Hargreaves, Roger	Fiction
Return Of The Native, The	Hardy, Thomas	Fiction
Revelations	Bible	Non-Fiction
Reverend James Currie And Friends	Currie, James	Fiction
Revolting Rhymes	Dahl, Roald	Fiction
Revolution Of 1848, The	Social Sciences	Non-Fiction
Revolutionary China	China	Non-Fiction
Revolutions Of 1848 In France And Central Europe	France	Non-Fiction
Rhinoceros	Ionesco, E	Non-Fiction
Rhyme Stew	Dahl, Roald	Fiction
Rhyming Words	Early Learning	Non-Fiction
Ribs Of Death, The	Aiken, Joan	Fiction
Richard Bolitho - Midshipman	Kent, Alexander	Fiction
Richard Eberhart Reading	Eberhart, Richard	Fiction
Richard II	A-Level	Non-Fiction
Richard II	Shakespeare, William	Fiction
Richard III	Shakespeare, William	Fiction
Riddle Of The Sands, The	Childers, Erskine	Fiction
Riddle Of The Third Mile, The	Dexter, Colin	Fiction
Ride A Pale Horse	Macinnes, Helen	Fiction
Riders Of The Purple Sage	Grey, Zane	Fiction
Riding High	Francombe, John	Fiction
Right Ho, Jeeves	Wodehouse, P.G.	Fiction
Right-Brain Solutions	Self Improvement	Non-Fiction
Rikki-Tikki-Tavi	Kipling, Rudyard	Fiction
Rime Of The Ancient Mariner, The	Poetry	Fiction
Ring Of Bright Water	Maxwell, Gavin	Fiction
Ring-A-Roses	Joseph, Marie	Fiction
Ringing The Changes	Rice, Nicky	Fiction
Rio Contract, The	Newton, William	Fiction
Ripley Under Ground	Highsmith, Patricia	Fiction
Ripley Under Water	Highsmith, Patricia	Fiction
Rise And Fall Of Sweden, The	Sweden	Non-Fiction
Rise And Fall Of The Dutch Republic, The	Holland	Non-Fiction
Rise Of The Labour Party 1885-1906, The	Social Sciences	Non-Fiction
Rise Of The Nazi Party, The	History	Non-Fiction
Rise Of The Spanish Empire, The	Spain...	Non-Fiction
Risk	Francis, Dick	Fiction
Risk / Bolt / The Fog	Francis, Dick	Fiction
Rites Of Passage	Golding, William	Fiction
Rivals	Dailey, Janet	Fiction
River Of Death	MacLean, Alistair	Fiction
Riviera Masquerade	Brayshaw, Margaret	Fiction
Road And The Miles, The	Boyce, Max	Fiction
Road Less Travelled, The	Self Improvement	Non-Fiction
Road Not Taken, The	Frost, Robert	Fiction
Road To Munich, The	Germany	Non-Fiction
Road To Omaha, The	Ludlum, Robert	Fiction
Road To Paradise Island, The	Holt, Victoria	Fiction
Road To Wigan Pier, The	Orwell, George	Fiction
Roald Dahl Collection, The	Dahl, Roald	Fiction
Roald Dahl Slipcase (Older)	Dahl, Roald	Fiction
Roald Dahl Slipcase (Younger)	Dahl, Roald	Fiction
Roarin' Game, The	Curling	Non-Fiction
Robbie Shepherd Reads Dufton Scott	Scott, Dufton	Fiction

TITLES INDEX

Title	Author	Category
Robert Browning	Browning, Robert	Non-Fiction
Robert Cecil, Lord Salisbury	History	Non-Fiction
Robert Frost Reads His Poems	Frost, Robert	Non-Fiction
Robert Graves Reads	Graves, Robert	Fiction
Robert Henryson Selections	Henryson, Robert	Fiction
Robert Lowell: A Reading	Lowell, Robert	Fiction
Robert Owen & New Lanark	Owen, Robert Dale	Non-Fiction
Robert Penn Warren Reads	Warren, Robert Penn	Fiction
Robert Raspberry And Grace Grape	Garden Gang	Fiction
Robert The Bruce	Robert The Bruce	Non-Fiction
Robin And His Merry Men	Traditional	Fiction
Robin Hood	Traditional	Fiction
Robin's Adventures With Little John	Traditional	Fiction
Robinson Crusoe	Defoe, Daniel	Fiction
Robinson Crusoe	Traditional	Fiction
Robots Of Dawn, The	Asimov, Isaac	Fiction
Rochdale Cowboy Rides Again, The	Harding, Mike	Non-Fiction
Rock A Bye Baby	Romer, Jane	Fiction
Rocking Horse Secret, The	Godden, Rumer	Fiction
Rodgers & Hammerstein	Rodgers & Hammerstein	Non-Fiction
Rodogune	Corneille, P	Fiction
Roland And Oliver	Traditional	Fiction
Roland, The Minstrel Pig	Steig, William	Fiction
Role Of Personality In Science, The	English Literature	Non-Fiction
Role Of The Church In Modern Italian History, The	Italy	Non-Fiction
Roll Over Cecil Sharpe	Harding, Mike	Fiction
Romancers, The	Saki	Fiction
Romans	Bible	Non-Fiction
Romans Et Contes	Voltaire	Non-Fiction
Romantic Hero, The	French Literature	Non-Fiction
Romantic Journey	Buckingham, Nancy	Fiction
Romantics, The	English Literature	Non-Fiction
Romany Tales	Traditional	Fiction
Romeo And Juliet	Shakespeare, William	Fiction
Ronald Reagan: An American Life	Reagan, Ronald	Non-Fiction
Room Of One's Own, A	Woolf, Virginia	Fiction
Room With A View, A	Forster, E.M.	Fiction
Rooney	Cookson, Catherine	Fiction
Rooted	Harding, Mike	Fiction
Roots Of Inflation	Social Sciences	Non-Fiction
Roots Of Marxism-leninism, The	Russia	Non-Fiction
Rose Storytape	Hughes, Shirley	Fiction
Rose Tattoo, The	Williams, Tennessee	Fiction
Rosencrantz And Guildenstern Are Dead	Stoppard, Tom	Fiction
Rough Cider	Lovesey, Peter	Fiction
Round The Horne	Radio	Fiction
Round Tower, The	Cookson, Catherine	Fiction
Rubaiyat Of Omar Khayyam, The	Khayyam, Omar	Non-Fiction
Ruined City	Shute, Nevil	Fiction
Rumpelstiltskin	Children's Stories..	Fiction
Rumpelstiltskin	Grimm	Fiction
Rumpole (1 & 2)	Mortimer, John	Fiction
Rumpole A La Carte	Mortimer, John	Fiction
Rumpole And The Golden Thread	Mortimer, John	Fiction
Rumpole For The Defence	Mortimer, John	Fiction
Rumpole Of The Bailey	Mortimer, John	Fiction
Rumpole's Return	Mortimer, John	Fiction
Runaway Heiress, The	March, Stella	Fiction
Runaway Train, The	Children's Stories..	Fiction
Runaways, The	Thomas, Ruth	Fiction
Running Blind	Bagley, Desmond	Fiction
Rupert And The Frog Song	Bestall, Alfred	Fiction
Rupert And The Magic Seeds	Bestall, Alfred	Fiction
Rupert And The Nutwood Stage	Bestall, Alfred	Fiction
Rupert And The Old Hat	Bestall, Alfred	Fiction
Rupert And The Wobbly Witch	Bestall, Alfred	Fiction
Rupert Bear	Bestall, Alfred	Fiction

TITLES INDEX

Title	Author	Category
Rupert Bear And The Chocolate Buttons Gang	Bestall, Alfred	Fiction
Rupert Bear And The Hidden Lake	Bestall, Alfred	Fiction
Rupert Bear And The Lonely Bird	Bestall, Alfred	Fiction
Rupert Bear And The Muddled Magic	Bestall, Alfred	Fiction
Rupert Bear And The Yellow Elephant	Bestall, Alfred	Fiction
Rupert Bear And The Young Dragon	Bestall, Alfred	Fiction
Rupert Bear - Stories From The 1982 Annual	Bestall, Alfred	Fiction
Rupert Bear's New Adventures	Bestall, Alfred	Fiction
Rush	Wonzencraft, Kim	Fiction
Russia 1917: Year Of Revolution	Russia	Non-Fiction
Russia House, The	Le Carre, John	Fiction
Russian And The Languages Of The U.S.S.R.	Russian	Non-Fiction
Russian Approach To Literature, The	Russian	Non-Fiction
Russian Cassette Course	Russian...	Non-Fiction
Russian Classicism	Russia	Non-Fiction
Russian Dialects	Russian	Non-Fiction
Russian Folk Theatre, The	Russia	Non-Fiction
Russian Hide-And-seek	Amis, Kingsley	Fiction
Russian Icons	Russia	Non-Fiction
Russian Language And People	Russian	Non-Fiction
Russian Listening Comprehension - Parts1 & 2	Russian	Non-Fiction
Russian Revolution, The	Russia	Non-Fiction
Russian Revolutionary Novel, The	Russian Literature	Non-Fiction
Russian Stress	Russian	Non-Fiction
Russian Travel Pack	Russian...	Non-Fiction
Russka	Rutherford, E	Fiction
Saddle Wolves, The	Floren, Lee	Fiction
Saddlebottom	King-Smith, Dick	Fiction
Sagittarius	Astrology	Non-Fiction
Sagittarius Rising	Lewis, Cecil	Non-Fiction
Sailing Alone Around The World	Slocum, Joshua	Non-Fiction
Sailor's Horse, The	England	Non-Fiction
Saint Errant	Charteris, Leslie	Fiction
Saint Joan	Shaw, George Bernard	Fiction
Saint Maybe	Tyler, A	Fiction
Saint Peters Fair	Peters, Ellis	Fiction
Saki	Saki	Fiction
Salzburg Connection, The	MacInnes, Helen	Fiction
Sam Smells A Rat	Wilmer, Diane	Fiction
Sam To The Rescue	Wilmer, Diane	Fiction
Samantha	Eden, Dorothy	Fiction
Sameep And The Parrots	Abrahams, Elaine	Fiction
Sam's Bumper Jumper	Wilmer, Diane	Fiction
Sam's Night Watch	Wilmer, Diane	Fiction
Sam's Rabbit Rescue	Wilmer, Diane	Fiction
Sam's Valley	Houston, Will	Fiction
Samuel Beckett	Beckett, Samuel	Non-Fiction
Samuel Pepys	History	Non-Fiction
San Andreas	MacLean, Alistair	Fiction
Sanaco	Grove, Fred	Fiction
Sanctuary Sparrow, The	Peters, Ellis	Fiction
Sanders Of The River	Wallace, Edgar	Fiction
Sands Of Time, The	Sheldon, Sidney	Fiction
Sangschaw	MacDiarmid, Hugh	Fiction
Santa Fe Trail	Hatton, Cliff	Fiction
Santorini	MacLean, Alistair	Fiction
Sarah, Plain And Tall	MacLachlan, Patricia	Fiction
Sarasnatichandra (Gujarati)	Tripathi, Gouardhanram Madhayram	Fiction
Satan Bug, The	MacLean, Alistair	Fiction
Satisfaction And Happiness	Self Improvement	Non-Fiction
Saturday City	Webster, Jan	Fiction
Savage Day, The	Higgins, Jack	Fiction
Savage Interlude	Mortimer, Carole	Fiction
Scales Of Justice	Marsh, Ngaio	Fiction
Scandal Of Father Brown, The	Chesterton, G.K.	Fiction
Scarlet Pimpernel, The	Baroness Orczy	Fiction
Scarlet Thread, The	Anthony, Evelyn	Fiction

TITLES INDEX

Title	Author	Category
Scattered Seed: Cords And Discords	Mosco, Maisie	Fiction
Scattered Seed: Relative Values	Mosco, Maisie	Fiction
Scattered Seed: Sticks And Stones	Mosco, Maisie	Fiction
Scend Of The Sea	Jenkins, Geoffrey	Fiction
Scenes De La Vie De Province	De Maupassant, Guy	Non-Fiction
Scenes From Watership Down	Adams, Richard	Fiction
Scent Of Heather, The	March, Stella	Fiction
Scent Of Oleander, A	Lea, Constance	Fiction
Schindler's Ark	Keneally, Thomas	Non-Fiction
Schizophrenia - A Viewpoint	Medical	Non-Fiction
School At Thrush Green, The	Read, Miss	Fiction
School Master, The	Burley, W.J.	Fiction
Science	G.C.S.E.	Non-Fiction
Science Fiction	Science Fiction	Non-Fiction
Science Fiction Adventures	Science Fiction	Fiction
Science Fiction Favourites	Asimov, Isaac	Fiction
Science Fiction Soundbook	Science Fiction	Fiction
Scientific View Of Meditation, A	Self Improvement	Non-Fiction
Scientists And Responsibility	Social Sciences	Non-Fiction
Sci-Fi And Futuristic	Sound Effects	Non-Fiction
Scoop	Waugh, Evelyn	Fiction
Scorpio	Astrology	Non-Fiction
Scorpius	Gardner, John	Fiction
Scotch And Full Of It	Nicol, Hector	Fiction
Scots Poems	Soutar, William	Fiction
Scottish Cup-1976	Football	Non-Fiction
Scottish Sketches	Cunningham Graham, R.B.	Non-Fiction
Scratch 'n' Sniff	Smith & Jones	Fiction
Screaming Skull, The	Ghost Stories	Fiction
Screwtape Letters, The	Lewis, C.S	Fiction
Sea Lord	Cornwell, Bernard	Fiction
Sea Wolf, The	London, Jack	Fiction
Seal Boy, The	Traditional	Fiction
Search Dog	Locke, Angela	Non-Fiction
Search The Shadows	Michaels, Barbara	Fiction
Season In Hell, A	Higgins, Jack	Fiction
Seasons Of My Life	Hauxwell, Hannah	Non-Fiction
Second Fiddle	Wesley, Mary	Fiction
Second Heaven	Guest, Judith	Fiction
Second Honeymoon	Young, Vivien	Fiction
Second Sickle, The	Curtiss, Ursula	Fiction
Second World War	Military History	Non-Fiction
Secret Agent, The	Conrad, Joseph	Fiction
Secret Armour, The	Andrews, Lucilla	Fiction
Secret Diary Of Adrian Mole	Townsend, Sue	Fiction
Secret Diary Of Adrian Mole Aged 13 & 3/4	Townsend, Sue	Fiction
Secret Garden, The	Hodgson Burnett, F.	Fiction
Secret Island, The	Blyton, Enid	Fiction
Secret Of Abbey Place	Young, Rose	Fiction
Secret Of Father Brown, The	Chesterton, G.K.	Fiction
Secret Of Kelly's Mill, The	Carus, Zena	Fiction
Secret Of The Glen	Charles, Cathy	Fiction
Secret Of The Indian, The	Reid Banks, Lynne	Fiction
Secret Policeman's Ball	Comedy...	Fiction
Secret Policeman's Other Ball	Comedy	Fiction
Secret Policeman's Third Ball	Comedy	Fiction
Secret Servant The	Lyall, Gavin	Fiction
Secret Seven Fireworks	Blyton, Enid	Fiction
Secret Seven Mystery	Blyton, Enid	Fiction
Secret Seven, The	Blyton, Enid	Fiction
Secret Seven Win Through	Blyton, Enid	Fiction
Secret Sorrow, A	Van Der Zee, Karen	Fiction
Secret Staircase, The	Barklem, Jill	Fiction
Secret Whispers, The	Allbeury, Ted	Fiction
Secrets Of Power Negotiating	Business	Non-Fiction
Secrets Of Success	Business	Non-Fiction
See Yourself Succeed	Business	Non-Fiction

TITLES INDEX

Title	Author	Category
Seeds Of Treason, The	Allbeury, Ted	Fiction
Selected Bosh	Lear, Edward	Fiction
Selected Poems	Warren, Robert Penn	Fiction
Selected Stories	Kazakov, Yu	Non-Fiction
Selected Stories Of John Buchan	Buchan, John	Fiction
Selection From Catullus And Horace	Latin...	Non-Fiction
Selection Of Favourite Poetry, A	Poetry	Fiction
Selection Of His Wartime Speeches	Churchill, Sir Winston	Non-Fiction
Selections	Dunbar, William	Fiction
Selections From Crow And Wodwo	Hughes, Ted	Fiction
Selections From The Greek Orators	Latin...	Non-Fiction
Selections From Virgil	Latin...	Non-Fiction
Self Defeating Behaviours	Self Improvement	Non-Fiction
Self Portrait, A	Dickinson, Emily	Fiction
Selfish Gene	Medical	Non-Fiction
Sell Your Way To The Top	Business	Non-Fiction
Sellers Market	Sellers, Peter	Fiction
Selling In The 90's	Business	Non-Fiction
Seminar For Murder	Gill, B.M.	Fiction
Senilita	Italian	Non-Fiction
Sense And Sensibility	Austen, Jane	Fiction
Sense Of Reality	Greene, Graham	Fiction
Sensible Life, A	Wesley, Mary	Fiction
Sentimental Journey	March, Stella	Fiction
Sentimental Journey, A	Sterne, Laurence	Fiction
Separation	Doddington, Paula	Fiction
Seperable And Inseperable Verbs, The	German	Non-Fiction
September	Pilcher, Rosamunde	Fiction
Serbo-Croat	Serbo Croat	Non-Fiction
Sergeant Lamb's America	Graves, Robert	Non-Fiction
Series Of Murders, A	Brett, Simon	Fiction
Set Up, The	Newton, William	Fiction
Seth: The Voice And The Message	Self Improvement	Non-Fiction
Seven Dwarfs And Their Diamond Mine	Disney	Fiction
Seven Habits Of Highly Effective People	Self Improvement	Non-Fiction
Seven Steps To Treason	Hartland, Michael	Fiction
Seventeenth Century Literature	English Literature	Non-Fiction
Seventh Secret, The	Wallace, Irving	Fiction
Severed Head, A	Murdoch, Iris	Fiction
Severn Valley Steam	Trains...	Non-Fiction
Shadow Of A Dream, A	March, Stella	Fiction
Shadow Of Clorinda	Wright, Katrina	Fiction
Shadow Of Shadows	Allbeury, Ted	Fiction
Shadow Of The Hunter	Kerr, Carole	Fiction
Shadow Of The Past	Ross, Stella	Fiction
Shadow The Sheepdog	Blyton, Enid	Fiction
Shakespeare Sonnets-1 & 2	Shakespeare, William	Fiction
Shakespeare's Women	A-Level	Non-Fiction
Shall We Tell The President	Archer, Jeffrey	Fiction
Shannon's Way	Cronin, A.J.	Fiction
Shap	Trains...	Non-Fiction
Shape Up And Dance	Health & Fitness	Non-Fiction
Shape Up For Motherhood	Health & Fitness	Non-Fiction
Shapiro Diamond, The	Legat, Michael	Fiction
Sharandel	Carr, Margaret	Fiction
Sharpe's Revenge	Cornwell, Bernard	Fiction
Sharpe's Waterloo	Cornwell, Bernard	Fiction
Sharpe's Eagle	Cornwell, Bernard	Fiction
Sharpe's Gold	Cornwell, Bernard	Fiction
Sharpe's Rifles	Cornwell, Bernard	Fiction
Sharpe's Siege	Cornwell, Bernard	Fiction
Shattered Silk	Michaels, Barbara	Fiction
She	Rider Haggard, H	Fiction
She Stoops To Conquer	Goldsmith, Oliver	Fiction
She Wolf	Saki	Fiction
Sheep-Pig, The	King-Smith, Dick	Fiction
Sheer Melodrama	Wallace, Edgar	Fiction

TITLES INDEX

Sheila Shallot And Benny	Garden Gang	Fiction
Shell Seekers, The	Pilcher, Rosamunde	Fiction
Sheltering Tree, A	Bromige, Iris	Fiction
Shepherd, The	Forsyth, Frederick	Fiction
She-Ra	Television	Fiction
Sheriff Of Bombay	Keating, H.R.F.	Fiction
Sherlock Holmes	Conan Doyle, Arthur	Fiction
Sherlock Holmes Adventures	Conan Doyle, Arthur	Fiction
Sherlock Holmes And The Dancing Men	Conan Doyle, Arthur	Fiction
Sherlock Holmes Soundbook	Conan Doyle, Arthur	Fiction
Sherlock Holmes Stories	Conan Doyle, Arthur	Fiction
Shikast (Urdu)	Chander, Krishan	Fiction
Shinel	Gogol, Nikolai Vasilievich	Non-Fiction
Ship Of Adventure, The	Blyton, Enid	Fiction
Shirley	Bronte, Charlotte	Fiction
Shock For The Secret Seven	Blyton, Enid	Fiction
Shock Tactics	Saki	Fiction
Shock To The System, A	Brett, Simon	Fiction
Shoe People, The	Driscoll, Jim	Fiction
Shoes Of The Fisherman, The	West, Morris	Fiction
Shoes Were For Sunday	Weir, Molly	Non-Fiction
Sholtie Burn, The	Paige, Frances	Fiction
Shona Basic Course	African...	Non-Fiction
Shooting The Actor	Callow, Simon	Fiction
Short Stories	Greene, Graham	Fiction
Short Stories	Hardy, Thomas	Fiction
Short Stories	Herriot, James	Fiction
Short Stories	Kipling, Rudyard	Fiction
Short Stories	Lawrence, D.H.	Fiction
Short Stories	Ludlum, Robert	Fiction
Short Stories	Maugham, W. Somerset	Fiction
Short Stories	Poe, Edgar Allan	Fiction
Short Stories	Sheldon, Sidney	Fiction
Short Stories	Stevenson, Robert Louis	Fiction
Short Stories	Wallace, Irving	Fiction
Short Stories	Wodehouse, P.G.	Fiction
Short Walk In The Hindu Kush, A	Newby, Eric	Non-Fiction
Shoscombe Old Place	Conan Doyle, Arthur	Fiction
Shout At The Devil	Smith, Wilbur	Fiction
Showboat And The Gay Old Dog	Ferber, Edna	Fiction
Showdown At Medicine Creek	Kincaid, J.D.	Fiction
Showdown At Mesa	Stokoe, E.G.	Fiction
Shower Of Gold	Driver, Grace	Fiction
Shrapnel Academy, The	Weldon, Fay	Fiction
Shrinking Of Treehorn, The	Heide, Florence Parry	Fiction
Shroud For A Nightingale, A	James, P.D.	Fiction
Shrouded Walls, The	Howatch, Susan	Fiction
Shuffle The Shoemaker	Children's Stories..	Fiction
Shunting The Yard	Trains...	Non-Fiction
Siamese Boyfriends	Langley, Gerard	Fiction
Sicilian World	Verga, Giovanni	Non-Fiction
Siege Of Troy, The	Greek Mythology	Fiction
Sigmund Freud	Freud, Sigmund	Non-Fiction
Sign Of Four, The	Conan Doyle, Arthur	Fiction
Sign Of Love, The	Cartland, Barbara	Fiction
Signalman, The	Dickens, Charles	Fiction
Signs Of The Times	Davidson, Peter	Fiction
Silas Marner	A-Level	Non-Fiction
Silas Marner	Eliot, George	Fiction
Silence In Hanover Close	Perry, Anne	Fiction
Silence Of The Lambs	Harris, Thomas	Fiction
Silent Partner	Kellerman, Jonathan	Fiction
Silicon Chips - Their Impact	Business	Non-Fiction
Silicon Chips - Their Uses	Business	Non-Fiction
Silk For My Lady	March, Stella	Fiction
Silk Maker, The	Legat, Michael	Fiction
Silken Trap, The	Lamb, Charlotte	Fiction

TITLES INDEX

Silmarillion ,the	Tolkien, J.R.R.	Fiction
Silva Mind Control Method Of Mental Dynamics	Self Improvement	Non-Fiction
Silver Chair, The	Lewis, C.S.	Fiction
Silver Falcon, The	Anthony, Evelyn	Fiction
Silver Fountain, The	Legat, Michael	Fiction
Silver Jackanory	Television	Fiction
Silver Skates, The	Dodge, Mary M.	Fiction
Silver Spitfire, The	Harvey, Roger	Fiction
Silver Sword, The	Serraillier, Ian	Fiction
Silver Wedding, The	Binchy, Maeve	Fiction
Silverhawks	Television	Fiction
Silverword	Whitney, Phyllis A	Fiction
Simon And The Witch	Stuart Barry, Margaret	Fiction
Simon Swede And Avril Apricot	Garden Gang	Fiction
Simple Adding Sums	Early Learning	Non-Fiction
Simple Spelling	Early Learning	Non-Fiction
Simple Take-Away Songs	Early Learning	Non-Fiction
Sinbad The Sailor	Traditional	Fiction
Sinbad Voyage, The	Severin, Tim	Non-Fiction
Sing High, Sing Low	March, Stella	Fiction
Sing No Sad Songs	Holland, Lys	Fiction
Singing Sands, The	Tey, Josephine	Fiction
Singing Spears	Thompson, E.V.	Fiction
Singing Stones, The	Traditional	Fiction
Singing Stones, The	Whitney, Phyllis A	Fiction
Sings A Golden Hour Of Nursery Rhymes	Bestall, Alfred	Fiction
Sinking Of The Lusitania	Military History	Non-Fiction
Sir Francis Drake	Drake, Sir Francis	Non-Fiction
Sir Gibbie	Macdonald, George	Fiction
Sir Henry At Rawlinson End	Stanshall, Vivian	Fiction
Sir Robert Peel	History	Non-Fiction
Sir Smasham Uppe	Rieu, E.V.	Fiction
Sister March's Secret	Lester, Jane	Fiction
Sittaford Mystery, The	Christie, Agatha	Fiction
Six Analyses	Rilke	Non-Fiction
Six Folk Tales	Traditional	Fiction
Six Little Ducks	Children's Stories..	Fiction
Six Plays	Plays	Fiction
Six Proud Walkers	Fraser, Anthea	Fiction
Six Thinking Hats	Self Improvement	Non-Fiction
Sixteenth Century France	France	Non-Fiction
Sixth Seal, The	Wesley, Mary	Fiction
Sixth Wife, The	Plaidy, Jean	Fiction
Skills For Success	Business	Non-Fiction
Skin For Skin	Rutherford, Douglas	Fiction
Skull Beneath The Skin, The	James, P.D.	Fiction
Skylark's Song, The	Howard, Audrey	Fiction
Slaughterhouse Five	Vonnegut, Kurt	Fiction
Slavonic Language, The	Slavonic	Non-Fiction
Slay-Ride	Francis, Dick	Fiction
Sleep Like A Baby	Self Improvement	Non-Fiction
Sleep Of Spies, A	Harcourt, Palma	Fiction
Sleep Peacefully	Self Improvement	Non-Fiction
Sleeping Beauty	Children's Stories..	Fiction
Sleeping Beauty	Perrault, Charles	Fiction
Sleeping Easy	Self Improvement	Non-Fiction
Sleeping Murder	Christie, Agatha	Fiction
Slim To Rhythm With Eileen Fowler	Health & Fitness	Non-Fiction
Slinky Jane	Cookson, Catherine	Fiction
Slow Awakening, The	Marchant, Catherine	Fiction
Slow Boats Home	Young, Gavin	Non-Fiction
Sly Fox And The Little Red Hen	Southgate, Vera	Fiction
Small Assassin, The	Bradbury, Ray	Fiction
Small House At Allington, The	Trollope, Anthony	Fiction
Small Woman, The	Burgess, Alan	Fiction
Smeddum, Clay, Greenden And Sim	Gibbon, Lewis Grassic	Fiction
Smell Of Money, The	Newton, William	Fiction

TITLES INDEX

Title	Author	Category
Smert' Ivana Il'icha	Tolstoy, Leo	Non-Fiction
Smile Of The Tiger	Charles, Caroline	Fiction
Smiley's People	Le Carre, John	Fiction
Smoke And Mirrors	Michaels, Barbara	Fiction
Smoke Without Fire	Ferrars, Elizabeth	Fiction
Smokescreen	Francis, Dick	Fiction
Snare Of The Hunter, The	MacInnes, Helen	Fiction
Snatching Of Bookie Bob, The	Runyon, Damon	Fiction
Sniff Stories, The	Whybrow, Ian	Fiction
Snitchnose Switch	Miscellaneous	Fiction
Snookered	Trelford, Donald	Fiction
Snow Goose, The	Milligan, Spike	Fiction
Snow Mountain	Gavin, Catherine	Fiction
Snow Queen, The	Andersen, Hans Christian	Fiction
Snow Spider, The	Nimmo, Jenny	Fiction
Snow Tiger, The	Bagley, Desmond	Fiction
Snow White	Grimm	Fiction
Snow White And Rose Red	Grimm	Fiction
Snow White And Rose Red	McBain, Ed	Fiction
Snow White And The Seven Dwarfs	Grimm	Fiction
Snowball	Allbeury, Ted	Fiction
Snowbird And The Sunbird	Traditional	Fiction
Snowman Postman	Cunliffe, John	Fiction
Snowman, The	Briggs, Raymond	Fiction
So Long, And Thanks For All The Fish	Adams, Douglas	Fiction
So You Think You Know About Football	Football	Non-Fiction
Soccer Tribe, The	Morris, Dr. Desmond	Fiction
Social And Economic History	G.C.S.E.	Non-Fiction
Social Change	Social Sciences	Non-Fiction
Social Change In The Sixteenth Century	Social Sciences	Non-Fiction
Social Impact Of The Industrial Revolution	Social Sciences	Non-Fiction
Society And Literature In The 1930's For Schools	English Literature	Non-Fiction
Soldier Tale, The	Traditional	Fiction
Soliloquy	Andi, Su	Fiction
Some Irish Loving	O'Brien, Edna	Fiction
Some More Of Me Poems And Songs	Ayres, Pam	Fiction
Some Of Me Poems And Songs	Ayres, Pam	Fiction
Some Problems In Reading Canterbury Tales	English Literature	Non-Fiction
Someone Has To Take The Fall	Newton, William	Fiction
Someone To Care	Weigh, Audrey	Fiction
Somerset And Dorset, The	Trains...	Non-Fiction
Something About Poetry	Auden, W.H.	Non-Fiction
Something Fresh	Wodehouse, P.G.	Fiction
Something In The Air	Lathen, Emma	Fiction
Something To Fall Back On	Lipman, Maureen	Non-Fiction
Something Wicked	Ferrars, Elizabeth	Fiction
Sometimes Hurts	Bible	Non-Fiction
Sonal Splash	Abrahams, Elaine	Fiction
Sonata De Otono	Valle-Inclan, R	Non-Fiction
Song In The Morning, A	Seymour, Gerald	Fiction
Song Of The Open Road	Whitman, Walt	Fiction
Songs And Dialogue	Laurel & Hardy	Fiction
Songs And Dialogue (Volume 2)	Laurel & Hardy	Fiction
Songs And Monologues Of Joyce Grenfell, The	Grenfell, Joyce	Fiction
Songs From The Deep	Whales	Non-Fiction
Songs Of Georges Brassens, The	Brassens, Georges	Non-Fiction
Songs Of The Humpback Whale	Whales	Non-Fiction
Sonnets	Shakespeare, William	Fiction
Sonnets From The Portuguese	Poetry	Fiction
Sons And Lovers	Lawrence, D.H.	Fiction
Sons Of The Wolf	Michaels, Barbara	Fiction
Sorcerer's Apprentice, The	Hosier, John	Fiction
Soria Moria Castle	Traditional	Fiction
Sound Effects And Lindrum Fills	Sound Effects	Non-Fiction
Sound Effects Nos. 1 - 13	Sound Effects	Non-Fiction
Sound Effects No.14	Trains...	Non-Fiction
Sound Effects Nos.15 - 29	Sound Effects	Non-Fiction

TITLES INDEX

Title	Subject/Author	Category
Sound Guide To British Waders	Bird Songs	Non-Fiction
Sound Of Classical Drama, The	Plays	Fiction
Sound Of Edna, The	Everage, Dame Edna	Fiction
Sound Of Modern Drama, The	Plays	Fiction
Sound Selling	Business	Non-Fiction
Sounds And Alphabet Of Czech, The	Czech	Non-Fiction
Sounds And Alphabet Of Polish, The	Polish	Non-Fiction
Sounds And Alphabet Of Romanian	Romanian	Non-Fiction
Sounds And Alphabet Of Russian, The	Russian	Non-Fiction
Sounds And Alphabet Of Serbo-Croatian, The	Serbo Croat	Non-Fiction
Sounds And Alphabet Of Spanish, The	Spanish	Non-Fiction
Sounds And Alphabet Of Welsh, The	Welsh	Non-Fiction
Sounds For Wargames	Sound Effects	Non-Fiction
Sounds Of Arabic, The - Parts 1 & 2	Arabic	Non-Fiction
Sounds Of Christmas	Christmas	Non-Fiction
Sounds Of Classical Latin, The	Latin...	Non-Fiction
Sounds Of Germany, The - Parts 1 And 2	Germany	Non-Fiction
Sounds Of Music	Early Learning	Non-Fiction
Sounds Of Poetry, The	English Literature	Non-Fiction
Sounds Of Severn Valley Railway	Trains...	Non-Fiction
Sounds Of Spanish, The	Spanish	Non-Fiction
Sources Of Energy	Social Sciences	Non-Fiction
South	Shackleton, Sir Ernest	Non-Fiction
South Atlantic Islands	Wildlife (Natural)	Non-Fiction
South To Java	Mack, William P.	Fiction
Southern Steam	Trains...	Non-Fiction
Soviet Economic Development 1917-1953	Russia	Non-Fiction
Soviet Economy: The Brezhnev Era	Russia	Non-Fiction
Soviet Economy Under Khrushchev, The	Russia	Non-Fiction
Soviet Jews	Russia	Non-Fiction
Soviet Political System, The	History	Non-Fiction
Soviet Union's Geographical Problems, The	Russia	Non-Fiction
Space Boat, The	Miscellaneous	Fiction
Spain	Spain...	Non-Fiction
Spanish Armada, The	Military History	Non-Fiction
Spanish At The Wheel	Spanish	Non-Fiction
Spanish Bride, The	Heyer, Georgette	Fiction
Spanish Cassette Course	Spanish	Non-Fiction
Spanish For Travel	Spanish	Non-Fiction
Spanish Gardener, The	Cronin, A.J.	Fiction
Spanish Language Basics	Spanish	Non-Fiction
Spanish Language In America, The	Spanish	Non-Fiction
Spanish Travel Pack	Spanish	Non-Fiction
Sparkling Cyanide	Christie, Agatha	Fiction
Speak Dutch Today	Dutch	Non-Fiction
Speak English Today	English	Non-Fiction
Speak French Today	French	Non-Fiction
Speak German Today	German	Non-Fiction
Speak Greek Today	Greek	Non-Fiction
Speak Ill Of The Dead	Chambers, Peter	Fiction
Speak Italian Today	Italian	Non-Fiction
Speak Portuguese Today	Portuguese	Non-Fiction
Speak Spanish Today	Spanish	Non-Fiction
Speak To Me Of Love	Eden, Dorothy	Fiction
Speak To Win	Business	Non-Fiction
Speak Up - Say What You Want To Say	Self Improvement	Non-Fiction
Speaker Of Mandarin, The	Rendell, Ruth	Fiction
Speaking Chinese In China	Chinese	Non-Fiction
Special Collection, The	Allbeury, Ted	Fiction
Special Present, The	Miscellaneous	Fiction
Specialist, The	Sale, Charles	Fiction
Specials In Steam	Trains...	Non-Fiction
Speckled Band, The	Conan Doyle, Arthur	Fiction
Spectacular Sound Effects Vols. 1 & 2	Sound Effects	Non-Fiction
Speed Reading	Self Improvement	Non-Fiction
Spell Me A Witch	Willard, Barbara	Fiction
Spella-Ho	Bates, H.E.	Fiction

TITLES INDEX

Title	Author/Subject	Category
Spencer's Hospital	Stuart, Alex	Fiction
Spend Your Life In Slender	Self Improvement	Non-Fiction
Spid	Moray Williams, Ursula	Fiction
Spirelli Names Names	Davison, Peter	Fiction
Spit In Your Ear	Spitting Image	Fiction
Splash Of Red, A	Fraser, Antonia	Fiction
Splintered Sword	Treece, Henry	Fiction
Spoken Egyptian Arabic	Arabic	Non-Fiction
Spoken Romanian	Romanian	Non-Fiction
Sport And Politics	Social Sciences	Non-Fiction
Sport In Soviet Society	Russia	Non-Fiction
Spot The Dog	Hill, Eric	Fiction
Spot's First Picnic	Hill, Eric	Fiction
Spot's Hospital Visit	Hill, Eric	Fiction
Spring Madness Of Mr Sermon	Delderfield, R.F.	Fiction
Spring Of The Tiger, The	Holt, Victoria	Fiction
Spy Hook	Deighton, Len	Fiction
Spy In Petticoats, The	Wright, Katrina	Fiction
Spy Story	Deighton, Len	Fiction
Spy Who Came In From The Cold, The	Le Carre, John	Fiction
Spy Who Came Of Age	Le Carre, John	Fiction
Spy Who Loved Me, The	Fleming, Ian	Fiction
Squib	Bawden, Nina	Fiction
Squirrel Of Wirral	Harvey, Richard	Fiction
St. Mawr	Lawrence, D.H.	Fiction
St. Thomas' Eve	Plaidy, Jean	Fiction
Staddlecombe	Winchester, Kay	Fiction
Stairs Of Sand	Grey, Zane	Fiction
Stalin	Russia	Non-Fiction
Stalin And Soviet Economic Development	Russia	Non-Fiction
Stalin And Stalinism	Russia	Non-Fiction
Stalker	Stalker, John	Non-Fiction
Stamboul Train	Greene, Graham	Fiction
Stamp Album	Stamp, Terence	Non-Fiction
Stand Up...Get Down	Henry, Lenny	Fiction
Standing Room Only	Duffus, George	Fiction
Stanley Bagshaw	Wilson, Bob	Fiction
Star Is Born, A	Radio	Fiction
Star Trek	Science Fiction	Fiction
Star Trek - Sound Effects: The TV Series	Sound Effects	Non-Fiction
Starch Of Aprons, A	Rayner, Claire	Fiction
Stare Back And Smile	Lumley, Joanna	Non-Fiction
Stark Truth, The	Freeborn, Peter	Fiction
Starlight Barking, The	Smith, Dodie	Fiction
Starlight Rider	Haycox, Ernest	Fiction
Start The Day With Colossians	Bible	Non-Fiction
Start The Day With Ephesians	Bible	Non-Fiction
Start The Day With Exodus	Bible	Non-Fiction
Start The Day With Galatians	Bible	Non-Fiction
Start The Day With Hebrews	Bible	Non-Fiction
Start The Day With Isaiah	Bible	Non-Fiction
Start The Day With James	Bible	Non-Fiction
Start The Day With Job	Bible	Non-Fiction
Start The Day With John	Bible	Non-Fiction
Start The Day With Luke	Bible	Non-Fiction
Start The Day With Mark	Bible	Non-Fiction
Start The Day With Matthew	Bible	Non-Fiction
Start The Day With Philippians	Bible	Non-Fiction
Start The Day With Psalms	Bible	Non-Fiction
Start The Day With Romans	Bible	Non-Fiction
Start The Day With Timothy	Bible	Non-Fiction
Starting School	Early Learning	Non-Fiction
State Funeral Of Sir Winston Churchill,	Churchill, Sir Winston	Non-Fiction
Staying On Top When Your World Turns Upside Down	Self Improvement	Non-Fiction
Steadfast Tin Soldier, The	Andersen, Hans Christian	Fiction
Steam And Harness	Trains...	Non-Fiction
Steam From A To V	Trains...	Non-Fiction

TITLES INDEX

Title	Author	Category
Steam Hauled By A Stanier Black 5	Trains...	Non-Fiction
Steam In All Directions	Trains...	Non-Fiction
Steam In Scotland	Trains...	Non-Fiction
Steam In The Fifties	Trains...	Non-Fiction
Steam In The Seventies	Trains...	Non-Fiction
Steam In Twilight	Trains...	Non-Fiction
Steam Locomotives On The Gradient	Trains...	Non-Fiction
Steam On The Lickey Incline	Trains...	Non-Fiction
Steam Over The Pennines	Trains...	Non-Fiction
Steam Railway Miscellany, A	Trains...	Non-Fiction
Steam Specials Of The 70s	Trains...	Non-Fiction
Steam Through All Seasons	Trains...	Non-Fiction
Steam Weekend, A	Trains...	Non-Fiction
Steam's Final Hours	Trains...	Non-Fiction
Steppenwolf	Hesse, Hermann	Fiction
Stepsisters, The	Street, Pamela	Fiction
Steptoe & Son	Radio	Fiction
Steptoe & Son	Steptoe & Son	Fiction
Stickit Minister, The	Crockett, S.R.	Fiction
Stig Of The Dump	King, Clive	Fiction
Still Further Up The Organisation	Business	Non-Fiction
Still On My Way To Hollywood	Wise, Ernie	Non-Fiction
Stockholm Syndicate, The	Forbes, Colin	Fiction
Stone Book	Garner, Alan	Fiction
Stone Leopard, The	Forbes, Colin	Fiction
Stonewalkers, The	Alcock, Vivien	Fiction
Storefield In The Rain	Trains...	Non-Fiction
Storefield Ssory	Trains...	Non-Fiction
Stories For Children	Andersen, Hans Christian	Fiction
Stories For Children	Wilde, Oscar	Fiction
Stories From Pippi Longstocking	Lindgren, Astrid	Fiction
Stories From The Allingham Casebook	Allingham, Margery	Fiction
Stories From The Science Fiction Magazine	Asimov & Ballard	Fiction
Stories Grandad Tells Me	Reid, George	Fiction
Stories Of Ernest Hemingway, The	Hemingway, Ernest	Fiction
Stories Of Franz Kafka	Kafka, Franz	Fiction
Stories Of Guy De Maupassant	De Maupassant, Guy	Fiction
Stories Of Muriel Spark, The	Spark, Muriel	Fiction
Stories Of Rupert Bear	Bestall, Alfred	Fiction
Storm In The Mountains	Buckingham, Nancy	Fiction
Storm Warning	Higgins, Jack	Fiction
Stormswift	Brent, Madeleine	Fiction
Storrington Papers, The	Eden, Dorothy	Fiction
Story Box (Vols. 1 - 4)	Bible	Non-Fiction
Story Of Babar	De Brunhoff, Jean	Fiction
Story Of Charles Dickens, The	Dickens, Charles	Non-Fiction
Story Of Hatim Tai, The	Traditional	Fiction
Story Of Peter Pan	Barrie, J.M.	Fiction
Story Of Robert Burns	Burns, Robert	Non-Fiction
Story Of Sir Galahad, The	Traditional	Fiction
Story Of Sir Lancelot, The	Traditional	Fiction
Story Of Star Wars	Science Fiction	Fiction
Story Of Swan Lake	Traditional	Fiction
Story Of The Empire Strikes Back	Science Fiction	Fiction
Story Of The Little Black Sambo	Bannerman, Helen	Fiction
Story Of The Nutcracker	Traditional	Fiction
Story Of The Return Of The Jedi	Science Fiction	Fiction
Story Of The Taj Mahal, The	Traditional	Fiction
Story Of The Three Kings	Bible	Non-Fiction
Story Of William Shakespeare, The	Shakespeare, William	Non-Fiction
Story, The	Superman	Fiction
Storybook	Children's Stories..	Fiction
Storytime	Lavitz, T	Fiction
Storytime For 2 Year Olds	Stimson, Joan	Fiction
Storytime For 3 Year Olds	Stimson, Joan	Fiction
Storytime For 4 Year Olds	Stimson, Joan	Fiction
Storytime For 5 Year Olds	Stimson, Joan	Fiction

TITLES INDEX

Storytime For 6 Year Olds	Stimson, Joan	Fiction
Storytime Top Ten	Berg, Leila	Fiction
Storytime Top Ten	Biro, Val	Fiction
Storytime Top Ten	Chapman, Elizabeth	Fiction
Storytime Top Ten	Children's Stories..	Fiction
Storytime Top Ten	Oldfield, Pamela	Fiction
Storytime Top Ten	Todd, H.E.	Fiction
Straight	Francis, Dick	Fiction
Straight Down The Middle	Golf	Non-Fiction
Strange Case Of Dr. Jekyll And Mr. Hyde	Stevenson, Robert Louis	Fiction
Strange Rapture	Robins, Denise	Fiction
Strange Riders At Black Pony Inn	Pullein-Thompson, Christine	Fiction
Stranger From The Tonto	Grey, Zane	Fiction
Stranger Is Watching, A	Higgins Clark, Mary	Fiction
Strategies For Stress Free Living	Self Improvement	Non-Fiction
Strategy Of Meetings	Business	Non-Fiction
Streetcar Named Desire, A	Williams, Tennessee	Fiction
Streetwise	Early Learning	Non-Fiction
Strega Nona's Magic Lessons	De Paola, Tomie	Fiction
Strengthen Your Ego	Self Improvement	Non-Fiction
Stress For Success	Business	Non-Fiction
Stress Proof Child	Self Improvement	Non-Fiction
Strike From The Sea	Reeman, Douglas	Fiction
Strode Venturer, The	Innes, Hammond	Fiction
Strong Poison	Sayers, Dorothy L.	Fiction
Study In Scarlet, A	Conan Doyle, Arthur	Fiction
Stuff And Nonsense	Cecil, Laura	Fiction
Subtext	Business	Non-Fiction
Success And Excellence	Self Improvement	Non-Fiction
Success And The Self-image	Business	Non-Fiction
Success Profile	Business	Non-Fiction
Success Secrets	McCormack, Mark	Non-Fiction
Success Through A Positive Mental Attitude	Business	Non-Fiction
Successful Independent Lifestyle	Self Improvement	Non-Fiction
Such Men Are Dangerous	Graham, Vanessa	Fiction
Sud'ba Cheloveka	Sholokhov, Michael	Non-Fiction
Sudden Departures	Ross, Jonathan	Fiction
Sullivan's Sting	Sanders, Lawrence	Fiction
Summer At Fairacre	Read, Miss	Fiction
Summer At The Haven	Moore, Katherine	Fiction
Summer Birdcage, A	Drabble, Margaret	Fiction
Summer Lightning	Wodehouse, P.G.	Fiction
Summer People, The	Stapleton, Maureen	Fiction
Summer Visitors	Sallis, Susan	Fiction
Summer's Flower, The	Stuart, Vivian	Fiction
Summer's Lease	Mortimer, John	Fiction
Summon The Bright Water	Household, Geoffrey	Fiction
Summoned By Bells	Betjeman, Sir John	Fiction
Sundowners, The	Cleary, Jon	Fiction
Sunset Of Steam	Trains...	Non-Fiction
Sunset Song	Gibbon, Lewis Grassic	Fiction
Super Gran	Wilson, Forrest	Fiction
Super Learning	Self Improvement	Non-Fiction
Superman And Nightmare	Children's Stories..	Fiction
Superted And Bubbles The Clown	Television	Fiction
Superted And The Lumberjacks	Television	Fiction
Superted And The Space Beavers	Television	Fiction
Superted In Superted's Dream	Television	Fiction
Sure Le Vif	French	Non-Fiction
Surgeon's Affair	Harrison, Elizabeth	Fiction
Surviving Loss	Self Improvement	Non-Fiction
Surviving The Great Depression Of 1990	Social Sciences	Non-Fiction
Surviving The Killing Fields	Ngor, Haing	Non-Fiction
Susan	Kennedy, Lena	Fiction
Susannah's Secret	Wright, Katrina	Fiction
Suspects	Canitz, William J.	Fiction
Suspense	Buchan, John	Fiction

TITLES INDEX

Title	Author	Category
Suspicious Death	Simpson, Dorothy	Fiction
Swahili, Active Introduction	African...	Non-Fiction
Swahili Basic Course	African...	Non-Fiction
Swallows And Amazons	Ransome, Arthur	Fiction
Swapping	Lowe & Ince	Fiction
Swedish Cassette Course	Swedish	Non-Fiction
Swedish Travel Pack	Swedish	Non-Fiction
Sweet Danger	Allingham, Margery	Fiction
Sweet Dreams	Frayn, Michael	Fiction
Sweet Rosemary	Chandos, Fay	Fiction
Sweet Sally Lunn	Oldfield, Pamela	Fiction
Sweet Thursday	Steinbeck, John	Fiction
Sweet Vengeance	Edwards, Rowan	Fiction
Swimmer, The	Cheever, John	Fiction
Swiss Family Robinson	Wyss, Johann	Fiction
Switch, The	Leonard, Elmore	Fiction
Switzerland In Question	Switzerland...	Non-Fiction
Sword In The Anvil, The	Traditional	Fiction
Sylvester, Or The Wicked Uncle	Heyer, Georgette	Fiction
Symphony Of The Body	Radio	Fiction
Syrian Arabic	Arabic	Non-Fiction
T S Elliot: Prufrock, Portrait Of A Lady ...	A-Level	Non-Fiction
Tailor Of Gloucester, The	Potter, Beatrix	Fiction
Tailors Of Penzance	Karlin, M.	Fiction
Take A Girl Like You	Amis, Kingsley	Fiction
Take Control Of Your Life	Self Improvement	Non-Fiction
Take It From Here	Radio	Fiction
Take My Life	Graham, Winston	Fiction
Take My Youth	Poetry	Fiction
Take Your Fingers Off It	Harding, Mike	Fiction
Taking Over	Lowe & Ince	Fiction
Taking Sides, Speaking Up	Levin, Bernard	Non-Fiction
Tale Of A Donkey's Tail	Children's Stories..	Fiction
Tale Of A One-Way Street	Aiken, Joan	Fiction
Tale Of Benjamin Bunny	Potter, Beatrix	Fiction
Tale Of Jemima Puddle-Duck	Potter, Beatrix	Fiction
Tale Of Mrs Tiggy-Winkle, The	Potter, Beatrix	Fiction
Tale Of Peter Rabbit, The	Potter, Beatrix	Fiction
Tale Of Scheherezade	Traditional	Fiction
Tale Of Squirrel Nutkin, The	Potter, Beatrix	Fiction
Tale Of The Cuddly Toys, The	Blyton, Enid	Fiction
Tale Of The Shining Princess, The	Gish, Lillian	Fiction
Tale Of Tom Kitten	Potter, Beatrix	Fiction
Tale Of Tuppeny	Potter, Beatrix	Fiction
Tale Of Two Bad Mice, The	Potter, Beatrix	Fiction
Tale Of Two Cities, A	Dickens, Charles	Fiction
Talented Mr. Ripley, The	Highsmith, Patricia	Fiction
Tales From A Country Practice	Jackson, Arthur	Non-Fiction
Tales From A Long Room	Tinniswood, Peter	Fiction
Tales From A Palm Court	Mawer, R.K.	Non-Fiction
Tales From Lavender Shoes	Uttley, Alison	Fiction
Tales From Moomin Valley	Jansson, Tove	Fiction
Tales From Shakespeare	Lamb, Mary	Fiction
Tales From Ten In A Bed	Ahlberg, Allan	Fiction
Tales From The Arabian Nights	Traditional	Fiction
Tales From The Jungle Book	Kipling, Rudyard	Fiction
Tales O A Gamie	Murray, Gordon K	Fiction
Tales Of Ancient Greece	Greek Mythology	Fiction
Tales Of Hans Christian Andersen	Andersen, Hans Christian	Fiction
Tales Of Horror	Poe, Edgar Allan	Fiction
Tales Of King Arthur	Traditional	Fiction
Tales Of Mystery And Imagination	Poe, Edgar Allan	Fiction
Tales Of Rupert Bear	Bestall, Alfred	Fiction
Tales Of Terror	Conan Doyle, Arthur	Fiction
Tales Of Terror	Ghost Stories	Fiction
Tales Of Terror	Poe, Edgar Allan	Fiction
Tales Of The Desert	Traditional	Fiction

TITLES INDEX

Tales Of Things That Go Bump In The Night	Symons, Julian	Fiction
Tales Of Toad	Grahame, Kenneth	Fiction
Tales Of Witches, Ghosts And Goblins	Ghost Stories	Fiction
Talking Bird, The	Traditional	Fiction
Talking Heads	Bennett, Alan	Fiction
Talking It Over	Barnes, Julian	Fiction
Talking To Strange Men	Rendell, Ruth	Fiction
Talking With The One Minute Manager	Blanchard, Kenneth	Fiction
Talyllyn Non Stop - Engine No.4	Thomas, Edward	Fiction
Tamarind Seed, The	Anthony, Evelyn	Fiction
Taming Of The Shrew	Shakespeare, William	Fiction
Tanya Moves House	Abrahams, Elaine	Fiction
Tapioca By Moonlight	Barras, Leonard	Fiction
Target 5	Forbes, Colin	Fiction
Tarka The Otter	Williamson, Harry	Fiction
Tartuffe	Moliere	Non-Fiction
Taste For Death, A	James, P.D.	Fiction
Tatty Apple	Nimmo, Jenny	Fiction
Taurus	Astrology	Non-Fiction
Teach Us To Pray	Religious	Non-Fiction
Team Yankee	Coyle, Harold	Fiction
Techniques For Greater Beauty & Greater Vitality	Health & Fitness	Non-Fiction
Techniques For Greater Energy And Vitality	Health & Fitness	Non-Fiction
Techniques For PMS Relief And Greater Vitality	Health & Fitness	Non-Fiction
Techniques For Weight Loss And Greater Vitality	Health & Fitness	Non-Fiction
Technology Two Edged Sword	King, Dr. Alexander	Non-Fiction
Teddy Bear's Picnic, The	Children's Stories..	Fiction
Teddy Ruxpin	Children's Stories	Fiction
Teenage Mutant Hero Turtles	Television	Fiction
Teenagers And Sexuality	Self Improvement	Non-Fiction
Teenagers In The Family	Social Sciences	Non-Fiction
Teenagers Under Stress	Self Improvement	Non-Fiction
Telling Tales	Davidson, Peter	Fiction
Telling The Time	Early Learning	Non-Fiction
Tell-Tale Heart, The	Poe, Edgar Allan	Fiction
Tempest, The	Shakespeare, William	Fiction
Tempest: Unity	A-Level	Non-Fiction
Temple Of My Familiar	Walker, Alice	Fiction
Tempo Favourite Poems	Poetry	Fiction
Tempt Her With Diamonds	Heaton, Dorothy	Fiction
Ten Kittle Quirks In Scottish History	History	Non-Fiction
Ten Poets Of The 20th Century	Poetry	Fiction
Ten Scottish Ballads	Traditional	Fiction
Tenant Of Wildfell Hall, The	Bronte, Anne	Fiction
Tender Loving, A	Slater, Elizabeth	Fiction
Tenement Tales	Weir, Molly	Non-Fiction
Tennis: Concentration,Timing,Strokes & Strategy	Self Improvement	Non-Fiction
Terminal	Forbes, Colin	Fiction
Terms Of Endearment	McMurty, Larry	Fiction
Terre Des Hommes	De Saint-Exupery	Non-Fiction
Terribly Plain Princess, The	Oldfield, Pamela	Fiction
Territorial Rights	Spark, Muriel	Fiction
Terror Stalks The Class Reunion	Higgins Clark, Mary	Fiction
Terror Tales, The	Poe, Edgar Allan	Fiction
Tess Of The D'urbervilles	Hardy, Thomas	Fiction
Testament Of Caspar Schultz, The	Higgins, Jack	Fiction
Testament Of Friendship	Brittain, Vera	Non-Fiction
Thai Travel Pack	Thai	Non-Fiction
Thank You, Jeeves	Wodehouse, P.G.	Fiction
Thanks For The Memory	Carrick, Peter	Non-Fiction
Thanks For The Memory	Hope, Bob	Non-Fiction
Thanks To The Saint	Charteris, Leslie	Fiction
That First Summer	McFadden, M	Fiction
That Year At The Office	Timperley, Rosemary	Fiction
Then Again, Maybe I Won't	Blume, Judy	Fiction
Theodore Roethke Reads	Roethke, Theodore	Fiction
There But For Fortune	Stuart, Alex	Fiction

TITLES INDEX

There Was This Bloke	Humour	Fiction
There's A Wolf In My Pudding	Wilson, David Henry	Fiction
There's Lovely	Morris, Johnny	Non-Fiction
Therese Desqueyroux	Mauriac, F	Non-Fiction
They All Laughed	Humour	Fiction
They And Mary Postgate	Kipling, Rudyard	Fiction
They Do It With Mirrors	Christie, Agatha	Fiction
Thief In The Village, A	Berry, James	Fiction
Thin Man, The	Hammett, Dashiell	Fiction
Thing On The Doorstep, The	Lovecraft H.P.	Fiction
Think Your Way To Success	Business	Non-Fiction
Thinking Room, The	Wynne-Jones, Tim	Fiction
Thinner	King, Stephen	Fiction
Thinner Than Water	Ferrars, Elizabeth	Fiction
Third Boat, The	MacKinlay, Leila	Fiction
Third Class Genie, The	Leeson, Robert	Fiction
Third Girl	Christie, Agatha	Fiction
Third Man, The	Greene, Graham	Fiction
Third Reich - A Social Revolution?	Germany	Non-Fiction
Thirteen Clocks, The	Thurber, James	Fiction
Thirteen Problems, Kiss Kiss	Mystery	Fiction
Thirteen Problems, The	Christie, Agatha	Fiction
Thirty Years War, The	Military History	Non-Fiction
Thirty-Nine Steps, The	Buchan, John	Fiction
This Is Hancock	Hancock, Tony	Fiction
This Is York	Trains...	Non-Fiction
This Rough Magic	Stewart, Mary	Fiction
This Sad Freedom	Fresson, I.M.	Fiction
This Side Of Heaven	Blair, Emma	Fiction
Thomas Alva Edison	Edison, Thomas Alva	Non-Fiction
Thomas And Bertie	Awdry, Rev. W.	Fiction
Thomas And Terence	Awdry, Rev. W.	Fiction
Thomas And The Missing Christmas Tree	Awdry, Rev. W.	Fiction
Thomas And Trevor	Awdry, Rev. W.	Fiction
Thomas Comes To Breakfast	Awdry, Rev. W.	Fiction
Thomas Goes Fishing	Awdry, Rev. W.	Fiction
Thomas Hardy 1	Hardy, Thomas	Non-Fiction
Thomas Hardy And Love	Hardy, Thomas	Fiction
Thomas Hardy And Music	Hardy, Thomas	Fiction
Thomas Jefferson	American...	Non-Fiction
Thomas, Percy And The Coal	Awdry, Rev. W.	Fiction
Thomas Wolsey	History	Non-Fiction
Thomas's Christmas Party	Awdry, Rev. W.	Fiction
Thoreau's World	Thoreau, Henry David	Fiction
Thornyhold	Stewart, Mary	Fiction
Those Of You With Or Without Children	Cosby, Bill	Fiction
Thoughts Of Chairman Alf	Mitchell, Warren	Non-Fiction
Three Bears, The	Traditional	Fiction
Three Billy Goats Gruff	Children's Stories..	Fiction
Three Billy Goats Gruff	Traditional	Fiction
Three Cheers Secret Seven	Blyton, Enid	Fiction
Three Day's Terror	Creasey, John	Fiction
Three Fat Women Of Antibes	Maugham, W. Somerset	Fiction
Three Father Brown Stories	Chesterton, G.K.	Fiction
Three Little Pigs	Children's Stories..	Fiction
Three Little Pigs	Traditional	Fiction
Three Men In A Boat	Jerome, Jerome K.	Fiction
Three Men On The Bummel	Jerome, Jerome K.	Fiction
Three Musketeers, The	Dumas, Alexandre	Fiction
Three Novels	Silone	Non-Fiction
Three Oak Mystery, The	Wallace, Edgar	Fiction
Three Of A Kind	Television	Fiction
Three On The Trail	Brand, Max	Fiction
Three Sisters	Chekhov, Anton	Fiction
Three Strangers, The	Hardy, Thomas	Fiction
Three Women In The House	Thompson, Estelle	Fiction
Three Women Of Liverpool	Forrester, Helen	Fiction

TITLES INDEX

Title	Author	Category
Thriving On Chaos	Peters, Tom	Non-Fiction
Thriving Self	Self Improvement	Non-Fiction
Through The Looking Glass	Carroll, Lewis	Fiction
Throwback, The	Sharpe, Tom	Fiction
Thumbelina	Andersen, Hans Christian	Fiction
Thumper's Race	Disney	Fiction
Thunder And Lightnings	Mark, Jan	Fiction
Thunder At Dawn	Evans, Alan	Fiction
Thunder Mountain	Grey, Zane	Fiction
Thunder On The Right	Stewart, Mary	Fiction
Thunder Valley	Paine, Lauren	Fiction
Thundercats	Television	Fiction
Thursday's Child	Forrester, Helen	Fiction
Ticket To Tenerife	Blake, Veronica	Fiction
Tickets, Please	Lawrence, D.H.	Fiction
Tied Up In Tinsel	Marsh, Ngaio	Fiction
Tiger In The Smoke	Allingham, Margery	Fiction
Tiger Man	Jordan, Penny	Fiction
Tiger Who Came To Tea, The	Kerr, Judith	Fiction
Tightrope Men, The	Bagley, Desmond	Fiction
Tilly Trotter	Cookson, Catherine	Fiction
Tilly Trotter Wed	Cookson, Catherine	Fiction
Tilly Trotter Widowed	Cookson, Catherine	Fiction
Time After Time	Keane, Molly	Fiction
Time For Tea	Miscellaneous	Fiction
Time Machine, The	Wells, H.G.	Fiction
Time Of Gifts, A	Fermor, Patrick Leigh	Non-Fiction
Time To Die, A	Smith, Wilbur	Fiction
Time To Love, A	Chard, Judy	Fiction
Time Without Shadows, A	Allbeury, Ted	Fiction
Timeless Moment, The	Street, Pamela	Fiction
Timon Of Athens	Shakespeare, William	Fiction
Timothy To Hebrews	Bible	Non-Fiction
Tinder Box, The	Andersen, Hans Christian	Fiction
Tinker Tailor Soldier Spy	Le Carre, John	Fiction
Tintin And The Picaros	Herge	Fiction
Tintin And The Seven Crystal Balls	Herge	Fiction
Tintin: The Broken Ear	Herge	Fiction
Tiny Lifeboat, The	Traditional	Fiction
Titmuss Regained	Mortimer, John	Fiction
Titus Andronicus	Shakespeare, William	Fiction
Titus Groan And Gormenghast	Peake, Mervyn	Fiction
Tnt For Two	Bates, Blaster	Fiction
To Be A Country Doctor	Duncan, Alex	Non-Fiction
To Be A Slave	Social Sciences	Non-Fiction
To Catch A Rainbow	Thompson, Estelle	Fiction
To Catch An Earl	Pyatt, Rosina	Fiction
To Give And To Hold	West, Sarah	Fiction
To Kill A Mockingbird	Lee, Harper	Fiction
To Kill The Potemkin	Joseph, Mark	Fiction
To Love Again	Pyatt, Rosina	Fiction
To Myself A Stranger	March, Stella	Fiction
To Play The King	Dobbs, Michael	Fiction
To The Navel Of The World	Somerville-Large	Non-Fiction
To The Quick	Childish, Wild Billy	Fiction
To The Victor, The Spoils	Gallagher, Jock	Fiction
Toast To Cousin Julian, A	Thompson, Estelle	Fiction
Tobermory	Saki	Fiction
Toby And The Stout Gentleman	Awdry, Rev. W.	Fiction
Toby Man, The	King-Smith, Dick	Fiction
Toledo Window Box	Carlin, George	Fiction
Tolkien Gift Set	Tolkien, J.R.R.	Fiction
Tolkien Soundbook	Tolkien, J.R.R.	Fiction
Tom And Jerry	Television	Fiction
Tom Brown's Schooldays	Hughes, Thomas	Fiction
Tom Fobbles Day	Garner, Alan	Fiction
Tom Jones	Fielding, Henry	Fiction

Title	Author	Category
Tom Sawyer	Twain, Mark	Fiction
Tom Thumb	Traditional	Fiction
Tombs Of Atuan	Le Guin, Ursula	Fiction
Tomorrow Is Too Late	Moore, Ray	Non-Fiction
Tomorrow, Jerusalem	Crane, Teresa	Fiction
Tomorrows Treason	Harcourt, Palma	Fiction
Tom's Midnight Garden	Pearce, Philippa	Fiction
Tonio Kroger	Mann, Thomas	Non-Fiction
Tony Ross' Fairy Tales	Ross, Tony	Fiction
Tony The Turtle	Poetry	Fiction
Too Few For Drums	Delderfield, R.F.	Fiction
Too Late The Phalarope	Paton, Alan	Fiction
Top Brain Anansi	Traditional	Fiction
Topiwalo The Hat Maker	Abrahams, Elaine	Fiction
Topsy And Tim Go Swimming	Adamson, Jean	Fiction
Topsy And Tim On Holiday	Adamson, Jean	Fiction
Torpedo Run	Reeman, Douglas	Fiction
Tottie	Godden, Rumer	Fiction
Touch	Leonard, Elmore	Fiction
Touch Not The Cat	Stewart, Mary	Fiction
Touch The Devil	Higgins, Jack	Fiction
Touching The Void	Simpson, Joe	Non-Fiction
Tough Ted	Bond, Simon	Fiction
Tough Times Never Last But Tough People Do	Self Improvement	Non-Fiction
Town Like Alice, A	Shute, Nevil	Fiction
Town Mouse And The Country Mouse, The	McKie, Anne	Fiction
Trade Union Movement And The General Strike	Social Sciences	Non-Fiction
Trade Unions In France	France	Non-Fiction
Traditional Stories Collection	Traditional	Fiction
Traditional Story Collection	Traditional	Fiction
Traffic Control	Social Sciences	Non-Fiction
Tragedy Of Richard III ,The	Shakespeare, William	Fiction
Trail Driver, The	Grey, Zane	Fiction
Trail Of The Hawks, The	Paine, Lauren	Fiction
Trail To San Triste, The	Brand, Max	Fiction
Trains In The Hills	Trains...	Non-Fiction
Trains In The Night	Trains...	Non-Fiction
Trains In Trouble	Trains...	Non-Fiction
Trains To Remember	Trains...	Non-Fiction
Traitor's Purse	Allingham, Margery	Fiction
Tramp In Armour	Forbes, Colin	Fiction
Transcendental Meditation	Health & Fitness	Non-Fiction
Transformation	Streiber, Whitley	Non-Fiction
Transformation: The Next Step For The No-Limit Person	Self Improvement	Non-Fiction
Transformers	Television	Fiction
Transit Of Earth	Clarke, Arthur C	Fiction
Transport Revolution, The	Social Sciences	Non-Fiction
Traveller's Joy	Allen, Maudie	Fiction
Traveller's Refresher, The	Self Improvement	Non-Fiction
Travelling Man, The	Joseph, Marie	Fiction
Travels Of Sir John Mandeville	Mandeville, John	Non-Fiction
Travels On My Elephant	Shand, Mark	Non-Fiction
Travels With My Aunt	Greene, Graham	Fiction
Tread Softly, My Heart	Ross, Stella	Fiction
Treasure Island	Stevenson, Robert Louis	Fiction
Treasure Upstairs, The	Powell, Margaret	Non-Fiction
Treasures Of Time	Lively, Penelope	Fiction
Treasury Of Fairy Tales	Traditional	Fiction
Tree Of Hands, The	Rendell, Ruth	Fiction
Tregaron's Daughter	Brent, Madeleine	Fiction
Trevayne	Ludlum, Robert	Fiction
Trial By Fury	Ferrars, Elizabeth	Fiction
Trial Of Mrs Maybrick (1889) & Mrs Merrifield ...	Lustgarten, Edgar	Non-Fiction
Trial Run	Francis, Dick	Fiction
Trials Of Life, The	Attenborough, David	Non-Fiction
Trials Of Rumpole, The	Mortimer, John	Fiction
Tribute To Fred Astaire, A	Carrick, Peter	Non-Fiction

Title	Author	Category
Tribute To The Kings Of Scottish Comedy	Beattie, Johnny	Fiction
Tricks	Mcbain, Ed	Fiction
Tricks	Whitman, Peter	Fiction
Trillions	Fisk, Nicholas	Fiction
Triple	Follett, Ken	Fiction
Triumph Of An A4 Pacific, The	Trains...	Non-Fiction
Troilius And Cressida	A-level	Non-Fiction
Troilus And Cressida	Shakespeare, William	Fiction
Troilus And Criseyde	Chaucer, Geoffrey	Fiction
Trois Contes	Flaubert, Gustave	Non-Fiction
Trojan Horse, The	Innes, Hammond	Fiction
Tropic Of Cancer	Miller, Henry	Non-Fiction
Trotsky And Trotskyism	Russia	Non-Fiction
Trouble At The Airport	Bond, Michael	Fiction
Trouble Is My Business	Chandler, Raymond	Fiction
Trouble With Product X, The	Aiken, Joan	Fiction
Trouble With The Fiend	Lavelle, Sheila	Fiction
Truant Heart, The	Farrant, Elizabeth	Fiction
True Blue Comedy Vols. 1, 2, 3	Lucky Grills	Fiction
True Britt	Ekland, Britt	Non-Fiction
True Stories Of The Supernatural	Ghost Stories	Non-Fiction
Trumpet Major, The	Hardy, Thomas	Fiction
Trust	Flanagan, Mary	Fiction
Try This One For Size	Chase, James Hadley	Fiction
Tshindao	Aardema, Verna	Fiction
TT Highlights	Motorcycling	Non-Fiction
Tuck Everlasting	Babbit, Natalie	Fiction
Tudor Foreign Policy	Social Sciences	Non-Fiction
Tudor Regime Reconsidered, The	Social Sciences	Non-Fiction
Tueur Sans Gages	Ionesco, E	Non-Fiction
Tuku Tuku And Samson	Berry, James	Fiction
Tumbleweed	King-Smith, Dick	Fiction
Tunnelling Into Colditz	Rogers, Jim	Non-Fiction
Turbulent Term Of Tyke Tiler, The	Kemp, Gene	Fiction
Turkish Cassette Course	Turkish	Non-Fiction
Turkish For Travel	Turkish	Non-Fiction
Turkish Language Basics	Turkish	Non-Fiction
Turkish Travel Pack	Turkish	Non-Fiction
Turn Of The Screw, The	James, Henry	Fiction
Turn Of Traitors, A	Harcourt, Palma	Fiction
Turning Your Stress Into High Energy Performance	Self Improvement	Non-Fiction
Twa Chiels And A Lass	Poetry	Fiction
Twa Leids And Da Chanan	Scottish	Non-Fiction
Twa Three Sangs And Stories	Graham, William	Fiction
Twain Soundbook	Twain, Mark	Fiction
Twelfth Juror, The	Gill, B.M.	Fiction
Twelfth Night	Shakespeare, William	Fiction
Twelve Dancing Princesses, The	Grimm	Fiction
Twelve Labours Of Heracles, The	Colum, Padraic	Fiction
Twelve Poets Of The 20th Century	Poetry	Fiction
Twentieth Day Of January, The	Allbeury, Ted	Fiction
Twenty One Stories	Greene, Graham	Fiction
Twi Basic Course	African...	Non-Fiction
Twice Shy	Francis, Dick	Fiction
Twinkle Twinkle Little Spy	Deighton, Len	Fiction
Twinkle Twinkle Little Star	Children's Stories..	Fiction
Twisted Tree, The	Harcourt, Palma	Fiction
Twits, The	Dahl, Roald	Fiction
Two Brothers, The	Traditional	Fiction
Two Dozen Red Roses	Hammond, Rosemary	Fiction
Two Gentlemen Of Verona	Shakespeare, William	Fiction
Two Little Rich Girls	Eberhart, Mignon G	Fiction
Two Mrs. Grenvilles, The	Dunne, Dominick	Fiction
Two Ronnies	Two Ronnies	Fiction
Two Stories From Button Moon	Parkinson, Robin	Fiction
Two Thousand Pound Goldfish, The	Byars, Betsy	Fiction
Two Views Of Italian Rural Society	Silone & Levi	Non-Fiction

TITLES INDEX

Two Worlds Of Joseph Race	Race, Steve	Non-Fiction
Twopence To Cross The Mersey	Forrester, Helen	Non-Fiction
Two-way Story	Michelmore, Cliff	Non-Fiction
Typewriting	G.C.S.	Non-Fiction
Ubu Roi	Jarry, A	Non-Fiction
UEFA Cup-1976	Football	Non-Fiction
Ugly Duckling, The	Andersen, Hans Christian	Fiction
Ugly Duckling, The	Children's Stories..	Fiction
Ukridge's Accident Syndicate	Wodehouse, P.G.	Fiction
Ultimate Relaxation	Self Improvement	Non-Fiction
Ultimate Secret To Getting Absolutely...	Self Improvement	Non-Fiction
Ulysses	Joyce, James	Fiction
Un Recteur De L'Ile De Sein	Queffelec, H	Non-Fiction
Unbaited Trap, The	Cookson, Catherine	Fiction
Uncle Fred In The Springtime	Wodehouse, P.G.	Fiction
Uncle Mort's North Country	Tinniswood, Peter	Fiction
Uncle Mort's South Country	Tinniswood, Peter	Fiction
Uncle Target	Lyall, Gavin	Fiction
Uncle Tom's Cabin	Beecher-Stowe, Harriet	Fiction
Unconquerable, The	MacInnes, Helen	Fiction
Unconscious Factors In Creativity	Koestler, Arthur	Non-Fiction
Uncooking Old Sherry	Thompson, John Cargill	Non-Fiction
Under A Monsoon Cloud	Keating, H.R.F.	Fiction
Under Milk Wood	Thomas, Dylan	Fiction
Under Milk Wood - A Play For Voices	Thomas, Dylan	Fiction
Under The Crab Apple Tree	Lustgarten, Edgar	Non-Fiction
Under The Eildon Tree	Goodsir Smith, Sydney	Fiction
Under The Eye Of The Clock	Nolan, Christopher	Non-Fiction
Under The Greenwood Tree	Hardy, Thomas	Fiction
Understanding And Coping With Anxiety	Self Improvement	Non-Fiction
Understanding And Managing Jealousy	Self Improvement	Non-Fiction
Understanding And Overcoming Loneliness	Self Improvement	Non-Fiction
Uneasy Terms	Cheyney, Peter	Fiction
Unexpected Guest	Christie, Agatha	Fiction
Unexpected Masterpiece, The	De Tormes, Lazarillo	Non-Fiction
Unexpected Mrs. Pollifax, The	Gilman, Dorothy	Fiction
Unfair Exchange	Babson, Marian	Fiction
Unfinished Clue, The	Heyer, Georgette	Fiction
Unicorn In The Garden, The	Thurber, James	Fiction
Unification Of Italy, The	Italy	Non-Fiction
Uninvited Ghosts	Lively, Penelope	Fiction
Unlikely Doctor, The	Pyatt, Rosina	Fiction
Unlimited Power	Self Improvement	Non-Fiction
Unnatural Causes	James, P.D.	Fiction
Unnatural Death	Sayers, Dorothy L.	Fiction
Unpleasantness At The Bellona Club, The	Sayers, Dorothy L.	Fiction
Unreliable Memoirs	James, Clive	Non-Fiction
Unspun Socks From A Chickens Laundry	Milligan, Spike	Fiction
Unsuitable Attachment, An	Pym, Barbara	Fiction
Unsuitable Job For A Woman, A	James, P.D.	Fiction
Unto The Fourth Generation: Part 4	Street, Pamela	Fiction
Unwilling To School	Social Sciences	Non-Fiction
Upper Hand, The	Self Improvement	Non-Fiction
Urban Geography	Social Sciences	Non-Fiction
Urgent Hangman, The	Cheyney, Peter	Fiction
Use Of Cases In Russian, The	Russian	Non-Fiction
USSR And Comecon, The	Russia	Non-Fiction
Utterly Utterly Live	Comedy...	Fiction
Vacillations Of Poppy Carew	Wesley, Mary	Fiction
Valiant Sailors, The	Stuart, Alex	Fiction
Valley Of Fear, The	Conan Doyle, Arthur	Fiction
Valley Of The Dolls	Susann, Jacqueline	Fiction
Valley Of The Ravens	Buckingham, Nancy	Fiction
Valuable As You Are	Self Improvement	Non-Fiction
Vampire's Holiday, The	Hall, Willis	Fiction
Vanishment Of Thomas Tull, The	Ahlberg, Janet	Fiction
Vanity Fair	Thackeray, William Makepeace	Fiction

TITLES INDEX

Variety Artistes, The	Wakefield, Tom	Fiction
Vassili Lackluck	Traditional	Fiction
Veil: The Secret Wars Of The Cia	Social Sciences	Non-Fiction
Veiled One, The	Rendell, Ruth	Fiction
Velveteen Rabbit, The	Williams, Margery	Fiction
Venetian Affair, The	MacInnes, Helen	Fiction
Venetian Romance	Sinclair, Clover	Fiction
Vengeance Is Mine	Spillane, Mickey	Fiction
Venus And Adonis	Shakespeare, William	Fiction
Verbs Of Motion	Russian	Non-Fiction
Vermont Hearth	Sound Effects	Non-Fiction
Vermont Stream	Sound Effects	Non-Fiction
Very Best Of Me And The Very Best Of Him, The	Two Ronnies	Fiction
Very Best Of Rowan Atkinson, The (Live)	Atkinson, Rowan	Fiction
Very Good Jeeves	Wodehouse, P.G.	Fiction
Very Private War, A	Cleary, Jon	Fiction
Very Quiet Place, A	Garve, Andrew	Fiction
Vet Among The Pigeons	Duncan, Alex	Fiction
Vet For All Seasons	Lasgarn, Hugh	Non-Fiction
Vet Has Nine Lives, The	Duncan, Alex	Fiction
Vet In A Storm	Lasgarn, Hugh	Non-Fiction
Vet In A Village	Lasgarn, Hugh	Non-Fiction
Vet In Green Pastures	Lasgarn, Hugh	Non-Fiction
Vet In The Manger	Duncan, Alex	Fiction
Vet's Choice	Duncan, Alex	Fiction
Vets In Congress	Duncan, Alex	Fiction
Vets In The Belfry	Duncan, Alex	Fiction
Vicar Of Wakefield, The	Goldsmith, Oliver	Fiction
Vice Versa	Anstey, F	Fiction
Victim Of Love	Buckingham, Nancy	Fiction
Victorian England	History	Non-Fiction
Victoria Plum	Hyks, Veronika	Fiction
Victoria Plum Gives Ben A Surprise	Hyks, Veronika	Fiction
Victoria Plum Has A Treasure Hunt	Hyks, Veronika	Fiction
Victoria Plum Helps The Badgers	Hyks, Veronika	Fiction
Victoria Plum Stories	Hyks, Veronika	Fiction
Victoria Wood	Wood, Victoria	Fiction
Victory In Europe	Military History	Non-Fiction
Vietnam - The History Of American Involvement	History	Non-Fiction
View From The Boundary	Cricket	Non-Fiction
Vile Bodies	Waugh, Evelyn	Fiction
Villa In France, A	Stewart, J.I.M.	Fiction
Village Diary	Read, Miss	Fiction
Village School	Read, Miss	Fiction
Villette	Bronte, Charlotte	Fiction
Vinegar Blossom, The	Peters, Maureen	Fiction
Vinegar Seed, The	Peters, Maureen	Fiction
Vinegar Tree, The	Peters, Maureen	Fiction
Vintage Archers	Radio	Fiction
Vintage Stuff	Sharpe, Tom	Fiction
Violent Enemy, The	Higgins, Jack	Fiction
Virago Book Of Ghost Stories	Ghost Stories	Fiction
Virago Victorian Ghost Stories	Ghost Stories	Fiction
Virgil, Dante Et Al	Poetry	Fiction
Virgin And The Gypsy, The	Lawrence, D.H.	Fiction
Virgin In The Ice, The	Peters, Ellis	Fiction
Virgin Soldiers, The	Thomas, Leslie	Fiction
Virginia Woolf	Woolf, Virginia	Non-Fiction
Virgo	Astrology	Non-Fiction
Virtuous Lady	Kerr, Madeleine	Fiction
Vishnyovyi Sad	Chekhov, Anton	Non-Fiction
Visionaries	Television	Fiction
Visit To America, A	Thomas, Dylan	Fiction
Visit To Morin, A	Greene, Graham	Fiction
Visit To The Dentist, A	Bond, Michael	Fiction
Vital Spark, The	Darke, Susan	Fiction
Vital Spark, The	Munro, Neil	Fiction

TITLES INDEX

Title	Author	Category
Vivero Letter, The	Bagley, Desmond	Fiction
Voice Of Churchill, The	Churchill, Sir Winston	Non-Fiction
Voice Of Cricket, The	Cricket	Non-Fiction
Voice Of Richard Dimbleby	Dimbleby, Richard	Non-Fiction
Voice Of The Dolls, The	Eden, Dorothy	Fiction
Voices In Summer	Pilcher, Rosamunde	Fiction
Voices In The Garden	Bogarde, Dirk	Fiction
Voices On The Stairheid	Humour	Fiction
Voices On The Wind	Anthony, Evelyn	Fiction
Voina I Mir	Tolstoy, Leo	Non-Fiction
Vortex	Cleary, Jon	Fiction
Voyage Of The Dawn Treader, The	Lewis, C.S	Fiction
Voyages Of Sinbad	Traditional	Fiction
Vremya Vperyod	Kataev, V	Non-Fiction
W B Yeates And The Romantic Tradition	A-Level	Non-Fiction
W B Yeats	Yeats, W.B.	Non-Fiction
W B Yeats: Poet Of Love, Politics And The Other	A-Level	Non-Fiction
W B Yeats: The Natural And The Supernatural	A-Level	Non-Fiction
Waiting For Godot	Beckett, Samuel	Non-Fiction
Waiting For Willa	Eden, Dorothy	Fiction
Waiting Game	Cadell, Elizabeth	Fiction
Waiting Sands, The	Howatch, Susan	Fiction
Wake-up Refresher, The	Self Improvement	Non-Fiction
Walden	Thoreau, Henry David	Fiction
Walking Tall	Weston, Simon	Non-Fiction
Wall Games	Dobbs, Michael	Fiction
Wallace Stevens Reading	Stevens, Wallace	Fiction
Wallis And Edward	Bloch, Michael	Non-Fiction
Wallpaper Man, The	Morgan, Katie	Fiction
Walpole, Pitt And Foreign Policy	Social Sciences	Non-Fiction
Walt Disney Stories For Children	Disney	Fiction
Waltz Of Hearts, The	Cartland, Barbara	Fiction
War: A Memoir	Duras, Marguerite	Non-Fiction
War And Society From 1914	Social Sciences	Non-Fiction
War Dog	Treece, Henry	Fiction
War Of 1812, The	American...	Non-Fiction
War Of The Worlds	Wells, H.G.	Fiction
Warblers	Bird Songs	Non-Fiction
Warden, The	Trollope, Anthony	Fiction
Warning To The Curious, A	James, M.R.	Fiction
Washington Square	James, Henry	Fiction
Waste Land	Eliot, T.S	Fiction
Watch Out For The Bits	Bates, Blaster	Fiction
Watching You, Watching Me	Weldon, Fay	Fiction
Water Babies, The	Kingsley, Charles	Fiction
Waterhole	Savarin, Julian Jay	Fiction
Waters Of The World	Self Improvement	Non-Fiction
Watership Down	Adams, Richard	Fiction
Watson's Apology	Bainbridge, Beryl	Fiction
Waving All Excuses	Campbell, Patrick	Fiction
Way I Say It, The	MacCaig, Norman	Fiction
Way Of The River, The: Part 2	Street, Pamela	Fiction
Way Of The World, The	Congreve, William	Fiction
Way To His Heart, The	Goodwin, Grace	Fiction
We All Had Doctors Papers	Boyce, Max	Fiction
We Are Still Married	Keillor, Garrison	Fiction
We Can Say No	Pithers & Greene	Non-Fiction
Web Of Dreams	Andrews, Virginia	Fiction
Webster: The White Devil	A-Level	Non-Fiction
Wee MacGreegor	Bell, John. S.	Fiction
Wee Willie Water Melon And Betty Beetroot	Garden Gang	Fiction
Weekend Sounds	Morecambe & Wise	Fiction
Weep No More My Lady	Higgins Clark, Mary	Fiction
Weeping And The Laughter, The	Barber, Noel	Fiction
Weight Lost	Self Improvement	Non-Fiction
Weimar Republic, The	Germany	Non-Fiction
Welcome To The Peach Tree Cottage	Kane, Charlotte	Non-Fiction

TITLES INDEX

Title	Author	Category
Well Done Secret Seven	Blyton, Enid	Fiction
We'll Meet Again	Lynn, Vera	Non-Fiction
Well Schooled In Murder	George, Elizabeth	Fiction
Well-Known Face, A	Bell, Josephine	Fiction
Wench Is Dead, The	Dexter, Colin	Fiction
West Of Exeter	Trains...	Non-Fiction
West Of Sunset	Bogarde, Dirk	Fiction
West Somerset Railway	Trains...	Non-Fiction
Western Steam In The Midlands	Trains...	Non-Fiction
Western Ways	Trains...	Non-Fiction
Westward Expansion	American...	Non-Fiction
W.H. Auden Reading	Poetry	Fiction
Whale Songs	Whales	Non-Fiction
What Bloody Man Is That?	Brett, Simon	Fiction
What Everyone In Business Better Know About The Law	Business	Non-Fiction
What Goes Up Might Come Down	Gunson, David	Fiction
What Katy Did	Coolidge, Susan M.	Fiction
What The Neighbours Did	Pearce, Philippa	Fiction
What's The Time?	Early Learning	Non-Fiction
Wheel Of Danger, The	Leeson, Robert	Fiction
Wheel Turns, The	LeMarchand, Elizabeth	Fiction
Wheels In The Dust	MacDonald, William Colt	Fiction
Wheels On The Bus, The	Children's Stories..	Fiction
When All You've Ever Wanted Isn't Enough	Self Improvement	Non-Fiction
When Eight Bells Toll	MaClean, Alistair	Fiction
When I Say No, I Feel Guilty	Self Improvement	Non-Fiction
When In France	French	Non-Fiction
When In Germany	German	Non-Fiction
When In Italy	Italian	Non-Fiction
When In Rome	Marsh, Ngaio	Fiction
When In Spain	Spanish	Non-Fiction
When Jenny Lost Her Scarf	Averill, Esther	Fiction
When Nightingales Sang	Hudson, Harriet	Fiction
When The Boat Comes In	Mitchell, James	Fiction
When We Were Very Young	Milne, A.A.	Fiction
Where Agents Fear To Tread	Harley Lewis, Roy	Fiction
Where All The Girls Are Sweeter	Allbeury, Ted	Fiction
Where Do We Go From Here?	Ferguson, Max	Fiction
Where Does The News Come From?	Morris, James D	Fiction
Where Have All The Bullets Gone?	Milligan, Spike	Non-Fiction
Where He Goes, There Go I	Heaton, Dorothy	Fiction
Where The Wild Things Are	Sendak, Maurice	Fiction
While I Work I Whistle	Cotswolds	Non-Fiction
While My Pretty One Sleeps	Higgins Clark, Mary	Fiction
While You're Here Doctor	Russell, Robert	Fiction
Whimpering In The Rhododendrons	Marshall, Arthur	Non-Fiction
Whip Hand, The	Canning, Victor	Fiction
Whip Hand, The	Francis, Dick	Fiction
Whipping Boy, The	Fleischman, Sid	Fiction
Whistle For The Crows	Eden, Dorothy	Fiction
White Guns, The	Reeman, Douglas	Fiction
White House Pantry Murder, The	Roosevelt, Elliott	Fiction
White Mischief	Fox, James	Non-Fiction
White Nile, The	Moorehead, Alan	Non-Fiction
White Orchid	McCall, Dina	Fiction
White Plague, The	Herbert, Frank	Fiction
White Seal, The	Kipling, Rudyard	Fiction
White Witch, The	Goudge, Elizabeth	Fiction
Whitehall Sanction	Gerson, Jack	Fiction
Whiteoaks Of Jalna, The	De La Roche, Mazo	Fiction
Whitton's Folly	Hill, Pamela	Fiction
Who Framed Roger Rabbit?	Wold, Gary K	Fiction
Who Needs God?	Religious	Non-Fiction
Whoever Heard Of A Fird?	Bach, Othello	Fiction
Whose Body?	Sayers, Dorothy L.	Fiction
Why Mosquitos Buzz In Peoples' Ears...	Aardema, Verna	Fiction
Why Overtime?	Social Sciences	Non-Fiction

TITLES INDEX

Title	Author	Category
Why Save Wild Animals	Mountford, G	Non-Fiction
Why The Whales Came	Morpurgo, Michael	Fiction
Wife In Waiting	Peters, Maureen	Fiction
Wilbur And Orville Wright	Wright Brothers	Non-Fiction
Wild And Crazy Guy	Martin, Steve	Fiction
Wild Animals (europe)	Environmental Sounds	Non-Fiction
Wild Freedom	Brand, Max	Fiction
Wild Island Affair	Edmunds, Karen	Fiction
Wild Island, The	Fraser, Antonia	Fiction
Wild Justice	Chard, Judy	Fiction
Wild Justice	Smith, Wilbur	Fiction
Wildcliffe Bird, The	Heaven, Constance	Fiction
Wilderness Of Mirrors, A	Allbeury, Ted	Fiction
Wilderness Tales	London, Jack	Fiction
Wildfire At Midnight	Stewart, Mary	Fiction
Wildtrack	Cornwell, Bernard	Fiction
Wilhelm Tell	Von Schiller, F	Non-Fiction
Willerby's And The Bank Robbers, The	Oldfield, Pamela	Fiction
William Blake	Blake, William	Non-Fiction
William Cecil, Lord Burghley	History	Non-Fiction
William Golding	Golding, William	Non-Fiction
William Styron Reads His Work	Styron, William	Non-Fiction
Willo The Wisp	Television	Fiction
Wind In The Willows	Grahame, Kenneth	Fiction
Windchill	McCaughna, David	Fiction
Windmills Of The Gods	Sheldon, Sidney	Fiction
Window In Thrums, A	Barrie, J.M.	Fiction
Windsor Secret, The	Fisher, Graham	Fiction
Winesburg, Ohio	Anderson, Sherwood	Fiction
Wingless Bird, The	Cookson, Catherine	Fiction
Wings Of History Vols. 1 - 4	Aviation	Non-Fiction
Wings Of The Morning	Chard, Judy	Fiction
Winnie The Pooh	Milne, A.A.	Fiction
Winnie The Pooh And Christopher Robin	Milne, A.A.	Fiction
Winnie The Pooh And Eeyore	Milne, A.A.	Fiction
Winnie The Pooh And Kanga And Roo	Milne, A.A.	Fiction
Winnie The Pooh And The Blustery Day	Milne, A.A.	Fiction
Winnie The Pooh And The Honey Tree	Milne, A.A.	Fiction
Winnie The Pooh And Tigger	Milne, A.A.	Fiction
Winnie The Pooh And Tigger Too	Milne, A.A.	Fiction
Winning Moves: The Body Language Of Selling	Business	Non-Fiction
Winston	Radio	Fiction
Winston Churchill	Churchill, Sir Winston	Non-Fiction
Winter And The White Witch	Gaston, Bill	Fiction
Winter's Tale, The	Shakespeare, William	Fiction
Win-Win Negotiator	Business	Non-Fiction
Wisdom Of Father Brown, The	Chesterton, G.K.	Fiction
Wise Children	Carter, Angela	Fiction
Wise Man From The West, The	Cronin, Vincent	Non-Fiction
Wish With The Candles	Neels, Betty	Fiction
Wit And Wisdom Of Ronald Reagan	Reagan, Ronald	Fiction
Witch Girl, The	Gater, Dilys	Fiction
Witches Revenge, The	Miscellaneous	Fiction
Witches, The	Dahl, Roald	Fiction
Witching Hour	Rice, A	Fiction
With A Little Help	Richardson, John	Fiction
Withered Arm, The	Hardy, Thomas	Fiction
Wizard Of Earthsea	Le Guin, Ursula	Fiction
Wizard Of Oz, The	Baum, L. Frank	Fiction
Wolf And The Seven Little Kids	Grimm	Fiction
Wolf To The Slaughter	Rendell, Ruth	Fiction
Wolfgang Amadeus Mozart	Mozart (Composer)	Non-Fiction
Wolfgang Amadeus Mozart 1756-1791	Mozart (Composer)	Non-Fiction
Wolves Of Willoughby Chase, The	Aiken, Joan	Fiction
Wolves, Witches And Giants	Milligan, Spike	Fiction
Woman In Black, The	Hill, Susan	Fiction
Woman In White, The	Collins, William Wilkie	Fiction

TITLES INDEX

Woman Of Leadenhall Street, The	Gibbon, Lewis Grassic	Fiction
Woman Of Singular Occupation, A	Gilliat, Penelope	Fiction
Woman Of Substance, A	Bradford, B.Taylor	Fiction
Woman Slaughter	Ferrars, Elizabeth	Fiction
Woman Writers In Italy 1943-1956	Italy	Non-Fiction
Woman's Hour Short Stories	Romance	Fiction
Woman's Hour, The	Austen, Jane	Fiction
Womble Stories	Beresford, Elizabeth	Fiction
Women Have Hearts	Cartland, Barbara	Fiction
Wonderful Story Of Henry Sugar, The	Dahl, Roald	Fiction
Wonderful What A Mess	Muir, Frank	Fiction
Wonderful World Of Children's Christmas	Christmas	Fiction
Wooden Horse	Williams, Eric	Fiction
Woodland And Garden Birds	Bird Songs	Non-Fiction
Woolly Rhino, The	Miscellaneous	Fiction
Wordbank	Business	Non-Fiction
Words And Music	Connolly, Billy	Fiction
Words Of Gandhi, The	Gandhi	Non-Fiction
Wordsworth	Wordsworth, William	Non-Fiction
Wordsworth: The Lyrical Ballads	A-Level	Non-Fiction
Wordsworth's 'the Prelude'	A-Level	Non-Fiction
Work That Body	Health & Fitness	Non-Fiction
Work That Body Into Ski Shape	Health & Fitness	Non-Fiction
Working On The Footplate	Trains...	Non-Fiction
Working Smarter	Business	Non-Fiction
Working With Jerks	Business	Non-Fiction
Workout Record New And Improved	Health & Fitness	Non-Fiction
World And Men	King, Dr. Alexander	Non-Fiction
World Apart, A	Joseph, Marie	Fiction
World Development And Europe's Long-term Rise	Social Sciences	Non-Fiction
World History	G.C.S.E.	Non-Fiction
World Of Colours, The	Early Learning	Non-Fiction
World Of Jack London, The	London, Jack	Fiction
World Of King Lear, The	Shakespeare, William	Fiction
World Of Minack, The	Tangye, Derek	Non-Fiction
World Of O. Henry	Henry, O	Fiction
World Of Paddy Roberts	Roberts, Paddy	Fiction
World Of Pete And Dud	Cook, Peter	Fiction
World Of Railways	Trains...	Non-Fiction
World Of Saki, The	Saki	Fiction
World Of Shakespeare, The	Shakespeare, William	Fiction
World Of Steam Vols 1 & 2	Trains...	Non-Fiction
World Of Stories	Children's Stories..	Fiction
World Of, The	Ashcroft, Peggy	Non-Fiction
World Of Tony Hancock, The	Hancock, Tony	Fiction
World War Ii	Military History	Non-Fiction
World Wars 1914/1939	Military History	Non-Fiction
World's Best Bird Songs	Bird Songs	Non-Fiction
Worst Witch, The	Murphy, Jill	Fiction
Worzel Gives A Lecture	Waterhouse, Keith	Fiction
Worzel Gummidge	Waterhouse, Keith	Fiction
Woulda, Shoulda, Coulda	Self Improvement	Non-Fiction
Woyzeck	Buchner, G	Non-Fiction
Wreck Of The Mary Deare, The	Innes, Hammond	Fiction
Wright Brothers	Wright Brothers	Non-Fiction
Writer In Wales Today, The	Wales...	Non-Fiction
Wrong Doctor, The	March, Stella	Fiction
Wu And The Dragon	Traditional	Fiction
Wuthering Heights	Bronte, Emily	Fiction
Wyatt's Hurricane	Bagley, Desmond	Fiction
Wychford Murders, The	Gosling, Paula	Fiction
Wycliffe And Death In A Salubrious Place	Burley, W.J.	Fiction
Wycliffe And Death In Stanley Street	Burley, W.J.	Fiction
Wycliffe And The Beales	Burley, W.J.	Fiction
Wycliffe And The Cycle Of Death	Burley, W.J.	Fiction
Wycliffe And The Dead Flautist	Burley, W.J.	Fiction
Wycliffe And The Four Jacks	Burley, W.J.	Fiction

TITLES INDEX

Title	Author	Category
Wycliffe And The Guilt Edged Alibi	Burley, W.J.	Fiction
Wycliffe And The Pea-green Boat	Burley, W.J.	Fiction
Wycliffe And The Quiet Virgin	Burley, W.J.	Fiction
Wycliffe And The Scapegoat	Burley, W.J.	Fiction
Wycliffe And The Schoolgirls	Burley, W.J.	Fiction
Wycliffe And The Tangled Web	Burley, W.J.	Fiction
Wycliffe And The Three Toed Mystery	Burley, W.J	Fiction
Wycliffe And The Windsor Blue	Burley, W.J.	Fiction
Wycliffe In Paul's Court	Burley, W.J.	Fiction
Wycliffe's Wild Goose Chase	Burley, W.J.	Fiction
Yankee Stranger	Thane, Elswyth	Fiction
Year In Provence, A	Mayle, Peter	Fiction
Yearling, The	Rawlings, Marjorie	Fiction
Yes Mama	Forrester, Helen	Fiction
Yes Minister	Radio	Fiction
Yesterday's Love	Ross, Stella	Fiction
York Collection, The	Trains...	Non-Fiction
Yoruba Basic Course	African...	Non-Fiction
You Are The Message	Business	Non-Fiction
You Are The Power	Self Improvement	Non-Fiction
You Can Become The Person You Want To Be	Self Improvement	Non-Fiction
You Can Do It	Self Improvement	Non-Fiction
You Can Get Anything You Want	Business	Non-Fiction
You Can If You Think You Can	Self Improvement	Non-Fiction
You Only Live Twice	Fleming, Ian	Fiction
Young Doctor Downstairs, The	Andrews, Lucilla	Fiction
Young Doctor Mason	Stuart, Alex	Fiction
Young Mrs. Burton, The	Penn, Margaret	Non-Fiction
Your Favourite Bird Songs	Bird Songs	Non-Fiction
Your Favourite Fairy Stories	Traditional	Fiction
Your Favourite Poems	Poetry	Fiction
Your First Animal Book And Safety First At Home	Early Learning	Non-Fiction
Your Last Cigarette - No Exceptions!	Self Improvement	Non-Fiction
Your Royal Hostage	Fraser, Antonia	Fiction
You're In Love, Charlie Brown	Schultz, Charles	Fiction
Yours Affectionately Peter Rabbit	Potter, Beatrix	Fiction
Yugoslav Travel Pack	Slavonic	Non-Fiction
Zadig, Man Of Destiny	Traditional	Fiction
Zapiski Iz Podpol'ya	Dostoyevsky, Fyodor	Non-Fiction
Zavist	Olesha, Yu	Non-Fiction
Zen: The Eternal Now	Social Sciences	Non-Fiction
Zero	Van Lustbader, Eric	Fiction
Zip Style Method	Cooper Clarke, John	Fiction
Zulu	Aardema, Verna	Fiction
Zulu	African...	Non-Fiction

NOTES

NOTES

NOTES

NOTES

NOTES

NOTES

NOTES

NOTES

NOTES

MUSIC MASTER

other titles available in this series:-

CD Catalogue

Tracks Catalogue

Country Music Catalogue

Price Guide for Record Collectors

Films and Shows Catalogue

Video Catalogue

Albums Catalogue

Jazz Catalogue

Master Catalogue (The Big Red Book)

To order any of the above titles, please use the order form on the facing page.

ORDER BY TELEPHONE 081 953 5433

MUSIC MASTER
SUBSCRIPTIONS & CATALOGUES ORDER FORM

SUBSCRIPTIONS

TITLE	CODE	PRICE (£)	QUANTITY	SUB-TOTAL
1992 MUSIC MASTER SUBSCRIPTION (Master Catalogue '92 (Available July '92), all supplements from July '92 to June '93 and 1992 Tracks Catalogue (4th edition))	C92	209.50		

CATALOGUES

TITLE	CODE	PRICE	QUANTITY	SUB-TOTAL
CD Catalogue 12th Edition	CD12	10.95		
Jazz Catalogue	J1	10.95		
Price Guide for Record Collectors	G1	9.95		
Albums Catalogue	P18	14.95		
Tracks Catalogue	T3	16.95		
Music on Video Catalogue (2nd Edition)	V2	9.95		
Films and Shows Catalogue	E1	7.95		
Country Music Catalogue	K1	9.95		

NEW FOR 1992

Directory of Popular Music (available now)	PM1	14.95		
Spoken Word Catalogue (available now)	SW1	14.95		
Master Catalogue '92 (available July '92)	H92	134.00		
			TOTAL	
		POSTAGE & PACKING		
		GRAND TOTAL		

POSTAGE & PACKING
SUBSCRIPTIONS   UK: no extra charge   EUROPE: add £25.00   REST OF WORLD: add £90.00
CATALOGUES   UK: add £1.50 per book (max order £5.00)   EUROPE: add £2.50 per book (Master Catalogue £8.50)   REST OF WORLD: add £7.00 per book (Master Catalogue £35.00)

☐ I enclose a cheque for the above amount made payable to MUSIC MASTER
☐ Please debit my credit card   ☐ Access/Mastercard   ☐ Visa/Eurocard   ☐ American Express
Credit Card Holder's Name . . . .
Address . . . .
Card No . . . . Expiry Date . . . .

Mr/Mrs/Miss/Ms . . . .
Company Name . . . .
Address . . . .
. . . .
Country . . . . Post Code/Zip Code . . . .
Telephone Number . . . . Fax Number . . . . Date . . . .

MUSIC MASTER, UNIT 4, DURHAM RD, BOREHAM WOOD, HERTS, WD6 1LW
TELEPHONE: 081 953 5433   FAX: 081 207 5814

☐ I would prefer not to receive literature about related products (Tick box as appropriate)